MW00461739

A GRAMMAR

OF THE

GREEK LANGUAGE,

CHIEFLY FROM THE GERMAN OF RAPHAEL KÜHNER.

BY

WILLIAM EDWARD JELF, M.A.

STUDENT OF CHRIST CHURCH.

SYNTAX.

OXFORD:

PRINTED BY T. COMBE, PRINTER TO THE UNIVERSITY, FOR

JOHN HENRY PARKER.

M.DCCC.XLII.

PREFACE.

THE want of a more philosophical arrangement and explanation of the phænomena of the Greek language, than is to be found in the Grammars at present within the reach of the English student, is the cause of the publication of the present volume. It has been judged advisable to publish the Syntax first, as it is in this that the philosophy of the language most requires explanation, and the present Grammars are most deficient. The first volume containing the Accidence is ready, and will shortly be put to press.

It is proper to state, that, while the greater part of the volume is taken from the German work of Professor Kühner, γ_ι much has been added which is not in the original. In particular the Professor is not accountable for the middle verb, the particle ἄν, the cases, the preposition παρά, or the compound verbs, as explained in the following pages, though his examples have been mostly retained where it was convenient to do so.

The publication of the present volume has been delayed by a great variety of College and University duties, the interruptions arising from which it is hoped will in some measure excuse any errors that may exist. It is but due to the Rev. John Barclay, of Christ Church, to take this opportunity of thanking him for the interest and trouble he has kindly taken in carrying this work through the press.

CHRIST CHURCH, May 1842.

SYNTAX.

INTRODUCTION.

Language :—Province of the Syntax.

§. 350. 1. LANGUAGE is the expression of thoughts, or combinations of notions in the mind[a]. Each of these notions is expressed by a *word*, a thought by a *sentence*, or combination of words; words are merely the materials of language, which receive their power by their combinations with each other.

Language is *subjective*, as it represents things only as they are conceived of in the mind.

2. Language does not consist in an arbitrary artificial arrangement of words, but is the expression of the previous internal arrangement of notions, by means of the words or forms of speech; therefore grammar, or the science of language, has rather to explain this arrangement of words than the nature of the words themselves; and its proper province is to trace the developement of a sentence from its most simple to its complete form, showing how, in the progress of this developement, the various phenomena of the language arose. But as each of these words has certain fixed properties of meaning which regulate its functions when combined with others in a sentence, and as some of the difficulties (to resolve which is an object of a modern grammar of an ancient language) consist in the right apprehension of these properties of single words, it follows that we must treat of words and their forms independently of each other, previously to the syntax, which treats of words and their forms in their connection with each other in a sentence.

[a] Arist. De Interp. l. i. ἔστι μὲν οὖν τὰ ἐν τῇ φωνῇ τῶν ἐν τῇ ψιχῇ παθημάτων σύμβολα.

Obs. In [a] the various theories on the origin of language, there are many attempts to decide whether the verb or the noun is the older form in which human thought expressed itself; but as such vague speculations depend on the assumption that these elements of language were arbitrary creations of the human mind, and moreover are apart from our purpose of investigating philosophically the facts of language, no notice will be taken of them, but the parts of speech will be treated of in the order which has been usually adopted by grammarians, the noun first, and then the verb.

Essential and Formal words :—Inflexion.

§. 351. 1. The essential notions of the mind are of things or persons, qualities, and actions or states : and these notions are capable of as great a variety of relations and combinations as the objects they represent in the world around us.

2. These notions are expressed by *Essential words ;* the relations in which they stand to each other, either by *Inflexion,* that is, certain changes in the word, or by *Formal words* used for that purpose—Thus in the sentence, τὸ καλὸν ῥόδον θάλλει ἐν τῷ τοῦ πατρὸς κήπῳ, the notions, beautiful—rose—flourish—father—garden, are expressed by the words καλόν, ῥόδον θάλλει, πατήρ, κῆπος, the relations between them partly by the inflexions, partly by the formal words ἐν, τό, τῷ, τοῦ.

3. The essential words therefore are, *noun substantive,* (things or persons,) *noun adjective,* (quality,) *verb,* (action or state,) and *adverbs derived from these three.* The formal words are, *pronoun, inflexions of essential words, numeral, pronominal adverb, preposition, conjunction,* and *the verb* εἶναι, when used only as a copula, with an adjectival predicate, and some other auxiliary verbs, expressing either the relations of time, as μέλλω γράφειν ; or, as δύνασθαι, χρή, βούλεσθαι, &c., the notion of possibility, necessity, &c.

Obs. Language in its earlier state expressed all the relations (which were afterwards expressed by prepositions, the verb εἶναι, and the other auxiliary verbs, &c.) by the inflexions alone [b]. As the full powers and meanings of the inflexions were by degrees lost sight of, and at the same time more accurate distinctions between the different relations were required, there arose the prepositions, which originally were themselves essential words, or inflexions thereof.—(*See* under *Prepositions.*)

---

[a] Smith's Moral Sentiments.   Kühner Gr. Gr. §. 386.   Donalds. New. Crat. 41.
[b] Donaldson New. Crat. p. 212.

PARTS OF SPEECH.

I. NOUNS.

A. *Substantive.*

§. 352. 1. The substantive expresses the notion of EXISTENCE.

2. Substantives express the notion of a person (names of persons), or of a thing (names of things).

3. The thing which is expressed as substantive has either an ideal existence independent of any subject-matter, as wisdom, virtue (*abstract substantives*), or an actual existence in subject-matter, as man, earth (*concrete substantives*); all names of persons are concrete.

4. Concrete substantives are divided into,

a. Proper names expressing the notion of individual persons; as, *Cyrus, Plato*, in which are included the names of states, or countries considered as individuals.

β. Names of individual things, as a *stick*, a *heart*.

γ. Appellative nouns, expressing the notion of a class; as, *man, tree.*

δ. Material nouns, expressing something not conceived of as an individual thing, but as made up of an infinite number of parts; as, *iron, milk.*

Remarks on the different meanings of the same Noun.

5. Many nouns have a variety of meanings, which often seem at first sight to be unconnected, but which can generally be traced to something in the original notion. This properly belongs to the lexicographer, but the following hints may be useful.

a. Some nouns signify the two contrary consequences of that action or state which they properly express; as, συμφορά, an event—for good or for evil.

b. Some nouns signify a notion which stands in a two-fold relation, so that, when these relations are separated, the noun is used for both. So ξένος, stranger and guest: ἄκρος, (the extremity) top and bottom: ὅσιος, in its relation to δίκαιος, things divine, to ἱερός, things human: πιθανός, probable and credible: κηδεστής, a mourner and a relation.

c. Some nouns embody in their twofold meaning the connection between the two notions they express; especially between two parts of man's nature or habits, &c. So λόγος, speech and reason: ἦθος, character and haunts: κοσμός, order and world.

d. When two notions coalesce, the noun which originally expressed only one, is used to express the other also; as, ἄτη, misfortune, and fault[*]; λαμπρός, light and rapid (wind): μαρμαρυγή, light, and quick motion.

e. Some nouns derive a secondary meaning from some well known custom, the way or mode, material or instrument with which any thing is done or made. So σφῦρα, a round stone, thence an hammer: δόρυ, a stick, thence ship: ἐπιστολή, something sent, thence a letter: σπονδή, a libation, thence a truce.

f. Some nouns substitute the generic notion for the specific; as, εἰρωνεία, any sort of pretext (Dem. 136.): ἀκήρατος, properly ἀκήρατος οἶνος, thence generally pure.

g. Or the specific for the generic; ὀργή, strong feeling, then anger.

h. Many nouns have a general primary meaning, which varies so as to suit the particular thought of the context; as, ἄγαλμα, something a person prides himself on, ornament, statue, &c. So ἄθυρμα, something with which a person is pleased, a plaything, trinkets, trifling; ἄκτη—δεινός, dreadful, clever, or wicked.

i. The abstract is used for the concrete; as, βίος, life, and means of life.

§. 353. 1. The use of the abstract for the concrete gives vigour and beauty to the sentence; it is naturally a poetic mode of expression, and therefore is more common in Greek than in other languages, as it grew up under the auspices of poetry. So in Homer: γένος, γενεή, γόνος for υἱός. Il. γ, 180 ἦ δ' ἄρ' ἔην θεῖον γένος, οὐδ' ἀνθρώπων. Il. τ, 124 Εὐρυσθεὺς—, σὸν γένος. Od. a, 216 γόνος. Il. ξ, 201 Ὠκεανόν τε, θεῶν γένεσιν, parentem, Cf. 245. Il. β, 235 ὦ πέπονες, κάκ' ἐλέγχε', 'Αχαιΐδες οὐκ ἔτ' 'Αχαιοί! Il. π, 422 αἰδώς, ὦ Λύκιοι, πόσε φεύγετε! Il. χ, 358 φράζεο νῦν, μή τοι τι θεῶν μήνιμα γένωμαι. Od. λ, 73. Il. ρ, 38 ἦ κέ σφιν δειλοῖσι γόου κατάπαυμα γενοίμην. Il. γ, 56 sq. γυναῖκ' εὐειδέ' ἀνῆγες πατρί τε σῷ μέγα πῆμα, πόληΐ τε, παντί τε δήμῳ, δυσμενέσιν μὲν χάρμα, κατηφείην δὲ σοὶ αὐτῷ; Il. ζ, 283 μέγα γάρ μιν 'Ολύμπιος ἔτρεφε πῆμα Τρωσί τε καὶ Πριάμῳ.—So in the tragic and other poets, applied to persons: πόνος, στύγος, ἄτη, πῆμα, νόσος, ἔρις, μῆνις, μῆτις, τιμαί, φλόξ (Eur. Bacch. 8. 599.), ποίμνη (Id. El. 726.), &c: also frequently in traged.: ἀγεμόνευμα for ἡγεμών, νύμφευμα for νυμφή, ὕβρισμα, βόσκημα, κώκυμα, ζηλώματα, πρεσβεύματα; so the following words of contempt in tragedy, comedy, and sometimes in prose: τρίμμα, παιπάλημα, ἄλημα (Soph. Aj. 382.), κρότημα —περίτριμμα δικῶν or ἀγορᾶς, Aristoph. Nub. 447, and Demosth. p. 269, 19.; ἐπίτριμμα ἐρώτων; κάθαρμα, an outcast, scape-goat, Demosth. Aristoph.; more rarely in a good meaning, as: μέλημα, beloved, Pind.—So also the expressions in the Attic writers: γέλως; λῆρος, nugæ for nugator, trifler; ὄλεθρος, pernicies for perniciosus homo, Demosth. 119. 8 ὀλέθρου Μακεδόνος (de Philippo): ubi v. Bremi; also Hdt. III. 142. extr. γεγονώς τε κακὸς καὶ ἐὼν ὄλεθρος; φθόρος Aristoph. Eq. 1151. Eur. Med. 1209 τὸν γέροντα τύμβον, a very grave (i. e. πλησίον ὄντα τοῦ θανάτου καὶ τοῦ τάφου)[a]; Lucian. Dial. Meretr. XI. Φιλημάτιον τὴν σορόν; βάραθρον, a debauchee: so in Latin[b]; very commonly in prose: ὁ βίος, subsistence, τὸ ὄφελος, Homer, &c. So Xen. Hell. V. 3, 6 παμπληθεῖς ἀπέκτειναν ἀνθρώπους, καὶ ὅ τι περ ὄφελος ἦν τοῦ τοιούτου στρατεύματος. So Thuc. IV. 133 ὅ

---

[*] Butt. Lex. 10.

[a] Pflugk ad loc. Elms. Med. 1178.   [b] Bentl. Horace, Od. I. 37. 9.

τι ἦ αὐτῶν ἄνθος, ἀπολώλει[a]. In historians and orators, especially the collective words : πρεσβεία for πρέσβεις, ξυμμαχία for ξύμμαχοι, ὑπηρεσία, remigium, ἑταιρία, δουλεία, φυγὴ for φυγάδες, φυλακή for φύλακες, ἡλικία for ἥλικες, &c[b]. Even τὴν πόλιν παίδευσιν εἶναι τῆς Ἑλλάδος for παιδευτρίαν.

2. In a similar way the name of a place is put for a person occupying that place; as, θέατρον for θεαταί, Σιδῶν, Ἄβυδος, for Σιδώνιοι, &c.; and on the other hand, the name of a people is very commonly used of a place, as in Latin. So Thuc. I. 107 Φωκέων στρατευσάντων ἐς Δωριᾶς τὴν Λακεδαιμονίων μητρόπολιν; see Thuc. VI. 4. Hdt. VIII. 127. So also the name of any thing is used for the place appropriated to or connected with it in any way; as, ἄγων, Hom. place for games; κέραμος, prison, Il. ε, 387; θῶκος, a market-place, Homer and Xen.: χίτων, weaving house: σίδηρος, iron mart, Hell. III. 3. 7; and in Attic, the name of any articles of life was used for the place where these were sold; as, ὄψον, ἔλαιον, λάχανα, σήσαμα, τυρός, κυρήβια, &c[c]. In poetry the use of this metonymy is still wider; as, πτέρον, a bird, Soph. and Eur.: κερκίδα, the weaving, Eur. &c.: and again, the idea of the part is sometimes expressed by the whole; as, βοῦς, ox-hide: ἀλώπηξ, λέων, fox-skin, lion-skin: so χείρ, like *manus*, for a work of art.

Remarks on the Number of a Substantive.

§. 354. The singular sometimes has a collective force, and stands for the plural; this arose from a poetical way of looking at plurality as unity :—

Il. π, 11 τέρεν κατὰ δάκρυον εἴβεις. Il. ξ, 16 ὡς δ' ὅτε πορφύρῃ πέλαγος μέγα κύματι κωφῷ. So Od. α, 162. μ, 169. So in tragic and other poets: ἀκτίς, σταγών, στάχυς, harvest, &c.—Prose: κῦμα (as Hdt. IV. 110. VII. 193.), πλίνθος, ἐσθής, λίθος, κέραμος, ἄμπελος, ἡ ἵππος cavalry, ἡ ἀσπίς=ὁπλῖται[d].

2. The singular is also used in a plural force to signify a whole nation. The nation being considered as a whole, and represented, as in despotic governments was natural, by its head :—

ὁ Πέρσης, ὁ Ἀράβιος, ὁ Λύδος, &c. This usage is mostly restricted to nations under monarchical institutions, though Thucyd. uses ὁ Ἀθηναῖος and ὁ Συρακόσιος[e].

Obs. In many combinations where we should expect the plural, the singular form is used, as for example, where a singular substantive is used to define a plural adjective; as, ἡδεῖς τὴν ὄψιν Plat., κακοὶ τὴν ψυχήν Æschyl.—Eur. El. 454 ταχυπόρος πόδα.—So also in the Trag. σῶμα is joined with plural words; as, σῶμα τέκνων Eur. Med. 1117. Conf. Cycl. 223. Id. H. F. 704 χρόνος γὰρ ἤδη δαρός, ἐξ ὅτου πέπλοις κοσμεῖσθε σῶμα.

[a] Bernh. p. 47. Valck. Phæn. 1498. Hipp. 406. Monk. Hipp. 406. Herm. Œ. R. 85. 1248. Blomf. Gloss. Sept. 599. Hemsterh. Luc. Timon. c. 55.

[b] Lobeck Phryn. 469.
[c] Bernh. 56. p.   Piers. Mœr. 351.
[d] Blomf. Gloss. Pers. 320.   Schaef. ad Longin. p. 373.   [e] Bernh. 60.

Plural.

§. 355. The plural properly belongs only to appellative nouns, not to abstract, proper, or material nouns; but these have also the plural when they assume a generic character.

a. Proper names, to signify persons resembling the person of the proper name; as, Plat. Theæt. p. 169. B οἱ Ἡρακλέες τε καὶ Θησέες, Hercules's and Theseus's, Æsch. Ag. 1439. Χρυσηίδων [a], but generally only in comic and the later prose writers [b]; as, Οἰδίποδες, Λάμαχοι. So still more frequently in Latin : *Scipiones, Lælii.*

b. Material names are often found in the plural; the plural parts which constitute the whole being considered rather than the singular whole. So Homer : κονίαι and κονίη (always κονίη when battle or danger is signified : as, ὑπῆγεν αὐτὸν ἐκ κονίης). Il. μ, 23 κάππεσον ἐν κονίησι; ψάμαθοι always; Att. πυροὶ καὶ κριθαί; Plat. Legg. p. 887 γάλαξι. Eur. Alc. 512 φάρνας ἴδοις ἂν αἵμασιν πεφυρμένας [c]: ἥλιοι, rays of sun, like *soles*, &c.

c. Abstract nouns are used in the plural when they signify the sorts or cases of the abstract notion—its particular circumstances or phænomena.

a. In Homer : when the several acts, or things differing in sort, time, or circumstances, whence an abstract notion springs, are considered, rather than the abstract notion which collects and unites them into one; the singular signifies an act or state, without considering the particulars whereof it is made up; as, Il. ν, 121 κακὸν ποιήσετε μεῖζον τῆδε μεθημοσύνῃ, i. e. by this carelessness which ye shew : Il. ν, 108 μάχονται ἡγεμόνος κακότητι, by the cowardice of one : μεθημοσύνῃσι τε λαῶν, by the careless actions of many. Od. α, 7 αὐτῶν γὰρ σφετέρῃσιν ἀτασθαλίῃσιν ὄλοντο. Il. χ, 104 νῦν δ' ἐπεὶ ὤλεσα λαὸν ἀτασθαλίῃσιν ἐμῇσιν, by my manifold follies ;—θάνατοι, *mortes*, sorts of death. Od. μ, 341. Cf. Il. β, 792 ποδωκείῃσιν. τ, 97 δυλοφροσύνης. χ, 216 συνημοσύνας. So ὑπεροπλίαι, ὑποθημοσύναι [d]. There are more abstracts in the Odyssey than the Iliad; though many of those in the former are to be taken as concrete.

β. In the Post-Homeric poets : μάνιαι, fits of madness, &c. So of feelings, thoughts, resolutions : Pindar. Pyth. III. 13 ἁ δ' ἀποφλαυρίξαισά νιν (*contemnens Apollinis iram*) ἀμπλακίαισι φρενῶν [e]. Ibid. VIII. 91 μεγάλας ἐξ ἐλπίδος πέταται ὑποπτέροις ἀνορέαις, *animosis consiliis, moliminibus fortibus* (ἀνορέα, *virtus, fortitudo*) : εὔνοιαι, Æsch. and orators.

γ. Prose : Hdt. VII. 158 ὑμῖν μεγάλαι ὠφελίαι τε καὶ ἐπαυρέσεις γεγόνασι. Id. III. 40 ἐμοὶ δὲ (Polycrati) αἱ σαὶ μεγάλαι εὐτυχίαι οὐκ ἀρέσκουσι. Ibid. 82 ἔχθεα, *inimicitiæ*, στάσεις, *seditiones*, φιλίαι. Id. VI. 11 ταλαιπωρίαι, *ærumnæ*. Ibid. 58 τῶν βασιλήων οἱ θάνατοι. As, Cicero Tuscul. I. 48, 116 *claræ mortes pro patria oppetitæ*; so also *neces* [f]. See Hdt. VI. 109 τὰ Ἀθηναίων φρονήματα, *animi*. Xen. Cyr. VIII. 8, 8 διὰ πόνων καὶ ἱδρώτων τὰ σώματα στερεοῦσθαι.—So in Isocrates we find : ἀλήθειαι, ἀργίαι, αὐθάδειαι, δυναστεῖαι, ἔνδειαι, εὐπορίαι, ἰσηγορίαι, ἰσότητες, καινό-

---

a Bl. Gloss. Ag. 1414.
b Lobeck Ajac. 190.
c Monk. ad loc. Blom. Gloss. Choeph.
60. Ellendt. Lex. Soph. ad V. Musgr.

Phœn. 1540.
d Nitzsch. Od. α, 7.
e Diss. ad loc.
f Stallb. Plat. Crito. 46. C.

τητες, καρτερίαι, μετριότητες, παιδεῖαι, πενίαι, πραότητες, σεμνότητες, φιλανθρωπίαι, χαλεπότητες[a], instances or sorts of truth, &c. Very commonly: ψύχη καὶ θάλπη; θυμοί, animi[b]; Plato Rep. p. 471. D φόβοι. Id. Phædon. p. 66. C ερώτων δὲ καὶ ἐπιθυμιῶν καὶ φόβων καὶ εἰδώλων παντοδαπῶν καὶ φλυαρίας ἐμπίπλησιν (τὸ σῶμα) ἡμᾶς πολλῆς. So σοφίαι, Arist. Ran. 670 φρονήσεις, φιλοσοφίαι, systems of philosophy: Plato Theæt. 172 C ἀπέχθειαι (Demosth. 127, 64.), ἀνδρίαι, deeds of valour, ὑγίειαι καὶ εὐεξίαι τῶν σωμάτων, (like *valetudines;*) So in Demosth. very often: πολλὰς ἐλπίδας ἔχω (p. 813, 2.): ἐπὶ ἐλπίσι καταλείπειν p. 841, 19.—πίστεις ἔχειν ἱκανάς, *testimonia,* p. 843. princ.—εὐνοίας δοῦναι, to give marks of favour, p. 96, 25. *ubi* v. Bremi: χάριτες, favours, gifts: 103. also, βοήθειαι, διάνοιαι, καιροί, πολιτεῖαι: p. 111, 3 αἱ τοιαῦται πολιτεῖαι, where Bremi: *Plural. indicat hanc rerum civilium rationem per longum jam tempus durantem, renovatam semper, adesse igitur eam in plurali.*

Obs. 1. In Attic and sometimes in other writers the plural was used with certain abstracts which might be considered in the plurality of their parts; as, γάμοι, nuptiæ: πλοῦτοι, divitiæ: νύκτες, horæ nocturnæ[c]: Plat. Symp. 217 D. Od. μ, 286. Hdt. IV. 181. Sapph. p. 28. Xen. Cyr. IV. 5. 13. So ὕπνοι, Plat. θρόνοι, the royal rights, Trag.[d]: τάφαι, a funeral, &c[e]. So of many concretes, the singular is not generally used, as in poetry: δώματα, κάρηνα, στέμματα, μέγαρα, κλίμακες, λέκτρα, πύλαι and τόξα, the two last in prose; and the names of feasts and games; as, τὰ Ὀλύμπια, &c.

Obs. 2. The poets often use the plural merely to give weight to the idea[f]: Eur. Hec. 403 χάλα τοκεῦσιν (for μητρί) εἰκότως θυμουμένοις. So in Lat.: parentes, liberi, filii. In the traged. to express fondness: τὰ φίλτατα, τὰ παιδεύματα &c.

Obs. 3. The Greeks use the plural both of abstracts and concretes, when the same thing is said of many persons; as, κακοὶ τὰς ψυχάς—οἱ τῶν ἀνθρώπων θάνατοι; but see §. 354. *Obs.*

II. ADJECTIVES.

Idea of Adjective.

§. 356. 1. Adjectives express the notion of QUALITY, and have a three-fold force.—1. *Attributive,* as τὸ κάλον ῥόδον.—2. *Possessive,* as βασιλικὸς κῆπος, the king's garden; or, 3. *Predicative,* τὸ ῥόδον ἐστὶ καλόν.

2. The original force of the adjective was probably only attributive, whereby some quality is represented as immediately residing in an object. It has the substantival relations of gender, number, and case, as in its character of attributive, it is always

a Bremi Excus. VII. ad Isocr. p. 210.
b Lobeck Aj. 716.
c Blomf. Gloss. Choeph. 282. Heind. Protag. 310 C.
d Ellendt. Lex. Soph. ad V.
e Bernh. 63.
f Arist. Rhet. III. 6 εἰς ὄγκον τῆς λέξεως (ad sermonis granditatem) συμβάλλεται τὸ ἐν πολλὰ ποιεῖν.

referred to a substantive. The use of adjectives as predicates instead of verbs, seems to have arisen from certain actions or energies of any thing being considered rather as qualities than energies; as τὸ δένδρον (θάλλει, energy)—ἐστὶ θαλερόν, (quality;) thus many primitive verbs are lost, and their derivative adjectives used in their place: as καλός, αἰσχρός, ἀγαθός, κακός &c. The possessive force arose from the notion of belonging to some one being considered as a distinctive quality.

3. With adjectives are classed participles, which express the action or passion of the verb (past, present, or to come), as a quality residing in the agent or patient. Many participles have from frequent use assumed a purely adjectival meaning; as, ὀλόμενος—πεπνυμένος.

4. Adjectives have either a transitive, or intransitive, or passive force; as, πρακτικός, active: ἐνεργητικός, operative: τρόφιμος, nutritious: καλός, κακός, ἰάσιμος, wholesome: σεμνός, honoured, &c.

Obs. Some verbal adjectives in τός, which generally have a passive force, are frequently in poetry, and sometimes in prose, used transitively [a]; as, ὕποπτος ὢν δὴ Τρωικῆς ἁλώσεως—suspecting, Hec. 1135. Thuc. VIII. 45. So πιστός, Æsch. Prom. 953. Soph. Œ. C. 1031. Plat. Legg. 824. B[b]. ἀλόγιστος, Arist. Rhet. II. 8. 6. μεμπτός, Soph. Trach. 446. περίρρυτος, Eur. Phœn. 209. ἀφόβητος, Soph. Œ. Rex. 885. ἄψαυστος, 996. ἀμφίπληκτος, Philoct. 688.

III. VERB.

Sorts of Verbs.

§. 357. 1. The verb expresses the notion of an ENERGY, ACTION, or STATE, and this action is conceived of as one of these three motions or directions in space—*whither—whence—where.*

2. The direction *whither* is expressed by those verbs, in which the action is represented as proceeding from the subject to the object of the verb; as, τύπτω τὸν παῖδα: or in which the object is represented as the effect produced by the action; as, γράφω τὴν ἐπιστολήν (verb t r a n s i t i v e): The direction *whence*, by the verbs in which the action is represented as coming to the subject from something else; as, τύπτομαι (ὑπό) τινος: The notion of *where*, (a state) in the verbs which represent the action as neither proceeding from nor to the subject, but merely residing in it; as, ἀνθῶ, I bloom—i n t r a n s i t i v e.

a Ellendt. Lex. Soph. ad V. μεμπτός. Schæf. Hec. Pors. 1117.
b R. P. Hec. 1117. Herm. Œ. R. 192—962.

3. There are various sorts of transitive actions : among them we may remark,—*a*. the c a u s a t i v e, which is conceived as placing its object in an intransitive state or action ; as, ἐγείρω, I waken; that is, I cause this person to be awake: φαίνω, I show; I make this to be seen. But many other transitive verbs are used in this sense, on the principle of *qui facit per alium facit per se ;* the person who caused the action to be done being conceived of as himself doing it. So Hdt. III. 39 ὁ Ἄμασις ἔφερε καὶ ἦγε πάντας. (*See also* §. 362. 6.)—*b*. t r a n s m i s s i v e. When the effect of the action is to transfer an immediate object to a more remote one, both of which are in some degree affected by the action ; as, δίδωμι ταῦτά σοι.

4. Intransitive verbs either express the state, as ἀνθέω, I bloom; or the motion of the subject, as ἔρχομαι, I am coming.

5. When the agent and patient of the verb is one and the same person, so that the action proceeds from and returns upon the subject,—as, τύπτεσθαι, to beat oneself: ἀπωθεῖσθαι, to repulse from yourself : κομίζεσθαι, to acquire for yourself,—this is called the r e f l e x i v e, or m i d d l e s e n s e, (m i d d l e v e r b.) Many verbs of the middle form, by a modification of their sense, whereby their reflexive notion, though implied, is lost, have assumed an intransitive force ; as, βουλεύομαι, I deliberate : and some even a transitive ; as, σοφίζομαί σε, I deceive you ; properly, I make myself wise : and in some, of which the active form is obsolete, all trace of the reflexive sense is lost ; as, μαίνομαι, I rage : ἥδομαι, I am pleased : (d e p o n e n t s.)

6. When the reflexive action is directed from two or more subjects to one another, it is called r e c i p r o c a l ; as, τύπτονται, they beat one another : διακελεύονται, they exhort one another.

7. Hence arises the following division of verbs :—

    1. Transitive Verbs.
    2. Reflexive Transitive Verbs.
    3. Reciprocal Transitive Verbs.
    4. Intransitive Verbs.
    5. Reflexive Intransitive Verbs.
    6. Passive Verbs.

8. For the expression of these different notions, the Greek language has, properly speaking, only two forms : the Active, for the transitive proper, and for many intransitive notions ; and the Middle, for the reflexive, reciprocal, and the rest of the intransitives. The Passive action is conceived of as reflexive, (as the action ends in the subject,) and hence is expressed by the middle

form, except in the future and aorist tenses which have peculiar passive forms.

Remarks on the Active, Middle and Passive Verbs.

A. ACTIVE.

§. 358. 1. The primary power of the verb was probably intransitive; and the form in μαι was probably the original form of the oldest verbs, expressing a state; but as a state may be conceived of as affecting others, the intransitive notion readily became transitive without any change in the word.

2. But the necessity of some distinction becoming evident as the language progressed, separate forms soon arose for the expression of each : the active (μι) for the transitive, the middle (μαι) for the passive and reflexive notions. This difference of sense is clear in the undoubtedly primary form in μι, as except εἰμί, sum, and εἶμι, eo. no verb in μι has a purely intransitive force—(for ἄημι, I blow, act. and neut. see Index to Vol. I.) The later active form in ω so little retained the proper transitive force of the older form in μι, that we find as many verbs in ω intransitive as transitive; as, θάλλειν, ἀνθεῖν, χαίρειν &c. : from transitive verbs in ω new reflexive notions were formed in the middle form μαι.

3. From this indefiniteness the following usages arose in the active voice.

Verbs Intransitive used as Transitive or Passive—or Transitive as Intransitive.

§. 359. 1. For the acc. after verbs intransitive, as βαίνειν πόδα, see *Accus. case.*

2. The state in which a person is represented by an intransitive verb, as ἐλεεῖν, to be in a state of pity, may be conceived of as directed towards an object, as ἐλεεῖν τινα, to pity some one, and thus have a partly transitive force; and in the construction of a sentence, when an intransitive action is considered as transitive, an equivalent transitive notion is substituted for the intransitive; as, ἐξιέναι (=λείπειν) τὴν γῆν, to leave the land.

3. Intransitive verbs are used as passive, when they are combined with words, generally ὑπό or πρός with gen., which represent the state or motion of the subject as caused by some one else; as, ἐκπίπτειν ὑπό τινος, *expelli ab aliquo :* Hdt. III. 65 οὗτος μὲν ἀνοσίῳ μόρῳ τετελεύτηκε ὑπὸ τῶν ἑωῦτοῦ οἰκηϊωτάτων: Id. VI. 92 ἐτελεύτησαν ὑπ' Ἀθηναίων, *interfecti sunt :* 106 πόλιν δουλοσύνη περιπεσοῦσαν πρὸς ἀνδρῶν βαρβάρων: VII. 18 μεγάλα πεσόντα (*eversa*) πρήγματα ὑπὸ ἡσσόνων. Very often φεύγειν ὑπό τινος, *fugari ab aliquo*, or in a legal sense, *accusatum esse ab aliquo ;* Il. σ, 149 Ἀχαιοὶ ὑφ' Ἕκτορος ἀνδροφόνοιο φεύγοντες : Plat. Apol. p. 12. G μήπως ἐγὼ ὑπὸ Μελήτου τοσαύτας δίκας φύγοιμι! Ibid. p. 35. D ἀσεβείας φεύγειν ὑπό τινος : Xen. Hell. IV. 1, 32 διακεῖσθαι ὑπό τινος : Plat. Apol. p. 30. E ἐὰν γάρ με ἀποκτείνητε, οὐ ῥᾳδίως ἄλλον τοιοῦτον εὑρήσετε—προσκείμενον τῇ πόλει ὑπὸ τοῦ θεοῦ (*urbi præpositum a deo*) : ὀφλεῖν ὑπό τινος, to be condemned, Plat. Apol. p. 39. B. : Demosth. p. 49, 33 ὁ τούτων καταστὰς ὑφ' ὑμῶν βουλεύσεται. So, πάσχειν ὑπό τινος, *affici ab aliquo.*

4. Many transitive verbs, especially such as express motion, are used intransitively. This usage extends from Homer downwards, and is found in other languages. So German: *ziehen, brechen, schmelzen.*—French: *décliner, changer, sortir.*—Latin: *vertere, mutare, declinare.*—English: *to move, turn,* &c. The common explanation of this has been to supply the personal pronoun, or some substantive; but this is both unfounded and unnecessary.

§. 360. The following Verbs commonly transitive are sometimes used as intransitive [a].

The Verbs marked † are of frequent occurrence.
———————— * *occur only in Poetry.*

ἄγειν, to move, Xen. Anab. IV. 2, 15, and compounds,

ἀνάγειν, to move back, Id. Cyr. I. 4, 24: to put out to sea, Hdt. VIII. 76 [b].

διάγειν, *perstare.*

αἴρειν, compounds of,

ἀνταίρειν, Demosth. p. 23, 20. 66, 5, to oppose.

ἀπαίρειν, Hdt. VI. 99, to sail away.

ἀνακαλύπτειν, to be uncovered, Eurip. Orest. 288.

ἀνακοντίζειν, to shoot forth, Od. ε, 113.

ἀναλαμβάνειν, *refici,* Plat. Rep. 467.

ἀνοίγειν, to stand out to sea, Xen. Hell. I. 1. ὡς ἕκαστοι ἤνοιγον.

ἀπαλλάττειν, to depart, Hdt. I. 16.

ἀφανίζειν, to disappear, Xen. Cyr. Exp. III. 4, 9.

* βάλλειν, Il. λ, 722. Æsch. Agam. 1172. and compounds,

† διαβάλλειν, to cross over, Hdt. VI. 44 [c].

† εἰσβάλλειν and ἐμβάλλειν, to invade.

ἐκβάλλειν, to spring forth.

ἐπιβάλλειν, to fall to the share of, Hdt. IV. 115.　St. Luke xv. 12.

† μεταβάλλειν, to change.

περιβάλλειν, to sail round, to double, Hdt. VI. 44.　Thuc. VIII. 95.

† προσβάλλειν, to fall on.

† συμβάλλειν, to engage.

† ὑπερβάλλειν, to surpass.

δηλοῖ, *patet,* Hdt. IX. 68.

διατρίβειν, *versari, colloqui,* Plat. Demosth. 93.

διέδεξε (δείκνυμι), Hdt. II. 134. III. 32, &c.

διδόναι, to yield, Eurip. Phœn. 21 [d].

† ἐκδιδόναι, to flow into, empty itself (of a river), Hdt. III. 9. VI. 76.

ἐπιδιδόναι, *proficere,* Hdt. II. 13.

ἀνταποδιδόναι, *respondere,* Plat. Phæd. 72. A. B.

* ἐγείρειν, to rouse yourself, Eurip. Iph. A. 624.

† ἐλαύνειν, to go, Xen. Cyr. I. 4, 20.

† προσελαύνειν, *adequitare,* Id.

διελαύνειν, to pass through, Hdt. III. 86.

ἐπελαύνειν, to advance against.

* ἐνιπλήττειν, to rush into, Il. μ, 72.

ἐπείγειν, to hasten, Eurip. Heracl. 732. Orest. 799.

† ἔχειν, to be, (that which a person has, often constituting his state, σχῆμα; so Lat. *habitus,*) Hdt. III. 82: with adverbs εὖ, καλῶς, κακῶς, &c. *bene, male habere :* and adjectives, Eurip. Med. 550: also more rarely, to come to land, Hdt. VI. 92: *domi se tenere,* Id. VI. 39.

ἀντέχειν, *resistere,* Hdt.

ἐξέχειν, to rise, (of the sun.)

ἐπέχειν, *se sustinere, expectare,* Hdt. VI. 102: *in mente habere,* Hdt. VI. 96.

κατέχειν, *se retinere;* also, to come to land.

παρέχειν, as τῇ μουσικῇ, *musicæ se dare,* Plat. Rep. 411. A.

παρέχει μοι, *licet mihi,* Hdt. III. 142.

---

[a] Monk. Alc. 922.　Herm. Œ. R. 153.　Bos. ἑαυτοῦ.
[b] Schweig. ad loc.　[c] Valck. Hdt. 114. 3.　[d] Valck. ad loc. Diatrib. p. 233.

προέχειν, *præstare*, Hdt. III. 142.
Demosth. 10.
προσέχειν, *attendere, appellere*, Hdt.
III. 48—and perhaps also μετέχειν, to cling to, Thuc. II. 15.
θαρσύνειν, to be of good cheer,
Soph. El. 917.
ἰέναι, to leave off, Il. τ, 402, &c.
and compounds [a],
ἐξιέναι, to empty themselves, (of
rivers,) Hdt. VI. 20.
ἀνιέναι, to remit.
ἐφιέναι ἰσχυρῷ γέλωτι, *indulgere*,
Plat. Rep. 388. E [b].
κατορθοῦν, to succeed, Demosth. 23.
κεύθειν, to be covered, Soph. Œ. R.
967.
κλίνειν, to bend towards, and compounds, like *declinare*,
ἐπικλίνω, to bend towards, Demosth. 30.
ἀποκλίνω, to turn to, Id. 13.
* κρύπτειν, to lie hid, Soph. El. 826.
Eurip. Phœn. 1117.
* κυκλοῦν, revolve, Soph. El. 1365.
Trach. 130.
μίσγειν, μιγνύναι, compounds of,
συμμίσγειν, *commisceri*.
προσμιγνύναι, to come to blows:
but more often in the historians
appropinquare, Hdt. VI. 95.
λείπειν, compounds of,
ἀπολιπεῖν, to be behind, Hdt. VII.
221.   Thuc. III. 10.   Plat.
Phæd. 78. B.
ἐλλείπειν, *officio suo deesse*, Demosth.
27. 30.   Hdt. III. 25, to fail.
νικᾶν, to prevail, Hdt. VI. 109, &c.
ξυντείνειν, to tend towards, Eurip.
Hec. 190.
οἰκεῖν, *habitari*, ἡ πόλις οἰκεῖ, Plat.
Rep. 462. D. 543. A: to live
(without any case,) Hdt. III. 99.
* παίειν [c], to dash against, Æsch.

Prom. Vinct. 855 : so ξυμπαίειν,
Eur. Hec. 118 : εἰσπαίειν, Eur.
Rhes. 560.   Soph. Œ. R. 1252.
— ἐπεισπαίειν, Aristoph. Plut.
806.
* πάλλειν, to shake, quake, Eur. El.
435.   Soph. Œ. R. 153.
* παύειν, to cease, in Imper. Od. δ,
659.   Eur. Helen. 1336.   Aristoph. Ran. 530.   So Plato.
καταπαύσας, Eur. Hec. 917.
ἀπόπαυε, Od. a, 340.
ποιεῖν, to make for, Thuc. II. 8.
IV. 12.
† πράττειν, with adverbs εὖ, κακῶς,
or neuter adj. κακά, &c.
† πταίειν, to stumble, Demosth. 23.
προσπταίειν, to be shipwrecked,
Hdt. VI. 95.
* σπέρχειν, to be excited, Il. ν, 334.
στρέφειν, and its compounds generally.
συνάπτειν, *manus conserere*.
συναρμόζειν, to suit.
σφακελίζειν, *carie corrodi*, Hdt. III.
66.
* τελεῖν, to be completed, Æsch. P.
V. 223.   Soph. El. 1419.
† τελευτᾶν, to die.
τήκειν, to pine, Soph. Elect. 124.
† τρέπειν, like *vertere*.
† ἐπιτρέπειν, *se permittere*, Hdt. III.
81.   Demosth. 92.
ὑποκύπτειν, *succumbere*, Hdt. VI. 96,
&c.
† φαίνειν, *splendere*, Theocr. II. 11.
φέρειν [d], compounds of,
† διαφέρειν, *differre*.
ὑπερφέρειν πλούτῳ, Xen. Rep. Lac.
XV. 3.   Thuc. I. 81.
* φύειν, to grow, Theocr. IV. 24.
† χαλᾶν [e], to yield, Eur. Hec. 403.
So also we must explain ἄγε,
ἄγε δή, πρόσαγε, φέρε δή, ἔχε δή.

Obs. 1. It is very important to remember the neuter usages of these
verbs, especially of ἔχω and its compounds, as the interpretation of a great
many passages depends upon this sense.
Obs. 2. In poetry sometimes the same word is used, even in the same

---

passage, both transitively and intransitively; as, Hesiod. Opp. 5 ῥέα μὲν
γὰρ βριάει (causes to swell), ῥέα δὲ βριάοντα (swelling) χαλέπτει:
Anacreont. XL. extr. εἰ τὸ κέντρον πονεῖ τὸ τῆς μελίσσης, πόσον δοκεῖς
πονοῦσιν, Ἔρως, ὅσους σὺ βάλλεις.

Obs. 3. Sometimes a double verbal notion, which naturally would be
expressed by two verbal forms, is expressed by a verb and a substantive;
so ἐξῆρχες λόγοις ἐμέ, instead of ἐξῆρχες λέγων ἐμέ, Soph. Elect. 556:
θεραπεύμασιν ἐμόχθει, Phœn. 1549=ἐμόχθει θεραπεύων: φυλακὰν κατασχεῖν,
Æsch. Ag. 236=φυλάσσων κατασχεῖν: τάκεις οἰμωγὰν Ἀγαμέμνονα, Soph.
El. 124=τάκεις οἰμώζουσα [a].

Obs. 4. Another form of expressing a verbal notion is by the verb εἶναι,
and an adjective cognate to the verb by which the verbal notion would
properly be expressed; as, Plato Charm. 117 ἐξάρνῳ εἶναι=ἀρνεῖσθαι:
Plato Alcib. 83 ἀνήκοον εἶναι=ἀνηκουστεῖν.

Remarks on the Tempora secunda.

§. 361. The Greek language has two forms for some tenses, which
are distinguished in grammar as primary and secondary tenses: the
secondary tenses are the older forms, and in many verbs retain the original
intransitive notion, while the stronger notion of the transitive was signified
by an augmented form; and so in fact we find many verbs, of which the
Aor. I. and the Pft. I. are transitive, the Aor. II. and Pft. II. intransitive.   So there is a similar distinction between the Aor. I. and II. Midd.,
and Aor. I. and II. Passive, as we shall see below.

B. MIDDLE VOICE.

§. 362. The middle voice has a twofold function; 1. it expresses
the reflexive and reciprocal, 2. some parts of the passive, notion.

a. *As Reflexive.*

1. The essential sense which runs throughout the middle reflexive
verb, is Self—the action of the verb has immediate reference to
self.   This is the proper generic notion of all middle verbs; and
the particular sense of each middle verb must be determined by
discovering the relation in which this notion of self stands to the
notion of the verb.

2. There are four relations in which this notion of self may stand
to the verb:—1. Genitive.—2. Dative.—3. Accusative.—4. Adjectival.

1. The "self" stands to the notion of the verb as Genitive:—

As, ἀπώσας, having pushed away: ἀπωσάμενος, having pushed from oneself, or repulsed: ἀποπέμπομαι, to send away from myself: ἀποσείσασθαι,
to shake off, *depellere*.   So ἀμύνεσθαι, (though this is rather for myself,
than from myself, as in the active voice it prefers the dative to the geni-

---

a Herm. Elect. 122.

tive) : παρέχεσθαι, to furnish from one's own means—οἱ μὲν γὰρ νέας παρείχοντο, but τοῖσι δὲ προσετέτακτο—νέας παρέχειν. So παρέχεσθαι ὀδμὴν —ἔργα : τὸ φρέαρ τριφασίας παρέχεται ἰδέας, from itself : ἐκδύεσθαι, to take off from oneself : ἀποθέσθαι, to put away from oneself : ἐπαγγέλλεσθαι, to declare from oneself; to promise : ἐκποιεῖσθαι υἱόν, to put away his son.

2. The " self " stands to the notion of the verb as the Dative :—
(Generally the Dat. Com. vel Incom.)—as, παρασκευάζεσθαί τι, *sibi parare :* αἱρεῖσθαί τι, *sibi sumere,* to choose : ἀφαιρεῖσθαι, to take away for oneself : αἵρεσθαι, to take on, or for oneself : αἵρειν, to take up, to lay on another : αἰτεῖσθαι, *sibi expetere :* πράττεσθαι χρήματα, *pecuniam sibi :* κτᾶσθαι, *sibi comparare :* μισθοῦσθαι, to hire for oneself, *conduco :* μισθοῦν, to hire out : ἄγεσθαι γυναῖκα, *ducere sibi uxorem,* to marry : βουλεύω (σοι), I advise : βουλεύομαι, I advise myself, deliberate. So ἐνδύεσθαι, to put on oneself : λείπεσθαι μνημοσύνα, to leave memorials for oneself : συλλέγεσθαι ; τιμωρεῖν τινι, to help a person : τιμωρεῖσθαι, to help myself. So ἀμύνεσθαι ; αἰτεῖσθαι and παραιτεῖσθαι, for myself : προσποιεῖσθαι *sibi subjicere :* δανείσασθαι and χρήσασθαι, to borrow : θέσθαι and παραθέσθαι ; μεταπέμψασθαι ; φέρεσθαι τὰ δευτεραῖα, to carry off for oneself the second prize : καταστρέφεσθαι, *sibi subvertere,* to reduce, so καταδουλοῦσθαι ; τίθεμαι, I take to myself—adopt : τιθέμενος βάσιν, Eur. Hec. So κληρώσασθαι. So θεῖναι νόμους, to make laws for others : θέσθαι νόμ. to make laws by which oneself is bound. So also γράφειν and γράφεσθαι νόμους [a] ; Xen. M. S. IV. 4, 19 ἔχεις ἂν οὖν εἰπεῖν, ὅτι οἱ ἄνθρωποι αὐτοὺς (τοὺς ἀγράφους νόμους) ἔθεντο ;— Ἐγὼ μὲν θεοὺς οἶμαι τοὺς νόμους τούτους τοῖς ἀνθρώποις θεῖναι : Id. Œcon. IX. 14 ἐν ταῖς εὐνομουμέναις πόλεσιν οὐκ ἀρκεῖν δοκεῖ τοῖς πολίταις, ἢν νόμους καλοὺς γράψωνται.

Obs. 1. Hence there is a difference between the active and middle sense of some verbs : the latter signifying that the action of the verb was done for one's own benefit, (Dat. Comm.) and thence signifying the corresponding contrary to the active voice ; as, λῦσαι, to set free ; λύσασθαι, to ransom : χρῆσαι, to lend or give an oracle ; -ασθαι, to borrow or consult an oracle : so δανεῖσαι, -ασθαι : τῖσαι, to pay ; τίσασθαι, to punish : the active signifying the giver, the middle the receiver [b] ; this may arise from the *receptive notion* proper to the middle verb.

3. The " self " stands to the verb as the Accusative. .
ἐπιτιθέναι, to place on ; -εσθαι, to place oneself on, to attack : χράω, I give or apply ; χράομαι, I apply myself to : τρέπω, I turn ; τρέπομαι, I turn myself : Od. α, 422 οἱ δ' εἰς ὀρχηστὺν—τρεψάμενοι τέρποντο : λούω, I wash ; λούομαι, I wash myself = I bathe : ἐπαίρω, I raise ; ἐπαίρομαι, I raise myself : ἀπέχω, I keep off ; ἀπέχομαι, I keep myself off = I abstain. Hdt. VI. 67 καλυψάμενος ᾔε ἐκ τοῦ θεήτρου, covering himself : ἀπάγξαι τινά, to throttle, hang ; ἀπάγξασθαι, to throttle, hang oneself : τύπτομαι, κόπτομαι, I beat myself : τήκειν, to melt, to melt away ; τήκεσθαι, to melt oneself away, *contabescere* = to pine : ἐγγυᾶσθαι, to pledge oneself : ἐπιβάλεσθαί τινι, to lay oneself on something, to attack. So κείρεσθαι, στεφανοῦσθαι, &c. : and ἀναμνήσασθαι, to remind oneself, *recordari* = to remember : λανθάνειν, to escape another person's notice ; λανθάνεσθαι, to forget : φυλάξασθαι, to guard oneself=to beware : φοβεῖσθαι, (φοβεῖν, *terrere :*) παύεσθαι, to cease, (παύω τινά τινος, *avocare ab :*) στέλλεσθαι, *proficisci,* (στέλλειν, *mittere :*) πλάζεσθαι, to wander, (πλάζειν, to make to wander :) περαίουσθαι

[a] Valck. Amm. p. 136. Kuster. Verb. Med. 58.   [b] Kuster. de Verb. Med. p. 61.

(ποταμόν), to pass over, (περαιοῦν τινα ποταμόν, *trajicere :*) φαίνεσθαι, to show oneself=appear, (φαίνειν, to show :) ἔλπεσθαι, to hope, (ἔλπω, to make to hope :) ἵστασθαι, to place oneself=to stand, (ἱστάναι, to place :) πήγνυσθαι, to congeal, (πηγνύναι, to fix :) γεύεσθαι, to taste, (γεύω, to make to taste :) πορεύεσθαι, to pass on, *proficisci*, (πορεύειν τινά, to pass a person on :) ἀπαλλάσσεσθαι, to remove oneself=to depart, (ἀπαλλάσσω τινά, to remove some one else :) ἐπείγεσθαι, to press on oneself=to hasten, (ἐπείγειν τινά, to press on some one :) εὐωχεῖσθαι, to feed oneself = to banquet, (εὐωχεῖν τινά, to feed any one :) κοιμᾶσθαι, to lull oneself to sleep=to go to sleep, (κοιμᾶν τινά, *consopire :*) ἀγάλλεσθαι, to adorn oneself, to plume oneself, (ἀγάλλειν, *ornare :*) ὀρέγεσθαί τινος, to stretch oneself at=to aim at a thing, (ὀρέγειν, to extend :) σκοπεῖσθαι, to look at oneself=consider, (σκοπέω, to look at :) and so in many verbs in όω; δηλόω, I show : δηλόομαι, I show myself.

Obs. 2. It will be seen from these instances, that in compound middle verbs the relation in which self stands to the verb is frequently determined by the preposition.

4. The "self" stands to the verb as a pronominal Adjective.

ὀνομάζεσθαι παῖδα, to call a person his son[a] : κείρεσθαι τὴν κεφαλήν : νίπτεσθαι τοὺς πόδας, to wash one's own feet, (νίπτειν τοὺς πόδας, to wash another's feet :) τύπτεσθαι τὴν κεφαλήν, to beat one's own head : Il. ε, 97 ἐπιταίνετο κάμπυλα τόξα : Od. α, 262 ὄφρα οἱ εἴη ἰοὺς χρίεσθαι χαλκήρεας : Demosth. p. 836, 3 Δημοχάρης—οὐκ ἀποκέκρυπται τὴν οὐσίαν : Id. p. 101, 46 ταύτην ῥαθυμίαν ἀποθέσθαι :—ἐγκαλύψασθαι τὴν κεφαλήν (*suum caput ;* ἐγκαλύπτειν, *alius c.*): περιρρήξασθαι χιτῶνα (*suam vestem ;* περιρρῆξαι, *alius v.*): θέσθαι τὰ ὅπλα.

Obs. 3. Verbs which have the self in the acc. relation, if they are followed by a substantive in the acc., transfer it to the subst. as a pronominal adject.; as, τύπτομαι, I beat myself; τύπτομαι τὴν κεφαλήν, I beat my head : λούομαι, I wash; ἐλούσατο χρόα (Eur. Alc. 160), she washed her body.

5. Some middle verbs have the self in more than one of these relations, in which case their sense generally differs accordingly :

αἴρεσθαι, acc. I raise myself : αἴρεσθαι, dat. I take on or for myself[b].

Or, the idea is the same, though the several parts of it stand in a different relation :—

τίθεμαι, I apply myself (acc.) to=1 adopt ; τίθεμαι, I apply to myself (dat.)=I adopt ; see Hec. 1059, 1074 : μεθίεσθαι, to remove myself from, followed by gen.; μεθίεσθαι, to remove from myself[c], followed by acc. So Eur. Med. 734 ἄγουσιν οὐ μεθεῖ' ἂν ἐκ γαίας ἐμέ. So Alc. 1111 οὐκ ἂν μεθείμην σοῖς γυναῖκα προσπόλοις, Mss. which editors have altered into μεθείην : Cf. Soph. Elect. 1277 τῶν σῶν προσώπων ἡδονὰν μεθέσθαι : Phœn. 529, where Mss. ἐκεῖνο, edd. ἐκείνου.

Obs. 4. It was laid down by Dawes, and adopted by almost all commentators, except Hermann and Pflugk, that μεθίεσθαι is always followed by a genitive, and to suit that dictum all the passages in which the acc. follows have been altered. It is true μεθίεσθαι generally has a gen., but in the

[a] Herm. Œ. R. 1014.   [b] Kuster. Verb. Med. 16.
[c] Pflugk. Eur. Alc. 1111. Herm. Electr. 1269. R. P. 734 Dawes Misc. Crit. 238. Elm. Med. 712. Valck. Phœn. 522.

passages above it will be seen (esp. in Med. 734) that the notion of dismissing from oneself is the one required by the sense.

6. The principle laid down (357. 3.), that the person who causes or allows an action to be done, is often conceived and spoken of as if he did it himself, is very frequently applied to middle verbs, with the additional notion of it being done for his especial benefit, so that the subject of the verb has a peculiar personal interest and anxiety therein.

So κείρασθαι[a], ἀνακρίνασθαι, διδάξασθαι, βιάσασθαι &c. i. e. *curo* or *permitto*, *ut quis me κείρει* &c. So γήμασθαι, to give in marriage, πρεσβεύομαι, *curo*, *ut quis in meis* or *mihi* πρεσβεύῃ, κηρυκεύομαι, ταγεύεσθαί τινα, ἄρχομαί τινος, *curo, ut quid* (ἄρχῃ) *primum sit* :—διδάξασθαι παῖδας, to send to be taught (διδάσκειν, to teach); as, Eur. Med. 295 παῖδας περισσῶς ἐκδιδάσκεσθαι σοφούς[b]: παραγράφεσθαι νόμους, *curare, ut leges excerpantur* : ἀρέσασθαί τινα, *curare, ut quis placetur* : Hdt. III. 88 τύπον (*monumentum*) π ο ι η σ ά μ ε ν ο ς λίθινον ἔστησε, having caused to be made: so I. 31 Ἀργεῖοι σφέων εἰκόνας ποιησάμενοι ἀνέθεσαν ἐς Δελφούς : γράφεσθαί τινα, properly, to cause the name of the accused to be entered in the accuser's name before the judge, *nomen differre*, hence to accuse : Hdt. VII. 101 παρέπλεε— ἀπογραφόμενος (sc. νέας), *naves consignari jubens* (100 ἀπέγραφον οἱ γραμματισταί).

Obs. 5. This sense of causing to be done is generally represented as arising from the power of the middle verb, but we see, both in the Greek and other languages, that it is merely a form of expression, (see §. 357. 3.) and applied no less to active than to middle verbs, and therefore cannot be said to arise from the middle verb; though the middle verb somewhat heightens the notion of personal interest in the action.

7. The self generally stands in the same relation to the middle as any other object would to the active verb: or it may be discovered from the context. If the case following the middle verb is in the genitive or dative, as ἐπιτίθεσθαι τοῖς πολεμίοις, the self must be in the acc.; if the case is acc., then the self must be in the genitive or dative, as ἀπωθοῦμαι τοὺς πολεμίους, I drive away the enemy from myself, ἀπωθέω ἀπὸ τοῦδε; ἀμύνομαι τούσδε, I repel these for my own advantage, ἀμύνω τόδε σοι, I drive this away for your advantage.

8. Some middle verbs have assumed a new transitive notion, deduced from or implied in the reflexive notion;

As, σοφίζομαι, I make myself cunning=I deceive: χράομαι, I use: ἐγγυᾶσθαι, to bail some one: ἀφαιρεῖσθαι, to deprive: τίσασθαι, to punish: ἐπίστασθαι, to know: ἀγάλλω, I adorn; ἀγάλλομαι, I adorn, plume myself, am proud of: λανθάνεσθαι, to forget.—(See also 3.)

Obs. 6. When the self stands in the relation of acc. the middle verb is generally intrans.; when as gen. or dat. the verb is generally transitive, or has some transitive force; as, λούομαι, I wash myself, acc.: ἀμύνομαι, I repel for myself=repulse.

a Lobeck Phryn. 319.   b Elm. Med. 290. Ruhnk. Tim. 71.

9. *Deponents.*—Many verbs exist only in the middle voice; and though we cannot discern the exact relation in which the self stands to the active notion of the verb, as the active form is no longer in existence, yet they mostly express notions in which self is very nearly interested: such as δέχομαι, ἡγέομαι, ἥδομαι, μαίνομαι, αἰσθάνομαι, γίγνομαι (*gigno*, Lat.), μάχομαι, ἀσπάζομαι. See vol. i. 216. They are divided as to their sense into middle deponents, such as μαίνομαι, and passive, such as γίγνομαι, I am born.

Remarks on the reflexive force of the Middle Verb.

363. 1. The reflexive sense of the middle is often so weak that it is scarcely discernible by us. It frequently consists in the notion of doing an action in which we are especially interested, for our own good or harm (self as *dativum commodi*), which we do not usually express; as, ῥηξάμενοι φάλαγγας, for their advantage: ποιησάμενος τὰς νῆας, making for himself a navy.

2. Hence sometimes the personal pronoun is used with the middle verb; as, Soph. Œ. R. 1143 ἐμαυτῷ θρεψαίμην: Eur. Hel. 1306 τρύχου σὺ σαυτήν. So Theocr. τί τὺ (for σέ) τάκεαι: Æschines ὑποκρυψάμενοι τοὺς ἑαυτῶν οἰκέτας: Plat. Protag. p. 349 σύγ' ἀναφανδὸν σεαυτὸν ὑποκηρυξάμενος.

3. The use of the reflexive or non-reflexive form often depends directly on the notion in the speaker's mind (*ex animo loquentis*, see 378). So, for example, φέρειν and πορίζειν are not unfrequently used where the middle would be rather expected, the speaker not regarding the action in its reflexive relation to the subject. So Pindar, Ol. VIII. 64 ἐξ ἱερῶν ἀέθλων—ποθεινοτάταν δόξαν φέρειν. So also μισθὸν φέρειν, *mercedem accipere*, as well as μ. φέρεσθαι: Xen. M. S. III. 14, 1 ὄψον φέρειν (φέρεσθαι): Plat. Rep. p. 468. C τἀριστεῖα φέρειν: Æsch. Pers. 197 πέπλους ῥήγνυσιν ἀμφὶ σώματι, on his body: Hdt. V. 40 ἐσάγειν γυναῖκα. And again, the middle form is sometimes used, from the reflexive character of the notion in the speaker's thoughts. So later writers used διακονεῖσθαι, ὑπηρετεῖσθαι (where the earlier writers used the active), to express the reciprocal notion which they conceived to exist in these verbs. Sometimes the middle is used only for rhetorical effect, as Plat. Protag. 324. C τιμωροῦνται καὶ κολάζονται[a].

4. The middle notion is sometimes expressed by the active verb and personal pronoun, as Demosth. p. 22 δύναμιν κατεσκεύασεν ἑαυτῷ. With some verbs this is always the case, as ἀπέκτεινεν ἑαυτόν, not ἀποκτείνεσθαι, ἐπαινεῖν ἑαυτόν, ἀπέσφαξεν ἑαυτόν. Those middle forms, which in other verbs are used both in a passive and middle sense, are in these verbs of course only used passively: ἐπαινεῖσθαι, to be praised, &c.

5. In the Homeric and post-Homeric dialect, there occur many intransitive verbs, especially those which express a perception of the mind or the senses, either in the middle voice only, or in the middle as well as the active; while the later writers used the form in ω; which confirms the notion that the middle form was originally the proper expression of intransitive and reflexive notions. And when the later form in ω arose, it followed that many intransitive verbs were used in both forms, without any difference of sense; as, Il. δ, 331 ἀκούετο λαὸς ἀϋτῆς: 343

---

[a] Stallb. ad loc.

ἀκουάζεσθαι: ὁρᾶσθαι Homer and other poets: Il. ο, 600 ἰδέσθαι: Soph. Trach. 103 ποθουμένᾳ φρενί: Phil. 852 αὐδῶμαι: Il. ο, 622 λαμπόμενος πυρὶ πάντοθεν: φλέγεσθαι and φλέγειν, μέλεσθαι and μέλειν, γηρύεσθαι and γηρύειν, γοάεσθαι and γοᾶν. So we may account for many verbs having some tenses in the middle form, especially the future, as ἀκούω, ἀκούσομαι (see 218); they almost all express an action of the mind or senses. So also πεφυγμένον εἶναι for πεφευγέναι. So κεχάρημαι Aristoph. for κεχάρηκα: κεκλαυμένος Æsch. and Soph.: ἐπιδεδράμημαι Xenoph. Œcon. XVI. for δεδράμηκα, &c. The more limited usage of prose generally adopted but one or the other of such forms, or used both with a difference of meaning. Some are found, however, with both forms, without any such difference, even in Attic prose; as, καλλιερέω -ομαι, εὐδοκιμέω -ομαι, στρατοπεδεύω -ομαι.

6. From this intransitive reflexive force of the middle a great difference of meaning arises between the active and middle sense of some verbs; a secondary sense having been adopted from the reflexive. The active form signifies an action as objective, that is, without any reference to the subject: the middle expresses the same action as subjective, that is, with especial reference to the mind of the subject; as, σκοπεῖν, to look at; σκοπεῖσθαι, to look mentally, to consider: τίθεσθαι, to place before one's mind = to think [a]: λανθάνω, I escape notice; λανθάνομαι, I escape my own notice = forget: θύειν, to sacrifice; θύεσθαι, to sacrifice with some particular object, for oneself: Xen. Anab. VII. 1. 40 ὁ Κοιρατάδης—εἱστήκει παρὰ βωμὸν ἐστεφανωμένος ὡς θύσων, but of Clearchus ἔτυχε γὰρ θυόμενος. So θηρᾶν, θηρᾶσθαι.—διοικεῖν, of external arrangement; διοικεῖσθαι, of mental: ποιεῖν λόγον, to write a speech; ποιεῖσθαι λόγον, to deliver a speech, harangue. So ποιεῖσθαι ὀργήν.—σπένδειν, to pour out a libation; σπένδεσθαι, to make a truce: ὁρίζειν, to bound; one's mind: πειρᾶν χωρίου, to attack a position; πειρᾶσθαί τινος, to experience any thing mentally: προτείνειν, of bodily actions; προτείνεσθαι (mental), to offer: Hdt. IX. 34 προετείνετο οἱ μισθόν ὁρίζεσθαι, to define: σταθμᾶν, to weigh; σταθμᾶσθαι, to weigh any thing in. And this distinction is very marked in those verbs in εύω, which in the active have merely an intransitive sense of being in a state, while the middle signifies to act the part of such a character—to live in such a state; as, βλακεύω, I am idle; βλακεύομαι, I behave idly: πονηρεύω, I am wicked; πονηρεύομαι, I behave wickedly: πολιτεύω, I am a burgher; πολιτεύομαι, I live as a burgher. So in Xen. στρατεύω, I undertake an expedition, of a general or state; -ομαι, I am engaged in an expedition, as a soldier [b]. And as the middle sense of such verbs is the most complete and expressive of the two, it is more commonly used than the active; as, εὐτραπελεύεσθαι, ἀκρατεύεσθαι, ἀνθρωπεύεσθαι, &c.; while others, which only express a state, and not the mental character implied in that state, are used only in the active; as, πρωτεύειν, ἀριστεύειν. So all derivatives from substantives in εύς, as βασιλεύω. The middle derivatives in ίζομαι correspond in meaning to those in εύομαι, as χαριεντίζομαι, ἀκκίζομαι ('Ακκώ, the name of a conceited woman), I dress finely. The derivatives from national names in ίζω have no middle form, as δωρίζω, I dorize. There is a peculiar reflexive sense appropriated to the middle forms of some verbs, which seems to have arisen from the arbitrary usages of language; as, αἰτεῖν, to ask for a gift; αἰτεῖσθαι, for a loan [c]: γαμεῖν, ducere uxorem; γαμεῖσθαι, nubere [d]. So τεκεῖν, properly of mother; τεκέσθαι, properly of father [e]:

[a] Valck. Diatrib. p. 8.
[b] Sturzii Lex. Xenoph. ad voc.
[c] Valck. Amm. 13.
[d] Elm. Med. 257. 593. Valck. Amm. 59.

[e] Herm. Trach. 831. but cf. Æsch. Eum. 660. Eur. Suppl. 1089 and 1092. Herc. 975. Soph. Œd. Col. 1110.

διδάσκειν, to teach ; διδάσκεσθαι, to send to be taught : ἐπιψηφίζειν, to put to the vote ; -εσθαι, to vote.

b. Reciprocal force of Middle.

§. 364. 1. When a middle verb refers to two or more subjects which act on each other, it has a reciprocal sense; as, ἀμείβεσθαι, to answer each other: τύπτονται, they beat each other : διακελεύονται, they exhort one another.

c. Passive force of Middle.

2. From the reflexive receptive sense of the middle (see especially §. 362. Obs. 1.) arose its passive receptive sense, whereby the subject is represented as receiving an action from some one else, and becoming the patient of it ; as, ζημιοῦμαι ὑπό τινος ; τετιμῆσθαι μετ' Ἀχαιοῖς, to receive honour among the Greeks, to be honoured : διδάσκομαι, I receive instruction, that is, I cause some one to teach me ; then pass. ὑπό τινος, I am taught : πείθομαι, I receive persuasion ; then pass. ὑπό τινος, I am persuaded by the arguments of some one.

3. There are especial passive forms for the expression of the passive sense in the Fut. and Aor.; which, however, are in many verbs frequently used as intransitive or reflexive : all other tenses are expressed by the tenses of the middle.

4. As the passive voice has a Future and Aorist of its own, it follows that, as a general rule, the Future and Aorist middle are almost always reflexive or intransitive (see 357. 5.), and only passive in particular cases. See below, Obs. All other middle forms are used equally in a passive sense.

Future and Aor. I. and II. Middle, used apparently in a passive, but really in a middle force.

a. Future middle.   Hdt. VIII. 113 οὗτος οὐκ ἔφη λείψεσθαι τοῦ βασιλῆος, he will not leave the king (λειφθήσεσθαι, be left): Thuc. VI. 18 τὴν πόλιν τρίψεσθαι, will wear itself away : Ibid. 64 οὐ βλάψονται, they will not injure themselves, receive any injury : Xen. Cyr. I. 6, 9 εἰ μὴ ἕξει ἡ στρατιὰ τὰ ἐπιτήδεια, καταλύσεταί σου εὐθὺς ἡ ἀρχή, will fall to pieces ; καταλυθήσεται, will be destroyed : Ibid. II. 1, 23 (προύφηνε) τῶν δεκαδάρχων τοὺς κρατίστους εἰς τὰς τῶν λοχαγῶν χώρας καταστήσεσθαι, to place themselves : Id. Anab. I. 3, 8 ἔλεγε θαρρεῖν, ὡς καταστησομένων τούτων εἰς τὸ δέον, the affair would (arrange itself) happen well : Ibid. V. 4, 17 τοῦτον (τετρωμένον)—ἔπεμπεν, ὅπως θεραπεύσοιτο, that he should take care of himself : Id. Anab. II. 3, 23 τούτου εἴς γε δύναμιν οὐχ ἡττησόμεθα εὖ ποιοῦντες, will not fall short of him : Plat. Rep. p. 376. C θρέψονται (grow up) δὲ δὴ ἡμῖν οὗτοι καὶ παιδευθήσονται τίνα τρόπον ; Id. Crit. p. 54. A σοῦ ζῶντος, βέλτιον θρέψονται καὶ παιδεύσονται, form themselves : Il. ν, 100 τελευτήσεσθαι, complete itself : Thuc. I. 142 κωλύσονται, will hinder themselves : Pind. Ol. VIII. 45 ἄρξεται, parebit. So λέξομαι ; as, Eur. Alc. 322 αὐτίκ' ἐν τοῖς οὐκέτ' οὖσι λέξομαι, will no longer call myself : Id. Or. 440 ψῆφος καθ' ἡμῶν οἴσεται τῇδ' ἡμέρᾳ, will bring itself out : Theocrit. I. 26 αἶγά τε σοι δωσῶ διδυματόκον ἐς τρὶς ἀμέλξαι, ἃ δύ' ἔχοισ' ἐρίφως ποταμέλξεται ἐς δύο πέλλας, give milk.

Obs. The Future middle is sometimes used passively, especially in Attic Greek, when the Fut. pass. is never or rarely used ; the receptive reflexive form being used for the passive receptive form, which, when considered *only* as receptive[a], differ but little; and the poets used the shorter form of the middle Future for the passive: thus, τιμήσεται (Plat. Xen. Soph., &c.), ζημιώσεσθαι, ὠφελήσεσθαι, ἀδικήσεσθαι, μαστιγώσεσθαι, &c.   So φιλήσεαι (Od. a, 123.), στερήσομαι, &c.[b]

b. The Aor. I. never, either in prose or poetry, has a passive sense: the following which seem to be passive will be seen to be in reality middle; Od. θ, 35 κούρω δὲ δύω καὶ πεντήκοντα κρινάσθων (let them divide themselves) κατὰ δῆμον: v. 48 κούρω δὲ κρινθέντε δύω κ. πεντ. (the divided) : Hesiod. Scut. H. 173 κάπροι δοιοὶ ἀπουράμενοι ψυχάς, lost their lives : Pindar. Olymp. VII. 15 εὐθυμάχαν ὄφρα πελώριον ἄνδρα παρ' Ἀλφειῷ στεφανωσάμενον αἰνέσω, *coronam sibi peperit :* Ibid. 81. Id. XII. 17. Nem. VI. 19 : Id. Pyth. IV. 243 ἤλπετο δ' οὐκέτι οἱ κεῖνόν γε πράξασθαι πόνον, *sibi effecturum esse :* Plat. Rep. p. 416. E τὰ δ' ἐπιτήδεια, ὅσων δέονται ἄνδρες ἀθληταὶ πολέμου σώφρονές τε καὶ ἀνδρεῖοι, ταξαμένους παρὰ τῶν ἄλλων πολιτῶν δέχεσθαι μισθὸν φυλακῆς, i. e. *apud se constitu-entes res ad vitam necessarias a reliquis civibus tanquam custodiæ merce-dem accipere :* Theocrit. III. 29 οὐδὲ τὸ τηλέφιλον ποτιμαξάμενον πλατάγησεν, sticking closely, when struck by the hand : Id. VII. 110 εἰ δ' ἄλλως νεύσαις, κατὰ μὲν χρόα πάντ' ὀνύχεσσι δακνόμενος κνάσαιο, allow them to tear your flesh. So Anthol. Epigr. XI. 33 τοίχων ὀρθὰ τιναξαμένων, vibrating ; J a c o b s, *dum parietes illum terræ tremorem et concussionem ita in se recipiebant, ut recti starent.*

§. 365. 1. *c.* The Aor. II. middle, also, is never used passively, and probably was originally distinguished from the Aor. I., in that the Aor. II. had rather an intransitive sense derived from the reflexive, the Aor. I. generally the reflexive or transitive sense ; as, ἐλειψάμην μνημόσυνα, I left for myself memorials ; ἐλιπόμην, I left myself, I remained : ἀνατρεψά-μην, I overturned myself ; ἀνετραπόμην, I fell : Plat. Cratyl. 395. D ἡ πατρὶς αὐτοῦ ὅλη ἀνετράπετο[c].

2. The use of the Aor. II. middle for the passive is only apparent, and arises from the affinity of the intransitive and passive notions : it fre-quently occurs in ἔχω and its compounds ; as[d], Il. η, 247 τῇ δ' ἑβδομάτῃ ῥινῷ σχέτο, stuck : Od. λ, κηληθμῷ δ' ἔσχοντο, were charmed : Id. γ, 284 κατέσχετ' ἐπειγόμενός περ ὁδοῖο, stopped : Hdt. VII. 128 ἐν θωύματι μεγάλῳ ἐνέσχετο, was fixed in great wonder : Id. I. 13 ἐν τελεῖ τούτῳ ἔσχοντο, rested in this end : Pind. Pyth. I. 10 τεαῖς ῥιπαῖσι κατασχόμενος, charmed by : Eur. Hipp. 27 ἰδοῦσα——καρδίας κατέσχετο, fixed her heart upon : Od. o, 384 κατάλεξον, ἠὲ διεπράθετο πόλις, fell.

Remarks on the use of the Middle forms for the Passive notion.

§. 366. It has been laid down above, that probably many of the forms usually called passive are in reality middle, and that the only real passive forms are the Future and Aor. To prove this we may observe, 1st, That the passive notion is nearly allied to the reflexive, as in both the subject is represented as receiving some action to itself—in the reflexive from itself,

a Bernh. 345.
b Monk. Hipp. 1458. Hermsterh. Thom. Mag. p. 852. R. P. Med. 336. Advers. 222. Piers. Mœr. 13, and 367—

though several futures given as passives in these commentators are in reality middle.
c Stallb. Plat. Crat. 395. D.
d Stallb. Plat. Phædr. 244. E.

in the passive from another[a]; so that originally, it is probable, no accurate distinction would be drawn between what may be called the accidents of the notion, or state, while the essence of it, the receiving some action on itself, remained the same. And the passive notion being conceived of as a sort of reflexive, would be represented in the reflexive form. 2nd, Those middle forms, Future and Aor. to which there are corresponding forms in the passive, have properly only a reflexive meaning; 3dly, We see that these are formed from the active by the addition of certain endings, while the really passive tenses are formed differently; so that it is probable that the other tenses usually termed passive, (Pres. Impft. Pft. Plpft.,) formed by the addition of the same endings, and used very frequently indeed in a reflexive sense, are likewise really reflexive forms; their use as passives arising from the affinity between the passive and reflexive notions, and the want of proper passive forms: as the passive notion of receiving from another became more defined, the form whereby it was already expressed still represented it in most of the tenses; while for its more accurate definition in past and future time fresh forms were quickly invented, partly from the middle, partly from the active (§. 367). So the Sclavonic language has no passive but uses the reflexive, and the Sanscrit has a transitive form (*Parasmaipadam*), and a reflexive (*Atmanêpadam*), the endings of which latter are used to express the passive, which is distinguished from the reflexive only by the addition of *ja* to the root of the verb.

C. PASSIVE VOICE.

§. 367. 1. The Aorist and Future of the passive seem to be formed from the active. The Aorist II. passive seems properly to be only an Aorist II. active, after the analogy of verbs in μι, with an intransitive sense, while the Aorist I. was transitive; as, ἐξέπληξα, I frightened; ἐξεπλάγην, I shuddered: ἵστησα, I placed; ἵστην, I stood, which accounts for the fact that few verbs have Aorist II. both active and passive; but as an intransitive notion properly only expresses a state consequent on a completed action, and not the performance or completion of that action, a letter (θ) was inserted in this Aorist II. to signify this performance or completion; as, ἐξεπλάγην, I shuddered; ἐξεπλήχ[θ]ην, I have been frightened: ἵστην, I stood; ἐστά[θ]ην, I have been placed; and from both these Aorists were formed Futures, with the middle endings; as, λιπή-σομαι, λειφθή-σομαι.

Obs. 1. The letter θ, which thus gives the passive force to the intransitive notion, answers to the *t* or *d* of the participle in the cognate languages: *da-tāh*, Sanscrit, from *dā* to give; *da-tus*, Latin; *da-déh*, Persian; *tavi-ts*, *tavi-da*, *tavi-th*, Gothic, from *tau*, to do: so, *fac-tus*, *bren-dur*.

Obs. 2. In the Homeric language, this difference between the Aorist I. and II. passive is yet clearer: Il. γ, 201 ὃς τράφη (grew up) ἐν δήμῳ Ἰθάκης—ἐθρέφθην, was brought up: compare Od. λ, 222. Il. ι, 158 δμηθήτω! *precibus se exorari patiatur!* but Il. β, 860 ἀλλ' ἐδάμη ὑπὸ χερσί, *prostratus jacuit:* compare Il. μ, 403. ο, 521. Il. π, 507 ἐπεὶ λίπεν ἅρματ' ἀνάκτων, left; λειφθῆναι, to be left behind: Hdt. IV. 84 Οἰόβαζος ἐδεήθη Δαρείου—ἵνα παῖδα αὐτῷ καταλειφθῆναι: ἐφάνην, I appeared, is in all writers distinguished from ἐφάνθην, I was shewn forth[b]. But in course of time the difference between these tenses was lost, so that most verbs formed only one or the other to express the passive notion.

[a] Elm. Heracl. 757.   [b] Cf. Soph. Ant. 103.

2. As the middle forms were used for the passive, so these passive forms were in many verbs used to express the reflexive and intransitive notion ; as, τραπῆναι, to turn oneself : φοβηθῆναι, to fear : ὁρμηθῆναι, to pass forth : καταπλαγῆναί τινα, to be alarmed at any one : ἀπαλλαγῆναι, to remove oneself : πορευθῆναι, ἀσκηθῆναι, εὐωχηθῆναι, κοιμηθῆναι, &c. When the Aorist both middle and passive was in use, as ἐχύμην and ἐχύθην, ταρπέσθαι and τερφθῆναι, ὁρμήσασθαι and ὁρμηθῆναι, the intransitive notion might be expressed by either, the passive only by the passive, form.

3. That all such verbs originally expressed these passive notions by the middle form is probable, from the fact, that of many verbs we find a middle form in the Homeric dialect, while the later writers use the passive ; as, ἄγαμαι, ἠγασάμην ep. ; ἠγάσθην Att. : ἔραμαι, ἠρασάμην ep. ; ἠράσθην Att.

Obs. Where both forms are in use, the Ionic and oldest Attic writers preferred the Aor. I., those of the later æra the more harmonious form of Aor. II. pass. [a]

Remarks on the Deponent Verbs.

§. 368. I. Deponent verbs are those verbs which exist only in the middle ; they are divided, as to their form, into deponents middle, and deponents passive, as their Aorist appears either in the middle or passive form ; as, χαρίζομαι, ἐχαρισάμην : ἐνθυμέομαι, ἐνεθυμήθην. See vol. i. §. 245.

2. In many deponent verbs the reflexive sense is apparently lost, at least to us, as we do not know what the active sense of the verb may have expressed ; so that they seem to have an independent transitive or intransitive sense ; as, βιάζομαί τι, ἐργάζομαί τι, δέχομαί τι, though it is probable that there was originally a corresponding active form. Of some verbs we find single instances of the active ; as, βιάζω, δωρέω, μηχανάω, ὠνέω. And some active forms may be traced through the Latin ; as, g i g n o, γίγνω, γίγνομαι.

3. From this original active form or active sense of the deponents it arose that many deponents have a passive meaning, corresponding to this existing or implied active notion, especially in the Pft., and some also a passive form of the Aor. I., besides the Aor. I. middle. So of the verbs mentioned in No. 1. we find βιάζομαι, βεβίασμαι, used passively : Hdt. VIII. 85 χώρη οἱ ἐδωρήθη πολλή (compare Soph. Aj. 1029[b] ἐδωρησάμην, I presented) : Id. V. 90 τὰ ἐκ τῶν Ἀλκμαιωνιδέων ἐς τὴν Πυθίην μεμηχανημένα, compare Demosth. p. 847, 10 : Plat. Phæd. p. 69. B ὠνούμενά τε καὶ πιπρασκόμενα [c] : Id. Soph. p. 224. A ὠνηθείσαν ; also, ἐωνῆσθαι. We subjoin also the following instances of passive forms of deponent verbs :

a. Pft. and Plpft. ἐργασμένα Hdt. VII. 53. Attic also, εἴργασμαι ; Hdt. I. 123 τάδε οἱ κατέργαστο : immediately afterwards, κατεργασμένου δέ οἱ τούτου, and κατεργασμένων τῶν πρηγμάτων, compare IV. 66 : Plat. Legg. p. 710. D πάντα ἀπείργασται τῷ θεῷ : Hdt. I. 207 χωρὶς τοῦ ἀπηγημένου, *præter id, quod expositum est*, compare IX. 26 : Id. II. 78. and 36 μεμιμημένος, *ad imitationem expressus :* οἰκεῖσθαι in Herodotus, and sometimes in other authors, means to dwell (compare Hdt. III. 91. 96. 97 : Thuc. V. 83 : Eur. Iph. A. 710), but Hdt. VII. 22 ὁ γὰρ Ἄθως ἐστὶ ὄρος μέγα — οἰκημένον ὑπὸ ἀνθρώπων (just before οἱ περὶ τὸν Ἄθων κατοικημένοι) : Thuc. VII. 70 κεκτημένος : Id. III. 61 ᾐτιαμένος : Plat. Gorg. p. 453. D ἀπεκέκριτο : Id. Crat. p. 404. sq. A εὖ ἐντε-

---

a R. P. Phœn. 986. and Valck. Phœn. 979.   b Ellendt Lex. Soph. ad voc.
                       c Stallb. ad loc.

θυμημένον, well considered: Id. Phædr. p. 279. C ἐμοὶ μὲν γὰρ μετρίως ηὖκται: Demosth. 576. 15 ἐσκεμμένα καὶ παρεσκευασμένα πάντα λέγω (though shortly afterwards, οὐχ ὁ ἐσκεμμένος οὐδ᾽ ὁ μεριμνήσας): λελωβῆσθαι ·Plat. Rep. 611. B.

b. A o r i s t ⁱ. ἀμιλληθέντα; Eur. Phœnix Fr. IV. 2 ὠνηθέν: Plat. Legg. 850. A. Soph. 224. A: Hdt. IX. 108 κατεργασθῆναι: Id. VII. 144 (νῆες) οὐκ ἐχρήσθησαν, adhibitæ sunt: Demosth. 519. 29. χρησθῇ [b]: Soph. Aj. 216 ἀπελωβήθη: Id. Phil. 330 ἐξελωβήθην; λωβηθῆναι. Plat. Men. 91. C: καταδερχθῆναι Pindar. Many deponent verbs have both the passive and middle Aorist, of which the passive has a passive sense, though not always; as for instance, μέμψασθαι and μεμφθῆναι do not differ in their meaning. But in the following this distinction regularly obtains: ἐδεξάμην, excepi; ἐδέχθην, exceptus sum (though Eur. Herc. 757 ὑποδεχθείς for the midd.): ἐβιασάμην, coëgi; ἐβιάσθην, coactus sum: ἐκτησάμην, mihi comparavi; ἐκτήθην, comparatus sum: ἰάσασθαι, sanare (Thuc. I. 123.); ἰαθῆναι, sanari (Hippocr.): θεάσασθαι, spectare; τὸ θεαθέν, the spectacle (Thuc. III. 38.): ὀλοφύρασθαι, to lament; ὀλοφυρθῆναι, to be lamented: λογίσασθαι, to reckon; ἐλογίσθην always pass.: αἰκίσασθαι, αἰκισθῆναι pass.: ἀκέσασθαι, ἀκεσθῆναι pass.: ἀποκρίνασθαι, to answer; ἀποκριθῆναι, to be divided; but in N. T. used for answered.

c. Present and Imperfect in very few verbs; as βιάζεσθαι frequently in Thucyd. and others[c]: προσεδέχετο Thucyd. IV. 19, &c.

d. The Future also very rarely, as Soph. Trach. 1220 ἐργασθήσεται: ἀπωνηθήσεται Bekk. Anecd. 432, 16[d].

Obs. In the decline of the language after the time of Aristotle, when the convenience of the form was rather looked to than the accuracy of the notion, the use of the middle in the passive sense was more extended.

Verbum finitum and infinitum.

§. 369. 1. In every verb the Greek language distinguishes the relations of person, time, and mode of expression, by the personal, temporal, modal forms.   When a verb is in one of these it is called *verbum finitum*.

2. When it assumes the form of a substantive (infinitive), or of an adjective (participle), it is called *infinitum.*

Unity of a Sentence.

§. 370. 1. The unity of a sentence consists in the relation in which a verbal notion of an action, or state (verb or adjective), stands to a substantival notion of a person, or thing, by means of which they form one thought[e].

Obs. 1. There are three relations in which a verbal (or adjectival) and a substantival notion may stand to one another: 1. the *predicative*, where the verbal or adjectival notion is referred to the substantive, so as to form one thought, τὸ ῥόδον θάλλει, τὸ ῥόδον ἐστι καλόν: 2. where the verbal or adjectival notion is referred to the substantive so as to form one thought

a Elm. Heracl. 757.

b Compare Herm. Ant. 23.   Ellendt χράομαι and χρῄζω.

c Ellendt Lex. Soph. ad voc. Toup. Longin. 365.

d Bernh. 341.

e Plato Soph. 262. B. οὐκοῦν ἐξ ὀνομάτων μὲν μόνων συνεχῶς λεγομένων οὐκ ἔστι ποτὲ λόγος, οὐδ᾽ αὖ ῥημάτων χωρὶς ὀνομάτων λεχθέντων.

(the *attributive*), θάλλον, καλὸν ῥόδον: 3. where the substantival notion is referred to the verbal, so as to form one thought (the *objective*), θάλλει ἐν τῷ κήπῳ: παίει τὸν παῖδα.

Obs. 2. The principal notion in the sentence is the one which grammatically depends on the other; in the predicative and attributive relation the verb or adjective, in the objective the substantive: and the word expressing this principal notion generally conveys by its inflexions the parcular nature of the relation between the two notions.

2. In all these relations the verbal and substantival notions differing from each other, form by these mutual relations a new complete thought: and as the dependent sentences are only substantival, adjectival, or adverbial, notions, expressed by many instead of one word, these same relations may exist between a leading word and one or more of these dependent sentences; as, ὁ ἀνὴρ (ὃν εἶδες) ἔφη: ὁ ὑπὸ σοῦ ὀφθεὶς ἀνὴρ ἀπήγγειλεν ὅτι ὁ Κῦρος ἐνίκησεν, sc. ἀπήγγειλε τὴν τοῦ Κύρου νίκην.

Obs. In combinations where two verbal forms, θαυμάζων εἶπε, or two substantival forms, as οἱ ἐν τῷ οὐρανῷ ἀστέρες, come together, the sentence is really composed of a verbal or adjectival and a substantival notion; as, θαυμάζων εἶπε = εἶπε μετὰ θαύματος: οἱ ἐν τῷ οὐρανῷ ἀστέρες = οἱ ἐν οὐρανῷ ὄντες (adjectival).

SYNTAX OF THE SIMPLE SENTENCE.

CHAP. I.

Of the Elements of a simple Sentence.

371. 1. In every thought there are three elements; two, as it were, the materials of the thought—the verbal and substantival notions; the third a mental act connecting the two, determining the connection between them. The verbal notion is expressed in language by the root of the verb, or an adjective derived from the root; the substantival notion by the substantive; the correspondence and connection between them by the personal forms of the verb, or the formal word εἶναι (*copula*) with an adjective; and the relation in which the verbal notion stands to the person speaking by the tenses and moods.

2. The verbal notion is called t h e   p r e d i c a t e, the thing spoken of another—*id quod prædicatum est.* The substantival notion, as the thing on which the verbal notion is as it were placed, is called t h e s u b j e c t—*id quod prædicato subjectum est.* The predicate is the essential part of the sentence, that which gives a character to it

the subject is subordinate to it, and can therefore be implied in the inflected forms of the verb, as δίδωμι, I give. So every finite form of the verb can stand as a perfect sentence, as γράφομεν: the root γράφ- expressing the predicate, and the inflexion ομεν both the subject, and the connexion between them.

3. As any sentence may either declare a fact, as τὸ ῥόδον θάλλει, ask a question, as τίς οἶδεν; or express a desire or wish, as γράφε, ἴωμεν, sentences are divided into categorical, interrogative, and imperative.

A. SUBJECT.

§. 372. 1. The subject is always

a. A substantive, or substantival pronoun: τὸ ῥόδον θάλλει: τρεῖς ἦλθον: ἐγὼ γράφω.

b. An adjective, used elliptically as a substantive: ὁ σόφος διδάσκει.

c. An adverb with the article, which have elliptically the force of a substantive; as, οἱ ἄνω ἀνέστησαν.

d. An infinitive, with or without the article, and with or without an objective case; as, διδάσκειν, or τὸ διδάσκειν, or τὸ διδασκειν τοὺς παῖδας—συμφέρει.

e. Any part of speech, or letter, or syllable, &c. not representing any notion, but considered merely as a combination of lines or letters; as, τὸ τύπτειν: τὸ Α: τὸ νῦν: τὸ " εἰ τοῦτο γενῆται" Ὁμηρικόν ἐστιν.

2. The subject is in the nominative case, as the relation of the sentence consists in the predicate being referred to the substantive, not the substantive to the predicate: and therefore the verb is inflected, not the substantive; as, τὸ ῥόδον θάλλει: ὁ ἄνθρωπος θνητός ἐστιν.

Obs. 1. The subject is sometimes expressed by the neuter article τό or τά, with the genitive plural of the substantive; as, Soph. Phil. 497 τὰ τῶν διακόνων = διάκονοι.

Obs. 2. In uncertain and distributive definitions of number, the subject is elliptically expressed by a preposition and the case of the numeral; as, εἰς τέσσαρας ἦσαν: Xen. Cyr. VIII. 3, 9 ἔστασαν δὲ πρῶτον μὲν τῶν δορυφόρων εἰς τετρακισχιλίους, ἔμπροσθεν δὲ τῶν πυλῶν εἰς τέσσαρας, δισχίλιοι δὲ ἑκατέρωθεν τῶν πυλῶν. Hence with the so called genitive absolute: Xen. Hell. 4, 5 ἤδη συνειλεγμένων εἰς τὴν Φυλὴν περὶ ἑπτακοσίους. So, καθ' ἑκάστους, *singuli,* κατὰ ἔθνη, *singulæ gentes :* Thuc. I. 3 καθ' ἕκαστους ἤδη τῇ ὁμιλίᾳ μᾶλλον καλεῖσθαι Ἕλληνας.

3. When the active form of the transitive verb is changed to the passive, if the transitive had an object in the accusative, this object becomes the subject of the passive verb in the nominative, and the former subject is put in the genitive, with prepos. ὑπό, παρά, πρός, διά: or sometimes in the instrumental dative; as, ὁ Ἀχιλλεὺς ἐφόνευσε τὸν Ἕκτορα, ὁ Ἕκτωρ ἐφονεύθη ὑπὸ τοῦ Ἀχιλλέως.

4. As in Greek the passive notion arises from the semi-reflexive notion of receiving something from some one else, it happens that in the passive voice of intransitive verbs also the same interchange between the subject and object takes place, while in languages which have only the proper passive form the genitive or dative remains, and the passive verb is used as an impersonal, as in Lat. *invidetur alicui;* act. *invidere alicui.* But in Greek, φθονοῦμαι ὑπό τινος (φθονεῖν τινι, *invidere alicui*), I receive envy from some one: πιστεύομαι and ἀπιστοῦμαι ὑπό τινος (πιστεύειν and ἀπιστεῖν τινι): Hdt. VII. 144 αἱ δὲ νῆες — οὐκ ἐχρήσθησαν (χρῆσθαί τινι): Thuc. I. 82 ἡμεῖς ὑπ' Ἀθηναίων ἐπιβουλευόμεθα (ἐπιβουλεύειν τινί): Plat. Rep. p. 417. B καὶ ἐπιβουλεύοντες, καὶ ἐπιβουλευόμενοι διάξουσι πάντα τὸν βίον: Thuc. V. 111 ἀλλ' ὑμῶν τὰ μὲν ἰσχυρότατα ἐλπιζόμενα μέλλεται, as Demosth. p. 50, 37 ἐν ὅσῳ ταῦτα μέλλεται: ubi v. Bremi. Plat. Rep. p. 551. A ἀσκεῖται δὴ τὸ ἀεὶ τιμώμενον, ἀμελεῖται δὲ τὸ ἀτιμαζόμενον: Xen. M. S. IV. 2, 33 Παλαμήδην πάντες ὑμνοῦσιν, ὡς διὰ σοφίαν φθονηθεὶς ὑπὸ τοῦ Ὀδυσσέως ἀπώλετο. So, καταψηφίζομαι θανάτου (καταψηφίζομαί τινος θάνατον), ἄρχομαι, κρατοῦμαι, ἡγεμονεύομαι, καταφρονοῦμαι ὑπό τινος (ἄρχειν, κρατεῖν, ἡγεμονεύειν, καταφρονεῖν τινος), ἐπιχειροῦμαι (ἐπιχειρεῖν τινι).

Ellipse of the Subject.

§. 373. The subject, as not being the principal member of the sentence, is sometimes not expressed by any especial word, though it may be easily supplied from the context, or from the elliptical usages of every day conversation; as, κακῶς ἔχει, it is ill, that is, this which you say.

1. The subject is indefinite, and must be conceived to be a neuter; as, καλῶς ἔχει, it is well: Xen. M. S. I. 2, 32 ἐδήλωσε δέ, it showed itself.

2. The subject is definite, and is implied in the predicate: as early as Homer; as, Od. φ, 142 ὄρνυσθ' ἐξείης ἐπιδέξια πάντες ἑταῖροι, ἀρξάμενοι τοῦ χώρου, ὅθεν τέ περ οἰνοχοεύει (sc. ὁ οἰνοχόος): Hdt. II. 47 θυσίη δὲ ἥδε τῶν ὑῶν τῇ Σελήνῃ ποιέεται· ἐπεὰν θύσῃ (sc. ὁ θυτήρ), τὴν οὐρὴν ἄκρην καὶ τὸν σπλῆνα καὶ τὸν ἐπίπλοον — ἐκάλυψε — τῇ πιμελῇ: Xen. Anab. III. 4, 36 ἐπεὶ δὲ ἐγίγνωσκον αὐτοὺς οἱ Ἕλληνες βουλομένους ἀπιέναι καὶ διαγγελλομένους, ἐκήρυξε (sc. ὁ κῆρυξ) τοῖς Ἕλλησι παρασκευάσασθαι: Ibid. VI. 5, 25 παρηγγέλλετο δὲ τὰ μὲν δόρατα ἐπὶ τὸν δεξιὸν ὦμον ἔχειν, ἕως σημαίνοι τῇ σάλπιγγι (sc. ὁ σαλπιγκτής). So ἐσάλπιγξεν in Xen. So we must explain

ὕει, νίφει, βροντᾷ, ἀστράπτει (sc. ὁ Ζεύς, ὁ θεός, who, as
being the only power which could perform this action, was, in the
notion of the ancients, implied in the verb). So Thuc. V. 52 ἔσεισε:
Xen. Cyr. IV. 5, 5 συσκοτάζει. Sometimes the subject was expressed; as, Il. μ, 25 ὗε δ᾽ ἄρα Ζεὺς συνεχές: Hdt. III. 117 τὸν
μὲν γὰρ χειμῶνα ὗει σφι ὁ θεός.

3. The subject is not implied in the predicate, but is easily supplied from the context: Hdt. III. 82 ἐξ ὧν στάσιες ἐγγίνονται, ἐκ
δὲ τῶν στασίων φόνος, ἐκ δὲ τοῦ φόνου ἀπέβη (sc. τὰ πρήγματα) ἐς
μουναρχίην. So in expressions of time; as, ἦν ἐγγὺς ἡλίου δυσμῶν
(sc. ἡ ἡμέρα). So in certain phrases the word θεός was omitted;
as, παρέχει μοι (sc. ὁ θεός), the god affords me the opportunity, per-
mits: Hdt. III. 73 ἡμῖν παρέξει ἀνασώσασθαι τὴν ἀρχήν. Then,
through the familiar and frequent use of this expression, it came to
have the force of the Latin *licet*: hence the accusative παρέχον,
quum liceat, or *liceret*; as, Hdt. V. 49 παρέχον (ὑμῖν) τῆς Ἀσίης
πάσης ἄρχειν. So προσημαίνει (sc. ὁ θεός): Hdt. VI. 27 φιλέει
δέ κως προσημαίνειν, εὖτ᾽ ἂν μέλλῃ μεγάλα κακὰ ἢ πόλι ἢ ἔθνεϊ
ἔσεσθαι (with the subject: Ibid. extr. ταῦτα μέν σφι σημήϊα ὁ θεὸς
προέδεξε). In expressions such as φασί, λέγουσι, &c. the subject
ἄνθρωποι is regularly omitted as intelligible of itself. So also in
the New Testament, προφητής, ἡ γραφή, πνεῦμα, &c. before φησί, λέγει, μαρτυρεῖ[a]. So also χρή, *oportet*, sc. ὁ θεός, ἡ πυθίη χρῇ, Ion.
χρᾷ (Hdt.), the god, the oracle, declares.

4. Frequently the subject is implied in and must be supplied from
some word in the sentence: Hdt. IX. 8 τὸν Ἰσθμὸν ἐτείχεον καί σφι
ἦν πρὸς τέλεϊ (sc. τὸ τεῖχος): Xen. Cyr. II. 4, 24 πορεύσομαι εὐθὺς πρὸς
τὰ βασίλεια, καὶ ἢν μὲν ἀνθίστηται (sc. ὁ βασιλεύς). Sometimes the
subject so implied is signified by a pronoun; as, Eur. Hec. 21 ἐπεὶ
δὲ Τροία θ᾽ Ἕκτορός τ᾽ ἀπόλλυται ψυχή, πατρῷα θ᾽ ἑστία κατεσκάφη
αὐτὸς δὲ (sc. πατήρ) βωμῷ πρὸς θεοδμήτῳ πίτνει: ubi v. Pflugk.
So ἕκαστος, where οὐδὲ εἷς precedes; as, Plat. Symp. 192. E οὐδ᾽ ἂν εἷς
ἐξαρνηθείη—ἀλλ᾽ οἴοιτ᾽ ἂν (sc. ἕκαστος)[b]. So also with other cases:
Il. ι, 383 Θῆβαι, αἵ θ᾽ ἑκατόμπυλοί εἰσι, διηκόσιοι δ᾽ ἀν᾽ ἑκάστην (sc. πύλην) ἀνέρες εἰσοιχνεῦσι: Od. ξ, 434 καὶ τὰ μὲν ἕπταχα
πάντα διεμοιρᾶτο δαΐζων· τὴν μὲν ἴαν (sc. μοῖραν) Νύμφῃσι
καὶ Ἑρμῇ, Μαιάδος υἱεῖ, θῆκεν ἐπευξάμενος, τὰς δ᾽ ἄλλας νεῖμεν
ἑκάστῳ: Hdt. IV. 110 ἐντυχοῦσαι δὲ πρώτῳ ἱπποφορβίῳ τοῦτο
διήρπασαν· καὶ ἐπὶ τούτων (sc. τῶν ἵππων) ἱππαζόμεναι ἐληΐζοντο
τὰ τῶν Σκυθέων: Id. VII. 34 ἐγεφύρουν—, τὴν μὲν (sc. γέφυραν): Aristoph. Plut. 502 πολλοὶ πλουτοῦσι—ἀδίκως αὐτὰ

---

[a] Viner. Gramm. p. 471.   [b] Stallb. ad loc.

(χρήματα, which is implied in πλουτοῦσι) συλλέγουσι : Eur. Phœn.
12 καλοῦσι δ' Ἰοκάστην με· τοῦτο (sc. ὄνομα, which is implied
in καλοῦσι) γὰρ πατὴρ ἔθετο : Plat. Leg. p. 864. D παιδιᾷ
χρώμενος, οὐδέν πω τῶν τοιούτων (sc. παίδων) διαφέρων : Id.
Phæd. p. 57. C πρὶν ἂν — ἀφίκηται τὸ πλοῖον —· τοῦτο δ'
ἐνίοτε ἐν πολλῷ χρόνῳ γίγνεται, ὅταν τύχωσιν ἄνεμοι ἀπολαβόντες
αὐτοὺς (sc. τοὺς πλέοντας) : ubi v. Stallbaum.

Obs. 1. So we frequently find a demonstrative pronoun in the neuter,
(sometimes also in the masculine,) without any substantive to which it
may be referred.   It supplies the place of a substantival notion implied in
some óne of the preceding words : Thuc. I. 122 οἱ τὴν Ἑλλάδα ἠλευθέρωσαν·
ἡμεῖς δὲ οὐδ' ἡμῖν αὐτοῖς βεβαιοῦμεν αὐτό (sc. τὴν ἐλευθερίαν) : Hdt. V. 92, 2
ἦν ὀλιγαρχίη, καὶ οὗτοι Βακχιάδαι καλεύμενοι ἔνεμον τὴν πόλιν : Plat. Phileb.
p. 58. E αἱ πολλαὶ τέχναι καὶ ὅσαι περὶ ταῦτα πεπόηνται : Rep. p. 422. B εἰς
πύκτης ὡς οἱόντε κάλλιστα ἐπὶ τοῦτο παρεσκευασμένος : cf. Xen. Cyr. III. 3, 50.
These demonstr. τοῦτο, ταῦτα, signify *of this sort.*   So the Platonic αὐτό
(sometimes τοῦτο) signifying abstracts.—Compare Cicero Tusc. I. 2, 4 *in
Græcia* m u s i c i *floruerunt, discebantque* i d *omnes.*

5. The indefinite pronoun τὶς (*one*) is frequently omitted.   The
very fact of the verb being without any expressed subject suggesting the indefinite τὶς, in answer as it were to the question
τίς ; who !   So Il. ν, 287 οὐδέ κεν ἔνθα τεόν γε μένος καὶ χεῖρας
ὄνοιτο (sc. τὶς) : Eur. Or. 418 μισούμεθ' οὕτως, ὥστε μὴ προσ-
εννέπειν (sc. τινά, *ut, nemo (nos) alloquatur*) : Plat. Gorg.
p. 456. D καὶ γὰρ τῇ ἄλλῃ ἀγωνίᾳ οὐ τούτου ἕνεκα δεῖ πρὸς ἅπαντας
χρῆσθαι ἀνθρώπους, ὅτι ἔμαθε (sc. τὶς) πυκτεύειν τε καὶ παγκρατιά-
ζειν καὶ ἐν ὅπλοις μάχεσθαι[a] : Id. Crit. p. 49. C οὔτε ἄρα ἀνταδι-
κεῖν δεῖ οὔτε κακῶς ποιεῖν οὐδένα ἀνθρώπων, οὐδ' ἂν ὁτιοῦν πάσχῃ
ὑπ' αὐτῶν : Id. Rep. 347. C[b] :   Id. Apol. p. 29. B ἡ τοῦ οἴεσθαι
εἰδέναι (ἀμαθία), ἃ οὐκ οἶδεν[c] : Æsch. Choeph. 592 αἰγίδων φράσαι
κότον : cf. Soph. Œ. R. 315[d]. and 611.   So often with infinitive ;
but when a participle is so used, as Eur. Med. 1018 κούφως φέρειν χρὴ
θνητὸν ὄντα συμφοράς, there is no ellipse of τινά, as the participle
must be considered as the subject.   This ellipse is used also in
Latin, Cic. de Orat. I. 8. 30 *neque vero mihi quidquam—præstabilius
videtur, quam posse dicendo tenere hominum cœtus, mentes allicere,
voluntates impellere, quo* v e l i t, *unde autem* v e l i t, *deducere.*

Obs. 2. Impersonal verbs, (in English, verbs with the indefinite *it,*) the
Greek language has not, since the expressions δεῖ, δοκεῖ, πρέπει, ἔξεστι,
ἐνδέχεται, ἔχει λόγον, λέγεται, were considered as personal ; the infinitive,
or substantival sentence, supplying the place of subject.   The indefinite
pronoun *one, they,* is in Greek expressed by τὶς or the III. plural, as λέγουσι, φασί,—or III. singular passive, λέγεται,—or II. singular, as φαίης ἄν.

Obs. 3. The real subject is sometimes supplied by τὶς, when there

---

[a] Stallb. ad loc.   [b] Ibid. ad loc.   [c] Ibid. ad loc.   [d] See Herm. ad loc.

is some reason for not naming expressly the person: Æsch. Choeph. 58 φοβεῖται δέ τις (sc. Clytæmnestra): Ag. 369 οὐκ ἔφα τίς. This also occurs with the object; as, Æsch. Eumen. 390 σπευδόμεναι δ᾽ ἀφελεῖν τινα τάσδε μερίμνας (sc. Jupiter).

B. PREDICATE.

§. 374. The predicate is always a verbal notion, and hence is expressed either

a. By a verb; as, τὸ ῥόδον θάλλει.

b. Or by an adjective. or substantive, with εἶναι, which, as connecting the predicate and subject, is called the copula; as, ὁ ἄνθρωπος θνητός ἐστιν: ὁ Κῦρος ἦν βασιλεύς.

c. Or a numeral with εἶναι; as, σὺ ἦς πάντων πρῶτος.

d. Sometimes by a pronoun with εἶναι; as, τοῦτο τὸ πρᾶγμά ἐστι τόδε: to this pronoun we must supply an essential word; as, τόδε τὸ πρᾶγμα.

Remarks on the Predicative Adjective, and the Copula εἶναι.

§. 375. 1. The predicate was originally expressed by a verb. On the origin of the predicative force of adjectives, see §. 356. 2.

2. The predicative adjective or substantive is capable of fully expressing the verbal notion, inasmuch as the relations of person, time, and mood are supplied by the inflexions of the verb εἶναι; as, εὐδαίμων εἰμί=εὐδαιμονέ-ω, εὐδαίμων εἶ=εὐδαιμον-εῖς: this copula expresses no real notion, but only the mental act whereby the two material notions are united; Man (is) mortal: hence it is called *verbum abstractum.*

3. We must distinguish between the formal sense of this verb and its essential sense, εἶναι, *to be,* expressing existence; as, ἔστι θεός, there is a God=θεός ἐστι ὤν: Hdt. III. 105 τοῦ θείου ἡ προνοίη—ἔστιν ἐοῦσα σοφή. In this essential sense, it may, like any other verb, be joined to an adverb, by which the existence, &c. is more clearly defined: Il. ξ, 130. sq. οὐδὲ γὰρ οὐδὲ Δρύαντος υἱὸς, κρατερὸς Λυκόοργος, δὴν ἦν, was (=lived) long: Il. η, 424 διαγνῶναι χαλεπῶς ἦν (*difficile sese habebat*) ἄνδρι ἕκαστον: Il. ι, 551 Κουρήτεσσι κακῶς ἦν: Il. λ, 762 ὧς ἔον (*sic eram*), εἴποτ᾽ ἔην γε μετ᾽ ἀνδράσιν! Hdt. III. 152 δεινῶς ἔσαν ἐν φυλακῇσι οἱ Βαβυλώνιοι, *cum diligentia versabantur in custodia:* Isocr. Paneg. c. I. §. 5 ὥστ᾽ ἤδη μάτην εἶναι τὰ μεμνῆσθαι περὶ αὐτῶν: Eur. Hec. 284 κἀγὼ γὰρ ἦν πόт᾽, ἀλλὰ νῦν οὐκ εἰμ᾽ ἔτι: Ibid. 626 ἄλλως (sc. ἐστὶ) φροντίδων βουλεύματα, *frustra sunt:* Ibid. 731 εἴ τι τῶνδ᾽ ἐστὶν καλῶς. So, ὁ Σωκράτης ἦν ἀεὶ σὺν τοῖς νέοις: so καλῶς, κακῶς ἔστι &c. So in Latin, Terent. Andr. I. 1, 35 *Sic vita erat.* The copula εἶναι is sometimes supplied by ὑπάρχειν, γίγνεσθαι, φῦναι, κυρεῖν (poet.), τυγχάνειν: hence the verbs γίγνεσθαι and φῦναι are found very frequently with adverbs, especially local and intensive, such as δίχα, χωρίς, ἐκάς, ἐγγύς: ἅλις, μᾶλλον, μάλιστα, οὐχ ἥκιστα &c.; as, Hdt. VI. 109 τοῖσι δὲ Ἀθηναίων στρατηγοῖσι ἐγίνοντο δίχα αἱ γνῶμαι: Thuc. IV. 61 οὐ γὰρ τοῖς ἔθνεσιν, ὅτι δίχα πέφυκε, τοῦ ἑτέρου ἔχθει προσίασιν: Demosth. p. 34. princ. τὰ δὲ πράγματα πολλάκις οὐχ οὕτω πέφυκεν: πέφυκε has, especially in Aristotle, the sense of, it is by nature: ταῦτα οὐχ οὕτως πέφυκε, this is not the nature of things: ἀγαθὸν πέφυκε, is by nature a good.

4. To give emphasis to the predicate, the verbal form is resolved into

the participle and εἶναι; this is rather poetical, though it is found also in prose, especially in Hdt.: Il. ε, 873 τετληότες εἰμέν : Æsch. Ag. 1178 καὶ μὲν ὁ χρησμὸς οὐκέτ' ἐκ καλυμμάτων ἔσται δεδορκὼς νεογάμου νύμφης δίκην: Eur. Alc. 124 δοδορκὼς ἦν: Soph. Phil. 1219 στείχων ἂν ἦν: Eur. Cycl. 381 πῶς, ὦ ταλαίπωρ', ἦτε πάσχοντες τάδε; Id. Hec. 117 ἢν σπεύδων[a] : Hdt. III. 99 ἀπαρνεόμενός ἐστι : Id. IX. 51 ἡ δέ (νῆσός) ἐστι ἀπὸ τοῦ Ἀσωποῦ δέκα σταδίους ἀπέχουσα: Plat. Legg. p. 860. E εἰ ταῦτα οὕτως ἔχοντά ἐστιν : Demosth. p. 11, 7 ταῦτ' ἂν ἐγνωκότες ἦσαν, compare p. 13, 14 : Id. p. 853, 29 ταῦτ' οὕτως ἔχοντ' ἐστίν : Hdt. III. 64 ἀπολωλεκὼς εἴη : so also with participles; Il. τ, 80 ἐπιστάμενόν περ ἐόντα. In an exactly similar way the verbs γίγνεσθαι and πέλεσθαι (poet.) are found with the participle ; as, Hdt. III. 76 ἐν τῇ ὁδῷ μέσῃ στείχοντες ἐγίνοντο.

5. The predicate is sometimes expressed by a verb and an adjective together, the verb expressing an action, and the adjective a state or effect consequent on the action; as, Soph. Œ. R. 166 ἠνύσατε ἐκτοπίαν φλόγα πήματος = ἐξετοπίσατε: Œ. C. 119 ποῦ κυρεῖ ἐκτόπιος συθείς; *quo secessit*[b] : Thuc. IV. 17 τοὺς δὲ λόγους μακροτέρους παρὰ τὸ εἰωθὸς οὐ μηκυνοῦμεν, i. e. so as to be longer. So also a substantive; as, ποιεῖσθαι λείαν χώραν = ληΐζεσθαι.

Ellipse of the Copula εἶναι.

§. 376. The predicate, as being the essential part of the sentence, can never be omitted ; but when it is expressed by the periphrasis with εἶναι, this copula, as expressing only the verbal relations, may be omitted when the time is present ; and sometimes εἶναι is omitted when it is the substantive verb. The following are the most frequent cases of this ellipse :

a. In general sentences, proverbs, &c. which in all languages take the shortest and most energetic forms : Eur. Or. 330 ὁ μέγας ὄλβος οὐ μόνιμος ἐν βροτοῖς : Ibid. 969 βροτῶν δ' ὁ πᾶς ἀστάθμητος αἰών : Xen. Cyr. II. 4, 27 στρατιᾷ γὰρ ἡ ῥᾴστη (ὁδὸς) ταχίστη. And in the first person plural: Æsch. Eumen. 382 εὐμήχανοι δὲ καὶ τέλειοι &c. (sc. ἔσμεν).

b. Very commonly with the verbal adjectives in τέος, and in other expressions of *necessity*, *duty*, as ἀνάγκη, χρεών, θέμις, εἰκός : Demosth. p. 129, 70 ἡμῖν γ' ὑπὲρ τῆς ἐλευθερίας ἀγωνιστέον. So frequently in Latin : Ibid. p. 112, 7 ἀνάγκη φυλάττεσθαι καὶ διορθοῦσθαι περὶ τούτου : Eur. Hec. 1275 καὶ σὴν γ' ἀνάγκη παῖδα Κασάνδραν θανεῖν. Also in certain formulas with καιρός and ὥρα, ἐστι is omitted ; as, ὥρα ἤδη ἀπιέναι.

c. With certain adjectives; as, ἕτοιμος, πρόθυμος, φροῦδος, οἷός τε, δυνατός, ῥᾴδιον, χαλεπόν : also in the constructions by attraction ; θαυμαστὸν ὅσον, *mirum quantum*, ἀμήχανον ὅσον, *immane quantum* : Eur. Med. 612 ἕτοιμος ἀφθόνῳ δοῦναι χερί : Id. Hel. 1543 εἰδέναι πρόθυμος

---

[a] See Pflugk ad Eur. Hec. 1179.   [b] Ellendt Lex. Soph. ad v. ἐκτόπιος.

(so. εἰμί) : Plat. Phædr. p. 252. A (ἡ ψυχὴ) δουλεύειν ἑτοίμη: Demosth. p. 48, 29 ἐγὼ — πάσχειν ὁτιοῦν ἕτοιμος : cf. Id. p. 111, 4. So φροῦδος γὰρ ὁ ἀνήρ, the man is gone; φροῦδα πάντα, all is gone.

d. Also in relative sentences, both when εἶναι is the copulative, and when the substantive verb : Od. v, 298 αἱ κατὰ δώματ' Ὀδυσσῆος θεῖοιο : Il. τ, 43 οἵ τε κυβερνῆται καὶ ἔχον οἰκῆϊα νηῶν. Regularly in the constructions by attraction : οὐδεὶς ὅς or ὅστις οὐ (*nemo non*); as, Soph. Œ. R. 372 οὐδεὶς ὃς οὐχὶ τῶνδ' ὀνειδιεῖ τάχα. See *Attraction of the Relative.*

Obs. The ellipse of the conjunctive of εἶναι after the relative ὅς ἄν, and after conjunctions, is but rare ; such as, ἔς τ' ἄν (Eur. Hipp. 659.), ὄφρ' ἄν (Theogn. 252.), ἕως ἄν (Hippocr. de aer. aq. loc. 101.) : also rare of the indicative after conjunctions; such as, ὁπότε (Il. θ, 230.) : frequent however after ὅτι; Il. ξ, 376 ὅς δέ κ' ἀνὴρ μενέχαρμος, sc. ᾖ : Plat. Rep. p. 370. E ὧν ἂν αὐτοῖς χρεία : Demosth. p. 529, 14 οἱ δὲ θεσμοθέται εἰσαγόντων εἰς τὴν Ἡλιαίαν τριάκοντα ἡμερῶν, ἀφ' ἧς ἂν ἡ γραφή. The ellipse of εἴην does not occur ; of the imperative very rarely : Il. ν, 95 αἰδώς, Ἀργεῖοι : Soph. Œ. C. 1477 ἵλαος, ὦ δαίμων. Of the participle it is very frequent ; of the infinitive in dependence on a governing verb far more rare.

Predicative construction of words.

A. OF AGREEMENT.

§. 377. The verb agrees with the subject in person and number ; the predicative adjective, or substantive, when it signifies a personal name, in gender, number, and case (nomin.) ; as, ἐγὼ γράφω, σὺ γράφεις, αὐτὸς γράφει : ὁ ἄνθρωπος θνητός ἐστιν, ἡ ἀρετὴ καλή ἐστι, τὸ πρᾶγμα αἰσχρόν ἐστιν, οἱ Ἕλληνες πολεμικώτατοι ἦσαν : ὁ Κῦρος ἦν βασιλεύς, ἡ Τόμυρις ἦν βασίλισσα.

Exceptions.

The exceptions to this agreement naturally are not confined to the predicative relation, but occur also with adjectives and participles in the objective and attributive constructions ; and therefore it will be convenient not to confine ourselves to the predicative exceptions, but to consider at the same time all cases of this sort which spring from the same principle. The disagreement of the relative however deserves a separate consideration, and therefore will be postponed to its proper place.

Constructio κατὰ σύνεσιν.

§. 378. *Principle.*—The Greek language in many of its constructions does not so much consider the grammatical form in which a notion is expressed, as the notion itself. This arose from the metaphysical spirit of the Greeks, which enabled them in the form of signification to see clearly the notion signified; and which, impressing itself strongly on the whole of their language, imparted to it a clearness and precision, in expressing the minutest shades of distinction, which are scarcely comprehensible to the moderns; while at the same time it creates a number of grammatical anomalies, which at first seem to be defects, but are in reality founded on the truest principles of grammar. The apprehension, retention, and application of this principle is most essential to the interpretation as well of particular passages, as of the general sense of an author. This construction is called κατὰ σύνεσιν, or *ad intellectum*, or σχῆμα πρὸς τὸ σημαινόμενον, or νοούμενον, or *ex animo loquentis* or *scribentis*.

a. Number of the verb: Il. β, 278 ὡς φάσαν ἡ πληθύς: Il. ο, 305 ἡ πληθὺς ἐπὶ νῆας Ἀχαιῶν ἀπονέοντο, the notion being πολλοὶ Ἀχαιοί: Il. ψ, 157 λαὸς Ἀχαιῶν πείσονται: Hdt. IX. 23 τὸ πλῆθος ἐπεβοήθησαν: Thuc. I. 20 Ἀθηναίων τὸ πλῆθος—οἴονται: Id. IV. 32 ὁ ἄλλος στρατὸς ἀπέβαινον: Id. V. 60 τὸ στρατόπεδον ἀνεχώρουν: Æsch. Ag. 588 Τροίην ἑλόντες δήποτ' Ἀργείων στόλος θεοῖς λάφυρα ταῦτα τοῖς καθ' Ἑλλάδα δόμοις ἐπασσάλευσαν. So in Latin; as, Liv. V. 40 *pars per agros dilapsi, pars urbes petunt finitimas:* and even Hesiod. Scut. 327 χαίρετε, Λυγκῆος γενεή. So St. John vii. 49 ὁ ὄχλος —— ἐπικατάρατοί εἰσι.

Obs. The phrase ἴβαν οἰκόνδε ἕκαστος does not belong to this class.

b. Gender and number of adjective, participle, and pronoun: τὸ μειράκιόν ἐστι καλός: τὸ γυναίκιόν ἐστι καλή: τὰ παιδικά ἐστι καλός: Xen. Cyr. V. 1, 14 τὰ μοχθηρὰ ἀνθρώπια πασῶν—τῶν ἐπιθυμιῶν ἀκρατεῖς εἰσι. So Plat. Phædr. p. 240. A ἔτι τοίνυν ἄγαμον, ἄπαιδα, ἄοικον ὅτι πλεῖστον χρόνον παιδικὰ ἐραστὴς εὔξαιτο ἂν γενέσθαι.

§. 379. In the attributive and objective constructions we find the following.

a. Adjective and participle not agreeing with the substantive of which they are the immediate attributives, only in poetry [a] :—

Il. χ, 84 φίλε τέκνον (Hector): Æsch. Choeph. 893 φίλτατ' Αἰγίσθου βία: Soph. Œ. R. 1215 ἰὼ Λαΐεε τέκνον: Eur. Bacch. 1305 ἕρνος κατθανόντα: Id. Troad. 757 (Seidl.) ὦ φίλτατ', ὦ περισσὰ τιμηθεὶς τέκνον: Aristoph. Ach. 880 κολλικοφάγε Βοιωτίδιον. So Soph. Œ. R. 1167 τίς γεννημάτων. Very commonly, in prose as well as poetry, participles do not agree with the substantive of which they are the remote attributives; as, Il. λ, 690 ἐλθὼν γάρ ῥ' ἐκάκωσε βίη Ἡρακληείη: Il. π, 281 ἐκίνηθεν δὲ φάλαγγες ἐλπόμενοι κ. τ. λ.: Pind. Nem. V. 43 ἔθνος μεταΐξαντα: Anacr. III. 16 βρέφος μὲν ἱσορῶ φέροντα τόξον: Soph. Phil. 356 καί μ' εὐθὺς ἐν κύκλῳ στρατὸς ἐκβάντα πᾶς ἠσπάζετ', ὀμνύντες βλέπειν τὸν οὐκ ἔτ' ὄντα ζῶντ' Ἀχιλλέα: Id. Antig. 1021 οὐδ' ὄρνις εὐσήμους ἀπορροιβδεῖ βοὰς ἀνδροφθόρου βεβρῶτες αἵματος λίπος: Eur. Hec. 39 κατέσχ' Ἀχιλλεὺς πᾶν στράτευμ' Ἑλληνικὸν πρὸς οἶκον εὐθύνοντας ἐναλίαν πλάτην: cf. Bacch. 1305. ubi v. Pflugk. Hdt. I. 87 ὡς ἄρα πάντα

[a] Elm. Œ. R. 1167. R. P. Phœn. 1730.

μὲν ἄνδρα σβεννύντα τὸ πῦρ, δυναμένους δὲ οὐκέτι καταλαβεῖν.
Thuc. III. 79 ἐπὶ μὲν τὴν πόλιν—ἐπέπλεον—ἐν πολλῇ ταραχῇ καὶ φόβῳ
ὄντας: Id. IV. 15 τὰ τέλη καταβάντας ἐς τὸ στρατόπεδον βουλεύειν πρὸς τὸ χρῆμα ὁρῶντας ὅτι ἂν δοκῇ: Xen. Cyr. VII. 3, 8 ὦ ἀγαθὴ
καὶ πιστὴ ψυχή, οἴχῃ δὴ ἀπολιπὼν ἡμᾶς: Id. I. 2, 12 αἱ μένουσαι
φυλαὶ—διαγωνιζόμενοι πρὸς ἀλλήλους διατελοῦσιν.

b. Very usually indeed with pronouns; as,

Hdt. IV. 125 ὑπῆγον ἐπὶ τὴν Νευρίδα, ταρασσομένων δὲ καὶ τούτων:
Id. VIII. 121 τρεπόμενοι ἐς Κάρυστον καὶ δῃώσαντες αὐτῶν τὴν χώρην:
Thuc. I. 136 φεύγει—ἐς Κέρκυραν ὡς αὐτῶν (sc. Κερκυραίων) εὐεργέτης:
Id. IV. 15 ἐς δὲ τὴν Σπάρτην ὡς ἠγγέλθη τὰ γεγενημένα περὶ Πύλον,
ἔδοξεν αὐτοῖς (sc. τοῖς Λακεδαιμονίοις): Xen. Cyr. III. 3, 14 συγκαλέσας
πᾶν τὸ στρατιωτικὸν ἔλεξε πρὸς αὐτοὺς τοιάδε: Id. M. S. I. 2,
62 ἐάν τις φανερὸς γένηται κλέπτων—τούτοις θάνατός ἐστιν ἡ ζημία,
cf. Cyrop. I. 2, 2. VII. 4, 5 : Plat. Rep. p. 370 ἐξ ἄλλης πόλεως—καὶ
ἐκεῖνοι (sc. οἱ πολῖται) δέονται, ubi v. Stallbaum ; cf. ibid. p. 374.
A.: Id. Lysid. p. 204. E ἃ χρὴ ἐραστὴν περὶ παιδικῶν πρὸς αὐτὸν
ἢ πρὸς ἄλλους λέγειν: Demosth. p. 23, 18 εἰ μὲν γάρ τις ἀνήρ ἐστιν
ἐν αὐτοῖς οἷος ἔμπειρος πολέμου καὶ ἀγώνων, τούτους μὲν φιλοτιμίᾳ πάντας
ἀπωθεῖν αὐτὸν (τὸν Φίλιππον) ἔφη.　　On this construction with relatives,
see *Adjectival Sentences.*

Obs. 1. Sometimes the attributive agrees in gender neither with the form
nor the implied notion of the substantive, but with another substantive,
which occurred to the author when he was writing, instead of the one he
had used before: Eur. Troad. 531 πᾶσα δὲ γέννα Φρυγῶν πρὸς πύλας
ὡρμάθη — ξεστὸν λόχον Ἀργείων καὶ Δαρδανίας ἄταν θεᾷ δώσων (as if
λαός, or some such word, had preceded). So Plato Phileb. p. 32. A
ἀπιόντων καὶ διακρινομένων, as if ὑγρῶν, not ὑγρότητος, had preceded. So
Æsch. Eum. 580 σὺ δ' εἴσαγε (Minerva) τήνδε κυρώσων δικήν (sc. acting
as θεσμοθέτης): Ibid. 960 κύρι' ἔχοντες θεαί, sc. gods.

Obs. 2. This anomaly is, in many cases, not properly to be explained
κατὰ σύνεσιν, but it arose rather from the carelessness of the writer in
not keeping in his mind the form he had used before.

Obs. 3. So in the number of the verb in the predicative sentence; as,
Æsch. Eum. 338 τοῖσιν ὁμαρτεῖν ὄφρ' ἂν γᾶν ὑπέλθῃ, sc. Orestes, who was
in the mind of the Chorus.

§. 380. 1. When the subject is expressed by the neuter article
τό or τά, with the gen. pl. of the substantive, the predicate is always
in the plural; and if it be an adjective, it agrees likewise in gender
with the attributive genitive; as, Soph. Phil. 497 τὰ τῶν διακόνων, τοὐμὸν ἐν σμικρῷ μέρει ποιούμενοι, τὸν οἴκαδ' ἤπειγον
στόλον: Plat. Rep. p. 563. C τὸ μὲν γὰρ τῶν θηρίων — ἐλευ-
θερώτερά ἐστιν (the sing. ἐστιν, is, on account of the neuter
plur. ἐλευθερώτερα): ubi v. Stallbaum.

2. Connected with this is the following: when a substantival
notion is expressed by a periphrasis of a substantive with another
attributive substantive in the genitive, as ψυχὴ Τειρεσίαο, the attributive participle agrees with the subject in case, but in gender and
number with the attributive genitive which expresses the principal

part of the compound notion; as, Od. λ, 90. sq. ἦλθε δ' ἐπὶ ψυχὴ
Θηβαίου Τειρεσίαο χρύσεον σκῆπτρον ἔχων: Il. β, 459
ὀρνίθων πετεηνῶν ἔθνεα πολλὰ — ἔνθα καὶ ἔνθα ποτῶνται
ἀγαλλόμεναι πτερύγεσσιν: Æsch. Ag. 770 θράσος ἄτας
— εἰδομέναν τοκεῦσιν[a]: Soph. Antig. 988. sq. ἀγνῶτ' ἀκούω
φθόγγον ὀρνίθων κακῷ κλάζοντας οἴστρῳ: Id. Aj. 168
πτηνῶν ἀγέλαι μέγαν αἰγυπιὸν ὑποδείσαντες: Xen. Cyr.
II. 4, 15 τὸ μὲν πλῆθος τῶν πεζῶν καὶ τῶν ἱππέων — ὡς
ἐπιόντες τὰ θηρία ἐξανισταῖεν. So Plat. Legg. p. 657. D τὸ
δὲ τῶν πρεσβυτέρων ἡμῶν ἐκείνους αὖ θεωροῦντες.

Obs. 1. The construction, so common in Latin, of a plural verb with
a singular subject, and *μετά, cum,* &c. is very rare in Greek : such as
Thuc. III. 112 Δημοσθένης μετὰ τῶν ξυστρατηγῶν — σπένδονται : Diphil. ap.
Athen. VII. p. 292 D πολυτελῶς 'Αδώνια ἄγουσ' ἑταίρα μεθ' ἑτέρων :
Lucian. D. D. XII. 1 ἐκείνη (ἡ 'Ρέα) — παραλαβοῦσα καὶ τοὺς
Κορύβαντας — ἄνω καὶ κάτω τὴν "Ιδην περιπολοῦσιν· ἡ μὲν ὀλολύ-
ζουσα ἐπὶ τῷ "Αττι, οἱ Κορύβαντες δέ κ. τ. λ.

Obs. 2. So in phrases such as ἄλλος ἄλλον, which imply at least two
subjects of the action, the plural verb is used ; as, Plat. Rep. 550. E
ἄλλος ἄλλον ὁρῶν — τὸ πλῆθος τοιοῦτον — αὐτῶν ἀπειργάσαντο ; though
generally there is a plural participle in the same sentence, which these
formulas define ; as, Æsch. Ag. 636 ἄλλος ἄλλοθεν — ἔλασκον εὐφημοῦντες [b].

Masculine or Feminine Subject, with the Adjective in Neuter Singular.

381. When the subjects, whether masculine or feminine, express
not any particular individual of a class, but merely the general
notion, the predicative adjective stands in the neuter singular.
This construction is used especially in sayings, proverbs, &c.: Il. β,
204 οὐκ ἀγαθὸν πολυκοιρανίη εἷς κοίρανος ἔστω : Eur.
Hipp. 110 τερπνὸν ἐκ (*post*) κυναγίας τράπεζα πλήρης : Id.
Or. 232 δυσάρεστον οἱ νοσοῦντες ἀπορίας ὕπο : Ibid. 224
μεταβολὴ πάντων γλυκύ : Ibid. 760 δεινὸν οἱ πολλοί,
κακούργους ὅταν ἔχωσι προστάτας : Id. Med. 329 πλὴν γὰρ τέκνων
ἔμοιγε φίλτατον πόλις : Ibid. 928 γυνὴ δὲ θῆλυ κἀπὶ
δακρύοις ἔφυ : Id. Herc. F. 1295 αἱ μεταβολαὶ λυπηρόν : Hdt.
III. 82 ἡ μουναρχίη κράτιστον : Id. VII. 10, 7 διαβολὴ (*calumnia*)
γάρ ἐστι δεινότατον. So we must explain Thuc. I. 10. princ.
Μυκῆναι μικρὸν ἦν, were a small thing: Plat. Rep. p. 354. A
οὐδέποτ' ἄρα — λυσιτελέστερον ἀδικία δικαιοσύνης : Ibid. p.
364. A καλὸν μὲν ἡ σωφροσύνη τε καὶ δικαιοσύνη,
χαλεπὸν μέντοι καὶ ἐπίπονον : Ibid. p. 375. D ἄμαχόν τε
καὶ ἀνίκητον θυμός : Id. Hipp. M. p. 288. B θήλεια ἵππος
καλὴ οὐ καλόν; ibid. C λύρα καλὴ οὐ καλόν; χύτρα καλὴ οὐ καλόν;

[a] Clausen Ag. 728.   [b] Matth. 301.

Here also belong these passages: εἰ ταῦτα ἀδύνατον Plat: Id.
Parmen. p. 260. Α ταῦτα δὴ ἀδύνατον ἐφάνη: Id. Sophist.
p. 252. Ε τά γε δύο ἀδύνατον εὑρέθη. Also, Xen. Anab. II.
1, 22 τί οὖν ταῦτ᾽ ἐστίν; Plat. Phæd. p. 58. C τί δὲ δὴ τὰ περὶ
αὐτὸν τὸν θάνατον; τί ἦν τὰ λεχθέντα καὶ πραχθέντα; Id.
Gorg. p. 58. C σκεπτέον τί τὰ συμβαίνοντα; (On the contrary, Phæd. p. 112. Α ἀλλὰ τίνα δὴ ἦν τὰ μετὰ ταῦτα λεχθέντα;) So Xen. M. S. III. 9, 3 φθόνον δὲ σκοπῶν, ὅτι
εἴη, *quid esset invidia;* but ὅστις, *quæ, qualis,* the neuter signifying the genus, the masculine the difference. So in Latin: Virg.
Æn. IV. 570 *varium et mutabile semper femina.* So also in abbreviated adjectival sentences: Hdt. III. 103 ἡ δὲ δὴ λέαινα, ἐὸν
ἰσχυρότατον καὶ θρασύτατον, ἅπαξ ἐν τῷ βίῳ τίκτει ἕν:
Thuc. I. 2. extr. παρ᾽ Ἀθηναίους οἱ δυνατώτατοι, ὡς βέβαιον
ὄν, ἀνεχώρουν: Plat. Rep. p. 420. C οἱ ὀφθαλμοὶ, κάλλιστον
ὄν, οὐκ ὀστρείῳ ἐναληλιμμένοι εἰσίν.

Obs. 1. The demonstrative pronoun deserves a separate consideration.
When the predicate is expressed by a demonstrative pronoun, it agrees
with its subject in gender, number, and case; as, οὗτός ἐστιν ὁ ἀνήρ — αὕτη
ἐστὶ πηγὴ καὶ ἀρχὴ πάντων τῶν κακῶν — τοῦτό ἐστι τὸ ἄνθος. So Plat. Phædr.
p. 245. Ε ὡς ταύτης οὔσης φύσεως ψυχῆς, *quum hæc sit natura animi:*
Id. Euthyphr. princ. οὗτοι δὴ Ἀθηναῖοί γε δίκην αὐτὴν καλοῦσιν, ἀλλὰ
γραφήν. But it very often stands in neut. sing.[a]: Plat. Rep. p. 344. A
ἔστι δὲ τοῦτο τυραννίς, *est autem hæc tyrannis*[b] (instances such as
Virg. III. 173, *nec sopor illud erat,* are very rare): Ibid. p. 432. B τοῦτό
ἐστιν ἡ δικαιοσύνη: Eur. Bacch. 305 μανία δὲ καὶ τοῦτ᾽ ἔστι: Plat.
Phædr. p. 245. C μόνον δὴ τὸ αὐτὸ κινοῦν — τοῦτο πηγὴ καὶ ἀρχὴ
γενέσεως: Demosth. p. 367 τοῦτο γάρ εἰσιν εὔθυναι: Id. p. 1141
τοῦτο γάρ ἐστιν ἡ αἰκία: Id. p. 96, 27 τοῦτ᾽ εἰσὶν οἱ λόγοι, *hæc
verborum est vis:* Id. p. 97, 28 τοῦτό γ᾽ ἐστὶν ὑπερβολὴ μανίας.
The plural form expresses yet more clearly the notion of general indefiniteness.

Obs. 2. The neuter demonstrative also is joined with a masculine or
feminine substantive when this expresses a general notion, as is most frequently the case in abstract substantives: Hdt. III. 82. princ. τριῶν γὰρ
προκειμένων, — δήμου τε —, καὶ ὀλιγαρχίης, καὶ μονάρχου, πολλῷ
τοῦτο (i. e. μόναρχον εἶναι) προέχειν λέγω: Demosth. p. 22, 15 (ὁ Φίλιππος)
δόξης ἐπιθυμεῖ καὶ τοῦτο (i. e. δόξαν λαμβάνειν) ἐζήλωκε. So Od. μ, 74.
sq. νεφέλη δέ μιν ἀμφιβέβηκε Κυανέη· τὸ μὲν (for ἡ) οὔποτ᾽ ἐρωεῖ.

Obs. 3. The pronouns οὐδείς and μηδείς agree generally with the subject
when they signify, *good for nothing, worthless;* as, Hdt. IX. 58 διέδεξαν —,
ὅτι οὐδένες ἄρα ἐόντες ἐν οὐδαμοῖσι ἐοῦσι Ἕλλησι ἐναπεδεικνύατο: Arist. Eq.
158 ὦ νῦν μὲν οὐδείς, αὔριον δ᾽ ὑπέρμεγας —; but stand in the neuter,
οὐδέν, μηδέν, when they signify the abstract notion of nothingness, bad-
ness, unworthiness; as, Plat. Rep. p. 556. D ἄνδρες ἡμέτεροι εἰσὶν οὐδέν:
ubi v. Stallbaum. So in abbreviated predicative sentences: Ibid. p.
341. C νῦν γοῦν, ἔφη, ἐπεχείρησας οὐδὲν ὤν, *quum nihil valeas, nullius mo-
menti sis:* Ibid. p. 562. D τοὺς δέ γε, εἶπον, τῶν ἀρχόντων κατηκόους προ-

[a] Stallb. ad loc. [b] Stallb. Gorgias 504.

Xen. Hell. III. 2, 19 δόξαντα δὲ ταῦτα καὶ περανθέντα, τὰ μὲν στρα-
τεύματα ἀπῆλθεν. The dual neuter is also joined with a singular verb; as,
Od. ζ, 131 ἐν δέ οἱ ὄσσε δαίεται, the neuter dual being considered as a
neuter plural: compare ὄσσε φαεινά Il. ν, 435, ὄσσε αἱματόεντα ibid. 617;
and Il. π, 139 εἵλετο δ᾽ ἄλκιμα δοῦρε : Lucian. Tox. 17 ἄμφω λέγεται :
Arist. Rhet. 1. 2. 19 ἄμφω ᾖ. But this construction does not appear to
have been usual.

Obs. 2. The principle of this construction is, that the neuter plural
was conceived to express a class as one individual thing, a whole collective unity; all notion of the individuality of the several members of the
whole being lost sight of; where the notion of individuality is meant to
be expressed the plural is used.

Exceptions.

§. 385. *a.* When the neuter plural signifies or stands for names of persons
or animate things, and the notion of individuality is intended to be expressed, the verb is in the plural[a]: Thuc. IV. 88 τὰ τέλη ὀμόσαντα
ἐξέπεμψαν : Id. VII. 57 τοσάδε μὲν μετὰ Ἀθηναίων ἔθνη ἐστρά-
τευον : Isocr. Panath. 90. 481 τὰ μειράκια—παραγεγενημένα—κατε-
φρόνησαν : Plat. Lach. p. 180. Ε τὰ μειράκια διαλεγόμενα ἐπιμέμ-
νηνται—καὶ—ἐπαινοῦσιν[b] : Eur. Cycl. 206 πῶς κατ᾽ ἄντρα νεόγονα
βλαστήματα (i. e. ἄρνες καὶ ἔριφοι), ἢ πρός γε μαστοῖς εἰσί; but Thuc.
I. 58 τὰ τέλη τῶν Λακεδαιμονίων ὑπέσχοντο αὐτοῖς, though the best
Mss. read ὑπέσχετο : if it is ὑπέσχοντο, τὰ τέλη signifies the magistrates
—if ὑπέσχετο, the cabinet. Of course the use of the plural or singular
number depends on the notion in the speaker's or writer's mind, *animo
loquentis*[c] : Plat. Rep. p. 353. Β ἆρ᾽ ἄν ποτε ὄμματα αὐτῶν ἔργον καλῶς
ἀπεργάσαιντο μὴ ἔχοντα τὴν αὐτῶν ἀρετήν : where the plural notion
ὀφθαλμοί was in the speaker's mind.

b. And also when the neuter plural does not express living objects, but
the individuality or the plurality of the parts is to be signified : Xen.
Anab. I. 7, 17 ταύτῃ μὲν οὖν τῇ ἡμέρᾳ οὐκ ἐμαχέσατο βασιλεύς, ἀλλ᾽ ὑποχω-
ρούντων φανερὰ ἦσαν καὶ ἵππων καὶ ἀνθρώπων ἴχνη πολλά : Id. Cyr. V.
1, 14 τὰ μοχθηρὰ ἀνθρώπια πασῶν οἶμαι, τῶν ἐπιθυμιῶν ἀκρατῆ ἐστι,
κἄπειτα ἔρωτα αἰτιῶνται : ἐστι, the whole class—mankind : αἰτιῶνται,
each for himself lays the blame on. So Hdt. II. 96 τὰ πλοῖα οὐ
δύνανται ἀνὰ πλέειν. So the idea of plurality of parts is signified by
the following plural verbs : Thuc. I. 126 ἐπειδὴ ἐπῆλθον Ὀλύμπια, the
Olympic (not festival but) games : Xen. Anab. I. 2, 23 ἐνταῦθα ἦσαν τὰ
Συεννέσιος βασίλεια : so c. 4, 10 : and when the neuter plural is defined
by a noun of number which gives it plurality ; as, Thuc. V. 62 καὶ ἐγένοντο
ἐξ αὐτῶν εἴκοσι καὶ ἑκατὸν τάλαντα : Xen. Anab. I. 4, 4 ἦσαν δὲ ταῦτα δύο
τείχη. So Thuc. V. 26 ἀμφοτέροις δὲ ἁμαρτήματα ἐγένοντο (ἁμαρτήματα is
predicated of each of the two). Xen. Cyr. III. 3. 15 ἀνέπαυον τὰ στρατεύ-
ματα, *Assyriorum et sociorum.*

Obs. 1. The singular number of the imperative is not used with
neuter plurals; as commands are not addressed to classes, but to the
individuals contained therein.

Obs. 2. The non-Attic poets from Homer downwards use the plural
very often merely for the metre : Il. λ, 310 ἀμήχανα ἔργα γένοντο : both
constructions occur together, Il. β, 135 καὶ δὴ δοῦρα σέσηπε νεῶ̣ καὶ σπάρτα

---

[a] R. P. Hec. 1149. Stallb. Cratyl. 425. A : cf. Heindorf. Herm. Elect. 430. Ast.
Plat. Legg. 46, and Rep. 353. Dobree Arist. Plut. 145.
    [b] Lobeck Phryn. 425.   [c] Stallb. Rep. 353. B. and 503. D.

λέλυνται. The Attic poets, except in the cases given under *a* and *b*, use
the singular.

Masculine or Feminine Noun in the Plural and Verb in the Singular.

§. 386. 1. A masculine or feminine subject in the plural is joined with
a singular verb. This construction is called σχῆμα Βοιωτικόν, or Πινδαρικόν [a],
probably because mostly used by the Doric poets. The instances of it
are rare : Pindar. Olymp. XI. (X.) princ. μελιγάρυες ὕμνοι ὑστέρων
ἀρχαὶ λόγων τέλλεται, where Dissen adds, "Hippon. Fragm. p. 41
Δύ' ἡμέραι γυναικός ἐστιν ἥδισται, ὅταν γαμῇ τις κἀκφέρῃ τεθνηκυῖαν,
quamquam Gaisfordius ad Hephæstion. p. 253. εἰσίν *scribat :*" Id. Fragm.
Dithyr. v. 16 sq. ἀχεῖταί τ' ὀμφαὶ μελέων σὺν αὐλοῖς, ἀχεῖται
Σεμέλαν ἑλικάμπυκα χοροί. In an oracle in Hdt. VI. 86 οὐδ' ἔπι χεῖρες :
Hom. Hymn. in Cerer. 279 ξανθαὶ δὲ κόμαι κατενήνοθεν : Pind. Pyth. X. 71
ἐν δ' ἀγαθοῖσι κεῖται—πολίων κυβερνάσεις : Fragm. Dithyr. IV. 15.

2. In Attic writers this construction is limited to ἔστι and ἦν, placed
at the beginning of a sentence, so that the subject follows the verb,
and the expression takes an impersonal form, like the French *Il est des*
hommes—Il est cent usages, &c. So Hesiod. Theog. 321 τῆς δ' ἦν τρεῖς
κεφαλαί : Soph. Trach. 520 ἦν δ' ἀμφίπλεκτοι κλίμακες : Eurip.
Ion. 1146 ἐνῆν δ' ὑφανταὶ γράμμασιν τοιαίδ' ὑφαί : Hdt. I. 26 ἔστι δὲ
μεταξὺ τῆς τε παλαιῆς πόλιος—καὶ τοῦ νηοῦ ἑπτὰ στάδιοι : Id. VII. 34
ἔστι δὲ ἑπτὰ στάδιοι ἐξ Ἀβύδου ἐς τὴν ἀπαντίον : Plat. Euthyd. p. 302.
C ἔστι γὰρ ἔμοιγε καὶ βωμοί : Id. Rep. p. 462. E. extr. ἔστι μέν που
καὶ ἐν ταῖς ἄλλαις πόλεσιν ἄρχοντές τε καὶ δῆμος : ubi v. Stallbaum.
So γίγνεται : Ibid. p. 363. A χρὴ δίκαιον εἶναι —, ἵνα δοκοῦντι δικαίῳ εἶναι
γίγνηται ἀπὸ τῆς δόξης ἀρχαί τε καὶ γάμοι. So in the dual: Plat.
Gorg. p. 500. D εἰ ἔστι τούτω διττὰ τὰ βίω : Arist. Vesp. 58 ἡμῖν γὰρ
οὐκ ἔστ' οὔτε—δούλω καταρίπτοντε.

Obs. 1. The passage in Eur. Bacc. 1350 αἴ! αἴ! αἴ! δέδοκται, πρέσβυ, τλήμονες φυγαί, is not an instance of this construction, δέδοκται being used
absolutely, *decretum est,* and τλήμονες φυγαί are merely an explanation
thereof; nor Id. Hipp. 1269 κέκρανται συμφοραί, as κέκρανται is III. plur.
with the anomalous ν.

Obs. 2. Similarly the regular phrase ἔστιν οἵ, *sunt qui.*

Subject in the Dual—Predicate in Plural.

§. 387. 1. The dual is not always used where two persons or things
are spoken of, but only where such two persons or things are either
really a pair, as πόδε, χεῖρε, &c., or in *animo loquentis* considered
as such, as two combatants.

2. Hence the dual in many cases is joined with the plural verb,
where the dual notion, as not requiring to be distinctly marked,
is merged in the plural of which it is a modification ; as, Il. ε, 275
τὼ δὲ τάχ' ἐγγύθεν ἦλθον ἐλαύνοντ' ὠκέας ἵππους : Il. π, 218
δύ' ἀνέρε θωρήσσοντο : Ibid. 337 τὼ δ' αὖτις ξιφέεσσι
συνέδραμον : Eur. Phœn. 69 τὼ δὲ ξυμβάντ' ἔταξαν.—

a Dissen Pind. Ol. X. VI. Herm. Trach. 517.

So attributives; as, Od. λ, 211 ὄφρα καὶ εἰν Ἀΐδαο φίλας περὶ χεῖρε βαλόντε ἀμφοτέρω κρυεροῖο τεταρπώμεσθα γόοιο: and participles as remote attributives; as, Plat. Euthyd. p. 273. D ἄμφω βλέψαντες. Compare §. 384. Obs. ὄσσε φαεινά, ἄλκιμα δοῦρε.

Obs. Very frequently, especially in poetry, the dual and plural are used indifferently in the same passage, especially with participles: Il. λ, 621 τοὶ δ᾽ ἱδρῶ ἀπεψύχοντο χιτώνων στάντε ποτὶ πνοίην: Pindar. Nem. X. 64 λαιψηροῖς δὲ πόδεσσιν ἄφαρ ἐξικέσθαν, καὶ μέγα ἔργον ἐμήσαντ᾽ ὠκέως: Plat. Euthyd. p. 273. D ἐγελασάτην γοῦν ἄμφω βλέψαντες εἰς ἀλλήλω: especially with the I. plur.; as, Eur. Iph. Taur. 777 ποῦ ποτ᾽ ὄνθ᾽ εὑρήμεθα[a].

Subject in Plural—Verb in Dual.

§. 388. 1. A dual verb is joined with a plural subject or with several subjects, when the persons or things signified by the plural or by the several subjects are spoken or conceived of as so opposed or arranged as to form a pair or two pairs[b]. There is a very simple case of this construction in Il. ε, 10 δύω δέ οἱ υἱέες ἤστην: Plat. Rep. p. 478. B δυνάμεις δὲ ἀμφότεραί ἐστον: again, Il. δ, 452. sqq. ὡς δ᾽ ὅτε χείμαρροι ποταμοὶ, κατ᾽ ὄρεσφι ῥέοντες, ἐς μισγάγκειαν συμβάλλετον ὄβριμον ὕδωρ,—ὡς τῶν μισγομένων γένετο ἰαχή τε φόβος τε (the streams being compared to two combatants): Il. θ, 185 sqq. Ξάνθε τε καὶ σὺ Πόδαργε, καὶ Αἴθων Λάμπε τε δῖε, νῦν μοι τὴν κομιδὴν ἀποτίνετον: 191 ἀλλ᾽ ἐφομαρτεῖτον καὶ σπεύδετον (two pairs). So Il. π, 371 πολλοὶ δ᾽ ἐν τάφρῳ ἐρυσάρματες ὠκέες ἵπποι ἄξαντ᾽ ἐν πρώτῳ ῥυμῷ λίπον ἄρματ᾽ ἀνάκτων: and Il. ρ, 427 ἵπποι δ᾽ Αἰακίδαο, μάχης ἀπάνευθεν ἐόντες, κλαῖον, ἐπειδὴ πρῶτα πυθέσθην ἡνιόχοιο ἐν κονίῃσι πεσόντος (pair of horses): Od. θ, 48 sq. κούρω δὲ κρινθέντε δύω καὶ πεντήκοντα βήτην: βήτην refers not to πεντήκ. but κούρω κρινθέντε δύω: Hom. Hymn. in Apoll. 456 τίφθ᾽ οὕτως ἧσθον τετιηότες, οὐδ᾽ ἐπὶ γαῖαν ἐκβῆτ᾽, οὐδὲ καθ᾽ ὅπλα μελαίνης νηὸς ἔθεσθε: v. 487 ἀλλ᾽ ἄγεθ᾽, ὡς ἂν ἐγὼ εἴπω, πείθεσθε τάχιστα᾽ ἱστία μὲν πρῶτον κάθετον, λύσαντε βοείας: v. 501 ἔρχεσθαί θ᾽ ἅμ᾽ ἐμοὶ, καὶ ἱηπαιήον᾽ ἀείδειν, εἰσόκε χῶρον ἵκησθον, ἵν᾽ ἕξετε πίονα νηόν: in this passage Apollo is speaking to the rowers, who must be considered as sitting in two rows, one on each side of the ship. Æschyl. Eum. 256 ὅρα, ὅρα μάλ᾽ αὖ, λεύσσετον πάντα, the Chorus being divided into two parts (ἡμιχόρια): Eur. Phœn. 1298 δίδυμοι θῆρες φόνιαι ψυχαὶ—αὐτίχ᾽ αἱμάξετον: Pind. Ol. II. 87 μαθόντες δὲ λάβροι παγγλωσσίᾳ, κόρακες ὡς, ἄκραντα γαρύετον Διὸς πρὸς ὄρνιχα θεῖον, "qui autem didicerunt inepte loquaces ut corvi inutili clamore certant adversus Jovis aquilam;" in γαρύετον the poet alludes to a couple of slanderous writers, Simonides and Bacchylides; see Schol. ad loc.: Plat. Theæt. p. 152. E περὶ τούτου πάντες ἑξῆς οἱ σοφοὶ πλὴν Παρμενίδου ξυμφέρεσθον, Πρωταγόρας τε καὶ Ἡράκλειτος καὶ Ἐμπεδοκλῆς, καὶ τῶν ποιητῶν οἱ ἄκροι: (here the notion of duality is produced by the opposition of philosophers and poets.) So Il. ε, 487 τύνη δ᾽ ἕστηκας, ἀτὰρ οὐδ᾽ ἄλλοισι κελεύεις λαοῖσιν μενέμεν —᾽ μήπως, ὡς ἀψῖσι λίνου ἁλόντε πανάγρου, ἀνδράσι δυσμενέεσσιν ἕλωρ καὶ κύρμα γένησθε (ἁλόντε sc. σὺ καὶ ἄλλοι λαοί): the explanation of the Scholiast, ὑμεῖς καὶ αἱ γυναῖκες, is too far-fetched. Il a, 567 is not an instance, as ἰόνθ᾽ is referable to ἐμέ.

---

[a] Elm. Iph. Taur. 777.
[b] Dissen Pind. Ol. II. 87.   Stallb. ad Theætet. 152. E.   Nitzsch Od. θ, 35.

2. In the attributive construction we may remark upon the dual:

a. A plural subst. is often joined with the dual pronominal adjectives, δύω, δύο, δυοῖν: Il. ε, 10 δύω υἱέες: Od. μ, 73 οἱ δὲ δύω σκόπελοι: Il. ι, 4 ἄνεμοι δύο: Æsch. Ag. 1395 δυοῖν οἰμώγμασιν: Id. Eum. 597 δυοῖν μιασμάτων: Theocr. V. 47 κρᾶναι δύω: Plat. Rep. p. 614. C δύο χάσματα ἐχομένω ἀλλήλοιν. But sometimes both the adjective and substantive are in the plural; as, Il. π, 326 δοιοῖσι κασιγνήτοισι.

b. In Attic a feminine substantive in the dual is often joined with a masculine attributive in the dual; as, Thuc. V. 23 ἄμφω τὼ πόλεε: Xen. Cyr. V. 5, 2 τὼ γυναῖκε: Ibid. I. 2, 11 καὶ μίαν ἄμφω τούτω τὼ ἡμέρα λογίζονται: Plat. Phæd. p. 71. E τοῖν γενεσέοιν. Τούτω τὼ τέχνα, τούτοιν τοῖν κινησέοιν, τὼ ὁδώ in Plato—especially with participles as remote attributives; this is also found as early as Homer: Il. θ, 455 οὐκ ἂν ἐφ᾽ ἡμετέρων ὀχέων πληγέντε κεραυνῷ ἂψ ἐς ῎Ολυμπον ἵκεσθον (*Minerva et Juno*): Hesiod. Opp. 195 καὶ τότε δὴ πρὸς ῎Ολυμπον — λευκοῖσιν φαρέεσσι καλυψαμένω χρόα καλόν, ἀθανάτων μετὰ φῦλον ἴτον προλιπόντ᾽ ἀνθρώπους Αἰδὼς καὶ Νέμεσις: Plat. Phædr. p. 237. D ἡμῶν ἐν ἑκάστῳ δύο τινέ ἐστον ἰδέα ἄρχοντε καὶ ἄγοντε, οἷν ἑπόμεθα — · τούτω δέ κ. τ. λ.[a] Eur. Alc. 925 δύο ψυχὰς—διαβάντε.

Obs. It seems probable that the dual of the article, pronoun, participle and adjective had originally only one form for the masculine and feminine. The feminine dual of the article, τά, is hardly ever found in good writers. In considering the use of the plural for the dual, it should be remembered that in the Æolic dialect and in Latin there is no dual.

IX. *Constructions by Attraction.*

§. 389. The verbs εἶναι, γίγνεσθαι, καλεῖσθαι, &c., when used for the copula, sometimes, by a sort of attraction, agree in number with the substantive which stands as the predicate: Hdt. I. 93 ἡ μὲν δὴ περίοδος — εἰσὶ στάδιοι ἕξ, like III. 60 τὸ μὲν μῆκος τοῦ ὀρύγματος ἑπτὰ στάδιοί εἰσι: Id. II. 15 αἱ Θῆβαι Αἴγυπτος ἐκαλέετο: Æsch. Choeph. 317 sq. Χάριτες δ᾽ ὁμοίως κέκληνται γόος εὐκλεὴς προσθοδόμοις ᾽Ατρείδαις (subj. γόος, predicate Χάριτες): Thuc. III. 112 ἐστὸν δὲ δύω λόφω ἡ ᾽Ιδομένη ὑψηλώ: Id. IV. 102 τὸ χωρίον τοῦτο, ὅπερ πρότερον ᾽Εννέα ὁδοὶ ἐκαλοῦντο: Isocr. Paneg. p. 54. B ἐστι γὰρ ἀρχικώτατα τῶν ἐθνῶν καὶ μεγίστας δυναστείας ἔχοντα Σκύθαι καὶ Θρᾶκες καὶ Πέρσαι: Plat. Gorg. p. 502. C λόγοι γίγνονται τὸ λειπόμενον[b]: Id. Rep. p. 422 E ἑκάστη γὰρ αὐτῶν πόλεις εἰσὶ πάμπολλαι[c]: Demosth. p. 817. princ. τῶν χρημάτων τὸ κεφάλαιον πλέον ἢ ὀκτὼ τάλαντα καὶ τριάκοντα μναῖ γίγνονται (sic Bekker e Codd., vulgo γίγνεται). So id. p. 877, 26 ἥ τε προὶξ ὀγδοήκοντα μναῖ γενήσονται. So especially the Latin; as, Terent. Andr. III. 3, 23 *Amantium iræ amoris integratio est.* The same thing occurs in participial constructions; the participle not agreeing with the substantive of which it is a remote attributive, but

---

[a] Heind. ad loc.   [b] Heind. and Stallb. ad loc.   [c] Stallb. ad loc.

with another, which is the proper predicate of the clause in which the participle stands: Plat. Legg. p. 735. E τοὺς γὰρ μέγιστα ἐξημαρτηκότας, ἀνιάτους δὲ ὄντας, μεγίστην δὲ οὖσαν βλάβην πόλεως, ἀπαλλάττειν εἰωθεν (for ὄντας): Id. Parmen. p. 134. B πάντα, ἃ δὴ ὡς ἰδέας αὐτὰς οὖσας ὑπολαμβάνομεν : Eur. Troad. 1221 σύ τ', ὦ ποτ' οὖσα καλλίνικε μυρίων μῆτερ τροπαίων, Ἑκτορος φίλον σάκος. So Plat. Parm. p. 153. A τἆλλα τοῦ ἑνὸς, εἴπερ ἕτερά ἐστιν, ἀλλὰ μὴ ἕτερον, πλείω ἐστὶν ἑνός· ἕτερον μὲν γὰρ ὂν ἐν ἂν εἴη (for ὄντα referring to τἆλλα τοῦ ἑνός)· ἕτερα δὲ ὄντα πλείω ἑνός ἐστι καὶ πλῆθος ἂν ἔχοι: Ibid. p. 145. C ᾗ μὲν ἄρα τὸ ἐν ὅλον ἐν ἄλλῳ ἐστίν, ᾗ δὲ τὰ πάντα μέρη ὄντα (for ὂν referring to τὸ ἕν) τυγχάνει, αὐτὸ ἐν ἑαυτῷ.

Especial Peculiarities of Number, Gender and Person.

§. 390. 1. The construction often changes from the singular to the plural, and *vice versa :*

a. Xen. M. S. II. 3, 2 θαυμαστὸν δὲ τοῦτο, εἴ τις τοὺς ἀδελφοὺς ζημίαν ἡγεῖται,—τοὺς δὲ πολίτας οὐχ ἡγεῖται ζημίαν, ὅτι—ἔχει—δύναται· ἐπὶ δὲ τῶν ἀδελφῶν τὸ αὐτὸ τοῦτο ἀγνοοῦσιν.

b. A singular verb is sometimes used after a plural subject implied in some part of the sentence, when the notion which might be predicated of them all is limited *in animo loquentis* to a single individual : as early as Homer : Od. δ, 691 sq. ἥτ' ἐστὶ δίκη θείων βασιλήων, ἄλλον κ' ἐχθαίρῃσι βροτῶν, ἄλλον κε φιλοίη. Plat. Protag. p. 319. E τούτοις οὐδεὶς τοῦτο ἐπιπλήττει, ὥσπερ τοῖς πρότερον, ὅτι οὐδαμόθεν μαθών, οὐδὲ ὄντος διδασκάλου οὐδενὸς αὐτῷ, ἔπειτα συμβουλεύειν ἐπιχειρεῖ[a]: Ibid. p. 334. C ἀπαγορεύ ουσι τοῖς ἀσθενοῦσι — ἐν τούτοις οἷς μέλλει ἔδεσθαι, *in iis, quæ edere vult* for *volunt:* Id. Gorg. p. 478. B. C ἆρ' οὖν τὸ ἰατρεύεσθαι ἡδύ ἐστι καὶ χαίρουσιν οἱ ἰατρευόμενοι ;—μεγάλου γὰρ κακοῦ ἀπαλλάττεται : Eur. Hec. 1189 ἀνθρώποισιν οὐκ ἐχρῆν ποτε τῶν πραγμάτων τὴν γλῶσσαν ἰσχύειν πλέον, ἀλλ' εἴτε χρήστ' ἔδρασε, χρήστ' ἔδει λέγειν, εἴτ' αὖ πονηρά, τοὺς λόγους εἶναι σαθρούς : Id. Androm. 421 οἰκτρὰ γὰρ τὰ δυστυχῆ βροτοῖς ἅπασι, κἂν θυραῖος ὢν κυρῇ.

c. When the gender of the persons signified is not to have especial stress laid upon it, but only the notion of personality is conveyed, the adjective, standing as the predicate, or as an attribute of a femin. subst., is in the masc. as the more indefinite form of expression : Xen. M. S. II. 7, 2 συνε ληλύθασιν ὡς ἐμὲ καταλελειμμέναι ἀδελφαί τε καὶ ἀδελφιδαῖ καὶ ἀνε ψιαὶ τοσαῦται, ὥστ' εἶναι ἐν τῇ οἰκίᾳ τεσσαρεσκαίδεκα τοὺς ἐλευ θέρους. In a tragic chorus the masc. is used when the individual female speaks of herself : Eur. Hipp. 1119 sqq. ξύνεσιν δέ τιν' ἐλπίδι κεύθων λείπομαι ἔν τε τύχαις θνατῶν καὶ ἐν ἔργμασι λεύσσων. The masc. is regularly used when a woman is spoken of in the plural number. In the abstract plural notion the difference of sex is lost sight of, and the masc. is used as a more general expression of personality ; as, Eur. Androm. 711 ἢ στεῖρος οὖσα μόσχος οὐκ ἀνέξεται τίκτοντας ἄλλους (for τίκτουσαν ἄλλην, *Andromacham*), οὐκ ἔχουσ' αὐτὴ τέκνα : Soph. Œ. T. 1184 ὅστις πέφασμαι φύς τ' ἀφ' ὧν οὐ χρῆν, ξὺν οἷς τ' (i. e. τῇ μητρί) οὐ χρῆν μ' ὁμιλῶν. And so an

---

a Heindorf. et Stallb. Protag. 319. E.   Pflugk Hec. 1189.   Heind. Phæd. 62. Stallb. Rep. 389. D.   Brunck Aj. 760.   Elm. Med. 215.

attributive or predicative adjective (or mostly a participle) is in the masc. gender when the woman to whom it refers speaks of herself, using the first person plural [a], or a plural participle; as, Eur. Hec. 509 οὐκ ἄρ' ὡς θανουμένους μετῆλθες ἡμᾶς: Soph. Trach. 491. (Dejanira) κοῦτοι νόσον γ' ἐπακτὸν ἐξαιρούμεθα θεοῖσι δυσμαχοῦντες: Id. Electr. 391. (Electra) πεσούμεθ', εἰ χρή, πατρὶ τιμωρούμενοι: Id. Aj. 266. (Tecmessa) ἡμᾶς δὲ τοὺς βλέποντας ἠνία ξυνών: Eur. Iph. Aul. 828 οὐ θαυμά σ' ἡμᾶς (Clytæmnestram) ἀγνοεῖν, οὓς μὴ πάρος κατεῖδες. Also in Aristoph. Eccles. 30 sq. a woman says, ὡς ὁ κήρυξ ἀρτίως ἡμῶν προσιόντων δεύτερον κεκόκκυκεν, as I came up.

Obs. We must not class here the anomalous instances of masculine adjectives with feminine substantives, which were sometimes used by poetical license or carelessness; as, Soph. Trach. 207 κοινὸς κλαγγά: Æschyl. Ag. 558 δρόσοι τιθέντες ἔνθηρον τρίχα: Nicand. Ther. 329 καταψυχθέντος ἀκάνθης: Ibid. 129 ψολόεντος ἐχίδνης: Orph. Arg. 263 ὑλήεντι κολώνη: Œ. C. 751 πτωχῷ διαίτῃ: Soph. El. 614. and Œ. C. 751. even τηλικοῦτος is used for the feminine.

d. The Greeks, like the Latins, frequently spoke of themselves in the plural number, to signify that the action or opinion spoken of was participated in by others in some way connected with themselves; hence the plural and singular were interchanged as the notion varied. Among the earlier writers however this idiom is almost exclusively confined to poets. The prose writers used it only when the speaker was really connected in some common bond with others: Il. ν, 257 τό νυ (sc. ἔγχος) γὰρ κατεάξαμεν, ὃ πρὶν ἔχεσκον: Eur. Iph. T. 349 οἷσιν ἠγριώμεθα, δοκοῦσ' Ὀρέστην μηκέθ' ἥλιον βλέπειν; ubi v. Seidler: Id. H. F. 858 Ἥλιον μαρτυρόμεσθα δρῶσ', ἃ δρᾶν οὐ βούλομαι: Id. Ion. 1250 διωκόμεσθα θανασίμους ἐπὶ σφαγὰς Πυθίᾳ ψήφῳ κρατηθεὶς ἔκδοτος δὲ γίγνομαι: Id. Hipp. 244 αἰδούμεθα γὰρ τὰ λελεγμένα μοι: Id. Bacch. 668 φράσω τὰ 'κεῖθεν ἢ λόγον στειλώμεθα; Id. Androm. 142 δεσποτῶν δ' ἐμῶν φόβῳ ἡσυχίαν ἄγομεν; ubi v. Pflugk: Id. Iph. Aul. 991 sq. οἰκτρὰ γὰρ πεπόνθαμεν, ἢ πρῶτα μέν σε γαμβρὸν οἰηθεῖσ' ἔχειν, κενὴν κατέσχον ἐλπίδ': Aristoph. Ran. 213 φθεγξώμεθ' εὔγηρυν ἐμὰν ἀοιδάν: Theocr. VIII. 75 ἀλλὰ κάτω βλέψας τὰν ἁμετέραν ὁδὸν εἷρπον [b]: but with reference to a real community or corporation; Plat. Sympos. 186. B ἄρξομαι δὲ ἀπὸ τῆς ἰατρικῆς λέγων, ἵνα καὶ πρεσβεύωμεν (i. e. τιμῶμεν) τὴν τέχνην, where the medical man Eryximachus speaks for the whole profession.

2. In an address directed to more than one person, the Greek language has several singular idioms :—

a. The imperative εἰπέ, and some others which express only exhortation or encouragement, as ἄγε, φέρε, ἴδε, are joined by the Attics with one plural subst. or several singulars. This arose from the idioms of every day conversation : Arist. Acharn. 318 εἰπέ μοι, τί φειδόμεσθα τῶν λίθων, ὦ δημόται: Id. Pac. 385 εἰπέ μοι, τί πάσχετ', ὦνδρες: Plat. Euthyd. p. 283. B εἰπέ μοι, ὦ Σώκρατές τε καὶ ὑμεῖς οἱ ἄλλοι: cf. Protag. p. 311. D. Demosth. p. 108, 74 εἰπέ μοι, βουλεύεσθε: Id. p. 43, 7 ἢ βούλεσθε, εἰπέ μοι, περιιόντες αὐτῶν πυνθάνεσθαι: Soph. Trach. 824 ἴδ', οἷον, ὦ παῖδες, προσέμιξεν ἄφαρ τοὔπος τὸ θεοπρόπον ἡμῖν.

β. In the old poets, and sometimes in prose, a plural predicate addressed to many persons is joined with one of the persons so addressed in the

---

[a] Dawes Misc. Crit. 549. Herm. Vig. 713. R. P. Hec. 509.   [b] Wüsteman ad loc.

vocative singular; this person being considered as the chief among them : Od. β, 310 Ἀντίνο᾽, οὕπως ἔστιν ὑπερφιάλοισι μεθ᾽ ὑμῖν δαίνυσθαι : Od. μ, 82 νῆα ἰθύνετε, φαίδιμ᾽ Ὀδυσσεῦ : Pind. Ol. VIII. 15 Τιμόσθενες, ὔμμι δ᾽ ἐκλάρωσεν πότμος Ζηνί : Soph. Œ. C. 1102 ὦ τέκνον, ἦ πάρεστον; 1104 προσέλθετ᾽, ὦ παῖ (Œdipus is thinking of Ismene and Antigone, but only addresses the latter) : Xen. Hell. IV. 1, 11 ἵτ᾽, ἔφη, ὑμεῖς ὦ Ἡριππίδα, καὶ διδάσκετε αὐτὸν βουληθῆναι ἅπερ ἡμεῖς· οἱ μὲν δὴ ἀναστάντες ἐδίδασκον. This and analogous idioms are very frequent in tragedy, especially where the chorus is addressed by another or speaks of itself, as at one time the whole chorus presents itself to the mind, at another the coryphæus : Soph. Œ. C. 167 ξεῖνοι, μὴ δῆτ᾽ ἀδικηθῶ σοι πιστεύσας καὶ μεταναστάς : see Æschyl. Eum. 174 sqq. 780 sqq. 837 sqq. Suppl. 179, 204 sqq. 710, 735, 910 sq., where the chorus is addressed in the singular or plural, as may seem fit to the speaker. So also the chorus speaking of itself : Æschyl. Eum. 247 uses the plural; 246 sqq. the singular. So 354 sq. 666 [a].

γ. In the Attic dialect we find a singular construction of the second person Imper. with the indef. pronoun τίς or πᾶς τις, with or without a substantive; as, Aristoph. Av. 1186 χώρει δεῦρο πᾶς ὑπηρέτης· τόξευε πᾶς τις ; hence the change from the third person to the second : Eur. Bacch. 327 (346.) στειχέτω τις ὡς τάχος, ἐλθὼν δὲ θάκους τούσδ᾽, ἵν᾽ οἰωνοσκοπεῖ, μοχλοῖς τριαίνου κἀνάτρεψον ἔμπαλιν, καὶ—μέθες. This also doubtlessly arises from common conversation ; the indefinite subject being addressed as if in the presence of the speaker : English, " go every one of you ;" hence we may see that probably the Imperat. originally was used only in the second person, as commands are issued most naturally in that form.

Predicate with more than one Subject.

I. *Adjective.*

§. 391. 1. If all the subjects are of the same gender, the adjective stands in that gender in the plural ; as, ὁ Σωκράτης καὶ ὁ Πλάτων ἦσαν σοφοί—ἡ μήτηρ καὶ ἡ θυγάτηρ ἦσαν καλαί—ἡ ὀργὴ καὶ ἡ ἀσυνεσία εἰσὶ κακαί. So also attributives, whether immediate or remote ; as, ὁ Σωκράτης καὶ ὁ Πλάτων σοφοί or σοφοὶ ὄντες.

2. When the subjects differ in gender the plural form is used ; and with names of persons the masculine is preferred to the feminine, the feminine to the neuter. With names of inanimate things the neuter plural is used frequently without any regard to the gender of the subjects : Ὁ ἀνὴρ καὶ ἡ γυνὴ ἀγαθοί εἰσιν : Il. σ, 567 παρθενικαὶ δὲ καὶ ἠΐθεοι, ἀταλὰ φρονέοντες : Il. β, 136 αἱ δέ που ἡμέτεραί τ᾽ ἄλοχοι καὶ νήπια τέκνα εἵατ᾽ ἐνὶ μεγάροις ποτιδέγμεναι : Xen. Cyr. III. 1, 7 ὡς δὲ εἶδε πατέρα τε καὶ μητέρα καὶ ἀδελφοὺς καὶ τὴν ἑαυτοῦ γυναῖκα αἰχμαλώτους γεγενημένους, ἐδάκρυσεν : Od. ξ, 226 ἄκοντες ἐΰξεστοι καὶ ὀϊστοί, λυγρά : Od. ν, 435 ῥάκος ἄλλο κακὸν βάλεν ἠδὲ χιτῶνα ῥωγα-

---

[a] Elm. Med. 552.

λέα: Hdt. III. 57 ἦν τότε ἡ ἀγορὰ καὶ τὸ πρυτανήϊον Παρίῳ λίθῳ
ἠσκημένα: Xen. M. S. III. 1, 7 λίθοι τε καὶ πλίνθοι και ξύλα
καὶ κέραμος ἀτάκτως ἐρριμμένα οὐδὲν χρήσιμά ἐστιν.

Obs. Sometimes an adjective which is common to several subjects is
referred only to one of them, which is to be distinguished as the most
significant or important: Il. a, 177 αἰεὶ γὰρ ἔρις τε φίλη, πόλεμοί
τε μάχαι τε: Il. o, 193 γαῖα δ' ἔτι ξυνὴ πάντων καὶ μακρὸς Ὄλυμπος. The
same holds good in apposition; as, Æsch. Ag. 41 μέγας ἀντίδικος Μενέλαος
ἄναξ ἠδ' Ἀγαμέμνων.   For the same purpose an attributive adjective
agrees sometimes, not with the substantive nearest to it, but with one
further off: Il. o, 344 τάφρῳ καὶ σκολόπεσσιν ἐνιπλήξαντες ὀρυκτῇ:
Od. ι, 222 ναῖον δ' ὀρῷ ἄγγεα πάντα, γαυλοί τε σκαφίδες τε, τετυγμένα,
τοῖς ἐνάμελγεν: Hesiod. Theog. 973 ἐπὶ γῆν τε καὶ εὐρέα νῶτα θαλάσσης,
πᾶσαν: Id. Opp. 403 οἶκον μὲν πρώτιστα γυναῖκά τε, βοῦν τ' ἀροτῆρα,
κτητὴν, οὐ γαμετήν: Thuc. I. 54 τά τε ναυάγια καὶ νεκροὺς ἀνείλοντο
τὰ κατὰ σφᾶς: Xen. Anab. I. 5, 6 ἑπτὰ ὀβολοὺς καὶ ἡμιωβόλιον Ἀττι-
κούς: Plat. Hipp. 290. C τοὺς ὀφθαλμούς—πρόσωπον—πόδας—χεῖρας—
εἴπερ χρυσοῦν γε δὴ ὂν κάλλιστον ἔμελλε φαίνεσθαι, sc. πρόσωπον.   Analogously to this the adjective belonging to two substantives is joined
with the latter; as, Eur. Suppl. 23 τό τ' ἔγχος τήν τε δυστυχεστάτην στέ-
νων στρατείαν.

II. *Verb and Copula.*

a. PERSON.

§. 392. When several subjects differing in person are joined
together, the verb is generally in the plural, and the first person
is preferred to the second, and the second to the third; as, ἐγὼ
καὶ σὺ γράφομεν, *ego et tu scribimus:* ἐγὼ καὶ ἐκεῖνος γράφομεν, *ego
et ille scribimus:* ἐγὼ καὶ σὺ καὶ ἐκεῖνος γράφομεν, *ego et tu et ille
scribimus:* σὺ καὶ ἐκεῖνος γράφετε, *tu et ille scribitis:* ἐγὼ καὶ ἐκεῖνοι
γράφομεν, σὺ καὶ ἐκεῖνοι γράφετε, ἡμεῖς καὶ ἐκεῖνοι γράφομεν, ὑμεῖς
καὶ ἐκεῖνος γράφετε: Demosth. Phil. III. p. 129, 72 (πρεσβείας)
ἐγὼ καὶ Πολύευκτος—καὶ Ἡγήσιππος καὶ Κλειτόμαχος καὶ Λυκοῦργος
καὶ οἱ ἄλλοι πρέσβεις περιήλθομεν.

Obs. 1. Sometimes the verb agrees in number with the most prominent
subject; as, Eur. Med. 1020 ταῦτα γὰρ θεοὶ κἀγὼ κακῶς φρονοῦσ' ἐμη-
χανησάμην.

Obs. 2. Or sometimes with the subject nearest to it: Xen. M. S. IV.
4. 7 περὶ τοῦ δικαίου πάνυ οἶμαι -νῦν ἔχειν εἰπεῖν, πρὸς ἃ οὔτε σὺ οὔτ' ἂν
ἄλλος οὐδεὶς δύναιτ' ἀντειπεῖν: Plat. Phæd. p. 77. D ὅμως δέ μοι
δοκεῖς σύ τε καὶ Σιμμίας ἡδέως ἂν καὶ τοῦτον διαπραγματεύσασθαι (*per-
tractare*) τὸν λόγον.   So Isæus p. 84. ἡμεῖς δὲ καὶ Στράτιος καὶ Στρατοκλῆς
παρεσκευάζοντο ἅπαντες.

b. NUMBER.

§. 393. When several subjects are joined with one verb, the
verb generally stands in the plural number; as, ὁ Σωκράτης καὶ ὁ

Πλάτων ἦσαν σοφοί—ὁ Φίλιππος καὶ ὁ Ἀλέξανδρος πολλά τε καὶ
θαυμαστὰ ἔργα ἀπεδείξαντο.

Exceptions.

1. The verb frequently stands at the beginning of the sentence, and
agrees with the subject nearest to it; as, Il. π, 844 σοὶ γὰρ ἔδωκε νίκην
Ζεὺς Κρονίδης καὶ Ἀπόλλων: Il. α, 255 ἦ κεν γηθήσαι Πρίαμος
Πριάμοιό τε παῖδες: Il. η, 386 ἠνώγει Πρίαμός τε καὶ ἄλλοι Τρῶες ἀγαυοί:
Plat. Lys. p. 207. D φιλεῖ σε ὁ πατὴρ καὶ ἡ μήτηρ: Hdt. V. 21 εἵπετο
γὰρ δή σφι καὶ ὀχήματα καὶ θεράποντες καὶ ἡ πᾶσα πολλὴ παρασκευή ; by this
construction the two subjects are represented as united under some common notion, such as father and mother : Xen. Anab. II. 4, 16 ἐπεμψέ με
Ἀριαῖος καὶ Ἀρτάοζος, πιστοὶ ὄντες Κύρῳ καὶ ὑμῖν εὖνοι, καὶ κελεύουσι
φυλάττεσθαι ; where the change of the number is remarkable. In poetry
sometimes the singular verb is placed after the first subject; as, Eur.
Suppl. 146 Τυδεὺς μάχην ξυνῆψε Πολυνείκης θ᾽ ἅμα : Aristoph. Vesp. 1450
Λᾶσός ποτ᾽ ἀντεδίδασκε καὶ Σιμωνίδης.
2. The verb stands at the end of the sentence, and agrees in number
with the nearest subject. By this construction, as in the last mentioned, a common notion of the two subjects is expressed : Xen. R. Ath.
691. E πένητες καὶ δῆμος πλέον ἔχει : Plat. Symp. p. 190. C αἱ τιμαὶ
γὰρ αὐτοῖς καὶ τὰ ἱερὰ τὰ παρὰ τῶν ἀνθρώπων ἠφανίζετο : Demosth.
307. D τριήρεις καὶ σκεύη καὶ κτήματα περίεστι : Diod. Sic. XX. c. 72
δάκρυα καὶ δεήσεις καὶ θρῆνος ἐγένετο συμφορητός : Strabo V. 350. A
Ἔρνικοι καὶ ἄλλα συστήματα ὑπῆρξε. The change of the number is
remarkable in Od. μ, 43 τῷ δ᾽ οὔτι γυνὴ καὶ νήπια τέκνα οἴκαδε νοστήσαντι
παρίσταται, οὐδὲ γάνυνται.
Obs. If the subjects are names of persons, the verb is properly used
in the singular only when it precedes, or stands between the subjects; but
sometimes is in the singular, when it stands after the subjects.
3. If all the subjects are neuter plurals, the verb is in the singular; as,
πολλά τε καὶ καλὰ καὶ θαυμαστὰ ἐγένετο.
4. If the subjects are names of things in the singular, the verb is
in the plural, when the subjects differ in species, or are opposed to
each other; as, ἡ τῆς ψυχῆς ἀρετὴ καὶ τὸ τοῦ σώματος κάλλος θαυμάζονται, but
in the singular when the subjects are conceived under one common notion ;
as, ἡ τῆς ψυχῆς ἀρετὴ καὶ τὸ τοῦ σώματος κάλλος θαυμάζεται.
5. σχῆμα Ἀλκμανικόν—the plural (or dual) verb is used with a singular noun, when some other noun follows to which it also refers. This
construction received its name from its being, according to the grammarians,
frequently used by Alcman : but it is found as early as Homer : Il. ε, 774
ἧχι ῥοὰς Σιμόεις συμβάλλετον ἠδὲ Σκάμανδρος : Od. κ, 513 ἔνθα μὲν
εἰς Ἀχέροντα Πυριφλεγέθων τε ῥέουσιν Κώκυτός τε : Il. υ, 138 εἰ
δέ κ᾽ Ἄρης ἄρχωσι μάχης ἢ Φοῖβος Ἀπόλλων. So also in construction
with a participle ; Pind. Pyth. IV. 179 τὸν μὲν Ἐχίονα κεχλάοντας ἥβᾳ, τὸν δ᾽
Ἔρυτον[a].
6. Sometimes the verb, though preceded by several subjects, agrees
with the first whereto the others are represented as subordinate : Il. ρ, 387
γούνατά τε καὶ κνῆμαί τε, πόδες θ᾽ ὑπένερθεν ἑκάστου χεῖρές τ᾽ ὀφθαλμοί τε
παλάσσετο μαρναμενοῖιν : Il. ψ, 380 πνοιῇ δ᾽ Εὐμήλοιο μετάφρενον

---

[a] Valck. Amm. p. 180 not. Welcker Alcm. p. 21. Diss. Pind. ad loc.

εὑρίε τ' ὥμω θέρμετ'.   Even with names of persons : Xen. Anab. I. 10, 1 βασιλεὺς δὲ καὶ οἱ σὺν αὐτῷ διώκων εἰσπίπτει: cf. Poppo. Here also we may refer Od. θ, 48. ἧ κούρω δὲ κρινθέντε δύω καὶ πεντήκοντα βήτην.

7. The verb stands sometimes in the singular, even when preceded by several names of things in the plural: Plat. Symp. p. 188 B καὶ γὰρ πάχναι καὶ χάλαζαι καὶ ἐρυσίβαι ἐκ πλεονεξίας καὶ ἀκοσμίας περὶ ἄλληλα τῶν τοιούτων γίγνεται ἐρωτικῶν, these things being conceived as component parts of one state.

8. If several subjects are disjunctively united by ἤ—ἤ, either—or, οὔτε —οὔτε, *neque—neque*, the verb is in the singular when an actual disjunction is intended, so that the predicate cannot be said of the one if it can be said of the other; as, ἢ οὗτος ἢ ἐκεῖνος ἀληθῆ λέγει, *aut hic, aut ille vera dicit*, like Cicer. N. D. III. 12 *omne corpus aut aqua aut aër aut ignis aut terra est, aut aliquid, quod est concretum ex iis, aut ex aliqua parte eorum:* or in the plural, when the predicate refers to all the subjects equally, at the same time and in the same manner; as, Il. υ, 138 εἰ δέ κ' Ἄρης ἄρχωσι μάχης ἢ Φοῖβος Ἀπόλλων, ἢ Ἀχιλῆ ἴσχωσι καὶ οὐκ εἰῶσι μάχεσθαι: Eur. Alc. 367 καί μ' οὔθ' ὁ Πλούτωνος κύων οὔθ' οὑπὶ κώπῃ ψυχοπομπὸς ἂν γέρων ἴσχουª: Demosth. p. 817, 12 ἃ μὲν οὖν Δημοφῶν ἢ Θηριππίδης ἔχουσι τῶν ἐμῶν: ubi v. Bremi Varr. Lectt. p. 25. So ibid. p. 814, 4 ἅπαντα ταῦτα ἐνεχείρισεν Ἀφόβῳ τε τούτῳ καὶ Δημοφῶντι, τῷ Δήμωνος υἱεῖ, τούτοιν μὲν ἀδελφιδοῖν ὄντοιν, τῷ μὲν ἐξ ἀδελφοῦ, τῷ δ' ἐξ ἀδελφῆς γεγονότοιν: Lucian. Ver. Hist. II. 19 πολλάκις γοῦν ὁ μὲν Ὑάκινθος ἢ ὁ Νάρκισσος ὡμολόγουν. So in Latin; as, Cicer. de Offic. I. 41, 148 *si quid Socrates aut Aristippus contra morem consuetudinemque civilem fecerint locutive sint*[b].

B.

THE TEMPORAL RELATIONS OF THE PREDICATE[c].

§. 394. 1. Every thing is considered by the speaker primarily with reference to the time present to himself, his present belief or conception, as being either coincident with it, or antecedent to it, or consequent upon it—present—past—future; a present belief that something has happened, is happening, or will happen; which relations are expressed by three forms, called tenses; γράφω, present: ἔγραψα, past: γράψω, future. And when these relations are by these forms expressed absolutely, without reference to any other action, they are called the *Absolute Tenses*.

2. But an action may not only be thus defined by its reference, whether as past, present, or future, to the time present to the speaker, but may also have a reference to some other action expressed by some other predicate, whether it be antecedent to, coincident with, or consequent on this action; that is, whether it be ended before this other action is going on, finished, or intended; whether

---

ª Monk ad loc.   b Matth. Eur. Hec. 84.   c Dissen Kleine Schriften, p. 1. 599.

both are, or were, or will be going on at the same time; or whether it is not yet begun, but only conceived as about to happen, while the other is going on, or finished, or intended.   For these also the Greek has forms, which are called the *Relative Tenses*.

3. As then the action itself is spoken of as past, present, or future, and in each of these relations may be conceived of in reference to some other action already past, or at that time going on, or as intended to be done, there are altogether nine relative tenses, of which those of time past and present are expressed by the inflexions of the verb, those of time future are sometimes supplied by the auxiliary verb μέλλω: the forms of the absolute present and future γράφω, γράψω, perform also the functions of the relative present and future; as, γράφω ἐπιστολὴν ἐν ᾧ σὺ παίζεις—ἐπεὶ οἱ βάρβαροι ἐγγὺς ἔσονται οἱ Ἕλληνες μαχοῦνται.

4. While the Absolute Tenses signify only the three notions of time, antecedent, coincident, consequent, without reference to any other predicate, the Relative Tenses express these temporal notions of the predicate, and also their relation to some other predicate, in past, present, or future time.

Obs. The difference between the absolute and relative tenses may be illustrated thus:

Pr. Abs.—The sun rises in the heavens; no definite notion of time, but extending through all time.

Pr. Rel.—The sun is rising in the heavens; now while I am speaking. This definition generally is not expressed, as it is implied in and suggested by the preposition.

Past Abs.—The sun rose; no definite time necessarily implied.

Past Rel.—The sun was rising, had risen, suggests the question, When? which is answered by the proper definition, When this happened, &c.

5. The relative tenses are divided into Principal (Present, Perfect, and Future) and Historic Tenses (Imperfect, Pluperfect, and Futurum exactum).   The Predicate of the Historic Tenses always has reference to some other predicate, either expressed or implied. The Predicate of the Principal Tenses often refers only to the time or act of speaking; as, νῦν γράφω—γέγραφα τὴν ἐπιστολήν, while I speak I am writing, have written.

6. The Præteritum absolutum (the Aorist) is opposed both to the Impft. and Plpft., and to the Perfect.   The Impft. and Plpft. signify a continued action in time past; the Aorist, a momentary action in time past; the Pft. a completed action in time past, but continuing in its effects; whereas the Aorist has no collateral notion of the effect.

7. Table of the Absolute and Relative Tenses:

	Present.	Past.	Future.
I. Absolute.	γράφω.	ἔγραψα.	γράψω.·
II. Relative. *a.* Coincidence. Action yet going on. Imperfect.	γράφω.	ἔγραφον.	γράψω.
b. Antecedence. Action past. Preterite.	γέγραφα.	ἐγεγράφειν.	γεγραφὼς ἔσομαι.
c. Consequence. Action yet to come. Future.	μέλλω γράφειν.	ἔμελλον γράφειν.	μελλήσω γράφειν.

8. Examples of the Relative Tenses:

I. *a.* Present Impf. (Pres.Proper) } γράφω τὴν ἐπιστολὴν ἐν ᾧ σὺ παίζεις.   Coincident with ⎫

   b. Present Perft. { γέγραφα τὴν ἐπ., the letter has been written, and is ready while I speak. } Antecedent to ⎬ a present action.

   c. Present Fut. { μέλλω γράφειν (γράψω), I intend to write while I am speaking. .... } Consequent on ⎭

II. *a.* Pret. Impft. (Impft.Proper) } ἔγραφον τὴν ἐπ. ἐν ᾧ σὺ ἔπαιζες ....   Coincident with ⎫

   b. Pret. Perfect ...ἐγεγράφειν τὴν ἐπ. ὅτε σὺ ἦλθες ....   Antecedent to ⎬ a past action. a fut. action.

   c. Pret. Future ...ἔμελλον γράφειν ὅτε σὺ ἦλθες ....   Consequent on ⎭

III. *a.* Future Impft....γράψω τὴν ἐπ. ἐν ᾧ σὺ παιξεῖ......... ..   Coincident with ⎫

   b. Future Perft. ...ἡ ἐπιστολὴ γεγράψεται ὅταν σὺ παραγένῃ   Antecedent to ⎬

   c. FutureFuture...μελλήσω γρ. ὅτε σὺ παραγενήσει ....   Consequent on ⎭

Explanation of names of the tenses given above.

I. An action which is still going on of course is not yet completed, and therefore the tense expressing such an action is termed generally Imperfect.

   a. Pres. Impft.—I am now doing this; action not completed now.

   b. Pres. Pft.—I have done this; action at present time past and completed.

   c. Pres. Fut.—I shall do it; I am at the present time in such a position that I shall do it.

II. *a.* Pret. Impft.—I was doing it; at some past time the action was going on, and imperfect.

    b. Pret. Pft.—I had done it; at some past time the action was completed.

    c. Pret. Fut.—I was about to do it; at some past time I was in such a position that I was about to do it.

III. *a.* Fut. Impft.—I shall do it; at some future time, the action will be going on and imperfect.

    b. Fut. Pft.—I shall have done it; at some future time the action will be completed.

    c. Fut. Fut.—I shall be about to do it; at some future time I shall be in such a position that I shall be about to do it.

Obs. The Infinitive and Participle express only the absolute time of the action as past, present, or future, λέξαι, λέγειν, λέξειν, without defining it by referring it to some other action, relatively to which it is past, present, or future ; so that the different forms of the Part. and Infin. past, present, or future, may be used indifferently with a past, present, or future verb ; as, βούλομαι λέγειν, ἠβουλόμην λέγειν, βουλήσεται λέγειν : γελῶν λέγει, γελῶν ἔλεγε, γελῶν λέξει : λέγει γεγραφέναι (γράψαι), ἔλεξε γεγραφέναι (γράψαι), λέξει γεγραφέναι (γράψαι) : γεγραφὼς (γράψας) λέγει, γεγραφὼς (γράψας) ἔλεξε, γεγραφὼς (γράψας) λέξει : ἐλπίζει εὖ πράξειν, ἤλπιζεν εὖ πράξειν, ἐλπίσει εὖ πράξειν : παρασκευάζεται ὡς λέξων, παρεσκευάζετο ὡς λέξων, παρασκευάσεται ὡς λέξων.

Present Absolute—Present Historic.

§. 395. 1. The Present properly signifies an incomplete action yet in course of performance, going on at the same time with another action then also going on—which is generally the act of speaking. But the notion of present is extended so as to comprehend indefinite spaces of time, as we say " the present age ;" and in this way the present is absolute, as referring to no particular moment when the action takes place ; as, φασί, aiunt. This absolute present is used in general propositions, proverbs, comparisons, and in speaking of manners and customs, or of any thing which frequently happens ; as, ὁ ἥλιος λάμπει: ὁ ἄνθρωπός ἐστι θνητός: Il. π, 364 ὡς δ' ὅτ' ἀπ' Οὐλύμπου νέφος ἔρχεται.

2. Another use of the absolute present is historic ; when to give animation to the narration past events are spoken of as present, and thus brought more vividly before the mind. This takes place even in dependent sentences, especially in adjectival sentences introduced by a relative pronoun ; as, Xen. Anab. I. 7, 16 ταύτην δὲ τὴν τάφρον βασιλεὺς μέγας π ο ι ε ῖ ἀντὶ ἐρύματος, ἐ π ε ι δ ὴ π υ ν θ ά ν ε τ α ι Κῦρον προσελαύνοντα: Eur. Med. 955 εὐδαιμονήσει δ' οὐχ ἕν, ἀλλὰ μυρία, ἀνδρός τ' ἀρίστου σοῦ τυχοῦσ' ὁμευνέτου, κεκτημένη τε κόσμον, ὅν ποθ' Ἥλιος πατρὸς πατὴρ δ ί δ ω σ ι ν ἐκγόνοισιν οἷς: Id. Hec. 1134 ἦν τις Πριαμιδῶν νεώτατος Πολύδωρος, Ἑκάβης παῖς, ὃ ν ἐκ Τροίας ἐμοὶ πατὴρ δ ί δ ω σ ι Πρίαμος ἐν δόμοις τρέφειν: Ibid. 963 τ υ γ χ ά ν ω γὰρ ἐν μέσοις Θρῄκης ὅροις ἀπὼν, ὅτ' ἦλθες δεῦρο.

Obs. 1. On the interchange of the Historic Pres. with the Impft. and Aor. see *Index.*

Obs. 2. This use of the absolute present is found also in the Infin. of which the Pres. is very often used in the *oratio obliqua* for the Aorist; as, Hdt. VI. 137 Ἀθηναῖοι λέγουσι, δικαίως ἐξελάσαι· κατοικημένους γὰρ τοὺς Πελασγοὺς ὑπὸ τῷ Ὑμησσῷ, ἐνθεῦτεν ὁρμεωμένους, ἀδικέειν τάδε· φοιτᾶν γὰρ αἰεὶ τὰς σφετέρας θυγατέρας τε καὶ τοὺς παῖδας ἐπ' ὕδωρ — · οὐ γὰρ εἶναι τούτον τὸν χρόνον σφίσι κω — οἰκέτας· ὅκως δὲ ἔλθοιεν αὐταί, τοὺς Πελασγοὺς ὑπὸ ὕβριος — βιᾶσθαί σφεας κ. τ. λ.: Xen. M. S. II. 6, 31 πέπυσμαι καὶ ἀπὸ τῆς Σκύλλης διὰ τοῦτο φεύγειν τοὺς ἀνθρώπους, ὅτι τὰς χεῖρας αὐτοῖς προσέφερε· τὰς δέ γε Σειρῆνας, ὅτι τὰς χεῖρας οὐδενὶ προσέφερον, ἀλλὰ πᾶσι πόρρωθεν ἐπῇδον, πάντας φασὶν ὑπομένειν καὶ ἀκούοντας αὐτῶν κηλεῖσθαι: Plat. Symp. p.175. C μετὰ ταῦτα ἔφη σφᾶς μὲν δειπνεῖν (*cœnasse*), τὸν δὲ Σωκράτη οὐκ εἰσιέναι (*introisse*) : Id. Rep. p. 614. C δικαστὰς δὲ μεταξὺ τούτων καθῆσθαι· οὕς, ἐπειδὴ διαδικάσειαν, τοὺς μὲν δικαίους κελεύειν πορεύεσθαι τὴν εἰς δεξιάν—ὁρᾶν δή κ. τ. λ.

§. 396. Several verbs have in their Pres. the sense of the Pft., as implying the action whence the present state arises ; as, οἴχομαι, I am gone=have departed ; or when a past action is expressed as past in time present, without distinct reference to its implied effects, the sense of the Aorist ; as, τίκτειν, *parentem esse* = *procreasse* (Aor.).   So always, ἥκω, *veni*, *adsum* (for ἐλήλυθα), and the following verbs of perception, ἀκούω, and the poetic κλύω, *audivi* (for ἀκήκοα), πυνθάνομαι, αἰσθάνομαι, γιγνώσκω, μανθάνω : Od. ο, 403 νῆσός τις Συρίη κικλήσκεται, εἴ που ἀκούεις (hear and have heard) : Il. ε, 472 πῇ δή τοι μένος οἴχεται, ὃ πρὶν ἔχεσκες (is gone = has departed): cf. ο, 223 : Od. π, 24 οὔ σ' ἔτ' ἔγωγε ὄψεσθαι ἐφάμην (*putabam*), ἐπεὶ ᾦχεο (*profectus fueras*) νηὶ Πύλονδε : Xen. Cyr. VI. 1, 45 μὴ λυποῦ, ὅτι Ἀράσπας οἴχεται εἰς τοὺς πολεμίους: Ibid. VIII. 3, 28 οὐ μετεστράφη, ἀλλ' ᾦχετο (as Aor.) ἐφ' ὅπερ ἐτάχθη. So ἀποίχεσθαι: Hdt. IX. 58 Μαρδόνιος, ὡς ἐπύθετο τοὺς Ἕλληνας ἀποιχομένους: Id. III. 72 φὰς ἄρτι τε ἥκειν (*adesse*, *venisse*) ἐκ Περσέων : Eur. Hec. princ. ἥκω νεκρῶν κευθμῶνα καὶ σκότου πύλας λιπών: Demosth. p. 28, 1 τὰ δὲ πράγματ' εἰς τοῦτο προήκοντα (ὁρῶ), ubi v. Schæfer: Plat. Gorg. p. 503 C Θεμιστοκλέα οὐκ ἀκούεις ἄνδρα ἀγαθὸν γεγονότα; Soph. Trach. 68 καὶ ποῦ κλύεις νιν, τέκνον, ἱδρύσθαι χθονός; Hdt. I. 69 πάντα πυνθανόμενος ὁ Κροῖσος ἔπεμπε ἐς Σπάρτην ἀγγέλους : Euripid. ἄρτι γιγνώσκεις τόδε ; ἄρτι μανθάνω (Bacch. 1297.).   Trag. and also other poets : θνήσκειν, *mortuum esse*, τίκτειν, τεκνοῦν, (Eur. Herc. 7) γεννᾶν τινα, *procreare et parentem esse.*

Obs. The Pres. of οἴχομαι seems in Homer always to have the sense of the Impft. or Aorist, but the Impft. is sometimes found in Homer in its proper sense ; as, Il. ε, 495 πάλλων δ' ὀξέα δοῦρα κατὰ στρατὸν ᾦχετο πάντῃ, ὀτρύνων μαχέσασθαι, ἔγειρε δὲ φύλοπιν αἰνήν.

§. 397. The Present is sometimes used for the Future, as in other languages; (*a*) when the future time need not be expressly marked; this is most plainly the case in the Inf. with such verbs as δοκῶ, νομίζω, ἡγοῦμαι, οἶμαι, ἐλπίζω, ὁμολογῶ, ὄμνυμι &c.; (*b*) when the certainty of the future event is to be signified, to which end it is represented as actually taking place:—

a. Lysias 145, 25 ὑμᾶς δὲ χρὴ τὴν αὐτὴν γνώμην ἔχοντας τὴν ψῆφον φέρειν, ἥνπερ ὅτε ᾤεσθε πρὸς τοὺς πολεμίους διακινδυνεύειν: Xen. M. S. I. 2, 3 οὐδὲ πώποτε ὑπέσχετο διδάσκαλος εἶναι τούτου: Id. Anab. VII. 7, 31 ἐὰν οἱ μὲν στρατιῶται ὑπισχνῶνται προθυμότερον αὐτοῖς συστρατεύεσθαι: Isocr. 130. B μὴ γὰρ οἴεσθ᾽ αὐτοὺς μένειν ἐπὶ τούτοις. So in general propositions where the time is not‛exactly defined : Eur. Troad. 1204 θνητῶν δὲ μωρὸς ὅστις εὖ πράσσειν δοκῶν βέβαια χαίρει: Id. Alc. 1091 μῶν τὴν θανοῦσαν ὠφελεῖν τι προσδοκᾷς. So the verb εἶμι and its compounds have, in Ionic prose and the Attic dialect, a future force,—*I will go.* The Inf. and Particip. of this verb have both a pres. and fut. force, and so in Homer have the Indic. and Opt.: Od. δ, 401 τῆμος ἄρ᾽ ἐξ ἁλὸς εἶσι γέρων —, ἐκ δ᾽ ἐλθὼν κοιμᾶται: Il. α, 426 καὶ τότ᾽ ἔπειτά τοι εἶμι Διὸς ποτὶ χαλκοβατὲς δῶ: Æsch. Prom. 325 εἶμι καὶ πειράσομαι: Eur. Hec. 1054 ἄπειμι κἀποστήσομαι: Ibid. 1196 πρὸς τόνδε δ᾽ εἶμι καὶ λόγοις ἀμείψομαι: Id. Med. 275 οὐκ ἄπειμι πρὸς δόμους πάλιν, πρὶν ἄν σε γαίας τερμόνων ἔξω βάλω: Xen. Cyr. I. 2, 15 ἵνα δὲ σαφέστερον δηλωθῇ πᾶσα ἡ Περσῶν πολιτεία, μικρὸν ἐπάνειμι (*paucis repetam*): Ibid. VI. 1, 5 ἄπειμι—στρατηγήσω: Plat. Apol. p. 29. E οὐκ εὐθὺς ἀφήσω αὐτὸν οὐδ᾽ ἄπειμι, ἀλλ᾽ ἐρήσομαι αὐτὸν καὶ ἐξετάσω καὶ ἐλέγξω. So Hdt. VIII. 60 παρέσονται—ἀπίασί τε[a]. Inf. and Particip.: Thuc. V. 7 ἐνόμιζεν ἀπιέναι, ὅταν βούληται, *se abiturum esse, quando vellet* : Plat. Phæd. p. 103. D καὶ τὸ πῦρ γε αὖ, προσιόντος τοῦ ψυχροῦ αὐτῷ, ἢ ὑπεξιέναι (*recessurum esse*) ἢ ἀπολεῖσθαι: Xen. Cyr. I. 3, 13 ἐπεὶ δὲ ἡ Μανδάνη παρεσκευάζετο ὡς ἀπιοῦσα πάλιν πρὸς τὸν ἄνδρα, ἐδεῖτο αὐτῆς ὁ Ἀστυάγης καταλιπεῖν τὸν Κῦρον: Thuc. V. 10 ἐξιόντων: Id. V. 65 ὡς ἰόντες.

b. Il. λ, 365 ἦ θήν σ᾽ ἐξανύω γε (*profecto te conficio*), καὶ ὕστερον ἀντιβολήσας, εἴ πού τις καὶ ἔμοιγε θεῶν ἐπιτάρροθός ἐστιν. Hence in oracles; as, Hdt. VII. 140 οὔτε γὰρ ἡ κεφαλὴ μένει ἔμπεδον, οὔτε τὸ σῶμα—λείπεται, ἀλλ' ἄζηλα πέλει &c. Infinitive : Soph. Trach. 170 τοιαῦτ' ἔφραζε πρὸς θεῶν εἱμαρμένα τῶν Ἡρακλείων ἐκτελευτᾶσθαι πόνων.

Imperfect.

§. 398. 1. The Impft. is to time past what the Pres. is to time present ; both express an action yet in course of performance, and not yet completed. By the Imperfect, an action is represented as going on in time past, relatively to another action also in time past. The Imperfect is never used absolutely, but always in relation to some other predicate expressed or implied. This predicate is in the Imperfect when its action is supposed to be coincident with the Imperfect ; as, ὅτε ἐγγὺς ἦσαν οἱ βάρβαροι, οἱ Ἕλληνες ἐμάχοντο : if the action is antecedent to the Impft. it is in the Plpft. or Aor. ; as, ὅτε οἱ βάρβαροι ἐπεληλύθεσαν οἱ Ἕλληνες ἐμάχοντο.

2. As both the Pres. and Impft. signify an action not yet completed, they are often used to express the attempt to do any thing. This is especially the case where the action is such that the consent or cooperation of another party is necessary to its completion. In this case the will is taken for the deed, which is therein commenced : Od. π, 431 τοῦ νῦν οἶκον ἄτιμον ἔδεις (consumis), μνᾷ δὲ γυναῖκα, παῖδά τ' ἀποκτείνεις, interficere conaris. So ἔκτεινον, ἀπωλλύμην, perdebar : Eur. H. F. 538 τἄμ' ἔθνησκε τέκν', ἀπωλλύμην δ' ἐγώ, liberi mei morituri erant &c. : Id. Phœn. 81 ἐγὼ δ' (Jocasta) ἔριν λύουσ', ὑπόσπονδον μολεῖν ἔπεισα παιδὶ παῖδα, πρὶν ψαῦσαι δορός : Id. El. 1024 κεἰ μὲν, πόλεως ἅλωσιν ἐξιώμενος ἢ δῶμ' ὀνήσων, τἄλλά τ' ἐκσώζων τέκνα, ἔκτεινε πολλῶν μίαν ὕπερ, συγγνώστ' ἂν ἦν : Ibid. 1298 ἐξένευσ' ἀποστῆναι, πρόσω Ἀγαμέμνονος παῖς, ὡς ἀπόρρητον φλόγα θύουσα : Hdt. VI. 82 πρὶν—μάθῃ, εἴτε οἱ ὁ θεὸς παραδιδοῖ, εἴτε οἱ ἐμποδὼν ἕστηκε : Xen. Cyr. I. 3, 14 ἔπειτα τά τε νῦν ὄντα ἐν τῷ παραδείσῳ θηρία δίδωμί σοι, καὶ ἄλλα παντοδαπὰ συλλέξω : Demosth. p. 849, 17 οὐδ' ἐμοῦ παραδιδόντος (τὸν παῖδα, quum traditurus non essem), παραλαβεῖν ἠθέλησεν, and so frequently in this oration. Hdt. III. 81 τὰ (i. e. ἃ) μὲν Ὀτάνης εἶπε, τυραννίδα παύων (aboliturus), λελέχθω κἀμοὶ ταῦτα : Xen. Hell. II. 1, 29 ἡ Πάραλος ἐς τὰς Ἀθήνας ἔπλευσεν, ἀπαγγέλλουσα τὰ γεγονότα. So often the Pr. Part. after verbs of motion : Eur. Suppl. 131 τούτους θανόντας ἦλθον ἐξαιτῶν πόλιν : Demosth. p. 69, 15 τοὺς μὲν ὄντας ἐχθροὺς Θηβαίων Λακεδαιμονίους ἀναιρεῖ, οὓς δ' ἀπώλεσεν αὐτὸς πρότερον Φωκέας νῦν σώζει ; καὶ τίς ἂν ταῦτα πιστεύσειεν ;

3. Hence arises the analogous usage of the Impft. or Aorist in sense of Inipft., where the Impft. with ἄν is more usual, in the sense of Fut. with ἔμελλεν, to express an action which was not completed, but would have been so under certain circumstances ; as, ἐβουλόμην, I would, that is, if I might: Eur. Iph. T. 26 ἐλθοῦσα δ᾽ Αὐλῖδ᾽ ἡ τάλαινα (Iphigenia)— ἐ κ α ι ν ό μ η ν ξίφει, ἀλλ᾽ ἐξέκλεψεν—᾿Αρτεμις (εἰ μὴ ἐξέκλεψεν): Id. Med. 1182 ἤδη—ταχὺς βαδιστὴς τερμόνων ἀ ν θ ή π τ ε τ ο, *assequuturus erat ; at assecutus non est :* Id. Bacch. 612 τίς μοι φύλαξ ἦ ν, εἰ σὺ συμφορᾶς τύχοις[a]. Sometimes the omission of ἄν gives irony to the verb : Arist. Nub. 1338 ἐδιδαξάμην μέντοι σε[b]. So χρῆν, *oportebat ;* ἔδει, *necesse erat ;* καλῶς εἶχε, &c.: hence the conditional usage of the Impft. with ἄν.

4. The Impft. is sometimes used for the Present, when the thought which the sentence expresses is not taken merely as an indefinite proposition, true at the present moment, but is referred in the speaker's mind to some time past ; as, Il. π, 29 τοὺς μέν τ᾽ ἰητροὶ πολυφάρμακοι ἀμφιπένονται, ἕλκε᾽ ἀκειόμενοι· σὺ δ᾽ ἀμή-χανος ἔ π λ ε ν, ᾿Αχιλλεῦ! cf. the preceding verse : Plat. Crit. p. 47. D διαφθεροῦμεν ἐκεῖνο καὶ λωβησόμεθα, ὃ τῷ μὲν δικαίῳ βέλτιον ἐ γ ί γ ν ε τ ο, τῷ δὲ ἀδίκῳ ἀ π ώ λ λ υ τ ο: for ὃ τῷ μὲν δικ. βέλτιον γίγνεσθαι, τῷ δὲ ἀδ. ἀπόλλυσθαι ἐ λ έ γ ε τ ο ἑκάστοτε ὑφ᾽ ἡμῶν περὶ τῶν τοιούτων διαλεγομένων: vide S t a l l b a u m. So especially the Impft. ἦν is used for ἐστί, referring to some past thought ; as, Il. ε, 331 Κύπριν ἐπῴχετο—γιγνώσκων, ὅτ᾽ ἄναλκις ἔ η ν θεός: Plat. Rep. p. 406. E ἆρ᾽, ἦν δ᾽ ἐγώ, ὅτι ἦ ν τι αὐτῷ ἔργον: S t a l l-b a u m ὅτι ἐστὶν αὐτῷ, ὡς ἄρτι ἐ λ έ γ ο μ ε ν, ἔργου τι : Ibid. p. 436. C εἰσόμεθα, ὅτι οὐ ταὐτὸν ἦ ν, ἀλλὰ πλείω, i. e. ὅτι οὐ ταὐτόν ἐστιν, ὥ σ π ε ρ ᾠ ό μ ε θ α : cf. ibid. p. 609. B. Id. Phædr. p. 230. A ἀτὰρ, ὦ ἑταῖρε, μεταξὺ τῶν λόγων, ἆρ᾽ οὐ τόδε ἦ ν τὸ δένδρον, ἐφ᾽ ὅπερ ἦγες ἡμᾶς, ubi v. S t a l l b a u m. Connected with this is the use of ἦν with ἄρα to express an opinion or expect-ation which has turned out to be wrong[c]. The Impft. refers to the moment when the mistake was made, when the thing was of the nature it has now turned out to be, though it seemed to be of a contrary nature : Od. π, 420 ᾿Αντίνο᾽, ὕβριν ἔχων, κακομήχανε, καὶ δέ σέ φασιν ἐν δήμῳ ᾿Ιθάκης μεθ᾽ ὁμήλικας ἔμμεν᾽ ἄριστον βουλῇ καὶ μύθοισι· σὺ δ᾽ οὐκ ἄ ρ α τοῖος ἔ η σ θ α: Soph. Phil. 975 ὅδ᾽ ἦ ν ἄ ρ α ὁ ξυλλαβών με : Eur. Med. 703 ξυγγνωστὰ μ έ ν τ ἄ ρ᾽ ἦ ν σε λυπεῖσθαι, γύναι: Plat. Gorg. p. 516. D ο ὐ κ ἄ ρ᾽ ἀγαθὸς τὰ πολι-τικὰ Περικλῆς ἦ ν ἐκ τούτου τοῦ λόγου, i. e. οὐκ ἄρ᾽ ἀγαθός ἐστιν, ὡ ς ἐ φ α ί ν ε τ ο.

[a] Elm. ad loc. Herm. Electr. 902. 1011. Elm. Med. 416. Lobeck Ajac. 634. Ellendt ad v. ἄν.   [b] Herm. Nub. 1344.   [c] Heind. Phædo, p. 75. §. 35. Bernh. 374.

Perfect.

§. 399. 1. The Perfect expresses a complete action, whether it be not completed till the very moment of speaking, as γέγραφα, I have (just) written; or a long time before, as ἡ πόλις ἔκτισται, it has been built, and there it is. But the Aorist is very often used for the Pft., and only in two cases is the Pft. always used:

a. When the completed action is to be expressly connected with the time present to the speaker. Hence in historic style the Pft. is not generally used, except by Herodotus, who loved to represent events not merely as we look at them when past, but as really happening before our eyes; and very frequently in the orators, who wished to connect every thing past with the moment in which they were speaking, and thus place it more vividly before the audience.

b. When the action is to be represented not only as completed, but as present in its effects and consequences; as, γέγραφα τὴν ἐπιστολήν, I have written the letter, and there it is, ready: ἔκτισται ἡ πόλις, the city has been built, and there it stands: Xen. Cyr. I. 3, 18 οὗτος μὲν γὰρ (sc. Astyages) τῶν ἐν Μήδοις πάντων δεσπότην ἑαυτὸν π ε π ο ί η κ ε ν: Ibid. IV. 2, 26 οὐδέν ἐστι κερδαλεώτερον τοῦ νικᾶν· ὁ γὰρ κρατῶν ἅμα πάντα σ υ ν ή ρ π α κ ε, καὶ τοὺς ἄνδρας καὶ τὰς γυναῖκας: Demosth. p. 834, 64 οἳ (sc. ἐπίτροποι) καὶ τὴν διαθήκην ἠ φ α ν ί κ α σ ι ν, — καὶ τὰς μὲν σφετέρας αὐτῶν οὐσίας ἐκ τῶν ἐπικαρπιῶν δ ι ῳ κ ή κ α σ ι, καὶ τἀρχαῖα τῶν ὑπαρχόντων ἐκ τῶν ἐμῶν πολλῷ μείζω π ε π ο ι ή κ α σ ι, τῆς δ' ἐμῆς οὐσίας — ὅλον τὸ κεφάλαιον ἀ ν ῃ ρ ή κ α σ ι ν. The same holds good of the Conj. and Inf. and Part. of the Pft., and of the Plpft.: Hdt. III. 75 ἔλεγε, ὅσα ἀγαθὰ Κῦρος Πέρσας π ε π ο ι ή κ ο ι: Xen. Cyr. VI. 2, 9 sqq. ἔλεγον, ὅτι Κροῖσος μὲν—ἠ ρ η μ έ ν ο ς εἴη—, δ ε δ ο γ μ έ ν ο ν δ' εἴη πᾶσι τοῖς συμμάχοις βασιλεῦσι, πάσῃ τῇ δυνάμει ἕκαστον παρεῖναι—· ἤδη δὲ καὶ μ ε μ ι σ θ ω μ έ ν ο υ ς εἶναι πολλοὺς—· π ε π ο μ φ έ ν α ι δὲ Κροῖσον καὶ εἰς Λακεδαίμονα περὶ συμμαχίας, συλλέγεσθαι δὲ τὸ στράτευμα — καὶ ἀγορὰν π α ρ η γ γ έ λ θ α ι.

Obs. 1. Hence arises the remarkable use of the III. sing. Pft. Imper. to express a strong command or exhortation, so that the action is represented as already completed, and as remaining in that complete state; as, λελείφθω, *reliquum esto*; πεπειράσθω, let it be tried; νῦν δὲ τοῦτο τετολμήσθω εἰπεῖν: Xen. M. S. IV. 2, 19 ὅμως δὲ ε ἰ ρ ή σ θ ω μοι, ἀδικώτερον εἶναι τὸν ἑκόντα ψευδόμενον τοῦ ἄκοντος: Plat. Rep. p. 561 sq. τετάχθω ἡμῖν κατὰ δημοκρατίαν ὁ τοιοῦτος ἀνήρ. So the Inf. in the *oratio obliqua:* Xen. Hell. V. 4, 7 ἐξιόντες δὲ εἶπον, τὴν θύραν κεκλεῖσθαι, be closed, and remain closed.

Obs. 2. This notion of continuance arises from the simple notion of the Pft.; a completed action implies and is the foundation of the permanent state which naturally follows such completion; hence we often translate a Pft. by a Present; as, τέθνηκα, I am dead—the action of dying is completed. So κέκτημαι, I have acquired=I do possess: οἶδα, *intellexi*=*scio:* μέμνημαι, I have called to mind=I remember: κέκλημαι, I have been called=I am named: τεθαύμακα (Xen. M. S. I. 4, 2 εἰπέ μοι — ἔστιν οὕστινας ἀνθρώπων τεθαύμακας ἐπὶ σοφίᾳ), I have wondered at = I am in wonder at: βεβούλευμαι, I have finished deliberating = am now determined: ἔρρωμαι, I have strengthened myself=*valeo*, am in health: ἔστηκα, I have placed myself=I stand: πέφυκα, I have been born=I am, like γέγονα: ἐγρήγορα, I have been awakened=I am awake: δέδοικα, πεφόβημαι, properly, I have been placed in fear=I am afraid: βέβηκα, I have walked=I now go on (Hdt. VII. 164 παραδεξάμενος τὴν τυραννίδα εὖ βεβηκυῖαν, *firmiter stantem*): πέποιθα, I have persuaded myself = I trust: μέμηλε, it has gone to my heart=it is a care to me (μέλει, it goes to my heart): πέφηνα, I have shewn myself = I appear: τέθηλα, I am in bloom (θάλλω, I blossom): κέκηδα, I am taken care of (κήδομαι, I take care of), &c. In many of these and other verbs the Pft. differs from the Present, in that the latter expresses the beginning of, the former the full operation and existence of the action, especially the following, which express a sound, or call, of which (except κλάζω) the Pres. is but little used: κέκραγα, λέλακα, κέκλαγγα, τέτριγα, βέβρυχα (βρυχάομαι), μέμυκα (μυκάομαι), μέμηκα (μηκάομαι). Of some Perfects the Pres. is either altogether lost, or only found in Epic: οἶδα, ἔοικα, εἴωθα, δέδοικα, δέδια, σέσηρα, τέθηπα, ΜΕΜΑΑ, μέμονα, I am minded; γέγωνα, I call; ἄνωγα, I order.

Obs. 3. These Pres. Perfects can express the frequency of an action like the simple Present; as, Il. a, 37 κλῦθί μευ, Ἀργυρότοξ, ὃς Χρύσην ἀμφιβέβηκας, Κίλλαν τε ζαθέην, Τενέδοιό τε ἶφι ἀνάσσεις.

2. The Pft., like the present, is used to express the future, but with an emphatical expression of the immediate occurrence of the action, and of its continuance, as if it were already done; as, Il. o, 128 μαινόμενε, φρένας ἠλὲ, διέφθορας! Soph. Phil. 75 εἴ με τόξων ἐγκρατὴς αἰσθήσεται, ὄλωλα, like *perii, interii, actum est de me:* Thuc. VIII. 74 ἵνα, ἢν μὴ ὑπακούσωσι, τεθνήκωσι, they will be straightway dead: Plat. Phæd. p. 80. D αὕτη δὲ δὴ ἡμῖν ἡ τοιαύτη καὶ οὕτω πεφυκυῖα, ἀπαλλαττομένη τοῦ σώματος, εὐθὺς διαπεφύσηται καὶ ἀπόλωλεν.

Pluperfect.

§. 400. 1. The Pluperfect stands to the Perfect as the Imperfect to the Present; it expresses, like the Perfect, a completed action, not with reference to time present, but to some other action in time past; as, ἐγεγράφειν τὴν ἐπιστολὴν ἐπεὶ ὁ ἑταῖρος ἦλθεν. This action, to which the Plpft. refers, is either consequent to it, and is expressed by the Impft.; as, ὅτε οἱ Ἕλληνες ἐγγὺς ἦσαν οἱ πολέμιοι ἀπεπεφεύγεσαν, or is coincident with it, and then stands in the Plpft.; as, ἐπειδὴ οἱ Ἕλληνες ἐπεληλύθεσαν οἱ πολέμιοι ἀπεπεφεύγεσαν.

2. What was said in the last section (1. *a. b.*) on the use of the Pft., holds good with the Plpft.; it is used only (*a*) when the actual completion of the two predicates is to be expressly signified: otherwise the Aorist is used; as, ἐπειδὴ οἱ Ἕλληνες ἐπῆλθον οἱ πολέμιοι ἀπέφυγον: (*b*) when the action is represented as continuing in its effects; as, Xen. Cyr. I. 4, 5 ταχὺ δὲ καὶ τὰ ἐν τῷ παραδείσῳ θηρία ἀ ν η λ ώ κ ε ι, διώκων καὶ βάλλων καὶ κατακαίνων, ὥστε ὁ ᾿Αστυάγης οὐκέτ᾿ εἶχεν αὐτῷ συλλέγειν θηρία. And where the Pft. has a present sense, the Plpft. is used as an Impft.; as, ᾔδην, *sciebam*— ἐκεκτήμην, &c.

Aorist.

§. 401. 1. The Aorist expresses an action simply past, neither having, like the Pft., any connexion with time present, nor, like the Impft., any reference to another action, nor any idea of continuance; as, ἔγραψα τὴν ἐπιστολὴν (no time defined): ἐκτίσθη ἡ πόλις, the city has been built, but at no definite time.

2. Hence the Aorist is used when any action is to be represented as *momentary*; and thus is opposed to the Impft. (c o n - t i n u a n c e).

3. In the narration of past events the Impft. and the Aor. are used. If the narration consists merely in a relation of the facts, the Aorist is used (*the narrative tense*); if the narrator places himself as it were in the midst of the facts he relates, and tells them as if he saw them with his own eyes, the Imperfect is used (*the descriptive tense*): ὁ Κῦρος πολλὰ ἔθνη ἐ ν ί κ η σ ε ν: Od. a, 106 οἱ μὲν ἔπειτα πεσσοῖσι προπάροιθε θυράων θυμὸν ἔ τ ε ρ π ο ν — οἱ μὲν ἄρ᾿ οἶνον ἔ μ ι σ γ ο ν ἐνὶ κρητῆρσι καὶ ὕδωρ, οἱ δ᾿ αὖτε σπόγγοισι πολυτρήτοισι τραπέζας ν ί ζ ο ν καὶ π ρ ο τ ί θ ε ν τ ο, ἰδὲ κρέα πολλὰ δ α - τ ε ῦ ν τ ο.

Obs. 1. The Impft. does not here denote the continued, nor the Aor. the momentary character of the action: the same event may be related by the Aorist in one place and the Impft. in another, accordingly as it is considered either merely as a completed action, or in course of completion, which the speaker is supposed to describe by the Impft. as he sees it going on.

4. When the Impft. and Aorist are interchanged and contrasted in the same passage, the latter represents the action as momentary, the former as continuing, so that the more or less important, the more or less transient actions are marked in the narration, by the use of the Impft. and Aorist. We find this usage in Homer applied with great effect: Il. ψ, 228 ἦμος δ᾿ Ἑωσφόρος εἶσι φόως ἐρέων ἐπὶ γαῖαν, τῆμος πυρκαϊὴ ἐ μ α ρ α ί ν ε τ ο, π α ύ σ α τ ο δὲ φλόξ: Il. ρ, 596 νίκην δὲ Τρώεσσι δ ί δ ο υ, ἐ φ ό β η σ ε δ᾿ ᾿Αχαιούς. (Cf. Il. a,

430 sqq. where the Impft. is used to express the principal event; and 453. 478. Od. a, 106. 112.)　Xen. Anab. V. 4, 24 τοὺς πελταστὰς ἐδέξαντο οἱ βάρβαροι, καὶ ἐμάχοντο· ἐπεὶ δ' ἐγγὺς ἦσαν οἱ ὁπλῖται, ἐτράποντο· καὶ οἱ μὲν πελτασταὶ εὐθὺς εἵποντο: Id. Cyr. I. 4, 1 τοιαῦτα μὲν δὴ πολλὰ ἐλάλει ὁ Κῦρος· τέλος δὲ ἡ μὲν μήτηρ ἀπῆλθε, Κῦρος δὲ κατέμενε, καὶ αὐτοῦ ἐτρέφετο.

5. A still greater effect is produced by the interchange of the Aor. and the historic Present; a continued action being held as it were before our eyes, as present to us, while the momentary one is suffered to pass rapidly by in the Aorist: Thuc. I. 95 ἐλθὼν (sc. Pausanias) δ' εἰς Λακεδαίμονα τῶν μὲν ἰδίᾳ πρός τινα ἀδικημάτων εὐθύνθη, τὰ δὲ μέγιστα ἀπολύεται μὴ ἀδικεῖν: Id. VII. 83 καὶ ἀναλαμβάνουσί τε τὰ ὅπλα, καὶ οἱ Συρακούσιοι αἰσθάνονται καὶ ἐπαιώνισαν: Xen. Cyr. I. 3, 11 πολλάκις γάρ με πρὸς τὸν πάππον ἐπιθυμοῦντα προσδραμεῖν οὗτος ὁ μιαρώτατος ἀποκωλύει: Xen. Anab. IV. 6, 22 ἐπεὶ δὲ ἐδείπνησαν καὶ νὺξ ἐγένετο, οἱ μὲν ταχθέντες ᾤχοντο (as Aor.) καὶ καταλαμβάνουσι τὸ ὄρος: Ibid. V. 8, 6 ἐνταῦθα δὴ ἀναγιγνώσκει τε αὐτὸν καὶ ἤρετο (as Aor.): Id. Hellen. II. 1, 15 προσβαλὼν πόλει — τῇ ὑστεραίᾳ προσβολῇ κατὰ κράτος αἱρεῖ καὶ ἐξηνδραπόδισε: Soph. El. 897 ἰδοῦσα δ' ἔσχον θαῦμα καὶ περισκοπῶ: Eur. Iph. T. 16 εἰς ἔμπυρ' ἦλθε καὶ λέγει Κάλχας τάδε[a].

Obs. 2. So the Infinitives of these tenses in the *oratio obliqua*: Plat. Rep. p. 358. D εἶναι μὲν γὰρ αὐτὸν (τὸν Γύγην) ποιμένα θητεύοντα παρὰ τῷ τότε Λυδίας ἄρχοντι· ὄμβρου δὲ πολλοῦ γενομένου καὶ σεισμοῦ, ῥαγῆναί τι τῆς γῆς καὶ γενέσθαι χάσμα κατὰ τὸν τόπον, ᾗ ἔνεμεν· ἰδόντα δὲ καὶ θαυμάσαντα καταβῆναι καὶ ἰδεῖν — ἵππον χαλκοῦν κ. τ. λ.: Id. Symp. p. 176. A ἔφη — σπονδάς τε σφᾶς ποιήσασθαι καὶ ᾄσαντας τὸν θεὸν καὶ τἆλλα νομιζόμενα τρέπεσθαι πρὸς τὸν πότον[b].

6. If the Aorist and Pft. (or Plpft.) are interchanged, the two latter represent the past action as continuing in its effects and consequences; the Pft. with reference to the act of speaking, the Plpft. with reference to some other past action: Hdt. VII. 8, 2 ἀλλ' ὁ μὲν τετελεύτηκε, καὶ οὐκ ἐξεγένετό (*contigit*) οἱ τιμωρήσασθαι: Isocr. p. 163. A ὁ μὲν πόλεμος ἁπάντων ἡμᾶς τῶν εἰρημένων ἀπεστέρηκε· καὶ γάρ τοι πενεστέρους πεποίηκε καὶ πολλοὺς κινδύνους ὑπομένειν ἠνάγκασε, καὶ πρὸς τοὺς Ἕλληνας διαβέβληκε καὶ πάντα τρόπον τεταλαιπώρηκεν ἡμᾶς.

Peculiar usages of the Aorist.

§. 402, 1. As the force of the Aorist extends over the whole space of past time, without reference to any single definite moment, it is used to

---

[a] Heind. Plat. Phæd. 84. D.　　　[b] Stallb. Plat. Symp. 172. D.

express an action which took place repeatedly in past time, or in the statement of some general truth, which operated at different indefinite moments of past time. The instances whence this general truth is derived are stated instead of the general truth which is deduced from them; which latter is expressed by the Present; so that the Present signifies a general inductive proposition, without any especial reference to the particulars of the induction; while the Aorist implies the general truth by the statement of the indefinite recurrence of the past instances: ὁ ἄνθρωπος θνητός ἐστι: Il. ν, 300 τῷ δὲ ("Αρηῖ) Φόβος, φίλος υἱός, ἅμα κρατερὸς καὶ ἀταρβής, ἕσπετο, ὅστ' ἐφόβησε (exterrere solet) ταλάφρονά περ πολεμιστήν: Il. ρ, 177 αἰεί τε Διὸς κρείσσων νόος αἰγιόχοιο, ὅστε καὶ ἄλκιμον ἄνδρα φοβεῖ, καὶ ἀφείλετο νίκην ῥηϊδίως. So Il. ι, 320 ἐν δὲ ἰῇ τιμῇ ἠμὲν κακός, ἠδὲ καὶ ἐσθλός· κάτθαν' ὁμῶς ὅ τ' ἀεργὸς ἀνήρ, ὅ τε πολλὰ ἐοργώς: Eur. Med. 130 τὰ δ' ὑπερβάλλοντ' (nimia) οὐδένα καιρὸν (parum opportune) δύναται θνατοῖς· μείζους δ' ἅτας ὅταν ὀργισθῇ δαίμων οἴκοις ἀπέδωκεν: Ibid. 245 ἀνὴρ δ' ὅταν τοῖς ἔνδον ἄχθηται ξυνών, ἔξω μολὼν ἔπαυσε καρδίαν ἄσης: Xen. Cyr. I. 2, 2 αἱ μὲν γὰρ πλεῖσται πόλεις προστάττουσι τοῖς πολίταις μὴ κλέπτειν, μὴ ἁρπάζειν, — καὶ τἄλλα τὰ τοιαῦτα ὡσαύτως· ἢν δέ τις τούτων τι παραβαίνῃ, ζημίας αὐτοῖς ἐπέθεσαν: Plat. Sympos. p. 181. Α ᾗ πίνειν, ἢ ᾄδειν, ἢ διαλέγεσθαι οὐκ ἔστι τούτων αὐτὸ καθ' αὑτὸ καλὸν οὐδέν, ἀλλ' ἐν τῇ πράξει, ὡς ἂν πραχθῇ, τοιοῦτον ἀπέβη, tale evenire solet: Ibid. p. 188. Β ὁ μετὰ τῆς ὕβρεως Ἔρως — διέφθειρέ τε πολλὰ καὶ ἠδίκησεν. So also the Perfect in Latin; as, Horat. Epist. I. 2, 48 Non domus et fundus, non æris acervus et auri Ægroto domini deduxit corpore febres, Non animo curas.

2. The Imperfect also has an iterative force, but with this difference, that it signifies the repetition of an action at some definite time or times marked out by the action to which the Impft. always refers (see §. 398. 1.), and therefore the frequency signified is not so general as that of the Aorist: Demosth. p. 834, 65 καὶ ὑμεῖς μὲν (sc. δικασταί) οὐδὲ τῶν εἰς ὑμᾶς ἁμαρτανόντων ὅταν τινὸς καταψηφίσησθε, οὐ πάντα τὰ ὄντα ἀφείλεσθε, ἀλλ' ἢ γυναῖκας, ἢ παιδί' αὐτῶν ἐλεήσαντες μέρος τι κἀκείνοις ὑπελείπετε· non omnem rem familiarem eripere sed partem aliquam illis relinquere solebatis. Here the Aorist ἀφείλεσθε is used because the action is supposed to have taken place an indefinite number of times; while in the Impft. ὑπελείπετε, the action is supposed to have taken place only as often as the former action took place.

Obs. 1. Where the idea of necessity, or inherent frequency, is to be especially signified. the verbs φιλεῖν or θέλειν are used. This is frequently the case in Herodotus, a writer who regarded the operation of things very much in the way in which nature or Providence had appointed them: Hdt. VII. 9, 3 αὐτόματον γὰρ οὐδέν, ἀλλ' ἀπὸ πείρης πάντα ἀνθρώποισι φιλέει γίνεσθαι: Ibid. 10, 5 φιλέει γὰρ ὁ θεὸς τὰ ὑπερέχοντα πάντα κολούειν: Ibid. 157 τῷ δὲ εὖ βουλευθέντι πρήγματι τελευτὴ ὡς τὸ ἐπίπαν χρηστὴ ἐθέλει ἐπιγίνεσθαι: φιλεῖν interchanged with the Pres. and Aor.: Hdt. III. 82 ἐν· δὲ ὀλιγαρχίῃ — ἔχθεα ἴδια ἰσχυρὰ φιλέει ἐγγίνεσθαι· αὐτὸς γὰρ ἕκαστος βουλόμενος κορυφαῖος εἶναι — ἐς ἔχθεα μεγάλα ἀλλήλοισι ἀπικνέονται· ἐξ ὧν στάσιες ἐγγίνονται, ἐκ δὲ τῶν στασίων φόνος, ἐκ δὲ τοῦ φόνου ἀπέβη ἐς μουναρχίην· καὶ ἐν τούτῳ διέδεξε (apparet). ὅσῳ ἐστὶ τοῦτο ἄριστον.

3. From this iterative use of the Aorist, it follows that it is used in comparisons or similes. As the object of a simile is to illustrate something to which it bears a resemblance, this resemblance is founded on a perception of an action indefinitely repeated; and therefore in poetry

the action is so represented by the Aorist, while the Present merely expresses the resemblance : Il. γ, 33–36 ὡς δ᾽ ὅτε τίς τε δράκοντα ἰδὼν παλίνορσος ἀπέστη οὔρεος ἐν βήσσῃς, ὑπό τε τρόμος ἔλλαβε γυῖα, ἄψ τ᾽ ἀνεχώρησεν, ὠχρός τε μιν εἷλε παρειάς· ὡς αὖτις καθ᾽ ὅμιλον ἔδυ Τρώων ἀγερώχων (sc. Πάρις) : Il. π, 482 ἤριπε δ᾽, ὡς ὅτε τις δρῦς ἤριπεν: Theocr. XIII. 61 sqq. ὡς δ᾽ ὁπόκ᾽ ἠϋγένειος — λῖς ἐσακούσας νεβρῶ φθεγξαμένας — ἐξ εὐνᾶς ἔσπευσεν ἑτοιμοτάταν ἐπὶ δαῖτα· Ἡρακλέης τοιοῦτος — παῖδα ποθῶν δεδόνατο κ. τ. λ.

Obs. 2. The future is also used in comparisons by the poets.

Obs. 3. The iterative Aor. and Impft. have in Ionic an especial form in σκον: Il. β, 198 ὃν δ᾽ αὖ δήμου τ᾽ ἄνδρα ἴδοι, βοόωντά τ᾽ ἐφεύροι, τὸν σκήπτρῳ ἐλάσασκε, ὁμοκλήσασκέ τε μύθῳ: Hdt. III. 119 ἡ δὲ γυνὴ τοῦ Ἰνταφέρνεος φοιτέουσα ἐπὶ τὰς θύρας τοῦ βασιλῆος κλαίεσκε καὶ ὀδυρέσκετο· ποιεῦσα δὲ ἀεὶ τωὐτὸ τοῦτο τὸν Δαρεῖον ἔπεισε οἰκτείραί μιν. So also of the same action taking place at the same time, but in a different place : Il. β, 271 ὧδε δέ τις εἴπεσκεν ἰδὼν ἐς πλησίον ἄλλον: Hdt. III. 117 ἄρδεσκε—in different places at the same time. Very often the iterative force of the form in σκον coincides with the notion of duration expressed by the Impft. : Il. γ, 388 φιλέεσκεν: ε, 708 ναίεσκεν: especially ἔσκε.

Use of the Aorist in the tragedians instead of the Present.—Aorist used to express future events.—Τί οὖν with the Aorist.

§. 403. 1. The tragedians often use the Aorist to express a determination, which is present indeed, but which is supposed to have been long and firmly conceived in the speaker's breast : Soph. Phil. 1434 καὶ σοὶ ταῦτ᾽, Ἀχιλλέως τέκνον, παρῄνεσα, I advise you this, and have advised you: Eur. Med. 707 (Medea) Κρέων μ᾽ ἐλαύνει φυγάδα γῆς Κορινθίας. (Ægeus) ἐᾷ δ᾽ Ἰάσων; οὐδὲ ταῦτ᾽ ἐπῄνεσα, nec id probatum volo: Ibid. 223 χρὴ δὲ ξένον μὲν κάρτα προσχωρεῖν (se accommodare) πόλει· οὐδ᾽ ἀστὸν ᾔνεσ᾽ ὅστις αὐθάδης γεγὼς πικρὸς πολίταις ἐστὶν ἀμαθίας ὕπο, nec laudo, nec unquam laudavi: Ibid. 272 σὲ τὴν σκυθρωπὸν καὶ πόσει θυμουμένην, Μήδειαν, εἶπον τῆσδε γῆς ἔξω περᾶν φυγάδα, dictum volo: Ibid. 791 ᾤμωξα δ᾽ οἷον ἔργον ἔστ᾽ ἐργαστέον τοὐντεῦθεν ἡμῖν, I have long with sorrow thought on the dreadful deed, &c. τέκνα γὰρ κατακτενῶ τἀμά : Id. Hec. 1276 (Polym.) καὶ σήν γ᾽ ἀνάγκη παῖδα Κασάνδραν θανεῖν. (Hecuba) ἀπέπτυσα, that thought is contrary to all my feelings and resolves.

2. The Aorist is also used, like the Pft., to express future events, which must certainly happen. The momentary force of the Aorist expresses yet more forcibly than the Pft. the inevitable, and as it were instantaneous developement of that which as yet is future : Il. δ, 160–162 εἴπερ γάρ τε καὶ αὐτίκ᾽ Ὀλύμπιος οὐκ ἐτέλεσσεν· ἔκ τε καὶ ὀψὲ τελεῖ, σύν τε μεγάλῳ ἀπέτισαν σὺν σφῇσιν κεφαλῇσι γυναιξί τε καὶ τεκέεσσιν, shall have done it, I consider it as done : Il. ρ, 99 ὁππότ᾽ ἀνὴρ ἐθέλῃ πρὸς δαίμονα φωτὶ μάχεσθαι, ὅν κε θεὸς τιμᾷ, τάχα οἱ μέγα πῆμα κυλίσθη: Il. ι, 412 sqq. εἰ μέν κ᾽ αὖθι μένων Τρώων πόλιν ἀμφιμάχωμαι, ὤλετο μέν μοι νόστος, ἀτὰρ κλέος ἄφθιτον ἔσται· εἰ δέ κεν οἴκαδ᾽ ἵκοιμι φίλην ἐς πατρίδα γαῖαν, ὤλετό μοι κλέος ἐσθλόν, ἐπὶ δηρὸν δέ μοι αἰὼν ἔσσεται: Eur. Med. 78 ἀπωλόμεσθ᾽ ἄρ᾽, εἰ κακὸν προσοίσομεν νέον παλαιῷ: Plat. Rep. p. 462. D ὅταν που ἡμῶν δάκτυλός του πληγῇ, πᾶσα ἡ κοινωνία ἡ κατὰ τὸ σῶμα πρὸς τὴν ψυχὴν — ᾔσθετό τε καὶ πᾶσα ἅμα ξυνήλγησε μέρους πονήσαντος ὅλη: ubi v. Stallb. So ταχὺ εἶπεν, statim dixerit, Plat. Rep. p. 406. D ibiq. Stallb. : Demosth. p. 20, 9 ὅταν δ᾽ ἐκ πλεονεξίας καὶ πονηρίας τις, ὥσπερ οὗτος (Phil.), ἰσχύσῃ, ἡ πρώτη

πρόφασις (*prætextus*) καὶ μικρὸν πταῖσμα ἅπαντα ἀ ν ε χ α ί τ ι σ ε καὶ δ ι έ λ υ-
σ ε ν: Ibid. p. 24, 21 οὕτω καὶ τῶν τυράννων, ἕως μὲν ἂν ἔξω πολεμῶσιν, ἀφανῆ
τὰ κακὰ τοῖς πολλοῖς ἐστιν, ἐπειδὰν δὲ ὅμορος πόλεμος συμπλακῇ, πάντα ἐ π ο ί η-
σ ε ν ἔκδηλα.   So the Inf. Aor. of an absolute assertion: Od. β, 171 καὶ
γὰρ ἐκείνῳ φημὶ τ ε λ ε υ τ η θ ῆ ν α ι ἅπαντα, ὡς οἱ ἐμυθεόμην.

Obs. Here also we must refer the passages in which the Aorist is improperly said to express *conatus rei faciendæ*. The Aorist, as an expression
of something absolutely past, or conceived to be so, cannot express
a mere intention of doing the action of the verb; but the action which was
only intended is spoken of as if it had really happened: Soph. Aj. 1105
sqq. (Teucer) ξὺν τῷ δικαίῳ γὰρ μέγ' ἔξεστιν φρονεῖν. (Menelaus) δίκαια
γὰρ τόνδ' εὐτυχεῖν, κ τ ε ί ν α ν τ ά με; (Teucer) κ τ ε ί ν α ν τ α; δεινόν γ'
εἶπας, εἰ καὶ ζῇς θανών. (Menelaus) θεὸς γὰρ ἐκσώζει με, τῷδε δ' οἴχομαι.
Menelaus, wishing to exaggerate the crime of Teucer, calls him an actual
murderer, at which Teucer remonstrates: so Eur. Ion. 1520 (Creusa)
ἐν φόβῳ καταδεθεῖσα, σὰν ψυχὰν ἀ π έ β α λ ο ν, τέκνον! ἔ κ τ ε ι ν ά σ' ἄκουσα.
(Ion) ἐξ ἐμοῦ τ' οὐχ ὅσι' (*non merito, immerito*) ἔθνῃσκες.

3. Analogously to this the Aor. is joined with τί οὖν, to express a command in the shape of a question: Xen. Cyr. II. 1, 4 τί οὖν, ἔφη ὁ Κῦρος, οὐ
καὶ τὴν δύναμιν ἔ λ ε ξ ά ς μοι; *quin igitur tu mihi—recenses?* why have you
not? instead of, do so directly. "*Hæc interrogatio alacritatem quandam
animi et aviditatem sciendi exprimit.*" W e i s k e ad h. l. Cf. B o r n e-
m a n n. Xen. Cyr. V. 4, 37 τ ί ο ὖ ν, ἔφη, ὦ Γαδάτα, οὐ χ ὶ τὰ μὲν τείχη φυλακῇ
ἐχυρὰ ἐ π ο ί η σ α ς; Ibid. VIII. 3, 46 τ ί ο ὖ ν, ἔφη, πρὸς τῶν θεῶν, ὁ Φεραύλας, οὐ χ ὶ σύ γε αὐτίκα μάλα εὐδαίμων ἐ γ έ ν ο υ, καὶ ἐμὲ εὐδαίμονα ἐ π ο ί η-
σ α ς; λαβὼν γὰρ, ἔφη, ταῦτα πάντα κέκτησο, καὶ χρῶ ὅπως βούλει αὐτοῖς:
Plat. Phæd. p. 86. D εἰ οὖν τις ὑμῶν εὐπορώτερος ἐμοῦ, τ ί ο ὐ κ ἀ π ε κ ρ ί-
ν α τ ο; *is quam celerrime respondeat:* Id. Gorg. p. 503. B εἴ τινα ἔχεις τῶν
ῥητόρων τοιοῦτον εἰπεῖν, τ ί ο ὐ χ ὶ καὶ ἐμοὶ αὐτὸν ἔ φ ρ α σ α ς τίς ἐστιν; *age
mihi protinus indica:* Id. Sympos. p. 173 B τ ί ο ὖ ν, ἔφη, οὐ δ ι η γ ή σ ω
μοι; *quin tu mihi narres?*[a]

The Aorist instead of the Imperfect, Perfect, and Pluperfect.

§. 404. The Aorist is sometimes used for one of these relative tenses:
in one case for the Impft., Pft., or Plpft., when the relations to some
other predicate implied or expressed proper to these tenses need not
be distinctly marked, or is sufficiently clear from the context: in another,
for the Pft. or Plpft., when the continuance of the action in its effects
may be omitted, and this not only in independent but in dependent sentences; as, Il. ν, 50 ἄλλῃ μὲν γὰρ ἔγωγ' οὐ δ ε ί δ ι α χεῖρας ἀάπτους
Τρώων, οἱ μέγα τεῖχος ὑ π ε ρ κ α τ έ β η σ α ν ὁμίλῳ (for Pft.): Od. α, 171
τίς, πόθεν εἶς ἀνδρῶν;—ὁπποίης δ' ἐπὶ νηὸς ἀ φ ί κ ε ο; πῶς δέ σε ναῦται
ἤ γ α γ ο ν εἰς Ἰθάκην; (for Pft.): Ibid. 194 ν ῦ ν δ' ἦ λ θ ο ν: Il. ρ, 173
ν ῦ ν δέ σευ ὠ ν ο σ ά μ η ν πάγχυ φρένας: Eur. Phœn. 4 sqq. Ἤλιε—ὡς
δυστυχῆ Θήβαισι τῇ τ ό θ' ἡμέρᾳ ἀκτῖν' ἐ φ ῆ κ α ς, Κάδμος ἡνίκ' ἦ λ θ ε
γῆν τήνδ', ἐκλιπὼν Φοίνισσαν χθόνα· ὃς παῖδα γήμας Κύπριδος Ἁρμονίαν ποτὲ
Πολύδωρον ἐ ξ έ φ υ σ ε (for Plpft.): Xen. M. S. 1. 6, 14 τοὺς θησαυροὺς
τῶν πάλαι σοφῶν, οὓς ἐκεῖνοι κ α τ έ λ ι π ο ν ἐν βιβλίοις γράψαντες, δ ι έ ρ χ ο-
μ α ι (for Pft.): Demosth. p. 859, 49 ἐκείνῃ τῇ ἡμέρᾳ κατωρύττετο, ὅτε εἰς

a Stallb. Symp. 173. B.

τὰς τούτων χεῖρας ἦλθεν (for Plpft.) : Ibid. p. 12, 14 νυνὶ δὲ Θετταλοῖς—
ἐβοήθησε (for Pft.).

Conjunctive, Optative, Imperative, Infinitive of the Aorist, and their inter-
change with the same moods of the Present, Imperfect, Perfect, and Future.
—Difference between the Present, Aorist, and Future Infinitive.

§. 405. The general force of this tense in the other moods, as opposed
to the Impft., Pft., and Plpft., is the same as in the Indicative ; but it is
especially used to express a momentary action without any relation to
any definite time, and thus is opposed to the Pres. and Future, which
express the continuance or extension of the action ; as, δός μοι τὸ
βιβλίον—ἀποθανεῖν ὑπὲρ τῆς πατρίδος καλόν ἐστι — κελεύω σε δοῦναι — λέγω, ἵνα μάθῃς — μέλλω γράψαι and μέλλω γράφειν or
γράψειν: Xen. Cyr. V. 1, 2 καλέσας ὁ Κῦρος Ἀράσπην Μῆδον, τοῦτον
ἐκέλευσε διαφυλάξαι αὐτῷ τήν τε γυναῖκα καὶ τὴν σκηνήν: Ibid. 3 ταύτην
οὖν ἐκέλευσεν ὁ Κῦρος διαφυλάττειν τὸν Ἀράσπην, ἕως ἂν αὐτὸς λάβῃ :
Demosth. p. 94, 19 χρὴ — οὐχ ἣν Διοπείθης πειρᾶται τῇ πόλει δύναμιν
παρασκευάζειν, ταύτην βασκαίνειν καὶ διαλῦσαι πειρᾶσθαι, ἀλλ'
ἑτέραν αὐτοὺς προσπαρασκευάζειν : Id. p. 44, 16 τριήρεις πεντήκοντα
παρασκευάσασθαί φημι δεῖν, εἶτ' αὐτοὺς οὕτω τὰς γνώμας ἔχειν: Ibid.
p. 45, 18 ἵν' ἡ διὰ τὸν φόβον—ἡσυχίαν ἔχῃ (ὁ Φίλιππος), ἡ παριδὼν ταῦτα
ἀφύλακτος ληφθῇ.   So when the notion of the verb is to be applied
to a single case, the Inf. Aor. should be used, as μαθεῖν, φυγεῖν, λαθεῖν ;
but in general precepts or statements the Imper. or Inf. Pres. is almost
always used.

Obs. 1. The rule for the choice of the Aor. or Pres. depends on the
animus loquentis. The same action may be expressed by either, as in
each case the speaker wishes to denote the continued or the momentary
nature of the action, and even in the same passage : so Demosth. p. 838,
10—14 λαβὲ δὴ τὰς μαρτυρίας καὶ ἀνάγνωθι—then λέγε, then λαβὲ
τὰς ἄλλας καὶ ἀναγίγνωσκε—λαβὲ ἑτέραν καὶ ἀνάγνωθι—λέγ' ἑτέραν.
The usage of the poets is very arbitrary : as, Eur. Phœn. 1712 τᾷδε
βᾶθί μοι, τᾷδε πόδα τίθει : Id. Hippol. 473 ἀλλ', ὦ φίλε παῖ, λῆγε
μὲν κακῶν φρενῶν, λῆξον δ' ὑβρίζουσ'.

Obs. 2. Verbs of intending, hoping, saying, swearing, willing, wishing,
refusing, delaying, praying, persuading, ordering, forbidding, hindering,
&c. whose object may be conceived of as future, take the Inf. of either
the Pr., Fut., or Aor., as the speaker regards the action either as simply
continuing, or continuing in future time, or has no regard either to its
continuance or its time, but only to its completion ; but the Present is
especially employed to signify that the event will either certainly take
place, or that it will follow immediately on the moment of speaking' :
Lysias p. 818, 4 οἶμαι—πάντας ὑμᾶς ὁμολογῆσαι: Demosth. p. 842,
21 (ἡ μήτηρ) νῦν μὲν οἴεται τυχόντα με τῶν δικαίων παρ' ὑμῖν ὑπο-
δέξασθαι (MSS., Reiske e conj. ὑποδέξεσθαι) καὶ τὴν ἀδελφὴν ἐκδώ-
σειν. (the Aor. here signifies the certainty of the hope, representing it as
fulfilled ; the Fut. that the portioning the daughter will take place when
the cause is won): Plat. Crit. p. 52. B ὡμολόγεις καθ' ἡμᾶς πολιτεύεσθαι: Hdt. IX. 106 πίστι τε καταλαβόντες καὶ ὁρκίοισι ἐμμένειν
τε καὶ μὴ ἀποστήσεσθαι: Xen. Cyr. VI. 2, 39 ἐμοὶ προσάγων ἐγγυητὰς
ἦ μὴν πορεύεσθαι: compare Plat. Legg. p. 937. B. Id. Anab. II. 3,
27 ὀμόσαι ἦ μὲν πορεύεσθαι: Id. Hellen. II. 4, 30 ὀμόσαντες

ὅρκους ἢ μὴν μὴ μνησικακήσειν: Demosth. p. 860, 54 ἐλπίζει ῥᾳδίως ὑμᾶς ἐξαπατήσειν: compare p. 852, 27. 853, 28. Od. γ, 320 ἔλποντο —ἐλθέμεν: Od. β, 280 ἐλπωρή τοι ἔπειτα τελευτῆσαι τάδε ἔργα: Plat. Symp. p. 193. D ἐλπίδας παρέχεται—ἡμᾶς εὐδαίμονας ποιῆσαι: Lysias p. 617, 8 ὑπόλοιπος ἐλπὶς ἦν ὑπὸ τοῦ πάππου ἐκτραφῆναι: Isocr. p. 291. C ἡμῖν ἐνδείξεσθαι βουλόμενος: Demosth. p. 850, 19 βούλομαι διεξελθεῖν: Ibid. p. 851, 22 βούλομαι εἰπεῖν: p. 852, 25 βούλομαι ἐξελέγξαι: Ibid. p. 850, 21 ἤθελον παραδοῦναι: Il. β, 39 θήσειν γὰρ ἔτ' ἔμελλεν ἐπ' ἄλγεα—Τρωσί: Od. τ, 95 τὸν ξεῖνον ἔμελλον ἀμφὶ πόσει εἴρεσθαι: Il. ψ, 773 ἔμελλον ἐπαίξασθαι. Even μέλλω ἐθελήσειν Plat. Rep. p. 347, A: Hdt. III. 72 οἱ μέν γε ψεύδονται τότε, ἐπεάν τι μέλλωσι—κερδήσεσθαι: and this idiom of the Fut. with μέλλω is the most usual. Id. VI. 86, 2 ταῦτα ὦν ὑμῖν ἀναβάλλομαι κυρώσειν ἐς τέταρτον μῆνα: Ibid. 88 Ἀθηναῖοι—οὐκέτι ἀνεβάλλοντο μὴ οὐ τὸ πᾶν μηχανήσασθαι ἐπ' Αἰγινήτησι: Demosth. p. 31, 9 ἀναβάλλεται ποιήσειν τὰ δέοντα: Hdt. VI. 61 ἐλίσσετο τὴν θεὸν ἀπαλλάξαι τῆς δυσμορφίης τὸ παιδίον: Id. VI. 5 ἔπεισε Λεσβίους δοῦναί οἱ νέας[a].

Future.

§. 406. 1. The simple Future, expressing a present belief that something will presently be, as γράψω, is used both as an absolute and relative tense; when used as the former, it signifies a simple future action; when as the latter, it signifies an action as future, in relation to and coincident with some other action in future time: ἐν ᾧ σὺ παιξεῖ, ἐγὼ γράψω: Il. δ, 164 ἔσσεται ἦμαρ, ὅτ' ἄν ποτ' ὀλώλῃ Ἴλιος ἱρή.

2. The absolute Future, like the Aorist and absolute Present, expresses repetition, that an action may happen at several future moments, but as not having yet happened, as only possible and supposable: Il. ε, 747 λάζετο δ' ἔγχος βριθὺ, μέγα, στιβαρόν, τῷ δάμνησι στίχας ἀνδρῶν ἡρώων, τοῖσίν τε κοτέσσεται ὀβριμοπάτρη: Od. δ, 208 ῥεῖα δ' ἀρίγνωτος γόνος ἀνέρος, ᾧτε Κρονίων ὄλβον ἐπικλώσει. The three iterative forms are found together in Soph. Antig. 348 κρατεῖ δὲ (scil. ἀριφραδὴς ἀνήρ) μηχαναῖς θηρὸς ὀρεσσιβάτα, λασιαύχενά θ' ἵππον ὑπάξεται ἀμφίλοφον ζυγόν — καὶ ἀστυνόμους ὀργὰς ἐδιδάξατο, — παντοπόρος, ἄπορος ἐπ' οὐδὲν ἔρχεται τὸ μέλλον· Ἄιδα μόνον φεῦξιν οὐκ ἐπάξεται· νόσων δ' ἀμαχάνων φυγὰς ξυμπέφρασται (as present). So in poetry the future is used in comparisons, as circumstances which are known to have happened frequently in past time, are supposed to be likely to happen in the same way in future time: Il. δ, 131 ἥ δὲ τόσον μὲν ἔεργεν (τὸ βέλος) ἀπὸ χροός, ὡς ὅτε μήτηρ παιδὸς ἐέργει μυῖαν, ὅθ' ἡδέϊ λέξεται ὕπνῳ.

---

[a] Lobeck. Phryn. 745. sqq. Stallb. Plat. Rep. 369. A. et Crit. 52, 6. Heind. Plat. Phæd. 67. B. Wunderlich ad Æsch. p. 175. Herm. Ajac. 1061. Elm. et Herm. Med. 1209.

3. The Future often expresses necessity—s h a l l—m u s t : Xen.
Cyr. III. 3, 52 νόμους ὑπάρξαι δεῖ τοιούτους, δι' ὧν τοῖς μὲν ἀγαθοῖς
ἔντιμος καὶ ἐλεύθερος ὁ βίος π α ρ α σ κ ε υ α σ θ ή σ ε τ α ι, τοῖς δὲ κακοῖς ταπεινός τε καὶ ἀλγεινὸς καὶ ἀβίωτος ὁ αἰὼν ἐ π α ν α κ ε ί σ ε τ α ι :
Id. M. S. II. 1, 17 οἱ εἰς τὴν βασιλικὴν τέχνην παιδευόμενοι — τι
διαφέρουσι τῶν ἐξ ἀνάγκης κακοπαθούντων, εἴ γε π ε ι ν ή σ ο υ σ ι καὶ
δ ι ψ ή σ ο υ σ ι καὶ ῥ ι γ ώ σ ο υ σ ι καὶ ἀ γ ρ υ π ν ή σ ο υ σ ι, if it is
determined that they shall fast, &c. : Plat. Rep. p. 372. C. D καὶ
ὁ Γλαύκων ὑπολαβών· Ἄνευ ὄψου ἔφη, ὡς ἔοικας, π ο ι ε ῖ ς τοὺς
ἄνδρας ἐστιωμένους. Ἀληθῆ, ἦν δ' ἐγώ, λέγεις· ἐπελαθόμην, ὅτι καὶ
ὄψον ἕ ξ ο υ σ ι ν· ἅλας τε δῆλον ὅτι καὶ ἐλάας καὶ τυρὸν — ἐ ψ ή σ ο υ-
τ α ι· καὶ τραγήματά πον παραθήσομεν αὐτοῖς —, καὶ μύρτα καὶ φηγοὺς
σποδιοῦσι πρὸς τὸ πῦρ, μετρίως ὑποπίνοντες· καὶ οὕτω διάγοντες τὸν
βίον ἐν εἰρήνῃ μετὰ ὑγιείας, ὡς εἰκός, γηραιοὶ τελευτῶντες ἄλλον τοιοῦτον βίον τοῖς ἐκγόνοις π α ρ α δ ώ σ ο υ σ ι.

4. The Pres. is sometimes elegantly expressed by the Future,
as the Future is by the Opt. with ἄν, when the action is not
represented as really taking place, but only as possible under
certain conditions : so the poetic form βουλήσομαι, *volo*, sc. *si
licet* : Soph. Œ. T. 1076 τοὐμὸν δ' ἐγώ, κεἰ σμικρόν ἐστι, σπέρμ'
ἰδεῖν β ο υ λ ή σ ο μ α ι : Eur. Med. 259 τοσοῦτον οὖν σου τυγχάνειν
β ο υ λ ή σ ο μ α ι, ἤν μοι πόρος τις μηχανή τ' ἐξευρεθῇ πόσιν δίκην
τῶνδ' ἀντιτίσασθαι κακῶν. So Plato, ἐθελήσω, προθυμήσομαι :
Phæd. p. 78. A ἀλλὰ ταῦτα μὲν δὴ, ἔφη, ὑπάρξει, *hœc igitur sic
erunt*, more elegantly than *sunt* ; hence the future is used for the
Imperative.

5. The Future, especially in the Part., is used in the force of
μέλλειν, likely, or intending to do any thing. So Thucyd. V. 90
πείσοντα ὠφεληθῆναι, should be profited by having the chance of—
μέλλοντα πείθειν. So in Euripides, the formula, τί λέξεις=τί
μέλλεις λέγειν, *what are you going to say*—when the speaker expects
to hear something worse than what is already said : Med. 1310
οἴμοι τί λέξεις; ὥς μ' ἀπώλεσας, γύναι [a].

Futurum III. or Exactum.

§. 407. 1. The Futurum exactum expresses an action which is conceived of as past in some future time ; Future in relation to time present, Past in relation to time future ; and expresses, like the Perfect,
the continuance of such an action in its consequences and effects :
Hesiod. Opp. 177 καὶ τοῖσι μ ε μ ί ξ ε τ α ι ἐσθλὰ κακοῖσιν : Plat.
Rep. p. 506. A οὐκοῦν ἡμῖν ἡ πολιτεία τελέως κ ε κ ο σ μ ή σ ε τ α ι,

---

[a] Elm Med. 1277. Pflugk. Eur. Hec. 55.

ἐὰν ὁ τοιοῦτος αὐτὴν ἐπισκοπῇ φύλαξ ὁ τούτων ἐπιστήμων : Ibid. p. 465. Α πρεσβυτέρῳ μὲν νεωτέρων πάντων ἄρχειν τε καὶ κολάζειν προστετάξεται. This notion is expressed in the active (and sometimes in the middle) by a periphrasis of the Part. and the Future of εἶναι : Demosth. p. 54, 50 τὰ δέοντα ἐσόμεθα ἐγνω-κότες καὶ λόγων ματαίων ἀπηλλαγμένοι. Where the Pft. has a Pres. sense, the Fut. exactum has the force of the simple Future : so κεκτήσομαι, μεμνήσομαι, τεθνήξω[a].

Obs. 1. In many verbs the Fut. III. supplies the place of the simple Fut. pass.; as in δύω, πιπράσκω, παύω, κόπτω; or is used together with it in the same sense; as in βάλλω, λέγω, &c.

Obs. 2. The notion of the momentary completion of the future action which in Latin is expressed by the Fut. exact., is expressed in dependent clauses by the Aor. Conj. with some conjunction compounded of ἄν, as ἐάν, ἐπάν, ἐπειδάν, ὅταν, πρὶν ἄν, ἔστ᾽ ἄν, ὃς ἄν, &c.; as, ἐὰν τοῦτο γένηται, si hoc factum fuerit; the Aorist expressing the completion, the Conj. the futurity. But in a principal clause the idea of this tense is expressed by the Aorist, either leaving out the notion of futurity, or supplying it from the context; or by the simple Fut., leaving the notion of completion to be supplied from the context : ὅταν ταῦτα γράψῃς, πορεύσομαι, cum epistolam scripseris, profectus fuero : ἐὰν ταῦτα λέξῃς, ἥμαρτες, you will have erred.

2. Sometimes the Fut. III. is used for the simple Future to express more vividly the immediate occurrence of some future action; as, Plat. Gorg. p. 469. D (of a tyrant) ἐὰν γὰρ ἄρα ἐμοὶ δόξῃ τινὰ τουτωνὶ τῶν ἀνθρώπων ὧν σὺ ὁρᾷς αὐτίκα μάλα δεῖν τεθνάναι, τεθνήξει οὗτος, ὃν ἂν δόξῃ· κἄν τινα δόξῃ μοι τῆς κεφαλῆς αὐτῶν κατεαγέναι δεῖν, κατεαγὼς ἔσται αὐτίκα μάλα, κἂν θοἰμάτιον διεσχίσθαι, διεσχισμένον ἔσται: so Aristoph. Plut. 1201 πάντα σοι πεπράξεται, all shall be done.

Remarks on the periphrasis with μέλλω for the Future.

§. 408. The periphrasis of μέλλω for the Future, as μέλλω γράφειν, ἔμελλον γράφειν, μελλήσω γράφειν, (γράψειν—γράψαι) represents the action in the moment of its beginning to be developed, as either in relation to the time present to the speaker, as μέλλω γράφειν, while I speak, I intend to write; or to the time present to some past action, as ἔμελλον γράφειν, when such an action, now past, was present, I intended to write; or to the time present to some future action; as, μελλήσω γράφειν, when some action, yet future, becomes present, I shall intend to write: but this last is often expressed by γράψω.

[a] Stallb. Gorg. 469. D. Dawes Misc. Crit. 149. Elm. Acharn. 590.

§. 409. Table of the Primary and Secondary powers of Present and Aorist Absolute, and the Relative Tenses :—

I. Present (Absolute), Primary : An action now going on—undefined by the time of any other action.

§. 395. 1.	Secondary :	*a.* Frequency—general statements.
§. 395. 2. 401. 5.	....	*b.* Historic Present.
§. 396.	....	*c.* For Pft. or Aor.
§. 397.	....	*d.* For Future — indefinite — or to mark certainty.
§. 398. 2.	....	*e.* An attempt to do something.

II. Aorist (Absolute), Primary : A past action, undefined by the time of any other action.

§. 401. 2, 4, 5.	Secondary :	*a.* A momentary action.
§. 402. 1, 2.	....	*b.* Frequency.
§. 402. 1, 2.	....	*c.* Induction.
§. 402. 3.	....	*d.* Comparison or Simile.
§. 403. 1.	....	*e.* Determination.
§. 403. 2.	....	*f.* Instantaneous Future.
§. 403. 2. *Obs.*	....	*g.* Attempt, already taken place.
§. 403. 3.	....	*h.* Command in shape of question.
§. 404.	....	*i.* For Pft. and Plpft.

III. Imperfect, Primary : Action in course of completion in time past, coincidently with another past action.

§. 398. 2.	Secondary :	*a.* Imperfect action—attempt.
§. 398. 3.	....	*b.* Conditional.
§. 398. 4.	....	*c.* For Present.
§. 398. 4.	....	*d.* An action which seemed different from what it really is.
§. 401. 4.	....	*e.* Continuance.
§. 402. 2.	....	*f.* Frequency.

IV. Perfect, Primary : An action completed at the present time.

§. 399. 1. *b.*	Secondary :	*a.* An action continuing in its effects.
§. 399. 1. *Obs.* 1.	....	*b.* Strong exhortation (in Imperative).
§. 399. 1. *Obs.* 2.	....	*c.* Pres. Pft.
§. 399. 1. *Obs.* 3.	....	*d.* Frequency, as Present.
§. 399. 2.	....	*e.* Future, as Present.

V. Plpft., Primary : An action completed at some past time.

§. 400. 2. Secondary : *a*. Past action continuing in its effects in time past.

§. 400. 2. .... *b*. Impft. of Pres. Pft.

VI. Future, Primary : An action about to go on coincidently with some future action.

§. 406. 2. Secondary : *a*. Probable repetition in future time.

§. 406. 2. .... *b*. Comparison.

§. 406. 3. .... *c*. Necessity.

§. 406. 4. .... *d*. For Pres.—Possibility for fact.

§. 406. 5. .... *e*. Intention.

VII. Fut. Exactum (III.), Primary : Action which will be past in time future.

§. 407. 1. Secondary : *a*. Continuance in time future.

§. 407. 2. .... *b*. For simple Future.

Moods.

Meaning of the term Mood.—Division of Moods[a].

§. 410. 1. The Predicate which, as we have seen, stands in certain relations to the subject, and to the time present to the speaker, stands thirdly in certain relations to the conception of the speaker. Our modes of conception are two, *direct*, arising from *perception* of something as really existing in time present or past ; *indirect*, arising from a *supposition* of such existence.

2. Hence arise the following moods :—

a. The Indicative, to express an act of perception of something conceived as *really* in existence in time present or past ; as, τὸ ῥόδον θάλλει—οἱ πολέμιοι ἀπέφυγον.

The Subjunctive, to express an act of supposition ; either present supposition, of things supposed now to exist or to be about to exist ; or past supposition, of things supposed to have existed, or to have been about to exist in time past ; so the Subjunctive is divided into

b. The Subjunctive of the principal tenses (Conjunctive), to express an act of supposition either present or future ; as, ἴωμεν, let us *now* go : τί ποιῶμεν ; what shall we do ? ἐπαγγέλλω, ἐπαγγελῶ, ἐπήγγελκα ἵνα εἰδῇς.

c. The Subjunctive of the historic tenses (Optative), to express a past act of supposition ; as, οὐκ εἶχον ὅποι τραποίμην, I did not know where I could go : ἐπήγγελλον, ἐπηγγέλκειν, ἐπήγγειλα ἵν' εἰδείης.

[a] Herm. de Part. &c 76. 599. Dissen Kleine Schriften, p. 23.

d. The Imperative is the proper expression of a wish delivered as a command to some one, either present or conceived of as present ; as, γραφέτω, *scribito.*

Obs. Properly speaking, the Indicative could have no Future tense, as things future are not objects of real perception; but as the mind of the speaker, throwing itself forward as it were into the future, conceives things future as if really existing, the Indicative has a Future tense.

Secondary meaning of the Conjunctive and Optative.

§. 411. 1. Primarily then the Conjunctive expresses a *present or future supposition, founded on present existing circumstances;* the Optative a *past supposition, founded on past circumstances.* Now as a supposition of the former kind presents itself more vividly to the mind, and approaches nearer to reality than the latter, the Conjunctive is used to express something which if not real is very near it ; something of which it may with very near certainty be expected that it will take place ; something more than a supposition—a very high degree of *probability ;* while the Optative is used to express a supposition of something which may take place, but with very little expectation of its really doing so— *possibility :* εἰ τοῦτο λέγοις, ἁμαρτάνοις ἄν, if you say this—but I have no expectation you will—ἁμαρτάνοις ἄν, you would be wrong ; but I have no expectation of your being wrong: ἐὰν τοῦτο λέγῃς, I expect that you will say so; hence the Optative is used to express a wish, this being considered as an indefinite possibility.— (See the *Optative.*)

Observations on the general power of the Moods.

2. There are three ways in which any thing may be spoken of ; as really existing—as contingent—as necessary. It is usually laid down [a] that these notions are expressed by the Present, Subjunctive, and Imperative, respectively : but this does not seem to be altogether true ; for though the Indicative may generally express a reality, and the Subjunctive contingency, yet the proper force of the Imperative is the expression of a wish in which no notion of necessity is implied. The notion of necessity is generally expressed in Greek by δυνατὸν εἶναι, μέλλειν, χρῆναι, δεῖν, ἀνάγκην εἶναι &c. or by verbal adjectives in τός or τέος, or modal adverbs, such as δή, μήν, ἴσως, ἄν &c., and these expressions are joined with all the moods; as, τοῦτο ποιεῖν ἀναγκαῖόν ἐστιν, ἀναγκαῖον ἂν

[a] Herm. de Emend. Gr. Gr. p. 204.

εἴη, ἀναγκαῖον ἔστω, δύναμαι, δυναίμην ἂν ποιεῖν, ἐὰν δύνωμαι ποιεῖν. The Indicative may express what is yet only a contingency; as, τὸ ῥόδον ἀνθήσει—while the Optative is often a mild way of expressing a certainty; as, λέγοιμ' ἄν, *dixerim*, for λέγω. The Conjunctive seems to come nearest to the notion of necessity, as expressing an action which, though not really existing, is conceived as almost certain to exist.

Indicative.

§. 412. The Predicate of the Indicative is represented as known, or conceived to be a real, certain fact, past or present; when future or contingent events are considered as certain, they may in respect of this certainty be expressed by the Indicative; as, τὸ ῥόδον ἀνθεῖ—ἤνθησεν—ἀνθήσει: εἰ τοῦτο λέγεις ἁμαρτάνεις: here λέγεις does not express an actual fact, but only something looked at for the time as a fact.

Obs. The use of the Indic. is very wide in Greek: it is frequently used instead of the Conj. and Opt., to place things more before one, as really happening, rather than as mere suppositions; to effect which was a principle which guided the Greeks in the choice of their expression. (See *Oratio Obliqua.*) So ὁ παῖς ἔλεξεν, ὅτι Σωκράτης ἐν τῷ τῶν γειτόνων προθύρῳ ἕστηκε καὶ οὐκ ἐθέλει εἰσιέναι: Xen. Cyr. II. 2, 1 ἀεὶ μὲν οὖν ἐπεμέλετο ὁ Κῦρος, ὁπότε συσκηνοῖεν, ὅπως εὐχαριστότατοι—λόγοι ἐμβληθήσονται.

Indicative Future.

§. 413. 1. The proper notion of the Future Indicative is of an action not as yet really happening, but conceived as certain to happen hereafter. Since therefore the notion of futurity implies a sort of contingency, while the Indicative expresses certainty, the Indicative Future is often used as a polite way of expressing a desire; the Future representing the action commanded as a contingency, depending in some sort on the will of the person to whom it is addressed, the Indicative expressing a confident expectation of its fulfilment: Il. κ, 88 ὦ Νέστορ—, γνώσεαι Ἀτρείδην: 235 Τυδείδη—, τὸν μὲν δὴ ἑταρόν γ' αἱρήσεαι: Od. β, 270 Τηλέμαχ', οὐδ' ὄπιθεν κακὸς ἔσσεαι, οὐδ' ἀνοήμων: cf. Xen. Cyr. I. 6, 35. Id. Hell. II. 3, 34 ὑμεῖς οὖν, ἐὰν σωφρονῆτε, οὐ τούτου, ἀλλ' ὑμῶν φείσεσθε: Plat. Rep. p. 432. C ὅρα οὖν καὶ προθύμου κατιδεῖν, ἐάν πως πρότερος ἐμοῦ ἴδῃς, καί μοι φράσεις[a]: Id. Protag. p. 338. A ὡς οὖν ποιήσετε, καὶ πείθεσθέ μοι.

2. Opposed to this polite way of expressing a desire is the use

---

[a] Stallb. ad loc.

of the Future Indicative, used interrogatively to express a strong command, accompanied with a sort of irony; as, οὐ παύσῃ λέγων; *non desines dicere?* for *desine dicere :* Eur. Androm. 1062 οὐχ ὅσον τάχος χωρήσεταί τις Πυθικὴν πρὸς ἑστίαν—; Plat. Symp. init. οὐ περιμενεῖς; (will you not wait?)[a] Demosth. p. 72. init. οὐ φυλάξεσθ᾽, ἔφην, ὅπως μὴ — δεσπότην εὕρητε[b]; When the command is negative, οὐ μὴ is used, and when a positive and negative command stand together, οὐ is used with the former, and μὴ added to the latter; as, οὐ μὴ φλυαρήσεις; οὐ μὴ λαλήσεις, ἀλλ᾽ ἀκολουθήσεις ἐμοί; Aristoph., for μὴ φλυάρει, μὴ λάλει, ἀλλ᾽ ἀκολούθει: Soph. Aj. 75 οὐ σῖγ᾽ ἀνέξει, μηδὲ δειλίαν ἀρεῖς; Plat. Symp. p. 175. A οὔκουν καλεῖς αὐτὸν καὶ μὴ ἀφήσεις;

3. This same interrogative form is sometimes used in the first person for the Conjunctive; as, Eur. Andr. 1212 οὐ σπαράξομαι κόμαν; οὐκ ἐπιθήσομαι δ᾽ ἐμῷ κάρᾳ κτύπημα χειρὸς ὀλοόν; for σπαράξωμαι, ἐπιθῶμαι.

Conjunctive and Optative.

§. 414. 1. The Predicate both of the Conjunctive and Optative is represented as something supposed, therefore uncertain, possible; and these words are divided, as to their relations of time, into the Subjunctive of the principal tenses (Conjunctive), and the Subjunctive of the historic tenses (Optative); the Optative standing to the historic, as the Conjunctive does to the principal tenses; the Pres. Opt. is the Conjunctive of the Impft., the Opt. Pft. is the Conjunctive of the Plpft.; hence it is seen how imperfect a notion the name Optative conveys of the nature and powers of the Mood to which it is applied.

2. The Conj. and Opt. represent their predicate as depending on an act of the mind; as, οὐκ οἶδα τί εἴπω, or on an expression of such an act; as, λέγε τί εἴπω: but this supposition or expression thereof is sometimes not expressly stated; as, τί εἴπω; *quid dicam?* and so in form is independent; this occurs in the following cases :—

Conjunctive for Indicative Future.

§. 415. 1. The Conjunctive is used mostly in dependent sentences; in independent sentences it is used for the Indicative Future, as a sort of Imperative (Conj. adhortativus), or to express deliberation (Conjunctivus deliberativus).

2. This Conjunctive expresses something future, the realisation

---

[a] Stallb. ad loc.   [b] Bremi ad loc.

of which is expected from the present position of circumstances, and differs from the Future, only in that the latter does not express the future action as merely something which we have reason to expect, but as (by anticipation) something certain.   The affinity between these two expressions is clear ; the Future in reality depends on a supposition as well as the Conj.   This use of the Conjunctive in positive sentences occurs only in epic writers, but in negative sentences it is found, though but rarely, in Attic Greek : Il. ζ, 459 καὶ ποτέ τις εἴπησιν, it may be expected that one would, will say ; (in verse 462 we find the Fut., ὥς ποτέ τις ἐρέει:) Il. η, 197 οὐ γάρ τίς με βίῃ γε ἑκὼν ἀέκοντα δίηται : Il. α, 262 οὐ γάρ πω τοίους ἴδον ἀνέρας, οὐδὲ ἴδωμαι, as things are at present, I may not expect to see (οὐδὲ ὄψομαι, I shall certainly not see) : Od. β, 201 οὐκ ἔστ᾽ οὗτος ἀνὴρ διερὸς βροτός, οὐδὲ γένηται [a], nor can he ever be, he will never be : Od. π, 437 οὐκ ἔστ᾽ οὗτος ἀνὴρ, οὐδ᾽ ἔσσεται οὐδὲ γένηται, it is not possible to conceive that he will be : Plat. Legg. p. 942. C οὔτ᾽ ἔστιν, οὔτε ποτὲ γένηται κρεῖττον.

Obs. 1. So in Attic the Conj. is used with οὐδὲ μή, where the predicate depends on the fear and anxiety of the speaker : Plat. Rep. p. 492. E οὔτε γὰρ γίγνεται, οὔτε γέγονεν, οὐδὲ οὖν μὴ γένηται, nor need we fear that.

Obs. 2. On the Homeric use of Conj. with ἄν, κέ, see §. 424. 3. ζ.

Conjunctivus Adhortativus.

§. 416. The first person Conj. expresses *exhortation, admonition.* The predicate expresses a desire of some supposed action which arises from the *present state* of things, (wherefore the Opt. is not used in this way ;) as, ἴωμεν, *eamus,* suppose we go, it is time to go : Od. χ, 77 ἔλθωμεν ἀνὰ ἄστυ : Il. χ, 450 ἴδωμ᾽, ὅτιν᾽ ἔργα τέτυκται : Eur. Heracl. 558 σαφῶς κελεύεις· μὴ τρέσῃς μιάσματος τοὐμοῦ μετασχεῖν, ἀλλ᾽ ἐλεύθερος θάνω.—In the *oratio obliqua,* ἄγε, φέρε, ἔα (also, though more rarely, δεῦρο), ἴωμεν. So mostly in the Post-Homeric dialect, especially in the first person singular, generally preceded by these words, as we find it also in Homer ; as, Il. ι, 60 ἀλλ᾽ ἄγ᾽, ἐγὼν ἐξείπω, καὶ πάντα διίξομαι : Hdt. VII. 103 φέρε, ἴδω : Plat. Phæd. p. 63. B φέρε δή, ἦ δ᾽ ὅς, πειραθῶ πρὸς ὑμᾶς—ἀπολογήσασθαι : Id. Soph. p. 239. B ἔα σκεψώμεθα. Sometimes also joined with the Imperative ; as, Il. ζ, 340 ἀλλ᾽ ἄγε νῦν ἐπίμεινον, ἀρήϊα τεύχεα δύω : Il. ψ, 71 θάπτε με ὅτι τάχιστα, πύλας Ἀΐδαο περήσω. And it is sometimes as Imper.

[a] Nitzsch ad loc.

in first person without φέρε, ἄγε: Soph. Phil. 1354 σχὲς, ἀνειρηκὸς σῶμ' ἀναπαύσω, let me rest my weary body [a].

Obs. In the second and third person this exhortation assumes the form of a wish, and therefore is expressed by the Opt.: Il. ν, 119 ἀλλ' ἄγεθ', ἡμεῖς πέρ μιν ἀποτρωπῶμεν ὀπίσσω αὐτόθεν, ἤ τις ἔπειτα καὶ ἡμείων Ἀχιλῆι παρσταίη, δοίη δὲ κράτος μέγα: Od. χ, 77 ἔλθωμεν δ' ἀνὰ ἄστυ, βοὴ δ' ὤκιστα γένοιτο.

Conjunctivus Deliberativus [b].

§. 417. The Conj. in all its persons is used to express a question implying doubt, deliberation, where the speaker considers with himself what, under present circumstances, it is best for him to do: Il. α, 150 πῶς τίς τοι πρόφρων ἔπεσιν πείθηται Ἀχαιῶν; Od. ε, 465 ὤ μοι ἐγώ, τί πάθω; τί νυ μοι μήκιστα γένηται; what shall I do now! Æsch. Eum. 791, 821 τί ῥέξω; γένωμαι; (for τί γεν.): Eur. Hec. 1057 πᾶ βῶ; πᾶ στῶ; πᾶ κέλσω; Id. Ion 758 εἴπωμεν ἢ σιγῶμεν; Id. Med. 1275 παρέλθω δομούς; 1271 οἴμοι, τί δράσω; ποῖ φύγω μητρὸς χέρας; So ποῖ τις ἔλθη; where shall one go to! Plat. Legg. p. 835. A ἄμιλλαι χορῶν — κοσμηθήσονται τότε, εἴτε τριετηρίδες εἴτε αὖ διὰ πέμπτων ἐτῶν — διανεμηθῶσι, whether they—will be. So in the *oratio obliqua:* οὐκ οἶδα, πότερον εἴπωμεν, ἢ σιγῶμεν: Il. π, 436 διχθὰ δέ μοι κραδίη μέμονε—, ἢ μιν—θείω, ἢ ἤδη—δαμάσσω: Xen. Cyr. VIII. 4, 16 τὰ δὲ ἐκπώματα—οὐκ οἶδ' εἰ Χρυσάντᾳ τούτῳ δ ῶ. So frequently after βούλει: Plat. Gorg. p. 454. C βούλει οὖν, δύο εἴδη θῶμεν πειθοῦς; Id. Phæd. p. 95. E εἴτε τι βούλει προσθῆς ἢ ἀφέλης.

Optative in its secondary sense.

§. 418. 1. The Optative, in its secondary sense, expresses a supposition, without any notion of its realisation; as arising in past time from past circumstances, it is represented as farther off from reality than the Conjunctive. The predicate is merely something supposed or assumed—a possibility; hence the Opt. is used to express

a. A supposition without any notion of the realisation thereof: Od. ξ, 193 εἴη μὲν νῦν νῶιν ἐπὶ χρόνον ἠμὲν ἐδωδή, ἠδὲ μέθυ γλύκερον — , ἄλλοι δ' ἐπὶ ἔργον ἔποιεν, ῥηιδίως κεν ἔπειτα καὶ εἰς ἐνιαυτὸν ἅπαντα οὔτι διαπρήξαιμι, λέγων ἐμὰ κήδεα θυμοῦ, i. e. *sit sane nobis satis cibi, aliique in opere occupati sint: ego tamen, ut res ita se habeat, haud facile omnia perficiam:* Plat. Phæd. p. 87. E ἀπολομένης δὲ τῆς ψυχῆς τότ' ἤδη τὴν φύσιν τῆς ἀσθενείας ἐπιδεικνύοι τὸ σῶμα καὶ ταχὺ σαπὲν διοίχοιτο, *animo exstincto tum sane corpus*

[a] Elm. Med. 1242. Heracl. 559.   [b] Herm. Part. ἄν 11. 4.

imbecillitatem suam ostendat et — intercidat: Id. Rep. p. 362. D
οὐκοῦν — ἀδελφὸς ἀνδρὶ παρείη, "*frater adesto viro*," Stallbaum.

b. A wish. (In negative wishes, with μή, never οὐ.) Od. a, 265
τοῖος ἐὼν μνηστῆρσιν ὁμιλήσειεν Ὀδυσσεύς! πάντες κ' ὠκύμοροί
τε γενοίατο πικρόγαμοί τε (κ' is κέν=εἰ τοῦτο γένοιτο): Od. a, 386
μή σέ γ' ἐν ἀμφιάλῳ Ἰθάκῃ βασιλῆα Κρονίων ποιήσειεν! Il. χ.
304 μὴ μὰν ἀσπουδί γε καὶ ἀκλειῶς ἀπολοίμην! Soph. Aj. 550 ὦ
παῖ, γένοιο πατρὸς εὐτυχέστερος, τὰ δ' ἄλλα ὅμοιος! καὶ γένοι' ἂν
οὐ κακός (ἂν = εἰ τοῦτο γένοιτο). This expression of a wish
commonly assumes the form of an hypothetical antecedent sentence, being prefaced by εἰ, εἴθε, εἰ γάρ: Od. γ, 205 εἰ γὰρ ἐμοὶ
τοσσήνδε θεοὶ δύναμιν παραθεῖεν! So in formulas of wishing and
conjuring prefaced by οὕτω: Il. ν, 825 εἰ γὰρ ἐγὼν οὕτω γε Διὸς
παῖς αἰγιόχοιο εἴην — , ὡς νῦν ἡμέρη ἥδε κακὸν φέρει Ἀργείοισι πᾶσι
μάλα. And in poetry the wish is expressed as a final sentence,
prefaced by ὡς (*ut, utinam*): Il. σ, 107 ὥς ἔρις ἔκ τε θεῶν ἔκ τ' ἀνθρώπων ἀπόλοιτο! Eur. Hipp. 405 ὡς ἀπόλοιτο παγκακῶς!

Obs. 1. When the speaker feels that his wish cannot be realised,
the historic tenses or Aor. Ind. are used; as, εἴθε τοῦτο ἐγίγνετο! *utinam
hoc fieret!* εἴθε τοῦτο ἐγένετο! *utinam hoc factum esset!* So, ὤφελες γράψαι! would that you had written! and also ὥς, εἴθε (αἴθε) ὤφελον
γράψαι! would that I had written!

Obs. 2. In English and German the wish is expressed as in Greek, by
the Ind. or Opt.: had he but written! would he but write! In Latin by
the Conj.; as, *utinam hoc fiat!* wherein is contained the notion of its
realisation; and in the Opt. only when such notion is to be excluded, as
utinam Deus essem!

c. A command is expressed in a civil way as a wish: Od. o, 24
ἀλλὰ σύ γ' ἐλθὼν αὐτὸς ἐπιτρέψειας ἕκαστα δμώάων ἥτις τοι ἀρίστη
φαίνεται εἶναι: Od. ξ, 408 τάχιστά μοι ἔνδον ἑταῖροι εἶεν: Il. ω, 144
κήρυξ τίς οἱ ἕποιτο γεραίτερος: Aristoph. Vesp. 1431 ἔρδοι τις
ἣν ἕκαστος εἰδείη τέχνην: Xen. Anab. III. 2, 37 εἰ μὲν οὖν ἄλλος
τις βέλτιον ὁρᾷ, ἄλλως ἐχέτω· εἰ δὲ μή, Χειρίσοφος μὲν ἡγοῖτο.

d. The Opt. is used vaguely to express a desire, willingness,
inclination, without any expectation of the realisation thereof:
Il. o, 45 αὐτάρ τοι καὶ κείνῳ ἐγὼ παραμυθησαίμην — τῇ ἴμεν
(*velim illi persuadere*): Æschin. p. 85, 2 ἐγὼ δὴ οὔτε τὰς Δημοσθένους
διατριβὰς ἐζήλωκα, οὔτ' ἐπὶ ταῖς ἐμαυτοῦ αἰσχύνομαι, οὔτε τοὺς εἰρημένους
ἐν ὑμῖν λόγους ἐμαυτῷ ἀρρήτους εἶναι βουλοίμην: Theocrit. VIII. 20
ταύταν (σύριγγα) κατθείην (I would be willing)· τὰ δὲ τῶ πατρὸς οὐ
καταθήσω. Preceded by a conditional sentence: Eur. Phœn. 1207
εἰ δ' ἀμείνον' οἱ θεοὶ γνώμην ἔχουσιν, εὐτυχὴς εἴην ἐγώ, I should be
content to be happy. So Pind. Ol. III. 46 κεινὸς εἴην, I would be
content to be held as vain. Cf. Ol. IX. 80. With a negative:

Hdt. VII. 11 μὴ γὰρ εἴην ἐκ Δαρείου —, μὴ τιμωρησάμενος 'Αθηναίους, I could not be sprung from Darius, &c.

e. In direct questions the Opt. is but rarely found. In Homer, when the question is used as if it were the antecedent to some sentence depending on a condition, expressed by the question: Il. δ, 93 sq. ἦ ῥά νυ μοί τι πίθοιο, Λυκάονος υἱὲ δαΐφρον; will you listen to me! Τλαίης κεν Μενελάῳ ἐπιπροέμεν ταχὺν ἰόν, πᾶσι δέ κε Τρώεσσι χάριν καὶ κῦδος ἄροιο (that is, εἴ τι μοι πίθοιο, τλαίης κεν &c.): Il. η, 43 ἦ ῥά νυ μοί τι πίθοιο; κασίγνητος δέ τοι εἰμί· ἄλλους μὲν κάθισον κ. τ. λ. (that is, εἰ πίθοιο, ἄλλους μὲν κάθισον). If the question is composed of two clauses, the first contains the condition, expressed by the Opt. without ἄν; the latter is the sentence depending on that condition, expressed by the Opt. with ἄν: Il. ξ, 191 ἦ ῥά νυ μοί τι πίθοιο, φίλον τέκος, ὅττι κεν εἴπω, ἠέ κεν ἀρνήσαιο κοτεσσαμένη τόγε θυμῷ; In Attic Greek, mostly however in poetry, the Opt. is used in questions to signify a supposed case, of the falsehood of which there is no doubt: Æsch. Choeph. 392 ἀλλ' ὑπέρτολμον ἀνδρὸς φρόνημα τίς λέγοι; who could say?—no one: Soph. Antig. 604 τέαν, Ζεῦ, δύνασιν τίς ἀνδρῶν ὑπερβασίᾳ κατάσχοι; who could restrain?—no one: Aristoph. Plut. 438 ἄναξ Ἄπολλον καὶ θεοί, ποῖ τις φύγοι[a]; where could a person fly?—nowhere: cf. ibid. 374. Demosth. p. 921, 1 καὶ ὅσα μὲν εἶπε μετὰ τῆς ἀληθείας, μὴ χρῆσθε τεκμηρίῳ· ἃ δ' ἐψεύσατο τὸ ὕστερον, ἐπειδὴ διεφθάρη, πιστότερα ταῦθ' ὑπολάβοιτε εἶναι; hæc vos veriora existimaturos quis putet?

f. In negative sentences also, where the notion of the predicate is such as could not take place, the Opt. is used with the negative to deny the remotest possibility of its taking place: Pind. Ol. X. 19 τὸ γὰρ ἐμφυὲς οὔτ' αἴθων ἀλώπηξ οὔτ' ἐρίβρομοι λέοντες διαλλάξαιντο ἦθος.

Remarks on the Opt. and Conj. in compound sentences.

§. 419. 1. When in a dependent sentence the notion of frequency or repetition is to be expressed, if the several actions be in present or future time, the Conj. is used; if in past, the Opt. These moods are used because actions which happen at different moments are not conceived of as definite perceived facts, but only as something supposed: Od. τ, 515 αὐτὰρ ἐπὴν νὺξ ἔλθῃ, ἕλῃσί τε κοῖτος ἅπαντας, κεῖμαι ἐνὶ λέκτρῳ, as often as night comes: Il. κ, 14 αὐτὰρ ὅτ' ἐς νῆάς τε ἴδοι καὶ λαὸν 'Αχαιῶν, πολλὰς ἐκ κεφαλῆς προθελύμνους ἕλκετο χαίτας, as often as he saw.

2. In comparisons either the Ind. or Conj. is used, as the thing was conceived of as really existing, or only imagined: Il. μ, 167 οἱ δ', ὥστε σφῆκες μέσον αἰόλοι, ἠὲ μέλισσαι οἰκία ποιήσωνται —, οὐδ' ἀπολεί-

---

[a] But see Dawes Misc. Crit. 375.

πουσιν κοῖλον δόμον, ἀλλὰ μένοντες ἄνδρας θηρητῆρας ἀμύνονται περὶ τέκνων, ὡς οἵγ' οὐκ εθέλουσι πυλάων — χάσσασθαι, πρίν γ' ἠὲ κατακτάμεν', ἠὲ ἁλῶναι: Il. ξ, 16 ὡς δ' ὅτε π ο ρ φ ύ ρ ῃ πέλαγος — · ὡς ὁ γέρων ὥρμαινε.

Obs. The Opt. is not used in comparisons, because the supposition implied therein is present.

3. For Opt. and Conjunctive after verbs of perceiving and saying, with the conj. ὅτι and ὡς, or in final sentences, see Index.

Imperative.

§. 420. 1. The Imperative expresses a desire or command, or even prayer or exhortation, addressed to some one present, or conceived of as present ; as, δός μοι τὸ βιβλίον: γράφε τὴν ἐπιστολήν.

Obs. 1. The Imperative, like the Conj., is used of the Present or Future, and the Conj. may, as we have seen, perform the functions of the Imperative. These two moods are also nearly allied in some of their forms, the III. dual in each being that of the principal tenses ον, but in the Imper. augmented into ων. The Optative also is allied in sense with the Imper., as by both is expressed a wish or desire : hence the construction is sometimes changed from the Imper. to the Opt.; as, Od. β, 230 μή τις ἔτι πρόφρων ἀγανὸς καὶ ἤπιος ἔ σ τ ω — ἀλλ' αἰεὶ χαλεπὸς ε ἴ η καὶ αἴσυλα ῥ έ ζ ο ι.

Obs. 2. The Imper. never depends on any other verb. The Inf. is used in this case, as κελεύω σοι γράφειν.

Obs. 3. The personal pronoun is added to the Imper. only when a peculiar emphasis is to be laid on the person; as, σὺ μὲν ἄπελθε, σὺ δὲ μένε.

2. Although the Imper. is always considered to be in the time present to the speaker, it has a Pft. and Aor.; but these are not applied to the predicate in their primary notions of time, but only in their secondary notions : the Present expresses the continuance, the Aorist the momentary character of some action, the Perfect that the action is now completed, and remaining in its effects ; as, γράφε τὴν ἐπιστολήν: δός μοι τὸ βιβλίον: τέθναθι, that is, κεῖσο τεθνηκώς.

3. In the negative or prohibitory forms with μή, the Greeks, as a general rule, use only the Imper. Pr., never the Imper. Aor., but instead thereof the Conjunc. Aor.[a] : μή μοι ἀντίλεγε, or μή μοι ἀντιλέξῃς (but not μή μοι ἀντίλεξον): Il. α, 363 ἐξαύδα μὴ κ ε ῦ θ ε νόῳ, ἵνα εἴδομεν ἄμφω: Od. π, 168 ἤδη νῦν σῷ παιδὶ ἔπος φάο, μήδ' ἐ π ί κ ε ν θ ε: Od. ο, 263 εἰπέ μοι εἰρομένῳ νημερτέα, μήδ' ἐ π ι κ ε ύ σ ῃ ς: Il. δ, 234 Ἀργεῖοι, μήπω τι μ ε θ ί ε τ ε θούριδος ἀλκῆς: Æsch. Eum. 797 ὑμεῖς δὲ τῇ γῇ τῇδε μὴ βαρὺν κότον σ κ ή ψ η σ θ ε, μὴ θ υ μ ο ῦ σ θ ε, μήδ' ἀκαρπίαν τ ε ύ ξ η τ ε : Soph. Œ. C. 735 ὃν μήτ' ὀ κ ν ε ῖ τ ε, μήτ' ἀ φ ῆ τ' ἔπος κακόν: Demosth. p. 494, 17 μὴ τοίνυν διὰ μὲν τοῦ τῶνδε κατηγορεῖν ὡς φαύλων ἐκείνους ἀ φ α ι ρ ο ῦ, δι' ἃ δ' αὖ καταλείπειν φήσεις, τούσδε ὃ μόνον λαβόντες ἔχουσι, τοῦτ' ἀ φ έ λ ῃ: Id. p. 582, 15 μὴ

a R. P. Hec. 1116.

κατὰ τοὺς νόμους δικάσητε, ὦ ἄνδρες δικασταί· μὴ βοηθήσητε
τῷ πεπονθότι δεινά· μὴ εὐορκεῖτε· ἡμῖν δότε τὴν χάριν ταύτην.

Obs. 4. The reason hereof may be, that by the Pres. Imper. (expressing
continuance) it is signified that the thing forbidden never will take place,
which is implied more or less in a prohibition. The Conj. rather expresses a wish that it may not take place, wherein is no notion of continuance; and this difference of meaning is found in those passages where
both the Imper. and Conj. occur.

Obs. 5. The II. Person Aor. Imper. with μή is however sometimes used
in Epic (though but rarely) to express a decided, energetic prohibition; as,
Il. δ, 410 τῷ μή μοι πατέρας ποθ' ὁμοίῃ ἔνθεο θυμῷ· Od. ω, 248 σὺ δὲ μὴ
χόλον ἔνθεο θυμῷ. So even Aristoph. Thesm. 877 μὴ ψεῦσον. We
oftener find the III. Person Aor. Imp. with μή, not only in poetry, but also
in Attic prose: Od. π, 301 μήτις ἔπειτ' Ὀδυσῆος ἀκουσάτω ἔνδον ἐόντος:
Æsch. Theb. 1044 μὴ δοκησάτω τινί, *ne quisquam hoc mente con-
cipiat:* Soph. Aj. 1334 μηδ' ἡ βία σε μηδαμῶς νικησάτω: Xen. Cyr. VII.
5, 73 καὶ μηδείς γε ὑμῶν ἔχων ταῦτα νομισάτω ἀλλότρια ἔχειν: Ibid. VIII.
7, 26 μηδεὶς ἰδέτω: Æschin. 62, 15 μήτ' ἀπογνώτω μηδὲν μήτε κατα-
γνώτω: Id. 23, 15 μὴ γὰρ ὑπ' ἐμοῦ λεγόμενον, ἀλλὰ γιγνόμενον τὸ πρᾶγμα
νομίσαθ' ὁρᾶν.

§. 421. The Attic formula οἶσθ' οὖν ὃ δρᾶσον, &c. seems to arise from
a change, so frequent in Greek, from the indirect to the direct construction.
(It is also explained by supposing a transposition for δρᾶσον, οἶσθ' ὅ, like
Plaut. Rudent. III. 5, 18 *tange, sed scin' quomodo?*) In the same way we
may account for the Imper. after ὥστε in a seemingly dependent construction; as, φρόνει ὥστε μὴ λίαν στένε, for στένειν. The Fut. is also used
in the place of the Imper. in the former formula, Eur. Cycl. 131 οἶσθ' οὖν
ὃ δράσεις ὡς ἀπαίρωμεν χθονός; and the III. Person Imper. is also used in
the same formula: Eur. Iph. Taur. 1203 οἶσθ' οὖν ἅ μοι γενέσθω; And the
III. Person is used not only in these dependent questions, but also in other
dependent sentences; as, Hdt. I. 89 νῦν ὦν ποίησον ὧδε, εἴ τοι ἀρέσκοι, τὰ
ἐγὼ λέγω· κάτισον τῶν δορυφόρων ἐπὶ πάσῃσι τῇσι πύλῃσι φυλάκους, οἳ λεγόντων —, ὥς σφεα (sc. χρήματα) ἀναγκαίως ἔχει δεκατευθῆναι τῷ Διΐ. Here the
relative sentence οἳ λεγόντων, though in form a dependent, is in sense
a principal clause = καὶ οὗτοι λεγόντων: Thuc. IV. 92 extr. πιστεύ-
σαντας δὲ τῷ θεῷ (sc. ἡμᾶς δεῖ) — ὁμόσε χωρῆσαι τοῖσδε, καὶ δεῖξαι, ὅτι,
ὧν μὲν ἐφίενται, πρὸς τοὺς μὴ ἀμυνομένους ἐπιόντες, κτάσθωσαν, i. e. *oportet
nos deo fretos — adversus hos tendere, et demonstrare, licere illis ea, quæ
concupiscant, si bellum non propulsantibus inferant, tenere,* Bauer p. 645:
Plat. Legg. p. 800. E τὸ δὲ τοσοῦτον ὑμᾶς αὐτοὺς ἐπανερωτῶ πάλιν, τῶν
ἐκμαγείων ταῖς ᾠδαῖς εἰ πρῶτον ἐν τοῦθ' ἡμῖν ἀρέσκον κείσθω. This idiom
seems to arise from the Greeks using the third person imperative as a
mild expression of a desire, where we use " shall" and " must."

Use of the Moods as Conditionals.

§. 422. 1. The predicate may also be conceived of in the mind
as depending, or as having depended, on certain conditions. A
sentence in which this conditional sense is expressed consists of
two parts; the condition, and that whereof it is the condition.

Obs. The condition by which the predicate is limited is frequently omitted, when it is contained or implied in the context, or readily supplied by the mind.

2. The conditional nature of the predicate is marked by its having the particle ἄν (Epic κέ, κέν) attached to it. And the notion thus limited almost invariably stands in the Historic tenses of the Ind., in the Opt. (or Conjunctive sometimes), in the Infin. or the Participle. And the forms with which it is never found are the Pres. or Pft. Indicative, and but rarely with the Fut. Ind. or the Imper., or the Conjunctive in independent sentences.

Theories on the Etymology of ἄν.

§. 423. *a.* ᾿Αν, ἀνά, *secundum;* κέ, κά, an old form of κατά as found in κάδδε, &c.[a]

b. ᾿Αν, connected with Latin *an;* κέ with Latin *quam*[b].

Nature and use of the Particle ἄν [c].

§. 424. 1. The proper force of the particle ἄν is the expression of a condition (either actually stated, implied in the context, or to be supplied by the mind[d]), on which the action of the verb to which it is attached depends; so that if the condition to which ἄν refers takes place, the action which depends on that condition will take place also[e]; and if the former does not take place, neither will (at least in this present case) the latter. Whether this condition will, or will not take place, is decided *animo loquentis,* by the mind of the speaker.

2. ᾿Αν therefore has a twofold force : the condition is supposed by the speaker to take place, and therefore the action is rendered more likely—(positive use of ἄν)—*probably;* or the condition is supposed by the speaker not to take place, and the action is rendered less likely—(negative use of ἄν)—*perhaps.*

3. Hence it is used with the Ind., Opt., and Conj., which express certainty, possibility, probability, respectively, as follows.

Indicative.

a. With the Historic tenses of Ind. expressing an absolute known fact, it renders the action thereof less likely, for the performance

---

[a] Donaldson's New Cratylus 244.
[b] Kühner Gr. Gr. 453. 2.   Hartung de Part. Græc. vol. ii. 225.
[c] Hermann de Part. ἄν. Opusc. vol. iv. Hartung de Part. Græc. vol. ii. 218.

Reisig. Comment. de vi et usu Part. ἄν. Ellendt Lex. Soph. ad voc.
[d] Ellendt ad voc. V.
[e] Herm. de Part. ἄν p. 165. Herm. Ajac. 1061.

of a condition cannot make a fact more probable ; but the addition of ἄν expresses that it is known to have taken place only on a certain condition; as, ἡμάρτανες, you were wrong, ἄν—but only supposing such or such a thing took place—but I know · it did not take place, therefore you are not wrong in this case; hence its derived sense, ἡμάρτανες ἄν, you would have been wrong, i. e. on such or such conditions.

Obs. On the Impft., or Aorist in Impft. sense, without ἄν in this sense, see §. 398. 3.

β. But when the Impft. (or Aorist, or Plpft. used as Impft.) is used to express an action not conceived of merely as absolutely past, but continuing in past time, ἄν being added to it expresses, *under such and such circumstances as often as they recurred:* ἡμάρτανες ἄν, you were wrong under such and such circumstances as often as they recurred; and these circumstances being supposed by the speaker's mind to have occurred at such and such times, the action is supposed to have taken place at those times likewise : so ἡμάρτανες ἄν, you were frequently wrong [a].

Obs. This use of ἄν with the Impft. to express frequency, is a proof that the condition expressed by ἄν is not, as laid down by most writers, always supposed not to take place; for if this were so, ἄν with the Impft. would only signify certain times when the action of the Impft. did not take place (the condition not being fulfilled), not certain times when (the condition being fulfilled) it did take place.

γ. ῎Αν is never used with the Pres. or Pft. Ind.[b], for that action which is represented as actually existing in the presence of the speaker, whether as actually going on and in course of completion, or already completed and existing before him, cannot be supposed to depend on a condition. In the few passages where ἄν is found with these tenses, either the reading is bad, ἄν being confused with ἄρα, αὖ, ἐν—κέ with καί; or ἄν is to be joined to some other verbal notion in the sentence (very often the Infin.) ; or the elided κ' is καί, and not κέ : so for instance :—

Od. β, 86 ἐθέλεις δέ κε μῶμον ἀνάψαι, Cod. Harlei. ἐθέλοις (see Nitzsch ad loc.): Il. ξ, 484 τῷ καί κε τις εὔχεται ἀνὴρ γνωτὸν ἐνὶ μεγάροισιν ἀρῆς ἀλκτῆρα λιπέσθαι (Cod. Clark. omits κέ with Eustath.) : Od. ω, 88. sq. κέν seems to have been originally καί : Od. γ, 255 ἤτοι μὲν τόδε κ' αὐτὸς ὀίεαι (κ' is καί) : see Nitzsch : Plat. Phæd. p. 102. init. σὺ δ', εἴ περ εἰ τῶν φιλοσόφων, οἶμαι ἂν ὡς ἐγὼ λέγω ποιοῖς (ποιοῖς ἄν) : Eur. Med. 930 οὐκ οἶδ' ἄν εἰ πείσαιμι, for εἰ πείσαιμι ἄν : Xen. Hell. VI. 1, 4 οἶμαι ἄν — οὐκ εἶναι ἔθνος κ. τ. λ. : immediately afterwards, οὐκ ἄν μοι δοκῶ — φιλίαν ποιήσασθαι· νομίζω γὰρ ἔτι ῥᾷον — παραλαβεῖν ἄν (in these passages ἄν belongs to the Infin.).

[a] Brunck Soph. Phil. 290.
[b] Monk Alc. 48. Dawes Misc. Crit. 106. Herm. p. 14.

δ. Sometimes, though but rarely, with the Ind. Fut.[a] This tense expresses a present belief that something will presently be; this *may* be supposed to depend on some condition; and if this is to be *expressly* marked, ἄν is joined to the Future. In Epic the weaker form κέ is frequently thus used; in Attic Greek it is very rare; and though in many passages the reading is bad or doubtful, yet we can hardly deny the existence of this construction altogether in Attic Greek[b]:—

Od. ρ, 540 εἰ δ' Ὀδυσσεὺς ἔλθοι—αἶψά κε σὺν ᾧ παιδὶ βίας ἀποτίσεται ἀνδρῶν. The conditional sentence however is generally wanting: Od. α, 268 ἀλλ' ἤτοι μὲν ταῦτα θεῶν ἐν γούνασι κεῖται· ἤ κεν νοστήσας ἀποτίσεται, ἠὲ καὶ οὐκί: Il. ο, 211 ἀλλ' ἤτοι νῦν μέν κε νεμεσσηθεὶς ὑποείξω: Od. γ, 80 εἴρεαι ὁππόθεν εἰμέν· ἐγὼ δέ κε τοι καταλέξω (if you will hear it): Il. δ, 176 καί κε τις ὧδ' ἐρέει Τρώων (so Pind. Nem. VII. 68 μαθὼν δέ τις ἂν ἐρεῖ): Il. ξ, 267 ἀλλ' ἴθ', ἐγὼ δέ κε τοι Χαρίτων μίαν ὁπλοτεράων δώσω ὀπυιέμεναι, dabo, si tibi lubuerit: Il. χ, 66 αὐτὸν δ' ἂν πύματόν με κύνες πρώτῃσι θύρῃσιν ὠμησταὶ ἐρύουσιν. So in dependent questions: compare Od. ο, 524. Il. ρ, 144. Hdt. III. 104 ὅκως ἂν—ἔσονται ἐν τῇ ἁρπάγῃ: Xen. Cyr. VI. 1, 45 ὑβριστὴν οὖν νομίζων αὐτὸν εὖ οἶδ' ὅτι ἄσμενος ἂν πρὸς ἄνδρα οἷος σὺ εἶ ἀπαλλαγήσεται (so Guelph. Paris. — Schneider c. vulg. ἀπαλλαγείη): Ibid. VII. 5, 21 ὅταν δὲ καὶ αἴσθωνται ἡμᾶς ἔνδον ὄντας, πολὺ ἂν ἔτι μᾶλλον ἢ νῦν ἀχρεῖοι ἔσονται ὑπὸ τοῦ ἐκπεπλῆχθαι (with no variation of Mss.): Plat. Phæd. p. 61. C σχεδὸν οὖν ἐξ ὧν ἐγὼ ᾔσθημαι, οὐδ' ὁπωστιοῦν ἄν σοι ἑκὼν εἶναι πείσεται (some Mss. omit ἄν): Id. Rep. p. 615. D ἔφη οὖν τὸν ἐρωτώμενον εἰπεῖν· Οὐχ ἥκει, φάναι, οὐδ' ἂν ἥξει δεῦρο (very few ἥξοι): *non venit, nec, si recte judico, veniet:* Æschin. 29, 30 οὕτω γάρ ἂν (omitted by Bekker) μάλιστα μεμνήσομαι καὶ δυνήσομαι εἰπεῖν, καὶ ὑμεῖς μαθήσεσθε (οὕτω, i. e. εἰ ταῦτα οὕτω ποιῶ or ποιήσω). Very often in questions, for here the Fut. expresses doubt: Eur. Bacch. 595 τί ποτ' ἂν ἐκ τούτων ἐρεῖ; Arist. Nub. 465 ἆρά γε τοῦτ' ἂν ἐγώ ποτ' ἐπόψομαι; Æschin. Ctes. §. 155 τί ποτ' ἂν ἐρεῖ;

ε. With the Imperative naturally it is not used[c], as the notion of immediate command excludes that of a condition. Where ἄν is found with the Imp. the reading is bad, or it belongs to some other word in the sentence, or implied therein:—

Xen. Anab. I. 8, 8 ἀλλὰ ἰόντων ἂν, εἰδότες, ὅτι κακίους εἰσὶ περὶ ἡμᾶς ἢ ἡμεῖς περὶ ἐκείνους, where ἄν probably arose from the various reading ἰέτωσαν[d]. In later writers, such as Theoc. XXIII. 35 ἀλλὰ τύ, παῖ, κἂν τοῦτο πανύστατον ἁδύ τι ῥέξον, there is an ellipse of κἂν τοῦτο πανύστατον ῥέξῃς, to which κἂν is to be referred.

ζ. When the Conjunctive is used for the Fut. Ind. (see §. 415), ἄν is sometimes in Homer[e] joined with it, when the future event is to be expressly marked as depending on a condition; as,

---

[a] Elm. Heracl. 769 not. Heind. Phæd. §. 13. Schæf. ad Greg. Cor. 66. Herm. Œ. R. 1055.

[b] Stallb. Rep. 615. D.

[c] For some seeming instances in Soph., see Ellendt ad voc. IV. 1.

see Ellendt ad voc. VI. Herm. Part. ἄν 170.

[d] Schneider ad loc.

[e] For some seeming instances in Soph., see Ellendt ad voc. IV. 1.

Il. a, 137 εἰ δέ κε μὴ δώωσιν, ἐγὼ δέ κεν αὐτὸς ἔλωμαι, in that case: Il. a, 205 ἧς ὑπεροπλίῃσι τάχ' ἄν ποτε θυμὸν ὀλέσσῃ, he would in certain circumstances: Il. γ, 54 οὐκ ἄν τοι χραίσμῃ κίθαρις: compare λ, 384. Il. ξ, 235 πείθευ· ἐγὼ δέ κε τοι ἰδέω χάριν ἤματα πάντα.

η. So also with the Conjunctivus deliberativus ἄν is joined, to signify that the action which is being deliberated upon depends on some condition, either expressed or implied:—

Od. β, 332 τίς δ' οἶδ', εἴ κε καὶ αὐτὸς ἰὼν κοίλης ἐπὶ νηὸς τῆλε φίλων ἀπόληται, ἀλώμενος ὥσπερ 'Οδυσσεύς; Il. ν, 742 ἔνθεν δ' ἄν μάλα πᾶσαν ἐπιφρασσαίμεθα βουλήν, ἤ κεν ἐνὶ νήεσσι — πέσωμεν, αἴ κ' ἐθέλῃσι θεὸς δόμεναι κράτος, ἤ κεν ἔπειτα πὰρ νηῶν ἔλθωμεν ἀπήμονες: Od. δ, 545 ἀλλὰ τάχιστα πεῖρα, ὅπως κεν δὴ σὴν πατρίδα γαῖαν ἵκηαι. Frequently we must supply a verb of trying or deliberating: Il. σ, 307 ἀλλὰ μάλ' ἄντην στήσομαι, ἤ κε φέρῃσι μέγα κλέος ἤ κε φεροίμην: Plat. Legg. p. 655. C τί ποτ' ἂν οὖν λέγωμεν; Id. Phædr. p. 231. D ὥστε πῶς ἂν εὖ φρονήσαντες ταῦτα καλῶς ἔχειν ἡγήσωνται; i. e. πῶς, ἐὰν εὖ φρονήσωσι, ταῦτα κ. ἐχ. ἡγήσωνται ἄν; Id. Protag. p. 319. B σοὶ δὲ λέγοντι οὐκ ἔχω ὅπως ἂν ἀπιστῶ: Xen. Anab. II. 4, 20 οὐχ ἕξουσιν ἐκεῖνοι ὅποι ἂν φύγωσιν. From εἰ ἄν is formed ἐάν: Xen. M. S. IV. 4, 12 σκέψαι, ἐὰν τόδε σοι μᾶλλον ἀρέσκῃ.

Ἄν with Optative.

§. 425. 1. With the Opt., which expresses an indefinite possibility, ἄν has likewise a twofold force: λέγοις you might say—ἄν, on this condition; 1st, if this condition is conceived of *in animo loquentis* as taking place, the action of the Optative is represented as more certain, one case being defined in which it will take place; hence its use for the Future and Imperative: λέγοις *you might say* —ἄν, *if you please*, &c.; but you do please, therefore, I think you will say: or, 2nd, the condition is conceived of *in animo loquentis* as not taking place, and then the action of the Optative is rendered less likely: λέγοις *you might say—ἄν, in such circumstances;* but as I do not think these circumstances will take place, there is one case at least where I know the action will not take place.

a. As a modest assertion of some action or fact[a], present or future, marking it as less certain than if it had been in the Present or Future, and depending on the will of the person who is addressed, or on some other condition which is supposed to be fulfilled: Xen. Cyr. I. 2, 11 καὶ θηρῶντες μὲν οὐκ ἂν ἀριστήσαιεν: Ibid. 13 ἐπειδὰν δὲ τὰ πέντε καὶ εἴκοσιν ἔτη διατελέσωσιν, εἴησαν μὲν ἂν οὗτοι πλείόν τι γεγονότες ἤ πεντήκοντα ἔτη ἀπὸ γενεᾶς: Plat. Gorg. p. 502. D Δημηγορία ἄρα τίς ἐστιν ἡ ποιητική: (Call.) Φαίνεται: (Socr.) Οὐκοῦν ἡ ῥητορικὴ δημηγορία ἂν εἴη. So very often in conclusions. There is often something ironical in this expression.

---

[a] Elm. Heracl. 972. Ellendt Lex. Soph. ad voc. VIII.

b. So for the Imperative; the action of the Opt. being supposed to depend on the will of the person addressed, who is
supposed to be willing, and therefore this milder form may be used
instead of a direct command: Soph. Elect. 1491 χώροις ἄν, if you
please. So Il. β, 250, Ulysses addresses Thersites with a certain
irony : Θερσῖτ'— ἴσχεο —! οὐ γὰρ ἐγὼ σέο φημὶ χερειότερον βροτὸν
ἄλλον ἔμμεναι—· τῷ οὐκ ἂν βασιλῆας ἀνὰ στόμ' ἔχων ἀγορεύοις,
καί σφιν ὀνείδεά τε προφέροις, νόστον τε φυλάσσοις ! do not
if you please. With οὐ as a question: Il. ε, 456 οὐκ ἂν δὴ
τόνδ' ἄνδρα μάχης ἐρύσαιτο μετελθών; so pronounced in a sharp
tone, as an earnest exhortation: Il. ω, 263 οὐκ ἂν δή μοι ἄμαξαν
ἐφοπλίσσαιτε τάχιστα, ταῦτά τε πάντ' ἐπιθεῖτε ἵνα πρήσσωμεν ὁδοῖο ;

c. When the condition is conceived of as not fulfilled, it expresses
a possibility yet more removed from reality than the simple Opt.
So Il. α, 271 κείνοισι δ' ἂν οὔτις τῶν, οἳ νῦν βροτοί εἰσὶν ἐπιχθόνιοι,
μαχέοιτο: Il. δ, 539 ἔνθα κεν οὐκέτι ἔργον ἀνὴρ ὀνόσαιτο:
Hdt. III. 82 ἀνδρὸς γὰρ ἑνὸς τοῦ ἀρίστου (i. e. εἰ ἄριστος εἴη) οὐδὲν
ἄμεινον ἂν φανείη: Id. IX. 71 ταῦτα μὲν καὶ φθόνῳ ἂν εἴποιεν,
this they *might* say: Id. I. 2 εἴησαν δ' ἂν οὗτοι Κρῆτες, they
might possibly be Cretans: Id. VII. 184 ἤδη ὦν ἄνδρες ἂν εἶεν
ἐν αὐτοῖσι τέσσερες μυριάδες καὶ εἴκοσι: Id. V. 9 γένοιτο δ' ἂν
πᾶν ἐν τῷ μακρῷ χρόνῳ, any thing *might* happen.

2. The most common uses therefore of this particle may be thus
arranged :

a. Past tenses. ἡμάρτανες ἄν, you would err, or have erred ; con-
     dition not fulfilled.

     ἡμάρτανες ἄν, you frequently erred ; condition
     fulfilled.

b. Optative. ἁμαρτάνοις ἄν, you would err ; condition not
     fulfilled.

     ἁμαρτάνοις ἄν, I think you will err ; condition
     fulfilled.

     ἁμαρτάνοις ἄν, as Imper.

On ἄν in Dependent sentences, see under that head.

Remarks.

§. 426. 1. The Opt. without ἄν is not generally used in independent
sentences, except in the senses given above ; but when the notion of the
Opt. is perfectly indefinite, represented as independent of all condition or
circumstances whatsoever, the Opt. without ἄν is sometimes used[a] in inde-

---

[a] Ellendt ad voc. IX.

pendent sentences, instead of the Opt. with ἄν. The supposed possible action is indefinite, depends on no conditions or circumstances, whether such as by their fulfilment would make it more likely, or by their non-fulfilment less likely, to take place; so that it is stated as something possible without any further notion of any definite time, place, circumstances, wherein it would be likely or unlikely to take place. This is called the Potential Optative. It is not used in Prose; for the matter-of-fact way of looking at things, natural to prose writers, could not separate a possibility from those circumstances and conditions which are implied in the very notion, while the more free genius of poetry could do so: Od. γ, 231 ῥεῖα θεὸς γ' ἐθέλων καὶ τηλόθεν ἄνδρα σαῶσαι, God can save (no notion of his doing so); σαῶσαι ἄν, might save if he would, or will save: Eur. Hippol. 1186 θᾶσσον ἢ λέγοι τις —, ἐστήσαμεν, quicker than one could speak (no notion of any one really speaking): Moschus I. 6 ἔστι δ' ὁ παῖς περίσαμος· ἐν εἴκοσι πᾶσι μάθοις νιν, you might or would know him (no notion of his really doing so); μάθοις ἄν, when you saw him. Hence in similes which are only imagined: Theocr. VIII. 89 οὕτως ἐπὶ ματέρα νεβρὸς ἄλοιτο (no notion of its taking place): 91 οὕτω καὶ νύμφα γαμεθεῖσ' ἀκάχοιτο. So Æsch. Choeph. 592 αἰγίδων φράσαι κότον: which is so indefinite, that the indefinite τίς is to be supplied as the natural subject. So in poetry; εἴποι τις, *dixerit quispiam ;* ἴδοι τις, *videas.* Often with τάχα, εἰκότως, &c. sometimes even in prose.

Obs. 1. With negatives the Opt. without ἄν seems to be a stronger negation: a supposition is denied absolutely and for itself, apart from any conditions or circumstances which might render it less likely to happen: Pind. Ol. X. 19 τὸ γὰρ ἐμφυὲς οὔτ' αἴθων ἀλώπηξ οὔτ' ἐρίβρομοι λέοντες διαλλάξαιντο ἦθος, cannot (absolutely), ἄν on no condition: Eur. Hipp. 468 οὐδὲ στέγην — καλῶς ἀκριβώσειαν: Id. Iph. Aul. 1210 οὐδεὶς πρὸς τάδ' ἀντείποι βροτῶν: Mosch. Id. III. 114 τῷ δ' ἐγὼ οὐ φθονέοιμι. τὸ γὰρ μέλος οὐ καλὸν ᾄδει: Æsch. Choeph. 854 οὗτοι φρένα κλέψειαν ὠμματωμένην[a]. So also with interrog. which have a negative force[b]; as, Plat. Rep. 352 C τί δ' ἀκούσαις ἄλλῳ ἢ ὠσὶ = οὐκ ἀκούσαις: Od. δ, 644. Soph. Ant. 604 τίς — κατάσχοι ; *quis vincat ?* ἄν, *quis vincere poterit* [c] ?

Obs. 2. Ἄν is also frequently omitted when a conditional adverb stands with the Opt., such as τάχα, εἰκότως, ἴσως, which express in some degree the conditional force of ἄν: Æsch. Aj. 1048 ἀπειθοίης δ' ἴσως[d]: Id. Suppl. 727 ἴσως — μόλοι. So Theocrit. XXII. 74 οὐκ ἄλλῳ γε μαχεσσαίμεθ' ἐπ' ἀέθλῳ, where ἐπ' ἄλλῳ ἀέθλῳ seem to be equivalent to ἄν.

2. The Opt. with ἄν differs from the Fut. Ind., in that the latter represents the future action as certain to happen, the former as only likely to happen, that is, under certain conditions. The Fut. and Opt. are sometimes interchanged to express this difference of sense: Il. ι, 416 αἰὼν ἔσσεται, οὐδέ κε μ' ὦκα τέλος θανάτοιο κιχείη: Hdt. IV. 97 ἔψομαί τοι καὶ οὐκ ἂν λειφθείην: Thuc. III. 13 οὔτε γὰρ ἀποστήσεται ἄλλος, τά τε ἡμέτερα προσγενήσεται, πάθοιμέν τ' ἂν δεινότερα ἢ οἱ πρὶν δουλεύοντες: Demosth. p. 356, 40 οὐ τοίνυν μόνον ἐκ τούτων ἂν γνοίητε, ὅτι δεινὸν οὐδ' ὁτιοῦν πέπονθε, — ἀλλὰ καὶ τὸ πρᾶγμα αὐτὸ εἰ σκέψεσθε[e].

[a] Monk Hipp. 482. Klaus. ad loc.
[b] But see Dawes Misc. Crit. 375.
[c] Herm. Ant. 601.
[d] Klaus. Ag. 973. See Hein. Part. ἄν, p. 164, where he says, "Quod id futurum putat esse Chorus;" and notes on Elms. Med. 310 fin., where he makes the ἄν in the former part of the sentence continue its force to ἀπειθοίης.
[e] Bremi ad loc.

Obs. 3. Many of the instances of the Potential (Opt. without ἄν) are to be explained by giving the Optative some one of the meanings—desire, wishing, willingness — given above[a] (§. 418.) ; and in some wrong readings may have arisen from an error in transcription[b].

Obs. 4. On the omission of ἄν in the second of two similar sentences, see §. 432. *Obs.* 2.

'Aν in Negative and Interrogative Sentences, &c.

§. 427. 1. So it is used in negative sentences to increase, in a manner exactly opposite to the Opt. alone, (§. 426. *Obs.* 1.,) the force of the negation : οὐκ ἂν λέγοιμι, I would not say on any condition, on any account, for the world, at all.   So with the Conj. : Il. γ, 54 οὐκ ἄν τοι χραίσμῃ κίθαρις, cannot at all.   It seems sometimes to have even a stronger force than the Future ; as, Æsch. Eum. 552 δίκαιος ὢν οὐκ ἄνολβος ἔσται, πανώλεθρος δ᾽ οὐ ποτ᾽ ἂν γένοιτο, he cannot possibly be.

2. So also in Interrog. sentences: Il. ω, 367 εἴ τις σε ἴδοιτο —, τίς ἂν δή τοι νόος εἴη; Il. τ, 90 ἀλλὰ τί κεν ῥέξαιμι; what in the world could I do! Soph. Phil. 1393 τί δῆτ᾽ ἂν ἡμεῖς δρῷμεν; Demosth. p. 43, 10 λέγεταί τι καινόν; γένοιτο γὰρ ἄν τι καινότερον ἢ Μακεδὼν ἀνὴρ 'Αθηναίους καταπολεμῶν;

Compare ποῖ τις φεύγει; whither does he fly!

ποῖ τις φύγοι; Arist. Plut. 438 whither should he fly[c]!

ποῖ τις ἂν φύγοι; Eur. Orest. 598 whither in the world!

ποῖ τις φύγῃ; Soph. Aj. 503 whither shall he fly!

3. So also with the Opt. in the formulas of wishing with πῶς, τίς, &c. to express the urgency of the wish : Soph. Aj. 338 ὦ Ζεῦ, — πῶς ἂν τὸν αἱμυλώτατον — ὀλέσσας τέλος θάνοιμι καὐτός! how in the world = would that by some means : Eur. Med. 97 ἰώ μοί μοι, πῶς ἂν ὀλοίμαν; quí fieri possit, ut peream! i. e. utinam peream! Id. Alc. 881 πῶς ἂν ὀλοίμην; Plat. Euthyd. p. 275 C πῶς ἂν καλῶς σοι διηγησαίμην; Æsch. Ag. 1457 φεῦ τίς (would that some one) ἂν ἐν τάχει μόλοι μὴ περιώδυνος μηδὲ δεμνιοτήρης μόλοι τὸν ἀεὶ φέρουσ᾽ ἐν ἡμῖν μοῖρ᾽ ἀτέλευτον ὕπνον;

'Aν with Conjunctive words.

§. 428. 'Aν is joined with Conjunctions or Relatives, followed by the Opt. and Conj.

a. With the Conj. the force of ἄν is generally thrown on the Conjunction or Relative, or Interrogative, and makes it indefinite, by giving it the notion of a contingent indefinite accomplishment, so that the speaker has not in his mind any definite person, time, place, &c.[d] ; as, ὃς ποιεῖ, the

---

[a] Herm. Part. ἄν, p. 162.   [b] Vid. Index Brunck Soph. ad voc. ἄν. R. P. Phœn. 412.
   [c] Dawes Misc. Crit. 375.   [d] Ellendt ad voc. IV. 2. a. b. c. d. e.

man who does, &c.; ὃς ἂν ποιῇ, the man, whosoever he is, who; where we may supply a participle to which ἂν belongs, (see below, *Obs.* 3.) so that ὃς ἂν often have the force of ἐάν τις, ἐάν ποτε, &c.[a]: ὅτε, when (definite time); ὅταν, whensoever (indefinite): Arist. Plut. 1151 πατρὶς γάρ ἐστι πᾶσ᾽ ἵν᾽ ἂν πράττῃ τις εὖ, wheresoever; ἵνα ἂν πράττοι, where he might possibly, under such or such conditions, fare well: Soph. Phil. 310 ἐκεῖνο δ᾽ οὐδεὶς ἡνίκ᾽ ἂν μνησθῶ θέλει, whensoever, at the different times when: Hdt. I. 182 ἡ γὰρ πρόμαντις τοῦ θεοῦ ἐπεὰν γένηται—οὐ γὰρ ὦν αἰεί ἐστι χρηστήριον αὐτόθι. From this close connection between the conjunction and ἂν arose the following compound conjunctions: ἐάν (from εἰ ἂν— ep. εἴκε), ἐπεάν, ἐπάν, ὅταν, ὁπόταν, εὖτ᾽ ἂν, πρὶν ἂν, ἕως ἂν, ἔνθ᾽ ἂν, ὅθι ἂν, οὗ ἂν, ὅπου ἂν, οἷ ἂν, ὅποι ἂν, ᾗ ἂν, ὅπη ἂν, ὅθεν ἂν, ὁπόθεν ἂν, &c. — ὃς ἂν (quicunque or si quis), οἷος ἂν, ὁποῖος ἂν, ὅσος ἂν, ὁπόσος ἂν, &c.

b. With the Opt. the force of ἂν is thrown on the verb, the sense of which it modifies, as in independent sentences: Plat. Euth. 293 A τίς πότ᾽ ἐστιν ἡ ἐπιστήμη ἧς τυχόντες ἂν (εἰ τυγχάνομεν) τὸν ἐπίλοιπον βίον διέλθοιμεν; Xen. Mem. II. 1, 23 ἐσθῆτα δι᾽ ἧς ἂν μάλιστα ἡ ὥρα διαλάμποι, may possibly: διαλάμπῃ, through which, whatever it may be.

(See also under Dependent sentences.)

Obs. 1. When the force of ἂν is thrown on the conjunctive word, the Conjunctive should be used[b]; when on the verb, the Opt.

Obs. 2. As a general rule, the Conjunctive is not used with these conjunctive words without ἂν; but when an indefinite sense is not intended to be affixed to the Conjunction, &c., so that ἂν is not required, the Opt. is used. This rule is more generally violated in poetry than in prose[c].

Obs. 3. With the Ind. also the force of the ἂν is sometimes thrown on the relative or interrog. word: Soph. Phil. 572 πρὸς ποῖον ἂν τόνδ᾽ αὐτὸς ὀδυσσεὺς ἔπλει; sc. πρὸς ποῖον ἂν ὄντα τόνδε — ἔπλει[d].

Ἂν with Infinitive and Participle.

§. 429. 1. When the construction changes from the *Verbum Finitum* to the Inf. or Part., ἂν is joined to these forms, if it would have been used in the construction with the *Verbum Finitum*[e]. Hence the Inf. and Part. in Greek have in some degree the power of moods, which in other languages they have not. This is especially the case after verbs of hoping, thinking, declaring, &c.[f]

a. Infinitive instead of the Opt. with ἂν, or Fut. Ind., which is equivalent to Opt. with ἂν; as, εἴ τι ἔχει or ἔχοι, ἔφη, δώσειν ἂν: Thuc. II. 30. extr. νομίζοντες, εἰ ταύτην πρώτην λάβοιεν, ῥᾳδίως ἂν σφίσι τἆλλα προσχωρήσειν: Id. V. 82 νομίζων μέγιστον ἂν σφᾶς ὠφελήσειν: Xen. Cyr. I. 5, 2 ἐνόμιζεν, εἰ τοὺς Μήδους ἀσθενεῖς ποιήσειε, πάντων γε ἂν τῶν πέριξ ῥᾳδίως ἄρξειν.

b. For the Ind. Hist. tenses and the Aorist with ἂν, as εἴ τι εἶχεν, ἔφη, δοῦναι ἂν.

c. For the Opt. of Impft. Plpft. and Aorist with ἂν, as εἴ τι ἔχοι, ἔφη, δοῦναι ἂν: Plat. Rep. p. 350 E εἰ οὖν λέγοιμι, εὖ οἶδ᾽, ὅτι δημηγορεῖν ἂν με φαίης.

2. But where in the construction with the *Verbum Finitum* ἂν would

---

a Stallb. Phædr. 68. B.　　　　　　b Dawes Misc. Crit. 127.
e Elm. Heracl. 959.　Herm. 113. R. P. Med. 222.　Elm. 215.　　　d Herm. Phil. 568.
e Herm. Aj. 1061.　　　　　　f Stallb. Phileb. 61.

not be used, neither will it be with the Inf.; as, εἴ τι ἔχει or ἔχοι, ἔφη, δώσειν = εἴ τι ἔχει, δώσει. The Inf. with ἄν is rendered in Latin as follows :—

γράφειν ἄν = scripturum esse,
γεγραφέναι ἄν = scripturum fuisse,
γράψαι ἄν = a. scripturum fuisse, or b. as Present, scripturum esse,
γράψειν ἄν = scripturum fore.

3. The same principle holds good in the Part. with ἄν, which frequently has the sense of future [a], and=μέλλων with Infin. : Soph. Œ. C. 761 ἀπὸ παντὸς ἂν φέρων λόγου δικαίου μηχάνημα, who would, &c. : Hdt. VII. 15 εὑρίσκω δὲ ὧδε ἂν γινόμενα ταῦτα, εἰ λάβοις τὴν ἐμὴν σκευήν, reperio, sic hæc futura esse, si sumas vestes meas: Thuc. VI. 33 οὔτε ὄντα, οὔτε ἂν γενόμενα λογοποιοῦσιν, i. e. ἃ οὔτε ἔστιν, οὔτ' ἂν γένοιτο : Isocrat. Archid. p. 129 A ἐπίσταμαι τοὺς Ἀθηναίους ὑπέρ γε τῆς σωτηρίας τῆς ἡμετέρας ὁτιοῦν ἂν ποιήσοντας : Plat. Legg. p. 781 A πολὺ ἄμεινον ἂν ἔχοντα, εἰ νόμων ἔτυχεν, i. e. ἃ πολὺ ἄμ. ἂν εἶχεν : Id. Crit. p. 48 C aliquis τῶν ῥᾳδίως ἀποκτιννύντων καὶ ἀναβιωσκομένων γ' ἄν, εἰ οἷοί τε ἦσαν : Eur. Hipp. 519 πάντ' ἂν φοβηθεῖσ' ἴσθι : Demosth. p. 859, 49 οὗτος δ' οὐκ ἔχων ἂν εἰπεῖν ὅπου τι τούτων ἀπέδωκεν : which Schæfer explains, εἰ καὶ πάντα ποιοίη, οὐκ ἂν ἔχοι : cf. p. 117, 25 : Id. p. 129. init. πάλαι τις ἡδέως ἂν ἴσως ἐρωτήσων κάθηται, i. e. κάθηταί τις ὃς ἡδέως ἂν ἴσως ἐρωτήσοι, scil. εἰ δύναιτο, vel simile quid : Arist. Pol. 334 C τὰ μὲν οὖν πλεῖστα τῶν ἐπιτιμηθέντων ἄν, which might be found fault with. So also in the so called Casus absoluti : Xen. Anab. V. 2, 8 ἐσκοπεῖτο, πότερον εἴη κρεῖττον ἀπάγειν τοὺς διαβεβηκότας, ἢ καὶ τοὺς ὁπλίτας διαβιβάζειν, ὡς ἁλόντος ἂν τοῦ χωρίου = νομίζων, ὅτι τὸ χωρίον ἁλοίη ἄν. Also to express repetition : Xen. Anab. IV. 7, 16 μαχαιρίῳ — ἔσφαττον, ὧν κρατεῖν δύναιντο· καὶ ἀποτέμνοντες ἂν τὰς κεφαλὰς ἔχοντες ἐπορεύοντο, that is, when it pleased them.

Obs. 1. 'Aν is frequently joined with a Participle standing in a gerundial or adverbial force with a verb already modified by ἄν; as, Xen. Cyr. I. 3, 11 στὰς ἄν — ἔπειτα λέγοιμ' ἄν. And sometimes ἄν is joined to a Participle which stands for a conditional sentence into which it may be resolved ; as, Soph. Œ. R. 446 συθείς τ' ἂν οὐκ ἂν ἀλγύναις πλέον : Hdt. VII. 139 ὁρῶντες ἂν ἐχρήσαντο ἄν. In both these cases ἄν does not modify the participle, but is used to prepare the mind for the conditional verb which follows.

Obs. 2. The Inf. and Part. of the Pres. or Aorist with ἄν have a future sense, inasmuch as a conditional action is at the present time uncertain; but are distinguished from the Inf. and Part. Fut. without ἄν, as the latter express the future as something certain to happen ; as, οἶδά σε πάντ' ἂν φοβηθέντα and πάντα φοβηθησόμενον.

'Aν without a Verb.

§. 430. 1. 'Aν is sometimes found without a verb [b], when it can be easily supplied from the context, generally from some former part of the sentence, or by the mind : Eur. Med. 1153 οὐ μὴ δυσμενὴς ἔσει φίλοις, — φίλους νομίζουσ', οὖσπερ ἂν (sc. νομίσαι) πόσις σέθεν : Soph. Phil. 493 ὃν δὴ παλαί, ἂν ἐξότου (sc. εἴη [c]) : Plat. Rep. p. 368 D δοκεῖ μοι—τοιαύτην ποιήσασθαι ζήτησιν αὐτοῦ, οἵανπερ ἂν (sc. ἐποιησάμεθα) εἰ προσέταξέ τις

[a] Elm. Med. 764. Dawes Misc. Crit. 128.   [b] Herm. Phil. 491. Ellendt ad voc. VIII.
   [c] Ellendt ad voc. IX. Schæf. Greg. Cor. 44.

γράμματα σμικρὰ πόρρωθεν ἀναγνῶναι μὴ πάνυ ὀξὺ βλέπουσιν. So especially the forms in Plato : πῶς γὰρ ἄν ; πῶς δ' οὐκ ἄν ; ὡς ἄν, and particularly, ὥσπερ ἄν εἰ, as if, in which ἄν belongs to the sentence introduced by εἰ, and generally is repeated therein (§. 431. *Obs.* 2.). The first ἄν prepares the mind for the conditional character of the sentence. From the frequent use of this formula it lost its proper force, and assumed an adverbial meaning (*quasi*) : Plat. Gorg. p. 479. Α φοβούμενος ὥσπερ ἄν εἰ παῖς, i. e. ὥσπερ ἄν φόβοιτο, εἰ παῖς εἴη : Demosth. p. 853 §. 30 ἐγὼ γὰρ — τὴν δίκην ἔλαχον τούτῳ τῆς ἐπιτροπῆς, οὐχ ἐν τίμημα συνθείς, ὥσπερ ἄν (sc. συνθείη) εἴ τις συκοφαντεῖν ἐπιχειρῶν (τὴν δίκην λάχοι).   The same is true of κἄν εἰ, where ἄν also belongs to the apodosis, and from frequent use this form assumed the adverbial force of, *at least;* and ἄν is sometimes joined to an adjective, to which the participle of εἶναι may be supplied : Eur. Alc. 179 σὲ δ' ἄλλη τις γυνὴ κεκτήσεται, σώφρων μὲν οὐκ ἄν μᾶλλον, εὐτυχὴς δ' ἴσως, for σώφρων οὐκ ἄν μᾶλλον οὖσα, i. e. ἡ οὐκ ἄν μᾶλλον σώφρων εἴη : Plat. Rep. p. 577 Β βούλει οὖν προσποιησώμεθα ἡμεῖς εἶναι τῶν δυνατῶν ἄν κρῖναι, sc. γενομένων, i. e. ἐκείνων, οἳ δυνατοὶ ἄν γένοιντο.

2. It is also attached to other words besides verbs, especially τάχα et simil. : Œ. R. 523 ἀλλ' ἦλθε μὲν δὴ τοῦτο τοὔνειδος τάχ' ἄν ὀργῇ βιασθέν, where ἄν seems to add doubt to the expression, (*haud dubie, opinor.*)

Position of ἄν.

§. 431. 1. When ἄν is joined with a conjunctive word and the Conjunctive, it either coalesces therewith, as ὅτ' ἄν into ὅταν ; (so ἐπάν, ἐπειδάν &c. ;) or follows it immediately, as πρὶν ἄν, ὃς ἄν. But sometimes particles, such as δέ, τέ, μέν, γάρ, are placed between them.

2. In the Ind. and Opt., as the force of ἄν is thrown on the predicate, it ought properly to be attached to it ; as, λέγοιμ' ἄν, ἔλεγον ἄν : but it is generally joined to that member of the sentence on which most emphasis is laid ; as, Hdt. III. 119 πατρὸς δὲ καὶ μητρὸς οὐκέτι μευ ζωόντων, ἀδελφεὸς ἄν ἄλλος οὐδενὶ τρόπῳ γένοιτο : Plat. Crit. p. 53 C καὶ οὐκ οἴει ἄσχημον ἄν φανεῖσθαι τὸ τοῦ Σωκράτους πρᾶγμα ; Demosth. p. 851, 23 οὐδὲ ταύτην ἄν τις ἐπενέγκοι δικαίως τὴν αἰτίαν. Hence it is regularly joined to those words which alter the nature of the sentence, as negative adverbs, and interrogatives ; as, οὐκ ἄν, οὐδ' ἄν, οὔποτ' ἄν, οὐδέποτ' ἄν &c. — τίς ἄν, τί ἄν, τί δ' ἄν, τί δῆτ' ἄν, πῶς ἄν, πῶς γὰρ ἄν, ἆρ' ἄν &c.—also to adverbs, such as place, time, &c. which modify and define the form and nature of the expression ; as, ἐνταῦθα ἄν, τότ' ἄν, εἰκότως ἄν, ἴσως ἄν, τάχ' ἄν, μάλιστ' ἄν, ἥκιστ' ἄν, μόλις ἄν, σχολῇ ἄν, ῥαδίως ἄν, ῥᾷστ' ἄν, τάχιστ' ἄν, σφόδρ' ἄν, ἡδέως ἄν, κἄν (for καὶ ἄν, *etiam, vel*).

Obs. 1. Expressions such as οἶμαι, ἔφη, &c. often stand between ἄν and the verb to which it belongs ; as, Plat. Rep. p. 333 A πρός γε ὑποδημάτων ἄν, οἶμαι, φαίης κτῆσιν [a] : Ibid. p. 438 A ἴσως γὰρ ἄν, ἔφη, δοκοῖ τι λέγειν : Id. Symp. p. 202 D τί οὖν ἄν, ἔφην, εἴη ὁ Ἔρως ;

Obs. 2. In some constructions ἄν is transposed from the Opt. in the dependent clause to which it really belongs, to the verb in the principal clause, especially in οὐκ οἶδ' ἄν with the Opt. : Eur. Med. 941 οὐκ οἶδ' ἄν εἰ πείσαιμι, for εἰ πείσαιμι ἄν : Id. Alc. 48 : Xen. Cyr. I. 6, 41 : Plat. Tim. p. 26 B ἐγὼ γὰρ ἃ μὲν χθὲς ἤκουσα, οὐκ ἄν οἶδα εἰ δυναίμην ἅπαντα ἐν μνήμῃ πάλιν λαβεῖν.

Obs. 3. In certain parenthetical sentences, ἄν which belongs to the Opt.

---

a Stallb. ad loc.

stands first: so especially ἄν τις εἴποι, φαίη: so Plat. Hipp. M. p. 299
A ταῦτα ἡμῶν λεγόντων, ὦ Ἱππία, μανθάνω (ἂν ἴσως φαίη) καὶ ἐγώ, ὅτι
πάλαι αἰσχύνεσθε ταύτας τὰς ἡδονὰς φάναι καλὰς εἶναι: Id. Phæd. p. 87 A
τί οὖν ἂν φαίη ὁ λόγος ὅτι ἀπιστεῖς; Demosth. p. 14, 20 τί οὖν ἄν τις
εἴποι σὺ γράφεις ταῦτ' εἶναι στρατιωτικά;

Obs. 4. The enclitic κέ sometimes, though far more rarely than ἄν, is
found at the beginning of the sentence; like ἄν, it is joined immediately
to adverbs and particles, but in these cases it does not generally admit
of being separated from the particle by another word; as, Il. η, 125 ἦ κε
μέγ' οἰμώξειε γέρων ἱππηλάτα Πηλεύς, for which an Attic writer would
have said, ἦ μέγα ἂν οἰμ.

Repetition of ἄν.

§. 432. Ἄν is sometimes found twice in a sentence [a], for which there
are two reasons.

a. It is used once at the beginning, to denote the conditional nature of
the whole sentence, and again with that part of the sentence which it
immediately modifies. This is especially the case when the sentence is
broken by other sentences, or a good many words precede the verb to
which ἄν belongs: Soph. Elect. 333 ὥστ' ἄν, εἰ σθένος λάβοιμι, δηλώ-
σαιμ' ἂν οἷ' αὐτοῖς φρονῶ. So when ὥσπερ ἂν εἰ is used with the Opt. or
Ind., ἄν is repeated with the Opt. or Ind. in the apodosis to which both
refer: Plat. Gorg. p. 447 D ὥσπερ ἂν εἰ ἐτύγχανεν ὢν ὑποδημάτων
δημιουργός, ἀπεκρίνατο ἂν δή που σοι: Dem. p. 293, 1 ὥσπερ ἂν
εἰ τις ναύκληρος — τῆς ναυαγίας αἰτιῷτο, — φήσειεν ἄν.

Obs. 1. When in a negative or interrogative sentence ἄν is found twice,
the former ἄν is joined to the neg. or interrog. on which it throws its
force, and the latter to the verb, so that it increases the negation or
question: so οὐκ ἂν φθάνοις ἄν: Æsch. Ag. 340 οὐκ ἄν γ' ἑλόντες
αὖθις ἀνθάλοιεν ἄν: Arist. Pac. 68 πῶς ἄν ποτ' ἀφικοίμην ἄν; Soph.
Œ. R. 772 τῷ γὰρ ἂν καὶ μείζονι λέξαιμ' ἂν ἢ σοί [b].

b. The second reason is rhetorical, ἄν being attached to the word on
which most emphasis is to be laid; if it is wanted to lay stress on more
than one word, it is repeated with every such word, and may be again
placed after the verb which it modifies, though no particular stress is to
be laid thereon: so Hdt. III. 35 δέσποτα, οὐδ' ἂν αὐτὸν ἔγωγε δοκέω τὸν
θεὸν οὕτω ἂν καλῶς βαλέειν: Thuc. I. 76. extr. ἄλλους γ' ἂν οὖν
οἰόμεθα τὰ ἡμέτερα λαβόντας δεῖξαι ἂν μάλιστα: Plat. Apol. p. 31 A
ὑμεῖς δ' ἴσως τάχ' ἂν ἀχθόμενοι, ὥσπερ οἱ νυστάζοντες ἐγειρόμενοι, κρού-
σαντες ἄν με, πειθόμενοι Ἀνύτῳ, ῥᾳδίως ἂν ἀποκτείναιτε, εἶτα τὸν λοιπὸν
βίον καθεύδοντες διατελοῖτ' ἄν: Ibid. p. 35 D σαφῶς γὰρ ἄν, εἰ
πείθοιμι ὑμᾶς —, θεοὺς ἂν διδάσκοιμι μὴ ἡγεῖσθαι ὑμᾶς εἶναι: Demosth. p.
849, 15 ὃν οὐκ ἂν δήπου, ψευδῆ μαρτυρίαν εἰ παρεσκευαζόμην, ἐνέγραψα
ἄν: Ibid. p. 852, 26 (τὴν μητέρα) μηδεὶς νομιζέτω καθ' ἡμῶν ποτ' ἂν ὀμνύναι
ταῦτ' ἂν ἐθέλειν, εἰ μὴ σαφῶς ᾔδει τὰ εὔορκα ὀμουμένη. Very frequently
with οὔτε—οὔτε: Soph. Antig. 69 οὔτ' ἂν κελεύσαιμ' οὔτ' ἂν εἰ θέλεις
ἔτι πράσσειν ἐμοῦ γ' ἂν ἡδέως δρῴης μέτα: Xen. Hier. V. 3 ἄνευ γὰρ τῆς
πόλεως οὔτ' ἂν σώζεσθαι δύναιτο, οὔτ' ἂν εὐδαιμονείν: Plat. Apol. p. 31
D πάλαι ἂν ἀπολώλη καὶ οὔτ' ἂν ὑμᾶς ὠφελήκη οὐδὲν οὔτ' ἂν ἐμαυτόν:
ubi v. Stallbaum. Also in poetry; as, Eur. Hipp. 957 τίνες λόγοι
τῆσδ' ἂν γένοιντ' ἄν; Id. Med. 250 τρὶς ἂν παρ' ἀσπίδα στῆναι
θέλοιμ' ἂν μᾶλλον, ἢ τεκεῖν ἅπαξ cf. 616 sq. Troad. 1252. Hec. 359.

[a] Elm. Med. 1257. Monk Hipp. 402. Herm. Op. iv. 188.   [b] Herm. Op. iv. 189.

Sometimes ἄν is used three times with a single verb : Arist. Ach. 216 ;
but here it seems to give a ludicrous turn to the sentence.

Obs. 2. When two sentences are but parallel parts of one thought, so
that the one is a repetition, continuation, enlargement, illustration of
the other, ἄν is properly used only with one; as, Xen. M. S. II. 1, 18 ὁ
μὲν ἑκὼν πεινῶν φάγοι ἄν, ὁπότε βούλοιτο, καὶ ὁ ἑκὼν διψῶν πίοι: but
not when one sentence is the Protasis, the other the Apodosis [a].

Obs. 3. Sometimes ἄν is repeated to repeat the verb with which it has
been already joined : Soph. Œ. C. 1528 ὡς οὔτ' ἄν ἀστῶν τῶνδ' ἄν ἐξείποιμι τῳ οὔτ' ἄν (ἐξείποιμι) τέκνοισι.

Obs. 4. Κέ is very seldom repeated, as in Od. δ, 733 τῷ κε μάλ' ἤ κεν
ἔμεινε.

Obs. 5. Sometimes in Homer ἄν is joined with κέ to give a greater
force to the conditional nature of the sentence ; as, Il. ν, 127 sq. ἵσταντο
φάλαγγες —, ἂς οὔτ' ἄν κεν Ἄρης ὀνόσαιτο μετελθών, οὔτε κ' Ἀθηναίη.

Obs. 6. The notion of possibility implies futurity ; for actions actually
past or present cannot properly speaking be conceived of as at the present
moment possible : so that the Opt. with ἄν gets its notion of futurity from
its proper force of possibility.   Hence ἄν is hardly ever used with the Opt.
Fut., since γίγνοιτ' ἄν or γένοιτ' ἄν express the notion of futurity in the
notion of possibility, while in γενήσοιτ' ἄν [b], the notion of futurity would
be needlessly repeated ; and the Opt. of the Impft. and Aorist may express a future possibility in any time (from their primary force of an indefinite supposition), but with this difference, that the Impft. Opt. signifies
a continued, the Aorist a momentary action [c].

CHAP. II.

Of the Attributive construction.

§. 433. The attributive construction is employed to define a
substantive; to add to it some quality.—(Attribute.)   And this
is done

a. By the adjective or participle ; as, τὸ καλὸν ῥόδον, τὸ θάλλον
ῥόδον.

b. By the genitive of a substantive ; as, οἱ τοῦ δένδρου καρποί.

c. By a preposition and its case ; as, ἡ πρὸς τὴν πόλιν ὁδός.

d. By an adverb ; as, οἱ νῦν ἄνθρωποι.

e. By a substantive in apposition ; as, Κροῖσος, ὁ βασιλεύς.

f. By a participle, with or without the article, separated from
the substantive (remote attributive); ὁ ἀνὴρ ταῦτα εἶπεν ἐλθών.

Remarks.

§. 434. 1. These attributive forms arise from, *a.* A verbal or
adjectival or a substantival notion, which in a predicative sentence

---

[a] Herm. Elm. Med. 310. fin.   Herm. Elect. 790.   [b] Dawes Misc. Crit. 167.
                                   [c] Herm. Ajac. 1061.

would stand as the predicate, becoming the attribute; as, τὸ ῥόδον θάλλει—τὸ θάλλον ῥόδον—τὸ ῥόδον ἐστὶ καλόν—τὸ καλὸν ῥόδον. Κροῖσός ἐστι βασιλεύς=Κροῖσος ὁ βασιλεύς. *b.* From a substantive standing as the subject of a simple sentence, and becoming the attribute of the object of the predicate in the genitive; as, τὸ δένδρον φέρει καρπούς—οἱ τοῦ δένδρου καρποί. *c.* From an article joined with the object of the sentence, consisting of an adverb or preposition with its case, which becomes the attribute of the subject, the verb being suppressed; as, ἡ πρὸς τὴν πόλιν ὁδός, sc. φέρουσα: ὁ μεταξὺ τόπος, sc. κείμενος.

Obs. Sometimes the verbal notion is expressed; as Hdt., οἱ τότε ἐόντες ἄνθρωποι, &c.

2. The principal difference between the predicative and attributive constructions is, that one expresses the notion as an operation then taking place, τὸ ῥόδον θάλλει; the other as having already taken place, as a fact or quality, τὸ θάλλον ῥόδον.

Interchange of the Attributive forms.

§. 435. Properly the attributive adjective expresses some quality residing in the subject. The attributive genitive denotes that which produces or creates the subject; as, οἱ τοῦ δένδρου καρποί: the attributive substantive (apposition) something identical with the subject; but as all these forms express the notion of a quality of that of which they are the attributes, they are frequently used for each other.

a. The adjective for the attributive genitive, especially in poetry: Il. β, 54 Νεστορέῃ παρὰ νηΐ: Il. ε, 741 Γοργείη κεφαλή. So βίη Ἡρακληείη: Od. γ, 190 Φιλοκτήτην, Ποιάντιον ἀγλαὸν υἱόν, for Ποίαντος: Il. ζ, extr. κρητῆρα ἐλεύθερον, for ἐλευθερίας: Il. π, 831 ἐλεύθερον ἦμαρ, day of freedom; 836 ἦμαρ ἀναγκαῖον, day of fate: Il. ρ, 511 νῶϊν δὲ ζωοῖσιν ἀμύνετε νηλεὲς ἦμαρ. So also often, νόστιμον ἦμαρ, the day of return: Pind. Ol. IX. extr. Αἰάντεος βωμός: Æsch. Pers. 8 νόστῳ τῷ βασιλείῳ: Id. Cho. 1063 ἀνδρὸς βασίλεια πάθη: Soph. Œ. T. 267 τῷ Λαβδακείῳ παιδί: Eur. Iph. T. 5 τῆς Τυνδαρείας θυγατρός, for Τυνδάρεω: Theocr. XV. 110 ἁ Βερενικεία θυγάτηρ. Prose: Hdt. VII. 105 τοῖς Μασκαμείοισι ἐκγόνοισι: Id. IX. 76 αἰχμαλώτου δουλοσύνης. So also Thucyd. II. 45 γυναικείας ἀρετῆς ὅσαι ἐν τῇ χηρείᾳ ἔσονται, sc. γυναικῶν ὅσαι: Aves 1198 δωροδόκοισιν ἄνθεσιν, for ἄνθεσιν δωροδοκίας.

Obs. The lyric and dramatic authors frequently use a compound adjective, either in the place of a simple substantive implied in that adjective; as, Æsch. Ag. 1529 ξιφοδηλήτῳ θανάτῳ, the death of the sword: Soph. Œ. T. 26 ἄγελαι βούνομοι, for βοῶν: Eur. Herc. Fur. 395 καρπὸν μηλοφόρον, for μήλων: Æsch. P. V. 148 ἀδαμανθέτοισι λύμαις, for ἀδαμαντίνων δεσμῶν: so Arist. Eq. 405 μητρόκτονον αἷμα, matricide; or, which is more usual, in the place of a subst. and attributive adjective, or subst. and attributive genitive, of which two notions the compound adjective is made up; as, Pindar. Ol. III. 3 Θήρωνος Ὀλυμπιονίκαν ὕμνον, for νίκης Ὀλυμπικῆς: Æsch. Ag. 272 εὐαγγέλοισιν ἐλπίσιν θυηπολεῖς, for ἀγαθῆς ἀγγελίας : Soph. Ant. 1022 ἀνδροφθόρον αἷμα, for ἀνδρὸς φθαρέντος : Id. Aj. 935 ἀριστόχειρ ἀγών : Eur. El. 126 ἄναγε πολύδακρυν ἡδονάν, for πολλῶν δακρύων : Id. El. 861 χαλαργοῖς ἁμίλλαις. Prose : Hdt. VII. 190 συμφορὴ παιδοφόνος. This is too poetic an usage for prose (except Hdt. whose style is very poetical) or comedy. Sometimes a substantive is added which is already implied in the compound adj.; as, Eur. Phœn. 1370 λευκοπήχεις κτύποι χεροῖν, for λεύκων πηχέων : or one part of the compound adj. refers to the substantive, while the other part stands for another subst. in the genitive ; as, Æsch. Choeph. 21 ὀξύχειρ κτύπος for ὀξὺς χειρῶν κτύπος : and sometimes besides the compound adj. another adj. is joined with the subst. which refers to some part of the notion of the compound adj. ; as, Soph. El. 858. sq. ἐλπίδες κοινότοκοι εὐπατρίδαι, for ἐλπίδες κοινοῦ τόκου (τοῦ κοινῇ ἐμοὶ τεχθέντος ἀδελφοῦ) εὐπατρίδου. So Herc. Fur. 1333 sq. ἡμᾶς ἔχεις παιδοκτόνους σούς (οἱ τοὺς σοὺς παῖδας ἔκτειναν).

b. The adjective is used instead of the subst. in apposition : so Richard Cœur de Lion, and the lion-hearted Richard ; as, Pind. Nem. I. 92 (B. 61.) ὀρθόμαντιν Τειρεσίαν, for T. ὀρθὸν μάντιν : Æsch. Prom. 301 σιδηρομήτωρ αἶα, for αἶα σιδήρου μήτηρ : Soph. Phil. 1338 Ἕλενος ἀριστόμαντις.

c. The attributive gen. instead of the material adj. ; as, ἔκπωμα ξύλου, τράπεζα ἀργυρίου : in the poets this idiom is very much used : Soph. El. 19 μέλαινά τ᾽ ἄστρων ἐκλέλοιπεν εὐφρόνη, for ἀστερόεσσα : Ibid. 757 καί νιν πυρᾷ κήαντες εὐθὺς, ἐν βραχεῖ χαλκῷ μέγιστον σῶμα δειλαίας σποδοῦ φέρουσιν ἄνδρες, for ἐσποδωμένον : Id. Antig. 114 λευκῆς χιόνος πτέρυγι στεγανός, for χιονέῃ : Id. Aj. 1003 ὦ δυσθέατον ὄμμα καὶ τόλμης πικρᾶς, for πικρότολμον : Eur. Phœn. 1529 στολὶς τρυφᾶς, for τρυφερά : Id. Bacch. 388 ὁ τᾶς ἡσυχίας βίοτος, for ἥσυχος.

d. The attributive genitive instead of the noun in apposition ; especially with the words ἄστυ, πόλις, as Ἀθηνῶν in the historians : Hdt. VII. 156 Καμαρίνης δὲ τὸ ἄστυ κατέσκαψε. So Homer Ἰλίου πτολίεθρον : so in Latin urbs Romæ : similarly Eur. Hipp. 646 θηρῶν δάκη, bestiæ mordaces : Id. Phœn. 307 παρηΐδων ὄρεγμα : Æsch. Choeph. 426 χερὸς ὀρέγματα.

e. The noun in apposit. is frequently used instead of the attributive gen. in definitions of measure and weight : Hdt. I. 14 ἑστᾶσι δὲ οὗτοι ἐν τῷ Κορινθίων θησαυρῷ σταθμὸν ἔχοντες τριήκοντα τάλαντα : Id. III. 89 τοῖσι — εἴρητο Βαβυλώνιον σταθμὸν τάλαντον ἀπαγινέειν : Id. VIII. 4 ἐπὶ μισθῷ τριήκοντα ταλάντοισι : Xen. Vect. III. 9 δέκα μναῖ εἰσφορά : Ibid. IV. 23 πρόσοδος ἑξήκοντα τάλαντα (but III. 10 δυοῖν μναῖν πρόσοδος) : Lys. Epit. p. 192, 27 ὁ τῆς Ἀσίας βασιλεὺς — ἔστειλε πεντήκοντα μυριάδας στρατιάν.

Ellipse of the Substantive of which the Adjective is the Attributive.

§. 436. When the subst. to which the attribute belongs expresses a general notion, or one which is easily supplied from the context or from the usages of common speech, as ἄνθρωπος, ἄνθρωποι, ἀνήρ, ἄνδρες, γυνή, γυναῖκες, πατήρ, μήτηρ, υἱός, παῖς, θυγάτηρ, ἀδελφός, πρᾶγμα, πράγματα, χρῆμα, χρήματα, ἔργον, ἔργα, χρόνος, ἡμέρα, χώρα, γῆ, ὁδός, οἰκία, οἶκος, μοῖρα, γνώμη, χείρ, χορδή (string in music), it is generally omitted, and the adj. with the article is used as a substantive.

a. Adjectives, participles, and pronominal adjectives, are used in this way. The participle frequently has so completely a substantival power, that the subst. which follows it is no longer in the case which the verb governs, but in the genitive ; and even takes the possessive pronoun as an attributive.

a. ἀνήρ or ἄνδρες: οἱ θνητοί, *mortales*, οἱ σοφοί : Hdt. I. 120 οἱ γει-νάμενοι (for γονεῖς) : Thuc. V. 32 οἱ ἡβῶντες (for ἔφηβοι) : so οἱ ἔχοντες, the rich : Xen. Apol. S. 20 οἱ φυλάσσοντες (φύλακες) : Demosth. p. 857, 44 οἱ δικάζοντες, the judges : Id. p. 53, 44 οἱ λέγοντες, the speakers, &c. Poetry : Eur. El. 337 ὅ τ' ἐκείνου τεκών.

β. Individual, personal, collective, and material names[a] : [*Those marked † are found in the New Testament.*]—

ἀδελφός, ἀδελφή : Isocr. Panath. 282.

ἄνεμος : Hdt. II. 20 ἐτησίαι.

ἄρτος : ζυμίτης, ἄζυμος, &c.

† αὔρα : Act. Apost. xxvii. 40 τῇ πνεούσῃ.

γάλα : Theocr. XXV.

† γῆ, (αἶα, χώρα, χθών) : ἡ οἰκουμένη : ἡ Μηδική : ἡ φιλία : ἡ βάρβαρος (Demosth.), &c.

γνώμη : Plat. κατάγε τὴν ἐμήν.

γυνή : Xen. Aristoph.

δῆμος : Arist. Eq. 79 ἐν Κλωπιδῶν.

δίκη : Hdt. IX. 78.

δίφρος : Plat. ἐπὶ χαμαιζήλου.

† δόμος, (οἶκος) : with attrib. genitive.

δορά : Hdt. V. 25. VII. 91.

δραχμή : with numerals, χιλίας, &c.

ἐσθής : Xen. ἤνθει δὲ φοινικίσι.

ἔτος : Theocr. XXVI. 29.

† ἡμέρα : ἡ αὔριον : ἡ ἐπιοῦσα : τρί-την : ἀγόραιοι Acts xix. 28.

ἱερά : Hdt. Κάρνεια : Ὀλύμπια, &c.

ἱμάτια : St. John xx. 12. λευκοῖς καθεζόμενος.

καιρός : Thuc. VI .35 ἐν τῷ παρ-όντι.

κόρη : Theocr. XVIII. 2.

μάζα : Hdt. VIII. 41.

μήτηρ : Soph. Ant. 512.

μοῖρα : Hdt. II. 135.

ναῦς : Thuc. IV. 9.

νεκρός : Hdt. IX. 85.

νῆσος : Hdt. IV. 85.

νόμισμα : Demosth. p. 1246.

† ὁδός : Hdt. V. 17, &c.

† οἴκημα : St. Luke xxii. 12.

† οἶκιον : Hdt. VI. 97. St. John xvi. 32.

οἰκία : Hdt. V. 20.

οἶνος : Theocr. Idyll. XIV. 15.

πέλαγος, (πόντος) : Thuc. I. 98 ἐν τῷ Αἰγείῳ.

περίοδος : Hdt. IV. 25.

† πληγή : Hdt. III. 64. Æsch. Ag. 1394. St. Luke xii. 47.

ποταμός : χείμαρρος.

† πύλη : St. John v. 2. προβατική.

σκευή : Hdt. VII. 62. 72.

στράτος, (στράτευμα) : πεζῷ, &c.

ταμεῖον : Thuc. VI. 8 τῷ κοινῷ.

τέχνη : χρηματιστική, ἰατρική, &c.

τιμή : Thuc. I. 27 ἐπὶ τῇ ἴσῃ.

† ὕδωρ : St. Matt. x. 42.

φυλακή : Polyb. I. 53.

† χείρ : ἡ δεξιά, ἀριστέρα, &c.

χορδή : ἡ ὑπάτη.

χρήματα : τὰ ἐμά, ὑμέτερα, &c.

χρόνος : ἐν τῷ τότε, &c.

χωρίον : Hdt. V. 50. Thuc. V. 65.

Obs. 1. Sometimes in tragedy, and occasionally in prose, τἀμά, τὸ ἐμόν, form a periphrasis for ἐγώ, when not only the person himself, but that which belongs to him, is signified ; as, Plat. Theæt. p. 161 E τὸ ἐμόν, seemingly for ἐμέ : Id. Rep. p. 533 A τό γ' ἐμὸν οὐδὲν ἂν προθυμίας ἀπολείποι. So Hdt. VIII. 140, 3 ὑμέτερον seemingly for ὑμεῖς.

γ. Abstract notions : τὸ καλόν, τὸ ἀγαθόν or τἀγαθόν, the beautiful, the good, often in Plato ; τὸ ταὐτόν, the same ; τὸ ἕτερον : and with ὄν, τὸ ἀνό-μοιον ὄν, Plat. — τὸ εὐτυχές, luck : τὸ ἀναίσθητον, want of feeling : τὸ κοινόν, the commonwealth : τῶν Σαμίων Hdt. VI. 14 : Id. VI. 113 τὸ μὲν τε-τραμμένον τῶν βαρβάρων φεύγειν. Thucydides abounds in neuter parti-ciples thus used ; as, τὸ δεδιός, fear : τὸ θαρσοῦν, confidence : τὸ τιμώ-

[a] Fisch ad Well. iii. p. 252. sqq.

μενον τῆς πόλεως II. 63, the honour paid to the state: Id. I. 142 ἐν τῷ μὴ μελετῶντι, in their not practising: Id. III. 43 ἐν τοιῷδε ἀξιοῦντι = ἐν τοιῇδε ἀξιώσει: Id. V. 7 τὸ ἐπίον, an attack. This answers to the English idiom, "his being afraid," &c.[a] : Xen. M. S. I. 2, 43 τὸ κρατοῦν τῆς πόλεως: Ibid. II. 6, 23 τὸ μεταμελησόμενον (for ἡ μέλλουσα μεταμέλεια). Poetry: Soph. Phil. 675 τὸ νοσοῦν (for ἡ νόσος): Id. Trach. 196 τὸ ποθοῦν (for ὁ πόθος): Id. Œ. C. 1604 τὸ δρῶν (for ἡ δρᾶσις): Ibid. 1220 τὸ θέλον = θέλημα: Eur. Iph. A. 1270 τὸ κείνου βουλόμενον[b].

Obs. 2. The singular neuter adj. expresses an abstract notion, but the plural the different elements or particulars which compose such notion ; as, τὸ κακόν, evil ; τὰ κακά, the evils[c].

δ. Collective names of persons : τὸ ἐναντίον, the enemy : τὸ ὑπήκοον, the subjects : τὸ λῃστικόν, the pirates[d], Thuc. Especially adjectives in ικόν : Hdt. VII. 103 τὸ πολιτικόν, the citizens — τὸ ὁπλιτικόν, τὸ οἰκετικόν (τὸ πεζικόν, non-Attic), — τὸ Ἑλληνικόν, τὸ βαρβαρικόν, τὸ ἱππικόν, &c. Thuc. Adjectives of this ending are also used in the plur. to express a series or circle of events ; as, τὰ Τρωικά, the Trojan war : τὰ Ἑλληνικά, the Grecian history : τὰ ναυτικά, naval affairs : Demosth. p. 21 extr. τὰ συμμαχικά.

b. The attributive genitive is also used, without the subst. to which it belongs : Ἀλέξανδρος ὁ Φιλίππου (υἱός) : Hdt. III. 88 Δαρεῖος ὁ Ὑστάσπεος : Id. VII. 204 Λεωνίδης, ὁ Ἀναξανδρίδεω, τοῦ Λέοντος, τοῦ Εὐρυκρατίδεω, &c. : Arist. Eq. 449 Βυρσίνης τῆς (γυναικὸς) Ἱππίου—εἰς ᾅδου (οἶκον) ἐλθεῖν — ἐν ᾅδου (οἴκῳ) εἶναι — εἰς διδασκάλου, εἰς Πλάτωνος φοιτᾶν, εἰς τὴν Κύρου ἐλθεῖν — τὰ τῆς τύχης, the events of fortune : τὰ τῆς πόλεως, the affairs of state : τὰ τοῦ πολέμου, the whole war : Eur. Phœn. 382 δεῖ φέρειν τὰ τῶν θεῶν, *ea quæ a diis proficiscuntur* : Plat. Gorg. p. 458 B τὸ τῶν παρόντων, present interests : Demosth. p. 47, 28 τὸ τῶν χρημάτων, money matters : Ibid. p. 49, 32 τὸ τῶν πνευμάτων, as it were the being of the wind : Id. p. 122, 45 τὰ τῶν Ἑλλήνων ἦν τῷ βαρβάρῳ φοβερά : ubi Bremi "*complectitur omnem Græcorum conditionem.*" So in the historians, τά τινος ; as, τὰ Ἀθηναίων φρονεῖν, *a parte stare.* Also, τὰ τῆς ὀργῆς Thuc. : τὰ τῆς ἐμπειρίας Id. : τὸ τῶν ἐπιθυμιῶν Plat. (the essentials of anger, &c.) : τό τινος, the custom, business, of any one : τὸ τῶν παίδων Plat. ; τὸ τῶν ἁλιέων Xen. — Trag. : τὰ τοῦδε, τὸ τῶνδε, seemingly for ὅδε, οἵδε.

c. The attributive adverb is also thus used : οἱ νῦν, οἱ τότε, οἱ πάλαι (ἄνθρωποι) — τὰ οἴκοι (πράγματα), *res domesticæ* — ἡ ἑξῆς (ἡμέρα), the following day, &c.

d. The attributive substantive (or substantival pronoun) with a preposition, as οἱ ἀμφὶ Πλάτωνα, οἱ καθ' ἡμᾶς, our contemporaries, signifies *a.* a person and his followers, of whatever sort : Hdt. I. 62 οἱ ἀμφὶ Πεισίστρατον, Pisistratus and his troops. So Hom. Il. μ, 137–140. Hdt. III. 76 (οἱ ἑπτὰ τῶν Περσέων) ἐδίδοσαν αὐτίς σφισι λόγους· οἱ μὲν ἀμφὶ τὸν Ὀτάνην, πάγχυ κελεύοντες ὑπερβαλέσθαι, μηδὲ, οἰδεόντων τῶν πρηγμάτων, ἐπιτίθεσθαι· οἱ δὲ ἀμφὶ τὸν Δαρεῖον, αὐτίκα τε ἰέναι καὶ τὰ δεδογμένα ποιέειν, μηδὲ ὑπερβάλλεσθαι, Otanes and those who voted with him— Darius and those who voted with him : Plat. Hipp. Maj. 281 C οἱ ἀμφὶ Θαλῆν, Thales and his school. *b.* Sometimes, but less frequently, the followers alone, without the person named. *c.* The principal person named alone, without his followers (i. e. his essence, properties which constitute him) ; but it is not so used till the Attic dial. : Xen. M. S. III.

---

[a] Arnold Thuc. I. 36.   [b] Herm. Trach. 195. Reisig. in Aristoph. p. 143.
[c] Stallb. Rep. 476. A.   [d] Lobeck Phryn. 242.

5, 10 οἱ περὶ Κέκροπα : Plat. Cratyl. p. 399 E οἱ ἀμφὶ Εὐθύφρονα : Id. Menon. extr. οἱ ἀμφὶ Θεμιστοκλέα. Also οἱ σύν τινι, οἱ μετά τινος, the hangers on; οἱ ὑπό τινι, the subjects of; οἱ ἀπό τινος, asseclæ, — οἱ ἐν ἄστει, οἱ περὶ φιλοσοφίαν, οἱ περὶ τὴν θήραν, οἱ ἀμφὶ τὸν πόλεμον. — Τὰ διὰ πλείστου, things at the greatest distance : τὰ τῆς πόλεως : τὰ κατά τινα, the position of any one; τὰ κατά τινος, res alicujus; τὸ κατὰ τοῦτον, ad hunc quod attinet; τὰ παρά τινος, the orders of any one : τὰ περί τινα, the circumstances : τὸ ἐπ' ἐμέ, τοῦπ' ἐμέ, τοὐπὶ σέ, quantum in me, te est, τὸ ἐπ' ἐμοί. So τὸ πρὸ τοῦδε, heretofore ; τὸ ἐπὶ τούτῳ (τῷδε), hereon.

Complex attributive Sentences.

§. 437. A simple attributive sentence may be enlarged by the addition of further attributive, or even objective forms, which define further some part of the sentence; as, π ο λ λ ο ὶ ἀγαθοὶ ἄνθρωποι — ὁ τοῦ τ ῶ ν Π ε ρ σ ῶ ν βασιλέως υἱός — Κῦρος, ὁ τῶν Περσῶν βασιλεύς, ὁ μ έ γ α ς — Σωκράτης, ὁ πάντων ἀνθρώπων μ έ γ α σοφώτατος ἀνήρ — Κῦρος, ὁ τῶν Περσῶν μ έ γ ι σ τ ο ς βασιλεύς — ὁ τῶν Ἑλλήνων π ρ ὸ ς τ ο ὺ ς Π έ ρ σ α ς πόλεμος.

The attributive Adjective.

§. 438. 1. The attributive adjective agrees with its subst. in gender, number, and case; and the two together represent one compound notion.

2. Attributive adj. are either e s s e n t i a l (adj. and participles), or f o r m a l (adjectival pronouns and numeral adj.); as, σοφὸς ἀνήρ, τὸ ῥόδον θάλλον, οὗτος ὁ ἀνήρ, τρεῖς ἄνδρες.

Obs. The part. λεγόμενος and καλούμενος are used in the sense of the Latin qui dicitur, vocatur, quem vocant, and the English s o c a l l e d : Hdt. VI. 61 ἐν τῇ Θεράπνῃ καλουμένῃ, i. e. in urbe, quæ Therapne vocatur : Isocr. ad Nicocl. p. 45 εἴ τις ἐκλέξειε καὶ τῶν προεχόντων ποιητῶν τ ὰ ς κ α-λ ο υ μ έ ν α ς γ ν ώ μ α ς, si quis excerpat præstantium poetarum quæ vocantur sententias : Plat. Rep. p. 493 D ἡ Δ ι ο μ η δ ε ί α λ ε γ ο μ έ ν η ἀ ν ά γ κ η ποιεῖν αὐτῷ πάντα, ἃ ἂν οὗτοι ἐπαινῶσιν, Diomedea quæ dicitur necessitas est illi omnia facere, quæcunque illi probarunt [a].

Remarks : Substantives used as attributive Adj.

§. 439. 1. Many personal nouns which express a station or profession are used as adj., and the word ἀνήρ is added to them when the person is viewed as belonging to such a station or profession, or omitted when he is regarded only as performing the functions of such a station or profession; as, ἀνὴρ μάντις, a man who is by profession a prophet ; μάντις, a man who acts as a prophet. So ἀνὴρ βασιλεύς, &c. ἄνδρες δικασταί, στρατιῶται. In expressions of contempt ἄνθρωπος is used ; as, ἄνθρωπος γεωργός : Lysias p. 186, 6 ἀνθρώπους ὑπογραμματίας : Plat. Gorg. p. 513 C διακόνους μοι λέ-γεις καὶ ἐπιθυμιῶν π α ρ α σ κ ε υ α σ τ ὰ ς ἀ ν θ ρ ώ π ο υ ς : although it is some-times used where ἀνήρ is more usual ; as, Xen. Cyr. VIII. 7, 14 πολῖ-ται ἄνθρωποι. So also we find ἀνήρ joined to national names, without any particular meaning ; as, ἄνδρες Ἀθηναῖοι : and also in the sing. ; ἀνὴρ

a Hoogev. Viger. p. 15.

Ἀθηναῖος, Ἀβδηρίτης.　　But these substantives are joined with other words
as adj., but mostly only in poetry, especially Ἕλλην, as masc. and poet.;
also as fem.; and Ἑλλάς only fem.; as, Soph. Phil. 223 Ἑλλὰς στολή :
also frequently in Hdt.; as, IV. 78 Ἑλλάδα γλῶσσαν : VII. 22 Σάνη, πόλις
Ἑλλάς : Eur. Iph. T. 342 Ἕλλην γῆ : Id. Heracl. 131 στολὴ Ἕλλην. In
Trag. we find other subst. used as adjectives : Æsch. Ag. 675 τύχη σωτήρ,
as fem. for σώτειρα. So also the words of reproach in which abstract
notions are applied to persons ; as, ἀνὴρ φθόρος, ὁ ὄλεθρος ἐκεῖνος, &c.
(§. 353. 1.)

Proleptic usage of attributive Adjectives.

2. An Adjective is sometimes applied to a substantive, though the
property expressed by it does not exist in the substantive till after the
action of the accompanying verb is completed.　In this construction the
verb and adjective generally form a compound predicative notion (see
§. 375. 5) : Il. ξ, 6 εἰσόκε θερμὰ λοετρὰ θερμήνῃ : Æsch. Ag. 1258
εὔφημον, ὦ τάλαινα, κοίμησον στόμα (i. e. ὥστε εὔφημον εἶναι) : Soph.
Œ. C. 1200 τῶν σῶν ἀδέρκτων ὀμμάτων τητώμενος[a]. So Virg. Æn. I.
70 age diversos : Pind. Pyth. 51 μιν φίλον ἔσανεν (i. e. ὥστε φίλον εἶναι).

An Adjective with a Substantive which is in construction with a second Substantive.

§. 440.　When a single substantival notion is expressed by a substantive joined with another subst. in the gen., the attributive adj. in poetry
frequently does not agree with the subst. in the gen. to which it properly
belongs, but with the other : the two words expressing one compound
notion being considered as one word[b] ; as, Od. ξ, 197 ἐμὰ κήδεα θυμοῦ,
the woes of my heart : Pind. Ol. VIII. 42 B Πέργαμος ἀμφὶ τεαῖς, ἥρως,
χερὸς ἐργασίαις ἁλίσκεται, by the work of thy hands : Id. Pyth. IV.
255 B ὑμετέρας ἀκτῖνος ὄλβου, for ὑμετέρου ὄλβου ἀκτῖνος (ἀκτὶς
ὄλβου=λαμπρὸς ὄλβος) : Id. Ol. XI. 5 ψευδέων ἐνιπὰν ἀλιτόξενον
(for ἐνιπὰν ψευδέων ἀλιτοξένων, reprehensionem mendacii adversus hospitem ;
ψευδέων ἐνιπή forms as it were one single notion) : ubi v. Dissen p. 128
ed. Goth. Id. Pyth. VI. 5 Πυθιόνικος ὕμνων θησαυρός : Æsch.
Theb. 709 περιθύμους κατάρας Οἰδιπόδα : Id. Ag. 512 δεκάτῳ
φέγγει τῷδ' ἔτους, in the light of the tenth year. So 96 πελάνῳ μυ-
χόθεν (=μυχοῦ) βασιλείῳ, the cake from the royal chamber : Soph.
Ant. 793 νεῖκος ἀνδρῶν ξύναιμον : Eur. Or. 225 ὦ βοστρύχων
πινῶδες ἄθλιον κάρα : Id. Andr. 585 οὑμὸς παῖς παιδός (παῖς
παιδός = υἱωνός, grandson) : Id. H. F. 449 γραῖαι ὄσσων πηγαί
(=γεραιά or γεραιᾶς δάκρυα) : Arist. Aves 1198 δίνης πτερωτὸς φθόγγος, for πτερωτοῦ δίνης : Id. Ran. 248 ἔνυδρον ἐν βυθῷ χόρειαν, for
ἐνύδρῳ ἐν βυθῷ : Æsch. Ag. 53 δεμνιοτήρη πόνον ὀρταλίχων[c] :
Ibid. 152 νεικέων τέκτονα σύμφυτον : Arist. Pac. 155 χρυσο-
χάλινον πάταγον ψαλίων : Eur. Herc. 1039 ἄκτερος τέκνων
ὠδίς : Id. Troad. 564 καράτομος ἐρημία νεανίδων : Soph. Trach.
817 ὄγκον ὀνόματος μητρῷον : Id. Aj. 176 νίκας ἀκάρπωτον
χάριν : Eur. Alc. 538 ξένων πρὸς ἄλλην ἑστίαν : Id. Phœn. 343
γάμων ἔπακτον ἄταν : Æsch. Eum. 325 ματρῷον ἄγνισμα
φόνου[d].

---

a Stallb. Protag. 327 C. Valck. Diatrib. 205.　　b Dissen Pind. Ol. XI. 5. Lobeck Aj. 7.
c Klausen ad loc.　　　　　d Bernh. 426.

Coordinate and subordinate Attributives.

§. 441. When more than one adj. belongs to the same subst. the attributive relation is either c o o r d i n a t e, when both apply equally to the subst., as σοφός τε καὶ ἀγαθὸς καὶ καλὸς ἀνήρ — καλὰ πέδιλα, ἀμβρόσια, χρυσεῖα : or s u b o r d i n a t e, when one of them forms with the substantive one notion, to which the other attributive is applied, as πολλοὶ—ἀγαθοὶ ἄνδρες : οὗτος ὁ ἀνήρ—ἀγαθός : τὸ πρῶτον—καλὸν πρᾶγμα. This is generally the construction of the numeral adj.; πολλοὶ, however, is often used as coordinate ; πολλὰ καὶ καλὰ ἔργα, where we usually say "many great deeds," *multa et praeclara facinora.*

Inversion of the members of the Attributive Sentence.

§ 442. The adj. not unfrequently assumes a substantival force, and the subst. to which the adj. properly belongs is put in the attributive genitive, defining the adj. instead of being defined by it. This occurs in the following cases.

a. The subst. stands with the plural adj., which retains the gender of the subst. (prose as well as poetry); οἱ χρηστοὶ τῶν ἀνθρώπων : Isocr. ad Nicocl. p. 24 D μηδὲ τὰ σπουδαῖα τῶν πραγμάτων, μηδὲ τοὺς εὖ φρονοῦντας τῶν ἀνθρώπων : Arist. Vesp. 95 τοὺς τρεῖς τῶν δακτύλων : Demosth. p. 44 τοῖς ἡμίσεσι τῶν ἱππέων.

b. The adj. is in the neuter sing., sometimes in the neuter plural : Od. ε, 277 ἐπ' ἀριστερὰ χειρός : Soph. Ant. 1265 ἐμῶν ἄνολβα βουλευμάτων : Hdt. VIII. 100 τὸ πολλὸν τῆς στρατιῆς : Id. VI. 113 τὸ τετραμμένον τῶν βαρβάρων : Id. I. 185 τὰ σύντομα τῆς ὁδοῦ : Id. V. 58 τὰ πολλὰ τῆς χώρας. Frequently in Attic, ἐπὶ πολύ, ἐπὶ μέγα with a Gen. : Thuc. I. 1 ἐπὶ πλεῖστον ἀνθρώπων : Id. I. 118 οἱ Ἀθηναῖοι ἐπὶ μέγα ἐχώρησαν δυνάμεως. Also τὶ, *aliquid*, and τί, *quid?* Id. IV. 130 ἦν τι καὶ στασιασμοῦ ἐν τῇ πόλει : Id. VII. 69 λαμπρότητός τι. (Cf. Soph. Ant. 1229 ἐν τῷ ξυμφορᾶς διεφθάρης ;) Id. I. 70 τῆς γνώμης τὰ βέβαια : Xen. Anab. I. 8, 8 καὶ ἤδη ἦν μέσον ἡμέρας. So ἡνίκα ἦν ἐν μέσῳ νυκτῶν, — ἔξω μέσου ἡμέρας Id. Cyr. V. 3, 52 : IV. 4, 1 : Id. Anab. I. 9, 26 ἄρτων ἡμίσεα : Plat. Legg. p. 806 C ἥμισυ βίου (but generally ἥμισυς is in the same gender as the substantive) : Id. Apol. p. 41 C ἀμήχανον ἂν εἴη εὐδαιμονίας, an inexpressible piece of luck[a] : Id. Rep. p. 405 B τὸ πολὺ τοῦ βίου : Id. Menex. p. 243 B δεινὸν τοῦ πολέμου (as Soph. Trach. 118 βιότου πολύπονον). So many phrases with πᾶν ; as, Hdt. VII. 118 εἰς πᾶν κακοῦ ἀφικνεῖσθαι : Thuc. VII. 55 ἐν παντὶ ἀθυμίας : Plat. Rep. p. 579 B ἐν παντὶ κακοῦ εἶναι : Demosth. p. 29, 3 εἰς πᾶν προελήλυθε μοχθηρίας. So πολὺ τῆς δόξης Thuc. And very often, especially in prose, the neut. pron. is joined with the gen. : Hdt. I. 84 τοῦτο τῆς ἀκροπόλιος : Id. VII. 38 ἐς τόδε ἡλικίης : Thuc. I. 49 ξυνέπεσον ἐς τοῦτο ἀνάγκης : Id. II. 17 ἐν τούτῳ παρασκευῆς ἦσαν : Id. VII. 36 ὥπερ τῆς τέχνης : Xen. R. Eq. IV. 1 ἐν τοιούτῳ τῆς οἰκίας : Id. Anab. I. 7, 5 ἐν τοιούτῳ τοῦ κινδύνου : Isocr. de Pac. p. 165 C εἰς τοῦτο γάρ τινες ἀνοίας ἐληλύθασιν : Plat. Gorg. p. 493 A τῆς δὲ ψυχῆς τοῦτο, ἐν ᾧ αἱ ἐπιθυμίαι εἰσί : Demosth. p. 51 princ. εἰς τοῦθ' ὕβρεως ἐλήλυθεν : p. 33, 47 εἰς τοῦθ' ἥκει

---

[a] Stallb. ad loc.

τὰ πράγματα αἰσχύνης: Id. p. 20, 8 καιροῦ — πρὸς τοῦτο πάρεστι Φιλίππῳ τὰ πράγματα, res Philippi ea conditione sunt.

c. The subst. is in the sing., and the adj., which should be in the neut., agrees with the gender of the subst.; as, ἡ πολλὴ τῆς Πελοποννήσου, for τὸ πολὺ τῆς Π.—This is a pure Attic construction, but used more in prose than in poetry. The word ἥμισυς is very often so used. So also πόλυς, πλείων, πλεῖστος, and other superlatives; ὁ ἥμισυς τοῦ χρόνου: Æsch. Eum. 422 ἥμισυς λόγου: Thuc. V. 31 ἐπὶ τῇ ἡμισείᾳ τῆς γῆς: Xen. Cyr. IV. 5, 1 πέμπετε ἡμῖν τοῦ πεποιημένου σίτου τὸν ἥμισυν: Hdt. I. 24 τὸν πολλὸν τοῦ χρόνου διατρίβειν: Id. III. 105 τὸν μὲν πλέω τοῦ χρυσοῦ οὗτω οἱ Ἰνδοὶ κτῶνται: Thuc. VII. 3 τὴν πλείστην τῆς στρατιᾶς παρέταξε: Xen. Cyr. III. 2, 2 πολλὴ τῆς χώρας: Isocr. Evag. p. 197 τὸν πλεῖστον τοῦ χρόνου: Thuc. I. 2 τῆς γῆς ἡ ἀρίστη ἀεὶ τὰς μεταβολὰς τῶν οἰκητόρων εἶχεν: Plat. Symp. p. 209 A μεγίστη καὶ καλλίστη τῆς φρονήσεως.

Obs. In poetry sometimes, very rarely indeed in prose, a masc. or fem. subst. in the gen. is joined with a neuter plural adj.; Soph. Œ. C. 923 φωτῶν ἀθλίων ἱκτήρια, for φῶτας ἀθλίους ἱκτηρίους: Eur. Phœn. 1500 ἁβρὰ παρηΐδος: Xen. Cyr. VIII. 3, 41 ἥκει δέ τις ἢ τῶν προβάτων λελευκω-μένα φέρων ἢ τῶν βοῶν κατακεκρημνισμένα. This is more common in Latin verse and post-Augustan prose. *Vilia rerum,* Horace.

d. A favorite construction of the poets is to express the adjectival property by a substantive, and put the person to whom the property belongs in the attributive genitive. This periphrasis is not a mere pleonasm for a personal name, but it expresses more than the personal name; it personifies that property or quality which is as it were the essence of the individual, that wherein the notion of him principally consists; so that it represents him in the light in which the mind would naturally either always, or for the time, view him. So κράτος was especially applied to the gods: Æsch. Eum. 27 Ποσειδῶνος κράτος: Eur. Hec. 88 Ἑλένου ψυχὰν ἢ Κα-σάνδρας, the inspired Helenus: Ib. 130 λέκτρα Κασάνδρας—'Αχιλείας λόγχης, the bride Casandra—the warrior Achilles. So Πισθέως γῆρας, the old Pitheus: Æsch. Prom. 1090 μητρὸς σέβας, honoured mother. So also Prom. 898 παρ-θενίαν 'Ιοῦς, the virgin Io: Hec. 1210 Ἕκτορος δόρυ: Orestes 991 Μυρτίλου φόνον: Æsch. Theb. 494 'Ιππομέδοντος μεγὰ σχῆμα καὶ τύπος. So in Epic, especially the words βία, ἴς, κῆρ, μένος, σθένος, are applied to heroes and warriors as their great characteristic: Αἰνείαο βίη. So also Pind. and Trag.; as, Κάστορος βία, Τυδέος βία, Πολυνείκεος βία — ἴς Τηλεμάχοιο, ἴς ἀνέμου, μένος 'Αλκινόοιο, "Αρηος, ἀνέμου, ἡελίου — σθένος 'Ηετίωνος. So Pind.: σθένος ἵππων, ἡμιόνων: Il. β, 851 Παφλαγόνων δ' ἡγεῖτο Πυλαιμένεος λάσιον κῆρ. So Hesiod. Scut. 144 ἐν μέσσῳ δὲ δράκοντος ἦην φόβος, the dreadful dragon. So Pind. Isthm. IV. 32 αἰχμὴ Κάστορος: Id. Isthm. IV. 53 Αἴαντος ἀλκάν. So also Soph. Œ. R. παιδὸς βλάστας = παῖδα βλαστάνοντα. In the tragic and lyric authors δέμας is applied to a person of high dignity or majesty: Eur. Hec. 713 ἀλλ' εἰσορῶ γὰρ τοῦδε δεσπότου δέμας 'Αγαμέμνονος: κάρα, ὄμμα, to objects of love: Soph. Œ. T. 1235 τέθνηκε θεῖον 'Ιοκάστης κάρα: Trach. 527 τὸ δ' ἀμφινεικητὸν ὄμμα νύμφας ἐλεεινὸν ἀμμένει. So ὄνομα, Eur. Or. 1088 ὦ ποθεινὸν ὄνομ' ὁμιλίας ἐμῆς χαῖρε. So in prose and poetry χρῆμα, to express size: Hdt. I. 36 συὸς χρῆμα μέγα: Aristoph. Vesp. 968 κλέπτον τὸ χρῆμα τἀνδρός: Id. Nub. 2 χρῆμα τῶν νυκτῶν: Theocr. XVIII. 4 μέγα χρῆμα Λακαιναν. The attributive adj. is also used in this way: Eur. Alc. 971 'Ορφεία γῆρυς, the melodious Orpheus. Things are sometimes periphrased in this way: πυρὸς σέλας, bright fire: Eur. Alc. 911 σχῆμα δόμων: Id. Hec. 619 σχῆματ' οἴκων: Soph. Phil. 952 σχῆμα πέτρας: Æsch. Pers. 543 εὐνὰς λέκτρων: Eur. Med. 1136 τέκνων γονή.

The Article.

§. 443. Of all the adjectival attributives the article ὁ, ἡ, τό, is the most important; to understand its nature we must trace it back to its original demonstrative force.

It had originally—1st, a demonstrative—2nd, a relative force.

The Article ὁ, ἡ, τό, as a Demonstrative.

§. 444. 1. In Homer it is used as pointing out some object as known or spoken of, and directing the mind of the reader to it: there are however in Homer some instances of an approach to the Attic use of. it, though Homer probably never used it quite as the simple article.

2. It has a purely demonstrative force, when it is used as a substantival pronoun: in this case it may be construed either as ὅδε, or οὗτος, or ἐκεῖνος, or αὐτός, is: Il. a, 9 ὁ γὰρ βασιλῆϊ χολωθεὶς νοῦσον ἀνὰ στρατὸν ὦρσε κακήν: Ibid. 12 ὁ γὰρ ἦλθε θοὰς ἐπὶ νῆας Ἀχαιῶν: 29 τὴν δ' ἐγὼ οὐ λύσω: 43 ὡς ἔφατ' εὐχόμενος· τοῦ δ' ἔκλυε Φοῖβος Ἀπόλλων: cf. 47. 55. 57. 58: Od. a, 9 αὐτὰρ ὁ τοῖσιν ἀφείλετο νόστιμον ἦμαρ.

3. It is used as an adjectival pronoun, to which a relative sentence refers: when thus used it is generally put after its subject: Il. ε, 320 οὐδ' υἱὸς Καπανῆος ἐλήθετο συνθεσιάων τάων, ἃς ἐπέτελλε βοὴν ἀγαθὸς Διομήδης: Od. β, 119 ἔργα τ' ἐπίστασθαι περικαλλέα, καὶ φρένας ἐσθλάς, κέρδεά θ', οἷ' οὔπω τιν' ἀκούομεν οὐδὲ παλαιῶν, τάων, αἳ πάρος ἦσαν ἐΰπλοκαμῖδες Ἀχαιαί: Od. κ, 74 οὐ γάρ μοι θέμις ἐστὶ κομιζέμεν οὐδ' ἀποπέμπειν ἄνδρα τόν, ὅς κε θεοῖσιν ἀπέχθηται μακάρεσσιν.

4. The demonstrative force is less strong where the pronoun is joined to a substantive without any relative sentence; but it serves in this case to bring the thing definitely before us, as something known, or spoken of before. In many passages the substantive stands in apposition with the demonstrative: Il. a, 20 παῖδα δ' ἐμοὶ λῦσαί τε φίλην, τά τ' ἄποινα δέχεσθαι (these things — sc. the ransom): 33 ὡς ἔφατ'· ἔδδεισεν δ' ὁ γέρων, the old man before mentioned: cf. 380: 35 πολλὰ δ' ἔπειτ' ἀπάνευθε κιὼν ἠρᾶθ' ὁ γεραιός: Il. η, 412 ὡς εἰπὼν τὸ σκῆπτρον ἀνέσχεθε πᾶσι θεοῖσιν, that sceptre—the well known sceptre: Il. δ, 1 οἱ θεοὶ, those who are gods, in opposition to those who are men: Il. ζ, 467 ἂψ δ' ὁ πάϊς, he, who is a boy, in opposition to Hector: (Il. ε, 554 οἵω τώγε λέοντε δύω ὄρεος κορυφῇσιν ἐτραφέτην, here the τώγε refers to both, and is substantival for τώγε, οἵω λέοντε δύω &c.:) Il. λ, 637 Νέστωρ ὁ γέρων, that old man, whom every one knows. So a, 11 τὸν Χρύσην ἀρητῆρα: Il. φ, 317 τὰ τεύχεα καλά, those famous arms: Od. φ, 10 τὸν ξεῖνον δύστηνον, that unhappy stranger, pointing to Ulysses: Od. ι, 378 ὁ μοχλὸς ἐλάϊνος, that—mentioned above, 319, sqq.: Il. ψ, 325 καὶ τὸν προΰχοντα δοκεύει, for τὸν δὲ ἕτερον τὸν προΰχοντα: Il. ρ, 80 τὸν ἄριστον, he who is the best: so οἱ ἄλλοι, these, the others; τἄλλα, this, the rest: Il. a, 107 αἰεί τοι τὰ κάκ' ἐστὶ φίλα φρεσὶ μαντεύεσθαι: Ibid. 70 ὃς ᾔδη τά τ' ἐόντα, τά τ' ἐσσόμενα, πρό τ' ἐόντα, that which

is, was, will be : 167 ἦν ποτε δασμὸς ἵκηται, σοὶ τὸ γέρας πολὺ μεῖζον &c.,
that, which is by far the most honourable gift, as Achilles points to that
which Agamemnon already had received : 217 ἦλθον ἐγὼ παύσουσα τὸ
σὸν μένος, that anger, which &c. : 340 τοῦ βασιλῆος ἀπηνέος, this
hateful monarch.

5. In the Post-Homeric writers also, ὁ, ἡ, τό has frequently a demonstrative force. In Hdt., the Doric writers, and Attic poets, it is not unfrequently
used as in Homer: Æsch. Suppl. 443 ἡ τοῖσιν ἡ τοῖς πόλεμον αἱρεσθαι μέγαν, πᾶσ’ ἔστ’ ἀνάγκη : Ibid. 1055 ὅ τι τοι μόρσιμόν ἐστιν, τὸ γένοιτ’
ἄν : Id. Agam. 7 κάτοιδα — ἀστέρας, ὅταν φθίνωσιν, ἀντολάς τε τῶν :
Soph. Œ. T. 200 τὸν (sc. Ἄρεα) —, ὦ Ζεῦ πάτερ, ὑπὸ σῷ φθίσον κεραυνῷ.
So especially with the particles, μέν, δέ, γάρ (ὁ γάρ, ἡ γάρ, τὸ γάρ often
in tragic) ; sometimes also with prepositions ; as, πρὸς δὲ τοῖσι, πρὸς τῷ,
ἐπὶ τοῖσι Eurip.   And even in Attic prose it retained its demonstrative
force in the following cases :—

a. Τό, therefore (as Il. ρ, 404.) : τό γε Plat. : τὸ δέ at the beginning of
a sentence—*whereas*, very frequent in Plato : ὁ μέν, or ὁ δέ, οἱ δέ, αἱ δέ,
at the beginning of a sentence very frequently : Thuc. I. 81 τοῖς δὲ
ἄλλη γῆ ἐστι πολλή : Demosth. p. 18, 3 ὁ μὲν γὰρ—θαυμαστότερος νομίζεται :
Id. p. 51 princ. ὁ δ’ εἰς τοῦτ’ ὕβρεως ἐλήλυθεν : p. 68, 15 ὁ δὲ ταῦτα μὲν
μέλλει.   So also, ὁ μέν or ὁ δέ is used, as in Homer, before its substantive,
to call attention to it : Thuc. VI. 57 καὶ ὁ μὲν τοὺς δορυφόρους τοσαυτίκα
διαφεύγει ὁ Ἀριστογείτων : also in Plur. ; as, Id. VIII. 77 : τῇ, τῇδε,
hac, there, here, on this side, wherefore : τῷ, even in Homer very frequently : Plat. Theæt. p. 179 D τῷ τοι, ὦ φίλε Θεόδωρε,—σκεπτέον.   With
prepos. ; as, ἐκ τοῦ, hence : διὰ τό, *wherefore*, Thucyd. : here belongs the
construction ἐν τοῖς, sometimes ἐν ταῖς, with a superlative ; as, Thuc. I.
6 ἐν τοῖς πρῶτοι δὲ Ἀθηναῖοι τὸν σίδηρον κατέθεντο, *omnium primi :* and
the adverbial formulas, πρὸ τοῦ (προτοῦ), before, almost always in the
sense of *ante illud modo definitum tempus :* cf. Hdt. I. 103. III. 62. Plat.
Alcib. II. p. 109 E.; and frequently the acc. is used with καί at the
beginning of a sentence in a demonstrative force : Xen. Cyr. I. 3, 9 καὶ
τὸν κελεῖσαι δοῦναι, *et eum ;* but in the nom. καὶ ὅς, καὶ ἥ, καὶ οἵ, are
used.

b. In the formula, τὸν καὶ τόν, τὸ καὶ τό, the one or the other, this or
that, τὰ καὶ τά, *varia, bona et mala*, these serve to signify indifferently
any variety of objects : Pind. Olymp. II. 53 ὁ μὰν πλοῦτος ἀρεταῖς δεδαι-
δαλμένος φέρει τῶν τε καὶ τῶν καιρόν, *variarum rerum opportunitatem :*
see Dissen T. II. p. 32. et ad Nem. I. 30 ; but far more usually in prose :
Lysias p. 157, 21 καί μοι κάλει τὸν καὶ τόν : Demosth. p. 128. §. 68
ἔδει γὰρ τὸ καὶ τὸ ποιῆσαι καὶ τὸ μὴ ποιῆσαι.   In the nomin. sing.
this formula is ὅς καὶ ὅς.

c. Immediately before a relative sentence, introduced by ὅς, ὅσος, or
οἷος, which expresses by a periphrasis either an adjectival, or, especially,
an abstract notion.   This idiom is peculiarly Platonic ; as, Protag. p.
320 D ἐκ γῆς καὶ πυρὸς μίξαντες καὶ τῶν ὅσα πυρὶ καὶ γῇ κεράννυται : Id.
Rep. p. 469 B ταὐτὰ δὲ ταῦτα νομιοῦμεν καὶ ὅταν τις γήρᾳ ἤ τινι ἄλλῳ
τρόπῳ τελευτήσῃ τῶν ὅσοι ἂν διαφερόντως ἐν τῷ βίῳ ἀγαθοὶ κριθῶσι ;
Ibid. p. 509 E λέγω δὲ τὰς εἰκόνας πρῶτον μὲν τὰς σκιάς, ἔπειτα τὰ ἐν
τοῖς ὕδασι φαντάσματα καὶ ἐν τοῖς ὅσα πυχνά τε καὶ λεῖα καὶ φανὰ ξυνέ-
στηκε : Id. Sophist. p. 241 E εἴτε μιμημάτων εἴτε φαντασμάτων αὐτῶν ἢ
καὶ περὶ τεχνῶν τῶν ὅσαι περὶ ταῦτά εἰσι[a] : Id. Phæd. p. 92 D

─────────

[a] Heindorf ad loc.

ὥσπερ αὐτῆς (sc. τῆς ψυχῆς) ἔστιν ἡ οὐσία ἔχουσα τὴν ἐπωνυμίαν τὴν τοῦ ὅ ἐστιν (abstract notion). This construction is also used as a periphrasis for an indefinite object, especially in the orators: Lysias p. 733 ταῦτ' οὖν ὡς ἀληθῆ ἐστι, τόν τε Εὐθύκριτον, ὃν πρῶτον ἠρόμην, καὶ τῶν ἄλλων Πλαταιέων ὅσοις προσῆλθον, καὶ τὸν, ὅς ἔφη δεσπότης τούτου εἶναι, μάρτυρας παρέξομαι: Demosth. p. 613, 9 σώζειν ὑμῖν τοὺς τοιούτους, ὦ ἄνδρες Ἀθηναῖοι, προσήκει καὶ μισεῖν τούς, οἷοσπερ οὗτος.

d. In the construction οἱ μέν — οἱ δέ, which properly signify some here —some there, part—part. This is found in Homer, and is very common both in prose and poetry. The use of the sing. ὁ μέν—ὁ δέ is Post-Homeric: very frequently τὸ μὲν—τὸ δέ, τὰ μὲν—τὰ δέ, τῇ μὲν—τῇ δέ, *partim—partim:* τὶς also is joined with this formula, ὁ μέν τις—ὁ δέ τις, *alius quis—alius quis,* properly, any one there—any one there; when the contrasted persons are uncertain or indefinite: Xen. Cyr. VI. 1, 1 ἐν τούτῳ οἱ φίλοι τῷ Κύρῳ προσῆγον οἱ μὲν Καδουσίους αὐτοῦ μένειν δεομένους, οἱ δὲ Ὑρκανίους, ὁ δέ τις Σάκας, ὁ δέ τις Γωβρύαν: here several individuals are signified by the indefinite singular τὶς: Plat. Phileb. p. 13 C τὰς μὲν εἶναί τινας ἡδονὰς ἀγαθάς, τὰς δέ τινας κακάς: Euthyphr. p. 12 A τὸ μὲν αὐτοῦ ὅσιον, τὸ δέ τι καὶ ἄλλο: interchanged with ἄλλος: Id. Legg. p. 658 B εἰκός που τὸν μέν τινα ἐπιδεικνύναι ῥαψῳδίαν, ἄλλον δὲ κιθαρῳδίαν, τὸν δέ τινα τραγῳδίαν: with τὶς preceding; Id. Gorg. p. 499 C ἡδοναί τινές εἰσιν αἱ μὲν ἀγαθαί, αἱ δὲ κακαί[a].

e. ὁ, ἡ, τό is used also as an attributive with a demonstrative force in all the Post-Homeric writers. Thus of objects well known, or mentioned before: Plat. Rep. p. 329 E τὸ τοῦ Θεμιστοκλέους εὖ ἔχει ὃς τῷ Σεριφίῳ (Seriphio isti) λοιδορουμένῳ—ἀπεκρίνατο: Id. Charmid. p. 155 D ἐνόμισα σοφώτατον εἶναι τὸν Κριτίαν τὰ ἐρωτικά, ὃς εἶπεν ἐπὶ τοῦ καλοῦ λέγων παιδός κ. τ. λ. (alluding to the well known story)[b]: Demosth. p. 850, 19 ἐξῄτει με τὸν ἄνθρωπον (sc. *Milyam, istum hominem*): so frequently in this orator: Id. p. 90, 3 ἐχθρὸς ὑπάρχων τῇ πόλει (*Athenis, huic urbi*) Φίλιππος: Theocrit. VIII. 43 ἔνθ' ἁ καλὰ παῖς ἐπινίσσεται: Ibid. 47 ἔνθ' ὁ καλὸς Μίλων βαίνει ποσίν.

The Article ὁ, ἡ, τό, as a Relative Pronoun.

§. 445. 1. In the Homeric dialect, the demonstrative ὁ, ἡ, τό frequently assumes the functions of the relative pronoun, ὅς, ἥ, ὅ: Il. *a,* 125 ἀλλὰ τὰ μὲν πολίων ἐξεπράθομεν τὰ δέδασται. This idiom may be accounted for by the consideration, that language originally makes no difference of form between principal and dependent sentences, but places them separately in similar parallel forms, as if standing in the same independent relations to the speaker.

2. This use of the article as the relative passed into the Ionic and Doric writers: Hdt. III. 81 τὰ μὲν Ὀτάνης εἶπε — λελέχθω κἀμοὶ ταῦτα· τὰ δ' ἐς τὸ πλῆθος ἄνωγε φέρειν τὸ κράτος, γνώμης τῆς ἀρίστης ἡμάρτηκε: cf. c. 82 princ. Ibid. πάντων τῶν λέγω ἀρίστων, *quæ dico.*

3. The Attic comic and prose writers do not admit this relative force of the article. The tragedians have adopted it only in the neuter, the oblique cases, and mostly to avoid an hiatus, or lengthen by position a final short syllable of the preceding word: Soph. Œ. T. 1379 δαιμόνων δ' ἀγάλμαθ' ἱερά, τῶν ὁ παντλήμων ἐγώ—ἀπεστέρησ' ἐμαυτόν.

---

a Stallb. ad loc.   b Heindorf p. 62.

The meaning and use of ὁ, ἡ, τό, as the Article proper.

§. 446. The article ὁ, ἡ, τό lost so much of its demonstrative force, that at last it was used merely to represent the notion expressed by the substantive, as viewed by the speaker as an individual, one of a class, and distinct from all the other members of that class. This usage of the article properly belongs to the æra of Attic prose: but as not only a single person, but also a whole class, may be considered as an individual, hence there arises a double and seemingly contrary use of the article.

a. The substantive without the article expresses the general notion without any limitation of individuality, but with the article a part of the general notion, an individual member or members of the class, contemplated as such by the speaker; as, ὁ ἄνθρωπος, *t h e* man, whom I am thinking of.

b. A second use of the article derived from the former is, that it expresses the notion of a whole and all its parts conceived of as one individual; as, ὁ ἄνθρωπος θνητός ἐστι, the man (the animal man = all men) is mortal.

Remarks on the Indefinite Article.

The English indefinite article *a* is used either to signify the whole class, where in Greek the substantive alone is frequently used—*a man,* ἄνθρωπος: or an individual, but not spoken of in a definite manner, *a man* —*any man,* where in Greek the indefinite τὶς is often used: γυνή τις ὄρνιν εἶχε. But sometimes the indefinite article is added; as, Soph. Œ. R. 107 τοὺς αὐτοέντας τινάς: τὶς in this case is generally placed after its substantive.

The Article with Collective, Abstract, Material and Personal Nouns.

§. 447. With collective nouns—it represents the notion of the substantives, either as an individual, or as a class in its full sense, comprehending all its parts logically distributed; from this latter usage there arose, that the article is used, (*a*) with distributives; as, Xen. Anab. I. 3, 21 προσαιτοῦσι δὲ μισθὸν ὁ Κῦρος ὑπισχνεῖται ἡμιόλιον πᾶσι δώσειν, οὗ πρότερον ἔφερον, ἀντὶ δαρεικοῦ τρία ἡμιδαρεικὰ τοῦ μηνὸς τῷ στρατιώτῃ (*singulis mensibus singulis militibus*); — (*b*) when any thing is represented as all that is requisite or possible in certain circumstances; as, Xen. Anab. VII. 6, 23 ἔδει τὰ ἐνέχυρα τότε λαβεῖν, all which the present state of affairs required: Ibid. 2, 8 ὡς τάχιστα Ξενοφῶντα προπέμψαι τοῖς ἵπποις (with the requisite horses) ἐπὶ τὸ στράτευμα: Plat. Menex. p. 235 A ὥστε καὶ τὰ προσόντα καὶ τὰ μὴ περὶ ἑκάστου λέγοντες, κάλλιστά πως τοῖς ὀνόμασι ποικίλλοντες, γοητεύουσιν ἡμῶν τὰς ψυχάς.

Obs. The article is sometimes omitted with collective nouns, though they are spoken of as individuals or as parts of a class; this happens, (*a*) in common speech, with words in every day use : πατήρ, μήτηρ, υἱός, παῖδες, γυνή, ἀδελφός, γονεῖς, θεός, ἄνθρωπος, ἀνήρ, πατρίς, πόλις, ἀγρός, &c. (*b*) When two or more independent substantives are joined in one notion, so that the individuality of each is lost ; as, παῖδες καὶ γυναῖκες : Plat. Rep. p. 574 γέροντός τε καὶ γραός, *senis patris et matris :* and even when a relative sentence follows ; as, Xen. Cyr. III. 3, 44 περὶ οἴκων ἐν οἶς ἐτράφητε, *the houses in which,* &c. (*c*) When the collective noun is used as a proper name ; as, ἥλιος, γῆ, &c. : so βασιλεύς, as the usual term for the king of Persia, Demosth. p. 114. (*d*) In certain phrases where the collective noun has an abstract or indefinite force ; as, Plato Euthy. p. 8 D ἡγεῖσθαι θεούς — ἰέναι ἐπὶ δεῖπνον — ἐφ' ἵππου εἶναι. If the article is used in these formulas, it is either demonstrative, *the particular one;* as, Eur. Hec. νόμῳ γὰρ τοὺς θεοὺς ἡγούμεθα, these particular gods mentioned in v. 799, ἀλλ' οἱ θεοί σθένουσι. or it signifies the concrete members of the abstract notion ; as, ἐπὶ τὸ δεῖπνον, *to the supper party.*

§. 448. Abstract nouns, when considered as such, do not take the article, as an abstract notion is not capable of individuality ; but the article is used sometimes either to define or particularise the abstract ; as, τὸ πρᾶγμα—ὁ βίος—ἡ φιλοσοφία, a particular branch of philosophy (φιλοσοφία, Philosophy generally) : τἀγαθόν, the good, good as conceived of by the speaker : or it gives it a collective force, so that the notion is taken in its widest extent ; as, Plat. Phæd. p. 69 C καὶ ἡ σωφροσύνη καὶ ἡ δικαιοσύνη καὶ ἡ ἀνδρεία, καὶ αὐτὴ ἡ φρόνησις μὴ καθαρμός τις ᾖ.

Obs. 1. The names of arts and sciences, virtues and vices, are generally without the article, as being familiar from every day use. So also πλῆθος, μέγεθος, ὕψος, εὖρος, have not the article when used adverbially, as definitions of space and size. So πρόφασιν γένος.

Obs. 2. When the inf. is used as an abstract subst., as it expresses the whole extent of the notion, it is generally introduced by the article : τὸ ὑπὲρ τῆς πατρίδος ἀποθανεῖν καλόν ἐστι.

§. 449. Material nouns, as expressing no idea of individuality, take the article only when the thing spoken of is to be represented as particularised in the speaker's mind ; as, τοῦ οἴνου πίνειν, *this* wine : or when it signifies the whole extent of the notion, τὸ γάλα ἐστι καλόν, *the* milk (all).

§. 450. Personal names, signifying individuals, but not individuals belonging to a class, and therefore requiring no further expression of their individuality, properly do not take the article ; as, Σωκράτης ἔφη : but they frequently take it in narratives, when the person is spoken of as regarded in some particular view by the speaker ; as, ὁ Σωκράτης ἔφη, the Socrates I just spoke of.

Obs. 1. When joined with an adject., the proper names generally take the article, as denoting an individual of a class ; as, ὁ σοφὸς Σωκράτης, *Socrates who is of the number of the wise.*

Obs. 2. When the proper name is followed by a substantive in apposition with the article, it has not itself the article ; as, Κροῖσος ὁ τῶν Λυδῶν βασιλεύς. If the article is added to it, it signifies that the person has been already named. When the word or sentence in apposition has not the article, the personal noun has it not ; as, Θουκυδίδης Ἀθηναῖος : but this idiom is not so common as, Θουκ. ὁ Ἀθην., and is only used when the attributive is unimportant ; but when the apposition is emphatic, and is used really to distinguish different persons of the same name, the article is always added. The same distinction exists with the personal pronoun, when used as a personal name, ἐγὼ ὁ τλήμων, I, *the* unlucky : ἐγὼ τάλας, I, an unlucky man. Names of rivers are generally joined to the word ποταμός, as adjectives, and stand between it and the article ; as, Hdt. I. 72 ὁ Ἅλυς ποταμός. So also hills and countries, sometimes islands, when they are of the same gender with the word in apposition, ὄρος, ἄκρον, γῆ, νῆσος, &c. ; as, τὸ Σούνιον ἄκρον, ἡ Θεσπρωτὶς γῆ, ἡ Δῆλος νῆσος. So Hdt. II. 106 ὁ Αἰγύπτου βασιλεὺς Σέσωστρις. When a participle, used as a substantive, stands in apposition, the article is always used with it ; and generally also with the substantive to which it is in apposition ; as, Hdt. VI. 47 οἱ Φοίνικες — οἱ κτίσαντες τὴν νῆσον.

The Article with Adjectives or Participles used as Substantives.

§. 451. 1. When, by the ellipse of a substantive, the adj. or part. stands as a substantive, the article is generally prefixed, when the whole of the notion is signified, and the whole is regarded as an individual ; as, οἱ ἀγαθοί—τὸ κακόν—οἱ ἔχοντες, *the rich* : ὁ βουλόμενος, *quivis* : ὁ τυχών, *the first who comes* : but when a part only of the whole notion is signified, the article is omitted ; as, κακὰ καὶ αἰσχρὰ ἔπραξεν.

2. The article is also used with participles when any individual is so conceived of by the speaker, that he is particularised ; this part. is expressed in Latin by, *Is qui* : English, *he, they who, one who* ; as, Hdt. IX. 70 πρῶτοι δὲ ἐσῆλθον Τεγεῆται ἐς τὸ τεῖχος, καὶ τὴν σκηνὴν τοῦ Μαρδονίου οὗτοι ἔσαν οἱ διαρπάσαντες : Id. III. 71 ἄνδρες οἱ παρεόντες, *viri, qui hic adestis* : Xen. Cyr. II. 2, 20 αἰσχρὸν ἀντιλέγειν, μὴ οὐχὶ τὸν πλεῖστα πονοῦντα καὶ ὠφελοῦντα τὸ κοινόν, τοῦτον καὶ μεγίστων ἀξιοῦσθαι : Id. Anab. II. 4, 5 αὖθις δὲ ὁ ἡγησόμενος οὐδεὶς ἔσται, *nemo statim erit, qui nobis viam monstret* : Id. Hell. VII. 5, 24 μάλα γὰρ χαλεπὸν εὑρεῖν τοὺς ἐθελήσοντας μένειν, ἐπειδάν τινας φεύγοντας τῶν ἑαυτοῦ ὁρῶσι : Isocr. p. 18 B πολλοὺς ἔξομεν τοὺς ἑτοίμως—συναγωνιζομένους : Plat. Menex. p. 236 B ἤκουσε —, ὅτι μέλλοιεν Ἀθηναῖοι αἱρεῖσθαι τὸν ἐροῦντα, *qui orationem haberet* : Demosth.

p. 101, 46 ἵν', ὥσπερ ἐκεῖνος ἕτοιμον ἔχει δύναμιν, τ ὴ ν ἀ δ ι κ ή σ ο υ-
σ α ν καὶ κ α τ α δ ο υ λ ω σ ο μ έ ν η ν ἅπαντας τοὺς Ἕλληνας, οὕτω
τ ὴ ν σ ώ σ ο υ σ α ν ὑμεῖς καὶ β ο η θ ή σ ο υ σ α ν ἅπασιν ἕτοιμον ἔχητε.
So εἰσὶν οἱ λέγοντες, *sunt, qui dicant,* instead of the obsolete form
εἰσὶν οἱ λέγουσιν, Plat. Gorg. 503 A.

Obs. There are however passages both in prose and poetry where the
article is wanting ; in these cases the person or thing is spoken of only
generally ; neither regarded as any *definite* part of a class, nor standing
for the collective unity of the whole class : Eur. Phœn. 270 ἅπαντα γὰρ
τ ο λ μ ῶ σ ι δεινὰ φαίνεται : Xen. Cyr. VI. 2, 1 ἦλθον δὲ ἐν τούτῳ τῷ χρόνῳ
καὶ παρὰ τοῦ Ἰνδοῦ χρήματα ἄ γ ο ν τ ε ς : Plat. Gorg. p. 498 A νοῦν ἔ χ ο ν τ α
(οὔπω εἶδες) λυπούμενον καὶ χαίροντα : Id. Legg. p. 795 B διαφέρει δὲ παμπολὺ
μ α θ ὼ ν μὴ μ α θ ό ν τ ο ς καὶ ὁ γυμνασάμενος τοῦ μὴ γεγυμνασμένου.

Article with the Pronoun, either with or without a Substantive.

§. 452. *a.* Personal pronouns :—*a.* Substantival pronouns have
an article only in a demonstrative force pointing to some preceding
subst.—(Frequent in Plato, much more seldom in later prose) :
Plat. Lys. p. 203 B δεῦρο δή, ἦ δ' ὅς, εὐθὺ ἡμῶν (*huc recta via veni
ad nos*). Οὐ παραβάλλεις ; (*Non accedis ?*) Ἄξιον μέντοι. Ποῖ,
ἔφην ἐγώ, λέγεις, καὶ παρὰ τίνας τ ο ὺ ς ὑ μ ᾶ ς ; Id. Theæt. p. 166 A
γέλωτα δὴ τ ὸ ν ἐ μ ὲ ἐν τοῖς λόγοις ἀπέδειξε. This construction
seems to be confined to the accusative.

β. With adjectival pronouns, the article is found as early as
Homer in a demonstrative sense : Il. λ, 608 τ ῷ ἐ μ ῷ κεχαρισμένε
θυμῷ, this my heart. If this demonstrative notion is not required,
the article is omitted ; as, Il. ε, 243. In Attic, the article is
regularly joined to the pronoun, the article standing first, then
the pronoun, lastly the subst. ; as, ὁ ἐμὸς πατήρ, as the subst. is
particularised by the pronoun ; but it may be omitted ; as, Lys.
Andoc. 54 πάππος ἡμέτερος, when the subst. is one of the common
words given in §. 447. *Obs. (a),* or expresses an indefinite person
or thing.

§. 453. *b.* Demonstrative pronouns :—*a.* Οὗτος, ὅδε, ἐκεῖνος, αὐτός
ipse,—regularly take the article in Attic Greek, in either of these
collocations : demonstrative, article, subst. ; or, article, subst.,
pronoun ; as,

  οὗτος ὁ ἀνήρ or ὁ ἀνὴρ οὗτος (not ὁ οὗτος ἀνήρ),

  ἥδε ἡ γνώμη or ἡ γνώμη ἥδε,

  ἐκεῖνος ὁ ἀνήρ or ὁ ἀνὴρ ἐκεῖνος,

  αὐτὸς ὁ βασιλεύς or ὁ βασιλεὺς αὐτός (but ὁ αὐτός = *idem*).

Obs. In poetry it is often omitted. Homer never joins the demonst.
pron. with ὁ, ἡ, τό : Il. ο, 206 τοῦτο ἔπος : Il. ν, 202 κεῖνος ἀνήρ. And in

prose it is sometimes omitted, when the substantive is either a proper name, or a collective noun used as a proper name; as, Thuc. II. 74 ἐπὶ γῆν τήνδε. It is always omitted when the pronoun stands as the subject, and the subst. as the predicate of the sentence; as, Thuc. I. 1 κίνησις αὕτη, i. e. *hic est motus :* Ibid. 65 αἰτία αὕτη: Plat. Gorg. p. 510 D αὕτη, ὡς ἔοικεν, αὐτῷ ὁδός ἐστι, this, as it seems, is his way: Id. Menon. p. 71 E αὕτη ἐστὶν ἀνδρὸς ἀρετή, this is the virtue of a man : Ibid. p. 75 B ἔστω γὰρ δὴ ἡμῖν τοῦτο σχῆμα: Id. Symp. p. 179 C εὐαριθμήτοις δή τισιν ἔδοσαν τοῦτο γέρας οἱ θεοί: Id. Apol. p. 24 B αὕτη ἔστω ἱκανὴ ἀπολογία.　So τούτῳ τῷ διδασκάλῳ χρῶνται, they have this teacher; τούτῳ διδ. χρ., they have this man as a teacher.　When the predicative subst. is joined with an attribute, and has the article, the demonst. pronoun, which stands as the subject (οὗτος), is sometimes placed between the article and its subst.; as, Thuc. VIII. 80 αἱ μὲν τῶν Πελοποννησίων αὗται νῆες, for αὗται (ἦσαν) αἱ τ. Π. ν.: Xen. Anab. IV. 2, 6 μαστὸς ἦν, παρ᾽ ὃν ἦν ἡ στενὴ αὕτη ὁδός, ἐφ᾽ ᾗ ἐκάθηντο οἱ φύλακες (for παρ᾽ ὃν αὕτη ἦν ἡ στενὴ ὁδ., ἐφ᾽ ᾗ κ. τ. λ.).　Αὐτός, *himself,* is also thus placed, when a participle and article are joined to a subst. instead of a relative sentence, in which αὐτός would be the subject; as, Demosth. p. 459 ἐν δὲ τῷ κοινῷ μὴ χρῆσθαι τῷ νόμῳ τούτῳ τὴν πόλιν τὴν αὐτὴν ἐπιτάξασαν τοῖς ἰδιώταις, for τὴν πόλιν, ἣ αὐτὴ ἐπέταξεν.　So also τοιοῦτος; see below.

β. The demonst. pronouns of quality and quantity—τοιοῦτος and τοσοῦτος—have the article, when the quality or quantity is conceived to belong to the whole class of individuals before named.　It is most usual with a demonstrative force, as referring to the object before named.　The article stands either between the pronoun and subst. or before them; as, τοιοῦτος ὁ ἀνήρ, τοσοῦτο τὸ χρῆμα, or ὁ τοιοῦτος ἀνήρ, τὸ τοσοῦτον χρῆμα.　In poetry we find other pronouns of this class in similar construction; as, ὁ τοιόσδε, οἱ τηλικοῦτοι Soph. Ant. 726 : Hdt. III. 82 ἔχω τοίνυν γνώμην, ἡμέας ἐλευθερωθέντας διὰ ἕνα ἄνδρα τὸ τοιοῦτο (*hanc talem imperii formam*) περιστέλλειν: Xen. M. S. I. 5, 2 διάκονον δὲ καὶ ἀγοραστὴν τὸν τοιοῦτον ἐθελήσαιμεν ἂν προῖκα λαβεῖν: Plat. Rep. p. 468 C καὶ καθ᾽ Ὅμηρον τοῖς τοιοῖσδε δίκαιον τιμᾶν τῶν νέων ὅσοι ἀγαθοί: Ibid. p. 476 C ἐγὼ γ᾽ οὖν ἂν — φαίην ὀνειρώττειν τὸν τοιοῦτον: Demosth. p. 42, 6 ἂν — ἐπὶ τῆς τοιαύτης ἐθελήσητε γενέσθαι γνώμης.　Τοιοῦτος also, like αὐτός, has the article in the constructions mentioned in the foregoing Obs., where it stands with a participle for the predicate of a relative sentence; as, Demosth. p. 467 τοῦτον τὸν τοιοῦτον περὶ ὑμᾶς γενόμενον, sc. ὃς γεγένηται τοιοῦτος.

c. Even relative pronouns have the article, as in the construction ὁ οἷος σὺ ἀνήρ.　See *Attraction of Relatives.*

d. For interrogative pronouns with the article, see *Interrogative Sentences.*

§. 454.　1. Indefinite Pronouns and Numerals.　The word πάντες is joined with the article, (a) when the pronoun stands first, the article second, and the subst. last, or the article first, the subst. second, and πάντες last. It expresses either the whole of a number of objects implied in the context, or the whole as opposed to other objects; or, in reference to some particular circumstances, we find both collocations together: Arist. Av. 444 πᾶσι τοῖς κριταῖς καὶ τοῖς θεαταῖς πᾶσι. In the sing. Thuc. VII. 59 ἑλεῖν τὸ στρατόπεδον ἅπαν. So ἀνὰ πᾶσαν τὴν ἡμέραν, *the whole day* (ἀνὰ πᾶσαν ἡ, *daily*). β. When πάντες stands between the article and the subst., or after both, as οἱ πάντες ἄνθρωποι, ἄνθρωποι οἱ πάντες, the notion of the *whole* is expressed: Thuc. τὰς ναῦς ἁπάσας πληρῶσαι, all the ships without exception: Thuc. V. 120 πεσόντων τῶν πάντων πολλῶν, the whole number which fell being great. So in definitions of number: Hdt. VII. 4 συνήνεικε αὐτὸν Δαρεῖον, βασιλεύσαντα τ ὰ π ά ν τ α ἔτεα ἕξ τε καὶ τριήκοντα, ἀποθανεῖν, thirty-six, all the years taken together. So Thuc. III. 66. ξυνεπληρώθησαν νῆες αἱ πᾶσαι δέκα μάλιστα καὶ ἑκατόν, about 110 in all. So also in sing.: Plat. Gorg. p. 470 E ἐν τούτῳ ἡ πᾶσα εὐδαιμονία ἐστίν. When the notion of "*all*" is merely general, neither signifying expressly the whole class, nor all the part of a class, the article is not used.

Obs. 1. Herodotus follows Homer (Od. ε, 244 εἴκοσι πάντα) in using in definitions of number πάντα without the article; as, I. 163 ἐβίωσε πάντα εἴκοσι καὶ ἑκατον ἔτεα.

2. Also with ἕκαστος, ἑκάτερος, the article is used to mark more strongly the notion of the individuality of each. Ἕκαστος generally stands first; as, Xen. Anab. VII. 4, 14 καὶ ἡγεμὼν μὲν ἦν ὁ δεσπότης ἑ κ ά σ τ η ς τ ῆ ς ο ἰ κ ί α ς: Ibid. III. 2, 36 ἐπὶ τῶν πλευρῶν ἑκατέρων: Plat. Rep. p. 338 D ἑκάστη ἡ ἀρχή.

3. The article with ἄλλοι signifies *the whole of the rest.* The singular is also joined with the article: ἡ ἄλλη Ἑλλάς, the rest of Greece. Ἕτερος takes the article, to denote more strongly the individuality implied in it. So οἱ ἕτεροι, the other of two parties; πολλοί, many; οἱ πολλοί, the most, the many, the *plebs*: πλείους, *plures*; οἱ πλείους, *plurimi*, the most: so in the sing.: Hdt. VI. 81 τὴν μὲν πλέω στρατίην ἀπῆκε: ὀλίγοι, *pauci*; οἱ ὀλίγοι, emphatically the oligarchy. So αὐτός, *ipse*; ὁ αὐτός, *idem*, his very self.

Obs. 2. Homer uses both πολλοί and οἱ πολλοί for *ceteri*, and αὐτός for ὁ αὐτός.

Obs. 3. The article is sometimes used with πλείους in an apparently comparative sense, but the comparative really refers to another notion in the sentence: Soph. Ant. 313 τ ο ὺ ς π λ ε ί ο ν α ς ἀτωμένους ἴδοις ἂν ἢ σεσωσμένους = τοὺς πλείστους ἀτωμένους μᾶλλον ἤ[a]: κ. τ. λ.

a Herm. Ant. 313.

The Article with numerals.

§. 455. 1. The article stands with cardinal numerals when the number is to be decidedly marked; as, Plat. Rep. p. 460 E ἆρ' οὖν σοι ξυνδοκεῖ μέτριος χρόνος ἀκμῆς τὰ εἴκοσιν ἔτη γυναικί, ἀνδρὶ δὲ τὰ τριάκοντα[a]. Or the article frequently has a demonstrative force, though here it is more properly joined with the subst., either expressed or implied, than the numeral; as, Hdt. VIII. 46 οἱ Χαλκιδέες τὰς ἐπ' Ἀρτεμισίῳ εἴκοσι παρεχόμενοι. Or it sometimes gives the notion of the whole; as, Xen. Anab. II. 6, 15 ἦν δὲ, ὅτε ἐτελεύτα, ἀμφὶ τὰ πεντήκοντα ἔτεα, *fifty years in all.*

2. Ἄμφω and ἀμφότεροι have the article either in an emphatic or demonstrative force; as, Thuc. V. 23 ἄμφω τὼ πόλεε: Id. III. 6 ἐπ' ἀμφοτέροις τοῖς λιμέσι.

3. The ordinal numerals are regularly joined with the article; as, ὁ πρῶτος στρατηγός. So τὸ πρῶτον, τὸ τρίτον, the first, third time.

Obs. The ordinals are used also in Homer with the article, which is here to be taken as a substantival pronoun with the numeral in apposition; as, Il. ψ, 265 τῷ πρώτῳ—τῷ δευτέρῳ—τῷ τριτάτῳ—τῷ δὲ τετάρτῳ—πέμπτῳ δὲ ἀμφίθετον φιάλην ἀπύρωτον ἔθηκεν, *him who was first, second,* &c.

The Article and Attributive Genitive, or Preposition and its cases, with an Adverb.

§. 456. 1. In the forms given, §. 436. *d.* as, οἱ ἀμφὶ τὸν πόλεμον, οἱ περί τινα, τὰ τῆς πόλεως, the article is used, partly because the substantival notion is particularised by the attributive with which it is joined, partly for the sake of clearness.

2. The article is used with adverbs of place and time, more rarely of quality and modality, when the adverb stands either for an adjective, οἱ νῦν ἄνθρωποι, or for a substantive, οἱ νῦν, τὰ νῦν, as,

a. Adverbs of place: Hdt. VIII. 8 ἡ ἄνω πόλις:—ὁ μεταξὺ τόπος—οἱ ἐνθάδε ἄνθρωποι, or οἱ ἐνθάδε — τὰ ἄνω, τὰ κάτω, the parts above, below: Æschin. p. 15, 21 τὸν Ἀθήνησιν ὑβριστήν.

b. Adverbs of time: ὁ νῦν βασιλεύς: Xen. M. S. I. 6, 14 οἱ πάλαι σοφοὶ ἄνδρες: — οἱ τότε (Il. ί, 559) — ἡ αὔριον (sc. ἡμέρα) — ἡ ἐξαίφνης μετάστασις — ὁ ἀεί, the perpetual: Soph. Œ. C. 1584 τὸν ἀεὶ βίοτον, *vitam perpetuam.* In these forms it points to the substantive or participle omitted, and thus defines the notion to

[a] Stallb. ad loc.

which it is joined. So many adverbial expressions with the neuter article, when the whole of a space of time is signified; as, τὸ, τὰ νῦν, the present; τὸ πάλαι, time gone by; τὸ πρὶν (Homer), τὸ πάρος, τὸ πρόσθεν, τὸ αὐτίκα, the immediate time; ἐκ τοῦ παραχρῆμα, immediately; τὸ ἐξαπίνης Thuc.: Hdt. VII. 17 οὔτε ἐς τὸ μετέπειτα, οὔτε ἐς τὸ παραυτίκα. So the adv. adjectives, τὸ ἀρχαῖον, τὸ πρῶτον, τὰ πρῶτα, τὸ λοιπόν, *in posterum*; τοῦ λοιποῦ, further.

c. Adverbs of quality and modality: σφόδρα, πάνυ, κάρτα, λίαν, ἄγαν, ἁπλῶς, ἀληθῶς, ὁμολογουμένως, φανερῶς: Thuc. VIII. 1 οἱ πάνυ τῶν στρατιωτῶν, the best of the soldiers: Hdt. III. 104 τὸ κάρτα ψῦχος: Demosth. p. 44, 17 ἐκ τῆς ἀμελείας ταύτης τῆς ἄγαν: Id. p. 848, 14 τὸν ὁμολογουμένως δοῦλον. Also, Plat. Legg. p. 667 C τὸ εὖ καὶ τὸ καλῶς, as an expression of abstract notions: Thuc. VI. 80 τὴν ἀκινδύνως δούλειαν. Many adverbial forms with the neuter article; as, τὰ μάλιστα and ἐς τὰ μάλ., *maxime* Hdt. VI. 63: τὸ πάμπαν and τὸ παράπαν, *omnino* — τὸ κάρτα Hdt. I. 191; τὸ παραπολύ Thuc. So many adjectives used adverbially in the Alexandrine writers; as, τὸ καρτερόν Theocrit. I. 41; τὸ καλόν Id. III. 3.

Obs. The article is very rarely omitted with these constructions. In Homer this omission is naturally more common than elsewhere: Il. δ, 310 πάλαι πολέμων εὖ εἰδώς: Hes. Theog. 486 μέγ' ἄνακτι: Ibid. 872 μάψ αὖραι: Hdt. I. 146 μᾶλλον Ἴωνες: Theocr. IX. 34 ἔαρ ἐξαπίνας (*subitum ver*). Even in prose: Demosth. p. 835 εἶτα τῶν ἐχθρῶν Φωκέων ἄρδην ὄλεθρος: Id. p. 245, 25 ἐν τοιαύτῃ δὲ καταστάσει καὶ ἔτι ἀγνοίᾳ. So in Latin: Plaut. Pers. III. 1, 57 *non tu nunc hominum mores vides.*

The Article before a single word or sentence.

§. 457. 1. The article may be prefixed to any word or sentence, which does not express the notion of the word, but only the grammatical form; as, τὸ τύπτω, τὸ τύπτεις: Demosth. p. 255, 4 ὑμεῖς, ὦ ἄνδρες Ἀθηναῖοι· — τ ὸ δ' ὑ μ ε ῖ ς ὅταν εἴπω, τὴν πόλιν λέγω.

2. This takes place also with sentences to which the article gives the form and power of an attributive: Plat. Rep. p. 341 B διόρισαι, ποτέρως λέγεις τὸν ἄρχοντά τε καὶ τὸν κρείττονα τ ὸ ν ὡ ς ἔ π ο ς ε ἰ π ε ῖ ν, ἢ τ ὸ ν ἀ κ ρ ι β ε ῖ λ ό γ ῳ, i. e. *utrum principem dicas eum, qui vulgari sermone dicatur, an eum, qui subtiliori sermone.*

3. So sentences assume a substantival force, and can perform all the functions of a substantive: Plat. Rep. p. 327 C ἓν ἔτι λείπεται, τ ὸ ἢν πείσωμεν ὑμᾶς, ὡς χρὴ ὑμᾶς ἀφεῖναι: Hdt. VII. 79 στασιάζειν — περὶ τ ο ῦ ὁκότερος ἡμέων πλέω ἀγαθὰ τὴν πατρίδα

ἐργάσεται. So the *dative*, Plat. Phæd. p. 102 C, and the *accusative*, Id. Gorg. p. 461 E. When a subst. precedes to which the sentence with the article refers, the gender of the preceding subst. is sometimes used instead of the neuter: Xen. M. S. I. 3, 3 καὶ πρὸς φίλους δὲ καὶ ξένους καὶ πρὸς τὴν ἄλλην δίαιταν καλὴν ἔφη παραίνεσιν εἶναι τὴν κὰδ δύναμιν ἔρδειν.

Position of the Article.

§. 458. In all the forms of the attributive sentence, the attributive stands either between the article and the subst.; as, ὁ ἀγαθὸς ἀνήρ — ὁ ἐμὸς πατήρ — οἱ τρεῖς ἄνδρες — ἡ ἄνω πόλις — ὁ τῶν Ἑλλήνων πόλεμος — ὁ πρὸς τοὺς Πέρσας πόλεμος, or after the subst., the article being repeated before it; as, ὁ ἀνὴρ ὁ ἀγαθός — ὁ πατὴρ ὁ ἐμός — οἱ ἄνδρες οἱ τρεῖς — ἡ πόλις ἡ ἄνω — ὁ πόλεμος ὁ τῶν Ἑλλήνων — ὁ πόλεμος ὁ πρὸς τοὺς Πέρσας : Isocr. p. 319 τήν τε διάνοιαν τὴν ἐκείνου — καὶ τὸν τρόπον τὸν ἐμαυτοῦ : Demosth. p. 861, 56 τὴν μητέρα τὴν ἐμαυτοῦ. The first article may be omitted ; as, πόλεμος ὁ μέγας : Hdt. V. 50 ἀπὸ θαλάσσης τῆς Ἰώνων : Τυραννὶς ἡ ἐν Χερσονήσῳ Id.

Obs. 1. Hence in constructions where two adjectives stand together, one of which has a substantival force ; as, τὰ ψευδῆ καλά, the latter is to be taken as the substantive, *false good tidings—not good falsehoods.*

Obs. 2. Hence when we find an article, substantive, and adjective, or an adjective, article, and substantive, standing together, we may generally know that the adjective is not an attribute, but forms part of the predicate ; as, Thuc. IV. 17 τοὺς λόγους μακροτέρους μηκυνοῦμεν : Id. I. 6 ξυνήθη τὴν δίαιταν μεθ᾽ ὅπλων ἐποιήσαντο, they made a habit of wearing arms in their daily life ; or it is in apposition to the subst., the participle of εἶναι being suppressed ; as, Soph. Phil. 942 τὰ τόξα μου ἱερὰ λαβὼν τοῦ Ζηνὸς Ἡρακλέους, which are sacred to Hercules. There are cases where this rule does not at first seem to apply ; as, Soph. Œ. R. 525 τοὺς λόγους ψευδεῖς λέγοι : Thuc. I. 10 οὐδὲ — τὰ πλοῖα καταφρακτὰ ἔχοντες : but *see following Section.*

Remarks on some peculiar collocations of the Article.

§. 459. 1. When the adjective has not an attributive but a predicative force, that is, where it represents a dependent sentence, such as ὅς ἐστι— ὥστε εἶναι, of which it would stand as the predicate, it is placed without the article prefixed either before, or after the article and the subst. ; as, ἀγαθὸς ὁ ἀνήρ, or ὁ ἀνὴρ ἀγαθός, that is ἀνὴρ ὃς ἀγαθός ἐστιν, or ἀνὴρ ἀγαθὸς ὤν : the former is the more emphatic : Soph. Aj. 1121 οὐ γὰρ βάναυσον τὴν τέχνην ἐκτησάμην (βάναυσον οὖσαν) ; Thuc. VI. 31 τήν τε τῆς πόλεως ἀνάλυσιν δημοσίαν, which came from the public treasury : Lysias Epitaph. p. 194, 10 ἃ ὑπὸ τῶν βαρβάρων εὐτυχησάντων τοὺς ὑπεκτεθέντας ἤλπιζον πείσεσθαι (i. e. εἰ εὐτυχήσειαν). So with μέσος, ἀκρός, ἔσχατος, &c., the same collocation is used, where in English we use a substantive with an attributive genitive, "through the middle of the city :" Hdt. I. 185 διὰ τῆς πόλιος μέσης : Id. V. 101 διὰ μέσης τῆς ἀγορᾶς : Demosth. p. 848, 12 ἐν τῇ ἀγορῇ μέσῃ.

2. The attributive genitive, beside the above given collocations—ὁ τῶν Ἑλλήνων πόλεμος, or ὁ πόλεμος ὁ τῶν Ἑλλήνων, is placed either before or after the subst. of which it is the attribute, without any repetition of the article belonging to that substantive ; as, τῶν Ἑλλήνων ὁ πόλεμος, or ὁ πόλεμος τῶν Ἑλλήνων : Hdt. I. 3 Μηδείης τὴν ἁρπαγήν : Id. I. 5 τῷ ναυκλήρῳ τῆς νηός : Thuc. I. 12 ἡ ἀναχώρησις τῶν Ἀθηναίων : Demosth. p. 41, 3 τῇ τότε ῥώμῃ τῶν Λακεδαιμονίων : Ibid. τῇ νῦν ὕβρει τούτου.

3. The article is sometimes not repeated before a preposition and its case, which is used as an attributive adjective : Thuc. I. 18 μετὰ δὲ τὴν τῶν τυράννων κατάλυσιν ἐκ τῆς Ἑλλάδος, for τὴν ἐκ τῆς Ἑ. In poetry, part of an attributive sentence is placed before the article ; as, Soph. Aj. 1166 βροτοῖς τὸν ἀείμνηστον τάφον καθέξει, for τὸν βροτοῖς ἀείμνηστον.

4. When the article is separated from its subst., all the words between are generally to be taken as an adjectival sentence standing as the attribute to the subst. So that where several articles refer to different members of the attributive sentence, they frequently stand together at the beginning of the sentence ; as, Plat. Soph. p. 254 A τὰ τῆς τῶν πολλῶν ψυχῆς ὄμματα καρτερεῖν πρὸς τὸ θεῖον ἀφορῶντα ἀδύνατα.

5. When two or more attributives are joined to a substantive, each of which has a peculiar force, the article is used with each. This is more rare where the attributives follow the subst. : Thuc. I. 108 τὰ τείχη τὰ ἑαυτῶν τὰ μακρὰ ἀπετέλεσαν : Arist. Nub. 764 τὴν λίθον ταύτην — τὴν καλὴν τὴν διαφανῆ :—more frequent when they precede it ; as, Thuc. I. 126 ἐν τῇ τοῦ Διὸς τῇ μεγίστῃ ἑορτῇ : Plat. Cratyl. p. 398 B ἔν γε τῇ ἀρχαίᾳ τῇ ἡμετέρᾳ φωνῇ : Id. Symp. p. 213 D τὴν τούτου ταυτηνὶ τὴν θαυμαστὴν κεφαλήν. Often ὁ ἄλλος : Lysias p. 281 ἐν τοῖς ἄλλοις τοῖς ἐμοῖς χωρίοις.

6. Ταὐτόν, θάτερον sometimes take the article, as their original article being lost in the crasis, they are regarded as simple words : Plat. Tim. p. 37 B περὶ τὸ ταὐτόν—ὁ τοῦ θατέρου κύκλος : Ibid. p. 44 B τό τε θάτερον καὶ τὸ ταὐτόν. In passages such as Xen. Hier. IX. 5 τἄλλα τὰ πολιτικά, τὰ πολιτικά must be taken as in apposition.

7. The article is sometimes divided from its substantive by the particles, μέν, δέ, γέ, τέ, ἄρα, τοί, τοίνυν, γάρ, καί, δή, rarely αὖ, — οἶμαι, τὶς Il. ε, 424 ; often in Hdt. and more frequently in the later writers, and even by Xenophon. So regularly when αὐτὸς ἑαυτοῦ, &c. are opposed to each other ; as, Æsch. Ag. 845 τοῖς αὐτὸς αὐτοῦ πήμασιν βαρύνεται.

8. When a substantive has two attributive genitives, it is not used with the latter, but the article alone is repeated ; sometimes the article is also omitted ; as, Eur. Bacch. 923 οὐχὶ τὴν Ἰνοῦς στάσιν, ἢ τῆς Ἀγαυῆς.

9. If several independent substantives occur, each of which requires to be distinctly brought into view, the article is repeated before each ; as, Plat. Phæd. p. 69 C καὶ ἡ σωφροσύνη καὶ ἡ δικαιοσύνη καὶ ἡ ἀνδρεία, καὶ αὐτὴ ἡ φρόνησις μὴ καθαρμός τις ᾖ :—but where this is not the case, the article is used only with the first, sometimes with the last : Hdt. IV. 71 καὶ τὸν οἰνοχόον καὶ μάγειρον καὶ ἱπποκόμον καὶ διήκονον : Xen. Anab. VII. 8, 9 λαβεῖν ἂν αὐτὸν καὶ γυναῖκα καὶ τὰ χρήματα.

The Article with the Subject and Predicate.

§. 460. The subject generally has the article, while the predicate generally is without it : Hdt. I. 102 νὺξ ἡ ἡμέρα ἐγένετο : Plat. Gorg. 4. §. 115. extr. ἆρ' οὖν παραπλησίως εἰσὶν ἀγαθοὶ καὶ κακοὶ οἱ ἀγαθοί τε καὶ οἱ κακοί :

Aristoph. Thesm. 733 ἀσκὸς ἐγένετο ἡ κόρη. The reason of this seems to be, that the subject is regarded definitely, and as it were individually by the speaker, and so becomes a particular instead of a general notion; while the predicate is the expression of some general class in which the subject is contained, and so has no individuality. When the subject however is spoken of generally, and indefinitely, it has not the article : Plat. Theæt. 8 πάντων χρημάτων μέτρον ἄνθρωπος, man (that is, mankind) is the standard of all other things : Isocr. p. 8 B καλὸς θησαυρὸς παρ' ἀνδρὶ σπουδαίῳ χάρις ὀφειλομένη : Id. p. 28 A λόγος ἀληθὴς καὶ νόμιμος καὶ δίκαιος ψυχῆς ἀγαθῆς καὶ πιστῆς εἰδωλόν ἐστι. The subject can also stand without the article as a general notion, while the predicate, as expressing something definite, has it; here the article is demonstrative : Philem. ap. Stob. Floril. Grot. p. 211 εἰρήνη ἐστὶ τἀγαθόν : Plat. Phæd. p. 78 ταῦτα μάλιστα εἶναι τὰ ἀξύνθετα. So Hdt. I. 68 συνεβάλλετο τὸν Ὀρέστην τοῦτον εἶναι, the long sought for : Id. V. 77 οἱ δ' ἱπποβόται ἐκαλέοντο οἱ παχέες, the rich have the definite name of " *the* ἱπποβόται :" Plat. Gorg. p. 491 E τοὺς ἠλιθίους λέγεις τοὺς σώφρονας. The article has its proper force before a predicative subst. after verbs of calling ; as, Xen. Cyr. III. 3, 4 ἀνακαλοῦντες τὸν εὐεργέτην, τὸν ἄνδρα τὸν ἀγαθόν : Id. Anab. VI. 6, 7 τὸν Δέξιππον ἀνακαλοῦντες τὸν προδότην. Here the article stands before the substantive, (τὸν εὐεργέτην, τὸν ἄνδρα τὸν ἀγαθόν, τὸν προδότην,) because the speaker regards each definitely, as standing in some particular relation to himself.

The Article with combinations of two Substantives.

§. 461. 1. The attributive genitive has the article, when the subst. of which it is the attributive has it ; as, τὸ τῆς ἀρετῆς κάλλος, but ἀρετῆς κάλλος : Plat. Phæd. p. 64 E ἀπὸ τῆς τοῦ σώματος κοινωνίας. But sometimes when one of the two substantives is to be particularised, the other has not the article ; as, Xen. Cyr. VI. 3, 8 συνεκάλεσε καὶ ἱππέων καὶ πεζῶν καὶ ἁρμάτων τοὺς ἡγεμόνας, these genitives expressing the several classes, of which the leaders are particularly selected.

2. In poetry the article is sometimes used only with the attributive genitive, as its omission before the other gives the whole notion a general force suitable to the context, or to the particular thought in the mind of the speaker : Soph. Œ. R. τέρμα τοῦ βίου, end of life : Arist. Nub. 852 ὑπὸ πλήθους τῶν ἐτῶν.

3. The rule given in 1. holds good whenever two substantives are dependent one on the other : Plat. Rep. p. 332 C ἡ τοῖς ὄψοις τὰ ἡδύσματα : Ibid. p. 354 A οὐδέποτ' ἄρα λυσιτελέστερον ἀδικία δικαιοσύνης : Ibid. B λυσιτελέστερον ἡ ἀδικία τῆς δικαιοσύνης : Ibid. p. 332 C ἡ σώμασι φάρμακα —ἀποδιδοῦσα τέχνη. The use or the omission of the article depends on whether the subst. is supposed to express a general indefinite, or a particular definite notion.

Use of the Article in the Post-Homeric writers.

§. 462. In tragedy it is used very sparingly, and generally, as in Homer, has somewhat of a demonstrative force, and is frequently used as a pure demonstrative. In comedy, the representation of every-day individual actions and persons, it was very much used. So also in the

Bucolic poets, and in the orators who wished to give their statements as much the colouring of individual realities as possible. In philosophy it has its full force—to define and limit notions, and distinguish general notions from particular; and it is but seldom that in these writers it has a rhetorical or purely demonstrative force.

Attributive Genitive.

§. 463. 1. The second attributive construction is the attributive genitive; as, οἱ τοῦ δένδρου καρποί, or οἱ καρποὶ οἱ τοῦ δένδρου, or τοῦ δένδρου οἱ καρποί, or οἱ καρποὶ τοῦ δένδρου — ἡ τοῦ Σωκράτους σοφία, or ἡ σοφία ἡ τοῦ Σ., or τοῦ Σ. ἡ σοφία, or ἡ σοφία τοῦ Σ. On the position of the Article see §. 458.

2. The most general power of the genitive is, *procession from, production, dependence on,* expressive of something, which is the cause of, creates (*gignit*), contains, possesses; so that the substantive to which an attributive genitive is annexed denotes something caused, created, contained, possessed by the person or thing signified by the attributive genitive.

3. Hence in the genitive is implied a verbal notion of creation, &c. whereby the two substantives are joined together, so as to form a perfect complex notion; as, τὰ τῶν ἀνθρώπων: which might be more fully expressed by τὰ τῶν ἀνθρώπων (πραχθέντα), ὁ τοῦ πατρὸς υἱός, the son springing from — produced by (verbal notion implied in gen.) the father: ἡ τοῦ τυράννου δύναμις, the power (proceeding from—residing in) the tyrant.

§. 464. The attributive genitive is either subjective—objective or causative—or passive, according to the place it would occupy if the complex notion were to be resolved by the verbal notion implied in the genitive.

Subjective—when it would stand for the subject: οἱ τοῦ δένδρου καρποί = τὸ δένδρον φέρει καρπούς — τὸ τῆς σοφίας κάλλος = ἡ σοφία παρέχει κάλλος. So, τὰ τοῦ Ὁμήρου ποιήματα — ὁ τοῦ βασιλέως υἱός. So Homer: τέλος θανάτοιο (Il. π, 502.), the end produced by death—ἡ τοῦ ἀνδρὸς ἀρετή—τὰ τῶν ἀνθρώπων πράγματα — τὸ τοῦ πατρὸς ῥόδον — ὁ τοῦ υἱοῦ πατήρ: Od. ι, 202 χρυσοῦ μέν μοι δῶκ᾽ εὐεργέος ἑπτὰ τάλαντα: — τὸ τοῦ πίθου μέλι — δέπας οἴνου = οἶνος πλήθει δέπας: Od. ι, 196 αἴγεον ἀσκὸν ἔχον μέλανος οἴνοιο: — σταγόνες ὕδατος.

Objective or causative—when it would occupy the place of the object of an intransitive verb; as, ἡ τῆς σοφίας ἐπιθυμία = (Σωκράτης) ἐπεθύμει τῆς σοφίας. It is called causative because that which it expresses is the cause of the notion of the verb. So πόθος υἱοῦ, *desiderium filii*, regret for a son: ἔχθος, ἔχθρα, φιλία, εὐμένεια, εὔνοιά τινος, enmity &c. against any one: Soph. Œ. C. 631 τίς δῆτ᾽ ἂν ἀνδρὸς εὐμένειαν ἐκβάλοι τοιοῦδε; Eur. Or. 422 τὸ Τροίας μῖσος, *odium propter Trojam susceptum*[a]: Id. Androm. 1060 γυναικὸς αἰχμαλωτίδος φόβος:— ἐπιμέλεια τῶν πολεμικῶν ἔργων. So Soph. Antig. 1185 εὔγματα Παλλάδος, prayers to P. (εὔχεσθαί τινι): Plat. Apol. p. 23 B ἡ τοῦ θεοῦ λατρεία[b]: Id. Phædr. p. 245 E καταφυγοῦσα πρὸς θεῶν εὐχάς τε καὶ λατρείας. Also, when the verb would be transmissive, and have an accusative of the thing but dative of the person; as, θύειν τί τινι, *sacra facere alicui:* Eur. Ion. 1234 θύματα νερτέρων: Id. Iph. T. 317 τὰ τῆς θεοῦ θύματα: Ibid. 443 νέον πρόσφαγμα θεᾶς. Also in prose: τὰ τῶν θεῶν θύματα Plat. Even when an intransitive verb would be joined with a preposition and its case: Eur. Or. 481 σοφίας ἀγών (περὶ σοφίας): Ibid. 812 χρυσέας ἔρις ἀρνός: Thuc. I. 108 ἐν ἀποβάσει τῆς γῆς=ἐπὶ τῆς γῆς: Id. II. 79 ἡ τῶν Πλαταιέων ἐπιστρατεία=πρὸς τοὺς Πλ.

Obs. For the sake of clearness, the preposition which was used to define the original powers of the cases is sometimes added to the objective genitive; as, ἐπιμέλεια περί τινος. So also in the verb ἐπιμελεῖσθαι περί τινος.

Double Genitive.

§. 465. 1. An objective and a subjective genitive may be derived from the same sentence; as, τοῦ πατρὸς πόθος τοῦ υἱοῦ=ὁ πατὴρ ποθεῖ τοῦ υἱοῦ—ἡ τοῦ Σωκράτους σοφίας ἐπιθυμία.

2. [c]The most satisfactory explanation of this double genitive seemingly dependent on one noun, is that the noun and one of the genitives together form one notion; and to that notion is attached a simple attributive genitive: Hdt. VI. 2 Ἱστιαῖος ὑπέδυνε τῶν Ἰώνων—τὴν ἡγεμονίην τοῦ πρὸς Δαρεῖον πολέμου: Thuc. III. 12 διὰ τὴν ἐκείνων—μέλλησιν τῶν εἰς ἡμᾶς δεινῶν: Plat. Rep. τὰς τῶν οἰκείων—προπηλακίσεις τοῦ γήρως. Or the two attributives together form one notion, which is attached as a simple attributive to the noun; as, ὁ τῶν τοῦ βασιλέως ἱππέων στρατηγός.

§. 466. Passive—when it stands as the object of a transitive verb; as, ἡ τῆς πόλεως κτίσις (= κτίζει τὴν πόλιν) — ὁ τῆς ἐπιστολῆς γραφεύς (= γράφει ἐπιστολήν) — ἡ τῶν καλῶν ἔργων πρᾶξις (= καλὰ ἔργα πράττει) — ἀγγελία, λόγος τινός, *de aliqua re:* Eur. Or. 244 λιταὶ θεῶν (λίσσεσθαί τινα).

---

[a] Matthiæ ad hunc loc.　　[b] Stallb. ad loc.　　[c] Darmstadt. Zeitschrift. Sept. 1837.

Obs. 1. This passive genitive is also joined with a subjective; as, ἡ τοῦ Ῥωμύλου τῆς πόλεως κτίσις = ὁ Ῥώμυλος κτίζει τὴν πόλιν.

Obs. 2. There are yet many other combinations of the attributive genitive; as, πρόβλημα, ἐπικούρημά τινος, *præsidium contra aliquid*, Prose: Xen. Anab. IV. 5, 13 ἐπικούρημα τῆς χιόνος. So Demosth. p. 41, 5 ἐπιτειχίσματα τῆς αὑτοῦ (*Philippi*) χώρας, against his land : Eur. Hipp. 716 εὕρημα συμφορᾶς, means against misfortune : Soph. Œ. C. 324 ὦ δισσὰ πατρὸς καὶ κασιγνήτης ἐμοὶ ἥδιστα προσφώνημαθ'. See Index—*Attributive Genitive*.

Obs. 3. For the objective and passive genitive the proper case of the verb is sometimes used; as, ἡ τοῖς φίλοις βοήθεια, ἡ ἑκάστῳ διανέμησις, πρὸς ἐπίδειξιν τοῖς ξένοις. This is always the construction of substantival infinitives : as, τὸ μισθοῦν τὸν οἶκον, τὸ τοῖς θεοῖς εὔχεσθαι.

Apposition.

§. 467. 1. The third attributive construction is apposition; as, Κῦρος ὁ βασιλεύς : Σωκράτης ὁ σοφός. Apposition is the identifying of one substantival notion with another, to define the latter more clearly. The two substantives agree in case and number, and when the noun apposed is a personal noun, in gender; as, Τόμυρις ἡ βασίλισσα.

2. Apposition arises from a verbal sentence, into which it may be resolved; as, Κῦρος ἦν βασιλεύς.

Obs. 1. In Greek the other attributive expressions assume the form of apposition when they are placed with the article after their substantive : ὁ πατὴρ ὁ ἀγαθός — οἱ ἄνθρωποι οἱ νῦν — τὸ κάλλος τὸ τῆς ἀρετῆς.

3. Apposition is used also with the substantival pronoun; as, ἡμεῖς οἱ σοφοί : ἐκεῖνος ὁ βασιλεύς : and even to the personal pronoun implied in the verb; as, Thuc. I. 137 Θεμιστοκλῆς ἥκω παρά σε : Eur. Andr. 1072 οἵας ὁ τλήμων ἀγγελῶν ἥκω τύχας : Lucian. D. D. XXIV. 2 ὁ δὲ Μαίας τῆς Ἀτλαντος διακονοῦμαι αὐτοῖς (for ἐγὼ ὁ Μαίας sc. υἱός).

4. When the apposition is used with a possessive pronoun, the apposed noun is in the genitive, to agree. with the gen. of the personal pronoun implied in the possessive : ἐμὸς τοῦ ἀθλίου βίος — τἀμὰ τοῦ δυστήνου κακά — σῇ τῆς καλλίστης εὐμορφία — ἐμὸς αὐτοῦ πατήρ — ἡμέτερος αὐτῶν πατήρ : Od. α, 7 αὐτῶν γὰρ σφετέρῃσιν ἀτασθαλίῃσιν ὄλοντο : Il. ρ, 226 ὑμέτερον δὲ ἑκάστου θυμὸν ἀέξω : Demosth. p. 42, 7 τὰ ὑμέτερ' αὐτῶν κομιεῖσθε (*recuperabitis*). So also with adj. derived from the names of persons : Il. β, 54 Νεστορέῃ παρὰ νηΐ Πυληγενέος βασιλῆος : Il. ε, 741 ἐν δέ τε Γοργείη κεφαλὴ δεινοῖο πελώρου : Plat. Lach. princ. παππῷον ὄνομ' ἔχει τοὐμοῦ πατρός, his grandfather, who was my father. So Id. Apol. p. 29 D Ἀθηναῖος ὢν πόλεως τῆς

μεγίστης. More remarkable is Xen. Anab. IV. 7, 22 γέρρα δασειῶν βοῶν ὠμοβοῖνα.

Obs. 2. There is an apposition, mostly poetic, when a word of wider signification is narrowed and defined by the apposition of another word of less wide signification : Il. ε, 122 γυῖα δ᾽ ἔθηκεν ἐλαφρὰ, πόδας καὶ χεῖρας ὕπερθεν : Il. θ, 48. ξ, 283 ῎Ιδην δ᾽ ἵκανεν πολυπίδακα, μητέρα θηρῶν, Γάργαρον, one of the peaks of Ida. (See Index, *Acc.*) In prose : Xen. Cyr. V. 4, 6 ἦσαν δὲ μάλα πάντες πιεζόμενοι——οἱ τοῦ Γαδάτα ἱππεῖς: V. 4, 16 οἱ δὲ Καδούσιοι ἐσώζοντο——ἀμφὶ δείλην οἱ πρῶτοι.

Obs. 3. ῾Ως is sometimes prefixed to the apposed word : Hdt. III. 86 οἱ δὲ καταθορόντες ἀπὸ τῶν ἵππων προσεκύνεον τὸν Δαρεῖον, ὡς βασιλῆα, ut regem.

Accusative in apposition to Sentence, see *Accusative Case.*

———◆———

CHAP. III.

Objective Construction.

§. 468. 1. In the objective construction a substantival notion is represented as standing in certain relations to a verbal notion. And as the substantival stands as it were over against the verbal notion, it is called the object ; as, ἐπιθυμῶ τῆς σοφίας—γράφω τὴν ἐπιστολήν — εὔχομαι τοῖς θεοῖς — ἔστη παρὰ τῷ βασιλεῖ — καλῶς ἐμαχέσατο — γελῶν εἶπε — ἐπιθυμῶ γράφειν.

2. The objective relations are,

   a. Local.
   b. Temporal.
   c. Causal.
   d. Modal.

a. The objective relations of place were originally expressed by the cases, afterwards by the prepositions and local adverbs ; as, Il. ρ, 372 νέφος δ᾽ οὐ φαίνετο πάσης γαίας (later ἀπὸ πάσης γ.) : Il. ι, 663 ᾽Αχιλλεὺς εὗδε μυχῷ κλισίης (later ἐν μυχῷ) : Il. α, 317 κνίσση δ᾽ οὐρανὸν ἷκε (later εἰς οὐρανόν). So later ἦλθε παρὰ τοῦ βασιλέως, &c.

b. Time—by the cases ; later by prepositions and temporal adverbs: τῆς ἡμέρας, τῇ ἡμέρᾳ, τὴν ἡμέραν — ἐν τῇ ἡμέρᾳ, παρὰ τὴν ἡμέραν, πρὸ τῆς ἡμέρας ἦλθεν. — νῦν ἦλθεν —. And by the participle (as Gerund) ; as, ἡμέρας ἐλθούσης ἀπέφυγον οἱ πολέμιοι, — ταῦτα ποιήσας (thereupon) ἀπέβη.

c. Causal—including the notions of the cause, origin, effect, object of the verb—by the cases, and sometimes by prepositions; as, ἐπιθυμῶ τῆς σοφίας, γράφω ἐπιστολήν, εὔχομαι θεοῖς, δίδωμι τὴν ἐπιστολὴν τῷ πατρί, ὑπὸ δέους ἀπέφυγεν. Also by the infin. and participle; as, ἐπιθυμῶ γράφειν — ταῦτα λέγων ἁμαρτάνοις ἄν, if you say this: ἦλθεν ἀγγελῶν, to inform &c.

d. Modal—generally by modal adverbs, but also by the cases, and sometimes by the participle; as, καλῶς ἔλεξεν — δίκῃ δημοσίᾳ ἔπραξεν—σὺν δίκῃ ἔπραξεν — γελῶν ἔλεξεν. The relation between the object and the verb is signified by the inflexion of the objective word, this being the principal feature of the sentence, as in the predicative construction the predicate is inflected.

Obs. 1. The objective construction always consists of a verbal and substantival notion, and when the objective notion is expressed by a part. or inf., these forms are to be considered as substantival expressions, like the supines and gerund in Latin: *venit nunciatum, ridendo dicere verum* — γελῶν (ridendo) εἰπεῖν τἀληθές, βούλομαι λέγειν (= τὸ λέγειν).

Obs. 2. As by the members of the predicative construction is formed one thought, and of the attributive one substantival notion, so the parts of the objective together form one verbal notion; as, οἶνον χέειν (= οἰνοχοεύειν)—ναῦς πηγνύναι (=ναυπηγεῖν)—καρποὺς φέρειν (=καρποφορεῖν)—καλῶς ἱερεύειν (= καλλιερεῖν).

Complex objective Sentence.

§. 469. A simple objective sentence, consisting of a predicate and an object, may stand in further relations to other objects, and may be manifoldly complex, inasmuch as there are four objective relations (place, time, cause, mood), and each of these may itself be expressed in different forms. But this combination of various forms, standing in different relations to the same predicate, expresses one verbal thought; as, οἱ Ἕλληνες παρεσκευάσαντο πόλεμον: and, another object being added, πρὸς τοὺς Πέρσας: and again, διὰ τὴν Ἑλλάδα—— τὸν αὐτὸν χρόνον — δεινῶς: as, οἱ Ἕλληνες τὸν αὐτὸν χρόνον διὰ τὴν Ἑλλάδα δεινῶς παρεσκευάσαντο πόλεμον πρὸς τοὺς Πέρσας. Each new object depends on the original one, so that the various objects are here linked together into one sentence; and the relation in which the several objects stand to each other depends on the importance of the element which each adds to the whole sentence, the less being always subordinate to the more important. The most usual order is—causal, local, temporal, modal notions; but, for the sake of clearness, the number of objects must be limited, so that the unity of the sentence may be easily perceived.

The simple Objective Relation.

PRELIMINARY REMARK.

§. 470. The four modes of expressing the objective relations—the cases, prepositions, adverbs, participials—will be treated of in their order;

but the prepositions are so mixed up with the cases, that it will be impossible not to touch upon them under that head, though the full development of their powers and usages will be reserved till its proper place.

The Cases standing as the Object of the Verb.

§. 471. 1. A sentence expresses a thought, or succession of notions, standing in certain relations and order to each other. Language, therefore, as being the expression of the operations of the mind, is the transcript of those notions represented in the relations, and in the order, in which they stand to each other in the mind.

2. The several objects of the verb, together with the verbal notion, make up the whole verbal thought, whereby the subject is represented to be engaged in some action, or to be in some state, more or less complex, as the objective notions attached to the verb are many or few.

·3. Every verbal thought is either of an action or a state, and in every such thought there is one principal notion expressing the essence of such action or state, to which the others which depend on it stand in certain relations ; and therefore in language there will be some principal word expressive of that principal notion, to which the other words will stand in relations analogous to their order in the mind. If this principal notion of the whole verbal thought be taken, any other notion must stand in one of three relations to it : it must either have preceded it,—or be implied in it as part of it,—or must follow it ; whence these three relations may be called, 1. *Antecedent*, 2. *Coincident*, 3. *Consequent* [a].

4. Hence, strictly speaking, no language can have more than three cases ; but as the development of the original powers of language kept pace with the requirements of a more civilized state of society, in which the various relations of things and persons were more accurately perceived and distinguished, it followed naturally that in many languages the original relation of each case was, as it were, split into several, and the parts so separated were expressed in language by a corresponding modification of form. In Greek,

---

[a] It is proper to state that Professor Kühner is in no way answerable for the principles or arrangement of the cases given in this and the following pages ; as his system, which makes the cases to depend on the external direction, or position, of *whence* (genitive), *whither* (accusative), *where* (dative), has been entirely departed from. His examples of the construction of the several verbs are, with some alterations, retained.

however, the original number was retained. The three cases in the Greek language are,

1. The *Genitive;* expressing the notion which in the mind precedes the principal notion of the thought, i. e. the *Antecedent notion;* as, ἐπιθυμέω σοφίας, the antecedent perception of σοφία being necessary to the conception of ἐπιθυμία. It mostly expresses the cause or origin of the notion; hence genitive, (γίγνομαι, *gigno.*)

2. The *Accusative;* expressing the notion which is implied in that principal notion as part of it, i. e. the *Coincident notion;* as, χαίρω χαράν.

3. The *Dative;* expressing the notion which follows on the principal notion, i. e. the *Consequent notion:* δίδωμί σοι, receiving being consequent on giving. It is mostly used in notions of transmission to another ; hence dative, (*do, dare.*)

Obs. It must be observed, that it is no explanation of the real power of the Greek cases to translate them by the English *of, to,* &c., which is frequently done; for these forms of expression being prepositions, cannot explain the true powers of a form which is independent of prepositions. But the English prepositions will be used in the following pages, e. g: *from,* not to account for the case, but to denote the notion of separation, which implies an antecedent notion.

Origin of Prepositions.

§. 472. 1. But as language expresses not only the order of internal thought, but also the circumstances of external things ; and as the relations in which these things stand to us in respect of their position were too manifold to be sufficiently defined by the simple powers of the cases, it happened that as men examined into and comprehended the position of external things, some further mode of expression became necessary, and cases of certain words, which from their original meaning were fitted for the expression of these relations, were so frequently used to express them, that at last they were appropriated to this function, and lost more or less their original meaning, as ἀπό, παρά, while χάριν, δίκην, which are, so to say, in the transition state between cases and prepositions, being sometimes used as one, sometimes as the other, will illustrate the mode by which prepositions arose.

2. But though a relation which was implied in the powers of the original cases might be, and generally was, for the sake of clearness, expressed by a preposition, yet it does not follow that the original power of the cases to express this relation was either in theory or practice wholly lost ; so that we find the same rela-

tion expressed sometimes by the original, more concise and vivid form of the case, at others by the later and more accurate form of the preposition.

3. Hence may be seen the mistake of explaining the construction of cases by the ellipse of a preposition, making the preposition the original and most perfect, the case the later and defective form; thus shutting out from view the real state of the case, and teaching the student to rest contented with an unphilosophical pretended explanation, instead of leading him to search out the abstract powers of the cases, which were entirely obscured by thus supplying a preposition whenever they most really came into play.

General Observations on the Greek Cases.

§. 473. There is a remarkable contrast between the Greek and the modern system of cases. The moderns, always taking a cold rationalistic view of things, look upon every thing as inanimate, produced or affected: the Greek language, with fresher, more poetical spirit, looked on every thing as more or less animate, as an agent, producing or working; and hence, where in modern languages we find a transitive verb with the acc. of the thing as a patient, the Greeks used an intransitive verb with the gen. of the thing as an agent, representing the action of the verb as proceeding from it. So, where in German the verb hören, *to hear*, has an accusative, the Greeks used the genitive. In their view, the object entered the mind rather as the antecedent cause than as the coincident effect; but in some verbs, either the former principle prevailed altogether, or sometimes; so that we find particular verbs with an accusative, while the other expressions of the same notion have a genitive, or the same verb sometimes with a genitive or an accusative *ex animo loquentis*.

Nominative and Vocative.

§. 474. The nominative and vocative cannot be termed, in a proper grammatical sense, cases, as they express no objective relations; but as they have certain peculiarities in Greek different from other languages, and as they do, in fact, perform certain objective functions (see §. 475. 2., §. 477. 3.), we must treat of them as belonging to the cases.

Nominative.

§. 475. 1. The Nominative expresses the subject of the sentence: τὸ ῥόδον ἀνθεῖ. When the predicate is not expressed by a verb, but by a noun with εἶναι, the noun is in the nominative; as, ἡ ἀρετή ἐστι καλή — ὁ Κῦρος ἦν βασιλεύς.

Obs. 1. The nominative, as expressing the subject, represents a thing independently existing, in and for itself; so that the name of any thing or person, which is to be represented as really independent of the other notions in the sentence, is often put in the nominative instead of an oblique case, generally in constructions with ὄνομα, ἐπωνυμία (especially in the phrases ὄνομά ἐστί μοι, ὄνομα ἔχω), or even with verbs of naming in the active voice; though in this construction the name can also stand in the accusative, as in apposition; as, Od. η, 54 Ἀρήτη δ᾽ ὄνομ᾽ ἐστιν ἐπώνυμον: Hdt. III. 85 Δαρείῳ δὲ ἦν ἱπποκόμος, τῷ οὔνομα ἦν Οἰβάρης: Ibid. 88. (in orat. obl. the Acc.; Id. VI. 52 τῇ οὔνομα εἶναι Ἀργείην: Ibid. καὶ οἱ οὔνομα τεθῆναι Εὐρυσθένεα, τῷ δὲ νεωτέρῳ Προκλέα. So ibid. 63 Δημάρητον δὲ αὐτῷ οὔνομα ἔθετο): Id. I. 199 Μύλιττα δὲ καλέουσι τὴν Ἀφροδίτην: Æschin. p. 41 προσείληφε τὴν τῶν πονηρῶν κοινὴν ἐπωνυμίαν συκοφάντης.

2. The following intransitive and passive verbs: εἶναι in the sense of *to be esteemed, valeo* ; δύνασθαι, *valeo* (in notions of value it has the acc.), ὑπάρχειν, γίγνεσθαι, φῦναι, κυρεῖν poet., αὐξάνεσθαι; μένειν, καταστῆναι; ἐοικέναι, φαίνεσθαι, δηλοῦσθαι; καλεῖσθαι, ὀνομάζεσθαι, λέγεσθαι, ἀκούειν (to be called, *audire ;* poet. κλύειν) &c.; αἱρεῖσθαι, ἀποδείκνυσθαι, κρίνεσθαι &c.; νομίζεσθαι, ὑπολαμβάνεσθαι &c. take the nominative to express the object of the verbal notion: Hdt. III. 132 ἦν δὲ μέγιστον πρῆγμα Δημοκήδης παρὰ βασιλέϊ: Ibid. 157 πάντα δὴ ἦν ἐν τοῖσι Βαβυλωνίοισι Ζώπυρος. So εἶναι, especially in definitions of size; as, Id. II. 29 τὸ δὲ χωρίον τοῦτο ἔστι ἐπὶ ἡμέρας τέσσερας πλόος: Id. III. 90 τριηκόσια ἦν τάλαντα φόρος: Thuc. I. 96 ἦν δὲ ὁ πρῶτος φόρος ταχθεὶς τετρακόσια τάλαντα καὶ ἑξήκοντα: Hdt. II. 30 δύναται δὲ τοῦτο τὸ ἔπος κατὰ τὴν Ἑλλήνων γλῶσσαν οἱ ἐξ ἀριστερῆς χειρὸς παριστάμενοι βασιλέϊ. Ὁ Κῦρος ἐγένετο βασιλεὺς τῶν Περσῶν: Eur. Or. 742 οὐ γὰρ αἰχμητὴς πέφυκεν (Menelaus), ἐν γυναιξὶ δ᾽ ἄλκιμος: Demosth. p. 19, 5 τούτοις ὁ Φίλιππος μέγας ηὐξήθη[a]: Id. p. 20, 8 διὰ τούτων ἤρθη μέγας: Demosth. p. 241 ἀντὶ γὰρ φίλων καὶ ξένων — νῦν κόλακες καὶ θεοῖς ἐχθροὶ — ἀκούουσιν (*audiunt*).

Obs. 2. These verbs in the active have a double accusative; the verbs ὀνομάζειν, ὀνομάζεσθαι, frequently add εἶναι to the nom. or acc.; as, Hdt. IV. 33 τὰς ὀνομάζουσι Δήλιοι εἶναι Ὑπερόχην τε καὶ Λαοδίκην: Xen. Apol. Socr. §. 13 μάντεις ὀνομάζουσι τοὺς προσημαίνοντας εἶναι: Plat. Rep. p. 428 E ὀνομάζονταί τινες εἶναι, *aliquod nomen habent*[b]: Similarly Hdt. II. 44 ἱρὸν Ἡρακλέος, ἐπωνυμίην ἔχοντος Θασίου εἶναι.

Nominative for the Vocative.

§. 476. The nominative is used for the vocative in the Attic and later poetry, and very frequently in prose.

a. Very commonly οὗτος, (rarely αὕτη) with a subst. in the nominative; also οὗτος without any nominative when a command is addressed to any one; οὗτος here has the force of the Latin *heus. a.* Without the article: Soph. Aj. 89 ὦ οὗτος Αἴας, δεύτερόν σε προσκαλῶ. So οὗτος, very frequently with the verbs καλῶ, φωνῶ &c., with an accusative of the person addressed:

a Bremi ad loc.   b Stallb. ad loc.

Soph. Aj. 71—73 οὗτος, σέ, τὸν — ἀπευθύνοντα, προσμολεῖν καλῶ, Αἴαντα φωνῶ· στεῖχε δωμάτων πάρος : Eur. Or. 1562 sq. οὗτος σύ, κλῄθρων τῶνδε μὴ ψαύσῃς χερί, Μενέλαον εἶπον, ὃς πεπύργωσαι θράσει : Id. Med. 922 αὕτη, τί χλωροῖς δακρύοις τέγγεις κόρας ; Id. Hec. 1127 οὗτος τί πάσχεις ; *heus tu, quid cœptas* [a] *?* Id. Alc. 776 οὗτος, τί σεμνὸν καὶ πεφροντικὸς βλέπεις ; Plat. Protag. p. 193 D καὶ ἐγὼ τὴν φωνὴν γνοὺς αὐτοῦ, Ἱπποκράτης, ἔφην, οὗτος, μή τι νεώτερον ἀπαγγέλλεις ; Id. Sympos. p. 213 B Σωκράτης οὗτος ἔλλοχῶν — ἐνταῦθα κατέκεισο. *b.* With the article : Plat. Symp. princ. ὁ Φαληρεύς, ἔφη, οὗτος Ἀπολλόδωρος, οὐ περιμενεῖς [b] ; Theocr. V. 102 οὐκ ἀπὸ τᾶς δρυὸς, οὗτος ὁ Κώναρος ἅ τε Κυναίθα, τουτεὶ βοσκησεῖσθε ποτ᾽ ἀντολάς ;

b. The nominative of substantives, without οὗτος, but with the article prefixed, is used in the same way : Arist. Acharn. 242 πρόϊθ᾽ ἐς τὸ πρόσθεν ὀλίγον ἡ κανηφόρος : Plat. Symp. p. 218 B οἱ δὲ οἰκέται, καὶ εἴ τις ἄλλος ἐστὶ βέβηλός τε καὶ ἄγροικος, πύλας πάνυ μεγάλας τοῖς ὠσὶν ἐπίθεσθε.

c. In addressing a person, when the substantive is defined by an attributive in apposition, the article is always prefixed to the attributive ; as, Xen. Cyr. IV. 5, 17 ἴθι μὲν οὖν σύ, ἔφη, ὁ πρεσβύτατος : Ibid. 22 σὺ δ᾽, ἔφη, ὁ τῶν Ὑρκανίων ἄρχων, ὑπόμεινον : Plat. Hipp. princ. Ἱππίας ὁ καλός τε καὶ σοφός, ὡς διὰ χρόνου κατῆρας ἡμῖν.

Obs. Distinct from these is the Homeric use of the nominative in passages such as Il. α, 231 δημοβόρος βασιλεύς, ἐπεὶ οὐτιδανοῖσιν ἀνάσσεις : ε, 403 σχέτλιος, ὀβριμοεργός, ὃς οὐκ ὄθετ᾽ αἴσυλα ῥέζων. These are predicative sentences expressed with emphatic brevity, by the ellipse of the copula εἶναι.

Especial Peculiarities in the use of the Nominative.

1. *Anacolouthon.*

§. 477. 1. Sometimes a word of especial significance in the sentence is placed at the beginning of the sentence in the nominative, to represent it emphatically as the fundamental subject of the whole sentence, though the grammatical construction requires a dependent case : Plat. Cratyl. p. 403 A ὁ δὲ Ἅιδης, οἱ πολλοὶ μέν μοι δοκοῦσιν ἀπολαμβάνειν τὸ ἀειδὲς προσειρῆσθαι τῷ ὀνόματι τούτῳ : Ibid. p. 404 C Περσέφαττα δέ, πολλοὶ μὲν καὶ τοῦτο φοβοῦνται τὸ ὄνομα : Id. Gorg. p. 474 E καὶ μὴν τά γε κατὰ τοὺς νόμους καὶ τὰ ἐπιτηδεύματα, οὐ δήπου ἐκτὸς τούτων ἐστὶ τὰ καλά.

2. Analogously to this the nominative is used, in seeming apposition to a substantive of a preceding sentence in an oblique case, (especially after οἷον.) The nominative is so placed to express the subject of a new thought suggested by the former substantive, the verb εἶναι being supplied by the mind : Il. ζ, 395 Ἀνδρομάχη, θυγάτηρ μεγαλήτορος Ἠετίωνος, Ἠετίων, ὃς ἔναιεν κ. τ. λ. : Il. κ, 437 τοῦ δὴ καλλίστους ἵππους ἴδον ἠδὲ μεγίστους· λευκότεροι χιόνος, θείειν δ᾽ ἀνέμοισιν ὁμοῖοι : Plat. Soph. p. 266 D τίθημι δύο διχῇ ποιητικῆς εἴδη· θεία μὲν καὶ ἀνθρωπίνη κατὰ θάτερον τμῆμα : Ibid. p. 218 E τί δῆτα προστάξαιμέ᾽ ἂν εὔγνωστον μὲν καὶ σμικρόν— ; οἷον ἀσπαλιευτής.

3. A participle in the nominative, either with or without the substantive, is sometimes referred as an attributive to an oblique case : the notion being grammatically the object, but logically (*ex animo loquentis*)

---

the subject of the verb; as, δοκεῖ μοι (= ἡγοῦμαι) ὁρῶν — αἰδώς μ' ἔχει (= αἰδοῦμαι) τάδε πράξας.

Obs. For this and other remarkable usages of the nominative participle, see *Index.*

2. Σχῆμα καθ' ὅλον καὶ μέρος.

§. 478. When the action of a whole body is attributed likewise to each individual of that body (σχῆμα καθ' ὅλον καὶ μέρος), the whole is put in the nominative instead of the genitive, each part thereof being considered as in apposition to the whole. So the nom. is used with ἕκαστος, ἑκάτερος, πᾶς, ἄλλος (espec. ἄλλος ἄλλοθεν), οἱ μέν — οἱ δέ. The whole subject is frequently not expressed, but only implied in the verb: Il. η, 175 οἱ δὲ κλῆρον ἐσημήναντο ἕκαστος: Il. ι, 311 ὡς μή μοι τρύζητε παρήμενοι ἄλλοθεν ἄλλος: Od. a, 424 δὴ τότε κακκείοντες ἔβαν οἰκόνδε ἕκαστος, i. e. *in suam quisque domum sese contulerunt:* Il. λ, 571 τὰ δὲ δοῦρα—ἄλλα μὲν ἐν σάκεϊ μεγάλῳ πάγεν—' πολλὰ δέ — ἐν γαίῃ ἵσταντο: cf. Od. a, 109 sqq. κήρυκες οἱ μέν —, οἱ δέ —: Hdt. III. 158 ἔμενον ἐν τῇ ἑωυτοῦ τάξι ἕκαστος, *in suo quisque ordine manserunt:* Thuc. I. 89 οἰκίαι αἱ μὲν πολλαὶ (for πολλ. μὲν) ἐπεπτώκεσαν, ὀλίγαι δὲ περιῆσαν: Xen. Rep. Lac. VI. 1 ἐν μὲν γὰρ ταῖς ἄλλαις πόλεσι τῶν ἑαυτοῦ ἕκαστος καὶ παίδων καὶ οἰκετῶν καὶ χρημάτων ἄρχουσιν, *suis quisque liberis imperant:* Xen. Cyr. III. 1. 3 διεδίδρασκον ἤδη ἕκαστος ἐπὶ τὰ ἑαυτοῦ, βουλόμενος τὰ ὄντα ἐκποδὼν ποιεῖσθαι: Plat. Charm. princ. καί με ὡς εἶδον εἰσιόντα ἐξ ἀπροσδοκήτου εὐθὺς πόρρωθεν ἠσπάζοντο ἄλλος ἄλλοθεν: Ibid. p. 153 D ἠρώτων δὲ ἄλλος ἄλλο: Id. Symp. p. 180 E ἀναγκαῖον δὴ καὶ Ἔρωτα τὸν μὲν—πάνδημον ὀρθῶς καλεῖσθαι, τὸν δὲ οὐράγιον: cf. Phædr. p. 255 C πηγή—ἡ μὲν ἐς αὐτὸν ἔδυ, ἡ δὲ—ἀπορρεῖ : Demosth. p. 54, 49 οἱ δὲ λόγους πλάττοντες ἕκαστος περιερχόμεθα. But sometimes the number of the verb is not regulated by the whole subject, but by the apposed particulars, ἕκαστος, πᾶς, &c.: Il. π, 264 οἱ δὲ (σφῆκες) ἄλκιμον ἦτορ ἔχοντες πρόσσω πᾶς πέτεται, καὶ ἀμύνει οἷσι τέκεσσιν: Xen. Anab. II. 1, 15 οὗτοι μὲν — ἄλλος ἄλλα λέγει: Ibid. I. 8, 9 πάντες δὲ οὗτοι κατὰ ἔθνη ἐν πλαισίῳ πλήρει ἀνθρώπων ἕκαστον ἔθνος ἐπορεύετο: Plat. Rep. p. 346 D καὶ αἱ ἄλλαι (τέχναι) πᾶσαι οὕτω τὸ αὑτῆς ἑκάστη ἔργον ἐργάζεται καὶ ὠφελεῖ ἐκεῖνο, ἐφ' ᾧ τέτακται: Id. Gorg. p. 503 E καὶ οἱ ἄλλοι πάντες δημιουργοὶ βλέποντες πρὸς τὸ αὑτῶν ἔργον ἕκαστος — προσφέρει (*confert*), ἃ προσφέρει πρὸς τὸ ἔργον τὸ αὑτοῦ[a].

Vocative.

§. 479. 1. The vocative is the expression of "calling" or "addressing" any one. It has no influence on the syntax, as it is inserted in the sentence without any grammatical connection with the other words. It is not at all essential to a language, as may be seen from its not existing in many languages, its place being supplied by the nominative, as is the case even in Greek, in the whole neuter gender, and in many masculine and feminine words, and even where there is a proper vocative form (II. Decl. in ος), the nominative is frequently used in its place; as, Il. γ, 277 Ζεῦ πάτερ, Ἠέλιός θ', ὃς πάντ' ἐφορᾷς: Od. a, 301 καὶ σύ, φίλος, — ἄλκιμος ἔσσι.

2. The vocative has the interjection ὦ prefixed to it; in prose almost invariably—in poetry less frequently, and generally with some pathetic force.

[a] Stallb. ad loc.

3. *Position of ὦ.*—When ὦ is joined to a substantive and adjective, either the substantive or adjective is placed first, as one or other of them is the more emphatic ; ὦ καλοὶ παῖδες : but Soph. El. 86 ὦ φάος ἁγνόν, *o lux pura,* "*quia lux, non quod pura, sed quod lux est, invocatur. Opponuntur enim statim tenebræ. Tum eodem modo, ubi substantivum et adjectivum quasi pro uno vocabulo sunt, ut* ὦ Ζεῦ πατρῷε [a]." Aristoph. Eq. 108 ὦ δαῖμον ἀγαθέ : Plat. Soph. p. 230 C ὦ παῖ φίλε. Sometimes (mostly Epic) it is placed between the adjective and substantive, as a pathetic expression : Il. δ, 189 φίλος ὦ Μενέλαε : ρ, 716 ἀγακλεὲς ὦ Μενέλαε. So in the Odyssey πάτερ ὦ ξεῖνε : Soph. Aj. 395 ἔρεβος ὦ φαεννότατον : Eur. Or. 1252 Μυκηνίδες ὦ φίλαι : El. 167 Ἀγαμέμνονος ὦ κόρα. Even Plat. Euthyd. p. 271 C θαυμάσι ὦ Κρίτων. Sometimes ὦ is repeated, but always with great emphasis : Soph. Phil. 799 ὦ τέκνον ὦ γενναῖον ὦ γενναῖον τέκνον. In forms of entreaty with πρός, the preposition with its case is sometimes placed between ὦ and the vocative : Plat. Apol. S. p. 25 C ἔτι δὲ ἡμῖν εἰπὲ ὦ πρὸς Διὸς Μέλιτε.

4. Sometimes in poetry an adjective belonging to the predicate, which should stand in the nominative, is in the vocative, by attraction to a foregoing vocative ; as, Soph. Aj. 695. ὦ Πάν, Πὰν ἀλίπλαγκτε — φάνηθι : Id. Phil. 671 ἰὼ δύστηνε σύ, δύστηνε δῆτα διὰ πόνων φανείς = ὃς ἐφάνης δύστηνος : Theocr. XVII. 66 ὄλβιε κῶρε γένοιο [b]. The foregoing vocative may even be omitted : Fragm. Callimach. (in Schol. Paris. ad Apoll. Rhod. II. 866) ἀντὶ γὰρ ἐκλήθης Ἴμβρασε Παρθενίου, *tu, Imbrase, Imbrasus vocatus es pro Parthenio.* So in Latin : Tibull. I. 7, 53 *Sic venias hodierne :* Horat. Sat. II. 6, 30 *Matutine pater, seu J a n e libentius audis.*

5. A vocative is very often followed by a particle which connects it with the following sentence, (a) by μέν with δέ following : Il. ε, 230 Αἰνεία· σὺ μὲν αὐτὸς ἔχ᾽ ἡνία καὶ τεὼ ἵππω — τόνδε δ᾽ ἐγὼν ἐπιόντα δεδέξομαι ὀξεῖ δουρί.—(β) δέ, generally in a transition from one thought to another : from a narration to an address to a person, or from one person to another : Il. a, 282 Ἀτρείδη, σὺ δὲ παῦε τεὸν μένος : Il. φ, 448 Φοῖβε, σὺ δ᾽ εἰλίποδας ἕλικας βοῦς βουκολέεσκες. Frequently in the tragedians : Eur. Hec. 372 μῆτερ, σὺ δ᾽ ἡμῖν μηδὲν ἐμποδὼν γένῃ [c] : Ibid. 1287 Ἑκάβη, σὺ δ᾽, ὦ τάλαινα, διπτύχους νεκροὺς στείχουσα θάπτε : Id. Or. 622 Μενέλαε, σοὶ δὲ τάδε λέγω [d] : Ibid. 1065 Πυλάδη, σὺ δ᾽ ἡμῖν τοῦ φόνου γενοῦ βραβεύς : Ibid. 1675 Ὀρέστα, σοὶ δὲ παῖδ᾽ ἐγὼ κατεγγυῶ. On the contrary : Ibid. 1643 sq. τὰ μὲν καθ᾽ Ἑλένην ὧδ᾽ ἔχει· σὲ δ᾽ αὖ χρεὼν, Ὀρέστα. Also in prose : Hdt. I. 115 ὦ δέσποτα, ἐγὼ δὲ ταῦτα τοῦτον ἐποίησα σὺν δίκῃ : Xen. M. S. II. 1, 26 ὦ γύναι, ἔφη, ὄνομα δέ σοι τί ἐστιν : Plat. Leg. p. 890 E ὦ προθυμότατε Κλεινία, τί δ᾽ οὐ χαλεπά τε ἐστί ; The orators and comic writers do not admit this idiom :—in Epic ἀτάρ : Il. ζ, 429 sqq. Ἕκτορ, ἀ τ ὰ ρ σύ μοι ἐσσὶ πατὴρ καὶ πότνια μήτηρ, ἠδὲ κασίγνητος, σὺ δέ μοι θαλερὸς παρακοίτης (ἀτάρ refers to what went before), I have lost all, father, mother, &c. ; but you are, &c. So ἀλλά also in other poets.—(γ) γάρ, very frequently in the Epic language ; the sentence of which γάρ gives the reason, either being supplied by the mind, or placed in an after part of the passage : Od. κ, 501 ὦ Κίρκη, τίς γὰρ ταύτην ὁδὸν ἡγεμονεύσει ; εἰς Ἄϊδος δ᾽ οὔπω τις ἀφίκετο νηῒ μελαίνῃ : Il. η, 328 Ἀτρείδη τε καὶ ἄλλοι ἀριστῆες Παναχαιῶν, πολλοὶ γὰρ τεθνᾶσι (331 τῷ σε χρὴ πόλεμον μὲν ἅμ᾽ ἠοῖ παῦσαι Ἀχαιῶν) : Hdt. III. 63 ὤνθρωπε, φῂς γὰρ ἥκειν παρὰ Σμέρδιος τοῦ Κύρου ἄγγελος· νῦν ὦν εἴπας τὴν

---

[a] Herm. Viger, 794. [b] Kiessling et Wüsteman ad loc. [c] Pflugk ad loc.
[d] Porson et Schæfer ad loc.

ἀληθηίην, ἄπιθι χαίρων· κότερα αὐτός τοι Σμέρδις φαινόμενος ἐς ὄψιν ἐνετέλλετο
ταῦτα, ἢ τῶν τις ἐκείνου ὑπηρετέων; Ibid. 83 ἄνδρες στασιῶται, δῆλα γὰρ
δή, ὅτι ἕνα γέ τινα ἡμέων βασιλέα γενέσθαι: where we must supply " Choose a
king." So ἐπεί: Od. a, 231 ξεῖν'· ἐπεὶ ἄρ δὴ ταῦτά μ' ἀνείρεαι ἠδὲ μεταλ-
λᾷς· (sc. I will tell you, since you ask.) cf. Il. ν, 68.

Dependent Cases.

GENITIVE.

§. 480. 1. The genitive expresses the *antecedent notion :* that
notion which precedes the principal verbal notion in the series
which forms the whole thought.

2. This notion is antecedent as being a notion of

I. C a u s e.—The notion of that, wherefrom any action, or emotion, or state arises, being necessarily antecedent in the mind to
the action or emotion or state itself; as, ἐπιθυμέω σοφίας : the
notion of σοφία must have existed before the feeling of ἐπιθυμία
could have arisen.

Obs. In verbs expressive of those states or energies, which arise from
the antecedent comprehension of the object to which they tend ; as,
ἐπιθυμέω σοφίας, in which ἐπιθυμία arises from the notion of σοφία, and
likewise tends towards it as its end, the antecedent notion, being likewise
the object, must be expressed to make up the objective construction :
ἐπιθυμέω for instance would be an imperfect expression ; but in notions
of action or states, in which there is some other object for the verb to
tend to and rest on, the antecedent cause need only be expressed in the
sentence, if it is wished clearly to state *what* the cause of the action is ;
as, εὐνοίας σοι δίδωμι, I give this to you, because of my good will; but
δίδωμί σοι is in itself a complete thought.

2. R e l a t i o n.—The notion of the correlative being necessary
to the conception of the relative ; as, μείζων τοῦδε.   If we have no
antecedent notion of the person or thing signified by ὅδε, we cannot say that any one is μείζων than him, so that the whole force of
μείζων arises from an antecedent consideration of that which ὅδε
represents.

3. P o s i t i o n.—Where the position (moral, or physical, or
temporal) of any thing is determined by its relation to something
else ; as, πέλας οἴκου : if πέλας is to give any notion at all, we must
antecedently know the situation of οἶκος, so that the whole force
of πέλας arises from an antecedent consideration of οἶκος : so ὡς
ποδῶν εἶχε, the meaning of ὡς arises from our knowledge or supposed knowledge of what were the powers of the πόδες.

4. P a r t i t i o n.—The notion of the whole being antecedently
necessary to the notion of a part ; that is, if we had no notion of
the whole, we could have no notion of the part as a part.

R 2

5. S e p a r a t i o n.—The point whence a motion, action, or state of separation begins, being (if conceived at all) antecedent to the notion of the motion, action, or state ; as, ἔρχομαι δόμων εἶς σε : here δόμων need not be expressed to make a perfect sentence ; but if it is expressed, it must be considered as antecedent to the notion of ἔρχομαι.

6. P r i v a t i o n.—The notion of a thing being antecedently necessary to any notion of being without it ; the whole force of the privative arising from the notion of the positive.

7. M a t e r i a l. —The notion of the material (if expressed) being properly antecedent to the thing made.

Causal Genitive.

§. 481. 1. All verbs *may* have a genitive of the antecedent notion whence their action arises ; as in the Homeric expressions, ἀγγελίης ἐλθεῖν &c.[a] ; as, Il. ν, 252 ἠέ τευ ἀγγελίης μετ᾽ ἔμ᾽ ἤλυθες : Il. ο, 640 ἀγγελίης οἴχνεσκε : Hesiod. Theog. 781 ἀγγελίης πωλεῖται. With some verbs it is *usual* to express the cause, though it is sometimes omitted, the objective sentence being perfect without it.

2. Those intransitive verbal notions, which either have no expressed object at all, or else an object which is likewise the cause of the verbal notion, require the expression of the cause in the genitive, the objective relation being imperfect without. These verbs are said to govern a genitive.

3. The causal genitive will then be treated of by considering

a. Those verbs which take a genitive of the object, as being likewise the cause.

b. Those verbs which very usually, though not always, take a genitive of the cause.

Obs. If (as in the case of the verbs mentioned in *a*) the cause is likewise the object, it follows, that if the objective notion is considered by the speaker rather as the object than the cause, the verb will be joined with an accusative, corresponding to the notion in the speaker's mind. Hence some verbs are constructed with a genitive and dative or accusative, as the thing or person is conceived of as the cause or the object.

§. 482. *a.* Verbs expressing intransitive or passive notions, where the verb has no definite object, or where the source whence the notion of the verb arises is also the object whither it tends,

---

[a] Buttmann (Lexil. ad voc. ἀγγελίη. 5.), who supposes a masc. substantive ἀγγελίης on the authority of some Alexandrian grammarians, but this seems to be needless.

and therefore is the proper case of the verb, which the verb is said, in common grammatical language, to govern. *b.* Where the verb has some other object whither it tends, and therefore the cause need not be expressed in the sentence, but if it is expressed it is in the genitive.

§. 483. Where the verb is *said* to govern a genitive.

Verbs of *proceeding from, becoming, arising, having become* or *arisen, being produced* or *created*, take a genitive of that whence they proceed, &c. ; as, γίγνεσθαι, φῦναι, εἶναι, and in poetry, φυτεύεσθαι, τεκνοῦσθαι: Od. δ, 611 αἵματος εἶς ἀγαθοῖο: cf. Il. τ, 111. Il. φ, 109 πατρὸς δ᾽ εἴμ᾽ ἀγαθοῖο: Il. α, 49 δεινὴ δὲ κλαγγὴ γένετ᾽ ἀργυρέοιο βιοῖο: Soph. Œ. C. 1324 τοῦ κακοῦ πότμου φυτευθείς: Eur. Or. 725 εἰκότως κακῆς γυναικὸς ἄνδρα γίγνεσθαι κακόν: Id. Hec. 383 ἐσθλῶν γενέσθαι. So often in tragedy γεγώς τινος: Eur. Iph. T. 4 τοῦ δ᾽ ἔφυν ἐγώ. (So in the transitive sense, where the cause *need* not be expressed: Eur. Ion 3 μιᾶς θεῶν ἔφυσε Μαῖαν: Id. Med. 800 οὔτε τῆς νεοζύγου νύμφης τεκνώσει παῖδα.) Hdt. III. 81 ἀρίστων δὲ ἀνδρῶν οἶκος (*consentaneum est*) ἄριστα βουλεύματα γίνεσθαι: Ibid. 160 Ζωπύρου δὲ τούτου γίνεται Μεγάβυζος: Xen. Cyr. I. 2, 1 πατρὸς μὲν δὴ λέγεται ὁ Κῦρος γενέσθαι Καμβύσου, Περσῶν βασιλέως· ὁ δὲ Καμβύσης οὗτος τοῦ Περσειδῶν γένους ἦν—μητρὸς δὲ ὁμολογεῖται Μανδάνης γενέσθαι: Plat. Menex. p. 239 A μιᾶς μητρὸς πάντες ἀδελφοὶ φύντες. So Arist. Acharn. 256 οἷσι παρ᾽ ἐμοῦ πόλεμος ἐχθοδοπὸς αὔξεται τῶν ἐμῶν χωρίων, grows from my farms: Plat. Phædr. p. 242 D τὸν Ἔρωτα οὐκ Ἀφροδίτης καὶ θεόν τινα ἡγῇ; — Here also belong the phrases (mostly poetical), κεκλῆσθαί τινος, *alicujus filium vocari (esse)*: Hdt. VI. 88 Νικόδρομος Κνοίθου καλεόμενος: cf. Theocr. XXIV. 102.

Obs. 1. Generally, and in prose almost invariably, the prepositions ἀπό, ἐκ, sometimes διά, are added to the genitive : Hdt. III. 159 ἐκ τουτέων δὲ τῶν γυναικῶν οἱ νῦν Βαβυλώνιοι γεγόνασι.

Obs. 2. Hence we may explain the elliptic attributive genitive (§. 463. 3.); as, ὁ τοῦ βασιλέως υἱός, i. e. ὁ τοῦ βασιλέως (γεννηθεὶς) υἱός : Hdt. III. 60 Εὐπαλῖνος Ναυστρόφου : Ibid. Ῥοῖκος Φίλεω : 123 Μαιάνδριος Μαιανδρίου : Id. VI. 52 Ἀριστόδημον τὸν Ἀριστομάχου, τοῦ Κλειοδαίου, τοῦ Ὕλλου : Ibid. Αὐτεσίωνος, τοῦ Τισαμενοῦ, τοῦ Θερσάνδρου, τοῦ Πολυνείκους : Thuc. I. 24 Φάλιος Ἐρατοκλείδου. Poetic : Διὸς Ἄρτεμις, Ὀϊλῆος ταχὺς Αἴας, Ovid. Met. XII. 622 *Oileos Ajax.* In the plural number with a preposition ; as, οἱ ἐκ Διός Soph. El. 659: οἱ ἐξ αὐτοῦ, *posteri ejus* Hdt. I. 56: οἱ ἀφ᾽ Ἡρακλέους Thuc. I. 24.

Obs. 3. In poetry, passive and intransitive verbs have a genitive of that antecedent notion which is conceived to have caused or produced the state expressed by the verb [a]: Soph. Phil. 3 κρατίστου πατρὸς Ἑλλήνων τραφείς: Id. Aj. 807 φωτὸς ἠπατημένη : Id. Œ. R. μερίμνης ὑποστραφείς: Id. Œ. C. 391 τίς δ᾽ ἄν τι τοιοῦδ᾽ ἀνδρὸς εὖ πράξειεν ἄν; Plat. Rep. 562 D μεθυσθῇ ἀκράτου αὑτῆς: Id. Symp. 203 B μεθυσθεὶς τοῦ νέκταρος: Soph. Œ. C. 274 εἰδότων ἀπωλλύμην. So Eur. Orest. 496 πληγεὶς θυγάτρος τῆς ἐμῆς: Id. Elect. 123 κεῖσαι σ ἆς ἀλόχου σφαγεὶς Αἰγίσθου τ᾽, Ἀγάμεμνον : Id. Or. 487 πληγεὶς θυγατρὸς τῆς ἐμῆς ὑπὲρ κάρα. So also verbal adjectives with a passive force; as, Soph. Elect. 343 ἅπαντα γάρ σοι τἀμὰ νουθετήματα κείνης διδακτά, κοὐδὲν ἐκ σαυτῆς λέγεις, *prœcepta a te mihi data sunt ab illa instillata;* generally this relation is expressed by the prepositions, ὑπό, παρά, πρός, ἐκ, διά.

Obs. 4. So the attributive genitive (§. 463.) is to be explained by some such notion implied in the substantive of which it is the attributive; as, τέχνημα ἀνδρός, i. e. τέχνημα ἀνδρὸς (πεποιημένον implied in τέχνημα), τὰ τῶν ἀνθρώπων πράγματα, τὰ τοῦ Ὁμήρου ποιήματα : Il. β, 397 τὸν δ᾽ οὔποτε κύματα λείπει παντοίων ἀνέμων, produced by : Æsch. Prom. 908 Ἥρας ἀλατεῖαι, *errores a Junone excitati* : Soph. Aj. 618 ἔργα χεροῖν μεγίστας ἀρετᾶς : Id. Trach. 113 Νότου ἢ Βορέα κύματα : Id. Phil. 1116 πότμος δαιμόνων : Xen. M. S. II. 1, 33 αἱ τῶν νέων τιμαί, the honours shewn by the young men. So also Thuc. IV. 92 θράσει ἰσχύος, confidence proceeding from strength : Demosth. p. 23, 18 πάντα αὑτοῦ ἔργα. Sometimes the relation is more accurately defined by a preposition : Hdt. II. 148 τὰ ἐξ Ἑλλήνων τείχεα : Soph. Phil. 106 τὰ ἐξ Ἀτρειδῶν ἔργα : Id. Antig. 1219 τὰ ἐκ δεσπότου κελεύσματα : Xen. Cyr. V. 5, 13 τὸ παρ᾽ ἐμοῦ ἀδίκημα : Ibid. III. 3, 2 ἥδεσθαι τῇ ὑπὸ πάντων τιμῇ.

§. 484. So verbs have a genitive of the source whence any action, physical or mental, arises; as this is conceived to be antecedent to that notion.

Verbs of " *smell* "—*breathing from any thing ;* as, πνέειν—ὄζειν— προσβάλλειν. Ὄζειν ἴων — ὄζειν κρομύων — προσβάλλειν μύρου — πνεῖν τράγου.   Anacr. XXVIII. 9 μύρου πνεῖν : Arist.· Pac. 180 πόθεν βροτοῦ με προσέβαλε : Id. Ran. 341 ὡς ἡδύ μοι προσέπνευσε χοιρείων κρεῶν : Id. Acharn. 190 ὄζουσι πίττης καὶ παρασκευῆς νεῶν : Theocr. I. 27 κισσύβιον—ἔτι γλυφάνοιο ποτόσδον : Id. VII. 143 πάντ᾽ ὦσδεν θέρεος μάλα πίονος, ὦσδε δ᾽ ὀπώρης : Id. XXIX. 19 ἀνδρῶν τῶν ὑπερηνορέων δοκέεις πνέειν. A genitive may also be used, of the spot where, as well as the thing whence, the smell proceeds, though here ἀπό is more usual; as, Hdt. III. 23 ὄζειν ἀπὸ κρήνης ὡσεὶ ἴων : τῆς κεφαλῆς ὄζειν μύρου. So Anacr. IX. 3 πόθεν μύρων πνέεις.

§. 485. Verbs expressing the reception of mental and physical perception, take the genitive of the source of that perception, that whence it proceeds and is received, this being necessarily antecedent to the perception : ἀκούειν, ἀκροᾶσθαι, κλύειν Poetic, ἀΐειν Poetic, ἀποδέχεσθαι, to assent to—to receive what he says : πυνθάνε-

---

[a] Herm. Phil. 3.

σθαι, αἰσθάνεσθαι, γιγνώσκειν generally with an accusative,—ὀσφραίνεσθαι—(sometimes ὀρᾶν, θεᾶσθαι, θεωρεῖν, σκοπεῖν, διασκοπεῖν et sim.)
—μανθάνειν, συνιέναι, to understand: more rarely, ἐπίστασθαι, εἰδέναι,
ἀγνοεῖν, ὑπονοεῖν, διανοεῖσθαι, ἐννοεῖν, ἐνθυμεῖσθαι: Il. a, 37 κ λ ῦ θ ί
μευ: Soph. Œ. C. 793 ὅσπερ καὶ σαφέστερον κλύω Φοίβου τε καὐτοῦ
Ζηνός: Od. ι, 401 οἱ δὲ β ο ῆ ς ἀ ί ο ν τ ε ς ἐφοίτων ἄλλοθεν ἄλλος:
Il. ρ, 686 ἄγε δεῦρο —, ὄφρα π ύ θ η α ι λυγρῆς ἀγγελίης: Il. δ, 357
ὡς γ ν ῶ χωομένοιο: Od. ψ, 109 γ ν ω σ ό μ ε θ' ἀλλήλων : Il. β, 26
νῦν δ' ἐ μ έ θ ε ν ξ ύ ν ε ς ὦκα: Il. a, 273 καὶ μέν μευ β ο υ λ έ ω ν
ξ ύ ν ι ο ν, πείθοντό τε μύθῳ: Od. δ, 76 ἀγορεύοντος ξ ύ ν ε τ ο:
Demosth. 67, 14 ἄλλου λέγοντος συνειῆτε: Il. ξ, 37 τῷ ῥ' οἵγ'
ὀ ψ ε ί ο ν τ ε ς ἀϋτῆς καὶ πολέμοιο — κίον ἀθρόοι: Æsch. P. V. 701
μαθεῖν τῆσδε: Soph. Aj. 1161 αἴσχιστον, κ λ ύ ε ι ν ἀνδρὸς ματαίου
φλαῦρ' ἔπη μυθουμένου: Id. Trach. 394 ἕρποντος ε ἰ σ ο ρ ᾷ ς ἐμοῦ:
Hdt. I. 47 καὶ κωφοῦ σ υ ν ί η μ ι, καὶ οὐ φωνεῦντος ἀ κ ο ύ ω: Id. I.
80 ὡς ὄ σ φ ρ α ν τ ο τάχιστα τῶν καμήλων οἱ ἵπποι, καὶ εἶδον αὐτὰς,
ὀπίσω ἀνέστρεφον: Thuc. V. 83 ὡς ἤ σ θ ο ν τ ο τειχιζόντων: Id.
IV. 6 ὡς ἐ π ύ θ ο ν τ ο τῆς Πύλου κατειλημμένης: Id. II. 81 οὐδέ-
τερον ᾔσθετο τῆς μάχης: Id. I. 68 τ ῶ ν λ ε γ ό ν τ ω ν μᾶλλον ὑ π ε-
ν ο ε ῖ τ ε, ὡς ἕνεκα τῶν αὐτοῖς ἰδίᾳ διαφορῶν λέγουσι: Xen. Cyr. I.
3, 10 οὐκ ἀ κ ρ ο ώ μ ε ν ο ι δὲ τοῦ ᾄδοντος ὠμνύετε ᾄδειν ἄριστα: Ibid.
VIII. 1, 40 κ α τ α μ α θ ε ῖ ν δὲ τ ο ῦ Κ ύ ρ ο υ δοκοῦμεν, ὡς οὐ τούτῳ
μόνον ἐνόμιζε χρῆναι τοὺς ἄρχοντας τῶν ἀρχομένων διαφέρειν: Id.
M. S. I. 1, 12 καὶ πρῶτον μὲν α ὐ τ ῶ ν ἐ σ κ ό π ε ι, πότερά ποτε
νομίσαντες ἱκανῶς ἤδη τ' ἀνθρώπινα εἰδέναι, ἔρχονται ἐπὶ τὸ περὶ
τούτων φροντίζειν κ. τ. λ.: Id. Œcon. XVI. 3 καὶ ἀ λ λ ο τ ρ ί α ς
γ ῆ ς τοῦτο ἔστι ‾ γ ν ῶ ν α ι, ὅ τι τε δύναται φέρειν: Id. Anab. III.
1, 19 δ ι α θ ε ώ μ ε ν ο ς α ὐ τ ῶ ν, ὅσην μὲν χώραν καὶ οἵαν ἔχοιεν:
Id. M. S. III. 6, 17 ἐ ν θ υ μ ο ῦ δὲ καὶ τ ῶ ν ε ἰ δ ό τ ω ν, ὅ τι τε
λέγουσι καὶ ὅ τι ποιοῦσιν: Plat. Apol. p. 27 A ἆρα γ ν ώ σ ε τ α ι
Σωκράτης ὁ σοφὸς ἐ μ ο ῦ χ α ρ ι ε ν τ ι ζ ο μ έ ν ο υ καὶ ἐναντί' ἐμαυτῷ
λ έ γ ο ν τ ο ς: Id. Phileb. p. 51 C εἴ μ ο υ μ α ν θ ά ν ε ι ς: Id. Gorg.
p. 463 D ἆρ' οὖν ἂν μ ά θ ο ι ς ἀποκριναμένου: Ibid. p. 517 C
ἀ γ ν ο ο ῦ ν τ ε ς ἀλλήλων, ὅ τι λέγομεν: Id. Rep. p. 375 E οἶσθα
γάρ που τ ῶ ν γ ε ν ν α ί ω ν κ υ ν ῶ ν, ὅτι τοῦτο φύσει αὐτῶν τὸ ἦθος,
πρὸς μὲν τοὺς συνήθεις τε καὶ γνωρίμους ὡς οἷόν τε πραοτάτους εἶναι,
πρὸς δὲ τοὺς ἀγνῶτας τοὐναντίον: Ibid. p. 525 D νῦν καὶ ἐ ν ν ο ῶ
ῥ η θ έ ν τ ο ς τ ο ῦ περὶ τοὺς λογισμοὺς μ α θ ή μ α τ ο ς, ὡς κομψόν
ἐστι κ. τ. λ.: Id. Charmid. p. 154 E τί οὖν, ἔφη, οὐκ — ἐ θ ε α-
σ ά μ ε θ α πρότερον τοῦ εἴδους: Id. Legg. p. 646 D καὶ τ ῆ ς περὶ
τὸν οἶνον ἄρα δ ι α τ ρ ι β ῆ ς ὡσαύτως διανοητέον: Id. Phæd. p.

92 D μήτε ἐμαυτοῦ μήτ' ἄλλου ἀποδέχεσθαι λέγοντος, ὡς ἡ ψυχή ἐστιν ἁρμονία: Demosth. p. 82, 3 ἀποδεχόμενοι τῶν συκοφαντούντων : Ἀκούειν δίκης, to listen to a cause, αἰσθάνεσθαι κραυγῆς, θορύβου, ἐπιβούλης.

Obs. The thing heard, &c. would properly, and not unfrequently does, follow the verb in the accusative; but as the Greeks loved to give a personal character to things, the genitive is not unfrequently used for the accusative, as in several of the above examples. So Arist. Ach. 306 τῶν δ' ἐμῶν σπονδῶν ἀκούσατε, listen to, as if the σπονδαί were speaking; while Ibid. 337 ἐμοῦ λέγοντος οὐκ ἠκούσατε.

§. 486. Here also belong the verbs of *examining, inquiring, saying*. The person or thing concerning whom any thing is said or asked, is sometimes considered as the source of the thing said or asked, whence it proceeds, and therefore, as being antecedent to it, takes the genitive: κρίνειν, ἐξετάζειν, εἰπεῖν, φράζειν, φάναι, δηλοῦν, &c.: Od. λ, 174 εἰπὲ δέ μοι πατρός τε καὶ υἱέος, ὃν κατέλειπον, ἢ ἔτι πὰρ κείνοισιν ἐμὸν γέρας, ἤέ τις ἤδη ἀνδρῶν ἄλλος ἔχει: Ibid. 493 εἰπὲ δέ μοι Πηλῆος ἀμύμονος, εἴ τι πέπυσαι: Soph. Trach. 1122 τῆς μητρὸς ἥκω τῆς ἐμῆς φράσων, ἐν οἷς νῦν ἐστιν: Id. El. 317 τοῦ κασιγνήτου τί φής; ἥξοντος ἢ μέλλοντος; Id. Phil. 439 ἀναξίου μὲν φωτὸς ἐξερήσομαι — τί νῦν κυρεῖ; Plat. Rep. p. 439 B τοῦ τοξότου οὐ καλῶς ἔχει λέγειν, ὅτι αὐτοῦ ἅμα χεῖρες τὸ τόξον ἀπωθοῦνταί τε καὶ προσέλκονται, ἀλλ' ὅτι ἄλλη μὲν ἡ ἀπωθοῦσα χείρ, ἑτέρα δὲ ἡ προσαγομένη: Ibid. p. 485 B μαθήματός γε ἀεὶ ἐρῶσιν, (*philosophi*) ὃ ἂν αὐτοῖς δηλοῖ ἐκείνης τῆς οὐσίας τῆς ἀεὶ οὔσης: Ibid. p. 576 D εὐδαιμονίας τε αὖ καὶ ἀθλιότητος ὡσαύτως ἢ ἄλλως κρίνεις; Demosth. p. 23, 20 εἰ δέ τι πταίσει, τότ' ἀκριβῶς αὐτοῦ ταῦτ' ἐξετασθήσεται. So perhaps we may explain, ibid. p. 19, 4 τούτων οὐχὶ νῦν ὁρῶ τὸν καιρὸν τοῦ λέγειν, *de his dicendi nunc non video tempus opportunum.*

Obs. 1. This notion is often more accurately defined by περί; as, Isocr. p. 614, 9 ἐνθυμηθῆναι περὶ τῶν κοινῶν πραγμάτων, to consider on.

Obs. 2. So the attributive genitive; as, Od. α, 409 ἀγγελίης πατρὸς φέρει οἰχομένοιο. — ἀγγελία τῆς Χίου Thuc., *de Chio :* Xen. M. S. II. 7, 3 τὸν τοῦ κυνὸς λόγον. — ἐρώτησίς τινος Plat., like *quæstio animorum* Cic. Tusc. I. 23. (generally περί) : Plat. Theæt. p. 164 D ὁ μῦθος ὁ τῆς ἐπιστήμης καὶ αἰσθήσεως.

§. 487. 1. Whether the genitive with the verbs in the two last paragraphs expresses the person or the thing, as ἀκούω Σωκράτους, or ἀκούω θορύβου, the principle of the construction is the same; when the thing heard is alone expressed, it is by a fiction of speech considered as the source whence the hearing, &c. proceeds; but when the person is likewise expressed, this fiction is no longer practicable, as the real source is expressly stated, and then the thing heard, &c. is in the accusative, and the source whence it proceeds in the genitive: Od. μ, 389 ταῦτα — Καλυψοῦς ἤκουσα: Xen. Cyr. III. 1, 1 ὁ Ἀρμένιος, ὡς ἤκουσε τοῦ ἀγγέλου τὰ παρὰ τοῦ Κύρου, ἐξεπλάγη, as in Latin *audire aliquid ex aliquo*: Eur. Rhes. 129 μαθόντες ἐχθρῶν μηχανὰς κατασκόπου βουλευσόμεθα. So συνιέναι τινός τι, as ἔπος — ὄπα θεᾶς: ὀσφραίνεσθαι ὀδμήν: Hdt. I. 80 κάμηλον ἵππος φοβέεται, καὶ οὐκ ἀνέχεται οὔτε τὴν ἰδέην αὐτῆς ὁρέων, οὔτε τὴν ὀδμὴν ὀσφραινόμενος. This is especially the case with the verbs of understanding, inquiring, examining, saying; as, ἐνθυμεῖσθαι, σκοπεῖν, λέγειν, δηλοῦν, which are rarely found with the genitive alone.

2. All these verbs are, properly speaking, intransitive; the subject being represented, not as acting upon, but as acted upon and receiving something from another. The construction with the genitive is most in harmony with their own force and the genius of the language; but they very frequently take an accusative in a transitive force, especially verbs of seeing, which, except in poetry, rarely have a genitive, as in Xen. M. S. I. 1, 10 οὐδεὶς δὲ πώποτε Σωκράτους οὐδὲν ἀσεβὲς οὐδὲ ἀνόσιον οὔτε πράττοντος εἶδεν, οὔτε λέγοντος ἤκουσεν.

3. Verbs of *hearing, perceiving, observing,* often take an accusative, as well of the person as of the thing: Il. κ, 354 ἔστη δοῦπον ἀκούσας: Od. κ, 147 ἐνοπήν τε πυθοίμην: Xen. Cyr. III. 1, 4 ὡς ᾔσθετο τὰ γιγνόμενα (but V. 3, 20 ἄρτι ᾐσθημένος τοῦ γεγενημένου): Thuc. V. 32 ἐνθυμούμενοι τὰς ἐν ταῖς μάχαις ξυμφοράς: Isocr. p. 15 D ἐπειδὰν ἐνθυμηθῶσι τοὺς φόβους καὶ κινδύνους.

4. The verbs of hearing take the genitive in the sense of "obey," as well as other verbs of obeying which are elsewhere joined with the dative; the person who is heard being considered as the source whence the obligation is derived; as, ἀκούειν, ὑπακούειν, κατακούειν, ἀνηκουστεῖν and νηκουστεῖν, κλύειν Poetic, πείθεσθαι seldom, ἀπειθεῖν. So the adjectives κατήκοος, ὑπήκοος rarely with a dative: Il. ο, 199 οἳ ἴθεν ὀτρύνοντος ἀκούσονται καὶ ἀνάγκη: Ibid. 236 οὐδ᾽ ἄρα πατρὸς ἀνηκούστησεν Ἀπόλλων: cf. π, 676. Od. η, 11 Φαιήκεσσιν ἄνασσε, θεοῦ δ᾽ ὣς δῆμος ἄκουεν [dative ἀκούειν τινί, to listen to, Il. π, 515, an unusual construction instead of a genitive]: Æsch. Prom. 40 ἀνήκουστεῖν δὲ τῶν πατρὸς λόγων οἷόν τε πῶς; Soph. Elect. 340 τῶν κρατούντων ἐστὶ πάντ᾽ ἀκουστέα: Eur. Or. 426 οὗτοί μ᾽ ὑβρίζουσ᾽, ὧν πόλις τανῦν κλύει (*quibus obedit*). Prose: Hdt. III. 61 Σμέρδιος τοῦ Κύρου ἀκουστέα (ἐστὶ) — ἀλλ᾽ οὐ Καμβύσεω: Ibid. 62 προαγορεύει ἡμῖν Σμέρδιος βασιλῆος ἀκούειν: Ibid. 101 Δαρείου βασιλῆος οὐδαμᾶ ὑπήκουσαν: Id. I. 126 νῦν ὢν ἐμέο πειθόμενοι γίνεσθε ἐλεύθεροι [a]: Id. VI. 12 μὴ πειθόμεθα αὐτοῦ: Thuc. VII. 73 πείθεσθαί τινος: Id. II. 62 ἄλλων ὑπακούειν: Xen. Cyr. IV. 5, 19 πῶς χρὴ καλοῦντος ἀπειθεῖν: Demosth. p. 15. extr. κατακούειν τινός. Adjective: Plat. Rep. p. 440 D ὑπηκόους τῶν ἀρχόντων.

§. 488. Verbs which express the notion of *grief, sympathy,* &c. take a genitive of those objects, the antecedent conception of which, as being that whence the feeling arises, is implied in the notion of grief; as, ἀλγεῖν, οἰκτείρειν, ὀδύρεσθαι, ὀλοφύρεσθαι: Od. δ, 104 ὀδύρεσθαί τινος: Od. φ, 250 οὔτι γάμου τοσσοῦτον ὀδύ-

---

[a] Schweigh. ad loc.

ρομαι: Il. χ, 169 ὀλοφύρεσθαι Ἕκτορος: Od. π, 17 Ἀργείων ὀλοφύρεαι: Æsch. Ag. 582 ἀλγεῖν τύχης παλιγκότου: Eur. Hec. 1256 παιδὸς οὐκ ἀλγεῖν δοκεῖς; (So στένω and οἰκτείρω with acc. of object in a transitive force: Xen. Cyr. V. 4, 32 ὁ Κῦρος ἀκούσας, τοῦ μὲν πάθους ᾤκτειρεν αὐτόν: Eur. Hipp. 1399 στένω σὲ μᾶλλον, ἢ 'μὲ, τῆς ἁμαρτίας.)—πενθικῶς ἔχειν τινός: Xen. Cyr. V. 2, 7 τὴν θυγατέρα, πενθικῶς ἔχουσαν τοῦ ἀδελφοῦ τεθνηκότος, ἐξάγων τάδε εἶπεν. Analogous to this is the construction, Soph. Phil. 715 πώματος ἥσθη, and the attributive genitive, ἡδοναὶ τέκνων &c.; the genitive expressing the cause whence the pleasure arises. So Soph. Œ. R. 234 δείσας φίλου, for his friend.

Obs. 1. So the attributive genitive (§. 464.): ἄλγος ἑταίρων (de amicis), ἄχος τινός Il. ξ, 458. τ, 581. χ, 428: Id. ο, 26 ὀδύνη Ἡρακλῆος: Soph. Phil. 966 οἶκτος — τοῦδ' ἀνδρός.

Obs. 2. Περί is sometimes added: Od. φ, 249 ἦ μοι ἄχος περί τ' αὐτοῦ καὶ περὶ πάντων.

Obs. 3. Most of these genitives of the cause or aim of the action, were formerly explained by a supposed ellipse of ἕνεκα or χάριν.

§. 489. Adjectives also which express the notion of *misery*, especially in exclamations[a]: Eur. Hipp. 344 ὦ τάλαινα τῶν δ' ἀλγέων! Ibid. 527 ὦ τλάμων ὑμεναίων! Ibid. 540 ὦ δυστάλαινα τῶν ἐμῶν παθημάτων! Id. Or. 1022 ὦ μέλεος ἥβης σῆς, Ὀρέστα, καὶ πότμου θανάτου τ' ἀώρου! Id. Med. 1028 ὦ δυστάλαινα τῆς ἐμῆς αὐθαδίας! Id. Hec. 661 ὦ τάλαινα σῆς κακογλώσσου βοῆς! Ibid. 783 ὦ σχετλία σὺ τῶν ἀμετρήτων πόνων! Id. Androm. 1179 ὦ σχέτλιος παθέων ἐγώ! So likewise interjections, either with or without corresponding expressions of feeling: Eur. Or. 402 οἴμοι διωγμῶν, οἷς ἐλαύνομαι τάλας! Id. Herc. 899 αἰαῖ κακῶν! Ibid. 1374 οἴμοι δάμαρτος καὶ τέκνων, οἴμοι δ' ἐμοῦ! Id. Hipp. 1444 ὦ μοι φρενὸς σῆς εὐσεβοῦς τε κἀγαθῆς! Xen. Cyr. III. 1, 39 φεῦ τοῦ ἀνδρός! Plat. Rep. p. 509 C Ἄπολλον, δαιμονίας ὑπερβολῆς! Even when the interjection is omitted: Theocr. XV. 75 χρηστῶ κᾠκτίρμονος ἀνδρός! Eur. Med. 1051 ἀλλὰ τῆς ἐμῆς κάκης, τὸ καὶ προέσθαι (scil. ἐμέ) μαλθακοὺς λόγους φρενί! Xen. Cyr. II. 2, 3 τῆς τύχης, τὸ ἐμὲ νῦν κληθέντα δεῦρο τυχεῖν!

Obs. 1. This idiom belongs to the Attic æra. The article is generally prefixed to this gen. in a demonstrative force, pointing out the presence of the misfortune, &c.

Obs. 2. The verbs expressing *sorrow for* and *sympathy with*, frequently take an acc. in the transitive sense of lamenting, pitying; the person or thing lamented, &c. being considered rather as the object or patient than

a Elm. Med. 996.

the cause or source of the sorrow, &c.   Hence they have a passive voice :
Plat. Apol. p. 34 C ἵνα—— ἐλεηθείη, that he might be pitied.

§. 490. So other verbs expressive of strong mental feeling take a
gen. of the antecedent notion of that thing or person which pro-
voked those feelings.   So verbs of *anger* and *annoyance*[a]; as,
χολοῦσθαι, χώεσθαι, μηνίειν, θυμοῦσθαι, κοτεῖν, ἄχθεσθαι, χαλεπαίνειν :
Il. ν, 660 τοῦ δὲ Πάρις μάλα θυμὸν ἀποκταμένοιο χολώθη : Il. ξ,
266 Ἡρακλῆος περιχώσατο, παιδὸς ἑοῖο : Il. π, 320 Μάρις——
Ἀντιλόχῳ ἐπόρουσε, κασιγνήτοιο χολωθείς : Il. π, 546 Δαναῶν
κεχολωμένοι : ν. 553 χωόμενος Σαρπηδόνος : Il. α, 429 χωόμενος κατὰ θυμὸν ἐϋζώνοιο γυναικός: Od. α, 69 Ποσειδάων—— Κύκλωπος κεχόλωται, ὃν ὀφθαλμοῦ ἀλάωσεν : Il. ε, 178 ἱερῶν μηνίσας.   So Plat. Rep. 501 E ἀγριανοῦσι λεγόντων ἡμῶν : Soph.
Antig. 1177 πατρὶ μηνίσας φόνου : Eur. Or. 739 ἴσως σοι
θυγατέρος θυμούμενος : Id. Alc. 3 οὗ δὴ χολωθείς.

Obs. 1. Περί is added sometimes to this gen., and also ἐκ : Il. ι, 566 ἐξ
ἀρέων μητρὸς κεχολωμένος.

Obs. 2. So in the attributive gen. : χόλος, κότος τινός, *de aliquo.*

§. 491. So verbs expressing a state of *benefit*, or *advantage*, or
enjoyment, stand with the genitive only of that whence the benefit is
received : ὀνίνασθαι, ἀπολαύειν, ἐπαυρέσθαι, ἀπαυρᾶν[b] (Post-Homeric;
see *Passow Lex. ad voc.*).   So Eur. Hec. 996 ὀναίμην τοῦ πα-
ρόντος, may I be benefited from : Hdt. VII. 180 τάχα δ' ἄν τι
καὶ τοῦ ὀνόματος ἐπαύροιτο : Xen. M. S. VI. 3, 11 ἀπολαύειν πάντων τῶν ἀγαθῶν.   So verbs of receiving, which
take an acc. of the thing received. (See *Acc. Case, Recipient Verbs.*)

Obs. 1. Sometimes μέρος is joined with ἀπολαύειν Isocr. 203 B; sometimes χάριν Soph. Œ. C. 1042.

Obs. 2. The prepositions ἀπό and ἐκ are sometimes joined with these
verbs; as, Plat. Rep. 395 ἀπολαύειν ἀπὸ τῆς μιμήσεως : Id. Lys. 210 B
ὀνησόμεθα γὰρ ἀπ' αὐτῶν[c]: always with ὠφελεῖσθαι ; καρποῦσθαι always has
the acc.

§. 492. We frequently find an infin. with the article in the gen.
used to express the *aim* or *intent* of an action, considered as its
final cause[d]: Thuc. I. 4 Μίνως τὸ λῃστικὸν καθῄρει ἐκ τῆς θαλάσσης
τοῦ τὰς προσόδους μᾶλλον ἰέναι αὐτῷ : Id. V. 27 τοῦ μὴ
καταφανεῖς γίγνεσθαι : Xen. Cyr. I. 6, 40 τοῦ μὴ διαφεύγειν τὸν
λάγων—σκόπους καθίστης. cf. Soph. Philoct. 297. So in Latin : Cæs.

---

[a] Mouk Alc. 5.
[b] Butt. Lexil. V. ἀπαυρᾶν. II.—"With
regard to the case which it governs, the
difference originally was this, that when
the relation of the object to the verb was
immediate, i. e. supposed to be an immediate taking, the acc. case followed ; on the

other hand, if rather the consequences or
fruits of any thing were to be enjoyed or
derived, the genitive; or, when the construction was complete, ἀπό with genitive."
[c] Ast Lex. Plat. ad voc.
[d] Vackn. Hipp. 48.

Bell. Gall. IV. *Naves dejiciendi operis a barbaris missæ.* So in N. T. St. Mark iv. 3 ἐξῆλθεν ὁ σπείρων τοῦ σπεῖραι: Acts xxvi. 18 ἀνοῖξαι τοὺς ὀφθάλμους τοῦ ἐπιστρέψαι: Rom. vi. 6 τοῦ μηκέτι δουλεύειν τῇ ἁμαρτίᾳ. And also frequently in the LXX[a].

§. 493. So also the notions of *knowing, being skilled in, experienced in, gaining experience in,* and the contrary, take a gen. of the thing in which the person is skilled or experienced, as being that from energising wherein the skill or experience proceeds, and therefore antecedently necessary to the conception of these notions. We cannot form a notion of experience without an antecedent notion of the things with which it has to do : ἔμπειρος, ἄπειρος, ἐπιστήμων, ἐπιστάμενος, ἀνεπιστήμων (rarely σοφός, συνειδέναι), τρίβων, συγγνώμων, ἀδαής, ἄϊδρις, ἀπαίδευτος, ἰδιώτης, also ἰδιωτεύειν (Plat. Protag. p. 327 A) &c., πειρᾶσθαι, διαπειρᾶσθαι, ἀποπειρᾶσθαι, πεπειραμένον εἶναι (also πειρᾶν Hdt.), ἀπείρως, ξένως ἔχειν. Ἔμπειρος or ἐπιστήμων εἰμὶ τῆς τεχνῆς: Hdt. II. 49 τῆς θυσίας ταύτης οὐκ—ἀδαὴς ἀλλ' ἔμπειρος.—Ἀπαίδευτος ἀρετῆς, μουσικῆς Xen.—Xen. Cyr. VI. I, 37 συγγνώμων τῶν ἀνθρωπίνων πραγμάτων: Lycurg. Leocr. p. 159 πάντων συνειδέναι: Æsch. Suppl. 448 θέλω δ' ἄϊδρις μᾶλλον ἢ σοφὸς κακῶν εἶναι (like σοφός τινος Plat. Soph. p. 230 A).— Τρίβων τῆς ἱππικῆς Aristoph.: Eur. Med. 870 Ἰᾶσον, αἰτοῦμαί σε τῶν εἰρημένων συγγνώμον' εἶναι: Id. Hec. 687 ἀρτιμαθὴς κακῶν. Ἀπείρως ἔχειν τινός Isocr.: Plat. Apol. p. 17 D ξένως ἔχω τῆς ἐνθάδε λέξεως.—Πειρᾶσθαί τινος Il. ω, 390: Hdt. III. 119 ἀποπειρᾶσθαι γνώμης: Ibid. 134 τῆς Ἑλλάδος ἀποπειρᾶσθαι: Id. VI. 86, 3 πειρηθῆναι τοῦ θεοῦ: Ibid. 128 διεπειρᾶτο αὐτέων τῆς δὲ ἀνδραγαθίης καὶ τῆς ὀργῆς καὶ παιδεύσιός τε καὶ τρόπου.

§. 494. Connected with this idea of skill are the notions of *capability of, power of, fitness for, talent for,* the notion of capacity, &c. arising from an antecedent notion of the thing, from the peculiar nature of which the notion of capacity for it is formed ; hence the genitive is used with verbal adj. in ικός, and others in which the notion of any capacity is implied: Xen. M. S. III. 1, 6 καὶ γὰρ παρασκευαστικὸν τῶν εἰς τὸν πόλεμον τὸν στρατηγὸν εἶναι χρὴ καὶ ποριστικὸν τῶν ἐπιτηδείων τοῖς στρατιώταις: Plat. Euthyph. p. 3 C διδασκαλικὸς τῆς αὑτοῦ σοφίας. So Hdt. I. 107 παρθένος ἀνδρὸς ὡραίη: Id. I. 196 γάμου ὡραίη: Ibid. VI. 122 (θυγατέρες) ἐγένοντο γάμου ὡραῖαι: Plat. Legg. p. 643 D τέλειος τῆς τοῦ πράγματος ἀρετῆς, perfectly versed in. Also verbal adj. which express a transitive action: Hdt. II. 174 ἱροὶ ὄφιες

a Viner. Gr. Gr. p. 269.

ἀνθρώπων οὐδαμῶς δ η λ ή μ ο ν ε ς, capable of injuring: Soph. Œ. T.
1437 θνητῶν — μηδενὸς π ρ ο σ ή γ ο ρ ο ς.

§. 495. The verbs of *wondering at, congratulating, praising,
blaming,* &c. take a genitive of the cause whence the feeling arises;
and the construction here is twofold: when the quality or action
which excites the feeling is distinctly stated, it is in the genitive,
and the person who is the patient or object of the feeling in the
accusative; as, ζηλῶ σε τῆς εὐτυχίας, τῆς ἀνοίας: but where the
quality is not stated, but is only implied, and represented as being
joined to or residing in the person, so that a consideration of
the person himself exercising the quality excites the feeling; as,
θαυμάζω σοῦ λέγοντος, or θαυμάζω σοῦ ἃ λέγεις, the person is put in
the genitive, and the patient or object of the feeling is supplied
from the genitive by the mind; as, ἄγασθαι, θαυμάζειν, ζηλοῦν, εὐδαιμονίζειν, ἐπαινεῖν, μέμφεσθαι (τινά τινος, acc. pers., gen. rei). Ἄγαμαί σε τῆς ἀνδρείας.—Θ α υ μ ά ζ ω σε τῆς σοφίας. — Ζ η λ ῶ σε τοῦ
πλούτου. — Ε ὐ δ α ι μ ο ν ί ζ ω σε τῶν ἀγαθῶν.—Α ἰ ν ῶ σε τῆς προθυμίας: Plat. Rep. p. 426 D τοὺς θέλοντας θεραπεύειν τὰς τοιαύτας
πόλεις καὶ προθυμουμένους οὐκ ἄγ α σ α ι τῆς ἀνδρείας τε καὶ εὐχερείας;
Hdt. VI. 76 ἄγ α σ θ α ι μὲν ἔφη τ ο ῦ 'Ε ρ α σ ί ν ο υ ο ὐ π ρ ο δ ι-
δ ό ν τ ο ς τοὺς πολιήτας: Thuc. I. 84 τὸ βραδὺ καὶ μέλλον, ὃ μ έ μ-
φ ο ν τ α ι μάλιστα ἡ μ ῶ ν, μὴ αἰσχύνεσθε: Æsch. Theb. 651 κηρυ-
κευμάτων μέμψει: Eur. Hec. 962 μέμφει τῆς ἐμῆς ἀπουσίας: Xen.
Cyr. III. 1, 15 εἰ μὲν ἄγ α σ α ι τ ο ῦ π α τ ρ ὸ ς, ἢ ὅσα βεβούλευται,
ἢ ὅσα πέπραχε, πάνυ σοι συμβουλεύω τοῦτον μιμεῖσθαι: Id. Ages.
II. 7 τάδ' α ὐ τ ο ῦ ἄγ α μ α ι, ὅτι—παρεσκευάσατο: Ibid. VIII. 4
ἐγὼ οὖν καὶ τοῦτο ἐ π α ι ν ῶ 'Α γ η σ ι λ ά ο υ, τὸ πρὸς τὸ ἀρέσκειν τοῖς
Ἕλλησιν ὑπεριδεῖν τὴν βασιλέως ξενίαν: Eur. Iph. A 28 οὐκ ἄγ α-
μ α ι ταῦτ' ἀ ν δ ρ ὸ ς ἀ ρ ι σ τ έ ο ς: Plat. Rep. p. 376 A καὶ τοῦτο —
ἐν τοῖς κυσὶ κατόψει, ὃ καὶ ἄξιον θ α υ μ ά σ α ι τ ο ῦ θ η ρ ί ο υ ᵃ: Id.
Men. p. 95 C καὶ Γ ο ρ γ ί ο υ μάλιστα—ταῦτα ἄγ α μ α ι: Thuc. VI.
36 θαυμάζω τῆς τόλμης: Plat. Theæt. p. 161 B ὃ θ α υ μ ά ζ ω τοῦ
ἑταίρου σου Π ρ ω τ α γ ό ρ ο υ: Id. Protag. p. 329 C ὃ δ' ἐ θ α ύ μ α σ ά
σου λέγοντος: Demosth. θαυμάζω τ ῶ ν ε ἰ ω θ ό τ ω ν λέγεσθαι: Plat.
Criton. p. 43 B ἀλλὰ καὶ σ ο ῦ πάλαι θ α υ μ ά ζ ω, αἰσθανόμενος ὡς
ἡδέως καθεύδεις: Id. Rep. 367 D τ ο ῦ τ' αὐτὸ ἐ π α ί ν ε σ ο ν δ ι-
κ α ι ο σ ύ ν η ς: Ibid. p. 383 A πολλὰ ἄρα 'Ο μ ή ρ ο υ ἐ π α ι ν ο ῦ ν-
τ ε ς ἄλλα τοῦτο οὐκ ἐπαινεσόμεθα. After this analogy we find the
transitive verb ὀνειδίζω: Hdt. I. 90 τούτων ὀνειδίσαι. So also adj.
which express or imply surprise: Plat. Phædon. p. 58 E ε ὐ δ α ί-

---

ᵃ Stallb. ad loc.

μων γάρ μοι ὁ ἀνὴρ ἐφαίνετο καὶ τοῦ τρόπου καὶ τῶν λόγων,
ὡς ἀδεῶς καὶ γενναίως ἐτελεύτα. So we must read in Xen. Anab.
II. 3, 15 θαυμάσιαι τοῦ κάλλους καὶ μεγέθους. And interjections or
exclamations; as, εὐδαίμων μοίρας! ὦ σχετλία τόλμης! Aristoph.
Av. 61 Ἄπολλον ἀποτρόπαιε τοῦ χασμήματος!

Obs. 1. Here also we find περί; as, ὀνειδίζειν περί τινος.

Obs. 2. There are two ways whereby the quality whence the feeling
arises may be joined to the person who is properly the immediate object or
patient thereof: 1. by a participle in the genitive; as, θαυμάζω σοῦ λέγοντος: 2. by an explanatory sentence, which gives the cause; as, Æsch.
Ag. 1399 θαυμάζομεν σοῦ, γλῶσσαν ὡς θρασύστομος: Plat. Hipp.
Maj. 27 ἄγαμαι σοῦ ὅτι &c.: Id. Crit. 100 ἀλλὰ καὶ σοῦ πάλαι θαυμάζω
αἰσθανόμενος ὡς ἡδέως καθεύδεις: Id. Legg. 190 Ῥαδαμάνθυος—
ἄγασθαι διότι &c.: Hdt. V. 92, 6 θαυμάζειν αὐτοῦ, παρ' οἷόν μιν
ἄνδρα ἀποπέμψειε.

Obs. 3. It is but seldom that we find a genitive of the person and the
thing, with verbs of admiration, as in Demosth. p. 296 ἀγάσαιτο τῶν
ἀνδρῶν ἐκείνων τῆς ἀρετῆς, both being considered at different moments of the thought as the cause of the feeling. Things are generally
rather regarded as the patient of the action or feeling than as the cause of it,
and therefore are generally in the acc.: Xen. Cyr. IV. 2, 28 τῶν δὲ πολεμίων,
ἐπεὶ φάος ἐγένετο, οἱ μὲν ἐθαύμαζον τὰ ὁρώμενα, οἱ δὲ ἐγίγνωσκον ἤδη. So
ἄγασθαι, ἐπαινεῖν, ψέγειν, μέμφεσθαί τι. Sometimes an accusative of the
person alone; as, ἐπαινεῖν, ψέγειν, μέμφεσθαί τινα: ἄγασθαι, θαυμάζειν τινά. So
also to wonder at a person, not at any particular quality in him: Od. ξ,
168 ὥς σε, γύναι, ἄγαμαί τε τέθηπά τε: Xen. M. S. II. 1, 19 πῶς οὐκ οἴεσθαι
χρὴ τούτους καὶ πονεῖν ἡδέως εἰς τὰ τοιαῦτα, καὶ ζῆν εὐφραινομένους, ἀγαμένους
μὲν ἑαυτούς, ἐπαινουμένους δὲ καὶ ζηλουμένους ὑπὸ τῶν ἄλλων; Id. Œcon. XXI.
10 ἐγὼ μὲν αὐτὸν οὐκ ἂν ἀγαίμην. Double acc.: Xen. Agesil. X. 1 ἐγὼ μὲν
οὖν τὰ τοιαῦτα ἐπαινῶ Ἀγησίλαον. (See *Double Acc.*)

§. 496. Verbs which express the notion of *caring for, thinking
much of,* or the contraries, which necessarily imply an antecedent
notion of the cause (person or thing) whence the case arises; as,
ἐπιμέλεσθαι or ἐπιμελεῖσθαι, φροντίζειν, κήδεσθαι, προνοεῖν, προορᾶν,
μέλει, μεταμέλει, ἀμελεῖν, ὀλιγωρεῖν, καταφρονεῖν, φείδεσθαι, φυλάττεσθαι, διευλαβεῖσθαι, and the poetic ἐμπάζεσθαι, ὄθεσθαι, ἀλέγειν,
ἀλεγίζειν, τημελεῖν: Od. ι, 275 οὐ γὰρ Κύκλωπες Διὸς αἰγιόχου ἀλέγουσιν, οὐδὲ θεῶν μακάρων: Il. α, 181 σέθεν δ' ἐγὼ οὐκ ἀλεγίζω,
οὐδ' ὄθομαι κοτέοντος: Od. α, 271 ἐμῶν ἐμπάζεο μύθων: Od. α,
415 οὔτε θεοπροπίης ἐμπάζονται: Hdt. III. 151 ἐπολιόρκεε
(Βαβυλωνίους) φροντίζοντας οὐδὲν τῆς πολιορκίης: Demosth.
p. 41, 8 οὐδὲν φροντίζειν ὧν ἔχρην: Plat. Gorg. 512 οὐδὲν
ἧττον αὐτοῦ καταφρονεῖς. So παραχρήσασθαι (to think
little of), τῶν μαχίμων Αἰγυπτίων Hdt. II. 141. But with
acc. Id. I. 108. VIII. 20: Ibid. I. 120 ἡμῖν τῆς σῆς ἀρχῆς προ-
οπτέον: Id. III. 159 τοῦ σίτου προορᾶν. cf. II. 121: Thuc. IV.

11 φυλάσσεσθαι τῶν νεῶν: Xen. Cyr. I. 2, 2 οἱ Περσῶν νόμοι (ἄρχονται) τοῦ κοινοῦ ἀγαθοῦ ἐπιμελούμενοι.—Μέλει μοί τινος:
Xen. Cyr. V. 1, 10 Γωβρύᾳ—πειράσομαι ποιεῖν μήποτε μεταμε-
λῆσαι τῆς πρὸς ἐμὲ ὁδοῦ: Id. Hell. VII. 3, 6 ὑπεριδόντας
τῆς πόλεως. In Hdt. and Thuc. ἀνακῶς ἔχειν τινός for ἐπιμελεῖσθαι: Theocr. I. 53 μέλεται δέ οἱ οὔτε τι πήρας, οὔτε φυτῶν:
Plat. Legg. p. 843 E διευλαβεῖσθαί τινος. So ἐπιτρέφεσθαι Soph. Phil. 595[a]: κινδυνεύειν τινός: Demosth. p. 835, 69 εἰ
αἴσθοιτο—ὑπὲρ τούτων τῆς ἐπωβελίας τὸν αὐτοῦ υἱὸν ἐμὲ κιν-
δυνεύοντα, where the gen. alone is used, instead of the more
usual construction with περί, apparently in consequence of the preceding ὑπέρ, as shortly before, we find περὶ ἀτιμίας κινδυνεύοντας:
Demosth. p. 96. §. 27 τῆς πατρίδος κήδεσθαι. Μελετᾶν also, in the
sense of *to care for*, has a gen. in Hesiod: Ἔργ. 316 μελετᾷς βίου
and 443 ἔργου μελετῶν: but in its usual sense of *to practise*, it
always has an acc.

Obs. 1. Many of these verbs take an accusative of the immediate object
rather than a genitive of the antecedent cause; as, Od. ζ, 268 ἔνθα δὲ
νηῶν ὅπλα μελαινάων ἀλέγουσιν.—φροντίζειν, to think on, Hdt. VII.
8, 16: ἐμιμελεῖσθαι Plat. Legg. p. 752 D: κήδεσθαι Soph. El. 1059: ἀμελεῖν Eur. Ion. 448: παραμελεῖν Xen. Cyr. I. 6, 14 παρημεληκότα — τὰ τῶν
θεῶν[b]: Plat. Phæd. p. 98 D ἀμελήσας τὰς ὡς ἀληθῶς αἰτίας: καταφρονεῖν
Thuc. and Hdt.

Obs. 2. Μέλει sometimes in poetry has the thing cared for as the
subject in the nominative: Il. κ, 481 μελήσουσιν δ' ἐμοὶ ἵπποι: Od. a, 358
μῦθος δ' ἄνδρεσσι μελήσει πᾶσι, μάλιστα δ' ἐμοί: Od. a, 159 τούτοισιν μὲν
ταῦτα μέλει, κίθαρις καὶ ἀοιδή: Eur. Hipp. 104 ἄλλοισιν ἄλλος θεῶν τε κἀν-
θρώπων μέλει. So μεταμέλει μοί τι Hdt. VI. 63 τῷ Ἀρίστωνι τὸ εἰρημένον
μετέμελε. Rarely μέλεσθαι: Od. κ, 505 μήτι τοι ἡγεμόνος γε ποθὴ παρὰ
νηΐ μελέσθω: Eur. Phœn. 785 γάμους—σοὶ χρὴ μέλεσθαι: Hipp. 60 Ἄρτεμιν
ᾷ μελόμεσθα.

Obs. 3. These verbs are sometimes further defined by the prepositions
περί and ὑπέρ. So in Attic prose: ἐπιμελεῖσθαι περί τινος, φροντίζειν περί
τινος.

Obs. 4. The attributive genitive: φροντὶς τῶν παίδων—κῆδός τινος: Hdt.
I. 4 μηδεμίην ὥρην ἔχειν τινος: Id. III. 155 (τῆς στρατιῆς) οὐδεμίη ἔσται ὥρη
ἀπολλυμένης. — ἐπιμέλεια τῶν πολεμικῶν ἔργων: Od. ο, 8 μελεδήματα πατρός.
So αἰδώς, πρόνοια, προμήθεια σοῦ — περί: Demosth. p. 110, 2 οὐδεμίαν περὶ
τῶν μελλόντων πρόνοιαν ἔχουσιν.—Ἐπιμέλεια, φρόντις περί τινος. So adjective; as, ἐπιμελής τινος.

§. 497. Verbs of *pouring libations* or *drinking* in honour of any
person. An antecedent conception of that person being that whence
the action of the verb arose: Arist. Equit. 106 σπονδὴν λαβὲ δή,
καὶ σπεῖσον ἀγαθοῦ Δαίμονος, *in Dæmonis honorem*. So
Aristoph. Ach. 985 φιλοτησίας προπίνειν: ἐπιχεῖσθαί τινος: Theocr.

---

[a] Ellendt ad voc.   [b] Bornemann ad loc.

II. 151 ἀτὰρ τόσον αἰὲν Ἔρωτος ἀκράτῳ ἐπεχεῖτο, *merum sibi infundi jussit in Amoris honorem :* Callimach. Epigr. XXXI. ἔγχει καὶ πάλιν εἰπέ, Διοκλέος: Meleagr. Ep. XCVIII. ἔγχει καὶ πάλιν εἰπέ, πάλιν, πάλιν, Ἡλιοδώρας.

§. 498. Verbs which signify a *desire* or *longing for*, take a gen. of that whence the desire arises, it being impossible to desire any thing without an antecedent notion of it ; as, ἐπιθυμεῖν, ἐρᾶν, ἔρασθαι, ἐρατίζειν poet., ἱμείρειν, ἱμείρεσθαι, λιλαίεσθαι poet., ἔλδεσθαι poet., ποθεῖν — διψῆν, πεινῆν : Il. ρ, 660 (λέων) κρειῶν ἐρατίζων : Il. ι, 64 πολέμου ἔραται ἐπιδημίου : Od. α, 315 λιλαίεσθαι ὁδοῖο : Il. ψ, 122 ἐλδόμεναι πεδίοιο : Hdt. III. 12 ἱμείρετο — χρημάτων : Plat. Rep. p. 403 A ὁ δὲ ὀρθὸς ἔρως πέφυκε κοσμίου τε καὶ καλοῦ σωφρόνως τε καὶ μουσικῶς ἐρᾶν : Ibid. p. 438 A οὐδεὶς ποτοῦ ἐπιθυμεῖ, ἀλλὰ χρηστοῦ ποτοῦ, καὶ οὐ σίτου, ἀλλὰ χρηστοῦ σίτου· πάντες γὰρ ἄρα τῶν ἀγαθῶν ἐπιθυμοῦσιν : Id. Symp. p. 181 B οἱ φαῦλοι τῶν ἀνθρώπων — τῶν σωμάτων μᾶλλον ἢ τῶν ψυχῶν — ἐρῶσιν : Ibid. p. 186 B τὸ ἀνόμοιον ἀνομοίων ἐπιθυμεῖ καὶ ἐρᾷ: Πεινῆν τῶν σίτων, τῶν ποτῶν, τοῦ ἐπαίνου : Odyss. υ, 137 σίτου πεινέμεναι. So in Aristoph. κιττᾶν τινος, *aliquid vehementer concupiscere,*—ἐπιτύφεσθαί τινος. Later writers : κνίζεσθαι, καίεσθαι, ἀλίσκεσθαί τινος : Theocr. IV. 59 τήναν τὰν κυανόφρυν ἐρωτίδα, τᾶς ποκ' ἐκνίσθη; Il. ξ, 37 ὀψείοντες ἀϋτῆς καὶ πολέμοιο.

Obs. 1. So also the attributive genitive : ἐπιθυμία, ἔρως, πόθος τῶν καλῶν Hdt. And also adjectives : Hdt. VII. 6 νεωτέρων ἔργων ἐπιθυμητής.

Obs. 2. These verbs sometimes take an accusative : ἱμείρειν Soph. Œ. T. 58.—ποθεῖν : Od. ι, 452 ἢ σύγ' ἄνακτος ὀφθαλμὸν ποθέεις ; Il. λ, 161 ἵπποι — ἡνιόχους ποθέοντες ἀμύμονας : Od. α, 343 τοίην γὰρ κεφαλὴν ποθέω : Hdt. III. 36 ἐπόθησέ τε δὴ ὁ Καμβύσης τὸν Κροῖσον (ἐπιζητεῖν) : Plat. Rep. p. 329 A ὀλοφύρονται —, τὰς ἐν τῇ νεότητι ἡδονὰς ποθοῦντες. — ἔλδεσθαι : Od. α, 409 ἦ ἑὸν αὐτοῦ χρεῖος ἐελδόμενος τόδ' (*huc*) ἱκάνει ; Il. ε, 481 κτήματα πολλά, τά τ' ἔλδεται ὃς κ' ἐπιδευής. Φιλεῖν, ἀγαπᾶν, στέργειν always have the accusative ; the object being considered not as the cause, but as the patient of the feeling ; this latter notion being for the time more immediately present to the mind of the speaker. The object in the accusative is represented as receiving the feeling, in the genitive as awakening it.

Verbs which take their object in the accusative or dative, but to which the cause is usually or frequently attached in the genitive.

§. 499. Verbs of *grudging,* &c. have a genitive of that from the antecedent perception of which the feeling proceeds : φθονεῖν, μεγαίρειν (τινί τινος, dat. pers., genit. rei) : Φθονεῖν τινι τῆς σοφίας : Thuc. I. 75 ἐπιφθόνως διακεῖσθαι ἀρχῆς τοῖς

Ἕλλησι: Æsch. Prom. 626 οὐ μεγαίρω τοῦδέ σοι δωρήματος: Eur. Hec. 238 τοῦ χρόνου γὰρ οὐ φθονῶ.

Obs. 1. So in the attributive genitive φθόνος τινός.

Obs. 2. This causal genitive is still more widely used in the attributive construction, being joined with many substantives, the verbs corresponding to which, though properly expressing an intransitive feeling arising from some person or thing, yet are used in a transitive force and take an object in the accusative or dative, the object being considered rather as the patient, than the cause of the action or the feeling expressed by the verb, while the substantive expresses not the action but the state of feeling: φόβοι πολεμίων, *metus ab aliquo* (but φοβεῖσθαί τινα): Eur. Or. 432 τὸ Τροίας μῖσος: Id. Troad. 376 ἡδοναὶ τέκνων, pleasure in the children: φιλία τινός.

§. 500. Verbs of *requital, revenge,* &c. take a genitive of that whence the desire of requital or revenge arises: τίσασθαι, τιμωρεῖσθαι (τιμωρεῖν trag.) τινά τινος (accus. pers. and gen. rei): Il. γ, 366 ἦτ' ἐφάμην τίσασθαι Ἀλέξανδρον κακότητος: Od. γ, 206 τίσασθαι μνηστῆρας ὑπερβασίης: Æsch. Aj. 1263 ἐμῆς ἀγαγῆς ἀντιτίσασθαι φόνον: Eur. Orest. 433 Παλαμήδους σε τιμωρεῖ φόνου—Τιμωρεῖσθαί τινα φόνου: Hdt. III. 145 τοὺς ἐπικούρους—τιμωρήσομαι τῆς ἐνθάδε ἀπίξιος, *ob hujus terræ incursionem:* Ibid. 47 τίσασθαι τῆς ἁρπαγῆς.

Obs. 1. The accusative δίκην, or dative δίκῃ, is often joined to the genitive; in which case the genitive becomes attributive: τῆς σῆς ἀνοίας—μέτειμι δίκην[a].—(See Index, τίσασθαι.)

Obs. 2. Some of these verbs have sometimes a derived sense of "avenging," and then the cause of the action of revenge, &c. is considered as the patient thereof.

Obs. 3. Attributive genitive; as, Od. a, 40 τίσις Ἀτρείδαο: Il. φ, 28 ποινὴ Πατρόκλοιο: Eur. Or. 415 πατρὸς δὲ δὴ τί σ' ὠφελεῖ τιμωρία.

Obs. 4. Ἀντί is sometimes added to this genitive: Hdt. VI. 135 Πάριοι—βουλόμενοί μιν ἀντὶ τουτέων (*hujus rei caussa*) τιμωρήσασθαι θεοπρόπους πέμπουσι ἐς Δελφούς.

§. 501. Judicial verbs of *prosecution,* and *sentencing;* as, αἰτιᾶσθαι, ἐπαιτιᾶσθαι, διώκειν, ἐπεξιέναι, εἰσάγειν, ὑπάγειν, γράφεσθαι, προσκαλεῖσθαι, ἐγκαλεῖν, ἐπισκήψεσθαι — φεύγειν — δικάζειν, κρίνειν — αἱρεῖν and ἁλῶναι. Ἐπαιτιᾶσθαί τινα φόνου: Hdt. VI. 104 (Μιλτιάδεα) οἱ ἐχθροὶ ἐδίωξαν τυραννίδος τῆς ἐν Χερσονήσῳ.— Ἐπεξιέναι τινὶ φόνου: Plat. Euth. 4 D ἐπεξέρχομαι τῷ πατρὶ φόνου.—Γράφεσθαί τινα παρανόμων.—Φεύγειν κλοπῆς, φόνου, ἀσεβείας.—Κρίνεσθαι ἀσεβείας: Xen. Cyr. I. 2, 7 δικάζουσι δὲ καὶ ἐγκλήματος, οὗ ἕνεκα ἄνθρωποι μισοῦσι μὲν ἀλλήλους μάλιστα, δικάζονται δὲ ἥκιστα, ἀχαριστίας: Id. M. S. I. 2, 49 κατὰ νόμον (ἔξεστι) παρανοίας ἑλόντι καὶ τὸν πατέρα

a Elm. Heracl. 852. Med. 256.

δῆσαι : Demosth. p. 846. extr. ἐπισκήψεσθαί τινι τῶν ψευδομαρτυριῶν : cf. Ibid. p. 857, 41. 848, 13. Ibid. p. 861, 58 φεύγειν ψευδομαρτυριῶν ὑπό τινος. Ἀλῶναι κλοπῆς. So Arist.
Rhet. I. 15, 17 οὐχ ἁλίσκεται ψευδομαρτυριῶν. So ἔνοχος δειλίας,
like *reus alicujus rei.*

Obs. 1. The fine or punishment is also in the genitive, the fine being
considered as the equivalent of the offence : Xen. Hell. II. 3, 12 ὑπάγειν
θανάτου : Plat. Rep. p. 558 A ἀνθρώπων καταψηφισθέντων (*damnatorum*)
θανάτου ἢ φυγῆς. — θανάτου κρίνειν, κρίνεσθαι, διώκειν θανάτου.

Obs. 2. Sometimes περί or ἕνεκα is added : Xen. Hell. VII. 3, 6
διώκειν τινὰ περὶ φόνου : Demosth. p. 53, 47 τῶν στρατηγῶν ἕκαστος δὶς καὶ
τρὶς κρίνεται παρ' ὑμῖν περὶ θανάτου. — ἕνεκα : Hdt. VI. 136 Ξάνθιππος —
Μιλτιάδεα ἐδίωκε τῆς Ἀθηναίων ἀπάτης εἵνεκεν. — γράφεσθαί τινά τινος ἕνεκα
Plat. : frequently also a substantive ; as, φεύγειν ἐπ' αἰτίᾳ φόνου Demosth.—
γράφεσθαί τινα γραφὴν φόνου, or δίκην φόνου.

Obs. 3. Recipient verbs take a genitive of the person or thing whence
any thing is received ; as, δέχομαι *et simil.* Eur. Hipp. 89 δέξαιό τι μοῦ :
Id. Sup. 848 τρῶμα λόγχης πολεμίων ἐδέξατο : Id. Phœn. 321 πῶς τέρψιν
παλαιᾶς λάβω χαρμονᾶς ;—(See *Accusative Case—Recipient Verbs.*)

Obs. 4. This causal genitive sometimes suffers attraction ; as, Soph.
Œ. C. 1291 ἃ δ' ἦλθον ἤδη σοι θέλω λέξαι, for ὧν ἦλθον.

Obs. 5. The preposition ἐκ is sometimes added : Soph. Œ. C. 1363 ἐκ
σέθεν ἀλώμενος.

Relative Genitive.

§. 502. Relative genitive.—When two things or notions are so
connected with each other, that the one is a necessary condition
of the existence or conception of the other, so that the notion of
the one is formed from an antecedent knowledge and consideration
of the other, or is conceived as depending on it, the verb takes a
genitive of the notion which is thus antecedent to it :

1. Every notion of *greater or less, superiority,* arises from the
antecedent consideration of that object to which it is superior, or
greater or less ; hence,

2. All *comparatives* take a genitive of that object from a comparison with which, the notion of greater or less (in whatever it
may consist) arises ; as, ὁ υἱὸς μείζων ἐστι τοῦ πατρός : Eur.
Med. 965 χρυσὸς δὲ κρείσσων μυρίων λόγων βροτοῖς : Ibid.
86 πᾶς τις αὑτὸν τοῦ πέλας μᾶλλον φιλεῖ : Plat. Symp. p. 188
D ὁμιλεῖν καὶ φίλους εἶναι καὶ τοῖς κρείττοσιν ἡμῶν θεοῖς.

3. Positive adjectives also, which imply a comparative notion,
as the numeral multiples in άσιος : as, διπλάσιος, τριπλάσιος, πολλαπλάσιος ; so also the numerals in πλοῦς, as διπλοῦς, τριπλοῦς &c. :
and δεύτερος, &c. ὕστερος ; περισσός, δὶς τόσος &c. : Il. ψ, 248 οἵ κεν

ἐμεῖο δεύτεροι ἐν νήεσσι πολυκλήϊσι λίπησθε: Hdt. VII. 48
τὸ Ἑλληνικὸν στράτευμα φαίνεται πολλαπλήσιον ἔσεσθαι τοῦ
ἡμετέρου: Id. VIII. 137 διπλήσιος ἐγένετο αὐτὸς ἑωῦτοῦ,
twice as great as before, marking increase in degree: Arist.
Equit. 285 τριπλάσιον κεκράξομαι σοῦ: cf. Hdt. VI. 133. Ibid. 120
ὕστεροι δὲ ἀπικόμενοι τῆς συμβολῆς (*prœlio*) ἱμείροντο ὅμως
θεήσασθαι τοὺς Μήδους: Id. I. 23 οὐδενὸς δεύτερος, as Plat. Tim.
p. 20 A οὐδενὸς ὕστερος: Xen. Cyr. VIII. 2, 21 τῇδέ γε μέντοι
διαφέρειν μοι δοκῶ τῶν πλείστων, ὅτι οἱ μὲν, ἐπειδὰν τῶν ἀρκούν-
των περιττὰ κτήσωνται, τὰ μὲν αὐτῶν κατορύττουσι, τὰ δὲ κατα-
σήπουσιν — ἐγὼ δὲ ὑπηρετῶ μὲν τοῖς θεοῖς καὶ ὀρέγομαι ἀεὶ πλειόνων·
ἐπειδὰν δὲ κτήσωμαι, ἃ ἂν ἴδω περιττὰ ὄντα τῶν ἐμοὶ ἀρκούν-
των, τούτοις τὰς ἐνδείας τῶν φίλων ἐξακοῦμαι. So ἡμιόλιος: Id.
Anab. I. 3, 21 μισθὸν ὁ Κῦρος ὑπισχνεῖται ἡμιόλιον πᾶσι δώσειν,
οὗ πρότερον ἔφερον.—δὶς τόσος Eur. Heracl. 294: δὶς τόσως
El. 1092. So also the superlative, when it expresses a very high
degree of superiority arising from a comparison: Od. λ, 481 σεῖο
δ' Ἀχιλλεῦ, οὔτις ἀνὴρ προπάροιθε μακάρτατος οὐδ' ἄρ' ὀπίσσω:
Eur. Iph. Aul. 1603 ταύτην μάλιστα τῆς κόρης ἀσπάζεται:
St. John i. 15 πρῶτος μοῦ γέγονεν, and xv. 18 ἐμὲ πρῶτον
ὑμῶν μεμίσηκεν. So probably St. Luke ii. 1 πρώτη Κυρηνίου
κ. τ. λ.

§. 503. Expressions of *difference*, which notion arises from an
antecedent conception and contemplation of that from which any
thing differs; as, διαφέρειν, διάφορος, ἄλλος, ἀλλοῖος, ἀλλότριος,
ἕτερος, — ἐναντίος, ἔμπαλιν, *e contrario:* Plat. Prot. 329 D οὐδὲν
διαφέρει τὰ ἕτερα τῶν ἑτέρων: Id. Phil. 69 D ἐπιστήμη
ἐπιστήμης διάφορος: Xen. Mem. Socr. I. 2, 37 ἄλλα τῶν
δικαίων: Hdt. IV. 126 ἐξόν τοι τῶνδε τὰ ἕτερα ποιεῖν: Plat.
Men. 87 ἀλλοῖον τῆς ἐπιστήμης: Id. Crat. 402 B ἀλλο-
τριώτερον Ἡρακλείτου: Id. Charm. 166 A ἑτέρου ὄντος
τοῦ περίττου—τῆς λογιστικῆς: Thuc. I. 28 φίλους ἑτέρους
τῶν νῦν ὄντων: Id. Euth. 3 D τὸ ὅσιον παντὸς ἀνοσίου
ἐναντίον: Demosth. p. 289, 14 οὐδὲν ἀλλότριον ποιῶν οὔτε
τῆς ἑαυτοῦ πατρίδος οὔτε τοῦ τρόπου.

Obs. 1. Sometimes πρό and ἀντί with the genitive, or παρά and πρός
with the accusative, are used instead of the comparative genitive, even after
ἄλλος.—(See these Prepositions.)

Obs. 2. Ἡ also is used instead of the genitive after comparative notions;
as, ὁ πατὴρ μείζων ἢ ὁ υἱός: Hdt. VI. 57 διπλήσια νέμονται ἑκατέρῳ τὰ
πάντα ἢ τοῖσι ἄλλοισι: so Att. prose: so Plat. Rep. p. 130 C οἱ δὲ κτησάμενοι
(sc. χρήματα) διπλῇ ἢ οἱ ἄλλοι ἀσπάζονται αὐτά: Hdt. IV. 50 πολλαπλή-
σιά ἐστι τοῦ θέρεος ἤπερ τοῦ χειμῶνος: cf. Id. IV. 50. Plat. Rep. p. 534

A.—ὕστερος ἢ Demosth. c. Timoth. p. 1193.—ἡμιόλιος, ἥμισυς ἢ: Xen. Hell. V. 3, 21 τὸν ἥμισυν σῖτον, ἢ πρόσθεν.—ἐναντίον: Plat. Phædr. p. 275 A τοὐναντίον εἶπες ἢ δύναται: Demosth. p. 98, 33 τοὐναντίον ἢ νῦν.—So the adverb ἔμπαλιν: Hdt. IX. 56 Ἀθηναῖοι ᾖσαν τὰ ἔμπαλιν ἢ Λακεδαιμόνιοι: Id. I. 207 ἐγὼ γνώμην ἔχω—τὰ ἔμπαλιν ἢ οὗτοι: Xen. Anab. III. 5, 13 ἐπανεχώρουν εἰς τοὔμπαλιν ἢ πρὸς Βαβυλῶνα.—διαφέρειν ἢ seldom: Plat. Phædr. p. 228 D διαφέρει τὰ τοῦ ἐρῶντος ἢ τὰ τοῦ μή. So ἄλλος ἢ.

§. 504. Verbs of *superiority*—*getting the better of*—*being prominent or eminent*, which arise from a comparison, and therefore imply an antecedent notion of some object or standard with which the comparison is made: προέχειν, ὑπερφέρειν, προφέρειν, ὑπερβάλλειν, ὑπερέχειν [a], περιγίγνεσθαι, περιεῖναι—πρωτεύειν, poet.: ἀριστεύειν, κρατιστεύειν, καλλιστεύειν (also prose), ὑπατεύειν,—πρεσβεύειν poet. and prose, διαφέρειν, βάλλειν: Plat. Euth. 4 D οὐδὲ ἂν διαφέροι τῶν πολλῶν: Eur. Med. 1092 προφέρειν ἐς εὐτυχίαν τῶν γειναμένων: Hdt. VIII. 138 ὀδμῇ ὑπερφέροντα τῶν ἄλλων: Thuc. I. 81 τοῖς ὅπλοις αὐτῶν ὑπερφέρομεν: Æsch. Prom. 921 βροντῆς ὑπερβάλλοντα: Soph. Phil. 137 τέχνα γὰρ τέχνας ἑτέρας προύχει: Od. σ, 247 περίεσσι γυναικῶν εἶδός τε μέγεθός τε: Il. ζ, 460 ὃς ἀριστεύεσκε μάχεσθαι Τρώων: Soph. Aj. 1389 Ὀλύμπου τοῦδ' ὁ πρεσβεύων πατήρ: Hdt. VI. 61 καλλιστεύσει (τὸ παιδίον) πασέων τῶν ἐν Σπάρτῃ γυναικῶν: (Cf. Eur. Hipp. 1009): Id. VII. 2 τῶν μὲν δὴ προτέρων (παίδων) ἐπρέσβευε Ἀρταβαζάνης, τῶν δὲ ἐπιγιγνομένων Ξέρξης: Xen. Cyr. III. 1, 19 τάχει—περιεγένου αὐτοῦ: Plat. Gorg. p. 475 B σκεψώμεθα, ἆρα λύπῃ ὑπερβάλλει τὸ ἀδικεῖν τοῦ ἀδικεῖσθαι, καὶ ἀλγοῦσι μᾶλλον οἱ ἀδικοῦντες ἢ οἱ ἀδικούμενοι: Id. Legg. p. 752 E πρεσβεύειν τῶν πολλῶν πόλεων: Id. Apol. p. 31 B ἀνέχεσθαι τῶν οἰκείων ἀμελουμένων: Demosth. p. 24, 23. (Phil.) στρατευόμενος καὶ πονῶν—ἡμῶν μελλόντων καὶ ψηφιζομένων καὶ πυνθανομένων περιγίγνεται: Ibid. θαυμαστὸν, εἰ μηδὲν ποιοῦντες ἡμεῖς—τοῦ πάντα ποιοῦντος, ἃ δεῖ, περιῆμεν: Thuc. V. 97 ἄλλως τε καὶ νησιῶται ναυτοκρατόρων εἰ μὴ περιγένοισθε.

Obs. 1. The particular point wherein one thing surpasses another is, generally in prose writers, in the instrumental dative; as, Hdt. I. 1 τὸ δὲ Ἄργος προεῖχε ἅπασι τῶν ἐν τῇ Ἑλλάδι, but is sometimes expressed by a preposition; as, ἔν τινι, εἴς τι, κατά τι, ἐπί τινι. In poetry it also stands in the accusative or infinitive.

Obs. 2. The verbs ἔχειν, φέρειν, βάλλειν, in the above compounds, are neuter (§. 360). The compound verb assumes sometimes a transitive force, and then the thing or person surpassed is considered

---

[a] Elm. Œ. T. 381.

rather as the object of the transitive, than the cause of the neuter notion of a state : So ὑπερβάλλειν generally; προέχειν, ὑπερέχειν frequently : Eur. Hipp. 1381.—(See *Compound Verbs*).

§. 505. Verbs which express *inferiority, submission, posteriority*, as these equally imply an antecedent standard : ἡττᾶσθαι, μειοῦσθαι, νικᾶσθαι poet., ὑστερεῖν, ὑστερίζειν, ὕστερον εἶναι, κρατεῖσθαι, ἐλαττοῦσθαι, μειονεκτεῖν, to come short; Ἡττᾶσθαι τῶν ἐπιθυμιῶν : Pind. Nem. IX. 2 ἔνθ᾽ ἀναπεπταμέναι ξείνων νενίκανται θύραι, *ab hospitibus vict.e patent* [a] : Eur. Med. 315 ἠδικημένοι σιγησόμεσθα, κρεισσόνων νικώμενοι [b]. So often in Eur. ; as, Iph. A. 1357. Cycl. 454. Id. Heracl. 233 τὴν εὐγένειαν τῆς τύχης νικωμένην : Xen. M. S. I. 3, 3 θυσίας δὲ θύων μικρὰς ἀπὸ μικρῶν οὐδὲν ἡγεῖτο μειοῦσθαι τῶν ἀπὸ πολλῶν καὶ μεγάλων πολλὰ καὶ μεγάλα θυόντων : Id. Hier. IV. 1 μεγάλου ἀγαθοῦ μειονεκτεῖ.—ὑστερίζειν τῶν καιρῶν, τῶν ἔργων Demosth. p. 50, 35. p. 51, 39. p. 93, 12. Id. p. 120, 36 οὔτε ναυμαχίας οὔτε πεζῆς μάχης οὐδεμιᾶς ἡττᾶτο (like ἡττᾶσθαι ἐπιθυμιῶν [c]).

Obs. Νικᾶσθαι is also joined with a dative, which represents the instrument whereby the defeat is produced : Eur. Hipp. 458 ξυμφορᾷ νικώμενοι [d]; and ἡττᾶσθαι is joined with ὑπό, frequently in Plato and the other Attic prose writers, which represents the genitive rather as the agent or cause of the inferiority or subjection.

§. 506. Verbs of *aiming at a mark*, real or imaginary ; as the apprehension of the object to be aimed at is necessarily antecedent to the notion of aiming at it, aiming implies an antecedent conception of the mark ; as, τοξεύειν, ἀκοντίζειν, στοχάζεσθαι (βάλλειν, ἰέναι, τιτύσκεσθαι [like τυγχάνειν τινός] poet.) : Il. ρ, 304 Ἕκτωρ δ᾽ αὖτ᾽ Αἴαντος ἀκόντισε δουρὶ φαεινῷ : Ib. 517 καὶ βάλεν Ἀρήτοιο κατ᾽ ἀσπίδα: Ib. 525 Ἕκτωρ δ᾽ Αὐτομέδοντος ἀκόντισε δουρὶ φαεινῷ: Ib. 608 ὁ δ᾽ Ἰδομενῆος ἀκόντισε Δευκαλίδαο, δίφρῳ ἐφεσταότος: Il. ν, 159 Μηριόνης αὐτοῖο τιτύσκετο δουρὶ φαεινῷ: Il. δ, 100 ὀΐστευσον Μενελάου κυδαλίμοιο: Il. θ, 118 τοῦ δ᾽ ἰθὺς μεμαῶτος ἀκόντισε Τυδέος υἱός: Il. ψ, 855 ἧς ἄρ᾽ ἀνώγει τοξεύειν : Soph. Aj. 154 τῶν γὰρ μεγάλων ψυχῶν ἱεὶς οὐκ ἂν ἁμάρτοι: Plat. Gorg. 465 A τοῦ ἡδέος στοχάζεται.

Obs. Τοξεύειν sometimes is used with κατά, to define more exactly the nature of the objective relation, and τοξεύειν and βάλλειν have a twofold sense, to cast, and to (cast at and) hit, in which latter sense they take an accus. of the patient of the transitive action : so ἔβαλεν αὐτοῦ, he cast at him ; ἔβαλεν αὐτόν, he (cast at and) hit him.

§. 507. Verbs which properly signify a rapid motion after some

a. Dissen ad loc.   b. Pflugk ad loc.   c. Bremi ad loc.   d. Monk ad loc.

object, and thence applied to the mental striving after an object : ἐπείγεσθαι, ὁρμᾶν (intransitive), and ὁρμᾶσθαι, ἐπιβάλλεσθαι, ἐπαΐσσειν, ἐσσύμενος Epic ; ἐφίεσθαι, ἐπιστρέφεσθαι (στρέφεσθαι and μεταστρέφεσθαι poet.), ἐντρέπεσθαι, ἐπιβατεύειν : Il. τ, 142 ἐπειγόμενός περ Ἄρηος : Od. a, 309 ἐπειγόμενός περ ὁδοῖο : Il. δ. 335 Τρώων ὁρμᾶν (intransitive) : Il. ξ, 488 ὡρμήθη δ᾽ Ἀκάμαντος : Il. ζ, 68 ὦ φίλοι, — μήτις νῦν ἐνάρων ἐπιβαλλόμενος μετόπισθεν μιμνέτω : Xen. Cyr. I. 2, 3 πονηροῦ τινος ἢ αἰσχροῦ ἔργου ἐφίεσθαι.—Ἐπιστρέφεσθαί τινος, to care for any one : Soph. Aj. 1117 τοῦ δὲ σοῦ ψόφου οὐκ ἂν στραφείην : Plat. Crit. p. 52 C οὔτε ἡμῶν τῶν νόμων ἐντρέπει.

Obs. Ἐφίεσθαι is sometimes used with an accusative, but very rarely.

§. 508. Verbs of *feeling, catching, reaching* after an object or aim ; as, ἐπιμαίεσθαι (to feel), μέμαα poet.[a], ὀρέγεσθαι (to stretch), as ἐπιμαίεσθαι σκοπέλου, δώρων, νόστου[b] : Il. ζ, 466 ὡς εἰπὼν οὗ παιδὸς ὀρέξατο φαίδιμος Ἕκτωρ : Il. π, 322 τοῦ δ᾽ ἀντίθεος Θρασυμήδης ἔφθη ὀρεξάμενος.—ὀρέγεσθαι τῶν καλῶν ἔργων.

Obs. Ἐπιμαίεσθαι with accusative : Od. λ, 531 ξίφεος ἐπεμαίετο κ ώ π η ν (he clasped) : Hymn. h. Merc. 108 ἐπεμαίετο τέχνην (to seek after).

§. 509. 1. Those verbs of *obtaining* or *reaching any thing,* which imply the notion of *aiming at* or *reaching after it ;* as, λαγχάνειν (seldom), τυγχάνειν, (συντυγχάνειν and ἐντυγχάνειν often in Soph.), κυρεῖν, προσήκει (μοί τινος) : Il. ω, 76 ὥς κεν Ἀχιλλεὺς δώρων ἐκ Πριάμοιο λάχῃ, ἀπό θ᾽ Ἕκτορα λύσῃ : Il. ε, 587 τύχε γάρ ῥ᾽ ἀμάθοιο βαθείης : Il. π, 609 ἔλπετο γὰρ τεύξεσθαι—προβιβῶντος : Isocr. p. 22 B C ἐπειδὴ θνητοῦ σώματος ἔτυχες, ἀθανάτου δὲ ψυχῆς, πειρῶ τῆς ψυχῆς ἀθάνατον μνήμην καταλιπεῖν.—Τυγχάνειν, λαγχάνειν χρημάτων, εὐτυχίας — τυχεῖν τελευτῆς, ὀνόματος &c. : Æsch. Prom. Vinct. 270 τυχόντ᾽ ἐρήμου : Id. 649. Eur. Hec. 359. 374. Xen. M. S. IV. 5, 11 δοκεῖς μοι λέγειν, ὡς ἀνδρὶ ἥττονι τῶν διὰ τοῦ σώματος ἡδονῶν πάμπαν οὐδεμιᾶς ἀρετῆς προσήκει.

Obs. Λαγχάνειν and τυγχάνειν[c] generally have the accusative, in the sense of *to find, meet with, gain.* So κυρεῖν in this sense in the tragedians ; as, Eur. Hec. 698 ἐπ᾽ ἀκταῖς ν ι ν κ υ ρ ῶ θαλασσίαις.

2. So the adverbs : εὐθύ, ἰθύ(ς), straight for any mark, μέχρι(s) Homer, ἄχρι(s), up to : Il. μ, 254 (θύελλα) ἰθὺς νηῶν κονίην φέρεν : Il. π, 584 ἰθὺς Λυκίων — ἔσσυτο : Il. ρ, 233 οἱ δ᾽ ἰθὺς Δαναῶν — ἔβησαν : Hdt. VI. 95 ἔχον (*dirigebant*) τὰς νέας ἰθὺ τοῦ Ἑλλησπόντου καὶ τῆς Θρῃΐκης.

§. 510. Verbs of *meeting with,* or *approaching ;* the notion of striving or reaching after something, as an aim, being implied therein : ἀντᾶν, ὑπαντᾶν, ἀπαντᾶν, ἀντιᾶν, ἀντιβολῆσαι — πελάζειν, (neuter) πελάζεσθαι, πλησιάζειν, ἐμπελάζεσθαι, ἐγγίζειν &c:: Il. π, 423 ἀντήσω γὰρ ἐγὼ τοῦδ' ἀνέρος, ὄφρα δαείω. So Homer, ἀντᾶν μάχης, ὀπωπῆς, δαίτης, to meet with, to hit upon: ἀντιᾶν πολεμοῖο, πόνοιο, μάχης, ἔργων, ἀέθλων, hence, to partake of, enjoy : Il. α, 66 αἴ κεν πως ἀρνῶν κνίσσης αἰγῶν τε τελείων βούλεται ἀντιάσας ἡμῖν ἀπὸ λοιγὸν ἀμῦναι. So ἀντιᾶν ἱρῶν, ἑκατόμβης: Od. π, 254 πάντων ἀντήσομεν ἔνδον ἐόντων, to meet with all as enemies[a]: Id. δ, 342 ἀντιβολῆσαι μάχης ; so τάφου, ἐδητύος Homer: γάμου Hesiod : ὑπαντᾶν Soph. Phil. 711 : Id. Aj. 695 πελάσαι νεῶν: Ibid. 1327 Χρύσης πελασθεὶς φύλακος: Xen. Cyr. III. 2, 4 μᾶλλον ἐπλησίαζον οἱ ἀμφὶ τὸν Κῦρον τῶν ἄκρων.

When these verbs have not the notion of striving after any thing, but the simple one of meeting, drawing nigh to, they take the dative; so always ὑπαντᾶν, ὑπαντιάζειν in Attic writers : ἀντᾶν τι Epic : ἀντιάζειν and ὑπαντιάζειν τινὰ, to lay hold on, Hdt., ἀπαντᾶν, to find : Il. α, 31 ἐμὸν λέχος ἀντιόωσα : Plat. Phil. p. 42 C ἀπαντᾶν ἡδονὰς καὶ λύπας.

§. 511. Words expressing the notion of *failing in, missing, deceived in,* which imply an antecedent notion of an object aimed at, or an opinion entertained : ἁμαρτάνειν, σφάλλεσθαι, ψεύδεσθαι, more rarely ψεύδειν, διαψεύδεσθαι: Il. ψ, 857 ὄρνιθος ἁμαρτών: Hdt. III. 81 γνώμης ἀρίστης ἡμάρτηκε. Ψεύδεσθαι, σφάλλεσθαι ἐλπίδος, δόξης, τύχης: Thuc. IV. 108 ἐψευσμένοις τῆς Ἀθηναίων δυνάμεως: Eur. Med. 1009 δόξης ἐσφάλην.

§. 512. So all verbs of *remembering* and *forgetting* take a genitive : these notions arising from and implying an antecedent notion of the thing remembered or forgotten ; as, μιμνήσκειν, μιμνήσκεσθαι, μνημονεύειν, μνᾶσθαι — λανθάνεσθαι, ἐπιλανθάνεσθαι, λήθειν poet., ληθάνειν Epic, to make to forget : Od. α, 29 μνήσατο γὰρ κατὰ θυμὸν ἀμύμονος Αἰγίσθοιο : Ibid. 321 ὑπέμνησέν τε ἑ πατρός: Od. η, 221 ἐκ δέ με πάντων ληθάνει, ὅσσ' ἔπαθον: Il. π, 357 οἱ δὲ φόβοιο δυσκελάδου μνήσαντο, λάθοντό τε θούριδος ἀλκῆς: Xen. Cyr. VIII. 3, 8 τοῦ μὲν φθόνου ἐπελέλησθο : Plat. Symp. p. 180 C λόγων οὐ πάνυ διεμνημόνευεν. So attributive genitive: μνήμη τῶν κακῶν.

Obs. Μνημονεύειν, *commemorare,* "to speak of," generally has an accusative, especially when the object is a thing ; a living person being sometimes considered as the source of the remembrance which is implied in the

notion of commemorating ; while a thing is regarded rather as the patient
of the verb, the thing spoken of or commemorated. So also the other
verbs take an accusative in the sense of "to keep in the memory;" as,
Il. ζ, 222 Τυδέα δ' οὐ μέμνημαι : Hesiod. Theog. 503 οἵ οἱ ἀπεμνήσαντο
χάριν εὐεργεσιάων : Hdt. VI. 21 ἀναμνήσαντα οἰκῆϊα κακά : Ibid. 86, 2 οὔτε
μέμνημαι τὸ πρῆγμα : Ibid. 136 (τοῦ Μιλτιάδου) ὑπεραπολογέοντο οἱ φίλοι τῆς
μάχης τε τῆς ἐν Μαραθῶνι γενομένης πολλὰ ἐπιμεμνημένοι καὶ τὴν Λήμνου ἅλωσιν
(genitive and accusative) : Id. VII. 18 μεμνημένος μὲν τὸν ἐπὶ Μασσαγέτας
Κύρου στόλον : Xen. Cyr. VI. 1, 24 ὅπως ἐν ταῖς ἀγωγαῖς τὰς τάξεις ὑπομιμνή-
σκοιντο : Id. Anab. III. 2, 11 ἀναμνήσω ὑμᾶς τοὺς τῶν προγόνων τῶν ὑμετέρων
κινδύνους : cf. Hell. II. 3, 30. Plat. Phædr. p. 241 A ὑπομιμνήσκων τὰ
πραχθέντα καὶ λεχθέντα : Id. Cratyl. p. 396 C ἐμεμνήμην τὴν Ἡσιόδου γενεα-
λογίαν : Demosth. p. 69 princ. οὐδ' ἀμνημονεῖ τοὺς λόγους οὐδὲ τὰς ὑποσχέσεις,
ἐφ' αἷς τῆς εἰρήνης ἔτυχεν. Λανθάνεσθαι always has the genitive, but ἐπιλανθάνεσθαι sometimes, even in prose, the accusative. — Μνᾶσθαι, to mention,
sometimes takes περί : Od. η, 191. Hdt. VII. 39. Demosth. p. 30, 6.

§. 513. So also the notions of *beginning something*, are formed
from and imply an antecedent conception of something not yet
begun, of a state different from that of which the verb expresses
the beginning : ἄρχειν, ἄρχεσθαι, ὑπάρχειν, κατάρχειν, ἐξάρχειν : Od.
α, 28 τοῖσι δὲ μ ύ θ ω ν ἦ ρ χ ε πατὴρ ἀνδρῶν : Eur. Alc. 814 π η μ ά-
τ ω ν ἄ ρ χ ε ι λ ό γ ο ς : Æsch. P. V. 199 ἦ ρ ξ α ν τ ο δαίμονες
χ ό λ ο υ : Arist. Pax, 605 ἦ ρ ξ ε ν ἄ τ η ς : Plat. Leg. 892 A
μ ε τ α β ο λ ῆ ς π ά σ η ς ἄ ρ χ ε ι : Od. δ, 19 μ ο λ π ῆ ς ἐ ξ ά ρ χ ε ι ν.
And in Attic prose : ὑ π ά ρ χ ε ι ν ἀ δ ί κ ω ν ἔ ρ γ ω ν, ε ὐ ε ρ γ ε-
σ ί α ς &c. This genitive must be distinguished from the separative, where a particular point whence the action proceeds is
taken.—(See *Separative Genitive*.)

Obs. These verbs are sometimes joined with the accusative, where the
accusative is conceived of as the object or patient of the action begun,
(implied in the substantive,) the notion of beginning being kept out of
sight. So Il. β, 273 ἐξάρχειν (βουλεύων) βουλάς : so Eur. Troad. ἐξῆρξω
(μέλπων) μολπάν : so Xen. Cyr. III. 3, 58. Plat. Euthyd. 283 B κατάρχειν (λέγων) λόγον : Eur. Hec. 685 κατάρχεσθαι νόμον : Orest. 960. Od. γ,
445. — κατάρχομαι is also used without any case, Eur. Iph. Taur. 40. —
ὑπάρχειν is always joined with a genitive in Attic Greek, except Æsch. p.
31, 32.

§. 514. So also verbs of *ceasing, stopping*, imply an antecedent
notion of something going on which is stopped : λήγειν, παύεσθαι
(παύειν τινά τινος). Sometimes τελευτᾶν, λωφᾶν (neuter, and also
τινά τινος), ἔχειν, to stop : Il. ζ, 107 Ἀργεῖοι — λ ῆ ξ α ν φ ό ν ο ι ο ;
so ἀναπνεῖν, to take breath from, to cease ; ἀ ν α π ν ε ῖ ν κ α κ ο τ ῆ-
τ ο ς, π ο ν ο ῖ ο : Eur. Med. 93 οὐδὲ π α ύ σ ε τ α ι χ ό λ ο υ : Thuc.
III. 59 τ ε λ ε υ τ ᾶ ν λ ό γ ο υ : Xen. Cyr. VIII. 7, 17 τ ε λ ε υ τ ᾶ ν
β ί ο υ : Thuc. I. 112 Ἑ λ λ η ν ι κ ο ῦ π ο λ έ μ ο υ ἔ σ χ ο ν οἱ Ἀθηναῖοι : Arist. Pax, 421 π ε π α υ μ έ ν α ι κ α κ ῶ ν : (Il. β, 595 Μοῦσαι — Θάμυριν π α ῦ σ α ν ἀ ο ι δ ῆ ς.)

Genitivus Pretii.

§. 515. 1. The price or value of any thing stands in the genitive, as it is only from an antecedent conception of the thing valued, and a comparison between the two, that the notion of equality implied in the notion of price or value arises.

2. Verbs of *selling* and *buying*; as, ὠνεῖσθαι, ἀγοράζειν, πρίασθαι, κτᾶσθαι, παραλαμβάνειν — πωλεῖν, ἀποδίδοσθαι, περιδίδοσθαι, διδόναι. As early as Homer: Il. ψ, 485 τρίποδος π ε ρ ι δ ώ μ ε θ ο ν ἠὲ λέβη-τος, to wager a tripod or a caldron: Od. ψ, 78 ἐμέθεν π ε ρ ι δ ώ-σ ο μ α ι αὐτῆς, I will wager the value of myself against the truth; as in Aristoph., π ε ρ ι δ ό σ θ α ι τῆς κεφαλῆς, to wager one's head: Hdt. III. 139 ἐγὼ ταύτην π ω λ έ ω μὲν οὐδενὸς χρήματος: Id. V. 6 (οἱ Θρῇκες) ὠ ν έ ο ν τ α ι τὰς γυναῖκας παρὰ τῶν γονέων χρημάτων μεγάλων: Xen. M. S. II. 1, 20 τῶν πόνων π ω λ ο ῦ σ ι ν ἡμῖν πάντα τἀγάθ᾽ οἱ θεοί: Id. Cyr. III. 1, 36 σὺ δὲ, ὦ Τιγράνη, λέξον μοι, πόσου ἂν π ρ ί α ι ο, ὥστε τὴν γυναῖκα ἀπολαβεῖν. — Ἐγὼ μὲν, ἔφη, ὦ Κῦρε, κἂν τῆς ψυχῆς π ρ ι α ί μ η ν, ὥστε μήποτε λατρεῦσαι ταύτην: Demosth. p. 113, 9 τοῦτο δ᾽ ἐστὶν, ὃ τῶν ἀναλισκομένων χρημάτων πάντων Φίλιππος ὠ ν ε ῖ τ α ι, αὐτὸς μὲν πολεμεῖν ὑμῖν, ὑφ᾽ ὑμῶν δὲ μὴ πολε-μεῖσθαι.

§. 516. Verbs of *exchange* and *barter*; as, ἀμείβειν, ἀμείβεσθαι, ἀλλάττειν, ἀλλάττεσθαι, λύειν &c.: Il. ζ, 236 τεύχε᾽ ἄ μ ε ι β ε ν, χρύσεα χαλκείων, ἑκατόμβοι᾽ ἐννεαβοίων: So Il. λ, 547 ὀλίγου γονὺ γουνὸς ἀμείβων: Il. λ, 106 υἷε δύω Πριάμοιο — ἔ λ υ σ ε ν (Ἀχιλ-λεὺς) ἀποίνων. So Od. λ, 326 Ἐριφύλην, ἣ χρυσὸν φ ί λ ο υ ἀ ν δ ρ ὸ ς ἐ δ έ ξ α τ ο τιμήεντα. So Xen. Cyr. III. 1, 37 καὶ σὺ δὲ, ὦ Ἀρμένιε, ἀπάγου τήν τε γυναῖκα καὶ αὐτοὺς παῖδας, μηδὲν αὐτῶν κ α τ α-θ ε ί ς [a], for them: Eur. Med. 967 sq. τῶν δ᾽ ἐμῶν παίδων φυγὰς ψ υ χ ῆ ς ἂν ἀλλαξαίμεθ᾽, οὐ χ ρ υ σ ο ῦ μόνον: Demosth. p. 68, 10 κέκρισθε — μηδενὸς ἂν κέρδους τὰ κοινὰ τῶν Ἑλλήνων π ρ ο έ σ θ α ι, μηδ᾽ ἀ ν τ α λ λ ά ξ α σ θ α ι μηδεμιᾶς χάριτος μηδ᾽ ὠφελείας τὴν εἰς τοὺς Ἕλληνας εὔνοιαν.

Obs. 1. So the attributive genitive, with a substantive expressing these notions: Eur. Or. 1149 sq. ἀλόγιστον δέ τι τὸ πλῆθος ἀντάλλαγμα γενναίου φίλου, for ἀλόγιστόν τι ἐστὶν τὸ ἀνταλλάττεσθαι τὸ πλῆθος τοῦ γενναίου φίλου.

Obs. 2. Sometimes ἀντί with a genitive, or πρός with an accusative, are joined with verbs of exchange. We also find the instrumental dative representing the thing exchanged as the means or instrument whereby the exchange is brought about; as, Il. η, 472 ἔνθεν ἄρ᾽ οἰνίζοντο καρηκο-μόωντες Ἀχαιοί, ἄλλοι μὲν χ α λ κ ῷ, ἄλλοι δ᾽ αἴθωνι σ ι δ ή ρ ῳ κ. τ. λ.: Eur. Troad. 355 δάκρυα τ᾽ ἀνταλλάσσετε τοῖς τῆσδε μ έ λ ε σ ι, Τρωάδες, γ α μ η-λ ί ο ι ς.

---

[a] Bornemann ad loc.

§. 517. Verbs and adjectives of *valuing* ; as, τιμᾶν, τιμᾶσθαι, ποιεῖσθαι, ἀξιοῦν, ἀξιοῦσθαι, ἀπαξιοῦν, ἄξιος, ἀνάξιος, ἀντάξιος : Il. ψ, 649 τιμῆς τετιμῆσθαι, to be considered worthy of honour. Βοὸς ἄξιος[a] : Il. λ, 514 ἰητρὸς γὰρ ἀνὴρ πολλῶν ἀντάξιος ἄλλων : Hdt. III. 53 ὁ δὲ Λυκόφρων οὐδὲ ἀνακρίσιος ἠξίωσε τὸν φέροντα τὴν ἀγγελίην : Ibid. 145 ἐμὲ — ἀδικήσαντα οὐδὲν ἄξιον δεσμοῦ δήσας γοργύρης ἠξίωσας. So ἀξίως : Hdt. VI. 112 ἐμάχοντο ἀξίως λόγου : Thuc. III. 39 ἐκολάσθησαν ἀξίως ἀδικίας. — Ἀξιοῦν τινα τιμῆς : Xen. Cyr. II. 2, 17 ἔγωγε οὐδὲν ἀνισώτερον νομίζω τῶν ἐν ἀνθρώποις εἶναι τοῦ τῶν ἴσων τόν τε κακὸν καὶ ἀγαθὸν ἀξιοῦσθαι. — Τιμᾶν τινί τινος and τινά τινος, to estimate a person's fine at such a sum ; τιμᾶν τινι δέκα ταλάντων, τοῦ θανάτου : Plat. Apol. S. p. 36 B τιμᾶταί μοι ὁ ἀνὴρ θανάτου. Εἶεν· ἐγὼ δὲ δὴ τίνος ὑμῖν ἀντιτιμήσομαι, ὦ ἄνδρες Ἀθηναῖοι ; ἢ δῆλον, ὅτι τῆς ἀξίας ; — So the midd. τιμᾶσθαί τινι ἀργυρίου, θανάτου, τῶν ἐσχάτων, to attach the penalty of fine, death, &c. to the indictment : Plat. Apol. p. 37. init. εἰ οὖν δεῖ με κατὰ τὸ δίκαιον τῆς ἀξίας τιμᾶσθαι, τούτου τιμῶμαι, ἐν πρυτανείῳ σιτήσεως. — Τιμᾶσθαι πολλοῦ. — Ποιεῖσθαι in the phrases, πολλοῦ, ὀλίγου ποιεῖσθαι (but often also with περί and the genitive) : Plat. Legg. p. 728 A πᾶς ὅ τ᾽ ἐπὶ γῆς καὶ ὑπὸ γῆς χρυσὸς ἀρετῆς οὐκ ἀντάξιος : Demosth. p. 862, 60 διὰ τούτῳ τῶν δέκα ταλάντων ἐτίμησαν.

§. 518. Verbs of *being superior to—being lords over—governing ;* these being relative notions, and arising from an antecedent conception of their correlatives, which stand in the genitive : κυριεύειν, κοιρανεῖν, δεσπόζειν, τυραννεῖν, τυραννεύειν, στρατηγεῖν, στρατηλατεῖν, ἐπιτροπεύειν, ἀνάσσειν, αἰσυμνᾶν, θεμιστεύειν poet., βασιλεύειν, ἐπιτάττειν (seldom)—ἄρχειν, ἀρχεύειν (poet.), ἐπιστατεῖν, σημαίνειν, κραίνειν (poet.), ἡγεμονεύειν, ἡγεῖσθαι, χορηγεῖν,—κρατεῖν : Il. α, 38 Τενέδοιο ἶφι ἀνάσσεις : Il. ξ, 84 σημαίνειν στρατοῦ : Od. ι, 114 θεμιστεύει δὲ ἕκαστος (τῶν Κυκλώπων) παίδων ἠδ᾽ ἀλόχων, οὐδ᾽ ἀλλήλων ἀλέγουσιν : Soph. Aj. 1050 κραίνει στρατοῦ : Eur. Med. 19 γήμας Κρέοντος παῖδ᾽, ὃς αἰσυμνᾷ χθονός : Hdt. VII. 7 Ἀχαιμένεα—ἐπιτροπεύοντα Αἰγύπτου—ἐφόνευσε Ἰνάρως : Ibid. 97 τοῦ δὲ ναυτικοῦ ἐστρατήγεον οἵδε. — 99 ἡγεμόνευε δὲ Ἁλικαρνησσέων : Id. III. 15 ἐπιτροπεύειν Αἰγύπτου : cf. 82. Ibid. 142 οὔτε γάρ μοι Πολυκράτης ἤρεσκε δεσπόζων ἀνδρῶν ὁμοίων ἑωυτῷ : Xen. Hell. III. 1, 10 ἐσατράπευε αὐτῷ τῆς χώρας : Æsch. Pers. 7 χώρας ἐφορεύειν : Thuc. I. 69 ὁ λόγος τοῦ ἔργου ἐκράτει, *fama superabat rem ipsam :* Xen. Cyr. I. 1, 2 ἄρχοντες μέν εἰσι καὶ οἱ βουκόλοι τῶν βοῶν, καὶ οἱ ἱππο-

[a] Vide Passow Lex.

φορβοὶ τῶν ἵππων, καὶ πάντες δὲ οἱ καλούμενοι νομεῖς ὧν ἂν ἐπιστατῶσι ζώων, εἰκότως ἂν ἄρχοντες τούτων νομίζοιντο: Plat.
Theæt. p. 179 D χορηγεῖν τοῦ λόγου: Demosth. p. 26, 30 εἰ
δὲ τοῖς μὲν ὥσπερ ἐκ τυραννίδος ὑμῶν ἐπιτάττειν ἀποδώσετε
κ. τ. λ.

Obs. 1. Κρατεῖν, to be superior to, or to get the upper hand of, or to
govern, from the relative notion κράτος, power, has a genitive—to conquer, from the positive notion κράτος, strength, it has an accusative;
rarely a local dative, as νεκύεσσιν Od. λ, 485 : ἀνδράσι καὶ θεοῖσι Od. π,
265.

Obs. 2. So the attributive genitive; as, Eur. Hec. 883 καὶ πῶς γυναιξὶν
ἀρσένων ἔσται κράτος; So the adjectives ἐγκρατής, ἀκρατής: Xen.
Cyr. IV. 1, 14 τῆς μεγίστης ἡδονῆς — ἐγκρατῆ εἶναι: Ibid. V. 1, 14 τὰ
μοχθηρὰ ἀνθρώπια πασῶν, οἶμαι, τῶν ἐπιθυμιῶν ἀκρατῆ ἐστι. So in Latin
impotens iræ.

Obs. 3. Many of these verbs of governing take a dative ; this is either
the dativus commodi, *for the benefit of,* or the local dative, to which the
local prepositions ἐν and μετά are sometimes added : *a.* στρατηγεῖν
(dat. commodi, seldom) : Hdt. VI. 72 ἐστρατήγησε Λακεδαιμονίοισι ἐς
Θεσσαλίην. So στρατηλατεῖν τινι. — *h.* ἀνάσσειν (dat. loci) ; in
Homer the dative is more usual than the gen. : Od. α, 181 Ταφίοισι φιλη-
ρέτμοισιν ἀνάσσω : Il. μ, 242 (Ζεὺς) ὃς πᾶσι θνητοῖσι καὶ ἀθανάτοισιν ἀνάσσει :
Il. α, 288 πάντων μὲν κρατέειν ἐθέλει, πάντεσσι δ' ἀνάσσειν. So in the sense
of "to be the master," in Od. α, 117 κτήμασιν οἶσιν ἀνάσσοι : cf. 402. δ,
309. So Od. α, 402 δώμασιν ἀνάσσειν. Also with dative and genitive :
Il. υ, 180 ἐλπόμενον Τρώεσσιν ἀνάξειν ἱπποδάμοισιν τιμῆς τῆς Πριάμου, among
the Trojans. With the preposition : μετ' ἀθανάτοισιν, μετ' 'Αργείοισιν ἀνάσσειν, as ἐν Θήβῃ ἀνάσσειν. *c.* βασιλεύειν. In Homer, dat. loci ; but
also, Il. λ, 285, genitive, which construction generally prevailed : βασιλεύειν ἐν 'Ιθάκῃ, κατὰ δῆμον in Homer. *d.* ἄρχειν, generally genitive (in
prose always) ; sometimes dative even in Homer : as, Il. ξ, 133 ἦρχε δ'
ἄρα σφιν ἄναξ ἀνδρῶν 'Αγαμέμνων : Il. π, 552 ἦρχε δ' ἄρα σφιν Ἕκτωρ : Od.
ξ, 230 ἀνδράσιν ἦρξα : Æsch. Prom. V. 940 δαρὸν γὰρ οὐκ ἄρξει θεοῖς, with
ἐν Il. ν, 690. So in Homer : ἀρχεύειν τινί, but later, τινός. *e.* ἐπιστατεῖν but seldom, and in prose never, the genitive. *f.* σημαίνειν
generally with dative : Il. κ, 58 σημαίνει φυλάκεσσι, (transmission.) *g.* θεμιστεύειν τινί Od. λ, 569. *h.* κραίνειν is not found with dative
till late Epic writers. *i.* ἡγεμονεύειν and ἡγεῖσθαι in the sense of,
to precede, shew the way, has the dative ; to rule, or lead, gen. ; ἡγεμονεύειν, has usually the dative in Homer only : Il. β, 816.—ἡγεῖσθαι in Homer
has both genitive and dative ; but in other writers, especially in prose, the
genitive. We find also, Od. ψ, 134 ἡγεῖσθαί τινι ὀρχηθμοῦ, to lead the
dance (dat. commodi) : so χορηγεῖν τινι (dat. commodi) ; ἡγεῖσθαι and
ἐξηγεῖσθαι Thuc., with accusative in the sense of, to conquer. So also
κραίνειν has the accusative : Soph. Trach. 127 ὁ πάντα κραίνων βασιλεύς.
So δεσπόζειν : Eur. H. F. 28 Λύκος τὴν ἑπτάπυργον τήνδε δεσπόζων πόλιν.

§. 519. Words expressing *relationship—connection—equality—
contraposition—community in,* and the contraries, all which notions
arise from a previous notion of the person or thing towards which
these relations exist : κοινός, ἴσος, ἰσόμοιρος poet., ἀντίπαλος, ἀντί-

U 2

φθόγγος Pind., ἰσόρροπος, — ὅμοιος and the poetic ὁμώνυμος, ὁμέστιος, ὁμόστολος—(προσφερής Eur. H. F. 130.)—συνεργός, σύντροφος, συμφυής, συνήθης, συγγενής, σύμψηφος, ξύμφωνος, ξύμφυτος and the Poetic, σύμφορος, σύννομος — also ἀδελφός — the Poetic, ἔννομος, ἔνθεος, ἔντροφος, κληρονομεῖν: Hdt. III. 37 ἔστι δὲ ταῦτα ὁμοῖα τοῦ Ἡφαίστου: Plat. Menex. p. 241 C ἔργον κοινὸν Λακεδαιμονίων τε καὶ Ἀθηναίων (as *communis alicujus rei*): Theocr. II. 88 καί μευ χρὼς μὲν ὁμοῖος ἐγίνετο πολλάκι θάψω: Demosth. p. 690, 14 κληρονομοῦσι τῆς ὑμετέρης δόξης: Soph. Ant. 192 ἀδελφὰ τῶνδε.

Obs. 1. Ἴσος, ὁμοῖος, κοινός generally take the dative; ἀδελφός generally the genitive.

Obs. 2. This genitive is sometimes more accurately defined by κατά, τοξεύειν κατά τινος (and τοξεύειν takes also ἐπί and εἰς with accusative: τοξεύειν has also the accusative in a transitive sense of, *to wound*.) So we find πλεῖν ἐπὶ Σάμου, to sail towards Samos, as it were, aiming at it: πῆξαι ὄμματα κατὰ χθονός.

Obs. 3. In the attributive construction, we find the object or aim of the substantive in the genitive; as, ὁδός, κέλευθος, νόστος τινός: Od. ε, 345 ἐπιμαίεο νόστου γαίης Φαιήκων: Eur. Iph. Taur. 1037 γῆς πατρῴας νόστος.

§. 520. So adjectives and adverbs, expressing *connection*, or *dependence*; as, ἐπιχώριος, φίλος, διάδοχος, (frequently with dative) δοῦλος (generally dative) ἀκόλουθος, ἑξῆς, ἐφεξῆς: So ἐχθρός Plat. Conv. 189 B ἡμετέρας Μούσης ἐπιχώριον: Id. Rep. 604 D δειλίας φίλον: Soph. Phil. 867 ὕπνου φέγγος διάδοχον: Arist. Ach. 438 τἀκολουθὰ τῶν ῥακῶν — τούτων ἑξῆς: Plat. Tim. 55 τῆς ἀμβλυτάτης — ἐφεξῆς γεγονυῖαν: Soph. Ant. 479 δοῦλος τῶν πέλας.

§. 521. 1. When any thing is spoken or conceived of as the *property*, or *possession* of, or *dependent* on another, this notion of property implies and arises from an antecedent notion of the person of whom it is the property, &c.

a. With the verbs, εἶναι, γενέσθαι; as, τῆς φύσεως μέγιστον κάλλος ἐστίν (certainly more correctly written ἔστιν) — τοῦ Σωκράτους πολλὴ ἦν ἀρετή: Il. ψ, 160 οἷσι μάλιστα κήδεός ἐστι (better ἔστι) νέκυς, the subject of mourning: Thuc. I. 113 τῆς αὐτῆς γνώμης εἶναι, *ejusdem sententiæ esse*: Demosth. p. 13, 16 τὸ μὲν ἐπιτιμᾶν (*vituperare*) ἴσως φῆσαί τις ἂν ῥᾴδιον καὶ παντὸς εἶναι (of any one), τὸ δ᾽ ὑπὲρ τῶν παρόντων ὅ τι δεῖ πράττειν ἀποφαίνεσθαι, τοῦτ᾽ εἶναι συμβούλου. So ἑαυτοῦ εἶναι, to be his own master: Demosth. p. 42, 7 ἦν ὑμῶν αὐτῶν ἐθελήσητε γενέσθαι, *non ex aliis pendere*. Also, εἶναί τινος, *alicujus esse*, *alicui addictissimum esse*, prose and poetry: Isocr. p. 185 τῆς πόλεως ὄντας καὶ τῶν τὰ βέλτιστα λεγόντων: Demosth.

p. 125, 56 εἶναι Φιλίππου[a]. So Ibid. εἶναι τοῦ βελτίστου, *studere rebus optimis.*

b. With many other verbs, though mostly there may be an ellipse of εἶναι: Il. γ, 457 νίκη μὲν δὴ φαίνετ' Ἀρηϊφίλου Μενελάου: Plat. Protag. p. 343 E εὔηθες γὰρ τοῦτό γε φανείη ἂν καὶ οὐ Σιμωνίδου: Demosth. p. 34, 21 δικαίου πολίτου κρίνω τὴν τῶν πραγμάτων σωτηρίαν ἀντὶ τῆς ἐν τῷ λέγειν χάριτος αἱρεῖσθαι: Eur. Hec. 279 ἐπιλήθομαι κακῶν. Even ποιοῦ σεαυτῆς Soph. Antig. 547.

2. The person or thing, to which belongs some quality essential or peculiar, is put in the genitive, since the notion of this quality is derived from an antecedent notion of that whereof it is the peculiar property; as, ἀνδρός ἐστιν (ἔστιν) ἀγαθοῦ εὖ ποιεῖν τοὺς φίλους: Hdt. I. 107 τρόπου ἡσυχίου ἐστί (ἔστι): Soph. El. 1054 πολλῆς ἀνοίας (sc. ἔστι) καὶ τὸ θηρᾶσθαι κενά: Eur. Hec. 844 ἐσθλοῦ γὰρ ἀνδρὸς τῇ δίκῃ θ' ὑπηρετεῖν καὶ τοὺς κακοὺς ὁρᾶν πανταχοῦ κακῶς ἀεί. So πολλοῦ χρόνου ἔστι τι, it is an affair of a long time: Demosth. p. 814, 4 ἐμὲ δ' ἔπτ' ἐτῶν ὄντα: Ibid. p. 54 princ. κακούργου μὲν γάρ ἐστι (ἔστι) κριθέντ' ἀποθανεῖν, στρατηγοῦ δὲ μαχόμενον τοῖς πολεμίοις: Ibid. p. 113, 12 συμμάχων δ' εἶναι καὶ φίλων ἀληθινῶν ἐν τοῖς τοιούτοις καιροῖς παρεῖναι: Ibid. p. 18, 2 ἔστι τῶν αἰσχρῶν (neuter), μᾶλλον δὲ τῶν αἰσχίστων, πόλεων—, ὧν ἡμέν ποτε κύριοι, φαίνεσθαι προϊεμένους: Ibid. p. 16, 26 τῶν ἀτοπωτάτων— ἂν εἴη, εἰ κ. τ. λ.: Ibid. p. 102, 48 δοκεῖ ταῦτα καὶ δαπάνης μεγάλης καὶ πόνων πολλῶν καὶ πραγματείας εἶναι.

Obs. 1. To this genitive however is frequently added the preposition πρός; as, πρὸς ἀνδρὸς ἀγαθοῦ ἔστιν εὖ ποιεῖν τοὺς φίλους.

Obs. 2. In poetry this genitive of the quality is used in the place of an adjective; as, Eur. Phœn. 1529 στολὶς κροκόεσσα τρυφᾶς for τρυφερά: Ibid. 1616 τραύματα αἵματος for αἱματόεντα: Id. Bacch. 388 ὁ τᾶς ἡσυχίας βίοτος for ἥσυχος. Compare (§. 435. *c.*)

3. So also with adjectives, which express the notion of being *sacred to, peculiar to, suitable to,* or the contraries: ἴδιος, οἰκεῖος, κύριος, ἱερός, πρέπων: as, Demosth. p. 26, 28 οἱ δὲ κίνδυνοι τῶν ἐφεστηκότων (*ducum*) ἴδιοι, μισθὸς δ' οὐκ ἔστιν: Id. p. 32, 16 καὶ ταύτης κύριος τῆς χώρας γενήσεται. So τοῦτό μου ἴδιον, or οἰκεῖόν ἐστι—ὁ τόπος ἱερός ἐστι τοῦ θεοῦ. Even πρεπόντως τῶν πραξάντων Plat. Menex. p. 239 C. instead of the usual dative. Cf. Lat. *proprius alicujus.*

Obs. 3. So the attributive genitive (§. 463.); as, ὁ τοῦ βασιλέως κῆπος, ἡ τοῦ Σωκράτους ἀρετή, πατὴρ Νεοπτολέμου, μήτηρ τοῦ Σωκράτους, Ἀθηνᾶς

---

[a] Bremi ad loc.

ἄγαλμα : Od. ν, 101 Διὸς τέρας : Il. ι, 579 τέμενος οἰνοπέδοιο.—τροπαῖα Διός
poet.—Ἡρακλέους Ἥβη Eur., as Virg. Æn. III. 319 *Hectoris Andro-*
mache.—Also with prepositions : Xen. M. S. II. 7, 9 ἡ ἀπὸ τούτων χάρις :
Demosth. p. 24, 22 τὴν παρὰ θεῶν εὔνοιαν : Id. p. 74, 34 τῇ παρ' ὑμῶν
ὀργῇ περιπεσεῖν.

Genitivus Loci.

§. 522. 1. The genitive of the place is almost wholly confined to
poetry. The place in this construction seems to be conceived by
the speaker as a *necessary condition* to the notion of the verb,
and therefore antecedent to it, whence it in some sort arose : Il. ρ,
72 νέφος δ' οὐ φαίνετο πάσης γαίης οὐδ' ὀρέων : Il. ι, 219
αὐτὸς δ' ἀντίον ἷζεν Ὀδυσσῆος θείοιο τοίχου τοῦ ἑτέρου : Od. α,
23 Αἰθίοπας, τοὶ διχθὰ δεδαίαται, ἔσχατοι ἀνδρῶν, οἱ μὲν δυσομένου
Ὑπερίονος, οἱ δ' ἀνιόντος : Od. γ, 251 ἢ οὐκ Ἄργεος ἦεν
Ἀχαιϊκοῦ, ἀλλά πῃ ἄλλῃ πλάζετ' ἐπ' ἀνθρώπους : Od. φ, 108 οἵη
νῦν οὐκ ἔστι γυνὴ κατ' Ἀχαιΐδα γαῖαν, οὔτε Πύλου ἱερῆς, οὔτ'
ἠπείροιο μελαίνης : Æsch. Ag. 1054 ἑστίας μεσομφά-
λου ἕστηκεν ἤδη μῆλα : Soph. El. 900 ἐσχάτης ὁρῶ πυρᾶς
νεωρῆ βόστρυχον τετμημένον : Plat. Symp. p. 182 B τῆς δὲ
Ἰωνίας καὶ ἄλλοθι πολλαχοῦ αἰσχρὸν νενόμισται.

Obs. 1. Hence the local adverbs in the genitive form : οὖ, πού, ποῦ,
ὅπου, αὐτοῦ, ὑψοῦ, τηλοῦ, ἀγχοῦ, ὁμοῦ, οὐδαμοῦ, ἀλλαχοῦ, and the local adverbs with the suffix θεν, apparently for the local adverbs with the suffix
θι ; as, ἔνδοθεν, ἐγγύθεν, τηλόθεν, ἕκτοσθεν, ὄπισθεν, πάροιθεν, πρόσθεν, ἄνωθεν
κάτωθεν, ἔνερθεν, ὕπερθεν, ἔξωθεν, ἔσωθεν ; as, Il. ρ, 582 Ἕκτορα δ' ἐγγύθεν
ἱστάμενος ὤτρυνεν Ἀπόλλων.

2. Hence, especially in Epic, we find verbs of motion with a
genitive of the way over which the motion proceeds, and which is
conceived of as a necessary condition of the motion : Il. δ, 244
ἔκαμον πολέος πεδίοιο θέουσαι : Il. β, 801 ἔρχονται πεδίοιο :
Il. β, 785 διέπρησσον πεδίοιο : Il. ν, 820 κονίοντες πεδίοιο :
Il. χ, 23 θέειν πεδίοιο : Il. ε, 597 ἰὼν πολέος πεδίοιο : Il.
κ, 353 ἑλκέμεναι νειοῖο βαθείης—ἄροτρον : Il. ν, 64 πεδίοιο
διώκειν ὄρνεον : Il. ω, 264 ἵνα πρήσσωμεν ὁδοῖο : Il. ζ, 38 ἵππω
ἀτυζομένω πεδίοιο : Æsch. Choeph. 705 ἡμερεύοντας μακρᾶς
κελεύθου : Soph. Œ. T. 1478 ἀλλ' εὐτυχοίης, καί σε τῆσδε τῆς
ὁδοῦ Δαίμων ἄμεινον ἢ 'μὲ φρουρήσας τύχοι ! So Hesiod. ἔργ. 577
ἠώς τοι προφέρει μὲν ὁδοῦ, προφέρει δὲ καὶ ἔργον. So in prose,
ἰέναι τοῦ πρόσω.

Obs. 2. There are various other ways of explaining this very difficult
construction, one of which is to take the genitive as partitive.

Obs. 3. So we may explain the genitive in the phrases as a genit.
loci : κατεάγη, ξυνετρίβη τῆς κεφαλῆς Arist. Vesp. 1248. Pac. 71. Plat.
Gorg. p. 469 D. : Eur. Troad. 1173 κρατὸς ὥς σ' ἔκειρε—βόστρυχον.

And so perhaps also the passage in Plat. Gorg. p. 496 E ἢ οὐχ ἅμα τοῦτο (sc. λυπούμενον χαίρειν, *cum voluptate dolorem esse conjunctum*) γίγνεται κατὰ τὸν αὐτὸν τόπον καὶ χρόνον (*eodem loco et tempore*), εἴτε ψυχῆς εἴτε σώματος βούλει, i.e. *sive illud* λυπούμενον χαίρειν *in animo, sive in corpore fieri vis.*

Genitivus Temporis.

§. 523. The moment of time in which an action takes place is sometimes conceived of as a necessary condition of the action, and therefore antecedent to it. This temporal genitive occurs both in prose and poetry : Ἄνθη θάλλει τοῦ ἔαρος, the spring being conceived of as a condition of the production of the flowers. So θέρους, χειμῶνος, ἡμέρας, τῆς αὐτῆς ἡμέρας, νυκτός, δείλης, ὀπώρης, μηνός, ἐνιαυτοῦ, &c. with the attributives, as τοῦ αὐτοῦ, τοῦ προτέρου, ἑκάστου &c.: hence the adverbial expressions, ἀρχῆς, at the beginning, and τοῦ λοιποῦ, for the future (in later writers generally λοιπόν, or τὸ λοιπόν): Od. η, 118 τάων οὔποτε καρπὸς ἀπόλλυται οὐδ᾽ ἀπολείπει χείματος οὐδὲ θέρους.—Poetic, ἠοῦς, νηνεμίης &c.: Il. ε, 522 (νεφέλας) Κρονίων νηνεμίης ἔστησεν ἐπ᾽ ἀκροπόλοισιν ὄρεσσιν: Il. θ, 470 ἠοῦς δὴ καὶ μᾶλλον ὑπερμενέα Κρονίωνα ὄψεαι: Hdt. IV. 48 Ἴστρος ἴσος ἀεὶ αὐτὸς ἑωυτῷ ῥέει καὶ θέρεος καὶ χειμῶνος: Id. VI. 12 τοῦ λοιποῦ μὴ πειθώμεθα αὐτοῦ: Eur. Iph. T. 1265 Chor. ὕπνου, *somni tempore*, Poetic: Plat. Phæd. p. 59 D ἐξήλθομεν τοῦ δεσμωτηρίου ἑσπέρας: Demosth. p. 44, 5 οὐκέτι τοῦ λοιποῦ πάσχοιμεν ἂν κακῶς.

A space of time is also considered as the necessary condition of the notion of the verb, and is in the genitive: Il. λ, 691 ἐλθὼν γὰρ ῥ᾽ ἐκάκωσε βίη Ἡρακληείη τῶν προτέρων ἐτέων: Æsch. Ag. 285 ποίου χρόνου δὲ καὶ πεπόρθηται πόλις; how long? Soph. El. 478 οὐ μακροῦ χρόνου, so συχνοῦ, πολλοῦ, πλείστου, ὀλίγου χρόνου (also χρόνου alone, Arist. Eq. 950.), πολλῶν ἡμερῶν, ἐτῶν &c.: Hdt. III. 134 ταῦτα ὀλίγου χρόνου ἔσται τελεύμενα: Id. VI. 58 ἐπεὰν δὲ θάψωσι, ἀγορὴ δέκα ἡμερέων οὐκ ἵσταταί σφι: Xen. Anab. I. 7, 18 βασιλεὺς οὐ μαχεῖται δέκα ἡμερῶν: Plat. Gorg. p. 516 D ἵνα αὐτοῦ δέκα ἐτῶν μὴ ἀκούσειαν τῆς φωνῆς: Id. Phæd. princ. οὔτε τις ξένος ἀφῖκται χρόνου συχνοῦ ἐκεῖθεν: Id. Symp. p. 172 C πολλῶν ἐτῶν Ἀγάθων ἐνθάδε οὐκ ἐπιδεδήμηκεν.

Obs. To define this relation more clearly, prepositions are sometimes used : ἐκ, ἀπό, ἐπί, which represent the time, as it were, on which the action rests : διά,—ἐντός and ἔσω, *intra* ; as, ἐκ νυκτός, like *de nocte*, ἐκ πολλοῦ χρόνου, ἐξ ἀρχῆς, ἀφ᾽ ἑσπέρας, ἐπὶ Κύρου, *Cyri ætate*, ἐπ᾽ ἐμοῦ, *mea ætate*, generally with a participle present ; as, ἐπὶ Κύρου ἄρχοντος Hdt. III. 89, διὰ πολλοῦ χρόνου, ἐντός, or ἔσω πολλοῦ χρόνου.

Position.

§. 524. 1. Closely connected with the relative genitive is the *Genitive of Position*, which is used when the notion of position (local, moral, or temporal), is determined by its relation to something else, which is in the genitive.

2. Adjectives and adverbs, which express the actual *local position*, take a genitive of the object from the existence or conception of which the notion of the particular position arises; as in πέλας οἴκου, the position of οἶκος must be in the mind before the notion of anything else, being either πέλας or τηλοῦ to it, can be conceived.

§. 525. So adjectives of being *opposite, corresponding in position to, near to*, take a genitive of the correlative spot or person; as, ἀντίος, ἐναντίος, μέσος, ἀντίστροφος (Plat.), παραπλήσιος (Plat. Soph. p. 217 B.): Il. λ, 214 ἐναντίοι ἔσταν Ἀχαιῶν: Ibid. 219 πρῶτος Ἀγαμέμνονος ἀντίος ἦλθεν: Il. ρ, 31 ἀντίος ἵστασ᾽ ἐμεῖο: Eur. Or. 1444 γυναικὸς ἀντίοι σταθέντες: Hdt. II. 34 ἡ Αἴγυπτος τῆς ὀρεινῆς Κιλικίης μάλιστά κη ἀντίη κέεται, so Id. VII. 36 ἐπικαρσίας τοῦ Πόντου, at right angles to the Pontus.

§. 526. So adverbs which express *position* or *proximity to*, or *distance from*; the notion of proximity, &c. being derived from the antecedent perception of the object to which it is near, &c.; as, ἄντα, ἄντην, ἄντα, ἀντία, ἀντίον (also with dative, Hdt. II. 34.) ἀντικρύ(s), ἀπαντικρύ(s), ἐναντίον, καταντίον, ἐνώπιον, πρόσθεν, ἔμπροσθεν, προπάροιθε — ὄπισθεν, πέλας (also with dative, poet.: See Passow Lex.), πλησίον, ἐγγύς (also with dative: Eur. Heracl. 37.), ἆσσον, ἐγγύθι, ἐγγύτατα, ἐγγυτάτω (also with dative), ἄγχι (also with dative), ἀγχοῦ, σχεδόν, χωρίς, τῆλε, τηλόθι, ἑκάς, ἀπόπροθεν, ἀπόπροθι, ἀνεύθε (at a distance), ἀπάνευθε, and also the prepositions, ἀντί, πρό. So also the genitive after ὑψόθεν, καθύπερθε, ἄνω, κάτω, νέρθε, ἀμφίς, ἔξω, ἔκτος, ἔσω (εἴσω), πέρα, πέραν (on the opposite side—beyond—opposite): Il. ρ, 29 εἴ κε μεῦ ἄντα στήῃς: Ibid. 69 ἀντίον ἐλθέμεναι Μενελάου κυδαλίμοιο: Od. κ, 156 ὅτε δὴ σχεδὸν ἦα κιὼν νεὸς ἀμφιελίσσης: Il. ρ, 468 στῆ δ᾽ ὄπιθεν δίφροιο: Hdt. III. 144 κατεναντίον τῆς ἀκροπόλιος ἑκατέατο: Id. VI. 77 ὡς δὲ ἀγχοῦ μὲν ἐγίνοντο τῆς Τίρυνθος: Soph. El. 900 τύμβον προσεῖπον ἆσσον: Eur. H. F. 1115 πέλας ἐλθεῖν τῶν κακῶν: Demosth. p. 117, 27 πλησίον Θηβῶν καὶ Ἀθηνῶν: Id. p. 99. init. ἀπαντικρὺ τῆς Ἀττικῆς: Il. ρ, 192 στὰς ἀπάνευθε μάχης: Il. π, 539 τῆλε φίλων καὶ πατρίδος αἴης: Plat. Apol. p. 38 C θανάτου ἐγγύς: Hdt.

VIII. 144 ἑκὰς χρόνου: Demosth. p. 49, 34 τοῦ πάσχειν —ἔξω γενήσεσθε: Od. π, 267 ἀμφὶς φυλοπίδος: Il. ψ. 393 ἵπποι ἀμφὶς ὁδοῦ δραμέτην: Il. θ, 444 ὁ Διὸς ἀμφίς: Æsch. Ag. 183 Χαλκίδος πέραν (opposite): Hdt. VI. 103 πέρην τῆς ὁδοῦ: Soph. Ant. 334 πολίου πέραν πόντου: Xen. Anab. VI. 5, 5 πέρα μεσούσης ἡμέρας. So Attic: ἐγγύτατα, or ἐγγυτάτω γένους expresses relationship.

§. 527. So also the adverbs[a] ποῦ, πού, πή, πόθεν, οὗ, ᾗ (ἵνα, τῇδε poet.), οὐδαμοῦ, πανταχῇ &c.: Od. a, 170 τίς, πόθεν εἶς ἀνδρῶν; *unde terrarum?* Od. β, 131 πατὴρ δ᾽ ἐμὸς ἄλλοθι γαίης ζώει ὅγ᾽ ἢ τέθνηκε: Soph. Aj. 386 οὐχ ὁρᾷς, ἵν᾽ εἶ κακοῦ; Hdt. I. 163 τῆς ἑωυτοῦ χώρης οἰκῆσαι ὅκου βούλονται: Id. II. 43 οὐδαμῇ Αἰγύπτου: Xen. Cyr. VI. 1, 42 ἐμβαλεῖν που τῆς ἐκείνων χώρας: Id. VI. 19 χρημάτων — μνήμην ἑτέρωθι τοῦ λόγου ἐποιησάμην: Plat. Rep. p. 403 E εἰδέναι ὅπου γῆς ἐστι: Id. Symp. p. 181 E τὸ γὰρ τῶν παίδων τέλος ἄδηλον, οἳ τελευτᾷ κακίας καὶ ἀρετῆς ψυχῆς τε πέρι καὶ σώματος. Ἐνταῦθα τῆς ἡλικίας, τοῦ λόγου, δεῦρο τοῦ λόγου Plat.: Demosth. p. 42, 9 ὁρᾶτε —, οἳ προελήλυθεν ἀσελγείας. — Πανταχοῦ τῆς γῆς, *ubique terrarum.* So ὀψὲ τῆς ἡμέρας, τοῦ χρόνου, τῆς ἡλικίας — τρὶς τῆς ἡμέρας — πολλάκις τῆς ἡμέρας — ἀωρὶ νυκτῶν, τῆς νυκτός &c.: Hdt. IX. 101 πρωὶ τῆς ἡμέρης: Plat. Protag. p. 326 C πρωϊαίτατα τῆς ἡλικίας, at a very early age: Theocr. II. 119 ἦνθον γὰρ — αὐτίκα νυκτός, h. e. *ut primum nox appetebat.*

Obs. This genitive might perhaps be considered also as partitive.

§. 528. So also the adverbs and adjectives εὖ, καλῶς, μετρίως, ὡς, πῶς, ὅπως, ᾗ, ὅπῃ, οὕτως, ὧδε, ὡσαύτως and others[b], when joined with the verb ἔχειν, (ἥκειν Hdt., less frequently Attic), sometimes also εἶναι and κεῖσθαι, take a genitive of that from the antecedent conception whereof, and relation whereto, the notion of the good or bad state or position arises; as in εὖ ποδῶν εἶχεν, it is from a notion of the properties of the πόδες that the notion of εὖ ἔχειν is formed. This construction is more common in poetry than in prose: Hdt. VI. 116 Ἀθηναῖοι δὲ ὡς ποδῶν εἶχον τάχιστα ἐβοήθεον ἐς τὸ ἄστυ: Id. V. 62 χρημάτων εὖ ἥκοντες. Also without εὖ Hdt. VII. 157 σὺ δὲ δυνάμιός τε ἥκεις μεγάλης, *magna præditus es potentia.* Εὖ, καλῶς, μετρίως ἔχειν βίου, φρενῶν, γένους, δυνάμεως: Thuc. I. 36 καλῶς παράπλου κεῖσθαι: Id. III. 92 τοῦ πρὸς πολέμου καλῶς αὐτοῖς ἐδόκει ἡ πόλις καθίστασθαι and immediately afterwards, τῆς τε ἐπὶ Θρᾴκης παρόδου χρησίμως κεῖσθαι. Οἱ Ἕλληνες

---

[a] Lobeck Phryn. 279.　　　[b] Ibid. 280.

οὕτως εἶχον ὁμονοίας πρὸς ἀλλήλους : Xen. Cyr. VII. 5, 56 οὕτω
τρόπου ἔχεις : Id. Hell. IV. 5, 15 ὡς τάχους ἕκαστος εἶχεν : Thuc.
I. 22 ὡς ἑκατέρων τις εὐνοίας — ἢ μνήμης ἔχοι (where
ἑκατέρων depends on εὐνοίας) : Plat. Rep. p. 576 D εὐδαιμονίας
ὡσαύτως ἔχεις : Id. Legg. p. 869 D κατὰ ταὐτὰ ἔστω τοῦ καθαρὸς
εἶναι : Lucian Somn. c. II. ὡς ἕκαστος γνώμης ἢ ἐμπειρίας
εἶχεν. Poetry : Eur. El. 751 πῶς ἀγῶνος ἥκομεν : Id. Hell.
321 πῶς δ' εὐμενείας τοῖσιδ' ἐν δόμοις ἔχεις : Ibid. 1273 ὡς
ἂν παρούσης οὐσίας ἕκαστος ᾖ : Arist. Lys. 1128 οὐ κακῶς
γνώμης ἔχω.

Privative Genitive.

§. 529. 1. The notion of being without any thing, implies and
arises from an antecedent conception of that thing : hence the
genitive is used after verbs, substantives, or adjectives, expressing
the notion of *being without, wanting, being deserted,* &c. ; also
after verbs expressing transitive actions, which produce such
state : as, στερεῖν, ἀποστερεῖν, χηροῦν, ἐρημοῦν, μουνοῦν (poet.),
and their middle forms, &c. : ἀπορεῖν, πένεσθαι, δεῖ, δεῖν, δεῖσθαι,
(to be in need of ; thence, to ask for ;) δεύεσθαι poet., λείπεσθαι
poet., λείπει, also ἐλλείπεσθαι, ἐπιλείπεσθαι, σπανίζειν, χρή, ἐλεύθερος, μόνος, καθαρός, κενός, ἔρημος, γυμνός, ὀρφανός, πένης, ψιλός :
and most compounds of a privative : Demosth. p. 845, 3 οὗτος
ἐμὲ τῶν πατρῴων ἁπάντων — ἀπεστέρηκε : Ibid. p. 108, 73
δεῖ δ' ἔργων τῇ πόλει καὶ πράξεώς τινος : Hdt. III. 65
τῆς βασιλητης ἐστέρημαι : Il. σ, 100 δῆσεν ἐμεῖο,
he wanted me : Soph. Œ. R. 406 εὐβουλίας δεῖ : Thuc.
VI. 14 ὠφελίας δεηθέντες : Id. VIII. 7 νῆες μιᾶς δεοῦ-
σαι τεσσαράκοντα, *forty minus one.* So Hdt. II. 2 καταδεῖ
πεντήκοντα σταδίων : Eur. Med. 960 σπανίζειν πέπλων.
Often Attic : πολλοῦ, ὀλίγου (seldom μικροῦ), δεῖ : Æsch. P. V.
993 γυμνὸς εἰμὶ προπόμπων : Eur. Med. 513 φίλων ἔρημος : Ibid. 51 σοῦ μόνη. So Id. Alc. 407 μονόστολος μα-
τρός : Id. Hec. 868 ἐλεύθερον φόβου : Plat. Epist. 332 C
πένης ἀνδρῶν φίλων : Hdt. II. 38 ἢν δὲ τουτέων πάντων
ᾖ καθαρός : Pind. Isthm. VI. 10 ὀρφανὸν ἐτάρων : Ibid.
III. 26 ὀρφανοὶ ὕβριος : Soph. El. 390 αἱ δὲ σάρκες αἱ κεναὶ
φρενῶν ἀγάλματ' ἀγορᾶς εἰσιν : Eur. Hec. 230 παρέστηκεν ἀγὼν
μέγας πλήρης στεναγμῶν, οὐδὲ δακρύων κενός : Hdt. I. 155
πόλιν — ἀναμάρτητον ἐοῦσαν τῶν τε πρότερον καὶ τῶν νῦν
ἐστεώτων : Id. I. 32 ; III. 147 ἀπαθὴς κακῶν : Soph. Ant. 583

κακῶν ἄγευστος αἰών: Eur. Supp. 82 ἄκλαυστος γόων:
Id. Troad. 1313 ἄτας ἄϊστος: Xen. Cyr. III. 3, 55 ἀπαίδευτος
μουσικῆς. So ἄτιμος ἐπαίνων. Substantives : Il. λ, 605 (and
elsewhere) τί δέ σε χρεὼ ἐμεῖο: Eur. Hec. 976 τίς χρεία σ᾽
ἐμοῦ (sc. ἔχει): Hdt. VI. 135 ἡσυχίη τῆς πολιορκίης : Ibid.
139 λύσις τῶν παρεόντων κακῶν : Plat. Rep. p. 329 C τῶν γε
τοιούτων ἐν τῷ γήρᾳ πολλὴ εἰρήνη γίγνεται καὶ ἐλευθερία.—
ἔνδεια χρημάτων, ἀπορία ἐφοδίων Demosth. So also participles
which express deprivation : Æsch. Ag. 479 φρενῶν κεκομμένος:
Eur. Hel. 274 φίλων τητωμένη : Æsch. P. V. 472 ἀποσφαλεὶς
φρενῶν: Id. Ag. 517 λελειμμένον δορός.

Obs. 1. Δεῖσθαι, to request, takes a genitive of the person only ; as,
Demosth. p. 67, 3 δεηθῆναι πάντων ὑμῶν, or a genitive of the person as well
as of the thing: Hdt. III. 157 τῶν ἐδέετο σφῶν, or the preposition παρά
is sometimes joined with the genitive of the person, and sometimes we
find an accusative of the person : Hdt. V. 37 ἐδέοντο Βοιωτούς; and an
accusative of the thing when it is considered, not as something wanted,
but as the request made : ἥν τι (δέημα) δεῶνται.—(See *Accusative*).

Obs. 2. Adjectives compounded with a privative in poetry, and sometimes in prose, take a cognate substantive in the genitive, and even, though
less frequently, where the substantive has no attributive. This fulness
of expression is very becoming to the lofty diction of tragedy, and
it is sometimes used even in prose : Soph. Œ. C. 1383 ἀπάτωρ ἐμοῦ:
Id. Aj. 314 ἀψόφητος ὀξέων κωκυμάτων: Id. Trach. 247 χρόνος ἀνήριθμος
ἡμερῶν: Id. El. 231 οὐδέποτ᾽ ἐκ καμάτων ἀποπαύσομαι ἀνάριθμος ὧδε θρήνων:
Ibid. 36 ἄσκευος ἀσπίδων: Id. Œ. C. 677 ἀνήνεμος πάντων χειμώνων : Ibid.
865 ἄφωνος ἀρᾶς: Eur. Phœn. 334 ἄπεπλος φαρέων λευκῶν: Id. Hipp. 546
ἄζυξ λέκτρων : Ibid. 146 ἀνίερος ἀθύτων πελάνων [a]: Id. Hel. 532 ἄφιλος
φίλων: Id. Herc. 114 πατρὸς ἀπάτορα: Id. Andr. 705 ἄπαις τέκνων. Prose:
Hdt. III. 66 ἄπαιδα—ἐόντα ἔρσενος καὶ θήλεος γόνου, and in other passages
in Hdt.: Id. VI. 12 ἀπαθέες ἐόντες πόνων τοιούτων : Thuc. II. 65 χρημάτων
ἀδωρότατος γενόμενος: Xen. M. S. II. 1, 31 τοῦ πάντων ἡδίστου ἀκούσματος,
ἐπαίνου σεαυτῆς, ἀνήκοος εἶ, καὶ τοῦ πάντων ἡδίστου θεάματος ἀθέατος: Id.
Cyr. IV. 6, 2 ἄπαις δέ εἰμι ἀρρένων παίδων.

Obs. 3. So also passive compounds with a privative : Soph. Œ. C. 1519
ἐγὼ διδάξω—ἅ σοι γήρως ἄλυπα (untouched by old age) τῇδε κείσεται
πόλει: Id. Antig. 847 φίλων ἄκλαυστος: Id. Œ. C. 1521 ἄθικτος ἡγητῆρος:
Id. Phil. 867 ἄπιστον ἐλπίδων : Eur. Hipp. 962 κακῶν ἄκρατος: Arist. Nub.
1413 ἀθῷος πληγῶν: Demosth. p. 316, 17 ἀθῷος τῆς Φιλίππου δυναστείας.

2. So adverbs which express *privation, absence, want,* or *exception from:* ἄνευ, ἄνευθεν, without: ἄτερ, ἄτερθε, νόσφιν, χωρίς, πλήν,
δίχα: Il. ε, 473 ἄτερ λαῶν : Soph. Œ. R. 1415 πλὴν τοῦ δαίμονος, *except:* Id. Phil. 115 οὔτ᾽ ἂν σὺ κείνων χωρὶς οὔτ᾽
ἐκεῖνα σοῦ: Ibid. 31 ὁρῶ κενὴν δόκησιν ἀνθρώπων δίχα.

---

[a] See Monk Hipp. 146.

Separative Genitive.

§. 530. 1. The notion of removal or separation implies the antecedent conception of a point whence the motion began; hence all verbs expressing any notion of *removal, separation, departure, rising from,* may have a genitive of the point whence these began: hence all verbs of motion: βαίνειν poet., ἀπιέναι, ἀναδῦναι poet., τρέπεσθαι (*se avertere*) poet., φέρειν, ἄγειν, ἀείρειν poet., χωρεῖν (*cedere*) poet., παραχωρεῖν, συγχωρεῖν rarely, ὑποχωρεῖν, εἴκειν and ὑπείκειν prose, χάζεσθαι and ἀναχάζεσθαι poet., ἀλύσκειν poet., φεύγειν often in the dramatists: ὑπανίστασθαι and ἐξίστασθαι Attic prose: νοσφίζειν, χωρίζειν, διορίζειν, διέχειν and ἀπέχειν (to be at a distance), &c. *a.* Poetic use: Il. μ, 262 οὐδέ νυ πω Δαναοὶ χάζοντο κελεύθου: Il. ρ, 129 Ἕκτωρ δ' ἄψ ἐς ὅμιλον ἰὼν ἀνεχάζεθ' ἑταίρων: Il. σ, 138 ὡς ἄρα φωνήσασα πάλιν τράπεθ' υἱὸς ἑοῖο: Il. α, 359 ἀνέδυ πολιῆς ἁλός: Il. ε, 348 εἶκε, Διὸς θύγατερ, πολέμου καὶ δηϊοτῆτος: Od. α, 18 οὐδ' ἔνθα πεφυγμένος ἦεν ἀέθλων (also with acc., Il. ζ, 488): Il. π, 629 νεκροῦ χωρήσουσι: cf. μ, 406: Il. ρ, 422 μήπω τις ἐρωείτω πολέμοιο! Here also belongs the Homeric δέχεσθαί τινος: cf. Il. ξ, 203; ω, 305. (So Eur. Hipp. 89 δέξαιό τι μοῦ: Æsch. Ag. 27 εὐνῆς ἐπαντείλασαν, from: Soph. Phil. 1030 τῆς νόσου πεφευγέναι: Id. El. 627 θράσους οὐκ ἀλύξεις: Id. Antig. 418 χθονὸς ἀείρας (from the earth): Id. Phil. 630 νεὼς ἄγοντα (from the ship): Id. El. 324 δόμων — φέρουσαν: Id. Œ. T. 24 ἀνακουφίσαι κάρα βυθῶν: Ibid. 152 Πυθῶνος βῆναι: Ibid. 229 γῆς ἀπιέναι. So Id. El. 324 ὡς δόμων ὁρῶ τὴν σὴν ὅμαιμον (from the house): Arist. Ran. 174 ὑπάγεθ' ὑμεῖς τῆς ὁδοῦ. *b.* Poetry and prose: Hdt. II. 80 οἱ νεώτεροι αὐτέων τοῖσι πρεσβυτέροισι συντυγχάνοντες εἴκουσι τῆς ὁδοῦ καὶ ἐκτράπονται: Id. VII. 161 συγχωρήσομεν τῆς ἡγεμονίης: Id. VI. 139 ἡ γὰρ Ἀττικὴ πρὸς νότον κέεται πολλὸν τῆς Λήμνου (*procul a Lemno*). So Ibid. 22 ἡ δὲ Καλὴ αὕτη Ἀκτὴ καλεομένη ἐστὶ μὲν Σικελῶν, πρὸς δὲ Τυρσηνίην τετραμμένη τῆς Σικελίης, *est Siciliæ tractus, Tyrrheniæ obversus a Sic.*, (from Sicily towards,) like Id. II. 112 τέμενός ἐστι — καλὸν — τοῦ Ἡφαιστηΐου πρὸς νότον ἄνεμον κείμενον, from the temple of Vulcan towards the south; the temple being the point whence it commenced: Xen. Cyr. II. 4, 24 ὑποχωρεῖν τοῦ πεδίου. (Cf. Arist. Ran. 798 :) Id. Hier. VII. 2 παραχωρεῖν ὁδοῦ: Id. Symp. IV. 31 ὑπανίστανται δέ μοι ἤδη καὶ θάκων καὶ ὁδῶν

ἐξίστανται οἱ πλούσιοι: Id. Vectig. IV. 46 ἀπέχει τῶν
ἀργυρείων ἡ ἐγγύτατα πόλις Μέγαρα πολὺ πλεῖον τῶν πεντακο-
σίων σταδίων: Plat. Menex. p. 246 E ἐπιστήμη χωριζομένη
δικαιοσύνης.

Obs. 1. Here also belong the expressions χειρός, as δεξιᾶς χειρός, or
δεξιᾶς alone, ἀριστερᾶς, λαιᾶς, from the right, left hand, right, left: Hdt.
V. 77 τὸ δὲ (τέθριππον χάλκεον) ἀριστερῆς χερὸς ἔστηκε: Æsch. Pr.
714 (Sch.) λαιᾶς δὲ χειρὸς οἱ σιδηροτέκτονες οἰκοῦσι Χάλυβες: Eur.
Cycl. 681 ποτέρας τῆς χειρός; but ἐκ is generally added.

Obs. 2. Some of these verbs, as φεύγειν, have an accusative, when the
notion is rather of the person whom they fly, than of the point whence
the motion begins; and very frequently, especially in poetry, the exact
point of the motion is further defined by the prepositions.—(See *Preposition.*)

Obs. 3. The adverbial genitive in θεν is sometimes used with these
verbs instead of the inflected genitive; as, οὐρανόθεν: but even to these
the prepositions ἀπὸ and ἐκ are added: Hesiod. Op. 763 ἐκ Διόθεν.

2. Here belongs the genitive after verbs of *beginning*, where the
point whence the action commences is expressly marked: Od. θ,
499 ὁρμηθεὶς θεοῦ ἤρχετο, from the god: Od. φ, 142 ἀρξάμενος τοῦ χώρου ὅθεν οἰνοχοεύει: Pind. Nem. V. 25 ὕμνησαν
Διὸς ἀρχόμεναι.

Obs. 4. The prepositions ἀπὸ and ἐκ are sometimes added to this
genitive, to define it more accurately: Xen. M. S. II. 1, 1 σκοπῶμεν
ἀρξάμενοι ἀπὸ τῆς τροφῆς, ὥσπερ ἀπὸ τῶν στοιχείων. So Latin *in-
cipere ab aliqua re:* Plat. Legg. 701 A ἦρξε—ἐκ μουσικῆς.

§. 531. All intransitive verbs of *leaving off, ceasing,* &c. which
imply the notion of *removal* or *departure from,* take a genitive of
that whence the motion, real or supposed, began; or transitive
verbs, of *driving away from, keeping off, delivering from, deviating
from,* may take a genitive, though it need not be expressed to make
up the objective construction, as these verbs take an accusative
of that which is the immediate patient of the transitive action:
ἰέναι, *desistere* Homer, μεθιέναι Homeric, dramatic, and prose:
μεθίεσθαι, ἀφιέναι τινά τινος, ἀφίεσθαι, ὑφιέναι in Hdt.: ὑφίεσθαι,
ἀνιέναι dramatic, in Thuc., and some other prose writers: παριέναι
Aristoph., Plat.: προίεσθαι Demosth. (generally acc.): κωλύειν,
ἐρητύειν, εἴργειν, βλάπτειν, εἴργεσθαι, ἔχειν and ἀπέχειν, to keep
off: ἀπέχεσθαι, ἀλαλκεῖν, ἀμύνειν, λύειν, ἐλευθεροῦν, ἀπαλλάττειν,
ῥύεσθαι (Eur.): σώζειν (Trag.): Il. δ, 130 μήτηρ παιδὸς ἐέργει
μυῖαν: Il. ν, 525 ἐεργόμενοι πολέμοιο: Od. ε, 397 τόνγε θεοὶ κακότητος ἔλυσαν: Od. α, 195 τόνγε θεοὶ βλάπτουσι κελεύθου: Od. α, 69 ὀφθαλμοῦ ἀλάωσεν ἀντίθεον Πολύφημον,
cæcando privavit: Il. ο, 731 Τρῶας ἄμυνε νεῶν: Od. κ. 288 ὃς
κρατὸς ἀλάλκῃσιν κακὸν ἦμαρ: Od. δ, 380 εἰπέ—, ὅστις μ'

ἀθανάτων πεδάᾳ καὶ ἔδησε κελεύθου: Æsch. Ag. 120 βλα-
βέντα λοισθίων δρόμων: Eur. Or. 1515 σ᾽ ἀπαλλάξει κακῶν:
Ibid. 767 σωθῆναι κακῶν. So Arist. Ach. 201 κακῶν ἀπαλ-
λαγείς: Hdt. V. 62 τυράννων ἐλευθερώθησαν: Thuc. VII.
43 ἀνιέναι τῆς ἐφόδου, to leave by advancing: Id. V. 83 κατέ-
κλησαν — Μακεδονίας Ἀθηναῖοι Περδίκκαν. Ἀφιέναι τινὰ
τῆς αἰτίας, τῶν ψευδομαρτυριῶν. Demosth. p. 18, 2 μὴ μόνον πόλεων
καὶ τόπων — φαίνεσθαι προϊεμένους, ἀλλὰ καὶ τῶν ὑπὸ τῆς
τύχης παρασκευασθέντων συμμάχων καὶ καιρῶν (αἰσχρόν
ἐστι).

Obs. 1. The verb φείδομαι takes a genitive, following, as it would seem,
the analogy of ἀπέχεσθαι; as, Eur. Med. 1057 φεῖσαι τέκνων; though from
our not knowing the force of the active voice, we cannot define its construction with any accuracy.

Obs. 2. In prose and not unfrequently in poetry, some of these verbs are
joined with ἐκ or ἀπό—ἐλευθεροῦν, λύειν, σώζειν—εἴργειν, ἀπείργειν, ἐξείργειν,
ἐρητύειν: Thuc. II. 71 Παυσανίας ἐλευθερώσας τὴν Ἑλλάδα ἀπὸ τῶν
Μήδων: Plat. Rep. p. 571 C ἀπὸ πάσης λελυμένον τε καὶ ἀπηλλαγ-
μένον αἰσχύνης: Id. Gorg. p. 511 C D ἐκ κινδύνων σώζειν. Even
παύειν, like Soph. El. 231, 987. Eur. Hec. 917. Med. 333. El. 1108.

Obs. 3. Ἀμύνω is more commonly found with the dat. commodi, (ἀμύνω
τόνδε σοι) than with the genitive; the notion attached to the verb being
rather that of benefit resulting to the person defended, than of the driving
away of the person attacking.

Temporal Separation.

§. 532. From this genitive of local separation is derived a genitive of
temporal separation—the point whence a space of time begins, but this is
rare; and the most usual construction is with ἐκ or ἀπό: Hdt. VI. 40
τρίτῳ γὰρ μὲν ἔτεῖ τούτων, in the third year from this—reckoning from
this point: Ibid. 56 δευτέρῳ ἔτεῖ τούτων, two years after this; whether it is
before or *after* the context will determine: Xen. Hell. I. 1, 2 μετ᾽ ὀλίγον
δὲ τούτων, after this; ἀπό is more frequently used: Hdt. VI. 69
νυκτὶ τρίτῃ ἀπὸ τῆς πρώτης: Ibid. 85 κατὰ τρίτην γενεὴν τὴν ἀπ᾽
ἐμέο. So also the suffix θεν is used of time: Xen. Anab. IV. 4, 8 ἕωθεν,
immediately from day-break. So *de tertiâ vigiliâ,* &c.

Partitive Genitive.

§. 533. The notion of the whole being antecedently necessary to
the very notion of part, those words which have or imply a partitive sense, take the word expressing the whole in the genitive:

1. The verbs εἶναι and γίγνεσθαι: Hdt. III. 141 ἀπέστελλε
—στρατηγὸν Ὀτάνεα, ἀνδρῶν τῶν ἑπτὰ γενόμενον: Thuc. I. 65
καὶ αὐτὸς ἤθελε τῶν μενόντων εἶναι: Xen. Anab. I. 2, 3 ἦν
δὲ καὶ ὁ Σωκράτης τῶν ἀμφὶ Μίλητον στρατευομένων: Id.
Cyr. I. 2, 15 οἳ δ᾽ ἂν αὖ ἐν τοῖς τελείοις (ἀνδράσι) διαγένωνται ἀνεπί-
ληπτοι, οὗτοι τῶν γεραιτέρων γίνονται: Demosth. p. 122

ἡ γὰρ Ζέλειά ἐστι τῆς ᾿Ασίας: Plat. Euthyd. p. 277 C τῶν
λαμβανόντων ἄρ᾿ εἰσὶν οἱ μανθάνοντες: Id. Phæd. p. 68 D
τὸν θάνατον ἡγοῦνται πάντες οἱ ἄλλοι τῶν μεγίστων κακῶν
εἶναι.

Obs. To distinguish more accurately the part from the whole, ἐκ is
sometimes used. This partitive relation is also more distinctly expressed
by τίς or εἷς, though there is no ellipse of either of these where the
genitive stands alone.

2. The verbs τιθέναι, τίθεσθαι, ποιεῖσθαι, ἡγεῖσθαι:
Plat. Rep. p. 376 E μουσικῆς δ᾿, εἶπον, τίθης λόγους; *ad
musicam refersne sermones* [a] ? Id. Phileb. p. 60 D φρόνησιν καὶ
ἀληθῆ δόξαν τῆς αὐτῆς ἰδέας τιθέμενος: Ibid. p. 66 D ἃ
τῆς ψυχῆς ἔθεμεν αὐτῆς, ἐπιστήμας τε καὶ τέχνας κ. τ. λ.:
Id. Rep. p. 424 C καὶ ἐμὲ τοίνυν — θὲς τῶν πεπεισμένων:
Ibid. p. 567 E ποιεῖσθαί τινα τῶν δορυφόρων. So ἀριθμεῖσθαι: Eur. Bacch. 1316 τῶν φιλτάτων ἀριθμήσει τέκνων:
Theocr. XIII. 72 οὕτω μὲν κάλλιστος ῞Υλας μακάρων ἀρι-
θμεῖται.

3. Any verb [b] whose operation extends only to part of the
objects signified by the objective substantive: Il. ξ, 121 ᾿Αδρήστοιο
δ᾿ ἔγημε θυγατρῶν: Od. ξ, 211 ἠγαγόμην δὲ γυναῖκα πολυκλή-
ρων ἀνθρώπων: Hdt. I. 67 ἐξ οὗ δὴ Λίχης τῶν ἀγαθοερ-
γῶν καλεομένων Σπαρτιητέων ἀνεῦρε: Id. III. 157 ὁ δὲ
ἐπιλεξάμενος τῶν Βαβυλωνίων ἐξήγαγε: Id. VII. 6 κατέλεγε
τῶν χρησμῶν, *recitabat vaticiniorum* sc. *partem*: Aristoph.
Ach. 181 ξυνελέγοντο τῶν λίθων.

§. 534. The attributive genitive—*a.* joined with a substantive;
as, στάγονες ὕδατος—σώματος μέρος: Hdt. III. 136 ἀπίκοντο τῆς
᾿Ιταλίας εἰς Τάραντα: Id. VI. 95 ἀπίκοντο τῆς Κιλικίας ἐς τὸ
᾿Αλήϊον πεδίον.—*b.* with adjectives used as substantives, especially
superlatives—pronouns and numerals used as substantives; as,
οἱ χρηστοὶ τῶν ἀνθρώπων. This construction is less frequent with
adj. than with participles and the article, (the article giving the
distinctive and partitive force,) and more in prose than poetry:
οἱ εὖ φρονοῦντες τῶν ἀνθρώπων: Xen. Cyr. I. 3, 2 Περσῶν μὲν
πολὺ κάλλιστος ὁ ἐμὸς πατήρ, Μήδων μέντοι — πολὺ οὗτος ὁ
ἐμὸς πάππος κάλλιστος: Eur. Med. 1228 θνητῶν γὰρ οὐδείς ἐστιν εὐδαίμων ἀνήρ: Æsch. Ag. 809 τόν τε δικαίως καὶ
τὸν ἀκαίρως πόλιν οἰκουροῦντα πολιτῶν: Eur. Heracl. 594 οἱ
θανούμενοι βροτῶν: Plat. Gorg. 525 C τοὺς ἀκριβῶς τῶν νόμων ἀνα-
γεγραμμένους. So especially superlatives: ἡ πλείστη γῆς, πλεῖστοι

---

[a] Stallb. ad loc.   [b] Stallb. Soph. 232 B. 247 B.

τῶν Ἑλλήνων: Hdt. III. 60 μέγιστα τῶν ἀπάντων Ἑλλήνων ἐξειργασμένα.—c. πολλοί, ὀλίγοι, τινὲς τῶν ἀνθρώπων, — εἷς,
ἕκαστος, πᾶς,—οἱ μὲν—οἱ δέ, ἄλλοι, ἕτεροι &c., with genitive ; often
οἱ τοιοῦτοι with genitive: Xen. M. S. II. 8, 3 τοῖς τοιούτοις τῶν
ἔργων. Relative : Hdt. VI. 8 Αἰολέων οἳ Λέσβον νέμονται :
Eur. Hec. 864 οὐκ ἔστι θνητῶν ὅστις ἔστ᾽ ἐλεύθερος. See also
§. 442. c.

Obs. 1. Of course the adjective signifies only a part of the whole, not
the whole itself : thus οἱ θνητοὶ ἄνθρωποι — πολλοί, or ὀλίγοι ἄνθρωποι, signifies a whole, composed of many or few individuals : πολλοί, ὀλίγοι ἀνθρώπων, a large or small part of the whole.

Obs. 2. Here belong also the Homeric phrases, wherein the adjective has
a partly superlative force : δῖα, πρέσβα, πότνα θεάων : Od. ξ, 443 δαιμόνιε
ξείνων. — ὦ φίλα γυναικῶν, ὦ τάλαινα παρθένων Eurip. : Od. ξ, 443 δαιμόνιε
ξείνων : Theog. 1307 ὄβριμε παίδων. The tragedians strengthen an adjectival notion by adding a genitive of the same adjective : δειλαία δειλαίων,
ἄρρητ᾽ ἀρρήτων, ἐχθροὶ ἐχθρῶν — ἔσχατ᾽ ἐσχάτων κακά Soph. Phil. 65.

§. 535. Verbs of *participation, share, communication, community,*
since all these notions imply part of something ; as, μετέχειν,
μέτεστί μοι, διδόναι, μεταδιδόναι, προσδιδόναι (sometimes προδιδόναι,
Eur. Suppl. 350.), διαδιδόναι, κοινωνεῖν, κοινοῦσθαι, ἐπαρκεῖν, to com-
municate : μεταλαμβάνειν — συλλαμβάνειν — sometimes συλλαμβάνε-
σθαι — συναίρεσθαι (the preposition giving to most of these verbs
their partitive force) : Soph. Œ. C 567 τῆς ἐς αὔριον οὐδέν — μοι
—μέτεστιν ἡμέρας : Eur. Med. 302 τῆσδε κοινωνῶ τύχης :
Id. Or. 439 sq. μετάδος φίλοισι σοῖσι τῆς εὐπραξίας : Xen.
Cyr. I. 2, 15 καὶ ἀρχῶν καὶ τιμῶν μετέχειν : Id. Rep. Lac. I. 9 τῆς
δυνάμεως κοινωνεῖν : Id. Cyr. VII. 5, 78 sq. θάλπους μὲν καὶ
ψύχους καὶ σίτων καὶ ποτῶν καὶ ὕπνου ἀνάγκη καὶ τοῖς δούλοις μεταδιδόναι—πολεμικῆς δ᾽ ἐπιστήμης καὶ μελέτης—οὐ μεταδοτέον:
Id. M. S. I. 2, 60 πᾶσιν ἀφθόνως ἐπήρκει τῶν ἑαυτοῦ : Id. Cyr.
I. 3, 7 τῶν κρεῶν διαδιδόναι τοῖς θεραπευταῖς. So Homer :
χαριζομένη παρεόντων, giving of what there was : Soph. Philoct.
282 ξυλλαμβάνειν νόσου, to take share in, to relieve by bearing
part of : Med. 946 ξυλλήψομαι δὲ τοῦδέ σοι κἀγὼ πόνου : Thuc.
IV. 10 ἄνδρες οἱ ξυναράμενοι τοῦδε τοῦ κινδύνου. Here belong also :
Med. 284 ξυμβάλλεται δὲ πολλὰ τοῦδε δείματος, *conferre aliquid.*
So Lysias 184, 31 τοῦ μὲν γὰρ καὶ φυγεῖν ὑμᾶς μέρος τι καὶ οὗτος
συνεβάλετο : Thuc. III. 36 προσυνεβάλετο τῆς ὁρμῆς.

Obs. 1. Sometimes the partitive notion is expressed by μέρος, or μοῖρα
in the accusative, the verb being no longer partitive with respect to its
object μέρος, which is itself partitive in relation to the substantive which
follows it in the genitive : a person who shares any thing with another,
takes the whole of part (μέρος in accusative), part of the whole (substantive in genitive) : Æsch. Ag. 518 μετέχειν φιλτάτου τάφου μέρος : Eur.

Iph. T. 1310 μέτεστιν ὑμῖν τῶν πεπραγμένων μέρος : Hdt. IV. 145 μοῖραν
τιμέων μετέχοντες : Id. VII. 157 μοῖρά τοι τῆς Ἑλλάδος οὐκ ἐλαχίστη μέτα :
Ibid. 16, 3 ἀλλά τι τοῦ θεοῦ μετέχον : Eur. Suppl. 1080 μετέλαχες τύχας
Οἰδιπόδα, γέρον, μέρος. So also ἴσος which implies μέρος in it : Arist. Plut.
1145 μετεῖχες τὰς ἴσας πληγάς. So also τι—something, or some part of,
κοινοῦσθαί τι — μεταδιδόναι τι Xen. Anab. IV. 5, 5. So another construction—the partitive is in the nominative : μέτεστί τι μοι.

Obs. 2. So also the phrases τί μοι τινός ; Il. φ, 360 τί μοι ἔριδος καὶ
ἀρωγῆς ; Eur. Hipp. 221 τί κυνηγεσίων καὶ σοὶ μελέτης ;

§. 536. Verbs of actual or imaginary contact, *to take hold of,
to be in dependence or connection with,* as it is a part and not the
whole which is touched ; as, θιγγάνειν, ψαύειν, ἅπτεσθαι, ἐφάπτεσθαι, δράττεσθαι — λαμβάνειν rather poet., λαμβάνεσθαι (λάζυσθαι
poet.) : ἐπιλαμβάνεσθαι, ἀντιλαμβάνεσθαι — ἔχεσθαι, ἀντέχεσθαι,
περιέχεσθαι (ἰσχανᾶν poet.), γλίχεσθαι (properly, to stick to)—
very rarely ἕπεσθαι, συνέπεσθαι (Eur. Troad. 569.) : Il. δ, 463 τὸν
δὲ πεσόντα ποδῶν ἔλαβεν : Il. θ, 371 ἔλαβε χειρὶ γενείου :
Il. π, 486 κόνιος δεδραγμένος αἱματοέσσης : Il. ω, 357 γούνων
ἀψάμενοι : Il. ι, 102 σέο δ' ἕξεται : Od. θ, 288 ἰσχανόων
φιλότητος : cf. Il. ψ, 300. Hdt. VI. 13 προφάσιος ἐπιλαβέ-
σθαι : Ibid. 91 ἐπιλαμβάνεσθαι τῶν ἐπισπαστήρων : Ibid.
31 ἀνὴρ ἀνδρὸς ἀψάμενος τῆς χειρός : Id. I. 93 λίμνη δ' ἔχεται
τοῦ σήματος μεγάλη : cf. VI. 8. Id. III. 72 ἔργου ἐχώμεθα,
opus aggrediamur : Id. VII. 5 τοιούτου λόγου εἴχετο, *amplexari.*
—Περιέχεσθαί τινος often in Hdt., *cupide aliquid amplecti :*
cf. Id. III. 53. Ibid. 72 τοῦ γὰρ αὐτοῦ γλιχόμεθα : Thuc. I.
140 τῆς γνώμης τῆς αὐτῆς ἔχομαι : Id. IV. 10 ἄνδρες οἱ ξυναράμενοι τοῦδε τοῦ κινδύνου : Xen. VI. 3, 17 κοινῇ τῆς σωτηρίας
ἔχεσθαι : Hdt. IV. 25 πάντα τὰ σιτίων ἐχόμενα : Plat. Rep. p.
329 A ἀλλ' ἄττα, ἃ τοιούτων ἔχεται (*quæ cum his conjuncta,
his similia sunt*)[a] : Ibid. p. 362 A ἀληθείας ἐχόμενον, *cum veri-
tate conjunctum :* Id. Symp. p. 217 D ἀνεπαύετο οὖν ἐν τῇ ἐχο-
μένῃ ἐμοῦ κλίνῃ, *lecto mihi proximo :* Eur. Med. 55 φρενῶν ἀν-
θάπτεται, *mentem tangit*[b] : Id. Or. 492 τοῦ νόμου ἔχεσθαι,
legi obedire : Ibid. 442 ἀντιλάζου καὶ πόνων ἐν τῷ μέρει : Ibid.
780 δυσχερὲς ψαύειν νοσοῦντος ἀνδρός : Demosth. p. 15, 20
ἀντιλάβεσθε τῶν πραγμάτων.

Obs. 1. Ἀντιποιεῖσθαι takes a genitive, seemingly after the analogy of
γλίχεσθαι.

Obs. 2. Here also belongs : Hdt. VIII. 90 προσεβάλετο πάθεος (*vulgata,*
e conj. προσελάβετο).

Obs. 3. In the phrases λαβεῖν τινα γούνων — ἅπτεσθαί τινα γενείου, we
must not conceive that the genitive signifies the part of the person

a Stallb. ad loc.   b Pflugk ad loc.

touched. The partitive genitive does not signify a part taken as the whole, but the whole considered in one of its parts; so that γούνων would not be the knee, which is part of a man, but some part_of the knee, viz. that from whence the touching object as it were hangs or depends.

Obs. 4. Many of these verbs have an accusative : the notion of touching or taking hold of the part, being exchanged for that of seizing or occupying the whole; as, Il. δ, 357 λάζυσθαι μῦθον. — ἐφάπτεσθαι Plat. Legg. p. 664 E. Demosth. p. 16, 24 συνάρασθαι τὰ πράγματα. — γλίχεσθαι Plat. Hipp. p. 226 E. — θιγγάνειν and ἅπτεσθαι are joined in Pindar with the local dative: Pyth. IV. 296 ἀσυχίᾳ θιγέμεν: Id. VIII. 24; IX. 43. Isthm. III. 30.

Obs. 5. The preposition ἐκ sometimes defines this relation of dependence more accurately : ἀνάπτεσθαι ἔκ τινος. So ἐπί with verbs of holding by, leaning on : ἐπὶ μελίης ἐρεισθείς Il. χ, 225 : ἔχεσθαι ἐπί τινος Hdt. VI. 11. Soph. Ant. 1142. Hence ἐφ' ἑαυτοῦ, ἑαυτῶν, leaning on oneself—independent. So γλίχεσθαι περί τινος.

Obs. 6. After this analogy verbs of praying or vowing are joined with a genitive of the person or thing by whom or which any one implores or vows; such as, λίσσεσθαι — ἱκετεύειν — ἱκνεῖσθαι : the person praying being conceived as touching the knee or the image of the divinity : Od. β, 68 λίσσομαι ἠμὲν Ζηνὸς Ὀλυμπίου ἠδὲ Θέμιστος. So λίσσεσθαι πατρός, τοκήων. So Hdt. VI. 68 ἐγὼ ὦν σε μετέρχομαι τῶν θεῶν (per deos te obsecro)[a]. The following passages support this explanation : Il. κ, 454 f. ὁ μέν μιν ἔμελλε γενείου χειρὶ παχείῃ ἀψάμενος λίσσεσθαι : Il. χ, 345 μή με, κύον, γούνων γουνάζεο, μηδὲ τοκήων : Il. ε, 451 ἠ δ' αἰὲν ἐμὲ λισσέσκετο γούνων : Il. ψ, 584 ἵππων ἁψάμενος γαιήοχον Ἐννοσίγαιον ὄμνυθι : Hdt. VI. 68 ὦ μῆτερ, θεῶν σε τῶν τε ἄλλων καταπτόμενος ἱκετεύω καὶ τοῦ Ἑρκείου Διὸς τοῦδε : Id. VIII. 65 Δημαρήτου τε καὶ ἄλλων μαρτύρων καταπτόμενος : Eur. Hec. 752 ἱκετεύω σε τῶνδε γουνάτων καὶ σοῦ γενείου δεξιᾶς τ' εὐδαίμονος. When ἀντί is added to the genitive it expresses the notion of the person being before the image of the god. The person or thing by which any one prays may be considered as the cause and origin of the prayer, in which case πρός or ὑπέρ is used with the genitive : Od. λ, 67 νῦν δέ σε τῶν ὄπιθεν γουνάζομαι, οὐ παρεόντων, πρός τ' ἀλόχου καὶ πατρός : Il. ο, 665 τῶν ὕπερ ἐνθάδ' ἐγὼ γουνάζομαι οὐ παρεόντων.

§. 537. Verbs of *eating, drinking,* have a partitive genitive ; as, ἐσθίειν, φάγειν, πίνειν, γεύεσθαι, γεύειν : as, ἐσθίειν κρεῶν : Od. ι, 102 μήπω τις λωτοῖο φαγὼν νοστοῖο λαθῆται : Xen. Cyr. I. 3, 4 (ἀνάγκη σοι) ἀπογεύεσθαι τούτων τῶν παντοδαπῶν βρωμάτων : Ibid. 10 καὶ τί δὴ, ὦ Κῦρε, τἀλλα μιμούμενος τὸν Σάκαν, οὐκ ἀπερρόφησας τοῦ οἴνου; Id. M. S. IV. 3, 11 γεύεσθαι τιμῆς — γεύειν τινὰ τιμῆς : Plat. Phædr. p. 227 B ἠ δῆλον ὅτι τῶν λόγων ὑμᾶς Λυσίας εἱστία ; for the usual dative : Id. Rep. 352 B εὐωχοῦ τοῦ λόγου, *fruere sermone* (like Theophr. c. 8 δοκῶ μοί σε εὐωχήσειν καινῶν λόγων for the usual καινοῖς λόγοις). Here perhaps is to be referred, Hdt. VII. 138 ἀρυσάμενος τοῦ ἡλίου, drawing in unto himself of the sun.

Obs. The verbs of eating and drinking not unfrequently take an accusative; the partitive notion arising from the particular action of eating and drinking being lost sight of, and the more vague notion of eating in general being substituted, as is clearly the case in the two first examples, of the means of subsistence : Il. μ, 319 ἔδουσί τε (ἡμέτεροι βασιλῆες) πίονα μῆλα, οἶνόν τ' ἔξαιτον μελιηδέα : Od. κ, 101 υἵτινες ἀνέρες εἶεν — σῖτον ἔδοντες: Od. ι, 347 Κύκλωψ, τῆ, πίε οἶνον, ἐπεὶ φάγες ἀνδρόμεα κρέα : Xen. Cyr. I. 3, 9 οὐκ ἐκπίομαι αὐτὸς τὸν οἶνον : Ibid. 6 κρέα γε εὐωχοῦ. So ἐσθίειν κρέα and κρεῶ, πίνειν οἶνον and οἴνου. As in English, he eats meat—he eat some meat, he drinks wine—he drank some wine; so in the old proverb : ὕδωρ δὲ πίνων οὐδὲν ἂν τέκοις καλόν (ὕδωρ πίνων = ὑδροπότης).

Material Genitive.

§. 538. The notion of any thing being made implies the antecedent existence of some material out of which it is made, which, if expressed, is accordingly in the genitive :

Verbs of *making, forming*, &c. : Il. η, 222 σκυτοτόμων ὄχ' ἄριστος — ἐποίησεν σάκος αἰόλον, ἑπταβόειον, ταύρων ζατρεφέων : Il. κ, 262 ἀμφὶ δέ οἱ κυνέην κεφαλῆφιν ἔθηκεν, ῥινοῦ ποιητήν : Hdt. V. 82 χαλκοῦ ποιέονται τὰ ἀγάλματα : Id. II. 138 ἐστρωμένη ἐστὶ ὁδὸς λίθου : Eur. Hel. 1380 κισσοῦ τε στεφθεῖσα χλόα.

Obs. 1. This construction is often expanded by the prepositions ἐξ, ἀπό, and διά; and the instrumental dative is also used. The view in which the speaker looks at it determines the case.

Obs. 2. The attributive genitive of the material belongs here ; as, ἔκπωμα ξύλου — τράπεζα ἀργυρίου — στέφανος ὑακίνθων : Theocr. I. 58 ἔδωκα —τυροέντα μέγαν λευκοῖο γάλακτος : Id. II. 73 βύσσοιο καλὸν σύροισα χιτῶνα.

§. 539. 1. Verbs of *being full*, or transitive verbs of *filling* ; as πλήθω, πληρόω, πίμπλημι, μεστόω rather Poetic : γέμειν, βρίθειν— νάσσειν, ἐπινάσσειν,—σάττειν, εὐπορεῖν : Il. ι, 224 πλησάμενος δ' οἴνοιο δέπας : Od. ι, 219 f. ταρσοὶ μὲν τυρῶν βρῖθον, στείνοντο δὲ σηκοὶ ἀρνῶν ἠδ' ἐρίφων : Il. α, 148 κοῦροι δὲ κρητῆρας ἐπεστέψαντο ποτοῖο : Od. σ, 22 στῆθος καὶ χείλεα φύρσω αἵματος : Hesiod. Sc. 290 βριθόμενα σταχύων : Æsch. Ag. 667 ὁρῶμεν ἀνθοῦν πέλαγος Αἰγαῖον νεκροῖς ἀνδρῶν Ἀχαιῶν ναυτικῶν τ' ἐρειπίων (both dative and genitive), like *florere frugum* Lucret. I. 256. Xen. Symp. IV. 64 σεσαγμένος — πλούτου τὴν ψυχὴν ἔσομαι : Plat. Apol. p. 26 D τὰ Ἀναξαγόρου βιβλία—γέμει τούτων τῶν λόγων: Demosth. p. 33, 29 τῶν ἀπόντων εὐπορῆσαι.

Obs. 1. So also the attributive genitive : as, πίθος μέλιτος, δέπας οἴνου : Od. ι, 196 αἴγεον ἀσκὸν ἔχον μέλανος οἴνοιο.

2. So also adjectives expressing fulness ; as, πλέος, ἔμπλεος,

πλήρης, μεστός, πλούσιος, δασύς—and the Poetic ἀφνειός, ἐπιστεφής, πολυστεφής, περιστεφής, ἄτος Epic: ἄπληστος Trag.: Od. α, 165 ἀφνειότεροι χρυσοῖό τε ἐσθῆτός τε: Od. β, 431 ἐπιστεφὴς οἴνου: Soph. Œ. R. 83 πολυστεφὴς δάφνης: Id. El. 895 περιστεφὴς ἀνθέων: Xen. Cyr. III. 1, 3 διαθεόντων καὶ ἐλαυνόντων τὸ πεδίον μεστόν: Id. Anab. II. 4, 14 δασὺς δένδρων. So Horace: *generosæ fertile testæ.*

Obs. 2. The instrumental dative is sometimes found with these words, especially βρύειν and δασύς.

§. 540. Verbs of *being satisfied,* or *satisfying*; as, ἆσαι, ἄσασθαι, κορέσασθαι: Il. ε, 289 αἵματος ἆσαι Ἄρηα: Il. ι, 489 ὄψου τ' ἄσαιμι: Il. λ, 562 ἐκορέσσατο φορβῆς. So Il. ι, 705 τεταρπόμενοι φίλον ἦτορ σίτου καὶ οἴνοιο: Hesiod. Sc. 255 ἀρέσαντο φρένας αἵματος: Plat. Symp. p. 203 B μεθυσθεὶς τοῦ νέκταρος.

Obs. The poets use a material genitive with many other verbs; the material being considered as the antecedent condition of the production or action. The Epic is very rich in this idiom, which is more and more lost in the later language; as while the Greek mind in its primitive freshness regarded the action as springing into life from the materials of which it was composed, the later Greeks regarded it rather as a mere lifeless work: Od. γ, 408 ἀποστίλβοντες ἀλείφατος: Plat. Phæd. p. 113 A λίμνην ποιεῖ — ζέουσαν ὕδατος καὶ πηλοῦ. Verbs of burning: Il. ι, 242 αὐτὰς δ' ἐμπρήσειν μαλεροῦ πυρός: Il. π, 81 μὴ δὴ πυρὸς αἰθομένοιο νῆας ἐνιπρήσωσι: Od. ρ, 23 ἐπεί κε πυρὸς θερέω: Il. ζ, 331 ἀλλ' ἄνα, μὴ τάχα ἄστυ πυρὸς δηίοιο θέρηται: cf. Il. λ, 667. Il. η, 410 (νέκυας) πυρὸς μειλισσέμεν. Verbs of bathing, washing: Il. ε, 6 λελουμένος Ὠκεανοῖο: Il. ζ, 508 λούεσθαι εὐρρεῖος ποταμοῖο: Od. β, 261 χεῖρας νιψάμενος πολιῆς ἁλός: though here the genitive may be local. Also Il. ι, 214 πάσσε δ' ἁλός.—καταπάσσειν Arist. Eq. 99: Plat. Lys. p. 210 A τοὺς ὀφθαλμοὺς ἐμπάσαι τῆς τέφρας.

Genitive Absolute.

§. 541. 1. The so called genitive absolute is also to be referred, either to the causal genitive—the action expressed by the substantive and participle in the genitive being considered as the antecedent cause, or condition, of the action of the verb or the sentence with which it is joined. So Thuc. IV. 11 ὁρῶν τοῦ χωρίου χαλεποῦ ὄντος τοὺς τριηράρχους—ἀποκνοῦντας, here τοῦ χωρίου χαλεποῦ ὄντος expresses the cause of the hesitation of the Trierarchs.

2. Or the genitive of time: Κύρου βασιλεύοντος, while Cyrus was reigning: Hdt. I. 190 ὄρθρου γενομένου, though this notion is frequently more accurately defined by ἐπί: ἐπὶ Κύρου βασιλεύοντος &c.

3. Or the genitive of place: Hdt. I. 208 ὡς αὐτοῦ διαβησομένου.

Genitive with Substantives and Adjectives.

§. 542. 1. When two substantives are so joined together, that the one seems to depend upon and derive its force and meaning from the other, in any one of the relations given above, that substantive on which the one depends is in the genitive, as being in some respect antecedent to its proper conception; and hence arises the rule, that when two substantives are joined together, the one that explains and more accurately defines the other is in the genitive. And when verbal notions, which take an accusative or dative, take the form of a substantive, they may have their object in the genitive.

2. The same holds good of adjectives; even many whose verb takes the accusative are joined with the genitive: Æsch. Ag. 1167 ἰὼ γάμοι Πάριδος ὀλέθριοι φίλων (which have ruined his friends): Eur. Hec. 235 καρδίας δηκτήρια: Ibid. 1135 ὕποπτος ὢν δὴ Τρωϊκῆς ἁλώσεως [a].

Double Genitive.

§. 543. 1. We sometimes find a substantive followed by two genitives. In this case the substantive and one of the genitives form one compound notion, on which the other genitive grammatically depends: Hdt. VI. 2 Ἱστιαῖος ὑπέδυνε τῶν Ἰώνων-τὴν-ἡγεμονίαν τοῦ πρὸς Δαρεῖον πολέμου: Ibid. 67 κατὰ μὲν δὴ τὴν Δημαράτου κατάπαυσιν-τῆς-βασιληΐης.

2. So also adjectives, derived from verbs which take a double accusative [b], are followed by a Genitive of each of these objects: Soph. Antig. 1185 Παλλάδος θεᾶς ὅπως ἱκοίμην εὐγμάτων προσήγορος.

ACCUSATIVE.

§. 544. 1. Every verbal expression of a state or action implies one or more notions as parts of the whole, necessary to and existing coincidently with itself as parts of the principal notion: thus the notion of beating contains in itself the notions of a person striking, of a blow, and of a person struck; and these two last notions are coincident with and implied in the notion of striking expressed by the verb, and are in the accusative.

2. This principle varies in its application according to the sense of the verb. All verbs imply coincidently their cognate notion— the feeling or state, or the act or thing done, or the effect or thing produced: but in those verbs which express the transition

---

[a] Pflugk ad loc. [b] Herm. Ant. 1170.

of this feeling or act or effect to some other person or thing, as
the patient thereof, there is a further coincident notion of this
patient, so that in these verbs there are two coincident notions, as
will be seen below.

Obs. A neuter verb sometimes has a transitive force when its effect on
some thing or person is considered; and a transitive verb is sometimes
neuter when it is not considered in its effect on its patient.

3. As the cognate notion, being already implied in the verb, is
readily supplied by the mind, it is not expressed in the sentence
except for the sake of emphasis, as βουλὰς βουλεύειν, or more generally when the nature, character, or manner of the verbal operation
is to be more exactly defined, as ἀρίστην βουλὴν βουλεύειν, or where
a relative represents the cognate substantive in a dependent sentence, as βουλὴν ἣν ἐβούλευον: hence verbs of state and feeling,
and neuter action, are not, except in such cases, joined with an
accusative.

4. So in transitive verbs also the objective sentence is perfect
without the accus. of the cognate notion; as, διδάσκω σε: but
where it is wished to define the nature or manner of the verbal
operation on the patient, the verb takes a double accusative.
This happens with different verbs more or less frequently according
to the requirements of language or the usages of speech; with
some verbs it is found once, with others oftener, others generally,
and some never; but where the verb is so general and vague, that
without further definition, it conveys no accurate notion of the way
in which the patient is affected, as ἐργάζομαί σε—διδάσκω σε, the
cognate accusative is used (except where the action is purposely
left indefinite); as, ἐργάζομαι κακόν σε, διδάσκω δικαιοσύνην σε. And
on the other hand, where the verbal notion is in itself express and
definite, so that it stands in need of no further definition, as νικάω
σε, the verb is frequently or always, found with a single accusative
of the patient.

5. So when no person is considered as the patient of the action
(the action of the verb being alone considered) a transitive verb is
joined with an accus. of the cognate notion only; as, αἰτέω τόδε,
I make this request. And some transitive verbs, though they are
not joined with a double accus. in any one passage of the writers
who remain to us, yet have an accus. of the cognate action in one
passage (the patient being omitted), as ἀρκεῖν τοῦτο; and of the
patient in another (the cognate notion not being expressly stated),
as, ἀρκεῖν ἄνδρα, and these separate uses of the two accus., together
with the double accus. being used with analogous verbs, shew that

such verbs are capable of being followed by the double accus., though language, as far as we know from the small portion of Greek authors which we possess, has not so used them.

§. 545. 1. The notion of *beating* implies as its parts—

Agent and his operation.   Act.   Patient.

The verbal form expresses the agent (by the ellipse of the pronoun) and his operation, while the other two notions, coincident with it, and together with it completing the whole notion, are in the accusative ; as,

Agent and operation,	Act or thing done,	Patient,
τύπτω.	τύμμα (πληγάς).	τυπτόμενον (σέ).

From which it is clear that every verb, which implies a patient as well as the act, *may* have a double accusative case.

Obs. 1. The notion of the act or thing done is not always, nor even generally, expressed by the noun cognate to the verb, as τύμμα, but more frequently by a word expressing the same or an equivalent notion ; as, πληγή = τύμμα, and very frequently it is represented by an adjective in the neuter singular or plural, agreeing with the neuter notion of the verbal act, (or sometimes in the feminine, if a feminine substantive suggests itself most readily to the mind of the speaker,) and expressing the mode or character thereof.

2. In neuter verbs and those which have no patient, there is only one coincident notion, viz. of the state, or act or thing done, &c.

The state of *joy* implies—

Subject and his operation,	State,
χαίρω.	χαράν.

The intransitive action of *labour* implies—

Subject and his operation,	Act or thing done,
πονῶ.	πόνους (or μοχθούς, or ταῦτα).

So production implies—

Agent and his operation,	Production or thing produced,
ποιῶ.	ταῦτα sc. ποιήματα.

3. In passive and middle verbs the agent and patient being one and the same, there remains only one coincident notion, viz. of the act—

Agent (Patient) and his operation,	Act,
τύπτομαι.	πολλάς (sc. πληγάς).

So Eur. Rhes. 5 τίς ἐκηρύχθη πρώτην φυλακήν : κηρύσσω φυλακήν

(= κήρυγμα). So Thuc. I. 126 ἐπιτετραμμένοι τὴν φυλακήν = ἐπιτροπήν : Id. V. 37 ταῦτα ἐπεσταλμένοι : so περιτίθεσθαι κυνῆν, ἐσθῆτα, &c.: Arist. Ach. 1 ὅσα δὴ δέδηγμαι.

Obs. 2. Neuter verbs have properly no accus. of the patient, as the agent and patient unite in the subject ; but many neuter verbs both of state and feeling, have an object wherein and whereon the state or feeling consists, operates, rests, and is completed ; as, φοβίομαί σε ; these semi-transitive verbs seldom have a double accusative, (only when it is required to mark the peculiar manner in which the verbal notion operates on the object) as in reality the object is substituted for the state or feeling which is the cognate notion of the verb ; this substitution may be clearly seen in such instances as Soph. Phil. 1250. ΟΔ. στράτον δ' 'Αχαιῶν οὐ φοβεῖ πράσσων τάδε ; where στράτον is the object on which the φόβος rests, which Philoctetes in his answer substitutes for it, ΦΙ. ξὺν τῷ δικαίῳ τὸν σὸν οὐ ταρβῶ φόβον : and in most languages the substantives, which primarily signify the feeling, are used equally for the object wherein the feeling for the time consists ; as, αἰδώς, ἔλπις, φόβος, χαρά &c.

4. In transmissive verbs, where something is spoken of as transmitted from one person to another, the notion of the person affected by the operation of the verb, is not coincident with but consequent on that operation, as receiving is consequent on giving ; and the grammatical patient of the verb, i. e. the passive participle, the thing given, is the same as the act of the verb or gift, so that there is only one accus., viz. of the gift or thing given.

Thus the notion of *giving* implies—

Agent and his operation,	Gift or thing given,
δίδωμι.	δῶρον or διδόμενον.

5. When the operation of the verb is more exactly defined by stating the exact part or parts where it operated, this is also in the accusative as being merely another way of expressing by a sort of apposition the operation of the verb ; as, τύπτω σε κεφαλήν, σε not being a sufficiently accurate expression for the patient (τυπτόμενον) κεφαλήν is added, as being the part really struck. So in neuter verbs ; as, τρέμουσα κῶλα = τρόμον κώλων, the accusative is of the equivalent notion, the part wherein the feeling, &c. consists, and is substituted for the feeling, &c. itself : Od. a, 208 ὄμματα ἔοικας αὐτῷ, the resemblance consisted in the eyes ; τὰ ὄμματα καλλιστεύει, the eyes were the κάλλος. So πόδας ὠκὺς 'Αχιλλεύς.

§. 546. Hence the following rules may be laid down :—

1. The accusative case represents the coincident notions of the verb.

2. All verbs which imply the two coincident notions of the act or

effect (or its equivalent), and of the patient, *may* have a double accus.; either of these notions may be omitted at the will of the speaker, and therefore these transitive verbs are frequently found with a single accus. of the patient, or, more rarely, of the act or effect.

3. All verbs which do not imply a patient have one coincident notion—the state, or act, or effect,—and therefore have one accus. case.

4. All passive verbs may have an accus. of the state, or act, or effect of the verb.

5. All transmissive verbs imply but one coincident notion, of the thing transmitted, and therefore have only one accus. case.

6. All verbs may have an accus. of the part to define more accurately the operation of the verb.

Obs. The cognate subst. is sometimes placed in a different part of the sentence from its verb; as, Plat. Rep. 567 C πολεμίῳ εἶναι καὶ ἐπιβουλεύειν ἕως ἂν καθήρῃ τὴν πόλιν—Καλόν γε, ἔφη, καθαρμόν.

§. 547. For the better examination of the functions of the acc. case the following division of verbs according to their notions will be useful :—

A. *Verbs with one Accusative case :—of Cognate notion.*

1. Neuter verbs of s t a t e or f e e l i n g, implying a cognate notion of that feeling or state : ἡδονὰς ἥδεσθαι, νόσον νοσεῖν.

2. Verbs of n e u t e r m o t i o n, implying a cognate notion of the road ; as, βαίνειν ὁδόν, or of the place arrived at, βαίνειν πόλιν.

3. Verbs of a c t i o n, implying a cognate notion of the act or thing done ; as, πράττω πρᾶγμα, πονέω πόνους.

4. Verbs of p r o d u c t i o n, implying a cognate notion of the production or thing produced ; as, ποιέω ποίημα, δέμω δόμον.

5. Verbs of t r a n s m i s s i o n, implying a cognate notion of the thing transmitted ; as, δωρέω δῶρον.

6. Verbs of r e c e p t i o n, implying a cognate notion of the receipt ; as, λαμβάνω λῆψιν.

7. Verbs of p e r c e p t i o n, implying a cognate notion of the perception or thing perceived ; as, αἰσθάνομαι αἴσθησιν.

8. Verbs of p o s s e s s i o n, implying a cognate notion of the possession or thing possessed ; as, κτήματα κέκτημαι.

B. *With two Accusative cases :—of Cognate notion, and patient.*

Verbs of a c t i o n or a c t i v e m o t i o n, implying an accus. of the p a t i e n t and a cognate acc. of the a c t ; as, διδάσκω σε διδάγματα.

Verbs with one Àccusative.

§. 548. 1. The accus. is used to define the operation of the verb, and in many of these constructions the Latin and modern languages would use an ablative or dative case, or an adverb. This is done either by the cognate substantive and an adjective, as ἀρίστην βουλὴν βουλεύειν, or by a neuter adjective ᾿agreeing with the verbal notion, as ἄριστα βουλεύειν, or by an equivalent substantive, which is to be resolved into a cognate substantive and an adjective, as τιτρώσκειν φόνον=φόνιον τραῦμα, or into a cognate substantive and genitive ; as, ῥέειν ὕδωρ=ῥόον ὕδατος.

Obs. 1. A good many verbs exchange their neuter for an equivalent transitive sense, and thus take an accus. of the patient ; as, ἀσεβεῖν εἰς θεούς, and ἀσεβεῖν (to dishonour) τοὺς θεούς ; so that, when they have an accus. of the patient, they must be explained by the corresponding transitive expression. So ἐξιέναι τὴν γῆν: Æsch. P.V. 713 ἐκπερᾶν χθόνα ; so ἀποδιδράσκειν τὸν δεσπότην. So Eur. Phœn. 874 θεούς ὑπεκδραμοῦσι: Thuc. VIII. 102 ἐκπλεῖν πολεμίους: Il. o, 227 νεμεσσηθεὶς ὑπόειξεν χεῖρας ἐμάς: ὑποχωρεῖν τὸν ὄχλον (cf. Thuc. II. 88.), ἀποχωρεῖν Xen. Cyneg. V. 18., ἐξαναχωρεῖν τὰ εἰρημένα Thuc. IV. 28. : ἐκστῆναι κίνδυνον, *reformidare,* ὑπεκστῆναι Plat. : ἀποστρέφεσθαι Xen. Eur. : ὑπεκτρέπεσθαι — ἐκτρέπεσθαι Demosth. : ἀφίστασθαι Xen. Cyneg. III. 3 ; ἐγκλίνειν τινά Id. Cyr. III. 3, 65. So Eur. Hec. 812 ποῖ μ᾿ ὑπεξάγεις πόδα: so ὑπέρχεσθαί τινα, and οἴχεσθαί τινα : Arist. Av. 86 ὁ κολοιός μ᾿ οἴχεται ὑπὸ τοῦ δέους: Theocr. XV. 8 τὺ δ᾿ ἑκαστοτέρω ἔμ᾿ ἀποικεῖς. So especially verbs of sound signify the action which that sound implies ; as, κτυπεῖν τὴν γῆν, to sound the ground, to beat it with a noise : Hom. κροτάλιζον ὄχεα, they rattled them along. So Theocr. τὸ χαλκίον ἤχει, sound the gong.

Obs. 2. Some verbs have a double sense arising from two different relations implied in the original idea (see §. 352. 5. *b.*) ; as, ἀμείβεσθαι, ἀλλάσσειν, to exchange ; hence to give and receive ; τίσασθαι, to avenge and to punish ; ἐρείδειν, to put one thing against another, to keep it up, or push it down.

Obs. 3. It is evident that the sense of the equivalent notion often reflects back a meaning to the verb, by defining in different ways its generic meaning ; thus τίνω, Æsch. Choeph. 650 τίνει μύσος Ἐρινύς, pays back the accursed deed, i. e. punishes it : τίνειν δίκην, to pay the penalty, to suffer punishment : τίνειν χάριν, to be grateful.

2. So that the accusative is either [a],

a. Accusative of cognate substantive ; as, βουλὴν βουλεύω, χαίρω χαράν :

Obs. 1. Many verbs which are not in good writers followed by their cognate substantives, are in later writers found with them [b].

b. Accusative of cognate notion, the proper cognate substantive being generally wanting or obsolete ; as, κειμένη θέσιν, κοιμήσατο ὕπνον :

---

[a] Lobeck Paral. 509.   [b] Lobeck, l. c.

Obs. 2. Adjectives also sometimes take this cognate accus.; as, Plat. Rep. 490 D κακοὺς πᾶσαν κακίαν: Ibid. 579 D δοῦλος μεγίστας θωπείας καὶ δουλείας: Id. Apol. 22 E σοφὸς τὴν ἐκείνων σοφίαν, μήτε ἀμαθὴς τὴν ἀμαθίαν.

c. Accusative of equivalent notion, the accus. not being the cognate subst., nor expressing the actual cognate notion of the verb, but a notion substituted for it, as being that wherein the action, or state, or effect of the verb for the time consists, and being in a sort of apposition to it; as, ἀντικατθανεῖν δίκην = θάνατον, which is the δίκην. As stated above, this equivalent substantive would follow the real cognate subst., if expressed, in the genitive; as, ἀντανγεῖ φόνον = αὐγὴν φόνου, or *vice versa*, as ἀντικατθανεῖν δίκην = δίκην θανάτου; or it would assume an adjectival form. And sometimes the cognate notion is joined in an adjectival form to the equivalent acc.; as, προρέειν καλλίρροον ὕδωρ = ῥόον ὕδατος. This equivalent accus. is very common with verbs of saying, &c.; the words spoken being substituted for the λόγος, (see verbs of saying) and is most generally used with verbs of production, reception, perception, transmission, possession, &c. where the act or effect implied in the verb requires to be especially defined:

d. Accusative cognate to a notion implied in the verb; as, σιγᾶ (= οὐ λέγει) λόγους:

Obs. 3. This accusative may either be the cognate substantive to the notion so implied, as σιγᾶ λόγους; or the equivalent notion to it, as σιγᾶ τύχας; or the elliptic accus., as σιγᾶ ταῦτα.

e. Elliptic accus., where an adjective in the neuter gender is joined to a verb, agreeing with the coincident state, or act, or effect implied therein; as, πράττειν τὰ ἐπεσταλμένα, sc. πράγματα, μέγα (sc. χάρμα) χαίρειν:

f. Derived from this is the *adverbial accus.*, which is joined to almost all verbs in a purely adverbial sense.

g. Accusative of duration in space or time—the duration being substituted for the act, or state, or effect in continuance.

Obs. 4. In verbs of action which have no patient, the cognate act or effect may be expressed by the passive voice as well as by a substantive; as, λέγω λόγον, or λεγόμενον; while in transitive verbs the passive voice is the proper expression of the patient; as, τύπτω σε τυπτόμενον, not τύμμα τυπτόμενον.

Obs. 5. On the use of the cognate substantive we may remark, that if the verb conveys a sufficiently definite notion, as χαίρω, πολεμέω, νοσέω, the cognate notion is added only when some further definition is required; and this is done in three ways: by affixing the adjective containing the required notion to the cognate substantive, as δεινὴν νόσον νοσεῖν; or the adjective alone agreeing with the neuter notion of the verb, as δεινὰ νοσεῖν; or by substituting for the cognate notion a substantive equivalent to it, but containing, besides, the notion whereby the verb is to be defined; as, νοσεῖν ἄλγος=ἀλγώδη νόσον. In most verbs which express indefinite production or action, the cognate or equivalent accus. is added to give to the verb a definite sense; as, ποιέομαι τεῖχος, or δόμον = ποίημα; κράτω τάφον, or εἰρήνην=πρᾶγμα.

Obs. 6. Instead of the cognate or equivalent accus. the instrumental dat. is sometimes used, expressing that whereby the feeling or action of the verb is produced, rather than the operation of the verb; as, Soph. Œ. R. 65 ὕπνῳ γ' εὕδοντα: Id. Trach. 168 ζῆν ἀλυπήτῳ βίῳ: Hdt. III. 130 ἐδωρέετο — δαψιλεῖ δωρεῇ[a]: Plat. Phil. p. 21 B μεγίσταις ἡδοναῖς χαίροις ἄν.

§. 549. Verbs of being *pleased, sorry, despondent,* of *pity, love, madness, content, discontent, displeasure, anger, envy, grudging, may* have an accus. of the feeling, or that wherein the feeling consists : ἥδομαι, χαίρω, γηθέω, ἐράω, ἄχθομαι, οἰκτείρω, οἰκτίζω, γελάω, μαίνομαι, &c.

a. Accus. of cognate subst.: Plat. Phil. p. 63 A ἡδονὰς ἥ δ ε σ θ α ι. (So Plaut. *mea gavisurum gaudia*): Eur. Alc. 31 ἐ ρ ῶ σ' ἔρωτα: Æsch. Eum. 490 οἶκτον ο ἰ κ τ ί σ α σ θ α ι: Eur. Med. 1041 τί π ρ ο σγ ε λ ᾶ τ ε τὸν πανύστατον γέλων: Arist. Thesm. 793 μανίας μ α ί ν εσ θ α ι: Eur. Bacch. 1259 ἀ λ γ ή σ ε τ' ἄλγος.

b. Accus. of cognate notion : Arist. Rhet. I. 2, 9 χ α ί ρ ε ι ν ἡδονήν : Æsch. P. V. 979 μ ε μ η ν ό τ' οὐ σμικρὰν νόσον : Xen. Eph. II. 1, 31 ἐ ρ ᾶ ν ἐπιθυμίαν.

c. Accus. of equivalent notion : ἄχθομαι ἕλκος=ἄχθος ἕλκεος: Eur. Hel. 831 τί χρῆμ' ἀθυμεῖς: Theocr. XIV. 26 κατατήκετο τῆνον ἔρωτα=τῆξιν ἔρωτος: Eur. Hipp. 1340 χ α ί ρ ω θνήσκοντας=χαρὰν θνησκόντων. The particular χαρά was their θάνατος: cf. Soph. Aj. 136. So Soph. Phil. 1314 ἤ σ θ η ν πατέρα τε τὸν ἐμὸν εὐλογοῦντά σε: Id. Œ. R. 936 τὸ δ' ἔπος τάχ' ἂν ἥ δ ο ῖ ο: Id. Aj. 136 σὲ μὲν εὖ πράσσοντ' ἐ π ι χ α ί ρ ω: Eur. Ion. 541 τοῦτο τ ε ρ φ θ ε ί ς, so χ α ί ρ ω τοῦτο: Ibid. 389 ἀ λ γ ε ῖ ν πρᾶξιν: Ibid. Phil. 906 ταῦτ' ἀ ν ι ῶ μ α ι. So Plat. Menex. p. 89 D δ υ σ χ ε ρ α ί ν ε ι ν αὐτό: Id. Legg. p. 908 B δ υ σ χ ε ρ α ί ν ε ι ν θεούς : Id. Soph. 229 E τὰ μὲν χ α λ ε π α ί ν ο ν τ ε ς : Demosth. p. 68, 24 τὸ λυσιτελοῦν ἀ γ α π ήσ ο ν τ α ς. So Xen. Cyr. I. 3, 5 μ υ σ α τ τ ό μ ε ν ο ν ταῦτα τὰ βρώματα: Soph. Œ. C. 110 φ θ ο ν ή σ α ς φάτιν. Plat. Euth. p. 4 D ἀ γ α ν α κ τ ῶ ταῦτα: Id. Phæd. p. 62 D ἀ γ α ν α κ τ ε ῖ ν τοὺς φρονιμωτάτους ἀπιόντας.

Obs. 1. Properly speaking, it is not the person which constitutes and is equivalent to the cognate feeling of joy, dislike, &c. but some thing or act; wherefore we do not find χαίρω, δυσχεραίνω, &c. with an accus. of a person, except with a participle or explanatory sentence introduced by ὅτι, &c. whereby his act is denoted, or unless the same is implied in the context, as δυσχεραίνειν θεούς: *the notion of the gods.* And the notions of *hating, loving, pitying,* as distinguished from *feeling dislike, desire,* &c. imply a person as the patient separate from the feeling, and hence they have an accus. of the patient, and some a double accus. case, while verbs of anger, envy, take the patient in the Dativus Incommodi.

Obs. 2. Some verbs signifying *contentment, acquiescence,* have an accus. derived from their primary sense; as, στέργειν, to love : Æsch. P. V. 10 τυραννίδα στέργειν: Id. Ag. 1551 στέργειν τάδε δύστλητα. So Demosth. 68, 24 τὸ λυσιτελοῦν ἀγαπήσοντας: Plat. Rep. p. 399 C ἀγαπῶντα τὰ ἀποβαίνοντα; so αἰνέω, I praise: Eur. Alc. 2 θῆσσαν τράπεζαν αἰνέσαι, to deign to; cf. Id. Phœn. 481.

d. Adverbial accus. : Arist. Nub. 817 τί δὲ τοῦτ' ἐγελάσας: Il. ς, 484 δακρυόεν γελάσασα: Od. β, 270 ἡδὺ γελᾶν: Il. ι, 77 τίς ἂν τάδε γηθήσειεν; so Arist. Ach. 7 ταῦθ' ὡς ἐγανώθην: Il. ε, 181 τάδε μαίνεται: Eur. Ion. 255 ἀνερεύνητα δυσθυμεῖ: Æsch. Theb. 373 τοιαῦτ' ἀλύων: Od. ε, 147 κοτεσσαμένη τόγε: Arist. Ach. 10 ὠδυνήθην ἕτερον αὖ τραγῳδικόν.

§. 550. Verbs expressing *fear, hope, confidence, wonder, shame,* &c. take an accus. of the feeling or that wherein it consists : φοβέομαι, δείδω, δειμαίνω, θαρρῶ, θαυμάζω, &c.

a. Accus. of cognate subst. : Plat. Prot. p. 361 B φόβους φοβοῦνται, cf. Eur. Suppl. 548: Plat. Symp. p. 198 A δέος δεδιέναι: Eur. Andr. 869 δεῖμ' ὃ δειμαίνεις: Plat. Prot. p. 360 B θάρρη θαρροῦσιν: Demosth. p. 426, 20 οὔτε ᾐσχύνοντο αἰσχύνην, they were not ashamed of the shame.

b. Accusative of equivalent notion : Soph. Phil. 1250 στράτον δ' Ἀχαιῶν οὐ φοβεῖ. The στράτος was the φόβος: then φοβεῖσθαί τι or τινα, considered as, and substituted for, the φόβος. So Soph. Œ. C. 604 πάθος δείσαντες: Plat. Rep. p. 382 D δεδιὼς τοὺς ἐχθρούς. (Cf. Demosth. p. 10, 2 τοῦτό ἐστι μάλιστα δέος; hence δεδιέναι τοῦτο = δέος, cf. Lys. 105, 9.): Eur. Hec. 54 φάντασμα δειμαίνουσα: Id. Med. 39 δειμαίνω νιν. (Cf. Eur. Herc. F. 700 πέρσας δείματα θηρῶν=δεινοὺς θῆρας.) Soph. Œ. R. 1010 τοῦτ' αὐτὸ μὴ φοβεῖ: Æsch. Eum. 38 οὐδὲν δείσασα: Eur. Andr. 362 ἐν δέδοικα: Id. Suppl. 179 τὰ οἰκτρὰ δεδοικέναι: Æsch. p. 42, 7 δεδιέναι τὰ δεινά: Plat. Phæd. p. 88 B θαρροῦντι θάνατον = θάρρος θανάτου. (Cf. Plat. Prot. p. 361 B οὐκοῦν αἰσχρὰ θάρρη θαρροῦσιν; Ὡμολόγει—θαρροῦσι δὲ τὰ αἰσχρὰ καὶ κακά. Hence θαρρεῖν τι or τινα.) So Eur. And. 994 θάρσει γέροντος χεῖρα: Od. θ, 197 θάρσει τόνδε γ' ἄεθλον: Xen. Cyr. V. 42 ἵνα σε θαρρήσωσι: Eur. Hec. 875 τὰ δ' ἄλλα θάρσει: Demosth. p. 30, 7 οὔτε Φίλιππος ἐθάρρει τούτους οὔθ' οὗτοι Φίλιππον: Soph. Trach. 110 ἐλπίζοντες αἶσαν: Id. Phil. 629 ταῦτ' ἐλπίσαι: Il. ο, 539 ἤλπετο νίκαν: Soph. Trach. 369 προσδόκα τάδε: Eur. Hipp. 244 αἰδού-

μεθα τὰ λελεγμένα = αἰδώ. (Cf. Passow ad voc.): Arist. Rhet.
I. 9, 20 τὰ αἰσχρὰ αἰσχύνονται: Plat. Symp. p. 216 B αἰσχύνομαι τὰ ὁμολογούμενα. So frequently Infin. with article:
Plat. Rep. p.414 E ᾐσχύνου τὸ ψεῦδος λέγειν: Soph. Œ. R. 1081
δυσγένειαν αἰσχύνεται: Eur. Med. 268 θαυμάζειν τύχας =
θαῦμα. (Cf. Id. Alc. 1126 θαῦμ' ἀνέλπιστον τόδε.) Demosth. p.
174 θαυμάζωμεν αὐτά: Plat. Gorg. p. 458 E ἃ (sc. θαύματα)
θαυμάζω: Id. p. 428 D θαυμάζω σοφίαν: Æsch. Ag. 853
θαυμάσῃς τόδε: so Eur. Orest. 878 ἐκπαγλούμενος πατέρα,
the person being the θαῦμα.

§. 551. 1. Verbs of *thinking, willing, caring, considering, calculating, deliberating, hesitating, shuffling, pretending*, &c. take an accus.
of the thought, &c. or that wherein it consists: σοφίζομαι, δοκέω,
δοξάζω, νοέω, φρονέω, λογίζομαι, βουλεύω, μήδομαι, μητίομαι, μερμηρίζω, μεριμνάω, ὁρμαίνω, μενοινάω &c.

a. Accus. of cognate subst.: Eur. Hel. 120 δοκεῖτε δόκησιν:
Plat. Rep. p. 493 A δόγματα ἃ δοξάζουσιν: Demosth. p. 1364,
17 λογισμὸν ἀνθρώπινον λογιζόμενος: Il. ι, 74 ἀρίστην βουλὴν
βουλεύειν: Il. ι, 104 νόον νοήσει: Plat. Parm. p. 132 C νόημα
νοεῖ: Id. Prot. p. 325 C ἐπιμελοῦνται ἐπιμέλειαν: Id. Rep.
p. 405 C πάσας στροφὰς στρέφεσθαι.

b. Accus. of cognate notion: Il. υ, 153 βουλὰς μητιόωντες:
Æsch. Choeph. 549 μήσατο πρόνοιαν.

c. Accus. of equivalent notion: Plat. Rep. p. 413 A τὰ ὄντα δοξάζειν: Id. Theæt. p. 209 B σὲ (=δόξαν σοῦ) δοξάσω: Xen. Hell.
VI. 1, 5 λογισάμενοι τὰς ἔξω μοίρας (which formed the λογισμός): Plat. Phil. p. 18 C τοῦτον τὸν δεσμὸν λογισάμενος: Hdt.
VIII. 4 ἐβούλευον δρησμόν (=βουλὴν δρησμοῦ): Æsch. Choeph.
985 τοῦτ' ἐμήσατο στύγος: Od. ζ, 14 νόστον μητιόωντες:
Soph. Trach. 289 φρόνει νιν ὡς ἥξοντα (his arrival was the
φρόνημα): Od. τ, 2 φόνον μερμηρίζων: Id. ω, 127 δόλον μερμήριζε: Soph. Œ. R. 1124 ἔργον μεριμνῶν: Od. δ, 732 ὁδὸν
ὁρμαίνειν, so πόλεμον, πλοῦν, φόνον: Od. β, 275 ὁδὸν ἣν συ
μενοινᾷς: Il. α, 549 μῦθον νοῆσαι: so σκήψασθαι νόσον
&c. the disease, &c. being the pretence.

d. Accus. of notion contained in verb: Thuc. V. 105 πιστεύει
(=πιστῶς δοκεῖ) δόξαν.

e. Elliptic accus.: Plat. Phædr. p. 228 C ἀληθῆ δοκῶ: Id. Rep.
p. 380 D τοιαῦτα δοκεῖν: Id. Menex. p. 243 ἀληθῆ (δόξαν preceding) ἔδοξε: Xen. Apol. I. 1, 3 ταῦτα δοξάζειν: Plat. Conv. p.
194 ἄγροικον (sc. δόγμα) δοξάσω: Od. ρ, 570 τοῦτ' ἐνόησε: Plat.
Prot. p. 347 E ἕτερα νοεῖ: Il. ξ, 221 ταῦτα μενοινᾷς: Od. δ,
533 ἀεικέα μερμηρίζει: Il. ξ, 20 διχθάδια (sc. ὁρμήματα)

ὥρμαινε: Xen. Ap. 15 ταῦτα πιστεύσητε: Plat. Tim. p. 90
C τὰ θεῖα φρονοῦντες: Soph. Phil. 77 αὐτὸ τοῦτο σοφισθῆναι:
Xen. Hell. VII. 5, 5 τὰ ἡμέτερα φρονοῦσαι: and Thuc. So
ταῦτα πάντα γιγνώσκειν: Hdt. V. 105 τὸ σκηπτόμενοι:
Plat. Rep. p. 533 A τόδε ἀμφισβητεῖ: Id. Lach. p. 196 B
τοιαῦτα στρέφεσθαι: so θέλω, βούλομαι ταῦτα.

f. Adverbial accus.: Plat. Phæd. p. 65 C λογίζεται κάλλιστα:
Xen. Apol. III. 5, 23 πολλὰ μεριμνῶν: Il. o, 703 ἀταλὰ φρονέοντες: Eur. Med. 1129 φρονεῖς ὀρθά: Soph. Phil. 1006
ἐλεύθερον φρονεῖν: Æsch. Ag. 214 τὸ παντότολμον φρονεῖν:
Hdt. VIII. 10 καταφρονήσαντες ταῦτα, thinking thus
meanly of them.

2. Verbs of *conceiving, knowing, believing, knowing from memory,
holding, concluding, or the contraries,* take an accus. of the knowledge, &c. or thing known, &c.: ἐπίσταμαι, γιγνώσκω, οἶδα, νομίζω,
ἡγοῦμαι, ἀπορῶ, ἀμηχανῶ &c.

Accus. of equivalent notion, of that wherein the knowledge, &c.
consists: Plat. Crat. p. 409 C τὸ πῦρ ἀπορῶ: Æsch. Ag. 1150
τέρμ' ἀμηχανῶ: Plat. Men. p. 93 A ἀρετὴν ἐπίσταντο: Id.
Gorg. p. 484 B ᾆσμα οὐκ ἐπίσταμαι (recollect): Id. Leg. p. 908
C νομίζων θεούς: cf. Eur. Suppl. 730. So Id. Hec. 790 ἡγεῖσθαι θεούς: cf. Arist. Eq. 32. Plat. Parm. p. 134 E γιγνώ-
σκουσι τὰ ἀνθρώπινα πράγματα: Id. Prot. p. 337 D εἰδέναι τὴν
φύσιν τῶν πραγμάτων: Æsch. Pers. 242 εἴσει λόγον: Id. Choeph.
101 ἔχθος νομίζομεν: Soph. Œ. R. 1525 αἰνίγματα ᾔδη:
Demosth. p. 69, 3 ἀμνημονεῖ τοὺς λόγους: Plat. Crat. p. 409 D ἃ
ἀπορῶ: Id. Euth. p. 301 B τοῦτο ἀπορῆσαι: Eur. 548 ταῦτ'
ἀμηχανῶ: Plat. Hipp. p. 285 C ἃ ἐπίστασαι: Id. Rep. p. 285 A
ὁμοῖα νομίσαντες: Id. Apol. p. 24 E τοῦτο αὐτὸ οἶδε: Id.
Euth. p. 2 B οὐκ ἐκεῖνο καταγνώσομαι, I will not believe this.

Obs. 1. In the usual construction of νομίζω, γιγνώσκω &c. the accus. of
the knowledge, or opinion, &c. is resolved either into a substantival sentence
with ὅτι, &c. (See *Substantival Sentences*); as, νομίζω ὅτι οἱ θεοί εἰσι =
νομίζω θεούς: or the accus. and infin.; as, νομίζω εἶναι θεούς.

Obs. 2. Νομίζω in Hdt. is used with a dat.—(See *Dative.*)

§. 552. Verbs of *living, faring well or ill, suffering, being ill,
being liable to, in danger, dying, perishing,* &c. take an accus. of the
state or that wherein it consists.

a. Accus. of cognate subst.: Plat. Rep. p. 444 C ζώειν ζωήν:
Æsch. 22, 35 διατριβὰς διέτριβον: Hdt. III. 147 πάθος μέγα
Πέρσας πεπονθότας: Il. ε. 386 πήματ' ἔπασχον: cf. Æsch.
P. V. 470. Soph. Œ. C. 361 παθήμαθ' ἃ ἔπαθον: Plat. Rep. p.
451 A κινδύνευμα κινδυνεύειν: Demosth. p. 139, 9 κινδυνεύ-

σαντες τοὺς ἐσχάτους κινδύνους: Plat. Alc. p. 139 E νόσον νοσεῖν:
cf. Eur. Andr. 220. Andoc. p. 114, 31. Arist. Aves 31. Od. ι,
303 ἀπωλόμεθ' αἰπὺν ὄλεθρον: Plut. Crass. XXV ὀξὺν θάνατον
ἀποθνήσκειν: Plat. Prot. p. 324 D ἀπορία ἣν ἀπορεῖς.

b. *Accus. of cognate notion :* Eur. Med. 248 ἀκίνδυνον βίον
ζῶμεν: cf. Soph. El. 589. Plat. Rep. p. 465 D. Isæus p. 36, 31
ἀσθενῶν νόσον: Plat. Rep. p. 408 E νόσους κάμνειν: Od. γ,
220 ἄλγεα πάσχομεν: Æsch. Choeph. 433 ἄλγεα πάθομεν:
Eur. Med. 581 ζημίαν ὀφλισκάνει: Æsch. Ag. 534 δίκην
ὀφλών: Plat. Apol. p. 39 B θανάτου δίκην ὀφλών: Od. a, 166
ἀπόλωλε κακὸν μόρον: Il. γ, 417 κακὸν οἶτον ὀλέσθαι: Il. ν,
384 φθίσεσθαι.

c. *Accus. of equivalent notion :* Isocr. 315 C βεβίωκα τὸν
παρελθόντα χρόνον = χρονὸν βίου: Demosth. p. 520 πράγματα αἴσχιστα
(= πάθη) ἐπάθομεν: Plat. Gorg. p. 495 E νοσεῖ ὀφθάλμους =
νόσον ὀφθάλμων: Soph. Phil. 1320 νοσεῖς ἄλγος = ἀλγώδη νόσον:
Eur. Ion. 620 ἀπαιδειαν νοσεῖν: Id. Phœn. 763 ὀφλισκάνεις
ἀμαθίαν = ὄφλημα ἀμαθίας: Id. Med. 404 γέλωτα ὀφλεῖν: Andoc. p.
18, 7 βλαβὴν ὀφλεῖν: Isæus p. 117, 7 ὤφλουν τὴν δίαιταν = δίκην
τῆς διαίτης: Plat. Apol. p. 36 A ὤφλε χιλίας δραχμάς: ζημίαν:
Demosth. p. 835, 15 κινδυνεύειν τὴν ἐπωβελίαν = κίνδυνον:
Ibid. p. 1033, 1 ψευδομαρτυρίαν: Eur. Hel. 76 ἀπόλαυσιν εἰκοῦς
ἔθανες ἂν Διὸς κόρης, ἀπόλαυσιν is in apposition to θάνατον, implied in ἔθανες.

d. *Accus. cognate to the notion implied in the verb :* Eur. Orest.
207 βίοτον ἕλκω = βίωμι ἕλκων, protract. So Id. Phœn. 1531
ἕλκεις μακρόπνουν ζόαν: Plat. Rep. p. 534 C ὀνειροπολοῦντα
(= ἐν ὀνείρῳ βιοῦντα) βίον, so ἄγειν βίον, ἡμέρας &c.

Obs. Ἄγω in its neuter sense signifies to do any thing continuously :
thus Soph. Aj. 382 ἄγεις γέλωτα.

e. *Elliptic accus.:* Demosth. p. 760, 14 ζῶμεν τὰ καθ' ἡμᾶς αὐτούς:
Eur. Troad. 615 νοσεῖς ἕτερα: Soph. Œ. C. 595 πέπονθα
δεινά: Plat. Rep. p. 318 A θεῖον πεπόνθατε. cf. Phædr. p. 238
C.: so ταὐτὰ πάσχειν, to be similarly affected : Eur. Med. 953
ἐν εὐδαιμονήσω, so πάντα εὐδαιμονεῖν: Eur. Hec. 429
πάντα δυστυχῶ: Demosth. p. 1460, 23 ἐν τοῦτο εὐτυχῆσαι:
Eur. Hel. 1213 τάδ' εὐτυχεῖν.

f. *Adverbial accus. :* Eur. Ion. 632 μέτρια ζῆν: Soph. Frag.
326 ζῆν ἄνοσον: Plat. Rep. p. 495 C οὐδ' ἀληθῆ ζῶσι: Od. χ,
472 οἴκτιστα θάνοιεν: Eur. Med. 349 πολλὰ διέφθορα.

§. 553. Verbs which express a man's *position*, or *condition in the
world*, *serving public offices*, *slavery*, *age*, &c. take an accus. of the

condition, &c. or that wherein it consists : ἄρχω, χορηγέω, τριηραρ-
χέω, λειτουργέω, πρεσβεύω, δουλεύω, βασιλεύομαι &c.

a. Accus. of cognate subst. : Arist. Av. 308 ἄρχειν ἀρχήν :
Demosth. p. 836 χορηγεῖ καὶ τριηραρχεῖ καὶ τὰς ἄλλας
λειτουργίας λειτουργεῖ : Ibid. p. 92, 11 πρεσβείας πρεσβεύειν :
Xen. Apol. 3, 12 δουλεύειν δουλείαν : Plaut. *servio servitutem* :
Plat. Legg. p. 676 B πολιτείας πεπολιτευμέναι : Ibid. p. 680
E βασιλείαν βασιλευόμενοι : Æschin. 3, 30 ἱερᾶσθαι ἱερωσύνην : Eur. Iph. A. 1364 αἱρεθεὶς αἵρεσιν. So Plat. Rep. p.
404 A μεταβολὰς μεταβάλλοντες. So Thuc. III. 13 ἀποστήσεσθαι διπλῆν ἀπόστασιν.

b. Accus. of cognate notion : Soph. Aj. 435 ἀριστεύσας
καλλιστεῖα.

c. Accus. of equivalent notion : Soph. Œ. C. 874 βίον (= γῆρας
βίου) γηρᾶναι : Eur. Herc. F. 436 ἥβων σθένος = σθεναρὰν
ἥβην : Eur. Electr. 131 τίνα οἶκον, τίνα πόλιν (=τίνος οἴκου λατρείαν)
λατρεύεις.

d. Elliptic accus. : Demosth. p. 62, 25 τὰ προσταττόμενα (λειτουρ-
γήματα) λειτουργῶν : Eur. Hel. 283 πολιὰ παρθενεύεται :
Soph. Electr. 950 ἄλεκτρα γηράσκουσαν : Demosth. p. 440,
16 τοιαῦτα πεπρεσβευκότος : Ibid. p. 535, 12 χορηγεῖν
Διονύσια.

e. Adverbial accus. : Antiph. p. 117 ἄριστα χορηγήσω : Eur.
Rhes. 405 ὑπηρετεῖν ταῦτα.

Obs. Λατρεύω also has a transitive sense of *waiting on*, like θεραπεύω.

§. 554. Verbs of *looking, having the aspect of,* &c. take an accus.
of the look, &c. or that wherein it consists.

a. Accus. of cognate notion : Eur. Cycl. 509 καλὸν ὄμμα δεδορ-
κότας : Æsch. Pers. 79 κυανοῦν λεύσσων δέργμα.

b. Accus. of equivalent notion : Od. τ, 446 πῦρ ὀφθάλμοισι δεδορ-
κώς=πυρὸς δέργμα. So the Homeric phrases : βλέπειν, δέρκεσθαι Ἄρην, ὁρᾶν ἀλκήν=ὅραμα ἀλκῆς : Æsch. Sept. c. Theb. 500
βλέπων φόβον = βλέμμα φόβου : Eur. Ion 1282 ἀναβλέπων
φλόγα = βλέμμα φλογός. So in the comedians : βλέπειν νᾶπυ,
ὑπότριμμα, ὄμφακας (sour grapes), αἰκίαν, ἀπιστίαν, συρμαίαν. Sometimes with the infin. used as a subst.: Arist. Vesp. 879 τιμᾶν
βλέπω.

c. Accus. cognate to notion implied in the verb : Eur. Med. 92
ταυρουμένην (=ταυρικῶς βλέπουσαν) δέργμα.

d. Adverbial accus. : φθονερὰ βλέπειν : Theocr. XX. 13 λοξὰ
βλέποισα : Hom., &c. δερκόμενος δεινόν, σμερδαλέον, τακερά,
so ἐλεεινὸν ὁρᾶν : Il. β, 269 ἀχρεῖον ἰδών : Eur. Alc. 773 τί σεμνὸν

οὕτω καὶ πεφροντικὸς βλέπεις. So Arist. Vesp. 900 κλέπτον βλέπει.

§. 555. Verbs which express the notion of *flowing, springing forth, flourishing in, shining, burning, breathing,* &c. take an accus. of the stream, &c. or that wherein it consists.

a. Accus. of cognate subst. : Plat. Alcib.: φύσημα φυσώντων. So Il. δ, 27 ἱδρῶσ' ἱδρῶτα.

b. Accus. of cognate notion : Eur. Phœn. 225 λάμπουσα σέλας=λαμπάδα: Hom. Hymn. Apol. προρέειν καλλίρροον ὕδωρ.

c. Accus. of equivalent notion : Soph. Aj. 1391 φυσῶσι μένος: Id. El. 1377 φυσῶν αἷμα: Eur. Orest. 1512 ἀνταυγεῖ φόνου= αὐγὴν φόνου: Hom. πνείοντες μένεα=πνεύματα μένεος, so Ἄρεα πνεῖν: Pind. Pyth. IV. 225 πνεῖν φλόγα = πνεῦμα φλογός. So Id. πῦρ πνεῖν: Soph. Ant. 1146 πῦρ πνεόντων ἄστρων: Id. Trach. 845 τέγγει ἄχναν: Anacr. XXXVII. 2 βρύειν ῥόδα : Æsch. Pers. 622 θαλλούσης βίον = θάλλος βίου: Pind. Ol. III. 23 δένδρε' ἔθαλλεν γῇ: Theocr. XXV. 16 ποίην θαλέθουσι λειμῶνες. (So elliptic : Eur. Frag. Dan. 10 γῇ τ' ἠρινὸν θάλλουσα.) Theocr. V. 124 ῥείτω γάλα : Ibid. 126 ῥείτω μέλι. So Æsch. P. V. 370 ἐξαναζέσει χόλον. So Eur. Bacch. 620 στάζων ἱδρῶτα : Id. Hipp. 122 πέτρα ὕδωρ στάζουσα.

d. Adverbial accus. : ὄζειν ἡδύ &c. : Eur. Iph. Aul. 381 δεινὰ φυσᾷς.

§. 556. Verbs expressing *bodily condition, position* or *motion, sleeping, sitting, standing, rising, falling, leaping, dancing,* &c. take an accus. of the position, &c. or that wherein it consists : εὕδω, ὑπνέω, κοιμάομαι, λαύω, ἀωτέω, ἵζω, καθίζω, ἔζω, ἧμαι, θακέω, θοάζω, θάσσω, ἅλλομαι, πίπτω, κεῖμαι, ἵσταμαι, χορεύω, ὀρχέομαι, ὁρμάω &c.

a. Accus. of cognate subst. : Eur. Bacch. 883 στάσιν ἑστάναι: Soph. Phil. 275 ἀνάστασιν στῆναι: Æsch. Ag. 1494 κεῖσαι κοίταν: Soph. Ant. 1045 πέπτωκε πτώματα. Cf. Eur. Elect. 606. Plat. Lach. p. 181 B. Eur. Andr. 654 πεσήματα πέπτωκε: Plat. Legg. p. 942 E χορείας χορεύειν.

b. Accus. of cognate notion : Eur. Herc. Fur. 1061 εὕδει ὕπνον: Ibid. 1034. Il. λ, 241 κοιμήσατο χάλκεον ὕπνον: Theocr. III. 49 ἄκροτον ὕπνον λαύων: Il. κ, 159 ὕπνον ἀωτεῖς: Æsch. Ag. 983 ἵζει θρόνον = ἕδραν : Eur. Orest. 954 καθίζων τρίποδα: Æsch. Ag. 190 σέλμα ἡμένων: Eur. Rhes. 547 ἡμένα κοίτας : Æsch. P. V. 389 θακοῦντι ἕδρας=θᾶκος: Soph. Œ. R. 2 ἕδρας θοάζετε : Arist. Thesm. 889 θάσσειν ἕδρας: Æsch. Pers. 303 πήδημα (=ἅλμα) ἀφήλατο: Thuc. I. 37 κειμένη θέσιν: Æsch.

Ag. 31 φροίμιον (πρῶτον χόρον) χ ο ρ ε ύ σ ο μ α ι : Hdt. VI. 129
ὅ ρ χ ή σ α τ ο σχημάτια = ὅρχους.

c. Accus. of equivalent notion : Soph. Phil. 249 ἐ ζ ό μ ε ν ο ν
ζυγόν: Eur. Orest. 861 θ ά σ σ ο ν τ' ἄκραν : Id. Iph. A. 141 ἵζου κρήνας :
Soph. Aj. 1183 ἐννυχίαν τέρψιν (=ὕπνον) λ α ύ ε ι ν : Eur. Rhes. 740
κοῖτον (= ὕπνον ἐν κοίτῳ) λ α ύ ε ι ν : Soph. Phil. 145 τόπον ὅντινα
κ ε ῖ τ α ι : Eur. Suppl. 987 ἕ σ τ η κ ε πέτραν, the πέτρα was the
στάσις : metaphor, Ibid. 1018 τελευτὰν ἢν ἕ σ τ α κ α : Id. Orest. 1256
σ τ ῆ θ' αἰ μὲν ἀμαξήρη τρίβον: Id. Phœn. 825 π ε ρ ι χ ο ρ ε ύ ο υ σ α
ἀδονάν = ἡδὺν χόρον: Id. Iph. A. 1058 γάμους (= γαμικὸν χόρον)
ἐ χ ό ρ ε υ σ α ν : Eur. Troad. 750 π ε σ ὼ ν πήδημα = πέσημα : Id.
Hipp. 829 ὁ ρ μ ή σ α σ α πήδημα.

d. Accus. cognate to the notion implied in the verb : Æsch.
Ag. 2 φυλακὴν ἢν κ ο ι μ ώ μ ε ν ο ς = ἐν κοίτῃ φυλάσσων : Arist.
Nub. 540 κόρδαχ' (χόρον), ε ἵ λ κ υ σ ε ν = ἑλκύσας ἐχόρευσεν, danced
slowly.

e. Adverbial accus. : Il. o, 684 ἀσφαλὲς θ ρ ώ σ κ ω ν : Il. φ, 266
σ τ ῆ ν α ι ἐναντίβιον : Eur. Hipp. 1079 ἐναντίον σ τ ά ν τ α : Soph.
Frag. 704, 2 φαιδρὰ χ ο ρ ε ύ ε ι : Id. Œ. R. 1300 μείζονα πηδήσας[a]. Cf. Trach. 1001. Id. Ant. 1325 λέχρια εἰσήλατο.

Obs. Χορεύω has a transitive sense of "to celebrate by dancing :" ἐχόρευσαν
τὸν θεόν : ἵζομαι has a transitive sense "to supplicate :" Soph. Œ. R. 30
ἐζόμεσθά σε.

Verbs of Motion.

§. 557. 1. Neuter verbs of motion have a twofold sense—1. Motion
along, *to go* ; 2. Motion to, *to arrive at* ; wherefore the accusative
after these verbs must be considered in its relation to each.

a. Motion along.—The notion of *going* implies, as coincident
with it, the notion of a space along which the motion takes place ;
as, βαίνειν ὁδόν, to go along a road.

b. Motion towards.—The notion of *going to, arriving at,* implies
the notion of the place arrived at, as coincident with its completion
—as the notion of "beating" implies the notion of a patient.

2. The use of the accusative however, with verbs of motion in
this latter sense, is confined to poetry, as the more accurate usage
of prose defined the direction more clearly by a preposition.

Obs. The notion of *arriving at,* is not communicated to the verbs of
motion by the accus. case, but is an independent and distinct sense of the
verb itself, called out by the notion with which it is joined ; in which sense
the verb is used, whether *motion along,* or *motion towards,* is determined
by the context, as in the two following instances : Od. a, 330 κλίμακα δ'

[a] Cf. Herm. ad loc.

ὑψηλὴν κατεβήσατο. Here the context shews that καταβαίνω means "to move along," or "down along;" but in Od. β, 337 θάλαμον κατεβήσατο, we see the verb signifies "to move towards," though the case used in both is the same, and therefore cannot determine the sense.

§. 558. 1. Verbs of *moving along.*—So βαίνειν, ἔρχεσθαι, περᾶν, ἕρπειν, πορεύεσθαι ὁδόν: Æsch. Ag. 81 τρίποδας ὁδοὺς στείχει (*itque reditque viam*): Plat. Rep. p. 405 διεξόδους διεξελθεῖν: Thuc. V. 10 ἴθει ὁδόν: Od. γ, 71 πόθεν πλεῖθ' ὑγρὰ κέλευθα: Il. ζ, 292 τὴν ὁδόν, ἣν Ἑλένην περ ἀνήγαγεν εὐπατέρειαν: Od. α, 330 κλίμακα δ' ὑψηλὴν κατεβήσατο: Od. ψ, 85 κατέβαιν' ὑπερῷα: Od. ξ, 350 ξεστὸν ἐφόλκαιον καταβῆναι, to creep down the rudder: Od. ι, 261 οἴκαδε ἱέμενοι ἄλλην ὁδόν, ἄλλα κέλευθα ἤλθομεν: Æsch. S. Th. 467 κλίμακος προσαμβάσεις στείχει πρὸς ἐχθρῶν πύργον: Id. Pers. 733 μολεῖν γέφυραν: Id. Cho. 727 πατεῖν πύλας: Soph. Aj. 845 διφρηλατεῖν τὸν οὐρανόν. So metaphor, ἀμαξεύω τὸν βίοτον: Soph. Œ. C. 1686 πόντιον κλύδων' ἀλώμεναι: Theocr. ἀλώμενος ὤρεα: Eur. Med. 1067 ἀλλ' εἶμι γὰρ δὴ τλημονεστάτην ὁδόν: Il. δ, 384 ἀγγελίην στεῖλαν: Soph. Œ. C. 20 προὐστάλης ὁδόν: ἐμβατεύειν τι (Æsch. Pers. 447.): Eur. Herac. 848 ἐμβῆσαι δίφρον: Id. Hipp. 1131 συζυγίαν πώλων ἐπιβήσει: Æsch. Pers. 447 νῆσον ἣν Πὰν ἐμβατεύει. So Eur. Iph. T. 398 ἔπλευσαν νάϊον ὄχημα: Hdt. VI. 119 τρέπεται τριφασίας ὁδούς: cf. Thuc. V. 10. Xen. Cyr. I. 6, 43 ἄγειν (στρατιὰν) ἢ στενὰς ἢ πλατείας ὁδούς: Demosth. p. 49, 34 ἄγων καὶ φέρων τοὺς πλέοντας τὴν θάλατταν. So Soph. Phil. 1027 πλεῖν στόλον = πλοῦν: cf. Id. Œ. R. 422. Il. λ, 140 ἀγγελίην (= ὁδὸν ἀγγελίης) ἐλθόντα: Il. ω, 235 ἐξεσίην ἐλθόντι: Demosth. p. 392 ἀπήραμεν πρεσβείαν=πλοῦν πρεσβείας: Soph. Phil. 163 στίβον ὀγμεύει: Æsch. Ag. 286 πόντον (=νῶτα πόντου) νωτίσαι: Soph. Œ. R. 193 παλίσσυτον δρόμημα νωτίσαι: Id. Œ. C. 1481 οἷον τέλος ὁδοῦ ἀφορμήθημεν = ὁδὸν οἵαν τελοῦσαν: Eur. Alc. 753 ἀμείψασθαι πύλας, to pass through: Xen. Hipp. VIII. 10 ὁ μὲν φεύγῃ παντοῖα χώρια, so γῆν πρὸ γῆς διώκων, passing quickly over: Æsch. P. V. 685 γῆν πρὸ γῆς ἐλαύνομαι, so ἐλαύνειν (to run) δρόμον: Demosth. p. 393 ὁδὸν ἐπειγόμενοι: Thuc. IV. 5 ἐπείγοντο τὸν πλοῦν, so φανῆναι (sc. ἐλθόντα) ὁδόν: Soph. Trach. 58 θρώσκει (passes quickly through) δόμους, so τόδ' ἱκάνεις, this journey, ἄντην (ὁδὸν) ἔρχεσθαι, ἀντίβιον ἐλθεῖν, and many other adverbial expressions of daily occurrence; as, τὴν ταχίστην (ὁδόν), *celerrime* (Xen. II. 1, 18.)—τὴν πρώτην, *primum* (Hdt. III. 134). Demosth. p. 28, 2[a]. Ibid. p. 34,

[a] Brenni ad loc.

21 τὴν ἄλλως—λέγειν, *frustra dicere :* Ibid. p. 73, 32 οὐδ' ἵνα τὴν ἄλλως ἀδολέσχω: Ibid. p. 34, 21 τὴν ἄλλως προήρημαι λέγειν, *non frustra statui dicere*—τὴν εὐθεῖαν, *rectâ*—μακράν, a long way, μακροτέραν Plat.—ἄλλην καὶ ἄλλην, now one way, now another —ἀντην, ἀντιβίην, ἀντίον, πλησίον, αὐτόδιον, properly *that same way, illico :* Od. θ, 449 αὐτόδιον δ' ἄρα μιν ταμίη λούσασθαι ἄνωγεν: Il. ψ, 116 πολλὰ δ' ἄναντα, κάταντα, πάραντά τε δόχμιά τ' ἦλθον.

2. Verbs of *stepping* take an accus. of the step or its equivalent; as, βαίνω πόδα=ποδὸς βάσιν: · Soph. Aj. 42 ἐπεμπίπτει (=ἐμπεσὼν βαίνει) βάσιν: Eur. Phœn. 1412 προβὰς κῶλον δεξιόν: Id. Orest. 1487 Μυκηνῶδ' ἀρβύλαν προβάς: Id. Heracl. 805 ἐκβὰς πόδα: Id. Hec. 1062 πᾶ πόδ' ἐπάξας: Ibid. 53 περᾷ πόδα: Æsch. Choeph. 676 δεῦρ' ἀπεζύγην πόδας, came on foot.

§. 559. Verbs expressing or implying *motion to :* Eur. Andr. 1120 χωρεῖ δὲ πρύμναν: Æsch. P. V. 708 στεῖχε γύας: Eur. Med. 668 ἐστάλης ὀμφαλόν: Ibid. 756 ἀφίξομαι πόλιν: Ibid. 1143 στέγας ἐσπόμην. So Il. θ, 195 κεκλήατο (sc. ἐλθεῖν) βουλήν. So Il. ζ, 87 ἡ δὲ ξυνάγουσα γεραιὰς νηὸν 'Αθηναίης: Soph. Œ. C. 1562 ἐκκατανύσαι νεκρῶν πλάκα, (Dind. ἐκτανύσαι): Od. γ, 162 οἱ μὲν ἀποστρέψαντες ἔβαν νέας ἀμφιελίσσας: Il. α, 317 κνίσσῃ δ' οὐρανὸν ἷκε: Od. α, 176 πολλοὶ ἴσαν ἀνέρες ἡμέτερον δῶ: Od. β, 337 θάλαμον κατεβήσατο: Od. ι, 351 σχέτλιε, πῶς κέν τις σε καὶ ὕστερον ἄλλος ἵκοιτο—; Od. ζ, 296 ἱκώμεθα δώματα πατρός: Il. ε, 291 βέλος δ' ἴθυνεν 'Αθήνη ῥῖνα: Soph. Œ. T. 35 ἄστυ Καδμεῖον μολών: Id. El. 893 ἦλθον πατρὸς ἀρχαῖον τάφον: Eur. Med. 7 Μήδεια πύργους γῆς ἔπλευσ' 'Ιωλκίας: Ibid. 12 φυγῇ—ἀφίκετο χθόνα: cf. 680. 682. 920. 1143. Id. Rhes. 289 δρυμὸν μολών. So we must explain ἱκνεῖσθαί τινα, to belong to a person; as, Hdt. IX. 26 ἡμέας ἱκνέεται.

Obs. 1. The sense of direction, *to,* contained in these verbs is usually (prose always) more definitely marked by the prepos. εἰς, ἀνά, κατά, ὑπέρ, ἐπί, περί, ἀμφί, μετά, πρός, παρά, ὑπό, ὡς, (see these prepos.) and by the local suffix δέ, as ἄστυδε ἔλθωμεν.

Obs. 2. Those verbs of motion which imply some further notion, as *departure, approach, pursuit, flight,* &c. take naturally a cognate accusative of that notion; as, Plat. Rep. p. 496 E τὴν ἀπαλλαγὴν ἀπαλλάξεται: Arist. Av. 854 προσόδια προσιέναι: Eur. Herc. F. 896 κυναγετεῖ διωγμόν: Id. Hel. 21 δίωγμα φεύγων: Plat. Symp. p. 197 D ξυνιέναι ξυνόδους.

Obs. 3. The distinction between the different cognate accusatives given in §. 548. 2., obtain with all verbs, though, for the sake of brevity, they will not in the following pages be classed under their separate heads as before; it being presumed that they are sufficiently illustrated in the foregoing pages, to enable the reader to determine for himself under which head they fall.

Verbs of Action.

§. 560. The notion of *doing* implies—

The Agent and his operation,	*The Deed or thing done,*
πράττω.	πρᾶγμα or τοῦτο.

So that all verbs of *doing* have an accusative of the coincident notion of the deed, or thing done.

1. Πράττω, ἐργάζομαι, ῥέζω, σπεύδω and σπουδάζω (to do eagerly) πραγματεύομαι &c. : Plat. Lach. p. 179 D πράγματα ἔπραττον, then ταῦτα, ἄριστα, πολιτικά, κοινά &c. (sc. πράγματα) πράττειν: Eur. Alc. 97 πράττειν τάφον: Xen. πράττειν εἰρήνην: Hes. Op. 404 χρῆμα πρήξεις: Il. ω, 733 ἔργα ἐργάζοιο : cf. Soph. Ant. 1227. Od. ρ, 321 ἐναίσιμα ἐργάζεσθαι: Od. ω, 457 ἔργον ἔρεζον: Soph. Trach. 288 θύματα ῥέξῃ: Eur. And. 837 τόλμαν ἂν (=τολμηρὸν ἔργον) ἔρεξα: Soph. Phil. 1206 παλάμαν ῥέξῃς: Il. λ, 502 μέρμερα ῥέζων: Od. σ, 138 πολλὰ ἀτάσθαλα ἔρεξα: Eur. Ion. 448 σπεύδοντες ἡδονάς: Æsch. Ag. 147 σπευδομένα θυσίαν: Eur. Supp. 161 εὐψυχίαν ἔσπευσας: Eur. Iph. T. 200 σπεύδει ἀσπούδαστα: Id. Hel. 1645 μεγάλα σπεύδεις κακά: Plat. Gorg. p. 481 B ταῦτα σπουδάζει: Id. Soph. p. 259 C οὐκ ἄξια ἐσπούδακας: Xen. Apol. VIII. 17 σπουδάζοντα τὰ ἑαυτοῦ ἡδέα.

2. Verbs of *accomplishing, bringing to an end, finishing, beginning (to do), endeavouring (to do), daring,* &c. : ἄνω, ἀνύω, ἀνύτω, περάω, πράσσω, περαίνω, τελέω, τελευτάω, τολμάω &c. : Od. γ, 490 ἤνον ὁδόν: Eur. Herc. Fur. 576 αὐτοὺς (sc. πόνους) ἤνυσα: Id. Hec. 936 οὐδὲν ἤνυσα: Æsch. Pers. 734 κέλευθον ἤνυσεν: Id. P. V. 702 χρείαν ἠνύσασθε: Soph. Œ. R. 1530 τέρμα βίου περάσῃ: Eur. Iph. A. 10 ἐξεπέρασε βίον: Od. ν, 83 πράσσειν κέλευθον: Od. ι, 491 πράσσειν ἅλα: Soph. Aj. 22 πρᾶγος περάνας: Id. Trach. 79 τελευτὴν τοῦ βίου τελεῖν: Id. Ant. 1114 βίον τελεῖν: Id. El. 726 τελοῦντες ἕβδομον δρόμον: Od. β, 280 τελευτῆσαι ἔργα, so ταῦτα τελευτᾶν: Arist. Plut. 149 τόλμημα τολμᾶτον: Soph. Elect. 470 πεῖραν (=τολμάν) τολμήσειν: Eur. Ion. 976 τὰ δυνατὰ τόλμησον: Id. Herc. F. 1184 τλὰς αἷμα=αἱματηρὸν ἔργον: Æsch. Ag. 1204 τοιαῦτα τολμᾷ. So Plat. Legg. p. 797 B καινοτομεῖν τι νέον. So Thuc. VI. 58 σπονδὰς σπένδεται: Hdt. VII. 148 σπεισάμενοι εἰρήνην, so τέμνειν (to make by sacrifice) ὅρκια πιστά, συνθεσίας, φιλότητα, Homer.

3. Verbs of *sacrificing* take an accus. of the sacrifice or that wherein it consists, the offering, victim, &c. : θύω, ῥέζω &c. : Eur. Iph. A. 721 θύσας θύματα : Plat. Rep. p. 362 C θυσίας θύειν : Od. ξ, 446 θῦσε ἄργματα θεοῖς : Æsch. Eum. 109 δεῖπνα ἔθυον : Eur. Iph. T. 1332 θύουσα φλόγα = θυσίαν φλογός : Æsch. Ag. 1391 ἔθυσε παῖδα : Arist. Av. 922 τὴν δεκάτην θύω = θυσίαν τῆς δεκάτης σελήνης, so εὐαγγέλια, διαβατήρια (θύματα) θύειν : Od. γ, 5 ἱερὰ ῥέζον : Il. ψ, 206 ῥέζουσι ἑκατόμβας.

§. 561. Verbs of *learning, concluding, studying, practising, being in the habit of,* &c. : μανθάνω, ἀσκῶ, μελετάω, ἐπιτηδεύω, νομίζω, *to have a custom,* &c. : Soph. Trach. 450 μάθησιν ἐκμανθάνεις, so μανθάνειν τι=μάθησιν : Plat. Lach. p. 184 E στάδιον ἀσκεῖν : Id. Legg. p. 795 B παγκράτιον ἠσκηκώς : Id. Gorg. p. 527 δικαιοσύνην καὶ ἄλλην ἀρετὴν (=ἄσκησιν ἀρετῆς) ἀσκοῦντας : Demosth. p. 799, 13 ἀσκοῦντες φθόνου : Æsch. P. V. 1068 κακότητ' ἀσκεῖν : Eur. Hel. 1110 ἔρωτας, ἀπάτας, δόλιά τ' ἐξευρήματα ἀσκοῦσα : Xen. Cyr. I. 5, 7 πολεμικὰ ἀσκεῖν : Hdt. II. 77 μνήμην ἐπασκεῖν : Plat. Gorg. p. 511 C μελετᾶν τέχνας = μελέτας : Demosth. p. 1129, 9 μελετᾶν τὴν ἀπολογίαν : Xen. Cyr. II. 3, 1 μελετᾶν τὰς τάξεις : Plat. Apol. p. 28 B ἐπιτήδευμα ἐπιτηδεύσας : Thuc. VI. 54 ἐπετήδευσαν ἀρετήν : Hdt. II. 51 ταῦτα Ἕλληνες νενομίκασι : cf. ch. 92 : so ch. 42 φωνὴν νομίζουσι : ch. 64 ἑορτὴν νενομίκασι : Id. I. 142 γλῶσσαν τὴν αὐτὴν νενομίκασι.

§. 562. Verbs of *eating, drinking,* &c. take an accusative of the cognate notion or its equivalent—food or thing eaten—drink or thing drunk : δειπνέω, βιβρώσκω, ἔδω, ἐσθίω, πατέομαι, φάγω, σιτέομαι, τρώγω, πίνω, ῥοφέω, δαίνυμαι &c. : Æschin. II. 13 δειπνῶν πολυτελῆ δεῖπνα : Xen. Cyr. I. 2, 11 ἄριστον δειπνήσαντες : Id. Conv. I. 11 τἀλλότρια δειπνεῖν : Il. χ, 94 βεβρωκὼς φάρμακα : Æsch. Theb. 1026 σάρκας πάσονται : Od. ι, 84 εἶδαρ ἔδουσι : Il. ε, 341 σῖτον ἔδουσι : Il. δ, 345 κρέα ἔδμεναι : Il. ο, 636 βοῦν ἔδει : metaph. οἶκον, κτήματα, θυμὸν ἔδειν : Od. κ, 460 ἐσθίετε βρώμην : Od. ν, 348 κρέα ἔσθιον : Od. ν, 19 ἑταίρους ἦσθιε : Il. α, 464 σπλάγχν' ἐπάσαντο : So Il. φ, 76 Δημήτερος ἀκτήν : Od. ι, 94 φάγοι καρπόν : Od. δ, 33 ξεινήϊα φαγόντε : Arist. Eq. 412 κυνὸς βορὰν σιτούμενος : so Id. Plut. 543 σοφίαν σιτήσομαι : Id. Ach. 801 τρώγοις ἂν ἐρεβίνθους : Od. ι, 354 ποτὸν πίνειν, so οἶνον, αἷμα, πίνειν : Arist. Vesp. 813 φακῆν ῥοφήσομαι : Id. Ach. 278 εἰρήνης ῥοφήσει τρυβλίον (= εἰρήνην ἐκ τρυβλίου) : Il. ω, 802 δαίνυντο δαῖτα : So Il. ψ, 201 εἰλαπίνην δαίνυντο : Il. τ, 299 δαίσειν γάμον=

γάμου δαῖτα : Il. ι, 531 θεοὶ δ α ί ν υ ν θ᾽ ἑκατόμβας : Od. ι, 162 δ α ι ν ύ μ ε ν ο ι κρέα.

§. 563. Verbs of *labouring, undertaking, toiling, playing, contending in games, enduring labour,* &c. take an accus. of the labour, &c. or that wherein it consists : πονέω, μοχθέω, μογέω, τλῆμι, τολμάω, καρτερέω, ἀθλεύω, ἀγωνίζομαι, ἁμιλλάομαι, παλαίω, τρέχω, παίζω &c. : Plat. Rep. p. 410 B πόνους π ο ν ή σ ε ι : cf. Æsch. Pers. 668. Eur. Orest. 777. 1615. Arist. Pac. 150. Demosth. p. 1443, 23. Plat. Rep. p. 410 B γυμνάσια (= πόνους) π ο ν ή σ ε ι : Eur. Hipp. 1369 ἐ π ό ν η σ α μόχθους : Id. Iph. A. 213 ἅμιλλαν ἐ π ό ν ε ι : Æsch. P. V. 44 τὰ μηδὲν ὠφελοῦντα μὴ π ό ν ε ι μάτην : Eur. Supp. 577 π ο ν ο ῦ σ α πολλά : Eur. Andr. 134 μόχθον μ ο χ θ ε ῖ ς : Xen. Œc. XVIII. 2 πόνον μ ο χ θ ο ῦ σ ι : Id. Apol. II. 1, 7 τἆλλα πάντα μ ο χ θ ή σ ο υ σ ι : Eur. Phœn. 1661 μάταια μ ο χ θ ε ῖ ς : Eur. Hel. 815 μ ο χ θ ο ῦ μ ε ν μαθήματα : Od. δ, 170 ἐ μ ό γ η σ ε ν ἀέθλους : Od. π, 19 ἄλγεα μ ο γ ή σ ῃ : Il. a, 162 πόλλ᾽ ἐ μ ό γ η σ α : Eur. Hel. 609 πόνους τ λ ῆ ν α ι : Id. Phœn. 1514 ἄχεα τ λ ῆ ν α ι : Ibid. 200 δουλοσύναν τ λ α ί η ν : Id. Herc. F. 1250 πολλὰ τ λ ᾶ σ α : Id. Iph. T. 615 τ ο λ μ ῶ σ ι πόνους : Æsch. P. V. 183 ὀ χ ή σ ω φρουράν. So Eur. Alc. 1071 κ α ρ τ ε ρ ε ῖ ν (= καρτερῶς τλῆναι) θεοῦ δόσιν : Id. Supp. 317 ἀ θ λ ή σ α ς πόνον : Id. Orest. 1125 ἀ γ ω ν ι ο ύ μ ε θ α ἀγῶνα : cf. Alc. 651. Suppl. 427. Arist. Ach. 481, &c. Hdt. V. 52 ἀ γ ω ν ί ζ ε σ θ α ι στάδιον (= ἀγῶνα σταδίου) : cf. Xen. Anab. IV. 8, 20. Arist. Eq. 617 πῶς τὸ πρᾶγμ᾽ ἠ γ ω ν ί σ ω ; Demosth. p. 653, 25 γραφὴν ἀ γ ω ν ί ζ ε σ θ α ι : Ibid. p. 194, 5 ἀ γ ω ν ί ζ ε σ θ α ι κίνδυνον : Xen. Anab. IV. 8, 7 κάλλιστα ἀ γ ω ν ι ο ῦ ν τ α ι, so ἁ μ ι λ- λ ᾶ σ θ α ι στάδιον, δίαυλον, λόγον : Eur. Hipp. 426 ταῦτα ἁ μ ι λ λ ῶ- μ α ι : Il. ψ, 733 τρίτον ἐ π ά λ α ι ο ν : Plat. Men. p. 94 C ἐ π ά- λ α ι σ α ν κάλλιστα : Hdt. VIII. 102 ἀγῶνας δ ρ α μ ε ῖ ν : So Id. VII. 57 θ ε ῖ ν τὸν περὶ ψυχῆς, so περὶ σωτηρίας &c. (sc. δρόμον), so τ ρ έ χ ω τὸν περί &c. : Soph. Ant. 898 ἠ ρ ό μ η ν πόνον : Id. Trach. 80 ἆθλον ἄ ρ α ς : Plat. Parm. p. 137 B παιδίαν π α ί ζ ε ι ν : Arist. Pac. 803 ξ ύ μ π α ι ζ ε τὴν ἑορτήν : Xen. Cyr. VI. 1, 4 τοιαῦτα ἔ π α ι ζ ε ν : Pind. Nem. III. 46 ἀ θ ύ ρ ω ν μεγάλα ἔργα. So Arist. Ach. 90 ταῦτ᾽ ἐ φ ε ν ά κ ι ζ ε ς.

§. 564. Verbs of *fighting, contending, going to war, going on an expedition, being victorious,* &c. take an accus. of the war or victory, &c. or that wherein it consists : μάχομαι, πολεμέω, πολεμίζω, ἐρίζω, στρατεύω, στρατεύομαι, νικάω &c. : Il. μ, 175 μάχην ἐ μ ά χ ο ν τ ο : cf. σ, 533. Xen. Ages. V. 5. Plat. Theæt. p. 123 A τοιαῦτα μ ά- χ ε τ α ι : Eur. Phœn. 1574 μ α ρ ν α μ έ ν ο υ ς κοινὸν ἐνυάλιον : Id. Rep. p. 551 D πόλεμον π ο λ ε μ ε ῖ ν : Il. γ, 433 πόλεμον π ο λ ε μ ί-

ζειν: Theocr. V. 23 ἔριν ἤρισε: Hes. Theog. 534 ἐρίζετο
βουλάς=ἔριν βουλῆς: Il. ι, 389 κάλλος (=ἔριν κάλλους) ἐρίζοι:
Demosth. p. 515, 15 στρατείας ἐστρατευμένος: cf. Æschin.
p. 50, 39. Isæus p. 76, 10. Thuc. I. 112 τὸν ἱερὸν πόλεμον ἐστράτευσαν: Xen. Ages. VI. 3 ὅσα ἐστρατεύσατο. So Demosth.
p. 1353 ἐξελθὼν στρατείαν: Od. κ, 544 νίκης ἣν νίκησα. Cf.
Eur. Suppl. 1060. Il. δ, 389 πάντα (sc. ἄεθλα) ἐνίκα: Eur.
Troad. 650 ἃ νικᾶν: Id. El. 955 νικᾶν τὴν δίκην: Id. Alc. 1034
τὰ μείζονα νικῶσι, so κρατέω (see *Double Accus.*): Thuc. I. 126
Ὀλύμπια νικᾶν, so στεφανοῦσθαι Ὀλύμπια, so νικᾶν γνώμην: Id. VII. 67 νικᾶν ναυμαχίας: Plat. Legg. p. 964 C ἀρετὴν
νικᾶν.

§. 565. Verbs of *being wrong, impious, pious,* &c. take an accus. of
the impiety, error, or that wherein it consists: ἀσεβέω, εὐσεβέω,
ἁμαρτάνω, ἀμπλακέω &c.: Plat. Legg. p. 910 ἀσεβήσας ἀσέβημα:
Soph. Phil. 1441 εὐσεβεῖν τὰ πρὸς θεούς: Eur. Hipp. 319 τίν'
ἡμάρτηκεν ἁμαρτίαν: Æschin. p. 26, 22 γυναικεῖα ἁμαρτήματα
ἁμαρτάνειν: cf. Lys. p. 189, 2. Plat. Legg. p. 730 A. Soph. Aj.
1096 ἁμαρτάνουσιν ἔπη: Arist. Pax 618 ἡμάρτομεν ταῦτα:
Od. χ, 154 τόδε ἤμβροτον: Xen. Cyr. III. 1, 22 ἀνθρώπινα
ἁμαρτάνειν: Æsch. Supp. 893 πολλὰ ἁμαρτών: Id. Ag.
1212 τάδ' ἤμπλακον.

Obs. The object of these verbs is generally denoted by εἰς, or περί.
Instrum. dat. as cause of error, is also used: Plat. ῥήμασι ἁμάρτῃ. In
Xen. Hell. I. 7, 10 ἁμαρτάνω is used with accus. of object. So Æsch.
Eum. 260 ἀσεβεῖν in the transitive sense of dishonouring.

§. 566. 1. Verbs of *saying, telling, uttering, proclaiming,* &c. or verbs
which imply these notions, take an accus. of the word, tale, &c. or
that wherein it consists: αἰνέω, ἀγγέλλω, κηρύσσω &c.: Soph. Phil.
1380 αἶνον αἰνέσας: Æsch. Choeph. 869 ἄκραντα βάζω: Id.
P. V. 585 ἐλεύθερα βάζειν: Hom. βάζειν πεπνυμένα, ἀνεμώλια,
νήπια: Od. ν, 100 φάσθαι φήμην: Il. β, 100 φάσθαι ἔπος:
Æsch. Choeph. 91 φάσκω τοῦπος: Il. σ, 17 φάτο ἀγγελίην: Il.
α, 106 εἶπας ἔπος: cf. Soph. Aj. 128. Plat. Ion. p. 538 B &c.
Soph. Aj. 1132 εἶπε λόγον: Il. α, 552 εἶπας μῦθον: Demosth.
p. 406, 11 ῥήματα εἰπεῖν: Od. ι, 555 εἰπὲ ὄνομα = ἔπος: Eur.
Orest. 415 μὴ "θάνατον" εἴπῃς: Pind. Nem. IX. 34 ἔειπα ἄπιστον:
Eur. Iph. Aul. 448 σῶφρον' εἶπας: Demosth. p. 226, 18 δυσχερὲς
εἰπεῖν: Æsch. Pers. 122 ἀπύων ἔπος: Eur. Suppl. 800 στενα-
γμὸν ἀπύσατε: Od. α, 273 φράζειν μῦθον: Od. θ, 142 λόγον:
Od. γ, 140 μῦθον μυθείσθην: Od. ι, 16 ὄνομα μυθήσομαι:
Od. δ, 829 κερτομίας μυθήσασθαι: Il. ζ, 382 ἀληθέα μυθήσα-

σθαι: Æsch. Suppl. 277.   Eur. Med. 321 λόγους λέγε : Plat.
Rep. p. 463 E ἐλέγομεν ῥῆμα: Ibid. p. 393 B λέγῃ ῥῆσιν:
Od. τ, 303 λέγων ἐτύμοισιν ὅμοια : Æsch. Ag. 611 οὐ ψευδῆ
λέγω : Eur. Med. 316 λέγεις ἀκοῦσαι μαλθακά : Od. ξ, 486
ἐκλέγων ἐμὰ κήδεα : Il. β, 182 θεᾶς ὄπα φωνήσασα : Soph.
El. 321 φωνεῖς φάτιν: Id. Aj. 73 Αἴαντα φωνῶ, the φωνὴ was
"Αἴας:" Id. Œ. C. 624 αὐδᾶν ἔπη: Demosth. p. 400, 17 ταῦτα
τραγῳδεῖ: Plat. Rep. p. 600 D Ὅμηρον (= Ὁμήρου ἔπη) ῥαψῳδεῖν:
Id. Ion p. 633 C ἃ ῥαψῳδεῖ: Eur. Hipp. 586 γεγωνεῖν ὄπα:
Demosth. p. 657, 3 δημηγορεῖν λόγον : Id. p. 441, 6 ἐκεῖνο δε-
δημηγορηκώς: Æsch. p. 83, 37 ῥῆμα φθεγξάμενοι : Æsch.
P. V. 33 φθέγξει γόους=φθογγὴν γόων: φθέγγεσθαι ταπεινόν,
ἀσθενές: Eur. Med. 1307 ἐφθέγξω λόγους: Id. Iph. T. 1385
βοὴν ἐφθέγξατο: Id. Ion 927 θέσπισμα ἐφθ.: Æschin. p.
387, 23 κηρύσσει κήρυγμα : Il. ρ, 701 κακὸν ἔπος ἀγγελέοντα :
Demosth. p. 849 μαρτυρίαν ἐμαρτύρησεν : Hdt. III. 147
ἐντολὰς ἐνετείλατο : Æsch. Eum. 716 μαντεῖα μαντεύσει:
cf. Æschin. p. 68, 41.   Eur. Ion 346 ταῦτα καὶ μαντεύομαι:
Ibid. 100 φήμας μαντεύεσθε: Il. τ, 420 θάνατον μαντεύεαι.
So Hdt. χρᾷ τάδε: Plat. Pol. p. 493 A ἀληθέστατα μαντεύει:
Soph. Aj. 757 ἐκόμπει μῦθον : Ibid. 1230 ὑψήλ' ἐκόμπεις:
cf. Œ. C. 1347.   Æsch. Eum. 180 μύζειν λευσμόν, the μύγμα
was "λευσμός." Æsch. P. V. 78 ὅμοια γηρύεται: Hdt. V. 30
αἰνίσσεσθαι (= ἠνιγμένως λέγειν) ἔπεα: Plat. Lys. p. 214 D
τοῦτο (αἴνιγμα) αἰνίττονται: Xen. Anab. IV. 4, 10 ἀληθεύ-
ουσα τοιαῦτα. So Plat. Apol. p. 19 C φλυαρίαν φλυαροῦντα.

So accus. cognate to the notion implied in the verb: Soph.
Trach. 753 σιγᾷ (=οὐ λέγει) λόγον : Æsch. P. V. 106 σιγᾶν
τύχας: Eur. Ion 868.   Plat. Theæt. p. 161 C τὸ δ' ἐμὸν σιγῶ :
Æschin. p. 15, 19 σιγᾶν τὴν ἑαυτοῦ συμφοράν : Eur. Frag. σιωπᾶν
τὰ δίκαια : Hdt. I. 85 ἔρρηξε (= ἐξαπίνως ἐφώνησε) φωνήν : Soph.
Aj. 1227 χανεῖν (= κεχηνὼς λέγειν, to speak open-mouthed)
ῥήματα.

2. Verbs of *praying, vowing, imprecating, swearing, cursing, threat-
ening, reproaching, ordering,* &c. take an accus. of the prayer, &c.
or that wherein it consists: εὔχομαι, εὐχετάω, λίσσομαι, ἀράομαι &c. :
Eur. Iph. T. 629 εὐχὴν ηὔξω: cf. Plat. Alc. p. 148 C. Æsch.
Theb. 248 εὔχου τὰ κρείσσω: Plat. Legg. p. 909 E θυσίας εὔχεσθαι: Id. Alc. p. 141 A κακὰ εὔχεσθαι: Il. ν, 219 ἀπειλαὶ τὰς
ἀπείλουν: Arist. Ach. 228 τί τοῦτο ἀπειλεῖ τοὔπος: Il. γ, 274
μεγάλ' εὔχετο: So Il. θ, 347 μεγάλα εὐχετόωντο: Eur. Med. 153
τόδε λίσσου: Ibid. 607 ἀρὰς ἀρωμένη: cf. Phœn. 67. Soph.

Œ. C. 902. Od. β, 135 ἀρήσεται Ἐρινῦς: Æsch. Theb. 615
ἀρᾶται τύχας: Eur. Rhes. 505 πολλὰ κακὰ ἤρᾱτο: Hom. πολλὰ
ἠρᾶτο: Eur. Orest. 672 ἱκετεύω τάδε: Plat. Legg. p. 800
βλασφημεῖν βλασφημίαν: Plat. Conv. p. 183 A ὅρκους ὀμνύναι: Il. τ, 133 ὅμοσεν ὅρκον, so ὅμνυμι πάσας τὰς θεοὺς=
ὅρκον: Il. ξ, 271 ὅμοσσον ἀάατον Στυγὸς ὕδωρ. So Hdt. VI. 74
ἐξορκοῦν Στυγὸς ὕδωρ: Id. IV. 172 ὀμνύουσι τοὺς παρὰ σφίσι
ἄνδρας δικαιοτάτους: Eur. Orest. 1510 τὴν ἐμὴν ψυχὴν κατώμοσ᾿,
ἣν ἂν εὐορκοῖμ᾿ ἐγώ: Id. Hipp. 708 ὄμνυμι σεμνὴν Ἄρτεμιν.
So frequently without the verb which is readily supplied by the
mind: Soph. Antig. 758 οὔ, τὸν Ὄλυμπον, hence μά, οὐ μά, ναὶ μά,
νή, νὴ Δία, ναὶ μὰ Δία, &c.: Il. β, 255 ἀλκήν μοι ὀνείδισας: Od.
σ, 379 γαστέρα ὀνειδίζων: Æsch. Choeph. 904 τοῦτ᾿ ὀνειδίσαι: Soph. Œ. C. 754 ὄνειδος ὠνείδισα: cf. Id. Phil. 523.
Eur. Andr. 979 ὀνειδίζειν τὰς θεοὺς ἐμοί: Id. Orest. 4 οὐκ ὀνειδίζω τύχας: Soph. Aj. 243 δεινάζων κακὰ ῥήματα: Plat.
Legg. p. 706 D αὐτῷ λοιδορεῖ τὸν Ἀγαμέμνονα: Il. ε, 528 πολλὰ
κελεύων.

8. Verbs of *singing, shouting, groaning, sounding,* &c. take an accus.
of the song, &c. or that wherein it consists: Æsch. Ag. 1164
ὑμνοῦσι ὕμνον: Id. 1463. Eur. Med. 543 ὑμνῆσαι μέλος:
Plat. Legg. p. 870 E νόμον ὑμνεῖν: Id. p. 822 C φήμην ὑμνούν-
των: Eur. Iph. T. 185 μοῦσαν τὰν ὑμνεῖ: Id. Herc. F. 688 παιᾶνα
ὑμνοῦσι: Id. Troad. 383 ὑμνήσει κακά: Æsch. Ag. 991
ὑμνωδεῖ θρῆνον: Id. Choeph. 385 ἐφυμνῆσαι ὀλολυγμόν: Il.
ζ, 570 ἱμερόεν κιθάριζε: Æsch. P. V. 574 ὀτοβεῖ νόμον: Id.
Ag. 1445 μέλψασα γόον: Eur. Med. 145 ἰαχάν, οἵαν μέλπει:
Id. Cycl. 70 ᾠδὰν μέλπω: Id. Ion 881 κιθάρας ἐνοπὰν μέλπων:
Soph. Aj. 335 θωΰσσει βοάν: Eur. Hipp. 168 ἄϋτεον Ἄρτε-
μιν, the ἀϋτή was "Ἄρτεμις." So Æsch. Ag. 48 κλάζοντες Ἄρη.
(So perhaps Soph. Ant. 110 ὃν Πολυνείκης κλάζων): Arist. Av. βοῶν
τὸν δεσπότην, the βοή was "ὦ Δεσπότα:" Æsch. Pers. 13 βαΰζει
ἄνδρα, the shout was "ἀνήρ:" Soph. Ant. 133 νίκην ἀλαλάξαι:
Æsch. Eum. 486 ἔπος θροούμενος: Id. Ag. 1112 θροεῖς
νόμον: Soph. Aj. 772 θροεῖς ἔπη: Id. Ant. 1287 θροεῖς λόγον:
Eur. Orest. 1248 θροεῖς αὐδάν: Soph. Phil. 1427 θάνατον θροεῖ:
Æsch. Choeph. 35 ἀμβόαμα ἔλακε: Ibid. 777 ἔπος ἔλακε:
Od. μ, 85 δεινὸν λελακυῖα: Æsch. P. V. 405 στονόεν λέλακε:
Id. Supp. 789 ἰΰζε ὀμφάν: Id. Pers. 272 ἰΰζε βοάν: Arist. Eq.
490 κραγὸν κεκράξεται: Æsch. Frag. 265 κέκραγα μέλος: Il.
π, 88 ὀξέα κεκληγώς: Il. σ, 280 μακρὰ μεμυκώς: Il. β, 314
ἐλεεινὰ τετρίγοντας: Eur. Alc. 763 ἄμουσ᾿ ὑλακτῶν: Æsch.

Eum. 299 τοιαῦθ' ὑλακτεῖ: Soph. Trach. 871 κωκυτὸν ἠχεῖ:
Eur. Rhes. 308 ἐκτύπει φόβον: Il. ρ, 593 μεγάλ' ἔκτυπε:
Eur. Troad. 520 οὐράνια βρέμοντα: Od. δ, 454 ἀζηχὲς μεμα-
κυῖαν: Æsch. Theb. 850 ὕμνον ἰαχεῖν: Soph. Trach. 639
ἀχῶν καναχάν: Eur. Hel. 1502 ὀλολύγματα ἰάχει: Il. ζ, 468
σμερδαλέα ἰάχων: Pind. Nem. IV. 26 κελάδησε ὕμνον: Eur.
El. 716 φθόγγον κελάδει: Id. Hel. 376 βοάν: Pind. Ol. II. 3
κόσμον ἡδυμελῆ κελαδήσομεν: Æsch. Ag. 920 προσχάνῃς
(= κεχηνὼς βοᾷς) βόαμα.

4. Verbs of *crying, mourning, groaning forth, lamentation*, &c. take
an accus. of the cry, groan, &c. or that wherein it consists: Il. ω,
722 ἀοιδὴν ἐθρήνεον: Arist. Av. 213 θρηνεῖν ὕμνους: Æsch.
Theb. 78 θρέομαι ἄχη: Eur. Orest. 1368 στένω ἁρματεῖον
μέλος: Æsch. Ag. 694 πολύθρηνον ὕμνον στένει: Id. P. V. 433
στένουσιν ἄλγος οἰκτρόν: Eur. Herc. F. 759 στενάζων φροίμιον φόνου: Id. Phœn. 336 στενάζων ἀράς: Eur. Med. 1184
δεινὸν στενάξασα: Soph. Trach. 51 γοωμένην ὀδύρματα:
Æsch. Ag. 1075 ταῦτα ἀνωτότυξας: Arist. Vesp. 555 οἰκτρο-
χοοῦντες φωνήν: Soph. Œ. R. πολλὰ δακρύσαντα: Eur. Andr.
1200 διάδοχα δακρύω: Od. ξ, 174 ἄλαστον ὀδύρομαι: Il. ω,
328 πόλλ' ὀλοφυράμενοι: Il. ψ, 12 ᾤμωξεν δ' ἐλεεινά:
Æsch. Ag. 1220 στυγνὸν ᾤμωξας: Il. σ, 37 κωκύσασα ὀξύ:
Soph. Phil. 695 ἀποκλαίω στόνον.

Obs. Almost all these verbs have the transitive sense of crying for,
lamenting, &c. and take an accus. of the patient or object; as, δακρύω σε:
στενάζω σε &c. So also τύπτομαι, κόπτομαι, τίλλομαι (to mourn for) τίνα.

§. 567. Verbs of *confessing, agreeing, admitting, yielding, denying,*
&c. take an accus. of the confession, &c. or that wherein it consists:
Soph. Phil. 980 ὁμολογῶ τάδε: Plat. Crit. p. 52 A ὁμολο-
γηκὼς ὁμολογίαν: Id. Conv. p. 195 B πολλὰ ἄλλα ὁμολογῶν:
Id. Alc. p. 151 B δέχομαι καὶ τοῦτο: Id. Legg. p. 781 A τοῦτο
εἴξαντος: Soph. Œ. C. 172 εἴκοντας ἃ δεῖ: Æsch. Ag. 1353
τάδ' οὐκ ἀρνήσομαι: Soph. Phil. 108 οὐκ ἂν ἀρνοίμην τὸ
δρᾶν: Eur. Ion 1026 ἀρνήσῃ φόνους.

§. 568. Verbs of *deciding, prosecuting, defending, determining, de-*
creeing, accusing, laying to the charge of, blaming, &c. take an accus.
of the decision, suit, blame, &c. or that wherein it consists: Plat.
Legg. p. 877 D τὴν δίκην κρίνῃ: Æsch. Eum. 652 πρώτας δίκας
κρίνοντες: Demosth. p. 1280, 23 δίκην δικάζονται. Cf.
Arist. Vesp. 414. Demosth. p. 632, 24 δικάζειν ψήφισμα. So
Soph. Aj. 449 ἐψήφισαν δίκην: Demosth. p. 327, 22 κρίνα-
σαν τὰ πράγματα: Id. p. 744 νομοθετεῖν τὰ αὑτοῖς συμφέ-

ροντα: Id. p. 1468 κρινάσης τὸν ἀγῶνα: Id. p. 575, 18 ἐψηφίσαντο τὴν βοήθειαν: Id. p. 988, 22 ἔγκλημα διώκουσιν:
Id. p. 1270, 3 δίκην διώκειν: Antiph. p. 115, 24 γράφας
διώκων: Id. p. 310 γράφην φεύγειν: Id. p. 1184 φεύγει
δίκην: Isaeus p. 37, 16 παρανομίαν κατηγοροῦσι: Demosth. p.
366, 21 κατηγορεῖν εὐθύνας: Plat. Gorg. p. 491 ταῦτα κατη-
γορεῖς: Id. Legg. p. 636 C Κρητῶν τὸν περὶ τὸν Γανυμήδη μῦθον
κατηγοροῦμεν: Arist. Vesp. 489 πρᾶγμα κατηγορῇ: Id. Plut.
10 μέμψιν μέμφεσθαι, 80 μέμφεσθαί τι = μέμψιν: Hdt.
VI. 88 μεμφόμενος τὴν ἑαυτῶν ἐξέλασιν: Eur. Med. 213 μή
μοι τι μέμψησθε: Arist. Pac. 643 ἄττα διαβάλοι.

Verbs of Production, or effect.

§. 569. The notion of producing implies—

The agent and his operation,—ποιέω.
The effect, production, or thing produced,—ποίημα (τεῖχος).

Hence all verbs of producing have an accus. of this effect. This is
not generally the cognate subst., but the cognate or equivalent
notion, defining the particular nature of the production.

1. Verbs of *making, forming, building, founding, contriving,
plotting, inventing, preparing,* &c. : ποιέω, τεύχω, δέμω, πλέκω,
πτύσσω, ῥάπτω, ἐλαύνω, (to work by beating, or to build in a line)
τειχέω, τειχίζω, πλινθεύω, σκευάζω, οἰκίζω, ἀρτύω, ἀρτύνω, τεκταίνω,
κτίζω, ξέω, ξύω, ἑτοιμάζω, πονέω, μηχανάομαι, ὁδοποιῶ &c. : Il. v,
147 τεῖχος (= ποίημα) ἐποίουν: Il. θ, 195 τεύχων θώρηκα:
Od. δ, 174 δώματ' ἔτευξε: Metaphorically τεύχειν δόλους,
βοήν, ἄλγος &c.: Od. ζ, 9 ἐδείματο οἴκους (δόμον): Il. ψ, 192
θάλαμον δέμον, 80 τεῖχος, πύργον &c. : Eur. Ion 826 ἔπλεκε
πλοκάς: Id. Iph. A. 578 μιμήματα πλέκων: Metaph. πλέκων
λόγους &c.: Od. α, 439 πτύξασα χιτῶνα: Hdt. VI. 1 ὑπόδημα
ἔρραψας: Metaph. κακόν, θάνατον, δόλον &c.: Il. μ, 296 ἐλαύνειν ἀσπίδα: ἐλαύνειν τεῖχος, σταύρους: Il. ι, ὄγμον: Pind. αὔλα-
κας: Arist. ὄρχον: Hdt. IX. 7 τεῖχος τὸ ἐτείχεον: Il. η, 449
τεῖχος ἐτειχίσαντο: Thuc. VI. 75. Hdt. VI. 100 σκευάζειν
προδοσίαν: Plat. Crat. p. 424 E ὅταν ἀνδρείκελον σκευάζωσιν.
So passive: Demosth. p. 319, 3 κατηγορίαν συνεσκευασμένον,
so πέμπειν πομπήν, to set forward the procession, so πέμπειν
ἑορτήν, Παναθήναια. So Hdt. V. 64 στόλον στείλαντες. So Pind.
πλόον στέλλειν: Hdt. III. 52 πλοῖον στέλλειν: Od. ξ, 648

ἐννέα νῆας ἔστειλα: Pass. Hdt. VII. 62 ἐσταλμένος σκευήν:
Il. ω, 190 ὅπλισον ἧια: Il. λ, 86 ὡπλίσσατο δόρπον: Plat. Rep.
p. 453 B οἰκίσειε πόλιν: Il. λ, 438 δόλον ἤρτυε: Il. ο, 303
ἀρτυνέουσιν ἔεδνα: Od. δ, 771 γάμον ἀρτύνει, so βουλήν,
ψεύδεα &c.: Il. ε, 62 τεκτήνατο νῆας: Metaph. μῆτιν: Od. λ,
262 Θήβης ἔδος ἔκτισαν: Æsch. P. V. 816 κτίσαι ἀποικίαν:
Soph. Ant. 1101 κτίζειν τάφον: Od. φ, 44 λέχος ἔξεον: Il.
ξ, 179 ἑανὸν ἔξυσε: Eur. Alc. 375 δῶμ᾽ ἐτοίμαζε: Il. ψ,
245 τύμβον πονέεσθαι: Xen. Cyr. I. 6, 19 μηχανὰς ἐμη-
χάνω: Ibid. I. 6, 10 μηχανᾶσθαι πόρον: Il. θ, 117 τάδε
τείχεα μηχανόωντο: Æschin. p. 13, 24 μηχανᾶσθαι τὴν ἀπολογίαν. So Demosth. πρεσβεύειν εἰρήνην, to bring about a
peace by an embassy. Xen. Anab. IV. 8, 6 τὴν ὁδὸν ὡδοποίουν:
cf. Ibid. V. 1, 7. Plat. Phædr. p. 230 D φάρμακον εὑρηκέναι:
Demosth. p. 187, 27 εὑρίσκειν λόγον: Eur. Andr. 28 πολλὰς
ἂν εὕροις μηχανάς: Æsch. P. V. 58 εὑρεῖν πόρους.

Obs. Οἰκίζω has two transitive senses : to settle, as οἰκίζειν τινά, and to
occupy by a settlement, as οἰκίζειν τὴν γῆν, so also κτίζειν τὴν γῆν.

2. Verbs of *creating, begetting, putting forth, bringing forth,
exhibiting, shewing*, &c. : γεννάω, τεκνόω, φιτύω, φύω, τίκτω, σπείρω,
to beget, φαίνω, δείκνυμι &c. : Æsch. Supp. 47 ἐγέννασε
Ἔπαφον, so γεννᾶν τρίχας, ὀδόντας, to put forth hair ; and
Metaph. νοῦν, δόξας &c.: Eur. Phœn. 19 τεκνώσεις παῖδα: Id.
Andr. 1236 τίκτειν τέκνα: Od. τ, 264. Eur. Her. 994 πόλλ᾽
ἔτικτον: Metaph. τίκτειν ὕβριν, φόβον &c.: Soph. Ant. 625
ἀνωφέλητα φιτύει τέκνα: Plat. Rep. p. 407 D ἔκγονα φυτεύειν:
Soph. Trach. 31 ἐφύσαμεν παῖδας : Il. α, 235 φύλλα φύσει,
will put forth ; so πώγωνα, γλῶσσαν ; and Metaph. φρένας &c. :
Soph. Elect. 74 σημεῖα φαίνεις : Id. Phil. 297 ἔφην᾽ ἄφαντον
φῶς : Plat. Pol. p. 514 B θαύματα δεικνυσιν = θαυμαστὰ δείγ-
ματα: Id. Legg. p. 764 B παράδειγμα δεικνύντα: Id. Symp. p.
179 D φάσματα δείξαντες : Soph. Aj. 1293 ὅς σ᾽ ἔσπειρε.

Obs. Δείκνυμι has also an active sense analogously to γράφω, of inform-
ing against. See *Double Accusative.*

3. Verbs of *writing, painting, engraving, spinning, working*, &c. :
γράφω, ἐντέμνω, ἐγκολάπτω, ἐγγλύφω, ὑφαίνω, πλάσσω, ποικίλλω,
τεχνάω &c. : Il. ζ, 169 σήματα γράψας: Thuc. V. 29 ἔγραψεν
ἐπιστολήν: Plat. Phædr. p. 278 C συγγράμματα ἔγραφεν: Ibid.
p. 258 C λόγους ἔγραφον: Id. Legg. p. 948 D ἄρησιν γρά-
ψαντα: Hdt. IV. 88 ζῷα γραψάμενος: Ibid. 87 ἐντέμνων
γράμματα: Id. I. 187 ἐνεκόλαψε γράμματα: Id. II. 4 ζῷα

ἐγγλύψαι: Eur. Ion 1417 ὕφην' ὕφασμα: Od. β, 96, &c.
ἱστὸν (= ὕφασμα) ὑφαίνει: Plat. Charm. p. 161 E ἱματίον
ὑφαίνειν: so Metaph. μῆτιν &c., ὑφαίνειν: Plat. Tim. p. 73
C σχήματα πλάσας ἐν χρύσῳ: Menand. Fr. πλάσματα πλάτ-
τειν: Metaph. λόγους &c., πλάσσειν: Il. σ, 590 χόρον ποί-
κιλλεν: Eur. Iph. T. 222 εἰκὼ Τιτάνων ποικίλλουσα: Od.
η, 110 ἱστὸν τεχνῆσαι: Metaph. Soph. Phil. 80 τεχνᾶσθαι
κακά.

§. 570. Verbs of *pouring, scattering,* &c. take an accus. of the
stream, &c. or that wherein it consists: χέω, σπένδω, ἐγκανάζω, ὕω,
δεύω, to pour; ἀστράπτω, στάζω, ἀρύω &c.: Od. κ, 518 χοὴν χεῖ-
σθαι: cf. Soph. Œ. C. 477. Il. ι, 15 χέει ὕδωρ: Il. π, 3 χέειν
δάκρυα: Æsch. Supp. 1007 πῶμα χέουσιν: Soph. El. 84 χέον-
τες λουτρά: Metaph. χέειν ἀχλύν, φύλλα, κάλλος &c.: Eur.
Electr. 511 σπονδὰς ἔσπεισα: Id. Or. 1322 σπείσασα χοάς:
Æsch. Eum. 269 σπένδοντα λοιβάς: Arist. Eq. 105 ἐγκάναξον
σπονδήν: Pind. Olymp. VII. 50 ὕσε χρυσόν: Soph. Aj. 369
ἐρεμνὸν αἷμ' ἔδευσα: Æsch. P. V. 356 ἤστραπτεν σέλας: Il.
τ, 38 νέκταρ στάξε: Æsch. Choeph. 1094 στάζουσιν αἷμα:
Eur. Iph. A. 1467 στάζειν δάκρυ: Id. Bacch. 620 στάζων
ἱδρῶτα: Eur. Hipp. 526 στάζεις πόθον: Id. Alc. 1015 ἐλειψάμην σπονδάς: Hdt. IV. 17 σπείρειν σῖτον: Od. ν, 352 αἷμα
ἐσκέδασε, so ἠέρα, ἀχλύν &c.

Obs. Σπείρω has a further transitive sense, as σπείρειν τὴν γῆν; and
σκεδάννυμι also signifies to divide, separate, as σκεδάσαι τὸν λαόν.

§. 571. Verbs of *heaping up, digging,* &c. take an accus. of the
heap, &c. or that wherein it consists: χόω, χέω, ὀρύσσω, νηέω &c.:
Hdt. I. 182 χώματα χοῦν: Soph. Ant. 81 τάφον χώσουσα
Ibid. 1204 τύμβον χώσαντες: Od. β, 222 σῆμα χεύσω—τύμβον
Od. δ, 584. Il. η, 440 τάφρον ὤρυξαν: Hdt. I. 186 ὤρυσσε
ἔλυτρον: Od. τ, 64 νήησαν ξύλα πολλά.

§. 572. Verbs of *preparing meat, drink,* &c. take an accus. of
the preparation, or meat or drink so prepared: μάττω, κεράννυμι,
ὁπλίζω, πέσσω &c.: Hdt. I. 200 μάττειν μάζαν: Il. δ, 260 οἶνον
κέρωνται: Od. γ, 393 κρητῆρα κεράσασθαι: Il. λ, 640
ὥπλισσε κυκεῶνα: Hdt. I. 161 οὐδεὶς πέμματα ἐπέσσετο:
Id. VIII. 137 ἔπεσσε σιτία. So Metaph. κεράσασθαι φιλίαν.

Verbs of Transmission.

§. 573. Verbs of transmission imply—

The agent and his operation.   *The thing transmitted or gift,*
δίδωμι.   δῶρον.

Verbs of *giving, contributing, granting, paying, selling*, &c. have an accus. of the gift, favour, payment, &c. : δίδωμι, τίνω, ἐκτίνω, τελέω, χαρίζομαι, νέμω &c. : Il. v, 299, &c. δῶρα δίδωσι : Hdt. VI. 89 δοῦναι δωτίνην : Od. ρ, 287 κακὰ δίδωσι : Od. a, 390 ἕδνα διδόντες. So person considered as a gift : Plat. Rep. p. 468 A τὸν ζῶντα δωρεὰν (in apposition) διδόναι : Hes. Op. 82 δῶρον ἐδώρησαν : Il. ι. 594 δῶρ' ἐτέλεσσαν : Plat. Protag. p. 311 D χρήματα τελεῖν : Id. Legg. p. 847 B τέλος τελεῖν : Id. Alc. 119 ἑκατὸν μνᾶς τελέσας : Demosth. p. 309, 20 χαρίζεσθαι χάριτας, then χαρίζεσθαί τι : Il. μ, 255 κῦδος ὅπαζε. So person considered as gift : Il. v, 416 ὦπασα πομπόν : Plat. Rep. p. 615 B ἐκτίνειν ἔκτισμα : Il. γ, 289 τιμὴν τίνειν : Od. β, 193 θωὴν τίνειν, so τίνειν δίκην &c., τίνειν φόνον = δίκην φόνου : Il. σ, 407 ζωάγρια τίνειν : Arist. Av. 191 φόρον φέρειν : Lys. p. 150, 1 εἰσφορὰς εἰσενηνόχασιν : Demosth. p. 1249 χιλίας δραχμὰς εἰσφέρειν. So Soph. Phil. 465 πλοῦν ἡμῖν εἴκῃ : Eur. Alc. 415 κοινοῦσθαι πένθος, so ἀλλάσσειν τι, to give in exchange : Plat. Legg. p. 862 B καπηλείας μήτε πωλείτω μήτε ὠνείσθω.

Obs. 1. Δωρέομαι also has a transitive sense *to gift*, δωρέομαι τινά τινι.

Obs. 2. So many verbs which have the patient in the Dativus Commodi have the act or commodum defined by an elliptic accus. ; as, βοηθῆσαι τὰ δίκαια, sc. βοηθήματα, so ἀρκέσαι ταῦτα. So Æsch. P. V. 362 τοῖσδ' ὑπουργῆσαι χάριν.

Verbs of Reception.

§. 574. The notion of receiving implies—

The agent and his operation,   *The receipt or thing received,*
δέχομαι.   δῶρον.

Hence all verbs of receiving have an accus. of this coincident notion. So δέχομαι, λαμβάνω &c. : Il. a, 20 κτήματα δεχέσθω : Il. η, 400 τοῦτο δέχομαι : Il. ω, 434 δῶρα δέχεσθαι. So of persons : Il. a, 446 ἐδέξατο παῖδα. So Plat. Rep. p. 416 E δέχεσθαι μισθόν : Ibid. p. 368 C λαμβάνουσι μισθόν : Ibid. p. 501 E τέλος λήψεται &c. ; so ἀλλάσσειν τι, to receive in exchange.

Verbs of Perception.

§. 575. Verbs of *seeing, hearing, receiving information from*, &c. have an accus. of the perception or thing perceived — the sight or thing seen—the hearing or thing heard ; εἴδω, αἰσθάνομαι, ἀκούω &c. : Eur. Med. 1167 ἰδεῖν θέαμα : Il. δ, 275 νέφος εἶδε : Eur. Hel. 71 τίν᾽ εἶδον ὄψιν ; cf. Plat. Phæd. p. 250 B. Eur. Hipp. 825 ἴδω θέαν : Id. Hel. 116 εἶδες σὺ τὴν δύστηνον : Æsch. Pers. 40 ὄψιν προσιδέσθαι : Id. P. V. 90 ὁρᾶν θέαμα : Plat. Legg. p. 887 D ὁρῶντες ὄψεις. Applied to persons ; as, Soph. Œ. C. 311 γυναῖχ᾽ ὁρῶ : or things ; as, Ibid. 1453 ὁρᾷ ταῦτα : Eur. Bacch. 1232 λεύσσω αὐτῆς ὄψιν : Plat. Theæt. p. 192 D αἴσθησιν αἰσθάνομαι : Id. Phæd. p. 75 τἆλλα αἰσθάνεσθαι : Soph. Œ. C. 301 τοὔνομ᾽ αἴσθηται : Id. Aj. 1318 ᾐσθόμην βοήν : Id. Œ. C. 241 ἀϊοντες αὐδάν : Il. κ, 532 κτύπον ἄϊε : Id. Orest. 1235 κλύειν βοήν : Id. Suppl. 1160 κλύων ἔπος &c. ; so ἀκούειν τι.—(See §. 487. 1.)

Obs. For the genitive after these verbs see §. 485.

Verbs of Possession.

§. 576. The notion of possessing implies—

| *The agent and his operation,* κέκτημαι. | *The possession or thing possessed,* χρήματα = κτῆμα. |

Hence all verbs of possessing have an accus. of this coincident notion ; these verbs are followed also by an accus. of a person, considered as a mere possession ; as, δοῦλον = κτῆμα.

1. Verbs of *inhabiting, possessing, finding, having, holding, occupying, enjoying, containing, wearing*, &c. take an accus. of the possession or thing possessed, &c. : οἰκέω, ναίω, ναιετάω, νέμω, νέμομαι, χανδάνω, χωρέω, κέκτημαι, ἔχω &c. : Eur. Phœn. 1231 οἶκον οἰκήσω : Æsch. Eum. 624 δώματ᾽ οἰκήσει : Eur. Iph. T. 699 οἰκεῖ δόμους : Id. Andr. 242 οἰκοῦμεν πόλιν : Id. Hel. 1102 οἰκεῖς ἀστέρων ποικίλματα = ποικίλους ἀστέρων οἴκους : Id. Iph. A. 1508 ἕτερον αἰῶνα καὶ μοῖραν (= ἑτέρους οἴκους) οἰκήσομεν : Id. El. 925 ἄλγιστα οἰκεῖς : Od. ρ, 419 οἶκον ἔναιον : Il. ρ, 308 οἰκία ναιετάασκε : Il. ο, 190 ναιέμεν ἅλα : Eur. Ion 1198 ἄτρεστα ναίουσι : Soph. Œ. R. 758 γῆν νέμειν : Il. ν, 8 ἄλσεα νέμονται, so Ἰθάκην νέμεσθαι : Il. ν, 185 νέμηαι τέμενος : Il. β, 751 ἔργα (agros) ἐνέμοντο : Il. ψ, 742 ἐξ μέτρα χάνδανε : Hdt. I. 51 χωρέων ἀμφορέας ἑξακοσίους : Id. IV.

61 χωρέουσι τὰ κρέα: Æsch. Ag. 1051 φωνὴν κεκτημένη:
Plat. Theæt. p. 175 κεκτημένος χρυσίον: Eur. Phœn. 558 χρήματα κέκτηνται: Id. Bacch. 514 δμωῖδας κεκτήσομαι: so
ἔχειν τι, or τινα, considered as a possession. So Æsch. Supp. 253
καρποῦται χθόνα: Soph. Œ. C. 1359 στολὰς φορεῖν: Id.
Elect. 420 σκῆπτρον οὐφόρει: Id. Ant. 705 ἦθος φόρει: Arist.
Eq. 757 θούριον λῆμα φορεῖν: Hdt. III. 12 ἀσθενέας φορέουσι
τὰς κεφαλάς.

2. Verbs of *obtaining, acquiring, finding, gaining, taking, catching,
buying, taking to oneself, choosing, gathering, reaping,* &c. take an
accusative of the acquisition, or thing acquired, gained, &c.: κτά-
ομαι, κερδαίνω, πλεονεκτέω, ἐμπολάω, αἴρομαι, ἄρνυμαι, δελεάζω, δρέπω,
δράσσομαι, ἀρπάζω, πρίαμαι, ζωγρέω, εὑρίσκω, κυρῶ and τυγχάνω
(sometimes) αἱρέω &c.: Il. ι, 400 τὰ (κτήματα) ἐκτήσατο: Od. ω,
192 ἐκτήσω ἄκοιτιν: Eur. Med. 1047 κτᾶσθαι κακά: Id. Hel.
903 τὰ κτητὰ κτᾶσθαι: Soph. Œ.R. 889 κέρδος κερδανεῖ: Id.
Œ. C. 72 κερδάνῃ μέγα: Id. Trach. 231 χρηστὰ κερδαίνειν
ἔπη: Thuc. VI. 61 πλεονεκτεῖν ταῦτα: Demosth. p. 1434
πλεονεκτεῖν ἄλλα: Od. o, 455 βίοτον πολὺν ἐμπολόωντο:
Soph. Trach. 93 κέρδος ἐμπολᾷ: Eur. Med. 710 εὕρημα οἷον
εὕρηκας: cf. Ibid. 553. Æsch. P.V. 267 αὐτὸς εὑρόμην πόνους:
Hdt. I. 195 πολλὸν χρυσίον εὑροῦσα: Soph. Aj. 1023 πάντα
ταῦτα εὑρόμην (acquired). So Hom. κῦδος ἀρέσθαι. So of a
person considered as a gain: Soph. Œ. C. 461 σωτῆρ' ἀρεῖσθε:
Id. Œ. R. 1225 πένθος ἀρεῖσθε: Id. Aj. 75 δειλίαν ἀρεῖς:
Eur. Alc. 56 ἄρνυμαι κλέος: Id. Iph. A. 995 ταῦτα τεύξομαι:
Id. Phœn. 493 ἃ μὴ κυρήσας: Id. Hec. 698 κυρῶ νιν: Id.
Bacch. 753 ἥρπαζον τέκνα=ἁρπαγήν. So Od. o, 174 ἥρπαξε
χῆνα: Eur. Hipp. 1427 πένθη καρπουμένῳ, so καρποῦσθαι τὴν
γῆν=καρποὺς τῆς γῆς: Id. Iph. Aul. 1299 ἄνθεα δρέπειν: so Id.
Hipp. 209 πῶμ' ἀρυσαίμην: Soph. Aj. 55 ἔκειρε φόνον, a
harvest of blood.

Accusative of Time.

§. 577. As verbs of motion imply a coincident notion of a space
over which the motion takes place, so all verbs imply a notion of
time over which the action extends, coincident and coextensive
with it; whence all verbs may have an accusative case of this coincident notion of time, if it be required definitely to express it: χρόνον,
τὸν χρόνον, during this time; different from χρόνῳ, σὺν χρόνῳ, with
time, as the instrument; νύκτα, ἡμέραν (poet. ἦμαρ): Od. κ, 142
ἔνθα τότ' ἐκβάντες δύο τ' ἤματα καὶ δύο νύκτας κείμεθα: Il.

β, 292 ἕνα μῆνα μένων: Il. κ, 312 οὐδ᾽ ἐθέλουσιν νύκτα φυλασ-
σέμεναι: Hdt. VI. 127 ἡ δὲ Σύβαρις ἤκμαζε τοῦτον τὸν χρόνον
μάλιστα: Id. IV. 181 τὸν ὄρθρον. (So τοὺς ὄρθρους Arist. Lysistr.
966.): Xen. Anab. IV. 5, 24 καταλαμβάνει τὴν θυγατέρα τοῦ κω-
μάρχου ἐννάτην ἡμέραν γεγαμημένην: Id. Cyr. VI. 3, 11 καὶ
χθὲς δὲ καὶ τρίτην ἡμέραν τὸ αὐτὸ τοῦτο ἔπραττον: Eur. Alc.
801 τὴν αὔριον μέλλουσαν εἰ βιώσεται: Demosth. p. 116,
23 ἴσχυσαν δέ τι καὶ Θηβαῖοι τοὺς τελευταίους τουτουσὶ
χρόνους μετὰ τὴν ἐν Λεύκτροις μάχην. Accus. of time and place
together: Soph. Œ. R. 1134 ἦμος τὸν Κιθαιρῶνος τόπον—ἐπλησίαζον τῷδε τἀνδρὶ τρεῖς ὅλους—μῆνας. The accus. of place marks
that the shepherds were wandering *over*, not merely *in*, Cithæron:
Arist. Ach. 141 τοῦτον ἔπινον τὸν χρόνον. So even with substantives, by an ellipse of εἶναι: Eur. Orest. 72 παρθένε μακρὸν
δὴ μῆκος χρόνου.

Obs. 1. When the time is in the genitive it is considered as the cause
or antecedent condition of the action (§. 523.) τοῦτο ἐγένετο ταύτης τῆς
ἡμέρας, on this day; ταύτην τὴν ἡμέραν, during this day; so νυκτός, at
night; νύκτα, during the night. Sometimes we find the point of time in
the accus., but this only in general notions of time, such as seasonably,
lastly, where the accus. stands for the cognate substantive; as, Arist.
Ach. 23 ἥκοντες δωρίαν=ἄωρον ἧξιν: Hdt. II. 2 τὴν ὥρην (=ὡραῖον,
neut. acc.) ἐπαγινέειν σφίσι αἶγας; so τὸ τέλος, τὸ τελευταῖον, καιρόν, οὐδένα
καιρόν.

Obs. 2. Hence arise many adverbial expressions; as, ἦμος, τῆμος, epic;
(=ἦμαρ and τῆμαρ), ἐννῆμαρ, παντῆμαρ, νύκτωρ, πάννυχα, σήμερον, αὔριον,
τῆτες, ὄναρ καὶ ὕπαρ, ἀκμήν, ἀρχήν, τὴν ἀρχήν (properly at first), omnino,
πέρας, τὸ πέρας, τέλος, τὸ τελευταῖον, νέον, ἔναγχος, nuper, πρότερον, τὸ
πρῶτον, τὸ πρίν (τὸ πάρος Il. κ, 309.), τὸ αὐτίκα, τανῦν—τὸ πάλαι (Hdt.
VII. 129.), τἀρχαῖον (Æsch. Suppl. 341.).—καιρόν, commodum (poet.).—
πρῶτον, τὸ παλαιόν, τὸ λοιπόν, τὸ ἑωθινόν (Hdt. III. 104 θερμότατος δέ ἐστι ὁ
ἥλιος τούτοισι τοῖσι ἀνθρώποισι τὸ ἑωθινόν), τὸ μεσημβρινόν (Theocr. I.
15.), δειλινόν, ὕστερον, πανύστατον, ἐξάπινα, δηρόν, (poet., δηρὸν χρόνον),—
εἰνάνυχες, εἰνάετες—ἔτος εἰς ἔτος Soph. Ant. 341.

Obs. 3. This notion of duration of time is also expressed by the prepositions διά, ὑπό, ἀνά, κατά &c.—(See *Prepos.*)

Accusative of Quantity.

§. 578. Those verbs of *space, distance, time, value,* &c. which are
defined by the mention of their parts, have an accusative of these
parts or measures, as being equivalent to the cognate notions of
space, distance, value, &c. which would be the proper accusative;
as, Il. ψ, 529 λείπετο δουρὸς ἐρωήν=λεῖμμα, the distance of a spear's
cast. So ἐπορεύσατο δύο σταδίους = ἐπορεύσατο τὴν ὁδὸν δυοῖν
σταδίων: Hdt. I. 31 σταδίους δὲ πέντε καὶ τεσσεράκοντα
διακομίσαντες ἀπίκοντο ἐς τὸ ἱρόν: Id. VI. 119 ἀπέχειν δέκα καὶ

διηκοσίους σταδίους: Ibid. 135 Μιλτιάδης ἀπέπλεε — Πάρον
—πολιορκήσας τε ἒξ καὶ εἴκοσι ἡμέρας: Xen. M. S. III. 6, 1
οὐδέπω εἴκοσιν ἔτη γεγονώς, like *viginti annos natus.*—So δύνασθαι, to be of the value of: Hdt. III. 89 τὸ δὲ Βαβυλώνιον
τάλαντον δύναται Εὐβοΐδας ἑβδομήκοντα μνέας: Xen. Anab. I. 5, 6
ὁ σίγλος δύναται ἑπτὰ ὀβολούς. So ἕλκειν, to weigh: Hdt. I.
50 ἕλκοντα τρίτον ἡμιτάλαντον—and even with the cognate
notion expressed: Ibid. ἕλκουσαν σταθμὸν τάλαντα δέκα.

Obs. 1. This definition of quantity is often more nearly defined by παρά;
and to define an uncertain quantity, εἰς, ἐπί, ἀμφί, περί, κατά, πρός.

Obs. 2. Here also must be classed the adverbial accusatives: πολλά,
sæpe, τὰ πολλά, *plerumque*, ὡς τὰ πολλά, πολύ (πολλόν), μέγα, μεγάλα, μέγιστα, ὀλίγον, μικρόν, μικρά, συχνά, μακρά, ἴσον, τοσοῦτο, ὅσον, πάντα, τὸ ἐπίπαν, in all (Hdt. VI. 46), ἅδην, enough, ἄχνην, the least, Arist. Vesp. 92.

Particular uses of the Equivalent Accusative as a means of defining the verbal notion.

§. 579. 1. It is clear from the foregoing examples, that the
particular object wherein any feeling, quality, or action consists,
is put in the accus., as being substituted for the cognate notion
of the verb. This is especially the case with verbs expressing
qualities or feelings: καλλιστεύει τὰ ὄμματα = καλλός, as the eyes
were the beauty. So Od. a, 208 ἔοικε αὐτῷ ὄμματα, the likeness
consisted in the eyes. So Hdt. II. 111 κάμνειν τοὺς ὀφθαλμούς: Id. III. 33 τὰς φρένας ὑγιαίνειν: Xen. M. S. I. 6,
6 ἀλγεῖν τοὺς πόδας: Ibid. IV. 1, 2 οἱ τὰ σώματα — τὰς
ψυχὰς εὖ πεφυκότες: Plat. Rep. p. 453 B διαφέρει γυνὴ ἀνδρὸς
τὴν φύσιν: Ibid. p. 462 D ὁ ἄνθρωπος τὸν δάκτυλον ἀλγεῖ.

2. Hence it is also used with adjectives expressing quality, &c.;
as, καλός, κακός, ἀγαθός, σοφός, φρόνιμος, χρήσιμος, χρηστός, δίκαιος,
ἴκελος &c. Ἀγαθὸς τέχνην τινά: Od. a, 164 ἐλαφρότερος
πόδας εἶναι: Il. ε, 801 Τυδεὺς μικρὸς μὲν ἔην δέμας: Od..a, 371
θεοῖς ἐναλίγκιος αὐδήν: Od. ε, 211 οὐ μέν θην κείνης γε χερείων
εὔχομαι εἶναι, οὐ δέμας, οὐδὲ φυήν· ἐπεὶ οὔπως οὐδὲ ἔοικε θνητὰς
ἀθανάτῃσι δέμας καὶ εἶδος ἐρίζειν: Ibid. 217 σεῖο περίφρων Πηνε-
λόπεια εἶδος ἀκιδνοτέρη μέγεθός τ᾽ εἰσάντα ἰδέσθαι: Il. ο, 642
ἐκ πατρὸς πολὺ χείρονος υἱὸς ἀμείνων παντοίας ἀρετάς, ἠμὲν πόδας,
ἠδὲ μάχεσθαι καὶ νόον ἐν πρώτοισι Μυκηναίων ἐτέτυκτο: Il. β, 478
ὄμματα καὶ κεφαλὴν ἴκελος Διῒ τερπικεραύνῳ, Ἄρεϊ δὲ ζώνην, στέρνον
δὲ Ποσειδάωνι: Æsch. Pers. 27 δεινοὶ μάχην: Eur. Hec. 269 ἡ
Τυνδαρὶς — εἶδος εὐπρεπεστάτη: Hdt. III. 4 Φάνης καὶ γνώμην
ἱκανός, καὶ τὰ πολέμια ἄλκιμος ἦν: Xen. Cyr. II. 3, 7 ἀνέστη

Φεραύλας τὸ σῶμα οὐκ ἀφυὴς καὶ τὴν ψυχὴν οὐκ ἀγεννεῖ ἀνδρὶ
ἐοικώς: Ibid. VIII. 4, 18 δεινὸς ταύτην τὴν τέχνην. So σοφὸς τὰ
τοιαῦτα: Arist. Nub. φιλόδημος τὴν φύσιν: θαυμαστὸς τὸ μέγεθος, τὸ
κάλλος Plat.

Obs. This is sometimes more accurately defined by the prepositions εἰς
(looking towards), πρός (with reference to), κατά (according to) : Il. γ,
158 εἰς ὦπα ἔοικεν — Eur. Orest. 529 μακάριος — πλὴν ἐς θυγατέρας, σοφὸς
πρός τι : Soph. Œ. R. 1087 κατὰ γνώμην ἴδρις. So sometimes we find
the local or instrumental dat. for the accus.: σώμασιν ἀδύνατοι—κακίστους
τοῖς ἤθεσι.

3. Hence arises the accus. with the verb εἰμί &c., denoting the
existence of some quality in some particular place or relation, such
as εὖρος, ὕψος, μέγεθος, βάθος, μῆκος, πλῆθος, ἀριθμόν, γένος, ὄνομα
—μέρος, τὸ σὸν μέρος, τὸ αὐτοῦ μέρος — πρόφασιν,—τὸ δ' ἀληθές—
γνώμην ἐμήν : Il. τ, 302 ἐπὶ δὲ στενάχοντο γυναῖκες Πάτροκλον
πρόφασιν, σφῶν δ' αὐτῶν κήδε' ἑκάστη : Hdt. VI. 83 Κλέανδρος
γένος ἐὼν Φιγαλεὺς ἀπ' Ἀρκαδίης : Plat. Euthyph. p. 2 A ἔστι
δὲ τὸν δῆμον Πιτθεύς : Hdt. VII. 109 λίμνη ἐοῦσα τυγχάνει ὡσεὶ
τριήκοντα σταδίων—τὴν περίοδον : Id. VI. 36 ἀπὸ δὲ τοῦ Ἰσθμοῦ
τούτου ἡ Χερσόνησος εἴσω πᾶσά ἐστι σταδίων εἴκοσι καὶ τετρακοσίων
τὸ μῆκος : Xen. Anab. II. 5, 1 μετὰ ταῦτα ἀφίκοντο ἐπὶ τὸν
Ζάβατον ποταμὸν τὸ εὖρος τεττάρων πλέθρων : Ibid. IV. 2, 2 οἱ
μὲν ἐπορεύοντο τὸ πλῆθος ὡς δισχίλιοι.

4. Here also belong some neuter accusatives denoting some
particular case or way in which any verbal notion operates, and
which from their frequent usage have generally a pure adverbial
sense; as, τοὐναντίον, τἀναντία, τἆλλα, λοιπόν, *de reliquo,* τὸ δ' ὅλον,
omnino, πότερον, πότερα, θάτερα, ἀμφότερον poet., ἀμφότερα prose,
δοιά epic, οὐδέτερα, τό, τοῦτο (ταῦτα) μὲν—τοῦτο (ταῦτα) δέ, ταῦτ' ἄρα,
ὅ, ὅτι, οἷον, ἅτε, οὐδέν (μηδέν) τι, πολλά, πάντα, τὸ κατά (εἰς, ἐπί)
τι (τινα) : Il. γ, 179 ἀμφότερον, βασιλεύς τ' ἀγαθὸς, κρατερός τ'
αἰχμητής : Il. δ, 145 βασιλῆϊ δὲ κεῖται ἄγαλμα, ἀμφότερον, κόσμος
θ' ἵππῳ ἐλατῆρί τε κῦδος : Il. η, 418 τοὶ δ' ὡπλίζοντο μάλ' ὦκα, ἀμφότερον νέκυάς τ' ἀγέμεν, ἕτεροι δὲ μεθ' ὕλην : Od. β, 46 ὅ μοι κακὸν
ἔμπεσεν οἴκῳ, δοιά· τὸ μὲν πατέρ' ἐσθλὸν ἀπώλεσα κ. τ. λ. : Plat.
Gorg. p. 524 C εἴ τινος μέγα ἦν τὸ σῶμα φύσει ἢ τροφῇ ἢ ἀμφότερα. Ἀμφότερα, ἕτερα : Id. Apol. p. 22 E μήτε τι σοφὸς ὢν τὴν
ἐκείνων, μήτε ἀμαθὴς τὴν ἀμαθίαν, ἢ ἀμφότερα [sc. σοφίαν καὶ ἀμαθίαν]:
Id. Euthyph. p. 9 D ὃ δ' ἂν οἱ μὲν φιλῶσιν, οἱ δὲ μισῶσιν, οὐδέτερα ἢ
ἀμφότερα : Id. Phæd. p. 68 C. Soph. Œ. R. 1197 ἐκράτησας τοῦ
πάντ' εὐδαίμονος ὄλβου : Id. Phil. 66 τούτων γὰρ οὐδέν μ' ἀλγυνεῖς.—Τὸ ἐπ' ἐμέ, τοὐπ' ἐμέ, τοὐπί σε, τὸ εἰς ἐμέ, *quantum ad me* :
Soph. Antig. τὸ ἐπὶ τήνδε τὴν κόρην : Plat. Phileb. p. 17 C τὸ κατ'
ἐκείνην τὴν τέχνην. So Xen. Anab. I. 6, 9 τὸ κατὰ τοῦτον εἶναι.

5. Some substantives, standing in the equivalent accus., have assumed from long usage a purely adverbial sense ; as, κράτος, strongly, (Æsch. Suppl. 763 χρὴ φυλάσσεσθαι κράτος = κρατερὰν φυλακήν,) τάχος—τάχος ἐλθεῖν (= ταχίστην ὁδὸν), μέγεθος : Hdt. II. 44 λάμποντος μέγεθος = μεγάλην λαμπάδα : Soph. Ant. 446 μῆκος = μακρὸν λόγον : Demosth. p. 367 τὸ μέρος : Plat. Crit. p. 45 τὸ τούτου μέρος. But generally this is more definitely expressed by κατά, ἀνά, εἰς &c.

Accusative in Apposition.

§. 580. 1. The accusative (frequently with a genitive depending on it) is put in apposition to the patient of the verb, or the cognate or equivalent notion, with which it agrees ; as, Il. λ, 27 ἄστε Κρονίων ἐν νέφεϊ στήριξε, τέρας μερόπων ἀνθρώπων : Eur. Med. 194 ὕμνους εὕροντο — βίου τερπνὰς ἀκοάς : Ib. 597 θέλων φῦσαι παῖδας ἔρυμα δώμασιν : Plat. Rep. p. 468 A δόντα αὐτὸν δ ω ρ ε ά ν : Eur. Orest. 715 εἰσορῶ φίλτατον βροτῶν, — ἡδεῖαν ὅ ψ ι ν : cf. Hec. 1074. Æsch. Choeph. 573 ἄκρατον αἷμα πίεται, τρίτην π ό σ ι ν : cf. Eur. Andr. 464. Ibid. 97. Arist. Eq. 9 ξυναυλίαν κλαύσωμεν. So especially we find many accusatives which from long usage have the force of prepositions or adverbs ; as, χάριν, gratia ; χάριν ἐμήν, σήν, mea, tua gratia (poet. also χρέος for χάριν Eur. Hec. 892.) ; δωρεάν, gratis ; δωτίνην (Hdt. VI. 89 δωτίνην γὰρ ἐν τῷ νόμῳ οὐκ ἐξῆν δοῦναι, g r a t i s dare per legem non licebat) ; προῖκα, μάτην, incassum ; μοῖραν, ἀρχὴν, omnino ; πέρας, lastly ; γνώμην ἐμὴν Aristoph., perhaps also ἕνεκα. So especially in similes and illustrations : τρόπον, τοῦτον τὸν τρόπον, hunc in modum ; πάντα τρόπον, τίνα τρόπον, δίκην, in morem ; δέμας poet., instar, ad instar : Plat. Phædr. 250 E τετράποδος νόμον, and also ὅμοια, ἐπιτηδές.

2. And even when there is no accus. of the cognate notion or its equivalent, an accusative stands in apposition to the verbal action contained in the sentence which precedes it, and which would stand, if expressed, in the cognate accusative or its equivalent ; as, Pind. Olym. IX. 79 ἐ π ω ν υ μ ί α ν χ ά ρ ι ν νίκας ἀγερώχου κελαδησόμεσθα, (ὕμνον) βροντᾶν : Il. ω, 735 ῥίψει ἀπὸ πύργου, λ υ γ ρ ὸ ν ὄ λ ε θ ρ ο ν = ὀλεθρίαν ῥίψιν : Eur. Hipp. 809 ὦ βιαίως θανοῦσ' ἀνοσίῳ τε συμφορᾷ, σ ᾶ ς χ ε ρ ὸ ς π ά λ α ι σ μ α μ ε λ έ α ς, sc. θάνατον, πάλαισμα : Id. Orest. 488 πληγεὶς θυγατρὸς τῆς ἐμῆς — (πληγὴν) υ.. ,ϊ σ τ ο ν ἔ ρ γ ο ν : cf. Id. Iph. A. 223. Id. Orest. 1098 Ἑλένην κτάνωμεν, Μ ε ν έ λ ε ῳ λ ύ π η ν π ι κ ρ ά ν : Æsch. Choeph. 199 εἴχε συμπενθεῖν ἐμοὶ, ἄ γ α λ μ α τ ύ μ β ο υ τ ο ῦ δ ε καὶ τιμὴν πατρός : cf. Plat. Gorg. p. 507 E. Eur. Alc. 7 καί με θητεύειν (δουλείαν) τ ῶ ν δ' ἄ π ο ι ν', ἠνάγκασεν : Id. Andr. 290 Κύπρις εἷλε λόγοις δολίοις — π ι κ ρ ὰ ν σ ύ γ χ υ σ ι ν Φρυγῶν πολεῖ : cf. Eur. Orest. 1495. So with δίκην and τρόπον, Æsch. Ag. 2 κοιμώμενος στέγαις Ἀτρειδῶν ἄγκαθεν κ υ ν ὸ ς δ ί κ η ν : Id. 48 μέγαν ἐκ θυμοῦ κλάζοντες Ἄρη, τ ρ ό π ο ν α ἰ γ υ π ι ῶ ν ; or it sometimes agrees with an indefinite notion of action implied in the definite verb of action in the sentence ; as, Xen. Cyr. VIII. 5, 32 τὰ μὲν γὰρ π α ρ ε λ θ ό ν τ α (πράγματα), Κῦρον η ὐ ξ ή σ α τ ε, in your former actions.

3. And when a verbal notion is resolved into a periphrasis for poetical effect, an accusative is used to define and illustrate the notion so resolved, standing seemingly independently, but in reality in apposition to the verbal notion in the speaker's mind, and implied in the sense : Æsch. Ag. 224 ἔτλα δ' οὖν θυτὴρ θυγατρὸς γενέσθαι (= ἐθυγατρόθυνε) γ υ ν α ι κ ο π ο ί ν ω ν π ο λ έ μ ω ν ἀ ρ ω γ ά ν = θυσίαν : Id. Theb. 289 μέριμναι ζωπυροῦσι τάρβος,

τὸν ἀμφιτειχῆ λεών: Eur. Phœn. 210 Ζεφύρου πνοιαῖς ἱππεύσαντος (= πνέοντος) κάλλιστον κελάδημα: Id. Orest. 951 τιθεῖσα λευκὸν ὄνυχα διὰ παρηΐδων (= τύπτουσα παρηΐδας) αἱματηρὸν ἄταν: Soph. Œ. R. 722 οὔτ᾽ ἤνυσεν φονέα γενέσθαι πατρός, οὔτε Λάϊον, τὸ δεινὸν οὐφοβεῖτο, πρὸς παιδὸς θανεῖν.

Obs. 1. In some cases a nomin. appears to take the place of the accus., but in reality it refers not to the whole sentence, but to the subject of the sentence: Eur. Heracl. 70 ἱκέται ὄντες βιαζόμεσθα καὶ στέφη μιαίνεται, πόλει τ᾽ ὄνειδος καὶ θεῶν ἀτιμία, sc. we ἱκέται ὄντες, being so shamefully treated, are ὄνειδος and ἀτιμία.

Obs. 2. So the expressions τὸ δὲ μέγιστον, τό γε μέγιστον, καὶ τὸ μέγιστον, τὸ δὲ δεινότατον, καὶ τὸ δεινότ., καὶ τὸ ἔσχατον, τό γε ἔσχ., τὸ κεφάλαιον, τὸ τελευταῖον, which are so frequently used in the Attic writers. The article is but rarely omitted: Thuc. I. 142 μέγιστον δὲ τῇ τῶν χρημάτων σπάνει κωλύσονται. When a greater emphasis is to be laid on one of these expressions, it assumes the form of a sentence, and the really primary sentence is made to depend on it; as, Plat. Phæd. 66 D τὸ δὲ μέγιστον πάντων ὅτι θόρυβον παρέχει καὶ ταραχήν.

Accusative Absolute.

§. 581. 1. Somewhat analogous to the accus. in apposition is the accus. which stands at the beginning of a sentence to mark the notion principally to be kept in view throughout, which has been called the accusative absolute, and explained by the ellipse of κατά: but this accus. either depends on some word carried on by the speaker's mind from the preceding sentence; as, Od. a, 274 μνηστῆρας μὲν ἐπὶ σφέτερα σκίδνασθαι ἄνωχθι μητέρα δ᾽, εἰ οἱ θυμὸς ἐφορμᾶται γαμέεσθαι, ἂψ ἴτω κ. τ. λ., where μητέρα depends on ἄνωχθι: or the accus. is in apposition to the proper accus. of some following verb; as, Arist. Nub. 1148 καί μοι τὸν υἱόν, εἰ μεμάθηκε τὸν λόγον ἐκεῖνον, εἴφ᾽, ὃν ἀρτίως εἰσήγαγες: where υἱόν is the patient of εἰπέ in the sense of "speak of:" or it is an accus. of time or quantity placed for emphasis at the beginning of the sentence; as, Xen. Cyr. VIII. 5, 32 τὰ μὲν γὰρ παρελθόντα ὑμεῖς μὲν Κῦρον ηὐξήσατε στράτευμα δόντες: or there is a change of construction in the sentence.—See *Anacolouthon.*

2. Sometimes this accus. depends on a verb in the speaker's mind, which is readily supplied by the nature of the passage, and is omitted for the sake of emphasis. So Soph. Ant. 441 σὲ δή, σὲ τὴν νεύουσαν ἐς πέδον κάρα, φῇς ἢ καταρνεῖ μὴ δεδρακέναι τάδε, where the fact of the passage being an address suggests λέγω.

Obs. The accusative stands also after adjectives derived from or compounded with verbs; as, Æsch. Ag. 1090 πολλὰ κακὰ ξυνίστωρ: Ibid. 103 ἐλπὶς ἀμύνει τὴν θυμοβόρον φρένα λύπην: Xen. Cyr. III. 3, 9 ἐπιστήμονες τὰ προσήκοντα: Eur. Med. 686 τρίβων τὰ τοιάδε: Id. Rhes. 625. Plat. Charm. p. 158 C ἔξαρνος εἶναι τὰ ἐρωτώμενα: Id. Alc. p. 141 D ἀνήκοον εἶναι ἔνια.

Accusative of the patient—Double Accusative.

§. 582. 1. Those verbs which, besides the notion of state or feeling, act, effect, motion, implied in the verb, imply further the operation of any of these on some person or thing, as the patient or object affected thereby, have an accusative of that patient or object as implied in the verb, and making up the notion of the whole verbal operation, as all such notions of action imply the notion of the patient. Thus verbs of striking, wounding, cutting, &c.; as, τύπτω σε, δέρω αὐτόν. Verbs of hurting, insulting, benefiting, deceiving, pleasing, &c.; as, βλάπτω σε. Verbs of depriving, taking from, stripping, killing, &c.; as, στέρομαί σε : it will be needless to enumerate all the verbs which imply a patient, as they will readily occur to the mind, or be recognised when met with.

Obs. 1. We must however be careful to distinguish between the accus. of the effect, δέμω δόμον, or act, θύω βοῦν = θυσίαν, διδάσκω γράμματα, and the real patient of a verbal notion, κτείνω σε, διδάσκω σε.

2. These verbs imply therefore two notions—the act, &c. and the patient, as making up the whole verbal notion; and hence such verbs may have a double accusative case, if it be necessary to define clearly both the act, &c. and the patient; as, διδάσκω σε καλά. (See §. 545. 1.)

3. But as this is not always necessary (with some verbs indeed never), it happens that the use of the double accusative case is mostly confined to certain verbs whose sense generally requires a definition of the act and the patient to convey a clear notion to the mind of the hearer, or to express the meaning of the speaker.

1. Verbs of *saying something of*, or *doing something to* another person; as, ἐργάζεσθαι, ποιεῖν, πράττειν &c.—λέγειν, εἰπεῖν &c.—κακά, ἀγαθά &c.: an accus. of the thing said or done, and of the patient.

2. Verbs of *asking, praying*, &c.; as, αἰτεῖν, αἰτεῖσθαι, ἀπαιτεῖν, ἐρωτᾶν, ἐρέσθαι, ἐξετάζειν, ἱστορεῖν &c.: accus. of the question asked and the patient.

3. Verbs of *teaching, reminding*, &c.; as, διδάσκειν, παιδεύειν, ἀναμιμνήσκειν &c.: accus. of the instruction and the patient.

4. Verbs of *dividing into parts*; as, δαίειν, τέμνειν &c.: accus. of the divisions and the patient.

5. Verbs of *concealing from*; as, κρύπτειν : accus. of the concealment, or that wherein it consists, and the patient.

6. Verbs of *advising, persuading, challenging, compelling*; as, πείθειν, ἐποτρύνειν, ἐπαίρειν, προκαλεῖσθαι, ἀναγκάζειν : accus. of the advice, &c. or that wherein it consists, and the patient.

7. Verbs of *depriving, taking away from, stripping, putting on*, &c.; as, ἀφαιρεῖσθαι, στερεῖν, ἀποστερεῖν, συλᾶν, ἐκδύειν, ἐνδύειν, &c.: accus. of the deprivation, &c. or that wherein it consists, and the patient.

Obs. 2. This double accus. with some of these verbs, as ἀφαιρέω, may arise from there being a twofold sense in the verb, thus ἀφαιρεῖν τι, to take away from some one, or to their loss ; and to deprive some one of something.

8. Analogously to these verbs, those also of *taking away some impurity*, &c. as καθαίρω, λούω, νίπτομαι, &c. are used with a double accus. case ; one of the cleansing, &c. or that wherein it consists, viz. the impurity &c., and the patient ; so also παύω.

4. It is not meant either that the verbs implying these notions always have a double accus. case, but only that generally or frequently in good writers they are so constructed, as both the notions more or less frequently require to be defined ; or that no verbs except those implying these notions ever have a double accusative. This construction is found with other verbs in good writers, when they may wish to define the exact nature of the verbal operation, as will be seen from the subjoined list, though it mostly happens that this is not required, the verb being already sufficiently definite in this respect ; and in later writers several verbs are found with a double accus. which are not so used in good writers ; and many verbs are found with the two accus. (of the act, &c. and the patient) separately, though not together, the objective sentence being sufficiently complete by the use of one of them only.

Obs. 3. Where the patient of any of these verbs is in the dative case, it arises from the notion of the benefit or harm resulting to him being the prominent feature in the thought ; as, Hes. Opp. 42 κρύψαντες βίον ἀνθρώ-ποισι, for their benefit ; ἀνθρώπους would simply be, concealing it from men.

Verbs which have a Double Accusative.

(*Those with an Asterisk prefixed are of common occurrence.*)

§. 583. 1. Ἄγω : Xen. Cyr. I. 6, 19 ἄγειν στενὰς ὁδοὺς στρατιάν.

Pass. Soph. Antig. 878 ἄγομαι ὁδόν. Very commonly acc. of person only. Acc. of cognate notion only : Hell. IV. 4, 13 ἦγε τὴν ἐπὶ Μέγαρα. So ἀνάγω : Il. ζ, 292 τὴν ὁδὸν ἣν Ἑλένην πὲρ ἀνήγαγεν.

2. Ἀδικέω : Demosth. p. 118, 19 ἀδικεῖν ἀδίκημα ἐκεῖνον : Thuc. III. 56 ἠδίκησαν πολλὰ ἡμᾶς : Pass. Eur. Med. 221 οὐδὲν (ἀδίκημα) ἠδικημένος : Id. Andr. 350 πόσας δ᾽ ἂν εὐνὰς (the ἀδίκημα) θυγατέρ᾽ ἠδικημένην.

Acc. of injustice, or unjust act alone ; as, Plat. Rep. p. 344 ἀδικίαν ἠδικηκότα : so οὐδέν, τοιαῦτα, πλεῖστα, μέγιστα &c. ἀδικεῖν : Eur. El. 920 ἠδίκεις λέχη. Acc. of person only ; as, Eur. Med. 692 ἀδικεῖ μ᾽ Ἰάσων.

3. Αἰδέομαι (to reverence) : Eur. Med. 326 αἰδέσει οὐδὲν λιτάς.

Generally with acc. of patient only : Id. Hipp. 1258 αἰδούμενος θεούς.

4. Ἀικίζω, αἰκίζομαι : Il. χ, 256 ἀεικιῶ ἔκπαγλόν σε : Xen. Anab. III. 1, 12 ἡμᾶς τὰ αἴσχιστα αἰκισάμενος.

Acc. of person only : Il. ω, 22 Ἕκτορα ἀείκιζεν. Thing as patient : Ibid. 54 γαῖαν ἀεικίζει.

5. Αἰνέω : Æsch. Ag. 1482 αἰνεῖς δαίμονα κακὸν αἶνον.

Acc. of cognate notion alone : Soph. Phil. 1380 αἶνον αἰνέσας : Ibid. 1398 ἃ δ᾽ ᾔνεσας : Æsch. Choeph. 78 δίκαια καὶ μὴ δίκαια αἰνέσαι. Acc. of person : Ibid. 1009 αὐτὸν αἰνῶ. Thing as patient : Æsch. Eum. 975 αἰνῶ μύθους.

6. Αἱρέω, I prosecute : Isæ. p. 64, 19 εἷλε δύο δίκας Εὔπολιν.

Acc. of thing only : Plat. Legg. p. 784 D ἕλῃ τὴν δίκην. Acc. of person only : Æschin. p. 75, 41 αἱρεῖτε τὸν δῆμον, accuse the people.

7. Αἴρω : Eur. Hipp. 1361 αἴρετε πρόσφορά με.

The patient of the verb is either a person, as Eur. Bacch. 942 αἴρειν νιν, or a thing, αἴρω χεῖρα &c.

8. *Αἰτέω : Od. β, 387 ᾔτεε νῆα αὐτόν, the ναῦς being the request ; so Arist. Av. 190 αἰτούμεθα δίοδον Βοιωτούς.

Also acc. of the request only : Il. ε, 358 ᾔτεε ἵππους : Æsch. Pers. 216 αἰτοῦ τάδε ; and acc. of person only : Soph. Ant. 1199 αἰτήσαντες ἐνοδίαν θεόν, so ἀπαιτέω : Eur. Phœn. 601 ἀπαιτῶ σκῆπτρά σε. Acc. of request only : Ibid. 81 πατρῷ᾽ ἀπαιτεῖ σκῆπτρα. Of person only : Id. Orest. 1586 ἀπαιτεῖ θεούς.

Obs. Αἰτεῖν τινός τι Eur. Very commonly αἰτεῖν, αἰτεῖσθαι παρά τινός τι.

9. Αἰτιάομαι : Arist. Ach. 514 αἰτιώμεθα ταῦτα (αἰτιάματα) τοὺς Λάκωνας : cf. Demosth. p. 250, 23.

Acc. of accusation only : Demosth. p. 1404, 23 αἰτιάσασθαι ταῦτα.—(See §. 568.) Acc. of person only : Il. λ, 78 ᾐτιόωντο Κρονίωνα : Eur. Med. 605 μηδέν᾽ ἄλλον αἰτιῶ. Thing substituted for person : Eur. Orest. 276 αἰτιᾶσθε θέσφατα : Demosth. p. 314, 20 αἰτιάσαιτο ἂν πενίαν.

10. Ἀλγύνω : Soph. Phil. 66 ἀλγυνεῖς οὐδέν με [a] : Pass. Soph. Phil. 1010 τοῦτο δ᾽ αὖτ᾽ ἀλγύνομαι.

Acc. of sorrow only : Soph. Œ. R. 446 ἀλγύναις πλέον. Acc. of person : Eur. Hipp. 798 ἀλγυνοῦσί σε. Of thing considered as patient : Id. Med. 398 ἀλγυνεῖ κέαρ.

11. Ἀλείφω : Od. ζ, 227 ἄλειψεν λίπα πάντα (τὸν χρόα).

Acc. of cognate notion only : Thuc. IV. 68 λίπα ἀλείψασθαι. Acc. of patient alone : Plat. Lys. p. 217 D τὰς τρίχας ἀλείψειε.

12. Ἀμείβομαι : Hdt. III. 52 ἀμείβεσθαι οὐδὲν πατέρα : cf. Id. VII. 135, and Od. λ, 278 : ρ, 393.

Acc. of answer : Eur. Suppl. 478 σφριγῶντ᾽ ἀμείψῃ μῦθον. Acc. of person alone : Od. ι, 272 μ᾽ αὖτις ἀμείβετο.

Obs. The words used in the answer are frequently put in the dative : ἀμείβεσθαι ἐπέεσσι &c.

---

[a] Herm. ad loc.

13. Ἀμέρδω : Hom. Hymn. Cer. 312 ἤμερσεν τιμὴν Ὀλύμπια δώματ᾽ ἔχοντας.

Acc. of thing lost : Eur. Hec. 1028 ἀμέρσας βίον. Acc. of person : Il. π, 53 ἀμέρσαι τὸν ὁμοῖον.

Obs. The thing lost is generally in the gen. : ἀμέρδειν βίου, ὀφθάλμων, αἰῶνος.

14. Ἀναγκάζω : Soph. Phil. 1366 ἀναγκάζεις τάδε ἐμέ : cf. Id. Electr. 256. Pass. Plat. Phædr. 254 A δεινὰ ἀναγκαζομένω.

Acc. of thing alone : Eur. Iph. T. 595 ἀναγκάζει τάδε. Acc. of person only : Eur. Hec. 364 μ᾽ ἀναγκάσει. So προσαναγκάζω Plat. Symp. p. 181.

15. Ἀναμνάω : Xen. Anab. III. 2, 11 ἀναμνήσω κινδύνους ὑμᾶς.

16. Ἀνιάω : Soph. Ant. 550 ἀνιᾷς ταῦτ᾽ ἐμέ : Pass. Soph. Phil. 906 τοῦτ᾽ ἀνιῶμαι.

Acc. of person only : Od. β, 115 ἀνιήσει υἷας Ἀχαιῶν.

17. Ἀπατάω : Thuc. V. 9 ἀπατήσας ἃ (κλέμματα) τὸν πολέμιον : Pass. Soph. Œ. R. 594 τοσοῦτον ἠπατημένος.

Acc. of deceit only : Soph. Phil. 929 οἷ᾽ ἠπάτηκας. So Il. γ, 399 ταῦτα ἠπεροπεύειν. Acc. of person only : Soph. Trach. 500 Κρονίδαν ἀπάτασεν. So ἐξαπατάω Demosth. p. 105, 62.

18. Ἀπαυράω : Il. ζ, 17 ἀπηύρα θυμὸν ἄμφω : Il. ψ, 291 ἀπηύρα ἵππους Αἰνείαν.

Acc. of thing taken only : Il. ι, 107 ἀπούρας κούρην. The person is sometimes put in the gen. : Od. σ, 272 τῆς ὄλβον ἀπηύρα. Also dative incomm. : Il. ρ, 236 πολέσσιν θυμὸν ἀπηύρα.

19. Ἀποκτείνω : Plat. Apol. p. 39 C ἀπεκτόνατε οἵαν τιμωρίαν (= θάνατον) ἐμέ.

Elsewhere with acc. of person only.

20. Ἀποσπάω : Soph. Œ. C. 866 ἀποσπάσας ὄμμ᾽ ἐμέ.

Generally acc. of thing only, or person considered as thing : ἀποσπᾶν τι or τινα.

21. Ἀπολιχμάω : Il. φ, 123 ἀπολιχμήσονται αἷμά σε.

22. Ἀποφεύγω : Demosth. p. 1014, 8 ἀπέφυγον δίκας αὐτούς : Id. p. 1021, 2, &c.

Acc. of suit only : Ant. p. 115, 32 ἀποφεύξεσθαι τὴν γραφήν. Of prosecutor only : Andoc. p. 16, 17 ἀποφεύξομαι αὐτόν.

23. Ἀπύω : Od. ι, 399 ἤπυεν μεγάλα τοὺς Κύκλωπας.

Acc. of thing said only : Eur. Supp. 800 στεναγμὸν ἀπύσατε : Il. ξ, 399 τόσσον ἤπυει : Æsch. Pers. 122 τοῦτ᾽ ἔπος ἀπύων.—(See §. 566. 1.) Acc. of patient only : Æsch. Theb. 130 σε ἀπύουσαι : Soph. Aj. 887,

24. Ἀπωθέομαι : Thuc. I. 32 ἀπεωσάμεθα τὴν γενομένην ναυμαχίαν Κορινθίους.

(See Κρατέω.)

25. Ἁρμόζω : Plat. Lach. p. 188 D ἡρμοσμένος καλλίστην ἁρμονίαν λύραν : cf. Arist. Eq. 995 : Plat. Pol. p. 591 D τὴν ἁρμονίαν ἁρμοττόμενος.

26. Ἀσπάζομαι : Plat. Lys. p. 133, 22 ἀσπασάμενοι τὰ ὕστατα τοὺς αὐτῶν : cf. Eur. Ion 1363.

Commonly acc. of person only ; as, Od. χ, 498 ἠσπάζοντο Ὀδυσῆα : or of a thing substituted for person ; as, Eur. Ion 587 τὴν συμφορὰν ἀσπάζομαι.

27. Ἀτιμάζω : Soph. Ant. 544 μήτοι μ' ἀτιμάσῃς τὸ μὴ θανεῖν (= ἀτιμίαν): cf. Id. Œ. R. 339. Pass. Eur. Iph. Aul. 943 ἀνάξι' ἠτιμασμένη.

Commonly acc. of patient only : Od. ψ, 116 ἀτιμάζει με : or thing considered as patient, Eur. Hipp. 611 ὅρκους ἀτιμάσῃς.

28. *Ἀφαιρέομαι : Il. α, 182 ἀφαιρεῖται Χρυσηΐδα ἐμέ : cf. Xen. Cyr. IV. 6, 4. Pass. Hdt. III. 65 ἀπαιρεθέω τὴν ἀρχήν : so Id. 137 ἐξαιρεθέντες τὸν Δημοκήδεα καὶ τὸν γαυλὸν ἀπαιρεθέντες.

So Eur. Hel. 95 βίον στερείς. With a gen. of person : Xen. Hell. III. 1, 7 ἀφαιρησόμενος τὸ ὕδωρ αὐτῶν : so Arist. Ach. 164 τὰ σκόροδα πορθούμενος.

29. Αὐδάω : Il. ε, 170 ἔπος μιν ηὔδα.

Acc. of person only : Od. ε, 28 Ἑρμείαν ηὔδα. Generally with acc. of thing spoken only.—(See §. 566. 1.)

30. Αὐξάνω, αὔξω : Æsch. Pers. 756 αὐξάνειν οὐδὲν ὄλβον : Pass. Plat. Rep. p. 328 D τοσοῦτον αὔξεται.

Generally with acc. of person only. Acc. of increase only : Eur. Iph. T. 413 φιλόπλουτον ἄμιλλαν (= αὔξημα) αὔξοντες μελάθροισι.

31. *Βάζω : Il. ι, 58 βάζεις πεπνυμένα βασιλῆας : Od. γ, 127. Eur. Rhes. 719. Æsch. Theb. 553.

Acc. of thing said only : Hom. ἀνεμώλια, νήπια βάζεις : Eur. Hipp. 119 μάταια βάζει : Æsch. Choeph. 869, &c.

32. Βάλλω (to hit): Od. ρ, 483 ἔβαλες καλὰ τὸν ἀλήτην : Il. δ, 480 ἔβαλε πρῶτον (βλῆμα) αὐτόν : Il. π, 511 βάλεν δ (ἕλκος) μιν.

Acc. of throw only : Eur. Suppl. 330 βλήματα βαλεῖν. Commonly with acc. of person only ; as, Il. λ, 410 ἔβαλε ἄλλον : or thing considered as patient ; as, Il. ζ, 17 ἔβαλε στῆθος.

33. Βάπτω : Arist. Ach. 112 βάψω βάμμα σε.

Acc. of dye only : Plat. Rep. p. 429 E χρώματα βάπτῃ. Commonly with acc. of patient only : Od. ι, 392 πέλεκυν βάπτει.

34. Βιάζομαι (to take away by force): Il. φ, 451 βιήσατο μισθὸν νῶϊ : Pass. Xen. Anab. VII. 6, 40 βιασθεῖσαι τοῦτο.

Generally acc. of patient only.

35. Βοάω (to call on): Eur. Med. 205 βοᾷ λιγυρὰ ἄχεα προδόταν: cf. Id. Troad. 351.

Acc. of cry only.—(See §. 566. 3.)

36. Γαμέω: Hdt. III. 88 ἐγάμεε τοὺς πρώτους γάμους Κύρου θυγατέρας: cf. Eur. Troad. 361.

Acc. of marriage only: Æsch. P. V. 766 γαμεῖ γάμον. Commonly acc. of person only; as, Od. o, 241 ἔγημε γυναῖκα: Il. ι, 388 κούρην οὐ γαμέω Ἀγαμέμνονος.

37. Γελάω, to laugh at: Theocr. XX. 14 ἐγέλαξε σεσαρὸς καὶ σοβαρόν με.

Generally dat. of person.

38. Γεύω: Eur. Cyc. 149 γεύσω ἄκρατον μέθυ σε.

39. Γοάω: Soph. Trach. 51 γοωμένην ὀδύρματα τὴν ἔξοδον.

Generally acc. of patient only.

40. Γράφω, γράφομαι (I prosecute): Plat. Euth. p. 2 E γέγραπται γραφήν σε: Demosth. p. 1296, 5 γράψασθαι αὐτοὺς ζημίαν: cf. Arist. Av. 1052.

Acc. of suit only: Plat. Legg. p. 928 E γράφεσθαι τὴν γραφήν, (with a gen. of the accusation of the crime.) Acc. of person only: Ibid. γράφεσθαι πατέρας.

41. Γυμνάζω: Eur. Hipp. 112 γυμνάσω τὰ πρόσφορα ἵππους.

Pass. Æsch. P. V. 594 δρόμους γυμνάζεται. Generally acc. of person only.

42. Δαίρω (δέρω): Arist. Nub. 441 δαίρειν ἀσκὸν (= δέρμα) σῶμα.

Acc. of skin only: Od. κ, 19 ἀσκὸν δείρας. Acc. of patient only: Ibid. 533 μῆλα δείραντας.

43. Δαίω (to divide): Hdt. VII. 121 δασάμενος τρεῖς μοίρας τὸν στρατόν. So Plat. Legg. p. 695 C ἑπτὰ μέρη τεμόμενος.

Generally only acc. of patient; as, δαίω γῆν.

44. Δεξιόομαι, to greet: Xen. Cyr. III. 2, 7 δεξιωσάμενοι πολλὰ τὸν Κῦρον.

Acc. of act only: Eur. Rhes. 419 πυκνὴν ἄμυστιν δεξιούμενοι. Of person only: Xen. Cyr. VIII. 7, 2 πάντας δεξιωσάμενος. With dat. Æsch. Ag. 852 θεοῖσι πρῶτα δεξιώσομαι.

45. Δέομαι: Thuc. V. 36 ἐδέοντο Πάνακτον (= δέημα) τοὺς Βοιωτούς: like αἰτέω.

More commonly with acc. of the thing requested, and gen. of person; as, Plat. Apol. p. 18 A τοῦτο ὑμῶν δέομαι. And the Infin. frequently stands for the request: Id. Rep. 338 A ἐδέοντο ὑμῶν μὴ ἄλλως ποιεῖν. Acc. of request only. Thuc. I. 32 ξύμφορα (sc. δήματα) δέονται: Isæus p. 78, 34 δέησιν δέομαι: Æsch. p. 328, 43 δέησιν ἐδεήθη: Arist. Ach. 1028 δέημα δ δεῖταί μου.

46. Δέχομαι, to greet: Eur. Iph. A. 1182 δεξόμεθα δέξιν ἥν σε δέξασθαι χρεών.

47. Δέω: Hdt. V. 72 κατέδησαν τὴν (δέσιν) ἐπὶ θανάτῳ τοὺς ἄλλους: cf. Id. III. 119. Pass. Eur. Hipp. 1237 δεσμὸν δεθείς.

Commonly acc. of patient only; as, Il. a, 406 τόν—οὐδ' ἔδησαν. Frequently a dat. of the bond, with ἐν: Od. μ, 161 ἀλλά με δεσμῷ δῆσατ' ἐν ἀργαλέῳ.

48. Διατρίβω, to put off: Od. β, 204 διατρίβῃ ὃν γάμον (=τριβήν) Ἀχαιούς.

Acc. of delay only: Od. υ, 341 διατρίβω γάμον: cf. β, 265.

49. * Διδάσκω: Il. ψ, 307 ἐδίδαξάν σε ἱπποσύνας: cf. Od. θ, 481. Æsch. Eum. 571. Eur. Hipp. 421. Arist. Ach. 656. Hdt. VI. 138. Midd. Soph. Ant. 356 ἐδιδάξατο ὄργας: cf. Eur. Andr. 740.

Acc. of instruction only: Eur. Hipp. 917 τέχνας μυρίας διδάσκετε. Acc. of person only: Id. Andr. 740 διδάξω γαμβρούς. So Hdt. II. 51 ὅστις τὰ Καβείρων ὄργια μεμύηται.

50. Δικάζω, to judge: Æsch. Suppl. 230 δικάζει ὑστάτας δίκας τἀμπλακήματα.

Generally acc. of suit.—(See §. 586.)

51. Διοικέω: Plat. Crit. p. 51 E διοικοῦμεν τἆλλα τὴν πόλιν: cf. Id. Prot. p. 318 E. Pass. Plat. Rep. p. 462 C ἄριστα διοικεῖται.

Acc. of thing only: Demosth. p. 332, 23 τοιαῦτα διοικεῖν. Acc. of patient only: Plat. Phædr. p. 240 E πάντα τὸν κόσμον διοικεῖ.

52. Διώκω, to pursue: Il. ρ, 75 διώκων ἀκίχητα (διώγματα) ἵππους Αἰακίδαο.

Acc. of pursuit only: Il. ε, 223 κραιπνὰ διώκειν. More commonly with acc. of person only; as, Il. ε, 672 Διὸς υἱὸν διώκοι. To pursue at law: Demosth. p. 1368, 8 ἐδίωκε γραφὴν Στέφανον. Acc. of suit only: Ant. p. 115, 24 γραφὰς διώξας: cf. Plat. Euthyd. p. 4 A.

53. * Δράω: Eur. Suppl. 1176 Ἀργείων χθόνα δέδρακας ἐσθλά: cf. Id. Iph. A. 371. Soph. Aj. 1384. Plat. Rep. p. 308 B, &c.

More commonly with acc. of act, or thing done only.—(See §. 560. 1.)

54. Δυστομέω: Soph. Œ. C. 985 δυστομεῖν ταῦτα ἐμέ.

55. Ἐγκωμιάζω: Plat. Legg. p. 753 E ἐγκωμιάζουσι τοιαῦτα δικαιοσύνην.

Generally acc. of patient only: Plat. Phædr. p. 258 A ἑαυτὸν ἐγκωμιάζων: Id. Rep. p. 568 B τὴν τυραννίδα ἐγκωμιάζει.

56. Ἐθίζω: Plat. Meno p. 70 B εἴθικεν ἔθος ἡμᾶς: Pass. Eur. Fr. Aut. I. 8 ἔθη ἐθισθέντες: Isocr. p. 343 C εἴθισμαι τρόπον (=ἔθος).

Acc. of habit alone: Plat. Rep. p. 469 B τοῦτο ἐθίζειν. Acc. of patient only: Ibid. p. 604 C ἐθίζειν τὴν ψυχήν.

57. Εἴδω, to look on: Eur. Or. 1020 ἰδοῦσα πρόσοψίν σε.
Generally acc. of sight only, either person or thing.

58. Εἴργω: Arist. Vesp. 334 εἴργων ταῦτά σε.
Generally acc. of patient only.

59. Ἐκδύω: Od. ξ, 341 ἐξέδυσαν εἵματά με: cf. Ag. 1269.
Midd. Il. γ, 114 τεύχεά τ᾽ ἐξεδύοντο.

60. Ἐκλέγω: Æschin. p. 17, 3 ἐξέλεγον τὰ τέλη τοὺς παραπλέοντας.
Acc. of exaction only: Demosth. p. 49 ἐξέλεξε χρήματα.

61. Ἐλάω (to strike): Od. φ, 219 οὐλὴν τὴν ποτέ με σῦς ἤλασε:
cf. Il. ψ, 74, &c.
Most commonly with acc. of patient: Od. δ, 507 ἤλασε πέτρην.

62. Ἐλέγχω: Plat. Lys. p. 222 D ἐξελέγξαι τοῦτο ἡμᾶς. So
Pass. Plat. Euth. p. 295 A ταῦτα ἐξελέγχομαι.
Acc. of thing only; as, Plat. Tim. p. 54 B τοῦτο ἐλέγξαντι. Acc. of
person only; as, Id. Gorg. p. 470 C ἐλέγξαι σε.

63. Ἐναρίζω (to spoil): Il. ρ, 187 ἐνάριξα τὰ (ἔντεα) Πατρόκλοιο
βίην: cf. Il. χ, 32, &c.
More commonly with acc. of person only, in the sense of "*to kill.*"

64. Ἐξετάζω: Xen. Cyr. VI. 2, 35 ἐξετάζετε τὰ δέοντα τοὺς ὑφ᾽
ὑμῖν.

65. Ἐπαινέω: Soph. Aj. 1381 ἐπαινέσαι πάντα σε.
Acc. of praise alone: Soph. Œ. C. 1009 ἐπαινῶν πολλά. Of patient:
Id. El. 1044 ἐπαινέσεις ἐμέ. Thing as patient: Ibid. 1047 τἄμ᾽ ἐπαινεῖν
ἔπη.

66. Ἐπισπέρχω (to exhort): Thuc. IV. 12 ἐπέσπερχε τοιαῦτα
ἄλλους.

67. Ἐπικνέομαι (to strike): Hdt. VII. 35 ἐπικέσθαι πληγὰς Ἑλλήσποντον.

68. *Ἔπω (to speak of): Eur. Med. 61 εἰπεῖν τόδε δεσπότας:
Arist. Ach. 649.
Acc. of person only: Il. a, 90 Ἀγαμέμνονα εἴπῃς; but generally with
acc. of thing said only.—(See §. 566. 1.)

69. *Ἐργάζομαι: Soph. Aj. 109 ἐργάσει κακὸν τὸν δύστηνον: Eur.
Hec. 264. Plat. Crito p. 96, &c.
Commonly with acc. of act only; as, Il. ω, 733 ἔργα ἐργάζοιο.—(See
§. 560. 1.)

70. Ἐπευφημέω: Æsch. ap. Plat. Rep. p. 383 B ἐπευφήμησεν
παιᾶνα τύχας.
Acc. of song of triumph only: Eur. Iph. A. 1468. Iph. Taur. 1403.
So Plat. Euthyd. p. 301 εὐφήμει τοῦτο. Acc. of person: Id. Epin.
p. 992 D εὐφημεῖν πάντας θεούς.

71. Ἔρδω: Il. γ, 351 ἔοργε κακά με: cf. Il. β, 12, &c. and Æsch. Pers. 236. Hdt. I. 137.

Commonly with acc. of act only.—(See §. 560. 1.)

72. Ἔρομαι: Od. η, 237 τὸ μέν σε εἰρήσομαι: cf. Od. τ, 46. γ, 243. Arist. Nub. 344. Eur. Andr. 603, &c.

Acc. of question only: Eur. Ion 541 κεῖν' οὐκ ἠρόμην. Acc. of person only: Eur. Troad. 945 οὔ σ', ἀλλ' ἐμαυτὴν ἐρήσομαι. Sometimes gen. of person: Eur. Herc. Fur. 177 Διὸς κεραυνὸν ἠρόμην.

73. Ἔρω (to say of): Eur. Alc. 957 ἐρεῖ τάδε με.

Acc. of person only: Eur. Hel. 824 ἐρεῖ με. Commonly with acc. of thing said.—(See §. 560. 1.)

74. Ἐρωτάω: Od. ι, 364 εἰρωτᾷς ὄνομά με: cf. Od. δ, 347, &c. Eur. Iph. Aul. 1129. Plat. Phil. p. 18 A.

Acc. of question only: Plat. Gorg. p. 466 B ἐρώτημα ἐρωτᾷς: Thuc. I. 5 τὰς πίστεις (=ἐρωτήσεις) ἐρωτῶντες: Eur. Iph. Taur. 501 οὐ τοῦτ' ἐρωτῶ. Acc. of person only: Od. ε, 97 εἰρωτᾷς με.

75. Ἑστιάω (to feast): Isæ. p. 46, 10 ἑστιᾶν θεσμοφόρια τὰς γυναῖκας.

Acc. of feast only: Eur. Herc. Fur. 483 ἑστιᾷ γάμους. Of person only: Id. Alc. 768 ἑστιῶ ξένον.

76. * Εὐεργετέω: Plat. Apol. p. 36 C εὐεργετεῖν εὐεργεσίαν ἕκαστον.

Acc. of benefit only: Plat. Pol. p. 615 B εὐργεσίας εὐεργηκότες. Acc. of patient only: Id. Crat. p. 428 A εὐεργέτει Σωκράτη.

77. Εὐλογέω: Arist. Ach. 372 εὐλογῇ δίκαια αὐτούς: Pass. Soph. Œ. C. 720 πλεῖστ' εὐλογούμενον.

Commonly acc. of person only: Eur. Ion 137 τὸν βόσκοντα εὐλογῶ.

78. Εὐφραίνω: Xen. Apol. II. 4, 6 εὐφραίνων πλεῖστα τοὺς εὖ πράττοντας: cf. Id. Cyr. IV. 2, 19.

Generally with acc. of person only: as, Soph. Aj. 469 Ἀτρείδας ἂν εὐφράναιμι.

79. Εὐωχέω: Plat. Gorg. p. 522 A εὐώχουν ἡδέα ὑμᾶς: Midd. Xen. Cyr. I. 3, 6 εὐωχοῦ κρέα.

Generally with acc. of person only; as, Eur. Cycl. 345 εὐωχῆτέ με.

80. Ἐχθαίρω: Soph. Elect. 1035 ἐχθαίρω ἔχθος σε.

Acc. of hatred alone: Soph. Phil. 59 ἔχθος ἐχθήρας. Generally with acc. of patient only.

81. *Ἔω (to put on): Od. ξ, 396 ἕσσας εἵματά με: cf. Od. ο, 337, &c.: Midd. Od. τ, 72 εἷμαι εἵματα: Od. ω, 249 ἀεικέα ἕσσαι. So Il. ξ, 181 ζώσατο ζώνην.

Acc. of garment only: Od. π, 457 εἵματα ἕσσε περὶ χροΐ. Generally double acc., so ἀμφιέννυμι: Xen. Cyr. I. 3, 17 ἠμφίεσε τὸν ἑαυτοῦ χιτῶνα ἐκεῖνον.

82. Ζημιόω : Xen. Cyr. III. 1, 17 ζημιώσῃς πλείω σαυτόν : Pass.
Plat. Legg. p. 843 E ζημίαν ζημιοῦσθαι : Hdt. VII. 39 ψυχὴν ζημιώσεαι : Thuc. III. 40 μεγάλα ζημιώσεται.

Generally with acc. of person only, and instrumental dat. of punishment.

83. Θεραπεύω : Plat. Euth. p. 13 D θεραπεύουσι ἣν (θεραπείαν)
τοὺς δεσπότας : cf. Id. Rep. p. 426 C. Pass. Plat. Menex. p. 249 C
θεραπείαν θεραπευόμενος : cf. Ant. 126, 18.

Generally with acc. of patient only.

84. Θοινίζω (to feast) : Hdt. I. 129 ἐθοίνισε τό (δεῖπνον) μιν :
Pass. Eur. Phil. Fr. VII. θοινᾶται σάρκας.

Generally with acc. of person only.

85. Ἱκετεύω : Od. λ, 529 ἱκέτευε πολλά με : cf. Eur. Hel. 945.

86. Ἱστορέω : Eur. Phœn. 624 ἱστορεῖς τόδε με : cf. Id. Andr.
1125. Soph. Trach. 404. So ἐξιστορέω : Eur. Hec. 234.

Acc. of question, or thing asked only : Soph. Œ. R. 1144 τοῦτος ἱστορεῖς.
Person, about whom the question is asked, put for the question : Ibid.
1150 ὃν ἱστορεῖ. Acc. of person to whom the question is put ; as, Eur.
Ion 1547 ἱστορήσω Φοῖβον.

87. Καθαίρω : Il. π, 667 κάθηρον αἷμα Σαρπηδόνα : Pass. Plat.
Legg. p. 868 C καθαίρεσθαι καθαρμούς : Ibid. καθάρσεις.

Acc. of impurity only : Id. Soph. 227 C ὅσα καθαίρει. Generally acc. of
patient : Plat. Rep. p. 403 D καθαίρων χρυσόν.

88. Κακουργέω : Xen. Cyr. VI. 3, 11 κακουργῇ τι τοὺς ἐναντίους.

89. Καλέω (to name) : Il. σ, 487 ἣν καὶ ἅμαξαν ἐπίκλησιν καλέουσιν. So Il. ε, 300 καλέουσιν κοτύλην (= ἐπίκλησιν) μίν : cf. Od. θ,
550. Xen. Œc. VII. 3. So ἀνακαλέω Plat. Rep. p. 471 D :
προσεννέπω Æsch. Ag. 162 : κλάζω Ibid. 174.

90. Κατασβέννυμι (to make to cease) : Soph. Aj. 1148 κατασβέσειε βοὴν τὸ σὸν στόμα.

Generally with acc. of patient only.

91. Κείρω : Eur. Troad. 1173 ἔκειρεν βόστρυχόν σε : Pass. Eur.
Hec. 910 ἀποκέκαρσαι στεφάναν : Arist. Vesp. 1313 σκευάρια
διακεκαρμένῳ.

Generally single acc. of thing cut ; as, Eur. Hel. 1124 κείραντες ἔθειραν :
Soph. Aj. 55 ἔκειρε φόνον.

92. Κελεύω : Il. ν, 87 κελεύεις ταῦτά με : Od. θ, 153.

Acc. of command only : Il. ε, 528 πολλὰ κελεύων. — (See §. 566. 2.)
Generally with acc. of person only.

93. Κερτομέω : Eur. Hel. 1229 κερτομεῖς τί με.

Generally acc. of person only : Eur. Bacch. 1292 ἐκερτόμει θεόν.

94. Κινέω : Aristot. Anim. I. 5 κινεῖν κίνησιν ζῶον.

So Lucret. *Moventur motus.* So Plat. Rep. p. 529 φέρεται φοράς.

95. Κολάζω : Soph. Aj. 1108 κόλαζε ἔπη ἐκείνους.

Elsewhere with acc. of patient only.

96. Κρατέω (to conquer) : Eur. Epig. II. 1 ἐκράτησαν ὀκτὼ νίκας Συρηκοσίους.

Acc. of conquest only : Eur. Hipp. 1016 κρατεῖν ἀγῶνας : cf. Demosth. p. 520, ult. Eur. Med. 120 πολλὰ κρατοῦντες : Æsch. P.V. 957 νέον κρατεῖτε : Thuc. IV. 18 τὰ νῦν προχωρήσαντα κρατῆσαι. Generally acc. of patient only ; as, Eur. Alc. 493 κρατήσας δεσπότην. So Pass. Hdt. III. τοῦτο ἐσσοῦνται.

97. Κρίνω (to try) : Eur. Hec. 645 κρίνει ἦν (ἔριν) τρισσὰς παῖδας : cf. Demosth. p. 781, 6. Midd. Eur. Med. 609 κρινοῦμαι πλείονα.

Acc. of suit alone ; Eur. Heracl. 180 δίκην κρίνειεν : cf. Æsch. Eum. 652. Acc. of person alone : Eur. Troad. 924 ἔκρινε τρισσὸν ζεῦγος.

98. Κρύπτω (to hide from) : Æsch. P.V. 628 κρύψῃς τοῦτό με : cf. Soph. Electr. 957, &c. Plat. Lys. p. 891, 1. Pass. κρύπτομαι τοῦτο.

Generally with acc. of thing concealed only ; as, Eur. Bacch. 953 κρύψω δέμας. Single acc. of person : Xen. Cyr. VII. 3, 4 σε κρύψω : Plat. Theæt. p. 130.

99. Κτυπέω (to strike) : Eur. Orest. 1451 κτύπησε πλαγὰν κράτα.

Generally acc. of patient only.

100. Κωλύω : Soph. Phil. 1242 ἐπικωλύσων τάδε με.

Generally acc. of person only.

101. Λανθάνω : Pind. Ol. I. 64 λαθέμεν τι θεόν.

Generally acc. of person only.

102. *Λέγω (to speak of) : Hdt. VIII. 61 ἔλεγε κακὰ τοὺς Κορινθίους.

To say, with acc. of thing said only.—(See §. 566. 1.) Frequently with acc. of person, and εὖ or κακῶς.

103. Λίσσομαι : Od. β, 210 λίσσομαι ταῦτα ὑμᾶς.

Acc. of prayer only.—(See §. 566. 2.) Of person only : Il. a, 174 σε λίσσομαι.

104. Λούω : Il. σ, 345 λούσειαν βρότον Πάτροκλον.

Acc. of thing only ; Il. ξ, 7 βρότον λούσῃ. Generally with acc. of person only.

105. Λοχεύω : Eur. Ion. 921 ἐλοχεύσατο λοχεύματά σε.

Generally with acc. of person only ; as, Eur. Ion 948 τίς λοχεύει σε ;

106. Λυμαίνομαι: Arist. Aves 100 λυμαίνεται τοιαῦτα ἐμέ.

Acc. of act only: Hdt. III. 16 τἆλλα πάντα λυμαίνεσθαι: cf. Eur. Bacch. 632, with dat. of person. Acc. of person only: Soph. Œ. C. 855 σε λυμαίνεται.

107. Λυπέω: Eur. Cycl. 337 λυπεῖν μηδὲν αὑτόν: cf. Plat. Apol. p. 41 E. Pass. Id. Gorg. p. 494, &c. Α λυποῖτο λύπας &c.

Generally with acc. of patient only.

108. Λωβάομαι: Il. ν, 623 λωβήσασθε ἣν (λώβην) ἐμέ: cf. Hdt. III. 154.

Acc. of insult only: Il. α, 232 ὕστατα λωβήσαιο. Generally acc. of person only.

109. Μαστιγόω: Æsch. p. 9, 12 ἐμαστίγουν πληγὰς Πιττάλακον.

Generally acc. of patient only.

110. Μέλπω (to sing): Eur. Alc. 448 μέλψουσι πολλά σε.

Generally with acc. of song only.—(See §. 566. 3.)

111. Μεταλλάω: Od. τ, 115 μετάλλα τὰ ἄλλα ἐμέ.

Acc. of question only: Od. π, 467 ταῦτα μεταλλῆσαι. Acc. of person only: Od. τ, 190 Ἰδομενῆα μετάλλα.

112. Μέτειμι: Eur. Bacch. 345 μέτειμι δίκην τόνδε: cf. Ibid. 516. Æsch. Eum. 231.

Generally with acc. of person only.

113. Μήδομαι (to plot against): Il. ψ, 176 μήδετο ἔργα (Ἕκτορα): cf. Il. κ, 52 κακὰ μήσατ' Ἀχαιούς.

Generally with acc. of thing plotted.—(See §. 551. 1.)

114. Μητίομαι: Od. σ, 27 μητισαίμην κακὰ ὄν.

Generally acc. of act only.

115. Μορμολύττομαι: Plat. Crit. p. 46 C μορμολύττηται πλείω ἡμᾶς.

Acc. of bugbear only: Plat. Ax. p. 364 B τοὺς μορμολύττοντας τὸν θάνατον.

116. Νίζω: Od. ζ, 224 νίζετο ἅλμην χρόα.

117. Νοσφίζω: Pind. Nem. VI. 106 ἐνόσφισεν ἄνθεά σε.

Acc. of thing taken only, (with gen. of person:) Eur. Iph. A. 1287 νοσφίσας βρέφος. Acc. of person only: Eur. Rhes. 56 ἐνόσφισάς με. (Often with gen. of thing.)

118. Ξυρέω: Hdt. V. 35 ξυρήσαντα τρίχας μιν.

(See Κείρω.)

119. Ὀδύρομαι: Soph. Aj. 693 ὀδύρεται οἷα (ὀδύρματα) παῖδα.

With acc. of person only: Od. δ, 110 ὀδύρονται αὐτόν. Acc. of lamentation only.—(See §. 566. 4.)

120. Ὀνειδίζω : Soph. Œ. C. 1002 ὀνειδίζεις τοιαῦτα ἐμέ.

Generally with dat. of person.   Acc. of act.—(See §. 566. 2.)

121. Ὀνίνημι : Od. ψ, 24 ὀνήσει τοῦτό σε : cf. Hdt. VII. 141.

Generally with acc. of patient only.

122. Ὀνομάζω : Eur. Ion. 800 ὀνομάζει ὄνομα αὐτόν : cf. Id. Hel.
1209, &c.

Often with acc. of person only.

123. Ὁρκόω : Thuc. VIII. 75 ὥρκωσαν ὅρκους πάντας : Arist.
Lys. 187.

Acc. of patient only : Isæ. V. 4, 17 ὁρκώσαντες ἡμᾶς : so ἐξορκόω
Hdt. VI. 74.   Acc. of oath : Id. III. 133.

124. Οὐτάζω : Il. ε, 361 οὔτασεν ὅ (ἕλκος) με.

Generally with acc. of patient only.   So τιτρώσκω, with acc. of wound
in Pass. Eur. Phœn. 1445 τετρωμένους σφαγάς=τραύματα.

125. *Παιδεύω : Plat. Hipp. Min. p. 364 παιδεύω αὐτὰ ἄλλους : cf.
Æschin. 74, 37.   Pass.   Plat. Legg. p. 695 A παιδευομένους τέχνην.

Acc. of thing taught only ; as, Demosth. p. 938, 10 παιδεύειν παιδείαν :
Soph. Phil. 1361 παιδεύει κακά.   Acc. of person only ; as, Eur. Andr. 602
γυναῖκας παιδεύετε.

126. Παίω : Soph. Ant. 1309 ἔπαισεν ἀνταίαν (πληγήν) με.

Acc. of blow only : Soph. Œ. C. 550 ἔπαισας νόσον (= πληγήν).   Acc.
of patient only : Id. Ant. 1274 μ' ἔπαισεν.

127. Παρακρούομαι : Demosth. p. 1062, 39 παρακρουόμενοι πρᾶγμα
δικαστάς : cf. Id. p. 844, 1.

128. Παύω : Pind. Nem. III. 39 ἔπαυσεν ἀκμὰν φρενῶν νιν.

129. *Πείθω : Hdt. I. 163 ἔπειθε τοῦτο τοὺς Φωκαίεας : Æsch.
Ag. 1185.   Soph. Œ. C. 797.   Eur. Hec. 1205.   Cf. Plat. Apol.
p. 37 A.   Xen. Hier. I. 16.   Pass.   Hdt. VI. 10 ταῦτα πείθοντο :
cf. Il. ψ, 157.   So ἀναπείθω : Arist. Nub. 77 ἀναπείσω ἦν
τουτονί.

Acc. of thing only : Soph. Œ. C. 1442 μὴ πεῖθ' ὃ μὴ δεῖ.   Generally
with acc. of person ; as, Ibid. 1516 πείθεις με.

130. Περαίνω (to do to) : Soph. Aj. 21 περάνας πρᾶγος ἡμᾶς.

Generally only acc. of act.—(See §. 560. 2.)

131. Πημαίνω : Plat. Legg. p. 932 E πημαίνει ὅσα ἄλλον.

Generally with acc. of person only.

132. Πιπίσκω (to give to drink) : Pind. Isth. V. 74 πίσω ὕδωρ
σφέ.   So ποτίζω St. Matt. x. 42.

133. *Ποιέω : Hdt. III. 59 ἐποίησαν κακὰ Αἰγινήτας : cf. Id.
IX. 113, &c.

Frequently with acc. of person only, with εὖ or κακῶς ; as, Hdt. II. 121
τοῦτον εὖ ποιοῦσι.

134. Πορεύω : Eur. Alc. 444 πορεύσας λίμναν (=πόρον) γυναῖκα :
Soph. Trach. 550 ἐπόρευε ποταμὸν (=πόρον) βροτούς : Midd. Plat.
Menex. p. 236 D πορεύονται πορείαν.

Generally with acc. of person only ; as, Eur. Hipp. 755 ἐπόρευσας
ἄνασσαν.

135. *Πράττω, -ομαι (to exact from) : Hdt. III. 58 ἐπρῆξαν τάλαντα αὐτούς : Pass. Thuc. VIII. 5 ὑπὸ βασιλέως πεπραγμένος
τοὺς φόρους. So πράττεσθαι : Æsch. Ag. 705 πρασσομένα ἀτίμωσιν
τίοντας : cf. Demosth. p. 845, 2. So εἰσπράττειν : Demosth. p.
1227, 9 εἰσπρᾶξαι τὰ ἀναλώματα τούτου.

Acc. of exaction only : Demosth. p. 1484, 2 τὰ ὀφειλόμενα εἰσπράξας.
Acc. of patient only : Id. p. 518, 9 τοὺς ὑπερημέρους εἰσπραττόντων.

136. Προΐστημι (to pray) : Soph. Elect. 1370 προὔστην πολλά σε.

137. Προκαλέομαι : Arist. Ach. 652 προκαλοῦνται εἰρήνην ὑμᾶς :
cf. Thuc. II. 72, &c. Plat. Euth. p. 5 A.

With acc. of proposition only : Plat. Legg. p. 855 E ἃ προκαλούμεθα.
Acc. of person only : Il. η, 39 προκαλέσσεται τινά.

138. Προσπίτνω (to entreat) : Eur. Phœn. 293 προσπίτνω ἕδρας σε.

139. Ῥέζω : Il. γ, 354 ῥέξαι κακὰ ξεινοδόκον : cf. Od. β, 72.

With acc. of act only.—(See §. 560. 1.) With acc. of patient, with εὖ,
καλῶς, or κακῶς ; as, Plat. Legg. p. 642 C ἡμᾶς οὐ καλῶς ἢ κακῶς ἔρεξε.

140. Σαίνω : Soph. Œ. C. 321 σαίνει φαιδρά με.

141. Σιτίζω : Xen. Symp. IV. 9 σιτίσαντες σκόροδα τοὺς ἀλεκτρυ-
όνας : Midd. Theocr. IV. 16 πρῶκας σιτίζεται.

142. Σκυλεύω : Hes. Sc. 468 σκυλεύσαντες τεύχεα Κύκνον.

Acc. of spoils only : Hdt. IX. 80 ἐσκύλευον ψέλια. Acc. of person
only : Eur. Phœn. 1426 ἐσκύλευέ νιν.

143. Στένω : Eur. Orest. 1368 στένω μέλος σε.

Acc. of lament only : Soph. Ant. 1249 πένθος στένει. Acc. of patient
only : Id. Œ. C. 1710 σε στένει.

144. Στερέω : Plat. Legg. p. 958 E στερείτω ὅσα (ἡ γῆ φέρει) τὸν
ζῶντα : Pass. Æsch. Eur. Hel. 95 βίον στερείς. So ἀποστερέω :
Demosth. p. 839, 13 ἀποστερεῖ τὴν τιμήν με : cf. Id. p. 54, 50. Pass.
Thuc. VI. 91 τὰς προσόδους ἀποστερήσονται. So ἀπορραίω Od. a,
403, and ἐρημόω Pind. Pyth. III. 97.

145. Στίζω : Hdt. VII. 233 ἔστιζον στίγματα βασιλήϊα.

146. Συλάω : Il. χ, 368 συλήσω τεύχεά σε : cf. Il. π, 500, &c.

Acc. of spoils only : Il. η, 78 τεύχεα συλήσας. Acc of person only : κ,
343 τινὰ συλήσων. So ἀποσυλάω : Æsch. P. V. 171 τιμὰς ἀποσυ-
λᾶται.

147. Ταράσσω : Soph. Œ. R. 483 ταράσσει δεινά (ταράγματα) με.

Acc. of thing only : Soph. Ant. 794 νεῖκος ταράξας, so πόλεμον, στάσεις. Acc. of patient only : Eur. Hipp. 969 ταράξῃ φρένα.

148. Τάσσω : Æsch. Theb. 284 τάξω τὸν μέγαν τρόπον (= τάξιν) ἀντηρέτας: Pass. Eur. Suppl. 657 δεξιὸν τεταγμένους κέρας (= τάξιν): Plat. Legg. p. 878 D ταττέσθω τάξεις: Æschin. p. 381, 7.

Generally with acc. of patient only.

149. Τεύχω (to do to) : Soph. Phil. 1173 τί σε τεύξω;

Generally acc. of act only.

150. Τίθημι : Plat. Rep. p. 479 C θήσεις καλλίονα θέσιν αὐτά.

Generally acc. of patient only.

151. Τιμάω : Xen. Cyr. VII. 3, 4 τιμήσω τἆλλα σε : Pass. Soph. Œ. R. 1223 μέγιστα τιμώμενοι: cf. Æsch. Choeph. 293.

Generally acc. of patient only.

152. * Τιμωρέομαι : Eur. Cycl. 691 ἐτιμωρησάμην φόνον σε : cf. Id. Alc. 733. Xen. Anab. VII. 1, 25.

Acc. of wrong only : Soph. El. 341 πάντα τιμωρουμένης. Acc. of patient : Eur. Hec. 882 τὸν ἐμὸν φονέα τιμωρήσομαι. With dat. to avenge : Soph. El. 391 πατρὶ τιμωρούμενοι.

153. Τίνομαι : (See §. 585.)

154. Τρέφω : Hdt. II. 2 τρέφειν τροφὴν παιδία : cf. Plat. Rep. p. 414 D. Eur. Elect. 509. Pass. Plat. Menex. 238 A. ἄριστα τρέφεται.

Generally with acc. of patient only.

155. Τύπτω : Ant. p. 127, 13 τύπτειν τὰς πληγὰς τὸν ἄνδρα : Pass. Arist. Nub. 972 τυπτόμενος πολλάς. So Il. ω, 421 ἕλκεα ὅσσ' ἐτύπη.

Generally with acc. of patient only.

156. Ὑβρίζω : Soph. El. 613 ὕβρισε τοιαῦτα τὴν τεκοῦσαν : cf. Eur. Elect. 264. Pass. Eur. Bacch. 1296 ὕβριν ὑβρισθείς.

Acc. of insult only : Eur. Bacch. 247 ὕβρεις ὑβρίζειν: Hdt. III. 118 ὑβρίσας τάδε : Soph. Aj. 954 ἐφυβρίζει θυμόν = θυμοῦ ὕβριν.—(See Ellendt ad voc.) Acc. of patient only : Eur. Phœn. 1638 ὑβρίζεις πατέρα.

157. Ὑμνέω : Eur. Bacch. 72 ὑμνήσω τὰ νομισθέντα Διόνυσον.

Acc. of song only.—(See §. 566. 3.) Acc. of patient : Eur. Iph. Taur. 1457 Ἄρτεμιν ὑμνήσουσι.

158. Ὑπομιμνήσκω : Thuc. VII. 64 ὑπομιμνήσκω τάδε Ἀθηναίους : Plat. Rep. p. 530 C, &c.

Acc. of thing only : Plat. Rep. p. 4, 427 E ἀληθῆ ὑπόμιμνήσκεις. Of person only : Id. Phil. p. 31 C ὑπομίμνησκε ἡμᾶς.

159. Φιλέω : Od. ο, 245 φιλεῖ φιλότητα ὅν.

Generally with acc. of person only.

160. Φοβέω : Thuc. VI. 11 ἐκφοβοῦσι ὃ ἡμᾶς.

Elsewhere with acc. of person only.

161. Χορτάζω : Plat. Rep. p. 372 D ἐχόρταζες ταῦτα αὐτάς : Pass.
Crat. in ap. Athen. 99 E χορταζόμενοι γάλα.

Acc. of patient only : Hes. Op. 454 βόας χορτάζειν.

162. Ψέγω (to find fault with) : Plat. Phædr. p. 243 C ψέγομεν
ἃ τὸν ἔρωτα.

Acc. of fault : Plat. Gorg. p. 483 τοὺς ψόγους ψέγουσιν : Id. Pol. p. 402
A τὰ αἰσχρὰ ψέγοι.   Acc. of person blamed : Id. Prot. p. 346 C σε ψέγω.

163. Ψεύδω : Eur. Protes. Fr. 6 ψεύδουσι πολλὰ βροτούς : Soph.
Œ. C. 1145 ἐψευσάμην οὐδέν σε :   Pass. Æsch. Choeph. 748
πολλὰ ψευσθεῖσα.

Acc. of falsehood only : Plat. Legg. p. 663 ψεῦδος ἐψεύσατο : Id. Hipp.
Min. p. 366 B πολλὰ ψεύδονται.   Acc. of person only : Soph. Œ. C. 634
ψεύσουσί με.

164. *Ὠφελέω : Eur. Alc. 878 ὠφελεῖς οὐδὲν τὰν νέρθεν : cf. Plat.
Phil. p. 58 C, &c.   Pass. Id. Rep. p. 346 C ὠφελίαν ὠφελοῦνται.

Acc. of benefit alone : Plat. Gorg. p. 520 B οὐδὲν ὠφελήκασι.   Acc. of
patient only : Id. Legg. p. 763 D ὠφελῇ τὴν πόλιν.

Obs. 1. Besides these, many verbs expressing the notions given in
§. 582. are found with a double accus. case in later writers; as, Achill.
Tat. I. 25 ῥαπίζει με πληγήν : and several verbs which in good writers are
found with an accus. of the patient only, are, in later writers, found with
an accus. of the cognate notion [a].

Obs. 2. Several verbs, though they are not found with both accusatives
of the cognate notion and the patient together, yet are found with each
separately ; as, νικάω σε, and νικάω νίκην.—(See Lexicons.)

Obs. 3. We must not confound with these classes of double accus. those
verbs compounded with a preposition, where one of the accusatives depends
on the preposition ; as, προσαυδᾶν τί τινα.

Use of Accusative to define the part—Σχῆμα καθ' ὅλον καὶ μέρος.

§. 584. 1. We must not confuse with the real double accus. case, the
accusatives of the patient and the part, which are frequently found with
all pure transitive verbs ; the part being put in apposition to the patient,
of which it is only a more accurate expression : Il. λ, 240 τὸν δ' ἄορι
πλῆξ' αὐχένα, λῦσε δὲ γυῖα : Ibid. 250 κρατερόν ῥα ἑ πένθος ὀφθαλμοὺς ἐκάλυψε, κασιγνήτοιο πεσόντος : Il. π, 465 τὸν βάλε νείαιραν κατὰ
γαστέρα : Ibid. 468 ὁ δὲ Πήδασον οὔτασεν ἵππον ἔγχεϊ δεξιὸν ὦμον : Il.

---

[a] Lobeck de Fig. Etym. Opusc. 501, sqq.

ρ, 83 Ἕκτορα δ' αἰνὸν ἄχος πύκασε φρένας ἀμφιμελαίνας : Il. ζ. 355 εἰ μάλιστα πόνος φρένας ἀμφιβέβηκεν : Il. γ, 438 μή με, γύναι, χαλεποῖσιν ὀνείδεσι θυμὸν ἔνιπτε : Od. a, 64 ποῖόν σε ἔπος φύγεν ἕρκος ὀδόντων : Od. κ, 161 τὸν (ἔλαφον) δ' ἐγὼ ἐκβαίνοντα κατ' ἄκνηστιν μέσα νῶτα πλῆξα : Il. ψ, 47 ἐμὲ ἵξετ' ἄχος κραδίην : Il. υ, 44 Τρῶας δὲ τρόμος αἰνὸς ὑπήλυθε γυῖα ἕκαστον : Il. υ, 406 ὡς ἄρα τόν γ' ἐρυγόντα λίπ' ὀστία θυμὸς ἀγήνωρ : Soph. Œ. C. 113 καὶ σύ μ' ἐξ ὁδοῦ πόδα κρύψον.

Obs. Sometimes we find the part substituted for the patient, which is put in the dat. commodi ; as, Il. ε, 493 δάκε δὲ φρένας Ἕκτορι μῦθος.

2. This accus. continues also in passive verbs, though the former patient has now become the subject of the verb, as it defines the exact operation of the affection or state, signified by the passive verb : Hdt. VI. 38 πληγεὶς τὴν κεφαλὴν πελέκεϊ : Id. VII. 69 Ἀράβιοι δὲ ζειρὰς ἐπεζωσμένοι ἦσαν — Αἰθίοπες δὲ παρδαλέας τε καὶ λεοντέας ἐναμμένοι : Ibid. 90 τὰς μὲν κεφαλὰς εἰλίχατο μίτρῃσι οἱ βασιλῆες αὐτέων : Xen. Anab. IV. 5, 12 ἐλείποντο δὲ καὶ τῶν στρατιωτῶν οἵτε διεφθαρμένοι ὑπὸ τῆς χιόνος τοὺς ὀφθαλμούς, οἵτε ὑπὸ τοῦ ψύχους τοὺς δακτύλους τῶν ποδῶν ἀποσεσηπότες : Eur. Helen. 1212 λύπῃ σὰς διέφθαρσαι φρένας : Id. Med. 8 Μήδεια — ἔρωτι θυμὸν ἐκπλαγεῖσ' Ἰάσονος (ἐκπλήττειν θυμὸν ἔρωτι) : Demosth. p. 247, 11 ἑώρων τὸν Φίλιππον — τὸν ὀφθαλμὸν ἐκκεκομμένον. So Eur. Hec. 1018 τυφλοῦμαι φέγγος : Arist. Ach. 18 ἐδήχθην τὰς ὀφρῦς : Eur. Phœn. 267 ὡπλισμένος χεῖρα : Æsch. V. P. 362 τυπεὶς ἐξεβροντήθη σθένος : Eur. Hipp. 199 λέλυμαι μελέων σύνδεσμα.

Construction of τίσασθαι.

§. 585. Τίνειν in the active voice means, to pay ; τίνειν τῷδε ταῦτα, to pay back, satisfaction, penalty, &c. In the middle voice, τίνομαι ταῦτα is properly, to pay satisfaction to myself—to take satisfaction for : Eur. Or. 322 αἵματος τινύμεναι δίκην : then if the equivalent notion of the injury received is substituted, it takes the sense of punishing, τινύμεναι φόνον ; thence it adopts two independent senses of punishing and avenging : Eur. Elect. 599 φονέα τισαίμην πατρός : Id. Troad. 1034 τίσαι δάμαρτα ; and then from these two senses it has a double accus. of the person punished, and the satisfaction : Eur. Med. 261 ἀντιτίσασθαι δίκην πόσιν ; or the act substituted for the satisfaction ; as, Od. o, 236 ἐτίσατο ἔργον ἀεικὲς ἀντίθεον Νηλῆα : so also τιμωρέομαι.

DATIVE.

§. 586. 1. As the Genitive expresses the antecedent, the Accusative the coincident, so the Dative expresses the *consequent* notions of the verb.

α. Those notions which are in the order of things and of conception, are actually consequent on the notion of the verb, as receiving is consequent on giving.

β. The accidents, accessories, circumstances, instruments, which are not conceived of as necessary causes or conditions, nor yet as coincident parts of the verbal notion, but which follow thereon in the speaker's mind, as notions of minor importance, are afterthoughts and additions to the essential parts of the objective sentence.

2. Hence it follows, that many uses of the dative depend on the place occupied by the notion in the speaker's mind. The same notion may be in the genitive, accusative, or dative, as it is conceived of as the cause, or the cognate notion, or the accident or instrument of the verbal notion.—Thus τέρπεσθαι τοῦδε, to derive pleasure from this (cause) ; τέρπεσθαι τοῦτο (sc. χάρμα), to be pleased in this (cognate notion) ; τέρπεσθαι τούτῳ, to feel pleasure produced by this (instrument).

3. The dative therefore will be treated of under the following heads :—

   a. 1. Transmissive Dative.
      2. Dativus Commodi.
      3. Dative of Reference.
      4. Dativus Incommodi.
   β. 5. Circumstantial or Modal Dative.
      6. Local Dative.
      7. Temporal Dative.
      8. Instrumental Dative.

a. Transmissive Dative.

§. 587. 1. Those verbs which express or imply the *transmission* or *communication of any thing, word, good or evil, pleasure or pain,* &c. which some person receives, or is conceived of as receiving, have a dative of that person ; the notion of receiving being consequent upon giving, as giving is antecedent to receiving : δέχομαι τόδε σοῦ : δίδωμι τοῦτό σοι.

2. It is clear from what has been said on the accusative, that the thing transmitted, the gift, aid, benefit, pleasure, pain, harm, &c. is in the accusative of the cognate notion.

§. 588. 1. Verbs of *giving, granting, indulging, offering, paying,* &c. or verbs which imply these notions : διδόναι, δωρεῖσθαι, τίνειν, χαρίζεσθαι, ὀπάζειν, παρέχειν, νομίζειν, to pay customarily ; διδόναι τί τινι, δωρεῖσθαί &c. τι τινί : Xen. Hell. III. 1, 8 χαρίσασθαι ταῖς παλλακίσιν αὐτοῦ : Il. ρ, 547 ἴριν θνατοῖσι τανύσσῃ Ζεύς : Hdt. II. 50 νομίζουσι ἥρωσι οὐδέν. So Arist. Av. 192 θύσωσιν θεοῖς : Il. η, 314 βοῦν ἱέρευσεν — Κρονίωνι : so ἐπιψηφίζειν τινί = ψῆφον διδόναι. So also καλεῖν τινι ὄνομα, Plato.

2. So words which denote that something is *allowed, allotted,*

decreed to any one, awaits any one : ἐστί μοι—ἔξεστί μοι; πεπρωμένον,
εἱμαρμένον, μοῖρά μοι ἐστί: Æsch. Ag. 1149 ἐμοὶ δὲ μίμνει
σχισμός. (but see §. 606. 3.)

Obs. So after substantives : Soph. Trach. 668 τῶν σῶν ꞌΗρακλεῖ δωρη-
μάτων : Arist. Nub. 305. (Chor.) οὐρανίοις θεοῖς δωρήματα : Thuc. V.
35 τὴν τῶν χωρίων ἀλλήλοις οὐκ ἀπόδοσιν : Plat. Apol. p. 30 D τὴν τοῦ
θεοῦ δόσιν ὑμῖν. This is very rarely found in the orators.

3. So verbs of *giving a share to, sharing with, transferring to,
selling,* &c.: μεταδίδοναι, ἀπονέμειν, κοινοῦν, κοινοῦσθαι, κοινωνεῖν &c.:
Xen. Mem Socr. II. 7, 1 μεταδιδόναι τοῖς φίλοις: Plat. Legg.
p. 906 D αὐτοῖς τῶν ἀδικημάτων τις ἀπονέμῃ : Ibid. p. 805 D μὴ
μετεχουσῶν ἀνδράσι γυναικῶν : Arist. Pax 1254 πώλει βαδίζων
αὐτὰ τοῖς Αἰγυπτίοις.

§. 589. 1. Verbs of *saying, conversing with,* or *conveying by words,
praying, swearing to,* &c. or which imply these notions : εἰπεῖν, λέγειν,
χρᾶν, διαλέγεσθαι, λαλεῖν, ληρεῖν, εὔχεσθαι, ἀπεύχ., κατεύχ., προσεύχ.,
ἀρᾶσθαι, καταρᾶσθαι, λαλεῖν, &c. τινί: Il. γ, 296 εὔχοντο θεοῖς:
Hdt. I. 55 οἱ χρᾷ τάδε : Soph. Aj. 509 θεοῖς ἀρᾶται : Eur. Alc. 714
ἀρᾷ γονεῦσιν; Il. β, 433 τοῖς ἄρα μύθων ἦρχε. So Æsch. Ag.
1570 δαίμονι ὅρκους θεμένα. So Arist. Nub. 1006 ὁπόταν πλάτανος πτελέᾳ ψιθυρίζῃ.

2. So after certain verbs which imply the notion of *praying* or
wishing, we find a dative of the person to whom the prayer or wish
is transmitted : Il. o, 369 πᾶσι θεοῖσιν χεῖρας ἀνίσχοντες (but
371 χεῖρ' ὀρέγων εἰς οὐρανὸν ἀστερόεντα): Od. ι, 294 ἡμεῖς δὲ κλαί-
οντες ἀνεσχέθομεν Διὶ χεῖρας: Il. κ, 16 ἕλκετο χαίτας ὑψόθ'
ἐόντι Διί: so ἀναβλέπω τινι.

Obs. In prose this relation is more commonly signified by ἐπί, πρός, εἰς,
with accus.

3. So verbs of *conveying reproach, praise, blame, counsel, orders,* &c.
to any one: ὀνειδίζειν, λοιδορεῖσθαι, μέμφεσθαι, ἐπιτιμᾶν, ἐγκαλεῖν,
ἐπικαλεῖν, ἐπιπλήσσειν, ἐπαινεῖν, κελεύειν, προστάσσειν, ἐπιτέλλεσθαι poet., ἐντέλλεσθαι, ἐπιστέλλειν, παραινεῖν, παρεγγυᾶν : Hdt.
III. 142 τὰ τῷ πέλας ἐπιπλήσσω : Plat. Legg. p. 706 D λοιδορεῖ
αὐτῷ ꞌΑγαμέμνονα : Isocr. p. 5 C ἄλλοις ἐπιτιμῴης. And analogously καταγελᾶν τινι: Hdt. III. 37 πολλὰ τῷγάλματι κατεγέλασε : Ibid. 38 οὐ γὰρ ἂν ἱροῖσί τε καὶ νομαίοισι ἐπεχείρησε
καταγελᾶν: cf. 155. IV. 79. VII. 9. (but with the more
usual construction with gen. V. 68.): Thuc. IV. 61 οὐ τοῖς ἄρχειν
βουλομένοις μέμφομαι, ἀλλὰ τοῖς ὑπακούειν ἑτοιμοτέροις οὖσιν : Il.
α, 295 ἄλλοισιν δὴ ταῦτ' ἐπιτέλλεο: Il. β, 50 αὐτὰρ ὁ κηρύκεσσι
λιγυφθόγγοισι κέλευσεν κηρύσσειν ἀγορήνδε καρηκομόωντας ꞌΑχαι-

ούς : Æsch. Ag. 28 εὐφημοῦντα τῇδε λαμπάδι : Eur. Alc. 701 ὀνειδίζω φίλοις. So Il. κ, 58 σημαίνει φυλάκεσσι.

Obs. 1. So in Pindar ὀτρύνειν : Pyth. IV. 40 ἡ μάν μιν ὤτρυνον θαμὰ λυσιπόνοις θεραπόντεσσιν φυλάξαι [a]. So Homer : ἐποτρύνειν ἑτάροισιν, ἱππεῦσιν, which generally have an accus. in the sense of urging.

Obs. 2. So μέμφεσθαι, to blame, without the notion of transmission of blame, has an accus. So βασκαίνειν : so ἐπιπλήττειν, to blame : Il. ψ, 580. Plat. Protag. p. 327 A ἐπίπληττε τὸν μὴ καλῶς αὐλοῦντα.

Obs. 3. The dative with κελεύειν, in Attic prose, is very doubtful, except in the sense of admonishing. The accus. and infin. is the common Attic construction.

Obs. 4. Even after substantives, such as παρακέλευσις, we find the dat., especially in Plato. So Symp. p. 182 D ἡ παρακέλευσις τῷ ἐρῶντι παρὰ πάντων θαυμαστή. So also Æsch. Theb. 891 διαλλακτῆρι ἀμεμφία. So Æsch. P. V. 444 μέμψιν ἀνθρώποις ἔχων.

§. 590. So verbs of *mingling oneself with, uniting oneself to, joining, holding converse with, clinging to,* or *causing others so to do* ; &c. as, ὁμιλεῖν, μίγνυσθαι, καταλλάττεσθαι, to be reconciled ; διαλλάττεσθαι, ξυναλλάττεσθαι, καταλύειν, ξενοῦσθαι. Ὁμίλει τοῖς ἀγαθοῖς ἀνθρώποις : Hdt. III. 131 ὁ δὲ Δημοκήδης—Πολυκράτεϊ ὡμίλησε : Id. VI. 21 πόλιες γὰρ αὗται μάλιστα—ἀλλήλῃσι ἐξεινώθησαν : Eur. Phœn. 673 ξυνῆψε γᾷ φίλᾳ νιν.

So adjectives, &c. expressing these notions—φίλος, κοινός, συγγενής, and many words compounded with σύν and μετά,—μίγδα, σύμμιγα— κοινωνία : Il. θ, 437 μίγδ' ἄλλοισι θεοῖσι : Hdt. VI. 58 σύμμιγα τῇσι γυναιξὶ κόπτονταί τε τὰ μέτωπα, καὶ κ. τ. λ. : Plat. Soph. p. 252 D ἀλλήλοις ἐπικοινωνία : Ibid. p. 257 A ἔχει κοινωνίαν ἀλλήλοις ἡ τῶν γενῶν φύσις : Ibid. p. 260 E τὴν κοινωνίαν αὐτῶν τῷ μὴ ὄντι κατίδωμεν.

Obs. 1. This relation is also expressed by σύν and μετά : so also ὁμιλεῖν ἐν, μετά, παρά τινι : so πρός and εἰς with the accus., ὁμιλεῖν, κοινοῦν εἴς τινα : and still oftener, κοινοῦσθαι εἴς τινα ; καταλλάττεσθαι πρός τινα Xen. So Demosth. p. 71, 21 οὐ γὰρ ἀσφαλεῖς ταῖς πολιτείαις (*rebus publicis*) αἱ πρὸς τοὺς τυράννους ὁμιλίαι.

Obs. 2. Hence the familiar interrogative phrase τί ἔστι (not ἐστὶ) μοί τινι ; what have I to do with ; the later prose writers add κοινόν. So also the phrase πρᾶγμά μοι καί τινι ἐστι : Hdt. V. 33 σοὶ δὲ καὶ τούτοισι τοῖσι πράγμασι τί ἔστι ; Arist. Eq. 1028 τί γάρ ἐστ' Ἐρεχθεῖ καὶ κολοιοῖς καὶ κυνί ; Dem. p. 320 μηδὲν εἶναί σοι καὶ Φιλίππῳ πρᾶγμα. So τί δέ μοι or σοι ; *quid ad me attinet ?* followed by an Infin., often in Arist., and even in Hesiod : Th. 35 ἀλλὰ τίη μοι ταῦτα περὶ δρῦν ἢ περὶ πέτρην ;

Obs. 3. On κοινός with gen., see §. 519.

§. 591. Verbs of *communicating* or *applying, giving up oneself to, adopting,* &c. : χράομαι, τρέπομαι, &c. : Eur. Med. 347 κείνους δὲ κλαίω ξυμφορᾷ κεχρημένους : Ibid. 240 ὅτῳ μάλιστα χρήσεται

a Dissen ad loc.

ξυνεννέτη : Hdt. III. 17 χρᾶσθαι τῷ ὕδατι: so χρᾶσθαι τῷ θεῷ, to apply to, or consult the god. So θέσθαι ταύτῃ τῇ ψήφῳ, γνώμῃ, or ταύτῃ θέσθαι.

Obs. In the construction of νομίζειν with the dat., such as Hdt. IV. 117 γλώσσῃ νομίζειν : Ibid 63 ὑσί : Thuc. III. 82 εὐσεβείᾳ νομίζειν, there seems to be a notion supplied by the mind, of χρῆσθαι, or some such word, to which νομίζειν added the notion of "habitually," "being accustomed," and was thence substituted for it.

§. 592. 1. So verbs of *going towards, meeting, approaching, falling on, causing to approach to, sending, pouring*, &c : ἀντᾶν, ἀντιᾶν, ἀντιάζειν, ἀπαντᾶν, ὑπαντιάζειν, πλησιάζειν, πελάζειν, ἐμπελάζεσθαι, ἐγγίζειν, &c. πέμπειν : Il. μ, 374 ἐπειγομένοισι δ' ἵκοντο : Thuc. I. 13 Σαμίοις ἦλθεν : Eur. Med. 91 πέλαζε μητρί : Id. Orest. 1433 νήματα θ' ἵετο πέδῳ : Soph. Trach. 101 δισσαῖσιν ἀπείροις κλιθείς : Il. ε, 709 λίμνῃ κεκλιμένος Κηφισίδι : Eur. Orest. 88 δεμνίοις πέπτωχ' ὅδε : Æsch. Choeph. 87 τύμβῳ χεοῦσα : so παρεῖναί τινι : Il. η, 218 προκαλέσσατο χάρμῃ : so πέμπειν τί τινι.

2. So adverbs, ἐγγύς, πέλας, ἀγχοῦ, when they express not so much the position of the objects in relation to something else, (see §. 526.) as their approach to something else.

§. 593. 1. Verbs of *giving oneself up to the guidance of, following, obeying, yielding, trusting*, &c. ; as, ἕπεσθαι, ἀκολουθεῖν, ὀπηδεῖν poet., ὁμαρτεῖν poet., διαδέχεσθαι — πείθεσθαι — ὑπακούειν, ἀπειθεῖν : Od. ι, 7 sq. οἵ ῥα (sc. Κύκλωπες) θεοῖσι πεποιθότες ἀθανάτοισιν οὔτε φυτεύουσιν χερσὶν φυτόν, οὔτ' ἀρόωσιν : Hdt. III. 88 Ἀράβιοι δὲ οὐδαμᾶ κατήκουσαν ἐπὶ δουλοσύνῃ Πέρσῃσι : Id. VI. 86, 5 Λευτυχίδης —, ὡς (*quum*) οἱ οὐδὲ οὕτω ἐσήκουον οἱ Ἀθηναῖοι, ἀπαλλάσσετο : Ibid. 14 ἐναυμάχεον ἀνηκουστήσαντες τοῖσι στρατηγοῖσι : Xen. Cyr. I. 1, 2 πάσας τοίνυν τὰς ἀγέλας ταύτας ἐδοκοῦμεν ὁρᾶν μᾶλλον ἐθελούσας πείθεσθαι τοῖς νομεῦσιν ἢ τοὺς ἀνθρώπους τοῖς ἄρχουσι : Ibid. VIII. 6, 18 τῷ ἡμερινῷ ἀγγέλῳ (φασί) τὸν νυκτερινὸν διαδέχεσθαι : Plat. Rep. p. 400 D εὐλογία ἄρα καὶ εὐαρμοστία καὶ εὐσχημοσύνη καὶ εὐρυθμία εὐηθείᾳ ἀκολουθεῖ. So Soph. Aj. 670 χειμῶνες ἐκχωροῦσιν εὐκάρπῳ θέρει, ἐξίσταται δὲ νυκτὸς αἰάνης κύκλος τῇ λευκοπώλῳ ἡμέρᾳ.

2. So also adjectives, adverbs, and sometimes substantives, expressing these notions ; as, ἀκόλουθος,—ως, ἀκολουθητικός, ἑπομένως, διάδοχος, διαδοχή, ἑξῆς, ἐφεξῆς : Eur. Andr. 803 κακὸν κακῷ διάδοχον : Xen. Cyr. I. 4, 17 ἡ διαδοχὴ τῇ πρόσθεν] φυλακῇ ἔρχεται ἐκ πόλεως : Demosth. p. 45. extr. (στρατεύεσθαι) ἐκ διαδοχῆς ἀλλήλοις : Plat. Cratyl. p. 399 D δοκεῖ τούτοις ἐξῆς εἶναι : Arist. Lys. p. 634 ἐξῆς Ἀριστογείτονι.

Obs. With verbs of "following." ἕπεσθαι, ὁμαρτεῖν, ὀπηδεῖν, ἀκολουθεῖν, this dative is sometimes more clearly defined by σύν, μετά, ἅμα, expressing two persons being together; or, ὄπισθεν, ἐπί, expressing the position of the person following: Od. η, 165 (Ζεὺς) ὅσθ' ἱκέτῃσιν ἅμ' αἰδοίοισιν ὀπηδεῖ: cf. Hesiod. Theog. 80. Id. Op. et D. 230 οὐδέποτ' ἰθυδίκῃσι μετ' ἀνδράσι λιμὸς ὀπηδεῖ: Hdt. I. 45 ὄπισθε δὲ εἵπετό οἱ ὁ φονεύς: Thuc. IV. 124 ξὺν Χαλκιδεῦσιν ἠκολούθουν: Xeu. Cyr. V. 2, 35 σὺν τοῖς νικῶσιν ἕπονται: Ibid. V. 5, 37 ἐπὶ μὲν τῷ Κυαξάρῃ οἱ Μῆδοι εἵποντο.—Ὁμαρτεῖσθαι with acc.: Il. μ, 400 τὸν δ' Αἴας καὶ Τεῦκρος ὁμαρτήσανθ'. So Pind. Nem. X. 37 ἕπεται δέ, Θεαῖε, ματρώων πολύγνωτον γένος, *adscendit ad illustre genus;* after the analogy of verbs of " going;" so in late Epic writers: ἕπεσθαί τινα.

§. 594. 1. So verbs of *agreeing with,* &c.: ὁμολογεῖν, συναινεῖν, ἐπαινεῖν &c.: Il. σ, 312 Ἕκτορι μὲν γὰρ ἐπήνησαν: so ὁμολογεῖν, συναινεῖν τί τινι.

Obs. Ἐπαινεῖν, to praise, has naturally an accusative.

2. Hence verbs, adjectives, and adverbs of *coincidence, equality, similarity,* &c.: ἐοικέναι, εἴδεσθαι poet., ὁμοιοῦν, ὁμοιοῦσθαι, ὅμοιος Attic, ὁμοῖος Ionic, ὁμοίως, ἴσος, ἴσως, ἐξ ἴσου, ἐν ἴσῳ, ὁμῶς Hom. &c. Ionic prose, ἐμφερής, παραπλήσιος, παραπλησίως, ὁ αὐτός, *idem,* ὡσαύτως espec. Ionic, ἅμα—ἀδελφός—and many compounds of ὁμοῦ, σύν, μετά: ὁμόγλωσσος, ὁμώνυμος, συμφωνεῖν, σύμφωνος, ξυνῳδός: Il. π, 716 ἀνέρι εἰσάμενος αἴζηῷ τε κρατερῷ τε, Ἀσίῳ: Od. α, 105 εἰδομένη ξείνῳ, Ταφίων ἡγήτορι, Μέντῃ: Soph. Antig. 644 τὸν φίλον τιμῶσιν ἐξ ἴσου πατρί: Hdt. VI. 69 ἦλθέ μοι φάσμα εἰδόμενον Ἀρίστωνι: Id. I. 123 τὰς πάθας τὰς Κύρου τῇσι ἑωυτοῦ ὁμοιούμενος, *comparans:* Id. III. 37 ἔστι γὰρ τοῦ Ἡφαίστου τὤγαλμα τοῖσι Φοινικηΐοισι Παταϊκοῖσι ἐμφερέστατον: Ibid. 48 κατὰ δὲ τὸν αὐτὸν χρόνον τοῦ κρατῆρος τῇ ἁρπαγῇ γεγονός: Id. II. 67 ὡς δ' αὔτως τῇσι κυσὶ οἱ ἰχνευταὶ (*Ichneumons*) θάπτονται: Xen. Cyr. I. 3, 4 ἡμᾶς μὲν γὰρ ἄρτος καὶ κρέας εἰς τοῦτο (sc. τὸ ἐμπλησθῆναι) ἄγει· ὑμεῖς δὲ εἰς μὲν τὸ αὐτὸ ἡμῖν σπεύδετε: Id. VII. 1, 2 ὡπλισμένοι δὲ πάντες ἦσαν οἱ περὶ τὸν Κῦρον τοῖς αὐτοῖς τῷ Κύρῳ ὅπλοις. (After the analogy of ὁ αὐτός we find εἰς with dat.: Il. γ, 238 τώ μοι μία γείνατο μήτηρ: Il. τ, 293 τρεῖς τε κασιγνήτους, τούς μοι μία γείνατο μήτηρ: Plat. Legg. p. 745 τὸ πρὸς τῇ πόλει μέρος τῷ πρὸς τοῖς ἐσχάτοις εἷς κλῆρος:) Demosth. p. 34, 21 τὸν ὁμώνυμον ἐμαυτῷ.

Obs. 1. So in the attributive construction after substantives: ὁμοιότης, ὁμοίωσις, ξυμφωνία: Od. γ, 49 ὁμηλικίη ἐμοὶ αὐτῷ: Plat. Rep. p. 401 D ὥσπερ αὔρα φέρουσα ἀπὸ χρηστῶν τόπων ὑγίειαν, καὶ εὐθὺς ἐκ παίδων λανθάνῃ εἰς ὁμοιότητά τε καὶ φιλίαν καὶ ξυμφωνίαν τῷ καλῷ λόγῳ ἄγουσα: Id. Phæd. p. 109 A ὁμοιότης ἑαυτῷ.

Obs. 2. Οἷος and τοιοῦτος are not found with a dative, though there are passages in which they seem to be: thus—Hes. Op. 314 δαίμονι δ' οἷος

ἦσθα τὸ ἐργάζεσθαι ἄμεινον—δαίμονι depends on ἄμεινον.   In many passages
an attraction takes place, as in Plat. Rep. p. 349 D τοιοῦτος ἄρα ἐστὶν
ἑκάτερος αὐτῶν, οἷσπερ ἔοικεν [a] : Ibid. p. 350 C ὡμολογοῦμεν, ᾧ γε ὅμοιος
ἑκάτερος εἴη, τοιοῦτον καὶ ἑκάτερον εἶναι, for τοιοῦτον ἑκάτερον εἶναι, οἷος ᾧ ὅμοιος
εἴη.   So Phæd. p. 92 B οὐ γὰρ δὴ ἁρμονία γέ σοι τοιοῦτόν ἐστιν, ᾧ ἀπεικάζεις, i. e. τοιοῦτόν ἐστιν, οἷον ᾧ ἀπεικάζεις.

Obs. 3. On gen. with ὅμοιος see §. 519.

Obs. 4. Instead of the construction with the dative, we sometimes find
the conjunction καί, whereby the two similar or equal things are placed as
it were parallel to each other.   This is more usual in prose than in poetry.
So τέ in Homer : Il. ε, 442 οὔποτε φῦλον ὁμοῖον ἀθανάτων τε θεῶν, χαμαὶ
ἐρχομένων τ᾽ ἀνθρώπων : Hdt. I. 94 Λυδοὶ δὲ νόμοισι μὲν παραπλησίοισι χρέωνται καὶ Ἕλληνες : Id. IV. 58 νόμος δὲ τοῖσι Λακεδαιμονίοισι κατὰ τῶν βασιλήων τοὺς θανάτους ἐστὶ ὡὐτὸς καὶ τοῖσι βαρβάροισι τοῖσι ἐν τῇ Ἀσίῃ.   So
ἐν ἴσῳ, ἴσα, ὁμοίως, ὡσαυτώς, κατὰ τωὐτὰ καί &c. : Plat. Ion. p. 500 D οὐχ
ὁμοίως πεποιήκασι καὶ Ὅμηρος.   This construction is also in Latin : *similis
et, ac, atque.*   We also find, especially in Attic prose writers, the comparative particles, ὡς, ὥσπερ, with ἴσος, ὁ αὐτός : Demosth. p. 119, 33 τὸν
αὐτὸν τρόπον, ὥσπερ κ. τ. λ.

3. Verbs, &c. of *being suitable to, proper for,* &c.; as, πρέπειν, ἁρμόττειν, προσήκειν followed by an infin., πρεπόντως, ἀπρεπῶς, εἰκός ἐστι,
εἰκότως : Xen. Cyr. VII. 5, 37 βασιλεῖ ἡγεῖτο πρέπειν : cf. V. 3,
47.   Plat. Apol. p. 36 D τί οὖν πρέπει ἀνδρὶ πένητι—; Id. Phædr.
p. 233 B πολὺ μᾶλλον ἐλεεῖν τοῖς ἐρωμένοις ἢ ζηλοῦν αὐτοὺς προσήκει : Id. Gorg. p. 479 E τούτῳ προσήκειν ἀθλίῳ εἶναι.   Here
also seem to belong the impersonal verbs δεῖ and χρή : Eur. Ion
1316 τοῖσι δ᾽ ἐνδίκοις ἱερὰ καθίζειν—ἐχρῆν : and ἀναγκαῖον &c.

4. So verbs, &c. of *pleasing :* ἁνδάνειν, ἀρέσκειν, ἀρέσκεσθαι,
ἐξαρέσκεσθαι : Hdt. IX. 79 μὴ ἅδοιμι, τοῖσι ταῦτα ἀρέσκεται, *iis
non acceptus ero, quibus hæc placent :* Ibid. Σπαρτιήτησι ἀρεσκό-
μενος : So Id. VI. 129 ἑωυτῷ μὲν ἀρεστῶς ὀρχέετο, *sibi placens.*
So Od. δ, 777 ἤραρεν ἡμῖν.

Obs. 1. This might perhaps be considered as the dativus commodi.

Obs. 2. Ἀρέσκειν, ἐπαρέσκειν, are also found with an accusative [b].

Dativus Commodi et Incommodi.

§. 595. From the dative expressing the notion of transmission,
it is also used when any good or evil is received by any one ; so
that all verbs *may* have this dative, when the action of the verb is
to be represented as *done for the harm, or benefit, guidance, instruction, sake, of any one.*   But there are also certain verbs whose sense
implies a *dativus commodi,* others a *dativus incommodi.*

---

[a] Stallb. ad loc.   [b] Elm. Med. 12.

Dativus Commodi.

§. 596. 1. Verbs of *helping, favouring,* &c. : ἀρήγειν, ἀμύνειν, ἀλέξειν, ἀλαλκεῖν, τιμωρεῖν, βοηθεῖν, ἐπικουρεῖν, et simil. ; as ἀπολογεῖσθαι, λυσιτελεῖν (λύειν τέλη poet.), ἐπαρκεῖν, χραισμεῖν, and many compounds of σύν, συμφέρειν, *conducere,* συμπράσσειν &c. — Χραισμεῖν τινι ὄλεθρον Homer : Eur. Or. 512 ἀμυνῶ δ', ὅσον περ δυνατός εἰμι, τῷ νόμῳ : Ibid. 912 ('Ορέστης) ἠθέλησε τιμωρεῖν πατρί, κακὴν γυναῖκα κάθεον κατακτανών : Plat. Apol. p. 28 C εἰ τιμωρήσεις Πατρόκλῳ τῷ ἑταίρῳ τὸν φόνον. So Il. ε, 433 οἱ αὐτὸς ὑπείρεχε χεῖρας : Æsch. Pers. 839 τοῖς θανοῦσι πλοῦτος οὐδὲν ὠφελεῖ. So Eur. Med. 813 ξυλλαμβάνουσα νόμοις βροτῶν : cf. Arist. Pax 417. So Soph. Œ. C. 1435 σφῷν δ' εὐοδοίη Ζεύς.

Obs. 1. Many of these verbs, such as ἀμύνω, ἀρήγω &c., signify properly, " to ward off ;" and with the dat. comm., " for the benefit of some one," τινί : " the benefit resulting to him" being considered rather than "the retreat of the enemy," τινός : Eur. Med. 1276 ἀρῆξαι φόνον τέκνοις. So ἀμύνειν τινί τι, and τινός, so εἴργειν τινί τι. Thence from this being the prominent notion, they assumed the independent notion of " *helping,*" but retained the construction with the dat., as it was on this that the notion of helping depended.

Obs. 2. So with substantives : Æsch. Prom. 501 ἀνθρώποισιν ὠφελήματα : Hdt. VII. 169 ἐκ τῶν Μενελέῳ τιμωρημάτων : Plat. Alc. p. 116 A τὴν ἐν τῷ πολέμῳ τοῖς φίλοις βοήθειαν : Id. Phileb. p. 58 C χρείαν τοῖς ἀνθρώποις. So τί πλέον ἐστί μοι ; Soph. Antig. 268 οὐδὲν ἦν ἐρευνῶσι πλέον.

2. So verbs of *serving as a slave, ministering to ;* the slave was considered as existing only for the benefit of his master : δουλεύειν, ὑπηρετεῖν, λατρεύειν, θητεύειν τινί : Eur. Med. 588 τῷδ' ὑπηρετεῖς λόγῳ.

So when the ruler or guide is supposed to act for the benefit of those under him : ἡγεῖσθαι, ἡγεμονεύειν τινί, to be his guide—for his benefit. So στρατηγῶν Eur. Andr. 325 : Hdt. VI. 72. So στρατηλατεῖν τινί—χορηγεῖν τινί.

Obs. 3. Ὑπηρετεῖν is used with a genitive, when the relation between master and servant, with a dative when the benefit of the master, is considered.

3. So adjectives which express kindly feelings or actions towards any one : φίλος, εὔνους, ὠφέλιμος—τινί. So subst. : Thucyd. V. 5 περὶ φιλίας τοῖς 'Αθηναίοις, so εἰρήνην τινί &c.

Obs. 4. The assistance, or that wherein it consists, is in the accus. ; as, βοηθεῖν δίκαια (βοηθήματά) τινι. So Soph. Aj. 439 ἔργα ἀρκέσας.

§. 597. So possessive and attributive notions, which usage arises from the thing possessed being conceived of as being for the owner's benefit or harm : dat. commodi aut incommodi. So after εἶναι and γίγνεσθαι : Τῷ Κύρῳ ἦν μεγάλη βασιλεία : Od. ι, 112 τοῖσιν (Κύκλωψι) δ' οὔτ' ἀγοραὶ βουληφόροι, οὔτε θέμιστες (sc. εἰσίν): Ibid. 366 Οὖτις ἔμοιγ' ὄνομα (sc. ἐστι) : Plat. Rep. p. 329 E τοῖς γὰρ πλουσίοις πολλὰ παραμύθιά φασιν εἶναι. So by an ellipse of εἶναι : Demosth. ὁρῶν ὑμῖν χιλίους μὲν ἱππότας. So Arist. Vesp. 240 ὡς ἔσται Λάχητι ννννί : Id. Ach. 446 Τηλέφῳ δ' (εἴη) ἀγὼ φρονῶ. So Hdt. II. 145 Ἡρακλεῖ εἶναι ἔτεα.

Obs. 1. So also substantives—but mostly only the personal pronouns : Il. μ, 174 Ἕκτορι γάρ οἱ θυμὸς ἐβούλετο κῦδος ὀρέξαι : Hdt. I. 31 οἱ δέ σφι βόες : Id. VII. 10, 8 κτεινέσθων οἱ ἐμοὶ παῖδες : Xen. Cyr. V. 1, 27 ἡ γάρ μοι ψυχή (Schneider wrongly, ἐμὴ ψ.), ἔφη, οὐχ ὡς βουλεύσουσα παρεσκεύασται : Plat. Rep. p. 431 B ἀπόβλεπε τοίνυν, ἦν δ' ἐγώ, πρὸς τὴν νέαν ἡμῖν πόλιν, this new city of ours : Id. Theæt. p. 210 B ἡ μαιευτικὴ ἡμῖν τέχνη. So Eur. Hec. 1276 ὁ Θρῃξὶ μάντις : Id. Orest. 363 ὁ ναυτίλοισι μάντις. So Æsch. Theb. 423 τῶν ἀνδράσιν φρονημάτων : Hdt. I. 92 ἀναθήματα Κροίσῳ : Thuc. VII. 50 ἡ τοῖς Συρακοσίοις στάσις : So Hdt. II. 17 τῶν ὁδῶν τῷ Νείλῳ.

Obs. 2. We find two datives in some cases, where we should expect a dative and a genitive. So personal pronouns are used seemingly for possessive ; as, Pind. Ol. VIII. 83 ἐνέποι κεν Καλλιμάχῳ λιπαρὸν κόσμον Ὀλυμπίᾳ, ὅν σφι Ζεὺς γένει ὤπασεν, their race : Ibid. II. 14 εὔφρων ἄρουραν ἔτι πατρίαν σφίσιν κόμισον λοιπῷ γένει, i. e. *serva regionem paternam futuro generi eorum* [a] : Eur. Heracl. 63 βούλει πόνον μοι τῇδε προσθεῖναι χερί. Though the real construction may be that the personal pronoun is in the dativus commodi, aut incommodi, while the other depends on the transmissive notion of the verb.

Obs. 3. In the σχῆμα καθ' ὅλον καὶ μέρος, we find, most commonly in Epic, the dative used in a seemingly possessive sense, where we should expect the genitive : Il. λ, 11 (ξ, 151) Ἀχαιοῖς δὲ μέγα σθένος ἔμβαλ' ἑκάστῳ καρδίῃ. In Il. λ, 447 τῷ δὲ μεταστρεφθέντι μεταφρένῳ ἐν δόρυ πῆξεν ὤμων μεσσηγύς, μεταστρεφθέντι depends on the verb, μεταφρένῳ is local.

§. 598. The dativus commodi is, as has been said above, joined with all verbs, to express that something is done, *for the sake, pleasure, honour, guidance, protection, safety, benefit, furtherance,* &c. of some person or thing. This is especially the case with δέχομαι, δέχεσθαι τινί τι, to receive it at his hands ; to please ; as a compliment to him ; for his sake, or benefit, &c. (σχῆμα Σικελικόν) : Il. ο, 87 Θέμιστι δὲ καλλιπαρήῳ δέκτο δέπας : Il. ρ, 207 οὔτι μάχης ἐκ νοστήσαντι δέξεται Ἀνδρομάχη κλυτὰ τεύχεα Πηλείωνος : Od. π, 40 ὡς ἄρα φωνήσας οἱ ἐδέξατο χάλκεον ἔγχος : Soph. Elect. 442 αὐτῇ, at her hands, at her request. So Æsch. Choeph. 762 πατρί. So Pind. So Arist. Ran. 1229 ἐγὼ πρίωμαι τῷδ', to serve him. So the dative

[a] Dissen ad loc.

μοί, for my sake, at my request, *prithee:* Eur. Hec. 535 δέξαι χοάς μοι τάσδε. So Hdt. VI. 86 σὺ δή μοι καὶ τὰ χρήματα δέξαι: Arist. Ach. 60 περὶ εἰρήνης πρυτανεύσητέ μοι: Id. Eccl. 726 ἵν' ἀποβλέπωμαι καὶ λέγωσί μοι (when I look); so κλῦθί μοι, *prithee* hear. So also Xen. Hell. III. 1, 15 Φαρναβάζῳ ἔσωζον αὐτάς: Soph. Œ. R. 1402 οἷ' ἔργα δράσας ὑμῖν: Eur. Hec. 460 ἀνέσχε πτόρθους Λατοῖ: Arist. Ran. 1134 ἐγὼ σιωπῶ τῷδ'; must I hold my tongue to please this fellow? So Il. ρ, 242 ἐμῇ κεφαλῇ περιδείδια: Il. ρ, 313 Ἱπποθόῳ περιβάντα: Il. κ, 16 πολλὰς ἐκ κεφαλῆς προθελύμνους ἕλκετο χαίτας ὑψόθ' ἐόντι Διΐ: Il. α, 159 τιμὴν ἀρνύμενοι Μενελάῳ: Ibid. 284 αὐτὰρ ἔγωγε λίσσομ' Ἀχιλῆϊ μεθέμεν χόλον: Il. τ, 290 ὥς μοι δέχεται κακὸν ἐκ κακοῦ αἰεί. — Δικάζειν τινί, as Hdt. VIII. 61 ἐπιψηφίζειν ἄπολι ἀνδρί.—Προαιδεῖσθαί τινι, ob *acceptum beneficium alicui reverentiam ostendere*; often in Hdt., as III. 140. — Φιλοφρονεῖσθαί τινι for the more usual τινά, to be gracious to any one: Soph. Aj. 1045 Μενέλαος, ᾧ δὴ τόνδε πλοῦν ἐστείλαμεν: Eur. Med. 6 ἀνδρῶν ἀρίστων, οἳ τὸ πάγχρυσον δέρος Πελίᾳ μετῆλθον: Eur. Heracl. 453 πέφευγεν ἐλπὶς τῶνδέ μοι σωτηρίας (cf. Xen. Œcon. II. 14 ἀποφεύγειν μοι): Demosth. p. 126, 59 Φιλιστίδης μὲν ἔπραττε Φιλίππῳ, *in Philippi gratiam res administrabat.* So Eur. Alc. 685 σαυτῷ γὰρ ἔφυς: Id. Her. 2 πέφυκε τοῖς πέλας: Æsch. Choeph. 728 ἐφοδεῦσαι ἀγῶσιν. So in acts done in honour of the gods; as, κωμάζειν, Pind. ὀρχεῖσθαι τοῖς θεοῖς, στεφανοῦσθαι θεῷ: Æsch. Ag. 586 θεοῖς λάφυρα ταῦτα—ἐπασσάλευσαν: Hdt. VI. 138 Ἀρτέμιδι ὁρτὴν ἄγειν: Id. II. 40 ἔπην προνηστεύσωσι τῇ Ἴσι: Arist. Av. 501 προκυλινδεῖσθαι τοῖς ἰκτίνοις: cf. Id. Thesm. 107. Hdt. IV. 34 τῇσι παρθένοισι κείρονται.

Obs. So with substantives; as, Æsch. Cho. 232 μέλημα δώμασιν: Plat. Rep. p. 607 A ὕμνους θεοῖς καὶ ἐγκώμια τοῖς ἀγαθοῖς ᵃ: Id. Symp. p. 194 D τοῦ ἐγκωμίου τῷ ἔρωτι: Id. Legg. p. 653 D ἑορτῶν ἀμοιβαὶ τοῖς θεοῖς: Demosth. p. 1313 ἱερωσύνη τῷ Ἡρακλεῖ.

Dative expressing reference to.

§. 599. 1. So when any thing is spoken of with especial reference to any person, as if he were interested and in some sort benefited therein, the *dativus commodi* is used; as, Hdt. I. 14 ἀληθῆ δὲ λόγῳ χρεωμένῳ οὐ Κορινθίων τοῦ δημοσίου ἔστιν ὁ θησαυρός, *recte æstimanti non est thesaurus Corinthiacus:* Id. VII. 143 ἐς τοὺς πολεμίους τῷ θεῷ εἰρῆσθαι τὸ χρηστήριον, συλλαμβάνοντι κατὰ τὸ ὀρθόν, ἀλλ' οὐκ ἐς Ἀθηναίους, *si quis recte intelligat.*—παραλιπόντι Thuc. II. 51.—συνελόντι, συντεμόντι εἰπεῖν, and without εἰπεῖν, especially in definitions of place: Hdt. VI. 33 ἀπὸ δὲ Ἰωνίης ὑπαλλασσόμενος ὁ ναυτικὸς στρατὸς τὰ ἐπ' ἀριστερὰ ἐσπλέοντι

ᵃ Stallb. ad loc.

τοῦ Ἑλλησπόντου αἴρεε πάντα [a] : Id. I. 51 ὁ μὲν—ἐκέετο ἐπὶ δεξιὰ ἐσ ιόντι: Id. III. 90 ἀπὸ δὲ Ἑλλησποντίων τῶν ἐπὶ δεξιὰ ἐσ π λ έοντι. So ὧδε, οὕτως ἔχειν τινι. So Soph. Œ. R. 616 καλῶς ἔλεξεν εὐλαβουμένῳ πεσεῖν.

2. And frequently, especially in Ionic, a participle is added expressing the circumstances, which make the person more or less interested in the action, &c. : Od. τ, 192 τῷ δ' ἤδη δεκάτη ἢ ἑνδεκάτη πέλεν ἠὼς οἰχο- μένῳ: Hdt. IX. 10 θυομένῳ δ' οἱ ἐπὶ τῷ Πέρσῃ ὁ ἥλιος ἀμαυρώθη : Id. I. 78 ταῦτα ἐπιλεγομένῳ Κροίσῳ τὸ προαστεῖον ὀφίων πᾶν ἐνεπλήσθη : Id. VI. 21 ποιήσαντι Φρυνίχῳ—καὶ διδάξαντι ἐς δάκρυα ἔπεσε τὸ θέατρον: Eur. Ion 1187 ἐν χεροῖν ἔχοντι δὲ σπονδάς — βλασφημίαν τις οἰκετῶν ἐφθέγξατο, spoke, not " to him," but " when he had the libation ready." So ἐκποδών : Eur. Orest. 547 ἀπελθέτω—ἐκ π ο δ ὼ ν ἡμ ῖ ν, out of our way : Id. Phœn. 40 τυράννοις ἐκποδὼν μεθίστασο.

3. Here also belongs the peculiar usage of certain participles of wishing, hoping, &c. such as βουλομένῳ, ἡδομένῳ, ἀσμένῳ, ἐλπομένῳ, generally with εἶναι and γίγνεσθαι: Il. η, 7 ὡς ἄρα τὰ Τρώεσσιν ἐελδομένοισι φανήτην : Il. ξ, 108 ἐμοὶ δέ κεν ἀσμένῳ εἴη: Od. γ, 228 οὐκ ἂν ἔμοιγε ἐλπο- μένῳ τὰ γένοιτο: Od. φ, 209 γιγνώσκω δ', ὡς σφῶιν ἐελδομένοισιν ἱκάνω οἷοισι δμώων: Æsch. P. V. 24 ἀσμένῳ δέ σοι—νὺξ ἀποκρύψει φάος: Id. Choeph. 517 θέλοντι—ἐμοὶ φράσον: Id. 461 εὐχομένοις ἂν ἔλθοι: Eur. Ion 642 ὁ εὐκτὸν ἀνθρώποισι κἂν ἄκουσιν ᾖ: Soph. Œ. C. 1505 ποθοῦντι προύφάνης: Hdt. IX. 46 ἡδομένοισιν ἡμῖν οἱ λόγοι γεγόνασι: Thuc. II. 3 τῷ πλήθει τῶν Πλαταιέων οὐ βουλο- μένῳ ἦν τῶν Ἀθηναίων ἀφίστασθαι: Id. VI. 46 τῷ Νικίᾳ προσδεχο- μένῳ ἦν τὰ περὶ τῶν Ἐγεσταίων : Plat. Rep. p. 358 D ἀλλ' ὅρα, εἴ σοι βουλομένῳ (sc. ἐστὶν), ἃ λέγω. This is not a Latin idiom, though it is sometimes adopted from the Greek ; as, Sall. Jug. 4 uti militibus exæ- quatus cum imperatore labos volentibus esset : Tac. Agric. 18 Quibus bellum volentibus erit.

4. So also the dative is used to signify that the thing is spoken of with especial reference to the circumstances, &c. of some one : Soph. Œ. C. 20 μακρὰν γάρ, ὡς γέροντι, προύστάλης ὁδόν : Id. Antig. 1161 Κρέων γὰρ ἦν ζηλωτός, ὡς ἐμοί, ποτε: Ibid. 904 καίτοι σ' ἐγὼ ἐτίμησα τοῖς φρονοῦ- σιν εὖ: Eur. Med. 580 ἐμοὶ γὰρ ὅστις ἄδικος ὢν σοφὸς λέγειν πέφυκε πλείστην ζημίαν ὀφλισκάνει, i. e. meo enim judicio [b] : Plat. Soph. p. 226 C ταχεῖαν, ὡς ἐμοί, σκέψιν ἐπιτάττεις.— So ὡς γ' ἐμοὶ κριτῇ (which may also be expressed by ὡς γ' ἐμοὶ χρῆσθαι κριτῇ): Plat. Rep. p. 536 C ὡς γ' ἐμοὶ ἀκροατῇ,—ὡς ἐμοὶ ῥήτορι. So Xen. Vect. V. 2 ὡς ἐμῇ δόξῃ.

Obs. Ὡς is used merely to mark that it is spoken of subjectively, only as conceived by the speaker.

§. 600. 1. So also after verbs which signify being, or seeming to be, a dative is used of the person, with reference to whom the thing is, or seems to be, in the opinion or estimation of. So δοκεῖ μοι τόδε, it appears to me to be so : Il. γ, 164 οὔτι μοι αἰτίη ἐσσί, θεοί νυ μοι αἴτιοι εἰσιν. So after adjectives without any verb : Hdt. III. 88 γάμους τοὺς πρώτους Πέρσῃσι, matrimonia ex Persarum judicio nobilissima : Æsch. Ag. 352 θεοῖς ἀμ- πλάκητός : Arist. Pax 1179 θεοῖσιν οὗτοι κἀνδράσιν ῥιψάσπιδες: Soph. Aj. 1358 τοιοίδε μέντοι φῶτες ἔμπληκτοι βροτοῖς: cf. Id. Œ. R. 40 κράτιστον πᾶσι. Very commonly in the phrase—ἄξιός εἰμί τινός τινι: or alone—ἄξιός εἰμί τινι, I am, in reference to such a person, worthy, &c.: Id. Œ. C. 1446 ἀνάξιαι γὰρ πᾶσίν ἐστι δυστυχεῖν (omnium *judicio) :* Eur. Hec. 309 ἡμῖν δ' Ἀχιλλεὺς ἄξιος τιμῆς, γύναι, *ita de nobis meritus est Achilles, ut nobis dignus honore videatur* [a] : Arist. Ach. 8 ἄξιον γὰρ Ἑλλάδι : Ibid. 205 ἄξιον γὰρ τῇ πόλει : Xen. M. S. I. 1, pr. ἄξιός ἐστι θανάτου τῇ πόλει : Ibid. §. 62 ἐμοὶ μὲν δὴ Σωκράτης τοιοῦτος ὢν ἐδόκει τιμῆς ἄξιος εἶναι τῇ πόλει μᾶλλον ἢ θανάτου : cf. §. 64. Plat. Symp. p. 185 B οὗτός ἐστιν ὁ τῆς Οὐρανίας θεοῦ ἔρως καὶ οὐράνιος καὶ πολλοῦ ἄξιος καὶ πόλει καὶ ἰδιώταις.

2. The datives of the I. and II. personal pronouns are very frequently thus used, to express that the person has some peculiar interest in the action—that it has some especial reference to him—the nature of which, and consequently the proper translation of it, must be determined from the context. This appears to have arisen from the simple and emphatic usages of every day speech : Od. ι, 42 ὡς μήτις μοι ἀτεμβόμενος κίοι ἴσης, as far as I am concerned : Xen. Cyr. I. 3, 2 ὁρῶν δὴ τὸν κόσμον τοῦ πάππου, ἐμβλέπων αὐτῷ, ἔλεγεν (ὁ Κῦρος)· Ὦ μῆτερ, ὡς καλός μοι ὁ πάππος : Ibid. 15 ἢν δέ με καταλίπῃς ἐνθάδε, καὶ μάθω ἱππεύειν, ὅταν μὲν ἐν Πέρσαις ὦ, οἶμαί σοι ἐκείνους τοὺς ἀγαθοὺς τὰ πεζικὰ ῥᾳδίως νικήσειν : Plat. Rep. p. 389 D τί δέ; σωφροσύνης ἄρα οὐ δεήσει ἡμῖν τοῖς νεανίαις; (where we must not join ἡμῖν with νεανίαις) : Ibid. p. 391 D μηδὲ ἡμῖν ἐπιχειρεῖν πείθειν τοὺς νέους : Id. Theæt. p. 143 E ἀκοῦσαι πάνυ ἄξιον, οἵῳ ὑμῖν τῶν πολιτῶν μειρακίῳ ἐντετύχηκα : Id. Soph. p. 216 E τοῦ μὲν ξένου ἡμῖν ἡδέως ἂν πυνθανοίμην : Id. Protag. p. 328 A εἰ ζητοῖς, τίς ἂν ἡμῖν διδάξεις τοὺς τῶν χειροτεχνῶν υἱεῖς αὐτὴν ταύτην τὴν τέχνην, — οὐ ῥᾴδιον οἶμαι εἶναι τούτων διδάσκαλον φανῆναι.—The III. personal pronoun is less frequently thus used : Plat. Rep. p. 343 A εἰπέ μοι, ἔφη ὁ Σωκράτης, τίτθη σοι ἔστι ; Τί δαί ; ἦν δ' ἐγώ· οὐκ ἀποκρίνεσθαι χρῆν μᾶλλον ἢ τοιαῦτα ἐρωτᾶν ; Ὅτι τοί σε, ἔφη, κορυζῶντα περιορᾷ καὶ οὐκ ἀπομύττει δεόμενον, ὅς γε αὐτῇ οὐδὲ πρόβατα οὐδὲ ποιμένα γιγνώσκεις, to her shame. "*Nimirum dativus significat, nutricem et ipsam in hujus turpitudinis societatem venire* [b]." So Soph. Aj. 1128 τῷδε δ' οἴχομαι, as far as he is concerned.

3. So we sometimes find a dative placed at the beginning of a sentence, of the person to whom the notion of the sentence refers, whether for his good or harm, or to denote that it holds good with regard to him. So Æsch. Ag. 1149 ἐμοὶ δὲ μίμνει σχισμός : Plat. Phileb. p. 253 τῷ τὸν τοῦ φρονεῖν ἑλομένῳ βίον—οὐδὲν ἀποκωλύει.

Dativus Incommodi.

§. 601. 1. Verbs expressing *hostility, vying with, opposing, fighting with, contending, standing up against in deeds or words, angry with, differing from,* &c. which express the notion of the speaker's *wishing* for the other person's harm : στῆναι poet., ὑποστῆναι and ὑφίστασθαι, μένειν poet., ἐρίζειν, μάχεσθαι, μάρνασθαι poet., πολεμεῖν — ἀγωνίζεσθαι, δικάζεσθαι, λαγχάνειν δίκην, ἀμφισβητεῖν — ἀείδειν, *cantando cum aliquo certare,* &c. ; χολοῦσθαι, νεμεσᾶν, θυμοῦσθαι, μενεαίνειν, κοτεῖν, χαλεπαίνειν, σπέρχεσθαι, (Ion.) &c. ; φθονεῖν, βασκαίνειν : Il. φ, 600 αὐτῷ—ἔστη, stood up against him : Il. δ, 509

μηδ' εἴκετε χάρμης (gen. separ.) 'Αργείοις: Æsch. Ag. 1150 μένειν
τινί.—ὑποστῆναι, ὑφίστασθαι πολεμίῳ, ξυμφοραῖς Thucyd. : Il. a, 277
ἐριζέμεναι βασιλῆϊ: Od. θ, 188 Φαίηκες. ἐδίσκεον ἀλλήλοισιν : Theocr.
I. 136 κῇ ὀρέων τοὶ σκῶπες ἀηδόσι δαρύσαιντο : Id. VIII. 6 λῆς μοι
ἀεῖσαι; Id. V. 22 ἀλλά γε τοι διαείσομαι : so ἐπαίρεσθαι, αἱρεσθαι δόρυ
τινί : Od. a, 20 ὁ δ' ἀσπερχὲς μ ε ν έ α ι ν ε ν ἀντιθέῳ 'Οδυσῆϊ : Hdt.
V. 33 ἐ σ π έ ρ χ ε τ ο τῷ 'Αρισταγόρῃ : Demosth. p. 30, 5 ἠ ν ώ χ λ ε ι
ἡμῖν ὁ Φίλιππος : Eur. Hipp. 426 ἁ μ ι λ λ ᾶ σ θ α ι βίῳ.

2. So adjectives; as, ἀντίος, ἐναντίος, ἐχθρός, πολέμιος, διάφορος,
διάφωνος : Hdt. VI. 77 ἴξοντο ἀ ν τ ί ο ι τοῖσι Λακεδαιμονίοισι :
Demosth. p. 72. princ. βασιλεὺς γὰρ καὶ τύραννος ἅπας ἐχθρὸς ἐλευθερίᾳ καὶ νόμοις ἐ ν α ν τ ί ο ς : so also ἐμποδών τινι.

Obs. 1. On these adjectives with the genitive see §. 525.
Obs. 2. Sometimes a substantive expressing these notions is followed by
a dative : Eur. Iph. A. 183 'Ηρᾳ Παλλάδι τ' ἔριν : Plat. Rep. p. 444 B
ἐ π α ν ά σ τ α σ ι ν μέρους τινὸς τῷ ὅλῳ : Thuc. I. 73 ἀ ν τ ι λ ο γ ί α ν τοῖς
ὑμετέροις συμμάχοις.
Obs. 3. So also διαβάλλεσθαί τινι, to quarrel ; and transitive, διαβάλλειν
τινά τινι, to make a person quarrel with another. Plat. Phæd. p. 67 E
εἰ γὰρ διαβέβληνται μὲν πανταχῇ τῷ σώματι, infensi sunt : Arist. ὡστίζεσθαί
τινι : Il. φ, 499 πληκτίζεσθαί τινι : Ibid. 225 πειρηθῆναί τινι, to measure
one's strength against a person : Thuc. I. 73 προκινδυνεῦσαι τῷ βαρβάρῳ.
So sometimes in Latin : Virg. Ecl. V. 8 tibi certet Amyntas : Ibid. VIII.
55 certent et cygnis ululæ.
Obs. 4. Sometimes this relation is defined by μετά : Il. ρ, 148 μάρνασθαι
μετ' ἀνδράσι, and it is also expressed by πρὸς and ἐπί with accus. So in
Latin : pugnare in aliquem : Cic. pro Ligar. 4 contra ipsum Cæsarem est
congressus.

§. 602. 1. So sometimes verbs of *taking away*, &c. ; the harm
and annoyance received by the patient being the point especially
in the speaker's mind : Od. a, 9 αὐτὰρ ὁ τοῖσιν ἀ φ ε ί λ ε τ ο νόστιμον ἦμαρ.

Obs. Sometimes the dative is *commodi* instead of *incommodi :* Xen. Cyr.
VII. 1, 44 τὸ μὲν ἐπὶ Κροῖσον συστρατεύειν ἀφελεῖν σφίσιν ἐδεήθησαν : Ibid.
II. 26 μάχας δέ σοι καὶ πολέμους ἀφαιρῶ.

2. Under the dativus incommodi is to be classed the construction βλάπτειν τινί : Hdt. III. 16 ᾧ λ υ μ α ι ν ό μ ε ν ο ι : so λωβᾶ-
σθαί τινι.

3. So also the dativus commodi et incommodi, is joined with all
sorts of substantives and adjectives, which, either from their own
meaning or the context, are conceived to *have a good or evil tendency*, to bring *good*, or *harm*, or *hinderance*, to any person or thing,
with or without εἶναι and γίγνεσθαι, such as χρήσιμον, ἀγαθόν, ῥάδιον,
χαλεπόν, ἐναντίον, καλόν, αἰσχρόν, φίλον, ἐχθρόν ἐστί μοι τι : Il. a,
188 Πηλείωνι δ' ἄχος γένετο : Eur. Or. 782 ὄκνος γὰρ τοῖς φίλοις

κακὸν μέγα (ἐστί).   So Soph. Antig. 571 κακὰς ἐγὼ γυναῖκας υἱέσι στυγῶ. So Æsch. Ag. 1115 ἀκόρετος γένει: Id. Choeph. 471 δώμασιν ἔμμοτον: Id. Supp. 148 ῥύσιος διωγμοῖς, against: Id. Theb. 996 κακὰ δώμασι καὶ χθονί, πρὸ πάντων δ᾽ ἐμοί: Eur. Hipp. 188 χερσὶν πόνος: Thuc. III. 10 οὐκ ἐπὶ καταδουλώσει τοῖς Ἀθηναίοις—ἀλλ᾽ ἐπ᾽ ἐλευθερώσει τοῖς Ἕλλησι: Ibid. 24 ἀναίρεσιν νεκροῖς. So Soph. Aj. 717 μετεγνώσθη θυμῶν Ἀτρείδαις. So Il. α, 284 χόλον Ἀχιλῆϊ.

β. *Circumstantial or Modal Dative.*

§. 603. The *circumstances*, or *accidents*, or *accessories* of any thing, are put in the dative.

1. The *circumstances* in which any thing took place; and when there are several, more than one dative may be used: Od. ξ, 253 ἐπλέομεν Βορέῃ ἀνέμῳ ἀκραέϊ καλῷ: Il. α, 418 τῷ σε κακῇ αἴσῃ τέκον ἐν μεγάροισιν: Soph. Trach. 1229 τὸ γάρ τοι μεγάλα πιστεύσαντ᾽ ἐμοὶ σμικροῖς (*quum res parvœ sunt*) ἀπιστεῖν, τὴν πάρος ξυγχεῖ χάριν: Id. Aj. 178 κλυτῶν ἐνάρων ψευσθεῖσα δώροις εἴτ᾽ ἐλαφηβολίαις: Hdt. VI. 139 ἐπεὰν βορέῃ ἀνέμῳ αὐτημερὸν νηῦς ἐξανύσῃ ἐκ τῆς ὑμετέρης ἐς τὴν ἡμετέρην, τότε παραδώσομεν: Thuc. I. 84 μόνοι—εὐπραγίαις τε οὐκ ἐξυβρίζομεν καὶ ξυμφοραῖς ἧσσον ἑτέρων εἴκομεν.

Obs. 1. Generally ἐπί is used to define this more accurately; as, ἐπὶ τούτῳ.

2. The *mode* or *manner* wherein any thing takes place is in the dative: Il. γ, 2 Τρῶες μὲν κλαγγῇ τ᾽ ἐνοπῇ τ᾽ ἴσαν, ὄρνιθες ὥς: Hesiod. Op. 91 αἱ (νόσοι) δ᾽ ἐπὶ νυκτὶ αὐτόματοι φοιτῶσι, κακὰ θνητοῖσι φέρουσαι, σιγῇ, ἐπεὶ φωνὴν ἐξείλετο μητίετα Ζεύς: Xen. Cyr. I. 2, 2 βίᾳ εἰς οἰκίαν παριέναι. So δίκῃ, ἐπιμελείᾳ, δημοσίᾳ (sc. ὁδῷ), ἰδίᾳ (ὁδῷ), πέζῃ (ὁδῷ), κοινῇ (ὁδῷ), together; τρόπῳ τοιῷδε Hdt. VI. 39 κομιδῇ, carefully; σπουδῇ, properly, with trouble, *œgre* ;—ἄλλῃ, ταύτῃ, ἅμα (Dor. ἀμῇ, v. ᾿ΑΜΟΣ, *unus, unâ viâ*) together; διχῇ, *duplici modo*; εἰκῇ, *frustra*; ἡσυχῇ. So τῷ ὄντι — τῇ ἀληθείᾳ — τῷ λόγῳ, τῷ ἔργῳ &c. So Eur. Alc. 712 μιᾷ ψυχῇ ζῆν.

Obs. 2. Σύν is sometimes joined hereto; as σὺν βίᾳ.

§. 604. 1. The *accessories*—that whereby any thing is accompanied. This is very common when the substantive is accompanied by αὐτός, "*very*," "*itself*," "*and all*," as this gives the notion of an accompaniment or an accessory: Il. ψ, 8 ἀλλ᾽ αὐτοῖς ἵπποισι καὶ ἅρμασιν ἆσσον ἰόντες Πάτροκλον κλαίωμεν: Il. ι, 541 πολλὰ

δ' ὅγε προθέλυμνα χαμαὶ βάλε δένδρεα μακρὰ αὐτῆσιν ῥίζῃσι καὶ
αὐτοῖς ἄνθεσι μήλων : Soph. Aj. 27 ἐφθαρμένας εὑρίσκομεν
λείας ἁπάσας αὐτοῖς ποιμνίων ἐπιστάταις : Eur. Med. 164 ὅν
(sc. *Jasonem*) ποτ' ἐγὼ νύμφαν τ' ἐσίδοιμ' αὐτοῖς μελάθροις
διακναιομένους (*cum ipsa domo pessumdatos*) : Hdt. III. 45 τὰ τέκνα
καὶ τὰς γυναῖκας ὁ Πολυκράτης ἐς τοὺς νεωσοίκους συνειλήσας εἶχε
ἑτοίμους—ὑποπρῆσαι αὐτοῖσι νεωσοίκοισι : Ibid. 126 ἀπο-
κτείνας δέ μιν ἠφάνισε αὐτῷ ἵππῳ : Id. VI. 32 τὰς πόλιας ἐνεπίμ-
πρασαν αὐτοῖσι τοῖσι ἱροῖσι : Ibid. 93 καί σφεων νέας
τέσσερας αὐτοῖσι ἀνδράσι εἷλον : Xen. Cyr. I. 4, 8 πολλοὺς
γὰρ (ἔλεγον) ἤδη αὐτοῖς τοῖς ἵπποις κατακρημνισθῆναι.   Here
also seem to belong, Hes. Theog. 742 φέροι πρὸ θύελλα θυέλλῃ :
Soph. Œ. R. 175 ἄλλον δ' ἂν ἄλλῳ προσίδοις, one after another :
Eur. Phœn. 1510 φόνῳ φόνος, in which construction ἐπί is
more usual.

Obs. 1. This dative is sometimes more accurately defined by σύν : Il. ξ.
498 Πηνέλεως — αὐχένα μέσσον ἔλασσεν, ἀπήραξεν δὲ χαμᾶζε αὐτῇ σὺν
πήληκι.

2. So very frequently with verbs of *coming, going ;* that whereby
the person comes or is accompanied is in the dative ; generally
collective nouns, such as στρατῷ, στόλῳ, πλήθει, or their comple-
ments, as στρατιώταις &c., in Homer very frequently : πέτετο πνοιῆς
ἀνέμοιο : Hdt. V. 99 οἱ Ἀθηναῖοι ἀπικέατο εἴκοσι νηυσί : Id. VI. 95
ἔπλεον ἑξακοσίῃσι τριήρεσι ἐς τὴν Ἰωνίην : Thuc. I. 102 Ἀθηναῖοι ἦλθον πλήθει οὐκ ὀλίγῳ : Id. II. 21 ἐσβαλὼν — στρατῷ
Πελοποννησίων : Xen. Cyr. I. 4, 17 αὐτὸς δὲ τοῖς ἵπποις προσ-
ελάσας πρὸς τὰ τῶν Μήδων φρούρια.

Obs. 2. Σύν and ἅμα are sometimes added to this dative : Hdt. VI. 118
Δᾶτις δὲ πορευόμενος ἅμα τῷ στρατῷ εἰς τὴν Ἀσίην — εἶδε ὄψιν ἐν τῷ ὕπνῳ : cf.
Ibid. 98.   So also in the Homeric ἅμα πνοιῆς ἀνέμοιο : Od. ω, 193 ἢ ἄρα
σὺν μεγάλῃ ἀρετῇ ἐκτήσω ἄκοιτιν, a wife accompanied by.   So
Plaut. Trin. IV. 5, 4 *amicus cum magna fide.*

Local Dative.

§. 605. 1. The accident of *place* is put in the dative, except
when, occasionally in poetry, the place is conceived of as the antecedent condition of the action of the verb.—(See §. 522. 1.)   So
that all verbs *may* be followed by a dative, when it is wished to define
the place : Il. ι, 663 αὐτὰρ Ἀχιλλεὺς εὗδε μυχῷ κλισίης εὐπήκτου :
so ρ, 36 μυχῷ θαλάμοιο : Il. π, 158 (λύκοι) ἔλαφον κεραὸν μέγαν
οὔρεσι δῃώσαντες δάπτουσιν : Ibid. 483 (πίτυν) οὔρεσι τέκτονες

ἄνδρες ἐξέταμον: 595 Ἑλλάδι οἰκία ναίων: Il. ρ, 473 τεύχεα δ'
Ἕκτωρ αὐτὸς ἔχων ὤμοισιν ἀγάλλεται Αἰακίδαο: Il. ε, 754 εὗρον
δὲ Κρονίωνα — ἥμενον — ἀκροτάτῃ κορυφῇ πολυδειράδος Οὐλύμποιο: Il. ω, 306 στὰς μέσῳ ἕρκεϊ: Il. β, 210 κῦμα πολυφλοί-
σβοιο θαλάσσης αἰγιαλῷ μεγάλῳ βρέμεται: Hesiod. ἔργ. 8
αἰθέρι ναίων: Soph. Trach. 171 τὴν παλαιὰν φηγὸν αὐδῆσαί ποτε
Δωδῶνι — ἔφη: Soph. Œ. R. 817 ᾧ μὴ ξένων ἔξεστι μηδ' ἀστῶν
τινα δόμοις δέχεσθαι.

Obs. 1. Here belong the dative adverbial forms, which are used both in
poetry and prose: Ἐλευσῖνι, Ῥαμνοῦντι, Πυθοῖ from Πυθώ, Σφηττοῖ, Ἰσθμοῖ,
οἴκοι,—ησι(ν).—ᾶσι(ν), Ἀθήνησιν, Θήβησιν, Πλαταιᾶσιν, Ὀλυμπίασι &c., ῇ,
τῇ, τῇδε, ταύτῃ &c.: Plat. Menex. p. 245 A Βασιλεῖ δὲ αὕτη μὲν οὐκ
ἐτόλμησε βοηθῆσαι, αἰσχυνομένη τὰ τρόπαια τά τε Μαραθῶνι καὶ Σαλαμῖνι καὶ
Πλαταιαῖς.—With ταύτῃ, τῇδε we often find αὐτοῦ (also αὐτῷ) joined ;
αὐτοῦ (αὐτῷ) ταύτῃ, τῇδε, *eo ipso loco* (Hdt. VII. 10, 8. and 44.).
Obs. 2. This use of the dative alone is confined mostly to poetry ; in
prose (and also in poetry) we find this dative more exactly defined by ἐν,
ἀνά poet., ἀμφί, περί, ἐπί, μετά (poet.), παρά, πρός, ὑπό.

2. Hence this dative is used to express the notion of *among:*
Il. δ, 95 πᾶσι δέ κε Τρώεσσι χάριν καὶ κῦδος ἄροιο (among): Il.
ζ, 477 ἀριπρεπέα Τρώεσσι: Il. α, 247 τοῖσι δὲ Νέστωρ ἡδυεπὴς
ἀνόρουσε: Il. β, 433 τοῖς ἄρα μύθων ἦρχε Γερήνιος Ἱππότα Νέστωρ:
Od. α, 71 ὅου κράτος ἐστὶ μέγιστον πᾶσιν Κυκλώπεσσι: Od.
ο, 227 Πυλίοισι μέγ' ἔξοχα δώματα ναίων: so ἀνθρώποις,
inter homines: Eur. Hec. 595 ἀνθρώποις δ' ἀεὶ ὁ μὲν πονηρὸς
οὐδὲν ἄλλο πλὴν κακός, ὁ δ' ἐσθλὸς ἐσθλός[a]: Id. Bacch. 310 μὴ τὸ
κράτος αὔχει δύναμιν ἀνθρώποις ἔχειν: Ibid. 402 ἵν' οἱ θελξίφρονες
νέμονται θνατοῖσιν Ἔρωτες (like Plat. Prot. p. 343 C εὐδοκιμεῖν
τοῖς τότε ἀνθρώποις): Eur. Phœn. 17 ὦ Θήβαισιν εὐίπ-
ποις ἄναξ: Ibid. 86 ὦ κλεινὸν οἴκοις Ἀντιγόνη θάλος πατρί:
Id. Hec. 1267 ὁ Θρῃξὶ μάντις εἶπε Διόνυσος τάδε. — In prose:
Hdt. VI. 70 Λακεδαιμονίοισι συχνὰ ἔργοισί τε καὶ γνώμῃσι ἀπολαμπρυνθείς, *inter Lac. et rebus gestis et consiliis clarus factus:*
Plat. Rep. p. 389 E οἷα καὶ Ὁμήρῳ (*apud H.*) Διομήδης λέγει.
So Æsch. Ag. 39 κοὐ μαθοῦσι λήθομαι, among us: Thuc. I. 6 οἱ
πρεσβύτεροι αὐτοῖς τῶν εὐδαιμόνων, among them : so τοῖσι δ' ἀνέστη:
Soph. Ant. 857 ἔψαυσας ἀλγεινοτάτας ἐμοὶ μερίμνας — κλεινοῖς Λαβ-
δακίδαισιν, that which is among : Hesiod. Th. 569 ὡς ἴδεν ἀνθρώποισι πυρὸς τηλέσκοπον αὐγήν: Soph. Œ. C. 966 οὐκ ἂν ἐξεύροις
ἐμοὶ ἁμαρτίας ὄνειδος οὐδέν: Plat. Rep. p. 421 E ἕτερα — τοῖς
φύλαξιν εὑρήκαμεν.

Obs. 3. The genitive represents the place as the antecedent condition

a Pflugk ad loc.

of the action. The accus. as the space over which the motion extends. The dative as the place wherein it happens. In αὐτοῦ ταύτῃ, *eo ipso loco*, the genitive and dative are united.

3. So also this local dative is sometimes found after verbs of *governing*, in Homer, more usually than the gen. with ἀνάσσειν: Od. a, 181 Ταφίοισιν ἀνάσσω: Il. μ, 242 Διὸς ὃς πᾶσι θνητοῖσι καὶ ἀθανάτοισιν ἀνάσσει: Il. a, 288 πάντεσσι δ' ἀνάσσειν: Od. a, 117 κτήμασιν οἶσιν ἀνάσσοι: Od. a, 402 δώμασιν ἀνάσσοις. (So with prepos. ἐν, μετά.) So βασιλεύειν, in Homer : Il. ξ, 134 ἦρχε δ' ἄρα σφιν: Od. ξ, 230 ἀνδράσιν ἦρξα (only in poetry): Æsch. P. V. 940 δαρὸν γὰρ οὐκ ἄρξει θεοῖς. So in Homer: ἀρχεύειν τινί: so ἐπιστατεῖν: Od. λ, 485 κρατέεις νεκύεσσι: cf. Ibid. 490. But several of these might be referred to the dativus commodi (§. 597, 598).

Obs. 4. And after substantives : Il. ε, 546 ἄνδρεσσιν ἄνακτα : Arist. Av. 1732 ἄρχοντα θεοῖς μέγαν.

4. Under the local dative, as expressing the particular point wherein any thing takes place, we must class such expressions as ὁ αὐτός εἰμὶ τῇ γνώμῃ—ψήφῳ, βουλεύματι Soph.: Thuc. πλεῖστος εἰμὶ τῇ γνώμῃ, I am of the same mind—I am mostly of this mind.

Obs. 5. The adverbial datives are used both in the transmissive as well as the local force of the dative ; as, χαμαί, *humi*, *humum*. So adverbs in η: Il. a, 120 γέρας ἔρχεται ἄλλῃ: Hdt. II. 29 τῇ ἂν (*quocunque*) κελεύῃ, ἐκεῖσε στρατεύονται: Plat. Gorg. p. 456 B εἰς πόλιν, ὅπῃ βούλει, ἐλθόντα. In ω, ἄνω, κάτω &c.; ᾧ, here, and hither often in Theocr. So ὧδε: Il. σ, 392 πρόμολ' ὧδε : Od. a, 182 νῦν δ' ὧδε ξὺν νηὶ κατήλυθον: cf. ρ, 545. Arist. Ach. 745 ὧδ' ἐσβαίνετε. In οι, as πεδοῖ, *humi*, *humum*, Æsch. P. V. 272 πεδοῖ βᾶσαι : ἐνταυθοῖ Hom. and Plat., *huc*; Attics, *hic* ; as, Plat. Prot. 310 A καθιζόμενος ἐνταυθοῖ (but οἶ, ὅποι, ποῖ always hither, &c.). In θα, ἔνθα, ἐνταῦθα, ἐνθάδε (Od. π, 204 ἐλεύσεται ἐνθάδ' Ὀδυσσεύς: Soph. El. 380 ἐνταῦθα πέμψειν, ἔνθα μήποτ' ἡλίου φέγγος προσόψει : Xen. Cyr. V. 4. 9 εἰς πόλιν, ἔνθα καὶ αὐτὸς κατέφυγεν: Id. Hell. I. 7, 16 ἀνέβην ἐνθάδε : Plat. Gorg. p. 494. extr. ἡ γὰρ ἐγὼ ἄγω ἐνταῦθα) ; further, ὕψι, *in alto* and *in altum* (Sappho: ὕψι δὴ τὸ μέλαθρον ἀείρατε, τέκτονες ἄνδρες): ἵνα, *ubi* and *quo* (Od. δ, 821 ἵν' οἴχεται), ἐκεῖ, κεῖθι, *illic* and *illuc* (Hdt. I. 209 ἐπεὰν ἐγὼ τάδε καταστρεψάμενος ἔλθω ἐκεῖ: Ibid. 121 ἐλθὼν δὲ ἐκεῖ).

Temporal Dative.

§. 606. The *accident of time* is considered as local, and is put in the dative, except when it is conceived of as the antecedent condition of the action.—(See §. 523.) Il. λ, 707 τρίτῳ ἤματι : Il. ν, 335 ἤματι τῷ, ὅτε κ.τ.λ.: Il. ο, 324 νυκτὸς ἀμολγῷ: Hdt. III. 131 τῷ πρώτῳ ἔτεϊ ὑπερβάλετο τοὺς πρώτους ἰητρούς — καί μιν δευτέρῳ ἔτεϊ ταλάντου Αἰγινῆται δημοσίῃ μισθεῦνται τρίτῳ δὲ ἔτεϊ

Ἀθηναῖοι ἑκατὸν μνέων· τ ε τ ά ρ τ ῳ δὲ ἔ τ ε ἴ Πολυκράτης δυῶν ταλάντων.—So prose: τῇδε τῇ νυκτί, ταύτῃ τῇ ἡμέρᾳ, ἐκείνῃ τῇ ἡμέρᾳ, τῇ
αὐτῇ νυκτί, πολλοῖς ἔτεσι: Xen. Hell. III. 2, 25 π ε ρ ι ι ό ν τ ι δὲ τ ῷ
ἐ ν ι α υ τ ῷ φαίνουσι πάλιν οἱ ἔφοροι φρουρὰν ἐπὶ τὴν Ἦλιν: Id.
Anab. IV. 8, 1 τῇ πρώτῃ ἡμέρᾳ ἀφίκοντο ἐπὶ τὸν ποταμόν.

Obs. 1. In prose generally, and in poetry frequently, ἐν is added ; and
sometimes ἐπί, as in Homer : ἐπ' ἤματι τῷδε, ἐπ' ἤματι, ἐπὶ νυκτί.

Obs. 2. The genitive, accusative, and dative, therefore, are all used to
express relations of time, and they differ as follows : the time is represented by the genitive as the antecedent condition of the action ; by the
dative as the space wherein the action took place ; while the accusative
expresses the duration of the action. So compare ταύτης τῆς ἡμέρας οἱ
Ἕλληνες ἐμαχέσαντο, this day giving them the occasion, with ταυτῇ τῇ ἡμέρᾳ,
on this day, and ταύτην τὴν ἡμέραν, throughout this day. So we find the
accusative and genitive, in the same sentence, expressing each its proper
notion ; as Hdt. II. 95 πᾶς ἀνὴρ αὐτέων ἀμφίβληστρον ἔκτηται, τῷ τ ῆ ς ἡ μ έ-
ρ η ς (by day) μὲν ἰχθῦς ἀγρεύει, τὴν δὲ νύκτα (throughout the night) αὐτῷ
χρᾶται, ἐν τῇ ἀναπαύεται κοίτῃ. The gen. and dative may express the same
actual point of time, but differing in the way in which it is looked at, as
in the above example. So the accusative differs from the dative as it
does from the genitive : Hdt. VII. 55 τ α ύ τ η ν μὲν τ ὴ ν ἡ μ έ ρ η ν οὗτοι·
τ ῇ δὲ ὑ σ τ ε ρ α ί ῃ πρῶτοι μέν κ. τ. λ.: Xen. Anab. II. 1, 3 καὶ λέγοι, ὅτι
τ α ύ τ η ν μὲν τ ὴ ν ἡ μ έ ρ α ν περιμείνειεν ἂν αὐτούς·— τ ῇ δὲ ἄ λ λ ῃ ἀπιέναι
φαίη ἐπὶ Ἰωνίας: Ibid. III. 4, 18 τ α ύ τ ῃ μὲν ἡ μ έ ρ ᾳ ἀπῆλθον οἱ βάρβαροι,
τ ὴ ν δὲ ἐ π ι ο ῦ σ α ν ἡ μ έ ρ α ν ἔμειναν οἱ Ἕλληνες, τ ῇ δὲ ὑ σ τ ε ρ α ί ᾳ
ἐπορεύοντο διὰ τοῦ πεδίου.

Instrumental Dative.

§. 607. The *instrument* or *means* whereby any thing is brought
about is in the dative, as being an afterthought in the mind of
the speaker, the conception of which is not necessary to the verbal
notion ; so that any verb *may* be followed by a dative, if it is
wished to express the instrument. If the instrument is considered
as the antecedent cause or condition of the action, it is in the
genitive (see §. 481, 599).

Verbs of *joy, sorrow,* and *similar feelings* or *states,* take a dative of
that whereby they are produced, when it is not conceived of as the
cause whence they spring, (see §. 488.) nor as that wherein they
consist, (see §. 549 :) χαίρειν, ἥδεσθαι, ἀγάλλεσθαι, ἐπαίρεσθαι (γελᾶν
Eur.), λυπεῖσθαι, ἀλγεῖν, στενάζειν : of *wonder,* as θαυμάζειν, ἄγασθαι :
rarely of *hope,* ἐλπίζειν — ; *contentment,* as στέργειν, rarely στέργε-
σθαι, ἀγαπᾶν, ἀρέσκεσθαι, ἀρκεῖσθαι, *contentum esse* — ; *discontent,*
as ἀγανακτεῖν, δυσχεραίνειν, δυσφορεῖν Eur., χαλεπῶς φέρειν,
ἄχθεσθαι, ἀσχαλᾶν Eur.— ; *shame,* as αἰσχύνεσθαι : Hdt. VI. 67
ἀ λ γ ή σ α ς τῷ ἐπειρωτήματι εἶπε : Id. III. 34 οὐκ ἀ ρ ε σ κ ό μ ε ν ο ς
(*contentus*) : Id. IV. 78 διαίτῃ οὐδαμῶς ἠρέσκετο Σκυθικῇ:

Id. IX. 33 ἔφη οὐκέτι ἀρκέεσθαι τούτοισι μούνοισι : Thuc. IV. 85 θαυμάζω τῇ ἀποκλείσει μου τῶν πυλῶν. —Ἐλπίζειν τῇ τύχῃ Thuc. III. 97: Στέργειν τοῖς παροῦσιν Isoc.: Ἀγαπᾶν τοῖς ὑπάρχουσιν ἀγαθοῖς Lysias p. 192, 26: Χαλεπῶς φέρειν τοῖς παροῦσι πράγμασι Xen. Anab. I. 3, 3: Αἰσχύνεσθαι τοῖς πεπραγμένοις Id. M. S. II. 1, 31: Plat. Hipp. maj. p. 285. extr. εἰκότως σοι χαίρουσιν οἱ Λακεδαιμόνιοι, ἅτε πολλὰ εἰδότι. —Ἀγάλλεσθαι τῇ νίκῃ. —Ἀγασθέντες τῷ ἔργῳ Plat. Symp. p. 179 C: Ἀγανακτεῖν τῷ θανάτῳ, δυσχεραίνειν τοῖς λόγοις Plat.: Demosth. p. 13, 14 ἀγαπήσας τοῖς πεπραγμένοις ἡσυχίαν σχήσει. So Eur. Hipp. 20 τούτοισι μέν νυν οὐ φθονῶ, am not made jealous by: Id. Hec. 251 κακύνει τοῖσδε τοῖς βουλεύμασιν.

So also verbs of *action*; as, Hdt. I. 87 ἔπρηξα τῇ σῇ μὲν εὐδαιμονίῃ, τῇ ἐμεωϋτοῦ δὲ κακοδαιμονίῃ: the good and bad luck being represented as the active instrument of the action.

§. 608. The actual *means* or *instrument*, by or with which any thing is done: Il. β, 199 τὸν σκήπτρῳ ἐλάσασκε: Il. κ, 121 βάλλειν χερμαδίοις. —Βάλλειν λίθοις, ἀκοντίζειν αἰχμαῖς. So Arist. Av. 619 θύραις θυρῶσαι: Od. ι, 82 ἔνθεν δ' ἐννῆμαρ φερόμην ὀλοοῖς ἀνέμοισιν πόντον ἐπ' ἰχθυόεντα: Xen. Cyr. IV. 3, 21 ὁ μὲν (ἱπποκένταυρος) γὰρ δυοῖν ὀφθαλμοῖν προεωρᾶτο καὶ δυοῖν ὤτοιν ἤκουεν· ἐγὼ δὲ τέτταρσι μὲν ὀφθαλμοῖς τεκμαροῦμαι, τέτταρσι δὲ ὠσὶ προαισθήσομαι· πολλὰ γάρ φασι καὶ ἵππον ἀνθρώποις τοῖς ὀφθαλμοῖς προορῶντα δηλοῦν, πολλὰ δὲ τοῖς ὠσὶ προακούοντα σημαίνειν: Ibid. 18 προνοεῖν μέν γε ἔξω πάντα τῇ ἀνθρωπίνῃ γνώμῃ, ταῖς δὲ χερσὶν ὁπλοφορήσω, διώξομαι δὲ τῷ ἵππῳ, τὸν δ' ἐναντίον ἀνατρέψω τῇ τοῦ ἵππου ῥώμῃ.—So φόβῳ, εὐνοίᾳ, ἀπειρίᾳ, φρονήματι, ὀργῇ, ὕβρει, ἀδικίᾳ &c., ποιεῖν τι.

Obs. 1. Also with adjectives, conceived as the instrument whereby the quality is produced; as, ποσὶ ταχύς, where the accus. is more usual (see §. 579): and even with subst., especially in Plato. So Soph. Œ. C. 1026 τὰ γὰρ δόλῳ τῷ μὴ δικαίῳ κτήματ' οὐχὶ σώζεται: Plat. Legg. p. 631 C κινήσεις τῷ σώματι: Id. Soph. p. 261 E τῶν τῇ φωνῇ περὶ τὴν οὐσίαν δηλωμάτων: Id. Polit. p. 280 D τὰς βίᾳ πράξεις: Id. Rep. p. 397 A διὰ μιμήσεως φωναῖς τε καὶ σχήμασιν, *imitatione per voces et gestus.*

Obs. 2. This is sometimes expressed by the preposition ἐν, the dative being considered local: Hesiod Scut. 199 ἔγχος ἔχουσ' ἐν χερσί, but Ibid. 214 εἶχε δὲ χερσίν (like *manu* and *in manu tenere*). — Θυμῷ ἕλπεσθαι and ἕλπεσθαι ἐν στήθεσσιν Homer, like *animo* and *in animo volvere*.— Διαφέρειν τινί and ἔν τινι or ἐπί τινι.—Ὀφθαλμοῖς and ἐν ὀφθαλμοῖς ἰδεῖν, or ἐν ὄμμασιν ἰδεῖν.—Σημαίνειν τί τινι and σημαίνειν ἐν ἱεροῖς, ἐν οὐρανίοις σημείοις, ἐν οἰωνοῖς, ἐν φήμαις (Xen.), πυρὶ καίειν and ἐν πυρὶ καίειν.

Obs. 3. Sometimes, though very rarely, a person is conceived of as an instrument: Soph. Elect. 226 τίνι γάρ ποτ' ἂν—ἀκούσαιμι ἔπος, by whom.

§. **609. 1.** With comparatives and analogous words, that whereby one thing exceeds another is in the dative, conceived of as the instrument whereby the difference is produced: Hdt. I. 184 Σεμίραμις γενεῆσι πέντε πρότερον ἐγένετο τῆς Νιτώκριος.—So πολλῷ, ὀλίγῳ μείζων, ὀλίγῳ πρότερον: Hdt. VI. 58 ἀριθμῷ, *certo numero:* Ibid. 89 ὑστέρισαν ἡμέρῃ μιῇ τῆς συγκειμένης, by one day: Ibid. 106 πόλι λογίμῃ ἡ Ἑλλὰς γέγονε ἀσθενεστέρη. So Thuc. V. 28 ἄριστα ἔσχον τοῖς πᾶσι: so διαφέρειν φρονήσει, ἰσχύειν τῷ σώματι: so ὑπερβάλλειν, προέχειν τινί.

2. So notions of *price* and *value, buying* and *selling:* Il. η, 473 ἔνθεν ἄρ' οἰνίζοντο—ἄλλοι μὲν χαλκῷ, ἄλλοι δ' αἴθωνι σιδήρῳ. So notions of *punishing, fining:* ζημιοῦν τινα χιλίαις δραχμαῖς: Hdt. VI. 136 ζημιώσαντος δὲ (τοῦ δήμου τὸν Μιλτιάδεα) κατὰ τὴν ἀδικίην πεντήκοντα ταλάντοισι: Thuc. IV. 73 τῷ βελτίστῳ τοῦ ὁπλιτικοῦ βλαφθῆναι. So Hdt. VIII. 60, 3 Μεγάροισι κερδανέομεν περιεοῦσι, *ex servata Megara lucrum capiemus.*

3. So that whereby any *judgment* or *opinion* concerning any thing is formed. So with verbs of *measuring, deciding,* &c.: σταθμᾶσθαι, γιγνώσκειν, εἰκάζειν, κρίνειν, τεκμαίρεσθαι: Il. ε, 182 ἀσπίδι γιγνώσκειν: Hdt. II. 2 τοιούτῳ σταθμησάμενοι πρήγματι, *ex tali re judicantes:* Id. VII. 11 εἰ χρὴ σταθμώσασθαι τοῖσι ὑπαργμένοισι ἐξ ἐκείνων, *ex iis, quæ ab illis fieri cœpta sunt:* Ibid. 237 τοῖσι λεγομένοισι σταθμώμενος: Id. III. 15 πολλοῖσι καὶ ἄλλοισι ἔστι σταθμώσασθαι, ὅτι κ.τ.λ.: Id. VII. 16, 3 τῇ σῇ ἐσθῆτι τεκμαιρόμενον, *ex veste tua judicium faciens:* Demosth. p. 113, 10 τοῦτ' ἐρεῖ, εἴπερ οἷς πρὸς τοὺς ἄλλους πεποίηκε δεῖ τεκμαίρεσθαι.—So γιγνώσκειν, εἰκάζειν τινί Thuc.—So the dative τῷ, wherefore, accordingly.

§. **610.** So also the *material* is put in the dative, when it is not conceived of as an antecedent condition of the thing made. (§. 538.) See Il. κ, 438 ἅρμα δέ οἱ χρυσῷ καὶ ἀργύρῳ εὖ ἤσκηται: Hdt. III. 57 ἀγορὴ καὶ τὸ πρυτανήϊον Παρίῳ λίθῳ ἠσκημένα.—So βρύειν ἄνθεσι.

§. **611.** So also passive verbs take a dative of the agent, considered as the instrument, whereby the state, &c. is produced, not as the cause whence it springs.—(See §. 483. *Obs.* 3:) Il. σ, 103 δάμεν Ἕκτορι δίῳ: Il. ε, 465 κτείνεσθαι Ἀχαιοῖς: Eur. Hec. 1085 σοὶ εἴργασται κακά: Hdt. VI. 123 μοὶ δεδήλωται: Isocr. Paneg. 1 εἰρῆσθαι τοῖς ἄλλοις: Demosth. p. 844, 1 τὰ τούτῳ πεπραγμένα.—So ταῦτά μοι λέλεκται.

Obs. Two or more datives may be joined to the same verb expressing different relations; as, Xen. Hell. III. 1, 13 ξενικῷ μὲν Ἑλληνικῷ προσβαλοῦσα τοῖς τείχεσιν: Hdt. VI. 70 Λακεδαιμονίοισι συχνὰ ἔργοισί τε καὶ γνώμῃσι ἀπολαμπρυνθείς.

§. 612. From the principles which have been laid down and the examples which have been given in the foregoing pages of the force and usages of the three Greek cases, it will be clear that when synonymous verbs are used with different cases, it arises from some slight difference in their notions, which, for the most part lost in the Latin and modern languages, was retained by the Greek. And where the same verb is found with different cases, it arises from a greater or less modification of their proper notion in the speaker's mind at the moment, so that by the use of one or the other of the cases, as was required, he was able to express the exact notion in his mind. And to observe and trace out these differences is a useful branch of the study of Greek, as it forms habits of accurately distinguishing and expressing notions differing slightly, yet often materially, from each other.

Verbal Adjectives in τέος, τέα, τέον.

§. 613. 1. These verbal adjectives are formed from all the sorts of verbs, as ἐπιθυμητέον (ἐπιθυμεῖν τινος), κολαστέον (κολάζειν τινά), ἀσκητέον (ἀσκεῖν τι), βοηθητέον (βοηθεῖν τινι), ἡσσητέον (ἡσσᾶσθαί τινος).

2. Verbal adjectives derived from neuter verbs are used as impersonal; from other verbs, either as personal or impersonal.

3. The impersonal verbal adjective is followed by the case of the verb from which it is derived: ἀσκητέον (or -τέα) ἐστὶ τὴν ἀρετήν—ἐπιθυμητέον (or -τέα) ἐστὶ τῆς ἀρετῆς—ἐπιχειρητέον (or -τέα) ἐστὶ τῷ ἔργῳ: Xen. Cyr. III. 1, 15 κολαστέον ἄρ' ἂν εἴη—τὸν πατέρα: Soph. Antig. 678 οὔτε γυναικὸς οὐδαμῶς ἡσσητέα (from ἡσσᾶσθαί τινος, *inferiorem esse aliquo*).

Obs. 1. From deponents also, such as βιάζομαι, ἐργάζομαι, considered as passives, as εἴργασται, *factum est*, are formed verbal adjectives, with the same force und construction as those given above; as, ἐργαστέος, *faciendus*, βιαστέον ἐστὶν αὐτούς, *ii cogendi sunt;* μιμητέον τοὺς ἀγαθούς, from μιμεῖσθαί τινα.

Obs. 2. Those verbs which in their middle voice assume a new sense, and consequently a new construction, have their verbal adjective in both of these senses and constructions: πειστέον ἐστὶν αὐτόν, one must persuade him, from πείθω τινά, and πειστέον ἐστὶν αὐτῷ, *obediendum ei est.* πειστέον τοῖς νόμοις, from πείθομαί τινι, *obedio alicui;* ἀπαλλακτέον ἐστὶν αὐτὸν τοῦ κακοῦ, from ἀπαλλάττειν τινὰ τοῦ κακοῦ, and ἀπαλλακτέον ἐστὶν ἡμῖν τοῦ ἀνθρώπου, from ἀπαλλάττεσθαί τινος, to free oneself, or depart; as, Plat. Phæd. p. 66 E ἀπαλλακτέον αὐτοῦ.

Obs. 3. Where the verb governs a double accus. case of the act and the patient, or a cognate accus. and dative, the verbal adjective is followed, when necessary, by the cognate accus.; as, Soph. Phil. 994 πειστέον τάδε, (πείθεσθαί τινί τι.)

4. The personal verbal adjective agrees, like other predicative adjectives, with its substantive, in gender, number, and case. It can also be used as an attributive; as, ἀσκητέα ἐστὶν ἡ ἀρετή, or ἡ ἀσκητέα ἀρετή: Xen. Mem. Socr. III. 6, 3 ὠφελητέα σοι ἡ πόλις ἐστίν.

5. The logical subject of the impersonal verbal adjective, the agent or person by whom the verbal operation is to be performed, stands in the instrumental dative as in the passive voice: 'Ασκη-τέον (or -τέα) ἐστί σοι τὴν ἀρετήν — ἀσκητέα ἐστί σοι ἡ ἀρετή, — ἐπιθυμητέον (or -τέα) ἐστὶ τοῖς ἀνθρώποις τῆς ἀρετῆς: Demosth. p. 14, 17 φημὶ δὴ — βοηθητέον εἶναι τοῖς πράγμασιν ὑμῖν.

Obs. 4. This dative is sometimes used with verbal adjectives in τός, which generally express possibility (English -ble): Hesiod Theog. 732 τοῖς οὐκ ἐξιτόν ἐστιν, *quibus non licet exire:* Aristoph. Lys. 636 ἆρα γρυκτόν ἐστιν ὑμῖν;

Obs. 5. In Attic Greek an accusative of the agent is sometimes used instead of the dative; as in the verbal adjective is implied the notion of δεῖ (on which the accus. depends) and the infinitive: Xen. M. S. III. 11, 1 ἰτέον ἂν εἴη θεασαμένους: Plat. Gorg. p. 5c7 D τὸν βουλόμενον εὐδαίμονα εἶναι σωφροσύνην διωκτέον καὶ ἀσκητέον: cf. Id. Rep. p. 413 E[a]: Id. Crit. p. 49 A οὐδενὶ τρόπῳ φαμὲν ἑκόντας ἀδικητέον εἶναι: Thuc. VIII. 65 ὡς οὔτε μισθοφορητέον εἴη τοὺς ἄλλους = οὐ δεῖ τοὺς ἄλλους μισθοφορεῖν. (The two constructions are sometimes found together: Plat. Rep. p. 453 D οὐκοῦν καὶ ἡμῖν νευστέον καὶ πειρατέον σώζεσθαι ἐκ τοῦ λόγου, ἤτοι δελφῖνά τιν' ἐλπίζοντας ἡμᾶς ὑπολαβεῖν ἄν —;) Eur. Phœn. 724 sq. ἐξοιστέον ἄρ' ὅπλα Θηβαίων πόλει — ἐκτὸς τάφρων τῶνδ' ὡς μαχουμένους τάχα: Id. Hipp. 491 sq. ὡς τάχος δυστέον (sc. ἡμᾶς) τὸν εὐθὺν ἐξειπόντας ἀμφὶ σοῦ λόγου, *celerrime explorandum nobis est rem aperte declarantibus):* Demosth. p. 21, 13 πολλὴν δὴ τὴν μετάστασιν καὶ μεγάλην δεικτέον τὴν μεταβολήν, εἰσφέροντας, ἐξιόντας, ἅπαντα ποιοῦντας ἑτοίμως. — And the verbal adjective is frequently changed into an infinitive: Xen. M. S. I. 5, 5 ἐμοὶ μὲν δοκεῖ — ἐλευθέρῳ ἀνδρὶ εὐκτέον εἶναι μὴ τυχεῖν δούλου τοιούτου, δουλεύοντα δὲ — ἱκετεύειν τοὺς θεούς κ.τ.λ.: Plat. Gorg. p. 492 D τὰς μὲν ἐπιθυμίας φῂς οὐ κολαστέον, εἰ μέλλει τις οἷον δεῖ εἶναι, ἑῶντα δὲ αὐτὰς ὡς μεγίστας πλήρωσιν ἀλλοθέν γε ποθὲν ἑτοιμάζειν.

Obs. 6. Difficult constructions of this nature may be generally explained by this resolution of the verbal into δεῖ and the infinitive.

Obs. 7. The personal verbal adjective has a purely passive sense: τόδε ποιητέον ἐστίν=δεῖ τόδε ποιεῖσθαι. The impersonal verbal adjective has also a passive force whenever it takes the person in the dative, as ποιητέον τάδε ἐστί σοι; but it has a partly active force, as it takes the object in the case proper to the active verb.

a Stallb. ad loc.

Prepositions.

§. 614. 1. As in the course of time the requirements of language on the one hand increased, and on the other, the metaphysical quickness by which the mind was able to recognise and distinguish between the several relations of the cases decreased, it became natural to represent those relations more accurately. In this way certain words (originally themselves cases of nouns) came into use, as definitions of the relations of the cases, by representing the substantival notion or object as standing in a certain *position* to the verbal notion : and as the Cases represent the internal order of notions in the mind, the Prepositions are derived from and represent the external position of things around.

2. The prepositions then properly express notions of the space or position in which one thing stands to another — either the parallel notions of *by—from the side of—in front of—round—with*, or the opposed notions of space—*above* and *below—in* and *out— before* and *behind—on this side* and *on that—on* and *off—thereon* and *therefrom—forwards* and *backwards—towards* and *from*.

3. Every notion of position must be conceived of as something either in motion — *whence* or *whither*, or at rest — *where*. Ἀπό and ἐκ imply in themselves a notion of " whence"—εἰς and ὡς a notion of " whither"—ἐν and σύν a notion of " where," while the rest have a general notion of position, and the sense of the verb, and the force of the cases which are joined to the prepositions determine in which of these three notions each is used. Thus the abstract force of the preposition παρά is not of motion, but only of position—" by the side of ;" but with a verb expressing motion, and a genitive expressing the point whence the motion begins, it signifies *from the side of,* ἦλθον παρὰ βασιλέως : joined with a verb of motion and an accus. signifying either the road traversed, or the place arrived at, it expresses the coming *to* a person, so as to be *by his side ;* as, ἦλθον παρὰ βασιλέα : or, with inanimate things, the travelling *by the side of,* or parallel to that thing, ἦλθον παρὰ ποταμόν : and with a verb which implies mere position, and a local dative, it defines the position, and signifies, *by the side of, at,* or *before,* παρὰ τῷ βασιλεῖ, in front of the king. In fact, prepositions being used principally to define more clearly the relations signified by the cases, naturally take their peculiar sense from the relations of the case to which they are joined—not altering, but merely expressing more clearly, that relation.

4. Thus the relations were so prescriptively defined by prepositions, that the construction with the case became a solecism—so not οἰκεῖν οἴκῳ, but οἰκεῖν ἐν οἴκῳ.

5. Every preposition is not joined with all three cases, but the original force of the preposition has in some cases made it inapplicable to the expression of one or more relations, as they were looked at by the Greeks. So that some prepositions only define the relation of the genitive, ἀντί, ἀπό, ἐκ, πρό: or only the relation of the dative, ἐν, σύν: or only the relation of the accus., ἀνά, εἰς (ὡς): or gen. and accus., διά, κατά, ὑπέρ: or all three, gen., dat. and accus., ἀμφί, περί, ἐπί, μετά, παρά, πρός, ὑπό.

§. 615. 1. Prepositions are divided as to their meaning :—

a. Juxtaposition : παρά, ἀμφί, by the side of; ἐπί, by and on; σύν and μετά, with. — *b.* Contraposition : ἐπί, on ; ἀνά, up, on ; ὑπέρ, above; ὑπό, below ; κατά, down ; πρό, πρός, ἀντί, before ; ὄπισθε (not properly a preposition), behind ; ἐν, εἰς, in, within ; ἐκ, ἐξ, out, without ; διά, through, within ; περί, round (about) ; ὡς, to ; ἀπό, from, away.

2. As the notion of time is nearly connected with the notion of space, time being considered as space, the relations of place and time in which a substantival stood to a verbal notion were expressed by the same preposition ; as, πρὸ τῶν πυλῶν ἔστη and πρὸ τῆς ἡμέρας ἀπῆλθεν: ἐκ τῆς πόλεως ἀπέφυγεν and ἐκ τοῦ πολέμου (immediately after the war) ἐγένετο εἰρήνη : ἐν ταύτῃ τῇ χώρᾳ and ἐν τούτῳ τῷ χρόνῳ πολλὰ καὶ καλὰ ἔργα ἀπεδείξατο &c.

§. 616. 1. As the increase of civilisation and exchange of thought required a greater variety and accuracy of expression, the notions of local relations expressed by prepositions were applied to represent, define, and specify more particularly the causal relations of things which were less accurately expressed by the cases, things being considered to stand in certain positions to each other ; thus, μάχεσθαι περί τινος expresses the cause, round which, as it were standing round it, the contest was going on ; which might be expressed in an equally correct but less defined form, μάχεσθαί τινος : so εἰμὶ δι' ὀργῆς, I am in a state of (passing through) anger. The poetic language, which loved to paint things as if actually and really existing, frequently expresses the causal relations by the preposition and the local dative, as if realising the actual position of the parties ; as, Il. π, 526 αὐτός τ' ἀμφὶ νέκυι κατατεθνηῶτι μάχωμαι : so δαμῆναι, τραφῆναι, κτείνεσθαι ὑπό τινι &c.

2. So on the contrary, the local notions of place and time sometimes lose their local force, and being regarded as causal, either

causing or suffering something, are expressed by the cases, as we have already seen; as, νέφος ἐφαίνετο ὀρέων, τρέχειν πεδίοιο, τῆς ἡμέρας; βαίνειν ὁδόν, πᾶσαν ἡμέραν.

§. 617. Every preposition has a proper original meaning, varying as it is joined with different cases or different verbal notions, but retained more or less in all its various applications; this is most discernible in the relations of place and time, while, in the causal usages, the original meaning is often difficult to trace, and sometimes wholly lost.

Obs. 1. All prepositions are originally adverbs of place, from which they differ, in as much as while the former refer to the substantive, the latter depend on the verb. There are some local adverbs which, as being seldom found except with a case, are used as prepositions, and are called *Prepositions improper.*—*a.* Local and other adverbs, used both alone and with substantives; as, ἄντα, ἄντην, ἀντία, ἀπόπροθεν, ἀποπρόθι, ἔξω, ἐκτός, ἄγχι, ἀντικρύ, ἀμφίς; ἄνευ, δίχα, τῆλε, νόσφιν &c.—ἅμα.—*b.* Substantives with a genitive; as, ἕνεκα, *caussa*; δίκην, *instar*; χάριν, *gratia*, &c.

Obs. 2. It not unfrequently happens that the force of the verbal notion is modified, or added to, by the preposition and its case with which it is joined; as, στὰς ἐπὶ συνεδρίον, going to the assembly and standing there; στὰς ἐπὶ συνεδρίῳ, standing by the assembly.

PREPOSITIONS CONSTRUCTED WITH *one* CASE.

1. *Genitive only.*

1. 'Αντί and πρό, before.

§. 618. *a.* 'Α ν τ ί [Sanscr. *a t i* (*super*, *supra*, *trans*, *ultra*); Lat. *a n t e*; Litth. *a n t*; Goth. *a n d, a n d a*]. Original meaning, "before," "face to face," "over against." 1. In its proper l o c a l force, as στῆναι ἀντί τινος. 2. C a u s a l (the object conceived as perceived by the senses in certain positions). *a.* In *adjurations*, &c. for the more usual πρός with gen.: Soph. Œ. C. 1326 ἀντὶ παίδων τῶνδε σ' ἱκετεύομεν (*per*), as it were, "standing before." *b.* In *comparisons, prizing, valuing, weighing*, &c. the one of the objects being considered as placed before the other: Il. φ, 75 ἀντί τοι εἴμ' ἱκέταο—αἰδοίοιο, I am to you as a suppliant. So ἓν ἀνθ' ἑνός Plat., one against the other. Hence with comparatives (§. 503. *Obs.* 1.), and the notions of *buying, selling, exchange, worth, similarity*, or *dissimilarity*; as, ὠνεῖσθαι, ἀλλάττεσθαι ἀντὶ χρυσοῦ, ἄξιος ἀντὶ πολλῶν, ἄλλος ἀντὶ σοῦ: Æsch. Prom. 467 θαλασσόπλαγκτα δ' οὔτις ἄλλος ἀντ' ἐμοῦ λινόπτερ' εὗρε ναυτίλων ὀχήματα: Soph. Aj. 439 οὐκ ἄν τις αὔτ' ἔμαρψεν ἄλλος ἀντ' ἐμοῦ. With the notions of *superiority* or *preference*, as the object spoken of, "a superior," is supposed to stand before the other; as, αἱρεῖσθαί τι ἀντί τινος (instead of the more usual τινός) Xen. From the notion of valuing, that of the cause or origin of any thing is derived ; as, ἀνθ' οὗ, ἀνθ' ὧν, wherefore—on this account: Soph. El. 585 δίδαξον, ἀνθ' ὅτου τανῦν αἴσχιστα πάντων ἔργα δρῶσα τυγχάνεις, and from the notion of valuing, equality in value, is derived the idea of substitution, standing as equivalent to—instead ; as, δοῦλος ἀντὶ βασιλέως : Hdt. VII. 37 ἀντὶ ἡμέρης—νὺξ ἐγένετο : Xen. Cyr. III. 1, 18 ἀντὶ τοῦ μάχεσθαι πείθεσθαι ἐθέλει.

Obs. As a general rule, the compounds of ἀντί are joined with the dative, but many in which the idea of substitution, as ἀντιπαρέχειν τί τινος, or of striving after something is contained, are construed with the genitive.

§. 619. *b.* Πρό [Sanscr. *pra;* Lat. *pro, præ;* Litth. *pro, pra-;* Goth. *faura, faur;* English *pre*] is used in the same way as ἀντί ; but, as having a more general meaning, is applied in a greater variety of relations. 1. L o c a l—*before,* *pro,* as στῆναι πρὸ πυλῶν, πρὸ οἴκου ; with the collateral notion of motion in the phrase : πρὸ ὁδοῦ ἐγένοντο Il. δ, 384, forward on the road—further on the way. So Æsch. Prom. Vinct. 887 γῆν πρὸ γῆς ἐλαύνομαι, I hurry through ; properly, from one land forward to another. So "forwards from" Hom., with gen. suffix θι : οὐρανόθι πρό, Ἰλιόθι πρό, forwards from Troy ; ἠῶθι πρό, forwards from the morning— that is, the whole morning forwards, Il. λ, 50. 2. T e m p o r a l— *before,* as πρὸ ἡμέρας : Hdt. VII. 130 πρὸ πολλοῦ, *multo ante.* 3. C a u s a l—*a.* but very nearly allied to the local force, in expressions of assistance, defence, *before, for,* προκαθῆσθαι : (Lat. *præsidium;*) as, μάχεσθαι πρό τινος—ὀλέσθαι πρὸ πόληος Hom., *pro patriâ mori.* —*b.* In comparisons, valuations, just as ἀντί ; as, πρὸ πολλοῦ ποιεῖ- σθαι, to value before much riches ; πρὸ πολλῶν χρημάτων τιμήσασθαι Isocr. c. Soph. p. 293 B. Hence with comparatives, and notions of superiority, for ἀντί ; as, αἱρεῖσθαί τι πρό τινος, to choose before the other : Plat. Phæd. p. 99 A εἰ μὴ δικαιότερον ᾤμην καὶ κάλλιον εἶναι πρὸ τοῦ φεύγειν : Id. Crit. p. 54 B μήτε παῖδας περὶ πλείονος ποιοῦ μήτε τὸ ζῆν μήτε ἄλλο μηδὲν πρὸ τοῦ δικαίου: Id. Rep. p. 361 E ἐπαινεῖν πρὸ δικαιοσύνης ἀδικίαν. — *c.* Hence *substitution, being equivalent,* like ἀντί ; as, δοῦλος πρὸ δεσπότου. — Lastly *d.* of the cause ; first, like ἀντί, properly of recompense, as πρὸ τῶνδε, " wherefore—for these things." Thence of internal causes : *præ;* as, Il. ρ, 667 πρὸ φόβοιο, *præ metu.*

Obs. The compounds of πρό are mostly followed by a genitive ; as, προαιρεῖσθαί τι χρήματός τινος, προορᾶν, προφυλάττειν, προνοεῖν τινος—προστα- τεύειν τινός.

2. 'Aπό, *from*—ἐκ, ἐξ. *out.*

§. 620. These prepositions differ, in that the former signifies rather external removal from something, the latter a motion from within of something ; and in the causal usage, the former signifies a more remote, the latter a more immediate cause.

a. 'A π ό [Epic ἀπαί ; Sancr. *apa* ; Lat. *ab* ; Goth. *af* ; German *aba, ab, abe, abo*], primary meaning *"from."* 1. L o c a l.— *a.* A removal from a place or object, with verbs of motion ; as, ἀπὸ τῆς πόλεως ἦλθεν. Very often with a notion of some elevated place or object whence something is supposed to proceed ; as, ἀφ' ἵππων μάχεσθαι ; further with verbs of loosing, delivering, &c. λύειν, ἐλευθεροῦν : of missing ; as, ἀπὸ σκοποῦ : thence applied to mental failures ; as, οὐχ ἅλιος σκοπὸς ἔσσομαι, οὐδ' ἀπὸ δόξης, wandering from the opinion of men, otherwise than men thought. So ἀπ' ἐλπίδων, ἀπὸ γνώμης, *aliter ac sperabam, putabam (aberrans ab exspectatione, ab opinione)*. It is written in these phrases, though without sufficient reason, ἄ π ο for ἀπό : ἄπο θυμοῦ, σκοποῦ, δόξης : Plat. Rep. p. 470 B ἄπο τρόπου λέγεις [a] : Theæt. p. 143 C καὶ οὐδέν γε ἄπο τρόπου : Ibid. p. 179 οὐκ ἄπο σκοποῦ εἴρηκεν, and elsewhere in Plato. *b.* Distance from a place or object, with verbs of rest. (Mostly Epic :) Il. β, 292 μένειν ἀπὸ ἧς ἀλόχοιο, far from : Il. μ, 70 ἀπ' Ἄργεος ἀπολέσθαι : cf. Il. ν, 227. Od. α, 49. 203. Xen. M. S. I. 2, 25 πολὺν χρόνον ἀπὸ τοῦ Σωκράτους γεγονότε. Here also ἄπο, not ἀπό. Hence also is derived the notion of *without* : Thuc. VI. 24 ἀπὸ τῶν ὅπλων (Schol. χωρὶς ὅπλων). So Soph. Œ. C. 900 ἀπὸ ῥυτῆρος [b]. 2. T e m p o r a l.—Departure from a point—*after :* Il. θ, 53 δεῖπνον ἕλοντο — ἀ π ὸ δ ε ί π ν ο υ θωρήσσοντο. So γενέσθαι ἀ π ὸ δ ε ί π ν ο υ Hdt. VI. 129 : ἀφ' ἡμέρας, *de die* ; ἀπὸ νυκτός, *de nocte* ; ἀφ' ἑσπέρας. So Plat. Rep. p. 365 E ἀδικητέον καὶ θυτέον ἀπὸ τῶν ἀδικημάτων. 3. C a u s a l.—*a.* The origin or birth ; as, εἶναι, γίγνεσθαι ἀπό τινος : Hdt. VI. 125 ἀ π ὸ δ ὲ 'Α λ κ μ α ί ω ν ο ς καὶ αὖτις Μ ε γ α κ λ έ ο ς ἐγένοντο καὶ κάρτα λαμπροί. *b.* The whole in relation to its parts, which are conceived as depending from it ; as, μήδεα ἀπὸ θεῶν (*divinam mentem*), κάλλος ἀπὸ Χαρίτων Od. : Hdt. I. 51 τὰ ἀπὸ τῆς δειρῆς, necklaces. So οἱ ἀπὸ βουλῆς, *qui sunt a consiliis* ; οἱ ἀπὸ τῆς σκηνῆς, players ; οἱ ἀπὸ Πλάτωνος, οἱ ἀπὸ τῆς 'Ακαδημίας &c. ; as, Cicer. Tusc. II. 3, 7 *quid sentiant ii, qui sunt a b e a d i s c i p l i n a* [c] : τὰ ἀπό τινος, *"complectitur omnia, quæ sunt in homine et ab eo exeunt, verba, sensus, facta."* Dem.

---

[a] Stallb. ad loc. et Schæfer. Melet. p. 51.   [b] Ellendt, Lex. ad voc. ἀπό.
[c] Vide adnott. ad loc.

p. 91, 5 τά γε ἀφ' ὑμῶν ἔτοιμα ὑπάρχοντα ὁρῶ [a]. *c.* The person who causes any thing, with passives instead of ὑπό with the genitive (but seldom): Hdt. II. 54 ζήτησιν μεγάλην ἀπὸ σφέων γενέσθαι: Thuc. I. 17 ἐπράχθη τε ἀπ' αὐτῶν οὐδὲν ἔργον ἀξιόλογον. *d.* The cause, occasion: Il. μ, 233 ἀπὸ σπουδῆς, in earnest. Nearly in the same force: Æsch. Eum. 671 ἀπὸ γνώμης: Id. Ag. 1303 τλήμων ἀπ' εὐτόλμου φρενός: Eur. Troad. 774 καλλίστων γὰρ ὀμμάτων ἄπο αἰσχρῶς τὰ κλεινὰ πεδί' ἀπώλεσας Φρυγῶν: Hdt. VII. 164 ἀπὸ δικαιοσύνης: Xen. Cyr. I. 1, 5 τῷ ἀφ' ἑαυτοῦ φόβῳ [b]: Ibid. III. 3, 53 τῷ ἀπὸ τῶν πολεμίων φόβῳ; as, *metus a b aliquo.* So ἀφ' ἑαυτοῦ, from one's own impulse. *e.* Material; as, ἀπ' ἀργυρίου.—(See §. §. 538. *Obs.* 1.) τρέφειν τὸ ναυτικὸν ἀπὸ προσόδων Thuc. I. 81. *f.* Way, means, and instruments: Il. ω, 605 ἀπὸ βιοῖο πέφνεν, from (with) the bow: Plat. Legg. p. 832 E ὀξύτης σώματος ἢ ἀπὸ τῶν ποδῶν: Demosth. p. 49, 34 ἀπὸ τῶν ὑμετέρων ὑμῖν πολεμεῖ (ὁ Φίλιππος) συμμάχων, i. e. *sociorum vestrorum ope.* Hence many adverbial expressions; as, ἀπὸ στόματος, ἀπὸ γλώσσης εἰπεῖν, ἀπὸ σπουδῆς, ἀπ' ἄκρας φρενός. *g.* In notions of conformity to; as, ἀπό τινος καλεῖσθαι: Hdt. VII. 74 ἀπ' Οὐλύμπου δὲ οὔρεος καλέονται Οὐλυμπιηνοί.—ἀπὸ ξυμμαχίας αὐτόνομοι.

Obs. The compounds with ἀπό take the genitive when they give to the verb the notion of removal.

§. 621. *b.* Ἐκ, ἐξ, *ex.* Primary meaning *out,* opposed to ἐν, *in.* 1. Local.—*a.* A removal, either from the interior of any thing, or from very near connection with any thing: with verbs of motion; as, ἐκ τῆς πόλεως ἀπῆλθεν, ἐκ τῆς μάχης ἔφυγεν (ἀπό on the contrary, signifies only a removal from the neighbourhood of the city, or battle): Od. λ, 600 κονίη δ' ἐκ κρατὸς ὀρώρει: Thuc. IV. 14 ἐκ γῆς ναυμαχεῖν, from the land (from an immediate contact with the land). Hence ἐκ is used to express the immediate succession of one object on another; as, *ex alio loco in alium:* Plat. Polit. p. 289 E οἱ δὲ πόλιν ἐκ πόλεως ἀλλάττοντες κατὰ θάλατταν καὶ πεζῇ: Id. Apol. Socr. p. 37 D καλὸς ἄν μοι ὁ βίος εἴη—ἄλλην ἐξ ἄλλης πόλεως ἀμειβομένῳ: cf. Soph. p. 224 B. *b.* Distance from, with verbs of rest, "*out of,*" Epic; as, ἐκ βελέων, *extra telorum jactum.* But also Hdt. III. 83 ἐκ τοῦ μέσου καθῆστο, instead of the more usual ἐκτός and ἔξω. 2. Temporal.—Immediate procession from a point of time; as, Hom.: ἐξ ἀρχῆς, from the very first beginning: Soph. El. 780 ἐξ ἡμέρας, *ex quo dies illuxit*—ἐκ νυκτός or ἐκ νυκτῶν Xenoph.—ἐκ παίδων—ἐξ ὑστέρου, ἐξ ὑστέρας,—ἐκ τοῦ λοιποῦ, *afterwards.* — Ἐκ is especially used of the immediate development of one thing from another — of the immediate succession in time, so that there is an unbroken connection between them.   First as in the local notion: Hdt. IX. 8 ἐξ ἡμέρης ἐς ἡμέρην ἀναβαλλόμενοι, *ex die in diem.*   Then Id. I. 50 ἐκ τῆς θυσίης γενέσθαι (far stronger than ἀπό): Ibid. 87 ἐκ δὲ αἰθρίης τε καὶ νηνεμίης συνδραμέειν ἐξαπίνης νέφεα: Thuc. I. 120 ἐκ μὲν εἰρήνης πολεμεῖν, ἐκ δὲ πολεμοῦ πάλιν ξυμβῆναι: Xen. Cyr. III. 1, 17 ὁ σὸς πατὴρ ἐν τῇδε τῇ μιᾷ ἡμέρᾳ ἐξ ἄφρονος σώφρων γεγένηται: Eur. Or. 269 ἐκ κυμάτων γὰρ αὖθις αὖ γαλήν' ὁρῶ: Id. Hec. 55 ὦ μῆτερ, ἥτις ἐκ τυραννικῶν δόμων δούλειον ἦμαρ εἶδες, ὡς πράσσεις κακῶς ᵃ: Ibid. 915 ἐκ δείπνων ὕπνος ἡδύς ᵇ: Soph. Œ. R. 454 τυφλὸς ἐκ δεδορκότος. 3. Causal.—*a.* Of the origin, but always in an immediate, while ἀπό is in a more remote notion; as, εἶναι, γίγνεσθαι ἔκ τινος.   *b.* Of the whole in relation to its parts separated from it, often with the collateral notion of selection; as, ἐξ Ἀθηναίων οἱ ἄριστοι.   So the singular expression ἐκ τρίτων, *one of three,* yourself the third: Plat. Gorg. p. 500 A σύμψηφος ἡμῖν εἶ καὶ σὺ ἐκ τρίτων ᶜ; So ἐκ τρίτου Eur. Or. 1180, which may be explained *"from the third place."*   *c.* The agent (for ὑπό) with passive or intransitive verbs, almost entirely Ionic, especially Hdt., rarely in Attic prose: Il. β. 669 ἐφίληθεν ἐκ Διός: Il. σ, 107 ἀπολέσθαι ἔκ τινος: Hdt. III. 62 τὰ ἐντεταλμένα ἐκ τοῦ Μάγου: Ibid. προδεδόσθαι ἐκ Πρηξάσπεος: Id. VI. 95 Ἀβυδηνοῖσι γὰρ προσετέτακτο ἐκ βασιλῆος — φύλακας εἶναι κ. τ. λ.   *d.* The cause, occasion: ἐξ ἔριδος μάχεσθαι, ἐκ καύματος Homer; but rarely of inanimate objects instead of the instrumental dative: Hdt. VI. 67 ἔφευγε δὲ Δημάρητος ἐκ Σπάρτης — ἐκ τοιοῦδε ὀνείδεος: Soph. Œ. C. 887 ἔκ τινος φόβου βουθυτοῦντά μ' ἔσχετε.— So ἐκ θυμοῦ φιλεῖν Hom.: Plat. Gorg. p. 510 D ἐκ παντὸς τοῦ νοῦ.   *e.* Material; as, ἔκπωμα ἐκ ξύλου.—(See §. 588. Obs. 1 :) Od. ζ 224 ἐκ τοῦ ποταμοῦ νίζεσθαι.   *f.* Means and instruments; as, ἐκ βίας and the like: Soph. Trach. 887 ἐξ ἀκινήτου ποδός: Id. Œ. C. 848 ἐκ σκήπτρων ὁδοιπορεῖν: Eur. Hec. 573 ἐκ χερῶν φύλλοις ἔβαλλον.   *g.* Conformity to—in consequence—by virtue of—according to; as, Hdt. II. 152 ἐκ τῆς ὄψιος τοῦ ὀνείρου: Plat. Crit. p. 48 B οὐκοῦν ἐκ τῶν ὁμολογουμένων τοῦτο σκεπτέον: Id. Charm. p. 160 B ἐκ τούτου τοῦ λόγου: Demosth. p. 91. extr. ἐκ τούτων τὰ δίκαια τίθενται: Id. p. 93, 16 εἴ γε ἐκ τῆς ἐπιστολῆς δεῖ σκοπεῖν: d. p. 114, 15 ἔστιν —, ὅστις εὖ φρονῶν ἐκ τῶν ὀνομάτων μᾶλλον ἢ τῶν πραγμάτων τὸν ἄγοντ' εἰρήνην ἢ πολεμοῦνθ' ἑαυτῷ σκέψαιτ' ἄν;

ᵃ Pflugk ad loc.   ᵇ Ibid.   ᶜ Heindorf et Stallb. ad loc.

—ἐξ ἴσου (see §.501. Obs. 5.) So ὀνομάζεσθαι ἔκ τινος, as *virtus ex viro appellata est* Cicer. Tuscul.—ἐκ τοῦ; why?

Obs. 1. Most compounds of ἐκ take the genitive.

Obs. 2. The improper adverbs which take a genitive are given under the gen.; besides these, the following substantives, when used as improper prepositions take a genitive.—(See *Acc. in App.*) *a.* δίκην (δέμας poet.), *instar:* See §. 580. 2. On ἄδην see §. 578. *Obs.* 2.—*b.* χάριν (poet. and late prose), *gratiâ,* for the sake of; generally after, but sometimes before, the genitive: Eur. Andr. 1235 χάριν σῶν τῶν πάρος νυμφευμάτων. For the gen. of the personal pronoun, ἐμοῦ, σοῦ, the possessive pronoun is joined with it as an attributive; as, ἐμήν, σὴν χάριν, *med, tuâ gratiâ.* — *c.* ἕνεκα (ἕνεκεν even before a consonant, and ἕνεκα before a vowel in Attic Greek; εἵνεκα and εἵνεκεν Ion., but found sometimes in Attic, οὕνεκα old poets), appears to be the acc. of an obsolete nom., Latin, *causâ* and *gratiâ.* The gen. may be placed either before or after it; it very often means, "as far as concerns"—"with regard to:" Hdt. III. 85 θάρσεε τούτου εἵνεκε, as far as this goes, be of good heart. It often gives the more remote cause, "by reason"—"in consequence of:" Plat. Rep. p. 329 B εἰ γὰρ ἦν τοῦτ᾽ αἴτιον, κἂν ἐγὼ τὰ αὐτὰ ταῦτα ἐπεπόνθη ἕνεκά γε γήρως, i. e. in consequence of my age [a]: Demosth. p. 17, 17. χρηστὰ δ᾽ εἴη παντὸς εἵνεκα, *utinam hæc prospere succedant, omnibus adjuvantibus.*—*d.* ἕκητι (only poetic), "after the will of." In Homer and Hesiod it is joined only to the names of the gods, as Διὸς ἕκητι, "by the favour and help of Jupiter"— "by God's blessing."—(See Pass. Lex.) In other poets it has the same sense as ἕνεκα. We even find an improper preposition joined with a proper one: Thuc. VIII. 92 ἀπὸ βοῆς ἕνεκα: cf. Xen. Hell. II. So Soph. Phil. 534 ἀμφὶ σοῦ ἕνεκα. So also Plat. Legg. 701 D τίνος δὴ χάριν ἕνεκα[b].

2. *Prepositions with Dative only.*

Ἐν *and* σύν (ξύν).

§. 622. *a.* Ἐν [ἐνί poet., εἰν and εἰνί Epic, both of which, as well as ἐς, εἰς, are formed from ἐντ, ἐνς] signifies *in, on, at, by,* corresponding to our *in,* as its especial force is union with something, and hence it is opposed to ἐκ. 1. L o c a l.—*a.* The notion of being in, enclosed within, contained by, a spot; as, ἐν νήσῳ, ἐν γῇ. With names of cities; as, ἐν Σπάρτῃ. Hence, being surrounded by; as, Il. o, 192 οὐρανὸς ἐν αἰθέρι καὶ νεφέλῃσι, enveloped in: Plat. Legg. p. 625 B ἀνάπαυλαι ἐν τοῖς ὑψηλοῖς δένδρεσίν εἰσι σκιαραί. So of clothing or arms (Post-Homeric); as, ἐν ἐσθῆτι— ἐν ὅπλοις, ἐν τόξοις διαγωνίζεσθαι — ἐν στεφάνοις, *corollis impeditus:* Xen. M. S. III. 9, 2 φανερὸν δ᾽ ὅτι καὶ Λακεδαιμόνιοι οὔτ᾽ ἂν Θρᾳξὶν ἐν πέλταις καὶ ἀκοντίοις, οὔτε Σκύθαις ἐν τόξοις ἐθέλοιεν ἂν διαγωνίζεσθαι. Then of persons— *among* —(the notion of being in a

number or crowd) ; as, ἐν προμάχοις Hom. : Plat. Legg. p. 879 B
ἔν τε θεοῖσι καὶ ἀνθρώποις. Hence *before, coram* (surrounded by a
number of hearers) : Od. β, 194 ἐν πᾶσι : Plat. Legg. p. 886 E
κατηγορεῖν ἐν ἀσεβέσιν ἀνθρώποις : Demosth. οἱ λέγοντες ἐν ὑμῖν ᵃ :
Id. p. 96, 27 οἱ κατηγοροῦντες ἐν ὑμῖν : Id. p. 108, 74 Τιμόθεός ποτ'
ἐκεῖνος ἐν ὑμῖν ἐδημηγόρησεν. Then applied secondarily to situa-
tions, both external and internal, in which a person is, or is caught,
or detained, whereby he is, as it were, surrounded ; as, ἐν πολέμῳ,
ἐν ἔργῳ, ἐν δαιτί, ἐν φόβῳ, ἐν ὀργῇ εἶναι : Soph. Aj. 270 ἤδεθ' οἷσιν
εἶχετ' ἐν κακοῖς : Plat. Crit. p. 43 C καὶ ἄλλοι — ἐν τοιαύταις ξυμφοραῖς ἁλίσκονται : Id. Phil. p. 45 C ἐν τοιούτοις νοσήμασιν ἐχόμενοι :
Id. Rep. p. 395 D ἐν ξυμφοραῖς τε καὶ πένθεσι καὶ θρήνοις ἐχομένην :
Id. Phæd. p. 108 B ἐν πάσῃ ἐχομένη ἀπορίᾳ : Ibid. δεδέμενος ἐν
ἀνάγκαις : Id. Gorg. p. 513 B ἐν πάσῃ εὐδαιμονίᾳ οἰκεῖν. — So of
occupations ; as, Soph. Œ. T. 570 τότ' οὖν ὁ μάντις ἦν ἐν τῇ τέχνῃ :
Hdt. II. 82 οἱ ἐν ποιήσει γενόμενοι : Thuc. III. 28 οἱ ἐν πράγμασι :
Xen. Cyr. IV. 3, 23 οἱ μὲν δὴ ἐν τούτοις τοῖς λόγοις ἦσαν : Plat.
Phæd. p. 59 A ἐν φιλοσοφίᾳ εἶναι ᵇ :—οἱ ἐν γεωργίαις, ἐν τέχνῃ εἶναι
Plat. Hence many adverbial expressions are developed ; as, ἐν
ἴσῳ εἶναι, to be equal ; ἐν ἡδονῇ μοί ἐστιν Hdt., it is pleasing to
me. So also with ἔχειν, ποιεῖσθαι, as ἐν ὁμοίῳ, ἐν ἐλαφρῷ ποιεῖσθαι
Hdt., to hold it in little value. Hence of persons, in whose hands
power resides : Od. χ, 69 δύναμις γὰρ ἐν ὑμῖν. So ἐν ἐμοί, σοί ἐστί
τι. Hence the phrase ἐν ἑαυτῷ εἶναι, to be in one's own power,
sui compotem esse. b. The notion of one thing being *on* another ;
as, ἔστη ἐν οὔρεσιν, ἐν ἵπποις, ἐν θρόνοις ᶜ. c. The notion of one
thing being *at,* or *by* another ; as, ἐν οὐρανῷ, ἐν ποταμῷ, ἐν τόξῳ,
ἐν ξίφει Hom. The Attics used it of names of cities, and especially with fields of battle ; as, ἡ ἐν Μαντινείᾳ μάχη, *at* : Demosth.
p. 116, 23 μετὰ τὴν ἐν Λεύκτροις μάχην. 2. T e m p o r a l (Post-
Hom.) ; as, ἐν τούτῳ τῷ χρόνῳ—ἐν ᾧ, in the time that, whilst :
Xen. M. S. III. 13, 5 ἐν πέντε ἡμέραις. 3. C a u s a l—a. Means
and instruments, when an object may be considered as received
into, contained, held, existing in the means. So of perceptions
of sense, in the phrases ὁρᾶν, ὁρᾶσθαι, ὄπτεσθαι ἐν ὀφθαλμοῖς (poet.) :
Il. α, 587 μή σε — ἐν ὀφθαλμοῖσιν ἴδωμαι, very frequently. Then
in other combinations in the poets : ἐν πυρὶ καίειν Il. ω, 38 : ἐν
δεσμῷ δῆσαι, ἐν χερσὶ λαβεῖν Hom., especially Pindar ; as, Nem.
XI. 17 ἐν λόγοις αἰνεῖσθαι, like ἐν μολπαῖς ὑμνεῖν, κελαδεῖν, and the
like : Id. Ol. I. 15 ἀγλαΐζεσθαι μουσικᾶς ἐν ἀώτῳ, *pulcherrimis car-*

ᵃ Bremi ad loc.   ᵇ Stallb. ad loc.   ᶜ Passow Lex.

minibus ornari: Id. Isth. IV. 30 κλέονται ἐν φορμίγγεσσιν ἐν αὐλῶν
τε παμφώνοις ὁμοκλαῖς. So δαμῆναι ἐν χερσί τινος: Pind. Pyth.
II. 8 ἀγαναῖσιν ἐν χερσὶν ἐδάμασσε πώλους, tamed them under his
hand. Prose, especially Xen., with δηλοῦν, δῆλον εἶναι, σημαίνειν
ἔν τινι: Xen. Cyr. I. 6, 2 ὅτι μὲν, ὦ παῖ, οἱ θεοί σε ἵλεῴ τε καὶ
εὐμενεῖς πέμπουσι, καὶ ἐ ν ἱ ε ρ ο ῖ ς δ ῆ λ ο ν καὶ ἐν οὐρανίοις σημείοις:
Ibid. VIII. 7, 3 ἐ σ η μ ή ν α τ έ μοι καὶ ἐ ν ἱ ε ρ ο ῖ ς κ α ὶ ἐ ν ο ὐ ρ α-
ν ί ο ι ς σ η μ ε ί ο ι ς καὶ ἐ ν ο ἰ ω ν ο ῖ ς καὶ ἐ ν φ ή μ α ι ς, ἅ τ' ἐχρῆν
ποιεῖν καὶ ἃ οὐκ ἐχρῆν. So also Anab. II. 5, 17 ὁπλίσεως ἐν ᾗ ὑμᾶς
βλάπτειν ἱκανοὶ εἴημεν ἄν. This mode of expression is frequently
employed by the poets; it brings the means more fairly before the
eyes than the mere instrumental dative. *b.* The mode and manner; as, ἐν δίκῃ, ἐν σιωπῇ. *c.* Conformity—after—according to:
Thuc. I. 77 ἐν τοῖς ὁμοίοις νόμοις τὰς κρίσεις ποιεῖν. So ἐν μέρει, in
turn. Then with names of persons: Eur. Alc. 735 κακὸν τὸ λῆμα,
κοὐκ ἐ ν ἀ ν δ ρ ά σ ι ν, τὸ σόν, not in the fashion of a man. So ἐν
ἐμοί, ἐν σοί, ἐν ἐκείνῳ (poet.): Eur. Hipp. 1335 σὺ δ' ἐν τ' ἐκείνῳ,
κἂν ἐμοὶ φαίνῃ κακός, *ex illius et meo judicio.*

Obs. The comp. of ἐν generally have the dat. or the acc. with εἰς, and
some the acc. alone; as, ἐμπίπτειν, occasionally in tragedy.

§. 623. *b.* Σ ύ ν [originally ΚΣΥΝ, then in the common dialect
σύν, and in Latin *c u m*; ξύν old Attic, but also Doric and Ionic;
Homer rarely, and only for the metre]. Original meaning—community and conjunction; Lat. *c u m*; Eng. *w i t h.* 1. L o c a l;
as, ὁ στρατηγὸς σὺν τοῖς στρατιώταις — ἄνεμος σὺν λαίλαπι. Frequently with the collateral notion of assistance or guidance; as,
Il. γ, 489 σὺν 'Αθήνῃ: Xen. Cyr. III. 1, 15 σὺν θεῷ. Hence to
express a league with, standing by a person to defend him; as,
σύν τινι εἶναι or γίγνεσθαι, *ab alicujus partibus stare:* Xen. Hell. III.
1, 18 σὺν τοῖς Ἕλλησι μᾶλλον ἢ σὺν τῷ βαρβάρῳ εἶναι: Σύν τινι
μάχεσθαι Id. Cyr. V. 3, 5, to fight on his side. 2. C a u s a l.—
a. Means and instruments—conceived as it were, in cooperation
with, and guiding the action—but almost entirely confined to real,
not moral, actions: Eur. Alc. 915 πεύκαις σὺν Πηλιάσιν σύν θ'
ὑμεναίοις ἔστειχον ἔσω: Æsch. Suppl. 119 Πολλάκι δ' ἐμπίτνω ξὺν
λακίδι. Also Od. ε, 293 σὺν δὲ νεφέεσσι κάλυψεν γαῖαν ὁμοῦ καὶ πόντον.
b. Mode and manner—considered as connected with, and guiding
the action; as, σὺν τάχει, σὺν βίᾳ ποιεῖν τι. *c.* Size—whereby the
action is limited and defined; as, Il. δ, 161 σύν τε μεγάλῳ ἀπέτισαν, σὺν σφῇσιν κεφαλῇσι, γυναιξί τε καὶ τεκέεσσιν: Xen. Cyr. III.
1, 15 πότερα δ' ἡγῇ, ὦ Κῦρε, ἄμεινον εἶναι, σὺν τῷ σῷ ἀγαθῷ τὰς
τιμωρίας ποιεῖσθαι, ἢ σὺν τῇ σῇ ζημίᾳ. *d.* Conformity—which is

considered as the coincidence of an action with some substantival notion ; as, σὺν τῷ νόμῳ τὴν ψῆφον τίθεσθαι—σὺν τῷ δικαίῳ.

Obs. The compounds of σύν almost invariably take a dative ; but where σύν gives to the verb the notion, that " the subject performs it with somebody else," it is followed by a partitive gen. ; and ξυντυγχάνειν has a genitive depending on the simple verb, while σύν refers to a dative expressed or supplied by the mind.

3. *Prepositions with Accusative only.*

'Ανά, εἰς, ὡς.

§. 624. *a.* 'Α ν ά [original meaning *o n, u p*]. In the Epic, Lyric, and Choral songs of the tragedians, ἀνά has also a dative ; as, ἀνὰ σκήπτρῳ, ὤμῳ, Γαργάρῳ ἄκρῳ in Homer. So εὕδει δ' ἀνὰ σκάπτῳ Διὸς αἰετός Pind. With the accus. it is exactly opposed to κατά with the accus. ; the one signifying a motion from above to below, the other from below to above. 1. L o c a l. — *a.* Direction towards some higher object : Il. τ, 212 ἀνὰ πρόθυρον τετραμμένος : Od. χ, 132. 143 ἀναβαίνειν ἀνά τι : v. 176 κίον' ἀν' ὑψηλὴν ἐρύσαι : Il. κ, 466 θῆκεν ἀνὰ μυρίκην. But this is confined mostly to the course of a river : ἀνὰ τὸν ποταμόν Hdt. II. 96. ἀνὰ ῥόον πλεῖν, up stream ; (κατὰ ποταμόν, down stream.) *b.* To express an extension of any thing—from bottom to top— *throughout* ; with verbs of rest, as well as motion : Il. ν, 547 (φλέψ) ἀνὰ νῶτα θέουσα διαμπερές (*ab infima dorsi parte usque ad cervicem*) : Il. a, 670 ἀνὰ δῶμα : Il. δ, 209 ἀνὰ στρατόν. — 'Ανὰ μάχην, ὅμιλον, νῆας, ἄστυ, πεδίον &c. in Homer [a]. So ἀνὰ στόμα ἔχειν Hom., Eurip. El. 80 (as it were to cast down and up in one's mouth), ἀνὰ θυμόν Hom., Hdt. VI. 131 καὶ οὕτω 'Αλκμαιωνίδαι ἐβώσθησαν ἀνὰ τὴν 'Ελλάδα. 2. T e m p o r a l.—Extension in time —duration—*throughout* ; in Homer, only Il. ξ, 80 ἀνὰ νύκτα : Hdt. VIII. 123 ἀνὰ τὸν πόλεμον τοῦτον. So ἀνὰ πᾶσαν τὴν ἡμέραν, ἀνὰ νύκτα : Id. VII. 10, 6 ἀνὰ χρόνον ἐξεύροι τις ἄν, with time — properly from a prior (as it were lower) to a later (as it were higher) point of time. 3. C a u s a l.—Mode and manner like κατά : the action being conceived of moving along in conformity to some higher object. So ἀνὰ κράτος, strongly ; ἀνὰ μέρος, in turn. Hence arises its distributive force in Hdt. ; as, Hdt. VII. 106 πέμπεσκε δὲ ἀνὰ πᾶν ἔτος, *quotannis* : Xen. Anab. IV. 6, 4 ἀνὰ πέντε παρασάγγας τῆς ἡμέρας, five parasangs every day. Lastly, in definitions of number, (first in Hdt. :) Engl. *about* ; Lat. *circa* ; as, Hdt. IV. 101 ἡ δὲ ὁδὸς ἡ ἡμερησίη ἀνὰ διηκόσια στάδια συμβέβληται.

[a] Passow Lex.

Obs. The compounds with ἀνά are joined with the acc. or gen. according to the verbal notion of the compound, as discernible in the elements thereof, or the context; as, ἀναβαίνειν τὸ ὄρος, to climb the mountain; but in Hom., like ἐπιβαίνειν (gen. partitive): Od. ι, 177 ὣς εἰπὼν ἀνὰ νηὸς ἔβην : Od. β, 416 ἂν δ' ἄρα Τηλέμαχος νηὸς βαῖνε, stepped on board ship; ἀνά expressing the stepping up the side of the ship; and the gen. being used, because the spot where Telemachus reached the deck is considered as *part* of the ship. So with the gen., where the compound notion is such as, by the ordinary rules, to require it so to be; as, Il. α, 359 ἀνέδυ πολιῆς ἁλός.— ἀναπνεῦσαι πόνοιο Hom.—So ἀνακουφίζειν, ἀνασώζειν Soph. : ἀναΐσσειν Eur., &c.

§. **625.** *b.* Εἴς (ἐς Ion., old Att., and poets for the metre, and in certain combinations ἐς retained its place) is only a modified form of ἐν. Whence the Dorians and Æolians use ἐς and ἐν in the same sense and constructions[a], and ἐς is found in inscriptions with dat. It expresses the same relations as ἐν, except that it has the notion of a direction—*whither*, while ἐν has the notion of rest—*where*. It is used to express the motion of an action—*into* an object, or *up* to an object—in its immediate neighbourhood; especially to express the reaching some definite point. 1. L o c a l.—*a.* An object in space; as, ἰέναι εἰς τὴν πόλιν : Il. α, 366 ᾠχόμεθ' ἐς Θήβην, ἱερὴν πόλιν Ἠετίωνος. So with persons, but with the collateral notion of their habitation (Epic, seldom pure Attic); as, Od. γ, 317 ἐς Μενέλαον ἐλθεῖν, to the tent of Menelaus: Od. ξ, 127 ἐλθὼν ἐς δέσποιναν ἐμήν : Plat. Apol. p. 17 C εἰς ὑμᾶς εἰσιέναι, i. e. εἰς τὸ δικαστήριον εἰσιέναι[b] : Demosth. p. 113, 11 εἰς Φωκέας ὡς π ρ ὸ ς συμμάχους ἐπορεύετο, ad εἰς *ponitur nomen* Φωκ. ut r e g i o n i s, ad πρὸς συμμ. *cogitandum ut nomen populi*[c]. In Attic writers also, in a hostile sense, *contra:* Thuc. III. 1 ἐστράτευσαν ἐς τὴν Ἀττικήν. *b.* To express a point of quantity; as, Thuc. I. 74 ναῦς ἐς τὰς τετρακοσίας. Hence also as a distributive—*up to:* εἰς ἑκατόν, *centeni;* εἰς δύο, *bini.* *c.* Extension through space; as, ἐκ θαλάσσης εἰς θάλασσαν : Plat. Gorg. p. 526 B εἷς δὲ καὶ πάνυ ἐλλόγιμος γέγονεν εἰς τοὺς ἄλλους Ἕλληνας, Ἀριστείδης. *d.* In the sense of *coram*, but with the notion of direction towards the object, as if it were reached or arrived at; as, λόγους ποιεῖσθαι εἰς τὸν δῆμον : Plat. Menex. p. 232 A οἱ πατέρες — πολλὰ δὴ καὶ καλὰ ἀπεφήναντο εἰς πάντας ἀνθρώπους. 2. T e m p o r a l.—*a.* A point of time — *until :* ἐς ἠέλιον καταδύντα Hom., till sunset. Hence εἰς ἑσπέραν, towards evening; properly to evening, as a boundary of time. *b.* Duration of time—until the end of some portion of time—*for;* as, Od. ξ, 384 ἐς θέρος, for the summer; properly to the end of the summer : εἰς ἐνιαυτόν, for a year—until the year be past. So in prose: εἰς

a Dissen Pind. Pyth. II. 11. and p. 638.　　Herm. Opusc. I. p. 265.
　　b Stallb. ad loc.　　　　　　　c Bremi ad loc.

τὴν ὑστεραίαν, for the following day ; εἰς τρίτην ἡμέραν. 3. C a u s a l.
—*a.* The mental aim, object, intention, purpose ; as, ἐχρήσατο τοῖς
χρήμασιν εἰς τὴν πόλιν : Il. ι, 102 εἰπεῖν εἰς ἀγαθόν, for good ;—εἰς
τι ; for what ?—εἰς κέρδος τι δρᾶν Soph. Phil. 111.　So *for* the purpose of producing, causing any thing.　It is also used in the New
Testament to express the point arrived at, the consequence of any
thing, without notion of purpose : Rom. i. 20 εἰς τὸ εἶναι αὐτοὺς
ἀναπολογήτους : I. Thess. ii. 16.　Hebr. xi. 3.　*b.* Mode and manner—being considered as objects which the action is endeavouring
to reach : Il. β, 379 ἐς μίαν βουλεύειν.　So Theocr. XVIII. 7 ἄειδον
δ᾽ ἄρα πᾶσαι ἐς ἓν μέλος. — εἰς καλόν, *opportune* ; εἰς τάχος, quickly ;
εἰς δύναμιν Plat., after his power : Xen. Anab. III. 3, 19 ἵππους
εἰς ἱππέας κατασκευάσωμεν, according to the sort of the riders.
c. Especially to express some particular reference to an object—
with respect to ; as, δυστυχεῖν, φοβεῖσθαι εἴς τι Soph.　Prose : θαυμάζειν, ἐπαινεῖν τινα εἴς τι, διαφέρειν τινὸς εἰς ἀρετήν—φρόνιμος, εὐδό-
κιμος εἴς τι—εἰς πάντα, in every respect : Xen. Œcon. II. 4 εἰς δὲ
τὸ σὸν σχῆμα—καὶ τὴν σὴν δόξαν—οὐδ᾽ ὡς ἂν ἱκανά μοι δοκεῖ εἶναί
σοι : Plat. Legg. p. 774 B εἰς μὲν οὖν χρήματα (*quod attinet ad*) ὁ
μὴ θέλων γαμεῖν ταῦτα ζημιούσθω.　So Thuc. IV. 18 ἐς ἀμφίβολον
ἀσφαλῶς, with respect to ; βλέπειν, ἀποβλέπειν εἰς τὰ πράγματα,
like πρός.　They are applied to different substantival notions : so
πρὸς τοὺς λόγους and εἰς τὰ πράγματα ἀποβλέπειν are joined in
Demosthenes.

Obs. The compounds of εἰς mostly take the acc. : εἰσέρχεσθαι and εἰσιέναι
acc. and dat.[a] So Soph. Trach. 297 ἐμοὶ γὰρ οἶκτος δεινὸς ε ἰ σ έ β η : Id.
Antig. 1325 sq. τὰ δ᾽ ἐπὶ κρατί μ ο ι πότμος δυσκόμιστος ε ἰ σ ή λ α τ ο.

§. 626. *c.* 'Ω s, *a d*, *t o*, is used by good authors only with
persons or things conceived of as such.　It is more common in
Attic Greek, though we find it as early as Homer : Od. ρ, 218 ὡς
αἰεὶ τὸν ὁμοῖον ἄγει θεὸς ὡς τὸν ὁμοῖον : Hdt. II. 121, 5 ἐσελθόντα
δὲ ὡς τοῦ βασιλέος τὴν θυγατέρα : Demosth. p. 54, 48 πρέσβεις
πέπομφεν ὡς βασιλέα : Id. p. 98, 35 πέμπετε ὡς ἡμᾶς—πρέσβεις.　It
is joined with names of towns, used instead of the inhabitants thereof ;
as, Thuc. VIII. 36 ἥκοντος ὡς τὴν Μίλητον : Ibid. 103 ὡς Ἄβυδον.

Obs. 1. We must distinguish between this ὡς and the ὡς joined with
εἰς, ἐπί, πρός, with acc. (ὡς εἰς, ὡς ἐπί, ὡς πρός τινα), which is no preposition, but merely expresses a supposed, and therefore intended, direction
towards something, *as if to* : Thuc. VI. 61 ἀπέπλεον μετὰ τῆς Σαλαμινίας ἐκ
τῆς Σικελίας ὡς ἐς τὰς Ἀθήνας : Soph. Phil. 58 πλεῖς δ᾽ ὡς πρὸς
ο ἶ κ ο ν.　Hence also in ὡς ἐπί with a dat. : Thuc. I. 126 κατέλαβε τὴν ἀκρό-
πολιν ὡς ἐπὶ τυραννίδι.

Obs. 2. 'Ωs is not used in composition.

[a] See Elm. Med. 56.

4. *Prepositions with Genitive and Accusative—διά, κατά, ὑπέρ.*

a. Διά, through.

§. 627. Δ ι ά (Æsch. διαί). Original force—*through*; properly —*asunder*, (perhaps connected with δίs) : with gen., in the direction —*whence* ; acc.—*whither.*

I. With gen. it expresses—1. L o c a l.—*a.* A motion extending through a space or object, and passing out of it, whence the genitive—*through*, and *out of*, then *throughout*—which notion Homer expresses yet more forcibly by a combination of διά with ἐκ or πρό ; as, Od. ρ, 460 δι᾽ ἐκ μεγάροιο ἀναχωρεῖν, through the house and out at the other side : Od. σ, 386 δι᾽ ἐκ προθύροιο θύραζε φεύγειν : Il. ξ, 494 δόρυ δ᾽ ὀφθαλμοῖο διὰ πρὸ—ἦλθεν. So Homer : διὰ ὤμου ἦλθεν ἔγχος, through the shoulder and out ; διὰ Σκαιῶν, out through the Scæan gate : Il. ρ, 281 ἴθυσεν δὲ διὰ προμάχων : Ibid. 293 ἐπαίξας δι᾽ ὁμίλου : 294 πλῆξε — κυνέης διὰ χαλκοπαρῄου : Hdt. VII. 8, 2 μέλλω — ἐλᾶν στρατὸν διὰ τῆς Εὐρώπης ἐπὶ τὴν Ἑλλάδα. Yet more forcibly : Ibid. 8, 3 διὰ πάσης διεξελθὼν τῆς Εὐρώπης : Ibid. 105 ἐξήλαυνε τὸν στρατὸν διὰ τῆς Θρῄκης ἐπὶ τὴν Ἑλλάδα : Id. III. 145 διακύψας διὰ τῆς γοργύρης, to creep out through the prison. *b.* An extension through a space — *throughout*, but without the above given collateral notion of the reappearance of the subject of the action. Mostly poetic ; as, Od. μ, 335 διὰ νήσου ἰών : διὰ πεδίον, *per campum :* Xen. Hier. II. 8 διὰ πολεμίας πορεύεσθαι. The difference between διὰ πεδίον ἰέναι and διὰ πεδίου is, strictly speaking, this—the genitive represents the space passed through (διά) as the antecedent condition of the notion ; the accus. is of the cognate notion of the space over which the motion takes place : διά in both cases marks that the motion extended throughout the space. This gen. is applied figuratively in the phrases : διὰ δικαιοσύνης ἰέναι, to pass through justice, i. e. to be just ; διὰ τοῦ δικαίου πορεύεσθαι,—διὰ φόβου ἔρχεσθαι Eur. Or. 747, to fear ; διὰ φιλίας ἰέναι τινί Xen. Anab. III. 2, 8, to be friendly to a person. 2. T e m p o r a l.—The course of some period of time ; properly, through it, and out of it ; as, δι᾽ ἔτους (διά here, as δι᾽ ὁμίλου, through and out again) ; διὰ πολλοῦ, μακροῦ, ὀλίγου χρόνου, also δι᾽ ὀλίγου, πολλοῦ, without χρόνου, or διὰ χρόνου ἦλθε, after long time he came ; διὰ παντὸς τοῦ χρόνου τοιαῦτα οὐκ ἐγένετο, during the whole course of time ; διὰ ἡμέρας, διὰ νυκτός : Hdt. VI. 118 ἀλλά μιν (τὸν ἀνδριάντα) δι᾽ ἐτέων εἴκοσι Θηβαῖοι αὐτοὶ ἐκ θεοπροπίου ἐκομίσαντο ἐπὶ Δήλιον, *post viginti annos.* So of any thing recurring at stated intervals of time; as, διὰ τρίτου ἔτους συνῇεσαν, every third year—after three years (inclusive of the year then current), διὰ πέμπτου ἔτους, διὰ πέντε ἐτῶν, quinto quoque anno, διὰ τρίτης ἡμέρας : Plat. Legg. p. 834 E διὰ πέμπτων ἐτῶν. So of intervals of space : Thuc. III. 21 διὰ δέκα ἐπάλξεων, every tenth battlement. The gen. expresses the time (or space), which is an antecedent condition of the action; and διά the extension of the action through that time or space. 3. Causal (direction whence).—a. The origin; as, διὰ βασιλέων πεφυκέναι. b. Property or quality (as if one were passing through it), in combinations with εἶναι and γίγνεσθαι; as, Thuc. IV. 30 διὰ προφυλακῆς : διὰ φόβου εἶναι Thuc. V. 59 : δι' ἔχθρας γίγνεσθαί τινι, δι' ἔριδος, ὀργῆς, ἀσφαλείας εἶναι or γίγνεσθαι. c. The agent or instrument; as, δι' ἑαυτοῦ often in prose, δι' ἐμοῦ Demosth. : δι' ἐκείνου Thuc. : Hebr. I. 2 δι' οὗ καὶ τοὺς αἰῶνας ἐποίησε, by= through whom (as an agent) He made the worlds[a]. d. The means or accompaniments, simply *with*; δι' ὀφθαλμῶν ὁρᾶν—ἔχειν τινὰ δι' ὀργῆς Thuc. : διὰ χειρῶν ἔχειν,—δι' οἴκτου λαβεῖν Eur. (i. q. οἰκτείρειν) : Plat. Apol. Socr. p. 17 D ἐὰν διὰ τῶν αὐτῶν λόγων ἀκούητέ μου ἀπολογουμένου δι' ὧνπερ εἴωθα λέγειν : Eur. Phœn. 261 εἰσεδέξατο δι' εὐπετείας : Arist. Nub. 583 βροντὴ ἐρράγη δι' ἀστραπῆς. e. Hence material; as, δι' ἐλέφαντος. f. Mode and manner; as, διὰ σπουδῆς —διὰ τάχους Thuc. II. 18. g. Value; as, Soph. Œ. C. 584 δι' οὐδενὸς ποιεῖσθαι, to esteem for nothing; and of superiority or comparison; as, Il. μ, 104 ὁ δ' ἔπρεπε καὶ διὰ πάντων (throughout, among all) : Hdt. I. 25 θέης ἄξιον διὰ πάντων τῶν ἀναθημάτων : Id. VII. 83 κόσμον δὲ πλεῖστον παρείχοντο διὰ πάντων Πέρσαι, *præcipuo cultu inter omnes eminebant.*

II. Accusative.—1. Local.—The extension of any thing throughout and over a space, (Homer, Pindar, Tragic chorus sometimes, but never in prose:) Æsch. Suppl. 15 φεύγειν διὰ κῦμ' ἅλιον.—διὰ δῶμα, διὰ κρατερὰς ὑσμίνας Hesiod : Eur. Hipp. 762 διὰ πόντιον κῦμα ἐπόρευσας ἐμὰν ἄνασσαν. 2. Temporal.—Extension through time; as, διὰ νύκτα. 3. Causal.—a. The cause, as well the antecedent as the final: δι' ἀτασθαλίας ἔπαθον κακόν Hom., (antecedent cause): διὰ ἕτερόν, for the sake of some further object (final cause): διὰ τοῦτο, ταῦτα, δι' ὅ or διό, wherefore ; διότι, because (for διὰ τοῦτο ὅτι), for this reason—*therefore*. So in the Att. formula: εἰ μὴ διὰ τοῦτον, were it not for him; especially when something has been prevented; Lysias p. 423, 60 ἀπολέσαι παρεσκευάζοντο τὴν πόλιν, εἰ μὴ δι' ἄνδρας ἀγαθούς[b] : Demosth. p. 680. I. 26 ψήφισμα τοιοῦτόν τι παρ' ὑμῶν εὕρετο, ἐξ οὗ κυρωθέντος

---

[a] Magee on the Atonement, Vol. I. p. 72.   [b] Bremi ad loc.

ἂν, εἰ μὴ δι' ἡμᾶς καὶ ταύτην τὴν γραφήν, ἠδίκηντο φανερῶς οἱ δύο τῶν βασιλέων. *b.* The means; as, διὰ βουλάς, διὰ μῆνιν.—νικῆσαι δι' Ἀθήνην Od.

Obs. The accus. follows most of the compounds of διά, except those implying the original notion of disunion (δίς), which take a dative.

b. Κατά, *from above, down.*

§. 628. Original meaning—Direction *from above to below, desuper.* Position *over against, contraposition to.* So that if two similar things were placed opposite to one another, each would be κατά to the other.

I. With gen.—1. L o c a l.— *a.* Motion from above to below, *desuper, deorsum;* as, Il. a, 44 βῆ δὲ κατ' Οὐλύμποιο καρήνων, from, down. The genitive expresses the point whence the motion begins, the κατά the direction of it—downwards. So κατ' ὀφθαλμῶν κέχυτ' ἀχλύς, from the eyes downwards. Hence Homer and Hdt. VIII. 53 ἐρρίπτεον ἑωυτοὺς κατὰ τοῦ τείχεος κάτω. Especially with κατ' ἄκρης: πόλιν αἱρέειν, to take a city by storm; properly from the highest point (citadel) to the lowest, i. e. altogether—*penitus.* Hence κατὰ παντός, καθ' ὅλου, for πάντως, ὅλως. So Hdt. III. 60 λιμένα βάθος κατὰ ὀργυιέων, where κατά seems otiose, but really expresses the measure from top to bottom. *b.* Direction towards an object— below (*sub, subter,* with acc.): κατὰ χθονὸς ὄμματα πῆξαι, on the earth which was below: Il. ψ, 100 ψυχὴ κατὰ χθονὸς ᾤχετο, *sub terram:* Hdt. VII. 6 ἀφανίζεσθαι κατὰ τῆς θαλάσσης: Ibid. 235 καταδεδυ- κέναι κατὰ τῆς θαλάσσης. So figuratively of some deep object; like τοξεύειν κατά τινος, παίειν κατά τινος, to strike at something; τύπτειν κατὰ κόρρης, on the head. The gen. here expresses the object aimed at, the preposition the direction, or supposed direction, of the blow.—(See §. 506.) *c.* Sometimes, but mostly in doubtful passages, κατά is used to express *rest in, on, at a place,* where the original force of the preposition is almost lost: Hdt. I. 9 ἐπεὰν κατὰ νώτου γένῃ, behind: Thuc. I. 75. VII. 78 κατὰ γῆς for κατὰ γῆν. The genitive is to be considered as the antecedent condition, as in διὰ γῆς ἰέναι. 2. C a u s a l.— *a.* The object or aim considered as the cause (hence the genitive); as, λέγειν κατά τινος, *dicere de aliquâ re.* The genitive expressing the subject of the λόγος (see §. 486.), the preposition the notion of its being below, subjected to the λόγος, as in the phrase λέγειν ἐπί τινι—especially used in the notion of a hostile intention; as, λέγειν, λόγος κατά τινος: Xen. Apol. S. 13 ψεύδεσθαι κατὰ τοῦ θεοῦ. But not exclusively: Demosth. p. 68,

9 ὃ καὶ μέγιστόν ἐστι καθ' ὑμῶν ἐγκώμιον: Æschin. c. Ctes. §. 50 οἱ κατὰ Δημοσθένους ἔπαινοι: §. 241 ἄνδρας ἀγαθούς, — ἐὰν τοὺς καθ' ἑαυτῶν ἐπαίνους λέγωσιν, οὐ φέρομεν ª. Also σκοπεῖν κατά τινος, where κατά may be translated by *secundum*; as, Plat. Phæd. p. 70 D μὴ τοίνυν κατ' ἀνθρώπων, ἦ δ' ὅς, σκόπει μόνον τοῦτο, εἰ βούλει ῥᾷον μαθεῖν, ἀλλὰ καὶ κατὰ ζώων πάντων καὶ φυτῶν. So also in Attic adjurations and oaths; as, εὔχεσθαι, ὀμόσαι κατά τινος &c.; the gen. expressing that whereupon the force of the oath or adjuration proceeds, the preposition signifying the laying (real or supposed) of the hands upon it. So also εὔχεσθαι καθ' ἑκατόμβης, βοός: Demosth. p. 852, 26 ἡ μήτηρ κατ' ἐμοῦ καὶ τῆς ἀδελφῆς — πίστιν ἠθέλησεν ἐπιθεῖναι.

§. 629. II. With acc.—1. L o c a l.—*a.* Κατά with gen. is exactly opposed to ἀνά in respect of the point whence the motion is supposed to begin, but with the accus. they agree in their notion of position, both signifying an extension over an object, and with verbs of, or implying, motion, direction towards it. The relative position of two parallel perpendicular lines as || would be expressed by either preposition with the accus.; ἀνά from bottom to top, κατά top to bottom. Most of the senses of κατά with accus. are derived from its notion of position, *over against* (*e regione*), *opposite to—at*: Hdt. III. 14 παρῆεσαν αἱ παρθένοι κατὰ τοὺς πατέρας, over against, opposite to: Id. VI. 19 ἐπεὰν κατὰ τοῦτο γένωμαι τοῦ λόγου, *quum ad hunc locum narrationis* i n f r a *sequuturum pervenero*. So in Hom., βάλλειν κατὰ γαστέρα &c. Then κατὰ ῥόον, down stream (see ἀνά). *b.* An extension through space—beginning from above and going downwards — along; as, καθ' Ἑλλάδα: Hdt. III. 109 αἱ ἔχιδναι κατὰ πᾶσαν τὴν γῆν εἰσί. — κατὰ γῆν, κατὰ θάλασσαν πορεύεσθαι. — κατὰ στρατόν, κατὰ νῆας Hom., as ἀνὰ στρατόν, ἀνὰ νῆας, both express extension, the supposed point of commencement being different. So κατὰ φρένα καὶ κατὰ θυμόν Hom., and ἀνὰ θυμόν Hom. 2. T e m p o r a l.—Extension through time, as ἀνά, the point of commencement being different — duration of time: Hdt. III. 131 κατὰ τὸν αὐτὸν χρόνον: Id. I. 67 κατὰ τὸν πρότερον πόλεμον: Id. II. 134 κατὰ Ἄμασιν βασιλεύοντα, ἀλλ' οὐ κατὰ τοῦτον: Id. III. 120 κατὰ τὴν Καμβύσεω νοῦσον ἐγένετο τάδε. So κατ' ἀρχάς, *initio*, Id. III. 153. —οἱ κατά τινα, the contemporaries of any one: Xen. M. S. III. 5, 10 οἱ καθ' ἑαυτοὺς ἄνθρωποι: Demosth. p. 70, 20 κατ' ἐκείνους τοὺς χρόνους, ὅτε κ. τ. λ. 3. C a u s a l—*Secundum.*—*a.* A model or rule for any action: the object being supposed to be placed lengthwise,

---

ª Bremi ad loc.

as a model would be, and the action directed according to it : ̓ κατ᾽
αἶσαν, κατὰ μοῖραν, κατὰ κόσμον, according to order : Hdt. I. 61
κατὰ νόμον : Ibid. 35 κατὰ νόμους τοὺς ἐπιχωρίους : Ibid. 134 κατὰ
λόγον, *ad rationem, pro ratione* : Id. II. 26 κατὰ γνώμην τὴν ἐμήν :
Demosth. p. 98, 34 χαρίζεσθαι καθ᾽ ὑπερβολήν, exceedingly ; καθό
(for καθ᾽ ὅ) or καθότι (καθ᾽ ὅτι), as far as—according to which ;
καθά or καθάπερ (καθ᾽ ἅπερ), as *prout.*   Hence generally of any
thing to which especial reference is made, as this is in some sense
the model or rule of the action ; as, Hdt. II. 3 κατὰ τὴν τροφὴν
τῶν παίδων τοσαῦτα ἔλεγον : Id. I. 85 κατὰ μέν νυν τὸν κρητῆρα
οὕτως ἔσχε. — διαφέρειν κατά τι Lysias : Soph. Trach. 379 ἢ κάρτα
λαμπρὰ καὶ κατ᾽ ὄμμα καὶ φύσιν : Id. Œ. T. 1087 κατὰ γνώμην ἴδρις.
—κατά τι, *quodammodo* Plat. Gorg. p. 527 B : κατ᾽ οὐδέν Id. Polit.
p. 302 B : κατὰ πάντα, in every respect ; κατὰ τοῦτο, *hoc respectu,
propter hoc,* very often Hdt. : Demosth. p. 90, 2 οὓς κατὰ τοὺς
νόμους ἐφ᾽ ὑμῖν ἔστιν, ὅταν βούλησθε, κολάζειν. So to express some
relation which the subject follows as its model — *in proportion
to* ; as, κατὰ φύσιν, *secundum naturam* — κατὰ δύναμιν, after one's
power ; κατὰ κράτος, according to strength — strongly ; κατὰ τὸ
μέγεθος.   *b.* Hence the object, at which any one looks and frames
any action : Od. γ, 72 ἢ τι κατὰ πρῆξιν — ἀλάλησθε ; Ibid. 106
πλαζόμενοι κατὰ ληῒδ᾽ : Hdt. II. 152 κατὰ ληΐην ἐκπλώσαντας :
Thuc. VI. 31 κατὰ θέαν ἥκειν, *spectatum venisse.* — κατά τί ; wherefore ? for what ?   *c.* An indefinite quantity — assimilation to a
number : Hdt. II. 145 κατὰ ἑξήκοντα ἔτεα καὶ χίλια : cf. Id. I. 121.
So κατὰ μικρόν, κατ᾽ ὀλίγον, κατὰ πολύ, πολλά, by far.   *d.* Mode
and manner — which is the model of the action — *according to —
after the fashion of* : Hdt. I. 9 κατ᾽ ἡσυχίην : 124 κατὰ τάχος : Id.
IX. 21 κατὰ συντυχίην, *casu* : κατὰ ἄνθρωπον : cf. Hdt. I. 121 extr.
So κατὰ τὸ ἰσχυρόν, *per vim,* κατὰ τὸ ὀρθόν Hdt. : Demosth. p. 92,
12 συμβαίνει τῷ μὲν (Φιλίππῳ), ἐφ᾽ ἃ ἂν ἔλθῃ, ταῦτ᾽ ἔχειν κατὰ
πολλὴν ἡσυχίαν : Eur. Andr. 554 κατ᾽ οὖρον, favourably.   And
hence any division, (as early as Homer,) these divisions serving as
models or rules for the distribution : κατὰ ἔθνεα Hdt., κατὰ φῦλα :
Id. VI. 79 ἄποινά ἐστι δύο μνέαι κατ᾽ ἄνδρα, *viritim* — κατὰ κώμας,
vicatim. — κατὰ μῆνα, *singulis mensibus,* καθ᾽ ἡμέραν, ἐν καθ᾽ ἕν, one
after the other—singly ; καθ᾽ ἑπτά, *septeni.*

Obs. The compounds of κατά take the genitive where the verbal action
is to be represented as aimed at some one ; which force is communicated distinctly to many simple verbs by κατά ; the gen. being considered
as the cause of the action, and κατά representing the superiority of the
agent. A cognate acc. of the act is found frequently both without this
gen., (where κατά is not the principal element, as κατηγορεῖν ταῦτα, to say

this openly) ; and with it, as κατηγορεῖν τί τινος, to say something against some one ; καταγιγνώσκειν τί (as ἄνοιαν, κλοπήν) τινος, κατακρίνειν τινὸς θάνατον, καταδικάζειν τινὸς θάνατον, καταψηφίζεσθαί τινος δειλίαν, καταψεύδεσθαί τινος ; καταφρονεῖν τινος, *despicere*, καταγελᾶν τινος ; κατασκεδάζειν, καταχεῖν, καταντλεῖν τί τινος. Sometimes the preposition is repeated : κατηγορεῖν and καταγιγνώσκειν κατά τινος Xenoph. Some of these verbs take an accus. of the patient instead of a genitive of the cause of the verbal notion : καταφρονεῖν τινα Eur. Bacch. 503. So cognate accus.: Thuc. VI. 43 καταφρονεῖν τι : Id. VIII. 12 καταλογεῖν τι. So καταγελᾶν with acc. in Eur., κατηγορεῖν τινα Plat., καταδικάζεσθαι with acc. Lysias, καταγιγνώσκειν τινά Xen. Cyr. VIII. 4, 9. Oecon. II. 18. So Demosth. p. 102, 52 ὑμᾶς ἔνιοι καταπολιτεύονται [a]. So dativus incommodi, instead of either accus. of patient, or genitive of cause of verbal action : καταχεῖν in Homer frequently; so also καταγελᾶν : Hdt. VII. 9 τοὺς ἐν τῇ Εὐρώπῃ κατοικημένους οὐκ ἐάσεις καταγελάσαι ἡμῖν. — καθυβρίζειν τινί Soph. Aj. 153. — κατακρίνειν in Hdt. VII. 146 τοῖσι μὲν κατακέκριτο θάνατος.

c. Ὑπέρ, *above*.

§. 630. Ὑπέρ, [Sanscrit *upari*; Lat. *super*, *above*.—] I. Genitive. — 1. Local. — *a*. Motion over an object. Mostly poetic : Il. o, 382 κῦμα — νηὸς ὑπὲρ τοίχων καταβήσεται. So in Homer : ὑπὲρ κεφαλῆς στῆναί τινι : Xen. M. S. III. 8, 9 ὁ ἥλιος τοῦ θέρους ὑπὲρ ἡμῶν καὶ τῶν στεγῶν πορευόμενος σκιὰν αὐτῶν παρέχει ; *b*. (Notion of position)—above (in rest) a place or object. The genitive signifies the relation of position (§. 524.), ὑπέρ defines it : Hdt. VIII. 69 Ἀραβίων δὲ καὶ Αἰθιόπων τῶν ὑπὲρ Αἰγύπτου οἰκημένων ἦρχε Ἀρσάμης : Ib. 115 οἱ ὑπὲρ θαλάσσης : Thuc. I. 46 ἔστι δὲ λιμὴν καὶ πόλις ὑπὲρ αὐτοῦ, of the position of a place on the sea ; situated above the sea—ὑπὲρ θαλάσσης οἰκεῖν. 2. Causal.—Ὑπέρ mostly agrees with περί : " *Id unum interest, quod* π ε ρ ί *usu frequentissimo teritur, multo rarius usurpatur* ὑ π έ ρ : *quod ipsum discrimen inter Lat. praep. d e et s u p e r locum obtinet. Sed Demosth. a vulgari usu sic deflectit, ut passim ponat* ὑπέρ, *ubi assuetus consuetudini positum malit* περί [b]." *a*. (Connected with its local force) in the notion of defending, helping, &c. for a person's good — to stand over, and defend or help a person ; as, μάχεσθαι ὑπὲρ τῆς πατρῖδος.—ὁ ὑπὲρ τῆς Ἑλλάδος θάνατος : Demosth. p. 19, 4 πολιτεύεσθαι ὑπέρ τινος (Φιλίππου), *in alicujus gratiam* : στρατηγεῖν ὑπὲρ Φιλίππου Ibid. p. 30, 6 : Ibid. p. 100, 43 ὑπὲρ τῶν πραγμάτων σπουδάζειν : Ibid. p. 116, 20 ὑπὲρ τῶν πραγμάτων—φοβοῦμαι. *b*. Substitution for—one thing being placed as it were over another and thus substituted for it : Eur. Alc. 700 εἰ τὴν παροῦσαν κατθανεῖν πείσεις ἀεὶ γυναῖχ' ὑπὲρ σοῦ. So Plat. Conviv. p. 179 B ὑπὲρ τοῦ αὐτῆς ἀνδρὸς ἀποθανεῖν. So Id. Gorg. p.

---

[a] Cf. Schæfer et Bremi ad hunc loc.   [b] Buttm. Ind. ad Midian. p. 188.

515 C ἐγὼ ὑπὲρ σοῦ ἀποκρινοῦμαι, in your stead : Xen. Anab. VII. 4, 9 ὑπὲρ τούτου ἀποθανεῖν. So in the New Test. : Rom. v. 8 Χριστὸς ὑπὲρ ἡμῶν ἀπέθανε[a].   *c.* Some mental cause of action, where ὑπό with gen. is more usual ; as, ὑπὲρ πένθους, ὑπὲρ παθέων : Eur. Suppl. 1129 βάρος μὲν οὐκ ἀβριθὲς ἀλγέων ὕπερ : Id. Andr. 490 κτείνει δὲ τὴν τάλαιναν—δύσφρονος ἔριδος ὕπερ. Also δεδιέναι ὑπέρ τινος, to be afraid for some one : Plat. Apol. Socr. p. 24 A ὑπὲρ ποιητῶν ἀχθόμενος.   *d.* With verbs of entreating, suppli- cating : Il. ω, 466 καί μιν ὑπὲρ πατρὸς καὶ μητέρος ἠϋκόμοιο λίσσεο καὶ τέκεος, for the sake of—*by*.   *e.* The object, considered as the cause, especially with the article and infin. : Demosth. p. 52, 43 ὑπὲρ τοῦ μὴ παθεῖν κακῶς ὑπὸ Φιλίππου.   *f.* Generally to express a special reference to something—*about*, for περί with genitive.

II. Accusative.—Motion above, over, beyond an object, whether in space, time, size, or number : 1. Hdt. IV. 188 ῥιπτέουσι ὑπὲρ τὸν δόμον, over the house ; ὑπὲρ Ἑλλήσποντον οἰκεῖν, on the other side the Hellespont : 2. ὑπὲρ τὴν ἡλικίαν.—3. ὑπὲρ αἶσαν, beyond, (contrary to) right ; ὑπὲρ μοῖραν — ὑπὲρ δύναμιν, ὑπὲρ ἄνθρωπον : 4. Hdt. V. 64 ὑπὲρ τὰ τεσσερήκοντα ἔτη.

Obs. The compounds of ὑπέρ take a genitive, when the notion of supe- riority is the prominent notion in the compound verb, as ὑπερφρονεῖν ; otherwise it does not materially alter the sense of the simple verb.

5. *Prepositions with Genitive, Dative, and Accusative :* ἀμφί, περί, ἐπί, μετά, παρά, πρός, ὑπό.

1. 'Αμφί *and* περί.

§. 631. 1. 'Α μ φ ί, π ε ρ ί, express the same position—*a b o u t, a r o u n d ;* ἀμφί, two sides only ; περί, all round. They agree also in their usage, except that ἀμφί is mostly confined to the Ionic dialect and pöetry, while περί is used in all the dialects, and there- fore has acquired a greater variety of meanings and more general usage.

a. 'Αμφί, *about.*

2. 'Α μ φ ί (ἀμπί) [Sans. *a p i* ; Lat. *a p u d* ; in Comp. *a m p, a m b, a m, a n*].   General force—the position of two things, so that one is bounded on two sides by the other.

I. Genitive.—1. L o c a l (Post-Homeric).—*a.* Removal of some- thing surrounded, from the thing surrounding it ; the gen. signi-

---

[a] Magee on Atonement, I. p. 245, sqq. Raphelius, Annot. II. p. 253-4. Schleusner Lex. ad voc. Viner Gramm. p. 328.

fying the removal, ἀμφί the relative position of the things : Eur.
Or. 1470 ἀμφὶ πορφυρέων πέπλων ξίφη σπάσαντες, drawing the
sword from the garments which enveloped it. b. Round any thing
—in rest : Hdt. VIII. 104 τοῖσι ἀμφὶ ταύτης οἰκέουσι τῆς πόλιος.
The gen. signifies an antecedent condition (§. 522.) of the notion
of the verb, ἀμφί defines the position. 2. C a u s a l.—The thing on
which a person is physically or morally employed, is considered as
the cause of such employment, and therefore is in the gen., while
ἀμφί defines the relation more clearly by adding the local notion
of " about ;" as, μάχεσθαι ἀμφί τινος, round—*for :* Od. θ, 267 ἀμφὶ
φιλότητος ἀείδειν (for the more usual περί), as it were, lingering
in song round love : Eur. Hec. 580 τοιάδ' ἀμφὶ σῆς λέγω παιδὸς
θανούσης : Hdt. VI. 131 ἀμφὶ μὲν κρίσιος τῶν μνηστήρων τοσαῦτα
ἐγένετο, as English *about.*

II. Dative—1. L o c a l.—Rest round, at, near ; as, τελαμὼν ἀμφὶ
στήθεσσιν Il. β, 388 : στῆσαι τρίποδα ἀμφὶ πυρί Homer, to place it
on the fire, so that it stood thereon ; then to express total envelop-
ment : Eur. Phœn. 1532 ἀμφὶ κλάδοις ἕζεσθαι, among—surrounded
by twigs. So ἀμφὶ Νεμέᾳ, at the Nemean games. So of time :
Pind. Ol. XIII. 37 ἀμφ' ἐνὶ ἁλίῳ, in one day. 2. C a u s a l.—*a.* The
cause or object, as with gen., with this difference—that the dative
expresses the cause by its position ; there is the notion of an actual
existence of the cause in some particular place : Il. π, 565 ἀμφὶ νέκυι
κατατεθνηῶτι μάχεσθαι : Il. γ, 157 ἀμφὶ γυναικὶ ἄλγεα πάσχειν :
Soph. El. 1180 τί δή ποτ', ὦ ξέν', ἀμφ' ἐμοὶ στένεις τάδε ; Hdt. VI.
129 οἱ μνηστῆρες ἔριν εἶχον ἀμφί τε μουσικῇ καὶ τῷ λεγομένῳ ἐς τὸ
μέσον. So with verbs of *fear, anxiety :* Od. a, 48 ἀλλά μοι ἀμφ'
Ὀδυσῆϊ δαΐφρονι δαίεται ἦτορ : Hdt. VI. 62 φοβηθεὶς ἀμφὶ τῇ γυναικί.
With verbs of *saying :* Hdt. III. 32 ἀμφὶ δὲ τῷ θανάτῳ αὐτῆς διξὸς
—λέγεται λόγος. *b.* Some mental cause ; as, Eur. Or. 825 ἀμφὶ
φόβῳ, *prœ metu* (as it were encircled by fear) : so ἀμφὶ θυμῷ, *prœ
râ ;* ἀμφὶ τάρβει, *prœ pavore.* *c.* The means or opportunity, considered as a local position, so that one thing is surrounded by
another, lingers round it (often in Pindar) : Pyth. I. 12 θέλγει
φρένας ἀμφί τε Λατοΐδα σοφίᾳ βαθυκόλπων τε Μοισᾶν, *demulcet mentes
per Apollinis et Musarum artem :* Ibid. VIII. 34 ἴτω τεὸν χρέος, ὦ
παῖ,—ἐμᾷ ποτανὸν ἀμφὶ μαχανᾷ, *tua res, tuum facinus divulgetur per
meam artem alatum.*

III. Accusative.—1. L o c a l.—Extension round any thing : ἀμφὶ
ῥέεθρα Il. β, 461. Thence an action in the interior (within the circle)
of anything : Il. λ, 706 ἀμφί τε ἄστυ ἔρδομεν ἱρὰ θεοῖσιν, around the
interior of the city. So also of those environing any one : οἱ ἀμφί τινα,

a person and those round him, i. e. his followers. 2. T e m p o r a l.
—An indefinite time ; as, ἀμφὶ τὸν χειμῶνα, about winter : Xen. Cyr.
V. 4, 16 ἀμφὶ δείλην.   Thence an indefinite number ; as, ἀμφὶ τοὺς
μυρίους, *circiter*. 3. C a u s a l.—A mental lingering round, employment, pains about something (also in Att. prose) ; as, εἶναι, ἔχειν
ἀμφί τι : Xen. Cyr. V. 8, 44 ἀμφὶ δεῖπνον ἔχειν : Ibid. VII. 5. 52
ἀμφ' ἵππους, ἅρματα, μηχανὰς ἔχειν.   Thence of any thing which
extends over and about, relates to something else ; as, τὰ ἀμφὶ
τὸν πόλεμον : Pind. Isth. VI. 9 θυμὸν εὐφραίνειν ἀμφ' Ἰόλαον :
Æsch. Sept. 845 μέριμνα ἀμφὶ πόλιν.

b. Περί, round—about.

§. 632. Π ε ρ ί (Æol. π έ ρ, Sansc. *p a r i*- (i. e. *circa*) ; Lat. and
Lith. *p e r* ; Goth. *f a i r*).   Original meaning—*round, in a circle.*
  I. Genitive.—1. L o c a l.—The position of one thing round, encircling another, (only in poetry, and but seldom.) The genitive expresses the antecedent condition (§. 522.), the preposition defines
it, by adding a notion of particular position.   Homer only Od. ε, 68
αὐτοῦ (there) τετάνυστο περὶ σπείους γλαφυροῖο ἡμερίς : and Ibid. 130
τὸν μὲν ἐγὼν ἐσάωσα περὶ τρόπιος βεβαῶτα, as it were riding on the
keel, encircling it with his legs : Eur. Troad. 824 (Chorus) τείχη περὶ
Δαρδανίας φονία κατέλυσεν αἰχμά : cf. Sapph. in Aphrod. 10. 2.
C a u s a l.—It is applied to denote a great variety of causes : the
gen. expresses some antecedent condition to the action, the prep.
defines it, and frequently represents the action as if it were actually
springing from the centre, so to say, of such condition. *a.* As
ἀμφί, but in a greater variety of relations : μάχεσθαι περὶ τῆς πατρίδος : Eur. Alc. 176 περὶ παίδων θνήσκειν.   With verbs of moral or
physical perception : ἀκούειν, εἰδέναι &c. ; of saying and asking ; as,
λέγειν περί τινος, λόγος περί τινος,—ἔρεσθαι περί τινος Od.[a] ; of care,
fright, and other passions ; as, φοβεῖσθαι περὶ πατρίδος, ἐπιμελεῖσθαι,
ἐπιμέλεια περί τινος.   *b.* Thence generally the cause, occasion, relation, reference in various combinations ; as, Eur. Phœn. 534 εἴπερ
γὰρ ἀδικεῖν χρὴ, τυραννίδος πέρι κάλλιστον ἀδικεῖν, about, for the sake
of : Dem. p. 52, 43 τὴν μὲν ἀρχὴν τοῦ πολέμου γεγενημένην περὶ τοῦ
τιμωρήσασθαι Φίλιππον. *c.* Some mental cause ; as, περὶ ἔριδος μάχεσθαι Hom., from strife ; περὶ ὀργῆς, *præ irâ*, Thuc. IV. 130. *d.* The
relation of an agent to that which belongs to and surrounds him,
as if he were the possessor thereof, as in the Attic formulas : τὰ
περί τινος, a person's affairs, &c. ; οἱ περί τινος, those belonging to

a Passow Lex.

any one : Demosth. p. 50, 36 ἐν δὲ τοῖς περὶ τοῦ πολέμου καὶ τῇ τούτου παρασκευῇ ἄτακτα ἄπαντα (sc. ἐστίν). *e.* Estimation, worth, superiority : Homer περὶ ἄλλων, *prœ ceteris* : Il. a, 287 περὶ πάντων ἔμμεναι ἄλλων, properly, from the midst of them : Od. ρ, 388 ἀλλ' αἰεὶ χαλεπὸς περὶ πάντων εἰς μνηστήρων, amidst them all. (The verb εἶναι is commonly found in these constructions with περί; as, περιεῖναι with gen. often has in Homer the sense of surpassing.) Then Hdt. and very frequently in Att. writers in certain phrases : περὶ πολλοῦ, περὶ πλείονος, περὶ πλείστου, περὶ ὀλίγου, περὶ ἐλάττονος, περὶ ἐλαχίστου, περὶ οὐδενὸς ποιεῖσθαι or ἡγεῖσθαί τι, to esteem one high, higher, &c. ; περὶ πολλοῦ ἔστιν ἡμῖν, of great value to us. The gen. signifies the antecedent notion of the value, as it is good Greek to say πολλοῦ ποιεῖσθαι, but περί represents the relation more visibly as arising from an actual circle of objects, as is clearly seen in the Homeric περὶ πάντων, περὶ ἄλλων.

II. Dative.—1. L o c a l.—A position in rest in a circle, environs, neighbourhood (like ἀμφί), but generally with the collateral notion of close connection [a], as, θώραξ περὶ τοῖς στέρνοις : Il. ν, 570 ἀσπαίρειν περὶ δουρί : Il. σ, 453 μάρναντο περὶ Σκαιῇσι πύλῃσι, at : Hdt. VII. 61 περὶ μὲν τῇσι κεφαλῇσι εἶχον τιάρας : Plat. Rep. p. 359 D περὶ τῇ χειρὶ χρυσοῦν δακτύλιον φέρειν. 2. C a u s a l, like ἀμφί with dat., *a.* as μάχεσθαι περί τινι poet.—δεδιέναι περί τινι : Hdt. III. 35 περὶ ἑωυτῷ δειμαίνοντα : Plat. Phæd. p. 114 D θαρρεῖν περί τινι, to be of good cheer about it. *b.* Some ground for an action, internal or external : Il. θ, 183 ἀτύζεσθαι περὶ καπνῷ (Wolf, ὑπὸ καπνοῦ).—περὶ χάρματι, φόβῳ, σθένει, ὀδύνῃ, *prœ* (as it were surrounded by).

III. Accusative.—1. L o c a l.—*a.* Motion into the circle, the vicinity of : Il. κ, 139 περὶ φρένας ἤλυθ' ἰωή, round his mind came the call. *b.* Frequently with verbs of rest, to express an extension through space — *round, at, through* : Il. σ, 374 ἑστάμεναι περὶ τοῖχον : Hdt. III. 61 Καμβύσῃ—χρονίζοντι περὶ Αἴγυπτον—ἐπανιστέαται ἄνδρες Μάγοι, in and round Egypt : Id. VII. 131 ὁ μὲν δὴ περὶ (*in*) Πιερίην διέτριβε ἡμέρας συχνάς, see ἀμφί with. accus. : Thuc. VI. 2 ᾤκουν Φοίνικες περὶ πᾶσαν τὴν Σικελίαν, *per Siciliam* : Demosth. p. 90, 3 Φίλιππος—περὶ Ἑλλήσποντον ὤν. Hence οἱ περὶ τινα, those who are about a person ; οἱ περὶ Πλάτωνα, Plato's scholars : cf. ἀμφί. 2. T e m p o r a l (Post-Homeric)—an indefinite period, like ἀμφί : Thuc. III. 89 περὶ τούτους τοὺς χρόνους. So an indefinite number ; as, περὶ μυρίους. 3. C a u s a l—ἀμφί, περὶ δόρπα πονεῖσθαι Hom. (as it were, running about.) Attic : ἀμελῶς ἔχειν περί τινα ; very often εἶναι περί τι, and so generally to express a

[a] Nitzsch. ad Od. p. 243.

particular reference to any thing; as, Xen. Anab. III. 2, 20 ἐξαμαρτάνειν περί τινα: Ibid. I. 6, 8 ἄδικος περί τινα: Id. M. S. I. 1, 20 σωφρονεῖν περὶ τοὺς θεούς: Plat. Rep. princ. πονηρὸς περί τι: Id. Gorg. p. 490 E περὶ σιτία λέγειν: αἱ περὶ τὸ σῶμα ἡδοναί—τὰ περὶ τὴν ἀρετήν, the essence of virtue. Also the subject matter of an argument, or treatise, or system: Plat. Phædr. p. 261 D περὶ δικαστήριά ἐστιν ἡ ἀντιλογική: Id. Crat. p. 408 A περὶ λόγου δύναμίν ἐστι πᾶσα ἡ πραγματεία.

Obs. 1. In the philosophical works of Aristotle, περί signifies "to be engaged in or upon," and takes its definite sense from the word on which it depends. So ἀρέτη ἐστὶν περὶ πάθη καὶ πράξεις, the subject matter of virtue; ἀρέτη ἐστὶν περὶ ἡδονὰς καὶ λύπας, virtue is the regulation of pleasure and pain.

Obs. 2. The compounds of περί generally follow the simple verb; as περί does not commonly form the principal part of the compound, except where a notion of superiority exists in the compound; as, περιγίγνεσθαι Thuc. I. 55. So the dat. with περιστῆναι Lys. p. 126, 4; and frequently in Demosth. in the sense of "to defend."

2. Ἐπί, *on.*

§. 633. Ἐπί (Sansc. *a b h i*). Original force *upon, on,* whence almost all its various meanings may be derived. It originally expresses the position of one thing *on* another, the latter being as it were the support or the foundation of the former, that whereon it rests. Thence, as an action is conceived to rest upon the motive or cause &c. for which it is done, (the motive being as it were the foundation of the action,) that whereon it rests expresses the *motive, cause,* &c. (like *on* in old English); and as this motive implies different relations with different verbal notions, ἐπί has a corresponding variety of meanings.

I. Genitive.—1. L o c a l.—*a.* Being on or at any thing. The genitive expresses an antecedent condition of the action, and ἐπί defines the peculiar position: Il. χ, 225 ἐπὶ μελίης ἐρεισθείς: Hdt. VII. 111 τὸ μαντήϊον τοῦτο ἔστι μὲν ἐπὶ τῶν οὐρέων τῶν ὑψηλοτάτων: Id. VI. 129 ἐπ᾽ αὐτῆς (τῆς τραπέζης) ὀρχήσατο: Demosth. p. 117, 26 τριάκοντα πόλεις ἐπὶ Θράκης ἐῶ. — ἐφ᾽ ἵππω ὀχεῖσθαι, on horse-back: Hdt. II. 35 τὰ ἄχθεα οἱ μὲν ἄνδρες ἐπὶ τῶν κεφαλέων φορέουσι, αἱ δὲ γυναῖκες ἐπὶ τῶν ὤμων. So also Id. VII. 10, 4 προσκεψάμενος ἐπὶ σεωυτοῦ, as it were resting on yourself, i. e. *tecum.* *b.* A motion towards a place or thing. The genitive represents the place as something aimed at, the desire antecedent to the notion (§. 507.); as early as Homer[a]. Thuc. I. 116 πλεῖν ἐπὶ Σάμον: Xen. Cyr. VII. 2, 1 ἐπὶ Σάρδεων φεύγειν: Demosth. p. 123, 48 ἀναχωρεῖν ἐπ᾽ οἴκου πάλιν. Also Hdt.

[a] Passow Lex.

VII. 31 ὁδοῦ—ἐπὶ Καρίης φερούσης. So Hom. ἐπὶ κόρρης τύπτειν.
2. T e m p o r a l.—The time when any thing happens or exists ; the
time being considered as a space or spot whereon the action rests—
as early as Homer : Il. β, 797 ἐπ᾿ εἰρήνης : Il. ε, 637 ἐπὶ προτέρων ἀνθρώπων : Hdt. VI. 98 ἐπὶ γὰρ Δαρείου—ἐγένετο πλέω κακὰ τῇ Ἑλλάδι : Xen. Cyr. I. 6, 31 ἐπὶ τῶν ἡμετέρων προγόνων : Demosth. ἐπὶ
τῶν κινδύνων, in the moment of danger. We often find the gen.
with a present participle expressing an action with which the action
of the sentence is coeval, whence ἐπί is said to express duration of
time : ἐπὶ Κύρου βασιλεύοντος. So also ἐφ᾿ ἡμῶν, *nostrâ memoriâ* :
Demosth. p. 28, 2 ἐπ᾿ ἐμοῦ γὰρ—γέγονε ταῦτα [a] : Ibid. p. 34, 21 ἐπὶ
τῶν προγόνων : Ibid. p. 23 τῶν τ᾿ ἐπὶ τῶν προγόνων ἔργων καὶ
τῶν ἐφ᾿ ὑμῶν : Id. p. 22, 14 οἷον ὑπῆρξέ ποθ᾿ ὑμῖν ἐπὶ Τιμοθέου,
duce Timotheo. 3. C a u s a l.—*a*. With verbs of saying, swearing,
affirming before some one : λέγειν ἐπὶ δικαστῶν, ἐπὶ μαρτύρων : Demosth. p. 273, 8 ἐπωμόσαντο ἐπὶ τῶν στρατηγῶν : the judges,
witnesses, generals being considered by the Greeks as that whence
the action proceeded, arising and having its force from their
authority, the antecedent cause of the action ; while ἐπί still further
defines the relation by representing it as resting on these persons.
So Hdt. IX. 11 εἶπαν ἐπ᾿ ὅρκου, *quasi substrato vel supposito jure-
jurando :* Soph. Œ. C. 476 ἐπὶ προσπόλου μιᾶς οἰκεῖν, with (as it
were depending on) one servant maid. *b.* The occasion, the
author of any thing—Καλεῖσθαι ἐπί τινος, to be named after some
one or something, whereon, as it were, the name rests : Hdt. VII.
40 Νισαῖοι δὲ καλέονται — ἵπποι ἐπὶ τοῦδε : Ibid. c. 74 ἐπὶ δὲ
Λυδοῦ τοῦ Ἄτυος ἔσχον τὴν ἐπωνυμίην : Id. IV. 45 ἔχειν ὄνομα ἐπί
τινος. — τὴν ἐπωνυμίην ποιεῖσθαι ἐπί τινος. So Ibid. ἐπ᾿ ὅτευ ; for
why ! — ἐφ᾿ ἑαυτοῦ, *sua sponte :* Id. VII. 151 ἐπὶ προφάσιος, *præ-
textu. c.* A cause. — The genitive expresses that whence the
action springs, and ἐπί represents the action as resting on
the object : λέγειν ἐπί τινος, *dicere de aliqua re :* Plat. Charm.
p. 155 D ἐπὶ τοῦ καλοῦ λέγων παιδός. *d.* Conformity to—after the
fashion of, in the case of ; with verbs of examining, deciding, saying,
shewing, &c. The genitive signifies the antecedent condition whence
the action springs ; ἐπί represents this condition as that whereon
the action rests : Ζητεῖν τι ἐπί τινος, κρίνειν τι ἐπί τινος, σκοπεῖν τι
ἐπί τινος, λέγειν τι ἐπί τινος, ἐπιδεῖξαί τι ἐπί τινος, &c.: Isocr.
p. 203 ἐπὶ τῶν ἐλαττόνων καὶ τοῦ βίου τοῦ καθ᾿ ἡμέραν ἐπιδείξειεν ἄν
τις κ. τ. λ.: Xen. Cyr. I. 6, 25 καὶ ἐπὶ τῶν πράξεων δέ, ἦν μὲν ἐν

[a] Bremi ad loc.

θέρει ὦσι, τὸν ἄρχοντα δεῖ τοῦ ἡλίου πλεονεκτοῦντα φανερὸν εἶναι:
Plat. Rep. p. 597 B βούλει οὖν, ἔφην, ἐπ᾽ αὐτῶν τούτων τὸν μιμητὴν
τοῦτον ζητήσωμεν, τίς ποτ᾽ ἐστίν; *visne, ad hæc ipsa imitatorem istum
exigamus* [a] *?* Ibid. p. 475 A εἰ βούλει, ἔφη, ἐπ᾽ ἐμοῦ λέγειν περὶ τῶν
ἐρωτικῶν, ὅτι οὕτω ποιοῦσι, συγχωρῶ τοῦ λόγου χάριν, *ita ut de me
rei exemplum petatur* [b]: Demosth. p. 18. 1 ἐπὶ πολλῶν (in
many cases) μὲν ἄν τις ἰδεῖν—δοκεῖ μοι τὴν παρὰ τῶν θεῶν εὔνοιαν
φανερὰν γιγνομένην τῇ πόλει.   *e.* Dependence on—ἐπὶ representing
a thing as resting on something else: ἐφ᾽ ἑαυτοῦ, ἑαυτῶν, ἡμῶν
αὐτῶν, ἑαυτῆς, by oneself— properly, resting or depending on oneself: Homer Il. η, 194 εὔχεσθε—σιγῇ ἐφ᾽ ὑμείων, ἵνα μὴ Τρῶές γε
πύθωνται: Hdt. V. 98 οἰκέοντας τῆς Φρυγίης χῶρόν τε καὶ κώμην ἐπ᾽
ἑωυτῶν: Id. IV. 114 οἰκέωμεν ἐπ᾽ ἡμέων αὐτῶν. So in Attic writers.
So also ἐπὶ ἑωυτοῦ βάλλεσθαι, *secum solo reputare*, in Hdt.: Id VII.
10 προσκεψάμενος ἐπὶ σεωυτοῦ.   Hence apparently the phrase so
frequent in Attic historians: ἐφ᾽ ἑνός, ἐπὶ τριῶν, τεττάρων τετάχθαι,
στῆναι, one, two, three men deep.   Hence also ἐπί is used to express a steady continuance on a thing; as Dem. p. 42, 6 ἂν—
καὶ ὑμεῖς ἐπὶ τῆς τοιαύτης ἐθελήσητε γενέσθαι γνώμης, *firmiter ad-
hærere huic rationi:* Ib. 9 οὐχ οἷός τ᾽ ἐστίν, ἔχων ἃ κατέστραπται,
μένειν ἐπὶ τούτων: Id. p. 66, 3 κωλύσαιτ᾽ ἂν ἐκεῖνον (*Philippum*)
πράττειν ταῦτα, ἐφ᾽ ὧν ἔστι νῦν, *quibus nunc studet:* Id. p. 93, 14
οἴεσθε τοὺς Βυζαντίους μενεῖν ἐπὶ τῆς ἀνοίας τῆς αὐτῆς: Ibid. p. 101,
47 μένειν ἐπὶ τῆς ἑαυτοῦ, *domi se continere;*   *f.* The object, conceived as the cause: Hdt. V. 109 ἐπ᾽ οὗ ἐτάχθημεν, over which:
super quâ re constituti sumus, that is *cui rei præfecti sumus.* Hence
οἱ ἐπὶ τῶν πραγμάτων, those entrusted with the management of
affairs.

§. 634. II. Dat.—1. Local.—Existence not only as with
gen. *on,* but also, and indeed more frequently, in a more remote
sense, *at,* or *by* a place or thing. *a. On* (rather more usual in
poetry than prose): Hdt. V. 77 κληρούχους ἐπὶ τῇ χώρῃ λείπουσι:
Id. VII. 217 ἐγένοντο ἐπὶ τῷ ἀκρωτηρίῳ τοῦ οὔρεος: Ibid. 41 τουτέων
χίλιοι μὲν ἐπὶ τοῖς δόρασι ἀντὶ τῶν σαυρωτήρων ῥοιὰς εἶχον χρυσέας:
cf. c. 74: Plat. Rep. p. 614 B κείμενος ἐπὶ τῇ πυρᾷ. *β. By—near:*
Hdt. III. 16 ἀποθανόντα ἔθαψεν ἐπὶ τῇσι θύρῃσι: Id. VII. 75 οἰκέ-
οντες ἐπὶ Στρυμόνι: Ib. c. 89 οὗτοι δὲ οἱ Φοίνικες τὸ παλαιὸν οἴκεον —
ἐπὶ τῇ Ἐρυθρῇ θαλάσσῃ.   Hence Xen. Cyr. VI. 3, 28 τῶν ἐπὶ
ταῖς μηχαναῖς, those stationed at the engines: εἶναι ἐπὶ τοῖς
πράγμασι, οἱ ἐπὶ τοῖς πράγμασι, Demosth.; though perhaps in these

---

a Stallb. ad loc.   b Ibid.

instances ἐπί has rather a causal force of the object. So λέγειν ἐπί τινί, to speak a panegyric on a person who is conceived to lie at the speaker's feet. So also when one thing is spoken of as being by or with another; as ἐσθίειν ἐπὶ τῷ σίτῳ ὄψον, with bread, Xen.: Arist. Ach. 835 παίειν ἐφ' ἁλὶ μάδδαν, with salt: ἐπὶ τῷ σίτῳ πίνειν, Xen.: ἐπὶ τῇ κύλικι ᾄδειν, Plat. Hence ἐπὶ τούτοις, on this. So Od. ρ, 308 ταχὺς ἔσκε θέειν ἐπὶ εἴδεῖ, in addition to his beauty. Hence a succession of things in space and time: Il. η, 163 ἐπὶ τῷδε ἀνέστη, on him—after him: Od. η, 120 ὄγχνη ἐπ' ὄγχνῃ γηράσκει, pear on pear: Xen. Cyr. II. 3, 7 ἀνέστη ἐπ' αὐτῷ Φεραύλας.—φόνος ἐπὶ φόνῳ, Eur., murder after murder. So Xen. Hell. I. τὰς ἐπὶ πᾶσι, those in all. 2. T e m p o r a l.—A period in which any thing is done; as ἐπὶ νυκτί Il. θ, 529, the time being considered as a space or spot on which the action is done. 3. C a u s a l.—a. The object or aim of an action, considered as the motive or foundation thereof, (mostly with verbs which do not imply a notion of motion, as with these the acc. is commonly used,) generally with a hostile force, *with a view to the harm of*, frequently found in Homer and other poets, and often in Ionic prose: Hdt. I. 61 μαθὼν τὰ ποιεύμενα ἐπ' ἑωυτῷ: Id. VI. 88 τὸ πᾶν μηχανήσασθαι ἐπ' Αἰγινήτῃσι. So simply with a view to: Id. I. 41 κλῶπες—ἐπὶ δηλήσει φανέωσι: Thuc. V. 45 οὐκ ἐπὶ κακῷ, not with any view to injure. So ἐπὶ τούτῳ, *hoc consilio*: Xen. Symp. I. 5 Πρωταγόρᾳ πολὺ ἀργύρεον ἐπὶ σοφίᾳ, *ad discendam sophiam*. Plat. Apol. p. 20 E ψεύδεταί τε καὶ ἐπὶ διαβολῇ τῇ ἐμῇ λέγει: Demosth. p. 68, 12 ἡγεῖτ' οὖν, εἰ μὲν ὑμᾶς ἕλοιτο φίλους, ἐπὶ τοῖς δικαίοις αἱρήσεσθαι[a]: Id. p. 92, 9 εἴπερ ὡς ἀληθῶς ἐπὶ πᾶσι δικαίοις ταῦτα συμβουλεύουσιν—νόμους θέσθαι ἐπί τινι (for) Plat. And so ὀνομάζειν or καλεῖν τι ἐπί τινι, *nomen alicui imponere*, in Thuc. and Plat. b. Dependence on any thing; as ἐπί τινι εἶναι, *penes aliquem esse*: Hdt. VIII. 29 ἐπ' ἡμῖν ἐστι ἠνδραποδίσθαι ὑμέας: Id. VII. 10, 3 ἀκοῦσαι δεινόν, ἐπ' ἀνδρί γε ἑνὶ πάντα τὰ βασιλέος πρήγματα γεγενῆσθαι: Plat. Rep. p. 460 A τὸ δὲ πλῆθος τῶν γάμων ἐπὶ τοῖς ἄρχουσι ποιήσομεν, i. e. *numerum nuptiarum rectoribus definiendum permittemus*[b]: Demosth. p. 90, 3 ἐφ' ὑμῖν ἐστι (τούτους) κολάζειν: Ibid. p. 103, 55 κολάζειν τοὺς ἀδικοῦντας ἐφ' ὑμῖν ἐστι. c. The condition of any thing—on these terms; the terms being considered as the foundation on which the whole rests. The dative is local. So especially ἐπὶ τούτῳ, ἐφ' ᾧ, ἐπὶ τούτοις, ἐπ' οὐδενί, *nulla conditione, nullo pacto*: Hdt. III. 83 ἐπὶ τούτῳ ὑπεξίσταμαι τῆς ἀρχῆς, ἐπ' ᾧτε ὑπ' οὐδενὸς ὑμέων ἄρξομαι. d. It expresses also the

---

[a] Cf. Bremi. [b] Stallb. ad loc.

antecedent as well as final cause: Thuc. VII. 46 ἐπὶ εὐπραγίᾳ
ἀναρρωσθέντες. *e.* The ground of any mental affection; as, γελᾶν
ἐπί τινι, μέγα φρονεῖν, μαίνεσθαι, ἀγανακτεῖν, &c., ἐπί τινι. (§. 607.)
So Demosth. p. 21, 10 ἀνθεῖ τι ἐπὶ ταῖς ἐλπίσιν: Id. p. 35. extr.
τὴν ἐπὶ (*propter*) τοῖς ἔργοις δόξαν. *f.* The means and instrument
conceived as the foundation of the action: Soph. El. 108 ἐπὶ
κωκυτῷ: Id. Antig. 759 ἐπὶ ψόγοισι δεννάσεις ἐμέ. *g.* Price, condition, reward, with a view to: Il. ι, 602 ἐπὶ δώροις ἔρχεο: Il. κ,
304 δώρῳ ἐπὶ μεγάλῳ: Hdt. III. 38 ἐπὶ τίνι χρήματι δεξαίατ᾽ ἂν
τελευτέοντας τοὺς πατέρας κατακαίειν πυρί. — ἐπ᾽ ἀργύρῳ τὴν ψυχὴν
προδοῦναι, ἐπὶ κέρδεσιν λέγειν Soph. — ἐπὶ μόσχῳ ᾆδειν Arist. Ach.
13, for the prize of a calf: Demosth. p. 103 init. μή ποθ᾽ ἡγήσησθε
ἐπὶ πολλῷ γεγενῆσθαι, *magno constitisse* [a].

§. 635. III. Accusative.—1. L o c a l.—*a.* The object in space
—of motion towards a place; as, ἀναβαίνειν ἐφ᾽ ἵππον, ἐπὶ θρόνον.
b. An extension in space over an object, as well with verbs of rest
as motion; as, πλεῖν ἐπὶ οἴνοπα πόντον Hom.: Od. λ, 577 ἐπ᾽ ἐννέα
κεῖτο πέλεθρα. — κλέος πάντας ἐπ᾽ ἀνθρώπους Hom. — τὸ κάλλιστον
καὶ ἄριστον γένος ἐπ᾽ ἀνθρώπους Plat. Hence the adverbial expressions ὡς ἐπὶ τὸ πλῆθος, ὡς ἐπὶ τὸ πᾶν εἰπεῖν Plat. — ὡς ἐπὶ τὸ πολύ.—
ἐπὶ δεξιά, ἐπ᾽ ἀριστερά Hom., &c. 2. T e m p o r a l.—*a.* The aim or
end of a period—*until ;* as, ἐπ᾽ ἠώ, until morning. *b.* Extension
over a space of time — *during* — till it is completed ; as, ἐπὶ πολλὰς
ἡμέρας, ἐφ᾽ ἡμέραν: Il. β, 299 ἐπὶ χρόνον, for a time. So an end
or limit of quantity ; as ἐπὶ τριηκόσια Hdt., until—as far as—
about: ἐπὶ μέγα, πολύ (also written ἐπιπολύ,) πλέον, μεῖζον, μᾶλλον,
μακρόν—ἐπὶ τόσον, ἐφ᾽ ὅσον—τετάχθαι ἐπὶ πολλούς (*many deep*) Xen.
3. C a u s a l.—*a.* The object—intention; with verbs either expressing or implying motion—a. as early as Homer: Od. γ, 421
ἐπὶ βοῦν ἴτω, *ad bovem petendum :* Il. δ, 384 στέλλειν ἐπ᾽ ἀγγελίην: ⋆
Hdt. I. 37 ἐπὶ θήραν ἰέναι, *venatum ire :* Id. III. 14 ἐπὶ ὕδωρ ἰέναι,
aquatum ire : Id. VII. 32 ἀπέπεμπε ἐπὶ γῆς αἴτησιν: Id. V. 12 πέμπειν ἐπὶ ὕδωρ. Hence ἐπὶ τί; wherefore? Arist. Aves 298 ἐπὶ τὸν
δίαυλον ἦλθον : so προτρέπειν ἐπ᾽ ἀρετὴν, so figuratively ἰέναι ἐπ.
β. With hostile intent—the end or object of ᾽an expedition being
the enemy—*against ;* as, Hdt. I. 71 στρατεύεσθαι ἐπὶ Λυδούς. —
ἐλαύνειν ἐπὶ Πέρσας Ibid. 90. Ibid. 153 ἐπὶ Ἴωνας ἄλλον πέμπειν
στρατηγόν. So Demosth. p. 62, 28 ταῦτα ἐφ᾽ ἑαυτοὺς ἡγοῦντο εἶναι:
b. Conformity — mode and manner: Od. ε, 245 ἐπὶ στάθμην, *ad
amussim.* So ἐπ᾽ ἴσα, in the same way: Hdt. III. 71 τὴν—ἐπιχεί-

* Bremi ad loc.

ρῆσιν ταύτην μὴ οὕτω συντάχυνε ἀβούλως, ἀλλ᾽ ἐπὶ τὸ σωφρονέστερον αὐτὴν λάμβανε, according to (bringing it to) prudence. *c.* Generally to express particular reference to any thing: Il. ζ, 79 ἄριστοι πᾶσαν ἐπ᾽ ἰθύν: Plat. Rep. p. 370 B διαφέρων ἐπὶ πρᾶξιν. — Τὸ ἐπ᾽ ἐμέ, *quod ad me attinet.*

Obs. The compounds of ἐπί are constructed with gen., dat., and acc., according to the sense of the compound verb.

3. Μετά, with.

§. 636. Μετά (Æol. πέδα), *with* ; connected with μέσος.

I. Genitive.—1. Local.—Connexion and community with, so that one thing is so intimately connected with the other that they are affected by the same action as one and the same thing: Od. κ, 140 μετὰ δμώων πῖνε καὶ ἦσθε: Eur. Hec. 209 μετὰ νεκρῶν κείσομαι, to lie among the dead, and oneself to be dead: Plat. Rep. p. 359 E καθῆσθαι μετὰ τῶν ἄλλων. Hence an active connexion, to aid a person; as, μετά τινος μάχεσθαι, to fight (in company) with a person: Demosth. p. 117, 24 μετὰ τῶν ἠδικημένων πολεμεῖν. — εἶναι μετά τινος Thuc., *ab alicujus partibus stare.*—ἔπεσθαι μετά τινος in Att.: Plat. Rep. p. 467 extr. σωθήσονται μετὰ πρεσβυτέρων ἡγεμόνων ἑπόμενοι, following with the older leaders. 2. Causal.—*a.* Mode and manner; the means being considered as accompaniments: Thuc. I. 18. extr. μετὰ κινδύνων τὰς μελέτας ποιούμενοι: Xen. M. S. III. 5, 8 μετ᾽ ἀρετῆς πρωτεύειν, *with*—as it were joined with virtue: Demosth. p. 29, 3 μετὰ παρρησίας ποιεῖσθαι λόγους : Id. p. 95, 21 μετὰ παρρησίας ἐξετάσαι τὰ παρόντα πράγματα: Id. p. 93, 13 μετὰ πλείστης ἡσυχίας ἄπανθ᾽, ὅσα βούλεται, Φίλιππος διοικήσεται: Id. p. 130, 74 ὑμῖν οἱ πρόγονοι τοῦτο τὸ γέρας ἐκτήσαντο καὶ κατέλιπον μετὰ πολλῶν καὶ μεγάλων κινδύνων. *b.* In conformity with—unity with : μετὰ τῶν νόμων Demosth., according to the laws—in union with the laws (τῶν νόμων ἐχόμενος, *legibus adhærens*): Plat. Apol. p. 32 C μετὰ τοῦ νόμου καὶ τοῦ δικαίου ᾤμην μᾶλλόν με δεῖν διακινδυνεύειν, ἢ μεθ᾽ ὑμῶν γενέσθαι.—μετὰ τοῦ λόγου Id. Phæd. p. 66 B: Demosth. p. 19 princ. μετ᾽ ἀληθείας σκοπεῖσθαι (ἐχόμενος τῆς ἀλ.).

II. Dative.—Only poetic, and especially epic.—*a.* To express a local union, where in prose σύν and ἐν are used. In general it is joined with the plural, or the singular of collective nouns, or with persons or things considered as such, or the parts of animate things: μετ᾽ ἀθανάτοις, with—among—in the midst of—between : μετὰ στρατῷ; μετὰ χερσί, ποσσί, γένυσσι, γαμφηλῇσι, μετὰ φρεσίν, in the mind: μετὰ νηυσί, κύμασι. *b.* Society—community; as μετὰ πνοιῇς ἀνέμοιο Hom., together with (so ἅμα πν. ἀ.). Hence to signify an addition to : Od. κ, 204 δίχα πάντας ἠρίθμεον, ἀρχὸν δὲ μετ' ἀμφοτέροισιν ὤπασσα, with, or to both.

III. Accusative.—1. L o c a l.—*a.* A motion. a. Into the midst of—*among*; as, ἱκέσθαι μετὰ Τρῶας καὶ 'Αχαιούς: Il. ρ, 460 ἀΐσσων ὥστ' αἰγυπιὸς μετὰ χῆνας. Seldom of things: Od. β, 308 ὅς με μετ' ἀπρήκτους ἔριδας καὶ νείκεα βάλλει, into the midst of. β. Generally direction or striving after, connection or union, whether friendly or hostile, with a person or thing ; as, βῆναι μετὰ Νέστορα, properly into union with, to join Nestor ; βῆ δὲ μετ' Ἰδομενῆα Il. ν, 297, to set after, to join him. Thence generally of succession in space—*behind, after :* Il. ν, 492 λαοὶ ἔπονθ' ὡσεί τε μετὰ κτίλον ἔσπετο μῆλα, behind the ram. Thence the same notion is applied to the relations of value, and rank, &c. *secundum*, after, next to, especially with superlatives ; as, κάλλιστος μετὰ Πηλείωνα : Il. β, 674. Il. ι, 54 μετὰ πάντας ὁμήλικας ἔπλευ ἄριστος : Hdt. IV. 53 ποταμὸς μέγιστος μετὰ Ἴστρον : Ibid. 49 ἔσχατοι—μετὰ Κύνητας οἰκέουσι, *post Cynesios.* *b.* A space between two objects, in the phrase μετὰ χεῖρας ἔχειν Hdt., between, in hand ; *occupatum esse in aliqua re :* Hdt. VII. 16, 2 ταύτην τὴν στρατηλασίην καὶ τὸ κάρτα (*quam maxime*) εἴχομεν μετὰ χεῖρας. 2. T e m p o r a l.—Succession in time, analogous to the succession in space ; as, μετὰ ταῦτα, after this. The subst. in the acc. is often joined with the part. ; as, Il. ρ, 605 μετὰ Λήϊτον ὁρμηθέντα : Hdt. I. 34 μετὰ Σόλωνα οἰχόμενον, after the departure of Solon ; μεθ' ἡμέρην Hdt. I. 150, and also Attic, *i n t e r d i u*, by day (properly after day rise). 3. C a u s a l. —*a.* Object : Od. a, 184 πλεῖν μετὰ χαλκόν, *ad aes petendum :* Eur. Alc. 67 Εὐρυσθέως πέμψαντος ἵππειον μετὰ ὄχημα. *b.* Accordance with,—according to a moral following after any thing : Il. ο, 52 τῷ κε Ποσειδάων γε — αἶψα μεταστρέψειε νόον μετὰ σὸν καὶ ἐμὸν κῆρ, according to your and my heart's desire.

Obs. The compounds of μετά, which denote "change," generally take a genitive of the old, an accusative of the new state, or position ; as, Eur. Med. 257 οὐχὶ συγγενῆ μ ε θ ο ρ μ ί σ α σ θ α ι τῆσδ' ἔχουσα συμφορᾶς.

4. Παρά, *by, and* πρός, *before.*

§. 637. These prepositions are nearly allied in their signification. The chief difference between them is, that παρά is used rather of external relations of space, πρός of internal relations of causation. This difference is perceived most strongly in the gen., where παρά generally expresses an external procession in space, πρός rather the procession of some energy or operation.

a. Παρά, *by.*

Many of the significations of παρά are apparently contradictory: such as *to, from, in consequence of, against,* but all of them are derived from the different relations of position which are signified by this preposition.

Παρά (Epic παραί: Sanscr. *parā* ; Litth. *pas, par-*; Goth. and German *fra, fram*). Original meaning — *by the side of.* Hence as every thing has four sides, the relations in which the object is viewed by the speaker will vary according to the position *by* one or other of these sides, and according to the power of the cases with which it is joined.

Obs. The letters refer to these lines to denote the position in which the object is supposed to stand.

I. With gen.—1. Local.—(A) *In front of,* and as the genitive with verbs of motion signifies the point whence the motion begins, it is used in the relations of space, to define more clearly this point which might have been denoted by the gen.: (§. 530.) *coming from the side of, motion from ;* as, ἐλθεῖν παρά τινος, like the French *de chez quelqu'un* ; φάσγανον ἐρύσσασθαι παρὰ μηροῦ: Hdt. VIII. 140 ἀγγελίη ἥκει παρὰ βασιλῆος. So always of an embassy, παρά, not πρός ; as, πεμφθῆναι παρά τινος Hom.—ἄγγελοι, πρέσβεις παρά τινος —ἀγγέλλειν παρά τινος, τὰ παρά τινος, &c. 2. Causal.—The person or thing whence knowledge or hearing. &c. proceeds ; as, μανθάνειν παρά τινος, ἀκούειν παρά τινος: Hdt. II. 104 παρ' Αἰγυπτίων μεμαθήκασι. So Demosth. p. 108, 75 τὰ μὲν ἔργα παρ' ὑμῶν αὐτῶν ζητεῖτε, τὰ δὲ βέλτιστα ἐπιστήμη λέγειν παρὰ τοῦ παριόντος (*apud oratorem*). a. παρ' ἑαυτοῦ, ἑαυτῶν, *sponte suâ.* β. With passive and intransitive verbs (especially in late prose) for ὑπό, when the energy is supposed to proceed immediately from (as it were, the side of) any one—by his means. (So above πεμφθῆναι παρά τινος): Plat. Symp. p. 175 C οἶμαι γάρ με παρὰ σοῦ σοφίας πληρωθήσεσθαι. γ. Hence with verbs of giving, &c.: παρ' ἑαυτοῦ, from his own resources: Hdt. VIII. 5 παρ' ἑωϋτοῦ διδούς: Id. VII. 29 παρ' ἐμωϋτοῦ: Ibid. 106 διὰ τοῦτο δέ οἱ τὰ δῶρα πέμπεται παρὰ τοῦ βασιλεύοντος ἀεὶ ἐν Πέρσῃσι. δ. *From*—of any feeling which is supposed to proceed from some one to its object ; as, ἡ παρά τινος εὔνοια, good will from some one towards some one.

II. Dative (A).—1. Local.—A point in front of, without motion (local dative); as, ἔστη παρὰ τῷ βασιλεῖ. So μέγας παρὰ βασιλεῖ, in the king's presence. 2. Thence Causal.—To express standing before a person as a judge, and submitting to his decision or sentence : Hdt. III. 160 παρὰ Δαρείῳ κριτῇ, *judice Dario* : Id. I. 33 παρ᾽ ἐμοί, *meo judicio* : Ibid. 86 τοὺς παρὰ σφίσι αὐτοῖσι δοκέοντας ὀλβίους : Plat. Rep. p. 529 A παρὰ σαυτῷ : Demosth. p. 18, 3 τοσούτῳ θαυμαστότερος παρὰ πᾶσι νομίζεται (ὁ Φίλιππος).

III. Accusative (A. B. C.).—1. Local.—*a.* (A) *In front of*, and with verbs of motion, defining more clearly the point whither the motion tends—*to the side of*—which might have been denoted by the simple acc., (§. 559.) In the sense of *to* it is only used with persons, or sometimes things considered as persons ; as a city, &c. Except Pind. Ol. II. 70 παρὰ τύρσιν : Hdt. I. 36 ἀπικέσθαι παρὰ Κροῖσον : Ibid. 86 ἤγαγον παρὰ Κῦρον. (B) Motion by the side of —parallel to—*along* ; as, παρὰ τὴν Βαβυλῶνα παριέναι Xen., παρὰ τὸν ποταμόν, by the side of the river. *b.* (B) An extension in space (without motion) alongside of an object—parallel to : Od. μ, 32 οἱ μὲν κοιμήσαντο παρὰ πρυμνήσια νηός : Hdt. IX. 15 παρὰ τὸν Ἀσωπόν : Demosth. p. 24, 22 ἡ τύχη παρὰ πάντ᾽ ἐστὶ τὰ τῶν ἀνθρώπων πράγματα, runs throughout all human things. Thence generally to express an indefinite vicinity — *by* — in the neighbourhood of. *c.* (C) On the other side of — *beyond* ; παρὰ τὸν ποταμὸν, on the other side of the river — transgression. Hence many figurative expressions : παρὰ μοῖραν, beyond, transgressing, contrary to ; παρὰ δόξαν, *præter opinionem*, παρ᾽ ἐλπίδα, παρὰ φύσιν, παρὰ τὸ δίκαιον, παρὰ τοὺς ὅρκους, παρὰ δύναμιν. (Contrary to κατά, as κατὰ μοῖραν, δύναμιν.) So Arist. Nub. 698 οὐκ ἔστι παρὰ ταῦτα ἄλλα, beyond these. 2. (B) Temporal.—Extension in time (Post-Homeric)—*during* ; as, παρ᾽ ἡμέραν, παρὰ τὸν πόλεμον,—παρὰ τὴν πόσιν, *inter potandum*. So of critical moments *during* which any thing happened ; as, παρ᾽ αὐτὸν τὸν κίνδυνον : Demosth. p. 49, 33 παρὰ τὸν καιρὸν — βουλεύσεται, *in ipso tempore*. 3. Causal.— *a.* (B) Possession — by the side of any one, *penes aliquem* : Hdt. VIII. 140 πυνθάνεσθε τὴν νῦν παρ᾽ ἐμὲ ἐοῦσαν δύναμιν. *b.* Accordance with—agreeing with—parallel to—according to ; with verbs of *trying, examining, estimating,* &c.: Plat. Rep. p. 550 A ὁρῶν τὰ ἐπιτηδεύματα αὐτῶν ἐγγύθεν παρὰ τὰ τῶν ἄλλων : Demosth. p. 224,

34 παρὰ τὸν λόγον, ὃν ἀποφέρουσιν,—ἐπιδείξω. *c. Besides;* springing up as the leaves from the stalk, ὡς παράφυές τι. So παρὰ ταῦτα, *præter hæc.* Hence through, by means of, according to; as the Latin *propter*, only used of the antecedent, not of the final cause, except perhaps Pindar: Demosth. p. 43, 15 οὐδὲ γὰρ οὗτος παρὰ τὴν αὑτοῦ ῥώμην τοσοῦτον ἐπηύξηται, ὅσον παρὰ τὴν ἡμετέραν ἀμέλειαν: Ibid. p. 110, 2 οὐ παρ᾽ ἓν οὐδὲ δύο εἰς τοῦτο τὰ πράγματα ἀφῖκται[a]. So παρὰ τοῦτο, παρό, *quapropter.* Thence generally, *d.* in comparisons (B): Hdt. VII. 20 ὥστε μήτε τὸν Δαρείου (στόλον) τὸν ἐπὶ Σκύθας παρὰ τοῦτον μηδὲν φαίνεσθαι: so παρ᾽ ὀλίγον ποιεῖσθαί τι, to esteem little—παρ᾽ ὀλίγον, μικρόν, βραχύ, by little—παρὰ πολύ (παραπολύ adv.), by much, by far—παρ᾽ οὐδὲν τίθεσθαι, as nothing: Plat. Rep. p. 348 A ἂν μὲν τοίνυν—ἀντικατατείναντες λέγωμεν αὐτῷ λόγον παρὰ λόγον. After comparatives or comparative expressions, as ἄλλος, ἕτερος, διάφορος: Thuc. I. 23 ἡλίου ἐκλείψεις πυκνότεραι παρὰ τὰ ἐκ τοῦ πρὶν χρόνου μνημονευόμενα: Plat. Phæd. p. 93 A οὐδὲ μὴν ποιεῖν τι οὐδέ τι πάσχειν ἄλλο παρ᾽ ἃ ἂν ἐκεῖνα ἢ ποιῇ ἢ πάσχῃ. *e.* Hence Proportion—according to: Demosth. p. 467, 6 παρὰ τὰς τριάκοντα μυριάδας δίδωσιν ὑμῖν μυρίους μεδίμνους, for, or on, every 300,000 bushels gives you 10,000: Ibid. p. 1402, 17 παρὰ τοὺς χρωμένους διαλλαττόντων. Often with the collateral notion of superiority, *præ, præter:* Xen. M. S. I. 4, 14 παρὰ τὰ ἄλλα ζῷα, ὥσπερ θεοί, οἱ ἄνθρωποι βιοτεύουσι, in comparison with, beyond other creatures. Hence of interchange: ἡμέρα παρ᾽ ἡμέραν, day by day, *alternis diebus*— also alone, παρ᾽ ἡμέραν, παρ᾽ ἦμαρ.— πληγὴν παρὰ πληγήν, blow upon blow, Arist. Ran. 643. *f.* Besides —within—except: Hdt. IX. 33 παρὰ ἓν πάλαισμα ἔδραμε νικᾶν Ὀλυμπιάδα, except one, within one.

b. Πρός, *before.*

§. 638. Πρός (or ποτί and originally προτί, both forms also Epic; Sans. *prati*) is derived from πρό, and has the same original meaning—*before;* but it is joined with all three cases, and with the genitive expresses a far greater variety of causal relations than πρό. While παρά expresses the relations of position on all four sides, πρός expresses only one, namely *in front of.*

I. Gen.—1. Local.—*a.* Before—in front of—this side of— coming from; the genitive expresses the point whence the motion is supposed to begin, and is further defined by the preposition,

---

[a] Bremi ad loc.

especially of the position of any spot: Hdt. III. 101 οἰκέουσι πρὸς
νότου ἀνέμου: Ibid. 102 πρὸς βορέου ἀνέμου: 107 πρὸς μεσημβρίης
'Αραβίη ἐστι, (as also in Latin, *ab oriente* for *versus orientem.*)
The same position may be expressed by the acc., a motion *towards*
being supposed; (as in Latin also, *versus* or *ad mentem*)—with
the genitive it is *from there* (*towards here*) — with accusative
(*from here*) *towards there*: ἔθνος οἰκημένον πρὸς ἠῶ τε καὶ
ἠλίου ἀνατολὰς Hdt. I. 201: πρὸς βορῆν τε καὶ νότον Id. II. 149.
Sometimes we find both constructions together; as, Hdt. II. 121
τὸν μὲν πρὸς βορέω ἑστεῶτα, τὸν δὲ πρὸς νότον: Id. VII. 126 οὔτε
γὰρ τὸ πρὸς τὴν ἠῶ τοῦ Νέστου—ἴδοι τις ἂν λέοντα, οὔτε πρὸς ἑσπέρης
τοῦ 'Αχελῴου.   *b.* The vicinity, or approach of one thing to another,
the preposition being used to define the particular relation which
the local genitive sometimes expresses alone (§. 522.) — near
thereto, and in front of: Il. χ, 198 αὐτὸς δὲ ποτὶ πτόλιος πέτετ'
ἀεί, he hovered over before the city: Hdt. II. 154 εἰσὶ οὗτοι οἱ
χῶροι πρὸς θαλάσσης.   The dative could also be used, but would
denote merely the actual vicinity, while the genitive represents the
place, as that whereon the verbal notion in some way depends.
2. C a u s a l. — The cause, occasion, author, generally any agent;
the action being considered to arise by virtue of the presence
of a person, or thing considered as a person.   *a.* Of descent; as,
οἱ πρὸς αἵματος, blood relations; πρὸς πατρός, πρὸς μητρός, from the
father's or mother's side.   *b.* Of properties which belong to any
one, or of the possessor of any thing, whence the action is supposed to arise; as, πρὸς γυναικὸς ἐστι, it is the property of a
female, it arises from the nature of a woman; πρὸς δίκης ἐστιν,
it is right.—See §. 521. 2.   So Od. ζ, 207 πρὸς Διὸς εἰσὶ ξεῖνοί
τε πτωχοί τε, they belong to, proceed from, are as it were his
children, and under his protection.   Further: εἶναι πρός τινος,
stare ab aliquo, facere pro aliquo, Hdt.: Eur. Alc. 58 πρὸς τῶν
ἐχόντων, Φοῖβε, τὸν νόμον τίθης, a law for the rich; proceeding from
regard to their interest.   *c.* The author or giver of any thing; as,
α. Il. α, 239 οἴτε θέμιστας πρὸς Διὸς εἰρύαται, *auctore, datore Jove:*
Hdt. II. 139 ἵνα κακόν τι πρὸς θεῶν ἢ πρὸς ἀνθρώπων λάβοι: Id.
IV. 144 εἶπας τόδε τὸ ἔπος ἐλείπετο ἀθάνατον μνήμην πρὸς Ἑλλησποντίων, *gloriam ab Hellespontiis omni tempore celebratam:* Id. VII.
5 στρατηλάτεε ἐπὶ τὰς 'Αθήνας, ἵνα λόγος—σε ἔχῃ πρὸς ἀνθρώπων
ἀγαθός, *ut lauderis ab hominibus (apud homines):* Id. VII. 139
γνώμην ἐπίφθονον πρὸς τῶν πλεόνων, *sententiam in invidia* or *odio
habitam a plerisque.*   β. With ἀκούειν *et sim.*, to define more clearly

the relation of genitive.   γ. With passive and intransitive verbs, even in Homer, frequently Hdt., and often in Attic writers, to define more clearly the relation of the simple genitive (§. 483. *Obs.* 3.) : Hdt. I. 61 ἀτιμάζεσθαι πρὸς Πεισιστράτου : Id. I. 73 ταῦτα πρὸς Κυαξάρεω παθόντες.   *d.* In oaths and adjurations : as, πρὸς θεῶν, *per deos,* properly before the gods ; but the genitive expresses that the oath derives its power from the gods.   *e.* The cause— defining the relation of the simple genitive : Hdt. II. 30 φυλακαὶ κατέστασαν πρὸς Αἰθιόπων, πρὸς ᾿Αραβίων, πρὸς Λιβύης, *custodiæ col- locatæ erant adversus Æthiopes &c.,* properly before the Æthiopians &c. ; but the genitive denotes them as the cause of the guard, as in Latin, *munimenta a b h o s t e* &c.   *f.* Sometimes of the reason (*per*) : Soph. Antig. 51 πρὸς αὐτοφώρων ἀμπλακημάτων διπλᾶς ὄψεις ἀράξας, *propter facinora.*

II. Dative.—To express a motionless position in front of a object ; as, πρὸς τοῖς κριταῖς.   So of employments : εἶναι, γίγνεσθαι πρὸς πράγμασι : Demosth. p. 92, 11 πρὸς τοῖς πράγμασι γίγνεσθαι. And *thereon,* in addition to ; as, πρὸς τούτῳ, πρὸς τούτοισι Hdt., *præter ea.*

III. Accus.—1. L o c a l.—A motion to the front of an object. Frequently in a hostile sense ; as, μάχεσθαι, πολεμεῖν πρός τινα, against ; properly, to go to his front and fight him : Thuc. I. 18 μάχη Μήδων πρὸς ᾿Αθηναίους.   Then with all verbs of *speaking* and *saying* ; as we say, " he spoke before me," that is, " to me :" λέγειν, ἀγορεύειν πρός τινα : Demosth. p. 95, 21 βούλομαι — πρὸς ὑμᾶς — ἐξετάσαι τὰ παρόντα πράγματα.   So λογίζεσθαι, σκέπτεσθαι, σκοπεῖν πρὸς ἑαυτόν, *secum cogitare.* Of its use in expressing the position of a place, see in its uses with genitive, *a.*   2. T e m p o r a l.—An inde- finite point of time ; as, Xen. Anab. IV. 5, 21 πρὸς ἡμέραν, towards day-break.   So also of number : πρὸς ἕκατον, towards an hundred. 3. C a u s a l.—*a.* The object : Demosth. p. 71, 23 παντοδαπὰ εὑρη- μένα ταῖς πόλεσι πρὸς φυλακὴν καὶ σωτηρίαν.   *b.* Accordance with, according to, in consequence of, after, on : Hdt. III. 52 πρὸς τοῦτο τὸ κήρυγμα.   So Id. I. 38 πρὸς ὧν τὴν ὄψιν ταύτην τὸν γάμον τοῦτον ἔσπευσα, in consequence of.   So κρίνειν τι πρός τι.   Also πρὸς βίαν, by force ; πρὸς ἀναγκήν, πρὸς ἡδονήν, πρὸς ἀκρίβειαν, according to necessity, &c.   Hence, on account of, *propter* ; as, πρὸς ταῦτα, pro- perly, looking to this, in these circumstances, hereon, for this reason.   Hence, *c.* (especially in Hdt.) comparison considered as placing one thing in opposition to another ; in Latin *contra.* Mostly with collateral idea of superiority—*præ, præter* ; it is used thus when an object is compared with several others, and either equals or surpasses them: Hdt. VIII. 44 Ἀθηναῖοι πρὸς πάντας τοὺς ἄλλους (συμμάχους) παρεχόμενοι νῆας ὀγδώκοντα καὶ ἑκατόν, equal to all the other members of the league: Id. III. 94 Ἰνδοὶ — φόρον ἀπαγίνεον πρὸς πάντας τοὺς ἄλλους, ἑξήκοντα καὶ τριηκόσια τάλαντα ψήγματος. So with comparatives: Thuc. III. 37 οἱ φαυλότεροι τῶν ἀνθρώπων πρὸς τοὺς ξυνετωτέρους ὡς ἐπὶ τὸ πλεῖστον ἄμεινον οἰκοῦσι τὰς πόλεις. So also of interchanges: Plat. Phæd. p. 69 A ἡδονὰς πρὸς ἡδονὰς καὶ λύπας πρὸς λύπας καὶ φόβον πρὸς φόβον καταλλάττεσθαι, καὶ μείζω πρὸς ἐλάττω, ὥσπερ νομίσματα. Generally to express a reference, regard to: σκοπεῖν, βλέπειν πρός τι Plat.: ἀποβλέψω εἰς τὰ πράγματα καὶ—πρὸς τοὺς λόγους Demosth.[a]: διαφέρειν πρὸς ἀρετήν Isocr.: καλὸς πρὸς δρόμον, πρὸς πάλην, τέλειος πρὸς ἀρετήν Plat.

5. Ὑπό, *under.*

§. 639. Ὑπό (poet. ὑπαί; Sanscr. *upa*; Lat. *sub*; Goth. *uf*). Original meaning—*under.*

I. Genitive.—1. Local.—*a.* A motion from under any thing—from below—from beneath—out of (as seen more apparently in the compound ὑπέκ with Gen.): Od. ι, 140 αὐτὰρ ἐπὶ κρατὸς λιμένος ῥέει ἀγλαὸν ὕδωρ, κρήνη ὑπὸ σπείους, from under the grotto: Il. ρ, 235 νεκρὸν ὑπ' Αἴαντος ἐρύειν, from under the hands of Ajax: Od. η, 5 ὑπὸ ἀπήνης λύειν ἵππους: Hesiod. Theog. 669 ὑπὸ χθονὸς ἧκε φόωσδε, from under the earth: Eur. Hec. 53 περᾷ γὰρ ἥδ' ὑπὸ σκηνῆς πόδα: Id. Andr. 442 ἢ καὶ νεοσσὸν τόνδ' ὑπὸ πτερῶν σπάσας. Here too the preposition is nearly adverbial; it belongs rather to the verb than to the substantive. *b.* Position without motion—under something; where the dative is more usual. But the dative signifies only the position, while the genitive denotes that some genitival relation is implied in the construction; as, Il. θ, 14 ῥίψω ἐς Τάρταρον —, ἧχι βάθιστον ὑπὸ χθονός ἐστι βέρεθρον, the deepest abyss *of* (possessive) the earth below; or, under the earth. So very frequently in Homer: Il. α, 501 δεξιτερῇ δ' ἄρ' ὑπ' ἀνθερεῶνος ἑλοῦσα (as θιγγάνειν τινός), catching him by the chin; or, under it. So with verbs of casting, hitting; as, Il. π, 606 τὸν βάλ' ὑπὸ γναθμοῖο καὶ οὔατος. The preposition here is almost adverbial. 2. Causal.—*a.* The author of an action, with passive and intransitive verbs—mostly the latter, used as passive; as, κτείνεσθαι ὑπό τινος—ἀποθανεῖν ὑπό τινος: Soph. Œ. C. 391 εὖ πράσσειν

---

[a] Bremi ad loc.

ὑπό τινος. b. The cause—occasion—actuating influence: a. Hdt. I. 85 ὑπὸ τῆς παρεούσης συμφορῆς, under the influence of; the calamity being as it were upon him, and he under its pressure: Id. III. 129 ὑπὸ τοῦ παρεόντος κακοῦ: Id. I. 131 ὑπὸ μεγάθεος τῆς πόλιος: Id. III. 104 ὑπὸ γὰρ τοῦ καύματος οἱ μύρμηκες ἀφανέες γίνονται ὑπὸ γῆν: Thuc. II. 85 extr. ὑπὸ ἀνέμων καὶ ὑπὸ ἀπλοίας ἐνδιέτριψεν οὐκ ὀλίγον χρόνον.—ὑπ' ἀνάγκης: Plat. Legg. p. 695 B ὑπὸ μέθης μαίνεσθαι.— ὑπὸ ῥίγους. β. Of a mental cause: Hdt. I. 85 ὑ π ὸ δ έ ο υ ς καὶ κακοῦ φωνὴν ἔρρηξε. So ὑπὸ χαρᾶς, φθόνου, ὀργῆς, ἀπειρίας, σωφροσύνης, ἀφροσύνης, &c.: Demosth. p. 107, 71 οὐδὲ προήχθην οὔθ' ὑπὸ κέρδους, οὔθ' ὑπὸ φιλοτιμίας. c. A mere intermediate cause—means or instrument—as it were a cause under the guidance, accompaniment, cooperation of which any thing happens; in some of which cases we use the word *under*: Hom. ὑπὸ Ζεφύροιο ἰωῆς ἔρχεσθαι: Hdt. VII. 21 ὤρυσσον ὑπὸ μαστίγων. Also c. 56. Also of persons: ἀϊσάντων ὑπ' Ἀχαιῶν Hom., under a shout from the Greeks: Hdt. IX. 98 ὑπὸ κήρυκος προηγόρευε, by the assistance of the herald, *præconis voce*; especially of the accompaniment of musical instruments; as, Hdt. I. 17 ἐστρατεύετο ὑπὸ συρίγγων. So ὑπ' αὐλοῦ χορεύειν, ὑπὸ φορμίγγων, ὑπὸ τυμπάνων. So ὑπ' αὐλητῆρος ἀείδειν: and Thuc. VI. 32 ὑπὸ κήρυκος ἐποιοῦντο εὐχάς, *præeunte præcone*, repeating them after the herald. So Eur. Hipp. 1299 ὑπ' εὐκλείας θανεῖν, under the auspices of good fame—famously. d. Subordination to: Od. τ, 114 ἀρετῶσι δὲ λαοὶ ὑπ' αὐτοῦ.

II. Dative.—1. L o c a l.—Position without motion under any thing; as, ὑπὸ γῇ εἶναι: applied to mountains, "at the foot;" Il. β, 866 ὑπὸ Τμώλῳ: Hdt. VI. 137 κατοικημένους γὰρ τοὺς Πελασγοὺς ὑπὸ τῷ Ὑμησσῷ. 2. C a u s a l.—a. The author, as with gen., especially poetic: δαμῆναι ὑπό τινι, πίπτειν ὑπό τινι. So Plato: πεπαιδευμένος, τεθραμμένος ὑπό τινι, e. g. ὑπὸ τῷ πατρί. b. The intermediate cause, &c., as gen., but rather poetic; as, ὑπὸ βαρβίτῳ χορεύειν, ὑπ' αὐλῷ, &c. c. Subordination; as, ποιεῖν τι ὑπό τινι, to subdue under some one: Hdt. VI. 121 βουλομένους ὑπὸ βαρβάροισί τε εἶναι Ἀθηναίους καὶ ὑπὸ Ἱππίῃ: Id. VII. 157 τὴν Ἑλλάδα ὑπ' ἑωυτῷ ποιήσασθαι. So Attics: εἶναι ὑπό τινι.

III. Accusative.—1. L o c a l.—a. Motion or direction under; as εἶναι ὑπὸ γαῖαν: of motion towards any lofty place, as we seem to go under it; as ὑπ' Ἴλιον ἦλθον: Hdt. VI. 44 ὑπὸ τὴν ἤπειρον ἐκόμιζοντο, passed under the shore. So Hdt. IX. 93 ὑπαγαγόντες μιν ὑπὸ δικαστήριον, the judgment-seat being raised. So. Id. VI. 136 ὑπάγειν τινὰ ὑπὸ τὸν δῆμον: Ibid. 82 ὑπὸ τοὺς ἐφόρους. b. Extension under an object: Hdt. II. 127 ὕπεστι οἰκήματα ὑπὸ γῆν:

Id. VII. 114 τῷ ὑπὸ γῆν λεγομένῳ εἶναι θεῷ ἀντιχαρίζεσθαι: Id.
V. 11 τὰ ὑπὸ τὴν ἄρκτον ἀοίκητα δοκέει εἶναι. 2. Temporal.—
a. An approximation to a point of time, as in Latin *sub*; as, ὑπὸ
νύκτα, *sub noctem*, towards: Hdt. I. 31 μετεκινήθησαν δὲ καὶ οὗτοι
ὑπὸ τὸν νηὸν κατακαέντα, at the time when the temple was burnt:
Id. VI. 2 ὑπὸ τὴν πρώτην ἐπελθοῦσαν νύκτα. So of an indefinite
measure in the Attic phrase: ὑπό τι, in some measure, *aliquatenus*:
Plat. Gorg. p. 493 C ταῦτ᾽ ἐπιεικῶς μέν ἐστιν ὑπό τι ἄτοπα, this is in
some measure wonderful ᵃ. *b.* Extension in time—which is conceived as extending under and parallel to the object: Hdt. IX. 5
ὑπὸ τὴν νύκτα, during: Ibid. 58 ὑπὸ τὴν παροιχομένην νύκτα, during
the preceding night. 3. Causal.—Subordination; as, ὑπὸ χεῖρα
ποιεῖν, ὑπὸ χεῖρα λαβεῖν: Hdt. VII. 108 καὶ ἦν ὑπὸ βασιλῆα
δασμοφόρος.

Remarks on some peculiarities of the Prepositions.

The original Adverbial force of Prepositions.

§. 640. 1. In Homer, the prepositions are used both in their primary
force, as local adverbs, and in their secondary force, as prepositions; that
is, as defining the local, and afterwards the causal relations of the cases.
They are also used adverbially in Ionic Greek, as Hdt., far less frequently
in Attic. The particle δέ is often joined to them, and they are frequently
placed first in the sentence for greater emphasis.

2. We find used as local adverbs—

᾿Αντί: Il. φ, 75 ἀντί τοι εἴμ᾽ ἱκέταο (τοί=σοί).

᾿Από: Il. φ, 594 πάλιν δ᾽ ἀπὸ χαλκὸς ὄρουσε βλημένου: Od. ζ, 40
πολλὸν γὰρ ἀπὸ πλυνοί εἰσι πόληος.

᾿Εκ: Il. σ, 480 περὶ δ᾽ ἄντυγα βάλλε φαεινήν — ἐκ δ᾽ ἀργύρεον τελαμῶνα
(and therefrom, ἐξ αὐτῆς).

Πρό, before: Il. ν, 800 ὡς Τρῶες πρὸ μὲν ἄλλοι ἀρηρότες, αὐτὰρ ἐπ᾽
ἄλλοι. Also Sophocles.

᾿Εν very frequently: Od. ι, 116—118 νῆσος — τετάνυσται ὑλήεσσ᾽, ἐν
δ᾽ αἶγες ἀπειρέσιαι γεγάασιν ἄγριαι: Ibid. 132 sqq. ἐν μὲν γὰρ λειμῶνες — ἐν
δ᾽ ἄροσις λείη — ἐν δὲ λιμὴν εὔορμος. Also Ionic: Hdt. III. 39 ἐν δὲ δὴ
καὶ Λεσβίους—εἷλε (among them, *in iis*). So also Soph. Œ. R. 27.

Σύν (σὺν δέ), at the same time: Il. ψ, 879 αὐτὰρ ἡ ὄρνις — αὐχέν᾽
ἀπεκρέμασεν, σὺν δὲ πτερὰ πυκνὰ λίασθεν. Also Traged., especially Soph.;
as, Ant. 85 κρυφῆ δὲ κεῦθε· σὺν δ᾽ αὔτως ἐγώ.

᾿Ανά, upon; generally *sursum* — only Homeric: Il. σ, 562 μέλανες δ᾽
ἀνὰ βότρυες ἦσαν. With accent thrown back, as interjection: ἄνα, up
then! Homer., and also Traged.; as, Soph. Aj. 192. Eur. Troad. 98.

Εἰς: Il. θ, 115 τὼ δ᾽ εἰς ἀμφοτέρω Διομήδεος ἅρματα βήτην.

Διά, through; Homer, especially διά πρό, see below, 3.

Κατά, down; *desuper* and *infra*, often in Homer: Il. ψ, 799. Od. ξ,
349. Hesiod. Sc. 173. Hdt. *prout*, III. 86 οἱ ἐξ κατὰ συνεθήκαντο,
παρῆσαν ἐπὶ τῶν ἵππων (where however we may read κατ᾽ ἅ); κατάπερ, so
as, Hdt. VII. 16, 1.

ᵃ Stallb. ad loc.

'Aμφί : Homeric, also Pind., Eur.

Περί : Od. ι, 184 περὶ δ' αὐλὴ ὑψηλὴ δέδμητο κατωρυχέεσσι λίθοισιν : Od. a, 66 ὃς περὶ μὲν νόον ἐστὶ βροτῶν. So very often in Homer. Also in Homer : περὶ κῆρι φιλεῖν τινα : Od. θ, 44 τῷ γάρ ῥα θεὸς περὶ δῶκεν ἀοιδήν : cf. Od. ξ, 433.

'Eπί, thereon—thereto : Il. σ, 529 κτεῖνον δ' ἐπὶ μηλοβοτῆρας. Also in Hdt. not unfrequently ἐπὶ δέ, thereupon, *tum :* VII. 219 ἐπὶ δὲ καὶ αὐτόμολοι ἦἰσαν : cf. 55. Also Soph. Œ. R. 183.

Mετά : Homer—*a.* Often together—thereto—besides. — *b.* Behind. —μετὰ δέ, *postea.* In Hdt., as III. 11, 39. VI. 125 πρῶτα μὲν— μετὰ δέ : VII. 12 μετὰ δή.

Παρά, thereby ; often Homer. So especially παρὰ δέ. Also Eur. Iph. A. 201.

Πρός, thereto — besides. So πρός γε, πρὸς δέ. So very frequently Homer, and also Attic writers : Hdt. III. 74 πρὸς δ' ἔτι : Id. VI. 125 καὶ πρός, *insuper.* —πρός alone Id. III. 6.—καὶ πρός γε : Eur. Med. 704 ὄλωλα καὶ πρός γ' ἐξελαύνομαι χθονός : Plat. Rep. p. 328 A[a]. Ibid. p. 466 E καὶ πρός γε ἄξουσι : Demosth. p. 835, 68 δίκαιοι δ' ἐστ' ἐλεεῖν — ἡμᾶς — στερομένους, καὶ πρὸς ὑπὸ τούτων ὑβριζομένους : Id. p. 491, 112 πρὸς δὲ καὶ οὐ δίκαιον. Often at the end of the sentence : Id. p. 47 extr. τάλαντα ἐνενήκοντα καὶ μικρόν τι πρός[b] : Eur. Or. 621 Μενέλαε, σοὶ δὲ τάδε λέγω, δράσω τε πρός : Id. Phœn. 613 καὶ κατακτενῶ γε πρός.

'Yπό, under ; often in Homer : ὑπὸ δέ Od. δ, 636. Also Æschylus.

3. In poetry we often find two prepositions joined together ; whereof the first is always adverbial, the second is followed by the case of the substantive. This is not a mere pleonasm, but gives a poetic fulness to the expression.—

Διὰ πρό : Il. ε, 66 ἡ δὲ διὰ πρὸ ἀντικρὺ κατὰ κύστιν ὑπ' ὀστέον ἤλυθ' ἀκωκή (where even ἀντικρύ is added :) Il. ρ, 393 τάνυται δέ τε πᾶσα (βοείη) διὰ πρό.

'Aμφὶ περί very frequently : Od. λ, 608 ἀμφὶ περὶ στήθεσσιν : Il. φ, 10 ὄχθιι δ' ἀμφὶ περὶ μεγάλ' ἴαχον : Il. β, 305 ἀμφὶ περὶ κρήνην.—So also Hymn. in Cer. 277 περί τ' ἀμφί τε. (Hence the Doric adverb περιαμπετίξ.)

Παρέκ : Od. ι, 116 παρὲκ λιμένος, from—by way of. Often Hdt. in sense of except. III. 91 πάρεξ τοῦ ἀργυρίου : Id. I. 14, 93 and elsewhere.

'Yπ' ἐκ Homer : and Hdt. III. 116 λέγεται δὲ ὑπ' ἐκ τῶν γρυπῶν ἁρπάζειν 'Αριμασπούς.

'Aπόπρο φέρων : Il. π, 669 and 679.

Περὶ πρό : Il. λ, 180 περὶ πρὸ γὰρ ἔγχεῖ θῦεν, round and forwards. Cf. π, 699.

Obs. A similar idiom to this occurs, when to a verb compounded with a preposition, this same preposition is prefixed as an adverb : Il. ψ, 709 ἂν δ' Ὀδυσεὺς πολύμητις ἀνίστατο : Od. ε, 260 ἐν δ' ὑπέρας τε κάλους τε πόδας τ' ἐνέδησεν ἐν αὐτῇ.

Prepositions in Composition.

§. 641. 1. Prepositions were not only used to define the relations of the cases, but were also compounded with simple verbs, not merely as local adverbs, but in one or more of their secondary powers, as expressions of cause, &c, : and being thus united to the

---

[a] Stallb. ad loc. 　　　[b] Bremi ad loc.

verb, they so added to or modified its sense, that a great variety of new verbs were formed, more or less differing from the simple verb, as the one or the other element of the compound prevailed therein.

2. The force and the construction of these compounds varies as the one or the other of the component notions, the preposition or the verb, has the predominant force in the new verb: they may be classed as follows;

a. Where the compound has essentially the same sense as the simple verb, more or less modified by the preposition, as αἱρεῖσθαι and προαιρεῖσθαι.

β. Where, instead of the usual construction of the verb, the preposition, and its case, the preposition is joined to the verb without affecting the meaning, but only perfecting the construction thereof, as εἰσιέναι δόμον = ἰέναι εἰς δόμον.

γ. Where a new notion results from the combined force of the preposition and the verb, so that, the preposition supplying the main notion of the compound, the construction of the simple verb is suspended; as μετέχω, I have with some one = I share; κατηγορέω, I accuse; καταφρονῶ, I despise; ἀπαλλάσσομαι, I depart; ἀντιβαίνω, I oppose.

§. 642. Some compound verbs are used in more than one of these ways, and the sense of the compound is to be determined by the case which follows; for which these rules may be laid down.

a. If the case be that of the simple verb, the compound has either the same essential sense as the simple verb, modified more or less by the pre-position, as προορᾶν τὸν πόλεμον, to foresee the war; or a new sense, which by the common rules of construction, requires or admits of the same case as the simple verb, as δοῦναι to give, and ἀποδόσθαι to sell: and this must be decided by the context, or by a lexicon: so ἐπέχειν τοῦτο, to hold this back.

Obs. 1. The preposition is never quite otiose, but always adds *something* to the verb.

b. If the case be that of the preposition, the compound verb must either be resolved into the simple verb, and the preposition followed by its case, as εἰσῆλθον δόμον = ἦλθον εἰς δόμον: or it has a new sense, in which the no-tion of the preposition, as determined by its case, predominates and is car-ried on to its case, as κατηγορεῖν σοῦ, to accuse you; προορᾶν τοῦ πολέμου, to take thought about the war; ἐπέχειν τούτου, to hold back from this; ἐπέχειν τούτῳ, to give one's attention to this.

c. If the case be neither that of the preposition, nor of the simple verb, then it depends on a new notion arising from their combination; as, προ-ορᾶν τῷ πολέμῳ, to provide for the war [a].

Obs. 2. Where the preposition is used with more than one case, the sense of the compound varies more or less with one or other of these

---

[a] Schol. Aristoph. Plut. 225. "Ὥσπερ γὰρ καὶ μεταλαμβάνω τ ο ύ τ ο υ καὶ τ ο ῦ τ ο φα-μὲν, οὕτω καὶ τὸ μετέχω διπλῶς συντάσσεται· καὶ ὅτε μέν ἐστι γενικὴ τὸ μ ε τ ὰ ἔχει τὴν δύναμιν, ὅτε δὲ αἰτιατικὴ τ ὸ ἔ χ ω ἢ τὸ λαμβάνω.

cases, as the sense of the preposition with the several cases, as παραστατέω τινι, to stand by a person; παραστατεῖν τινα, to go and stand near a person.

Obs. 3. When two cases follow a compound verb, as κατηγορεῖν ταῦτα σοῦ, one of them properly depends on the verb (ταῦτα), the other on the preposition (σοῦ); or if the compound be looked upon as expressing a simple notion, (*accuse*) and not a compound one, (*speak against*) the two cases depend on the common principles for the construction of simple verbs. (See §. 501.)

Obs. 4. Sometimes two datives follow a compound verb, one of which depends on the verb, the other on the preposition : Æsch. Ag. 1323 ἡλίῳ δ' ἐπεύχομαι, πρὸς ὕστατον φῶς, τοῖς ἐμοῖς τιμαόροις ἐχθροῖς φονεῦσι τοῖς ἐμοῖς τίνειν ὁμοῦ := ἡλίῳ εὔχομαι (§. 589. 1.) ἐπὶ τοῖς ἐμοῖς ἐχθροῖς τίνειν, &c. [b] Id. Choeph. 828 ἐπαύσας πατρὸς ἔργῳ θροούσῃ πρός σε, τέκνον, πατρὸς αὐδάν= αὐτῇ θροούσῃ—αὔσας πατρὸς αὐδὰν, ἐπὶ πατρὸς ἔργῳ.

Obs. 5. Prepositions also compounded with adjectives are followed by their proper case: Æsch. Ag. 17 ὕπνου ἀντίμολπον ἄκος : Eur. Hec. 152 τύμβου προπετῆ : Id. Alc. 314 συζύγου τῷ σῷ πατρί.

Tmesis in Compound Verbs.

§. 643. As prepositions are properly merely local adverbs, the older dialects, which commonly used them as such, would naturally place the preposition apart from the verb, in many cases where the Attics always used the compound : and even where Homer uses the compound in the same sense as the simple verb, we are not to suppose an actual Tmesis wherever we find the verb and the preposition used instead of the compound ; for Homer would use both the old forms of speech and those which, in his time recently introduced, were in later periods of the language universally adopted. We must distinguish the following cases.

a. Where the preposition seems to be separated from the verb, but really is used alone in its original force of a local adverb : Il. γ, 34 ὑπό τε τρόμος ἔλλαβε γυῖα : Il. γ, 135 παρὰ δ' ἔγχεα μακρὰ πέπηγεν : Il. δ, 63 ἐπὶ δ' ἔψονται θεοὶ ἄλλοι : Il. δ, 161 ἔκ τε καὶ ὀψὲ τελεῖ : Il. ν, 368 τῷ δ' ὁ γέρων Πρίαμος ὑπό τ' ἔσχετο καὶ κατένευσεν δωσέμεναι, properly he held himself under (=bound) : Od. δ, 6 ὑπέσχετο καὶ κατένευσεν δωσέμεναι): Od. δ, 525 ὑπὸ δ' ἔσχετο μισθόν (pregnant construction), he held himself under, and promised : Il. θ, 108 οὓς (ἵππους) ποτ' ἀπ' Αἰνείαν ἑλόμην (ἑλέσθαι τινά τι, Il. π, 59) : Il. ν, 394 ἐκ δέ οἱ ἡνίοχος πλήγη φρένας (πλήττεσθαι φρένας can be used as well as ἐκπλήττεσθαι φρένας : Od. μ, 312 μετὰ δ' ἄστρα βεβήκει : Il. α, 67 ἀπὸ λοιγὸν ἀμῦναι. The adverbial preposition sometimes, though but rarely, follows ; as, Il. μ, 195 ἐνάριζον ἀπ' ἔντεα.

Obs. 1. Here belongs an abbreviated form of expression; when the same compound should be repeated in each of several succeeding sentences, the verb is used only in the first, and the preposition stands alone in the others : Il. ψ, 799 κατὰ μὲν δολιχόσκιον ἔγχος θῆκ' ἐς ἀγῶνα φέρων, κατὰ δ' ἀσπίδα καὶ τρυφάλειαν.—Hdt. often ; as, II. 141 κατὰ μὲν φαγέειν τοὺς φαρετρεῶνας αὐτέων, κατὰ δὲ τὰ τόξα : Id. VIII. 33 κατὰ μὲν ἔκαυσαν Δρυμὸν πόλιν, κατὰ δὲ Χαράδρην : Id. IX. 5 κατὰ μὲν ἔλευσαν αὐτοῦ τὴν γυναῖκα, κατὰ δὲ τὰ τέκνα : (but Id. III. 36 καὶ ἀπὸ μὲν σεωυτὸν ὤλεσας — ἀπὸ δὲ ὤλεσας Κῦρον with the verb repeated.)   Here we must refer such instances as Il. γ,

268 ὤρνυτο δ' αὐτίκ' ἔπειτα ἄναξ ἀνδρῶν Ἀγαμέμνων, ἀν δ' Ὀδυσεὺς πολύμητις (as if ἀνώρνντο had preceded) : Il. ε, 480 sq. ἔνθ' ἄλοχόν τε φίλην ἔλιπον καὶ νήπιον υἱόν, καδ' δὲ κτήματα πολλά (as if κατέλιπον had preceded.)

Obs. 2. The Tmesis cannot be properly spoken of, till in the later dialects, especially the Attic, the preposition coalesced so closely with the verb that the new word took its place in the language as such. It is found pretty frequently in Herodotus, more rarely in the Attic chorus, and still more rarely in the Dialogue, and only where a particle is the dividing word, so that the connection between the two parts or the unity of the compound notion is not utterly destroyed : Hdt. VII. 15 Ξέρξης — ἀνά τε ἔδραμε ἐκ τῆς κοίτης καὶ πέμπει ἄγγελον : Id. VIII. 89 ἀπὸ μὲν ἔθανε ὁ στρατηγός : Id. VII. 164 extr. ἀπὸ πάντα τὰ χρήματα ἄγων : Æsch. Pers. 455 ἀμφὶ δὲ κυκλοῦντο : Soph. Trach. 565 ἐκ δ' ἧϋσ' : Eur. Iph. T. 1371 δι' ἄρ' ὀλώλαμεν : Id. Hec. 1172 ἐκ δὲ πηδήσας. In Attic prose, Tmesis, except in one or two singular instances, is not found : Thuc. III. 13 μὴ ξὺν κακῶς ποιεῖν αὐτοὺς μετ' Ἀθηναίων ἀλλὰ ξυνελευθεροῦν (to increase the antithesis :) Plat. Gorg. p. 250 E ἀντ' εὖ ποιεῖν : and immediately after, εἰ εὖ ποιήσας ταύτην τὴν εὐεργεσίαν ἀντ' εὖ πείσεται. " *Nam* τὸ εὖ *καὶ* τὰ στερητικὰ μόρια *n o n componuntur cum verbis primitivis, sed cum nominibus et verbis inde derivatis :*" Demosth. p. 105, 65 οὐκ ἦν ἀσφαλὲς λέγειν ἐν Ὀλύνθῳ τὰ Φιλίππου, μὴ σὺν εὖ πεπονθότων τῶν πολλῶν Ὀλυνθίων τῷ Ποτίδαιαν καρποῦσθαι.

b. Where the preposition seems to be separated from the case of a substantive. Here also in Homer, the preposition retains its adverbial force, and belongs to the verb ; these two together form one notion, and this, and not the preposition alone, governs the case. *a.* Genitivus separativus : Il. ι, 292 τοῦ δ' ἀπὸ μὲν γλῶσσαν τάμε : Il. ε, 694 ἐκ δ' ἄρα οἱ μηροῦ δόρυ—ὦσε θύραζε : Od. ζ, 140 ἐκ δέος εἵλετο γυίων : Od. θ, 149 σκέδασον δ' ἀπὸ κήδεα θυμοῦ, away from the mind.—Gen. as expressing the spot as the antecedent condition of the action (§. 522. 1.), or a reaching towards and after the object (§. 508.) : Od. β, 416 ἂν δ' ἄρα Τηλέμαχος νηὸς βαῖν' : Od. ι, 177 ἀνὰ νηὸς ἔβην. — Gen. originis or auctoris : Od. ζ, 29 ἐκ γάρ τοι τούτων φάτις ἀνθρώπους ἀναβαίνει ἐσθλή : Il. λ, 831 τά σε προτί φασιν Ἀχιλλῆος δεδιδάχθαι, where προτί seems to mean " before," " formerly."—Gen. comparativus : Il. ν, 631 ἦ τέ σε φασὶ περὶ φρένας ἔμμεναι ἄλλων, more than : Il. φ, 75 ἀντί τοι εἴμ' ἱκέταυ, I am in the place of.—*β.* Dativus localis : Il. ι, 382 πλεῖστα δόμοις ἐν κτήματα κεῖται, lie within, in the house : Il. ο, 266 ἀμφὶ δὲ χαῖται ὤμοις ἀΐσσονται, on the shoulders, around : Od. θ, 343 ἐν δὲ γέλως ὦρτ' ἀθανάτοισι, in the midst, among the gods : Od. ο, 440 μετὰ γάρ τε καὶ ἄλγεσι τέρπεται ἀνήρ, in the midst, among sorrows. — Dativus commodi : Il. ε, 566 περὶ γὰρ δίε ποιμένι λαῶν.—Transmissive Dative (§. 587.) : Il. τ, 394 ἐν δὲ χαλινοὺς γαμφηλῆς ἔβαλον : Od. ξ, 520 ἐπὶ δὲ χλαῖναν βάλεν αὐτῷ : Il. π, 291 ἐν γὰρ Πάτροκλος φόβον ἧκεν ἄπασιν, to all he infused fear : Il. θ, 485 ἐν δ' ἔπεσ' Ὠκεανῷ λαμπρὸν φάος ἠελίοιο.—*γ.* Accus. of place (§. 559.) : Il. θ, 115 τὼ δ' εἰς ἀμφοτέρω Διομήδεος ἅρματα βήτην. — Of the patient (§. 566. 1.) : Il. β, 156 Ἀθηναίην Ἥρη πρὸς μῦθον ἔειπεν.

Obs. 3. This sort of tmesis exists only when a particle, such as μέν, δέ, τέ, ῥά, γάρ, μὲν ἄρ', δ' ἄρα, intervenes between the subst. and the preposition, as is very often found in the Post-Homeric authors, and even in Attic Greek.

Prepositions joined with Adverbs.

§. 644. Prepositions are often joined with local adverbs, which however in such composition assume a sort of substantival force. Many of these compounds are also written as one word, so closely are they united. This species of composition seems to have been more frequently used from the time of Herodotus, than before him. So ὑποκάτω, ὑπεράνω; ἔμπροσθεν (*inante*, contrary to, *exante*), κατοπισθέν, ἐξοπίσω, εἰσοπίσω or ἐσοπίσω; ἐξόθεν (*exinde*), ἐκτόσθεν, ἐξ ὁμόθεν, ἀπεντεῦθεν, παραυτόθεν; καταυτόθι, παρ' αὐτόθι; ἐπιπρόσω; εἰς τότε (pure Attic, often in Plato), ἐς τῆμος Od. η, 318: εἰς νῦν Plat. Tim. p. 20 B: ἐκ τότε not till Aristotle: εἰς ὅτε Od. β, 99: ἐν οὗ Hdt. I. 67: μέχρι τότε Hdt. VI. 34: πρόπαλαι Aristoph. Eq. 1155, (jokingly) and thence in later writers: εἰσοψέ Thuc. VIII. 23. Demosth. p. 1303, 13: προπέρυσι Plat., Demosth.: ἐς αὐτίκα Aristoph. Pax, 367: παραυτίκα very commonly: ἐφ' ἅπαξ, εἰσάπαξ (Ionic ἐσάπαξ, Hdt. VI. 125): καθάπαξ: εἰς πρόσθεν Eur. Hec. 960: Plat., Isocrates εἰς τὸ πρόσθεν: ἐπίπροσθεν and ἔμπροσθεν very commonly: ἐπίπαγχυ Hesiod. Opp. 264. Theocr. XVII. 104: ἐπὶ μᾶλλον.

Obs. Such prepositions compounded with ἔτι take their cases: προσέτι τούτῳ, ἐξέτι πατρῶν Od. θ, 245: εἰσέτι που χθιζόν Apoll. Rhod. IV. 1397. And even with a particle between them; as, ἐνγεταυθί, ἐνμεντευθενί in comedy.—(See *Index*.)

Pregnant Construction of Prepositions.

§. 645. Prepositions with dative are sometimes joined to verbs of motion, *whither*, and with the accus. to verbs of rest, especially in the Homeric dialect: this is called the pregnant construction. In the former case, the speaker regards the state of rest following on the completed motion; in the latter, the motion which precedes, and is implied in, the state of rest; so that the two parts, which in other languages require two verbs to express them, are in Greek signified by one.

The verb of motion is considered rather as implying the notion of rest. The dative is used with the preposition instead of the accus.; this occurs with the following prepositions:—

a. Ἐν: Especially in Epic dialect: Il. ε, 370 ἡ δ' ἐν γούνασι πίπτε Διώνης δῖ' Ἀφροδίτη, fell and lay: Od. α, 200 ἐγὼ μαντεύσομαι, ὡς ἐνὶ θυμῷ ἀθάνατοι βάλλουσι: Il. λ, 743 ἤριπε δ' ἐν κονίῃσιν. So βάλλειν ἐν κονίῃσι Hom.: Il. ψ, 131 ἐν τεύχεσσιν ἔδυνον (but Od. ω, 428 ἐς τεύχε' ἔδυνον). Prose, τιθέναι ἐν χερσίν, as in Latin, *ponere et collocare in manibus:* Thuc. IV. 14 ταῖς ἐν τῇ γῇ καταπεφευγυίαις (on account of the past tense); and even Ibid. 42 ἐν Ἀμπρακίᾳ καὶ ἐν Λευκαδίᾳ ἀπῄεσαν: Xen. Hell. IV. 5, 5 first ἐς δὲ τὸ Ἥραιον κατέφυγον, and then οἱ δ' ἐν τῷ Ἡραίῳ καταπεφευγότες (as a completed action) ἐξῇεσαν: Plat. Euthyd. p. 292 E ἐν ταύτῃ τῇ ἀπορίᾳ ἐνεπεπτώκειν. Very frequent in late writers. So also sometimes in Latin; as, Ovid. Fast. III. 664 *in sacri vertice montis abit:* Cæs. B. G. V. 10 *naves in littore ejectas esse:* Sall. Jug. 5 *in amicitiā receptus.*

Obs. 1. Instances such as Od. ι, 164 πολλὸν γὰρ (οἶνον) ἐν ἀμφιφορεῦσιν ἕκαστοι ἠφύσαμεν: Il. ο, 229 ἐν χείρεσσι λάβ' αἰγίδα: Eur. Hec. 527 λαβεῖν ἐν χεροῖν: Hdt. III. 23 ἐν πέδῃσι χρυσέῃσι δεδέσθαι et simil., do not seem to belong here. The dative seems to express the notion of the means or instrument.—(§. 608, *Obs.* 2.)

b. Ἀμφί, περί, with accus. for dat.: Il. λ, 17 κνημῖδας μὲν πρῶτα περὶ κνήμῃσιν ἔθηκεν, placed on the shin bones, so that they fitted firmly on them: Ibid. 19 δεύτερον αὖ θώρηκα περὶ στήθεσσιν ἔδυνεν: Od. θ, 434 ἀμφὶ πυρὶ στῆσαι τρίποδα.

Obs. 2. In the Homeric phrase, κρέα ἀμφὶ ὀβελοῖς ἔπειραν (e. g. Il. a, 465), where we say, " on the spit," the dat. seems to express the means or instrument, with the collateral notion however, of the meat being around the spit (§. 632. ii).

c. Ἐπί: Il. a, 55 τῷ γὰρ ἐπὶ φρεσὶ θῆκε θεὰ λευκώλενος Ἥρη (so ἐν φρεσὶ θεῖναι).

d. Πρός: Od. ι, 284 νέα μέν μοι κατέαξε Ποσειδάων ἐνοσίχθων, πρὸς πέτρῃσι βαλών: Ibid. 289 σὺν δὲ δύω μάρψας, ὥστε σκύλακας, ποτὶ γαίῃ κόπτε. So βάλλειν ποτὶ γαίῃ.

e. Παρά very rare: Xen. Anab. II. 5, 27 ἰέναι παρὰ Τισσαφέρνει, to go to (and stay with) Tissaphernes.

f. Ὑπό in the phrases, ὑπό τινι γίγνεσθαι, to come into a person's power; ποιεῖν τι ὑπό τινι, *alicui aliquid subjicere;* ποιεῖσθαι ὑφ' ἑαυτῷ, *sibi subjicere:* Demosth. p. 104, 60 οὐ γὰρ ὑφ' αὑτῷ τὴν πόλιν ποιήσασθαι βούλεται Φίλιππος: Ibid. 116, 21 τὰ λοιπὰ ὑφ' αὑτῷ ποιήσασθαι: ὑπό si notionem habet subjectionis c. dat. constr. non solum verborum, quæ indicant subjectionem esse finitam. sed eorum etiam, quæ fieri eam significant ᵃ.

Obs. 3. As the dative frequently expresses the aim or object of the operation of the verb, it is in many cases uncertain whether we must suppose a pregnant construction, or take the dative as transmissive and denoting the aim of the verb. In the following cases it is clearly the latter; the dative referring not so much to the motion of the verb, as the intention of the agent: χεῖρας ἰάλλειν ἐπὶ σίτῳ, ἧκαι βέλος ἐπί τινι, πέμψαι ὄνειρον ἐπί τινι, ἐλαύνειν ἵππους ἐπὶ νηυσίν, τιταίνεσθαι τόξα ἐπί τινι, ἄλλεσθαι ἐπί τινι, μάχεσθαι ἐπί τινι, πέτεσθαι ἐπ' ἄνθεσιν.

§. 646. *a.* The verb of rest is considered as signifying the notion of the previous motion implied in it, when the preposition εἰς with the accus. is used instead of ἐν with the dative: Il. o, 275 ἐφάνη λῖς εἰς ὁδόν: Od. δ, 51 ἐς θρόνους ἕζοντο: Eur. Iph. T. 624 ἀλλ' εἰς ἀνάγκην κείμεθ': Id. Or. 1315 ἀνάγκης δ' ἐς ζυγὸν καθέσταμεν: Hdt. III. 11 (τοὺς παῖδας) ἔσφαζον ἐς τὸν κρητῆρα. So Cato R. R. 156, 5 *in aquam macerare:* Ibid. 39, 2 *in fornacem coquere:* Hdt. III. 62 προηγόρευε στὰς ἐς μέσον τὰ ἐντεταλμένα: Ibid. 64 ὃς ἐδόκεε ἐν τῷ ὕπνῳ ἀπαγγεῖλαί τινά οἱ, ὡς Σμέρδις ἱζόμενος ἐς τὸν βασιλήϊον θρόνον ψαύσειε τῇ κεφαλῇ τοῦ οὐρανοῦ. So εἶναι εἰς Id. I. 21, especially παρεῖναι εἰς: Id. VI. 1 παρεῖναι ἐς Σάρδις: Id. IV. 14 φανῆναι εἰς Προκόννησον.—κεῖσθαι εἰς (so Plaut. Casin. II. 3, 26 *ubi in lustra jacuisti?*): Id. VIII. 60, 2 ἐς τὴν Σαλαμῖνα ὑπέκκειται ἡμῖν τέκνα τε καὶ γυναῖκες (carried into safety in): Id. III. 31 πάντα ἐς τούτους ἀνακέαται (i. q. ἀνατεθειμένα ἐστί): Id. VI. 100 ἐβουλεύοντο ἐκλιπεῖν τὴν πόλιν ἐς τὰ ἄκρα τῆς Εὐβοίης, *relictâ urbe se recipere in:* Plat. Rep. p. 468 A τὸν δὲ ζῶντα εἰς τοὺς πολεμίους ἁλόντα, i. e. εἰς τοὺς πολεμίους πεσόντα ἁλῶναι: Demosth. p. 834, 67 καὶ νῦν κομίσασθαι τἀμαυτοῦ ζητῶν εἰς κίνδυνον καθέστηκα τὸν μέγιστον.

b. So ἐπί with acc. instead of dat.: Arist. Pax 342 ἐς πανηγύρεις θεωρεῖν: Hdt. VIII. 79 στὰς ἐπὶ τὸ συνέδριον: Hdt. III. 111 καταρρήγνυσθαι ἐπὶ γῆν. So πρός: Arist. Vesp. 773 πρὸς τὸ πῦρ καθήμενος, going and sitting by the

---

ᵃ Bremi ad loc.

fire. Παρά : Eur. Alc. 238 μαραινομέναν νόσῳ παρ' ῾Αδην. Sometimes the verb implies a motion which usually or necessarily follows it, as ἑάλωσαν ἐς ᾿Αθήνας.

c. The verbs of *standing, sitting, suspending, holding,* are joined with ἀπό and ἐκ, and denote a motion from their objects which is implied therein : Il. λ, 130 τὼ δ' αὖτ' ἐκ δίφρου γουναζέσθην : Il. ξ, 153 ῞Ηρη δ' εἰσεῖδε χρυσόθρονος ὀφθαλμοῖσι στᾶσ' ἐξ Οὐλύμποιο ἀπὸ ῥίου : Il. ε, 131 τὼ μὲν ἀφ' ἵπποιϊν, ὁ δ' ἀπὸ χθονὸς ὤρνυτο πεζός : Od. φ, 420 αὐτόθεν ἐκ δίφροιο καθήμενος ἧκε δ' οἰστόν : Soph. Antig. 411 καθήμεθ' ἄκρων ἐκ πάγων ὑπήνεμοι : Od. θ, 67 καθ' δ' ἐκ πασσαλόφι κρέμασεν φόρμιγγα λίγειαν, he hung it on, so that it hung down from it.   So in prose : φέρειν ἐκ τῶν ζωστήρων, to carry at the girdle ; ἐκ χειρὸς λαμβάνεσθαι : Hdt. IV. 10 ἐκ τῶν ζωστήρων φορέειν φιάλας, hanging from the girdle.

Obs. Local adverbs admit also of this pregnant construction.

a. Adverbs of rest, joined with verbs of motion (*whither*), to signify the place of rest after the motion : Soph. Trach. 40 κεῖνος δ' ὅπου (for ὅποι, *quo*) βέβηκεν, οὐδεὶς οἶδε.   (So Id. Philoct. 256 μηδαμοῦ διῆλθέ που : Arist. Lys. 1233 πανταχοῦ πρεσβεύσομεν.)   Xen. Hell. VII. 1, 25 ὅπου βουληθείεν ἐξελθεῖν.   So Tacit. Ann. I. 22 *responde, ubi cadaver abjeceris*.   b. Adverbs of motion (*whither*), joined with verbs of rest, to bring out the notion of the motion implied in the state of rest : Æsch. Suppl. 603 δήμου κρατοῦσα χεὶρ ὅποι (for ὅπου, *ubi*) πληθύεται : Id. Choeph. 1008 τοῦτ' ἄρ' οἶδ' ὅποι τελεῖ, *quorsum evasurum sit :* Soph. Œ. C. 23 ἔχεις διδάξαι δή μ' ὅποι καθέσταμεν, *quo progressi simus et ubi stemus :* Ibid. 383 τοὺς δὲ σοὺς ὅποι θεοὶ πόνους κατοικτιοῦσιν οὐκ ἔχω μαθεῖν : Eur. Herc. F. 74 ποῖ πατὴρ ἄπεστι γῆς; Ibid. 1160 ποῖ κακῶν ἐρημίαν εὕρω; *quo me vertam, ut requiem inveniam ?* Id. Hipp. 371 ἄσημα δ' οὐκ ἔτ' ἐστὶν οἷ φθίνει τύχα Κύπριδος : Id. Iph. T. 349 οἶ μ' ὥστε μόσχον Δαναΐδαι χειρούμεναι ἔσφαζον : Arist. Av. 9 ὅποι γῆς ἐσμέν ; whither (have we come and) are we ? Demosth. p. 102, 50 ποῖ ἀναδυόμεθα; *quo nos vertamus, ut perniciem vitemus ?* Id. p. 51, 40 ὁ πληγεὶς ἀεὶ τῆς πληγῆς ἔχεται, κἂν ἑτέρωσε πατάξῃ τις, ἐκεῖσε εἰσὶν αἱ χεῖρες.   So also Æsch. Eum. 80 ἄγκαθεν λαβὼν βρέτας, taking into the arms, so that it hangs therefrom.

Attraction of Prepositions with the Article.

§. 647. Another species of pregnant construction occurs when the article with a preposition (with or without a substantival object) expresses a substantival notion, as, οἱ ἐκ τῆς ἀγορᾶς ; since there is no motion implied here, the preposition ἐν, as the proper expression for a state of rest, ought to be used ; but instead, either ἀπό, ἐκ, or εἰς, is joined with the preposition, by virtue of a notion of motion (*whence, or whither*) drawn from a verb of motion either in the sentence, or to be supplied from it : this is called the attraction of prepositions.   So οἱ ἐκ τῆς ἀγορᾶς ἀπέφυγον, those who were *in* the forum ; ἐκ is used for ἐν, because the notion of motion in the mind of the speaker is communicated from ἀπέφυγον to the whole of the sentence, which therefore requires the preposition signifying motion.

a. ᾿Από, ἐκ for ἐν : Hdt. III. 6 τοὺς δὲ ἐκ Μέμφιος ἐς ταῦτα δὴ τὰ ἄνυδρα τῆς Συρίης κομίζειν : Thuc. II. 34 θάπτουσι τοὺς ἐκ τῶν πολέμων : Id. III. 22 ᾐσθοντο οἱ ἐκ τῶν πύργων φύλακες : Id. VI. 32 ξυνεπεύχοντο δὲ καὶ ὁ ἄλλος ὅμιλος ὁ ἐκ τῆς γῆς : Id. VII. 70 οἱ ἀπὸ τῶν καταστρωμάτων τοῖς ἀκοντίοις — ἐχρῶντο : Soph. El. 135 ἀλλ' οὔτοι τόν γ' ἐξ ῾Αΐδα παγκοίνου λίμνας πατέρ' ἀνστάσεις [a] : Plat. Apol. p. 32 B ὅτε ὑμεῖς

---

[a] Herm. ad loc.

τοὺς δέκα στρατηγοὺς τοὺς οὐκ ἀνελομένους τοὺς ἐκ τῆς ναυμαχίας ἐβούλεσθε ἀθρόους κρίνειν ᵃ : Id. Phæd. p. 109 E οἱ ἐκ τῆς θαλάττης ἰχθύες ἀνακύπτοντες : Demosth. p. 53, 45 τὰς ἀπὸ τοῦ βήματος ἐλπίδας ἐκπέμπειν : Id. p. 114, 15 τοὺς ἐκ Σερρίου τείχους — στρατιώτας ἐξέβαλεν.

Obs. This also takes place with local adverbs, ἐκεῖθεν, ἔνδοθεν being used for ἐκεῖ, ἔνδον : Arist. Av. 1168 ὅδε φύλαξ τῶν ἐκεῖθεν ἄγγελος ἐσθεῖ πρὸς ἡμᾶς δεῦρο : Id. Plut. 227 τοῦτο δὲ τὸ κρεᾳδίον τῶν ἔνδοθέν τις εἰσενεγκάτω λαβών ; Eur. Or. 838 ἔοικε — ὅδ' ἄγγελος λέξειν τὰ κεῖθεν σοῦ κασιγνήτου πέρι : Plat. Apol. p. 40 C καὶ μετοίκησις τῇ ψυχῇ τοῦ τόπου τοῦ ἐνθένδε εἰς ἄλλον τόπον : Demosth. p. 13, 15 ἀγνοεῖ τὸν ἐκεῖθεν πόλεμον δεῦρο ἥξοντα.

b. Eἰς for ἐν (far more rarely) : Hdt. II. 150 ἔλεγον δὲ οἱ ἐπιχώριοι καὶ ὡς ἐς τὴν Σύρτιν τ ὴ ν ἐ ς Λ ι β ύ η ν ἐκδιδοῖ ἡ λίμνη αὕτη.

Construction of Prepositions with different cases.

§. 648. The same preposition sometimes occurs in one sentence or paragraph with different cases. The reason of this is either, that although the sense is the same, yet the two relations in which the two objects are viewed are slightly different, as πρὸς βορέου, and πρὸς νότον : thus A | β, the position of A may be regarded either as from or towards the line β : or a different case is used for the sake of variety : Pind. Isthm. VI. 8 sq. τίνι τῶν πάρος, ὦ μάκαιρα Θήβα, καλῶν ἐπιχωρίων μάλιστα θυμὸν τεὸν εὔφρανας ; ἦ —; ἦ ὅτ' ἀ μ φ ὶ π υ κ ν α ῖς Τειρεσίαο β ο υ λ α ῖς ; ἢ ὅτ' ἀ μ φ' Ἰ ό λ α ο ν ἱ π π ό μ η τ ι ν ; (θυμὸν εὐφραίνειν ἀμφί τινι and ἀμφί τινα ᵇ.) Or, thirdly, with a real difference of sense : Hdt. VII. 61 περὶ μὲν τῇσι κεφαλῇσι εἶχον τιάρας —περὶ δὲ τὸ σῶμα κιθῶνας : Demosth. p. 478 εἰ αἱ μὲν παρὰ τοῖς ἄλλοις δωρεαὶ βέβαιοι μένουσιν αὐτῷ, τῆς δὲ παρ' ὑμῶν (granted by you) μόνης τοῦτ' ἀφαιρεθήσεται. Often in late authors.

Interchange of Prepositions.

§. 649. Sometimes prepositions are interchanged, either (*a*) without, or (*b*) with a difference of meaning : *a.* Hdt. VI. 86, 1 ἀ ν ὰ πᾶσαν μὲν τὴν ἄλλην Ἑλλάδα, ἐν δὲ καὶ π ε ρ ὶ Ἰωνίην τῆς σῆς δικαιοσύνης ἦν λόγος πολλός : Demosth. p. 74, 35 τῆς ἐ π ὶ τὴν Ἀττικὴν ὁδοῦ καὶ τῆς ε ἰ ς Πελοπόννησον κύριος γέγονε. Demosth. frequently περί and ὑπέρ with genitive (see above, ὑπέρ). Demosth. p. 621, 7 sqq. ὑ π ὲ ρ τοῦ Χερρονήσου ἔχειν ὑμᾶς ἀσφαλῶς— π ε ρ ὶ τούτου μοί ἐστιν ἅπασα ἡ σπουδή : Id. p. 74, 35 καὶ πεποίηχ' ὑμῖν μὴ π ε ρ ὶ τῶν δικαίων μηδ' ὑ π ὲ ρ τῶν ἔξω πραγμάτων εἶναι τὴν βουλήν, ἀλλ' ὑ π ὲ ρ τῶν ἐ ν τῇ χώρᾳ. *b.* Demosth. princ. ἐ π ὶ π ο λ λ ῶ ν μὲν ἄν τις ἰδεῖν — δοκεῖ μοι τὴν παρὰ τῶν θεῶν εὔνοιαν φανερὰν γιγνομένην τῇ πόλει, οὐχ ἥκιστα δὲ ἐ ν τ ο ῖ ς π α ρ ο ῦ σ ι π ρ ά γ μ α σ ι : Id. p. 35, 25 ἐ π ὶ μὲν δὲ τῶν Ἑλληνικῶν ἦσαν τοιοῦτοι· ἐ ν δὲ τοῖς κατὰ τὴν πόλιν αὐτὴν θεάσασθε ὁποῖοι ἔν τε κοινοῖς καὶ ἐν τοῖς ἰδίοις.

Repetition and Omission of Prepositions.

§. 650. 1. In a string of substantives joined by τέ and καί, the preposition is either repeated before every one, as Plat. Tim. p. 18 C κατά τε πόλεμον καὶ κατὰ τὴν ἄλλην δίαιταν. So where τέ and καί are omitted (Asynd.): Demosth. p. 129, 71 ἐκπέμπωμεν πρέσβεις πανταχοῖ, εἰς Πελοπόννησον, εἰς

ᵃ Stallb. ad loc.   ᵇ Dissen ad loc.

'Ρόδον, εἰς Χίον. Or placed only before the first subst.: Xen. Hell. I. 1, 3 ἀπό τε τῶν νεῶν καὶ τῆς γῆς: Plat. Phæd. p. 99 A ἡ περὶ Μέγαρα ἢ Βοιωτούς. In Asynd. it is scarcely ever omitted, except in poetry: Theocr. I. 83 κώρα πᾶσας ἀνὰ κράνας, πάντ' ἄλσεα ποσσὶ φορεῖται: Ibid. 117 ὁ βώκολος ὕμμιν ἐγὼ Δάφνις οὐκ ἔτ' ἀν' ὕλαν, οὐκ ἔτ' ἀνὰ δρυμώς, οὐκ ἄλσεα.

2. In poetry it is sometimes omitted before the first, and placed before the second only: Od. *a,* 247 ἢ ἁλὸς ἢ ἐπὶ γῆς: Pind. Isthm. I. 29 ῥεέθρωσί τε Δίρκας ἔφανεν καὶ π α ρ' Εὐρώτᾳ: Id. Nem. X. 38 Χαρίτεσσί τε καὶ σὺν Τυνδαρίδαις: "*quum in continuatâ constructione facilius languescat oratio, hoc artificio poetico nova vis et alacritas secundo membro conciliatur, eaque vera causa est hujus collocationis*[a]." So also traged., as Æsch. Suppl. 313 καὶ μὴν Κάνωβον κἀπὶ Μέμφιν ἵκετο: Eur. Hec. 146 (Chor.) ἀλλ' ἴθι ναούς, ἴθι πρὸς βωμούς[b]: Id. Helen. 872 Τροίας δὲ σωθεὶς κἀπὸ βαρβάρων χθονός. Cf. Id. Alc. 509.

3. When a relative follows the substantive joined with the preposition, and is in the same construction with it, the preposition is often repeated before it. Frequently, however, and almost generally in Attic (especially prose) writers it is omitted: Xen. Vectigg. IV. 13 ἀπ' αὐτῶν μὲν οὖν ἔγωγε ἀφ' ὧν μέλλω λέγειν οὐδέν τι ἀξιῶ θαυμάζεσθαι. But Thuc. I. 28 δίκας ἤθελον δοῦναι ἐν Πελοποννήσῳ παρὰ πόλεσιν, οἷς ἂν ἀμφότεροι ξυμβῶσιν: Xen. Symp. IV. 1 ἐν τῷ χρόνῳ, ᾧ ὑμῶν ἀκούω: Plat. Rep. p. 402 A ἐν ἅπασιν οἷς ἐστι: Id. Phæd. p. 76 D ἐν τούτῳ ἀπόλλυμεν, ᾧπερ καὶ λαμβάνομεν[c]: Demosth. p. 848 extr. περὶ μέν τινων, ὧν αὐτὸς βούλεται[d]. So in Latin; as, Cicer. de Fin. IV. 20 *Zeno negat Platonem, si sapiens non sit, eâdem esse in causâ, qu â tyrannum Dionysium.*

4. A less frequent omission of the preposition takes place in the second of two antithetical sentences; as, Thuc. I. 141 ἐν βραχεῖ μὲν μορίῳ σκοποῦσί τι τῶν κοινῶν, τῷ δὲ πλέονι τὰ οἰκεῖα πράσσουσι: Xen. M. S. I. 3, 8 τοιαῦτα μὲν περὶ τούτων ἔπαιζεν ἅμα σπουδάζων, ἀφροδισίων δ ὲ παρήνει τῶν καλῶν ἰσχυρῶς ἀπέχεσθαι.

5. The preposition is frequently omitted in the questions and answers of the dialogue of Aristophanes, and (especially) Plato, but not in tragedy: Arist. Pax, 1080 ποῖον γὰρ κατὰ χρησμὸν ἐκαύσατο μῆρα θεοῖσιν: — ὅ ν π ε ρ κάλλιστον δήπου πεποίηκεν Ὅμηρος: Plat. Soph. p. 243 D περὶ δὲ τοῦ μεγίστου τε καὶ ἀρχηγοῦ πρώτου νῦν σκεπτέον: Theat. Τίνος δὴ, λέγεις[e]; Id. Polit. p. 283 C περὶ δὴ τούτων αὐτῶν ὁ λόγος ἡμῖν — ὀρθῶς ἂν γίγνοιτο. Ε. Τίνων; X. Μήκους τε πέρι κ. τ. λ.: Id. Rep. p. 456 D πῶς οὖν ἔχεις δόξης τοῦ τοιοῦδε πέρι; Τίνος δή; Τοῦ ὑπολαμβάνειν παρὰ σαυτῷ κ. τ. λ.: Id. Protag. §. 110 ὑπὸ τίνος, φήσει. Τοῦ ἀγαθοῦ, φήσομεν, νὴ Δία.

6. Lastly, a preposition is omitted in the second member of a comparison, after ὡς rarely; after ὥσπερ, ἢ frequently in Attic writers; less frequently when the two members of the comparison are distinctly drawn out, as in Isocr. Pac. 161 E πρὸς δὲ τοὺς ἐπιπλήττοντας καὶ νουθετοῦντας ὑμᾶς οὕτω διατίθεσθε δυσκόλως, ὡς τοὺς κακόν τι τὴν πόλιν ἐργαζομένους (for ὡς πρὸς τούς κ. τ. λ.): Plat. Rep. p. 330 C περὶ τὰ χρήματα σπουδάζουσιν, ὡς ἔργον ἑαυτῶν: Demosth. p. 127, 63 ἥδιον πρὸς τοὺς ὑπὲρ Φιλίππου λέγοντας ἔχειν ἢ τοὺς ὑπὲρ ἑαυτῶν for ἢ πρὸς τούς[f]: but very frequently where the two members of the comparison are joined together and coalesce, since the repetition of the preposition would destroy the unity which it is the purpose of such a collocation to produce: Hom. Od. δ, 413 λέξεται ἐν μέσ-

---

a Dissen ad loc.	b Pflugk ad loc.	c Stallb. ad loc.
d Bremi ad loc.	e Heind. ad loc.	f Bremi ad loc.

σησι νομεύς ὡς πόεσι μήλων : Thuc. VI. 50 ὡς παρὰ φίλους καὶ εὐεργέτας Ἀθηναίους ἀδεῶς ἀπιέναι : Plat. Rep. p. 520 E ὡς ἐπ᾽ ἀναγκαῖον αὐτῶν ἕκαστος εἰσι
τὸ ἄρχειν (i. e. ἕκαστος αὐτῶν εἰσι ἐπὶ τὸ ἄρχειν ὡς ἐπ᾽ ἀναγκαῖον) : Ibid.
p. 545 E ὡς πρὸς παῖδας ἡμᾶς παιζούσας (i. e. πρὸς ἡμᾶς ὡς πρὸς παῖδας) : Id.
Protag. p. 337 E συμβῆναι ὑμᾶς ὥσπερ ὑπὸ διαιτητῶν ἡμῶν συμβιβαζόντων.
When the object of comparison is placed before the thing compared, the
preposition is seldom repeated, as in Plat. Phædr. p. 250 D ὥσπερ δὲ ἐν
κατόπτρῳ ἐν τῷ ἐρῶντι ἑαυτὸν ὁρῶν λέληθε : Id. Rep. p. 553 B πταίσαντα ὥσπερ
πρὸς ἕρματι πρὸς τῇ πόλει (for πρὸς ἕρματι τῇ πόλει).

Obs. When a verb, compounded with a preposition, is to be repeated,
either the verb is omitted, and the preposition alone repeated, §. 643. *Obs.*1.
or, *vice versâ*, the verb repeated and the preposition omitted : Eur. Bacch.
1018 λαβὼν γὰρ ἐλάτης οὐράνιον ἄκρον κλάδον, κ α τ ή γ ε ν, ἦ γ ε ν, ἦ γ ε ν εἰς
μέλαν πέδον : Plat. Phæd. p. 59 B π α ρ ῆ ν καὶ Κριτόβουλος καὶ ὁ πατὴρ αὐτοῦ
—ἦ ν δὲ καὶ Κτήσιππος κ. τ. λ.[a]

Collocation of Prepositions.

§. 651. The nature of the preposition requires that it should stand in
immediate connection with its substantive. There are the following exceptions.

a. When a particle would follow the substantive, as γέ, μέν, γάρ, μὲν
γάρ, δέ, οὖν, also μὲν οὖν, αὖ, καί, *etiam*, τοίνυν, ἴσως, and the adverbial
οἶμαι (Plato), which frequently, in prose, as well as in poetry, intervene between the preposition and substantive ; as, ἐν μὲν εἰρήνῃ, ἐν μὲν γὰρ εἰρήνῃ.
So also Hdt. VI. 69 ἐν γάρ σε τῇ νυκτὶ ταύτῃ ἀναιρέομαι.

Obs. We rarely find such a separation as Xen. Symp. IV. 55 ἐπ ὶ νὴ Δία
τ ο ῖ ς ἄ φ ρ ο σ ι ν : Demosth. p. 859,51 π ε ρ ὶ μὲν τοίνυν, ἔφην ἐγώ, τ ο ύ τ ο υ.

b. On rhetorical grounds : a. when different cases of the same word
follow one another ; as, Od. ε, 155 παρ᾽ οὐκ ἐθέλων ἐθελούσῃ : — β. Πρός in
oaths and exclamations : Soph. Phil. 467 πρὸς νῦν σε πατρός, πρός τε μητρός,
πρός τ᾽ εἴ τι σοι κατ᾽ οἶκον ἔστι προσφιλές, ἱκέτης ἱκνοῦμαι : Id. O. C. 1333
πρός νυν σε κρηνῶν, πρὸς θεῶν ὁμογνίων αἰτῷ πιθέσθαι : so in Latin, *p e r t e
d e o s oro.*

c. Sometimes the preposition (with the accent thrown back on the first
syllable) is placed after its case, as Ἰθάκην κάτα κοιρανέουσι : in Attic prose
only περί, with gen. (very frequently), even when divided by other words :
Hdt. VI. 101 τούτου σφι ἔμελε πέρι : Plat. Apol. p. 19 C ὧν ἐγὼ οὐδὲν οὔτε
μεγὰ οὔτε σμικρὸν πέρι ἐπαΐω.

d. If the subst. is joined with an attributive, the preposition stands
either before both ; as, ἐν τῷ πολέμῳ τῷ μακρῷ, or ἐν τῷ μακρῷ πολέμῳ, ἐν τῷ
τοῦ Κ. Κύρου πράγματι or ἐν τῷ πράγματι τῷ τοῦ : or between the two, in
which case, if the substantive precedes, the accent is thrown back ; as,
μάχῃ ἔνι κυδιανείρῃ (but θοὰς ἐπὶ νῆας) : or is placed after both, and then, of
course, the accent is thrown back ; as, τῆς ἐμῆς ψυχῆς πέρι.—Ἀ ν τ ί, ἀ μ φ ί,
δ ι ά, never throw back their accent ; πρό never follows its case, and ἐν only
in Epic.

---

[a] Elms. ad Eur. Med. 1219.

PRONOUNS.

Use of the Pronouns.

§. 652. 1. The substantival (ἐγώ, σύ, αὐτός), and adjectival or possessive personal pronouns are only used when particular emphasis is laid upon them; hence especially in antithesis ; as, καὶ σὺ ταῦτα ἔπραξας ; — καὶ ὁ σὸς πατὴρ ἀπέθανεν ; — ἐγὼ μὲν ἄπειμι, σὺ δὲ μένε. Otherwise substantival pronouns are supplied by the inflexions of the verb, the adjectival by prefixing the article to the substantive ; as, γράφω, γράφεις — ἡ μήτηρ εἶπέ μοι—οἱ γονεῖς στέργουσι τὰ τέκνα, their children.

Obs. 1. In the Homeric dialect, however, ἐγώ and σύ are used where no emphasis is meant : Il. a, 207 ἦλθον ἐγὼ παύσουσα τὸ σὸν μένος.

2. Of the accented and enclitic forms ἐμοῦ, μου, ἐμοῦ is emphatic, μου is used where no emphasis is intended. Hence in antithesis the accented form is always used ; as ἐμοῦ μὲν κατεγέλασε, σὲ δὲ ἐπήνεσεν.

Obs. 2. In poetry, however, we sometimes find the enclitic even where emphasis is required, in the same way as poetry also expresses an emphatic nominative by the mere inflexions of the verb : Soph. Œ. C. 726 καὶ γὰρ εἰ γέρων (ἐγὼ) κυρῶ, τὸ τῆσδε χώρας οὐ γεγήρακε σθένος : Eur. Andr. 237 ὁ νοῦς ὁ σός μοι μὴ ξυνοικοίη : Id. Med. 464 καὶ γὰρ εἰ σύ με στυγεῖς, οὐκ ἂν δυναίμην σοὶ (ἐγὼ) κακῶς φρονεῖν ποτε. This is less surprising, when the pronoun is the first of two persons in the same sentence ; as, Eur. Suppl. 3 εὐδαιμονεῖν με Θησέα τε : Id. Or. 736 κάκιστος εἶς μ ε καὶ κασιγνήτην ἐμήν.

3. Instead of the adjectival pronouns ἐμός, σός &c. the gen. of the substantival are used ; both the simple (in singular and dual always the enclitic forms) μου, σου (σέθεν) and the reflexive ἐμαυτοῦ, &c. with the simple pronouns. The article is placed before the subst. or the gen. ; as, ὁ πατήρ μου (σου, ἡμῶν, ὑμῶν, νῷν, αὐτοῦ, αὐτῆς, αὐτῶν) : or between them, as, μου (σου, ἡμῶν, ὑμῶν, αὐτοῦ, αὐτῆς, αὐτῶν) ὁ πατήρ : with the reflexive before the genitive and subst. ; as, ὁ ἑαυτοῦ (ἐμαυτοῦ, σεαυτοῦ) πατήρ : or repeated if the gen. is placed after the substantive ; as, ὁ πατὴρ ὁ ἑαυτοῦ (ἐμαυτοῦ, σεαυτοῦ.) Αὐτοῦ, αὐτῶν are sometimes, contrary to the rule, placed between the article and the subst. ; as, Isocr. p. 151 A ταῖς αὐτῶν ἐπιμελείαις : and sometimes ἑαυτοῦ is placed after it without the article : Arist. Nub. 516. Isocr. p. 103 D, or placed before the article, (Arist. Ran. 424.)

Obs. 3. When besides the gen. μου &c. any attributive is joined to the subst., both are placed between the article and substantive ; as, Aristoph. Ran. 485 εἰς τὴν κάτω μου κοιλίαν.

Obs. 4. The personal pronoun in gen. is sometimes placed before the subst. and even separated from it by another subst. or verb, when it stands in the place of and supplies the notion of the Dat. commodi or incommodi. Plat. Phæd. p. 117 B οὐδὲν ἄλλο (sc. χρὴ ποιεῖν) ἢ πιόντα περιϊέναι, ἕως ἂν σου βάρος ἐν τοῖς σκέλεσι γένηται : Id. Symp. p. 215 E οὐδὲ τεθορύβητό μου ἡ ψυχὴ οὐδ' ἀγανακτεῖ.

Obs. 5. Sometimes, but seldom, ἐμοῦ is used for ἐμαυτοῦ ; as, Aristoph. Vesp. 1398 ἐμοῦ τὰ φορτία : Id. Lys. 301 τὰς λημὰς ἐμοῦ.

Obs. 6. Sometimes the adjectival personal pronoun supplies the place of the genitive of the object ; as, Od. λ, 201 σὸς πόθος : as Terent. Heaut. II. 3, 66 *desiderio tuo* for *tui :* Il. τ, 321 σῇ ποθῇ : Xen. Cyr. III. 1, 28 εὐνοίᾳ καὶ φιλίᾳ τῇ ἐμῇ, *benevolentiâ et amore mei :* Id. VIII. 3, 32 τῆς ἐμῆς δωρεᾶς (*doni mihi dati*[a]) : Id. Anab. VII. 7, 29 οὐ φιλίᾳ τῇ σῇ ἐπείσθησαν ὑπὸ σοῦ ἄρχεσθαι : Plat. Gorg. p. 486 A εὐνοίᾳ γὰρ ἐρῶ τῇ σῇ.

[a] Bornemann ad loc.

Reflexive Pronouns.

§. 653. The reflexive pronouns ἑαυτοῦ, &c. always refer to the word on which they depend, as ἀπέκτεινεν ἑαυτόν; but in a dependent clause, or a clause with an acc. and inf., they refer either to some word in the clause wherein they stand, or to the governing word of the principal clause; as, ἔφη πάντας τοὺς ἀνθρώπους τὰ ἑαυτῶν (sua) ἀγαπᾶν—νομίζει τοὺς πολίτας ὑπηρετεῖν ἑαυτῷ. In the last case, however, the pronoun αὐτός can stand, and this is always the case when the dependent clause is not conceived in the mind of the person to whom the pronoun refers, but by the writer: Xen. Cyr. I, 1, 5 (ὁ Κῦρος) τῶν ἐθνῶν τούτων ἦρξεν, οὔθ' ἑαυτῷ ὁμογλώττων ὄντων, οὔτε ἀλλήλοις· καὶ ὅμως ἠδυνήθη ἐφικέσθαι μὲν ἐπὶ τοσαύτην γῆν τῷ ἑαυτοῦ φόβῳ, ὥστε καταπλῆξαι πάντας καὶ μηδένα ἐπιχειρεῖν αὐτῷ· ἐδυνήθη δὲ ἐπιθυμίαν ἐμβαλεῖν τοσαύτην τοῦ πάντας αὐτῷ χαρίζεσθαι, ὥστε ἀεὶ τῇ αὐτοῦ γνώμῃ ἀξιοῦν κυβερνᾶσθαι.

Reflexive Pronoun of III. Person for that of I. and II. Person.

§. 654. 1. a. The simple reflexive pronoun of III. for I. and II. Pers. only Epic; as, Il. κ, 398 φύξιν βουλεύοιτε μετὰ σφίσιν (for μεθ' ὑμῖν): Apoll. Rhod. II. 635 αὐτὰρ ἔγωγε εἷο (for ἐμοῦ) οὐδ' ἠβαιὸν ἀτύζομαι.

b. The compound reflexive subst. pronoun ἑαυτοῦ for ἐμαυτοῦ and σεαυτοῦ (frequent both in poetry and prose, but commonly only in plural; the instances in sing. are mostly uncertain readings): Soph. Œ. T. 138 οὐχ ὑπὲρ τῶν φίλων, ἀλλ' αὐτὸς αὑτοῦ τοῦτ' ἀποσκεδῶ μύσος, med ipse causâ (unless here αὐτὸς αὐτοῦ is the reading, see §. 656. Obs.1.): Thuc. I. 82 τὰ αὑτῶν ἅμα ἐκποριζόμεθα: Xen. M. S. I. 4, 9 οὐδὲ γὰρ τὴν ἑαυτοῦ σύγε ψυχὴν ὁρᾷς (var. σεαυτοῦ and σαυτοῦ, see Schneider): Ibid. II. 6, 35 ἐπί τε τοῖς καλοῖς ἔργοις τῶν φίλων ἀγάλλῃ οὐχ ἧττον ἢ ἐπὶ τοῖς ἑαυτοῦ, καὶ ἐπὶ τοῖς ἀγαθοῖς τῶν φίλων χαίρεις οὐδὲν ἧττον ἢ ἐπὶ τοῖς ἑαυτοῦ (var. σαυτοῦ, see Schneider): Plat. Phædon. p. 78 B δεῖ ἡμᾶς ἀνερέσθαι ἑαυτούς.

c. Reflexive adjectival pronoun ἑός, σφέτερος for ἐμός, σός, ἡμέτερος, ὑμέτερος (epic): Od. ι, 28 ἔγωγε ἧς γαίης δύναμαι γλυκερώτερον ἄλλο ἰδέσθαι: Od. α, 402 δώμασιν οἷσιν ἀνάσσοις: Od. ν, 320 ἀλλ' αἰεὶ φρεσὶν ᾗσιν ἔχων δεδαϊγμένον ἦτορ ἠλώμην: Il. τ, 174 σὺ δὲ φρεσὶν ᾗσιν ἰανθῇς: Cf. Hesiod. Opp. 391.

Obs. 1. On the Homeric use of αὐτοῦ, &c. for the reflexive pronoun of all three persons, see §. 656. Obs. 1.

Obs. 2. This interchange may be thus explained; a general reflexive notion is expressed by III. person. pronoun, while the particular person to whom the notion applies is defined by the person of the verb, or a pronoun attached.

Obs. 3. As σφέτερος is used in the plural and singular, so it is sometimes used for ἐμός, σός: Theocr. XXV. 163 ὡσεί περ σφετέρῃσιν ἐνὶ φρεσὶ βάλλομαι (mente meâ): Ibid. XXII. 67 σφετέρης μὴ φείδεο τέχνης (arti tuæ noli parcere.)

Reflexive instead of Reciprocal Pronoun.

2. The reciprocal pronoun ἀλλήλων is often represented by the reflexive, as Hes. Scut. 403 ἀλλήλοις κοτέοντες ἐπί σφεας ὁρμήσωσι: then

also in Traged., Pindar, and other poets; very commonly in Attic and modern writers : Thuc. IV. 25. VI. 77 : Soph. Ant. 145 πατρὸς ἑνὸς μητρός τε μᾶς φύντε, καθ' αὑτοῖν δικρατεῖς λόγχας στήσαντ' ἔχετον κοινοῦ θανάτου μέρος ἄμφω : Plat. Lys. p. 215 B πῶς οὖν οἱ ἀγαθοὶ τοῖς ἀγαθοῖς ἡμῖν φίλοι ἔσονται τὴν ἀρχήν, οἳ μήτε ἀπόντες ποθεινοὶ ἀλλήλοις, ἱκανοὶ γὰρ ἑαυτοῖς καὶ χωρὶς ὄντες, μήτε παρόντες χρείαν αὑτῶν ἔχουσι [a]; Dem. p. 43, 10 ἢ βούλεσθε—περιιόντες αὐτῶν πυνθάνεσθαι, each other : Id. p. 124, 50 ἐπειδὰν δὲ ἐπὶ τούτοις πρὸς νοσοῦντας ἐν αὑτοῖς προσπέσῃ : but ἀλλήλων can never stand for ἑαυτῶν: so in Thuc. III. 81. we must explain οἱ πολλοὶ τῶν ἱκετῶν—διέφθειραν αὐτοῦ ἐν τῷ ἱερῷ ἀλλήλους, one another.

Obs. The subst. pronouns of I. and II. person are also used for ἀλλήλων : Dem. p. 30, 7 ἐπράξαμεν ἡμεῖς κἀκεῖνος πρὸς ἡμᾶς (i. e. ἀλλήλους) εἰρήνην [b].

Demonstrative Pronoun.

§. 655. 1. The pronouns ὅδε, ὅγε, οὗτος, ἐκεῖνος, express a pointing to the scene (near or distant) of some action; hence they are used in an animated address, and even are applied emphatically to the speaker himself ; so especially in the speeches of Homer : Il. κ, 82 τίς δ' οὗτος κατὰ νῆας ἀνὰ στρατὸν ἔρχεαι οἶος : Od. a, 76 ἀλλ' ἄγετ', ἡμεῖς οἵδε περιφραζώμεθα πάντες, let us here debate : Ibid. 186 νηῦς δέ μοι ἥδ' ἕστηκεν ἐπ' ἀγροῦ νόσφι πόληος : Il. τ, 344 Ἀχιλλεύς—κεῖνος ὅγε προπάροιθε νεῶν ὀρθοκραιράων ἧσται (he there) : Od. φ, 207 ἔνδον μὲν δὴ ὅδ' αὐτὸς ἐγὼ κακὰ πολλὰ μογήσας ἤλυθον : so τόδε in Homer frequently *huc*, Od. a, 409 : in the dramatists and Hdt. ὅδε is especially thus used : Eur. Suppl. 1048 ἥδ' ἐγὼ πέτρας ἔπι—δύστηνον αἰώρημα κουφίζω, πάτερ : Id. Or. 374 ὅδ' εἴμ' Ὀρέστης, *en! adsum Or.* : but also οὗτος in Attic prose ; as, Plat. Rep. I. init. ἠρόμην, ὅπου εἴη. Οὗτος, ἔφη, ὄπισθεν προσέρχεται, there he comes behind me.

2. So also in poetry ὅδε for ἐμός ; as, Soph. Ant. 43 εἰ τὸν νεκρὸν ξὺν τῇδε κουφιεῖς χερί (τῇ ἐμῇ θάψεις) : hence οὗτος is used generally for every known object to which the speaker points as before him ; so in Plato ταῦτα, this world and all therein ; and so especially of any famous or notable, much spoken of object, whether person or thing : Xen. Anab. I. 5, 8 ἔχοντες τούτους τε τοὺς πολυτελεῖς χιτῶνας καὶ τὰς ποικίλας ἀναξυρίδας : Plat. Menon. p. 80 A καὶ δοκεῖς μοι παντελῶς—ὁμοιότατος εἶναι τό τε εἶδος καὶ ἄλλα ταύτῃ τῇ πλατείᾳ νάρκῃ τῇ θαλαττίᾳ.

3. The notion of "something lying before us" is also apparent in the phrase οὐ τάδ' ἐστίν, εἰσίν, which occurs as early as Homer (Od. a, 226 οὐκ ἔρανος τάδε γ' ἐστίν), but is especially used in the Attic dramatists : Eur. Androm. 168 οὐ γάρ ἐσθ' Ἕκτωρ τάδε, οὐ Πρίαμος, οὐδὲ χρυσός, ἀλλ' Ἑλλὰς πόλις : also Thuc. VI. 77 οὐκ Ἴωνες τάδε εἰσὶν οὐδὲ Ἑλλησπόντιοι : so τάδε πάντα ; as, Plat. Theæt. p. 168 D τάδε πάντα πλὴν σοῦ παιδία ἐστίν : also ταῦτα πάντα.

4. From the sense of something lying before the speaker, the use of οὗτος and ὅδε for ἐγώ and σύ has arisen : Plat. Gorg. p 489 B οὑτοσὶ ἀνὴρ οὐ παύσεται φλυαρῶν for σὺ οὐ παύσει : thus in tragedy frequently ἀνὴρ ὅδε for ἐγώ (in this construction the article is always wanting.)

5. When joined with adverbs of time and place, τοῦτο, τόδε, ταῦτα,

---

[a] Cf. Heindorf. p. 32.　　　　　[b] Vide Schäfer p. 284.

τάδε denote more forcibly the time and place, as it were, by pointing at them, as αὐτοῦ τῆδε, exactly here: Hdt. VII. 104 ἐγὼ τυγχάνω τανῦν τάδε ἐστοργὼς ἐκείνους, at this very time: Eur. Ion 566 τοῦτ' ἐκεῖ, exactly there.

6. Οὗτος generally refers to what immediately precedes, ὅδε to what immediately follows: Hdt. VI. 53 ταῦτα (what I have just spoken of) μὲν Λακεδαιμόνιοι λέγουσι—τάδε (what follows) δὲ—ἐγὼ γράφω: Ibid. 58 ταῦτα μὲν (quæ dicta sunt) ζῶσι τοῖσι βασιλεῦσι δέδοται ἐκ τοῦ κοινοῦ τῶν Σπαρτιητέων· ἀποθανοῦσι δὲ τάδε (quæ sequuntur): Cf. VII. 133: Plat. Menon. p. 93 B εἰ διδακτόν ἐστιν ἀρετή, πάλαι σκοποῦμεν τοῦτο δὲ σκοποῦντες, τόδε σκοποῦμεν, ἆρα κ. τ. λ. The same distinction obtains also in τοιοῦτος and τοιόσδε, οὕτως and ὧδε, but not unfrequently the reverse is the case, οὗτος, τοιοῦτος, οὕτως referring to what follows; ὅδε, τοιόσδε, ὧδε to what has gone before.

Obs. 1. Before a relative sentence we generally find οὗτος, seldom ὅδε; as, οὗτός ἐστιν ὃν εἶδες ἄνδρα: Plat. Legg. p. 627 E πότερος οὖν ἀμείνων; ὅστις—προστάξειεν, ἢ ὅδε, ὃς ἂν τοὺς χρηστοὺς ἄρχειν ποιήσειε.

Obs. 2. In Epic, when the same subject belongs to two sentences, ὅγε is often used emphatically in the second sentence, to mark distinctly the identity of the subject: Il. β, 664 αἶψα δὲ νῆας ἔπηξε, πολὺν δ' ὅγε (idemque) λαὸν ἀγείρας βῆ φεύγων ἐπὶ πόντον: Il. o, 586 Ἀντίλοχος δ' οὐ μεῖνε, θόος περ ἐὼν πολεμιστής, ἀλλ' ὅγ' ἄρ' ἔτρεσε. So in Epic, and especially in Hdt., ὁ δέ is used in a series of actions referring to the same subject, as we should say, *and then he; but he,* &c.: Il. θ, 302 καὶ τοῦ μέν ῥ' ἀφάμαρθ'· ὁ δ' ἀμύμονα Γοργυθίωνα—κατὰ στῆθος βάλεν ἰῷ, idemque: Cf. 320. Od. χ, 85, 431: Hesiod. Theog. 491 ἔμελλε—ἐξελάαν, ὁ δ' ἐν ἀθανάτοισιν ἀνάξειν, to overthrow him and then to reign: Hdt. VI. 3 τὴν μὲν γενομένην αὐτοῖσι αἰτίην οὐ μάλα ἐξέφαινε, ὁ δὲ ἔλεγέ σφι (but he). Rarely in Attic Greek; as, Eur. Or. 35 νοσεῖ τλήμων Ὀρέστης, ὁ δὲ πεσὼν ἐν δεμνίοις κεῖται.—This repetition of the subject by ὁ δέ is often called by the mention of another person in the preceding sentence, which makes it necessary that the subject should be distinctly stated: Il. ν, 321 αὐτίκα τῷ μὲν ἔπειτα κατ' ὀφθαλμῶν χέεν ἀχλὺν (Ποσειδάων) Πηλεΐδῃ Ἀχιλῆϊ· ὁ δὲ (Ποσειδάων), μελίην εὔχαλκον ἀσπίδος ἐξέρυσεν μεγαλήτορος Αἰνείαο: Cf. Il. α, 190: Od. ε, 13. This idiom is much used by Hom. and Hdt. in disjunctive sentences: ἢ— ἢ ὅγε: Od. β, 327 ἤ τινας ἐκ Πύλου ἄξει ἀμύντορας—, ἢ ὅγε καὶ Σπάρτηθεν: Cf. Od. δ, 789: Il. μ, 239: Hdt. II. 173 λάβοι ἂν ἤτοι μανείς, ἢ ὅγε ἀπόπληκτος γενόμενος: so Lat. ille; as, nunc dextrâ ingeminans ictus, nunc ille sinistrâ (Virg.).

Obs. 3. Sometimes οὗτος is used twice in the same sentence of one and the same object: Plat. Lach. p. 200 C τὸν Νικήρατον τούτῳ ἥδιστ' ἐπιτρέποιμι, εἰ ἐθέλοι οὗτος: Demosth. p. 846. extr. πριάμενοι παρὰ τούτου τούτῳ τὰς τιμὰς διέλυσαν (where instead of τούτῳ we should expect αὐτῷ). If ἐκεῖνος is used, αὐτός generally follows, though sometimes even ἐκεῖνος is used twice of one object: Soph. Trach. 605 ὅπως μηδεὶς βροτῶν κείνου πάροιθεν ἀμφιδύσεται χροΐ,—πρὶν κεῖνος αὐτὸν—δείξῃ θεοῖσιν: Id. Aj. 1039 κεῖνος τὰ κείνου στεργέτω, κἀγὼ τάδε: but Plat. Cratyl. p. 430 E δεῖξαι αὐτῷ, ἂν μὲν τύχῃ, ἐκείνου εἰκόνα: Lys. p. 429 ἕως ὁ λεγόμενος ὑπ' ἐκείνου καιρὸς ἐπιμελῶς ὑπ' αὐτοῦ ἐτηρήθη.

Obs. 4. Οὗτος is sometimes omitted: a. Before relatives—(see *Relative Sentences*): b. In poetry—in animated passages, and expressions of feeling: Od. δ, 292 ἄλγιον, (this is) bad enough! Theocr. XV. 79 τὰ ποικίλα πρᾶτον ἄθρησον· λεπτὰ καὶ ὡς χαρίεντα (sc. ταῦτα)· θεῶν περονάματα φασείς: cf. Ibid. 83. *c.* In prose—where it is wished to sum up what has been said in a brief conclusion: Plat. Phæd. p. 89 E οὐκουν, ἦ δ᾽ ὅς, αἰσχρόν; *nonne hoc turpe est?* *d.* By orators — in the rhetorical phrases: τεκμήριον δέ, κεφάλαιον δέ, σημείον δὲ μέγιστον, αἴτιον δέ &c., which arises from the animated character of the oration.

7. When ἐκεῖνος and οὗτος are used in opposition to each other, the latter signifies the object nearer, either in time or space, to the speaker, the former the more remote. Sometimes this is reversed, but generally only when οὗτος refers to the more important, ἐκεῖνος to the less important object: Xen. M. S. I. 3, 13 τοσούτῳ δεινότερόν ἐστι τῶν φαλαγγίων, ὅσῳ ἐκεῖνα μὲν ἀψάμενα, τοῦτο δὲ οὐδ᾽ ἀπτόμενον: Demosth. p. 107, 72 καὶ (δεῖ) τὸ βέλτιστον ἀεί, μὴ τὸ ῥᾷστον ἅπαντας λέγειν· ἐπ᾽ ἐκεῖνο (τὸ ῥᾷστον) μὲν γὰρ ἡ φύσις αὐτὴ βαδιεῖται, ἐπὶ τοῦτο (τὸ βέλτιστον) δὲ τῷ λόγῳ δεῖ προάγεσθαι διδάσκοντα τὸν ἀγαθὸν πολίτην· "*relationem dicas logicam, non grammaticam: quippe τὸ ῥᾷστον removendum, τὸ βέλτιστον amplexandum [a].*" So in Latin, *hic* and *ille.*

8. Ἐκεῖνος is sometimes (like in Latin *ille,* though more rarely) used emphatically of well known objects, or famous persons; as, Soph. Ant. 384 ἥδ᾽ ἐστ᾽ ἐκείνη τοὔργον ἡ 'ξειργασμένη: Eur. Troad. 1188 τὰ πόλλ᾽ ἀσπάσμαθ᾽ αἵ τ᾽ ἐμαὶ τροφαὶ ὕπνοι τ᾽ ἐκεῖνοι φροῦδά μοι (that restless sleep): Demosth. p. 301 Καλλίστρατος ἐκεῖνος: so often in late prose. So especially in Aristoph. Plat., &c.: τοῦτ᾽ ἐκεῖνο, τόδ᾽ ἐκεῖνο, where ἐκεῖνο signifies some common expression or proverb, and τοῦτο or τόδ᾽ denotes its application to the present case; as, Eur. Or. 804 τοῦτ᾽ ἐκεῖνο, κτᾶσθ᾽ ἑταίρους, μὴ τὸ συγγενὲς μόνον: Arist. Ach. 41 τοῦτ᾽ ἐκεῖν᾽ οὑγὼ ᾽λεγον.

Obs. 5. The nomin. οὗτος (rarely αὕτη) is used as a vocative in Attic Greek; as, ὦ οὗτος: Soph. Aj. 89 ὦ οὗτος Αἴαν, δεύτερόν σε προσκαλῶ: Lat. *heus tu.*

The Demostrative Pronoun Αὐτός.

§. 656. The original meaning of αὐτός is αὖ τός, *again he = the same;* in which sense it is found frequently in Homer: afterwards ὁ αὐτός signified *idem* (opposed to ἕτερος), and from its original sense of *idem,* was derived the sense of *ipse, he the same and no other,* (opposed to ἄλλος,) and this is its general force. So ὁ υἱὸς αὐτός, or αὐτὸς ὁ υἱός. So αὐτὸ τοῦτο, τοῦτ᾽ αὐτό, *hoc ipsum, just this, no other.* If joined with ἕκαστος, it is always placed first: Hdt. VII. 19 θέλων αὐτὸς ἕκαστος τὰ προκείμενα δῶρα λαβεῖν. On the collocation of αὐτός, and a substantive and article, see §. 453.

Obs. 1. Αὐτός, *ipse,* can be referred to any personal pronoun implied in the verb: Il. a, 133 ἦ ἐθέλεις, ὄφρ᾽ αὐτὸς ἔχῃς γέρας, αὐτὰρ ἔμ᾽ αὔτως ἧσθαι δευόμενον; Thus Homer often used it for the reflexive pronoun of all three persons: Od. δ, 247 ἄλλῳ δ᾽ αὐτὸν (for ἑαυτόν) φωτὶ κατακρύπτων ἤϊσκεν: Od. ζ, 27 σοὶ δὲ γάμος σχεδόν ἐστιν, ἵνα χρὴ καλὰ μὲν αὐτὴν (for σαυτήν) ἕννυσθαι: cf. ξ, 389 αὐτόν for σαυτόν: α, 27 αὐτῶν γὰρ ἀπωλόμεθ᾽ ἀφραδίῃσιν. So also Hdt. and sometimes the Trag., wherefore perhaps the readings, αὐτοὶ κατ᾽ αὐτῶν, αὐτὸς πρὸς αὐτοῦ, (for αὑτῶν, αὑτοῦ) αὐτὴ πρὸς αὑτὴν (for ἐμαυτήν) Soph. El. 277, &c. are correct.

Obs. 2. Since the αὐτός, *ipse,* separates as it were the object from every thing else, it is especially used in the neuter in Attic Greek to express the

a Schæfer ad loc.

abstract idea; as, αὐτὸ τὸ καλόν, αὐτὸ τὸ δίκαιον, the *very* just; or, and indeed more commonly, without an article: αὐτὸ καλόν, the idea of beauty —beauty taken by itself in the abstract. So Plat. Menon. p. 87 D αὐτὸ τὴν ἀρετήν: (cf. Symp. p. 199 E ἀδελφός, αὐτὸ τοῦτο, ὅπερ ἐστιν.) The plural αὐτά is more rarely used of generic notions: Xen. M. S. IV. 5, 7 αὐτὰ ἐναντία: Plat. Soph. p. 225 C περὶ δικαίων αὐτῶν. (Hence we find in Aristotle a variety of compounds, such as αὐτοβούλησις, αὐτοεπιθυμία.)

Obs. 3. From this separative and exclusive power of αὐτός, the following meanings are derived: *a. Alone*, s o l u s (*ipse, non alius*): Il. ν, 729 ἀλλ' οὗπως ἅμα πάντα δυνήσεαι αὐτὸς ἑλέσθαι: Xen. Laced. III. 5 αὐτὰ τὰ πρὸ τῶν ποδῶν ὁρᾶν, *ea sola, quæ sunt ante pedes:* Plat. Phæd. p. 63 C πότερον αὐτὸς ἔχων τὴν διάνοιαν ταύτην ἐν νῷ ἔχεις ἀπιέναι [a]: hence the Attic phrase, αὐτοί ἐσμεν "*de iis, qui ut soli cum amicis et familiaribus liberius loqui solent.*" *b.* But also *himself* (*ipse*); as, αὐτὸς ὁ Σωκράτης ἐδάκρυσεν. *c. Of himself*—*sponte*, like *ipse*, since a person can hardly be said to do that *himself* which another compels him to do: Il. ρ, 254 ἀλλά τις αὐτὸς ἴτω. *d.* In Homer it is very often used in opposition to some person or thing, which is to be distinguished from the object signified by αὐτός, as the soul in opposition to body (Od. λ, 602), or body to soul (Il. α, 4 αὐτοὺς δὲ ἑλώρια τεῦχε κύνεσσιν), or a man to his goods (Od. τ, 329. 332), or his relations (Il. θ, 4). Hence αὐτός, as in Latin *ipse*, is used of a lord—master; as, αὐτὸς ἔφη. *e.* Αὐτός, as in Lat. *ipse*, is used of that which is spoken of, and supplies the place of αὐτὸς οὗτος. So especially the neuter: Plat. Rep. p. 362 D αὐτό, ἦ δ' ὅς, οὐκ εἴρηται, ὃ μάλιστα ἔδει ῥηθῆναι [b]: Id. Char. p. 166 B ἐπ' αὐτὸ ἥκεις ἐρευνῶν, ὅτῳ διαφέρει. *f.* Joined with ordinal numerals, it means *himself and no other*, and is generally used of the chief of an expedition: Thuc. I. 46 Κορινθίων στρατηγὸς ἦν Ξενοκλείδης — πέμπτος αὐτός, he with four subordinate generals.

Obs. 4. When the verb is followed by a reflexive pronoun in gen., dat., or acc., the subject is opposed to itself by the use of the nom. αὐτός, as it represents the subject of the verb as something distinct from the object thereof: Od. α, 33 οἱ δὲ καὶ αὐτοὶ σφῇσιν ἀτασθαλίῃσιν ὑπὲρ μόρον ἄλγε' ἔχουσιν, just as in Latin, s u d i p s i *temeritate* (they themselves, no others); while v. 7 αὐτῶν γὰρ σφετέρῃσιν ἀτασθαλίῃσιν ὄλοντο signifies, s u d i p s o r u m *temeritate*, by their own, not that of another: Soph. Antig. 1177 (Αἵμων ὄλωλεν) αὐτὸς πρὸς αὐτοῦ: Plat. Phæd. p. 94 E οὔτε γὰρ ἂν Ὁμήρῳ ὁμολογοῖμεν, οὔτε αὐτοὶ ἡμῖν αὐτοῖς. In this idiom, αὐτός is placed between the preposition (or the article) and the reflexive pronoun; as, Æsch. Ag. 845 τοῖς αὐτὸς αὐτοῦ πήμασιν βαρύνεται: Id. Prom. 929 τοῖον παλαιστὴν νῦν παρασκευάζεται ἐπ' αὐτὸς αὐτῷ.

Obs. 5. Αὐτός is sometimes followed by a relative sentence, and then stands instead of οὗτος or ἐκεῖνος: Eur. Troad. 668 ἀπέπτυσ' αὐτὴν, ἥτις ἄνδρα τὸν καινοῖσι λέκτροις ἀποβαλοῦσ' ἄλλον φιλεῖ. Especially Plato; as, Charm. p. 166 B ἐπ' αὐτὸ ἥκεις ἐρευνῶν, ὅτῳ διαφέρει—ἡ σωφροσύνη: Parm. p. 130 C ἐν ἀπορίᾳ—περὶ αὐτῶν γέγονα, πότερα χρὴ φάναι ὥσπερ περὶ ἐκείνων ἢ ἄλλως. This is rarely found in other good authors: cf. Eur. Iph. A. 1025. Thuc. VII. 34 νομίσαντες δι' αὐτὸ οὐχ ἡσσᾶσθαι, δι' ὅπερ οὐδ' οἱ ἕτεροι νικᾶν: Xen. M. S. III. 10, 14.

Obs. 6. Αὐτός, in composition, sometimes signifies "*together with.*" So αὐτότοκος, *cum ipso fetu*, young and all: cf. Eumen. 404 [c].

a Stallb. ad loc.   b Ibid.   c Blomfield Gloss. Ag. 134.

Prospective use of the III. Personal and the Demonstrative Pronouns.

§. 657. I. The III. personal pronoun, οὗ, οἷ, ἕ, μίν, and the demonstrative, ὁ, ἡ, τό, are often used in Homer to direct the reader's attention to some substantive which is to follow, and as it were to prepare the way for it : Il. a, 488 αὐτὰρ ὁ μήνιε, νηυσὶ παρήμενος ὠκυπόροισιν, Διογενὴς Πηλέος υἱός, πόδας ὠκὺς Ἀχιλλεύς : Il. υ, 321 αὐτίκα τῷ μὲν ἔπειτα κατ' ὀφθαλμῶν χέεν ἀχλὺν, Πηλείδῃ Ἀχιλῆϊ : Il. φ, 249 ἵνα μιν παύσειε πόνοιο, δῖον Ἀχιλλῆα : Od. a, 125 ἡ δ' ἕσπετο Παλλὰς Ἀθήνη. In the Post-Homeric writers more rarely, sometimes in Attic in the formula, ὁ (οἱ, τό) μέν, and ὁ (οἱ, τό) δέ.

2. Similarly the neuter demonstrative, ταῦτα, τοῦτο, rarely ἐκεῖνο is used (a) to prepare the way for a following substantive ; as, Od. a, 159 τούτοισιν μὲν ταῦτα μέλει, κίθαρις καὶ ἀοιδή : Plat. Gorg. p. 478 C οὐ γὰρ τοῦτ' ἦν εὐδαιμονία, ὡς ἔοικε, κακοῦ ἀπαλλαγή, ἀλλὰ τὴν ἀρχὴν μηδὲ κτῆσις : Id. Apol. p. 37 A τούτου τιμῶμαι, ἐν πρυτανείῳ σιτήσεως : Id. Rep. p. 583 D τοῦτο γὰρ τότε ἡδὺ ἴσως καὶ ἀγαπητὸν γίγνεται ἡσυχία : Ibid. p. 606 B ἐκεῖνο κερδαίνειν ἡγεῖται, τὴν ἡδονήν. (b) For a whole sentence (τοῦτο, more rarely τόδε,) : Plat. Gorg. p. 515 E ἀλλὰ τόδε μοι εἰπὲ ἐπὶ τούτῳ, εἰ λέγονται Ἀθηναῖοι διὰ Περικλέα βελτίους γεγονέναι : Demosth. p. 41, 5 ἀλλ' οἶδεν, ἄνδρες Ἀθ., τοῦτο καλῶς ἐκεῖνος, ὅτι ταῦτα μέν ἐστιν ἅπαντα τὰ χωρία ἆθλα τοῦ πολέμου κείμενα ἐν μέσῳ. This usage is very common before infinitives, generally without the article, as early as Hom. ; as, Od. a, 82 εἰ μὲν δὴ νῦν τοῦτο φίλον μακάρεσσι θεοῖσιν, νοστῆσαι Ὀδυσῆα δαΐφρονα : Plat. Apol. S. p. 38 C ἀπὸ τοῦ αὐτομάτου ἂν ὑμῖν τοῦτο ἐγένετο, ἐμὲ τεθνάναι δή. So also in gen., dat., and acc. ; as, Plat. Gorg. p. 474 E οὐ δήπου ἐκτὸς τούτων ἐστὶ τὰ καλά, τοῦ ἢ ὠφέλεια εἶναι ἢ ἡδέα ἢ ἀμφότερα : Id. Ap. S. p. 35 C οὐ γὰρ ἐπὶ τούτῳ κάθηται ὁ δικαστὴς, ἐπὶ τῷ καταχαρίζεσθαι τὰ δίκαια. Even before a participle with article : Plat. Legg. p. 680 D μῶν οὐκ ἐκ τούτων, τῶν κατὰ μίαν οἴκησιν καὶ κατὰ γένος διεσπαρμένων (τοιαῦται πολιτείαι γίγνονται).

Retrospective Power of the Demonstrative and Personal Pronouns.

§. 658. On the other hand, after a substantive or pronoun, between which and its verb another sentence intervenes, or on which emphasis is to be laid, it is not unusual to place οὗτος or (especially) αὐτός, to recall the preceding substantive to the mind, or to bespeak especial attention to it. As early as Homer, though but rarely : Il. a, 300 τῶν δ' ἄλλων ἅ μοι ἔστι, τῶν οὐκ ἄν τι φέροις. Also rarely in dramatists ; as, Soph. Œ. R. 386 εἰ τῆσδέ γ' ἀρχῆς οὕνεχ', ἣν ἐμοὶ πόλις — εἰσεχείρισεν, ταύτης Κρέων ἐκβαλεῖν ἱμείρεται. Very frequently in prose, especially Herodotus ; as, III. 63 ὁ δέ μοι Μάγος, τὸν Καμβύσης ἐπίτροπον τῶν οἰκίων ἀπέδεξε, οὗτος ταῦτα ἐνετείλατο : Ibid. 85 τῶν θηλέων ἵππων μίην, τὴν ὁ Δαρείου ἵππος ἔστεργε μάλιστα, ταύτην ἀγαγὼν ἐς τὸ προάστειον κατέδησε : Thuc. IV. 69 αἱ οἰκίαι τοῦ προαστείου ἐπάλξεις λαμβάνουσαι, αὗται ὑπῆρχον ἔρυμα : Id. VIII. 61 Λέοντα —, ὃς — ξυνεξῆλθε τοῦτον κεκομισμένοι : Plat. Rep. p. 398 A ἄνδρα δὴ, ὡς ἔοικε, δυνάμενον ὑπὸ σοφίας παντοδαπὸν γίγνεσθαι καὶ μιμεῖσθαι πάντα χρήματα, εἰ ἡμῖν ἀφίκοιτο εἰς τὴν πόλιν — προσκυνοῦμεν ἂν αὐτόν, (for the sake of clearness :) Xen. Cyr. VI. 1, 17 ὑμεῖς δὲ τὰ πρόσ-

ὅρα ὑμῖν αὐτοῖς τῆς Ἀσσυρίας, ἐκεῖνα κτᾶσθε καὶ ἐργάζεσθε: Demosth.
p. 837, 6 αὐτὴν δὲ τὴν διαθήκην — ταύτην δ᾽, where also δέ is repeated
to increase the emphasis. So in Antithesis: Xen. M. S. I. 2, 24 Ἀλκιβιάδης — ὥσπερ οἱ τῶν γυμνικῶν ἀγώνων ἀθληταὶ ῥᾳδίως πρωτεύοντες ἀμελοῦσι
τῆς ἀσκήσεως, οὕτω κἀκεῖνος ἠμέλησεν αὐτοῦ. So also personal pronouns
are there repeated (the enclitic form being always used in the second):
Soph. Œ. C. 1407 μήτοι με — μή μ᾽ ἀτιμάσητέ γε: Eur. Phœn. 507 ἐμοὶ
μὲν, εἰ καὶ μὴ καθ᾽ Ἑλλήνων χθόνα τεθράμμεθ᾽, ἀλλ᾽ οὖν ξυνετά μοι δοκεῖς λέγειν:
Xen. Cyr. IV. 5, 29 σκέψαι δὲ καί, οἵῳ ὄντι μοι περὶ σὲ οἷος ὢν περὶ ἐμὲ
ἔπειτά μοι μέμφῃ.

Obs. For Relative Pronoun, see *Syntax of Relative Sentences.*

Indefinite Pronoun τὶς, τὶ.

§. 659. 1. The indefinite pronoun often has in its substantival force a
collective sense: even in Homer very usually; as, οὐκ ἄν τις εὕροι ἄνδρα
σοφώτερον. It often has an ironical force, and signifies a great number;
as, Demosth. p. 42, 8 ἀλλὰ καὶ μισεῖ τις ἐκεῖνον (Φίλιππον), ὦ ἄνδρες Ἀθ.,
καὶ δέδιεν καὶ φθονεῖ [a]:

2. It is also used in all its cases for ἐγώ, σύ: Arist. Thesm. 603 ποῖ
τις τρέψεται; (for ἐγώ): Soph. Aj. 1138 τοῦτ᾽ εἰς ἀνίαν τοὔπος ἔρχεταί τινι
(for σοί): Plat. Alc. II. init. Socr. φαίην γέ τι ἐσκυθρωπακέναι τε καὶ εἰς γῆν
βλέπειν ὥς τι συννοούμενος: Alc. καὶ τί ἄν τις συννοοῖτο; (for ἐγώ).

3. When joined with substantives, it supplies the place of the indefinite
article (see §. 446, *Remark*).

4. When joined with adjectives, indefinite numerals, and adverbs, it
brings the notion of these words more prominently forward, by either
increasing or weakening the notion, according as the meaning of the word
or the context requires; as, μέγας τις, μικρός τις, πᾶς τις, ἕκαστός τις, οὐδείς
τις, ὀλίγοι τινές, ποῖός τις, πόσος τις: Plat. Rep. p. 432 C δύσβατός τις
ὁ τόπος φαίνεται καὶ κατάσκιος, as in Lat. Cic. Acad. II. 1 *incredibilis
quædam ingenii magnitudo —; habuit enim divinam quandam memo-
riam rerum.*—βραχύ τι, ὁμοῦ τι, ἐγγύς τι, σχεδόν τι, πάνυ τι, παντάπασί τι,
πολύ τι, οὐδέν τι, πάλαι τι, διαφερόντως τι: Hdt. III. 38 οὕτω νομίζουσι
πουλύ τι καλλίστους τοὺς ἑωυτῶν νόμους ἕκαστοι εἶναι. A word may also
intervene: Plat. Phæd. p. 63 E ἀλλὰ σχεδὸν μέν τι ᾔδειν [b]: Id. Lysid.
p. 204 E οὐ γὰρ πάνυ, ἔφη, τι αὐτοῦ ὄνομα λέγουσιν: Id. Lachet. p. 192 C
σχεδὸν γάρ τι οἶδα.

Obs. 1. Hence the substantival sense of τὶς: *eximius quidam,
eximium quiddam,* as the Latin, *aliquis, aliquid.* In this
meaning τὶς is always accented, and generally placed before its verb:
Eur. El. 939 ηὔχεις τις εἶναι: Plat. Amat. p. 133 C τὸ μὲν πρῶτον ἔδοξε
τὶ εἰπεῖν. So also δρᾶν τί, to do some wrong.

5. When joined with pronouns and cardinal numerals, τὶς expresses indefiniteness; as, Plat. Symp. p. 175 B ἔθος τι τοῦτ᾽ ἔχει: Id. Gorg.
p. 522 D αὕτη τις βοήθεια. So οὕτω δή τι, *sic fere.* — Τρεῖς τινες,
some three. So Shakespeare, "*We four set upon some dozen:*" Plat.
Rep. p. 601 D ταύτας τινὰς τρεῖς.

Obs. 2. The phrase adopted from common life by Herodotus and the
Attic writers ἤ τις ἢ οὐδείς signifies "scarcely any one:" Hdt. III. 140
ἀναβέβηκε δ᾽ ἤ τις ἢ οὐδείς κω παρ᾽ ἡμέας αὐτῶν: Xen. Cyr. VII. 5, 45 τούτων

τῶν περιεστηκότων ἤ τινα ἤ οὐδένα οἶδα : Plat. Apol. p. 17 B οὗτοι μὲν οὖν, ὥσπερ ἐγὼ λέγω, ἤ τι ἤ οὐδὲν ἀληθὲς εἰρήκασιν, i. e. *nihil propemodum veri dixerunt* [a], they have said nearly no word of truth.

Position of τὶς.

§. 660. The regular position of τὶς is as an enclitic after the word to which it belongs, as ἀνήρ τις, καλός τις ἀνήρ, but it is sometimes in closely connected combinations of words placed before it ; as, Il. π, 406 ὡς δ' ὅτε τις φώς : Demosth. p. 123, 47 ἔστι τοίνυν τις εὐήθης λόγος. When τὶς refers to two members of the sentence, it is sometimes joined to the latter ; as, Plat. Phileb. p. 43 A οὔτε ἡδονὴ — οὔτ' ἄν τις λύπη. The Ionic frequently places it between the genitive depending on it, and the article belonging to the genitive ; as, τῶν τις ἱερέων for τῶν ἱερέων τις.

Obs. 1. The enclitic τὶς seems never to have been placed at the beginning of the sentence by the old writers. In such passages as Æsch. Choeph. 111, 650. Eur. Phœn. 1097. Bacch. 69. Suppl. 1186. τὶς must be taken as interrogative, and written τίς.

Obs. 2. Τὶς is sometimes found at the beginning of a member of a sentence, or of an abbreviated dependent sentence : such sentences, according to the ancient system of punctuation, not being considered as separate sentences ; as, Theocr. I. 32 ἔντοσθεν δὲ γυνά, τι θεῶν δαίδαλμα, τέτυκται.

Obs. 3. Τὶς is sometimes omitted, where it is very indefinite, the very indefiniteness suggesting τὶς. See §. 373. 5. Soph. Ant. 1068 τῶν ἄνω κάτω βαλών [h].

Syntax of the Infinitive and Participle.

§. 661. 1. The same relations of time, cause, mode (not place), which are expressed by the cases, are also expressed by the infinitive and participle.

2. The relation of time is expressed either by the simple participle, or the participle in construction with a substantive ; as, ταῦτα ποιήσας ἀπέβη, after this act ; τοῦ ἔαρος ἐλθόντος τὰ ἄνθη θάλλει, on the approach of spring : the causal relation (of cause and effect), either by infin., as μέλλω γράφειν, or by a participle, as τιμώμενος χαίρει — θεοῦ διδόντος πάντα ἂν γίγνοιτο — παρεσκευάζοντο πολεμήσοντες : the modal relation by the simple participle, as γελῶν εἶπε.

Remarks on the notions expressed by the Infinitive and Participle.

§. 662. 1. The Infinitive expresses the notion of the verb in a substantival, the Participle in an adjectival form, abstractedly, without the relations of mood or person ; but they retain the temporal relations of the verb, and follow its construction ; as, πάντα τὰ προσήκοντα εὖ πράττειν καλόν ἐστιν — ὁ τὴν ἐπιστολὴν καλῶς γράψας παῖς.

2. The adjectival nature of the participle is clearly seen in its

---

[a] Stallb. ad loc.   [b] Herm. Ant. 1056.

agreement with the form of the adjective, and also in its use as an attributive of the subst. And though the infinitive differs from the substantive in its form, yet its substantival character is apparent in its use, and also from the fact that it is joined with the article. In Sanscrit also the infinitive is used as a substantive, though it retains the government of its verb.

3. The infinitive without the article also differs from the substantive, in that it always depends on some verbal notion, (verb, adjective or substantive with ἐστί); even when apparently it is used as the subject; as, οὐ κακόν ἐστι βασιλεύειν, it is not bad that one should be king; and therefore always has the nature of an object in government, as the equivalent notion of the verb, the effect, &c. (ἐλπίζω νικήσειν = *spero victoriam* — ἥκω μανθάνειν, πείθω σε ταῦτα ποιεῖν). The Indian infinitive, which is always the object, has the accusative termination.

4. In course of time the article was prefixed to the infinitive, to mark more clearly its substantival character; and by this form, which differs from the substantive only as expressing abstract notions, and retaining the government of its verb, may be expressed all the relations signified by the cases, or by the cases with a preposition.

INFINITIVE.

Without the Article.

§. 663. *a.* As subject: Il. κ, 173 ἐπὶ ξυροῦ ἵσταται ἀκμῆς ἢ μάλα λυγρὸς ὄλεθρος Ἀχαιοῖς ἠὲ βιῶναι: Od. α, 393 οὐ μὲν γάρ τι κακὸν βασιλεύεμεν: Il. μ, 243 εἷς οἰωνὸς ἄριστος, ἀμύνεσθαι περὶ πάτρης: Æsch. Ag. 595 ἀεὶ γὰρ ἡβᾷ τοῖς γέρουσιν εὖ μαθεῖν: Eur. Med. 652 μόχθων δ' οὐκ ἄλλος ὕπερθεν, ἢ γᾶς πατρίας στέρεσθαι: Hdt. III. 81 ὁ μὲν γὰρ, εἴ τι ποιέει, γινώσκων ποιέει· τῷ δὲ οὐ γινώσκειν (*intelligentia*) ἔνι.

Obs. The verbal element in the infin. does not allow of its taking an attributive adjective, as καλὸς θάνατος, but in place thereof the adverb is used, as καλῶς θνήσκειν.

b. Object.—The infinitive expresses the notion of the thing done, effected, resulting from — or something to be done, or effected— the aim, purpose, consequence, &c. and stands as an accus., whether the verb would have the object, if expressed by a substantive, in acc., or gen., or dat. If the particular relations of the gen. or dat. are to be distinctly signified, the article is added, as it always is when a preposition is joined to an infinitive.

§. 664. The infinitive occurs as the object with the following classes of verbs and adjectives.

A. Verbs which signify any sensual or mental energy of the subject, or some expression of such energy:

1. Verbs which denote a motion of the will; as, βούλομαι, θέλω, ἐθέλω, μέλλω, ἐπιθυμῶ, μέμονα, δικαιῶ, σπουδάζομαι, προθυμοῦμαι,

πρόθυμός εἰμι, ἐπιχειρῶ, πειρῶμαι, βουλεύομαι, παρασκευάζομαι, μηχανῶμαι, τολμῶ, ἀνέχομαι, ὑπομένω, ἔτλην, εἴωθα, — δέομαι (I pray), λίσσομαι, ἱκετεύω, παραινῶ, ἐπιτέλλω, παροξύνω, πείθω, ἀναγιγνώσκω (*persuadeo*, Ion.), συμβουλεύω, νουθετῶ, κελεύω, προστάττω, λέγω (*jubeo*) — ἐῶ, περιορῶ, ἐπιτρέπω, (allow), συγχωρῶ, ἀμελῶ &c. So also the contraries thereof; as, δέδοικα, φοβοῦμαι, φοβερόν or φόβος ἐστί, φεύγω, ἀναβάλλομαι, ὀκνῶ, αἰσχύνομαι, αἰσχρόν ἐστιν, — ἔχω (hold of), κατέχω, κωλύω, εἴργω, ἀπαγορεύω &c. Βούλομαι, μέλλω γράφειν—ἐπιθυμῶ πορεύεσθαι—τολμῶ ὑπομένειν τὸν κίνδυνον—παραινῶ σοι γράφειν: Il. λ, 783 Πηλεὺς μὲν ᾧ παιδὶ γέρων ἐπέτελλ' Ἀχιλῆι, αἰὲν ἀριστεύειν καὶ ὑπείροχον ἔμμεναι ἄλλων: Hdt. VI. 75 τὴν Πυθίην ἀνέγνωσε τὰ περὶ Δημάρητον γενόμενα λέγειν: Ibid. 83 οὗτος τοὺς δούλους ἀνέγνωσε ἐπιθέσθαι τοῖσι δεσπότῃσι: Id. V. 49 ἀναβάλλομαί τοι ἀποκρίνεσθαι: Id. VII. 11 τοῦτό με ῥύσεται μηδένα ἄξιον μισθὸν λαβεῖν: Thuc. III. 110 τῇ ἄλλῃ στρατιᾷ ἅμα παρεσκευάζετο βοηθεῖν ἐπ' αὐτούς. — Κωλύω σε ταῦτα ποιεῖν: Eur. Hec. 762 πατήρ νιν ἐξέπεμψεν ὀρρωδῶν θανεῖν: Id. Troad. 718 λέξας ἀρίστου παῖδα μὴ τρέφειν πατρός, that one should not bring up: Id. Or. 257 σχήσω σε πηδᾶν: Id. Alc. 11 ὃν θανεῖν ἐρρυσάμην: Plat. Gorg. p. 457 E φοβοῦμαι διελέγχειν σε: Id. Lys. p. 207 E διακωλύουσι τοῦτο ποιεῖν, ὃ ἂν βούλῃ: Id. Phaed. p. 98 D ἀμελήσας τὰς ὡς ἀληθῶς αἰτίας λέγειν: Demosth. p. 16, 23 τίς ἂν αὐτὸν ἔτι κωλύσει δεῦρο βαδίζειν.

Obs. 1. Here also belongs μένειν and its compounds—to wait for, to expect, (wherein is implied the notion of "wishing") followed by the infin.: Il. o, 599 τὸ γὰρ (*quapropter*) μένε μητιέτα Ζεύς, νηὸς καιομένης σέλας ὀφθαλμοῖσιν ἰδέσθαι: Od. a, 422 μίνον δ' ἐπὶ ἕσπερον ἐλθεῖν, like μένειν Ἠὼ δῖαν: Æsch. Ag. 460 μένει δ' ἀκοῦσαί τι μου μέριμνα νυκτηρεφές, expects to hear: Plat. Rep. p. 375 C οὐ περιμενοῦσιν ἄλλους σφᾶς διολέσαι, ἀλλ' αὐτοὶ φθήσονται αὐτὸ δράσαντες.

Obs. 2. Πείθειν, to persuade, generally takes its object in a substantival sentence expressed by ὡς and the verb, rarely the infin. (see §. 665.): Xen. M. S. princ. πολλάκις ἐθαύμασα, τίσι ποτὲ λόγοις Ἀθηναίους ἔπεισαν οἱ γραψάμενοι Σωκράτην, ὡς ἄξιος εἴη θανάτου τῇ πόλει.

Obs. 3. To mark the notion of "something to be done," &c. more clearly, the old writers added ὥστε to the infinitive with these verbs. Homer once: Il. ι, 44 εἰ δέ σοι αὐτῷ θυμὸς ἐπέσσυται, ὥστε νέεσθαι: Soph. Œ. C. 1350 δικαιῶν, ὥστ' ἐμοῦ κλύειν λόγους: Eur. Hipp. 1342 Κύπρις γὰρ ἤθελ', ὥστε γίγνεσθαι τάδε. Often after πείθειν; as, Soph. Phil. 389 ἔπεισεν, ὥστε—ἄγειν: Hdt. VII. 6 ἀνέπεισε Ξέρξεα, ὥστε ποιέειν ταῦτα: cf. VI. 5. Sometimes also to mark yet more distinctly the notion of "intention" or "purpose," ὅπως or ὡς is used with the conj. or opt., or ind. fut., instead of the infin.: Od. θ, 344 λίσσετο δ' αἰεὶ Ἥφαιστον κλυτοεργόν, ὅπως λύσειεν Ἄρηα: Hdt. III. 44 ἐδεήθη, ὅκως ἂν δέοιτο στρατοῦ and elsewhere: Xen. Cyr. I. 4, 13 βουλεύομαι, ὅπως σε ἀποδρῶ; γλίχεσθαι also is followed by ὡς with ind. fut. So in Attic prose, προθυμεῖσθαι, διανοεῖσθαι, μηχανᾶσθαι, παρακελεύεσθαι, διακελεύεσθαι, παρασκευάζεσθαι with indic. fut. Also συγχωρεῖν ὥστε in Thucyd.

§. 665. II. Verbs which signify the notion of the operation of some power of thought, or the expression thereof: ἡγεῖσθαι, νομίζειν, ἔλπεσθαι, ἐλπίζειν, εὔχεσθαι, λογίζεσθαι, δοκεῖν, κινδυνεύειν, φαίνεσθαι (*videri*)—δοκεῖ (*placet*)—διανοοῦμαι (like *cogito facere*), προαιροῦμαι (*statuo*) — εἰδέναι, μανθάνειν, γιγνώσκειν — λέγειν, φάναι, ἀγγέλλειν, πείθειν (to persuade), &c.; and their contraries, ἀρνεῖσθαι, ἀπιστεῖν, καταρνεῖσθαι &c.: Hdt. III. 53 συνεγινώσκετο ἑωῦτῷ οὐκέτι εἶναι δυνατὸς τὰ πρήγματα ἐπορᾶν τε καὶ διέπειν: Id. VIII. 108 δοκεῖ ἐπιδιώκειν: Thuc. III. 74 ἡ πόλις ἐκινδύνευσε πᾶσα διαφθαρῆναι.—Ἔφη εἶναι στρατηγός.—Ὁ Ἀλέξανδρος ἔφη εἶναι Διὸς υἱός.—Λέγω εἰδέναι ταῦτα—μανθάνω ἱππεύειν: Xen. M.S. I. 2, 49 Σωκράτης τοὺς πατέρας προπηλακίζειν ἐδίδασκε, πείθων μὲν τοὺς ξυνόντας αὑτῷ σοφωτέρους ποιεῖν τῶν πατέρων: Plat. Prot. p. 346 B Σιμωνίδης ἡγήσατο καὶ αὐτὸς ἢ τύραννον ἢ ἄλλον τινὰ τῶν τοιούτων ἐπαινέσαι, thought that he must: Eur. Or. 555 ἐλογισάμην μ' ἀμῦναι, I considered that I must help.

Obs. Ὥστε is also used with the infinitive after these verbs to denote more clearly the effect or consequences: Eur. Or. 52 ἐλπίδα δὲ δή τιν' ἔχομεν, ὥστε μὴ θανεῖν. And also a substantival sentence with ὡς or ὅτι is used instead of infin.

§. 666. III. After verbs which express the notion of *ability, efficacy, power, capacity, causing,* or their contraries; as, δύναμαι, δυνατός, ἀδύνατος, οἷός τ' εἰμί, also οἷός εἰμι (οὐχ οἷός εἰμι), ἔχω—ἔστι, πάρεστιν, ἔξεστιν, ἔνεστι (*licet*),—ποιῶ, δεινός (strong, clever), ἱκανός, ἐπιτήδειος, κακός, ἥσσων εἰμί &c.;—so τοιόσδε, τοιοῦτος, ποῖός εἰμι &c. (but rarely and rather poetic), — αἴτιός εἰμι (*auctor sum*),— κατεργάζομαι, διαπράττομαι, and hence after verbs of *choosing, naming, educating, teaching*; Δύναμαι ποιεῖν ταῦτα: Od. ι, 411 νοῦσον γ' οὔπως ἔστι Διὸς μεγάλου ἀλέασθαι: Il. ν, 483 ὃς μάλα καρτερός ἐστι μάχῃ ἔνι φῶτας ἐναίρειν: Od. φ, 173 οὐ γάρ τοι σέ γε τοῖον ἐγείνατο πότνια μήτηρ, οἷόν τε ῥυτῆρα βιοῦ τ' ἔμεναι καὶ ὀϊστῶν: Od. β, 271 εἰ δή τοι σοῦ πατρὸς ἐνέστακται μένος ἠΰ, οἷος ἐκεῖνος ἔην τελέσαι ἔργον τε ἔπος τε: Il. ζ, 463 τοιοῦδ' ἀνδρὸς ἀμύνειν δούλιον ἦμαρ: cf. Od. β, 60. Od. φ, 195 ποῖοί κ' εἶτ' Ὀδυσῆϊ ἀμυνέμεν. (So Od. ρ, 20 τηλίκος; Hdt. III. 34 κοῖος:) Il. ω, 369 γέρων δέ τοι οὗτος ὀπηδεῖ ἀνδρ' ἀπαμύνασθαι, too weak to: Hdt. VI. 109 ὀλίγους γὰρ εἶναι στρατιῇ τῇ Μήδων συμβαλέειν: Id. II. 20 τοὺς ἐτησίας ἀνέμους εἶναι αἰτίους πληθύειν τὸν ποταμόν: cf. III. 12. Id. VII. 129 ἀνωνύμους τοὺς ἄλλους εἶναι ποιέει: Id. V. 97 στρατηγὸν ἀποδέξαντες αὑτῶν εἶναι Μελάνθιον: cf. V. 55. Id. II. 44 τὰς ὀνομάζουσι Δήλιοι εἶναι Ὑπερόχην τε καὶ Λαοδίκην: Plat. Prot. p. 311 E σοφιστὴν — ὀνομάζουσί γε τὸν ἄνδρα εἶναι. —

Οἷός τ' εἰμὶ ποιεῖν ταῦτα : Xen. Cyr. I. 4, 12 τίς γὰρ ἂν — σοῦ γε
ἱκανώτερος πεῖσαι ; Ibid. δεινότατος λαλεῖν : Ibid. III. 18
δεινότερος διδάσκειν. — διδάσκω σε γράφειν — ποιῶ σε γελᾶν.

Obs. Ὥστε is also joined with the infin. after these verbs: Soph.
Phil. 656 ἆρ' ἔστιν, ὥστε κἀγγύθεν θεὰν λαβεῖν ; Id. El. 1446 πάρεστ' ἆρ'
ἡμῖν, ὥστε—μαθεῖν : Plat. Legg. p. 709 E ἕξεις, ὥστε—διοικῆσαι : Id. Prot.
p. 338 C ἀδύνατον ὑμῖν, ὥστε Πρωταγόρου τοῦδε σοφώτερόν τινα ἑλέσθαι[a] :
Id. Phædr. p. 269 D τὸ μὲν δύνασθαι, ὦ Φαῖδρε, ὥστε ἀγωνιστὴν τέλεον γενέσθαι[b]. So often Plat. ἱκανὸς ὥστε : Xen. Ages. I. 37 ἐποίησεν (sc. Agesi-
laus), ὥστ' ἄνευ φυγῆς καὶ θανάτων — τὰς πόλεις διατελέσαι. After ποιεῖν,
instead of infin., we sometimes find ὅπως with ind. fut., when the notion of
" taking care," is to be expressed : Hdt. I. 8 ποίεε ὅκως ἐκείνην θεήσεαι.

§. 667. *B.* The infin. is also used,

a. After various adjectives and even subst., to limit or define the
operation of the notion thereof : ἄξιος, δίκαιος (worthy), ἡδύς, ῥᾴδιος,
χαλεπός &c., θαῦμα, φόβος. Ἄξιός ἐστι θαυμάζεσθαι : Il. κ, 437
ἀλεγεινοὶ δαμήμεναι, *difficiles ad domandum :* Hdt. IV. 53 Βορυ-
σθένης πίνεσθαι ἥδιστός ἐστι, *dulcissimus ad bibendum,* (πίνεσθαι
defines the ἥδιστος:) Id. VI. 112 τέως δὲ ἦν τοῖσι Ἕλλησι καὶ τὸ
οὔνομα τὸ Μήδων φόβος ἀκοῦσαι, a horror to hear.—Θαῦμα
ἰδέσθαι, a wonder to see : Plat. Symp. p. 185 D δίκαιος εἶ ἢ
παῦσαί με τῆς λυγγὸς ἢ λέγειν ὑπὲρ ἐμοῦ.

Obs. 1. Homer also uses the infin. with adjectives in the same way as
the accus. (§. 579.) : Il. κ, 437 θείειν (= πόδας) δ' ἀνέμοισιν ὁμοῖοι
(ἵπποι) : Od. θ, 123 θείειν ἄριστος : Il. ο, 570 οὔτε ποσὶν θάσσων, οὔτ'
ἄλκιμος, ὡς σύ, μάχεσθαι. So also in the phrase, καίνυσθαί τινα, to
surpass a person in ; Od. γ, 283 ἐκαίνυτο φῦλ' ἀνθρώπων νῆα κυβερνῆσαι.
The phrase ἑκὼν εἶναι must be explained by this analogy, " willing
(εἶναι=οὐσίαν) according to his real nature," that is *really :* Hdt. VII.
104 ἑκών τε εἶναι οὐδ' ἂν μουνομαχέοιμι : Ibid. 164 ὁ δὲ Κάδμος—ἑκών
τε εἶναι καὶ δεινοῦ ἐπιόντος οὐδενός, ἀλλ' ἀπὸ δικαιοσύνης, ἐς μέσον Κώοισι
καταθεὶς τὴν ἀρχήν, οἴχετο ἐς Σικελίην : Id. I. 8, 30 (Φωκέες ἔφασαν) οὐκ
ἔσεσθαι ἑκόντες εἶναι προδόται τῆς Ἑλλάδος : Plat. Phædr. p. 242 A
ὅθεν δὴ ἑκοῦσα εἶναι οὐκ ἀπολείπεται ἡ ψυχή. Also with the gen.:
Id. Gorg. p. 499 C καίτοι οὐκ ᾤμην γε κατ' ἀρχὰς ὑπὸ σοῦ ἑκόντος εἶναι
ἐξαπατηθήσεσθαι, ὡς ὄντος φίλου. This phrase rarely occurs in affirmative
sentences ; as, Hdt. VII. 164 : Plat. Legg. p. 646 B.

Obs. 2. After the analogy of θαῦμα ἰδέσθαι, we find the infin. after
verbs of " appearing," " shewing oneself :" ὁρᾶν, εἰσορᾶν, ἰδεῖν, ἰδέσθαι :
Od. ι, 143 οὐδὲ προὐφαίνετ' ἰδέσθαι, *non apparebat ad conspiciendum,* i. e.
nec se præbebat conspiciendum : Hesiod. Theog. 700 εἴσατο δ' ἄντα ὀφθαλμοῖσιν ἰδεῖν ἠδ' ὄμμασιν ὅσσαν ἀκοῦσαι αὔτως, ὡς ὅτε γαῖα καὶ οὐρανὸς
εὐρὺς ὕπερθεν πίλνατο : Ibid. 216 τοῖος ἰδεῖν ἐφάνη : Plat. Phæd. p. 84
C ὁ Σωκράτης, ὡς ἰδεῖν ἐφαίνετο.

Obs. 3. With the adjectives and substantives of this and the preceding
paragraph, the infin. act. or midd. is joined ; as, καλός ἐστιν ἰδεῖν, he is
fair to look upon. The subject of the infin. is either easily supplied from
the context ; as, Il. σ, 258 τόφρα δὲ ῥηίτεροι πολεμίζειν ἦσαν Ἀχαιοί, *Achivi*

        [a] Stallb. ad loc.   [b] Heindorf ad loc.

faciles erant (sc. *nobis*) *ad devincendum,* or is indefinite, in which case we may supply τινί: Hdt. VII. 59 ἔδοξε—τῷ Ξέρξη ὁ χῶρος εἶναι ἐπιτήδεος ἐνδιατάξαι τε καὶ ἐξαριθμῆσαι τὸν στρατόν, *idoneus, in quo ordinaret* &c. : Thuc. I. 138 ἄξιος θαυμάσαι : Plat. Phæd. p. 62 B λόγος δυνατὸς κατανοῆσαι (sc. *cuivis*): Id. Phæd. p. 92 D ὑπόθεσις ἀξία ἀποδέξασθαι, *digna quam quis accipiat :* Id. Rep. p. 368 E ῥᾴων καταμαθεῖν : Id. Phæd. p. 110 B λέγεται εἶναι τοιαύτη ἡ γῆ αὐτὴ ἰδεῖν. With the dative : Id. Rep. p. 599 A ῥᾴδια ποιεῖν μὴ εἰδότι τὴν ἀλήθειαν : Eur. Med. 316 λέγεις ἀκοῦσαι μαλθάκ', *dulcia ad audiendum* (sc. ἀκούοντι, *ei qui audit*). Id. Or. 1146 sq. πάσαις γυναιξὶν ἀξία στυγεῖν ἔφυ ἡ Τυνδαρὶς παῖς.

§. **668. *b.*** After the verbs εἶναι, πεφυκέναι, with a substantive to signify the object, or define the nature of the states expressed by those verbs : Il. ν, 312 νηυσὶ μὲν ἐν μέσσῃσιν ἀμύνειν εἰσὶ καὶ ἄλλοι. Often in Homer and other poets, and sometimes in prose : Soph. Phil. 80 ἔξοιδα καὶ φύσει σε μὴ πεφυκότα τοιαῦτα φωνεῖν, μηδὲ τεχνᾶσθαι κακά : Ibid. 88 ἔφυν γὰρ οὐδὲν ἐκ τέχνης πράσσειν κακῶς : Demosth. p. 100, 42 ἐστὲ γὰρ ὑμεῖς οὐκ αὐτοὶ πλεονεκτῆσαι καὶ κατασχεῖν ἀρχὴν εὖ πεφυκότες.

c. After abstract substant. which, with εἶναι or γίγνεσθαι, express a verbal notion, to signify the operation or effect thereof, as early as Homer with subst., which express some mental state ; Il. μ, 245 σοὶ δ' οὐ δέος ἔστ' ἀπολέσθαι : Il. ν, 175 ἐπεί τοι θυμὸς ἀναίτιον αἰτιάασθαι : Od. ζ, 314 ἐλπωρή τοι ἔπειτα φίλους τ' ἰδέειν καὶ ἱκέσθαι. Also Il. ν, 98 νῦν δὴ εἴδεται ἦμαρ ὑπὸ Τρώεσσι δαμῆναι. In Attic, πράγματα, ἀσχολίαν, ὄχλον παρέχειν τινὶ &c., in infin. ; as, Thuc. I. 16 ἐπεγίγνετο δὲ ἄλλοις τε ἄλλοθι κωλύματα μὴ αὐξηθῆναι : Xen. Ages. I. 7 ἀσχολίαν αὐτῷ παρέξειν στρατεύειν ἐπὶ τοὺς Ἕλληνας : cf. Cyr. IV. 5, 46. Anab. III. 2, 27. Plat. Phæd. p. 115 A. Demosth. p. 102, 53 ἡσυχίαν δὲ ποιοῦσιν ἐκείνῳ *πράττειν*, ὅτι βούλεται.

Obs. The article τό is often added after substantives by writers after Homer : Plat. Rep. p. 465 B δέος δὲ τὸ τῷ πάσχοντι τοὺς ἄλλους βοηθεῖν : Xen. Anab. II. 5, 22 τῆς δοκήσεως προσγεγενημένης αὐτῷ τὸ κρατίστους εἶναι. And also as an attributive ; as, Thuc. I. 44 ἐς ἐλπίδα τοῦ περιέσεσθαι.

§. **669. *d.*** This infin. is also used with single words or phrases, or whole sentences, to complete or define the notion involved therein ; and expresses the operation, effect, or intended effect.

a. After συμβαίνει, συνήνεικεν (Hdt.), *accidit,* κατέλαβε (Hdt.), *accidit,* ἔστι in the same sense, δεῖ, χρή, ἀνάγκη, δίκαιον, ὠφέλιμόν ἐστιν &c. ; also after ἀφίκετο, ἦλθεν, it came to : Hdt. VII. 166 συνέβη Γέλωνα νικᾶν : Id. VI. 117 συνήνεικε δ' αὐτόθι θῶμα γενέσθαι τοιόνδε : Ibid. 103 καί μιν—κατέλαβε ἀποθανεῖν ὑπὸ τῶν Πεισιστράτου παίδων : Id. III. 71 ἐπεί τε δὲ ἐς Δαρεῖον ἀπίκετο γνώμην ἀποφαίνεσθαι : Thuc. VIII. 76 ἡ Σάμος παρ' ἐλάχιστον ἦλθε τὸ Ἀθηναίων κράτος ἀφελέσθαι.

Obs. 1. Ὥστε is often used to define these notions of effect, &c. more clearly: Hdt. III. 14 συνήνεικε ὥστε : Thuc. V. 14 ξυνέβη ὥστε. So ἔστω ὥστε Plat. Phæd. p. 103 Eᵃ: γέγονεν ὥστε Isocr. p. 124 A : compare *est, ut* with conjunct.

β. After subst.: Hdt. I. 32 εἰ μή οἱ τύχη ἐπίσποιτο, πάντα καλὰ ἔχοντα τελευτῆσαι εὖ τὸν βίον.

γ. After a demonstrative, either alone or with an adj. or subst.: Od. α, 370 ἐπεὶ τόγε καλὸν ἀκουέμεν ἐστὶν ἀοιδοῦ : cf. δ. 197. Hdt. VI. 23 μισθὸς δέ οἱ ἦν εἰρημένος ὅδε ὑπὸ τῶν Σαμίων, πάντων— τὰ ἡμίσεα μεταλαβεῖν : Id. VII. 52 ἐπὶ τούτοισι ἡ πᾶσα Περσικὴ στρατιὴ ἐγένετο διαφθεῖραι καὶ περιποιῆσαι.

e. Lastly, the infin. is used with verbs of *giving, taking, going, sending,* &c. to express the aim or object, and answers to the Latin Supine: Il. η, 251 Ἑλένην δώομεν Ἀτρείδῃσιν ἄγειν.—Βῆ δ' ἰέναι he stept forth to go—ἥκομεν μανθάνειν—: Il. ι, 442 τοὔνεκά με προέηκε διδασκέμεναι τάδε πάντα : Od. α, 138 χέρνιβα δ' ἀμφιπόλος προχόῳ ἐπέχευε φέρουσα νίψασθαι : Hdt. VI. 23 τοὺς δὲ κορυφαίους (*principes*) — ἔδωκε τοῖσι Σαμίοισι κατασφάξαι : Thuc. II. 27 τοῖς Αἰγινήταις οἱ Λακεδαιμόνιοι ἔδοσαν Θυρέαν οἰκεῖν καὶ τὴν γῆν νέμεσθαι : Plat. Apol. p. 33 B ὁμοίως καὶ πλουσίῳ καὶ πένητι παρέχω ἐμαυτὸν ἐρωτᾶν : cf. Arist. Nub. 441.

Obs. 2. After a verb of "giving," when a dative of the person, to whom any thing is given, is not expressed, the infin. pass. should properly be used; and sometimes, though very seldom, this construction is found ; as, Plat. Charm. p. 157 B ὃς ἂν μὴ τὴν ψυχὴν παράσχῃ τῇ ἐπωδῇ ὑπὸ σοῦ θεραπευθῆναι : cf. §. 667. *Obs.* 3.

Remarks on the use of the Infinitive with the Article for the Infinitive without it.

§. 670. From the substantival use of the infin. it would naturally follow that the article would be attached to it, when especial emphasis was to be laid on the notion expressed by the infin.; and as this infin. always stands to the preceding verb in the relation of the accus., (effect, or operation, or intention, &c. as the verbal notion may require,) this article is always the neuter τό, even when the preceding verb is constructed with a substantive in genitive. This construction, as being emphatical, is very often used in antithesis; it most frequently occurs in tragedy: Æsch. Ag. 15 τὸ μὴ βε- βαίως βλέφαρα συμβαλεῖν ὕπνῳ : Id. Eum. 220 τὸ μὴ γενέσθαι : cf. Id. Pers. 292 : Soph. Œ. C. 441 οἱ δ' ἐπωφελεῖν, οἱ τοῦ πατρὸς, τῷ πατρὶ δυνάμενοι, τὸ δρᾶν οὐκ ἠθέλησαν : Id. Antig. 79 τὸ γὰρ βίᾳ πολιτῶν δρᾶν ἔφυν ἀμήχανος : Ibid. 264 ἦμεν δ' ἕτοιμοι—καὶ ὀρκωμοτεῖν τὸ μήτε δρᾶ- σαι, μήτε τῷ ξυνειδέναι τὸ πρᾶγμα βουλεύσαντι : Ibid. 1106 μόλις μὲν, καρ- δίας δ' ἐξίσταμαι τὸ δρᾶν, *ægre quidem, sed cedam, ut fariam*: Id. Phil. 1241 ἔστιν τις, ἔστιν, ὅς σε κωλύσει τὸ δρᾶν : Eur. Iph. A. 452

τὸ μὴ δακρῦσαι αἰδοῦμαι : Thuc. II. 53 τὸ μὲν προσταλαιπω-
ρεῖν τῷ δόξαντι καλῷ οὐδεὶς πρόθυμος ἦν : Xen. Apol. S. 13 τὸ προει-
δέναι τὸν θεὸν τὸ μέλλον πάντες λέγουσι : Id. M. S. III. 6, 6 τὸ μὲν
πλουσιωτέραν τὴν πόλιν ποιεῖν ἀναβαλούμεθα : Id. Symp. III. 3
οὐδείς σοι, ἔφη, ἀντιλέγει τὸ μὴ οὐ λέξειν : Id. Hell. V. 2, 36 οὐ μέντοι ἔπειθε τὸ μὴ πολυπράγμων τε καὶ κακοπράγμων εἶναι (πείθειν τινά τι) :
Plat. Soph. p. 247 C αἰσχύνονται τὸ τολμᾶν ὁμολογεῖν : Id. Legg.
p. 943 D χρὴ φοβεῖσθαι τὸ μήτε ἐπενεγκεῖν ψευδῆ τιμωρίαν. Where the
verb is generally constructed with the genitive : Hdt. V. 101 τὸ μὴ λεη-
λατῆσαί σφεας ἔσχε τόδε : Thuc. III. 1 τὸν πλεῖστον ὅμιλον τῶν ψιλῶν
εἶργον τὸ μή,—τὰ ἐγγὺς τῆς πόλεως κακουργεῖν : Xen. Rep. Lac.
V. 7 τὸ ὑπὸ οἴνου μὴ σφάλλεσθαι ἐπιμελεῖσθαι : Plat. Rep. extr.
οὐκ ἀπεσχόμην τὸ μὴ οὐκ ἐπὶ τοῦτο ἐλθεῖν ἀπ' ἐκείνου[a] : Id. Criton.
p. 43 C οὐδὲν αὐτοὺς ἐπιλύεται ἡ ἡλικία τὸ μὴ οὐχὶ ἀγανακτεῖν τῇ παρούσῃ
τύχῃ (*neque senectus eos liberos præstat a mortis metu*[b]) : Id. Lach. p. 190
E ἐγὼ αἴτιος τό σε ἀποκρίνασθαι : Demosth. p. 392 οὐδ' ἄρνησίς
ἐστιν αὐτοῖς τὸ μή—πράττειν : and even when τούτου has preceded : Xen.
Anab. II. 5, 22 ὁ ἐμὸς ἔρως τούτου αἴτιος, τὸ τοῖς Ἕλλησιν ἐμὲ πιστὸν
γενέσθαι.

The Elliptical use of Inf. in commands and wishes.

§. 671. From the use of the infin. after verbs of *willing, wishing, praying,* &c. we may explain the following apparent anomalies.

a. The inf. is used (in Epic, and sometimes other poets, and even in
Attic prose) in the place of the imperative, to express a command or wish
that the person addressed would do something. It depends on a verb of
" wishing" or " desiring" in the mind of the speaker, but can only stand
for the second person sing. or plur. The subject of the infin. itself, and of
the verb on which it depends, (such as ἔθελε : Il. α, 277 μήτε σὺ, Πη-
λείδη, θέλ' ἐριζέμεναι βασιλῆϊ) is the person addressed, which is
sometimes placed before the inf. in the nom. or vocative ; wherefore if a
predicative adjective follows the inf. it is likewise in the nominative :
Il. ρ, 501 Ἀλκίμεδον, μὴ δή μοι ἀπόπροθεν ἰσχέμεν ἵππους, ἀλλὰ μάλ'
ἐμπνείοντε μεταφρένῳ· Od. α, 290 sqq. νοστήσας δὴ ἔπειτα φίλην ἐς πατρίδα
γαῖαν σῆμά τε οἱ χεῦαι, καὶ ἐπὶ κτέρεα κτερεΐξαι — καὶ ἀνέρι μητέρα
δοῦναι : Il. β, 75 ὑμεῖς δ' ἄλλοθεν ἄλλοι ἐρητύειν ἐπέεσσιν : Hdt. VI.
86 extr. σὺ δή μοι καὶ τὰ χρήματα δέξαι, καὶ τάδε τὰ σύμβολα σῷζε λαβών· ὃς δ'
ἂν ἔχων ταῦτα ἀπαιτέῃ, τούτῳ ἀποδοῦναι, εἰ redde : Id. VII. 159 εἰ μὲν βού-
λεαι βοηθέειν τῇ Ἑλλάδι, ἴσθι ἀρξόμενος ὑπὸ Λακεδαιμονίων· εἰ δ' ἄρα μὴ δικαιοῖς
ἄρχεσθαι, σὺ δὲ μὴ βοηθέειν : Plat. Rep. p. 473 A ἐὰν οἷοί τε γενώμεθα
εὑρεῖν ὡς ἂν ἐγγύτατα τῶν εἰρημένων πόλις οἰκήσειε, φάναι ἡμᾶς εὑρηκέναι
κ. τ. λ.[c] : Ibid. p. 508 B τοῦτον τοίνυν, ἦν δ' ἐγώ, φάναι : Ibid. p. 509 B
καὶ τοῖς γιγνωσκομένοις τοίνυν μὴ μόνον τὸ γιγνώσκεσθαι φάναι : Ibid. p. 580
B καὶ σὺ οὕτω, τίς πρῶτος κατὰ τὴν σὴν δόξαν εὐδαιμονίᾳ καὶ τίς δεύτερος, καὶ
τοὺς ἄλλους—κρῖναι : Id. Soph. p. 218 A ἂν δ' ἄρα τι τῷ μήκει πονῶν ἀχθῇ,
μὴ ἐμὲ αἰτιᾶσθαι τούτων : Id. p. 262 E λέξω τοίνυν σοι λόγον—ὅταν δ' ἂν
ὁ λόγος ᾖ, σύ μοι φράζειν : Demosth. p. 99, 39 πρῶτον μὲν, ὦ ἄνδρες Ἀθ.,
τοῦτο παρ' ὑμῖν αὐτοῖς βεβαίως γνῶναι, ὅτι τῇ πόλει Φίλιππος πολεμεῖ[d].

b. The infin. is used in forms of wishing or praying, in invocations and
entreaties that the person addressed would cause some one else to do

a Stallb. ad loc.   b Stallb. ad loc.   c Stallb. ad loc.   d Bremi ad loc.

something; the accus. is joined with the infin. and the two together stand
as the object of a verb, expressing or implying the notion of wishing, or
desiring, such as ἤθελε or εὔχομαι, δός (Æsch. Choeph. 16 ὧ Ζεῦ, δός με
τίσασθαι μόρον πατρός), ποίει, cause: Il. β. 412 Ζεῦ κύδιστε—, μὴ πρὶν ἐπ'
ἠέλιον δῦναι καὶ ἐπὶ κνέφας ἐλθεῖν, πρίν με κατὰ πρηνὲς βαλέειν Πριάμοιο μέλαθρον: Il. η, 179 sq. ὧδε δέ τις εἴπεσκεν, ἰδὼν εἰς οὐρανὸν εὐρύν· Ζεῦ
πάτερ, ἢ Αἴαντα λαχεῖν, ἢ Τυδέος υἱόν, ἢ αὐτὸν βασιλῆα πολυχρύ-
σοιο Μυκήνης! Æsch. Suppl. 255 θεοὶ πολῖται, μή με δουλείας τυχεῖν:
Hdt. V. 105 ὧ Ζεῦ, ἐκγενέσθαι μοι Ἀθηναίους τίσασθαι, may it be granted
me. Interchanged with the imp. III. person: Il. γ, 285 Ζεῦ πάτερ—Ἠέλιός
θ—ὑμεῖς μάρτυροι ἔστε, φυλάσσετε δ' ὅρκια πιστά· εἰ μέν κεν Μενέλαον Ἀλέξανδρος καταπέφνῃ, αὐτὸς ἔπειτ' Ἑλένην ἐχέτω καὶ κτήματα πάντα·—εἰ δέ κ'
Ἀλέξανδρον κτείνῃ ξανθὸς Μενέλαος, Τρῶας ἔπειτ' Ἑλένην καὶ κτήματα πάντ'
ἀποδοῦναι (but if Menel. kills Paris, then grant that &c.)

c. Hence the infin., either alone or with subj. and predicate in acc., can
be used of all three persons, as a general expression of necessity, or of
something to be done.   a. I. Pers.: Hdt. VIII. 109 νῦν μὲν ἐν τῇ Ἑλλάδι
καταμείναντας ἡμέων τε αὐτέων ἐπιμεληθῆναι καὶ τῶν οἰκετέων (i. e.
ἡμᾶς χρὴ or δεῖ καταμείναντας ἐπιμεληθῆναι).   β. II. Pers., as Hesiod. Opp.
391 γυμνὸν σπείρειν, γυμνὸν δὲ βοωτεῖν (i. e. χρή σε γ. σπ.).   γ. III.
Pers.: Hdt. I. 32 πρὶν δ' ἂν τελευτήσῃ, ἐπισχέειν, μηδὲ καλέειν κω
ὄλβιον, ἀλλ' εὐτυχέα, where τίνα must be supplied as the subst. " men."

d. Thence it is used, of I. and II. person, in questions expressing reluctance.   a. I. Pers.: Hdt. I. 88 ὦ βασιλεῦ, κότερον λέγειν πρὸς σὲ τὰ
νοέων τυγχάνω, ἢ σιγᾶν ἐν τῷ παρέοντι χρόνῳ, shall I (must I) speak or be
silent? Bion V. 4 εἰ δ' οὐχ ἀδέα ταῦτα, τί μοι πολὺ πλήονα μοχθῆν.   β. II.
Pers.: Od. κ, 431 ἃ δειλοί, πόσ' ἴμεν ; τί κακῶν ἱμείρετε τούτων; whither
are ye (fated) to go?

e. Lastly, it stands with αἲ γάρ, εἴθε, as an expression of a wish, in the
place of the optative, with the nominative, the verb to be supplied being ὤφελον, -ες, -ε, &c.[a]: Od. η. 311 sqq. αἲ γὰρ, Ζεῦ τε πάτερ καὶ Ἀθηναίη καὶ Ἄπολλον, τοῖος ἐὼν οἷός ἐσσι, τά τε φρονέων ἅ τ' ἐγώ περ, παῖδά τ' ἐμὴν ἐχέμεν καὶ
ἐμὸς γαμβρὸς καλέεσθαι αὖθι μένων! (for ἔχοις—καλέοιο): Od. ω, 375 sqq.
αἲ γὰρ, Ζεῦ τε πάτερ—, τοῖος ἐών τοι χθιζὸς ἐν ἡμετέροισι δόμοισι, τεύχε'
ἔχων ὤμοισιν, ἐφεστάμεναι καὶ ἀμύνειν ἄνδρας μνηστῆρας. This construction occurs in Homer only in the Odyssey[b], and does not appear to
have been much used elsewhere: Eur. Hel. 262 εἴθ' ἐξαλειφθεῖσ' ὡς ἄγαλμ'
αὖθις πάλιν αἴσχιον εἶδος ἀντὶ τοῦ καλοῦ λαβεῖν (for λάβοι or ἔλαβε[c]).

Nominative, Genitive, Dative, and Accusative, with the Infinitive.

§. 672. 1. Most of the verbs which take this inf. have also a
personal object on which the infinitive depends; as, ἡγοῦμαί σε
ἁμαρτεῖν or ἡγοῦμαί σε εὐδαίμονα εἶναι: this object is in the case
which the usual construction of the verb requires, accus. gen. or
dat.; as, δέομαι σοῦ ἐλθεῖν—συμβουλεύω σοὶ σωφρονεῖν—
ἐποτρύνω σε μάχεσθαι.

2. But when the same person is both the subject and object of

---

[a] Klausen. Choeph. 349. λείπει τὸ ὤφελον Schol.   [b] Buttm. Lexil.   [c] Pflugk ad loc.

the verb, this verb being *declarandi* or *sentiendi*, governing an accus., the object is not, as in Latin, expressed by the personal pronoun, but altogether omitted, so that the nominative stands with the inf., as οἴομαι (οἴει, οἴεται) ἁμαρτεῖν (for οἴομαι ἐμαυτὸν ἁμαρτεῖν, οἴει σαυτὸν ἁμ., οἴεται ἑαυτὸν ἁμ., *credo me errasse, credis te errasse, credit se errasse*) οὐκ ἔφη αὐτὸς λέγειν = αὐτὸς οὐκ ἔφη ἑαυτόν λέγειν.

3. When an adjective or a subst. follows the inf. as part of the predicate, it is in the same case as the personal subject which precedes, gen. dat. or acc.; when the subject is omitted as above, (§. 2.), in nominative. This construction is called the attraction of the infinitive.

Nom. with Inf. Od. a, 180 Μέντης Ἀγχιάλοιο δαΐφρονος εὔχομαι εἶναι υἱός, cf. 418. Ibid. 187 ξεῖνοι δ' ἀλλήλων πατρώϊοι εὐχόμεθ' εἶναι.—Gen. with Inf. Δέομαί σου προθύμον εἶναι: Hdt. I. 176 τῶν δὲ τῶν Λυκίων φαμένων Ξανθίων εἶναι, *se esse Xanthios*: Id. III. 75 φαμένου δὲ καὶ ταῦτα ἑτοίμου εἶναι ποιέειν τοῦ Πρηξάσπεω: Xen. Hier. III. 8 εὑρήσεις—πολλοὺς τυράννους—διεφθαρμένους—ὑπὸ ἑταίρων γε τῶν μάλιστα δοκούντων φίλων εἶναι: Plat. Apol. p. 21 Β ἦλθον ἐπί τινα τῶν δοκούντων σοφῶν εἶναι.—Dat. with Inf. Xen. Anab. II. 1, 2 ἔδοξε τοῖς τῶν Ἑλλήνων στρατηγοῖς συσκευασαμένοις ἃ εἶχον καὶ ἐξοπλισαμένοις προϊέναι: Demosth. p. 35. princ. οὐ γὰρ ἀλλοτρίοις ὑμῖν χρωμένοις παραδείγμασιν, ἀλλ' οἰκείοις, ὦ ἄνδρες Ἀθηναῖοι, εὐδαίμοσιν ἔξεστι γενέσθαι. —Acc. with Inf. Ἐπώτρυνεν αὐτὸν πρόθυμον εἶναι. —Ἔφη σε εὐδαίμονα εἶναι: Hdt. VII. 136 Ξέρξης οὐκ ἔφη ὁμοῖος ἔσεσθαι Λακεδαιμονίοισι· κείνους μὲν γὰρ συγχέαι τὰ πάντων ἀνθρώπων νόμιμα, ἀποκτείναντας κήρυκας, αὐτὸς δὲ ταῦτα οὐ ποιήσειν.

Remarks on these Constructions.

§. 673. 1. Sometimes, however, instead of the nom. with inf. we find the full construction as in Latin; as, οἴομαι ἐμαυτὸν ἁμαρτεῖν, *credo me errasse* (for οἴομαι ἁμ.), νομίζει ἑαυτὸν εἶναι εὐδαιμονέστατον, *putat se beatissimum esse* (for νομ. εὐδαιμονέστατος εἶναι); but almost always for some definite reason. The principal reason is to lay emphasis on the subject, especially in antithesis; as, Od. θ, 221 τῶν δ' ἄλλων ἐμὲ φημι πολὺ προφερέστερον εἶναι: Il. η, 198 ἐπεὶ οὐδ' ἐμὲ νήϊδά γ' οὕτως ἔλπομαι ἐν Σαλαμῖνι γενέσθαι τε τραφέμεν τε (*that I also*, opposed to preceding words οὐ γάρ τις με βίῃ γε ἑκὼν ἀέκοντα δίηται, οὐδὲ μὲν ἰδρείῃ): Il. ν, 269 οὐδὲ γὰρ οὐδ' ἐμὲ φημι λελασμένον ἔμμεναι ἀλκῆς (opposed to the words of Idomeneus): Hdt. II. 2 οἱ Αἰγύπτιοι—ἐνόμιζον ἑωυτοὺς πρώτους γενέσθαι πάντων ἀνθρώπων (*s e, non alios homines*) : Id. I. 34 Κροῖσος ἐνόμιζε ἑωυτὸν εἶναι πάντων ὀλβιώτατον. In other instances the accusatives, ἐμαυτόν, σεαυτόν, ἑαυτόν, are used on rhetorical grounds, or to define more clearly

the person meant, or to round off the sentence; as, Xen. Cyr. V. 1, 21
νομίζοιμι γὰρ ἐμαυτὸν ἐοικέναι λέγοντι ταῦτα κ. τ. λ.[a] : Id. VIII. 2, 26
ταῦτα μὲν δὴ καὶ τοιαῦτα πολλὰ ἐμηχανᾶτο πρὸς τὸ πρωτεύειν παρ' οἷς ἐβούλετο
ἑαυτὸν φιλεῖσθαι. The enclitic pronouns are sometimes thus used without
any particular emphasis being intended : Hesiod. Opp. 656 ἔνθα μέ φημι
ὕμνῳ νικήσαντα φέρειν τρίποδ' ὠτώεντα : Plat. Rep. p. 400 B οἶμαι δέ με ἀκηκοέναι[b] : Id. Symp. p. 175 E οἶμαι γάρ με παρὰ σοῦ πολλῆς καὶ καλῆς σοφίας
πληρωθήσεσθαι : Id. Charmid. p. 173 A οἶμαι μέν, ἦν δ' ἐγώ, ληρεῖν με.

2. The acc. pers. pron. which is thus joined to the infin., as the object
of the verb, sometimes, though but rarely, becomes the nom., by attraction
to the suppressed subject of the verb : Thuc. VIII. 76 (*in orat. obliqua*)
πόλιν τε γὰρ σφίσιν ὑπάρχειν Σάμον οὐκ ἀσθενῆ (*scil.* ἔφησαν οἱ ἐν Σάμῳ)—
καὶ δυνατώτεροι εἶναι σφεῖς (for καὶ δυνατωτέρους εἶναι ἑαυτούς),
ἔχοντες τὰς ναῦς, πορίζεσθαι τὰ ἐπιτήδεια τῶν ἐν τῇ πόλει. So we must
read Xen. Cyr. II. 4, 25 νόμιζε δ', ὥσπερ ἐν θήρᾳ, ἡμᾶς μὲν τοὺς ἐπιζητοῦντας
ἔσεσθαι, σὺ δὲ τὸν ἐπὶ ταῖς ἄρκυσι. (*Schneider cum Castalione et Stephano,*
σὲ δέ; Edd. primæ, σὺ δέ.) Id. M. S. II. 3, 17 τί γὰρ ἄλλο, ἔφη ὁ
Σωκράτης, ἢ κινδυνεύσεις ἐπιδεῖξαι, σὺ μὲν χρηστός τε καὶ φιλάδελφος
εἶναι, ἐκεῖνος δὲ (sc. κινδυνεύσει ἐπιδεῖξαι) φαῦλός τε καὶ οὐκ ἄξιος
εὐεργεσίας ;— Demosth. p. 579 νομίζεις — ἡμᾶς μὲν ἀποψηφιεῖσθαι, σὺ δὲ οὐδὲ
παύσεσθαι, Ibid. p. 130, 74 εἰ δ' οἴεσθε Χαλκιδέας τὴν Ἑλλάδα σώσειν ἢ
Μεγαρέας, ὑμεῖς δ' ἀποδράσεσθαι τὰ πράγματα, οὐκ ὀρθῶς οἴεσθε[c]. Exactly
similar : Il. τ. 258 ἴστω νῦν Ζεὺς πρῶτα, θεῶν ὕπατος καὶ ἄριστος. μὴ μὲν ἐγὼ
κούρῃ Βρισηΐδι χεῖρ' ἐπενεῖκαι, οὔτ' εὐνῆς πρόφασιν κεχρημένος οὔτε τευ
ἄλλου. (After ἴστω νῦν Ζεύς, we must supply ὅτι ὄμνυμι; as, Od. ε, 184
ἴστω νῦν τόδε Γαῖα καὶ Οὐρανὸς εὐρὺς ὕπερθεν — μήτι σοι αὐτῷ πῆμα κακὸν
βουλευσέμεν ἄλλο, but ἐγώ, though really belonging to the suppressed
ὄμνυμι, is expressed with the infinitive, for the sake of emphasis.

Obs. The nom. pronoun or adj. is joined sometimes with the inf., even
where δεῖν requires the accus. : Plat. Protag. p. 316 C σκόπει, πότερον περὶ
αὐτῶν μόνος οἴει δεῖν διαλέγεσθαι πρὸς μόνους ἢ μετ' ἄλλων : Demosth.
p. 414, 15 (R) ἡγούμην ἐν τούτοις πρῶτος αὐτὸς περιεῖναι δεῖν αὐτῶν καὶ
μεγαλοψυχότερος φαίνεσθαι.

---

*Remarks on the use of the Accusative with Infinitive instead of
Genitive and Dative with Infinitive.*

§. 674. It is remarkable, that verbs which are followed either always or
generally by a dative of the personal object, take an accusative of this
object in construction with the infinitive. The reason of this seems to be,
that the accusative in reality no longer stands as the personal object of the
verb, but coalesces with the infinitive, so as together to make up one
compound notion of the *action* of that *person*. So in κελεύω σοι τοῦτο, the
σοί is in the dative, as being the personal object of a verb of transmission ;
but in κελεύω σε-τοῦτο-ποιεῖν, these three last words together (σέ being
joined with ποιεῖν) = κέλευσμα, as in λέγει σε χαίρειν, the λόγος is χαῖρε σύ.
Wherefore, as the person in the accus. and infin. together represents the
cognate substantive, the person takes the form of the accusative, according
to the common principles of accusative construction. So εἰπεῖν, λέγειν,
φράζειν (σοί τι), κελεύειν, which sometimes takes dat., sometimes acc.

---

a Bornemann ad loc.　　　b Stallb. ad loc.　　　c Bremi ad loc.

with infin. With those verbs which take both cases with infin., the difference is, that when the dative is used, it is considered as the personal object of the verb; when the acc., as part of the compound cognate notion. So Il. β, 50 αὐτὰρ ὁ κηρύκεσσι λιγυφθόγγοισι κέλευσε κηρύσσειν ἀγορήνδε καρηκομόωντας Ἀχαιούς, he gave an order to the heralds: but, Hdt. VI. 81 ὁ δὲ Κλεομένης τὸν ἱρέα ἐκέλευε τοὺς εἵλωτας ἀπὸ τοῦ βωμοῦ ἀπάγοντας μαστιγῶσαι, he ordered, "that the priest should;" the order being, ὁ ἱερεὺς τοὺς εἵλωτας —— μαστιγούτω = κέλευσμα: Xen. Cyr. I. 3, 9 κέλευσον δή, ὦ πάππε, τὸν Σάκαν καὶ ἐμοὶ δοῦναι τὸ ἔκπωμα: Soph. Œ. T. 350 ἐννέπω σε τῷ κηρύγματι — ἐμμένειν (= ἔπος). Hence χαίρειν λέγειν τινά (like *aliquem valere jubere, aliquem missum facere, non curare*) and χαίρειν εἰπεῖν, λέγειν, φράζειν τινί, both Attic. Here belong the following verbs: μεγαίρω (σοί τι): Od. γ, 55 κλῦθι, Ποσείδαον γαιήοχε, μηδὲ μεγήρῃς ἡμῖν εὐχομένοισι τελευτῆσαι τάδε ἔργα, grudge not to us; but, Od. β, 235 ἀλλ᾽ ἤτοι μνηστῆρας ἀγήνορας οὔτι μεγαίρω ἔρδειν ἔργα βίαια κακορραφίῃσι νόοιο, grudge not that they: Od. α, 346 φθονέω with acc. and inf., νεμεσίζομαι Il. β, 296. So προσήκει, πρέπει, ἔξεστι, σύμφορόν ἐστι, with dat., or acc. with infin.; συμβαίνει, δεῖ, χρή Æsch. Suppl. 218 θρασυστομεῖν γὰρ οὐ πρέπει τοὺς ἥσσονας: Thuc. II. 36 νομίζων — τὸν πάντα ὅμιλον ἀστῶν — ξύμφορον εἶναι αὐτῶν ἐπακοῦσαι: Plat. Gorg. p. 479 E τούτῳ προσήκειν ἀθλίῳ εἶναι. Æsch. Ag. 1551 οὔ σε προσήκει λέγειν. But Id. Ion. p. 539 extr. οὐκ ἂν πρέποι γε ἐπιλήσμονα εἶναι ῥαψῳδὸν ἄνδρα.

Obs. If a predicative word follows the infin., referring to the object of the verb, this predicate, by coalescing with the infin., frequently forms with it the compound cognate notion; while the object, thus being (so to say) released from the infin., returns to its proper government as the object of the verb; as, Hdt. III. 36 ἐνετείλατο τοῖς θεράπουσι λαβόντας (sc. τοὺς θεράποντας) μιν ἀποκτεῖναι. And sometimes the proper construction of the verb obtains in an after part of the sentence: Soph. Œ. R. 350 ἐννέπω σὲ (σοὶ) τῷ κηρύγματι — ἐμμένειν ὡς ὄντι γῆς μιάστορι. Cf. Eur. Med. 56 [a].

§. 675. Hence we may see how it happens that participles after infin., which ought to be in the same case as the object of the verb to which they refer (§. 672. 3), are often in the accus., because they are not considered as referring to that object, but as forming with the infin. the compound notion cognate to the verb.

a. The object of the verb in the genitive.—Hdt. VI. 100 Ἀθηναίων ἐδεήθησαν σφίσι βοηθοὺς γενέσθαι (but Id. V. 80 δέεσθαι τῶν Αἰγινητέων τιμωρητήρων γενέσθαι): Thuc. I. 120 ἀνδρῶν σωφρόνων μέν ἐστιν, εἰ μὴ ἀδικοῖντο, ἡσυχάζειν, ἀγαθῶν δέ, ἀδικουμένους, ἐκ μὲν εἰρήνης πολεμεῖν.

b. In the dative.—Il. ο, 115 sq. μὴ νῦν μοι νεμεσήσετ᾽, Ὀλύμπια δώματ᾽ ἔχοντες, τίσασθαι φόνον υἷος, ἰόντ᾽ ἐπὶ νῆας Ἀχαιῶν: Od. κ, 531 ἑτάροισιν ἐποτρῦναι καὶ ἀνῶξαι μῆλα—δείραντας κατακῆαι: Æsch. Choeph. 136 καὶ σὺ κλῦθί μου, πάτερ, αὐτῇ τέ μοι δὸς εὐτυχεστέραν πολὺ μητρὸς γενέσθαι χεῖρά τ᾽ εὐσεβεστέραν: Eur. Med. 815 σοὶ δὲ συγγνώμη λέγειν τάδ᾽ ἔστι, μὴ πάσχουσαν ὡς ἐγὼ κακῶς [b]: Hdt. VI. 78 παραγγέλλει σφι, ὅταν σημήνῃ ὁ κῆρυξ ποιέεσθαι ἄριστον, τότε ἀναλαβόντας τὰ ὅπλα χωρέειν ἐς τοὺς Ἀργείους: Ibid. 109 ἐν σοὶ νῦν — ἔστι ἢ καταδουλῶσαι Ἀθήνας, ἢ ἐλευθέρας ποιήσαντα μνημόσυνα λιπέσθαι ἐς τὸν ἅπαντα ἀνθρώπων βίον: Id. III. 36 ἐνετείλατο τοῖσι θεράπουσι λαβόντας μιν ἀποκτεῖναι: Thuc. IV. 2

---

[a] Elmsl. Med. 56.   [b] Pflugk ad loc.

εἶπον δὲ τούτοις καὶ Κερκυραίων ἅμα παραπλέοντας τῶν ἐν τῇ πόλει ἐπιμεληθῆναι : Id. VII. 75 οἷς ἀντὶ μὲν τοῦ ἄλλους δουλωσομένους ἥκειν, αὐτοὺς τοῦτο μᾶλλον δεδιότας μὴ πάθωσι ξυνέβη ἀπιέναι : Lys. Epitaph. p. 129 (R) εἰ μὲν γὰρ οἷόν τε ἦν τοὺς ἐν τῷ πολέμῳ κινδύνους διαφυγοῦσιν ἀθανάτους εἶναι : Ibid. p. 86 ἐνόμιζον αὐτοῖς προσήκειν ἀγαθοὺς εἶναι : Xen. M. S. II. 6, 26 εἰ ἐξῆν τοῖς κρατίστοις συνθεμένους ἐπὶ τοὺς χείρους ἰέναι : Id. Anab. I. 2, 1 Ξενίᾳ— ἥκειν παρήγγειλε λαβόντα τοὺς ἄνδρας. And even the two constructions are found in the same passage : Il. χ, 109 ἐμοὶ δὲ τότ᾽ ἂν πολὺ κέρδιον εἴη, ἄντην ἢ Ἀχιλῆα κατακτείναντα νέεσθαι, ἠὲ καὶ αὐτῷ ὀλέσθαι εὐκλειῶς πρὸ πόληος : Soph. El. 958 ᾗ πάρεστι μὲν στένειν πλούτου πατρῴου κτῆσιν ἐστερημένῃ, πάρεστι δ᾽ ἀλγεῖν εἰς τοσόνδε τοῦ χρόνου ἄλεκτρα γηράσκουσαν ἀνυμέναιά τε : Eur. Med. 1236 sqq. φίλαι, δέδοκται τοὔργον ὡς τάχιστά μοι παῖδας κτανούσῃ τῆσδ᾽ ἀφορμᾶσθαι χθονός, καὶ μὴ σχολὴν ἄγουσαν ἐκδοῦναι τέκνα ἄλλῃ φονεῦσαι[a].

Obs. Sometimes, by a singular attraction, the noun preceding the infin. is in the case of the subject of a parenthetical sentence; as, Thuc. V. 50 αὖθις τάδε ἠξίουν (οἱ Ἠλεῖοι), Λέπρεον μὲν μὴ ἀποδοῦναι (τοὺς Λακεδαιμονίους), εἰ μὴ βούλονται· ἀναβάντες δὲ ἐπὶ τὸν βωμὸν τοῦ Διὸς τοῦ Ὀλυμπίου, ἐπειδὴ προθυμοῦνται χρῆσθαι τῷ ἱερῷ, ἀπομόσαι κ.τ.λ. : Id. VII. 48 (ὁ Νικίας οὐκ ἐβούλετο) ἐμφανῶς σφᾶς ψηφιζομένους μετὰ πολλῶν τὴν ἀναχώρησιν τοῖς πολεμίοις καταγγέλτους γίγνεσθαι· λαθεῖν γὰρ ἄν, ὁπότε βούλοιντο, τοῦτο ποιοῦντες πολλῷ ἧσσον.

Accusative with Infinitive, as Subject of a Sentence.

§. 676. 1. From this substantival usage of the accus. and infin. as representing together the cognate notion of the verb, it arose that they performed other substantival functions, and stood with some verbs as the subject : thus in λέγουσι τὸν Κῦρον νικῆσαι, the τὸν Κῦρ. νικῆ. = the victory of Cyrus ; then the form of the sentence being altered into " the victory of Cyrus is reported," the compound notion retains the form whereby it originally derived its substantival power as the compound object of the verb, and stands in that form as a compound subject to the verb which would otherwise be impersonal — τὸν-Κῦρον-νικῆσαι λέγεται. If the nomin. were used it would immediately destroy the substantival power of the expression, and the compound would separate itself into the subject and predicate of the verb, as ὁ Κῦρος, (subj.) λέγεται νικῆσαι : and it must be observed that this use of the accus. and infin. as a subject depends on the original form of the thought, which is implied in its altered expression; as, λέγεται τὸν Κῦρον νικῆσαι = λέγουσι ; πέπρωται τὸν βασιλέα ἀποθανεῖν=fatum constituit ; δοκεῖ μοί σε ἁμαρτεῖν=ἡγοῦμαι ; ἀγαθόν ἐστί σε τοὺς γονεῖς ἀγαπᾶν=probo &c.

2. It is used as the subject,

a. After passive verbs, λέγεται, ἀγγέλλεται, ὁμολογεῖται &c., for which however we often find the active form used : Hdt. III. 9 λέγεται τὸν βασιλέα—ἀγαγεῖν : Ibid. 26 ἐς μὲν δὴ τοῦτον τὸν χῶρον λέγεται ἀπικέσθαι τὸν στρατόν : Xen. Cyr. I. 4, 26 καὶ Κῦρον δὲ αὐτὸν σὺν πολλοῖς δακρύοις λέγεται ἀποχωρῆσαι. Immediately afterwards, πολλὰ δὲ δῶρα διαδοῦναί φασιν αὐτὸν (τὸν Κῦρον) τοῖς ἡλικιώταις —. Τοὺς μέντοι λαβόντας καὶ δεξαμένους τὰ δῶρα λέγεται Ἀστυάγει ἀποδοῦναι· Ἀστυάγην δὲ δεξάμενον ἀποπέμψαι· τὸν δὲ πάλιν τε ἀποπέμψαι εἰς Μήδους : Plat. Phæd. p. 72 A ὁμολογεῖται δὲ καὶ ταύτῃ,

---

[a] Pflugk ad loc.

τοὺς ζῶντας ἐκ τῶν τεθνεώτων γεγονέναι.—But Xen. Cyr. V. 3, 30 ὁ Ἀσσύριος εἰς τὴν χώραν ἐμβάλλειν ἀγγέλλεται: Ibid. I. 2. princ. πατρὸς μὲν δὴ λέγεται Κῦρος γενέσθαι Καμβύσου. Both constructions, Plat. Charm. princ. καὶ μὴν ἤγγελταί γε ἡ μάχη ἰσχυρὰ γεγονέναι καὶ πολλοὺς τεθνάναι.

b. After πέπρωται, ἔοικε, προσήκει, πρέπει, δοκεῖ, ξυμβαίνει &c.: Il. σ, 329 ἄμφω γὰρ πέπρωται ὁμοίην γαῖαν ἐρεῦσαι αὐτοῦ ἐνὶ Τροίῃ: Il. a, 126 λαοὺς δ' οὐκ ἐπέοικε παλιλλόγα ταῦτ' ἐπαγείρειν: Hdt. III. 124 ἐδόκεέ οἱ τὸν πατέρα—λοῦσθαι μὲν ὑπὸ τοῦ Διός, χρίεσθαι δὲ ὑπὸ τοῦ ἡλίου: Thuc. IV. 3. extr. τῷ δὲ ἐδόκει—τοὺς Μεσσηνίους ἂν βλάπτειν κ. τ. λ.: Plat. Phæd. p. 74 A ἆρ' οὖν οὐ κατὰ πάντα ταῦτα συμβαίνει τὴν ἀνάμνησιν εἶναι μὲν ἀφ' ὁμοίων κ. τ. λ.

Obs. Δοκεῖν is sometimes used as a personal, as in Lat., *videri:* Xen. Anab. III. 1, 21 λελύσθαι μοι δοκεῖ καὶ ἡ ἐκείνων ὕβρις, καὶ ἡ ἡμετέρα ὑποψία. So also συμβαίνειν, there being no connection between the infin. and subst.: Plat. Phæd. p. 67 C κάθαρσις δὲ εἶναι οὐ τοῦτο ξυμβαίνει κ. τ. λ. for ξυμβαίνει κάθαρσιν τοῦτο εἶναι[a]: Id. Rep. p. 438 E ἐπιστήμη—ποιά δή τις συνέβη καὶ αὐτή γενέσθαι.

c. After adj. and subst. with εἶναι, (a) when the infin. signifies something to be done, or (β) when it signifies an object of a mental emotion, expressed by an adj. or subst.: α. After ἀγαθόν, κακόν, καλόν, φίλον, ἐπιεικές ἐστιν &c. — μοῖρά ἐστιν &c. — οὐκ ἔστιν, οὕπως ἔστιν &c.; Od. η, 159 sq. οὐ μέν τοι τόδε κάλλιον, οὐδὲ ἔοικεν, ξεῖνον μὲν χαμαὶ ἧσθαι ἐπ' ἐσχάρῃ ἐν κονίῃσιν: Il. ν, 226 sq. μέλλει δὴ φίλον εἶναι ὑπερμενεῖ Κρονίωνι, νωνύμνους ἀπολέσθαι ἀπ' Ἄργεος ἐνθάδ' Ἀχαιούς: Il. ρ, 421 μοῖρα παρ' ἀνέρι τῷδε δαμῆναι πάντας ὁμῶς: Il. ν, 114 ἡμέας γ' οὔπως ἔστι μεθιέμεναι πολέμοιο; β. Il. τ, 182 οὐ μέν γάρ τι νεμεσσητὸν βασιλῆα ἄνδρ' ἀπαρέσσασθαι, ὅτε τις πρότερος χαλεπήνῃ: Il. γ, 156 οὐ νέμεσις, Τρῶας καὶ ἐϋκνήμιδας Ἀχαιοὺς τοιῇδ' ἀμφὶ γυναικὶ πολὺν χρόνον ἄλγεα πάσχειν: Il. ρ, 336 sq. αἰδὼς μὲν νῦν ἥδε γ', Ἀρηϊφίλων ὑπ' Ἀχαιῶν Ἴλιον εἰσαναβῆναι ἀναλκείῃσι δαμέντας!

Change of the Impersonal into the Personal Construction.

§. 677. In the instances given under *a.* and *b.* §. 676. 2, we see the Greeks avoid the impersonal construction, by placing the acc. and infin. as the subject of the passive or impersonal verbs. Another mode of avoiding this construction with the verb εἶναι is, by separating the noun in the accus. from the infin., placing it in the nom. as the subject of the verb εἶναι, and making the adjective, which with ἔστι makes up the verbal notion, agree with it. This is especially the case with the adj.: δίκαιος, ἄξιος, ἐπίδοξος, δυνατός, ἀμήχανος, χαλεπός &c.; as, δίκαιός εἰμι τοῦτο πράττειν, for δίκαιόν ἐστί με ταῦτα πράττειν.—Δίκαιός εἰμι εἶναι ἐλεύθερος: Il. a, 107 ἀεί τοι τὰ κάκ' ἔστι φίλα φρεσὶ μαντεύεσθαι: Il. ν, 726 Ἕκτορ, ἀμήχανός ἐσσι παραρρητοῖσι πιθέσθαι: Hdt. VI. 12 ἐπίδοξοι τωὐτὸ τοῦτο πείσεσθαι εἰσι: Xen. Cyr. V. 4, 20 ἄξιοί γε μέντοι ἐσμὲν τοῦ γεγενημένου πράγματος τούτου ἀπολαῦσαί τι ἀγαθόν: Id. Anab. I. 2, 21 ὁδὸς ἀμήχανος εἰσελθεῖν στρατεύματι: Ibid. IV. 1, 17 δυνατὴν καὶ ὑποζυγίοις πορεύεσθαι ὁδόν: Plat. Rep. p. 471 C δυνατὴ αὕτη ἡ πολιτεία γενέσθαι[a]: Id. Phædr. p. 256 B οὗ μεῖζον ἀγαθὸν οὔτε σωφροσύνη ἀνθρωπίνη οὔτε θεία μανία δυνατὴ πορίσαι ἀνθρώπῳ: Id. Rep. p. 559 B δυνατὴ δὲ κολαζομένη—ἀπαλλάττεσθαι: Ibid. p. 330 C (οἱ χρηματισάμενοι) χαλεποὶ—ξυγγενέσθαι εἰσίν, οὐδὲν ἐθέλοντες ἐπαινεῖν ἀλλ' ἢ τὸν πλοῦτον.

---

[a] Heindorf ad loc.   [b] Stallb. ad loc.

Obs. The construction with certain verbs compounded with ἐν affords a
remarkable instance of this attraction, where even the object of the infin.
is made the subject of the verb : Hdt. IX. 7 τῆς ἡμετέρης ἐπιτηδεώτατόν ἐστιν
ἐμμαχέσασθαι τὸ Θριάσιον πεδίον (i. e. ἐπιτηδεώτατον ἦν μαχέσασθαι ἐν τῷ
Θριασίῳ πεδίῳ : Eur. Phœn. 739 ἐνδυστυχῆσαι δεινὸν εὐφρόνης κνέφας. And
this occurs not only with adj. but with verbs : Demosth. p. 294, 13 τὰ τῶν
Ἑλλήνων ἀτυχήματα ἐνευδοκιμεῖν ἀπέκειτο, for ἀπέκειτο εὐδ. ἐν τοῖς ἀτυχήμασι :
Plat. Phædr. p. 228 E ἐμαυτόν σοι ἐμμελετᾶν παρέχειν οὐ πάνυ δέδοκται.

Infinitive with the Article.

§. 678. 1. The Infin. with the article (τό) is treated as a substantive, capable of declension by means of the inflexions of the
article, and thereby of expressing all the relations of the cases of a
substantive. It retains however so much of its verbal nature as
to admit the objective relations : τὸ ἐπιστολὴν γράφειν, τὸ καλῶς γράφειν ἐπιστολήν &c., τὸ καλῶς θνήσκειν, τὸ ὑπὲρ τῆς πατρίδος θνήσκειν.

2. In this way whole sentences, by prefixing the article, may
assume the character of one lengthened substantival notion. The
unity of this notion is often marked by the position of the article
first, and the infinitive last, so that all the words between them
are marked as belonging to the infinitive, and making up with it
one notion. This collocation however is not always observed, and
in poetry is not unfrequently violated; as, Soph. Ant. 723 καὶ τῶν
λεγόντων εὖ καλὸν τὸ μανθάνειν for τὸ τῶν εὖ λεγόντων μανθάνειν
καλόν.

3. If a noun is joined with the infin. as the subject thereof, it is
in the accus., unless it is the same as the principle subject of the
sentence, when it is in the nomin.—(See §. 672. 1, 2.)

a. Nominative (subject).— Τὸ θνήσκειν τινὰ ὑπὲρ τῆς πατρίδος
καλή τις τύχη : Xen. Cyr. V. 4, 19 τὸ ἁμαρτάνειν ἀνθρώπους ὄντας
οὐδὲν, οἶμαι, θαυμαστόν. As an explanation : Plat. Rep. p. 590 E
ἡ τῶν παίδων ἀρχή, τὸ μὴ ἐᾶν ἐλευθέρους εἶναι.

b. Genitive—whether as attribute of another subst., or object
of a verbal notion : Hdt. I. 86 εἴ τις μιν δαιμόνων ῥύσεται τ ο ῦ μὴ
ζῶντα κατακανθῆναι : Xen. Anab. I. 3, 2 Κλέαρχος μικρὸν ἐξέφυγε
τ ο ῦ μὴ καταπετρωθῆναι : Xen. Cyr. I. 4, 4 ὡς δὲ προῆγεν ὁ χρόνος
αὐτὸν (τὸν Κῦρον) σὺν τῷ μεγέθει εἰς ὥραν τοῦ πρόσηβον γενέσθαι :
Id. M. S. I. 2, 55 παρεκάλει ἐπιμελεῖσθαι τ ο ῦ ὡς φρονιμώτατον
εἶναι καὶ ὠφελιμώτατον : Plat. Rep. p. 354 B οὐκ ἀπεσχόμην τοῦ μὴ οὐκ
ἐπὶ τοῦτο ἐλθεῖν ἀπ᾽ ἐκείνου : Demosth. p. 16. princ. δοκεῖ τὸ φυλάξαι
τἀγαθὰ τ ο ῦ κτήσασθαι χαλεπώτερον εἶναι. The genitive is very
often used to define a preceding subst.: Plat. Legg. p. 657 B ἡ—
ζήτησις τοῦ καινῇ ζητεῖν ἀεὶ μουσικῇ χρῆσθαι : (cf. Ibid. p. 776 D ἡ

τε τῶν Ἡρακλεωτῶν δουλεία τῆς τῶν Μαριανδυνῶν καταδουλώ-
σεως.) With prepos.; as, ἀντί, *instead of*, χωρὶς, μέχρι, ἐκ, especially ὑπέρ and ἕνεκα with μή: Thuc. I. 45 προεῖπον δὲ ταῦτα τοῦ
μὴ λύειν ἕνεκα τὰς σπονδάς, *ne fœdera frangerent*: Xen. Hier.
IV. 3. δορυφοροῦσιν ἐπὶ τοὺς κακούργους ὑπὲρ τοῦ μηδένα τῶν
πολιτῶν βιαίῳ θανάτῳ ἀποθνήσκειν: Plat. Crit. p. 44 B χωρὶς μὲν
τοῦ ἐστερῆσθαι τοιούτου ἐπιτηδείου[a]: Demosth. p. 101, 45 κἀ-
κεῖνα ὑπὲρ τοῦ τούτων γενέσθαι κύριος καὶ τἆλλα πάντα πρα-
γματεύεται. The genitive is especially used to denote something to
be done—an object, aim, purpose, (in a negative sense most commonly,) this object, &c. being considered as the cause of the action
(§. 492.). This was an Attic idiom, not usual in the old orators,
but very usual in Demosth. and still more so in the later writers:
Xen. Cyr. I, 3, 9 οἱ γὰρ τῶν βασιλέων οἰνοχόοι — εἰς τὴν ἀριστερὰν
(οἶνον) ἐγχεάμενοι καταρροφοῦσι, τοῦ δὴ, εἰ φάρμακα ἐγχέοιεν, μὴ
λυσιτελεῖν αὐτοῖς: Plat. Gorg. p. 509 D ἐὰν δύναμιν παρασκευά-
σηται τοῦ μὴ ἀδικεῖσθαι. Without any negation: Ibid. p.
457 E φοβοῦμαι οὖν διελέγχειν σε, μή με ὑπολάβῃς οὐ πρὸς τὸ πρᾶγμα
φιλονεικοῦντα λέγειν τοῦ καταφανὲς γενέσθαι, ἀλλὰ πρὸς σέ, i. e.
*ne suspiceris me non rei caussâ contendentem dicere, ut manifesta fiat,
sed tuâ caussâ*[b].

c. Dative.—Xen. Cyr. IV. 5, 9 ἐβριμοῦτό τε τῷ Κύρῳ καὶ τοῖς
Μήδοις τῷ καταλιπόντας αὐτὸν ἔρημον οἴχεσθαι: Plat. Phæd.
p. 71 C τῷ ζῆν ἔστι τι ἐναντίον ὥσπερ τῷ ἐγρηγορέναι τὸ
καθεύδειν: Demosth. p. 92, 11 οὐδενὶ τῶν πάντων πλέον κεκράτηκε τῆς
πόλεως Φίλιππος ἢ τῷ πρότερος πρὸς τοῖς πράγμασι γίγνεσθαι.
With the nom. in attraction for acc.: Thuc. II. 42 καὶ παθεῖν μᾶλλον ἡγησάμενοι ἢ τῷ ἐνδόντες σώζεσθαι: Plat. Hipp. Maj.
p. 299 D ἐρωτῶ, εἴ τις (ἡδονὴ) αὐτῷ τούτῳ διαφέρει, τῷ ἢ μὲν
ἡδονὴ εἶναι, ἡ δὲ μὴ ἡδονὴ εἶναι τῶν ἡδονῶν. With prepositions; as, ἐν, ἐπί: Soph. Aj. 554 ἐν τῷ φρονεῖν ἥδιστος
βίος: Plat. Gorg. p. 456 E ἐκεῖνοι μὲν γὰρ παρέδοσαν ἐπὶ τῷ δικαίως
χρῆσθαι τούτοις.

d. Accusative.—Xen. Cyr. I. 4, 21 ὁ Κῦρος ἐφέρετο, μόνον ὁρῶν
τὸ παίειν τὸν ἁλισκόμενον: Plat. Gorg. p. 512 E αὐτὸ μὲν γὰρ τὸ
ἀποθνήσκειν οὐδεὶς φοβεῖται: Id. Apol. S. p. 28 D πολὺ μᾶλλον
δείσας τὸ ζῆν. Frequently, as more accurate explanation of a preceding accusative: Xen. Cyr. V. 1, 28 δαίμονος ἂν φαίην τὴν
ἐπιβουλὴν (*alii* βούλησιν) εἶναι τὸ μὴ ἐᾶσαι ὑμᾶς μέγα εὐδαίμονας γενέσθαι. With prepositions, as πρός, especially διά. With the
nominative in attraction with the infin.: Xen. Cyr. I. 4, 3 ὁ

---

[a] Stallb. ad loc. [b] Stallb. ad loc.

Κῦρος διὰ τὸ φιλομαθὴς εἶναι πολλὰ—τοὺς παρόντας ἀνηρώτα —, καὶ ὅσα αὐτὸς ὑπ' ἄλλων, διὰ τὸ ἀγχίνους εἶναι ταχὺ ἀπεκρίνετο.

Obs. 1. With many verbs the infin. is used both with and without the article, as may be seen by a comparison of the instances given of each; but when a preposition is joined with the infin., as if it were actually a substantive, it must have the article, as without it it is not capable of inflexion. Herodotus alone uses ἀντὶ with the infin. without the article: as, I. 210 ὃς ἀντὶ μὲν δούλων ἐποίησας ἐλευθέρους Πέρσας εἶναι, ἀντὶ δὲ ἄρχεσθαι ὑπ' ἄλλων, ἄρχειν ἁπάντων, apparently for antithesis. In other passages, as VI. 32, VII. 170, the reading is doubtful.

Obs. 2. For the Infin. with Acc., for Infin. with Gen., see §. 675, *a.*

Infinitive with the Article (a) *in exclamations and questions,* (b) *in adverbial expressions.*

§. 679. 1. As the equivalent acc. is used to express the annoyance, or object of pain, dislike, &c., so the infin. with the article (which, however, is sometimes omitted in poetry) is used in similar expressions and questions: Xen. Cyr. II. 2, 3 ἐκεῖνος πάνυ ἀνιαθεὶς εἶπε πρὸς ἑαυτόν· τῆς τύχης, τὸ ἐμὲ νῦν κληθέντα δεῦρο τυχεῖν! Soph. Phil. 234 ὦ φίλτατον φώνημα· φεῦ τὸ καὶ λαβεῖν πρόσφθεγμα τοιοῦδ' ἀνδρὸς ἐν μακρῷ χρόνῳ! Without the article: Æsch. Eum. 835 ἐμὲ παθεῖν τάδε, φεῦ, ἐμὲ παλαιόφρονα κατὰ γᾶν οἰκεῖν, ἀτίετον, φεῦ, μύσος!

2. Many phrases, in which the article τό precedes the infin. εἶναι, joined with an adverb or prepos. and its case, are used adverbially. These are to be considered as accusatives, as this is the proper form of adverbial expressions of this sort (§. 548. 2. *f.*); the infin. signifies the state; as, τὸ νῦν εἶναι, the present state; and is used adverbially, " with respect to the present state," *pro præsenti temporis conditione;* τὸ τήμερον εἶναι, *pro hodierni diei conditione:* Thuc. IV. 48 ἐκέλευεν ἥντινα βούλεται δύναμιν λαβόντα τὸ ἐπὶ σφᾶς εἶναι ἐπιχειρεῖν.—τὸ ἐπ' ἐκείνοις εἶναι Thuc.: Xen. Anab. I. 6, 9 τὸ κατὰ τοῦτον εἶναι, as far as belongs to him: (Plat. Protag. p. 317 princ. ἐγὼ δὲ τούτοις ἅπασι κατὰ τοῦτο εἶναι οὐ ξυμφέρομαι, *ego vero cum his omnibus, quantum quidem ad hoc attinet, non consentio,* it should probably be read with Ast, τὸ κατὰ τοῦτο εἶναι [a]. Τὸ νῦν is also used without εἶναι, which must be supplied by the reader. The following passages grammarians generally class here improperly: Hdt. I. 153 καὶ τοὺς Ἴωνας ἐν οὐδενὶ λόγῳ ποιησάμενος τὴν πρώτην εἶναι. Εἶναι is here the predicate of Ἴωνας, and the construction is correct without it; cf. Id. VII. 143 extr. Ἀθηναῖοι ταῦτά σφι ἔγνωσαν αἱρετώτερα εἶναι μᾶλλον ἢ τὰ τῶν χρησμολόγων, οἳ οὐκ ἔων ναυμαχίην ἀρτέεσθαι, τὸ δὲ σύμπαν εἶναι, οὐδὲ χεῖρας ἀνταείρεσθαι, ἀλλὰ ἐκλιπόντας χώρην τὴν Ἀττικήν, ἄλλην τινὰ οἰκίζειν, i. e. *censuerunt Athenienses potiorem esse rationem, quam illam, quæ erat ab oraculorum interpretibus proposita, qui, apparatum navalis pugnæ dissuadentes, summam rei in eo verti aiebant, ut ne manus quidem tollerent* &c.: Id. VI. 137, where the infin. ἰδεῖν stands (as elsewhere) in the *oratio obliqua* for the opt.: Soph. Œ. C. 1184 (1191) ἔφυσας αὐτὸν, ὥστε μή γε δρῶντά σε τὰ τῶν κάκιστα δυσσεβεστάτων, πάτερ, θέμις σέ γ'

[a] Cf. Stallb.

εἶναι κεῖνον ἀντιδρᾶν κακῶς: join ὥστε θέμις εἶναι (not ὥστε ἀντιδρᾶν;
θέμις εἶναι is here a predicate of the sentence σε κεῖνον ἀντιδρᾶν: θέμις
is here indeclinable).

PARTICIPLE.

§. 680. 1. The use of the participle for the object of the verb
differs from that of the infin., inasmuch as the latter expresses
either the immediate object of the verb, or end or result thereof,
while the former is used not only, as the infin., to add to the verbal
notion the accessories which are required to give it a definite
meaning, as χαίρω, I rejoice, τῷ πατρὶ ἐλθόντι (or τὸν πατέρα ἐλθεῖν);
but also adverbially, to express notions of time, cause, mode and
manner, which are the accidents of the verbal notion, and not
actually necessary to its definite meaning, as τοῦ ἔαρος ἐλθόντος τὰ
ἄνθη θάλλει.

2. The essential force of the participle is attributive, which it
retains throughout: hence it must always be joined with a subst.
which it represents as being in the action or state expressed by
the participle, while the infin. signifies the effect, or result, or aim
of the action or state of the governing verb.

Participle as the completion of the verbal notion.

§. 681. The participle with a substantive completes the notion
of an action or state by expressing the exact circumstances under
which the action or state took place, as χαίρω, I rejoice, is an
imperfect notion, as we do not know the cause of the joy—χαίρω
τῷ πατρὶ ἐλθόντι is a complete notion, as we know of what nature
the joy is.

It is not used with verbs where these circumstances express
the consequent aim or the effect of the action, but where the notion of the participle is conceived, as either actually existing, or
as having taken place antecedently to the notion of the verb; as,
ἁμαρτάνων ὁρῶ, erring I (now) see it; or (more rarely) coincidently
with it; as, ἐπειρᾶτο κατιών, he endeavoured to come back—or,
coming back he endeavoured; the endeavour consisted in beginning κατιέναι. So ὁρῶ τὸν ἄνθρωπον τρέχοντα—χαίρω τῷ φίλῳ
ἐλθόντι—οἶδα ἄνθρωπον θνητὸν ὄντα—ἀκούω αὐτοῦ λέγοντος—παύω
αὐτὸν γράφοντα. In many of these constructions in Latin, *quod*,
that, with the subjunctive would be used.

1. The part. of course stands in the same case as its subst., and
this in the case of the governing verb; as, ἀκούω Σωκράτους and

ἤκουσά ποτε αὐτοῦ περὶ φίλων διαλεγομένου.—Χαίρω σοι and χαίρω σοι ἐλθόντι.—Ὁρῶ ἄνθρωπον and ὁρῶ ἄνθρωπον τρέχοντα.

2. But when the subst. or pers. pronoun following the verb refers to the subject of the verb, as οἶδα (ἐγώ) ἐμὲ θνητὸν ὄντα—; the subst. or pronoun is suppressed, and the participle by attraction to the subj. is in the nomin.; as, οἶδα θνητὸς ὤν : Thuc. VII. 47 ἐώρων οὐ κατορθοῦντες (*se rem non prospere gerere*) καὶ τοὺς στρατιώτας ἀχθομένους. So also must the part. be in the nom. when it refers to the subject of a passive or reflexive verb; as, ὁρῶμαι, φαίνομαι, φανερός εἰμι, δῆλός εἰμι ἡμᾶς εὖ ποιήσας.— Ἐπαύοντο ἀδικοῦντες.

Obs. Sometimes this construction occurs with a seemingly future notion, when the participle is in the future, as Isocr. p. 311 C. ἐώρων οὔτε—οἷός τε γενησόμενος; but the future expresses here not the future fact, but the existing fact of something being about to happen. So also with present or past perceptions of a future fact; the future here equals μέλλων with the infin., as in many other constructions.

Remarks on this construction.

§. 682. 1. This attraction sometimes does not take place when it is to be expressly marked that the subject of the verb is also the object of it, and the participle and pronoun follow the verb in the acc. : Xen. Cyr. I. 4, 4 οὐχ, ἃ κρείττων ᾔδει ὤν, ταῦτα προὐκαλεῖτο τοὺς συνόντας, ἀλλ᾽ ἅπερ εὖ ᾔδει ἑαυτὸν ἥττονα ὄντα, ταῦτα ἐξῆρχε : Ibid. 5, 10 περιεῖδον αὐτοὺς γήρᾳ ἀδυνάτους γενομένους : Demosth. p. 817 extr. ἀπέγραψε ταῦτα— ἔχοντα ἑαυτόν.

2. With σύνοιδα, συγγιγνώσκω ἐμαυτῷ the participle may either agree with the subject or with the personal pronoun following the verb; as, σύνοιδα (συγγιγνώσκω) ἐμαυτῷ εὖ ποιήσας, or σύνοιδα ἐμαυτῷ εὖ ποιήσαντι : Plat. Apol. p. 21 B ἐγὼ — ξύνοιδα ἐμαυτῷ σοφὸς ὤν : Id. p. 22 D ἐμαυτῷ ξυνῄδειν οὐδὲν ἐπισταμένῳ. But when the object of these verbs is not the same person as the subj., then the part. and subst. are either in the dat., as σύνοιδά σοι εὖ ποιήσαντι, or both in acc., as σύνοιδά σε εὖ ποιήσαντα, or the subst. in dat., and participle in acc., where the dat. depends upon σύν, and the acc. on οἶδα : Xen. Œc. III. 7 ἐγώ σοι σύνοιδα ἐπὶ μὲν κωμῳδῶν θέαν καὶ πάνυ πρωὶ ἀνιστάμενον, καὶ πάνυ μικρὰν ὁδὸν βαδίζοντα καὶ ἐμὲ ἀναπείθοντα προθυμῶς συνθεᾶσθαι. Also with ἐοικέναι, *to be like*, and ὅμοιον εἶναι, the part. agrees either with the subj. or object : Plat. Cratyl. p. 419 C ὀδύνη δὲ ἀπὸ τῆς ἐνδύσεως τῆς λύπης κεκλημένη ἔοικεν : Xen. Hell. VI. 3, 5 ἐοίκατε τυραννίσι μᾶλλον ἢ πολιτείαις ἡδόμενοι : Id. M. S. IV. 3, 8 ταῦτα παντάπασιν ἔοικεν ἀνθρώπων ἕνεκα γιγνόμενα : But Xen. Anab. III. 5, 13 ὅμοιοι ἦσαν θαυμάζοντες : Plat. Menon. p. 97 A ὅμοιοί ἐσμεν οὐκ ὀρθῶς ὡμολογηκόσι : Id. Rep. p. 414 C ἔοικας, ἔφη, ὀκνοῦντι λέγειν : Id. Apol. p. 26 extr. ἔοικε γὰρ ὥσπερ αἴνιγμα ξυντιθέντι, διαπειρωμένῳ κ. τ. λ., the partic. being omitted (see 3.) : Id. Phæd. p. 62 C ὁ μέντοι νῦν δὴ ἔλεγες, τὸ τοὺς φιλοσόφους ῥᾳδίως ἂν ἐθέλειν ἀποθνήσκειν, ἔοικε τοῦτο, ὦ Σώκρατες, ἀτόπῳ (sc. ὄντι).

3. The participle ὤν is often omitted with predicative adj. and subst. : Soph. Œ. C. 783 φράσω δὲ καὶ τοῖσδ᾽, ὥς σε δηλώσω κακόν (sc. ὄντα):

Ibid. 1210 σῶς ἴσθι (sc. ὤν) : Id. Antig. 471 δηλοῖ τὸ γέννημ' ὠμὸν ἐξ ὠμοῦ πατρὸς τῆς παιδός (sc. ὄν) : Eur. Hipp. 903 σὴν δάμαρθ' ὁρῶ, πάτερ, νεκρόν (sc. οὖσαν) : Ibid. 1074 σαφῶς τόδ' ἔργον — σε μηνύει κακόν : cf. 1288 : Id. Hec. 348 κακὴ φανοῦμαι καὶ φιλόψυχος γυνή : Ibid. 423 ἄγγελλε πασῶν ἀθλιωτάτην ἐμέ [a]. So also after ἡγεῖσθαι, νομίζειν : Eur. El. 67 ἐγὼ σ' ἴσον θεοῖσιν ἡγοῦμαι φίλον : Demosth. p. 45, 18 εἰδὼς εὐτρεπεῖς ὑμᾶς. And even when **εἶναι** is the substantive verb : Ibid. p. 51, 41 ἐὰν ἐν Χερρονήσῳ πύθησθε Φίλιππον (sc. ὄντα, i. e. *versantem*). So probably we must explain Eur. Hec. 1215 καπνῷ δ' ἐσήμην' (intrans.) ἄστυ πολεμίων ὕπο (sc. ὄν, the city appeared to be in flames (καπνῷ), under the hand of the enemy, i. e. fired by them.

4. Where the participle is in the nom. by attraction, the Latins would use either the pronoun with infin., as *sensit se errasse ;* or in fut. time, the future in *rus* with *esse*, as *sensit se lapsurum esse ;* or sometimes the Greek construction, *sensit medios delapsus in hostes.* In similar cases, in English we should use either the pronoun and infin. ; as, I know myself to be mortal ; or the finite verb with "that," I know that I am mortal. And, as a general rule, such Latin and English expressions may be translated into Greek by this construction, when the verbal notion of the part. is conceived to exist antecedently or coincidently with the notion of the verb.

§. 683. The verbs which admit of this construction are,

I. Verbs of sensual or mental perception (as the action or state must always be antecedent to, or coincident with, the perception) ; as, ὁρᾶν, ἀκούειν, κλύειν poet. : νοεῖν, ἐννοεῖν, ἀγνοεῖν, εἰδέναι, ἐπίστασθαι ; μανθάνειν, γιγνώσκειν ; φρονεῖν, ἐνθυμεῖσθαι ; πυνθάνεσθαι, αἰσθάνεσθαι ; μιμνήσκεσθαι, ἐπιλανθάνεσθαι &c. : Thuc. I. 32 καὶ ἡμεῖς ἀδύνατοι ὁ ρ ῶ μ ε ν ὄ ν τ ε ς περιγενέσθαι. Ὁ ρ ῶ σε τρέχοντα. Seldom with the genitive : Soph. Trach. 394 δίδαξον, ὡς ἕ ρ π ο ν τ ο ς εἰσορᾷς ἐμοῦ. — Ἀ κ ο ύ ε ι ν : Xen. M. S. II. 2, 4 ἤ κ ο υ σ α δέ ποτε α ὐ τ ο ῦ καὶ περὶ φίλων δ ι α λ ε γ ο μ έ ν ο υ : Eur. Phœn. 1341 ὦ δώματ' εἰσηκούσατ' Οἰδίπου τάδε π α ί δ ω ν ὁμοίαις ξυμφοραῖς ὀ λ ω λ ό τ ω ν : Soph. El. 293 ὅταν κ λ ύ ῃ τινὸς ἥ ξ ο ν τ' Ὀ ρ έ σ τ η ν. — Ο ἶ δ α θνητὸς ὤν — ο ἶ δ α ἄνθρωπον θνητὸν ὄντα : Hdt. III. 1 ὦ βασιλεῦ, διαβεβλημένος ὑπὸ Ἀμάσιος οὐ μ α ν θ ά ν ε ι ς [a] ; Ibid. 40 ἡδὺ μὲν π υ ν θ ά ν ε σ θ α ι ἄνδρα φίλον καὶ ξεῖνον εὖ πρήσσοντα : Id. VI. 23 οἱ Ζαγκλαῖοι ὡς ἐ π ύ θ ο ν τ ο ἐ χ ο μ έ ν η ν τ ὴ ν π ό λ ι ν ἑωϋτῶν ἐβοήθεον αὐτῇ : Ibid. 100 Ἐρετριέες δὲ π υ ν θ α ν ό μ ε ν ο ι τ ὴ ν σ τ ρ α τ ι ὴ ν τ ὴ ν Π ε ρ σ ι κ ὴ ν ἐ π ι π λ έ ο υ σ α ν Ἀθηναίων ἐδεήθησαν κ. τ. λ. (More rarely with gen. ; as, Il. ρ, 426 κλαῖον, ἐπειδὴ πρῶτα π υ θ έ σ θ η ν ἡ ν ι ό χ ο ι ο ἐν κονίῃσι π ε σ ό ν τ ο ς :) Eur. Med. 26 πρὸς ἀνδρὸς ᾖ σ θ ε τ' ἠ δ ι κ η μ έ ν η : Xen. M. S. II. 2, 1 α ἰ σ θ ό μ ε ν ο ς δέ ποτε Λ α μ π ρ ο κ λ έ α πρὸς τὴν μητέρα χ α λ ε π α ί ν ο ν τ α. And with gen. : Ibid. IV. 4, 11 ᾔ σ θ η σ α ι οὖν π ώ π ο τ έ μ ο υ ἢ ψ ε υ δ ο μ α ρ τ υ ρ ο ῦ ν τ ο ς ἢ σ υ κ ο φ α ν τ ο ῦ ν τ ο ς ;

[a] Pflugk ad loc.

Obs. As the action of the part. must be supposed to exist antecedently to or coincidently with the verb, it follows naturally that when the object is not conceived of as actually existing, but only as possible, or where a consequent object is to be expressed, the infin., not the part., is used. So with the verbs εἰδέναι, ἐπίστασθαι, to understand how to do something; μανθάνειν, not to perceive, but to learn; γιγνώσκειν, to learn, decide, determine; μιμνήσκεσθαι, to remember to do a thing, the object is in infin. : Eur. Hipp. 993 ἐπίσταμαι—θεοὺς σέβειν, I understand how to honour the gods (consequence of understanding) ; but ibid. 1244 ἐπεί νιν ἐσθλὸν ὄντ᾽ ἐπίσταμαι, I know that he is good (antecedent to knowledge) : Soph. Aj. 666 εἰσόμεσθα μὲν θεοῖς εἴκειν : Xen. Cyr. IV. 1, 18 εἰ μαθήσονται ἐναντιοῦσθαι : ἔμαθε ἀγαθὸς ὤν, he knew that he was : Soph. Antig. 1089 ἵνα — γνῷ τρέφειν τὴν γλῶσσαν ἡσυχωτέραν : ἔγνω τρέφων : Isocr. p. 361 D ἔγνωσαν Πασίωνα ἐμοὶ παραδοῦναι τὸν παῖδα, they determined that he should : Xen. Cyr. II. 1, 22 ἀγῶνάς τε αὐτοῖς προεῖπεν ἁπάντων, ὁπόσα ἐγίγνωσκεν (judicabat) ἀσκεῖσθαι ἀγαθὸν εἶναι ὑπὸ στρατιωτῶν : Xen. Anab. III. 2, 39 μεμνήσθω ἀνὴρ ἀγαθὸς εἶναι, remember to be ; ἔμαθε ἀνὴρ ἀγαθὸς ὤν, he felt that he was. After εἰδέναι and ἐπίστασθαι, in the sense of *to know*, the infin. follows, but very seldom after πυνθάνεσθαι and αἰσθάνεσθαι, *to observe*, when the action of the dependent verb is future, and perceived as such, or where these verbs express only a *supposition* of the notion of the verb having taken place, or taking place, as the part. gives the notion of its actually being past, or present : Soph. Phil. 1329 καὶ παῦλαν ἴσθι τῆσδε μήποτ᾽ ἐντυχεῖν νόσου βαρείας : Hdt. VII. 171 ἐπίστασθε ἡμέας ὁμολογήσειν τῷ Πέρσῃ : Thuc. VI. 59 αἰσθανόμενος (opinans) αὐτοὺς μέγα παρὰ βασιλεῖ Δαρείῳ δύνασθαι : Plat. Phæd. p. 235 C πλήρές πως, ὦ δαιμόνιε, τὸ στῆθος ἔχων αἰσθάνομαι (opinor) παρὰ ταῦτα ἂν ἔχειν εἰπεῖν ἕτερα μὴ χείρω.

§. 684. II. The verbs which imply or produce perception of the mind or senses also have the participle in this construction; as, before any perception can be roused, the object which is perceived must exist ; as, δεικνύναι, δηλοῦν, δῆλον ποιεῖν, φαίνειν, to shew; φαίνεσθαι, to appear, *apparere*; ἐοικέναι, to appear—to resemble—be like; ὅμοιον εἶναι, ὁμολογεῖν, δῆλον and φανερὸν εἶναι, and sometimes ἀγγέλλειν; ἐλέγχειν, ἐξελέγχειν, to prove; ἁλίσκεσθαι, to be convicted; ποιεῖν, to represent; εὑρίσκειν, to find; εὑρίσκεσθαι, be found, &c. : Hdt. VII. 18 Ἀρτάβανος, ὃς πρότερον ἀποσπεύδων μοῦνος ἐφαίνετο, τότε ἐπισπεύδων φανερὸς ἦν : Id. VI. 21 Ἀθηναῖοι — δῆλον ἐποίησαν ὑπεραχθεσθέντες τῇ Μιλήτου ἁλώσει : Thuc. III. 84 ἡ ἀνθρωπεία φύσις — ἀσμένη ἐδήλωσεν ἀκρατὴς μὲν ὀργῆς οὖσα, κρείσσων δὲ τοῦ δικαίου, πολεμία δὲ τοῦ προὔχοντος : Eur. Med. 84 κακὸς ὢν ἐς φίλους ἁλίσκεται : Isocr. p. 190 D τοῖς ποιηταῖς — τοὺς θεοὺς οἴόντ᾽ ἐστὶ ποιῆσαι καὶ διαλεγομένους καὶ συναγωνιζομένους, οἷς ἂν βουληθῶσιν : Plat. Criton. p. 50 A ἐμμένομεν οἷς ὡμολογήσαμεν δικαίοις οὖσιν : Demosth. p. 846, 5 ἐπιδείξω δὲ τοῦτον οὐ μόνον ὡμολογηκότα εἶναι τὸν Μιλύαν ἐλεύθερον, ἀλλὰ καὶ φανερὸν τοῦτ᾽ ἔργῳ πεποιηκότα, καὶ πρὸς τούτοις

ἐκ βασάνου περὶ αὐτῶν πεφευγότα τοῦτον τοὺς ἀκριβεστάτους
ἐλέγχους, καὶ οὐκ ἐθελήσαντ' ἐκ τούτων ἐπιδεῖξαι τὴν ἀλήθειαν,
ἀλλ' ἀεὶ πανουργοῦντα καὶ μάρτυρας ψευδεῖς παρεχόμενον
καὶ διακλέπτοντα τοῖς αὐτοῦ λόγοις τὴν ἀλήθειαν τῶν πεπραγμένων : Id. p. 818, 16 φανήσεται — ταῦθ' ὡμολογηκώς : Ibid. p. 819,
20 ῥᾳδίως ἐλεγχθήσεται ψευδόμενος.

Obs. 1. Instead of the impersonal forms, δῆλόν ἐστι, φανερόν ἐστι, φαίνεται, *apparet*, the Greeks used the personal ; as, δῆλός εἰμι, φανερός εἰμι,
φαίνομαι, τὴν πατρίδα εὖ ποιήσας : and the part. is constructed with the
subject thus created : Soph. Aj. 326 δῆλός ἐστιν ὥς τι δρασείων κακόν :
Hdt. III. 26 ἀπικόμενοι μὲν φανεροί εἰσι ἐς Ὄασιν πόλιν : Xen. Anab. II. 6,
23 στέργων δὲ φανερὸς μὲν ἦν οὐδένα, ὅτῳ δὲ φαίη φίλος εἶναι, τούτῳ ἔνδηλος
ἐγίγνετο ἐπιβουλεύων : Plat. Apol. p. 23 D κατάδηλοι γίγνονται προσποιούμενοι
μὲν εἰδέναι, εἰδότες δὲ οὐδέν.

Obs. 2. Many of these verbs in a different signification take the infin. :
a. Δεικνύναι, to teach ; what is learnt being consequent on teaching :
Eur. Androm. 707 δείξω δ' ἐγώ σοι μὴ τὸν Ἰδαῖον Πάριν μείζω νομίζειν Πηλέως
ἐχθρόν ποτε : Ibid. 1002 ὁ μητροφόντης — δείξει γαμεῖν σφε μηδέν' ὧν ἐχρῆν ἐμέ.
So when the object is represented not as something actually perceived
as in existence, but only supposed as possible : Xen. M. S. II. 3, 17 τί
γὰρ ἄλλο, ἔφη ὁ Σωκράτης, ἢ κινδυνεύσεις ἐπιδεῖξαι σὺ μὲν χρηστός τε καὶ φιλάδελφος εἶναι, ἐκεῖνος δὲ φαῦλός τε καὶ οὐκ ἄξιος εὐεργεσίας ; Ἀλλ' οὐδὲν οἶμαι
τούτων ἔσεσθαι.

b. Ἀγγέλλειν. Demosth. p. 29, 4 ἀπηγγέλθη τεθνεώς ; but Xen. Cyr.
I. 5, 30 ὁ Ἀσσύριος εἰς τὴν χώραν ἐμβάλλειν ἀγγέλλεται (it is not expressed
whether he has really entered the country). And other verbs of this class,
which are generally constructed with infin., sometimes take the part. ; as,
λέγω, φράζω, ἐννέπειν Trag., λέγεσθαι Plat. Phileb. p. 22 E : μαρ-
τυρέω Soph. Ant. 995 : ὁμολογεῖσθαι Isocr. Paneg. p. 47 B : ἀναίνομαι Trag.

c. Φαίνεσθαι, to seem, has the infin. ; *apparere*, to shew oneself, the
part. : Hdt. III. 53 κατεφαίνετο εἶναι νωθέστερος, he seemed to be : but ἐφαίνετο ἀνὴρ ἀγαθὸς ὤν, he shewed himself a brave man ; because the seeming
does not imply the reality of the fact : Plat. Criton. p. 52 E μηδὲ δίκαιαι
ἐφαίνοντό σοι αἱ ὁμολογίαι εἶναι.

d. Ποιεῖν, *facere, efficere*, takes infin., as ποιῶ σε γελᾶν,
efficio ut : signifying *to represent*, the part. See examples given above.

§. 685. III.

Verbs of mental feelings and affections (as that
action which caused the feeling must have existed before it or
coincidently with it) ; as, χαίρειν, ἥδεσθαι, γηθεῖν ; ἀγαπᾶν, to be
content ; ἄχθεσθαι, ἀγανακτεῖν, ἀσχαλᾶν ; αἰδεῖσθαι, αἰσχύνεσθαι ;
μεταμελεῖν ; ῥᾳδίως φέρειν &c. : Il. ν, 352 ἤχθετο — δαμναμέ-
νους (τοὺς Ἀχαιούς) : Hdt. IX. 98 ἤχθοντο ἐκπεφευγότων :
Id. VII. 54 μετεμέλησέ οἱ τὸν Ἑλλήσποντον μαστιγώσαντι :
Thuc. V. 35 τοὺς δ' ἐκ τῆς νήσου δεσμώτας μετεμέλοντο ἀποδεδω-
κότες : Eur. Med. 244 ἀνὴρ δ' ὅταν τοῖς ἔνδον ἄχθηται ξυνών,
ἔξω μολὼν ἔπαυσε καρδίαν ἄσης : Id. Hipp. 8 τιμώμενοι χαίρουσιν (οἱ θεοὶ) ἀνθρώπων ὕπο : Plat. Rep. p. 328 E χαίρω γε
διαλεγόμενος τοῖς σφόδρα πρεσβύταις. — χαίρω σοι ἐλθόντι.

But often with acc. (see §. 549. c.). Soph. Aj. 136 σὲ μὲν εὖ πράσσοντ' ἐπιχαίρω: Id. Phil. 1314 ἥσθην σε εὐλογοῦντι πατέρα τὸν ἐμόν: Plat. Rep. p. 475 B ὑπὸ σμικροτέρων καὶ φαυλοτέρων τιμώμενοι ἀγαπῶσιν: Id. Phæd. p. 62 E τοὺς μὲν φρονίμους ἀγανακτεῖν ἀποθνήσκοντας πρέπει, τοὺς δὲ ἄφρονας χαίρειν.

Obs. When the object expresses the consequent effect of these feelings, the infin. is used. Αἰσχύνεσθαι and αἰδεῖσθαι take the infin. when the feelings prevent the person from acting, the part. when the person has done something which causes them : Xen. Cyr. V. 1, 20 καὶ τοῦτο μὲν (sc. ἀποδιδόναι χάριν μήπω με δύνασθαι) οὐκ αἰσχύνομαι λέγων· τὸ δέ· Ἐὰν μένητε παρ' ἐμοί, ἀποδώσω, τοῦτο, εὖ ἴστε, αἰσχυνοίμην ἂν εἰπεῖν: Plat. Apol. p. 22 B αἰσχύνομαι οὖν ὑμῖν εἰπεῖν — τἀληθῆ : Eur. Hec. 967 αἰσχύνομαί σε προσβλέπειν ἐναντίον, shame prevents me : Xen. de Rep. Lac. I. 5 ἔθηκε γὰρ (Λυκοῦργος) αἰδεῖσθαι μὲν εἰσιόντα ὀφθῆναι, αἰδεῖσθαι δ' ἐξιόντα. But Soph. Aj. 506 αἴδεσαι μὲν πατέρα τὸν σὸν ἐν λυγρῷ γήρᾳ προλείπων.

§.686. IV. The verbs of *satisfying oneself, enjoying the possession of, being full of any thing* (as that which satisfies, is possessed, or which fills, must have existed antecedently to these states) ; as, τέρπεσθαι, ἐμπίπλασθαι, μεστὸν εἶναι &c.: Od. a, 369 νῦν μὲν δαινύμενοι τερπώμεθα: Il. ω, 633 ἐπεὶ τάρπησαν ἐς ἀλλήλους ὁρόωντες: Soph. Œ. C. 768 μεστὸς ἦν θυμούμενος : Eur. Ion. 943 οὔ τοι σὸν βλέπων ἐμπίπλαμαι πρόσωπον : Hdt. VII. 146 ἐπεὰν ταῦτα θηεύμενοι ἔωσι πληρέες.

§. 687. V. The verbs of *permitting, allowing to happen, tolerating, persevering, continuing,* &c.; and the contrary, *being weary of* ; as, περιορᾶν (poet., ἰδεῖν), κατιδεῖν, εἰσιδεῖν, οὐ φροντίζειν, ἐπιτρέπειν, (seldom); ἀνέχεσθαι, καρτερεῖν, ὑπομένειν (seldom) ; τλῆναι and τολμᾶν (both seldom, usually with infin.) ; λιπαρεῖν, *perseverare*, κάμνειν ; διατελεῖν, διαγίγνεσθαι, διάγειν: Od. ω, 162 ἐτόλμα ἐνὶ μεγάροισιν ἐοῦσιν βαλλόμενος καὶ ἐνισσόμενος τετληότι θυμῷ, like Eur. Hipp. 476 τόλμα δ' ἐρῶσα: Hdt. VII. 101 εἰ Ἕλληνες ὑπομενέουσι χεῖρας ἐμοὶ ἀνταειρόμενοι: Id. IX. 45 λιπαρέετε μένοντες: Id. III. 65 (ὑμῖν ἐπισκήπτω) μὴ περιιδεῖν τὴν ἡγεμονίην αὖτις ἐς Μήδους περιελθοῦσαν: Isocr. p. 268 E ἡ πόλις αὐτοῖς οὐκ ἐπιτρέψει παραβαίνουσι τὸν νόμον, permit them to overstep: Xen. Cyr. V. 1, 26 ὁρῶντές σε ἀνεξόμεθα καὶ καρτερήσομεν ὑπὸ σοῦ εὐεργετούμενοι: Eur. Or. 736 μή μ' ἰδεῖν θανόνθ' ὑπ' ἀστῶν: Id. Hec. 256 τοὺς φίλους βλάπτοντες οὐ φροντίζετε: Id. Hipp. 354 οὐκ ἀνέξομαι ζῶσα: Id. Med. 74 Ἰάσων παῖδας ἐξανέξεται πάσχοντας. Also with the gen.: Plat. Apol. p. 31 B ἀνέχεσθαι τῶν οἰκείων ἀμελουμένων. (See §. 504.): Demosth. p. 112, ὁ ἀνέχεσθαί τινων ἐν ταῖς ἐκκλησίαις λεγόντων πολλάκις, ὡς κ. τ. λ.: Id. p. 118, 29 μείζω γιγνόμενον τὸν ἄνθρωπον περιορῶμεν.

Obs. The verbs ἀνέχεσθαι, ὑπομένειν, τλῆναι, τολμᾶν, in the
sense of to dare (*audere*), have the infin.: Hdt. VII. 139 extr. καταμεί-
ναντες ἀνέσχοντο τὸν ἐπιόντα ἐπὶ τὴν χώρην δέξασθαι. — Ἐπιτρέπειν, usually the infin. So περιορᾶν, when the notion is not of permitting something already existing, but something which may exist hereafter. So often Hdt., and Thuc.: Hdt. VII. 16, 1 πνεύματα ἀνέμων ἐμπί-
πτοντα οὐ περιορᾶν τὴν θάλασσαν φύσει τῇ ἑωυτῆς χρῆσθαι: Thuc. II.
20 τοὺς Ἀθηναίους ἤλπιζεν τὴν γῆν οὐκ ἂν περιιδεῖν τμηθῆναι —Ἀποκάμνειν
in the sense of to cease to strive after something, infin.: Plat. Crit.
p. 45 μήτε—ἀποκάμῃς σαυτὸν σῶσαι.

§. 688. VI. Verbs of *beginning*, and *ceasing, making to cease*, &c. ;
(as the beginning is coincident with the action begun, ceasing is consequent on that from which one ceases;) as, ἄρχεσθαι, ὑπάρχειν ;
παύειν, παύεσθαι, λήγειν, διαλλάττειν, ἀπαλλάττεσθαι ; *of relaxing in
any thing*, as μεθίεσθαι, μεθιέναι poet., λείπεσθαι, ἐκλείπειν, ἐπιλείπειν: Il. ω, 48 κλαύσας μεθῆκε, having wept he left off (weeping)
= he ceased to weep: Hdt. VI. 75 Κλεομένης δὲ παραλαβὼν τὸν
σίδηρον, ἄρχετο ἐκ τῶν κνημέων ἑωυτὸν λωβώμενος: Eur.
Hipp. 701 παῦσαι λέγουσα. — Παύω σε ἀδικοῦντα. — Παύομαί σε
ἀδικῶν: Xen. Œc. I. 23 (αἱ ἐπιθυμίαι) αἰκιζόμεναι τὰ σώματα
τῶν ἀνθρώπων καὶ τὰς ψυχὰς καὶ τοὺς οἴκους οὔποτε λήγουσιν,
ἔστ᾽ ἂν ἄρχωσιν αὐτῶν. —Ἐλλείπεται εὖ ποιῶν τοὺς εὐεργετοῦντας
ἑαυτόν Id.: Plat. Phæd. p. 60 C ὁ θεὸς βουλόμενος αὐτὰ (τὸ ἡδὺ καὶ
τὸ λυπηρὸν) διαλλάξαι πολεμοῦντα, ἐπειδὴ οὐκ ἠδύνατο, ξυνῆψεν
εἰς ταὐτὸν αὐτοῖς τὰς κορυφάς: Id. Symp. p. 186 B ἄρξομαι δὲ ἀπὸ
τῆς ἰατρικῆς λέγων.

Obs. Ἄρχεσθαι is used with infin. when the notion of the dependent
verb is only in intention, not in act; as, Thuc. I. 107 ἤρξαντο καὶ τὰ μακρὰ
τείχη Ἀθηναῖοι οἰκοδομεῖν: οἰκοδομοῦντες, when it is actually begun. Παύειν
is also sometimes joined with the infin. when the ceasing from the action,
is to be represented as the effect of the active verb: Il. λ, 442 ἔμ᾽ ἔπαυσας
ἐπὶ Τρώεσσι μάχεσθαι, *effecisti, ut ego pugnare desinerem.* So Hdt. V. 67.
VII. 54.   Plat. Rep. p. 416 C ἥτις (οὐσία) μήτε τοὺς φύλακας ὡς ἀρίστους
εἶναι παύσοι, *quæ neque custodes impediat, quominus quam optimi sint.*

§. 689. VII. Verbs of *being in luck*, or *success, distinguishing
oneself, doing well, being deficient, being in error*, take a participle
of the notion which preceeds any of these states ; as, εὐτυχεῖν, εὖ
ποιεῖν, ἁμαρτάνειν, ἀδικεῖν &c., so καταπροΐξεσθαι, *impune facturum
esse*: Eur. Or. 1218 εἴπερ εὐτυχήσομεν ἑλόντες, if we shall be suc-
cessful enough to take it—if having taken it, we shall be: Hdt. V.
24 εὖ ἐποίησας ἀφικόμενος: Id. VII. 17 οὔτε—νῦν καταπροΐξεαι
ἀποτρέπων τὸ χρεὸν γενέσθαι, *nec impune feres, qui infecta red-
dere studeas, quæ fieri oportet*: Thuc. I. 53 ἀδικεῖτε — πολέμου ἄρχοντες καὶ σπονδὰς λύοντες.—Ἁμαρτάνει ταῦτα ποιῶν: Plat. Phæd.
p. 60 C εὖ γ᾽ ἐποίησας ἀναμνήσας με: Id. Euthyd. p. 282 C καὶ εὖ
ἐποίησας ἀπαλλάξας με σκέψεως πολλῆς: Xen. Cyr. I. 4, 13 καλῶς

ἐποίησας προειπών: Aristoph. Eccles. 1045 κεχάρισαί γε μοι, ὦ γλυκύτατον, τὴν γραῦν ἀπαλλάξασά μου.

§.690. VIII. Πειρᾶσθαι, very frequently in Hdt. (as the notion of attempting any action generally may be taken to imply that this action is begun, "doing it he tried it," or "he tried to do it"): and also sometimes in Attic, and the Ionic phrases, πολλός ἐστι, παντοῖός ἐστι, e. g. ποιῶν τι, which imply the notion of endeavouring: so παρασκευάζεσθαι, but generally with ὡς and fut. part.: Hdt. VII. 158 ὁ Γέλων πολλὸς ἐνέκειτο λέγων: Id. IX. 90 πολλὸς ἦν λισσόμενος ὁ ξεῖνος: Id. I. 98 ὁ Δηιόκης ἦν πολλὸς ὑπὸ παντὸς ἀνδρὸς καὶ προβαλλόμενος καὶ αἰνεόμενος: Id. IX. 109 παντοῖος ἐγένετο οὐ βουλόμενος δοῦναι, *nihil non tentavit, quo efficeret, ut non daret:* Id. VII. 10, 3 παντοῖοι ἐγένοντο Σκύθαι δεόμενοι Ἰώνων λῦσαι τὸν πόρον. (So after this analogy: Plat. Euth. p. 8 C πάντα ποιοῦσι καὶ λέγουσι φεύγοντες τὴν δίκην:) Hdt. VII. 9, 1 ἐπειρήθην—ἐπελαύνων ἐπὶ τοὺς ἄνδρας τούτους: Ibid. 139 οὐδαμοὶ ἂν ἐπειρῶντο ἀντιεύμενοι βασιλέι: cf. Id. VI. 5, 9.—Thuc. II. 7 οἱ Ἀθηναῖοι παρεσκευάζοντο ὡς πολεμήσοντες. So ἐπείγεσθαι is, in Hdt., joined with part.; as, VIII. 68, 2 ἢν μὲν μὴ ἐπειχθῆς ναυμαχίην ποιεύμενος.

Obs. 1. The infin. is also used with παντοῖος ἐγένετο in Hdt., as III. 124 παντοίη ἐγένετο μὴ ἀποδημῆσαι τὸν Πολυκράτεα. Πειρᾶσθαι and παρασκευάζεσθαι take the infin. usually, when the part of the action yet remaining to be done, or its completion, is more especially considered; so also ἐπείγεσθαι, Hdt. VIII. 68, 3 ἢν δὲ αὐτίκα ἐπειχθῆς ναυμαχῆσαι, though shortly before the part. occurs with this verb.

Obs. 2. In παρασκευάζεσθαι with ὡς and fut. part., the fut. expresses the intention, which exists before the verb, and gives rise to its action; that the action itself of the part. does not yet exist is marked by ὡς. So we must look at ἔρχομαι, ἥκω φράσων; as, Hdt. III. 6 τοῦτο ἔρχομαι φράσων, with the intention of saying I am present here: Id. VI. 70 ἐς Δελφοὺς χρησόμενος τῷ χρηστηρίῳ πορεύεται: Xen. M. S. III. 7, 5 σέ γε διδάξων ὥρμημαι. So generally when the fut. part. is joined with the verb, it expresses an intention: Hdt. III. 36 ἐλάμβανε τὸ τόξον ὡς κατατοξεύσων αὐτόν. So πέμπω σε λέξοντα. The pres. part. is joined with verbs of "going," when the subject of the verb is supposed to continue a state of real or metaphorical motion already begun: Hdt. I. 122 ἤιε ταύτην (τὴν γυναῖκα) αἰνέων διὰ παντός, he proceeded to praise.

§. 691. IX. Certain expressions (mostly impersonal); *it is fitting, useful, profitable, good, agreeable, shameful, to my mind,* &c.; but they have the infin. as frequently, and even more so than the participle, the notion of the dependent verb being conceived to follow from the notion of the governing verb, not to have preceded it as already attached to the subject; Πρέπει μοι ἀγαθῷ ὄντι, to me who am good it suits well; and ἀγαθῷ εἶναι, it suits

well that I should be good: Xen. Œc. IV. 1 αἲ δοκοῦσι κάλλισται
τῶν ἐπιστημῶν καὶ ἐμοὶ πρέποι ἂν μάλιστα ἐπιμελομένῳ sc.
αὐτῶν: Plat. Phæd. p. 114 D τοῦτο καὶ πρέπειν μοι δοκεῖ—
οἰομένῳ οὕτως ἔχειν[a]. (So perhaps we may explain Od. ζ, 193
οὔτ᾽ οὖν ἐσθῆτος δευήσεαι, οὔτε τευ ἄλλου, ὧν ἐπέοιχ᾽ ἱκέτην ταλα-
πείριον ἀντιάσαντα.) So φίλον ἐστίν: Æsch. Ag. 169 εἰ
τόδ᾽ αὐτῷ φίλον κεκλημένῳ.—Λυσιτελεῖ: Lysias p. 174,
14 οἷς οὐδὲ ἅπαξ ἐλυσιτέλησε πειθομένοις: Soph. Œ. R.
316 φρονεῖν ὡς δεινὸν, ἔνθα μὴ τέλη λύει φρονοῦντι.—Ἀμεινόν ἐστιν &c.: Thuc. I. 118 ἐπηρώτων τὸν θεὸν, εἰ (sc. αὐτοῖς)
πολεμοῦσιν ἄμεινον ἔσται: Plat. Apol. p. 41 B ἀντι-
παραβάλλοντι (sc. μοί, *conferenti*) τὰ ἐμαυτοῦ πάθη πρὸς τὰ
ἐκείνων οὐκ ἂν ἀηδὲς εἴη: Id. Rep. p. 458 B (ταῦτα) ξυμφο-
ρώτατ᾽ ἂν εἴη πραχθέντα τῇ τε πόλει καὶ τοῖς φύλαξι (and ξυμφο-
ρώτατ᾽ ἂν εἴη ταῦτα πραχθῆναι): Id. Phil. p. 42 D ἅπανθ᾽ ὁπόσα
τοιαῦτ᾽ ὀνόματ᾽ ἔχει ξυμβαίνει γιγνόμενα: Id. Alcib. p.
113 D σκοποῦσιν ὁποτέρα συνοίσει πράξασιν. So ἔστι, ὕπεστι, ξύνεστί μοι τι: Soph. Œ. C. 648 εἰ σοί γ᾽ ἅπερ φῂς ἐμμένει τελοῦντί μοι: Id. Œ. T. 296 ᾧ μή ᾽στι δρῶντι τάρβος,
οὐδ᾽ ἔπος φοβεῖ: Id. El. 480 ὕπεστί μοι θράσος ἀδυπνόων κλύουσαν ἀρτίως ὀνειράτων. Also Æsch. Choeph. 408 πέπαλται δ᾽
αὐτέ μοι φίλον κέαρ τόνδε κλύουσαν οἶκτον.

Obs. 1. On the accus. ἀντιάσαντα, κλύουσαν, for dat. see below, §. 711. 1.

Obs. 2. When the part. is applied generally, not to any definite subject,
the article may be joined with it: Plat. Legg. p. 656 A μῶν οὖν τι βλαβὴν
ἔσθ᾽ ἥντινα φέρει τῷ χαίροντι πονηρίας ἢ σχήμασιν ἢ μέλεσιν: that any
one should rejoice, &c.

§. 692. X. Ἔχειν, in the sense of *to be, to hold oneself,* forms
when joined with a participle agreeing with the subject, an apparent
periphrasis for the simple verb, as it cannot be said to supply any
definite form thereof, but expresses the continuance of the action
when already begun, (as in Latin *habere* with a passive part. in
acc.; as, *rem aliquam pertractatam habere*): Soph. Antig. 22 τὸν
μὲν προτίσας, τὸν δ᾽ ἀτιμάσας ἔχει: Eur. Med. 33 ἀφίκετο
μετ᾽ ἀνδρὸς, ὅς σφε (i. e. αὐτήν) νῦν ἀτιμάσας ἔχει: Id. Bacch.
302 Ἄρεως τε μοῖραν μεταλαβὼν ἔχει τινά: Id. Hecub. 1013
πέπλων ἐντὸς ἢ κρύψασ᾽ ἔχεις; Id. Med. 90 σὺ δ᾽ ὡς μάλιστα
τούσδ᾽ ἐρημώσας ἔχε: Hdt. III. 65 δόλῳ ἔχουσι αὐτὴν (τὴν
ἡγεμονίην) κτησάμενοι: Id. VI. 12 ἀνδρὶ Φωκαέϊ ἀλαζόνι-ἐπι-
τρέψαντες ἡμέας αὐτοὺς ἔχομεν[b]: Demosth. p. 818. extr. τὴν μὲν
τοίνυν προῖκα — ἔχει λαβών: Id. p. 113, 12 καὶ μὴν καὶ Φερὰς πρῴην
ὡς φίλος—εἰς Θετταλίαν ἐλθὼν ἔχει καταλαβών.

[a] Cf. Heindorf.   [b] Valckenar. ad loc.

Obs. On the contrary : ἔχω λέγειν, I can say, *habeo dicere.*

§. 693. XI. Another sense in which the participle may be said to complete a verbal notion is, where it explains and defines a demonstrative, which is joined to a preceding verb: Plat. Phæd. p. 59 A καὶ πάντες οἱ παρόντες σχεδόν τι οὕτω διεκείμεθα, ὁτὲ μὲν γελῶντες, ἐνίοτε δὲ δακρύοντες: Xen. Anab. IV. 1, 4 τὴν δὲ — ἐμβολὴν ὧδε ποιοῦνται, ἅμα μὲν λαθεῖν πειρώμενοι, ἅμά δὲ φθάσαι. So Soph. Œ. T. 10 τίνι τρόπῳ καθέστατε ; δείσαντες ἢ στέρξαντες.

§. 694. XII. Lastly, the part. stands with τυγχάνω, *I happen*; κυρῶ, *I am there, I chance*; λανθάνω, *I escape notice*; (the thing which is not observed being antecedent or coincident with the escaping observation ;) φθάνω, *I anticipate*; οἴχομαι, *I hasten away*, and expresses the notions to which these several actions refer: Hdt. I. 44 ὁ Κροῖσος φονέα τοῦ παιδὸς ἐλάνθανε βόσκων: Id. III. 83 καὶ νῦν αὕτη ἡ οἰκίη διατελέει μούνη ἐλευθέρη ἐοῦσα Περσέων. — Διάγω, διατελῶ, διαγίγνομαι, δίειμι καλὰ ποιῶν: Id. I. 157 ᾤχετο φεύγων (*celeriter fugiebat*). (So Hom. : βῆ φεύγων, βῆ ἀΐξασα:) Id. VI. 138 οἴχοντο ἀποπλέοντες. — Οἴχομαι φέρων, *celeriter aufero*: Thuc. IV. 113 ἔτυχον ὁπλῖται ἐν τῇ ἀγορᾷ καθεύδοντες ὡς πεντήκοντα (there chanced to be sleeping): Plat. Rep. p. 412 κήδοιτο δέ γ' ἄν τις μάλιστα, ὃ τυγχάνοι φιλῶν: Eur. Alc. 957 ὅστις ἐχθρὸς ὢν κυρεῖ: Xen. Cyr. I. 3, 12 χαλεπὸν ἦν ἄλλον φθάσαι τοῦτο ποιήσαντα. — So οὐκ ἂν φθάνοις λέγων ; Plat. Symp. p. 185. extr. *quin statim loqueris*, i. e. will you not be quick in saying this ? *quantocius dicas*: Id. Phæd. p. 106 B οὐκ ἂν φθάνοις περαίνων; i. e. *statim reliqua conclude.*

Obs. 1. With τυγχάνειν and κυρεῖν the part. ὤν is sometimes omitted; as, Soph. El. 46 ὁ γὰρ μέγιστος αὐτοῖς τυγχάνει δορυξένων. Sometimes where there is no adj.: Ibid. 313 νῦν δ' ἀγροῖσι τυγχάνει : Eur. Hipp. 1411 ὃς ἂν μάλιστα φίλτατος κυρῇ βροτῶν: Plat. Rep. p. 369 B τυγχάνει ἡμῶν ἕκαστος οὐκ αὐτάρκης, ἀλλὰ πολλῶν ἐνδεής[a]: Id. Apol. Socr. p. 38. princ., and Gorg. p. 502 B εἰ δέ τι τυγχάνει ἀηδές. Sometimes also after διατελεῖν: Thuc. I. 34 ἀσφαλέστατος ἂν διατελοίη: Xen. Hell. VII. 3, 1 ἄλυποι διετέλεσαν.

Obs. 2. Φθάνειν, *antevertere*, often has an acc. of the person anticipated or present: Hdt. VI. 115 βουλόμενοι φθῆναι τοὺς Ἀθηναίους ἀπικόμενοι ἐς τὸ ἄστυ. The comparison implied therein is sometimes expressed by ἤ : Od. λ, 58 ἔφθης πεζὸς ἰὼν ἢ ἐγὼ σὺν νηὶ μελαίνῃ ; So with ἤ and infin.: Hdt. VI. 108 φθαίη τε πολλάκις ἂν ἀνδραποδισθέντες ἤ τινα πυθέσθαι ἡμέων. Also πρὶν ἤ: Ibid. 116 ἔφθησάν τε ἀπικόμενοι πρὶν ἢ τοὺς βαρβάρους ἥκειν. Similarly to οὐκ ἂν φθάνοις λέγων; we find οὐκ ἂν φθάνοις without a question, "You cannot be too quick in saying it," where

a Stallb. ad loc.

φθάνειν signifies *nimis cito aliquid facere, nimis properare*: Hdt. VII. 162 οὐκ ἂν φθάνοιτε τὴν ταχίστην ὀπίσω ἀπαλλασσόμενοι, si quam primum abieritis, non nimis cito abieritis, non nimis properaveritis, i. e. *nullá interpositá morá, e vestigio hinc abire maturate!* Οὐ φθάνειν followed by καί, καὶ εὐθύς, may be translated by, *scarcely—not so soon as*: Isocr. p. 58 B οἱ Λακεδαιμόνιοι οὐκ ἔφθησαν πυθόμενοι τὸν περὶ τὴν Ἀττικὴν πόλεμον, καὶ πάντων τῶν ἄλλων ἀμελήσαντες ἧκον ἡμῖν ἀμυνοῦντες.

Obs. 3. The construction of λανθάνειν and φθάνειν is sometimes reversed, so that they are placed in the participle and seem to be accessories to the action of another verb: Il. μ, 390 ἂψ δ' ἀπὸ τείχεος ἆλτο λαθών: Hdt. III. 71 οὐκ ἄλλος φθὰς ἐμεῦ κατήγορος ἔσται, ἀλλά σφεας αὐτὸς ἐγὼ κατερέω. So in Homer φθάμενος, as ὅς μ' ἔβαλε φθάμενος[a]: Xen. Cyr. III. 3, 18 φθάνοντες ἤδη δῃοῦμεν τὴν ἐκείνων γῆν.

Obs. 4. Φθάνειν is but rarely joined with infin.: Arist. Nub. 1384 οὐκ ἔφθης φράσαι. It is wrong to class here Il. π, 860 τίς δ' οἶδ' εἴ κ' Ἀχιλεὺς—φθήῃ ἐμῷ ὑπὸ δουρὶ τυπεὶς ἀπὸ θυμὸν ὀλέσσαι; here ὀλέσσαι θυμὸν is the consequence of τυπείς, and does not depend on φθήῃ.

The Participle used as the Latin Gerund.

§. 695. 1. From the use of the participle just gone through, whereby some essential part of the whole verbal action is supplied, we must distinguish the same form when used to express certain accidents of the verbal action, such as are expressed by adverbs; which though not necessary to a full conception thereof, yet add distinctness to the notion of it, by stating the circumstances, conditions, &c. under which it took place, or by which it was accompanied. When thus used the participle is called, for the sake of distinction, the *gerund*, as it answers to that form in another language: ὁ ἀνθῶν κῆπος—ὁρῶ σε τρέχοντα, οἶδα θνητὸς ὤν.

2. Of the gerundial use of the part., there are two sorts—*a.* Where the part. has the same subject as the verb of the sentence, in which case it agrees with it in gender, number, and case; as, ὁ Κῦρος γελῶν εἶπε, οἱ παῖδες γελῶντες εἶπον.—*b.* Where the subject of the participle is not the same as that of the verb, in which case the partic. and its subject are in the gen.; as, τοῦ παιδὸς γελῶντος, ὁ Κῦρος εἶπεν, which construction is termed *Casus absoluti*.

Obs. For the reason why the gen. is used, see §. 541.

3. The adverbial notions which are expressed by the partic. are,

a. Temporal.

b. Causal, including the notion of the conditions under which any thing happened.

c. Modal.

[a] Passow Lex.

a. Temporal.

§. 696. The participle is used to express the time which is defined by some action or state: Xen. M. S. I. 2, 22 πολλοὶ τὰ χρήματα ἀναλώσαντες, ὧν πρόσθεν ἀπείχοντο κερδῶν, αἰσχρὰ νομίζοντες εἶναι, τούτων οὐκ ἀπέχονται, after spending; so we frequently find a periphrasis with ποιήσας,=*thereon* : Hdt. VI. 96 ἐνέπρησαν καὶ τὰ ἱρὰ καὶ τὴν πόλιν· ταῦτα δὲ ποιήσαντες ἐπὶ τὰς ἄλλας νήσους ἀνάγοντο, or a repetition of the preceding verb, in the participle, without ταῦτα: Ibid. 108 Ἀθηναίοισι—ἐπεθήκαντο Βοιωτοί· ἐπιθέμενοι δὲ ἐσσώθησαν τῇ μάχῃ : Id. VII. 60 πάντας τούτῳ τῷ τρόπῳ ἐξηρίθμησαν· ἀριθμήσαντες δὲ κατὰ ἔθνεα διέτασσον. Gen. absol. : Il. a, 88 οὔτις ἐμεῦ ζῶντος καὶ ἐπὶ χθονὶ δερκομένοιο σοὶ κοίλῃς παρὰ νηυσὶ βαρείας χεῖρας ἐποίσει.

Obs. 1. Here also belong the following participles, which we translate by adverbs, or adverbial expressions ; a. ἀρχόμενος, at the beginning, at first: Thuc. IV. 64 ἅπερ καὶ ἀρχόμενος εἶπον. We must distinguish this from ἀρξάμενος ἀπό τινος, which may be translated "especially." This participle ἀρξάμενος generally agrees in gender, case, and number, with the substantive, of which it defines and limits the sense; as, Plat. Rep. p. 600. extr. οὐκοῦν τίθωμεν ἀπὸ Ὁμήρου ἀρξαμένους πάντας τοὺς ποιητικοὺς μιμητὰς εἰδώλων ἀρετῆς εἶναι, all the poets, (subst. defined) especially Homer; but sometimes with the subject of the verb : Plat. Symp. p. 173 D δοκεῖς μοι ἀτεχνῶς πάντας ἀνθρώπους ἀθλίους ἡγεῖσθαι πλὴν Σωκράτους, ἀπὸ σοῦ ἀρξάμενος: Cf. Xen. Cyr. VII. 5, 65 :—β. τελευτῶν, at last, finally ; Plat. Rep. p. 362 A τελευτῶν πάντα κακὰ παθὼν ἀνασκινδυλευθήσεται [a] : Id. Apol. p. 22 C τελευτῶν (at last) οὖν ἐπὶ τοὺς χειροτέχνας ᾖα : Demosth. p. 125, 57 δυστυχεῖς Ἐρετριεῖς τελευτῶντες ἐπείθησαν τοὺς ὑπὲρ αὐτῶν λέγοντας ἐκβαλεῖν.—γ. διαλιπὼν χρόνον, after some time, or διαλ. πολὺν, ὀλίγον χρ., ἐπισχὼν πολὺν χρόνον, μικρόν: Plat. Phaedon. extr. ὀλίγον χρόνον διαλιπὼν ἐκινήθη: Id. p. 59 E οὐ πολὺν δ᾽ οὖν χρόνον ἐπισχὼν ἧκε [b] : Cf. Hdt. VI. 129.—δ. ἀνύσας, immediately, quickly : Arist. Lys. 438 ἀνύσαντε δήσετον, *illico colligate.*

Obs. 2. We often find participles of "coming" and "going" joined with the verb, to put the whole action in a clear distinct light, most commonly in poetry, but also in prose, as Xen. Cyr. II. 2, 6 οὕτω καὶ ἐγὼ ἐλθὼν ἐδίδασκον ἕνα λόγον.

Obs. 3. The gen. part. sometimes stands alone, without its subject, which is either supplied from the context, or, when it is wholly indefinite, a demonstrative pronoun or the indefinite words πράγματα, χρήματα, ἄνθρωποι, &c. are without difficulty supplied by the mind : Il. o, 190 ἤτοι ἐγὼν ἔλαχον πολιὴν ἅλα ναιέμεν αἰεὶ παλλομένων, when they cast lots: Hdt. III. 13 οἱ δὲ Αἰγύπτιοι—ἔφευγον—· κατειληθέντων δὲ (sc. αὐτῶν) ἐς Μέμφιν ἔπεμπε—Καμβύσης (κήρυκα): Thuc. I. 116 Περικλῆς—ᾤχετο κατὰ τάχος ἐπὶ Καύνου καὶ Καρίας, ἐσαγγελθέντων, ὅτι Φοίνισσαι νῆες ἐπ᾽ αὐτοὺς πλέουσιν: Xen. Cyr. I. 4, 18 σημανθέντων δὲ τῷ Ἀστυάγει ὅτι πολέμιοί εἰσιν ἐν τῇ χώρᾳ, ἐξεβοήθει καὶ αὐτὸς πρὸς τὰ ὅρια: Ibid. III. 1, 38 διασκηνούν-

---

[a] Stallb. ad loc.   [b] Stallb. ad loc.

τ ω ν δὲ (sc. αὐτῶν) μετὰ τὸ δεῖπνον, ἐπήρετο ὁ Κῦρος : also in sing. Thuc. I. 74 σαφῶς δ η λ ω θ έ ν τ ο ς, ὅτι ἐν ταῖς ναυσὶ τῶν Ἑλλήνων τὰ πράγματα ἐγένετο : so οὕτως ἔχοντος Plat. *quum res ita se habeat* : so in Latin, *cognito, edicto, petito,* &c. for *postquam cognitum erat,* &c.

Obs. 4. To define more distinctly the notion of time, ἐπί is often joined with the gen. and the part. present (only) ἐπὶ Κύρου βασιλεύοντος (see §. 633. I.) : the notion of past time is sometimes expressed by μετά, with acc., as Hdt. VI. 98 μετὰ δὲ τοῦτον ἐνθεῦτεν ἐξαναχθέντα Δῆλος ἐκινήθη : Ibid. 132 μετὰ δὲ τὸ ἐν Μαραθῶνι τρῶμα γενόμενον Μιλτιάδης—αὔξετο : and of indefinite time, by ὑπό with acc., as ὑπὸ τὴν πρώτην ἐπελθοῦσαν νύκτα. (See §. 639. III. 2. *a.*)

Obs. 5. The time is also more accurately expressed by the addition of the temporal adverbs, α ὐ τ ί κ α, ε ὐ θ ύ ς (Ion. ἰθέως), ἐ ξ α ί φ ν η ς, μ ε τ α ξ ύ, ἅ μ α, to the genitive absolute, or the simple participle, as Hdt. I. 179 ὀ ρ ύ σ σ ο ν τ ε ς ἅμα τὴν τάφρον ἐπλίνθευον : Id. VI. 10 ταῦτα μέν νυν ἰ θ έ ω ς ἀ π ι κ ο μ έ ν ω ν ἐς τὴν Μίλητον τῶν Περσέων ἐγίνετο : Xen. Anab. III. 3, 7 φ ε ύ γ ο ν τ ε ς ἅμα ἐτίτρωσκον : Plat. Phædon. p. 60 B κ α ὶ τ ρ ί β ω ν ἅ μ α—ἔφη ª : Ibid. p. 77 B ὅπως μή, ἅμα ἀ π ο θ ν ή σ κ ο ν τ ο ς τοῦ ἀνθρώπου, διασκεδάννυται ἡ ψυχή : Ibid. p. 70 A ὅρα, μὴ ε ὐ θ ὺ ς ἀ π α λ λ α τ τ ο μ έ ν η (ἡ ψυχὴ) τοῦ σώματος—διασκεδασθεῖσα οἴχηται : Id. Rep. p. 238 C ε ὐ θ ὺ ς οὖν με ἰ δ ὼ ν ὁ Κέφαλος ἠσπάζετό τε καὶ εἶπεν, *sinul ut me conspexit* : Id. Lys. p. 207 A ὁ Μενέξενος ἐκ τῆς αὐλῆς μ ε τ α ξ ὺ π α ί ζ ω ν εἰσέρχεται, whilst he was playing : Id. Rep. p. 336 B καὶ ὁ Θρασύμαχος πολλάκις μὲν καὶ δ ι α λ ε γ ο μ έ ν ω ν ἡμῶν μ ε τ α ξ ὺ ὥρμα ἀντιλαμβάνεσθαι τοῦ λόγου. On ἅμα with dat., see §. 669. *Obs.* 2.

Obs. 6. To express more clearly and emphatically any sequence, whether of time, or otherwise, on the action of the partic., the adverbs ἐ ν τ α ῦ θ α, ο ὕ τ ω, ο ὕ τ ω δ ή, ὧ δ ε, are joined to the verb of the sentence, as Hdt. VI. 23 πειθομένων δὲ τῶν Σαμίων καὶ σχόντων τὴν Ζάγκλην, ἐ ν θ α ῦ τ α οἱ Ζαγκλαῖοι ἐβοήθεον (as Virgil. Æn. II. 391 *sic fatus, deinde comantem Androgei galeam clipeique insigne decorum induitur*) : Id. VI. 104 ἀποφυγὼν δὲ καὶ τούτους, στρατηγὸς ο ὕ τ ω᾽ Ἀθηναίων ἀπεδέχθη, *ita demum imperator creatus est* : Id. VII. 174 Θεσσαλοὶ δὲ ἐρημωθέντες συμμάχων ο ὕ τ ω δ ὴ ἐμήδισαν προθύμως.—In poetry the part. is often joined to the verb by καί : Il. χ, 247 ὡς φαμένη καὶ κερδοσύνῃ ἡγήσατ᾽ Ἀθήνη.

Obs. 7. We find a curious change of construction in the form ἅπερ ἔχων ἦλθε, *which he had when he came ;* the principal verb being in the partic., and the verb expressing the time being made the predicate of the sentence.

b. Causal.

§. 697. *a.* The cause or reason : Xen. M. S. I. 2, 22 πολλοὶ τὰ χρήματα ἀναλώσαντες, ὧν πρόσθεν ἀπείχοντο κερδῶν, αἰσχρὰ ν ο μ ί ζ ο ν τ ε ς εἶναι, τούτων οὐκ ἀπέχονται : Plat. Phædon. p. 102 D λέγω δὲ τοῦδ᾽ ἕνεκα β ο υ λ ό μ ε ν ο ς (i. e. ὅτι βούλομαι) δόξαι σοι ὅπερ ἐμοί. Very common in interrogatory and relative sentences : Plat. Phædon. p. 63 A τί γὰρ ἂν β ο υ λ ό μ ε ν ο ι (i. e. *cur*) ἄνδρες σοφοὶ ὡς ἀληθῶς δεσπότας ἀμείνους αὐτῶν φεύγοιεν ; For τί μαθών and τί παθὼν ταῦτα ἐποίησας ; *cur hæc fecisti?* see interrogatory sentences.

—Gen. abs. Thuc. VII. 13 τὰ δὲ πληρώματα δ ι ὰ τ ό δ ε ἐφθάρη τε ἡμῖν καὶ ἔτι νῦν φθείρεται, τ ῶ ν ν α υ τ ῶ ν τῶν μὲν διὰ φρυγανισμὸν καὶ ἁρπαγὴν μακρὰν καὶ ὑδρείαν ὑπὸ τῶν ἱππέων ἀ π ο λ λ υ μ έ ν ω ν, οἱ δὲ θεραπεύοντες—αὐτομολοῦσι.

Obs. Here also ο ὕ τ ω is sometimes added to the verb, to mark the sequence more distinctly : Plat. Lach. in. ὑμᾶς δὲ ἡμεῖς ἡγησάμενοι καὶ ἱκανοὺς γνῶναι, καὶ γνόντας ἁπλῶς ἂν εἰπεῖν ἃ δοκεῖ ὑμῖν, ο ὕ τ ω παρελάβομεν.

b. The conditions : Plat. Symp. p. 193 D οὗ δὴ τὸν αἴτιον θεὸν ὑ μ ν ο ῦ ν τ ε ς δικαίως ἂν ὑμνοῖμεν Ἔρωτα : Ibid. p. 194 C οὐ μέντ' ἂν καλῶς ποιοίην—, ὦ Ἀγάθων, περὶ σοῦ τι ἐγὼ ἀγροῖκον δ ο ξ ά ζ ω ν : Ibid. p. 196 C κ ρ α τ ῶ ν δὲ ἡδονῶν καὶ ἐπιθυμιῶν ὁ Ἔρως διαφερόντως ἂν σωφρονοῖ : Id. Phileb. p. 43 C αἱ μεταβολαὶ κάτω τε καὶ ἄνω γ ι γ ν ό μ ε ν α ι λύπας τε καὶ ἡδονὰς ἀπεργάζονται : Demosth. p. 122, 45 οὐ γὰρ ἂν αὐτοῖς ἔμελεν—, μὴ τοῦθ' ὑ π ο λ α μ β ά ν ο υ σ ι ν, i. e. εἰ μὴ τοῦθ' ὑπελάμβανον [a]. In questions : Plat. Gorg. p. 509 B τίνα ἂν βοήθειαν μὴ δ υ ν ά μ ε ν ο ς ἄνθρωπος βοηθεῖν ἑαυτῷ καταγέλαστος ἂν τῇ ἀληθείᾳ εἴη ;—G e n i t. a b s o l. Od. a, 390 καί κεν τοῦτ' ἐθέλοιμι, Δ ι ό ς γ ε δ ι δ ό ν τ ο ς, ἀρέσθαι (*Deo volente*) : Eur. Hipp. 1424 ἀνθρώποισι δὲ, θ ε ῶ ν δ ι δ ό ν τ ω ν (*si dii auctores sunt*), εἰκὸς ἐξαμαρτάνειν : Demosth. p. 130. extr. καὶ οἴομαι καὶ νῦν ἔτι ἐπανορθωθῆναι ἂν τὰ πράγματα, τ ο ύ τ ω ν γ ι γ ν ο μ έ ν ω ν.

c. Limitation, which is generally signified by the addition of the limiting particles κ α ί, κ α ί τ ο ι, π έ ρ (which in Homer are often strengthened by ἔ μ π η ς) κ α ί π ε ρ or κ α ί—π ε ρ, ὅ μ ω ς, ἔ π ε ι τ α, ε ῖ τ α poet., κ ᾆ τ α prose, also κ α ὶ τ α ῦ τ α to the participle. Without any particle : Xen. Cyr. III. 2, 15 ὡς ὀλίγα δ υ ν ά μ ε ν ο ι προορᾶν ἄνθρωποι περὶ τοῦ μέλλοντος πολλὰ ἐπιχειροῦμεν πράττειν !—With it, καί : Il. ε, 651 Ἕκτορα κ α ὶ μ ε μ α ῶ τ α μάχης σχήσεσθαι ὀίω : —π έ ρ : Il. a, 241 τοῖς δ' οὔτι δυνήσεαι, ἀ χ ν ύ μ ε ν ό ς π ε ρ, χραισμεῖν : with ἔ μ π η ς, Il. o, 399 : Il. π, 638 φράδμων π ε ρ ἀνήρ (sc. ὤν) : Æsch. Ag. 1051 μένει τὸ θεῖον δουλίᾳ π ε ρ ἐν φρενί (sc. οὔσῃ) : Ibid. 1051 ἐγὼ δ' οὖν ἐθέλω—τάδε μὲν στέργειν, δύστλητά π ε ρ ὄ ν τ α) :—κ α ί π ε ρ, divided in Homer, κ α ὶ—π ε ρ (only Od. η, 224 καί περ), so that π έ ρ is placed beside the word on which emphasis is to be laid ; but joined in Attic Greek, κ α ί π ε ρ ; so also in Attic, ο ὐ δ έ π ε ρ : Il. β, 270 καὶ ἀχνύμενοί περ : Xen. Anab. I. 6, 10 προσεκύνησαν κ α ί π ε ρ ε ἰ δ ό τ ε ς, ὅτι ἐπὶ θανάτῳ ἄγοιτο : Eur. Phœn. 1667 οὐκ ἂν προδοίην ο ὐ δ έ π ε ρ π ρ ά σ σ ω ν κακῶς :—κ α ί τ ο ι : Plat. Prot. p. 339 C οὐδέ μοι ἐμμελέως τὸ Πιττάκειον νέμεται, κ α ί τ ο ι σοφοῦ παρὰ φωτὸς εἰρημένον :—ὅ μ ω ς (which

---

[a] Schäfer. ad loc.

though it properly belongs to the verb of the sentence, yet generally is attached to the partic., and often is even placed before it):
Hdt. VI. 120 ὕστεροι δὲ ἀπικόμενοι τῆς συμβολῆς (*prœlio*) ἱμείροντο
ὅμως θεήσασθαι τοὺς Μήδους: Eur. Or. 679 κᾀγώ σ' ἱκνοῦμαι, καὶ
γυνή περ οὖσ' ὅμως: Id. Med. 280 ἐρήσομαι δὲ καὶ κακῶς π ά-
σχουσ' ὅμως: Xen. Cyr. V. 1, 26 οὕτως ἔχομεν, ὡς σὺν σοὶ μὲν
ὅμως καὶ ἐν τῇ πολεμίᾳ ὄντες θαρροῦμεν: Id. Œcon. XVI. 8 οὓς
ἂν αἰσθάνωμαι ὅμως καὶ εὖ πάσχοντας ἔτι ἀδικεῖν πειρωμένους:
—ἔπειτα, εἶτα: Plat. Charmid. p. 163 A ὑποθέμενος σωφροσύνην εἶναι τὸ τὰ ἑαυτοῦ πράττειν, ἔπειτα οὐδέν φησι κωλύειν
καὶ τοὺς τὰ τῶν ἄλλων πράττοντας σωφρονεῖν: Xen. M. S. I. 1, 5 εἰ
προαγορεύων ὡς ὑπὸ θεοῦ φαινόμενα κᾆτα ψευδόμενος ἐφαίνετο:—
καὶ ταῦτα: Plat. Rep. p. 404 B Ὅμηρος—ἐν ταῖς τῶν ἡρώων
ἑστιάσεσιν οὔτε ἰχθύσιν αὐτοὺς ἑστιᾷ, καὶ ταῦτα ἐπὶ θαλάττῃ ἐν Ἑλλη-
σπόντῳ ὄντας, although they were: Demosth. p. 922, 5 θανάτῳ
ζημιώσαντες εἰσαγγελθέντα ἐν τῷ δήμῳ, καὶ ταῦτα πολίτην ὑμέτερον
ὄντα, *capitis eum damnantes delatum ad populum, quamvis civis vester
esset:* so that it sometimes has the sense of *especially:* cf. Hdt. II.
120. Rarely after the participle: Plat. Rep. p. 341 C νῦν γοῦν, ἔφη,
ἐπεχείρησας, οὐδὲν ὢν καὶ ταῦτα, *quamvis nullus et impotens sis* [a].

§. 698. *d.* Means : Xen. Cyr. III. 2, 25 ληϊζόμενοι ζῶσιν,
raptu vivunt: Id. M. S. III. 5, 16 προαιροῦνται μᾶλλον οὕτω κερδαίνειν ἀπ' ἀλλήλων, ἢ συνωφελοῦντες αὐτούς: Isocr. p. 241
D τοὺς Ἕλληνας ἐδίδαξαν, ὃν τρόπον διοικοῦντες τὰς αὑτῶν πατρίδας καὶ πρὸς οὓς πολεμοῦντες μεγάλην τὴν Ἑλλάδα ποιήσειαν:
so very commonly χρώμενος with dat. where we use "with:"
as πολλῇ τέχνῃ χρώμενος τοὺς πολεμίους ἐνίκησεν.

e. Mode or manner: γελῶν εἶπε: so λαθών, secretly, φθάμενος, φθάσας, ἀνύσας, quickly: Hom., Hdt., Thuc.

Obs. 1. Here also certainly belong the forms which introduced themselves from the colloquial dialect, ληρεῖς ἔχων, or as a question, τί
ληρεῖς ἔχων, you trifle so—properly, you trifle conducting yourself so:
φλυαρεῖς ἔχων Aristoph.: Plat. Gorg. p. 490 E ποῖα ὑποδήματα φλυαρεῖς ἔχων; what shoes are you thus continually chattering about?
Aristoph. Nub. 509 τί κυπτάζεις ἔχων περὶ τὴν θύραν; what are you
about stooping so unceasingly about the door ? — also φερόμενος, and
(used intransitively) φέρων, *summo studio, maximo impetu:* with verbs
of motion: Hdt. VIII. 91 ὅκως δέ τινες τοὺς Ἀθηναίους διαφύγοιεν, φερόμενοι (*cum impetu delati*) ἐσέπιπτον ἐς τοὺς Αἰγινήτας: Id. IX. 102 διωσά-
μενοι γὰρ τὰ γέρρα οὗτοι φερόμενοι ἐσέπεσον ἁλέες ἐς τοὺς Πέρσας: Id. VIII.
87 (ναῦς) διωκομένη γὰρ ὑπὸ τῆς Ἀττικῆς φέρουσα ἐνέβαλε νηῒ φιλίῃ, *cum
impetu aggressa est amicam navem.*

Obs. 2. So also where we use "with," the Greeks use ἔχων, ἄγων,
φέρων, λαβών: of animate or inanimate things or possessions, ἔχων and

λ α β ώ ν : of animate, ἄγων : of inanimate φέρων; as, Xen. Cyr. I. 3, 1 ἔρχεται—ἡ Μανδάνη πρὸς τὸν πατέρα καὶ τὸν Κῦρον τὸν υἱὸν ἔχουσα : so ὁ Κῦρος
ξίφος φέρων προσῆλασε—ἵππον ἄγων ἦλθεν—ἱππέας λαβὼν τοὺς πολεμίους κατε-
δίωξεν. The Homeric and poetic dialects use ἔχων, φέρων, λαβών and ἄγων,
frequently with verbs of *giving*, or *placing*, to bring the action immediately
preceding the giving or placing before the eyes : Il. η, 302 δῶκε ξίφος ἀρ-
γυρόηλον σὺν κολεῷ τε φέρων καὶ ἐϋξέστῳ τελαμῶνι.

Dative absolute.

§. 699. We also find, though but very seldom, the dative
in the absolute construction with the part., as expressing the
notion of " *when*" defined by some action or state (see Dat.
§. 606) :   Xen. Hell. III. 2, 25 περιϊόντι δὲ τῷ ἐνιαυτῷ,
φαίνουσι πάλιν οἱ ἔφοροι φρουρὰν ἐπὶ τὴν Ἦλιν : Theocrit. XIII. 29
κοίλαν δὲ καθιδρυνθέντες ἐς Ἀργὼ Ἑλλάσποντον ἵκοντο, νότῳ τρίτον
ἆμαρ ἀέντι.

Obs. 1. We must distinguish these cases from those given §. 599. 2.
Obs. 2. To define more clearly the notion of coincident time, ἅμα is
added to the dat. absolute : Hdt. III. 86 ἅμ' ἡμέρῃ διαφωσκούσῃ : Ibid. 86
ἅμα δὲ τῷ ἵππῳ τοῦτο ποιήσαντι, ἀστραπὴ ἐξ αἰθρίης καὶ βροντὴ ἐγένετο : Thuc.
IV. princ. ἅμα τῷ σίτῳ ἀκμάζοντι, *simulac frumentum adultum est ;* also ἐπί,
either in notion of *after*, ἐπ' ἐξειργασμένοις ἐλθεῖν Hdt. VIII. 95, or to
express a consequence or sequence on, Hdt. II. 22 ἐπὶ χιόνι πεσούσῃ ἀνάγκη
ἐστὶ ὗσαι ἐν πέντε ἡμέρῃσι.

Accusative absolute[a].

§. 700. 1. Lastly, in Hdt. and Attic writers, the accus. is used
in the same construction as the genitive, but scarcely ever except
when the participle has no definite subject, as in impersonal verbs,
as ἐξόν (from ἔξεστι, it is lawful), or impersonal phrases, as αἰσχρὸν
ὄν (from αἰσχρόν ἐστιν, it is shameful).

2. Since the acc., as we have seen, signifies extension or parallelism in time (§. 577), as ταῦτα ἐγένετο ταύτην τὴν νύκτα, the
action, therefore, during which another action takes place defines
the time, and is conceived of as parallel to and coincident with
that action, and may be translated by *whilst*, as ἐξόν, whilst it
is allowed, and thence it is used in the sense of our " while," as
expressing a state of things which exists coincidently with the
action of the principal verb, while the genitive expresses the state
of things conceived of as the antecedent cause or condition thereof.
a. Accusative absolute : Hdt. I. 129 εἰ, π α ρ ε ὸ ν αὐτῷ βασι-

λέα γενέσθαι,—ἄλλῳ περιέθηκε τὸ κράτος: Id. VI. 72 π α ρ ε ὸ ν δ έ
οἱ ὑποχείρια πάντα ποιήσασθαι, ἐδωροδόκησε ἀργύριον πολύ: Id. V. 49
extr. π α ρ έ χ ο ν (*quum liceat*) δὲ τῆς Ἀσίης πάσης ἄρχειν εὐπετέως,
ἄλλο τι αἱρήσεσθε; Ibid. 50 χ ρ ε ὼ ν γάρ μιν μὴ λέγειν τὸ ἐὸν—
λέγει: Id. III. 65 ἀδελφεοκτόνος τε, οὐδὲν δ έ α ν (*quum fas non
esset, fieri deberet*), γέγονα: Thuc. I. 76 π α ρ α τ υ χ ὸ ν ἰσχῦί τι κτήσασθαι: Ibid. 126 ὑ π ά ρ χ ο ν ὑμῖν πολεμεῖν: Id. VIII. 79 δ ό ξ α ν
αὐτοῖς, *quum iis visum esset*: Id. IV. 125 δ ο κ ο ῦ ν (*quum videretur*)
ἀναχωρεῖν: Demosth. p. 832, 59 π ρ ο σ ῆ κ ο ν, *quum deceret*: Id.
p. 25, 24 πολλὰ ἰδίᾳ πλεονεκτῆσαι πολλάκις ὑμῖν ἐ ξ ὸ ν οὐκ ἠθελήσατε.—Also passive partic.; Thuc. I. 125 δ ε δ ο γ μ έ ν ο ν δὲ αὐτοῖς,
εὐθὺς μὲν ἀδύνατα ἦν ἐπιχειρεῖν ἀπαρασκεύοις οὖσιν: Id. V. 30 ε ἰ ρ η-
μ έ ν ο ν, *quum dictum esset*: Ibid. 56 γ ε γ ρ α μ μ έ ν ο ν.—And thirdly, an adjective with ὄν, as α ἰ σ χ ρ ὸ ν ὄ ν: Xen. Cyr. II. 2, 20 *quum
turpe esset*; ἄ δ η λ ο ν ὄ ν Thuc. I. 2: δ υ ν α τ ὸ ν ὄ ν, ἀ δ ύ ν α τ ο ν
ὄ ν: Plat. Criton. p. 46 A ο ἷ ό ν τε ὂ ν καὶ δ υ ν α τ ό ν: also without ὄν, as δ ῆ λ ο ν, Plat. Rep. p. 449 C: Id. Protag. p. 323 B ὡς
ἀ ν α γ κ α ῖ ο ν οὐδένα—μετέχειν αὐτῆς: Hdt. II. 66 ταῦτα δὲ γ ι-
ν ό μ ε ν α, πένθεα μεγάλα τοὺς Αἰγυπτίους καταλαμβάνει: Thuc. IV.
125 ὥστε, ἤδη ἀμφοτέροις μὲν δοκοῦν ἀναχωρεῖν,—κ υ ρ ω θ ὲ ν δὲ ο ὐ-
δ ὲ ν (*sed quum nihil decretum esset*),—ἐχώρουν ἐπ᾽ οἴκου: Plat.
Gorg. p. 495 C ἄλλο τι οὖν (i. e. *nonne igitur*), ὡς ἕ τ ε ρ ο ν (sc. ὄν)
τ ὴ ν ἀ ν δ ρ ε ί α ν τῆς ἐπιστήμης, δύο ταῦτα ἔλεγες; *nonne, quia di-
versa esset fortitudo a scientiâ, duo hæc ponebas?* Xen. Hellen. III.
2, 19 δ ό ξ α ν τ α δὲ τ α ῦ τ α καὶ π ε ρ α ν θ έ ν τ α, τὰ μὲν στρατεύ-
ματα ἀπῆλθεν: Soph. Œ. C. 1119 μὴ θαύμαζε—, τ έ κ ν᾽ εἰ φ α ν έ ν τ᾽
ἄ ε λ π τ α, μηκύνω λόγον.

Obs. 1. In many of the examples which are brought of the accusative
absolute, we shall find that the accusative either depends, in apposition or
government, on some word in another part of the sentence, more or less
distant, as Soph. Electr. 881 οὐχ ὕβρει λέγω τάδ᾽, ἀλλ᾽ ἐκεῖνον (sc. λέγω) ὡς
παρόντα νῷν: or on a word supplied from the context, Eur. Ion. 964 ΠΑΙΔ.
σοὶ δ᾽ ἐς τί δόξης ἦλθεν, ἐκβαλεῖν τέκνον (=τί δόξασα ἐξέβαλες τέκνον;) ΚΡ. ὡς
(δόξασα) τὸν θεὸν σώσοντα τόν γ᾽ αὑτοῦ γόνον.

Obs. 2. Where the subject is implied in the impersonal verb, the gen. is
used; as, ὕοντος, σαλπίζοντος (§. 373): otherwise the gen. is seldom used
with impersonal verbs or phrases, as δόξαντος τούτου. Sometimes the gen.
and dat. are interchanged: Thuc. VII. 25 ὡς Ἀ θ η ν α ί ω ν π ρ ο σ δ ο κ ί μ ω ν
ὄ ν τ ω ν καὶ τ ὸ π α ρ ὸ ν σ τ ρ ά τ ε υ μ α αὐτῶν δ ι α π ο λ ε μ η σ ό μ ε ν ο ν:
Plat. Euthyphr. p. 4 D ὡς ἀνδροφόνου ὄντος καὶ οὐδὲν ὂν πρᾶγμα: Id. Rep.
p. 604 B λέγει πού ὁ νόμος, ὅτι κάλλιστον ὅτι μάλιστα ἡσυχίαν ἄγειν ἐν ταῖς
ξυμφοραῖς καὶ μὴ ἀγανακτεῖν, ὡς οὔτε δ ή λ ο υ ὄ ν τ ο ς τοῦ ἀγαθοῦ τε καὶ
κακοῦ τῶν τοιούτων (*talium casuum*), οὔτε εἰς τὸ πρόσθεν οὐδὲν π ρ ο β α ῖ ν ο ν
τῷ χαλεπῶς φέροντι, οὔτε τι τῶν ἀνθρωπίνων ἄ ξ ι ο ν ὂ ν μεγάλης σπουδῆς, ὅ
τε δεῖ ἐν αὐτοῖς ὅτι τάχιστα παραγίγνεσθαι ἡμῖν, τούτῳ ἐ μ π ο δ ὼ ν γ ι γ ν ό μ ε-

νον τὸ λυπεῖσθαι ᵃ: Xen. M. S. II. 2, 13 ὡς οὔτε ἂν τὰ ἱερὰ εὐσεβῶς θυόμενα—οὔτε ἄλλο καλῶς καὶ δικαίως οὐδὲν ἂν τούτου πράξαντος.

Obs. 3. It is evident that the uses of gen., dat. and acc. absolute spring from the simple power of the cases, and that as definitions of time, they properly have a meaning analogous to the power of each case.

1. Gen. abs. Time considered as a cause: τοῦ ἔαρος ἐλθόντος τὰ ἄνθη θάλλει; hence it is rarely used with impersonal verbs, as the agent of a verb is conceived of as the cause.

2. Dat. abs. Time considered as a point: περιιόντι τῷ ἐνιαύτῳ, at the return of the year.

3. Acc. abs. Duration in time—whilst.

The Comparative Particle ὡς *with the Participle and Absolute Cases.*

§. 701. Ὡς is joined to the simple participle, or with the gen. and acc. absolute, when it is to be signified that the action of the participle does not really exist, or when its real existence is to be kept out of view, and represented only as something supposed or thought of, referring to the opinion which a person formed, or was to form of it.

a. With simple part.: Xen. Cyr. I. 1, 1 οἱ δὲ, κᾂν ὁποσονοῦν χρόνον ἄρχοντες διαγένωνται, θαυμάζονται, ὡς σοφοί τε καὶ εὐτυχεῖς γεγενημένοι: Plat. Rep. p. 329 A ἀγανακτοῦσιν, ὡς μεγάλων τινῶν ἀπεστερημένοι (i. e. ἡγούμενοι μεγ. τ. ἀπεστερῆσθαι, like Isocr. p. 52 B ἦλθον—οἱ Ἡρακλέους παῖδες — τὰς μὲν ἄλλας πόλεις ὑπερορῶντες, ὡς οὐκ ἂν δυναμένας βοηθῆσαι, τὴν δ' ἡμετέραν ἱκανὴν νομίζοντες εἶναι).

b. Genitive absolute: Plat. Alcib. p. 106 B οὐκοῦν ὡς διανοουμένου σοῦ ταῦτα ἐρωτῶ, ἃ φημί σε διανοεῖσθαι (i. e. νομίζων σε διανοεῖσθαι): Xen. Hell. VII. 5, 20 παρήγγειλεν αὐτοῖς παρασκευάζεσθαι, ὡς μάχης ἐσομένης (i. e. νομίζων μάχην ἔσεσθαι): Ibid. V. 4, 9 ἐκήρυττον ἐξιέναι πάντας Θηβαίους, ὡς τῶν τυράννων τεθνεώτων, *quia tyranni mortui essent.* The reason of κηρύττειν is not the actual fact of the tyrant's death, but the persuasion of the οἱ κηρύττοντες that it was so—ἡγούμενοι τοὺς τυρ. τεθνάναι.

§. 702. A singular use of the gen. abs. with ὡς occurs with the verbs εἰδέναι, ἐπίστασθαι, νοεῖν, ἔχειν γνώμην, διακεῖσθαι τὴν γνώμην, φροντίζειν, and sometimes λέγειν and the like, where we should expect to find the accus. with the infin. The gen. signifies that the action of the participle is the cause of the state or action expressed by the verb. This relation is marked even in the position, as the genitive absol. almost always precedes the verb. The connection of the verb (as a consequence) with the gen. absol. is also generally marked by the addition of οὕτω: Xen. Cyr. I. 6, 11. extr. ὡς οὖν ἐμοῦ, ἔφη, μηδέποτε ἀμελήσοντος τοῦ τὰ ἐπιτήδεια τοῖς στρατιώταις συμμηχανᾶσθαι, μήτ' ἐν φιλίᾳ μήτ' ἐν πολεμίᾳ, οὕτως ἔχε τὴν γνώμην: Id. Anab. I. 3, 6 ὡς ἐμοῦ οὖν ἰόντος, ὅπῃ ἂν καὶ ὑμεῖς, οὕτω τὴν γνώμην ἔχετε: Plat. Rep. p. 327. extr. ὡς τοίνυν μὴ ἀκουσομένων, ἔφη, οὕτω διανοεῖσθε ᵃ: Ibid. p. 470 E. Ibid. p. 437 A ὑποθέμενοι ὡς τούτου οὕτως ἔχοντος: Id. Cratyl. p. 439 C διανοηθέντες—ὡς ἰόντων τε ἁπάντων ἀεὶ καὶ ῥεόντων: Id. Menon. p. 95 E οἶσθ', ὡς ἐν τούτοις μὲν, ὡς διδακτοῦ οὔσης τῆς ἀρετῆς, λέγεις; Eur. Med. 1311 ὡς οὐκέτ' ὄντων σῶν τέκνων, φρόντιζε δή.

Obs. Ὡς is never used with the dat. absol., as this is confined to its original force of a definition of time.

ᵃ Stallb. ad loc.   ᵇ Stallb. ad loc.

§. 703. *c.* Accusative absolute: Plat. Rep. p. 425. princ. τοῖς ἡμετέροις παισὶν ἐννομωτέρου εὐθὺς παιδιᾶς μεθεκτέον, ὡς, παρανόμου γιγνομένης αὐτῆς,—ἐννόμους τε καὶ σπουδαίους — ἄνδρας αὐξάνεσθαι ἀδύνατον ὄν : Ibid. p. 427 E σὺ γὰρ ὑπέσχου ζητήσειν, ὡς οὐχ ὅσιόν σοι ὂν μὴ οὐ βοηθεῖν δικαιοσύνῃ. So ὡς ἐξόν, ὡς παρόν &c. For some other examples see above (§. 700.) : Plat. Rep. p. 345 E τί δέ ; ἦν δ᾽ ἐγώ, ὦ Θρασύμαχε, τὰς ἄλλας ἀρχὰς οὐκ ἐννοεῖς ὅτι οὐδεὶς ἐθέλει ἄρχειν ἑκών, ἀλλὰ μισθὸν αἰτοῦσιν, ὡς οὐχὶ αὐτοῖσιν ὠφέλειαν ἐσομένην ἐκ τοῦ ἄρχειν, ἀλλὰ τοῖς ἀρχομένοις ; cf. Ibid. p. 426 C. Ibid. p. 468 D Ὅμηρος τὸν εὐδοκιμήσαντα ἐν τῷ πολέμῳ νώτοισιν Αἴαντα ἔφη διηνεκέεσσι γεραίρεσθαι, ὡς ταύτην οἰκείαν οὖσαν τιμὴν τῷ ἡβῶντί τε καὶ ἀνδρείῳ : Xen. M. S. I. 2, 20 διὸ καὶ τοὺς υἱεῖς οἱ πατέρες εἴργουσιν ἀπὸ τῶν πονηρῶν ἀνθρώπων ὅμως, ὡς τὴν μὲν τῶν χρηστῶν ὁμιλίαν ἄσκησιν οὖσαν τῆς ἀρετῆς, τὴν δὲ τῶν πονηρῶν κατάλυσιν : Ibid. I. 3, 2 εὔχετο δὲ πρὸς τοὺς θεοὺς ἁπλῶς τ᾽ ἀγαθὰ διδόναι, ὡς τοὺς θεοὺς κάλλιστα εἰδότας.

Obs. We must not class here those instances in which the partic. stands with a subst. in accus., as the object of a verb of thinking or saying : Hdt. II. 1 Καμβύσης Ἴωνας μὲν καὶ Αἰολέας ὡς δούλους πατρωίους ἐόντας ἐνόμιζε : Æsch. Ag. 683 λέγουσιν ἡμᾶς ὡς ὀλωλότας : Soph. Œ. T. 625 ὡς οὐχ ὑπείξων οὐδὲ πιστεύσων λέγεις ; So with ὥστε (§. 704.) : Id. Antig. 242 δηλοῖς δ᾽ ὥστε σημανῶν νέον.

The Comparative Particles ὥστε, ἅτε, οἷα, οἷον, *with the Participle or Genitive absolute.*

§. 704. Instead of ὡς we find, not so often in Attic as in Ionic dialect, ὥστε, ὥστε δή (only Hdt.), ἅτε, ἅτε δή, οἷα, οἷον, when the reason of any action is brought forward, not as the certain and actual reason, but as supposed or represented to be the probable reason by the speaker, or some one of whom he is speaking—where we should frequently use the word "probably :" Hdt. VI. 79 ἅτε γὰρ πυκνοῦ ἐόντος τοῦ ἄλσεος, οὐκ ὥρων οἱ ἐντὸς τοὺς ἐκτός : Ibid. 107 οἷα δέ οἱ πρεσβυτέρῳ ἐόντι τῶν ὀδόντων οἱ πλεῦνες ἐσείοντο : Ibid. 136 ἦν γὰρ ἀδύνατος (Μιλτιάδης ἀπολογέεσθαι), ὥστε σηπομένου τοῦ μηροῦ : Plat. Protag. p. 321 B ἅτε δὴ οὖν οὐ πάνυ τι σοφὸς ὢν ὁ Ἐπιμηθεὺς ἔλαθεν αὑτὸν καταναλώσας τὰς δυνάμεις εἰς τὰ ἄλογα. In Attic ὥσπερ with the partic. has often merely a comparative force ; as, Lysias p. 178, 39 ὧν αὐτοὶ λαμβάνετε χάριν ἴστε, ὥσπερ ὑμεῖς τὰ τούτων μισθοφοροῦντες, ἀλλ᾽ οὐ τούτων τὰ ὑμέτερα κλεπτόντων.

Remarks on the general use and some peculiar Constructions of the Participle.

§. 705. 1. It will be evident from what has been said, that the participial construction has a far wider range than in most other languages, and that great clearness, precision, and neatness of expression results from this use.

2. Although the Greeks make great use of the participle to express the accidental accompaniments of an action, and thus distinguish it from that action itself, yet this is sometimes reversed ; the principal action is expressed in the participle as a mere accompaniment, while the accompaniment assumes the character of the principal verb of the sentence : Soph. El. 345 ἑλοῦ γε θάτερ᾽, ἢ φρονεῖν κακῶς, ἢ τῶν φίλων φρονοῦσα μὴ μνήμην ἔχειν, i. e. ἢ τῶν φίλων μὴ μνήμην ἔχουσα (εὖ) φρονεῖν.

3. By a peculiar Greek idiom there is attached to the verb of the sentence a participle of the same root and similar meaning—this is exactly analogous to the constructions, μάχην μάχεσθαι, φυγῇ φεύγειν &c. : Hdt. VII. 10, 1 τὴν ἀμείνω (γνώμην) αἱρεόμενον ἐλέσθαι : Id. VI. 34 ἰόντες δὲ τὴν ἱρὴν ὁδὸν διὰ Φωκέων τε καὶ Βοιωτῶν ᾖσαν : Plat. Theæt. p. 183 D ἱππέας εἰς πεδίον προκαλεῖ Σωκράτη εἰς λόγους προκαλούμενος: Id. Euthyd. p. 288 D τίνα ποτ' οὖν ἂν κτησάμενοι ἐπιστήμην ὀρθῶς κτησαίμεθα; what knowledge (acquiring), should we rightly acquire (it)? Xen. Cyr. VIII. 4, 9 ἀλλ' ὑπακούων σχολῇ ὑπήκουσα; So also when a participle with the article prefixed is used as a substantive: Plat. Apol. p. 19 B τί δὴ λέγοντες διέβαλλον οἱ διαβάλλοντες;

4. Sometimes we find a participial construction changed in a succeeding and connected sentence into that of the verb and nomin. case : even in Homer ; as, Od. a, 162 ὀστέα πύθεται ὄμβρῳ, κείμενα ἐπ' ἠπείρου, ἢ εἰν ἁλὶ κῦμα κυλίνδει : Thuc. IV. 100 ἄλλῳ τε τρόπῳ πειράσαντες καὶ μηχανὴν προσήγαγον : Plat. Soph. p. 222 B θὲς δὴ ὅπη χαίρεις, εἴτε μηδὲν τιθεὶς ἥμερον, εἴτε ἄλλο μὲν ἥμερόν τι, τὸν δὲ ἄνθρωπον ἄγριον, εἴτε ἥμερον μὲν λέγεις αὖ τὸν ἄνθρωπον, ἀνθρώπων δὲ μηδεμίαν ἡ γῆ θήραν [a].

5. The Greeks generally are very accurate in their use of participles of the same or of different time with the verb of the sentence. So Homer: ὡς εἰπὼν ὤτρυνε μένος (English, *saying*), because the words are already spoken. But when a continued action is to be expressed, the part. pres. is used: Xen. M. S. I. 2, 61 (ὁ Σωκράτης) βελτίους—ποιῶν τοὺς συγγιγνομένους ἀπέπεμπεν. So also when one action precedes another, but is considered as intimately and necessarily connected with it : Od. a, 127 ἔγχος ἔστησε φέρων πρὸς κίονα. The aorist part. is often used for perfect ; as, στρατηγήσας ἐποίει, having assumed the generalship, that is, as a general.

6. When an adj. or subst. occurs, not in dependence on, but in the same construction with, the participle, the participle ὤν is used with them : Hdt. I. 35 ἀνὴρ σύμφορῃ ἐχόμενος καὶ οὐ καθαρὸς χεῖρας ἐών. But ὤν is often omitted, especially in poetry, the verbal notion of existence being reflected from the accompanying participle to the adj. or subst.; Plat. Rep. p. 393 D ἦλθεν ὁ Χρύσης—λύτρα φέρων καὶ ἱκέτης.

Asyndeton in the Participial Construction.

§. 706. 1. Two or more participles stand in the same sentence without being connected by a copulative conjunction καί or τέ. This is the case when the two participles are opposed to each other, or in a climax, or where two or three parts of an action, independent of each other, are brought before the mind in rapid succession, as is frequently the case in poetry : Il. φ, 324 ἦ καὶ ἐπῶρτ' Ἀχιλῆϊ κυκώμενος, ὑψόσε θύων, μορμύρων ἀφρῷ τε καὶ αἵματι καὶ νεκύεσσιν : Il. χ, 414 πάντας δ' ἐλλιτάνευε κυλινδόμενος κατὰ κόπρον, ἐξονομακλήδην ὀνομάζων ἄνδρα ἕκαστον : Il. θ, 231 sq. ἔσθοντες κρέα πολλὰ βοῶν ὀρθοκραιράων, πίνοντες κρητῆρας ἐπιστεφέας οἴνοιο : Od. μ, 256 sq. αὐτοῦ δ' εἰνὶ θύρῃσι κατήσθιε κεκλήγοντας, χεῖρας ἐμοὶ ὀρέγοντας.

2. We must distinguish a sentence thus constructed from that where, in a succession of participles, one stands subordinate to, and explanatory of another, or where they stand in different relations to the verb ; (for instance, one expressing the cause, the other defining the nature of

---

[a] Heindorf ad loc.

the action :) Od. δ, 114 δάκρυ δ' ἀπὸ βλεφάρων χαμάδις βάλε, πατρὸς ἀ κ ο ύ-
σ α ς (postquam audiv.), χλαῖναν πορφυρέην ἄντ' ὀφθαλμοῖιν ἀ ν α σ χ ώ ν: Od.
ε, 374 αὐτὸς δὲ πρηνὴς ἀλὶ κάππεσε, χεῖρε π ε τ ά σ σ α ς νηχέμεναι μ ε μ α ώ ς,
(the latter is an explanatory definition of the former :) Il. λ, 212 π ά λ λ ω ν
ὀξέα δοῦρα κατὰ στρατὸν ᾤχετο πάντη, ὀ τ ρ ύ ν ω ν μαχέσασθαι. In prose such
a combination of participles is a favourite method of expressing briefly
but forcibly a number of single actions : Plat. Apol. p. 31 A ὑμεῖς δ' ἴσως
τάχ' ἂν ἀ χ θ ό μ ε ν ο ι, ὥσπερ οἱ νυστάζοντες ἐγειρόμενοι, κ ρ ο ύ σ α ν τ ε ς ἄν
με, π ε ι θ ό μ ε ν ο ι Ἀνύτῳ, ῥᾳδίως ἂν ἀποκτείναιτε : Id. Phæd. p. 70 A εὐθὺς
ἀ π α λ λ α τ τ ο μ έ ν η τοῦ σώματος καὶ ἐ κ β α ί ν ο υ σ α ὥσπερ πνεῦμα ἢ καπνὸς
δ ι α σ κ ε δ α σ θ ε ῖ σ α οἴχηται δ ι α π τ ο μ έ ν η καὶ οὐδὲν ἔτι οὐδαμοῦ ᾖ [a].

Seeming and real Anacolouthon in the Participial Construction.— Exchange of Cases.

§. 707. A participle in nomin. refers to a subst. in gen., dat., or acc.,
when the thing or person expressed by any one of these cases is
grammatically the object, but really the subject of the verbal notion,
as in the phrase δ ο κ ε ῖ μ ο ι = ἐ γ ὼ ἡγοῦμαι.—a. Dative : Thuc. III. 36
ἔ δ ο ξ ε ν α ὐ τ ο ῖ ς (i. e. ἐψηφίσαντο) οὐ τοὺς παρόντας μόνον ἀποκτεῖναι, ἀλλὰ
καὶ τοὺς ἄπαντας Μιτυληναίους — ἐ π ι κ α λ ο ῦ ν τ ε ς κ. τ. λ. (like Sallust. Jug.
112 p o p u l o R o m a n o melius v i s u m — r a t i [b]): Id. IV. 108 καὶ γὰρ
ἐ φ α ί ν ε τ ο α ὐ τ ο ῖ ς (i. q. ἡγοῦντο), ἐ ψ ε υ σ μ έ ν ο ι ς μὲν τῆς Ἀθηναίων δυνάμεως ἐπὶ τοσοῦτον, ὅση ὕστερον διεφάνη, τὸ δὲ πλέον βουλήσει κ ρ ί ν ο ν τ ε ς
ἀσαφεῖ ἢ προνοίᾳ ἀσφαλεῖ : Id. VI. 24 καὶ ἔ ρ ω ς ἐ ν έ π ε σ ε π ᾶ σ ι ν (=ἐπε-
θύμουν πάντες) ὁμοίως ἐκπλεῦσαι· τ ο ῖ ς μὲν π ρ ε σ β υ τ έ ρ ο ι ς ὡ ς—καταστρε-
ψομένοις ἐφ' ἃ ἔπλεον—τ ο ῖ ς δ' ἐ ν ἡ λ ι κ ί ᾳ—ε ὐ έ λ π ι δ ε ς ὄ ν τ ε ς σωθήσεσθαι:
Id. VII. 42 τ ο ῖ ς μ ὲ ν Σ υ ρ α κ ο υ σ ί ο ι ς καὶ ξ υ μ μ ά χ ο ι ς κ α τ ά π λ η ξ ι ς
ἐ ν τ ῷ αὐτίκα οὐκ ὀλίγη ἐ γ έ ν ε τ ο (= οἱ Συρακούσιοι κατεπλήχθησαν)—ὁ ρ ῶ ν-
τ ε ς κ. τ. λ.: Xen. Cyr. VIII. 8, 10 ἦ ν δ ὲ α ὐ τ ο ῖ ς ν ό μ ι μ ο ν (=νόμιμον
ἡγοῦντο) μηδὲ προχοΐδας εἰσφέρεσθαι εἰς τὰ συμπόσια, δηλονότι ν ο μ ί ζ ο ν τ ε ς
τῷ μὴ ὑπερπίνειν ἧττον ἂν καὶ σώματα καὶ γνώμας σφάλλειν : Eur. Cycl. 330
δοραῖσι θηρῶν σῶμα π ε ρ ι β α λ ὼ ν ἐμὸν καὶ πῦρ ἀ ν α ί θ ω ν, χιόνος ο ὐ δ έ ν
μ ο ι μ έ λ ε ι (=οὐδὲν φροντίζω) : Plat. Legg. p. 686 D ἀ π ο β λ έ ψ α ς γὰρ
πρὸς τοῦτον τὸν στόλον—ἔ δ ο ξ έ μ ο ι πάγκαλος — εἶναι.   b. Accusative :
Il. ζ, 510 ὁ δ' ἀγλαΐηφι π ε π ο ι θ ὼ ς ῥίμφα ἑ γ ο ῦ ν α φ έ ρ ε ι (=ῥίμφα φέρεται) : Il. ε, 135 καὶ πρίν περ θυμῷ μ ε μ α ὼ ς Τρώεσσι μάχεσθαι, δὴ τότε μιν
τρὶς τόσσον ἕ λ ε μ έ ν ο ς (=ἐχώσατο) : Eur. Hec. 970 αἰδώς μ' ἔχει (=αἰδοῦ-
μαι) ἐν τῷδε πότμῳ τ υ γ χ ά ν ο υ σ', ἵν' εἰμὶ νῦν [c] : Id. Hipp. 23 τὰ πολλὰ δὲ
πάλαι π ρ ο κ ό ψ α σ' οὐ πόνου πολλοῦ μ ε δ ε ῖ (= οὐ πολλοῦ πόνου δέομαι).
c. Genitive : Æsch. Eum. 100 π α θ ο ῦ σ α δ' οὕτω δεινὰ πρὸς τῶν φιλτάτων,
ο ὐ δ ε ὶ ς ὑ π έ ρ μ ο υ δ α ι μ ό ν ω ν μ η ν ί ε τ α ι (= οὐδενὸς δαίμονος μῆνιν
ἔχω) : Eur. Iph. T. 695 sqq. σ ω θ ε ὶ ς δ ὲ, παῖδας ἐξ ἐμῆς ὁμοσπόρου κ τ η-
σ ά μ ε ν ο ς,—ὄ ν ο μ ά τ' ἐ μ ο ῦ γ έ ν ο ι τ' ἄν (= ὄνομα ἐμοῦ σώσαις) : Hdt.
IV. 132 Δ α ρ ε ί ο υ ἡ γ ν ώ μ η ἔ η ν (= ἐγίγνωσκε) — ε ἰ κ ά ζ ω ν.
§. 708. 1. So we find also a subst. and partic. in nom. where we should
expect a gen. absolute, so that it appears to be a nom. absolute. This
nom. is considered as the subject of a verb implied in the form which
grammatically requires the gen. absolute; and by the use of the nom., *the
real agent* of the verbal notion is brought forward in the sentence : Thuc.
IV, 23 καὶ τὰ περὶ Πύλον ὑπ' ἀ μ φ ο τ έ ρ ω ν κατὰ κράτος ἐ π ο λ ε μ ε ῖ τ ο

---

a Stallb. Apol. p. 27 A.   b Cf. Stallb. Apol. p. 21 C.   c Pflugk ad loc.

(= ἀμφότεροι ἐπολέμουν), Ἀθηναῖοι μὲν—τὴν νῆσον περιπλέοντες—, Πελοποννήσιοι δὲ ἐν τῇ Ἠπείρῳ στρατοπεδευόμενοι: Id. V. 70 καὶ μετὰ ταῦτα ἡ ξύνοδος ἦν (= ξυνῆλθον)· Ἀργεῖοι μὲν καὶ οἱ ξύμμαχοι ἐντόνως καὶ ὀργῇ χωροῦντες, Λακεδαιμόνιοι δὲ βραδέως: Soph. Antig. 259 sq. λόγοι δ' ἐν ἀλλήλοισιν ἐρρόθουν κακοί (= κακοὺς λόγους εἶπον ἀλλήλους), φύλαξ ἐλέγχων φύλακα [a].

2. An anomalous construction, closely connected with this, occurs when two subjects stand together in a sentence without any copulative particle, and a participle in the nom. is joined thereto: one of the two subjects is contained under the other as a part, and both belong to the same verb. The participle is joined either with the whole, and the verb refers to the part, or the part has the participle, and the verb is joined to the whole: (Σχῆμα καθ' ὅλον καὶ μέρος: cf. §. 478.): Il. γ, 211 ἄμφω δ' ἑζομένω γεραρώτερος ἦεν Ὀδυσσεύς: Il. κ, 224 σύν τε δύ' ἐρχομένω καί τε πρὸ ὃ τοῦ ἐνόησεν: Od. ω, 483 ὅρκια πιστὰ ταμόντες ὁ μὲν βασιλευέτω αἰεί: Od. ι, 462 sq. ἐλθόντες (sc. ἡμεῖς) δ' ἠβαιὸν ἀπὸ σπείους τε καὶ αὐλῆς, πρῶτος ὑπ' ἀρνειοῦ λυόμην, ὑπέλυσα δ' ἑταίρους: Thuc. I. 49 αἱ Ἀττικαὶ νῆες— φόβον μὲν παρεῖχον τοῖς ἐναντίοις, μάχης δὲ οὐκ ἦρχον, δεδιότες οἱ στρατηγοὶ τὴν πρόρρησιν τῶν Ἀθηναίων: Id. IV. 118 ἐκκλησίαν δὲ ποιήσαντας τοὺς στρατηγοὺς—βουλεύσασθαι Ἀθηναίους: Id. VI. 73 οἱ γὰρ Μεγαρῆς—ἡσύχαζον, λογιζόμενοι καὶ οἱ ἐκείνων στρατηγοί. So particularly with οἱ μέν, οἱ δέ: Xen. Cyr. III. 1, 25 ἔνιοι γὰρ φοβούμενοι, μὴ ληφθέντες ἀποθάνωσιν, ὑπὸ τοῦ φόβου προαποθνήσκουσιν, οἱ μὲν ῥιπτοῦντες ἑαυτούς, οἱ δὲ ἀπαγχόμενοι, οἱ δὲ ἀποσφαττόμενοι: Eur. Or. 1470 sqq. τότε διαπρεπεῖς ἐγένοντο Φρύγες, ὅσον Ἄρεως ἀλκὰν ἥσσονες Ἑλλάδος ἐγενόμεθ' αἰχμᾶς, ὁ μὲν οἰχόμενος φυγὰς, ὁ δὲ νέκυς ὢν, ὁ δὲ τραῦμα φέρων, ὁ δὲ λισσόμενος. And also frequently with ἕκαστος, ἑκάτερος: Il. ι, 656 οἱ δὲ ἕκαστος ἑλὼν δέπας σπείσαντες παρὰ νῆας ἴσαν: Hdt. III. 82 αὐτὸς γὰρ ἕκαστος βουλόμενος κορυφαῖος εἶναι γνώμῃσί τε νικᾶν, ἐς ἔχθεα μεγάλα ἀλλήλοισι ἀπικνέονται: Thuc. VI. 62 οἱ λοιποὶ τῶν Ἀθηναίων στρατηγοὶ—δύο μέρη ποιήσαντες τοῦ στρατεύματος καὶ λαχὼν ἑκάτερος ἔπλεον: Id. VII. 70 ἦρχον δὲ—Σικανὸς μὲν καὶ Ἀγάθαρχος, κέρας ἑκάτερος τοῦ παντὸς ἔχων: cf. Plat. Rep. p. 488 B. Demosth. p. 118, 29 [b].

3. A rhetorical anacolouthon occurs when a person considered as the principal agent (as opposed to another subject which is subordinate) in the action which the whole sentence expresses, is placed with a participle in the nomin., in the beginning of the sentence, and followed immediately by the other subject with μέν and its proper verb; after which the principal subject, being repeated by the particle δέ, follows with the proper *verbum finitum*: Thuc. III. 34 ὁ δὲ (Πάχης) προκαλεσάμενος ἐς λόγους Ἱππίαν—, ὁ μὲν (Ἱππίας) ἐξῆλθε παρ' αὐτόν, ὁ (Πάχης) δ' ἐκεῖνον μὲν ἐν φυλακῇ ἀδέσμῳ εἶχεν: Id. IV. 80 καὶ προκρίναντες (οἱ Λακεδαιμόνιοι) ἐς δισχιλίους, οἱ μὲν (Εἵλωτες) ἐστεφάνωσαν τότε καὶ τὰ ἱερὰ περιῆλθον, ὡς ἠλευθερωμένοι· οἱ δὲ (Λακεδαιμόνιοι) οὐ πολλῷ ὕστερον ἠφάνισαν—αὐτούς: cf. Xen. Cyr. IV. 6, 3.

Nominative Participle without any Verbum Finitum.

§. 709. The partic. sometimes stands in the nom. without any *verbum finitum*, which however is to be supplied either by what has gone before

---

[a] Cf. Elmsl. Œ. R. 60.   [b] Bremi ad loc.

or what follows: Hdt. I. 82 Λακεδαιμόνιοι δὲ τὰ ἐναντία τούτων ἔθεντο
νόμον· οὐ γὰρ κομῶντες πρὸ τούτου ἀπὸ τούτου κομᾶν (scil. νόμον ἔθεντο):
Thuc. I. 25 Κορίνθιοι δὲ κατά τε τὸ δίκαιον ὑπεδέξαντο τὴν τιμωρίαν, ἅμα δὲ καὶ
μίσει τῶν Κερκυραίων, ὅτι αὐτῶν παρημέλουν ὄντες ἄποικοι· οὔτε γὰρ ἐν
πανηγύρεσι ταῖς κοιναῖς διδόντες (scil. παρημέλουν) γέρα τὰ νομιζόμενα, οὔτε
Κορινθίῳ ἀνδρὶ προκαταρχόμενοι τῶν ἱερῶν κ. τ. λ. So also with conjunctions; as, εἰ, ἐάν, ὅταν, &c.: Xen. M. S. II. 1, 23 ὁρῶ σε ἀποροῦντα,
ποίαν ὁδὸν ἐπὶ τὸν βίον τράπῃ· ἐὰν οὖν ἐμὲ φίλην ποιησάμενος (scil. τὴν ἐπὶ
τὸν βίον ὁδὸν τράπῃ). And in dialogues, in reference to what some one else
has said: Plat. Phædr. p. 228 D ἐν κεφαλαίοις ἕκαστον ἐφεξῆς δίειμι, ἀρξάμενος ἀπὸ τοῦ πρώτου. ΣΩ. δείξας γε πρῶτον, ὦ φιλότης, τί ἄρα ἐν τῇ
ἀριστερᾷ ἔχεις. But in very many passages the verb εἰμί must be supplied.

Genitive Participle for some other case.

§. 710. We sometimes find the genitive absolute, even where we should
expect it to agree with the subject of the verb, or some object thereof.
It must be observed, that the subject of the gen. absolute is frequently
supplied from the context.

a. Gen. abs. instead of nomin.: Hdt. I. 178 πόλις κέεται ἐν πεδίῳ
μεγάλῳ μέγεθος ἐοῦσα μέτωπον ἕκαστον εἴκοσι καὶ ἕκατον σταδίων ἐούσης
τετραγώνου: Ibid. 208 Κῦρος προηγόρευε Τομύρι ἐξαναχωρέειν αὐτοῦ
διαβησομένου ἐπ' ἐκείνην: Id. II. 111 τοῦ ποταμοῦ κατελθόντος
μέγιστα δὴ τότε ἐπ' ὀκτωκαίδεκα πήχεας — κυματίης ὁ ποταμὸς ἐγένετο:
Thuc. II. 83 παρὰ γῆν σφῶν κομιζομένων καὶ — πρὸς τὴν ἀντιπέρας
ἤπειρον διαβαλλόντων — κατεῖδον (sc. αὐτοί) τοὺς Ἀθηναίους: Id. III. 13
βοηθησάντων ὑμῶν προθύμως πόλιν προσλήψεσθε: Ibid. 70 καὶ ἐς
λόγους καταστάντων (Κερκυραίων) ἐψηφίσαντο Κερκυραῖοι: Xen.
Cyr. I. 4, 20 ταῦτα εἰπόντος αὐτοῦ ἔδοξέ τι (sc. αὐτός) λέγειν τῷ
Ἀστυάγει: Ibid. VI. 1, 37 μή τι πάθω ὑπὸ σοῦ ὡς ἠδικηκότος ἐμοῦ
μεγάλα. So sometimes in Latin: Ovid. Amor. II. 12, 13 *Me duce ad
hanc voti finem, me milite veni.*

b. Gen. abs. instead of accus.: Hdt. IX. 99 οἱ γὰρ ὦν Σάμιοι, ἀπικο-
μένων Ἀθηναίων αἰχμαλώτων — τούτους λυσάμενοι πάντας ἀπο-
πέμπουσι — ἐς τὰς Ἀθήνας: Thuc. II. 8 ἐς τοὺς Λακεδαιμονίους,
ἄλλως τε καὶ προειπόντων (Λακεδαιμονίων), ὅτι τὴν Ἑλλάδα ἐλευθεροῦσιν:
Id. III. 22 προσέμιξαν δὲ τῷ τείχει τῶν πολεμίων λαθόντες τοὺς φύλακας, .
ἀνὰ τὸ σκοτεινὸν μὲν οὐ προϊδόντων αὐτῶν, ψόφῳ δὲ — οὐ κατακου-
σάντων: Id. IV. 18 σφεῖς δὲ—ἐκπολιορκήσειν τὸ χωρίον κατὰ τὸ εἰκὸς,
σίτου τε οὐκ ἐνόντος καὶ δι' ὀλίγης παρασκευῆς κατειλημμένου (sc. αὐτοῦ):
Id. V. 31 ἔπειτα παυσαμένων — οἱ Ἠλεῖοι ἐπηνάγκαζον (αὐτούς): Id.
V. 33 Λακεδαιμόνιοι δὲ — ἐστράτευσαν — τῆς Ἀρκαδίας ἐς Παρρασίους —
κατὰ στάσιν ἐπικαλεσαμένων σφᾶς: Id. V. 56 ἦλθον ἐπὶ τὴν Ἐπίδαυρον ὡς ἐρήμου οὔσης.

c. Gen. abs. instead of dative: Hdt. III. 65 τὸν μέν νυν μάλιστα χρῆν,
ἐμεῦ αἰσχρὰ πρὸς τῶν Μάγων πεπονθότος, τιμωρέειν ἐμοί: Id. VI. 85
μελλόντων δὲ ἄγειν τῶν Αἰγινητέων τὸν Λευτυχίδεα, εἶπέ σφι Θεα-
σίδης: Id. VII. 235 μὴ τῆς ἄλλης Ἑλλάδος ἁλισκομένης ὑπὸ
τοῦ πεζοῦ βοηθέωσι ταύτῃ (sc. Ἑλλάδι): Id. IX. 58 καὶ ὑμῖν μὲν ἐοῦσι
Περσέων ἀπείροισι πολλὴ ἔκ γε ἐμεῦ ἐγίνετο συγγνώμη, ἐπαινεόντων
τούτους, τοῖσί τι καὶ συνῃδέατε: Thuc. I. 114 καὶ ἐς αὐτὴν διαβεβηκότος
ἤδη Περικλέους — ἠγγέλθη αὐτῷ (Περικλεῖ): Eur. Med. 910 εἰκὸς

γὰρ ὀργὰς θῆλυ ποιεῖσθαι γένος, γάμους παρεμπολῶντος ἀλλοίαις, πόσει[a].

Obs. We must distinguish from these instances the Homeric construction, where the genitive partic. follows on a dat. pron. ; as, Il. ξ, 26 λάκε δέ σφι περὶ χροΐ χαλκὸς ἀτειρὴς νυσσομένων ξίφεσιν : Od. ι, 257 ἡμῖν δ᾿ αὖτε κατεκλάσθη φίλον ἦτορ δεισάντων φθόγγον τε βαρὺν αὐτόν τε πέλωρον : Ibid. 458 sq. τῷ κέ οἱ ἐγκέφαλός γε διὰ σπέος ἄλλυδις ἄλλῃ θεινομένου ῥαίοιτο πρὸς οὔδεϊ. Here the gen. part. agrees with ἡμῶν &c., which is the proper case after ἦτορ, but Homer frequently uses the dat. instead of the gen. of pronouns. So ἡμῖν κατεκλάσθη φίλον ἦτορ is the same, as ἡμῶν φίλον ἦτορ. Hence the dat. part. sometimes follows a pronoun or substantive in gen. (§. 712.) Nor must we class here those instances where the gen. abs. is joined with a verb, which requires the dative, but in this construction is used without a case ; as, Demosth. p. 71, 20 ἢ λέγοντος ἄν τινος πιστεῦσαι οἴεσθε (τὸν Φίλιππον); where we might also say, ἢ λέγοντι ἄν τινι πιστεῦσαι οἴεσθε ;

Accusative Participle for other cases.

§. 711. 1. Sometimes an accus. is used though it refers to a substantive in another case. The ground of this anomaly may be, that in the speaker's mind it depends on a verbal notion equivalent to the phrase on which the subst. depends, but which requires an accus. instead of a dative : Æsch. Choeph. 396 sq. πέπαλται δ᾿ αὖτί μοι φίλον κέαρ (=τρόμος ἔχει με) τόνδε κλύουσαν οἶκτον : Id. Pers. 909 λέλυται γὰρ ἐμοὶ γυίων ῥώμη τήνδ᾿ ἡλικίαν ἐσιδόντ᾿ ἀστῶν : Soph. El. 479 s. ὑπεστί μοι θράσος ἀδυπνόων κλύουσαν ἀρτίως ὀνειράτων : cf. Plat. Alc. p. 148 D[b].

2. Sometimes the accus. partic. stands at the beginning of the sentence, though the verb thereof requires another case. The accus. then follows the construction of a preceding sentence, whether from carelessness or on some rhetorical ground : Hdt. V. 103 ἐκπλώσαντές τε ἔξω τὸν Ἑλλήσποντον, Καρίης τὴν πολλὴν προσεκτήσαντο σφίσι σύμμαχον εἶναι· καὶ γὰρ τὴν Καῦνον πρότερον οὐ βουλομένην συμμαχέειν, ὡς ἐνέπρησαν τὰς Σάρδις, τότε σφι καὶ αὕτη προσεγένετο (as if the construction went on, καὶ τὴν Καῦνον —προσεκτήσαντο) : Plat. Phædr. p. 233 B τοιαῦτα γὰρ ἔρως ἐπιδείκνυται· δυστυχοῦντας μὲν, ἃ μὴ λύπην τοῖς ἄλλοις παρέχει, ἀνιαρὰ ποιεῖ νομίζειν· εὐτυχοῦντας δὲ καὶ τὰ μὴ ἡδονῆς ἄξια παρ᾿ ἐκείνων ἐπαίνου ἀναγκάζει τυγχάνειν : " quum sic procedere deberet structura, καὶ τὰ μὴ ἡδονῆς ἄξια ἐπαίνου ἀναγκάζει, quo rotundior exeat periodus, subito convertitur oratio[c]." Here there is clearly a rhetorical force in this construction ; the accus. εὐτυχοῦντας being placed in antithesis to δυστυχοῦντας.

3. In other instances the accus. is placed with the partic. as the object of the speaker's words, coincident with the whole paragraph which is concerning it, without any reference to the grammatical construction of the sentence ; (we should preface the sentence with—" as for :") Plat. Legg. p. 819 D περὶ ἅπαντα ταῦτα ἐνοῦσάν τινα φύσει γελοίαν τε καὶ αἰσχρὰν ἄνοιαν ἐν τοῖς ἀνθρώποις πᾶσι, ταύτης ἀπαλλάττουσι : Ibid. p. 761 E καὶ δὴ καὶ τοὺς ἀγρονόμους—ὀνείδη φερέσθωσαν.

---

[a] Pflugk ad loc.   [b] Elmsl. Heracl. 693.   [c] Heindorf ad loc.

Dative Participle for another case.

§. 712. A dative participle follows where some other case is required, by virtue of some notion implied in the verb on which it depends; but far more rarely than the nomin. or accus.: Thuc. I. 62 ἦν δὲ γνώμη τοῦ Ἀριστέως (=ἔδοξεν αὐτῷ) τὸ μὲν μεθ᾽ ἑαυτοῦ στρατόπεδον ἔχοντι ἐν τῷ Ἰσθμῷ ἐπιτηρεῖν τοὺς Ἀθηναίους. So Eur. Iph. A. 491 ἄλλως τέ μ᾽ ἕλεος τῆς ταλαιπώρου κόρης ἐσῆλθε συγγένειαν ἐννοουμένῳ.

Obs. For the Homeric passages.: Il. κ, 188 ἀπό τε σφίσιν ὕπνος ὄλωλεν· ὡς τῶν νήδυμος ὕπνος βλεφάροιιν ὀλώλει νύκτα φυλασσομένοισι κακήν: Il. ξ, 141 Ἀτρείδη, νῦν δή που Ἀχιλλῆος ὀλοὸν κῆρ γήθει ἐνὶ στήθεσσι φόνον καὶ φύζαν Ἀχαιῶν δερκομένῳ see above (§. 710. Obs.).

ADVERBS.

§. 713. 1. The adverbs express the notion of the place, the time, or the mode and manner of a predicate or attribute; as, ἐγγύθεν ἦλθεν— χθὲς ἀπέβη — καλῶς ἀπέθανεν, and are analogous to the cases of substantives which also express these notions; as, πεδίοιο θέειν, βαίνειν ὁδοῦ, ταῦτα ἐγένετο τῆς ἡμέρας, βαίνειν ὁδόν, πᾶσαν τὴν ἡμέραν, τούτῳ τῷ τόπῳ, ταύτῃ τῇ ἡμέρᾳ. Hence it arises, that most adverbs are relics of inflexions which are become obsolete; as, οὗ, where, ἄνω, κάτω, οἷ, οἴκοι, πῇ, ὅπη &c.

2. In its widest sense, the term "adverbs," "adverbial expressions," includes all the forms (whether single words or phrases) whereby these notions are expressed; such as, γελῶν εἶπε—διὰ τάχους—σπούδῃ—τρίτῃ ἡμέρᾳ &c.

Remarks on the use of Adjectives for Adverbs.

§. 714. The poets especially are fond of signifying the adverbial notions of place, still more frequently of time, sometimes of mode or manner, and causality, by adjectives; a greater energy is hereby given to the expression, the attributive of the verb (adverb) being considered as the attributive of the substantive.

a. Adjectives used instead of adverbs of place : Il. ρ, 361 τοὶ δ᾽ ἀγχηστῖνοι ἔπιπτον for ἄγχι ἀλλήλων: Od. φ, 146 ἷζε μυχοίτατος αἰεί for ἐν μυχοιτάτῳ. So the adjectives κρηναῖος, ὄρειος, οὐράνιος, ὑλαῖος, ἀγοραῖος &c., are joined with the subject instead of the predicate : Arist. Vesp. ῥίπτειν σκέλος οὐράνιον. So also πρῶτος, ὕστατος, μέσος, πλάγιος, μετέωρος, ἄκρος, ἄφορρος, ἐπιπόλαιος, πρυμνός, παράθυρος, θυραῖος, θαλάσσιος, ὑπερπόντιος &c.: Soph. Œ. T. 1411 θαλάσσιον ἐκρίψατε for εἰς θάλασσαν : Ibid. 32 ἐφέστιοι ἑζόμεθα for ἐπὶ τῇ ἑστίᾳ : Id. Antig. 785 φοιτᾷς ὑπερπόντιος for ὑπὲρ τὸν πόντον.

Obs. 1. Πρῶτος, ὕστατος, and many others of those here mentioned, are also applied to time.

Obs. 2. Here also belongs the use of the demonstratives ὅδε, οὗτος, ἐκεῖνος, mentioned above (§. 655. 1.). Other adjectival pronouns are also used as adverbs. — a. Ἄλλος, on the other side : Il. φ, 22 ὡς δ᾽ ὑπὸ δελφῖνος μεγακήτεος ἰχθύες ἄλλοι φεύγοντες πιμπλᾶσι μυχοὺς λιμένος εὐόρμου: Od. a, 132 πὰρ δ᾽ αὐτὸς κλισμὸν ἔθετο ποικίλον ἔκτοθεν ἄλλων μνηστήρων, apart from the suitors on the other side: cf. ζ, 83. So with the article in Attic, *in alterd parte*, and without it, *in alid parte*, then *præterea*, *pariter*, otherwise: Thuc. VII. 61 ἄνδρες στρατιῶται Ἀθηναῖοι τε καὶ τῶν ἄλλων ξυμμάχων, and their allies on the other hand. *b.* Πᾶς, as οἱ στρατιῶται πάντες or οἱ πάντες στρατιῶται for τὸ πᾶν, τὰ πάντα, altogether. *c.* Ἕκαστος or ὡς ἕκ., each one, singly, every time; and in this case it is placed either before the article, or after the subst.

b. Adjectives for adverbs of time; as, σημερινός, σήτειος, ἑωθινός, ἡέριος, ὑπηοῖος, ὄψιος, νύχιος, μεσονύκτιος, θερινός, χθιζός, ἐαρινός, χειμερινός &c.; especially those in αἶος, as δευτεραῖος, τριταῖος &c. (When?)—ἡμερήσιος, σκοτιαῖος, δεχήμερος, ὡριαῖος, μηνιαῖος, δίμηνος, ἐνιαύσιος, πανημέριος, ἡμάτιος &c.—Also χρόνιος, μακρός, δηρός, too long, &c. ; Il. *a*, 497 ἠερίη δ' ἀνέβη μέγαν οὐρανόν for ἦρι, early: Ib. 423 Ζεὺς, χθιζὸς ἔβη κατὰ δαῖτα for χθές: Il. θ, 530 ὑπηοῖοι θωρηχθέντες for ὑπὸ τὴν ἠῶ : Xen. Anab. IV. 1, 5 σκοτιαίους διελθεῖν τὸ πεδίον, in the twilight. — τεταρταῖος, πεμπταῖος ἀφίκετο, on the 4th, 5th day. — εὗδον παννύχιοι Homer. —χρόνιος ἦλθεν, after long time.

c. Adjectives instead of adverbs of mode, and other causal relations: ὀξύς, ταχύς, αἰφνίδιος, βραδύς, ὑπόσπονδος, ἄσπονδος, ὅρκιος,—ἑκών, ἄκων, ἄσμενος, ἄοκνος, ἐθελόντης — ἥσυχος — συχνός, πολύς, ἀθρόος, πυκνός, σπάνιος, μόνος ; as, ὑπόσπονδοι ἀπῇεσαν=ὑπὸ σπονδαῖς: Hdt. VI. 103 κατῆλθε ἐπὶ τὰ ἑωυτοῦ ὑπόσπονδος: Soph. Phil. 808 ἥδε (νόσος) μοι ὀξεῖα φοιτᾷ καὶ ταχεῖ' ἀπέρχεται for ὀξέως, ταχέως: Id. Œ. C. 1637 κατήνεσεν τάδ' ὅρκιος δράσειν for ὅρκῳ.

Obs. 3. The difference between πρῶτος and πρῶτον, μόνος and μόνον τὴν ἐπιστολὴν ἔγραψα is clear ; πρῶτος, μόνος, I am the first, the only one, who ever did so ; *primus scripsi*; πρῶτον, μόνον, it is the first, the only thing which I did ; or, I wrote it first, before I did something else ; I only wrote it.

Local Adverbs.

§. 715. 1. The adverbial notion of place is expressed, as we have seen, by (*a*) the cases: gen. (§. 522.), dat. (§. 605.), accus. (§. 577.) : (*b*) the prepositions with their cases ; and (*c*) by local adverbs. The prepositions with their cases and the local adverbs differ only that, in the former, the position is determined by its reference to something else ; as, ἔστη πρὸ τῆς πόλεως : in the latter, it is arbitrarily determined by the speaker's mind without reference to any thing but his own position ; as, ἔστη ταύτῃ, ἐκεῖ, except where two adverbs are opposed ; as, ἐνταῦθα, οὗ, there, where.

2. Local adverbs are derived either from pronouns, or from essential words (§. 351. 3.). The former only signify motion or rest, *whence, whither, where*; as, ἐνταῦθα, τόθεν, ἐνταυθοῖ : the latter express, besides these notions, that of position ; as, ὄπισθεν, ἐγγύθεν &c.

Adverbs of Time.

§. 716. The adverbial notion of time is expressed (*a*) by the cases: gen. (§. 523.), dat. (§. 606.), accus. (§. 577.) ; (*b*) prepos. with cases ; (*c*) participle as gerund (§. 696.), and (*d*) the adverbs of time. The prepositions express it relatively, as in notions of place the adverbs positively.

Obs. 1. As the prepositions express notions of time by a metaphorical application of the notions of place, considering time as a space, it follows naturally that many local adverbs express notions of time.

Obs. 2. Those adverbs which express frequency (repetition in time), as ἅπαξ, δίς, τρίς, πολλάκις, or intensity (quantity in time), as πολύ, σχεδόν, belong to the class of temporal adverbs.

Adverbs of Mode and Manner.

§. 717. The notion of mode and manner is generally expressed by adverbs, though frequently by partic. as gerund, and sometimes by substantives, with or without a preposition. These adverbs are mostly derived from essential words, and so closely connected with the verb that they form but one notion; as, κακῶς λέγειν (κακολογεῖν), εὖ λέγειν (εὐλογεῖν) &c.

Modal Adverbs.

§. 718. 1. There are also other adverbs which do not (as these given above) belong immediately to the predicate, but to the whole thought of the sentence which they define. These are called Modal Adverbs.

2. They signify an affirmation (ναί) or negation (οὐ, μή), the certainty, credibility (ἦ, μήν, πάντως &c.), the uncertainty, doubt (ἄν, πού, ἴσως &c.), of the thought.

Obs. Only those adverbs will be treated of here which are of grammatical importance; for the others, see the Lexicons.

The Temporal Adverbs νῦν, νύν—ἤδη.

a. Νῦν, νύν.

§. 719. 1. Νῦν (formed from νέξον, Lat. *num, etiamnum,* formed from *novum, num* scil. *tempus;* English *now* formed from *nûwa*), expresses the continuance of something present, but can be joined with the imperf., when the speaker considers the time just past as present to him: Eur. Hec. 1144 κακὸν Τρώων, ἐν ᾧπερ νῦν—ἐκάμνομεν: Demosth. p. 847, 9 νῦν — αὐτὸ καθ᾽ αὑτὸ διδάξειν ἐμέλλομεν. But the form, lengthened by the demonst. ι, νυνί (*numce*), is not so applied, as the demonst. ι points to what is really present, and hence is joined only with present, perfect, and future; as, νυνὶ γράφω, γέγραφα, γράψω or μέλλω γράφειν.

2. The notion of time is applied secondly to the notion of causality, and then νῦν, or, at the beginning of a sentence, νῦν δέ, signifies *now=therefore,* as the Latin, *nunc, nunc vero, nunc autem, rebus sic stantibus, quæ quum ita sint:* Eur. El. 979 μητροκτόνος νῦν φεύξομαι, τόθ᾽ ἁγνὸς ὤν. So often with imper. with μή: Il. o, 115 μὴ νῦν μοι νεμεσήσετ᾽—τίσασθαι φόνον υἷος—, εἴπερ μοι καὶ μοῖρα, Διὸς πληγέντι κεραυνῷ, κεῖσθαι.

3. Νῦν, when used in this sense of *therefore,* became enclitic (νύν); this is only used in poetry (from Homer downwards): but the compound form μίννυν is used in Ionic prose to denote a transition from one

sentence to another, or in a string of sentences; and in its form τοίνυν (see τοί) is used generally. This νύν is sometimes used as an adverb of time; as, Il. κ, 105 οὐ θην Ἕκτορι πάντα νοήματα — Ζεὺς ἐκτελέει, ὅσα πού νυν ἐέλπεται, but more usually as a weak illative conjunction.

b. Ἤδη.

4. Ἤδη, *already*, answers both in etymology and its whole use, to the Latin *Jam*.

a. Time. 1. The immediate and momentary presence of that which is spoken of, without any notion of duration; as, νῦν ἤδη, or ἤδη νῦν, *jam nunc*, even now: with the perfect, or with a past tense, it may be translated by "*just*," with the future, by "*immediately*," as ἤδη ἀπῆλθεν, or ἀπελήλυθεν— ἤδη ἀπελεύσεται. With participles it denotes something which begins the moment the action of the participle ends: so also in commands, exhortations, impatient questions, (*quid jam?*) Pind. Ol. VI. 22 ὦ Φίντις, ἀλλὰ ζεῦξον ἤδη μοι σθένος ἡμιόνων, ᾷ τάχος. When applied to space it denotes the point where a new country or territory immediately begins, and may be translated by *immediately after*, or *from this point*: Hdt. III. 5 ἀπὸ ταύτης ἤδη Αἴγυπτος: so Thuc. III. 95 Φωκεῦσιν ἤδη ὅμορος ἡ Βοιωτία ἐστίν.—2. If an action is supposed to extend from time past into time present, ἤδη signifies *adhuc*, as yet; if from time present into time future, *posthac*: so ἤδη οὐκ, no longer, no further; as, πυθέσθαι ἤδη τὰ ὀνόματα αὐτῶν οὐκ εἴχομεν— ἤδη οὐχ ἕξομεν πυθέσθαι.—3. Of unexpected, or long expected things, *at last, not till now*; as, ἀναπαύσωμεν ἤδη ποτέ, *jam tandem, tandem aliquando* —ἤδη ποτ' ἐν μακρῷ χρόνῳ.—4. Sometimes it is used indefinitely, *before this*: ἤδη ποτέ: Il. γ, 134 ἤδη καὶ Φρυγίην εἰσήλυθον, many times before this.

b. The secondary senses of ἤδη arise immediately from this temporal force. It denotes reality, certainty, definiteness of any thing, implied in the notion of its being immediately present to us, *now then—at this very moment, already, immediately, without difficulty, without ceremony:* Eq. 210 τὸν οὖν δράκοντά φησι —ἤδη κρατήσειν: Eur. Troad. 236 δοῦλοι γὰρ δὴ Δωρίδος ἐσμὲν χθονὸς ἤδη, at this very moment: Xen. Hell. VII. 1, 12 ἤδη γὰρ ἡγήσεσθε κατὰ θάλατταν, now then ye shall. In this sense it refers to the preceding sentence, and denotes an immediate consequence therefrom, wherefore it is sometimes employed merely to connect the sentence with a preceding one, on which it depends; as, Xen. Cyr. VII. 5, 58 ποιήσας δὲ τοῦτο, τὰ ἄλλα ἤδη ἤρχετο διοικεῖν.—It frequently expresses the completion of a climax, *but now, at last, jam, jam vero*; as, ἤδη δ' ἀκούσατε: hence it is frequently joined to demonstrative pronouns, (though as an adverb, it should be joined to the verb) as οὗτος ἤδη, τότ' ἤδη, ἐνταῦθ' ἤδη, οὕτως ἤδη, &c. So also καὶ ἤδη, and even: Plat. Symp. 204 B δῆλον δή, ἔφη, τοῦτό γε ἤδη καὶ παιδί.

Obs. Ἤδη, with the article is also joined, as an attribute, to a subst.; as, ἡ ἤδη χάρις, the present favour.

•

Δή, δῆτα, θήν, δῆθεν, δήπουθεν, δαί.

a. Δή.

§. 720. 1. Δή supposed by some to be a shortened form of ἤδη, by others a lengthened form of δέ, can never stand at the beginning of a sentence,

(except in Epic, δὴ τότε, *tum vero*, δὴ γὰρ, *jam enim*,) but generally immediately after the word to which it belongs. It is used to express the
exactness, reality, certainty, of the notion of the word or sentence to which
it belongs: in many of its significations, it answers to our word *just,* or
sooth, in sooth, forsooth.

2. It is applied in its sense of *exactness* to words of time; and by thus
laying emphasis on the time implied by the word, repeats the notion of
that time, as it were, in an adverbial form, and thus has a great number of
significations, most of which may be expressed by *now, just now, but now,
lately, immediately, then.*   *a.* So with present time: Plato Phædon. p. 60
C ἐπειδὴ ὑπὸ τοῦ δεσμοῦ ἦν ἐν τῷ σκέλει πρότερον τὸ ἀλγεινόν, ἥκειν
δ ὴ φαίνεται ἐπακολουθοῦν τὸ ἡδύ—then follows: so νῦν δὴ, just now.
b. Past time—but now, just now: περὶ τούτων ὧν δὴ σὺ ἔλεγες, which you
just now were saying; so also *hitherto*, οὐδὲν δὴ κακὸν προπεπονθώς, *nihil
dum.*   *c.* Future time—immediately; τοῦτο δὴ δηλώσω, νῦν δὴ δηλώσεις:
so with imperatives, and conjunctives used as imper., as ἴωμεν δὴ, let us go
now: so μὴ δή, after verbs of fear; δείδω μὴ δή (lest now) μοι τελέσῃ ἔπος
ὄβριμος Ἕκτωρ: οὐδὲν δὴ κακὸν πείσεται.   *d.* At length—now at least—then;
of something unexpected, (*then;*) or of something long expected, (*at
length;*) these senses arise from the emphatic nature of the "now," or
"then," expressed by δή, as in English;) ὦ πάτερ σὺ δ᾽ ἐν Ἅιδᾳ δὴ κεῖσαι.
e. With expressions of number: Il. ω, 107 ἐννῆμαρ δὴ νεῖκος ἐν ἀθανάτοισιν
ὄρωρεν, for now nine days: so πολλάκι δή, *jam sæpe*; νῦν δή, τέλος δή, ὀψὲ
δή, νεωστὶ δή, ὕστερον δή, ἐς ὃ δή, ὅτε δή, ὁπότε δή, ἐξ οὗ δή; like *donec jam.*

Secondary sense of δή.

§. 721. 1. From these notions of "*now*" and "*then*" is derived the use
of δή, as a conjunction, to signify *at once, without hesitation, straightway,
now then,* &c.: so in Homer we find μὲν (=μὴν) δή: Il. ι, 309 χρὴ μὲν δὴ
τὸν μῦθον ἀπηλεγέως ἀποειπεῖν, *now then:* hence, with the imper., *now then:*
Il. ω, 650 ἕκτος μὲν δὴ λέξο: so τότε δή, οὕτως δή, ἐνταῦθα δή—οἱ δ᾽ ὅτε δή—
when they then; hence ἔνθα δή Hdt., here then=thereupon: ἐπειδή, *since
then=whereas*, (*quoniam=quum jam*:) so ὡς δή, *as then*; εἰ δή, *if then*; and
even for ἤδη—καὶ δή, *and now*, in the middle of a sentence; sometimes
attached to the last of a string of subst. to express *lastly:* Plat. Meno p. 87
E ὑγίεια, φαμέν, καὶ ἰσχὺς καὶ κάλλος καὶ πλοῦτος δή.   Hence it is used
generally in a rapid string of sentences—*immediately—shortly;* often with
a notion of a climax, as μή τι γε δή, or μήτι δή—or μήτοι γε δή, *nedum*—
or to resume a sentence after an interruption, especially after a parenthesis,
and very frequently to express a logical conclusion: Plat. Rep. p. 494 A ἐκ
δὴ τούτων τίνα ὁρᾷς σωτηρίαν φιλοσόφῳ φύσει; so also in Aristotle, when he
sums up an argument, Cf. Eth. III. 5: he uses it also to mark a new
point in an argument, like in English, *now:* here belongs also the use of
μὲν δή, with a reference to what has gone before, followed by δέ, which
marks a new thought; as, Hdt. I. 32 Σόλων μὲν δή, Solon then, (as I have
told,) Κροῖσος δέ, and Crœsus &c.; so also τοιαῦτα μὲν δὴ ταῦτα, *hæc hactenus*;
and the combinations δὲ δή, ἀλλὰ δή, εἶτα δή, &c., which are used to connect sentences; so the questions πῶς δή, τί δή, ποῦ δή, *how now,* &c., as
expressions of impatience, astonishment, τί δὴ πότε, πῶς οὖν δή, τί οὖν δή.

2. Exactness applied to other notions: *a.* often joined with a pronoun,
in explanatory sentences, when reference is made to something well known;
as, Plat. Rep. p. 467 B κίνδυνος οὐ σμικρὸς σφαλεῖσιν οἷα δὴ ἐν πολέμῳ φιλεῖ.

just as. b. With a pronoun, which is used to recall an object in the former part of a sentence, whose immediate connection with the latter part has been interrupted; as, Il. ζ. 395 Ἀνδρομάχη θυγάτηρ μεγαλήτορος Ἠετίωνος, Ἠετίων ὃς ἔναιεν ὑπὸ Πλάκῳ ὑληέσσῃ, τοῦπερ δὴ θυγάτηρ ἔχεθ᾽ Ἕκτορι χαλκοκορυστῇ: comp. Il. η, 155. c. Sometimes with the collateral notion of excluding every thing else—*exactly this, and nothing else :* and in this sense we often find μὴ δή, with imper.: Il. κ, 447 μὴ δή μοι φύξιν γε Δόλων ἐμβάλλεο θυμῷ, just do not think of flight; so σκόπει δή, only just look: ἄγε δή, φέρε δή, ἴθι δή.

3. With particles, *just :* ὡς δή, ἵνα δή, *just that :* with explanatory particles, γὰρ δή, ὡς δή, (mostly ironical) οἷα δή, ἅτε δή, ἀλλὰ δή, *for just,* &c.

§. 722. 1. The certainty, reality of any thing, in which sense it may often be translated by *in sooth, forsooth :* Plat. Apol. p. 27 C οὐχ οὕτως ἔχει; ἔχει δή, is it not so ἔ in sooth is it : and it is sometimes used with a collateral notion of *at least :* Soph. Phil. 866 ἐπειδὴ τοῦδε τοῦ κακοῦ δοκεῖ λήθη τι εἶναι κἀνάπαυλα δή; if not λήθη, at least certainly ἀνάπαυλα.

2. This notion of certainty or reality is frequently used ironically, *forsooth :* Thuc. VI. 80 τοὺς Ἀθηναίους φίλους δὴ ὄντας μὴ ἐᾶσαι ἁμαρτεῖν, as being friends forsooth ; hence it is frequently used to denote that something pretends or appears to be that which it really is not ; as, Xen. Hell. V. 4, 6 εἰσήγαγε τὰς ἑταιρίδας δή, and so very often in Hdt. and Thuc. (as δῆθεν), to express the pretence on which something is done : that the reason which is given is either not in itself true, or not the one on which the party really acted.

3. Somewhat analogous to this ironical force is its use in suppositions, *supposing this were really so :* Thuc. VIII. 52 εἰ δὴ ἔλθοιεν, supposing they were really to come: Eur. Med. 388 καὶ δὴ τεθνᾶσι, suppose them then to be actually dead.

§. 723. 1. By the addition of these notions of certainty and reality the force of the word is heightened, and δή is to be translated so to express this heightened force according to the meaning of the word ; μόνος δή, quite alone : ἐν βραχεῖ δή—ἀσθενὴς δή, decidedly weak : Il. σ, 95 ὠκύμορος δή μοι τέκος ἔσσεαι : πολλοὶ δή—πολλάκις δή : especially with superlatives; κράτιστοι δή, decidedly, *by far, the greatest :* so also with pronouns, of which it increases the personal or demonstrative force, so as to denote the greatness, or dignity, or importance of the person or thing spoken of, or referred to ; ἐκεῖνος δή, that well known man. Hence also with indefinite pronouns, it increases the indefiniteness : Hdt. I. 86 θεῶν ὅτεῳ δή, *Deorum nescio cui :* ἄλλοι δή, others, be they who they may : Il. α, 295 ἄλλοισιν δὴ ταῦτ᾽ ἐπιτέλλεο, to others I care not whom : so ὅσος δή—ὁπόσον δή—ὅστις δή, *nescio quandam, quis :* ὅπου δή, ζῆν ὁπόσον δὴ χρόνον, I know not how long ; with τὶς or πότε, δή comes first ; δή τις, *quidam nescio quis :* δή ποτε *quondam nescio quando.*

2. With interrogatives, to increase the force of the question, and often denotes that a definite answer is expected to this point : Od. φ, 362 τῇ δὴ κάμπυλα τόξα φέρεις, where then ? answer me this : Plat. Phæd. p. 61 E κατὰ τί δὴ οὖν ποτε οὔ φασι, why in the world then ? Id. Theat. p. 148 A τίς δὴ οὖν ὦ παῖ, λείπεται λόγος ; so often with οὖν.

3. With numerals, it either heightens or limits their force, according to the context.

§. 724. 1. Hence it arises that καὶ δή is used to introduce the most important member of a sentence—καὶ τὸ δὴ μέγιστον, or when a particular follows an universal—ἄλλοι δέ—καὶ δὴ καί : Hdt. I. 30 ἀπίκετο παρὰ Ἄμασιν καὶ δὴ καί—παρὰ Κροῖσον; as negative οὐδὲ δή—μηδὲ δή : so Hdt. III. 39 ἐν δὲ δὴ καὶ Λεσβίους, and among them the Lesbians.

2. It is also used with various adverbs and particles, to express the certainty of the sentence to which they are attached : ἦ δή—ἦ μάλα δή—καὶ δή, οὐ δή, δήπου, *surely ;* οὐ δή που, *surely not ;* both post-Homeric ; and sometimes they have a certain irony : Xen. M. S. ii. 3, 1 οὐ δήπου καὶ οὐ εἰ τῶν τοιούτων ἀνθρώπων.

b. Δῆτα.

§. 725. 1. Δῆτα, formed from δή, as ἐνθαῦτα from ἔνθα, &c. has the same notion of exactness with δή, *now then,* but with a greater force, corresponding to its lengthened form. It is not found in Epic or Doric, nor often in Hdt., but very frequently in Attic.

2. *a.* Very often after interrogatives : a. to increase their force, *j a m, d e m u m :* and to mark a conclusion or consequence : Aristoph. Acharn. 1011 τί δῆτ', ἐπειδὰν τὰς κίχλας ὀπτωμένας ἴδητε; *quid tum demum dicetis, quum :—β.* to qualify them, when a person asks with somewhat of impatience, how something which appears contradictory can happen ; as, Æsch. Sept. 93 τίς ἄρα ῥύσεται, τίς ἄρ' ἐπαρκέσει θεῶν ἢ θεᾶν ; Πότερα δῆτ' ἐγὼ ποτιπέσω βρέτη δαιμόνων ;—after οὔκουν, μῶν, εἶτα, ἔπειτα, and ἄρα, δῆτα is used both to increase or qualify the question. *b.* In questions, to give emphasis to the word with which it stands : Eur. Iph. A. 856 οἶσθα δῆτά γ', ὅστις ὢν σοὶ καὶ τέκνοις εὔνους ἔφυν ; do you really know ? *c.* Very frequently with answers, to express the exact correspondence of the answer to the question, *just so, exactly so,* like δή, but stronger : Plat. Rep. p. 333 A ξυμβόλαια δὲ λέγεις κοινωνήματα, ἤ τι ἄλλο ;—Κοινωνήματα δῆτα :—*d.* ἦ δῆτα, certainly ; οὐ δῆτα, *m i n i m e v e r o,* μὴ δῆτα, only not this, to give emphasis to the negative entreaty : μὴ δῆτα δράσῃς ταῦτα, only do not this.—*e.* With wishes, commands, exhortations, it expresses "*just,*" as an expression of impatience, like δή : Aristoph. Nub. init. ἀπόλοιο δῆτ', ὦ πόλεμε, πολλῶν ἕνεκα ! may you just perish, and nothing else :—σκόπει δῆτα, just but look. *f.* With ἀλλά, or γάρ, it belongs not to these conjunctions, but it adds the notion of exactness to some part of the sentence ; this is often ironical : Eur. El. 930 ᾔδησθα γὰρ δῆτ' ἀνόσιον γήμας γάμον. *g.* It is used as a conjunction, generally with a notion of a climax : hence with conjunctions and relatives ; as, ὅτε δῆτα, *when at length :* Hdt. IV. 69 ἀπολλῦσι δῆτα αὐτοὺς τρόπῳ τοιῷδε.—Καὶ δῆτα, *and just, and in sooth.*

c. Θήν, δῆθεν, δήπουθεν.

§. 726. 1. Θήν is a collateral form of δή, which prevailed mostly in the Sicilian dialect, (hence so frequent in Theocr.) but it is also found in Epic, as an enclitic, whence it was introduced in its enclitic form θεν, as a mere suffix, into Attic : (θήν only Æsch. P. V. 964.) This particle is less independent than δή, and can only affect the sense of the single word with which it is joined, and not of the whole sentence. Its use varies in the different dialects : in the Mimes of Sophron it has the temporal force of δή, and is accentuated ; in Theocritus it is also accentuated ; it is most frequently joined with a pronoun : ἐγὼ θήν, I for my part : τὺ θήν.— In a demonstrative sense, as Adoniaz. 15. *Shortly, d e n i q u e, u t p a u c i s d i c a m :* Ibid. 63 ἐς Τροίαν πειρώμενοι ἥνθον Ἀχαιοί, κάλλιστοι παίδων· πείρᾳ θ ὴ ν πάντα τελεῖται. In Homer θήν is always ironical, as in Attic δήπου: it is very frequently joined with οὐκ (ο ὐ μ έ ν θ η ν — γ έ, but certainly not—at least: Od. ε, 211 οὐ μέν θην κείνης γε χερείων εὔχομαι εἶναι), ἤ, ἐπεί, γάρ.

2. In Attic it is found in its shortened form: θεν (θε Eur. El. 266.) only in the two compounds, δ ῆ θ ε ν, δ ή π ο υ θ ε ν.

a. Δ ῆ θ ε ν is used, almost always, in the ironical sense of δή, (forsooth, *scilicet*,) (§. 722. 2.) especially to express that the writer does not believe that the account he is giving is the true one, but only the one given by others—and it but seldom has a more explanatory force: Hdt. I. 59 (Πεισίστρατος) τρωματίσας ἑωυτόν τε καὶ ἡμιόνους, ἤλασεν ἐς τὴν ἀγορὴν τὸ ζεῦγος, ὡς ἐκπεφευγὼς τοὺς ἐχθρούς, οἵ μιν ἐλαύνοντα ἐς ἀγρὸν ἠθέλησαν ἀπολέσαι δῆθεν.

b. Δ ή π ο υ θ ε ν, certainly, clearly: Xen. Cyr. IV. 3, 20 ἐγὼ δέ, ἢν ἱππεύειν μάθω, ὅταν μὲν ἐπὶ τοῦ ἵππου γένωμαι, τὰ τοῦ ἱπποκενταύρου δ ή π ο υ θ ε ν διαπράξομαι.

Obs. A still shorter form of θήν appears in ε ῖ θ ε, where θε has the force of δή in emphatic questions and addresses (if only that).

d. Δ α ί.

§. 727. Δαί is a lengthened form of δή, as ναί of νή, it is frequent in the language of common life, rare in traged. It is found only in the combinations τί δαί, πῶς δαί; and seems, a. to express astonishment in a question, what else then? what then? when the speaker answers to an objection, by asking, "if not this, what can it be?" Aristoph. Av. 64 ἀλλ' οὐκ ἐσμὲν ἀ-θρώπω.—Τ ί δ α ί; Id. Vesp. 1212 ὡδὲ κελεύεις προσκλιθῆναι ;—Μηδαμῶς.— —Πῶς δαί ;— b. A rapid, unexpected transition from one person to another: Plat. Phæd. p. 71 A καὶ μὴν ἐξ ἰσχυροτέρου γε τὸ ἀσθενέστερον καὶ ἐκ βραδυτέρου τὸ θᾶττον — Πάνυ γε.—Τί δαί; ἄν τι χεῖρον γίγνηται, οὐκ ἐξ ἀμείνονος, καὶ, ἐὰν δικαιότερον, ἐξ ἀδικωτέρου ;

Confirmative Adverbs.

a. Μ ή ν (Doric and Epic, μάν.)

§. 728. 1. Μήν signifies certainty, assurance, *surely*, and answers to the Lat. *vero*. It can never stand first in the sentence, but generally depends on that word which gives the general force to the whole sentence—especially particles ; so in addresses it is joined with the imper., as ἄγε μήν, ἔπου μήν: in questions it is joined with the interrogative word; as, τί μήν, qui v e r o, πῶς μήν, &c. : Plat. Phædon. p. 229 A B ὁρᾷς οὖν ἐκείνην τὴν ὑψηλοτάτην πλάτανον ; Τ ί μ ή ν, *quid quæso ?*

2. The other uses are three.

1. A simple assurance of what is said.

2. In an antithesis either to what has gone before, or follows ; to express the certainty, *therefore*, when there is not a real, but only apparent opposition between the two sentences; in which case it has a further power of laying emphasis on what is said ; as, Plat. Rep. p. 465 B πανταχῇ δὴ ἐκ τῶν νόμων εἰρήνην πρὸς ἀλλήλους οἱ ἄνδρες ἄξουσι; Πολλήν γε. Τ ο ύ τ ω ν μὴν ἐν ἑαυτοῖς μὴ στασιαζόντων οὐδὲν δεινόν, μή ποτε ἡ ἄλλη πόλις πρὸς τούτους ἢ πρὸς ἀλλήλους διχοστατήσῃ. these then.

3. In antithesis, where the opposition is real.

3. It is combined with the following particles :

a. Ἦ μήν, strong assurance — truly — surely. Hence commonly in oaths, and a. simply : Xen. Cyr. IV. 2, 8 τὰ πιστὰ δίδωσιν αὐτοῖς, ἦ μὴν — ὡς φίλοις καὶ πιστοῖς χρήσεσθαι αὐτοῖς : Plat. Crit. p. 51 E ὁμολογήσας ἦ μ ὴ ν πείθεσθαι οὔτε πείθεται οὔτε πείθει ἡμᾶς. β. Opposed to what has gone before : Il. ι, 57 ἀτὰρ οὐ τέλος ἵκεο μύθων· ἦ μ ὴ ν καὶ νέος ἐσσὶ, ἐμὸς δέ κε καὶ παῖς εἴης, you are assuredly. γ. Opposed to what follows : Il. ν, 354 ἦ μ ὰ ν ἀμφοτέροισιν ὁμὸν γένος ἠδ' ἴα πάτρη, ἀ λ λ ὰ Ζεὺς πρότερος γεγόνει καὶ πλείονα ᾔδη.

b. Ο ὐ μήν, μ ὴ μ ή ν, certainly not. α. In a simple sentence : Il. μ, 318 οὐ μ ὰ ν ἀκλεεῖς Λυκίην κάτα κοιρανέουσιν ἡμέτεροι βασιλῆες : cf. Il. ρ, 41, 448. β. Opposed to what has gone before : Il. ο, 16 σὸς δόλος, Ἥρη, Ἕκτορα δῖον ἔπαυσε μάχης, ἐφόβησε δὲ λαούς : Ο ὐ μ ὰ ν οἶδ' εἰ αὖτε κακορραφίης ἀλεγεινῆς πρώτη ἐπαύρηαι, and truly I know not. So ἀ λ λ' ο ὐ μ ὰ ν ο ὐ δ έ Il. ψ, 441 : Soph. Œ. C. 694 οὐδὲ Μουσᾶν χοροί νιν ἀπεστύγησαν, ο ὐ δ ὲ μ ὰ ν (neque vero) χρυσάνιος Ἀφροδίτα.

c. Κ α ὶ μ ή ν : α. In a simple sentence, where καί is merely the copula, (Attic more commonly καὶ μέντοι) : Il. ψ, 410 ὧδε γὰρ ἐξερέω, κ α ὶ μ ὴ ν τετελεσμένον ἔσται, or where καί refers to something implied in the context, ὥσπερ καὶ λέγεις, ὥσπερ καὶ δοκεῖ, yes truly : Plat. Phæd. p. 58 E κ α ὶ μ ὴ ν ἔγωγε θαυμάσια ἔπαθον παραγενόμενος. β. Opposed to what has gone before, where καί means also *vel*, as κ α ὶ μ ὴ ν, *et vero*; καί belongs either to the word following μήν, or to the whole sentence. Καὶ μήν is often used when some new paragraph is begun : Od. λ, 582 κ α ὶ μ ὴ ν Τάνταλον εἰσεῖδον. In the dramatists it is often used on the entrance of a new character. Also κ α ὶ μ ὴ ν κ α ί, *et vero etiam*, and indeed also ; κ α ὶ μ ὴ ν ο ὐ δ έ, and indeed not.

d. Ἀ λ λ ὰ μ ή ν : α. In a simple sentence — assurance, (these words are sometimes divided by the word to which they convey an emphasis : Il. ρ, 448 ἀ λ λ' οὐ μ ὰ ν ὑμῖν γε καὶ ἅρμασι δαιδαλέοισιν Ἕκτωρ Πριαμίδης ἐποχήσεται· οὐ γὰρ ἐάσω), when the person wishes to express his willingness to comply with the demand, "but in truth ;" or where any one hastily takes up what another has said ; Eur. Hec. 498 τῆσδ' ἑκοῦσα παιδὸς οὐ μεθήσομαι, — Ἀ λ λ' οὐδ' ἐγὼ μ ὴ ν τήνδ' ἄπειμ' αὐτοῦ λιπών, and I in truth also. β. Opposed to what has gone before ; *but surely also, sed vero* Xen. Cyr. V. 3, 31 καὶ ἅμα δίκαια ποιοῖμεν ἂν, χάριν ἀποδιδόντες· ἀ λ λ ὰ μ ὴ ν καὶ ξυμφορά γ' ἄν. Often in logical arguments ; as Lucian, εἰ εἰσὶ βωμοί, εἰσὶ καὶ θεοί· ἀ λ λ ὰ μ ὴ ν (atqui) εἰσὶ βωμοί· εἰσὶν ἄρα θεοί.

Obs. When joined with the imper. it increases the urgency of the request.

b. Μέν (confirmativum).

§. 729. 1. Instead of μήν, the Ionic uses the shortened form μ έ ν, which occurs in Homer also, besides μήν and μάν. It is never placed at the beginning of a sentence, but is joined to the leading word in the sentence : Il. η, 89 καί ποτέ τις εἴπῃσι — · ἀ ν δ ρ ὸ ς μ ὲ ν τόδε σῆμα πάλαι κατατεθνηῶτος, of a hero in truth : Il. ο, 203 ἤ τι μεταστρέψεις; στρεπταὶ μ έ ν τε φρένες ἐσθλῶν, are surely to be turned.

2. Μέν is also used, (as μήν) either in a simple sentence, or when a sentence is opposed to what has gone before, or what follows : Od. ν, 154 ὦ πέπον, ὣς μὲν ἐμῷ θυμῷ δοκεῖ εἶναι ἄριστα, *immo vero sic*. So fre-

quently after a vocative, it marks the sentence to be opposed to something: Od. φ, 344 μῆτερ ἐμή, τόξον μὲν Ἀχαιῶν οὔτις ἐμεῖο κρείσσων ᾧ κ' ἐθέλω δόμεναί τε καὶ ἀρνήσασθαι, *immo vero arcum.*

3. It is combined with the following particles:

a. Ἦ μέν, which Homer uses exactly as ἦ μήν (§. 728. 3. *a.*) in oaths and asseverations. α. In a simple sentence: Od. ξ, 160 ἦ μέν τοι τάδε πάντα τελεῖεται, ὡς ἀγορεύω: Hdt. IV. 154 ἐξορκοῖ, ἦ μέν οἱ διηκονήσειν, ὅτι ἂν δεηθῇ. β. With reference to what has gone before: Od. λ, 447 λίην γὰρ πινυτή τε καὶ εὖ φρεσὶ μήδεα οἶδεν—Πηνελόπεια· ἦ μέν μιν νύμφην γε νέην κατελείπομεν ἡμεῖς ἐρχόμενοι πόλεμόνδε, and truly she was young. γ. In opposition to what follows: Il. ω, 416 ἦ μέν μιν — ἕλκει, οὐδέ μιν αἰσχύνει.

b. Οὐ μέν, μὴ μέν (= οὐ μήν, μὴ μήν §. 728. 3. *b.*). α. In a simple sentence: Il. ξ, 472 οὐ μέν μοι κακὸς εἴδεται, οὐδὲ κακῶν ἔξ, ἀλλὰ κασίγνητος Ἀντήνορος ἦ παῖς: Hdt. II. 118 καὶ ὀμνύντας καὶ ἀνωμοτί, μὴ μέν ἔχειν Ἑλένην: so οὐ μέν γάρ, ἐπεὶ οὐ μέν, since in truth not; μὴ μέν δή, οὐ μέν τοι. β. With reference to what has gone before: Il. ο, 735 ἠέ τινάς φαμεν εἶναι ἀοσσητῆρας ὀπίσσω, ἠέ τι τεῖχος ἄρειον, ὅ κ' ἀνδράσι λοιγὸν ἀμύναι; Οὐ μέν τι σχεδόν ἐστι πόλις, but truly there is no city near. So οὐδὲ μέν for ἀλλ' οὐ μήν. Also οὐ μέν δή, οὐ μέν τοι, οὐ or οὐδέ—οὐ μέν or οὐδὲ μέν—οὐδὲ μέν οὐδέ = ἀλλ' οὐ μὲν οὐδέ. γ. In a sentence referring to what follows—(rare): Od. δ, 31 οὐ μέν νήπιος ἦσθα — τὸ πρίν· ἀτὰρ μὲν νῦν γε παῖς ὡς νήπια βάζεις.

c. Καὶ μέν (= καὶ μήν §. 728. 3. *c.*). α. In a simple sentence: Il. ω, 488 καὶ μέν που κεῖνον περιναιέται ἀμφὶς ἐόντες τείρουσ', and surely. β. In a sentence referring to what has gone before, when a new paragraph is introduced; and also when there is an emphatic reference to the former sentence: Il. ι, 499 The gods are mighty, καὶ μέν τοὺς θυέεσσι — παρατρωπῶσ' ἄνθρωποι, but even these.

d. Γέ μέν is used in a sentence which is opposed to another: Hdt. VII. 234 ἔστι ἐν τῇ Λακεδαίμονι Σπάρτη, πόλις ἀνδρῶν ὀκτακισχιλίων μάλιστά κη· οὗτοι πάντες εἰσὶ ὁμοῖοι τοῖς ἐνθάδε μαχεσαμένοισι· οἵ γε μὲν ἄλλοι Λακεδαιμόνιοι τούτοισι μὲν οὐκ ὁμοῖοι, ἀγαθοὶ δέ.

e. Ἀτὰρ μέν, ἀλλὰ μέν. α. Simply: Od. μ, 156 ἀλλ' ἐρέω μέν ἐγώ. β. With reference to what has gone before: Od. ο, 405 νῆσος —οὔτι περιπληθὴς λίην τόσον, ἀλλ' ἀγαθὴ μέν, εὔβοτος κ. τ. λ.

f. Νῦν μὲν δή with fut. at the beginning of a speech, in which any thing is spoken of as being now at last determined for certain: Od. τ, 253 Νῦν μὲν δή μοι, ξεῖνε, πάρος περ ἐὼν ἐλεεινός, ἐν μεγάροισιν ἐμοῖσι φίλος τ' ἔσῃ αἰδοῖός τε.

g. Εἰ μὲν δή at the beginning of a sentence, if it might once be. Very often in Homer: Od. α, 82. δ, 831.

Obs. 1. It is used with the imper., as μήν.

Obs. 2. Μέν is very often placed after a pronoun, whereby some aforementioned person is repeated, and thus it signifies the identity of the person thus introduced again: Od. λ, 51 πρώτη δὲ ψυχὴ Ἐλπήνορος ἦλθεν — v. 55 τὸν μὲν ἐγὼ δάκρυσα κ. τ. λ. Μέν in this repetitive force may be used more than once in a succession of sentences: Od. ι, 319 sq. (ῥόπαλον) τὸ μὲν ἔκταμεν, τὸ μὲν ἄμμες εἴσκομεν, τοῦ μὲν ὅσον τ' ὀργυιαν ἐγὼν ἀπέκοψα παραστάς. It is also used in this force with adverbs; as, ἔνθα μέν, there, where. But μέν is frequently used with pronouns in an adversative sentence: Il. β, 324 τίπτ' ἄνεω ἐγένεσθε —; ἡμῖν μὲν τόδ' ἔφηνε τέρας μέγα.

Obs. 3. Sometimes μέν is followed by another μέν, the one having an adversative force, the other joined to a pronoun to mark the identity of the person : Il. σ, 432 sq. ἐκ μέν μ' ἀλλάων ἀλιάων ἀνδρὶ δάμασσεν — ὁ μὲν δὴ γήραϊ λυγρῷ κεῖται ἐνὶ μεγάροις ἀρημένος· ἄλλα δέ μοι νῦν.

c. Μέντοι, μενοῦν, μενδή.

§. 730. In the other dialects μέν is found for μήν only in the compounds, μέντοι, μενοῦν, μενδή.

a. Μέντοι strengthens or qualifies the notion (especially in answers), sometimes ironically. So καὶ μέντοι, οὐ μέντοι, ἀλλὰ μέντοι (especially in answers). It is also used in reference to another sentence, and generally signifies, that although from what has gone before it might not be expected, yet such or such a thing is so : especially μέν—μέντοι, *indeed—yet :* but also where there is no such contradiction between the sentences : Plat. Phæd. 87 E εἰ γὰρ ῥέοι τὸ σῶμα καὶ ἀπολλύοιτο—, ἀναγκαῖον μέντοι ἂν εἴη κ.τ.λ., it would in truth. So καὶ μέντοι, καὶ μέντοι καί, ἀλλὰ μέντοι, ἐπεί γε μέντοι.

b. Μενοῦν, which seems to answer to the Latin *immo*, is almost entirely confined to replies, either affirmative, or negative, or corrective (see *Interrogative Sentences*). Οὖν gives decision to what is said. So οὐ or μὴ μενοῦν, *immo non :* Plat. Symp. p. 201 C σοὶ οὐκ ἂν δυναίμην ἀντιλέγειν, ἀλλ' οὕτως ἐχέτω, ὡς σὺ λέγεις. Οὐ μενοῦν τῇ ἀληθείᾳ, φάναι, δύνασαι ἀντιλέγειν, i. e. *immo vero contra veritatem non potes disputare*[a]; or rather, you cannot fight against truth. Sometimes μενοῦν is used where a person replies to himself, or corrects a reply : Æsch. Choeph. 999 δίκτυον μὲν οὖν, nay it is rather : Eur. Hipp. 1009 μάταιος ἄρ' ἦν, οὐδαμοῦ μενοῦν φρενῶν, I was foolish, or rather out of my mind : Aristoph. Equit. 911 ἐμοῦ μὲν οὖν, no, rather on mine.

c. Μενδή always in the combinations, ἢ μενδή, οὐ μενδή, ἀλλὰ μενδή, καὶ μενδή, γὲ μέν—δή for ἢ μὴν δή &c. : Xen. Cyr. I. 6, 8 τί δέ, ἔφη, οἶσθα, ὁπόσα αὐτῷ ἔστι ; Μὰ τὸν Δία, ἔφη ὁ Κῦρος, οὐ μενδή.

d. Ἤ — ἤτοι.

§. 731. 1. *a.* Ἤ, like μήν, expresses confirmation, assurance (Hesych. ἤ = ἀληθῶς, ὄντως), but it is never, as μήν is, used as a conjunction. For ἢ μήν in strong asseverations, see §. 728. *a.* §. 729. *a.* It is also joined frequently with πού, τοί, γέ : ἢ πού, *to be sure,* denotes that the assertion has a certain degree of doubt. It is often ironically applied in this sense to things which are quite clear. So ἢ πού is used in conclusions of which no doubt can be entertained : Isocr. p. 164 A ὅπου γὰρ Ἀθηνόδωρος καὶ Καλλίστρατος — οἰκίσαι πόλεις οἷοί τε γεγόνασι, ἢ πού βουληθέντες ἡμεῖς πολλοὺς ἂν τόπους τοιούτους δυνηθείημεν κατασχεῖν.

Obs. For ἀλλ' ἤ, at *profecto,* we often find a false reading ἀλλ' ἤ, it being supposed that ἀλλ' ἤ is only used in questions.

2. *b.* Ἤτοι, which is only used in Epic writers, appears to be a combination of the confirmative ἤ and the restricting particle τοί. It expresses certainty, and often accompanies μέν in the same sense. In all those forms mentioned above, μέν appears to be used only to strengthen ἤτοι : Od. π, 309 ὦ πάτερ, ἤτοι (in truth) ἐμὸν θυμὸν καὶ ἔπειτά γ' ὀΐω γνώσεαι :

<hr>

[a] Stallb. ad loc.

Il. ω, 460 ὦ γέρον, ἤτοι ἐγὼ θεὸς ἄμβροτος εἰλήλουθα Ἑρμείας· σοὶ γάρ με πατὴρ ἅμα πόμπον ὅπασσεν: Il. φ, 446 ἤτοι ἐγὼ Τρώεσσι πόλιν πέρι τεῖχος ἔδειμα. So ἀλλ' ἤτοι, ἀλλ' ἤτοι μέν: Od. ξ, 259 ἔνθ' ἤτοι (then in truth) μὲν ἐγὼ κελόμην ἐρίηρας ἑταίρους αὐτοῦ παρ' νήεσσι μένειν καὶ νῆα ἔρυσθαι: Il. η, 451 τοῦ δ' ἤτοι κλέος ἔσται, ὅσον τ' ἐπικίδναται ἠώς: Il. ς, 191 ὦ φίλοι, ἤτοι κλῆρος ἐμός: Od. μ, 165 ἤτοι ἐγὼ τὰ ἕκαστα λέγων ἑτάροισι πίφαυσκον, surely: Od. ζ, 86 ἔνθ' ἤτοι πλυνοὶ ἦσαν, there in truth. Ἤτοι is often used, where two things are contrasted, either with the first sentence, on which some contrast follows; as, Il. θ, 323 ἤτοι ὁ μὲν (Teucer) φαρέτρης ἐξείλετο πικρὸν ὀϊστόν, θῆκε δ' ἐπὶ νευρῇ· τὸν δ' αὖ κορυθαίολος Ἕκτωρ—βάλεν λίθῳ ὀκριόεντι, or with the second, so that it introduces the contrast, where it = καίτοι, quamquam : Od. φ, 98 τῷ δ' ἄρα θυμὸς — ἐώλπει νευρὴν ἐντανύσειν διοϊστεύσειν τε σιδήρου· ἤτοι ὀϊστοῦ γε πρῶτος γεύσεσθαι ἔμελλεν ἐκ χειρῶν Ὀδυσῆος ἀμύμονος, ὃν ποτ' ἀτίμα.

3. From this power of expressing certainty it arises that ἤτοι as well as μέν (μήν) is used with the first of two assertions, to mark its reality, which from the second assertion might be doubted : Od. ο, 6 εὗρε δὲ Τηλέμαχον καὶ Νέστορος ἀγλαὸν υἱόν — · ἤτοι Νεστορίδην μαλακῷ δεδμημένον ὕπνῳ· Τηλέμαχον δ' οὐχ ὕπνος ἔχε γλυκύς: Od. ω, 154 ἵκοντο προτὶ ἄστυ περικλυτόν· ἤτοι Ὀδυσσεὺς ὕστερος, αὐτὰρ Τηλέμαχος πρόσθ' ἡγεμόνευεν. Ἤτοι is more emphatic than μέν (μήν): both however can be used with the second also of two assertions to mark its reality, though somewhat contrary to the former sentence : ἀλλ' ἤτοι, but yet : Od. ο, 486 Εὔμαι', ἦ μάλα δή μοι ἐνὶ φρεσὶ θυμὸν ὄρινας, ταῦτα ἕκαστα λέγων, ὅσα δὴ πάθες ἄλγεα θυμῷ· ἀλλ' ἤτοι σοὶ μὲν παρὰ καὶ κακὸν ἐσθλὸν ἔθηκεν Ζεύς. Ἤτοι, as well as μέν, is joined to the imperative, to make the request more urgent: Od. δ, 238 ἤτοι νῦν δαίνυσθε — καὶ μύθοις τέρπεσθε.

4. Ἤτοι is joined with a conjunction which introduces a dependent clause to give the notion of certainty thereto; as, Od. ε, 23 οὐ γὰρ δὴ τοῦτον μὲν ἐβούλευσας νόον αὐτή, ὡς ἤτοι κείνους Ὀδυσεὺς ἀποτίσεται ἐλθών : so ὃς δ' ἤτοι — ὄφρ' ἤτοι Od. γ, 418.

e. Νύ, (Epic) *Enclitic.*

§. 732. Νύ expresses an asseveration, but is seldom used seriously, to increase the force of the sentence, but has somewhat of an ironical bitterness ; *surely, forsooth, nempe, scilicet :* Od. α, 347 μῆτερ ἐμή, τί τ' ἄρα φθονέεις ἐρίηρον ἀοιδὸν τέρπειν, ὅπῃ οἱ νόος ὄρνυται ; οὐ νύ τ' ἀοιδοὶ αἴτιοι, ἀλλά ποθι Ζεὺς αἴτιος.—So ἐπεί νυ, since surely, as men know too well : Cf. Il. α, 416: we also find ἦ ῥά νυ, μή νυ τοι, οὔ νυ τι, surely not : and with a past tense indic., after an hypothetical sentence also expressed by a past tense indic. καί νυ κε : Od. δ, 363 καί νυ κεν ᾖα πάντα κατέφθιτο καὶ μένε' ἀνδρῶν, εἰ μήτις με θεῶν ὀλοφύρατο, *et nimirum — periissent, nisi — commisseratus fuisset :* but sometimes it is used to give certainty to the sentence: Il. σ, 392 Ἥφαιστε, πρόμολ' ὧδε ! Θέτις νύ τι σεῖο χατίζει: Od. β, 320 ὥς νυ πού ὔμμιν ἐείσατο κέρδιον εἶναι, "*sic nimirum,* opinor (πού), *vobis satius videbatur :*" so also in questions; as Od. α, 62 τί νυ οἱ τόσον ὠδύσαο, Ζεῦ; *quid nam ?* Cf. Il. α, 414.

f. Νή, ναί, μά.

§. 733. Νή, Lat. *næ,* expresses an asseveration, but only in affirmative sentences—especially in oaths, νὴ τὸν Δία, truly by Jupiter ; ναί is a length-

ened form of νή, as δαί of δή, and has the same force, but is often joined
with μά, as ναὶ μὰ τὸν Δία, which is only used in negative sentences : Il.
α, 86 οὐ μὰ γὰρ Ἀπόλλωνα, &c.; sometimes the negation follows at some
distance : Eur. Med. 1067 μὰ τοὺς παρ' ᾅδην νερτέρους ἀλάστορας, οὔτοι
ποτ' ἔσται τοῦτο.

Intensive particles : γέ, πέρ.

a. Π έ ρ.

§. 734. 1. Πέρ, Lat. *per, nuper,* &c., is an enclitic form of the adverb
περί, *through and through, throughout, throughly :* hence *very,* of which
a lengthened form is περίσσως; whence πέρ (like δή) increases the force of
the word to which it is attached, and if the word be that which gives a
character to the whole sentence, it modifies the meaning thereof, according
to the proper force of the word.

2. With single words, of which it increases the force : (Lat. *per gratus
perque jucundus.*)

ı. With participles, or more commonly with an adjective, and the participle of εἶναι, it either increases the force of the verbal or adjectival notion,
as Il. γ, 201 Ἰθάκης κραναῆς περ ἐούσης, very rough : Il. α, 132 ἀγαθός περ
ἐών, very good : or of the time of the verb ; Il. ψ, 79 γενόμενόν περ, at the
very moment of his birth.

2. With subst., (or adj. without ἐών), adverbs, ἀμφότεροί περ, both together, οὐκ ὀλίγον περ — μινυνθά περ — πρῶτόν περ — ὕστατόν περ, quite the
first, last, πύκα περ, very wisely. It sometimes expresses a contrast to
another notion not expressed, by laying a strong emphasis on the word : Il.
κ, 70 ἀλλὰ καὶ αὐτοί περ πονεώμεθα, we ourselves, (not leaving it to others :)
Il. β, 236 οἴκαδέ περ σὺν νηυσὶ νεώμεθα, to our *proper* home, (and not stay
here :) Od. γ, 236 θάνατον μὲν—οὐδὲ θεοί περ, not *even* the gods, (let alone
men ;) or the notion, the contrast to which πέρ denotes, is expressed, in
which case it may be translated " at least :" Il. ι, 301 εἰ δέ τοι Ἀτρείδης—
ἄλλους περ Παναχαιούς; and sometimes in this last case πέρ is joined with
both the words : Il. α, 353 μῆτερ ἐπεί μ' ἔτεκες μινυνθαδιόν περ ἐόντα τιμήν
περ μοι, very short time, very great glory.

3. With relative nouns, or adverbs. In Homer it defines exactly the
relative notion ; in Attic it generally calls out more strongly the indefinite
notion ; Lat., *cunque ;* English, *soever.* Ὅσπερ, exactly the same who ;
ὅσοσπερ, exactly as large as, or how large soever ; οἷός περ, exactly such a
person ; οἷά περ, just such as ; ὅπου περ, just where, wherever ; ὅθεν περ,
just whence, or whence soever ; οἵ περ, ἔνθα περ, ἵνα περ, &c. ; ὥσπερ, just
as ; ἥ περ, ὅτε περ, ἡνίκα περ, πρίν περ ; so with reference to a demonstrative, Œd. R. 1498 τὴν τεκοῦσαν ἤροσεν, ὅθεν περ αὐτὸς ἐσπάρη.

3. With sentences.— 1. When laying emphasis on the word (generally
a conjunction) which gives the character to the sentence, it modifies that
character according to the sense in which the conjunction is used : Soph.
Elect. 583 ἐάν περ καὶ λέγῃς : if emphatic=even if—lessens the probability
of its happening : Soph. Œd. Col. 1212 ἐάν περ κἀμέ τις σώζῃ θεῶν, if it
pleases the gods to save me ; as long as they save me : so ὅταν περ Soph.
Phil. 767 =*dummodo,* until : Elect. 378 =*ut primum :* so εἴπερ, if in reality, even if : ἕως περ, up to the very moment, until : τῆπερ, Il. ω, 603
Νιόβη ἐμνήσατο σίτου τῆπερ δώδεκα παῖδες—ὄλοντο, although to her. 2. And
even where there is no conjunction, if the participle, or adj. with ἐών, is felt

to express something which might be expected to counteract something just spoken of, or about to be spoken of, and thus gives a peculiar character to the action, πέρ, by laying emphasis on the participle, draws out this latent force, and takes the sense of "*although.*" Homeric, except Philoct. 1068 γενναῖος πέρ ἐών, though so noble : so ἱμερτός πέρ, though desirous ; and Homer, *passim.*

b. Γέ (Dor. γά) enclitic.

§. 735. The proper force of γέ is (like πέρ) intensive. It lays an emphasis on the word to which it is attached, and thus derives various significations, according to the sense of the word, or its relation to the context : its most general use is when two things, or persons, or notions are contrasted, or supposed to be contrasted, in the sense of *at least — at all events.* The object of the contrast frequently must be supplied by the mind.

1. Where something is represented as resulting from the character of the one, as contrasted with the character of the other : Il. ο, 48 εἰ μὲν δὴ σύ γ' ἔπειτα, βοῶπις πότνια Ἥρη, ἴσον ἐμοὶ φρονέουσα μετ' ἀθανάτοισι καθίζεις, τῷ κε Ποσειδάων γε, καὶ εἰ μάλα βούλεται ἄλλῃ, αἶψα μεταστρέψειε νόον, since he is only Neptune : Xen. Cyr. VIII. 1, 30 ὅταν γὰρ ὁρῶσιν ᾧ μάλιστα ἔξεστιν ὑβρίζειν τοῦτον σωφρονοῦντα, οὗτω μᾶλλον οἵ γε ἀσθενέστεροι ἐθέλουσιν οὐδὲν ὑβριστικὸν ποιοῦντες φανεροὶ εἶναι—argument *a majori.*

2. Where one alternative is contrasted with the other, γέ is used with the one on which the emphasis is to be laid : Hdt. IV. 120 εἰ δὲ μὴ ἑκόντες γε —, ἀλλ' ἄκοντες κ. τ. λ., if you will not do it *voluntarily,* you shall involuntarily : one alternative sometimes is to be supplied, ἐγώγε ταῦτα ποιήσω, I myself, (since others will not.) So in disjunctive sentences with ἤ—ἤ, ἤτοι—ἤ, εἴτε—εἴτε, where of two persons one must suffer or do something, γέ is joined to the one which is to make the greatest impression : Hdt. I. 11 ἤτοι κεῖνόν γε, τὸν ταῦτα βουλεύσαντα, δεῖ ἀπόλλυσθαι, ἢ σὲ, τὸν ἐμὲ γυμνὴν θηησάμενον : so in urgent questions, where the alternative is to be supplied ; as, Aristoph. Vesp. init. ἆρ' οἶσθά γ', οἶον κνώδαλον φυλάττομεν, do you not, at all events, (surely) know, (or not) ? If the γέ is meant to give emphasis to the whole question, it is joined to the interrogative word : Plat. Criton. p. 44 E ἆρά γε μὴ ἐμοῦ προμηθεῖ ; do you surely, (at all events) take some thought for me, (or not) ? Od. ω, 259 ὄφρ' εὖ εἰδῶ, εἰ ἐτεόν γ' Ἰθάκην τὴν δ' ἱκόμεθα.

3. When in disjunctive sentences a pronoun is to be repeated, γέ is added to it in the second sentence : Od. γ, 214 εἰσί μοι, ἠὲ ἑκὼν ὑποδάμνασαι, ἢ σέ γε λαοὶ ἐχθαίρουσ', or do the people hate you, I say : so Soph. Œ. R. 1098 τίς σ' ἔτικτεν—ἢ σέ γε.—So also when a pronoun is used in the first member of a disjunctive sentence, to repeat a person before mentioned, γέ is used with it : Od. β, 131 πατὴρ δ' ἐμὸς ἄλλοθι γαίης, ζώει ὅγ' ἢ τέθνηκεν : Il. κ, 504 αὐτὰρ ὁ μερμήριζε—· ἢ ὅγε δίφρον ἐξερύοι, ἢ ἔτι τῶν πλεόνων Θρηκῶν ἀπὸ θυμὸν ἕλοιτο,—whether he, I say : Il. χ, 33 ᾤμωξεν δ' ὁ γέρων, κεφάλην δ' ὅγε κόψατο χερσίν, he groaned, and (he I say) beat his head ;—and where we do not use the pronoun — ἄρα ὅγε, οἵγε, τοίγε, &c., and ὅγε after a pronoun, which also repeats the foregoing subject ; so Il. μ, 171—κεῖνός γε, οὗτός γε, he I say, with emphasis on the person to whom the demonstrative refers.

4. Γέ is often used to give the reason or character of an action expressed

in a preceding sentence: Eur. Iph. A. 1373 οὐ δεῖ τόνδε διὰ μάχης μολεῖν πᾶσιν Ἀργείοις γυναικὸς οὕνεκ', οὐδὲ κατθανεῖν· εἷς γ' ἀνὴρ κρείσσων γυναικῶν μυρίων ὁρᾶν φάος, as *quidem :* so γάρ (i. e. γ' ἄρα), γέ τοι, γοῦν (i. e. γε οὖν), μένγε.

5. It frequently limits the assertion of a sentence, by annexing certain conditions on which it would be true: Od. *a*, 229 νεμεσσήσαιτό κεν ἀνήρ, αἴσχεα πόλλ' ὁρόων, ὅστις πινυτός γε μετέλθοι, a man would be angry *that is to say*, if any one of good sense should come; or an expression in a sentence: Od. *ι*, 529 κλῦθι, Ποσείδαον γαιήοχε—, εἰ ἐτεόν γε σός εἰμι : hear, O father, *that is*, if I am indeed your son.

6. It is used when an assertion is followed by a statement which would imply a contradiction — *nevertheless in truth :* Eur. Med. 84 δεσπότης γάρ ἐστ' ἐμός· ἀτὰρ κακός γ' ὢν ἐς φίλους ἁλίσκεται. It is often accompanied by ἀλλά—καὶ μήν—καίτοι—μέντοι—ἦτοι : Æsch. Prom. 1018 ἀλλ' ἐκδιδάσκει πάνθ' ὁ γηράσκων χρόνος.—Καὶ μὴν σύγ' οὔπω σωφρονεῖν ἐπίστασαι, and yet, *nevertheless :* so Od. *τ*, 86 εἰ δ' ὁ μὲν ὡς ἀπόλωλε καὶ οὐκέτι νόστιμός ἐστιν, ἀλλ' ἤδη παῖς τοῖος Ἀπόλλωνός γε ἕκητι Τηλέμαχος, yet nevertheless he has a son.

7. Γέ is sometimes ironical : Eur. Iph. Aul. 1212 εὖ γε κηδεύεις πόλιν! you *forsooth* take good care of the city.

8. Γέ in the tragedians is also used in answers, to express an assent and an extension of the notion signified by the question, *certainly and moreover.*

9. Γέ is also joined with relatives and other conjunctions; it either gives the reason of what has preceded : so ὅσγε, ὅστις γε, οἷός γε, ὅσος γε, &c. who indeed, *qui quidem :* —ὥσπερ γε, as indeed : ὅπου γε, ἐπεί γε, *quandoquidem*, ὥς γε, ὅτε γε—εἴγε, *siquidem :* γάρ, i. e. γ' ἄρα : Xen. M. S. II. 1, 17 τί διαφέρουσιν (οἱ εἰς τὴν βασιλικὴν τέχνην παιδευόμενοι) τῶν ἐξ ἀνάγκης κακοπαθούντων, εἴγε πεινήσουσι καὶ διψήσουσι κ. τ. λ.; *si quidem :* — or limits the assertion; so ὅσγε, ὅστις γε, that is to say : (=οὗτός γε, ὃς γε), *qui quidem :*—εἰ γε, *si quidem* (= τότε γε, εἴ γε—οὕτως γε, εἴ γε) — πρίν γε, *prius quidem*, *quam*, οὐ—πρίν γε, *non prius quidem*, *quam*, that is to say, not before ; as, Il. *ε*, 303 μέγα ἔργον, ὅγ' οὐ δύο ἄνδρε φέροιεν : Eur. Alc. 511 πώλους ἀπάξω κοιράνῳ Τιρυνθίῳ—, εἰ μή γε πῦρ πνέουσι, *nisi quidem*, that is to say, unless : so also καίτοι γε, ἀλλά γε, when the latter of two sentences seems to contradict the former, *quamquam quidem*, *verum quidem :* Eur. Iph. T. 703 ἀτὰρ τὸ τοῦ θεοῦ γ' οὐ διέφθορέν σε πω μάντευμα, καίτοι γ' ἐγγὺς ἔστηκας φόνου, although at all events, *quamquam quidem.*

10. In καί—γέ, (only Attic,) *et quidem*, γέ qualifies or explains the preceding sentence : Plat. Phædon. p. 58 D ἀλλὰ παρῆσάν τινες, καὶ πολλοί γε, and indeed many : cf. p. 65 D δίκαιον— ; καὶ καλόν γε τι καὶ ἀγαθόν. Where a number of objects are strung together, γέ is used with the last, or one of the last, to prevent the sentence lagging : Plat. Criton. p. 47 B ταύτῃ ἄρα αὐτῷ πρακτέον καὶ γυμναστέον καὶ ἐδεστέον γε καὶ ποτέον, and to eat surely, (at all events) : so οὐδέ—γε, μηδέ—γε (in Homer, *at least not :* Il. ξ, 221.) Τέ γε, οὔτε γε is used only where γέ has a purely adversative force ; as, Xen. Cyr. II. 4, 13 μήτ' αὐτός γε ὑποχείριος γενέσθαι.—Δέ γε, like καί γε, is often used in logical forms ; εἰ ἡμέρα ἐστί, φῶς ἐστιν· ἡμέρα δέ γέ ἐστιν, but at all events it is day : in γέ μήν, καὶ μήν—γε ἢ μήν—γε, it qualifies or explains the sentence preceding.

Obs. 1. Of course if the explanatory or limiting sentence is expressed by a participle, γέ is used as with other sentences ; Od. *a*, 390 Διός γε διδόντος, that is, God willing.

Obs. 2. Γέ naturally is placed after the word to which it belongs. It sometimes however stands between a preposition and its case, or an article and its substantive ; or when two or more words form a whole notion, as βίος γε ἀνθρώπινος, or βίος ἀνθρωπίνος γε. If it refers to the whole sentence, it generally stands next to the governing conjunction, but Homer often allows the pronoun ὁ, ἡ, τό to come between them, and also other words, as may be seen from examples given above.

Τοί, *Enclitic.*

§. 736. Τοί lays an emphasis on the word or sentence to which it is attached, to denote that what is said especially applies to that word.

1. In the confirmative sense of the Latin *sane—verily—of a truth, indeed :* Eur. Rhes. 567 ὅρα κατ᾽ ὀρφνην μὴ φύλαξιν ἐντύχῃς.——Φυλάξομαί τοι, I will verily : Soph. Phil. 245 ἐξ Ἰλίου τοι δῆτα νῦν γε ναυστολῶ, a Trojá *sane.* Sometimes it conveys a notion of wonder, or impatience [a] : Plat. Gorg. p. 499 B πάλαι τοί σου ἀκροῶμαι, ὦ Σώκρατες, for a long time *in truth,* have I been listening to you. It is especially used with general propositions, maxims, assertions to confirm them—*sane* [b] : Od. θ, 329 οὐκ ἀρετᾷ κακὰ ἔργα· κιχάνει τοι βραδὺς ὠκύν : 351 δειλαί τοι δειλῶν γε καὶ ἐγγύαι ἐγγυάσθαι : Theogn. 74 παῦροί τοι πολλῶν πιστὸν ἔχουσι νόον : Soph. Phil. 475 τοῖσι γενναίοισί τοι τό τ᾽ αἰσχρὸν ἐχθρὸν καὶ τὸ χρηστὸν εὐκλεές : Ibid. 637 ἵ τοι καίριος σπουδή, πόνου λήξαντος, ὕπνον κἀνάπαυλαν ἤγαγεν : Xen. Cyr. VIII. 7, 14 καὶ πολίταί τοι ἄνθρωποι ἀλλοδαπῶν οἰκειότεροι καὶ σύσσιτοι ἀποσκήνων : Id. Anab. VI. 3, 24 ἡδύ τοι ἀνδρεῖόν τι καὶ καλὸν νῦν εἰδώτα καὶ ποιήσαντα μνήμην — παρέχειν ἑαυτοῦ : Il. ψ, 315 μῆτιν ἐμβάλλεο θυμῷ παντοίην· μῆτί τοι δρυτόμος μέγ᾽ ἀμείνων, ἠὲ βίηφιν· μῆτι δ᾽ αὖτε κυβερνήτης—νῆα θοὴν ἰθύνει—, μῆτι δ᾽ ἡνίοχος περιγίγνεται ἡνιόχου.

2. With a less definite emphasis to denote that what is said especially applies to the word to which τοί is attached ; *he (for his part* emphatic) will do this. Where we use the more emphatic tone, τοί may be used by the Greeks *for his part* [c]. So ἐγώ τοι, ἐγώγε τοι, ἡμεῖς τοι : Xen. M. S. I. 6, 11 ὦ Σώκρατες, ἐγώ τοι σε δίκαιον μὲν νομίζω : Id. Cyr. V. 2, 23 ἐγὼ τοι, ἔφη, ὦ Περίκλεις, ἐλπίδα ἔχω : so σύ τοι, σέ τοι &c. in addresses to a person who seems to pay no heed, that his attention may be awakened by hearing himself particularly addressed : Arist. Plut. 1100 σέ τοι, σέ τοι λέγω, Καρίων, ἀνάμεινον : Id. Av. 406 ἰὼ ἔποψ, σέ τοι καλῶ : Soph. Aj. 1228 σέ τοι τὸν ἐκ τῆς αἰχμαλωτίδος λέγω. So Id. Phil. 1084. And in prayers and entreaties, to signify that the person addressed is the only person to whom one can apply ; as, πρός σε τοι ἤλθομεν [d]. Hence frequently in addresses to the Deity : so ταῦτά τοι, this verily ; ὁπόσα τοι βούλει, in truth what you will.

Obs. It will easily be seen that in English we express many of these notions by an emphasis on the word, while in Greek this emphasis is distinctly embodied in the form of τοί.

3. Τοί is also used when two sentences are seemingly opposed, and may be translated by " yet," marking the truth of the one, though somewhat contradictory to the other : Æsch. Suppl. 78 Διὸς ἵμερος οὐκ εὐθήρατος ἐτύχθη· πάντα τοι φλεγέθει κἂν σκότῳ : so μέντοι, *tamen* (§. 730. *a.*).

---

[a] Stallb. Plat. Gorg. p. 499 B.
[b] Ellendt ad voc.   Stallb. Plat. Sympos. p. 219 A.   Heindorf Plat. Prot. p. 346. C.
[c] Stallb. Prot. p. 316 B.   [d] Heindorf Plat. Prot. p. 316 B.

4. It is subjoined with a number of particles [a], to most of which it gives an intensive force—*verily* [b] : ἀλλά τοι, when something is suddenly introduced, "*but verily*," Soph. Trach. 1239: γάρ τοι very common, γέ τοι, αὐτάρ τοι, ἀτάρ τοι, καίτοι, οὖτοι, μήτοι, τοιγάρτοι &c. τοίνυν &c.

5. It is frequently found in crasis with ἄν [c] and ἄρα, in its simple as well as its compound forms.

Οὖν.

§. 737. 1. Οὖν (Ion. ὦν) (probably a contraction from ἐόν, *quæ quum ita sint*) is used by Homer and Pindar only as a suffix to pronouns and conjunctions: ὅστις οὖν, ὅσπερ οὖν, ὅσοι οὖν, μενοῦν, γοῦν, οὔκουν, μῶν (μὴ οὖν), δ' οὖν, ἀλλ' οὖν, εἶτ' οὖν, γὰρ οὖν. Its strictly illative force (which will be treated of under the *Illative Particles*) was not fully developed till after Homer, though he uses it in certain combinations, such as ἐπεὶ οὖν, ὡς οὖν.

2. The proper adverbial force of οὖν seems to be *really, truly* [d], *then* ; and like that word in English, it is used for referring to a state of things whence something follows—generally marking an inference from something which has gone before, or is supposed to be known : εἰ δ' ἐστὶν, ὥσπερ οὖν ἐστι, θεός, as there is then truly : Æsch. Choeph. 95 ὥσπερ οὖν ἀπώλετο πατήρ, as then (as is well known) my father died. So Soph. Aj. 991. Æsch. Ag. 590 γυναῖκα πιστὴν — οἵανπερ οὖν ἔλειπε, as in truth he left her : Soph. Phil. 1306. Id. Œ. C. 1199 ἔχεις γὰρ οὖν βίαια τἀνθυμήματα : Eur. Med. 585 ἐν γὰρ οὖν ἐκτενεῖ [e] σ' ἔπος, one word then. So it is used to confirm a statement of which there is some doubt : Hdt. III. 80 καὶ ἐλέχθησαν λόγοι ἄπιστοι μὲν ἐνίοισι — ἐλέχθησαν δ' ὦν [f]. So when a statement is repeated and confirmed in spite of contradiction : Eur. Alc. 72 πόλλ' ἂν σὺ λέξας οὐδὲν ἂν πλέον λάβοις, ἡ δ' οὖν γυνὴ κάτεισιν εἰς Ἅδου δόμους, the lady I say. So in the commencement of a new sentence, it expresses something of wonder or feeling as if the person doubted it : σὺ δ' οὖν τέθνηκας, you are dead then !

3. It is used also as a conjunction to mark the continuation of a sentence—*then*—*thus then :* Soph. Elect. 299 ἐν οὖν τοιούτοις οὔτε σωφρονεῖν κ.τ.λ.: Id. Aj. 28. Æsch. Ag. 217 ἔτλα δ' οὖν θυτὴρ γενέσθαι, thus he endured then : Plat. Prot. p. 316 A ἡμεῖς μὲν οὖν εἰσήλθομεν : Arist. Thesm. 755. In the continued narrations of Hdt. it is found in its Ionic form ὦν, in the sense of "*straightway* [g]," and between a preposition and the verb with which it is compounded : ἀπ' ὦν ἔδοντο, they sell it then = straightway. So Hdt. IV. 60 καὶ ἔπειτα βρόχῳ περὶ ὦν ἔβαλε τὸν αὐχένα. It sometimes expresses an impatient permission to a person to do what he will : Soph. Œ. R. 669 ὅδ' οὖν ἴτω, let him go then.

4. In interrogative forms it very often expresses deduction from what has gone before, with a notion of objection thereto [h] : Soph. Phil. 100 τί οὖν μ' ἄνωγας ἄλλο πλὴν ψευδῆ λέγειν, why then do you (as you do) require of me nothing else, but &c. : cf. Id. 102. Æsch. Sept. 686 τί οὖν ἔτ' ἂν σαίνοιμεν ὀλέθριον μόρον ;

5. It is also used after an interruption in a sentence [i], to take up the thread, *I say, as I said,* (*inquam* [k] :) Thuc. VI. 44.

a Ellendt Lex. Soph. ad voc.
b Pass. Lex. τοί.
c Elmsley Œd. Col. 1351, and Acharn. 323.
d Pass. ad voc.
e R. P. Med. 585.

f Matth. Gr. Gr. 625.
g Ellendt Lex. Soph. ad voc. 3.
h Ellendt Lex. Soph. ad voc. 2.
i Matth. Gr. Gr. 611.
k Passow Lex. ad voc.

6. It is often used in a dialogue to express a wish for, or in a question which is meant to elicit, further information : ᵃ Æsch. Choeph. 171 τὰς οὖν παλαιὰ παρὰ νεωτέρας μάθω ; ᵇ Soph. Phil. 568 : so Æsch. Sept. 810 βαρέα δ' οὖν ὅμως φράσον : or merely to connect the question with what has gone before.

7. It is also used as a suffix to pronouns and pronominal adverbs, laying emphasis on the indefinite notion, in the sense of the Latin *cunque*: ὁστισοῦν, ὁπωσοῦν, &c.

Negative Particles, οὐκ *and* μή.

§. 738. 1. There are two sorts of negation : *a.* Negative proper, where the sentence is negative, the agreement of the subject and predicate, as, *he is not learned,* being denied. *b.* Privative, where the predicate is negative, expressing the absence of some quality, and the presence of the contrary, as, *he is not learned*=*unlearned ;* with which predicate the subject is said to agree.

2. The former is properly expressed by οὐ, (οὐκ before an unaspirated, οὐχ before an aspirated vowel, Attic also οὐχί, like ναιχί) and its compounds, such as οὐδέ, οὔτε, &c., and by μή and its compounds, as μηδέ, μήτε, &c. ; the latter, properly by the inseparable privative adverbs, ἀν-, νη-.

Obs. 1. Οὐ and μή sometimes appear to be, and indeed practically are, privative ; as, ἀνὴρ οὐ μέγας : Thuc. VIII. 100 οὐχ οἱ ἀδυνατώτατοι ; but this privative force really belongs to the original negative notion, as may be seen, when these words are resolved into their full form, ἀνὴρ δὲ οὐ μέγας ἐστίν.

Obs. 2. This seemingly privative use frequently arises from the negative being generally joined to the word to which the force of the negation especially applies : Eur. Hipp. 1254 οὐκ ὠμὸς ἐς σὸν παῖδα δυστυχοῦντ' ἔσει : so οὐ πάνυ μέμνημαι, not at all, &c. ; and it even sometimes separates a preposition and its adjective ; as, Eur. Rhes. 925 ἐς οὐ βροτείαν ἐσχάραν.

Obs. 3. Sometimes οὐ seems to have the force of the privative ἀν-, as it so affects the predicate, as to convey exactly the contradictory thereof to the mind ; as, τὰ οὐ καλά, *inhonesta,* οὐ καλῶς, *turpiter,* οὐχ εἷς, οὐκ ὀλίγοι = πολλοί ; οὐχ ἥκιστα=μάλιστα ; οὐκ ἀφανής=ἔνδοξος : Xen. Hell. VI. 4. 18 οἱ οὐκ ἐλάχιστον δυνάμενοι ἐν τῇ πόλει : so especially with verbs of *saying* and *thinking ;* as, οὔ φημι, *nego* ; οὐχ ὑπισχνοῦμαι, I refuse ; οὐκ ἐῶ, *prohibeo* ; οὐ κελεύω, *veto :* so οὐ στέργω, I hate. If the nature of the sentence requires it, μή can be used in the same way ; as, Soph. Phil. 444 ὅπου μηδεὶς ἐῴη : so ἔφη ἐκεῖνον ταῦτα μὴ καλῶς πρᾶξαι : but here also the negation rests on the sentence, not on the single word ; for this idiom must be classed among the instances of the much used figure of the Greek language, called λιτότης, whereby more is meant than is actually said. These negative forms imply, though they do not express, the contradictory to the predicate which is denied of the subject ; as, οὐ στέργω, not only I love not, but (by implication) I hate.

Obs. 4. Sometimes, though rarely, the elements of the compounds of οὐ or μή change places, but always for the sake of particular emphasis : Eur. Alc. 196 οὔ ποτ' οὔ : Hdt. VIII. 119 ἐν μυρίῃσι γνώμῃσι μίαν οὐκ ἔχω= οὐδεμίαν, as in English *I have not one,* =*none.*

ᵃ Well. Lex. Æsch. ad voc.   ᵇ Ellendt Lex. Soph. ad voc. 3.

Difference between οὐ *and* μή.

§. 739. Οὐ conveys an *independent* and *immediate* negation ; he is *not* good : μή, a negation depending on a supposition ; *I do not think* that he is good. The force of οὐ is complete, in the sentence in which it stands— μή always points out of the sentence to a preceding supposition, either actually expressed in some other sentence, or implied in the context.

Οὐκ *in independent Sentences.*

§. 740. 1. Οὐ therefore is a positive negation, whether of an actual fact in the ind., or of a supposed fact in the opt. ; as, ο ὐ γίγνεται, ο ὐ κ ἐγένετο, ο ὐ γενήσεται τοῦτο—ο ὐ κ ἂν γίγνοιτο ταῦτα. So also Homer uses it with the conjunct. used as the fut. ind. ; as, οὐ γάρ πω τοίους ἴδον ἀνέρας, ο ὐ δ ὲ ἴδωμαι (§. 415.).

2. It is used also in questions, *is it not?* *non, nonne*, when an affirmative answer is expected or required : οὐ δράσεις τοῦτο ; *nonne facies?* οὐ περιμενεῖς ; will you not wait=wait : and where the questions are suggested by strong feeling, τίς οὐ, πῶς οὐ, signify *every one, every way* ; as, τίς ἂν οὐκ ἐτόλμησεν ; who would not dare ?

Obs. Οὐ may be attached to single notions, to deny their existence, and to convey the contrary notion also in questions ; as, ο ὐ δ ρ ά σ ε ι ς τοῦτο ; *omittes hoc?* ο ὐ τ ο ῦ τ ο δράσεις : *non hoc facies?*=*aliud facies?* ἆρ' ο ὐ φ ε ύ ξ ε τ α ι ; *itane? manebit?* οὐ τέθνηκεν ; *estne inter vivos?* ἆρ' ο ὐ χ ὑ π ὸ σ ο ῦ τέθνηκεν ; *itane? ab alio occisus est?*

Μή *in independent sentences.*

§. 741. *a.* In sentences which express a command, either in the imper. or conjunctive, as this negation depends on the fancy or desire of another person ; μ ὴ γράφε—μ ὴ γράψῃς.

Obs. If the command is expressed by opt. with ἄν, either as a question or not, οὐ is used, not μή, as the negation is still positive, conditionally on the circumstances referred to by ἂν taking place : Il. β, 250 τῷ οὐκ ἂν βασιλῆας ἀνὰ στόμ' ἔχων ἀγορεύοις, do not be always having the king's name on your lips, properly, if you were sane you would not (positive negation) &c. : so in a question ; Od. ζ, 57 πάππα φίλ', οὐκ ἂν δή μοι ἐφοπλίσσειας ἀπήνην ;) so also οὐ is used with fut. ind., to forbid any thing ; as, οὐ δράσεις τοῦτο : you will not do it?=do it not ; or in a question to command, οὐ δράσεις τοῦτο ; will you not do it?=do it.

b. In sentences which express a wish, whether in opt. or historic ind., as the negation depends entirely on the fancy or desire of another person : Od. η, 316 μ ὴ τοῦτο φίλον Διὶ πατρὶ γένοιτο ! Il. ι, 698 μ ὴ ὄφελες λίσσεσθαι ! Soph. Antig. 682 ο ὔ τ' ἂν δυναίμην μ ή τ' ἐπισταίμην λέγειν : Demosth. p. 387, 13 ὑμῖν δὲ τοιοῦτο μὲν οὐδὲν ο ὔ τ' ἦν (assertion), μ ή τ ε γένοιτο τοῦ λοιποῦ.

c. With a conjunctive, expressing deliberation or exhortation ; as, μὴ γράφωμεν ! *ne scribamus !* Xen. M. S. I. 2, 45 πότερον βίαν φῶμεν εἶναι ἢ μὴ φῶμεν ; *utrumne dicamus, an non dicamus?*—(Οὐ can only be used in this construction, when it belongs to a single word, with which it forms one notion ; as, οὐ φῶμεν, *negemus*) : so in a sentence to which an affirmative answer is expected : Plat. Rep. p. 335 B ἀνθρώπους δέ, ὦ ἑταῖρε, μ ὴ οὕτω

354 *Syntax of the simple Sentence:* §. 742.

φῶμεν βλαπτομένους εἰς τὴν ἀνθρωπείαν ἀρετὴν χείρους γίγνεσθαι; πῶν μὲν οὖν: Ibid. p. 337 B πῶς λέγεις; μὴ ἀποκρίνωμαι; must I not answer you?=I will answer you.

d. In questions to which a negative answer is expected; as, μὴ δράσεις τοῦτο; you will not do this? *anne hoc facies?* μὴ τέθνηκεν ὁ πατήρ; — μὴ δειλοὶ ἐσόμεθα; we will not be cowards? Od. ζ, 200 ἢ μή πού τινὰ δυσμενέων φάσθ᾽ ἔμμεναι ἀνδρῶν; Plat. Prot. p. 310 E μή τι νεώτερον ἀγγέλλεις; In such questions the negation depends on a certain anxiety in the person's mind, to be assured that such or such a thing is not so, mixed with apprehension lest it be; in reference to which μή is used. The conjunctive also may be used in such questions, when the negation depends not on the anxiety of the person who asks the question, but of him to whom it is addressed: Od. ι, 405 τίπτε τόσον, Πολύφημ᾽, ἀρημένος ὧδ᾽ ἐβόησας—; ἦ μή τις σευ μῆλα βροτῶν ἀέκοντος ἐλαύνει; ἦ μή τίς σ᾽ αὐτὸν κτείνῃ δόλῳ ἠὲ βίηφιν; surely no one is driving away your flocks? you are not afraid lest some one should kill you?"

e. In oaths μή is sometimes used with ind., in place of the positive negation οὐ, as the negation is conceived to depend on the oath, and the determination arising therefrom in the mind;—as surely as there is a God, I am determined not: or it may be referred to the knowledge of the God who is invoked as a witness; as, Il. κ, 330 ἴστω νῦν Ζεὺς αὐτός—μὴ μὲν τοῖς ἵπποισιν ἀνὴρ ἐποχήσεται ἄλλος Τρώων, ἀλλὰ σέ φημι διαμπερὲς ἀγλαϊεῖσθαι. Cf. Il. ο, 41. Aristoph. Eccl. 991 μὰ τὴν Ἀφροδίτην—μὴ ᾽γώ σ᾽ ἀφήσω: Id. Av. 194 μὰ γῆν—μὴ ᾽γὼ νόημα κομψότερον ἤκουσά πω.

Οὐκ and μή in dependent Sentences.

§. 742. 1. In dependent clauses introduced by ὅτι and ὡς, " that," οὐ is sometimes used, as these clauses assume an independent force; as, ἔλεγεν, ὅτι (ὡς) οὐχ ἥμαρτεν—οἶδα, ὅτι τοῦτο οὐχ οὕτως ἔχει.

2. For the same reason οὐ is always used in modal or temporal dependent clauses; as, ὅτε οὐκ ἦλθεν: Il. φ, 95 μή με κτεῖν᾽, ἐπεὶ οὐχ ὁμογάστριος Ἕκτορός εἰμι.

§. 743. In relative clauses both are used, though μή is the more usual.

1. Οὐ is used (a) when the notion of the relative clause is denied directly without reference to the principal clause; as, ἀνὴρ, ὃν οὐκ εἶδες—ἀνὴρ, ὃν οὐκ ἂν θαυμάζοις. (b) When the negation applies to some particular notion in the relative clause: Isocr. p. 71 B λαβόντες ἑξακισχιλίους τῶν Ἑλλήνων — οἱ ἐν ταῖς αὑτῶν οὐχ οἷοί τ᾽ ἦσαν ζῆν. Hence in such combinations as οὐδείς ὅστις οὐ, οὐδενὸς ὅτου οὐ. So also οὐκ ἔσθ᾽ ὅπως οὐ. These expressions being as it were but one word; as, *nullus non.* (c) Where an antithesis makes the negation to rest on some single notion instead of the whole relative clause: Soph. Phil. 1010 ὃς οὐδὲν ἤδη πλὴν τὸ προσταχθὲν ποιεῖν: Thuc. I. 39 ἦν γε οὐ τὸν προὔχοντα—, ἀλλά κ. τ. λ. This antithesis may be supplied by the mind.

2. Μή on the other hand is used when the relative clause, whether it expresses a fact or a supposition, depends immediately on the principal, so that it is introduced by and completes it; especially therefore where the relative clause expresses the condition or aim of the principal, or may be resolved into the Latin *is qui* with the conjunctive=*ita comparatus, ut:* Soph. Phil. 409 ἔξοιδα γάρ νιν παντὸς ἂν λόγου κακοῦ γλώσσῃ θιγόντα καὶ πανουργίας, ἀφ᾽ ἧς μηδὲν δίκαιον ἐς τέλος μέλλει ποιεῖν: Id. El. 380 μέλ-

λουσι γάρ σε—ἐνταῦθα πέμψαι, ἔνθα μή ποτ' ἡλίου φέγγος πρυσόψει: Hdt. I. 32 ἐν γὰρ τῷ μακρῷ χρόνῳ πολλὰ μὲν ἔστι ἰδέειν, τὰ μή τις ἐθέλει, πολλὰ δὲ καὶ παθέειν: Eur. Hipp. 689 ὅλοιο καὶ σὺ χώστις ἄκοντας φίλους πρόθυμός ἐστι μὴ καλῶς εὐεργετεῖν: Plat. Phæd. p. 65 A δοκεῖ, ᾧ μηδὲν ἡδὺ τῶν τοιούτων, μηδὲ μετέχει αὐτῶν, οὐκ ἄξιον εἶναι ζῆν (=εἴ τινι μηδέν &c.): Thuc. I. 40 ἀλλ' ὅστις (=εἴ τις) μὴ πόλεμον ἀντ' εἰρήνης ποιήσει. Thence ὅτι μή, except, besides, nisi (properly οὐδὲν ὅτι μή, then generally for εἰ μή): Plat. Phæd. p. 67 A ἐὰν τῷ σώματι μὴ κοινωνῶμεν, ὅτι μὴ πᾶσα ἀνάγκη: Hdt. I. 18 τοῖσι δὲ Μιλησίοισι οὐδαμοὶ Ἰώνων τὸν πόλεμον τοῦτον συνεπελάφρυνον, ὅτι μὴ Χῖοι μοῦνοι.

§. 744. 1. In all final and conditional clauses, introduced by ἵνα, ὡς, ὅπως, ὄφρα, or εἰ, ἐάν, ἤν, ὅταν, ὁπόταν, ἐπειδάν, ἕως ἂν &c. μή is always used, as these clauses depend entirely on the principal; as, εἰ μὴ λέγεις, ἐὰν μὴ λέγῃς, ὅταν (ὁπόταν) ταῦτα μὴ γένηται.

Obs. Οὐ may be used either where the negation rests on some particular notion, or where there is an antithesis: Xen. Cyr. VI. 2, 30 μὴ δείσητε, ὡς οὐχ ἡδέως καθευδήσετε: Il. ω, 296 εἰ δέ τοι οὐ δώσει (recusabit): Soph. Aj. 1131 εἰ τοὺς θανόντας οὐκ ἐᾷς (prohibes) θάπτειν. But ibid. 1183 (1163. Herm.) ἀλλ' ἀρήγετ', ἔστ' ἐγὼ μόλω τάφου μεληθεὶς τῷδε, κἂν μηδεὶς ἐᾷ (even if no one allows it). Οὐ is used with εἰ after θαυμάζω &c., since εἰ here is used for ὅτι; as, θαυμάζω, εἰ ταῦτα οὐ ποιεῖς.

2. In clauses expressing consequence, οὐ is used when ὥστε is joined with the indicative, that is, when the consequence does not follow necessarily and immediately from the principal clause: μή when ὥστε is joined with infin., that is, when the consequence does so follow, as in this latter case the negation depends on the former clause: Xen. Cyr. I. 4, 5 ταχὺ τὰ θηρία ἀνηλώκει, ὥστε ὁ Ἀστυάγης οὐκέτ' εἶχεν αὐτῷ συλλέγειν θηρία: Plat. Phæd. p. 66 D ἐκπλήττει (τὸ σῶμα), ὥστε μὴ δύνασθαι ὑπ' αὐτοῦ καθορᾶν τἀληθές.

3. In indirect questions μή is used, as these depend on the principal clause; οὐ is only used as in §. 743. 1. b., c.

Οὐκ and μή with the Infinitive and Participle.

§. 745. With infinitives or infinitival clauses, whether with or without the article, μή is generally used, as these depend on some verb, or verbal thought, expressed or understood: Xen. M. S. II. 1, 3 τί δέ; τὸ μὴ φεύγειν τοὺς πόνους, ἀλλὰ ἐθελοντὴν ὑπομένειν, ποτέρῳ ἂν προσθείημεν; Eur. Troad. 638 τὸ μὴ γενέσθαι τῷ θανεῖν ἴσον λέγω: Plat. Phæd. p. 93 D προωμολόγηται, μηδὲν μᾶλλον μηδ' ἧττον ἑτέραν ἑτέρας ψυχὴν ψυχῆς εἶναι: Id. Apol. p. 18 D ἀνάγκη — ἐλέγχειν μηδενὸς ἀποκρινομένου (but ibid. C εἰσὶ πολλοὶ κατηγοροῦντες ἀπολογουμένου οὐδενός). So especially after verbs of believing, physical or mental perception, willing, determining, ordering, shewing, making known, proving, swearing, assenting, denying; and expressions of necessity and the like; as, ἀνάγκη, χρή, εἰκός, ἀδύνατον, δίκαιόν ἐστιν.

Obs. 1. After verbs of saying and narrating, οὐ is very often used, when the infinitival clause assumes the character of the *oratio recta*, the fact expressed therein being conceived of as independent of the speaker's mind; as, Plat. Phæd. p. 63 D φησὶ δεῖν οὐδὲν τοιοῦτον προσφέρειν τῷ φαρμάκῳ (= ὅτι οὐδὲν δεῖ,) he says, that "one must not," but μηδὲν — προσφέρειν would denote that the notion expressed, resulted from the view taken of it by the speaker, depending on φησί, he says one must not.

Obs. 2. Οὐ can also stand with the infin. when it defines some particular notion ; as, Eur. Rhes. 801 μηδὲν δύσοιζ᾽ οὐ πολεμίους δρᾶσαι τάδε, those who are not—enemies ; or where a negative notion stands in antithesis to a positive one of equivalent meaning ; the positive notion may be supplied by the mind : Arist. Eccles. 581 ἀλλ᾽ οὐ μέλλειν, ἀλλ᾽ ἄττεσθαι καὶ δὴ χρὴ τῆς διανοίας : Eur. Andr. 587 δρᾶν εὖ, κακῶς δ᾽ οὔ. But if both the notions are negative, μή must be used ; as, Xen. Hell. III. 2, 19 ἐνόμισαν αὐτὸν μὴ βούλεσθαι μᾶλλον ἢ μὴ δύνασθαι.

Obs. 3. When the infin. is supplied by an abstract subst., or adject. used as a subst., either οὐ or μή is used, according to the dependent clause into which the subst. or adj. may be resolved : Thuc. I. 137 γράψας τὴν τῶν γεφυρῶν οὐ διάλυσιν = ὅτι or ὡς (that) αἱ γέφυραι οὐ διελύθησαν : Id. V. 50 κατὰ τὴν οὐκ ἐξουσίαν τῆς ἀγωνίσεως = ὅτι (because) ἡ ἀγώνισις οὐκ ἐξῆν. On the other hand : Id. I. 22 καὶ ἐς μὲν ἀκρόασιν ἴσως τὸ μὴ μυθῶδες αὐτῶν ἀτερπέστερον φανεῖται, *scripta mea fortasse, quia nullæ in iis exstent fabulæ, lectoribus minus jucunda videbuntur* (*ex mente lectorum*; but τὸ οὐ μυθ., *quia nullæ in iis exstant fabulæ* (really, actually, without reference to any supposition) : Arist. Eccles. 115 δεινὸν δ᾽ ἐστὶν ἡ μὴ ἐμπειρία (= εἰ μή τις ἐστὶν ἔμπειρος ; but ἡ οὐκ ἐμπ. = ὅτι τις οὐκ ἔμπειρός ἐστιν). Οὐ must also be used when it is joined with the subst., so as to form an equivalent positive notion ; Eur. Hipp. 195 δι᾽ ἀπειροσύναν ἄλλου βιότου κοὐκ ἀπόδειξιν τῶν ὑπὸ γαίας.

Obs. 4. To these abstracts belong τὸ μηδέν = τὸ τοιοῦτον εἶναι, οἷον μηδὲν εἶναι, a nonentity, not actual but supposed : Hdt. I. 32 ἡ δὲ ἡμετέρη εὐδαιμονίη οὕτω τοι ἀπέρριπται ἐς τὸ μηδέν, ὥστε οὐδὲ ἰδιωτέων ἀνδρῶν ἀξίους ἡμέας ἐποίησας.

Οὐκ and μή with *Participles and Adjectives.*

§. 746. 1. Οὐ is used (*a*) when a participle or adjective is denied directly without reference to any supposition, or changed by the addition of the negative into its contrary ; as, οὐ δυνάμενος, like οὐ δύναμαι (*nequeo*), οὐ βουλόμενος, *nolens*, οὐκ ἀναγκαῖον (*unnecessary*), τὰ οὐ καλὰ βουλεύματα, *turpia consilia* : Plat. Phæd. p. 63 B εἰ μὲν μὴ ᾤμην ἥξειν παρὰ θεοὺς — ἠδίκουν ἂν οὐκ ἀγανακτῶν τῷ θανάτῳ (= ὀλιγωρῶν τοῦ θαν.). Hence when a participle may be resolved into a relative, or causal, or temporal dependent clause ; as, ὁ οὐ πιστεύων, *is qui non credit*, or *quia non credit*, ὁ οὐ φιλοσοφῶν, *is qui non philosophatur*. (*b*) When the participle or adjective with οὐ is in an antithesis : Eur. Andr. 703 ἡ στεῖρος οὖσα μόσχος οὐκ ἀνέξεται τίκτοντας ἄλλους, οὐκ ἔχουσ᾽ αὐτὴ τέκνα : Arist. Eccles. 187 ὁ μὲν λαβὼν — ὁ δ᾽ οὐ λαβών : Thuc. I. 124 ξυνελθόντες μὲν, ἀμύνεσθαι δ᾽ οὐ τολμῶντες : Xen. Cyr. II. 4, 27 οὐχ ἡγεμόνας ἔχων ἀνθρώπους πλανᾷ ἀνὰ τὰ ὄρη, ἀλλ᾽ ὅπῃ ἂν τὰ θηρία ὑφηγῆται.

2. Μή on the other hand, when they can be resolved into a conditional clause ; as, ὁ μὴ πιστεύων, *si quis non credat* : Soph. Œ. C. 1154 δίδασκέ με ὡς μὴ εἰδότ᾽ αὐτὸν μηδὲν ὧν σὺ πυνθάνει : Id. Trach. 727 οὐκ ἔστιν ἐν τοῖς μὴ καλοῖς βουλεύμασιν οὐδ᾽ ἐλπίς, if they are not good : Eur. Heracl. 283 μάτην γὰρ ἥβην ὧδέ γ᾽ ἂν κεκτῴμεθα πολλὴν ἐν Ἄργει, μή σε τιμωρούμενοι, *frustra tantam Argivorum pubem coëgissemus, nisi te puniremus* : Xen. Anab. IV. 4, 15 οὗτος γὰρ ἐδόκει καὶ πρότερον πολλὰ ἤδη ἀληθεῦσαι τοιαῦτα, τὰ ὄντα τε ὡς ὄντα, καὶ τὰ μὴ ὄντα ὡς οὐκ ὄντα (if anything was not, he represented it as not being). So also in antithesis : Hdt. IV. 64 ἀπενεί-

κ α ς . μὲν γὰρ κεφαλήν, τῆς ληίης μεταλαμβάνει, τὴν ἂν λάβωσι· μ ὴ ἐ ν ε ί κ α ς δὲ, οὔ, *if* he does not, &c.

3. After verbs of perceiving and saying, either οὐ or μή may be used; the former marks that the thought is independent of any supposition, the latter represents it as depending on the mind of the subject of the governing verb ; as, οἶδά σε ταῦτα οὐ ποιήσοντα — ἤγγειλε τὴν πόλιν οὐ πολιορκηθεῖσαν : Xen. Cyr. I. 2, 7 καὶ ὃν ἂν γνῶσι δυνάμενον μὲν χάριν ἀποδιδόναι, μ ὴ ἀποδιδόντα δὲ, κολάζουσι τοῦτον ἰσχυρῶς : Plat. Rep. p. 486 A καὶ τόδε δεῖ σκοπεῖν, ὅταν κρίνειν μέλλῃς φύσιν φιλόσοφόν τε καὶ μ ή (sc. φιλόσοφον οὖσαν) : Ibid. B ψυχὴν σκοπῶν φιλόσοφον καὶ μ ή.

Repetition of the Negative.

§. 747. 1. When in a negative sentence there occur indefinite pronouns, such as *any one, any how, any where, at any time*, &c. they are all negative : these negatives neither neutralise nor strengthen each other, but each one is independent of the rest. The negative must be of the same character, either οὐ or μή throughout ; as, Plat. Rep. p. 495 B σμικρὰ φύσις ο ὐ δὲν μέγα ο ὐ δέποτε ο ὐ δένα ο ὔ τε ἰδιώτην, ο ὔ τε πόλιν δρᾷ : Id. Phileb. p. 19 B ο ὐ δεὶς εἰς οὐδὲν οὐδενὸς ἂν ἡμῶν οὐδέποτε γένοιτο ἄξιος. So also the negative is added to a part of a sentence which is already negative ; as, ο ὐ δ ύ ν α τ α ι ο ὔ τ' εὖ λέγειν ο ὔ τ' εὖ ποιεῖν τοὺς φίλους, though in poetry it is sometimes omitted ; as, Od. ι, 293 οὐδ' ἀπέλειπεν ἔγκατά τε σάρκας τε καὶ ὀστέα. So also ο ὐ δ έ, μ η δ έ, *ne quidem*, *not even*, are used in a negative sentence ; as, ο ὐ δύναται ο ὐ δ ὲ νῦν εὖ ποιεῖν τοὺς φίλους. Hence we find in the beginning of a sentence the following formulas : ο ὐ — ο ὐ, οὐ μ ὴ ν ο ὐ δ έ, ο ὐ δ ὲ μ ὲ ν ο ὐ δ έ, οὐ γ ὰ ρ ο ὐ δ έ, ο ὐ δ ὲ γ ὰ ρ ο ὐ δ έ : Il. ζ, 130 ο ὐ δ ὲ γὰρ οὐδὲ Δρύαντος υἱὸς, κρατερὸς Λυκόοργος, δὴν ἦν.

Obs. The phrase οὐδὲ πολλοῦ δεῖ, after a negative sentence, in the sense of *multum abest*—*minime gentium*, is remarkable, wherein the οὐδέ, instead of neutralizing, increases the force of the phrase πολλοῦ δεῖ : Demosth. p. 117, 24 ὅμως οὔθ' ὑμῖν οὔτε Θηβαίοις οὔτε Λακεδαιμονίοις οὐδεπώποτε—συνεχωρήθη τοῦθ' ὑπὸ τῶν Ἑλλήνων, ποιεῖν ὅ τι βούλοισθε, ο ὐ δ ὲ π ο λ λ ο ῦ δ ε ῖ, ἀλλὰ κ. τ. λ. Id. p. 100, 42 οὔκουν βούλεται τοῖς ἑαυτοῦ καιροῖς τὴν παρ' ὑμῶν ἐλευθερίαν ἐφεδρεύειν, ο ὐ δ ὲ π ο λ λ ο ῦ δ ε ῖ, οὐ κακῶς—ταῦτα λογιζόμενος.

2. Sometimes the negative of the principal is repeated in the dependent clause : Plat. Apol. p. 31 E ο ὐ γὰρ ἔστιν ὅστις ἀνθρώπων σωθήσεται ο ὔ τ ε ὑμῖν ο ὔ τ ε ἄλλῳ ο ὐ δ ε ν ὶ πλήθει γνησίως ἐναντιούμενος, *nemo est, qui se servare possit, si vel vobis v e l alii plebi libere adversatur.*

Seeming Pleonasm of μή, οὐ—οὐ μή—μὴ οὐ.

a. Οὐ μή.

§. 748. 1. Οὐ μή is frequently joined with the future indicative, or the aorist, rarely the present, conjunctive—in the former case it has the force of the imperative, in the latter of the future—οὐ μὴ ποιήσεις, *do not do this* ; οὐ μὴ ποιήσῃς, *you shall not do this.*

2. There are two ways of explaining this construction—

a. By supposing, after οὐ, an ellipse of some expression of anxiety or fear, on which the clause introduced by μή depends, so that οὐ μὴ ποιήσῃ =

οὐ δεινὸν μὴ ποιήσῃ, *haud vereor ne faciat,* and we sometimes find the usually omitted notion expressed by δεινόν, δέος, φόβος, &c.: Arist. Eccl. 646 οὐχὶ δέος, μή σε φιλήσῃ : Xen. M. S. II. 1, 25 οὐ φόβος, μή σι ἀγάγω ἐπὶ τὸ ταῦτα πορίζεσθαι : Plat. Rep. p. 465 B οὐδὲν δεινὸν μήπστι ἡ ἄλλη πόλις—διχοστατήσῃ [a] : Id. Apol. p. 28 B οὐδὲν δεινὸν μὴ φοβηθῇ.

b. [b] Another way of explaining it is by making it into a question, which, in the future, is equivalent to the imperative; as, οὐ μενεῖς ; will you not stay ?=μένε : οὐ μὴ μενεῖς ; will you not not-stay ?=do not stay : or with the conjunctive is equivalent to a future ; μὴ μενῇς ; must you not stay ?=you must stay, you shall stay : οὐ μὴ μένῃς ; must you not not-stay ?=you shall not stay : with the first person singular of the future, it has the force of a simple strong negative, as there is no first person singular imper. for it to represent ; so Soph. El. 1052 ἀλλ' εἴσιθ', οὔ σοι μὴ μεθέψομαί ποτε : Arist. Ran. 508 μὰ τὸν Ἀπόλλω, οὐ μή σε περιόψομαι ἀπελθόντα ; and sometimes also with the third person : Soph. Œ. C. 176 οὗτοι μήποτέ σ' ἐκ τῶν δ' ἑδράων ὦ γέρον ἄκοντά τις ἄξει [c] : Hdt. III. 62 οὐ μὴ ἀναβλαστήσεις. In this construction we sometimes find several futures following one another, some with a negative, others with an affirmative sense, for which the following rules may be laid down : οὐ runs through the whole sentence, and applies to each clause ; μή is continued by a conjunctive, but dropped by a disjunctive particle ; and if after an affirmative future, one of the later futures requires to be negative, μή must be again used with it ; as, Eur. Bacch. 342 οὐ μὴ προσοίσεις χεῖρα (do not) βακχεύσεις δ' ἰών ("do," the μή being dropped) μηδ' ἐξομόρξει, (do not,) μωρίαν τὴν σὴν ἐμοί. Sometimes οὐ stands in one clause with the future, and μή follows with another future, so that the first sentence is affirmative, the other negative : Eur. Hipp. 498 οὐχὶ συγκλείσεις στόμα, shut your mouth ; καὶ μὴ μεθήσεις αὖθις αἰσχίστους λόγους. The following are examples of both constructions : Eur. Hipp. 601 οὐ μὴ προσοίσεις χεῖρα, μηδ' ἅψει πέπλων : Id. Hec. 1039. ἀλλ' οὔ τι μὴ φύγητε λαιψηρῷ ποδί [d] : Plat. Rep. p. 341 C ἀλλ' οὐ μὴ οἷός τ' ᾖς : Id. Criton. p. 44 B τοιούτου ἐπιτηδείου, οἷον ἐγὼ οὐδένα μή ποτε εὑρήσω : Ibid. p. 486 D ἀλλ' οὐ μὴ φῶμεν : Id. Rep. p. 492 E οὔτε γὰρ γίγνεται, οὔτε γέγονεν οὐδὲ οὖν μὴ γένηται ἀλλοῖον ἦθος, πρὸς ἀρετὴν παρὰ τὴν τούτων παιδείαν πεπαιδευμένον : Ibid. p. 597 C οὔτε ἐφυτεύθησαν ὑπὸ τοῦ θεοῦ οὔτε μὴ φυῶσιν : Id. p. 473 D οὐδὲ αὕτη ἡ πολίτεια μήποτε πρότερον φυῇ τε καὶ φῶς ἡλίου ἴδῃ : Id. Phædr. p. 260 E οὔτε ἔστιν οὔτε μήποτε ὑστέρου γένηται : Id. Legg. p. 492 C οὔτ' ἔστιν, οὔτε ποτὲ γένηται κρεῖττον : Id. Phileb. p. 21 E οὐδέτερος ὁ βίος —ἔμοιγε τούτων αἱρετός, οὐδ' ἄλλῳ μήποτε—φανῇ : Ibid. p. 15 E ἀλλ' οὔτε μὴ παύηταί ποτε οὔτε ἤρξατο νῦν.

Obs. 1. Sometimes the construction is changed from οὐ μή, with the conjunct., to a simple future : Soph. El. 43 οὐ γάρ σε μὴ γήρᾳ τε καὶ χρόνῳ μακρῷ γνῶσ' οὐδ' ὑποπτεύσουσιν : Id. Œd. C. 450 ἀλλ' οὔ τι μὴ λάχωσι τοῦδε συμμάχου, οὔτε σφιν—ὄνησις ἥξει.

Obs. 2. In the *oratio obliqua,* where the future would be used in the *oratio recta,* οὐ μή is (though but rarely) joined with the opt., in the same way as with the first and third persons of the future ind. ; as, Soph. Phil. 510 sq. ἐθέσπισε, τἀπὶ Τροίᾳ πέργαμ' ὡς οὐ μή ποτε πέρσοιεν.

Obs. 3. Dawes has restricted this use of οὐ μή, with the conjunctive, to the second aorist only, but without reason, as there are many instances to the contrary [e] : Plat. Rep. p. 29 D οὐ μὴ παύσωμαι, the best MSS. : Id.

a Stallb. ad loc.   b Elm. et Herm. Med. 1120.   c Elm. ad loc.
d Pflugk ad loc.   e Elm. Œ. C. 177.

Phædon. p. 66 B οὐ μήποτε κτησώμεθα : Id. **Rep.** p. 609 A οὐ γὰρ τόγε ἀγαθὸν μήποτέ τι ἀπολέσῃ (fut. ἀπολεῖ) : Xen. **Anab.** IV. 8, 13 οὐδεὶς μηκέτι μείνῃ
(fut. μενεῖ :) Soph. **Phil.** 381 οὐ μήποτ' ἐς τὴν Σκῦρον ἐκπλεύσῃς (fut. ἐκπλευσεῖ).

b. Μή—οὐκ.

§. 749. 1. With verbs expressing fear, anxiety, care, doubt, distrust,
denial, forbidding, preventing, &c. the infinitive is used with μή, instead of
without it, as we might expect : so that the negative notion of the verb
is increased thereby : Hdt. I. 158 'Αριστόδικος—ἔσχε μὴ ποιῆσαι ταῦτα
Κυμαίους : Id. III. 128 Δαρεῖος ἀπαγορεύει ὑμῖν μὴ δορυφορέειν 'Οροίτεα :
Thuc. III. 6 καὶ τῆς μὲν θαλάσσης εἶργον μὴ χρῆσθαι τοὺς Μιτυληναίους :
Id. V. 25 ἀπίσχοντο μὴ ἐπὶ τὴν ἑκατέρων γῆν στρατεῦσαι : Eur. **Hec.**
867 νόμων γραφαὶ εἴργουσι χρῆσθαι μὴ κατὰ γνώμην τρόποις [a] : Id. 'Androm. 664 τοῦτο δ' οἱ σοφοὶ βροτῶν ἐξευλαβοῦνται μὴ φίλοις τεύχειν
ἔριν : Id. **Iph. T.** 1391 φόβος δ' ἦν, ὥστε μὴ τέγξαι πόδα : Demosth.
p. 813, 1 ἔφυγε μηδὲν διαγνῶναι περὶ αὐτῶν [b]. Μὴ is rarely omitted,
as with the verbs of preventing—'Αρνοῦμαι μὴ εἰδέναι : Hdt. III.
66 δεινῶς—ὁ Πρηξάσπης ἔξαρνος ἦν μὴ μὲν ἀποκτεῖναι Σμέρδιν : Thuc.
IV. 40 ἀπιστοῦντες μὴ εἶναι τοὺς παραδόντας τοῖς τεθνεῶσιν ὁμοίους :
Demosth. p. 818, 16 μὴ λαβεῖν ἐξαρνούμενος : Ibid. 15 ἠμφισβή-
τησε μὴ ἔχειν [c].

2. And even after verbs of doubt and denial, the negation is repeated
by οὐ, even when the finite with ὅτι is used instead of the infin. : Plat.
Menon. p. 89 D ὅτι δ' οὐκ ἔστιν ἐπιστήμη, σκέψαι ἐάν σοι δοκῶ εἰκότως
ἀπιστεῖν : Id. **Prot.** p. 350 D τοὺς δὲ ἀνδρείους ὡς οὐ θαρραλέοι εἰσί, τὸ
ἐμὸν ὁμολόγημα, οὐδαμοῦ ἀπέδειξας, ὡς οὐκ ὀρθῶς ὡμολόγησα : Demosth. p. 871,
14 ὡς δ' οὐκ ἐκεῖνος ἐγεώργει τὴν γῆν, οὐκ ἠδύνατ' ἀρνηθῆναι : Id. **Phil.**
p. 124, 54 ὧν οὐδ' ἂν ἀρνηθεῖεν ἔνιοι, ὡς οὐκ εἰσὶ τοιοῦτοι : so also
in French, after *empêcher*, *prendre garde*, *craindre*, *avoir
peur*, *appréhendre*, *ne nier pas*, *ne douter pas*, *ne discon-
venir pas, que* with *ne* is used ; *il craint que sa maladie ne soit
mortelle*. So Italian ; as, *guardarsi di non credere alle favole—
io temo che Lidia questo non faccia.*

3. So after ἤ, *quam*, after comparatives, or comparative expressions, οὐ
is sometimes used, as these expressions imply the negative notion of disjunction : Hdt. IV. 118 ἥκει γὰρ ὁ Πέρσης οὐδέν τι μᾶλλον ἐπ' ἡμέας, ἢ
οὐ καὶ ἐπὶ ὑμέας : Id. V. 94 ἀποδεικνύντες τε λόγῳ οὐδὲν μᾶλλον Αἰολεῦσι
μετεὸν τῆς 'Ιλιάδος χώρης, ἢ οὐ καί σφι καὶ τοῖσι ἄλλοισι κ. τ. λ. : Id. VII.
26, 3 φανῆναι δὲ οὐδὲν μᾶλλόν μοι ὀφείλει ἔχοντι τὴν σὴν ἐσθῆτα, ἢ οὐ καὶ
τὴν ἐμήν· οὐδέ τι μᾶλλον ἐν κοίτῃ τῇ σῇ ἀναπαυομένῳ, ἢ οὐ καὶ ἐν τῇ
ἐμῇ : Thuc. II. 62 οὐδ' εἰκὸς, χαλεπῶς φέρειν αὐτῶν μᾶλλον ἢ οὐ κήπιον
καὶ ἐγκαλλώπισμα πλούτου πρὸς ταύτην νομίσαντας ὀλιγωρῆσαι : Id. III. 36
μετάνοιά τις εὐθὺς ἦν αὐτοῖς καὶ ἀναλογισμός, ὠμὸν τὸ βούλευμα καὶ μέγα ἐγνῶ-
σθαι, πόλιν ὅλην διαφθεῖραι μᾶλλον ἢ οὐ τοὺς αἰτίους : compare the French, as,
*il n'écrit pas mieux cette année-ci qu'il ne fuisait l'année passé—il faut
plus d'esprit pour apprendre une science qu'il n'en faut pour s'en moquer
—on méprise ceux qui parlent autrement qu'ils ne pensent.*

---

[a] Pflugk ad loc.　　　　　[b] Bremi ad loc..　　　　　[c] Bremi ad loc.

c. μὴ οὐκ.

§. 750. 1. Μὴ οὐ is used with the indic. or conjunctive, after notions of fear, anxiety, doubt, &c. to mark that the object of fear, &c. does not, or will not happen. Μὴ performs the functions of a conjunction, *lest or whether,* while οὐ belongs to the clause depending on that conjunction. Compare δέδοικα μὴ ἀποθάνῃ, I doubt that he will die; δέδ. μὴ οὐκ ἀποθ., I doubt that he will not die: Plat. Phæd. p. 76 B φοβοῦμαι, μ ὴ αὖριον τηνικάδε οὐκέτι ᾖ ἀνθρώπων οὐδεὶς ἀξίως οἷός τε ποιεῖν: Id. Menon. p. 89 D πρὸς τί βλέπων δυσχεραίνεις καὶ ἀπιστεῖς, μὴ οὐκ ἐπιστήμη ᾖ ἡ ἀρετή; that virtue is not a science. Very often the expression of fear, &c. is supplied by the mind or context; as, Plat. Crit. p. 48 C ἡμῖν δ', ἐπειδὴ ὁ λόγος οὗτως αἱρεῖ, μὴ οὐδὲν ἄλλο σκεπτέον ᾖ, ἢ ὅπερ νῦν δὴ ἐλέγομεν, *vide, ne non aliud quid spectandum sit.* So Il. α, 28 μή νυ τοι οὐ χραίσμῃ σκῆπτρον καὶ στέμμα θεοῖο.

Obs. 1. Μὴ οὐκ with the infinitive is rarely used except after verbs expressing negative notions, so that μή strengthens the former negative, while the negation of οὐ belongs to the infinitive.

Obs. 2. Instead of μὴ οὐ we find μὴ μή; as, Xen. M. S. I. 2, 7 φοβοῖτο, μὴ ὁ γενόμενος καλὸς κἀγαθὸς τῷ τὰ μέγιστα εὐεργετήσαντι μὴ τὴν μεγίστην χάριν ἕξοι, *metueret,* n e—n o n *maximam gratiam habiturus esset* = I think he will. So that the former μή is a conjunction, the latter a repetition of the negative notion in the principal clause.

2. Μὴ οὐ is also used in the sense of *quominus quin,* with the infin. *a.* After verbs of preventing, denying, distrusting, when a negation is joined with them. *b.* After δεινὸν εἶναι, αἰσχρόν, αἰσχύνην εἶναι, αἰσχύνεσθαι, which imply a negative notion. *c.* After all negative notions where, in Latin, *quin* with conjunct. would be used.

a. Οὐδὲν κωλύει μὴ οὐκ ἀληθὲς εἶναι τοῦτο: or as a question, τί ἐμποδὼν μὴ οὐκ ἀποθανεῖν; *nihil impedit,* q u o m i n u s *id verum sit—quid impedit,* q u o m i n u s *moriar?* Hdt. VI. 88 Ἀθηναῖοι—οὐκέτι ἀνεβάλλοντο μὴ οὐ τὸ πᾶν μηχανήσασθαι ἐπ' Αἰγινήτῃσι: Plat. Rep. p. 354 D οὐκ ἀπεσχόμην τὸ μὴ οὐκ ἐπὶ τοῦτο ἐλθεῖν ἀπ' ἐκείνου, *mihi non temperabam, quin illo relicto ad hoc accederem* [a]: Id. Menon. p. 89 D τὸ μὲν γὰρ διδακτὸν αὐτὸ εἶναι, εἴπερ ἐπιστήμη ἐστίν, οὐκ ἀνατίθεμαι, μὴ οὐ καλῶς λέγεσθαι, *non repugno, quin hoc recte dicatur:* Xen. Symp. III. 3 οὐδείς σοι, ἔφη, ἀντιλέγει τὸ μὴ οὐ λέγειν: Soph. Trach. 88 οὐδὲν ἐλλείψω τὸ μὴ οὐ πᾶσαν πυθέσθαι τῶνδ' ἀλήθειαν, *nihil prætermittam, quin — cognoscam:* Lucian D. M. p. 94 νῦν μέν, ὦ Ἀλέξανδρε, οὐκ ἂν ἔξαρνος γένοιο, μὴ οὐκ ἐμὸς υἱὸς εἶναι, *non negabis, quin filius meus sis:* Id. Lapith. p. 440 οὐκ ἂν ἔξαρνος γένοιο, μὴ οὐχὶ φάρμακον ἀποδεδόσθαι Κρίτωνι ἐπὶ τὸν πατέρα, *non negabis, quin venenum vendideris.*

b. Hdt. I. 187 Δαρείῳ δὲ δεινὸν ἐδόκεε εἶναι μὴ οὐ λαβεῖν τὰ χρήματα: Xen. Cyr. VIII. 4, 5 τὸν δὲ πρωτεύοντα ἐν ἕδρᾳ ᾐσχύνετο μὴ οὐ πλεῖστα καὶ ἀγαθὰ ἔχοντα παρ' αὑτοῦ φαίνεσθαι: Plat. Prot. p. 352 D αἰσχρόν ἐστι καὶ ἐμοὶ σοφίαν καὶ ἐπιστήμην μὴ οὐχὶ πάντων κράτιστον φάναι εἶναι [b].

c. Hdt. VII. 5 οὐκ οἰκός ἐστι, Ἀθηναίους μὴ οὐ δοῦναι δίκας τῶν ἐποίησαν. — Οὐ δύναμαι, ἀδύνατός εἰμι, οὐχ οἷός τ' εἰμὶ μὴ οὐ λέγειν, *non possum non dicere, non possum quin dicam:* Hdt. III. 82 δήμου —ἄρχοντος ἀδύνατα μὴ οὐ κακότητα ἐγγίνεσθαι: Plat. Phæd. p. 72 D

---

[a] Stallb. ad loc.   [b] Heindorf ad loc.

τίς μηχάνη (= ἀδύνατον), μὴ οὐχὶ πάντα καταναλωθῆναι εἰς τὸ τεθνάναι: Id. Gorg. p. 462 B ᾐσχύνθη σοι μὴ ὁμολογῆσαι (= ἀρνηθῆναι), τὸν ῥητορικὸν ἄνδρα μὴ οὐχὶ καὶ τὰ δίκαια εἰδέναι: Soph. Ant. 97 πείσομαι γὰρ οὐ τοσοῦτον οὐδὲν, ὥστε μὴ οὐ καλῶς θανεῖν.

3. Μὴ οὐ is also used with participles after negative expressions: Hdt. VI. 106 εἰνάτῃ δὲ οὐκ ἐξελεύσεσθαι ἔφασαν μὴ οὐ πλήρεος ἐόντος τοῦ κύκλου: Soph. Œ. R. 12 δυσάλγητος γὰρ ἂν εἴην, τοιάνδε μὴ οὐ κατοικτείρων ἕδραν, *nisi vestra me supplicatio tangat.*

Obs. 3. There are very few instances of the infin. being used without μὴ οὐ after negative verbs: Plat. Lysis. p. 209 B οὐ διακωλύουσί σε οὔτε ὁ πατὴρ οὔτε ἡ μήτηρ ἐπιτεῖναί τε καὶ ἀνεῖναι ἣν ἂν βούλῃ τῶν χορδῶν, καὶ ψῆλαι καὶ κρούειν τῷ πλήκτρῳ.—And not many of μὴ being used alone with such verbs: Soph. Aj. 96 κόμπος πάρεστι κοὐκ ἀπαρνοῦμαι τὸ μή: Plat. Parm. §. 41 οὐ πάντῃ ἂν ᾖδη ἐκφύγοι τὸ μὴ ἕτερα εἶναι ἀλλήλων: Xen. M. S. IV. 8, 9 ἐμοὶ δὲ τί αἰσχρόν (= οὐκ αἰσχρ.), τὸ ἑτέρους μὴ δύνασθαι περὶ ἐμοῦ τὰ δίκαια μήτε γνῶναι, μήτε ποιῆσαι.

Obs. 4. Μή may be used instead of μὴ οὐ after οὐ δύναμαι, ἀδύνατος, οὐχ οἷός τ᾽ εἰμι, οὔ φημι, οὐ λέγω &c. It may be that these verbs may be considered, when separated from their negatives, as conveying positive notions; though perhaps this idiom is to be attributed rather to the arbitrary anomalies of common speech, as these expressions are practically negative: οὐ δύναμαι μὴ ποιεῖν, *non possum non facere:* Æsch. Prom. 106 ἀλλ᾽ οὔτε σιγᾶν, οὔτε μὴ σιγᾶν τύχας οἰόντε μοι τάσδ᾽ ἐστί, *nec tacere, nec non tacere possum.* — Οὔ φημι τοῦτο μὴ οὕτως ἔχειν, *non dico id sic se non habere.* Μή and μὴ οὐ are found together: Xen. Apol. extr. οὔτε μὴ μεμνῆσθαι δύναμαι αὐτοῦ, οὔτε μεμνημένος μὴ οὐκ ἐπαινεῖν.

Obs. 5. Hermann [a] holds that μὴ οὐκ denies somewhat doubtfully, while μή is an emphatic negative; but whence the doubt can arise in μὴ οὐ is not clear. The use of μὴ οὐ seems to arise from the Greek practice of applying the negative to all the members of the negative sentence. Thus in ἀπαρνοῦμαι μὴ δρᾶν ταῦτα, the μή is the repetition of the negative notion of denial applying to the dependent clause; in ἀπαρνοῦμαι μὴ οὐ δρᾶν ταῦτα, the negative οὐ is applied to the member of the negative clause δρᾶν, so that μὴ οὐ is a more, instead of a less, emphatic negation.

SYNTAX OF THE COMPOUND SENTENCE.

CHAP. IV.

Compound Sentences.

§. 751. 1. It is not improbable that in the simpler ages of language the successive thoughts in the mind were represented by successive sentences, as it were parallel to and unconnected with each other; as, *winter is gone—the spring is come—the fields are green.*

2. But as language was more and more developed by the increasing intercourse of common life, the unity which really exists

[a] Ad Viger. 797.

between successive thoughts in the mind was more and more realised in language, so that in course of time certain words were appropriated to the expression thereof, which were termed *Conjunctions.*

3. Sentences are connected in two ways—either they are properly independent of each other (*coordinate*), but united by a conjunction (*coordinate* or *copulative conjunctions* καί, τέ, δέ &c.); or dependent the one on the other, so that the one is incomplete without the other; as, δένδρα θάλλει, ὅτε τὸ ἔαρ ἦλθε (*subordinate*). and this connection is expressed by the *subordinate conjunctions* ὅτε, ὅτι, ὡς, &c.

4. Each sentence to which these conjunctions are attached, should properly be a complete simple sentence; but when the same members belong to two or more sentences, they are generally only expressed once; as, ὁ Σωκράτης ἦν σοφὸς καὶ ὁ Σ. ἦν ἀγαθός = ὁ Σ. ἦν σοφὸς καὶ ἀγαθός—ὁ Σ. ἦν σοφὸς καὶ ὁ Πλάτων ἦν σοφός = ὁ Σ. καὶ ὁ Πλ. ἦσαν σοφοί. — Ὁ Σ. σοφὸς ἦν κ. ἀγ. καὶ ὁ Πλ. σοφ. ἦν κ. ἀγ. = ὁ Σ. καὶ ὁ Πλ. ἦσαν σοφοὶ καὶ ἀγαθοί.

5. The grammatical arrangement of sentences does not always represent their actual logical relations to each other. Thus it is possible so to connect two sentences, one of which depends on the other, that as far as the form of expression goes they are exactly the same : τὸ ἔαρ ἦλθε καὶ τὰ ῥόδα θάλλει for ὅτε τὸ ἔαρ ἦλθε, τὰ ῥ. θ.

Coordinate thoughts expressed in a coordinate form.

§. 752. 1. In Homer we find many instances of this ; as, Il. ζ, 147 φύλλα τὰ μέν τ' ἄνεμος χαμάδις χέει, ἄλλα δέ θ' ὕλη τηλεθόωσα φύει· ἔαρος δ' ἐπιγίγνεται ὥρη (for ὅτε ἔαρος ἐπιγίγνεται ὥρη) : Il. ο, 551 ναῖε δὲ πὰρ Πριάμῳ· ὁ δέ μιν τίεν ἶσα τέκεσσιν (for ὅς μιν ἔτιεν) : Il. ρ, 300 sq. ὁ δ' ἄγχ' αὐτοῖο πέσε πρηνὴς ἐπὶ νεκρῷ, τηλ' ἀπὸ Λαρίσσης ἐριβώλακος· οὐδὲ τοκεῦσιν θρέπτρα φίλοις ἀπέδωκε, μινυνθάδιος δέ οἱ αἰὼν ἔπλεθ' ὑπ' Αἴαντος μεγαθύμου δουρὶ δαμέντι (for ὅτι μινυνθ. οἱ αἰὼν ἔπλετο) : Il. χ, 235 νῦν δ' ἔτι καὶ μᾶλλον νοέω φρεσὶ τιμήσασθαι, ὃς ἔτλης ἐμεῦ εἵνεκ', ἐπεὶ ἴδες ὀφθαλμοῖσιν, τείχεος ἐξελθεῖν, ἄλλοι δ' ἔντοσθε μένουσιν (for ἐπειδὴ ἄλλοι ἐντ. μένουσιν) : Od. ψ, 37 sq. (ἄγε δή μοι, μαῖα φίλη, νημερτὲς ἐνίσπε) ὅππως δὴ μνηστῆρσιν ἀναιδέσι χεῖρας ἐφῆκεν, μοῦνος ἐών, οἱ δ' αἰὲν ἀολλέες ἔνδον ἔμιμνον (for ὅτε οἱ ἄλλοι αἰὲν—ἔνδον ἔμιμνον) : Il. κ, 185 πολὺς δ' ὀρυμαγδὸς ἐπ' αὐτῷ ἀνδρῶν ἠδὲ κυνῶν· ἀπό τε σφισιν ὕπνος ὄλωλεν (for οἷς ὕπνος ἀπόλωλεν).

2. So in Herodotus, to whose loose and careless style this form of expression was particularly agreeable : Hdt. I. 36 νεόγαμός τε γάρ ἐστι, καὶ τοῦτό οἱ νῦν μέλει. Many of these combinations came into common use even in Attic Greek ; as, τέ—καί, or καί alone, for ὅτε, of things that happened at the same time ; ἅμα—καί, so soon as : Id. III. 76 (οἱ ἑπτὰ τῶν

Περσῶν) ᾖσαν εὐξάμενοι τοῖσι θεοῖσι, τῶν περὶ Πρηξάσπεα εἰδότες οὐδέν· ἕν τε δὴ τῇ ὁδῷ μέσῃ στείχοντες ἐγίνοντο, καὶ τὰ περὶ Πρηξάσπεα γεγονότα ἐπυνθάνοντο (= ὅτε — ἐπυνθάνοντο) : Id. VII. 217 ἧός τε δὴ διέφαινε καὶ ἐγένοντο ἐπὶ τῷ ἀκρωτηρίῳ τοῦ οὔρεος : Id. IV. 199 συγκεκόμισταί τε οὗτος ὁ μέσος καρπός, καὶ ὁ ἐν τῇ κατυπερτάτῃ τῆς γῆς πεπαίνεταί τε καὶ ὀργᾷ, ὥστε ἐκπέποταί τε καὶ καταβέβρωται ὁ πρῶτος καρπός, καὶ ὁ τελευταῖος συμπαραγίνεται : Thuc. I. 50 ἤδη δὲ ἦν ὀψὲ καὶ οἱ Κορίνθιοι ἐξαπίνης πρύμναν ἐκρούοντο : Hdt. I. 112 ἅμα δὲ ταῦτα ἔλεγε καὶ ἀπεδείκνυε : Isocr. Paneg. p. 73 C ἅμα διαλλάττονται καὶ τῆς ἐχθρᾶς ἐπιλανθάνονται.

3. It is also a peculiarity of Herodotus, that when he wishes to express a negative motive, he prefixes it coordinately with οὔκων (οὔκουν) to the consequences which result from it, while the sentence expressing those consequences is not connected by any conjunction, as it is referred back to the οὖν in οὔκουν : Hdt. I. 11 οὔκων δὴ (ὁ Γύγης) ἔπειθε, ἀλλ᾿ ὥρα ἀναγκαίην ἀληθέως προκειμένην, ἢ τὸν δεσπότεα ἀπολλύναι, ἢ αὐτὸν ὑπ᾿ ἄλλων ἀπόλλυσθαι, αἱρέεται αὐτὸς περιεῖναι for οὐ πείθων δέ, ἀλλ᾿ ὁρῶν — αἱρέεται : or οὐκ ἔπειθε — αἱρέεται οὖν &c. : Hdt. IV. 118 οὔκων ποιήσετε ταῦτα, ἡμεῖς μὲν πιεζόμενοι ἢ ἐκλείψομεν τὴν χώρην κ. τ. λ. for ὑμῶν οὖν μὴ ποιούντων ταῦτα, ἡμεῖς μὲν ἢ ἐκλείψομεν κ. τ. λ. : so γάρ, which is placed before the sentence on which it depends, as a cause.

4. And sometimes the subordinate clause is placed coordinately in order to give it emphasis, by making it seem as important as the principal clause : so Pind. Pyth. X. 45 θρασείᾳ δὲ πνέων καρδίᾳ μόλεν Δανάας ποτὲ παῖς, ἁγεῖτο δ᾿ Ἀθάνα, ἐς ἀνδρῶν μακάρων ὅμιλον (for ὅτε ἡγεῖτο Ἀθηνᾶ, or ἡγουμένης Ἀθηνᾶς).

Different forms of coordinate Sentences.

Sentences logically coordinate, expressed in a coordinate form.

§. 753. 1. A sentence logically coordinate with another is either an extension or limitation of the thought ; in the former case the connection is *copulative*, in the other *adversative*.

Copulative.

2. This consists in the joining into one thought two or more sentences, which are, as it were, parallel and independent of each other, so that the coordinate clause gives a wider application to the thought of the preceding sentence. This is either by simply stringing them together, (*connexive*) or when the statement applies more strongly to the latter than to the former clause (*incressive*).

Connexive.

3. This is expressed by the conjunctions τέ, τέ — τέ, καί, τέ — καί, καί — καί.

Τέ.

§. 754. 1. The proper mode of uniting two clauses into one thought, is, by placing the connecting particle in both ; so that in the first it points forward to the following, and in the last backward to the preceding.

2. The original and most general copula is τέ, and from its general use it may supply the place of many other conjunctions. It seems to be connected with τίς, as its corresponding Latin copula *que* with *quis*.

Τέ—τέ.

3. Τέ—τέ signifies that the two sentences are parallel to each other, *as—so;* thus frequently in antithesis : ἔργον τε ἔπος τε, as the deed, so the word: πατὴρ ἀνδρῶν τε θεῶν τε. So used frequently in a succession of notions : Il. a, 177 αἰεὶ γὰρ ἔρις τε φίλη πόλεμοί τε μάχαι τε. Hence οὔτε—οὔτε, εἴτε—εἴτε, ἐάντε—ἐάντε. In prose we find τέ—τέ far more rarely, and generally only when whole sentences, or at the least, complete portions of sentences are to be connected : Thuc. II. 64 φέρειν χρὴ τά τε δαιμόνια ἀναγκαίως τά τε ἀπὸ τῶν πολεμίων ἀνδρείως : Xen. Cyr. VIII. I. 5 παρῶμέν τε οὖν—ἐπὶ τάδε τὸ ἀρχεῖον, ἀσκῶμέν τε, δι' ὧν μάλιστα δυνησόμεθα κατέχειν ἃ δεῖ, παρέχωμέν τε ἡμᾶς αὐτοὺς χρῆσθαι Κύρῳ ὅτι ἂν δέῃ. In antithetical words or sentences, τέ approaches in sense to ἤ—ἤ, *vel—vel;* whence sometimes they are interchanged, either τέ—ἤ, or ἤ—τέ : Plat. Ion. p. 535 D ὃς ἂν—κλάῃ τ' ἐν θυσίαις καὶ ἑορταῖς—ἢ φοβῆται : Il. β, 289 ἢ παῖδες νεαροὶ χῆραί τε γυναῖκες.

4. Τέ — τέ are frequently used as μέν — δέ, so that when in the first clause something is allowed or stated, the first τέ prepares the mind for something following thereon, while the second τέ refers the mind back to the former statement ; but μέν—δέ separate the two clauses, (*on the one hand—on the other,*) while τέ—τέ, by virtue of their primary force, unite them as part of one whole ; so Hdt. I. 22 καὶ δύο τε ἀντὶ ἑνὸς νηοὺς τῇ Ἀθηναίῃ ᾠκοδόμησε ὁ Ἀλυάττης, αὐτός. τε ἐκ τῆς νούσου ἀνέστη.

5. Hence (*a*) τέ—δέ are often found in two successive clauses, especially where one of the clauses, generally the first, is negative ; or where the second clause is to be opposed to the former, as the more important : Eur. Or. 192 σύ τε γὰρ ἐν νεκροῖς, τὸ δ' ἐμὸν οἴχεται βίου τὸ πλέον μέρος ὁ στοναχαῖσι: so ἔπειτα δὲ καί—ἅμα δὲ καί—ὡσαύτως δὲ καί, &c. : or when some notions in the two clauses are opposed ; or when the second clause conveys not merely a notion equivalent to the former, but something more : Hymn. Hom. Ven. 110 οὔτις τοι θεός εἰμι· τί μ' ἀθανάτῃσιν ἐΐσκεις ; ἀλλὰ καταθνητή τε, γυνὴ δέ με γείνατο μήτηρ ;—(*b*) and also μέν—τέ, which will be treated of under μέν—δέ.

Τέ alone.

6. In all the cases where τέ—τέ may be used, τέ may be used in the second clause alone. The two clauses are naturally less closely connected ; the second clause is not represented as necessarily following on the first, which is supposed to have an existence independent of it : so *senatus populusque Romanus ita censuit,* the senate is the principal : πατὴρ ἀνδρῶν θεῶν τε, father of men, and moreover of gods : Il. a, 5 αὐτοὺς δὲ ἑλώρια τεῦχε κύνεσσιν οἰωνοῖσί τε πᾶσι: Hdt. VI. 107 ἐς τὸν Μαραθῶνα τὰς νέας ὅρμιζε οὗτος, ἐκβάντας τε ἐς γῆν τοὺς βαρβάρους διέτασσε.

7. In prose, especially Thucydides, sentences separated by a stop are connected by τέ, where δέ would generally be used ; this τέ generally signifies *itaque, and so,* or it may be translated *for example* : Thuc. I. 9 Ἀγαμέμνων τέ μοι δοκεῖ—τὸν στόλον ἀγεῖραι, Agamemnon for example. Ibid. 22 κτῆμά τε ἐς ἀεὶ μᾶλλον ἢ ἀγώνισμα ἐς τὸ παραχρῆμα ἀκούειν ξύγκειται, and so κτῆμα ἐς ἀεί, &c.

8. When an expression is common to two clauses, it is used only once, either in the first or second clause, and when τέ is used to carry it on from one to the other, it is used either with both, or with the latter of the two clauses : Soph. O. R. 253 ὑπέρ τ' ἐμαυτοῦ (sc. ὑπέρ) τοῦ θεοῦ τε : Hdt.

VII. 106 οἵ τε ἐκ Θρᾴκης καὶ (sc. οἱ ἐξ) Ἑλλησπόντου: Eur. Phœn. 96
ἅ τ᾽ εἶδον (sc. ἅ) εἰσήκουσά τε: Xen. M. S. III. 5, 3 προτρέπονταί
τε ἀρετῆς ἐπιμελεῖσθαι καὶ (sc. προτρέπονται) ἄλκιμοι γίγνεσθαι: Arist. Vesp.
1277 ἅπασι φίλον ἄνδρα τε σοφώτατον (for φίλον ἄνδρα σοφώτατόν τε
ἄνδρα.)

Remarks on the Epic use of τέ.

§. 755. 1. In Epic poets, (and in Lyric, though but rarely, and in Attic
only in some few fragments,) τέ is joined frequently to conjunctions and
relatives, to denote more distinctly the opposition and connection of the
clauses of a sentence; *so as—so.* This idiom seems to arise from the old
practice of expressing subordinate clauses as coordinate, and it remained
after the more logical form of expression had been developed by the
conjunctions.

2. This τέ is either in both clauses, pointing forward to the one, and
backward to the other, or only in one. It occurs less frequently where
the clauses are connected by a demonstrative in one, and a relative in the
other, and only where the demonstr. and relative do not correspond: Il.
a, 218 ὅς κε θεοῖς ἐπιπείθηται, μάλα τ᾽ ἔκλυον αὐτοῦ, but more frequently in
other clauses; so frequently εἴπερ τε—τέ, or εἴπερ—τέ, εἴπερ τε
—also εἴπερ τε, with the apodosis suppressed, Il. δ, 160 εἴπερ γάρ
τε καὶ αὐτίκ᾽ Ὀλύμπιος οὐκ ἐτέλεσσεν, ἔκ τε καὶ ὀψὲ τελεῖ: or ἤ τε, so certainly, Od. β, 62 ἦ τ᾽ ἂν ἀμυναίμην, εἴ μοι δύναμίς γε παρείη. — μέν τε—
δέ τε, or ἀλλά τε, *as on one side, so on the other:* but in either of the
clauses τέ may be omitted; as, τέ—δέ τε, ἀλλά τε (Il. a, 82): μέν
τε—δέ or ἀλλά: or even the former clause may be supplied from the
context; as, δέ τε, ἀλλά τε; — also without μέν: δέ—τέ, τέ—δέ,
τέ—αὐτάρ, frequently answer to each other; καί τε, *atque* (=ad
que, yet to that), where the former clause is implied in the context, *so as,
so also:* Il. ι, 509 τὸν δὲ μέγ᾽ ὤνησαν, καί τ᾽ ἔκλυον εὐξαμένοιο:—γάρ τε,
then so as—so: Il. ω, 602 νῦν δὲ μνησώμεθα δόρπου· καὶ γάρ τ᾽ ἠύκομος
Νιόβη ἐμνήσατο σίτου, τῇπερ δώδεκα παῖδες ἐνὶ μεγάροισιν ὄλοντο;—so also
sometimes ἤ τε, or even ἤ τε—ἤ τε. See *Disjunctive Sentences.*

3. From this idiom another has arisen, whereby τέ is added to relatives
in dependent clauses, to denote more forcibly the relation between the
principal and dependent clauses; ὅστε, *he who* (not only in Homer, but in
lyric poets, and the chorus of tragedy, and even here and there in Herodotus): ὅστις τε, οἷός τε, ὅσος τε (=τοῖος, οἷος; τόσος, ὅσος; just of
such a nature, such a size, such a quantity, as); ὥστε, *so as, so that;* ὡσεί
τε, ἄτε, ἠύτε, ὅπως τε, ὅτε τε, then when, ἵνα τε, there where.

4. In Attic prose the following formulas occur: οἷός τε εἰμί, I am
able = *queo,* properly τοιοῦτός εἰμι οἷος, the τέ supplying the suppressed
τοιοῦτος: also ὥστε, ὡσείτε, and ἔστε (i. e. ἐς ὅ, τε), *quoad,* and
also, ἔπειτε, *postquam.*

Position of τέ.

§. 756. As being an enclitic, τέ cannot stand at the beginning of a
sentence or a clause, but must always depend on some word—generally
that to which its force applies, but from this there are the following
exceptions:

a. When the word to which τέ properly belongs is very closely connected with another word, so that they form as it were one notion, as

the article and substantive, dependent genitives, preposition and its case, and then τέ is placed between them: Il. γ, 54 οὐκ ἄν τοι χραίσμη κίθαρις, τά τε δῶρ' 'Αφροδίτης, ἥ τε κόμη, τό τε εἶδος.

b. When τέ belongs to the whole sentence, or clause, it is placed after the first word thereof: Hdt. VI. 123 οἵτινες ἔφευγόν τε τὸν πάντα χρόνον τοὺς τυράννους, ἐκ μηχανῆς τε τῆς τούτων ἐξέλιπον οἱ Πεισιστρατίδαι τὴν τυραννίδα: τέ belongs not to μηχανῆς, but to the predicate ἐξέλιπον.

Καί.

§. 757. 1. Καί signifies repetition, union, and emphasis, and occurs not only as a conjunction, but also in its original force as an adverb; in which it has its full meaning of *too*, while as a conjunction it has a weaker force, like *et*, formed from ἔτι, *yet*.

Καί *as a copulative Conjunction.*

Καί—καί.

2. Καί—καί, properly *too—too, et—et, as well—as also, not only—but also*, gives the clauses to which it is joined a more forcible and independent meaning than τέ—τέ; wherefore it is used when clauses of a different nature, or opposed to each other, are to be connected; as, ἄνθρωποι καὶ ἀγαθοὶ καὶ κακοί—καὶ πένητες καὶ πλούσιοι—καὶ ταχὺς καὶ ἄγριος (but not καὶ κακοὶ καὶ πονηροί)—καὶ χρήματα καὶ ἄνδρες—καὶ νῦν καὶ ἀεί—καὶ πρῶτα καὶ ὕστατα: Xen. Cyr. I. 1, 2 ἄρχοντες μέν εἰσι καὶ οἱ βούκολοι τῶν βοῶν καὶ οἱ ἱπποφορβοὶ τῶν ἵππων καὶ πάντες δὲ οἱ καλούμενοι νομεῖς ὧν ἂν ἐπιστατῶσι ζώων. Hence also it means *sive—sive;* see τέ—τέ (§. 754. 3.) and τέ—καί: Eur. Hec. 734 τολμᾶν ἀνάγκη, κἂν τύχω κἂν μὴ τύχω; and sometimes ἤ in the second clause answers to καί in the first: Plat. Lach. 191 E καὶ μένοντες ἢ ἀναστρέφοντες.

Τέ—καί.

§. 758. 1. Τέ—καί, *que—et, so as—so also*, mark that the two clauses are in close or necessary connection: Il. α, 17 'Ατρεῖδαί τε καὶ ἄλλοι ἐϋκνήμιδες 'Αχαιοί. — καλός τε κἀγαθός; even numbers, as τρεῖς τε καὶ δέκα. In most points the use of τέ—καί corresponds with that of τέ—τέ, except that it expresses a more intimate connection, and that καί implies the greater emphasis of its clause. Thus τέ — καί is used like τέ — τέ in opposed sentences which are coordinate and are conceived of as one whole: ἀγαθά τε καὶ κακά, χρηστοί τε καὶ πονηροί, τά τε ἔργα ὁμοίως καὶ οἱ λόγοι—νῦν τε καὶ τότε Soph., as now, so also then; νῦν τε καὶ πάλαι Id.: Xen. Hier. I. 2 πῇ διαφέρει ὁ τυραννικός τε καὶ ὁ ἰδιωτικὸς βίος. Hence in the sense of *sive—sive*, ἤ—ἤ, *vel—vel* (§. 757, 2.), ἅ τε δεῖ φίλια καὶ πολέμια νομίζειν: Plat. Legg. p. 831 D πᾶσαν τέχνην καὶ μηχανὴν καλλίω τε καὶ ἀσχημονεστέραν, *sive honestam, sive turpem;* then for μέν—δέ: Eur. Rhes. 335 σύ τ' εὖ παραινεῖς καὶ σὺ καιρίως σκοπεῖς.

2. Two actions which are coincident in point of time, or stand as antecedent and consequent to each other (as one takes place — so the other), are connected by τέ—καί.

3. The increasive force of καί is seen clearly in the combinations, πολλά τε καὶ καλὰ ἔργα ἀπεδείξατο: · Hdt. VI. 114 ἄλλοι 'Αθηναίων

πολλοί τε καὶ οὐνομαστοί : and yet more so when it connects the universal and particular (*quum — tum*) ; as, ἄλλοι τε καὶ ὁ Σωκράτης — ἄλλως τε καί, *quum aliter, tum, especially :* Hdt. VI. 136 Μιλτιαδέα — ἔσχον ἐν στόματι οἵ τε ἄλλοι καὶ μάλιστα Ξάνθιππος : Plat. Symp. p.176 D ἔγωγέ σοι εἴωθα πείθεσθαι ἄλλως τε καὶ ἅττ' ἂν περὶ ἰατρικῆς λέγῃς. So τά τε ἄλλα, καί—, especially. So ἄλλως τε πάντως καὶ κασιγνήταις πατρός Æsch. Prom. 637. So, instead of καί, a strong emphasis is given to the second clause by καὶ δὴ καί, *tum vero etiam :* Hdt. VI. 137 ἄλλα τε σχεῖν χωρία καὶ δὴ καὶ Λῆμνον : Plat. Rep. p. 357 A ὁ γὰρ Γλαύκων ἀεί τε ἀνδρειότατος ὢν τυγχάνει πρὸς ἅπαντα, καὶ δὴ καὶ τότε τοῦ Θρασυμάχου τὴν ἀπόρρησιν οὐκ ἀπεδέξατο[a]. (But ἄλλως τε without καί expresses a mere addition, *prætereaque, adde quod :* Plat. Phæd. p. 87 D ἀλλὰ γὰρ ἂν φαίη ἑκάστην τῶν ψυχῶν πολλὰ σώματα κατατρίβειν, ἄλλως τε εἰ καὶ πολλὰ ἔτη βιῴη.)

Obs. Καί may be used several times after τέ ; or in the first clause the conjunction may be omitted, and the following clauses united by the repetition of καί ; or in Epic τέ is used with several clauses, καί only with the last : Od. γ, 413. f. Ἐχέφρων τε Στρατίος τε Περσεύς τ' Ἀρητός τε καὶ ἀντίθεος Θρασυμήδης : Xen. Cyr. I. 4, 7 ἄρκτοι τε πολλοὺς ἤδη πλησιάσαντας διέφθειραν καὶ λέοντες καὶ κάπροι καὶ παρδάλεις· αἱ δὲ ἔλαφοι καὶ δορκάδες καὶ οἱ ἄγριοι ὄιες καὶ οἱ ὄνοι οἱ ἄγριοι ἀσινεῖς εἰσιν. And between καὶ—καί, there may be placed two distinct notions united by τὲ καί : Hdt. VII. 1 (ἐπέταξε ἑκάστοισι) καὶ νέας τε καὶ ἵππους καὶ σῖτον καὶ πλοῖα. But καὶ—τέ are not thus used, because the first clause may not be more emphatic than the second.

Καί alone.

§. 759. 1. Καί like τέ may be used alone, without another καί preceding, when the emphasis is to be more decided ; but it marks the intimate connection of the two clauses when ὁ Σωκράτης καὶ ὁ Πλάτων σοφοὶ ἦσαν, the two are as one (*τέ adjungit, καί conjungit*) : Xen. Cyr. I. 4, 7 αἱ δὲ ἔλαφοι καὶ δορκάδες καὶ οἱ ἄγριοι ὄιες καὶ οἱ ὄνοι οἱ ἄγριοι ἀσινεῖς εἰσιν : Ibid. VII. 5, 39 ὁ δ' ὄχλος πλείων καὶ πλείων ἐπέρρει. So it has often the sense of *atque* or *ac, et quidem*, the latter clause being either emphatic, or limiting and defining the former : Plat. Apol. p. 23 A ἡ ἀνθρωπίνη σοφία ὀλίγου τινὸς ἀξία ἐστὶ καὶ οὐδενός[b], (*parvo digna ac nullo.*) So πολλὰ καὶ πονηρά Xen., πολλὰ καὶ ἐσθλά Hom. : Demosth. c. Aphob. II. princ. πολλὰ καὶ μεγάλ' ἐψευσμένου : Cic. Legg. III. 14, 32 *pauci atque admodum pauci.* So καὶ ταῦτα, *idque*, that too.

2. Καί has this force at the beginning of a question wherein the speaker takes up what some one has said, and makes it into an *argumentum ad absurdum :* Plat. Theæt. p. 188 D καὶ τίς ἀνθρώπων τὸ μὴ ὂν δοξάσει ; Xen. Cyr. IV. 3, 11 ἀλλ' εἴποι τις ἄν, ὅτι παῖδες ὄντες ἐμάνθανον. Καὶ πότερα παῖδές εἰσι φρονιμώτεροι, ὥστε μαθεῖν τὰ φραζόμενα καὶ δεικνύμενα ἢ ἄνδρες ; = *ac multo minus prudentes sunt.* So especially καὶ πῶς : Plat. Alc. p. 134 C δύναιτο δ' ἄν τις μεταδιδόναι ὃ μὴ ἔχει ; — Καὶ πῶς ; = *ac minime quidem.*

3. In this way καί gets an adversative force, and sometimes seems to stand for καίτοι : Eur. Herc. F. 508 ὁρᾶτέ μ' ὅσπερ ἦν περίβλεπτος βροτοῖς, ὀνομαστὰ πράσσων. Καὶ μ' ἀφείλεθ' ἡ τύχη—ἡμέρᾳ μιᾷ.

---

[a] Stallb. ad loc.   [b] Stallb. ad loc.

4. Lastly, its increasive power is used in imperative clauses, which it connects with the preceding, as well as generally in expressions of some action following suddenly and forcibly on what goes before ; as, καί μοι δὸς τὴν χεῖρα!—καί μοι λαβὲ τὸ ψήφισμα : Il. a, 584 ὡς ἄρ' ἔφη, κ α ὶ ἀναίξας δέπας—μητρὶ φίλῃ ἐν χερσὶ τίθει.

Obs. 1. Kaί is used often instead of τέ—καί, when the latter clause is to be suddenly and unexpectedly connected with the former by ἴσος, ὁ αὐτός, ἄμα &c.; as, σεβίζω σ' ἴσα καὶ μάκαρας. So also in two coincident actions. See §. 758. 2.

Obs. 2. In English we say many great men, but in Greek generally, πολλοί is considered as a substantival word and is joined to the word following, either by καί or τέ alone (rare and only poetic), Eur. Hec. 620 ὃ πλεῖστ' ἔχων κάλλιστά τε : or by τ έ κ α ί, or (Homeric) by τ έ—τ έ, in which case πολλοί stands after the adjective : Il. β, 213 ἄκοσμά τε πολλά τε ἤδη. So in Latin, multæ et præclaræ res.

Obs. 3. When Homer after a temporal conjunction such as ὅτε, ἦμος &c., joins the sentence depending thereon by καί, this arises from the old fashion of coordinate clauses (see §. 752. 1., and δέ in Dependent Sentences) : Il. a, 478 ἦμος δ' ἠριγένεια φάνη ῥοδοδάκτυλος Ἠώς, κ α ὶ τ ό τ' ἔπειτ' ἀνάγοντο μετὰ στρατὸν εὐρὺν Ἀχαιῶν.

Obs. 4. Coordinate sentences ought to be alike as to the mood and tense of their verbs, but sometimes in poetry, and even in prose, they differ; and especially we find a participle in one sentence and the finite verb in another : Il. θ, 347 ἐρητύοντο μένοντες ἀλλήλοισί τε κ ε κ λ ό μ ε ν ο ι κ α ὶ πᾶσι θεοῖσιν χεῖρας ἀνίσχοντες μεγάλ' ε ὐ χ ε τ ό ω ν τ ο ἕκαστος : Thuc. IV. 100 ἄλλῳ τε τρόπῳ π ε ι ρ ά ζ ο ν τ ε ς κ α ὶ μηχανὴν π ρ ο σ ή γ α γ ο ν.

Kaί, e t i a m, as an Adverb.

§. 760. 1. Kaί like ἔτι is properly an adverb, even, e t i a m. But this emphatic force of κ α ί implies a connection with another clause, and hence καί derives its power as a conjunction. When καί is used in this sense, it often refers back to a principal sentence introduced by οὐ μόνον, οὐ μᾶλλον, or ὥσπερ καί, εἴπερ καί &c., or this clause is supplied by the mind ; as, καὶ ὁ Σωκράτης ταῦτα ἔλεξεν (sc. οὐ μόνον οἱ ἄλλοι, or ὥσπερ καὶ οἱ ἄλλοι).

2. According to the nature of this former clause, whether expressed or implied, καί has either a strengthening or a weakening power. In the first case, καί with verbs, subst., and numerals, means even, quite, yet ; with adject. and adverbs of quantity and intensity—entirely, certainly, very ; with temporal and conditional expressions—already, even already, yet, even yet ; as, καὶ καταγελᾷς μου — καὶ σὺ ταῦτα ἔλεξας : Il. λ, 654 τάχα κεν καὶ ἀναίτιον αἰτιόωτο. Also with comparatives : Il. κ, 556 θεὸς καὶ ἀμείνονας ἵππους δωρήσαιτο.—καὶ τρίς—καὶ λίην, καὶ κάρτα, καὶ πάνυ, καὶ πολύς, καὶ πᾶς—καὶ πρίν, καὶ πάλαι, καὶ χθές, καὶ αὐτίκα, καὶ δή or ἤδη, καὶ ὀψέ, καὶ πάλιν, καὶ νῦν or ἔτι καὶ νῦν — καὶ ὡς, καὶ οὕτως, vel sic. b. In the last case, even but, but even : Od. a, 58 ἱέμενος καὶ καπνὸν ἀποθρώσκοντα νοῆσαι. So with μόνος, εἷς, the indefinite and demonstrative pronouns, after relatives, interrogatives, and μή ; as, Plat. Rep. p. 335 B ἔστιν ἄρα δικαίου ἀνθρώπου βλάπτειν καὶ ὁντινοῦν ἄνθρωπον : Ibid. p. 445 C δεῦρο νῦν — ἵνα καὶ ἴδῃς, ὅσα κ α ὶ εἴδη ἔχει ἡ κακία : Demosth. p. 46 τί χρὴ κ α ὶ προσδοκᾶν ; What shall one but expect ? (= n i h i l p l a n e exspectandum est :) Eur. Hec. 515

πῶς καί νιν ἐξεπράξατο[a]; Ibid. 1064 ποῖ καί με φυγᾷ πτώσσουσι μυχῶν: Id. Hippol. 1171 πῶς καὶ διώλετ᾽, εἰπέ: " Qui τί χρὴ λέγειν interrogat, is, quid dici, non, an aliquid dici debeat, quærit; sed qui τί χρὴ καὶ λέγειν, is non solum quid, sed etiam an aliquid dicendum sit, dubitat (plene: quid dicendum est, si omnino aliquid dicendum est ?" [b])

Remarks on καί which belongs to another καί in a dependent clause, such as ὥσπερ καί &c.

§. 761. 1. If καί, *etiam*, belongs to another καί in a dependent clause; as, καὶ ὁ Σωκράτης ταῦτ᾽ ἔλεξεν, ὥσπερ καὶ οἱ ἄλλοι; it frequently is omitted in the former or latter clause: in the former, when the speaker is not at the moment thinking of the latter, or does not mean to point forward to the latter; as, ὁ Σωκράτης ταῦτ᾽ ἔλεξεν, ὥσπερ καὶ οἱ ἄλλοι;—in the latter, when the former is to be more emphatic; as, καὶ ὁ Σωκράτης ταῦτ᾽ ἔλεξεν, ὥσπερ οἱ ἄλλοι.

2. The relative or demonstrative sentence to which καί refers is frequently omitted, and must then be supplied from the context; as, καὶ ὁ Σωκράτης ἔλεξεν (scil. ὥσπερ or ἅπερ καὶ οἱ ἄλλοι): Xen. M. S. III. 10, 11 πῶς οὖν, ἔφη, τῷ ἀρρύθμῳ σώματι ἁρμόττοντα τὸν θώρακα εὔρυθμον ποιεῖς; Ὥσπερ καὶ ἁρμόττοντα, ἔφη, scil. οὕτω καὶ εὔρυθμον.

3. It is a curious feature in this use of καί that it is transferred from the clause to which it more properly belongs, to the other clause where it is not so much wanted, so that the unity of the two is more strongly marked; as, ὁ Σωκράτης εἴπερ τις καὶ ἄλλος, for καὶ ὁ Σ., εἴπερ τις ἄλλος: Hdt. I. 2 διαπραξαμένους καὶ τἆλλα, τῶν εἵνεκεν ἀπίκατο, ἁρπάσαι τοῦ βασιλῆος τὴν θυγατέρα Μηδείην, for καὶ ἁρπάσαι. So in temporal and conditional dependent clauses it is transferred to the principal clause, to mark that one action follows immediately on the other: Thuc. II. 93 ὡς δὲ ἔδοξεν αὐτοῖς, καὶ ἐχώρουν εὐθύς for ὡς καὶ ἔδοξ., and ὡς καί may be translated by *simulatque; simulac decretum est ab iis, continuo discesserunt.* So often in Homer: ὅτε—καὶ τότε; εἰ—καί; ἐπεί—καί.

Incressive or Emphatic Adverbs.

§. 762. Emphasis is expressed by καί, *et*, or the adverb καί, *etiam*, but more forcibly by οὐ μόνον—ἀλλὰ καί, or οὐχ ὅτι—ἀλλὰ καί &c.

Οὐ μόνον—ἀλλὰ καί.

1. Ὁ Σωκράτης οὐ μόνον σοφὸς ἦν, ἀλλὰ καὶ ἀγαθός. Καί is sometimes dropped in the second clause, whereby that clause is more emphatically contrasted with the former, while οὐ μόνον—ἀλλὰ καί denotes rather that the two clauses are of equal weight in the thought: Xen. M. S. I. 6, 2 καὶ ἱμάτιον ἠμφίεσαι οὐ μόνον φαῦλον, ἀλλὰ τὸ αὐτὸ θέρους τε καὶ χειμῶνος.

2. Here belong the following elliptic phrases: οὐχ ὅτι or μὴ ὅτι—ἀλλὰ καί or ἀλλά; οὐχ ὅπως or μὴ ὅπως—ἀλλὰ καί or ἀλλά; οὐ μόνον, ὅτι—ἀλλὰ καί; οὐχ οἷον—ἀλλά.—Οὐχ ὅτι, ὅπως,

that is οὐκ ἐρῶ, ὅτι, ὅπως as in Latin *non dico*; οὐχ οἶον, i. e. οὐ τοίω, οἶον; μὴ ὅτι, ὅπως, i. e. μὴ λέγε or λέγῃς, ὅτι, ὅπως, *not to say*, as in Latin, *ne dicam*.

3. According to the nature of the two opposed clauses, these forms, οὐχ ὅτι &c., mean *non solum*, or *non solum non*, or *nedum*. If they be directly and equally opposed to one another, οὐχ ὅτι = *non solum non*; as, οὐχ ὅτι ἔφυγεν, ἀλλ' ἐνίκησε, *non solum non fugit, sed vicit*, properly οὐκ ἐρῶ, ὅτι ἔφ., ἀλλ' ἐν., *non dicam eum fugisse, sed vicit*. If the latter is stronger than the former, οὐχ ὅτι = *non solum*; as, οὐχ ὅτι ἔτρεσεν, ἀλλ' ἔφυγεν, *non solum extimuit, sed fugit*; if the former is the more important, and is followed by οὐχ ὅτι, οὐχ ὅπως, these = *nedum*; as, ἔφυγεν, οὐχ ὅπως ἔτρεσεν, *fugit, nedum extimuerit*: Xen. Cyr. I. 3, 10 λέγω δὲ (*prædicans*) ἕκαστος ὑμῶν τὴν ἑαυτοῦ ῥώμην, ἐπεὶ ἀνασταίητε ὀρχησόμενα, μὴ ὅπως ὀρχεῖσθαι ἐν ῥυθμῷ, ἀλλ' οὐδ' ὀρθοῦσθαι ἐδύνασθε, *non solum non saltare, sed ne rectis quidem pedibus stare poteratis*: Plat. Apol. p. 40 D μὴ ὅτι ἰδιώτην τινά, ἀλλὰ τὸν μέγαν βασιλέα, *ne dicam privatum aliquem*: Id. Symp. p. 179 B καὶ μὴν ὑπεραποθνήσκειν γε μόνοι ἐθέλουσιν οἱ ἐρῶντες, οἱ μόνον ὅτι ἄνδρες, ἀλλὰ καὶ γυναῖκες: Demosth. p. 67. extr. (τὼ Θηβαίους ἡγεῖτο) οὐχ ὅπως ἀντιπράξειν καὶ διακωλύσειν, ἀλλὰ καὶ συστρατεύσειν, ἂν αὐτοὺς κελεύῃ (scil. συστρατεύειν), *non solum non, sed etiam*.

Obs. So also μή τι, μή τοι are used, generally accompanied by γέ and δή: Demosth. p. 24, 23 οὐκ ἔνι δ' αὐτὸν ἀργοῦντα οὐδὲ τοῖς φίλοις ἐπιτάττειν ἐπὲρ αὑτοῦ τι ποιεῖν, μή τι γε δὴ τοῖς θεοῖς, *ne dicam, nedum.*

Two adversative clauses standing coordinately to each other.

§. 763. 1. Two adversative clauses may be coordinate when the latter *limits* or *denies* some notion or thought in the former, as, *he is poor, but brave—he is not bold, but cowardly*; the former clause, as it allows or concedes something, is called the *concessive*, the clause coordinate to it, the *adversative* clause.

Limitation.

Δέ.

2. Δέ is the most general expression of opposition, and expresses every sort thereof. As uniting the force of the copulative conjunctions (τέ, καί), and the adversative (ἀλλά), it is used in both forces.

Μέν—δέ.

§. 764. 1. As the adversative clause is marked by δέ, so is the concessive by μέν, which gives to the former clause the notion of allowing *something*, and thus points forward to the disallowing something else, that is to the limitation in the second clause, and the force both of δέ and μέν is weaker or stronger as the case may be.

2. The derivation and original force of μέν and δέ is of course very doubtful: μέν is by some derived from μήν, *vero*, and δέ from δέω, *to bind*: it seems better to consider μέν as the neuter of εἷς, *one*, as if it were μεῖς, μία, μέν, and δέ as connected with δίς, δύο[a]; so that they would mean *in the first place,—in the second place*, and these meanings may perhaps be

---

[a] R. P. Tracts, p. 303. Sewell Hor. Philol. 128.

traced in all the uses of these particles; we may translate them very often *indeed—but,* or *on the one hand—on the other.*

3. *a.* Mέν and δέ are used in distinctions or divisions of *place, time, number, order, person;* the single members being placed in contrast to each other by μέν—δέ, so that the one is separated from the other; as, ἐνταῦθα μέν—ἐκεῖ δέ, ἔνθα μέν—ἔνθα δέ, ὁτὲ μέν—ὁτὲ δέ, τοτὲ μέν—τοτὲ δέ (ὅτε and τότε in this sense are accented like ποτέ) ποτὲ μέν—ποτὲ δέ—ἄλλοτε μέν—ἄλλοτε δέ, ἅμα μέν—ἅμα δέ, πρῶτον μέν—ἔπειτα δέ, τῇ μέν—τῇ δέ, πῇ μέν—πῇ δέ, τὸ μέν—τὸ δέ, τὰ μέν—τὰ δέ, and τοῦτο μέν—τοῦτο δέ (especially in Hdt.): and from the original distinction of place is derived the distinction of person; ὁ μέν—ὁ δέ, *hic—ille,* properly *he here—he there.* —Hence frequently the whole is followed by two parts distinguished by μέν—δέ, in the same case with the whole, especially nomin. and accus.: Plat. Legg. p. 838 A τέχνην—τὴν μὲν ῥᾳδίαν ἔχω, τὴν δ' αὖ—χαλεπωτάτην : Id. Phædr. p. 248 A αἱ δὲ ἄλλαι ψυχαὶ ἡ μέν—ἡ δέ : so in Homer, but only when the whole is in the dual or plural; as, Il. η, 306 τὼ—ὁ μέν—ὁ δέ.

Obs. 1. Sometimes the two clauses do not correspond in their forms; as, ὁ μέν—ἄλλος δέ, οἱ μέν—ἔνιοι δέ or ἔστι δ' οἵ, οἱ μέν—ἄλλος δέ, οἱ μέν— ἕτεροι δέ, οἱ μέν—καὶ οἱ, ὁτὲ μέν—ἐνίοτε δέ, &c.: Thuc. VII. 73 καὶ οἱ μὲν εἰπόντες ἀπῆλθον, καὶ οἱ ἀκούσαντες διήγγειλαν τοῖς στρατηγοῖς : Plat. Phædon. p. 59 A ὁτὲ μὲν γελῶντες, ἐνίοτε δὲ δακρύοντες : Id. Protag. p. 334 A ἔγωγε πολλὰ οἶδ' ἃ ἀνθρώποις μὲν ἀνωφελῆ ἐστι—τὰ δέ γε ὠφέλιμα (for πολλὰ οἶδα, ἃ ἀνθρώπ. τὰ μὲν ἀνωφ. ἐστι—τὰ δέ γε ὠφ.) : Demosth. p. 117, 24 τοῦτο μὲν ὑμῖν—καὶ πάλιν Λακεδαιμονίοις : Ibid. p. 123, 48 πρῶτον μὲν—οὕτω δ' ἀρχαίως εἶχον : Ibid. p. 125, 58 τοτὲ μέν—πάλιν δέ.

Obs. 2. In the second clause the proper contrary subst. is sometimes used instead of the article: Plat. Rep. p. 366 E ὡς τὸ μὲν (ἡ ἀδικία) μέγιστον κακῶν, ὅσα ἴσχει ψυχὴ ἐν αὐτῇ, δικαιοσύνη δὲ μέγιστον ἀγαθόν : Id. Theæt. p. 157 E ἀδικεῖν δ' ἐστὶν ἐν τῷ τοιούτῳ, ὅταν τις μὴ χωρὶς μὲν ὡς ἀγωνιζόμενος τὰς διατριβὰς ποιῆται, χωρὶς δὲ διαλεγόμενος, καὶ ἐν μὲν τῷ παίζῃ—ἐν δὲ τῷ διαλέγεσθαι σπουδάζῃ. Sometimes, for the sake of emphasis or clearness, the substantive is expressed, as well as the article, with μέν or δέ: Thuc. VII. 86 ξυνέβαινε δέ, τὸν μὲν πολεμιώτατον αὐτοῖς εἶναι, Δημοσθένην, διὰ τὰ ἐν τῇ νήσῳ καὶ Πύλῳ, τὸν δὲ διὰ τὰ αὐτὰ ἐπιτηδειότατον.

b. When the same word is repeated, or an equivalent word used in two sentences, the sameness of the common notion is somewhat lessened, and its importance increased by the use of μέν—δέ, which by separating them, makes it seem as if they were different notions placed in contrast to each other : Hesiod. Th. 655 περὶ μὲν πραπίδας, περὶ δ' ἐσσὶ νόημα : Hdt. III. 52 καὶ εἷλε μὲν τὴν Ἐπίδαυρον, εἷλε δὲ αὐτὸν Προκλέα καὶ ἐζώγρησε: Id. VI. 112 πρῶτοι μὲν γὰρ Ἑλλήνων—δρόμῳ ἐς πολεμίους ἐχρήσαντο, πρῶτοι δὲ ἀνέσχοντο ἐσθῆτά τε Μηδικὴν ὁρέωντες, καὶ τοὺς ἄνδρας ταύτην ἐσθημένους : Id. VII. 9, 1 τῶν ἐπιστάμεθα μὲν τὴν μάχην, ἐπιστάμεθα δὲ τὴν δύναμιν, cf. 18. Xen. M. S. II. 1, 32 ἐγὼ δὲ σύνειμι μὲν θεοῖς, σύνειμι δ' ἀνθρώποις τοῖς ἀγαθοῖς.

c. When different predicates belong to the same subject, or different actions to the same person : Soph. Phil. 239 ἐγὼ γένος μέν εἰμι τῆς περιρρύτου Σκύρου, πλέω δ' ἐς οἶκον, αὐδῶμαι δὲ παῖς Ἀχιλέως Νεοπτόλεμος : so in a principal and dependent clause; Hdt. I. 103 οἱ ἐσέβαλον μὲν ἐς τὴν Ἀσίην, Κιμμερίους ἐκβαλόντες ἐκ τῆς Εὐρώπης, τούτοισι δὲ ἐπισπόμενοι φεύγουσι οὕτω ἐς τὴν Μηδικὴν χώρην ἀπίκοντο. It is a peculiar idiom of Homer and Herodotus, when two predicates belong to the same subject, to use

μέν with the first, then οἱ δέ with the second predicate, as it were to
repeat it : Hdt. I. 66 οἱ Λακεδαιμόνιοι Ἀρκάδων μὲν τῶν ἄλλων ἀπείχων,
οἱ δὲ (sc. Λακεδ.)—ἐπὶ Τεγεήτας ἐστρατεύοντο : Id. VI. 9 εἰ δὲ ταῦτα μὲν
οὐ ποιήσουσι, οἱ δὲ πάντως διὰ μάχης ἐλεύσονται, τάδε σφι λέγετε : Id. VII.
13 ὀνείρου μὲν τούτου λόγον οὐδένα ἐποιέετο, ὁ δὲ—ἔλεγε.

d. So actions connected in place, time, or causation are joined by μέ—
δέ as by τέ—καί; only that in this latter a more intimate connection, while
by the former a more external connection is intimated : Soph. Œ. C. 1619
ἦν μὲν σιωπή, φθέγμα δ' ἐξαίφνης τινὸς θώϋξεν αὐτόν.

e. So two clauses of the same construction are opposed to each
other by μέν—δέ, in order to connect the former, which ought to have
been expressed by a dependent clause, to the context, by putting it in
contrast to the latter. This occurs in Homer, though probably not
with this rhetorical intent, but from the old practice of placing subordinate
thoughts in a coordinate form ; it may be often translated by " whilst :"
Il. a, 165 οὐ μὲν σοί ποτε ἴσον ἔχω γέρας, ὁππότ' Ἀχαιοὶ Τρώων ἐκπέρσωσ' εὐ-
ναιόμενον πτολίεθρον· ἀλλὰ τὸ μὲν πλεῖον πολυάϊκος πολέμοιο χεῖρες ἐμαὶ διέπουσ'·
ἀτὰρ ἤν ποτε δασμὸς ἵκηται, σοὶ τὸ γέρας πολὺ μεῖζον, ἐγὼ δ' ὀλίγον τε φίλον τε
ἔρχομ' ἔχων ἐπὶ νῆας = οὐ μὲν σοί ποτε ἴσον ἔχω γέρας—, ἀλλὰ, χειρῶν
ἐμῶν πλεῖον πολέμοιο διεπουσῶν, σοὶ τὸ γέρας πολὺ μεῖζον γίγνεται :
Ibid. 182 ὡς ἔμ' ἀφαιρεῖται Χρυσηΐδα Φοῖβος Ἀπόλλων, τὴν μὲν ἐγὼ σὺν νηΐ
τ' ἐμῇ καὶ ἐμοῖς ἑτάροισιν πέμψω, ἐγὼ δέ κ' ἄγω Βρισηΐδα—κλισίηνδε (while I
send away, &c.): Il. θ, 270 αὐτὰρ ὅγ' ἥρως παπτήνας, ἐπεὶ ἄρ' τιν' ὀϊ-
στεύσας ἐν ὁμίλῳ βεβλήκειν, ὁ μὲν (sc. βληθείς) αὖθι πεσὼν ἀπὸ θυμὸν ὄλεσσεν,
αὐτὰρ ὁ αὖτις ἰὼν, παῖς ὡς ὑπὸ μητέρα, δύσκεν εἰς Αἴανθ' (=since the man had
lost his life, he &c.): Eur. Iph. T. 115 οὗτοι μακρὸν μὲν ἤλθομεν κατὰ
πόρον, ἐκ τερμάτων δὲ νόστου ἀροῦμεν πόλιν, since we have made so long
a voyage : Demosth. p. 281 αἰσχρόν ἐστιν, εἰ ἐγὼ μὲν τοὺς πόνους, ὑμεῖς δὲ
μηδὲ τοὺς λόγους αὐτῶν ἀνέξεσθε, that whilst I, &c. ; but the blame also implied in the latter clause is here brought out more strongly by its contrast with the former clause.

Remarks on μέν and δέ.

Position.

§. 765. 1. Sometimes μέν—δέ belong to the predicate of the whole
clause, and not to the word to which they are joined : Il. a, 183 τὴν μὲν
ἐγὼ—πέμψω, ἐγὼ δέ κ' ἄγω Βρισηΐδα. So especially δέ is used with personal or demonstrative pronouns at the beginning of the clause, though
the opposition resides in some other word, generally the predicate : Il.
θ, 119 καὶ τοῦ μέν ῥ' ἐφάμαρτεν, ὁ δ' ἡνίοχον θεράποντα—βάλε. In this case,
if the substantive or adjective is joined with the article or a preposition,
the μέν or δέ come between these : Demosth. p. 815, 6 τὰ μὲν ἄλλα
πάντα ἀπεστερήκασι, τὴν οἰκίαν δὲ καὶ ἀνδράποδα—παραδεδώκασιν[a]: Isocr.
Paneg. c. 41 πρὸς μὲν τοὺς φίλους—πρὸς δ' ἐχθρούς. In poetry, δέ
is frequently placed third in the sentence, not only after a preposition or
the article, as sometimes in prose, but also after two or even three words
which are closely connected ; as, Æsch. Pers. 725 πεζὸς ἢ ναύτης δὲ
πεῖραν τήνδ' ἐμώρανεν τάλας.

---

[a] Bremi ad loc.

Disparity or disjunction of the Clauses.

2. One of the opposed clauses may be expressed by the *verbum finitum*, while the other either takes the form of a participle or a periphrasis; as, ταῦτα καλῶς μὲν πρᾶξαι δόξας, σφόδρα δὲ ἁμαρτάνεις.

3. Sometimes a periphrasis intervenes; as, Il. β, 494 Βοιωτῶν μέν. Πηνέλεως καὶ Λήϊτος ἦρχον—511 οἳ δ᾽ Ἀσπληδόνα ναῖον ἰδ᾽ Ὀρχομενὸν Μινύειον, τῶν ἦρχ᾽ Ἀσκάλαφος καὶ Ἰάλμενος.

Μέν—, μέν—.

4. If μέν is used in adjectival (relative) or adverbial sentences, it is often repeated in a following demonstrative sentence, for the sake of emphasis: Hdt. II. 121 καὶ τὸν (i. e. ὅν) μὲν καλέουσι θέρος, τοῦτον μὲν προσκυνέουσί τε καὶ εὖ ποιοῦσι· τὸν δὲ χειμῶνα κ. τ. λ.

Μέν—μέν— ; δέ—δέ.

5. Thus μέν—μέν are often followed by corresponding δέ—δέ, which gives force to the expression: Plat. Apol. p. 28 E ἐγὼ οὖν δεινὰ ἂν εἰργασμένος, ὦ ἄνδρες Ἀθηναῖοι, εἰ, ὅτε μέν με οἱ ἄρχοντες ἔταττον, οὓς ὑμεῖς εἵλεσθε ἄρχειν μου, καὶ ἐν Ποτιδαίᾳ καὶ ἐν Ἀμφιπόλει καὶ ἐπὶ Δηλίῳ, τότε μὲν οὗ ἐκεῖνοι ἔταττον ἔμενον—καὶ ἐκινδύνευον ἀποθανεῖν, τοῦ δὲ θεοῦ τάττοντος, ὡς ἐγὼ ᾠήθην τε καὶ ὑπέλαβον, φιλοσοφοῦντά με δεῖν ζῆν καὶ ἐξετάζοντα ἐμαυτὸν καὶ τοὺς ἄλλους, ἐνταῦθα δὲ φοβηθεὶς ἢ θάνατον ἢ ἄλλο ὁτιοῦν πρᾶγμα λίποιμι τὴν τάξιν[a]: Isocrat. Areopag. 18 παρ᾽ οἷς μὲν γὰρ μήτε φυλακὴ μήτε ζημία τῶν τοιούτων καθέστηκε, μήθ᾽ αἱ κρίσεις ἀκριβεῖς εἰσι, παρὰ τούτοις μὲν διαφθείρεσθαι καὶ τὰς ἐπιεικεῖς τῶν φύσεων· ὅπου δὲ μήτε λαθεῖν τοῖς ἀδικοῦσι ῥᾴδιόν ἐστι, μήτε φανεροῖς γενομένοις συγγνώμης τυχεῖν, ἐνταῦθα δ᾽ ἐξιτήλους γίγνεσθαι τὰς κακοηθείας. But this form of parallelism is seldom found so perfectly drawn out; either the second μέν is omitted, as Xen. Cyr. VI. 2, 14. or both; or the second δέ is dropped, or the two latter clauses are joined into one, so that there is only one δέ: Hdt. III. 108 ὅσα μὲν ψυχήν τε δειλὰ καὶ ἐδώδιμα, ταῦτα μὲν πάντα πολύγονα πεποίηκεν—, ὅσα δὲ σχέτλια καὶ ἀνιηρά, ὀλιγόγονα κ. τ. λ.

Obs. In Homer we do not find μέν—μέν— ; δέ—, but where μέν is twice used, the second is not a repetition of the first, but is opposed to the following δέ, while the first μέν belongs to the protasis of which the two clauses (μέν—δέ) are the apodosis: Il. υ, 41—47 εἵως μέν ῥ᾽ ἀπάνευθε θεοὶ θνητῶν ἔσαν ἀνδρῶν, τέως Ἀχαιοὶ μὲν μέγα κύδανον—, Τρῶας δὲ τρόμος αἰνὸς ὑπήλυθε γυῖα ἕκαστον—. Αὐτὰρ ἐπεὶ κ. τ. λ. To the first (εἵως μέν), αὗταρ corresponds; to the second, δέ (Τρῶας δέ).

Μέν—ἀλλά, &c.—Μέν—τέ or καί, or ἤ, or εἴτε.

6. Of course instead of δέ any other adversative copula may be used; as, ἀλλά, αὖ, αὐτάρ, ἀτάρ, μέντοι, ὅμως, μήν, &c. But instead of such a copula we sometimes find *a.* τέ, καί, and in Homer, ἠδέ; or *b.* the construction is entirely changed, no regard being had to μέν.

a. In this construction, though the sentence begins as if the clauses were to be distinguished from and opposed to each other, afterwards they are represented as parts of a whole; Od. χ, 475 τοῦ δ᾽ ἀπὸ μὲν ῥῖνάς τε καὶ οὔατα νηλέϊ χαλκῷ τάμνον· μήδεά τ᾽ ἐξέρυσαν (for ἀπὸ μὲν ῥῖνας τάμνον, ἐκ δὲ μήδεα ἔρυσαν :) Od. ι, 49 ἐπιστάμενοι μὲν ἀφ᾽ ἵππων ἀνδράσι μάρ-

---

[a] Stallb. ad loc.

νασθαι, καὶ ὅθι χρὴ πεζὸν ἐόντα: Od. γ, 351 αὐτὰρ ἐμοὶ πάρα μὲν χλαῖνα καὶ (for πάρα δέ) ῥήγεα καλά: Il. α, 267 κάρτιστοι μὲν ἔσαν, καὶ καρτίστοις ἐμάχοντο: Od. μ, 168 ἄνεμος μὲν ἐπαύσατο ἠδὲ γαλήνη ἔπλετο: Eur. Or. 22, 24 ('Αγαμέμνονι) παρθένοι μὲν τρεῖς ἔφυμεν ἐκ μιᾶς, Χρυσόθεμις, 'Ιφιγένειά τ', 'Ηλέκτρα τ' ἐγώ, ἄρσην τ' 'Ορέστης, μητρὸς ἀνοσιωτάτης: Cf. Med. 13: Hipp. 712 sq.: Andr. 8 sq. 467. 643. 645: Suppl. 1040. 1042.: Iph. T. 73 sq.: Troad. 48 sq.: Eur. Or. 489 sq. χρῆν αὐτὴν ἐπιθεῖναι μὲν αἵματος δίκην ὁσίαν διώκοντ', ἐκβαλεῖν τε δωμάτων μητέρα: Thuc. III. 46 τίνα οἴεσθε ἥντινα οὐκ ἄμεινον μὲν ἢ νῦν παρασκευάσασθαι, πολιορκίᾳ τε παρατενεῖσθαι ἐς τοὔσχατον: Xen. M. S. I. 1, 10 ἐκεῖνός γε ἀεὶ μὲν ἦν ἐν τῷ φανερῷ—, καὶ ἔλεγε μὲν ὡς τὸ πολύ, τοῖς δὲ βουλομένοις ἐξῆν ἀκούειν.—And subdivisions which intervene between μέν and δέ are connected by τέ.

b. Il. θ, 374 ἀλλὰ σὺ μὲν νῦν νῶϊν ἐπέντυε μώνυχας ἵππους, ὄφρ' ἂν ἐγὼ— τεύχεσιν ἐς πόλεμον θωρήξομαι: Il. σ, 134 ἀλλὰ σὺ μὲν μήπω καταδύσεο μῶλον Ἄρηος, πρίν γ' ἐμὲ δεῦρ' ἐλθοῦσαν ἐν ὀφθαλμοῖσιν ἴδηαι.

Obs. In many passages the use of μέν—τέ or καί, instead of μέν—δέ is only seeming, each particle being used in its proper sense. In such passages μέν stands alone, (§. 766. 2.) the corresponding clause with δέ being supplied, and the τέ or καί is a mere copula, and does not belong to the μέν: Od. δ, 190 'Ατρείδη, περὶ μέν σε βροτῶν πεπνυμένον εἶναι Νέστωρ φάσχ' ὁ γέρων, ὅτ' ἐπιμνησαίμεθα σεῖο. Καὶ νῦν, εἴ τι που ἔστι, πίθοιό μοι: Od. ω, 24 'Ατρείδη, περὶ μέν σε φαμὲν Διὶ τερπικεραύνῳ ἀνδρῶν ἡρώων φίλον ἔμμεναι — ἦ τ' ἄρα καὶ σοὶ πρῶτα παραστήσεσθαι ἔμελλεν Μοῖρ' ὀλοή: Il. θ, 274 ἔνθα τίνα πρῶτον Τρώων ἕλε Τεῦκρος ἀμύμων; 'Ορσίλοχον μὲν πρῶτα καὶ Ὅρμενον ἠδ' 'Οφελέστην κ. τ. λ.

Μέν without any adversative Copula.

§. 766. 1. The adversative copula which should answer to μέν is sometimes wanting, when the word to which δέ would be attached, in itself implies the opposition sufficiently; as, ἐνταῦθα μέν—ἐκεῖ, and very often πρῶτον μέν—ἔπειτα: Eur. Med. 548 ἐν τῷδε δείξω πρῶτα μὲν σοφὸς γεγώς, ἔπειτα σώφρων, εἶτα σοὶ μέγας φίλος[a]: cf. Id. Hec. 357: Xen. M. S. III. 11, 14 εἰ πρῶτον μὲν τοῖς κεκορεσμένοις μήτε προσφέροις, μήτε ὑπομιμνήσκοις, —ἔπειτα τοὺς δεομένους ὑπομιμνήσκοις: Demosth. p. 836, 3. p. 40, 2. p. 18, 1 πρῶτον μὲν ἀπίστους, εἶτα: Xen. Cyr. I, 2, 4 τούτων (sc. μέρων) δ' ἐστιν ἐν μὲν παισὶν, ἐν δὲ ἐφήβοις, ἄλλο τελείοις ἀνδράσιν, ἄλλο τοῖς ὑπὲρ τὰ στρατεύσιμα ἔτη γεγονόσι.

2. The adversative clause is often wholly omitted, and must be supplied; this especially occurs with personal and demonstrative pronouns : Od. η, 237 ξεῖνε, τὸ μέν σε πρῶτον ἐγὼν εἰρήσομαι: Hdt. III. 3 λέγεται δὲ καὶ ὅδε ὁ λόγος, ἐμοὶ μὲν οὐ πιθανός, to me indeed incredible (but to others perhaps not so): Xen. Cyr. II. 2, 10 ἐγὼ μὲν οὐκ οἶδα.— So ὡς μὲν λέγουσιν: Plat. Apol. p. 21 D ἐλογισάμην, ὅτι τούτου μὲν τοῦ ἀνθρώπου ἐγὼ σοφώτερός εἰμι: Id. Phæd. p. 58 A ταῦτα μὲν ἡμῖν ἤγγειλέ τις[b]. Also the forms οἶμαι μέν, ἡγοῦμαι μέν, δοκῶ μέν, οὐκ οἶδα μέν &c., I indeed think so=surely. And this μέν may stand after any word, as the adversative clause to it may be supplied. So in questions, where it may be translated by *but certainly, to be sure,* &c : Plat. Charm. p. 153 C παρεγένου μέν, ἦ δ' ὅς, τῇ μάχῃ; but were you really ? &c.

[a] Pflugk ad loc   [b] Stallb. ad loc.

Δέ *without* μέν.

§. 767. 1. Δέ often stands alone :—*a.* When the second clause is not in the speaker's mind when he conceives the first. *b.* When he purposely refrains from pointing forward to any second clause. *c.* When the former clause is but slightly opposed to the second. *d.* When the first clause is not expressed, but supplied by the mind.

2. Hence δέ can be used alone in all cases where μέν—δέ might be used ; the opposition being of course partial and imperfect : Xen. Cyr. IV. 5, 46 ὁρᾶτε ἵππους, ὅσοι ἡμῖν πάρεισιν, οἱ δὲ προσάγονται (for ὅσοι οἱ μέν—). Cf. Plat. Apol. p. 18 D[a]. Xen. Hell. I. 2, 14 οἱ αἰχμάλωτοι — ᾤχοντο ἐς Δεκέλειαν, οἱ δ' ἐς Μέγαρα : and so ὁ μέν is often omitted before ὁ δέ. In poetry μέν is sometimes omitted, where a perfect opposition between the two sentences might be looked for : Eur. Or. 100 ὀρθῶς ἔλεξας, οὐ φίλως δέ μοι λέγεις : Ibid. 414 οὐ σοφὸς, ἀληθὴς δ' ἐς φίλους ἔφυν φίλος : Ibid. 444. sq. ὄνομα γὰρ, ἔργον δ' οὐκ ἔχουσιν οἱ φίλοι, οἱ μὴ 'πὶ ταῖσι συμφοραῖς ὄντες φίλοι.

Obs. Of course δέ can belong to other conjunctions as well as μέν ; as, γέ, τέ, καί, ἤ &c.: Xen. Cyr. IV. 4, 3 ὁ δὲ διήκουέ τε ἡδέως πάντων ὅσα ἐβούλοντο λέγειν, ἔπειτα δὲ καὶ ἐπῄνεσεν αὐτούς.

3. We find then δέ without μέν in the following cases :

a. Where a word is used twice, or its equivalent is in the second clause (§. 764, 3. *b.*) : Il. ω, 484 ὡς Ἀχιλεὺς θάμβησεν, ἰδὼν Πρίαμον θεοειδέα· θάμβησαν δὲ καὶ ἄλλοι : Eur. Med. 98 μήτηρ κινεῖ κραδίαν, κινεῖ δὲ χόλον. In prose, μέν is placed in the former clause.

b. When several predicates belong to the same subject (§. 764, 3. *c.*) : Hdt. VII. 8, 2 Ἀρισταγόρη τῷ Μιλησίῳ, δούλῳ δὲ ἡμετέρῳ.

c. Where actions are coincident in time, place, or causation (§. 764, 3. *d.*) : Eur. Phœn. 426 νὺξ ἦν· Ἀδράστου δ' ἦλθον εἰς παραστάδας.

d. After negative sentences : Thuc. IV. 86 οὐκ ἐπὶ κακῷ, ἐπ' ἐλευθερώσει δὲ τῶν Ἑλλήνων παρελήλυθα.

e. As μέν is often used twice alone, so is δέ, especially to take up an interrupted sentence, and also to sum up thoughts already separately and loosely stated (*ut paucis complectar*) : Hdt. I. 28 χρόνου δὲ ἐπιγινομένου καὶ κατεστραμμένων σχεδὸν πάντων τῶν ἐντὸς Ἅλυος ποταμοῦ οἰκημένων (πλὴν γάρ κ. τ. λ.), κατεστραμμένων δὲ τούτων κ. τ. λ. So δέ is often placed in opposition to a parenthesis : Hdt. VII. 67 ἐπεὶ ὦν ἀπίκατο ἐς τὰς Ἀθήνας πάντες οὗτοι πλὴν Παρίων (Πάριοι δὲ ὑπολειφθέντες ἐν Κύθνῳ ἐκαραδόκεον τὸν πόλεμον κῇ ἀποβήσεται), οἱ δὲ λοιποὶ ὡς ἀπίκοντο ἐς τὸ Φάληρον κ. τ. λ. But frequently the sentence which δέ thus takes up, is contained in the preceding context.

f. As we sometimes find μέν, μέν—δέ, δέ, so δέ, δέ is sometimes found alone : Plat. Phæd. p. 78 C οὔκουν ἅπερ ἀεὶ κατὰ ταὐτὰ καὶ ὡσαύτως ἔχει, ταῦτα μάλιστα εἰκὸς εἶναι τὰ ἀξύνθετα, τὰ δὲ ἄλλοτ' ἄλλως καὶ μηδέποτε κατὰ ταὐτὰ, ταῦτα δὲ εἶναι τὰ ξύνθετα ;

4. An idiomatic construction in which δέ alone has a very good effect, is in exclamations of displeasure, &c. where δέ forms a strong contrast to the thought which the mind supplies : Demosth. p. 582, 1 ἀλλ' οὐκ ἂν εὐθέως εἴποιεν· τὸν δὲ βάσκανον ! τὸν δὲ ὄλεθρον ! τοῦτον δὲ ὑβρίζειν ! ἀναπνεῖν δέ !

---

[a] Stallb. ad loc.

Δέ as a Copula.—Δέ for γὰρ, οὖν.—Δέ in Questions and Answers.

§. 768. 1. From this weaker adversative use of δέ its use as a copula is
derived, *in the second place :* whereby sentences are connected, though the
thoughts are to a certain degree hereby opposed to each other, the thought
which follows being represented as new and distinct from the old one
which preceded : one may translate this by *and.*

2. Hence δέ is used when the speaker passes from one object to
another : Il. a, 43–49 ὡς ἔφατ' εὐχόμενος· τοῦ δ' ἔκλυε Φοῖβος Ἀπόλλων· βῆ
δὲ κατ' Οὐλύμποιο καρήνων —, ἔκλαγξαν δ' ἄρ' ὀϊστοὶ ἐπ' ὤμων χωομένοιο —· ὁ
δ' ἤιε νυκτὶ ἐοικώς· ἕζετ' ἔπειτ' ἀπάνευθε νεῶν, μετὰ δ' ἰὸν ἕηκεν· δεινὴ δὲ κλαγγὴ
γένετ' ἀργυρέοιο βιοῖο.

3. Even clauses which are properly subordinate, are often joined by δέ,
it being left to the hearer or reader to make out the real relation of the
sentences from the context (§. 761, 2). Thus δέ often expresses the reason
and stands for γάρ : except that γάρ makes the clauses logically subordinate
—one the cause of the other—as δέ makes them logically coordinate, as if
both were of the same separate character and importance : Il. ι, 496 sq.
ἀλλ', Ἀχιλεῦ, δάμασον θυμὸν μέγαν· οὐδέ τί σε χρὴ νηλεὲς ἦτορ ἔχειν· στρεπτοὶ
δέ τε καὶ θεοὶ αὐτοί : Il. ξ, 416 τὸν δ' οὔπερ ἔχει θράσος, ὃς κεν ἴδηται, ἐγγὺς
ἐὼν χαλεπὸς δὲ Διὸς μεγάλοιο κεραυνός : Il. α. 259. Eur. Hipp. 175 δυσέ-
ρωτες δὴ φαινόμεθ' ὄντες τοῦδε (τοῦ ζῆν) — δι' ἀπειροσύνας ἄλλου βιότου κοὐκ
ἀπόδειξιν τῶν ὑπὸ γαίας· μύθοις δ' ἄλλως φερόμεσθα. So in Latin, a u t e m.
And δέ is used for οὖν, when an imperative clause, the reason whereof
is contained in what goes before, is joined on by δέ : Il. θ, 204 (Ἐννοσί-
γαιε, οἱ Δαναοὶ) τοι—δῶρ' ἀνάγουσιν πολλά τε καὶ χαρίεντα· σὺ δέ σφισι
βούλεο νίκην !

4. And in questions and answers δέ is used, and marks the transition
from and continuation of the dialogue, as the person who asks or answers the question is supposed to interrupt the other person, take up
what he is saying, and join thereto his own thought : Xen. Cyr. V. 1, 4
κελευόμενος δὲ ὁ Ἀράσπης ἐπήρετο· Ἑώρακας δ', ἔφη, τὴν γυναῖκα, ὦ Κῦρε, ἣν
με κελεύεις φυλάττειν ; Id. M. S. II. 9, 2 καὶ ὁ Σ., εἰπέ μοι, ἔφη, ὦ Κρίτων,
κύνας δὲ τρέφεις, ἵνα σοι τοὺς λύκους ἀπὸ τῶν προβάτων ἀπερύκωσι ; *And do
you keep hounds, (since you are unprotected from bad men ?)* Hdt. I. 116 ὁ
δὲ ἀμείβετο ὧδε· Ὦ δέσποτα, ἐγὼ δὲ ταῦτα τοῦτον ἐποίησα σὺν δίκῃ, (*you are
right,*) *but,* &c. : Soph. Œ. T. 378 Κρέοντος, ἢ σοῦ, ταῦτα τἀξευρήματα ;—
Κρέων δέ σοι πῆμ' οὐδέν, ἀλλ' αὐτὸς σὺ σοί.

Adverbial use of δέ.—Καὶ δέ.

§. 769. 1. Δέ besides its copulative has also an adverbial force, whereby
sentences are placed in contrast to each other, but not united into one
thought. It is used thus in οὐδέ, μηδέ, *also not,* and in κ α ὶ δ έ.

2. Κ α ὶ δ έ (divided, except in Epic, by the word in which the contrast
resides) may be translated by *and on the other side, also, then,* which is
derived from its original force of *in the second place.* Sometimes μέν precedes : Il. ψ, 80 ἀλλ' ἐμὲ μὲν κὴρ ἀμφέχανε στυγερή, ἥπερ λάχε γεινόμενόν
περ· καὶ δὲ σοὶ αὐτῷ μοῖρα — τείχει ὑπὸ Τρώων — ἀπολέσθαι : Od. π, 418
Ἀντίνο', ὕβριν ἔχων, κακομήχανε ! Καὶ δέ σε φασὶν ἐν δήμῳ Ἰθάκης μεθ'
ὁμήλικας ἔμμεν' ἄριστον βουλῇ καὶ μύθοισι ! and *then :* Eur. El. 1125 καὶ σὺ

δ' αὐθάδης ἔφυς, you *also*, not only Ægisthus: Xen. Hell. V. 2, 37 καὶ οἱ
τε ἄλλοι προθύμως τῷ Τελευτίᾳ ὑπηρέτουν — κ α ὶ ἡ τῶν Θηβαίων δ ὲ πόλις —
προθύμως ξυνέπεμπε καὶ ὁπλίτας καὶ ἱππέας.

Δέ in the Apodosis.

§. 770. 1. Δέ has here also a double force, adversative or copulative.
Sometimes μέν stands in the former clause.

a. The adversative δέ, which in sense approaches to αὖ, marks that
the apodosis is opposed to its protasis. It is used (*a*) often after an hypothetical protasis — (β) after a comparative or relative protasis.—*a*. Il. *a*,
135 ἀλλ' εἰ μὲν δώσουσι—, εἰ δέ κε μὴ δώωσιν, ἐγὼ δέ κεν αὐτὸς ἕλωμαι, so
on the contrary—: Il. μ, 245 εἴπερ γάρ τ' ἄλλοι γε περικτεινώμεθα πάντες—,
σοὶ δ' οὐ δέος ἔστ' ἀπολέσθαι: Od. μ, 54 αἱ δέ κε λίσσηαι ἑτάρους—, οἱ δέ σ'
ἔτι πλεόνεσσι τότ' ἐν δεσμοῖσι δεόντων. (For δὲ, ἀλλά and αὐτάρ are used, as in
Latin, a t after si : Il. a, 82 εἴπερ γάρ τε χόλον γε καὶ αὐτῆμαρ καταπέψῃ,
ἀ λ λ ά τε καὶ μετόπισθεν ἔχει κότον, ὄφρα τελέσσῃ : Il. θ, 153 εἴπερ γάρ σ'
Ἕκτωρ γε κακὸν καὶ ἀνάλκιδα φήσει, ἀ λ λ' οὐ πείσονται Τρῶες καὶ Δαρδανίωνες :
Il. τ, 164 εἴπερ γὰρ θυμῷ γε μενοινάᾳ πολεμίζειν, ἀ λ λ ά τε λάθρῃ γυῖα βαρύνεται : Il. χ, 390 εἰ δὲ θανόντων περ καταλήθοντ' εἰν Ἀίδαο, α ὐ τ ὰ ρ ἐγὼ καὶ
κεῖθι φίλου μεμνήσομ' ἑταίρου :) Xen. Cyr. V. 5, 21 ἀλλ' εἰ μηδὲ τοῦτ', ἔφη,
βούλει ἀποκρίνασθαι, σὺ δ ὲ τοὐντεῦθεν λέγε, εἰ κ. τ. λ.—β. Il. ζ, 146 οἵη περ
φύλλων γενεή, τοίη δ έ καὶ ἀνδρῶν : Od. η, 108 ὅσσον Φαίηκες περὶ πάντων
ἴδριες ἀνδρῶν νῆα θοὴν ἐνὶ πόντῳ ἐλαυνέμεν, ὣς δ έ (so on the contrary)
γυναῖκες ἱστὸν τεχνῆσαι : Il. β, 716 οἱ δ' ἄρα Μηθώνην καὶ Θαυμακίην ἐνέμοντο—,
τῶν δὲ Φιλοκτήτης ἦρχεν, these *another*, namely Philoctetes, led. (So αὖτε :
Il. β, 738 οἱ δ' Ἄργισσαν ἔχον —, τῶν α ὖ θ' ἡγεμόνευε — Πολυποίτης. The
corresponding clauses are not always fully or equally developed ; as, Il.
ψ, 319 ἀλλ' ὃς μέν θ' ἵπποισι — πεποιθὼς ἀφραδέως ἐπὶ πολλὸν ἑλίσσεται ἔνθα
καὶ ἔνθα, ἵπποι δ ὲ πλανόωνται ἀνὰ δρόμον (for τούτῳ δέ, to him *also*) : Il. ω,
255 ἐπεὶ τέκον υἷας ἀρίστους—, τῶν δ' οὔτινά φημι λελεῖφθαι :) Soph. Phil.
86 ἐγὼ μὲν οὓς ἂν τῶν λόγων ἀλγῶ κλύειν, Λαερτίου παῖ, τοὺς δ ὲ καὶ πράσσειν
στυγῶ : Xen. Cyr. VIII. 5, 12 ὥσπερ οἱ ὁπλῖται, οὕτω δ ὲ καὶ οἱ πελτασταὶ
καὶ οἱ τοξόται.

Obs. Thus δ έ stands, especially in Attic, after a protasis, which is
shortly expressed by a participle ; as, Xen. M. S. III. 7, 8 θαυμάζω σου, εἰ
ἐκείνους, ὅταν τοῦτο ποιῶσι, ῥᾳδίως χ ε ι ρ ο ύ μ ε ν ο ς, τούτοις δ ὲ (so in the
common edition) μηδένα τρόπον οἴει δυνήσεσθαι προσενεχθῆναι, that although,
—*yet* to these, &c.

b. The copulative δ έ joins together the protasis and apodosis, as if
they were coordinate, which seems to arise from the old idioms of the
language, which loved to give an independent character to subordinate
clauses. Hence mostly in Epic and Herodotus, but very rarely in the
more accurate Attic idiom. It is used after a protasis expressive of a relation of time : Od. λ, 387 αὐτὰρ ἐπεὶ ψυχὰς μὲν ἀπεσκέδασ' ἄλλυδις ἄλλῃ
ἁγνὴ Περσεφόνεια γυναικῶν θηλυτεράων, ἦλθε δ' ἐπὶ ψυχὴ Ἀγαμέμνονος Ἀτρείδαο :
Il. π, 199 αὐτὰρ ἐπειδὴ πάντας ἅμ' ἡγεμόνεσσιν Ἀχιλλεὺς στῆσεν εὖ κρίνας,
κρατερὸν δ' ἐπὶ μῦθον ἔτελλεν : Il. φ, 53 τὸν δ' ὡς οὖν ἐνόησε ποδάρκης δῖος
Ἀχιλλεὺς —, ὀχθήσας δ' ἄρα εἶπε πρὸς ὃν μεγαλήτορα θυμόν. So ὄφρα — τόφρα
δέ, ὁπότε — δέ, ἕως—δέ : Hdt. IX. 70 ἕως μὲν γὰρ ἀπῆσαν οἱ Ἀθηναῖοι, οἱ δ'
ἠμύνοντο.

2. Frequently a sentence composed of such a protasis and apodosis is opposed to another similar pair of clauses by δέ—δέ, so that the second protasis answers to the first, and the second apodosis belongs to the second protasis. This is very common in Homer. In the first apodosis the δέ may be omitted: Il. a, 53–58 ἐννῆμαρ μὲν ἀνὰ στρατὸν ᾤχετο κῆλα θεοῖο· τῇ δεκάτῃ δ' ἀγορήνδε καλέσσατο λαὸν Ἀχιλλεύς·— οἱ δ' ἐπεὶ οὖν ἤγερθεν ὁμηγερέες τ' ἐγένοντο, τοῖσι δ' ἀνιστάμενος μετέφη πόδας ὠκὺς Ἀχιλλεύς: Il. ε, 436–439 τρὶς μὲν ἔπειτ' ἐπόρουσε κατακτάμεναι μενεαίνων τρὶς δέ οἱ ἐστυφέλιξε φαεινὴν ἀσπίδ' Ἀπόλλων· ἀλλ' ὅτε δὴ τὸ τέταρτον ἐπέσσυτο δαίμονι ἶσος, δεινὰ δ' ὁμοκλήσας προσέφη ἑκάεργος Ἀπόλλων: Od. γ, 470–474 οἱ δ' ἐπεὶ ὤπτησαν κρέ' ὑπέρτερα καὶ ἐρύσαντο, δαίνυνθ' ἑζόμενοι· ἐπὶ δ' ἀνέρες ἐσθλοὶ ὄροντο, οἶνον ἐνοινοχοεῦντες ἐνὶ χρυσέοις δεπάεσσιν. Αὐτὰρ ἐπεὶ πόσιος καὶ ἐδητύος ἐξ ἔρον ἕντο, τοῖσι δὲ μύθων ἦρχε Γερήνιος ἱππότα Νέστωρ: Od. ι, 56 ὄφρα μὲν ἠὼς ἦν—τόφρα δ' ἀλεξόμενοι μένομεν—· ἦμος δ'—καὶ τότε δή—: Il. ι, 550 ὄφρα μὲν—τόφρα δέ—· ἀλλ' ὅτε δὴ—ἤτοι ὁ—: Il. μ, 10–17 ὄφρα μὲν—καὶ—καὶ—, τόφρα δέ—· αὐτὰρ ἐπεὶ—πολλοὶ δ'—οἱ μὲν—οἱ δὲ—πέρθετο δὲ— Ἀργεῖοι δὲ—δὴ τότε—. In such sentences the first δέ is copulative, with a certain adversative force; the second δέ (in the second protasis) is adversative, as placing the second pair of clauses in opposition to the first; and the last δέ (in the second apodosis) is again copulative, but frequently with a certain adversative force.

Αὖ—αὖτε—αὖθις (αὖτις)—αὐτάρ, ἀτάρ.

§. 771. 1. The original force of αὖ as an adverb is doubtlessly local, *back, retro* (cf. αὐερύειν): although it so soon passed into a temporal notion that it is not used as a local adverb; (so in Homer νῦν αὖ, δεύτερον αὖ, τὸ τρίτον αὖ, &c.; in Attic, αὖ πάλιν, πάλιν αὖ, also αὖθις πάλιν, αὖθις αὖ πάλιν, αὖθις αὖ; as in poetic questions, and exclamations of displeasure, it expresses the repetition of a similar, if not the same thing: Il. a, 540 τίς δ' αὖ τοι, δολομῆτα, θεῶν συμφράσσατο βουλάς; so also τίπτ' αὖτε in Homer,) and then like *rursus*, it denotes opposition, on the other side, *contra*; as, Xen. Hell. IV. 8, 1 καὶ ὁ μὲν δὴ κατὰ γῆν πόλεμος οὕτως ἐπολεμεῖτο· ἐν ᾧ δὲ πάντα ταῦτα ἐπράττετο, τὰ κατὰ θάλατταν αὖ καὶ τὰς πρὸς θαλάττῃ πόλεις γενόμενα διηγήσομαι.

2. From the notion of repetition and opposition is derived its copulative force, whereby it can join together two clauses, and place them in opposition like δέ. In Homer it sometimes answers to μέν, but the adverbial force of αὖ was so strong that this use of it never became usual; hence it generally in such cases is supported by δέ: Xen. M. S. I. 2, 12 Κριτίας μὲν γὰρ τῶν ἐν τῇ ὀλιγαρχίᾳ πάντων πλεονεκτίστατός τε καὶ βιαιότατος ἐγένετο, Ἀλκιβιάδης δὲ αὖ τῶν ἐν τῇ δημοκρατίᾳ πάντων ἀκρατέστατος καὶ ὑβριστότατος.

3. Of the same sense with αὖ is the Homeric and poetic αὖτε (that is, αὖ . . τέ, like πότε, τότε, ἄλλοτε, ἐνίοτε,) the poetic αὖθις, and the Ionic αὖτις, (another form of αὖτε,) αὐτάρ (epic), and ἀτάρ (from αὖτε and ἄρ=ἄρα. These two last are always at the beginning of the sentence, and express an unexpected, or strange contrast, or a rapid change and continuation of the subject: Hdt. VI. 133 τοῦτο μὲν δὴ πρόσχημα λόγου ἦν· ἀτάρ τινα καὶ ἔγκοτον εἶχε τοῖσι Παρίοισι.

Καίτοι.

§. 772. 1. Καίτοι, *and yet, verum, sed tamen,* is used when an objection to what is said or proposed comes across the speaker's mind, so that he either gives up or thinks of giving up his intention; as in Latin, *quamquam :* Eur. Hippol. 1287 ἄκουε, Θησεῦ, σῶν κατάστασιν κακῶν· κ α ί τ ο ι προκόψω γ' οὐδέν, ἀλγυνῶ δέ σε, this being an objection to her going on : where also, as elsewhere, it is strengthened by γέ : Cf. Eur. Phœn. 690 χώρει σὺ καὶ κόμιζε τὸν Κρέοντα—καίτοι (but) ποδῶν σῶν μόχθον ἐκλύει παρών: Arist.Ach. 466. Thus it is also very frequently used concessively, when the speaker wishes to mark that the statement he has made holds good in spite of some seeming contradictory fact, which he allows to be true, and which is introduced by καίτοι, *and yet, although :* Soph. Aj. 1069 οὐ γὰρ ἴσθ' ὅπου λόγων ἀκοῦσαι ζῶν ποτ' ἠθέλησ' ἐμῶν· καίτοι κακοῦ πρὸς ἀνδρός κ. τ. λ. Ajax's character seemingly contradicted Menelaus' statement; and so Eur. Orest. 75 προσφθέγμασιν γὰρ οὐ μιαίνομαι σέθεν εἰς Φοῖβον ἀναφέρουσα τὴν ἁμαρτίαν· κ α ί τ ο ι στένω γε τὸν Κλυταιμνήστρας μόρον ἐμῆς ἀδελφῆς : *quamquam sane doleo fatum Clytæmnestræ;* Helen's grief for Clytemnestra was a seeming contradiction to any sympathy for Orestes : Thuc. II. 64 κ α ί τ ο ι ταῦτα ὁ μὲν ἀπράγμων μέμψαιτ' ἄν, ὁ δὲ δρᾶν τι βουλόμενος καὶ αὐτὸς ζηλώσει.

2. Hence also it is used to introduce an objection to an argument or action of somebody else : Thuc. I. 86 ἐπαινέσαντες πολλὰ ἑαυτούς, οὐδαμοῦ ἀντεῖπον ὡς οὐκ ἀδικοῦσι τοὺς ἡμετέρους ξυμμάχους, κ α ί τ ο ι εἰ πρὸς τοὺς Μήδους ἐγένοντο ἀγαθοὶ τότε, πρὸς δὲ ἡμᾶς κακοὶ νῦν, διπλασίας ζημίας ἄξιοί εἰσιν.

Obs. When a word intervenes between καὶ and τοί, they are not taken as καίτοι, but τοί belongs to the word which it follows : Xen. Cyr. VII. 3, 10 καὶ τἄλλά τοι, ὦ Κῦρε, οὕτως ἔχει.

Ὅμως.

3. Ὅμως (from ὁμός equal), *equally, nevertheless, yet,* denies the consequences which might be expected to follow from what has gone before : Thuc. VI. 50 Λάμαχος μὲν ταῦτα εἰπὼν ὅ μ ω ς προσέθετο καὶ αὐτὸς τῇ Ἀλκιβιάδου γνώμῃ. The opposition is often more strongly marked by ἀλλά— ἀ λ λ' ὅ μ ω ς : and ἀ λ λ' ὅ μ ω ς is often found by itself in the dramatists, especially Euripides, at the end of a line, to denote that something will happen, though contrary to what might be expected : Eur. Elect. 753 ἤκουσα κἀγώ, τηλόθεν μὲν, ἀλλ' ὅμως; so in entreaties, where a person is asked to do something which seems unreasonable or unnecessary : Eur. Hec. 842 παράσχες χεῖρα—τιμωρόν, εἰ καὶ μηδέν ἐστιν, ἀλλ' ὅ μ ω ς: so Arist. Ach. 408 Dic. ἀλλ' ἐκκυκλήθητ'. Eur. ἀλλ' ἀδύνατον. — Dic. ἀ λ λ' ὅ μ ω ς. It is also sometimes strengthened by ὅμως γε μήν—ὅμως γε μέντοι.

Εἶτα, ἔπειτα.

4. Εἶτα and ἔπειτα (ἐπ' εἶτα) sometimes have the force of ὅ μ ω ς : Plat. Gorg. p. 519 E μέμφεσθαι τούτῳ, ὅτι ἀφ' ἑαυτοῦ ἀγαθὸς γεγονώς τε καὶ ὢν ἔπειτα πονηρός ἐστιν.

Limitation and denial.

'Αλλά.

§. 773. 1. 'Αλλά, neut. plur. of ἄλλος, the accent being changed, expresses *difference, division, separation.*

2. Its powers vary according to the nature of the preceding clause.—
It either marks the direct contrary thereof, (*but*) so that both cannot be
true together, and thus denies it : this happens *a.* with a negative clause
preceding, where the second clause is affirmative; as, οὐχ οἱ πλούσιοι εὐδαίμονές εἰσιν, ἀλλ' οἱ ἀγαθοί:—or *b.* where an affirmative clause precedes, and
the second clause is negative; as, Plat. Phædr. p. 229 D ἐκεῖθεν, ἀλλ'
οὐκ ἐνθένδε ἡρπάσθη.

3. Or it denotes that the second clause differs from the first sufficiently
to *limit* its truth ; the two are supposed to be true together, though differing from each other: this occurs both with affirmative and negative
concessive sentences, and may be translated by *yet, but ;* in the last case
the opposition is pointed out in the first clause by μέν, ἤτοι, γέ, &c.:
Il. π, 240 αὐτὸς μὲν γὰρ ἐγὼ μενέω νηῶν ἐν ἀγῶνι, ἀλλ' ἕτερον πέμπω:
Il. a, 284 ναὶ δὴ ταῦτά γε πάντα, γέρον, κατὰ μοῖραν ἔειπες, ἀλλ' ὅδ' ἀνὴρ
ἐθέλει περὶ πάντων ἔμμεναι ἄλλων : Il. γ, 214 παῦρα μὲν (*Menelaus dixit*),
ἀλλὰ μάλα λιγέως : Il. a, 22 ἔνθ' ἄλλοι μὲν πάντες ἐπηυφήμησαν Ἀχαιοί,
αἰδεῖσθαι ἱερῆα καὶ ἀγλαὰ δέχθαι ἄποινα, ἀλλ' οὐκ Ἀτρείδῃ Ἀγαμέμνονι ἥνδανε
θυμῷ: Xen. Cyr. VII. 1, 16 τὰ μὲν καθ' ἡμᾶς ἐμοίγε δοκεῖ καλῶς ἔχειν,
ἀλλὰ τὰ πλάγια λυπεῖ με: Plat. Gorg. p. 448 D καλῶς γε—φαίνεται Π.
παρεσκευάσθαι εἰς λόγους· ἀλλὰ γὰρ, ὃ ὑπέσχετο Χαιρεφῶντι, οὐ ποιεῖ.

4. But ἀλλά is used also after other negative clauses, when the universal negative is to be limited by a particular exception—here ἀλλά=
πλήν or εἰ μή, *nisi.* It denotes something different from, and not comprehended in the negative first clause— generally we find ἄλλος, (as οὐδεὶς
ἄλλος, ἀλλά,) in the first clause, which points forward to the ἀλλά, which
answers to it: Od. φ, 70 οὐδέ τιν' ἄλλην μύθου ποιήσασθαι ἐπισχεσίην
ἐδύνασθε, ἀλλ' ἐμὲ ἱέμενοι γῆμαι θέσθαι τε γυναῖκα : Il. φ, 275 ἄλλος δ'
οὔτις μοι τόσον αἴτιος Οὐρανιώνων, ἀλλὰ φίλη μήτηρ: Od. θ, 311 οὔτι μοι
αἴτιος ἄλλος, ἀλλὰ τοκῆε δύω : Soph. Œ. R. 1355 ἔπαισε δ' αὐτόχειρ νιν
οὔτις ἀλλ' ἐγώ: Eur. Hipp. 633 ῥᾷστον δ' ὅτῳ τὸ μηδὲν ἀλλ' ἀνωφελὴς εὐηθίᾳ κατ' οἶκον ἵδρυται γυνή: Xen. Vectig. III. 6 εἰς μὲν οὖν τὰς τοιαύτας
αὐξήσεις τῶν προσόδων οὐδέπως δαπανῆσαι δεῖ οὐδὲν ἀλλὰ ψηφίσματά τε
φιλάνθρωπα καὶ ἐπιμελείας: Id. Anab. VI. 4, 2 ἐν δὲ τῷ μέσῳ ἄλλη μὲν
πόλις οὐδεμία οὔτε φιλία, οὔτε Ἑλληνίς, ἀλλὰ Θρᾷκες καὶ Βιθυνοί: Plat.
Symp. p. 192 E οὐδ' ἄλλο τι ἂν φανείη βουλόμενος, ἀλλ' ἀτεχνῶς οἴοιτ'
ἂν κ. τ. λ. Instead of ἄλλος, also ἕτερος : Demosth. p. 554 (R.) μηδένα ἕτερον εἶναι τὸν Νικομήδου φονέα, ἀλλ' Ἀρίσταρχον: so in a question, as Plat. Protag. p. 354 B ἢ ἔχετέ τι ἄλλο τέλος λέγειν, εἰς ὃ ἀποβλέψαντες αὐτὰ ἀγαθὰ καλεῖτε, ἀλλὰ (Stephan. e conj. ἀλλ' ἢ) ἡδονάς τε καὶ
λύπας ; after τίς ἄλλος there regularly follows ἤ, or ἀλλ' ἤ, or πλήν: and
moreover we find πλήν, or sometimes πλὴν ἤ, instead of ἄλλα, both
after a simple negation, as after οὐδεὶς ἄλλος : Demosth. p. 1073
οὐδενὸς αὐτοῖς μέλει πλὴν τοῦ πλεονεκτεῖν: Plat. Tim. p. 30 A θέμις δὲ
οὔτ' ἦν οὔτ' ἔστι τῷ ἀρίστῳ δρᾶν ἄλλο πλὴν τὸ κάλλιστον. When δέ is
used for ἀλλά, the preceding ἄλλος is accompanied by μέν: Plat. Rep.
p. 359 E τοῦτον δὲ ἄλλο μὲν ἔχειν οὐδέν, περὶ δὲ τῇ χειρὶ χρυσοῦν
δακτύλιον.

5. We should especially observe the phrase ἀλλ' ἤ after a negation, or a question which implies a negative (either after the interrogative pronoun, or an indefinite ἄλλό τι joined with some other interrogative), and even when ἕτερος or ἄλλος is joined to the negation; οὐκ, οὐδὲν ἀλλ' ἤ; οὐδὲν ἄλλο, ἀλλ' ἤ; οὐδὲν ἕτερον, ἀλλ' ἤ; τί ἄλλο, ἀλλ' ἤ; ἄλλο τι, ἀλλ' ἤ: Xen. Anab. VII. 7, 53 ἀργύριον μὲν οὐκ ἔχω, ἀλλ' ἢ μικρόν τι: Id. Œcon. 13 οὔτε ἄλλος πώποτέ μοι παρέσχε τὰ ἑαυτοῦ διοικεῖν ἀλλ' ἢ σὺ νυνὶ ἐθέλεις παρέχειν: Plat. Protag. p. 329 D τὰ τοῦ χρυσίου μόρια οὐδὲν διαφέρει τὰ ἕτερα τῶν ἑτέρων, ἀλλήλων καὶ τοῦ ὅλου, ἀλλ' ἢ μεγέθει καὶ σμικρότητι: Id. Phæd. p. 97 D οὐδὲν ἄλλο σκοπεῖν προσήκειν ἀνθρώπῳ, ἀλλ' ἢ τὸ ἄριστον καὶ τὸ βέλτιστον: Id. Rep. p. 429 B τίς ἂν εἰς ἄλλο τι ἀποβλέψας ἢ δειλὴν ἢ ἀνδρείαν πόλιν εἴποι, ἀλλ' ἢ εἰς τοῦτο τὸ μέρος; Id. Protag. p. 354 B ἢ ἔχετέ τι ἄλλο τέλος λέγειν—ἀλλ' ἢ ἡδονάς τε καὶ λύπας: Id. Rep. p. 553 D τὸ μὲν οὐδὲν ἄλλο ἐᾷ λογίζεσθαι οὐδὲ σκοπεῖν ἀλλ' ἢ ὁπόθεν ἐξ ἐλαττόνων χρημάτων πλείω ἔσται: Arist. Eqq. 779 ὡς δ' οὐχὶ φιλεῖ σ' οὐδ' ἔστ' εὔνους, τοῦτ' αὐτό σε πρῶτα διδάξω, ἀλλ' ἢ διὰ τοῦτ' αὖθ' ὅτι σου τῆς ἀνθρακιᾶς ἀπολαύει.

Obs. 1. This form arises from the confusion of two cognate phrases, οὐδὲν ἄλλο—ἀλλά and οὐδὲν ἄλλο—ἤ: ἀλλά and ἤ agree in sense; ἀλλά does not express *opposition*, but only a *difference* and *limitation* of the former clause, as is evident from ἄλλος being used in the first clause—so ἤ expresses not only *exclusion*, but also a mere difference. Thus in οὐδὲν ἄλλο—ἀλλά, ἀλλά belongs rather to οὐδέν, and in οὐδὲν ἄλλο—ἤ, ἤ belongs rather to ἄλλο, so that the two phrases coalesced, and in course of time were used after a negation or negative question, (without ἄλλο), the proper force of each particle being unregarded; like οὗ ἕνεκα, οὕνεκα, for ἕνεκα.

Obs. 2. In many passages there is doubt whether we should read ἀλλ' or ἄλλ', when ἄλλο suits the sense and ἄλλος does not precede; as, Plat. Rep. p. 330 C οὐδὲν ἐθέλοντες ἐπαινεῖν ἀλλ' (*alii* ἄλλ') ἢ τὸν πλοῦτον: Arist. Ran. 227 οὐδὲν γὰρ ἔστ' ἄλλ' (Brunck.) ἢ κοάξ. If 'ΑΛΛ' is at a great distance from the negation, ἀλλ' is preferable, but if it is near or at least not very far off, we should naturally write ἄλλ'. But in the elliptic expression οὐδὲν ἄλλο (sc. ποιῶ) ἤ, or τί ἄλλο (sc. ποιῶ) ἤ, which are never followed by ἀλλ' ἤ, but only by ἤ alone, it is always better to write οὐδὲν ἀλλ', τί ἀλλ'—though writers do not agree on this point.

Obs. 3. In many passages the use of ἀλλ' ἤ arises from the union of two phrases, οὐκ ἀλλά and οὐδὲν ἄλλο (sc. γίγνεται &c.) ἤ: Arist. Pac. 476 οὐ δ' οἶδε γ' εἷλκον οὐδὲν 'Αργεῖοι πάλαι, ἀλλ' ἢ κατεγέλων τῶν ταλαιπωρουμένων (formed from οὐδὲ εἷλκον — ἀλλὰ κατεγέλων, *non trahebant, sed ridebant* and οὐδὲν ἐποίουν, ἢ κατεγ. *nihil aliud faciebant, quam ridebant:*) Demosth. p. 45, 19 μή μοι μυρίους μηδὲ δισμυρίους ξένους, μηδὲ τὰς ἐπιστολιμαίους ταύτας δυνάμεις, ἀλλ' ἢ τῆς πόλεως ἔσται, *exercitus noster non ex mercenariis etc. debet esse compositus, sed ex civibus,* and *non ex mercenariis, neque—, neque ex aliis, quam,* μηδὲ λέγε ἄλλας δυνάμεις, ἢ τῆς πόλεως.

Obs. 4. This ἀλλά is very nearly allied to πλήν. Πλήν is used as ἀλλά, as is clear from what has been already said. So πλήν as well as ἀλλά is used before a negation: Hdt. VII. 84 πλὴν οὐ πάντα παρείχετο ἵππον: Xen. Hier. I. 18 πάντες προσδέχονται πλὴν οὐχ οἱ τύραννοι: Demosth. p. 1290 πλείουσα πανταχόσε πλὴν οὐκ εἰς 'Αθήνας: so πλὴν ἤ: Plat. Apol. fin. ἄδηλον παντὶ πλὴν ἢ θεῷ: also πλὴν ἀλλά: Lucian. Dial. Deor. XVI. fin. μέγα, ὦ Ἥρα, φρονεῖς, ὅτι ξύνει τῷ Διί, καὶ συμβασιλεύεις αὐτῷ, καὶ διὰ τοῦτο ὑβρίζεις ἀδεῶς· πλὴν ἀλλ' ὄψομαί σε μετ' ὀλίγον αὖθις δακρύουσαν. Preceded by a negation: Id. Prom. c. 20 οὐ ῥᾴδιον, ὦ Προμηθεῦ, πρὸς οὖς γενναῖον σοφιστὴν ἀμιλλᾶσθαι· πλὴν ἀλλὰ ὤνησο, διότι μὴ καὶ ὁ Ζεὺς ταῦτ' ἐπήκουσέ σου. Even πλὴν ἀλλ' ἤ after a negation, in Aristot. Metaph. 1. *nisi quod*.

Obs. 5. After a comparative, such as μᾶλλον, τὸ πλέον, joined with a negative, ἀλλά is often used in a different sense from ἤ. Ἢ marks the equality of the two clauses (*non magis quam*), but ἀλλά denotes the contrary to that which is denied in the first clause: the two clauses being compared, the latter is preferred to the former, and hence is opposed to it: Thuc. II. 44 οὐκ ἐν τῷ ἀχρείῳ τῆς ἡλικίας τὸ κερδαίνειν — μᾶλλον τέρπει, ἀλλὰ τὸ τιμᾶσθαι, i. e. *non in senectute lucrum magis juvat* (sc. *quam honor*), *sed honor* (sc. *magis, quam lucrum*) : Id. I. 83 καὶ ἔστιν ὁ πόλεμος οὐχ ὅπλων τὸ πλέον (sc. ἡ δαπάνης), ἀλλὰ δαπάνης (sc. τὸ πλέον ἢ ὅπλων) : Id. II. 43 ἐλάμβανον τὸν τάφον ἐπισημότατον, οὐκ (i. e. οὐ τοῦτον, ἐν ᾧ) ἐν ᾧ κεῖται μᾶλλον (sc. ἢ ἐκεῖνον, ἐν ᾧ ἡ δόξα αὐτῶν καταλείπεται, i. e. ἡ πᾶσαν τὴν γῆν), ἀλλ' ἐν ᾧ ἡ δόξα αὐτῶν ἀείμνηστος καταλείπεται (sc. μᾶλλον ἢ τοῦτον, ἐν ᾧ κεῖται). Πλὴν is also thus used, even where no negative accompanies the comparative. (See §. 779. *Obs.* 2.)

6. Lastly we must mention some elliptic forms : οὐ μὴν ἀλλά or οὐ μέντοι ἀλλά,—οὐ γὰρ ἀλλά (frequent in Attic), *no indeed! but.* The two former may be translated by *yet*, *verumtamen*, the latter by *then surely*, or *surely*. The ellipse must be supplied by the verb of the foregoing sentence, or something in its place (such as, τοῦτ' ἐγένετο, τοῦτ' ἐστίν) after the negation : Xen. Cyr. I. 4, 8 ὁ ἵππος πίπτει εἰς γόνατα, καὶ μικροῦ κἀκεῖνον ἐξετραχήλισεν· οὐ μὴν (sc. ἐξετραχήλισεν) ἀλλ' ἐπέμεινεν ὁ Κῦρος μόλις πως, καὶ ὁ ἵππος ἐξανέστη : Arist. Ran. 463 φέρε δὴ ταχέως αὔτ'· οὐ γὰρ ἀλλὰ πειστέον, for I cannot refuse, but must obey = I must certainly obey. It then gives the notion that the agent is reluctant, but cannot help himself.

§. 774. Ἀλλά is also used to express opposition between the sentences without connecting them—it signifies the transition to different or contrary thoughts. Hence it is used in exhortations, addresses—generally when there is a break in the sentence, and some new thought suddenly introduced ; ἀλλ' εὐτυχοίης — ἀλλ' ἄνα! — ἀλλ' εἶα!—Also when the speaker interrupts or answers quickly and decidedly ; as, ἀλλὰ βούλομαι, *well, I will*; and it is frequently used in a question with great emphasis, to mark a strong contradiction to, and contrast with, the foregoing clause : Æsch. Cheoph. 762 ἀλλ' ἦ φρονεῖς εὖ τοῖσι νῦν ἠγγελμένοις ;

Obs. 1. The clause to which ἀλλά is opposed is sometimes in the form of an hypothetical protasis (§. 770. *a.*) : Il. θ, 153 εἴπερ γάρ σ' Ἕκτωρ γε κακὸν καὶ ἀνάλκιδα φήσει, ἀλλ' οὐ πείσονται Τρῶες. So also after ἐπεί : Hdt. IX. 41 ἐπεὶ (since) ὑμεῖς ἡ οὐκ ἴστε οὐδέν, ἡ οὐ τολμᾶτε λέγειν, ἀλλ' ἐγὼ ἐρέω. So ἀλλ' οὖν, when the consequences of the former clause are to be signified : Plat. Phæd. p. 91 B εἰ δὲ μηδέν ἐστι τελευτήσαντι, ἀλλ' οὖν τοῦτόν γε τὸν χρόνον ἧττον ἀηδὴς ἔσομαι. Hence arose the elliptic use of ἀλλά in the middle of a sentence, the hypothetical protasis being suppressed : Soph. Œ. C. 1276 πειράσατ' ἀλλ' ὑμεῖς γε κινῆσαι πατρὸς — στόμα, *si nullus alius, at vos certe*, = at least do you try.

Obs. 2. Ἀλλά can also stand at the beginning of a sentence, without any clause before it to which it refers ; but in this case it refers to something in the speaker's mind, or something commonly and generally known. So Xenophon's Symposium begins : ἀλλ' ἐμοὶ δοκεῖ τῶν καλῶν κἀγαθῶν ἀνδρῶν ἔργα οὐ μόνον μετὰ σπουδῆς πραττόμενα ἀξιομνημόνευτα εἶναι, ἀλλὰ καὶ ἐν ταῖς παιδιαῖς.

Connection and Opposition of Negative clauses.

a. Οὔτε — οὔτε, μήτε — μήτε.

§. 775. 1. Οὔτε — οὔτε (μήτε — μήτε), *nec — nec, neither — nor,* are to negative clauses what τέ — τέ are to affirmative, joining them into one thought ; as, Il, *a,* 548 οὔτε θεῶν τις, οὔτ' ἀνθρώπων.

Obs. 1. In poetry sometimes we find οὔτε — τε οὔ for οὔτε — οὔτε : Eur. Hipp. 304 sq. οὔτε γὰρ τότε λόγοις ἐτέγγεθ' ὅδε, νῦν τ' οὐ πείθεται.

2. Besides these usual forms there occur the following ;

a. Οὐ — οὔτε (mostly poetry) : Il. ζ, 450–454 ἀλλ' οὔ μοι Τρώων τόσσον μέλει ἄλγος ὀπίσσω, οὔτ' αὐτῆς Ἑκάβης οὔτε Πριάμοιο ἄνακτος, οὔτε κασιγνήτων —, ὅσσον σεῖο. Also οὐ — οὔτ' οὖν : Od. ι, 147 ἔνθ' οὔτις τὴν νῆσον ἐσέδρακεν ὀφθαλμοῖσιν, οὔτ' οὖν κύματα μακρὰ κυλινδόμενα προτὶ χέρσον εἰσίδομεν.

Obs. 2. But negative clauses may follow one another without any connecting particle, especially in pathetic passages : Hymn. h. in Merc. 265 οὐκ ἴδον, οὐ πυθόμην, οὐκ ἄλλον μῦθον ἄκουσα, οὐκ ἂν μηνύσαιμ', οὐκ ἂν μήνυτρον ἀροίμην, οὔτε βοῶν ἐλατῆρι, κραταιῷ φωτί, ἔοικα.

b. Οὐδέ — οὔτε, like οὐ — οὔτε, except that it connects the former clause with what went before, οὐδέ being used instead of οὐ : Hymn. Cer. 22 οὐδέ τις ἀθανάτων οὔτε θνητῶν ἀνθρώπων ἤκουσεν φωνῆς.

c. Οὔτε — οὐ (rarely in prose). The speaker begins with οὔτε, as though another οὔτε were to follow ; but then the next clause is added ἀσυνδέτως, without any copula, in order to make it emphatic by giving it an independent character : Hdt. VIII. 98 τοὺς οὔτε νιφετός, οὐκ ὄμβρος, οὐ καῦμα, οὐ νὺξ ἔργει : Eur. Or. 41 sq. ὧν οὔτε σῖτα διὰ δέρης ἐδέξατο, οὐ λούτρ' ἔδωκε χρωτί.

Obs. 3. In poetry, the first οὔτε is altogether dropped in a short sentence, so that the latter οὔτε is referred back to its former clause as well as its own : Æsch. Ag. 532 Πάρις γὰρ οὔτε συντελὴς πόλις : Id. Choeph. 294 δέχεσθαί τ' οὔτε συλλύειν τινά. Similarly Juvenal, *qud fornace graves quå non incude catenæ :* Pind. Pyth. VI. 48 ἄδικον οὔθ' ὑπέροπλον ἥβαν δρέπων.

d. Οὔτε — οὐδέ (also strengthened into οὐδ' αὖ, οὐδὲ μήν, οὐδέ γε) stand to each other as τέ — δέ (§. 754. 5.), and hence signify *neither — nor yet,* since οὐδέ gives its clause an adversative or emphatic force, as *nec — neque* or *neque vero :* Plat. Apol. p. 19 D ἀλλὰ γὰρ οὔτε τούτων οὐδέν ἐστιν, οὐδέ γ' εἴ τινος ἀκηκόατε, ὡς ἐγὼ παιδεύειν ἐπιχειρῶ ἀνθρώπους καὶ χρήματα πράττομαι, οὐδὲ τοῦτο ἀληθές[a] : Xen. Cyr. I. 6, 6 καὶ οἶδά σε ἐπιτιθέντα αὐτῷ, ὡς οὐδὲ θέμις εἴη αἰτεῖσθαι παρὰ τῶν θεῶν οὔτε ἱππεύειν μὴ μαθόντας ἱππομαχοῦντας νικᾶν, οὔτε μὴ ἐπισταμένους τοξεύειν τοξεύοντας κρατεῖν τῶν ἐπισταμένων, οὔτε μὴ ἐπισταμένους κυβερνᾶν, σῴζειν εὔχεσθαι ναῦς κυβερνῶντας, οὐδὲ μὴ σπείροντάς γε [σῖτον] εὔχεσθαι, καλὸν αὐτοῖς σῖτον φύεσθαι, οὐδὲ μὴ φυλαττομένους [γε] ἐν πολέμῳ σωτηρίαν αἰτεῖσθαι : Plat. Legg. p. 840 A οὔτε τινὸς πώποτε γυναικὸς ἥψατο, οὐδ' αὖ παιδός.

Obs. 4. Also after οὔτε (sometimes after οὐ) we find οὐδέ — οὔτε when subdivisions, definitions, and explanations are to be added to the clause

---

[a] Stallb. ad loc.

introduced by οὔτε, *neither—and not—nor*; as, Plat. Gorg. p. 500 B μήτε αὐτὸς οἴου δεῖν πρὸς ἐμὲ παίζειν, μηδ' ὅτι ἂν τύχῃς παρὰ τὰ δέοντα ἀποκρίνου, μήτ' αὖ τὰ παρ' ἐμοῦ οὕτως ἀποδέχου ὡς παίζοντος. So Il. a, 115 ἐπεί οἱ ἔθεν ἐστὶ χερείων οὐ (for οὔτε) δέμας, οὐδὲ φυήν, οὔτ' ἄρ φρένας, οὔτε τι ἔργα.

3. And a negative and positive clause may be joined together as follows :

a. Οὔτε—τέ (seldom καί), neq*u$—que* (*et*) Hdt. V. 49: οὔτε γὰρ οἱ βάρβαροι ἄλκιμοί εἰσι, ὑμεῖς τε τὰ ἐς τὸν πόλεμον ἐς τὰ μέγιστα ἀνήκετε ἀρετῆς πέρι : Id. VII. 8, 1 οὔτ' αὐτὸς κατηγήσομαι νόμον τόνδε ἐν ὑμῖν τιθείς, παραδεξάμενός τε αὐτῷ χρήσομαι : Eur. Iph. T. 595 sq. εἰ γὰρ οὔτε δυσγενής, καὶ τὰς Μυκήνας οἶσθα : Plat. Prot. p. 361 E οὔτε τἆλλα οἶμαι κακὸς εἶναι ἄνθρωπος, φθονερός τε ἥκιστ' ἂν ἀνθρώπων. Cf. Ibid. p. 347 E.

β. Οὔτε—δέ, when the second clause is opposed to the first : Xen. Anab. VI. 1, 16 ἀλλὰ δὴ ἐκεῖ μὲν οὔτε πλοῖά ἐστιν οἷς ἀποπλευσόμεθα, μένουσι δὲ αὐτοῦ οὐδὲ μιᾶς ἡμέρας ἐστι τὰ ἐπιτήδεια : Plat. Rep. p. 388 extr. οὔτε ἄρα ἀνθρώπους ἀξίους λόγου κρατουμένους ὑπὸ γέλωτος ἄν τις ποιῇ, ἀποδεκτέον, πολὺ δὲ ἧττον, ἐὰν θεούς : Id. Legg. p. 627 E μήτε ἀπολέσειε μηδένα, διαλλάξας δὲ εἰς τὸν ἐπίλοιπον χρόνον—διαφυλάττειν δύναιτο.

b. Οὐδέ, μηδέ.

§. 776. 1. Οὐδέ either expresses opposition, or connects a new clause.

a. Adversative : Il. ω, 25 ἔνθ' ἄλλοις μὲν πᾶσιν ἑήνδανεν, οὐδέ ποθ' Ἥρῃ, *neque* (*but not*) *Junoni :* Od. γ, 141 ἔνθ' ἤτοι Μενέλαος ἀνώγει πάντας Ἀχαιούς — οὐδ' Ἀγαμέμνονι πάμπαν ἑήνδανε. So οὐδέ is used (not οὔτε) when the same notion is expressed, first in a positive, then in a negative, form : μνήσομαι οὐδὲ λάθωμαι : Od. ι, 408 Οὔτις με κτείνει δόλῳ οὐδὲ βίηφιν : Soph. El. 997 γυνὴ μὲν οὐδ' ἀνὴρ ἔφυς. Generally, when a negative clause is to be joined to a positive one : Od. a, 369 νῦν μὲν δαινύμενοι τερπώμεθα, μηδὲ βοητὺς ἔστω.

Obs. 1. But when the opposition does not rest on the negation, but on some other notion, this is signified by placing this word before δέ, and then using afterwards the negative οὐ or μή.

b. Copulative : Il. a, 330 οὐδ' ἄρα τώγε ἰδὼν γήθησεν Ἀχιλλεύς. Οὐ—οὐδέ, *not — and* or *also not :* Eur. Med. 474 οὔτοι θράσος τόδ' ἐστὶν οὐδ' εὐτολμία. Οὐ—οὔτε is used when the speaker in the first clause implies or intends the second ; οὐ—οὐδέ when the second comes in as an addition to the first, without being intended when the first clause was formed in the mind.

2. Also οὐδέ—οὐδέ, *also not—and not* (never *neither—nor*) : Il. ι, 372 sqq. οὐδ' ἂν ἔμοιγε τετλαίη—εἰς ὦπα ἰδέσθαι· οὐδέ τι οἱ βουλὰς συμφράσσομαι, οὐδὲ μὲν ἔργον. The first οὐδέ often = *ne quidem*, and the second is merely copulative : Isocr. p. 64, 115 καὶ μὴν οὐδὲ τὴν παροῦσαν εἰρήνην οὐδὲ τὴν αὐτονομίαν—ἀξίαν ἑλέσθαι, *ne pacem quidem neque libertatem.*

Obs. 2. Οὐδέ (μηδέ) are used for καὶ οὐ (καὶ μή) : but when the negative follows καί, it belongs to the following word, and καί only denotes the completion of the former thought, *and thereto, and in sooth,* as is very clear when the same notion is stated positively and negatively for the sake of emphasis, so that the one is intended to explain and strengthen the other : Od. θ, 307 δεῦθ' ἵνα ἔργα γελαστὰ καὶ οὐκ ἐπιεικτὰ ἴδησθε (i. e. *et intolerabilia*) : Hdt. I. 91 συνέγνω ἑωυτοῦ εἶναι τὴν ἁμαρτάδα, καὶ οὐ τοῦ θεοῦ, *and in sooth not.* Οὐδέ marks that the clauses formally answer to each other, but not any connection between them : Demosth. p. p. 254, 85 φαίνομαι τοίνυν ἐγὼ χάριτος τετυχηκὼς τότε καὶ οὐ μέμψεως οὐδὲ τιμωρίας : Id. p. 255, 89 ὧν διαμάρτοιεν καὶ μὴ μετάσχοιεν ὧν ὑμεῖς —τοὺς θεοὺς αἰτεῖτε, μηδὲ μεταδίδοιεν ὑμῖν ὧν αὐτοὶ προῄρηνται.

Obs. 3. Sometimes the negation in the first clause seems to be separated from the predicate, and to attach itself to some other word : Od. ξ. 223 ἔργον δέ μοι οὐ φίλον ἔσκεν οὐδ' οἰκωφελίη. And sometimes it is wanting and must be supplied from the second clause. So Æsch. Choeph. 472 τῶν δ' ἑκὰς οὐδ' ἀπ' ἄλλων : Hdt. I. 215 σιδήρῳ δὲ οὐδ' ἀργύρῳ χρέωνται οὐδέν.

3. If οὔτε — οὔτε come between οὐδέ — οὐδέ, they denote the minor clauses which are subdivisions of or subordinate to the first clause : Æschin. p. 44 ἄν τις Ἀθηναίων ἑταιρήσῃ, μὴ ἐξέστω αὐτῷ τῶν ἐννέα ἀρχόντων γενέσθαι, μηδ' ἱερωσύνην ἱεράσασθαι, μηδὲ συνδικησάτω τῷ δημοσίῳ μηδὲ ἀρξάτω ἀρχὴν μηδεμίαν μηδέποτε μήτ' ἔνδημον, μήτ' ὑπερόριον, μήτε κληρωτὴν, μήτε χειροτονητὴν, μηδὲ κηρυκευσάτω —, μηδὲ γνώμην εἰπάτω μηδέποτε μήτε ἐν τῷ δήμῳ, μήτε ἐν τῇ βουλῇ, μηδ' ἂν δεινότατος ᾖ λέγειν Ἀθηναίων.

4. If a negative clause is to be joined to a positive, τέ in the first clause may be followed by οὐδέ in the second : Od. φ, 310 πῖνέ τε μηδ' ἐρίδαινε. But if τέ or καί follow οὐδέ, they do not carry on its negative force to the words to which τέ or καί are joined, but belong to some other word in the first clause which they connect with the second ; Hymn. Cer. 95 οὐδέ τις ἀνδρῶν εἰσορόων γίγνωσκε βαθυζώνων τε γυναικῶν (ἀνδρῶν τε γυναικῶν τε). In such passages as Hdt. VII. 8, 1 χώρην τε τῆς νῦν ἐκτήμεθα οὐκ ἐλάσσονα οὐδὲ φλαυροτέρην παμφορωτέρην τε, τέ does not refer to οὐδέ, but to the positive notion implied in οὐκ ἐλάσσονα=ἴσην.

Adverbial use of οὐδέ.

5. Οὐδέ as an adverb is to negative sentences what the adverb καί is to positive, *ne quidem*, *not even*. It may, like καί, stand in both the opposed clauses ; as, Xen. Cyr. I. 6, 18 ὥσπερ οὐδὲ γεωργοῦ ἀργοῦ οὐδὲν ὄφελος, οὕτως οὐδὲ στρατηγοῦ ἀργοῦ οὐδὲν ὄφελος εἶναι, *not even —, so too not even :* but very often it is used only once, and generally it follows the usages of καί (§. 760.) So like καί it has an emphatic force ; as, οὐδ' ὁ κράτιστος ἐτόλμησεν αὐτῷ μάχεσθαι. So οὐδείς, οὐδὲ εἷς, *ne unus quidem*, οὐδ' ὥς, *ne sic quidem*, οὐδ' ὅσον, οὐδ' ὁπωστιοῦν &c. In these phrases the negative may be repeated with the predicate ; Soph. Trach. 279 ὕβριν γὰρ οὐ στέργουσιν οὐδὲ δαίμονες, *non amant ne dii quidem*.

Disjunctive Coordination.

§. 777. 1. Clauses are said to be disjunctively coordinate when one of them excluding the other, so that they cannot be true together, they are joined together as one whole. The disjunctive conjunctions are ἤ — ἤ (Epic ἠέ — ἠέ), εἴτε — εἴτε, ἐάντε — ἐάντε.

a. Alternatives ἤ — ἤ — ἤ.

2. Ἤ has a twofold force : it expresses either that one thing is excluded from the other, so that if one is true the other is not (*alternative*), or that one thing differs from the other (*comparative*).

3. *Alternative:* ἤ—ἤ, *either—or, a u t—a u t, v e l—v e l :* Od. ξ, 330
ἢ ἀμφαδὸν ἠὲ κρυφηδόν : Il. a, 138 ἢ τέον ἢ Αἴαντος—γέρας, ἢ ᾿Οδυσῆος.

4. The first ἤ may be omitted: Il. a, 62 μάντιν ἐρείομεν ἢ ἱερῆα ἢ καὶ
ὀνειροπόλον : Eur. Or. 1145 ἕξομεν κλέος, καλῶς θανόντες ἢ καλῶς σεσωσμένοι.

Obs. 1. Homer sometimes marks the coordinate relations of the two
clauses by adding τέ (§. 755. 2.), so that ἤ is nearly the same as εἴτε : Il.
ρ, 42 πόνος ἔσται—ἤτ᾿ ἀλκῆς ἤ τε φόβοιο : Il. τ, 148 δῶρα μέν, αἴ κ᾿ ἐθέλῃσθα,
παρασχέμεν, ὡς ἐπιεικές, ἤτ᾿ ἐχέμεν.

5. In Attic, the first ἤ often takes the separative particle τ ο ί, whereby
the disjunctive force is increased and made to seem necessary, so that ἤ
takes the sense of *a u t, either surely, either only*—or γέ is often added to
strengthen τοί : Plat. Parm. p. 131 A οὐκοῦν ἤτοι ὅλου τοῦ εἴδους ἢ μέρους
ἑκάστου τὸ μεταλαμβάνον μεταλαμβάνει : Id. Phæd. p. 76 A ἤτοι ἐπιστάμενοί
γε αὐτὰ γεγόναμεν—ἢ ὕστερον—ἀναμιμνῄσκονται : Id. Gorg. p. 460 A ἤτοι
πρότερόν γε ἢ ὕστερον μαθόντα παρὰ σοῦ.　This τοί is but rarely added to
the second ἤ, as it is more natural to express the necessity of the alternative
in the first clause—it here means *or at least, or surely :* Pindar. Nem. VI.
5 sq. ἀλλά τι προσφέρομεν ἢ μέγαν νόον ἤτοι φύσιν ἀθανάτοις [a] : Plat. Rep.
p. 344 E ἔοικας (sc. οἴεσθαι τουτὶ ἄλλως ἔχειν), ἢν δ᾿ ἐγώ, ἤτοι ἡμῶν γε
οὐδὲν κήδεσθαι, *videris aliter existimare, aut certe nostri quidem curam habere
nullam.*

Obs. 2. We must distinguish between the disjunctive ἤτοι, *or surely,* and
the Epic ἤτοι, which expresses certainty—*surely* (§. 731.).

Obs. 3. If the clause to which ἤ refers is suppressed, it has the force of
otherwise, a l i a s, a l i o q u i n, that is — *if this is not so :* Plat. Phædr. p.
245 E τοῦτο δὲ οὔτ᾿ ἀπόλλυσθαι οὔτε γίγνεσθαι δυνατόν, ἢ πάντα τε οὐρανὸν
πᾶσάν τε γένεσιν συμπεσοῦσαν στῆναι, *alioquin omne cælum collapsum stare.*

Obs. 4. The disjunctive conjunctions ἤ—ἤ are in Epic (very rarely in
Tragedy), joined with μέν and δέ, ἠμέν—ἠδέ, and then have a copulative instead of a disjunctive sense, like καί—καί, τέ—τέ.　᾿Ιδέ is also used,
for the sake of the metre, for ἠδέ, of which it is a weakened form : Il. ς,
128 ὄφρ᾿ εὖ γιγνώσκῃς ἠμὲν θεόν, ἠδὲ καὶ ἄνδρα, as well on one side, as
on the other.　So we say, "You would know *either* God *or* man," meaning both ; so that it is not necessary to suppose with some writers, that
the copulative ἤ has a root different from the disjunctive ἤ — it means
both, be it one, or the other : Il. δ, 257 πέρι μέν σε τίω — ἠμὲν ἐπὶ πτο-
λέμῳ, ἠδ᾿ ἀλλοίῳ ἐπὶ ἔργῳ, ἠδ᾿ ἐν δαιτί.　Καί is often added to ἠδέ, and
sometimes, though rarely, is used instead of it after ἠμέν — sometimes
τέ, and still more rarely δέ : Il. o, 664 μνήσασθε—παίδων ἠδ᾿ ἀλόχων—,
ἠμὲν ὅτεῳ ζώουσι κ α ὶ ᾧ κατατεθνήκασιν : cf. Od. θ, 575 (ἠμέν—τε) and Il.
μ, 428 (ἠμέν—δέ).　And on the other hand ἠδέ sometimes answers to μέν,
or τέ, or καί in the first clause : Od. μ, 168 αὐτίκ᾿ ἔπειτ᾿ ἄνεμος μὲν
ἐπαύσατο, ἠδὲ γαλήνη ἔπλετο : Od. a, 12 πόλεμόν τε πεφευγότες ἠδὲ
θάλασσαν.　And it is often used without any corresponding particle before
it : Il. a, 334 Διὸς ἄγγελοι ἠδὲ καὶ ἀνδρῶν : Eur. Hec. 320 γραῖαι γυναῖκες
ἠδὲ πρεσβῦται σέθεν.

b. Εἴτε—εἴτε, ἐάν τε (ἤν τε)—ἐάν τε (ἤν τε).

§. 778. If the disjunctive relation is hypothetically expressed, the hypothetical conjunctions ε ἰ and ἐ ά ν are accompanied by τέ, as in Latin
s i v e—s i v e, though not till after Homer.

---

[a] Dissen ad loc.

a. Εἶτε—εἶτε. We often find either clause strengthened by the particle δή or the suffix οὖν: Hdt. I. 86 ἐν νόῳ ἔχων, εἶτε δὴ ἀκροθίνια ταῦτα καταγιεῖν θεῶν ὅτεῳ δή, εἶτε καὶ εὐχὴν ἐπιτελέσαι θέλων: Plat. Rep. p. 493 D εἶτ' ἐν γραφικῇ, εἶτ' ἐν μουσικῇ, εἶτε δὴ ἐν πολιτικῇ: Id. Apol. p. 27 C εἶτ' οὖν καινὰ εἶτε παλαιά. Οὖν may be used in both clauses: Ibid. p. 34 E εἶτ' οὖν ἀληθὲς, εἶτ' οὖν ψευδές.

Obs. Sometimes εἶτε—ἤ: Plat. Rep. p. 364 B εἶτε τι ἀδίκημά του γέγονεν αὐτοῦ ἢ προγόνων. Or ἤ—εἶτε, but scarcely found any where but in poetry: Eur. Alc. 112 ἢ Λυκίας εἶτ' ἐπὶ τὰς ἀνύδρους Ἀμμωνιάδας ἕδρας.—Εἶτε only in one clause, almost wholly poetic: Soph. Œ. T. 517 λόγοισιν εἶτ' ἔργοισιν: Æsch. Ag. 1403: also εἰ—εἶτε: Id. Eum. 459 σὺ δ', εἰ δικαίως, εἶτε μή, κρῖνον δίκην. So the Latin comedians; as, Plaut. Curs. I. 1, 4 *Si media non est, sive est prima vespera, tamen est eundum.* Lastly, εἶτε—εἰ δέ: Plat. Apol. p. 40 C καὶ εἶτε δὴ μηδεμία αἴσθησίς ἐστιν—E εἰ δ' αὖ οἷον ἀποδημῆσαι, after a long interruption. So in Latin, *sive—si vero.*

b. Ἐάν τε—ἐάν τε, ἤν τε—ἤν τε, ἄν τε—ἄν τε, always with the conjunctive. This differs from εἶτε—εἶτε &c. as the simple conjunctions εἰ and ἐάν: Plat. Euth. c. 6 ἐάν τε πατὴρ ὢν τυγχάνῃ, ἐάν τε μήτηρ, ἐάν τε ἄλλος ὁστισοῦν. Instead of this formula, we find in Sophocles ἐὰν δέ—καὶ μή: Soph. Ant. 327 ἐάν δέ τοι ληφθῇ καὶ μή.

Comparative ἤ.

§. 779. Ἤ is not only disjunctive, but is also used in comparisons. As ἤ disjunctive answers to another ἤ, so as a comparative it refers to some word which expresses *difference* or *distinction ;* as, ἄλλος, οὐδεὶς ἄλλος, ἀλλοῖος, ἐναντίος, ἴδιος, διαφέρω &c.: also to comparatives, and all words implying comparative notions ; as, διπλήσιος, ὑπερθεν, πρίν, φθάνω &c. So that ἤ here also retains its original *exclusive* power: Hdt. III. 37 ἐσῆλθε δὲ καὶ ἐς τῶν Καβείρων ἱρόν, ἐς τὸ οὐ θεμιτόν ἐστι ἐσιέναι ἄλλον γε ἢ τὸν ἱρέα: Plat. Phæd. p. 64 A οὐδὲν ἄλλο αὐτοὶ ἐπιτηδεύουσιν ἢ ἀποθνῄσκειν τε καὶ τεθνάναι: Id. Gorg. p. 481 C ἀλλά τις ἡμῶν ἴδιόν τι ἔπασχε πάθος ἢ οἱ ἄλλοι: Eur. Med. 647 μόχθων δ' οὐκ ἄλλος ὑπέρθεν ἢ γᾶς πατρίας στερέσθαι. So ἔξω ἤ Hdt. VII. 228.—See §. 503. *Obs.* 2.

Obs. 1. Ἤ also stands sometimes after an interrogative τίς, τί without ἄλλος: Plat. Crit. p. 53 E τί ποιῶν ἢ εὐωχούμενος ἐν Θετταλίᾳ; Xen. Œcon. III. 3 ἀλλὰ τί οὖν τούτων ἐστὶν αἴτιον, ἢ ὅτι κ. τ. λ. So in indirect questions we sometimes find τί instead of ἄλλο τί: Xen. M. S. IV. 3, 9 ἐγὼ μὲν ἤδη τοῦτο σκοπῶ, εἰ ἄρα τι ἐστὶ τοῖς θεοῖς ἔργον, ἢ ἀνθρώπους θεραπεύειν;

Obs. 2. As the disjunctive ἤ nearly approaches in sense to the adversative ἀλλά, we find after μᾶλλον sometimes ἀλλ' οὐ: Isocr. p. 23 B μᾶλλον αἱροῦνται συνεῖναι τοῖς ἐξαμαρτάνουσιν, ἀλλ' οὐ τοῖς ἀποτρέπουσι. —On μᾶλλον ἢ οὐ see §. 749. 3. And πλήν, whose sense is cognate to ἤ and ἀλλά, can supply the place of ἤ, as οὐδὲν ἄλλο πλήν: Eur. Heracl. 232 ταῦτ' ἐστὶ κρείσσω πλὴν ὑπ' Ἀργείοις πεσεῖν. Also the comparative adverbs ὡς or ὥσπερ can stand after comparatives: Lysias p. 572, 5 μᾶλλον ὥς μοι προσῆκε: Plat. Rep. p. 526 C ἄ γε μείζω πόνον παρέχει μανθάνοντι καὶ μελετῶντι, οὐκ ἂν ῥᾳδίως οὐδὲ πολλὰ ἂν εὕροις, ὡς τοῦτο: Xen. Hell. II. 3, 16 εἰ δὲ, ὅτι τριάκοντά ἐσμεν καὶ οὐχ εἷς, ἧττόν τι οἴει ὥσπερ τυραννίδος ταύτης τῆς ἀρχῆς χρῆναι ἐπιμελεῖσθαι, εὐήθης εἶ. Also ἢ ὡς, *than as* : Plat. Rep. p. 410 D μαλακώτεροι αὖ γίγνονται ἢ ὡς κάλλιον αὐτοῖς.

Obs. 3. The comparative ἤ stands sometimes after positive adjectives, or where μᾶλλον is omitted. *a.* After expressions of *will, preference, &c.* as in them is implied the notion of *difference, separation, superiority:* βούλεσθαι, ἐθέλειν, αἱρεῖσθαι, αἵρεσιν δοῦναι, ἐπιθυμεῖν, δέχεσθαι, ζητεῖν &c.: Il. a, 117 βούλομ' ἐγὼ λαὸν σόον ἔμμεναι, ἢ ἀπολέσθαι: Il. λ, 319 Τρωσὶν δὴ βόλεται δοῦναι κράτος ἠέπερ ἡμῖν: Lysias de aff. tyr. §. 1 ζητοῦσι κερδαίνειν ἢ ἡμᾶς πείθειν: Xen. Cyr. I. 4, 3 ὥστ' ἐπιθυμίαν τις εἶχεν πλείω ἀκούειν αὐτοῦ ἢ σιωπῶντι παρεῖναι; So Thuc. VII. 49 ἢ πρότερον θαρσήσει κρατηθείς, which has a comparative notion implied in it. *b.* After δίκαιόν ἐστι, λυσιτελεῖν &c., when they are used in doubtful cases, where the justice, expediency, &c. of two things are compared: Hdt. IX. 26 extr. οὕτω οὖν ἡμᾶς δίκαιον ἔχειν τὸ ἕτερον κέρας, ἤπερ Ἀθηναίους: Soph. Aj. 945. H. (966.) Tecmessa says, ἐμοὶ πικρὸς τέθνηκεν (Ajax), ἢ κείνοις γλυκύς, αὐτῷ δὲ τερπνός = ἐμοὶ πικρὸς τέθνηκεν, καὶ μᾶλλον πικρὸς, ἢ κείνοις γλυκύς.

Obs. 4. Πέρ which is often joined with ἤ (§.734. 2. 3) has a double force, as the second clause of the comparison is conceived of as positive or negative. In itself this second clause is negative, (ὁ πατὴρ μείζων ἐστὶν ἢ ὁ υἱός, the father is the greater, not the son,) but it also may be considered as positive, when the quality is not directly denied in the second clause, but only as compared with the first clause—the father is greater than the son, though he is great—in the former clause πέρ increases the negative force of ἤ, so that ἤπερ almost equals οὔπερ: Il. π, 688 ἀλλ' αἰεί τε Διὸς κρείσσων νόος ἠέπερ ἀνδρῶν (=ἀλλ' οὔπερ ἀνδρῶν :) Il. σ, 302 τῶν τινα βέλτερόν ἐστιν ἐπαυρέμεν, ἤπερ Ἀχαιούς: Hdt. IX. 28 Ἀθηναίους ἀξιονεικοτέρους εἶναι ἔχειν τὸ κέρας, ἤπερ Ἀρκάδας. In the second case πέρ brings out the positive force of the clause, and means *much*; as, Od. δ, 819 τοῦ δὴ (Τηλεμάχου) ἐγὼ καὶ μᾶλλον ὀδύρομαι, ἤπερ ἐκείνου sc. Ὀδυσσέως, I mourn Telemachus yet more than Ulysses, much as I lament him.

Remarks on the use of ἤ, and the Genitive, with a Comparative.

§. 780. The object of comparison may be denoted by the disjunctive ἤ, or by the genitive; but it is not in every case that these may be interchanged so that one may be used instead of the other.—The following will hold good:

a. If both the subjects have the same verb, either the genitive may be used, or ἤ with the same case as in the first clause : Eur. Or. 715 sq. πιστὸς ἐν κακοῖς ἀνὴρ κρείσσων γαλήνης ναυτίλοισιν εἰσορᾶν (or ἢ γαλήνη): Ibid. 1148 οὐκ ἐστιν οὐδὲν κρεῖσσον, ἢ φίλος σαφής, οὐ πλοῦτος, οὐ τυραννίς (or οὐδὲν κρεῖσσον τοῦ φίλου.)

b. If the two things compared are the objects of the same verb, the genitive is not generally used, but only ἤ: (Genit.) Hdt. VII. 26 ἵνα πηγαὶ ἀναδιδοῦσι Μαιάνδρου ποταμοῦ καὶ ἑτέρου οὐκ ἐλάσσονος ἢ Μαιάνδρου : Thuc. II. 13 οὐκ ἐλάσσονος ἦν ἢ πεντήκοντα ταλάντων : Id. VII. 77 ἤδη τινὲς καὶ ἐκ δεινοτέρων ἢ τοιῶνδε ἐσώθησαν : (Dat.) Il. a, 260 ἤδη γάρ ποτ' ἐγὼ καὶ ἀρείοσιν ἠέπερ ὑμῖν (sc. ὁμιλῶ) ἀνδράσιν ὡμίλησα. (Accus.) Hdt. VII. 10, 1 σὺ δὲ μέλλεις ἐπ' ἄνδρας στρατεύεσθαι πολὺ ἀμείνονας ἢ Σκύθας. But if the object in the first clause is in the accusative, the genitive is frequently used ; as, Od. ι, 27 οὔτοι ἔγωγε ἧς γαίης δύναμαι γλυκερώτερον ἄλλο ἰδέσθαι : Od. σ, 130 οὐδὲν ἀκιδνότερον γαῖα τρέφει ἀνθρώποιο.

Obs. 1. With the neuter words πλέον, πλείω, ἔλαττον if joined

with a numeral, ἤ is in general omitted, without any change in the case
following; so in Latin, after *plus* and *amplius, decem amplius homines :*
Plat. Apol. S. p. 17 D νῦν ἐγὼ πρῶτον ἐπὶ δικαστήριον ἀναβέβηκα, ἔτη γεγονὼς
πλείω ἑβδομήκοντα, *annos plus septuaginta natus* [a]. These words also
stand as an adverbial accus. of quantity (§. 578.) joined with substantives
of different gender and form : Xen. Cyr. II. 1, 5 ἵππους μὲν ἄξει οὐ μεῖον
δισμυρίων. §. 6 ἱππέας μὲν ἡμῖν εἶναι μεῖον ἤ τὸ τρίτον μέρος : Ibid. πελταστὰς καὶ τοξότας πλέον ἤ εἴκοσι μυριάδας. So the neuter plural : Plat.
Menex. p. 235 B αὕτη ἡ σεμνότης παραμένει ἡμέρας πλείω ἤ τρεῖς : Demosth. p. 846, 7 μαρτυριῶν γὰρ πλέον ἤ πάνυ πολλῶν τῶν ἁπασῶν ἀναγνω-
σθεισῶν, *more than very many.* This idiom is Attic, which seldom made
πλείων, μείων, &c. agree with their substantives in gender, number, and
case, as in Xen. Cyr. II. 1, 5 τοξότας πλείους ἤ τετρακισμυρίους, λογχοφόρους
οὐ μείους τετρακισμυρίων, πελταστὰς οὐ μείους τρισμυρίων.

Obs. 2. Sometimes the particle is used as well as the genitive. This
may be explained in two ways; either the genitive is independent of the
comparative, and expresses some one of the relations of the genitive ; as,
Plat. Legg. p. 765 A μὴ ἔλαττον ἤ τριάκοντα γεγονὼς ἐτῶν (as γίγνεσθαι τριάκοντα ἐτῶν (§. 521. 2.). Or the genitive is a demonstrative pronoun, depending on the comparative, the former clause being of such a nature
that it represents a substantival notion, to which the demonstrative refers. The genitive is used to denote beforehand the importance of the
following clause introduced by ἤ, which is then only a further explanation
and enlargement upon the demonstrative ; — so an infinitival sentence
which has a substantival force often has τοῦτο prefixed ; as, τοῦτο καλόν
ἐστιν, ἀποθανεῖν περὶ τῆς πατρίδος. This idiom is universal, from Homer
downwards : Il. ο, 509 sq. ἡμῖν δ' οὔτις τοῦδε (sc. νοῦ) νόος καὶ μῆτις ἀμείνων,
ἢ αὐτοσχεδίῃ μῖξαι χεῖράς τε μένος τε : Od. ζ, 182 οὐ μὲν γὰρ τοῦγε κρεῖσσον
καὶ ἄρειον, ἢ ὅθ' ὁμοφρονέοντε νοήμασιν οἶκον ἔχητον ἀνὴρ ἠδὲ γυνή (=τοῦ ὅτε—
ἔχητον) : Lysias de affect. tyr. §. 23 οὐδὲν γὰρ εἴη αὐτοῖς χαλεπώτερον
τούτων ἢ πυνθάνεσθαι μὲν ἡμᾶς μετέχοντας τῶν πραγμάτων ; Demosth. p. 847
extr. ᾠήθην δεῖν μηδὲν ἄλλο τούτου πρότερον ἤ τούτον παρακαλούμενος
ἐλέγξαι. And sometimes ἤ is dropped after the demonstrative genitive :
Æsch. Ag. 613 τί γὰρ γυναικὶ τούτου φέγγος ἥδιον δρακεῖν, ἀπὸ στρατείας
ἄνδρα σώσαντος θεοῦ, πύλας ἀνοῖξαι : also Plat. Gorg. p. 519 D καίτοι
τούτου τοῦ λόγου τί ἄν ἀλογώτερον εἴη πρᾶγμα, ἀνθρώπους ἀγαθοὺς καὶ
δικαίους γενομένους—ἀδικεῖν. But very rarely do we find the demonstrative
genitive omitted as well as ἤ : Eur. Alc. 896 τί γὰρ ἀνδρὶ κακὸν μεῖζον,
ἁμαρτεῖν πιστῆς ἀλόχου. In these cases the infin. is to be taken as a genitive without the article ; in poetry sometimes ἤ is used before the genitive,
as a pleonasm : Soph. Antig. 1281 τί δ' ἐστὶν αὖ κάκιον ἤ κακῶν ἔτι ;

§. 781. *c.* If two objects are compared together in respect of their partaking of the quality or operation of some verb, to which, however, they do
not stand in the same grammatical relation, the proper and clearest construction is to use ἤ with the nomin., supplying εἶναι, or the verb, from the
other part of the sentence ; but the genitive is often used instead thereof :
Isocr. Pac. extr. τοῖς νεωτέροις καὶ μᾶλλον ἀκμάζουσιν, ἤ ἐγὼ (sc. ἀκμάζω),
παραινῶ : Ibid. p. 176 A πλείοσι καὶ μείζοσι κακοῖς περιέπεσον ἐπὶ τῆς ἀρχῆς
ταύτης τῶν ἐν ἅπαντι τῷ χρόνῳ τῇ πόλει γεγενημένων : Demosth. p. 287, 27
ἡμῶν ἄμεινον, ἤ ἐκεῖνοι, τὸ μέλλον προορωμένων.

d. (Comparatio compendiaria.) If two things compared have a common

---

verb, and one of them is accompanied by an attributive genitive; as, Διὸ γενεὴ κρείσσων τέτυκται ἢ ποταμοῖο γενεή, or κρείσσων τ. τῆς ποταμοῖο γενῆς, the object of comparison (as γενεή) is not compared with the proper corresponding object (as γενῆς), but is directly referred to the thing or person of which that object would be, if expressed, the attribute, as ποταμοῖο for γενῆς ποταμοῖο: Il. φ, 191 κρείσσων δ' αὖτε Διὸς γενεὴ Ποταμοῖο τέτυκται: Pindar. Ol. I. princ. μηδ' 'Ολυμπίας ἀγῶνα φίρτερον αὐδάσομεν: Eur. Med. 1343 λέαιναν, οὐ γυναῖκα, τῆς Τυρσηνίδος Σκύλλης ἔχουσαν ἀγριωτέραν φύσιν: Id. Androm. 220 χείρον' ἀρσένων νόσον ταύτην νοσοῦμεν: Xen. Cyr. III. 3, 41 χώραν ἔχετε οὐδὲν ἥττον ἡμῶν (for τῆς ἡμετέρας) ἕντιμον: Theocrit. VI. 37 τῶν δὲ τ' ὀδόντων λευκοτέραν αὐγὰν Παρίας ὑπέφαινε λίθοιο.

Obs. This short form of comparison occurs in all languages, but not so universally as in Greek, as here it is used not only with comparatives, but in all other expressions of comparison; so Il. ρ, 51 αἵματί οἱ δεύοντο κόμαι Χαρίτεσσιν ὁμοῖαι. See §. 519. §. 594. 2.

§. 782. *e.* If the comparative word belongs to the verb of the clause, either form may be used; as, οὗτος ἀπελίπετο πολλὸν ἐλάσσω πυραμίδα ἢ ὁ πατήρ: Hdt. II. 134 πυραμίδα δὲ καὶ οὗτος ἀπελίπετο πολλὸν ἐλάσσω τοῦ πατρός: Soph. Antig. 74 πλείω (ἐστὶ) χρόνος, ὃν δεί μ' ἀρέσκειν τοῖς κάτω τῶν ἐνθάδε (*diutius me oportet placere inferis, quam iis, qui hic sunt*): Thuc. VII. 63 καὶ ταῦτα τοῖς ὁπλίταις οὐχ ἧσσον τῶν ναυτῶν παρακελεύομαι (for ἢ τοῖς ναύταις:) Id. I. 85 ἔξεστι δ' ἡμῖν μᾶλλον ἑτέρων (καθ' ἡσυχίαν βουλεύειν) for ἢ ἑτέροις.

f. If any two properties of the same object are compared, they are signified by the comparatives of their proper adjectives, and connected by ἤ, θάττων ἢ σοφώτερος, that is, *rash man*, in a higher degree than *wise*, but not wise in a higher degree=not equally wise as rash; Od. α, 164 πότνα κ' ἀρησαίατ' ἐλαφρότεροι πόδας εἶναι ἢ ἀφνειότεροι χρυσοῖό τε ἐσθῆτός τε: Plat. Rep. p. 409 D πλεονάκις δὲ πονηροῖς ἢ χρηστοῖς ἐντυγχάνων σοφώτερος ἢ ἀμαθέστερος δοκεῖ εἶναι αὐτῷ τε καὶ ἄλλοις: so when the comparative belongs to a verb: Hdt. III. 65 ἐποίησα ταχύτερα ἢ σοφώτερα:—and also with μᾶλλον and a positive adjective: Eur. Med. 471 πρόθυμος μᾶλλον ἢ σοφωτέρα.

g. If the subject at one time is compared with itself at another, so that an increase in degree is signified, the genitive of the reflexive pronouns ἐμαυτοῦ, σεαυτοῦ, ἑαυτοῦ is used; and after this last αὐτός is added. This is not found in Homer, and rather in prose than poetry: 'Αρείων εἰμὶ ἐμαυτοῦ—ἀρείων εἶ σεαυτοῦ—ἀρείων ἐστὶν αὐτὸς ἑαυτοῦ: Thuc. III. 11 δυνατώτεροι αὐτοὶ αὑτῶν ἐγίγνοντο. The following passage of Plato will illustrate this construction: Rep. p. 431 A B φαίνεταί μοι βούλεσθαι λέγειν οὗτος ὁ λόγος, ὥς τι ἐν αὐτῷ τῷ ἀνθρώπῳ περὶ τὴν ψυχὴν τὸ μὲν βέλτιον ἔνι, τὸ δὲ χεῖρον, καὶ ὅταν μὲν τὸ βέλτιον φύσει τοῦ χείρονος ἐγκρατὲς ᾖ, τοῦτο λέγειν τὸ κρείττω αὑτοῦ—, ὅταν δὲ ὑπὸ τροφῆς κακῆς ἤ τινος ὁμιλίας κρατηθῇ ὑπὸ πλήθους τοῦ χείρονος σμικρότερον τὸ βέλτιον ὄν, τοῦτο δὲ—καλεῖν ἥττω ἑαυτοῦ καὶ ἀκόλαστον τὸν οὕτω διακείμενον.——κρείττω——(τὴν νέαν ἡμῖν πόλιν) αὐτὴν αὑτῆς δικαίως φήσεις προσαγορεύεσθαι, εἴπερ οὗ τὸ ἄμεινον τοῦ χείρονος ἄρχει, σῶφρον κλητέον καὶ κρεῖττον αὐτοῦ. Sometimes the difference of time is marked by ἤ, and an expression of time: Hdt. II. 25 ὁ δὲ Νεῖλος—τοῦτον τὸν χρόνον αὐτὸς ἑωυτοῦ ῥέει πολλῷ ὑποδεέστερος ἢ τοῦ θέρεος. It is used in Aristotle to denote a change in degree, not in kind. Sometimes these genitives are accompanied by ἤ and a clause signifying the time or circumstances under which the increase is conceived: so the superlative is joined with αὐτός and the genitive of the reflexive pronouns (ἐμαυτοῦ, σεαυτοῦ, ἑαυτοῦ) to mark that the subject possesses the quality in the highest degree, higher, that is, than at any other time: ἄριστος αὐτὸς ἑαυτοῦ—ἀρίστη αὐτὴ ἑαυτῆς: Xen. M. S. I. 2, 46 εἴθε σοι, ὦ Περίκλεις, τότε συνεγενόμην, ὅτε δεινότατος σαυτοῦ ταῦτα ἦσθα, when you so entirely surpassed yourself. So also when the superlative belongs to the verb: Plat. Legg. p. 715 D νέος ἂν πᾶς ἄνθρωπος τὰ τοιαῦτα ἀμβλύτατα αὐτὸς αὑτοῦ ὁρᾷ.

§. 783. *h.* A peculiar form of comparison is found, when any thing is compared in respect of some property with a whole thought or sentence. In this case the thought is contracted into a single substantival notion, which stands in the genitive after the comparative: Hdt. II. 148 ἦσαν—αἱ πυραμίδες λόγου μέζονες, *grandiores, quam ut oratione explicari possit:* Thuc. II. 50 γενόμενον κρεῖσσον λόγου τὸ εἶδος τῆς νόσου: Soph. Œ. T. 1361 κρεῖσσον' ἀγχόνης εἰργασμένα: so πρᾶγμα ἐλπίδων κρεῖσσον: so adverbs: Xen. Hellen. VII. 5, 13 ἐδίωξαν πορρωτέρω τοῦ καιροῦ: and even participles are used instead of substantives, to represent the whole thought, as δέοντος: Plat. Rep. p. 410 D οἱ μὲν γυμναστικῇ ἀκράτῳ χρησάμενοι ἀγριώτεροι τοῦ δέοντος ἀποβαίνουσιν.

Obs. But sometimes the thought is expressed in full by ἢ ὥστε and the infinitive of the verb, sometimes without ὥστε, or by ἢ ὡς with the opt. and ἄν: Demosth. p. 68, 11 ἔστι γὰρ μείζω τἀκείνων ἔργα ἢ ὡς τῷ λόγῳ τις ἂν εἴποι.

i. When the notion of inequality between two objects is denoted, so that the properties of the one are too different or too great to exist in or with the other, the comparative of the adjective is used with ἢ κατά, or more rarely ἢ πρός, with the accus.: Thuc. VII. 75 μείζω ἢ κατὰ δάκρυα πεπονθότας: Id. IV. 39 ὁ γὰρ ἄρχων Ἐπιτάδας ἐνδεεστέρως ἑκάστῳ παρεῖχεν ἢ πρὸς τὴν ἐξουσίαν: Plat. Rep. p. 359 D νεκρὸς μείζων ἢ κατ' ἄνθρωπον. The Latin uses *quam pro* with the ablative: Liv. XXI. 29 *prælium atrocius, quam pro numero pugnantium, editur.* Sometimes an infinitive is used to define the property more clearly: Eur. Med. 675 σοφώτερ' ἢ κατ' ἄνδρα συμβαλεῖν ἔπη, *voces sapientiores ad intelligendum, quam pro homine, h. e. quam ut homo ea intelligere possit:* Plat. Cratyl. p. 392 A ταῦτα μείζω ἐστὶν ἢ κατ' ἐμὲ καὶ σὲ ἐξευρεῖν, *majora ad inveniendum quam pro me et te.*

k. It sometimes happens that the comparative notion is formally contained in the word πλείονας, while in reality it applies to another notion in the sentence: Soph. Ant. 312 ἐκ τῶν γὰρ αἰσχρῶν λημμάτων τοὺς πλείονας ἀτωμένους ἴδοις ἂν ἢ σεσωσμένους=τοὺς πολλοὺς ἴδοις ἂν ἀτωμένους μᾶλλον ἢ σεσωσμένους: Id. Œ. C. 795 κάκ' ἂν λάβοις τὰ πλείον' ἢ σωτήρια=τὰ πολλὰ λάβοις ἂν κακὰ μᾶλλον ἢ σωτήρια [a].

The Comparative without the second clause of the Comparison.

§. 784. We often find in Greek the comparative used without any object of comparison, so that where we use the positive, they use the comparative. The cause thereof seems to be that the Greek had the power, by a sort of instinct, or by experience, of defining in his mind the proper or usual size or degree of any thing; so that whatever went beyond, or fell short of this size or degree, presented itself to his mind in

[a] Herm. Ant. 312.

the relation of greater or less : hence the comparative is used in Greek where we use the positive, and the adverbs *too, very, rather, somewhat :* the comparison being made with reference to some such thought as —*than it was before*—*usual*—*fitting*—*right*, &c., more or less clearly present to the speaker's mind, and sometimes expressed in words; as, Hdt. VI. 84 Κλεομένεα δὲ λέγουσι, ἡκόντων τῶν Σκυθέων—, ὁμιλέειν σφι μεζόνως· ὁμιλέοντα δὲ μᾶλλον τοῦ ἰκνευμένου (*quam par erat* μαθεῖν τὴν ἀκρητοποσίην παρ' αὐτέων*: Ibid. 107 πταρεῖν τε καὶ βῆξαι μεζόνως ἢ ὡς ἐώθεε : Id. VII. 13 ἡ νεότης ἐπέζεσε, ὥστε ἀεικέστερα ἀπορρίψαι ἔπεα ἐς ἄνδρα πρεσβύτερον ἢ χρεών*: Hdt. I. 91 μητρὸς ἀμείνονος, πατρὸς δὲ ὑποδεεστέρου : Id. III. 145 Μαιανδρίῳ δὲ τῷ τυράννῳ ἦν ἀδελφεὸς ὑπομαργότερος, *hebetioris ingenii* : Id. VI. 108 ἡμεῖς ἑκαστέρω οἰκέομεν, *too far* (sc. ἢ ὥστε ὑμᾶς δέχεσθαι) : Id. I. 116 ἐδόκεε — ἡ ἀπάκρισις ἐλευθερωτέρη εἶναι (*justo liberior*)* : Id. VI. 38 πολέμιος ὑποθερμότερος, *hostis ferventior :* Ibid. 46 τεῖχος ἰσχυρότερον περιβαλλόμενοι : Ibid. 51 ἐὼν—οἰκίης ὑποδεεστέρης, *familiæ inferioris :* Ib. 75 ὑπέλαβε μανίη νοῦσος ἐόντα καὶ πρότερον ὑπομαργότερον : Ibid. 92 Αἰγινῆται δὲ οὔτε συνεγινώσκοντο ἔσαν τε αἰδεστέροι, *pertinaciores :* Isocr. Paneg. 14. p. 38 sq. ἡρούμεθα τοῖς ἀσθενεστέροις—βοηθεῖν μᾶλλον, ἢ τοῖς κρείττοσι—συναδικεῖν. So two comparatives frequently answer to one another, as we use the words *better, weaker*, &c.: Plat. Apol. p. 18 D τὸν ἥττω λόγον κρείττω ποιῶν : Arist. Ach. 681 μῖλος εὔτονον ἀγροικότερον, *very rustic*—that is, more than usual. So especially, ἄμεινον, βέλτιον, κέρδιον Hom. κάλλιον, μᾶλλον, χεῖρον, αἴσχιον, κάκιον, νεώτερον. more rarely, καινότερον, (as the positive καινός is synonymous with νεώτερος) &c., especially with a negative ; as, οὐ κάλλιον, οὐκ ἄμεινον, οὐ κάκιον, οἱ κρεῖττον, οὐ χεῖρον, οὐ ῥᾷον, not so easy as it seems : Il. ω, 52 Ἕκτορα—περὶ σῆμ' ἑτάροιο φίλοιο ἕλκει· οὐ μήν οἱ τόγε κάλλιον οὐδέ τ' ἄμεινον, than if this were not done : Il. λ, 469 ἀλλ' ἴομεν καθ' ὅμιλον ἀλεξέμεναι γὰρ ἄμεινον, than if we did it not : Hdt. III. 71 ποιέειν αὐτίκα μοι δοκέει καὶ μὴ ὑπερβαλέσθαι· οὐ γὰρ ἄμεινον, than if we did it straightway : Eur. Hipp. 1455 τῶν γὰρ μεγάλων, *magnorum virorum*, ἀξιοπενθεῖς φῆμαι μᾶλλον κατέχουσιν (*magis percrebescit, quam fama de interitu ignobiliorum*) : Plat. Phædon. p. 105 A πάλιν δὲ ἀναμιμνήσκου· οὐ γὰρ χεῖρον πολλάκις ἀκούειν : Xen. Œcon. VIII. 25 πρὸς τὸ φυλάσσειν οὐ κάκιόν ἐστι φοβερὰν εἶναι τὴν ψυχήν : Hdt. III. 62 οὐ μή τι τοι ἐκ γε ἐκείνου νεώτερον ἀναβλαστήσει, *newer than before*[a] : (Cf. IV. 127 οὐδέ τι νεώτερόν εἰμι ποιήσας ἢ καὶ ἐν εἰρήνῃ ἐώθεα ποιέειν :) Eur. Or. 1312 εὔφημος ἴσθι· τί δὲ νεώτερον λέγεις, than we wished : Plat. Phædon. p. 115. B οὐδέν καινότερον : Id. Euthyphr. princ. τί νεώτερον, ὦ Σώκρατες, γέγονεν ; so νεώτερα πράσσειν, and hence νεωτερίζειν (but καινῶν, not καινοτέρων, πραγμάτων ἐφίεσθαι).

Coordination of Sentences logically subordinate.

§. 785. 1. This consists not in the connection of sentences which logically have no connection, but in joining together, so as to form one thought and one grammatical sentence, those clauses which stand in the logical relation of conclusion and premiss, antecedent and consequent.

2. The second clause expresses,

   a. The cause or reason, (conjunction γάρ.)

   b. The consequence of the former clause, (οὖν, ἄρα, τοίνυν, τοιγαροῦν.)

---

a Valcken. ad loc.

Cause, or reason.

Γάρ, for.

§. 786. Γάρ is a combination of γέ and ἄρα ; so that as γέ denotes
the reason or complement of something, (§. 735.) ἄρα an explanation, or
consequence, (§. 789. a.) γάρ, as combining the two, has either a causal and
explanatory (*argumentative*), or complementary and consequential force
(*consequential*). Γέ confirms the clause to which it is joined, and thus confirms and suggests a sort of reason or ground for that which precedes :
λέγε· σύ γε οἶσθα, say—*you at least* (*certainly*) *know :* to this ἄρα adds
an explanation of that which precedes, and thus gives a reason for it :
λέγε· σύ ἄρα οἶσθα, say—*you know now :* λέγε· σύ γὰρ οἶσθα, say—*you now
certainly know.* It cannot stand at the beginning, and generally is the
second word of a sentence.

1. Γάρ causal and explanatory—either one of these forces prevails over
the other.

a. The causal being the prominent notion : Plat. Phædr. p. 230 B νὴ
τὴν Ἥραν, καλή γε ἡ καταγωγή· ἥ τε γὰρ πλάτανος αὕτη μάλ' ἀμφιλαφής τε
καὶ ὑψηλή.

Obs. 1. It very often happens that the sentence whereof γάρ gives the
premiss is suppressed, and must be supplied by the mind : Plat. Symp.
p. 194 A καλῶς γὰρ αὐτὸς ἠγώνισαι (sc. σὺ μὲν δύνασαι θαρρεῖν.)

β. The explanatory force being the prominent notion. Here a demonstrative pronoun generally stands in the clause to be explained, which
points forward to the clause with γάρ : Lysias Epit. p. 192, 6 τοσοῦτον
δὲ εὐτυχέστεροι παῖδες ὄντες ἐγένοντο τοῦ πατρός· ὁ μὲν γὰρ—τοὺς μὲν ἄλλους
ἀδικοῦντας ἐκόλασεν : so after a superlative, τὸ δὲ μέγιστον, τὸ δὲ σχετλιώ-
τατον &c. : Isocr. Pac. p. 170 B τὸ δὲ πάντων σχετλιώτατον· οὓς
γὰρ ὡμολογήσαμεν ἄν. Lastly, after such expressions as τεκμήριον δέ, μαρτύ-
ριον δέ, σημεῖον δέ, δῆλον δέ sc. ἐστί, δείκνυμι δέ, ἐδήλωσε δέ, σκέψασθε δέ
&c. Plat. Protag. p. 320 C δοκεῖ τοίνυν μοι, ἔφη, χαριέστερον εἶναι μῦθον ὑμῖν
λέγειν· ἦν γὰρ ποτε χρόνος κ. τ. λ.

Obs. 2. This γάρ after the demonstratives τόσος, τοῖος, τοιοῦτος, ὧδε,
is often omitted ; as in Latin *enim* after *tantus, talis, sic,* and also the
phrases given above : Plat. Legg. p. 821 E τεκμήριον δέ· ἐγὼ τούτων
οὔτε νέος οὔτε πάλαι ἀκήκοα σφῶν.

Obs. 3. Very often, especially in Herodotus, the explanatory clause with
γάρ is placed first : Hdt. VI. 102 καί, ἦν γὰρ ὁ Μαραθὼν ἐπιτηδεώτατον
χωρίον τῆς Ἀττικῆς ἐνιππεῦσαι—, ἐς τοῦτό σφι κατηγέετο Ἱππίης : Ib. 118 καί,
ἀπίκατο γὰρ τηνικαῦτα οἱ Δήλιοι ὀπίσω ἐς τὴν νῆσον, κατατίθεταί τε ἐς τὸ ἱρὸν
τὸ ἄγαλμα, καὶ ἐντέλλεται τοῖσι Δηλίοισι ἀπαγαγεῖν τὸ ἄγαλμα ἐς Δήλιον τὸ
Θηβαίων.

Obs. 4. The clause which thus follows the explanatory clause with γάρ is
often connected therewith, as a consequence, by οὖν, (in Homer τῷ,
wherefore) Hdt. VI. 11 (λέγει τάδε·) Ἐπὶ ξυροῦ γὰρ ἀκμῆς ἔχεται ἡμῖν τὰ
πρήγματα—ἢ εἶναι ἐλευθέροισι ἢ δούλοισι, καὶ τούτοις ὡς δρηπέτησι· νῦν ὦν
ὑμίες, ἢν μὲν βούλησθε ταλαιπωρίας ἐνδέκεσθαι, τὸ παραχρῆμα μὲν πόνος ὑμῖν
ἔσται, οἷοί τε δὲ ἔσεσθε, ὑπερβαλόμενοι τοὺς ἐναντίους, εἶναι ἐλεύθεροι.

Obs. 5. The two clauses are often so compressed together that the subject
of the former is placed in the latter, and even follows the government
thereof : Hdt. IX. 109 τῇ δὲ κακῶς γὰρ ἔδεε πανοικίῃ γενέσθαι, πρὸς ταῦτα
εἶπε Ξέρξη : Id. IV. 200 τῶν δὲ πᾶν γὰρ ἦν τὸ πλῆθος μεταίτιον, οὐκ ἐδέκοντο
τοὺς λόγους (for οἱ δὲ (πᾶν γὰρ ἦν τὸ πλῆθος [αὐτῶν sc.] μεταίτιον) οὐκ ἐδέ-

χοντο τοὺς λόγους): Id. I. 24 καὶ τοῖσι ἐσελθεῖν γὰρ ἡδονὴν, εἰ μέλλοιεν ἀκούσεσθαι τοῦ ἀρίστου ἀνθρώπων ἀοιδοῦ, ἀναχωρῆσαι. Cf. I. 114. II. 101. Thuc. VIII. 30 τοῖς ἐν τῇ Σάμῳ Ἀθηναίοις προσαφιγμέναι γὰρ ἦσαν καὶ οἴκοθεν ἄλλαι νῆες—καὶ στρατηγοὶ—, καὶ τὰς ἀπὸ Χίου πάσας καὶ τὰς ἄλλας ξυναγαγόντες ἐβούλοντο &c.: Id. I. 115 τῶν δὲ Σαμίων ἦσαν γάρ τινες οἳ οὐχ ὑπέμενον—, ξυνθέμενοι—ξυμμαχίαν,—διέβησαν ὑπὸ νύκτα εἰς τὴν Σάμον.

Obs. 6. The premiss is often placed first, when, as being opposed to the conclusion, it is introduced by ἀλλά: Hdt. IX. 27 ἀλλ' οὐ γὰρ ἐν τοιῷδε τάξιος εἵνεκα στασιάζειν πρέπει, ἄρτιοί εἰμεν πείθεσθαι ὑμῖν. We generally find ἀλλὰ γάρ, *at enim, sed enim*: Plat. Apol. p. 19 C μή πως ἐγὼ ὑπὸ Μελήτου τοσαύτας δίκας φύγοιμι! ἀλλὰ γὰρ ἐμοὶ τούτων —οὐδὲν μέτεστι,= *but I have no share*, and *for I have no share*: Ibid. p. 20 C ἐγὼ γοῦν καὶ αὐτὸς ἐκαλλυνόμην τε καὶ ἡβρυνόμην ἄν, εἰ ἠπιστάμην ταῦτα ἀλλ' οὐ γὰρ ἐπίσταμαι, but indeed I know not: so especially in Plato we find νῦν δέ—γάρ used, which however stands after the sentence it explains: Plat. Symp. p. 180 C εἰ μὲν γὰρ εἷς ἦν ὁ Ἔρως, καλῶς ἂν εἶχε νῦν δὲ οὐ γάρ ἐστιν εἷς.

2. Γάρ is used as explanatory and consequential together, in addresses, wishes, orders, questions: Arist. Ran. 248 τουτὶ παρ' ὑμῶν λαμβάνω; Δεινὰ γὰρ πεισόμεθα! then we shall suffer monstrous things! Κακῶς γὰρ ἐξόλοιο! may you then perish! so εἰ γάρ, εἴθε γάρ.

Obs. 7. In καὶ γάρ, καί belongs to the word next following, and signifies *even;* γάρ has attached itself to καί, being the first word in the sentence, though γάρ in poetry sometimes takes the third place; as, ἀπὸ γάρ Eur.: Hdt. I. 77 καὶ γὰρ πρὸς τούτους αὐτῷ ἐπεποίητο συμμαχίη, i. e. καὶ πρὸς τούτους.

Consequence.

a. Ἄρα.

§. 787. 1. Ἄρα (Epic ἄρα and ἄρ; enclit. ῥά; never stands in the beginning of a sentence, but in the first part thereof;) is connected with the verb ΑΡΩ, *to answer, to suit,* and expresses the intimate connection and coincidence of two thoughts or notions, so that one exactly suits and answers to the other; it signifies, *exactly, precisely, just.*

2. Hence Homer uses ἄρα,

a. In correlative sentences of place, time, mode or manner, *exactly, that, which—there, where—then, when—so, as*: Il. η, 182 ἐκ δ' ἔθορε κλῆρος κυνέης, ὃν ἄρ' ἤθελον αὐτοί, just the one which: Il. ν, 594 Ἀτρεΐδης—τῷ (χεῖρα) βάλεν, ᾗ ῥ' ἔχε τόξον, just the one in which: Il. λ, 149 ὁ δ', ὅθι πλεῖστοι κλονέοντο φάλαγγες, τῇ ῥ' ἐνόρουσ', just there: Il. ω, 788 ἦμος δ' ἠριγένεια φάνη ῥοδοδάκτυλος Ἠώς, τῆμος ἄρ' ἀμφὶ πυρὴν κλυτοῦ Ἕκτορος ἔγρετο λαός, just then; so εὖτ' ἄρα, ὅτ' ἄρα, just as, just when: τότ' ἄρα, just then: εἰ μὴ ἄρα, if not exactly: ὡς ἄρα, just so.

b. If by means of a pronoun a preceding object is again brought forward as the commencement of a new thought, ἄρα is used to refer back to it—*exactly him who*: Il. ν, 170 Τεῦκρος δὲ πρῶτος Τελαμώνιος ἄνδρα κατέκτα Ἴμβριον αἰχμητήν: v. 177 τόν ῥ' υἱὸς Τελαμῶνος ὑπ' οὔατος ἔγχεϊ μακρῷ νύξ': so ταῦτ' ἄρα, τοῖος ἄρα, τόσος ἄρα, τῷ ἄρα, τῇ ἄρα, ἔνθ' ἄρα, ὡς ἄρα, e. g. φωνήσας ἀπέβη, ὃς ῥα, he who, in a demonstrative force. Often the confirmative μέν (§. 729. *Obs.* 2.) comes between the pronoun and ἄρα: Il. β, 867 Νάστης αὖ Κιρῶν ἡγήσατο: v. 870 τῶν μὲν ἄρ' Ἀμφίμαχος καὶ Νάστης ἡγησάσθην: and sometimes ῥά is thus used with other words, as ἦ ῥα.

c. In the following combination of particles, ἄρα expresses the union of two thoughts, by marking that a sentence is immediately connected with what went before, and expresses exactly what it has expressed: a. τὰ μὲν ἄρ—ἀλλά, that is just so, but: Od. λ, 139 Τειρεσίη, τὰ μὲν ἄρ που ἐπέκλωσαν θεοὶ αὐτοί. Ἀλλ' ἄγε μοι τόδε εἰπέ—. β. οὐκ—, ἀλλ' ἄρα, not—but just; negative, οὐδ' ἄρα, but precisely not. The thing spoken of is represented as holding good without any reference to circumstances which might accompany any event: Od. κ, 214 οὐδ' οἵγ' (leones et lupi Circæ) ὡρμήθησαν ἐπ' ἀνδράσιν, ἀλλ' ἄρα τοίγε οὐρῇσιν μακρῇσι περισσαίνοντες ἀνέσταν (it was just so): Il. ψ, 670 ἦ οὐχ ἅλις, ὅττι μάχης ἐπιδεύομαι; οὐδ' ἄρα πῶς ἦν, ἐν πάντεσσ' ἔργοισι δαήμονα φῶτα γενέσθαι, but it was just not possible: so οὔτ' ἄρα—οὔτε: Il. ζ, 349 sqq. αὐτὰρ ἐπεὶ τάδε γ' ὧδε θεοὶ κακὰ τεκμήραντο, ἀνδρὸς ἔπειτ' ὤφελον (debebam) ἀμείνονος εἶναι ἄκοιτις—· τούτῳ δ' οὔτ' ἄρ νῦν φρένες ἔμπεδοι, οὔτ' ἄρ' ὀπίσσω ἔσονται, but my present spouse has just neither—nor. Οὔτ' ἄρα—οὔτε begins a speech when the speaker opposes some false notion: Il. α, 93 οὔτ' ἄρ' ὅγ' εὐχωλῆς ἐπιμέμφεται, οὔθ' ἑκατόμβης, ἀλλ' ἕνεκ' ἀρητῆρος—. γ. ἀλλ' εἰ δή ῥα, with the finite verb; as, ἐθέλεις, if it is in sooth (δή) just (ἄρα) your will: δ. ἐπεὶ ῥα, since just, γάρ ῥα, for just.

§. 788. 1. From this notion of immediate connection and coincidence of two things, ἄρα has the further force of the progression and continuation of any action—hence it is used in Epic in narratives, to connect the several thoughts and events thereof: Il. ε, 592 ἅμα δὲ Τρώων εἵποντο φάλαγγες καρτεραί· ἦρχε δ' ἄρα σφιν Ἄρης καὶ πότνι' Ἐνυώ: so καὶ ῥα; οὐδ' ἄρα; οὔτ' ἄρ—οὔτε; μέν ῥα—ἀλλά, αὐτάρ, δέ; τίς τ' ἄρ, τί τ' ἄρ, πῶς τ' ἄρ &c. when the narration is continued by a question; also in explanations or illustrations, which are connected immediately with that which they explain, and are, as it were, a drawing out and development thereof: Il. μ, 152 μάλα γὰρ κρατερῶς ἐμάχοντο λαοῖσιν καθύπερθε πεποιθότες ἠδὲ βίηφιν· οἱ δ' ἄρα (λαοὶ) χερμαδίοισιν εὐδμήτων ἀπὸ πύργων βάλλον, these to wit: Il. ε, 333 οὐδὲ θεάων τάων, αἵ τ' ἀνδρῶν πόλεμον κάτα κοιρανέουσιν, οὔτ' ἄρ' Ἀθηναίη, οὔτε πτολίπορθος Ἐνυώ: Od. ε, 175 τῶν δ' ἀνδρῶν πειρήσομαι, οἵτινές εἰσιν· ἦ ῥ' οἵγ' ὑβρισταί—ἠὲ φιλόξεινοι. Often in relative sentences used to explain or illustrate: Il. β, 20 στῆ δ' ἄρ' ὑπὲρ κεφαλῆς, Νηληΐῳ υἷι ἐοικώς, Νέστορι, τόν ῥα μάλιστα γερόντων τῖ' Ἀγαμέμνων: so ὅτι ῥα, ἐπεὶ ῥα, οὕνεκ' ἄρα, since to wit—hence: γάρ (from γὲ ἄρ) and even γάρ ῥα.

2. In this use of ἄρα is often implied the notion of *quickness*; hence there arises a second sense of ἄρα, *so soon, so forth, as soon as*; and thus it is often joined to the adverbs, αἶψα, αὐτίκα, καρπαλίμως, θοῶς, ἐσσυμένως. (Hence the compounds, αὐτάρ, at, = αὖτ' ἄρ—εἶθαρ = εὖθα from εὐθύς and ἄρα—ἄφαρ.) This usage also belongs to Homer: Il. κ, 349 sqq. ὡς ἄρα φωνήσαντε παρὲξ ὁδοῦ ἐν νεκύεσσιν κλινθήτην· ὁ δ' ἄρ' ὦκα παρέδραμεν ἀφραδίῃσιν· ἀλλ' ὅτε δή ῥ' ἀπέην, ὅσσον τ' ἐπίουρα πέλονται ἡμιόνων —, τὼ μὲν ἐπιδραμέτην· ὁ δ' ἄρ' ἔστη δοῦπον ἀκούσας —, ἀλλ' ὅτε δή ῥ' ἄπεσαν δουρηνεκές —, γνῶ ῥ' ἄνδρας δηΐους. So very commonly, δ' ἄρ, καὶ ῥα.

3. Ἄρα also has this force in the combinations of (a) ἐπεί ῥα, ὅτε ῥα, as soon as (both in the protasis and apodosis); ὅτε δή ῥα—, καὶ τότ' ἄρ, so soon—then straightway; or in the apodosis alone, ὅτε δή —, δή ῥα τότε, then straightway; ἦμος —, καὶ τότε δή ῥα;—(b) μέν ῥα—, αὐτάρ, ἀλλὰ δέ; where by the use of μέν, which points forward to the following clause, it is denoted that this clause is a continuance of the former one: Od. β, 148-150 τὼ δ' ἕως (= τέως) μέν ῥ' ἐπέτοντο —,

ἀλλ' ὅτε δή κ. τ. λ.—(c) οὐδ' ἄρα, where οὐ either belongs to the ἄρα (*not so soon*), or to the predicate (*straightway—not*) : Od. ι, 92 οὐδ' ἄρα Λωτοφάγοι μήδονθ' ἑτάροισιν ὄλεθρον, *but not straightway* : Od. μ, 16 ἡμεῖ μὲν τὰ ἔκαστα διείπομεν· οὐδ' ἄρα Κίρκην ἐξ Ἀΐδεω ἐλθόντες ἐλήθομεν, ἀλλὰ μάλ' ὦκα ἦλθ', and straightway we did not remain any longer.

4. The notion of quickness suggests the notion of *suddenness, surprise*, and therefore ἄρα is used to denote things, that from their size, beauty, sublimity, singularity, &c. come suddenly and unexpectedly upon the mind, so as to produce surprise and wonder thereat. So when an error, delusion, or any other strange thing is spoken of. In English this is frequently expressed by *then* : Il. π, 33 νηλεές ! οὐκ ἄρα σοί γε (sc. Achilli) πατὴρ ἦν ἱππότα Πηλεύς, οὐδὲ Θέτις μήτηρ· γλαυκὴ δέ σε τίκτε θάλασσα.

5. Ἄρα is very often used in this latter sense in Ionic and Attic prose: Plat. Rep. p. 375 D οὐκ ἐνενοήσαμεν, ὅτι εἰσὶν ἄρα τοιαῦται φύσεις, οἵας ἡμεῖς οὐκ ᾠήθημεν, "*ἄρα significat, aliquid praeter opinionem accidere* [a]." So without a negative : Xen. Cyr. l. 4, 11 ὦ παῖδες, ὡς ἄρα ἐφλυαροῦμεν, ὅτε τὰ ἐν τῷ παραδείσῳ θηρία ἐθηρῶμεν· ὅμοιον ἔμοιγε δοκεῖ εἶναι, οἷόνπερ εἴ τις δεδεμένα ζῶα θηρῴη. So when the writer is narrating what produced surprise at the time. The discovery of a mistake is also expressed by ἄρα, when a person finding it out from some one else, does something which signifies that he also feels it, so that ἄρα is used nearly in its Epic force of αὐτίκα : Xen. Cyr. VII. 3, 6 ταῦτα ἀκούσας ὁ Κῦρος ἐπαίσατο ἄρα τὸν μηρόν, he straightway : Ibid. VIII. 3, 25 Σάκαν δὲ ἰδιώτης ἀνὴρ ἀπέλιπεν ἄρα τῷ ἵππῳ τοὺς ἄλλους ἐγγὺς τῷ ἡμίσει τοῦ δρόμου (then, would one have thought it ?) Here also belong the combinations εἰ ἄρα, *if at all events;* εἰ μὴ ἄρα, often ironical, *nisi forte.*

§. 789. Ἄρα as an expression of something unexpected is especially applied (*a*) in explanations and illustrations (ἄρα *explicativum*) ; (*b*) in sentences expressing the consequences of any thing (ἄρα *conclusivum*).

a. The explicative ἄρα denotes that some explanation or information is conveyed suddenly and unexpectedly, *now* : Il. α, 96 τοὔνεκ' ἄρ' ἄλγε' ἔδωκεν Ἑκηβόλος: Xen. Cyr. I. 3, 9 ὦ Σάκα, ἀπόλωλας· ἐκβαλῶ σε ἐκ τῆς τιμῆς· τί τε γὰρ ἄλλα—σοῦ κάλλιον οἰνοχοήσω καὶ οὐκ ἐκπίομαι αὐτὸς τὸν οἶνον· οἱ δ' ἄρα τῶν βασιλέων οἰνοχόοι—καταρροφοῦσι. Hence γάρ, which is also accompanied by ἄρα when a strange or surprising thought is to be expressed : Plat. Rep. p. 358 C πολὺ γὰρ ἀμείνων ἄρα ὁ τοῦ ἀδίκου ἢ ὁ τοῦ δικαίου βίος, ὡς λέγουσιν, *scilicet :* Ibid. p. 438 A οὐδεὶς ποτοῦ ἐπιθυμεῖ, ἀλλὰ χρηστοῦ ποτοῦ—· πάντες γὰρ ἄρα τῶν ἀγαθῶν ἐπιθυμοῦσω, *omnes scilicet etc.*

b. The conclusive force of ἄρα was not developed till the Attic aera. It marks an unexpected consequence ; for emphasis sake it sometimes stands at the end of a sentence : Hdt. III. 64 τὸ δὲ χρηστήριον τοῖσι ἐν Συρίῃ Ἀγβατάνοισι ἔλεγε ἄρα : Xen. Hell. VII. 1, 32 οὕτω κοινόν τι ἄρα χαρᾷ καὶ λύπῃ δάκρυά ἐστιν !—δὲ ἄρα signifies *contradiction* : Plat. Apol. p. 34 C ἐγὼ δὲ οὐδὲν ἄρα τούτων ποιήσω : "*δὲ ἄρα indicat contrarium illud, quod ex praecedentibus colligitur, esse absurdum neque ullo modo probandum, contineique deductionis ad absurdum quam dialectici vocant significationem, sive quis suam ipsius sententiam enuntiet, sive ex alius cujusdam mente loquatur* [a] :" Id. Rep. p. 600 D ἀλλὰ Πρωταγόρας μὲν ἄρα — καὶ Πρόδικος— ἐπὶ ταύτῃ τῇ σοφίᾳ οὕτω σφόδρα φιλοῦνται—, Ὅμηρον δ' ἄρα οἱ ἐπ' ἐκείνου— ἢ Ἡσίοδον ῥαψῳδεῖν ἂν περιϊόντας εἴων ;

---

[a] Stallb. ad loc.

Obs. The lyric, tragic, and comic poets used the lengthened ἄρα for ἄρα : Eur. Phœn. 1669 νὺξ ἄρ᾽ ἐκείνη Δαναΐδων μ᾽ ἕξει μίαν : so εἰ ἄρα, εἶτ᾽ ἄρα for εἰ ἄρα, εἶτ᾽ ἄρα. For ἄρα, and ἄρα interrogative see *Index.*

Τοίνυν.

§. 790. 1. Τοίνυν (from τῷ, *wherefore,* and νύν, *then,* §. 719. 3.) is used in (*a*) transitions—(*b*) conclusions—*wherefore then.* Often in transitions, καὶ τοίνυν, ἔτι τοίνυν, are found : Xen. Cyr. I. 3, 16 ὅτι —ὁ διδάσκαλός με ὡς ἤδη ἀκριβοῦντα τὴν δικαιοσύνην καὶ ἄλλοις καθίστη δικάζειν· καὶ τοίνυν — ἐπὶ μιᾷ ποτε δίκῃ πληγὰς ἔλαβον, *et, ut paucis me expediam :* Ibid. I. 2 πάσας τοίνυν τὰς ἀγέλας ταύτας ἐδοκοῦμεν ὁρᾶν μᾶλλον ἐθελούσας πείθεσθαι τοῖς νομεῦσιν ἢ τοὺς ἀνθρώπους τοῖς ἄρχουσι, *omnes igitur g r e g e s, ut rem paucis complectar.*

2. Τοίνυν is also used to mark a transition when a person takes up another person quickly, and replies to him decidedly : Plat. Rep. p. 450 A δέδοκται ἡμῖν τοῦτο, ὃ σὺ ἤκουσας, τὸ σὲ μὴ μεθιέναι, πρὶν ἂν ταῦτα πάντα ὥσπερ τἆλλα διέλθῃς. Καὶ ἐμὲ τοίνυν, ὁ Γλαύκων ἔφη, κοινωνὸν τῆς ψήφου ταύτης τίθετε. So οὐ τοίνυν, μὴ τοίνυν, μὲν τοίνυν in transitions, where οὐ, μή, μέν mark an opposition in the new thought.

Τοίγαρ.

3. Τοίγαρ (from τῷ and γάρ) answers to the Latin *e r g o, therefore :* Il. a, 76 ὦ Ἀχιλεῦ, κέλεαί με—μυθήσασθαι μῆνιν Ἀπόλλωνος—᾽ τοίγαρ ἐγὼν ἐρέω. It generally stands at the beginning of the sentence.

Τοιγάρτοι.

4. Τοιγάρτοι (from τῷ, *wherefore,* γάρ, and the restrictive τοί) *just so, and on no other ground.* It always stands first in the sentence : Plat. Gorg. p. 471 C τοιγάρτοι νῦν, ἅτε μέγιστα ἠδικηκὼς τῶν ἐν Μακεδονίᾳ, ἀθλιώτατός ἐστι πάντων Μακεδόνων.

Obs. This τοί used in τοίνυν, τοίγαρ, τοιγάρτοι is to be distinguished from the restrictive τοί, which is never used by itself to express transitions or conclusions, but is so used with other particles ; and we may observe that it always follows the particle with which it is joined. Τοί joined with καί expresses a transition — with γάρ, ἐπεί, sometimes with γέ, a conclusion : Xen. Cyr. VIII. 7, 17 οὐδὲ γὰρ νῦν τοι τὴν γ᾽ ἐμὴν ψυχὴν ἑωρᾶτε. In οὔτοι and ἤ τοι, τοί expresses a transition with a further adversative notion which arises from οὐ and ἤ : Il. γ, 65 οὔτοι ἀπόβλητ᾽ ἐστὶ θεῶν ἐρικυδέα δῶρα, *no, truly not :* Soph. Œ. C. 1366 εἰ δ᾽ ἐξέφυσα τάσδε μὴ 'μαυτῷ τροφοὺς τάσδε παῖδας, ἤ τἂν οὐκ ἂν ἦν, τὸ σὸν μέρος. So οὔτοι (μήτοι) more generally have an adversative force, *yet not—not only.*

Οὖν.

§. 791. 1. Οὖν is used as an illative particle very rarely in Homer, and only in certain combinations, as ἐπεὶ οὖν, ὡς οὖν. It never stands first, but generally second in the sentence. As οὖν properly dwells and lays emphasis on the circumstances under which the thing to which it is attached took place (§. 737. 2.), so as an illative particle it points strongly to what has gone before, so that the premises and conclusion are represented as one thought.   So οὖν, illative, is used by Homer with ἐπεί and ὡς (ἐπεὶ οὖν, ὡς οὖν), because these conjunctions introduce sentences which lead us back to what has gone before, so that the mind dwells thereon : Od. π, 453 οἱ δ᾽ ἄρα δόρπον ἐπισταδὸν ὡπλίσαντο—v. 478 οἱ δ᾽ ἐπεὶ οὖν παύσαντο πόνου τετύκοντό τε δαῖτα : Il. θ, 249 πὰρ δὲ Διὸς βωμῷ περικαλλῆ κάββαλε νεβρόν, ἔνθα πανομφαίῳ Ζηνὶ ῥέζεσκον Ἀχαιοί.   Οἱ δ᾽ ὡς οὖν εἶδον ὅτ᾽ ἄρ᾽ ἐκ Διὸς ἦλυθεν ὄρνις.

2. It often means *denique, without more to say* ; so that it is used especially to resume a sentence which has been broken by a parenthesis. The following combinations also occur, τοιγαροῦν, οὐκ οὖν, οὐδ᾽ οὖν, καὶ οὖν &c.

Obs. It is generally laid down that οὔκουν means *not*, οὐκοῦν *therefore*, the accent being placed over that part of the word the sense of which prevails ; but this is not right.   When it is negative it should be written οὐκ οὖν, when it means *therefore*, οὐκοῦν, with a note of interrogation, *Is it not then?* whence arises its ironical force of *s c i l i c e t*, the question being dropped in the pronunciation : Demosth. p. 104, 59 ἢ καὶ τότε τοὺς ἀμύνεσθαι ἐθέλοντας πόλεμον ποιεῖν φήσομεν ; οὐκοῦν ὑπόλοιπον δουλεύειν, does not then slavery await us ?=therefore slavery awaits us.

Remarks on the Asyndeton.

§. 792. 1. From the general rule, that sentences which are logically one thought should be also represented as one in language by conjunctions, there are certain exceptions ; sentences, which are really connected together following one another, without any conjunction to denote the connection : this is called *Asyndeton* (ἀσύνδετον).

a. An asyndeton can properly only take place when sentences, which are in the same logical and grammatical relations to each other, are not connected by a conjunction.   By the omission of the conjunction, the successive thoughts are represented as following one another so rapidly that they are but one thought, and are taken in as it were by one glance of the mind.   So repeatedly in Homer after αὐτίκα, and after εὗρεν following βῆ : Od. ι, 154 ὦρσαν δὲ Νύμφαι, κοῦραι Διὸς αἰγιόχοιο, αἶγας ὀρεσκῴους, ἵνα δειπνήσειαν ἑταῖροι. Αὐτίκα καμπύλα τόξα καὶ αἰγανέας δολιχαύλους εἱλόμεθ᾽ ἐκ νηῶν : Il. λ, 196 βῆ δὲ κατ᾽ Ἰδαίων ὀρέων εἰς Ἴλιον ἱρήν· εὗρ᾽ υἱὸν Πριάμοιο δαΐφρονος Ἕκτορα δῖον.   And as here the notion of αὐτίκα produces the asyndeton, so in pathetic passages also, the rapidity of the whole speech throws out the conjunctive particles.   In an animated description also, the thoughts are crowded together into one.   The Lyric, which loved pathetic, and often unconnected and sudden, turns of construction, frequently uses asyndeton, but more rarely the more stately and equable Epic.   But even prose writers, especially the orators, sometimes allow themselves in animated descriptions to drop the conjunction : Il. χ, 295 (of Hector) στῆ δὲ κατηφήσας, οὐδ᾽ ἀλλ᾽ ἔχε μείλινον ἔγχος· Δηΐφοβον δ᾽ ἐκάλει λευκάσπιδα, μακρὸν ἀΰσας, ἦ τε ἕ μιν δόρυ μακρόν— : Ibid. 450 sq. (of Andromache) δεῦτε, δύω μοι ἕπεσθον, ἴδωμ᾽, ὅτιν᾽ ἔργα τέτυκται.   Αἰδοίης ἑκυρῆς ὀπὸς ἔκλυον κ. τ. λ. : Eur. Hippol. 352 sqq. οἴμοι τί λέξεις, τέκνον ; ὡς μ᾽ ἀπώλεσας· γυναῖκες, οὐκ ἀνάσχετ᾽, οὐκ ἀνέξομαι ζῶσ᾽· ἐχθρὸν ἦμαρ, ἐχθρὸν εἰσορῶ φάος· ῥίψω, μεθήσω σῶμ᾽· ἀπαλλαχθήσομαι βίου θανοῦσα· χαίρετ᾽· οὐκ ἔτ᾽ εἴμ᾽ ἐγώ.

b. The asyndeton also takes place between two sentences which are grammatically coordinate, but one of which is logically subordinate.   By the omission of the conjunction the second clause is represented as a new, important, unexpected point in the narration : Il. ρ, 50 δούπησεν δὲ πεσὼν, ἀράβησε δὲ τεύχε' ἐπ' αὐτῷ. Αἵματί οἱ δεύοντο κόμαι, Χαρίτεσσιν ὁμοῖαι, πλοχμοί θ', οἳ χρυσῷ τε καὶ ἀργύρῳ ἐσφήκωντο.   So the end of a long train of thought is given with a beautiful emphasis by the asyndeton : Il. χ, 391 (*Achilles Hectore interempto*) νῦν δ' ἄγ' ἀείδοντες παιήονα — νεώμεθα, τόνδε δ' ἄγωμεν. Ἠράμεθα μέγα κῦδος· ἐπέφνομεν Ἕκτορα δῖον, ᾧ Τρῶες κατὰ ἄστυ θεῷ ὣς εὐχετόωντο : Pind. Pyth. II. 49 after relating the punishment of Ixion, θεὸς ἅπαν ἐπὶ ἐλπίδεσσι τέκμαρ ἀνύεται, θεὸς ὃ καὶ πτερόεντ' αἰετὸν κίχε &c.

c. It is very common in explanatory sentences, which would be introduced by ἄρα, or γάρ. The second clause defines or explains that which is generally or unclearly stated in the first ; so Il. φ, 654 πυγμαχίης ἀλεγεινῆς θῆκεν ἄεθλα· ἡμίονον ταλαεργὸν ἄγων κατέδησ' ἐν ἀγῶνι : Il. β, 217 αἴσχιστος δὲ ἀνὴρ ὑπὸ Ἴλιον ἦλθεν· φολκὸς ἔην, χωλὸς δ' ἕτερον πόδα κ. τ. λ. : Il. ω, 608 οὕνεκ' ἄρα Λητοῖ ἰσάσκετο καλλιπαρῄῳ· φῆ δοιὼ τεκέειν, ἡ δ' αὐτὴ γείνατο πολλούς : Il. ν, 46 ἀλλὰ Ποσειδάων — Ἀργείους ὤτρυνε — Αἴαντε πρώτω προσέφη : Pind. Ol. II. 44 ἕπεται δὲ λόγος εὐθρόνοις Κάδμοιο κούραις, ἔπαθον αἱ μεγάλα, πένθος δ' ἐπιτνεν βαρὺ κρεσσόνων πρὸς ἀγαθῶν. Ζώει μὲν ἐν Ὀλυμπίοις ἀποθανοῖσα βρόμῳ κεραυνοῦ τανυέθειρα Σεμέλα κ. τ. λ.   So especially when a demonstrative stands in the first clause ; as, τοῦτο, τόδε, οὕτως, ὧδε &c. : Plat. Gorg. p. 450 A καὶ μὴν καὶ αἱ ἄλλαι τέχναι οὕτως ἔχουσιν, ἑκάστη αὐτῶν περὶ λόγους ἐστι : Xen. Anab. III. 2, 19 ἐνὶ μόνῳ προέχουσιν ἡμᾶς οἱ ἱππεῖς, φεύγειν αὐτοῖς ἀσφαλέστερόν ἐστιν, ἢ ἡμῖν. But here also the real cause of the asyndeton may be the animation of the speech : Demosth. p. 44 princ. καὶ δὲ πειράσομαι λέγων, δεηθεὶς ὑμῶν, ὦ ἄνδρες Ἀθηναῖοι, τοσοῦτον· ἐπειδὰν ἅπαντα ἀκούσητε, κρίνατε, μὴ πρότερον προλαμβάνετε. Generally after such a demonstrative we find γάρ (§. 786. l. β.). But it is used also with supplementary clauses, where γάρ would not be used : Xen. Anab. I. 8, 9 καὶ ἦσαν ἱππεῖς μὲν λευκοθώρακες ἐπὶ τοῦ εὐωνύμου τῶν πολεμίων· Τισσαφέρνης ἐλέγετο τούτων ἄρχειν.

d. So when the same thoughts are emphatically repeated in other words : Pindar Pyth. III. 107 σμικρὸς ἐν σμικροῖς, μέγας ἐν μεγάλοις ἔσσομαι· τὸν ἀμφέποντ' αἰεὶ φρασὶν δαίμον' ἀσκήσω κατ' ἐμὰν θεραπεύων μαχανάν).

e. Cognate to this is the asyndeton, which occurs in the beginning of a new sentence, which is begun to explain a preceding one : Plat. Phædon. p. 91 C Ἀλλ' ἰτέον, ἔφη. Πρῶτόν με ὑπομνήσατε ἃ ἐλέγετε, ἐὰν μὴ φαίνωμαι μεμνημένος.

f. Often the conjunction, though not expressed, is to a certain degree implied in some other words ; especially in demonstratives, which point back to what has preceded, and thus connect the sentences—so very often in Homer, ὣς ἔφατ'.   That the demonstratives οὕτως, τόσος, τοῖος, &c. often imply γάρ, as in Latin, *sic, talis, tantus* imply *enim*, we have seen, (§. 786. *Obs.* 2.)

g. The asyndeton naturally occurs when the unconnected sentence is opposed to what has gone before, or comes after : Od. μ, 426 sqq. ἔνθ' ἤτοι Ζέφυρος μὲν ἐπαύσατο—ἦλθε δ' ἐπὶ Νότος ὦκα· παννύχιος φερόμην, ἅμα δ' ἠελίῳ ἀνιόντι ἦλθον ἐπὶ Σκύλλης σκόπελον : Od. δ, 605 sq. ἐν δ' Ἰθάκῃ οὔτ' ἂρ δρόμοι εὐρέες, οὔτε τι λειμών· αἰγίβοτος sc. ἐστίν : Il. ψ, 352 sq. ἂν δ' ἔβαν ἐς δίφρους, ἐν δὲ κλήρους ἐβάλοντο· πάλλ' Ἀχιλεύς. So in Homer the adversative conjunction is often dropped when the opposition of a sentence introduced by εὖτε=ὅτε or ὄφρα is expressed : Od. ω, 146 sqq. ὡς τὸ μὲν ἐξετέλεσσε καὶ οὐκ ἐθέλουσ', ὑπ' ἀνάγκης.   Εὖθ' ἡ φᾶρος ἔδειξεν, ὑφήνασα μέγαν ἱστόν—, καὶ τότε δή ῥ' Ὀδυσῆα κακός κτλ ἤγαγε δαίμων, (but) when she &c.

2. Besides these general cases of asyndeton, there are the following:

h. Very commonly before τὰ τοιαῦτα, *cetera*, ἄλλα, οἱ ἄλλοι, in the enumeration of many objects καί is omitted, as in Latin *et* before *ceteri, alii, reliqui*, when these signify collectively all the objects which yet remain to be mentioned: Plat. Gorg. p. 503 E οἶον εἰ βούλει ἰδεῖν τοὺς ζωγράφους, τοὺς οἰκοδόμους, τοὺς ναυπηγούς, τ ο ὺ ς ἄ λ λ ο υ ς πάντας δημιουργούς.

i. When several objects, especially if they run in pairs, are enumerated: Plat. Protag. p. 319 D πλούσιος, πένης, γενναῖος, ἀγεννής: Cic. Tusc. I. 26, 64 *ut omnia, supera, infera, prima, ultima, media videremus*[a].

k. When the same word is to be emphatically repeated (*anaphora*): Plat. Gorg. p. 510 C ο ὗ τ ο ς μέγα ἐν ταύτῃ τῇ πόλει δυνήσεται, τ ο ῦ τ ο ν οὐδεὶς χαίρων ἀδικήσει.

l. The phrase ἐ δ ό κ ε ι τ α ῦ τ α, *et simil.* is always inserted without any conjunction, after a question, or address, the result whereof is signified by these words:—generally the same word which is used in the first is used in the second unconnected clause: Xen. Anab. III. 2, 38 ἐπεὶ δὲ οὐδεὶς ἀντέλεγεν, εἶπεν· Ὅτῳ δοκεῖ ταῦτα, ἀνατεινάτω τὴν χεῖρα. Ἔδοξε τ α ῦ τ α : Ibid. VI. 3, 9 ἐνταῦθα ὁ Ξενοφῶν λέγει· Δοκεῖ μοι, ὦ ἄνδρες στρατηγοί—. Συνεδόκει ταῦτα πᾶσι: Ibid. VII. 3, 6 καὶ ὅτῳ, ἔφη, ταῦτα δοκεῖ, ἀράτω τὴν χεῖρα. Ἀνέτειναν πάντες.

m. In poetry, (especially Epic) two or four adjectives, each pair whereof forms one whole notion, or also three adjectives belonging to one substantive, follow one another without any conjunction, if they are merely epithets and ornaments of the substantive. The greatest effect is produced by the adjectives being divided into pairs, as the sentence is broken off suddenly, and contrary to our expectation, while, on the other hand, three adjectives form a natural and pleasing period : Il. π, 140. 802 ἔγχος βριθύ, μέγα, στιβαρόν, κεκορυθμένον: Od. a, 97 καλὰ πέδιλα, ἀμβρόσια, χρύσεα: Od. ι, 205 οἶνον — ἡδὺν, ἀκηράσιον, θεῖον ποτόν: Ibid. 319 sq. Κύκλωπος γὰρ ἔκειτο μέγα ῥόπαλον παρὰ σηκῷ, χλωρόν, ἐλαΐνεον: Ibid. 322 sq. ἱστὸν νηὸς ἐεικοσόροιο μελαίνης, φορτίδος, εὐρείης, ἥτ' ἐκπεράᾳ μέγα λαῖτμα: Od. o, 406 (νῆσος) εὔβοτος, εὔμηλος, οἰνοπληθής, πολύπυρος : Æsch. Sept. 861 ἐρατῶν ἐκ βαθυκόλπων στηθέων: Soph. Trach. 770 φοινίας ἐχθρᾶς ἐχίδνης: Eur. Hipp. 668 τάλανες ὦ κακοτυχεῖς γυναικῶν πότμοι.

THE SUBORDINATE SENTENCE.

Substantival Clauses.

§. 793. 1. When sentences, which together represent but one thought in the speaker's mind, stand in such a relation to each other, that one expresses merely the causes, results, circumstances, accidents, &c. which accompany the other, and therefore has of itself no definite meaning or place in the passage independent of the other, there are two different ways of expressing this con-

---

[a] Vid. Adnot. ad loc.

nection; either the real logical relation is overlooked, and they are joined by a copula, which probably would be the original method before the niceties of language had developed themselves, as τὸ ἔαρ ἦλθε, τὰ δὲ δένδρα θάλλει: or their true logical relation is expressed in the form of the connection, by using a word which represents the one as depending on the other, as ὅτε τὸ ἔαρ ἦλθε, τὰ δένδρα θάλλει. This is called the *subordinate construction.*

2. The essence then of the subordinate construction is, that two or more thoughts are represented as forming one compound thought, the parts whereof are likewise represented in their pro-per relation to each other. The sentence on which the rest de-pend is called the *principal clause,* the dependent sentence or sen-tences *dependent clauses.* Thus in, *The man who came from the enemy's camp informed Cyrus, when the night broke, that the enemy had fled;—the man informed Cyrus,* is the principal, the others the dependent clauses. These may be increased to any number, though necessarily they have a tendency to interrupt and confuse the whole thought.

3. Every dependent sentence expresses a thought, and con-tains the same elements as a principal sentence, (subject and predicate) only that this thought by itself has no definite meaning; as, *when the spring came,* conveys no definite idea to the mind.

§. 794. 1. The compound sentence is in reality nothing more than a development and resolution of the several parts of a simple sentence, which, as we have seen, when complete, consists of sub-ject, predicate, attribute, object; each of which, except the pre-dicate, which is as it were the essential part of the sentence, may be resolved into a fresh sentence, dependent on the predicate; as, *The victory of the famous Cyrus over the enemy was made known to the Persians,* may be resolved into *That Cyrus, who was so famous, had conquered the enemy, was made known to those who dwelt in Persia*: so in ἄνδρα μοι ἔννεπε Μοῦσα πολύτροπον, ὅς μάλα πολλὰ πλάγχθη, the epithet πολύτροπον is resolved into ὅς μάλα &c.: Plat. Rep. p. 496 C τῶν πολλῶν ἱκανῶς ἰδόντες τὴν μανίαν καὶ ὅτι οὐδεὶς αὐτῶν οὐδὲν ὑγιὲς πράττει (=τὴν μανίαν καὶ τὸ μηδὲν ὑγιὲς πράττειν).

2. So long as these members of the sentence (subject, attribute, object) are in a simple form, as the *mortal* man, they generally are not resolved into dependent sentences; or if so, it is for the purpose of giving emphasis to the sentence: but when they stand in a compound form, as *The complete victory of Cyrus over his enemies*—the expansion of one or more of these elements is natural,

and if the compound subject, attribute, or object comprehends many notions within itself, the clearness and flow of the whole sentence is improved by its being resolved into clauses.

3. The subordinate construction is not so frequently used in Greek as it is in English, and most modern languages: our participles do not possess the same powers, so that where the Greeks use with great brevity and facility of expression a participle, we use a dependent sentence, which perhaps is more accurate, as giving the nature of the relation, and the notion of mode and time—though probably the Greeks did not feel this want themselves, from the wonderful power they possessed, of determining from the context the particular nature and properties of any part or member of a sentence. Compare "when he had done this he departed" with "ταῦτα πράξας ἀπέβη"—"when spring is come" with "ἔαρος ἐλθόντος" &c.

Sorts of dependent Sentences.—Conjunctions.

§. 795. 1. As the subject, attribute, object, are expressed by substantives, infinitives, adjectives, participles, and adverbs, it follows that dependent sentences are resolutions of

α. A substantive, or infinitive used as a substantive.—*Substantival sentences.*

β. An adjective or participle.—*Adjectival sentences.*

γ. Adverbs, or cases of substantives used as adverbs.—*Adverbial sentences.*

Under substantival sentences we must class interrogative dependent sentences, as being in reality the object of the governing verb; as, *he asked me whether he was returned*=*he asked after his return.*

2. Though the cases of substantives express the adverbial notions of place, time, reason, means, mode and manner; as, αἰθέρι ναίει, τοῦ Κύρου βασιλεύοντος τοῦτο ἐγένετο, ὕβρει, yet we consider as substantival sentences, those sentences only which are resolutions of substantives forming the subjects or the immediate objects of the action of the verb, and without which its meaning is indefinite; as, ἤγγειλε τὸν τοῦ πατρὸς θάνατον : while those which express any of the above-mentioned adverbial notions are termed *adverbial sentences.*

3. This subordinate relation of one sentence to another is signified by the conjunctions, as opposed to the copulative particles : these conjunctions stand to sentences in the same relation as prepositions to single notions, as defining the relations between them:

to these we must add the relative pronoun, which represents the
inflexions of an adjective or participle. The conjunctions as well
as the relative pronouns are properly correlatives, or words used
as correlatives, referring to some demonstrative, or word used as
demonstrative, in the principal clause ; and as these two, the demonstrative and the relative, as it were, dovetail into each other,
they represent very well the logical unity of the two sentences:
οὗτός ἐστιν ὁ ἀνὴρ, ὃν εἶδες—τὸ ῥόδον, ὃ ἀνθεῖ ἐν τῷ κήπῳ, κάλ-
λιστόν ἐστιν—ἔλεξε τοῦτο, ὅτι (Homer, δ) ὁ ἄνθρωπος ἀθάνατός
ἐστιν; τοῖος, οἷος; ὅσῳ—τοσούτῳ; ὡς προέλεξα, οὕτως
ἐγένετο—οὕτω καλῶς πάντα ἔπραξεν, ὥστε ἐπαίνου μεγίστου ἄξιος
ἦν — ὅτε ὁ Κῦρος ἦλθε, τότε πάντες μεγάλως ἐχάρησαν — ἔμεινε
μέχρι τούτου, οὗ ὁ βασιλεὺς ἐπῆλθεν: so τόφρα, ὅτε—τότε, ὄφρα,
&c. ἐν τούτῳ τῷ χρόνῳ, ὅτε: but when no particular emphasis is
required, the demonstrative is omitted ; as, ἔλεξεν, ὅτι ὁ ἄνθρωπος
ἀθάνατός ἐστιν — καλῶς πάντα ἔπραξεν, ὥστε—ὅτε ὁ Κῦρος ἦλθε,
πάντες μεγάλως ἐχάρησαν — ἔμεινε μέχρις οὗ ὁ βασιλεὺς ἐπῆλθεν:
and even both the pronouns are omitted ; as, ἔμεινε μέχρι ὁ βασιλεὺς
ἐπῆλθεν—ἀπέβη πρὶν ὁ βασιλεὺς ἐπῆλθεν.

Means of distinguishing the sorts of dependent Sentences.

§. 796. The dependent sentences are known one from the
other partly by the demonstrative, either expressed or supplied,
in the principal clause, (a substantival demonstrative denoting
a substantival sentence, &c.) or by the conjunctions by which the
dependent clause is introduced — but these last are not certain
guides—for instance ὥστε may introduce an adverbial, as οὕτω καλός
ἐστιν, ὥστε θαυμάζεσθαι (=θαυμασίως καλός ἐστιν), or
a substantival sentence, as Hdt. VII. ὁ ἀνέπεισε Ξέρξεα, ὥστε
ποιέειν ταῦτα = ἀνέπεισε Ξέρξεα ποιεῖν (accusative, as in
ἀνέπεισε Ξ. τοῦτο). In this case we must determine by the context
what sort of demonstrative is to be supplied in the principal
clause, and thence determine the nature of the dependent :
οὕτω (adverbial demonst.) καλός ἐστιν, ὥστε θαυμάζεσθαι,—ἀνέπεισε Ξέρξεα τοῦτο (substantival demonst.) ὥστε ποιέειν ταῦτα.
The exact force of each conjunction will be elsewhere explained.
It will be sufficient to say at present that

I. Substantival sentences are introduced *a.* by ὅτι and ὡς,
that; *b.* by the final conjunctions ἵνα, ὅπως, ὡς, ὄφρα, ὅπως

μή, and *c.* the interrogative substantival sentences by ἤ, ἆρα, πότερον, ὅστις, ὁποῖος, ὁπόσος, &c.

II. Adjectival sentences by the relative pronouns ὅς, ὅστις, οἷος, ὅσος, &c.

III. Adverbial sentences by *a.* local adverbs; as, οὗ, ὅθεν, οἷ, &c. *b.* temporal conjunctions, as ἐπεί, ἐπειδή, ὡς (when) ὅτε, ἐπήν, ἐπειδάν, ὅταν, &c. — ἡνίκα, ὁπότε, ἕως, πρίν, ὄφρα; *c.* by the causal conjunctions, ὅτι, διότι: *d.* hypothetical conjunctions, εἰ, ἐάν (ἤν, ἄν); *e.* consequential, ὥστε, ὡς, *so that;* *f.* comparative, ὡς, ας, ὅπως, ὥσπερ— (οὕτως); ὅσῳ—(τοσούτῳ.)

Moods and Tenses in the dependent Sentences.

§. 797. 1. Of course the moods have the same force and meaning in the dependent as in the principal clauses, (§. 410.) but there are certain peculiarities of construction of the moods, applicable to the different sorts of dependent sentences, which will be treated of here.

2. With regard to the tenses it may be laid down as a general rule — that the time in the dependent clause refers to and is determined, not by the time present to the speaker, but by the time of the principal clause; so that if the verb of the principal clause express a time present, past, or future to the time then present to the speaker, and hence is either in pres. pft. or fut., the verb of the dependent clause is also in the pres., pft., or fut., as the case may be; as, ἀγγέλλεται, ἤγγελται, ἀγγελθήσεται, ὅτι οἱ πολέμιοι φεύγουσιν—ὅτι οἱ πολέμιοι πεφεύγασιν—ὅτι οἱ πολέμιοι φεύξονται. The pft. may be supplied by the aorist (§. 404.) ἔφυγον.— When a future dependent verb should stand in the conjunct., the pres. or aor. conj. supplies the place of the fut. conj., which does not exist: τοῦτο λέγω, τοῦτό μοι λέλεκται, τοῦτο λέξω, ἵνα γιγνώσκῃς or γνῷς.

3. When the verb of the principal clause is in an historic tense, (impft., plpft., or aorist used as plpft.) the verb of the dependent clause is either in the impft. (ind. or opt.) or plpft., (ind. or opt.) or aorist (ind. or opt.), or the future opt., (for which, however, the fut. ind. is very often used,) according as the verb is to represent the action as present, perfect, or future to past time. The impft. opt., and the aorist opt., are generally used instead of the future opt.: thus ἠγγέλλετο, ἤγγελτο or ἠγγέλθη, ὅτι οἱ πολέμιοι ἔφευγον,

ἐπεφεύγεσαν or ἔφυγον, ὅτι οἱ πολέμιοι φεύξοιντο or φεύξονται—τοῦτο
ἔλεγον, τοῦτό μοι ἐλέλεκτο, ἵν' εἰδείης—ἐδίδουν, ἐδεδώκειν, ἔδωκά σοι
τὸ βιβλίον, ἵνα λάβοις.

Obs. When the principal verb is in the future, and the dependent
verb is to express something which will be past in reference to that future
verb, it does not stand, as in Latin, in the *fut. exactum*; but if the thing is to
be represented as really in existence, in the aorist ind.; or in the fut. ind.,
as if the notion were simply future, and the notion of the perfection of the
action lost sight of; or if merely a supposition is to be signified, in the conj.
aor.; as, εἰ τοῦτο ἐποίησας, εἰ τοῦτο ποιήσεις, ἐὰν τοῦτο ποιήσῃς, πορεύσομαι.
Cf. §. 407. *Obs.* 2.

4. Very often however the tense of the dependent verb is not
determined by the time of the principal verb, but by the time
present to the speaker, so that the same tense follows an historic
tense which would follow one of the principal tenses : Xen. Anab.
II. 1, 3 οὗτοι ἔλεγον, ὅτι Κῦρος—τέθνηκεν: Id. Cyr. I. 2, 3
ἐπεμέλετο ὁ Κῦρος, ὁπότε συσκηνοῖεν, ὅπως εὐχαριστότατοι—λόγοι
ἐμβληθήσονται: Hdt. I. 29 Σόλων ἀπεδήμησε ἔτεα δέκα,
ἵνα δὴ μή τινα τῶν νόμων ἀναγκασθῇ λῦσαι τῶν ἔθετο: (see *Oratio
obliqua*). By this construction a certain vigour is imparted to the
sentence, that which is past being represented as in our presence,
that which has happened as happening before our eyes.

5. But also after the principal tenses we find an historic tense
in the dependent clause. *a.* When the dependent clause stands
in such relations to another dependent clause, that its time is
decided by it, not by the time of the principal verb: Demosth. p.
118, 30 ἴστε, ὅτι, ὅσα μὲν ὑπὸ Λακεδαιμονίων ἢ ὑφ' ἡμῶν ἔπασχον οἱ Ἕλληνες, ἀλλ' οὖν ὑπὸ γνησίων γε ὄντων τῆς Ἑλλάδος ἠδι-
κοῦντο. This also takes place when the verb of the dependent
clause has conditions annexed to it by another sentence : φημὶ, ὅτι,
εἰ τοῦτο λέγοις, ἁμαρτάνοις ἄν — φημὶ, ὅτι, εἰ τοῦτο ἔλεγες
(ἔλεξας), ἥμαρτες ἄν.   *b.* When a past action is to be represented as being in present continuance: Demosth. p. 41, 4 λογι-
σάσθω (taken as present) μέντοι τοῦθ', ὅτι εἴχομέν ποτε ἡμεῖς
—Πύδναν—καὶ πολλὰ τῶν μετ' ἐκείνου νῦν ὄντων ἐθνῶν αὐτονομούμενα
καὶ ἐλεύθερα ὑπῆρχε, καὶ μᾶλλον ἡμῖν ἐβούλετ' ἔχειν οἰκείως ἢ 'κείνῳ:
Hdt. III. 89 λέγουσι Πέρσαι, ὡς Δαρεῖος μὲν ἦν κάπηλος· Καμβύσης δὲ, δεσπότης· Κῦρος δὲ, πατήρ· ὁ μὲν, ὅτι ἐκαπήλευε πάντα
τὰ πρήγματα· ὁ δὲ, ὅτι χαλεπός τε ἦν καὶ ὀλίγωρος· ὁ δὲ, ὅτι ἤπιός τε
καὶ ἀγαθά σφι πάντα ἐμηχανήσατο.

Remarks.

Interchange of the Clauses.

§. 798. 1. *a.* A substantival sometimes assumes the form of a principal clause, the word expressing the dependent relation being omitted, but only when the verbs οἶμαι, οἶδα, δοκῶ, ὁρᾷς, ὁρᾶτε precede : Thuc. l. 3 δοκεῖ δέ μοι, οὐδὲ τοὔνομα τοῦτο ξύμπασά πω εἶχεν : Plat. Protag. p. 336 B ἀλλ᾽ ὁρᾷς, ἔφη, ὦ Σώκρατες, δίκαια δοκεῖ λέγειν Πρωταγόρας : Xen. Hieron. I. 16 ἀλλ᾽ ὁρᾷς, ἐκεῖνό γ᾽ οὐκ ἂν ἔτι πείσαις ἀνθρώπων οὐδένα. We must not include here the passages where οἶμαι, &c. are little more than adverbs.

b. An adverbial for a substantival clause : θαυμάζω, εἰ σὺ ταῦτα ποιεῖς for ὅτι ταῦτα ποιεῖς = θαυμάζω σε ποιοῦντα : Eur. Hipp. 424 f. δουλοῖ γὰρ ἄνδρα (τοῦτο), κἂν θρασύσπλαγχνός τις ᾖ, ὅταν ξυνειδῇ μητρὸς ἢ πατρὸς κακά.

c. An adjectival clause is used for a substantival : ἦλθον οἱ ἄριστοι ἦσαν (for ἦλθον ἄνδρες, οἱ ἄριστοι ἦσαν), subject ; ἔπεμψεν οἱ ἄριστοι ἦσαν (for ἐπ. τοὺς ἄνδρας, οἱ ἄρ. ἦσαν), object.

Parenthesis.

2. We must not include in the dependent sentences those words or clauses which are inserted in a passage without in any way influencing the construction ; they form indeed part of the whole thought, as expressed in language, but seem to represent an idea or ideas which did not belong to it as it was originally formed, but come into the mind as the thought is passing through, to explain, or modify, or lay emphasis on it, and interrupt for a time the original train of thought, which however returns when the interruption is over ; they are not really connected with either what goes before or follows, and standing as it were alone in the mind, in the middle of the thought, they stand alone in the sentence without in any way influencing its construction : Plat. Phæd. p. 60 A κατελαμβάνομεν τὸν μὲν Σωκράτη ἄρτι λελυμένον, τὴν δὲ Ξανθίππην — γιγνώσκεις γάρ — ἔχουσάν τε τὸ παιδίον αὐτοῦ καὶ παρακαθημένην. Here belong οἶμαι, οἶδα, δοκῶ, ὁρᾷς, ὁρᾶτε : Arist. Thesmoph. 490 ταῦτ᾽ οὐδεπώποτ᾽ εἶφ᾽, ὁρᾶτ᾽, Εὐριπίδης : 496 ταῦθ᾽, ὁρᾷς, οὐδεπώποτ᾽ εἶπεν. Interjections also and the vocative may be looked upon as in a parenthesis.

Substantival Clauses.

§. 799. 1. The substantival clause supplies the place of the subject (nom.), or object of the verb in gen., instrumental dat., and accus. In many instances a demonstrative in the principal clause marks for which of these cases the substant. clause stands, in others it must be discovered from the context ; as, (Nom.) ὅτι ὁ ἄνθρωπος θνητός ἐστι, (τοῦτο) δῆλόν ἐστιν. — (Gen.) (τούτου) πολλάκις ὁ Σωκράτης ὑπέμνησε τοὺς αὐτῷ συνόντας, ὅτι ὁ ἄνθρωπος θνητός ἐστιν.—(Acc.) πάντες ἴσασι (τοῦτο), ὅτι ὁ ἄνθρωπος θνητός ἐστιν.—(Instrumentalis) ἐλυπήθη (τούτῳ), ὅτι ὁ ἄνθρωπος θνητός ἐστιν.

2. The substantive which is resolved into the substantival clause, would stand generally in the cognate accusative (§. 548. 2.); and substantival clauses are divided into those introduced by ὅτι or ὡς (*that*), and those introduced by the final conjunctions ἵνα, ὅπως, ὡς (*so that*), ὄφρα.

Substantival Clauses with ὅτι, ὡς.

§. 800. Substantival clauses introduced by ὅτι (for which Homer also uses ὅ) and ὡς, sometimes ὅπως (and poet. οὕνεκα, trag. ὁθούνεκα for ὅτι, *that*), all of which we translate by *that*, stand for the cognate accusative which follows verbs of mental or sensual perception; as, ὁρᾶν, ἀκούειν, νοεῖν, μανθάνειν, γιγνώσκειν &c. (§. 561. 575.), or the setting forth the same ; as, λέγειν, δηλοῦν, δεικνύναι, ἀγγέλλειν (§. 566.).

Construction of ὅτι, ὡς &c.

§. 801. The verb of the substantival clause may be in

a. Any tense of the Indicative.

b. In the Subjunctive of the Historic Tenses (Optative).

c. In the Subjunctive of the Principal Tenses (Conjunctive).

d. In the Historic Tenses of the Indicat., and in the Conj. or Opt. with ἄν.

Obs. As in these sentences the thing spoken of, though it really exists, is represented not in its character of a really existing thing, as τοῦτό ἐστι, but only as a persuasion, existing or produced in the mind of the speaker, of something past, as λέγει ὅτι τοῦτό ἐστι, it would seem natural that the mood should always be the optative ; but the use of these moods is not only regulated by the strict primary, but also by the secondary powers, the indic. being used to signify a *certain* persuasion considered as an actual fact (§. 412.), the optative an uncertain fact, considered as a mere supposition or persuasion (§. 418.).

Indicative and Optative.

§. 802. 1. The indicative is used in any of its tenses, when a fact or certainty is spoken of.

2. The optative, where the thing spoken of is represented as an uncertainty, a supposition.

3. After verbs of *saying* or *telling, shewing, setting forth :*

a. The indicative is used, when the principal verb being in the present (not the historic present), the notion of the dependent verb is spoken of as a fact, as if it were in the speaker's presence, of which therefore he can speak with certainty ; as, οἴεται or λέγει, ὅτι νοσεῖ — ὅτι οἱ πολέμιοι πεφεύγασιν (ἀπέφυγον) — ὅτι μάχη γενήσεται.

b. The indicative is used, when the writer introduces a person making some statement, and proceeds to give it as a fact stated in that person's own words ; the thing so spoken of being considered in the view in which the speaker looked at it, viz. as a fact, of the certainty of which he had no doubt ; as, Xen. Cyr. I. 4, 7 οἱ δ᾽ ἔλεγον, ὅτι ἄρκτοι—πολλοὺς ἤδη διέφθειραν.

The optative is used, when the writer introduces a person making some assertion, which he adopts, but works it up in his own words, representing it in the relation in which it stands to himself ; not expressly as a fact of which he has personal knowledge, but as an assertion of another, on the certainty or uncertainty of which he can of himself decide nothing ; as, οἱ δ᾽ ἔλεγον, ὅτι ἄρκτοι πολλοὺς ἤδη διαφθείρειεν.

c. So the ind. is used, when the speaker wishes to express some former thought or saying of his own, of the truth of which he had no doubt ; as, ἔλεξά ποτε, ὅτι οἱ Ἕλληνες τοὺς Πέρσας νικήσουσιν. The optative is used, when the speaker repeats some former saying of his own as if it were another person's, so that he means to express nothing as to the certainty thereof: Plat. Gorg. p. 461 A ἐκείνους εἶπον τοὺς λόγους, ὅτι εἰ μὲν κέρδος ἡγοῖο εἶναι — ἄξιον εἴη διαλέγεσθαι [a].

d. Hence in a sentence where two assertions depend on the same verb, if one is to be represented as certain, the other merely as something probable, the indicative and optat. are interchanged ; Thuc. II. 80 λέγοντες ὅτι— κρατήσουσι, καὶ ὁ περίπλους οὐκέτι ἔσοιτο Ἀθηναίοις ὅμοιος: Plat. Phæd. p. 95 D πάντα ταῦτα μηνύειν ὅτι δὲ πολυχρόνιόν ἐστι ἡ ψυχὴ καὶ—ταλαιπωρουμένη δὴ τοῦτον τὸν βίον ζῴη.

Obs. 1. The same rules hold good also with words which imply saying or telling, &c.: γνώμη Hdt. IX. 41 : λόγος Plat. Phæd. p. 86 : χρῆσμος Hdt. VII. 6 ; verbs of blaming, κακίζω Thuc. II. 21 ; or with words used metaphorically, as δηλοῦν, μηνύειν, of things without speech.

4. With verbs of *hearing, receiving in answer that—learning that :*

a. The indicative is used, when the writer wishes to express the thing heard, the answer given, in the shape of a fact, just as he heard it from his informant ; as, Hdt. VII. 157 τὸν γὰρ ἐπιόντα πάντως κου πυνθάνεαι ὅτι Πέρσης ἀνὴρ μέλλει κ. τ. λ.

b. The optative is used, when the writer adopts the thing heard, or the answer given, and works it up in his own words, not repre-

a Stallb. ad loc.

senting it as a fact in the words of the informant, but as an assertion of another person, on the certainty of which he wishes to express nothing; as, Hdt. III. 140 πυνθάνεται (hist. pres.) ὁ Συλοσῶν ὡς ἡ βασιληίη περιεληλύθοι ἐς τοῦτον τὸν ἄνδρα.

Obs. 2. The same interchange takes place between the ind. and opt. as with verbs of saying, &c. See examples of this interchange below, γ.

5. With verbs of *mental persuasion, understanding,* or words which imply the same, as δῆλος, ἀληθής &c.

The indic. is used, when the persuasion amounts to a certain conviction: εὖ ᾔδει, ὅτι ταῦτα ἔπραξας or πράξεις—δῆλον ἦν, ὅτι οἱ βάρβαροι ὑπὸ τῶν Ἑλλήνων ἐνικήθησαν or νικηθή-σονται. The optative, when it is only a suspicion, or a persuasion of the probability of any thing; as, Hdt. III. 68 ὁ Ὀτάνης πρῶ-τος ὑπόπτευσε τὸν μάγον, ὡς οὐκ εἴη ὁ Κύρου Σμέρδις, ἀλλ᾽ ὅσπερ ἦν.

Obs. 3. The same interchange also takes place here. See examples, γ.

a. Ind.: Il. o, 248 οὐκ ἄιεις, ὃ (i. q. ὅτι) με βάλεν Αἴας: Il. θ, 140 ἦ οὐ γιγνώσκεις, ὅ τοι ἐκ Διὸς οὐχ ἕπετ᾽ ἀλκή; Il. λ, 408 οἶδα γὰρ, ὅτι κακοὶ μὲν ἀποίχονται πολέμοιο: Hdt. III. 74 κεῖνον δ᾽ ἐκέ-λευον ἀναβάντα ἐπὶ πύργον ἀγορεῦσαι, ὡς ὑπὸ τοῦ Κύρου Σμέρδιος ἄρχονται: Ibid. 62 οὐκ ἔστι ταῦτα ἀληθέα, ὅκως (i. q. ὡς) ποτέ σοι Σμέρδις ἀδελφεὸς ὁ σὸς ἐπανέστηκε: Xen. Cyr. I. 4, 7 οἱ δ᾽ ἔλεγον, ὅτι ἄρκτοι—πολλοὺς ἤδη πλησιάσαντας διέφθειραν; Ibid. 3, 11 εἶθ᾽ ὁπόταν ἥκῃ ἐπὶ τὸ δεῖπνον, λέγοιμ᾽ ἂν, ὅτι λοῦται (ὁ Ἀστυάγης)· εἰ δὲ πάνυ σπουδάζοι φαγεῖν, εἴποιμ᾽ ἂν, ὅτι παρὰ ταῖς γυναιξίν ἐστιν.

β. Opt.: Hdt. III. 148 πυνθάνεται (hist. pres.) ὁ Συλοσῶν, ὡς ἡ βασιληίη περιεληλύθοι ἐς τοῦτον τὸν ἄνδρα: Id. VI. 23 ἀνα-πείθει (hist. pres.), ὡς χρεὼν εἴη Καλὴν μὲν Ἀκτὴν — ἐᾶν χαίρειν: Ibid. 29 Περσίδα γλῶσσαν μετεὶς καταμηνύει ἑωυτὸν, ὡς εἴη Ἱστιαῖος ὁ Μιλήσιος: Id. VII. 6 χρησμὸν, ὡς αἱ ἐπὶ Λήμνου ἐπικείμεναι νῆσοι ἀφανιζοίατο (for ἀφανίζοιντο) κατὰ τῆς θαλάσσης: Ibid. ἔλεγε τόν τε Ἑλλήσποντον ὡς ζευχθῆναι χρεὼν εἴη ὑπ᾽ ἀνδρὸς Πέρσεω: Thuc. I. 72 ἔδοξεν αὐτοῖς παριτητέα ἐς τοὺς Λακεδαιμονίους εἶναι, δηλῶσαι περὶ τοῦ παντὸς, ὡς οὐ ταχέως αὐτοῖς βουλευτέον εἴη: Xen. M. S. II. 6, 13 ἄλλας δέ τινας οἶσθα ἐπῳδάς; οὔ· ἀλλ᾽ ἤκουσα, ὅτι Περικλῆς πολλὰς ἐπίσταιτο: Id. Cyr. I. 1, 3 ὅτε μὲν δὴ ταῦτα ἐνεθυμούμεθα, οὕτως ἐγιγνώσκομεν περὶ αὐτῶν, ὡς ἀνθρώπῳ πεφυκότι πάντων τῶν ἄλλων ῥᾷον εἴη ζῴων ἢ ἀνθρώπων ἄρχειν.

γ. Ind. and Opt.: Hdt. III. 43 ἐπιλεξάμενος δὲ ὁ Ἄμασις τὸ βιβλίον τὸ παρὰ τοῦ Πολυκράτους ἧκον ἔμαθε, ὅτι ἐκκομίσαι τε ἀδύνατον εἴη ἀνθρώπῳ ἄνθρωπον ἐκ τοῦ μέλλοντος γίνεσθαι πρήγματος, καὶ ὅτι

οὐκ εὖ τελευτήσειν μέλλει Πολυκράτης: Ibid. 61 οὗτος δὴ ὤν ὁ
ἐπανέστη, μαθών τε τὸν Σμέρδιος θάνατον, ὡς κρύπτοιτο γενόμενος
καὶ ὡς ὀλίγοι τε ἦσαν οἱ ἐπιστάμενοι αὐτὸν Περσέων, οἱ δὲ πολλοὶ
περιεόντα μιν εἰδείησαν: Thuc. II. 80 λέγοντες, ὅτι—κρατήσουσι, καὶ ὁ περίπλους οὐκέτι ἔσοιτο Ἀθηναίοις ὅμοιος: Xen.
Anab. II. 1, 3 οὗτοι ἔλεγον, ὅτι Κῦρος μὲν τέθνηκεν, Ἀριαῖος δὲ
πεφευγὼς—εἴη καὶ λέγοι, ὅτι ταύτην τὴν ἡμέραν περιμείνειεν ἂν
αὐτούς: Hdt. III. 71 ἐγὼ ταῦτα ἐδόκεον αὐτὸς μοῦνος ἐπίστασθαι,
ὅτι τε ὁ μάγος εἴη ὁ βασιλεύων, καὶ Σμέρδις ὁ Κύρου τετελεύτηκε.

Obs. 4. Sometimes in these interchanges ὡς or ὅτι is omitted before the
optative [a], even where it stands at some distance from the ind.; as, Plat.
Phæd. p. 95 C. This is especially the case, where the writer after giving
some statement, answer, information, or conviction, as it was given or
conceived by the person himself, goes on to give the probable grounds on
which it was or might be supported, introducing the opt. by γάρ [b]: Plat.
Phileb. ἤκουον—ὡς ἡ τοῦ πείθειν δύναμις πολὺ διαφέρει πασῶν τεχνῶν· πάντα
γὰρ ὑφ᾽ αὑτῶν δουλοῖ: so Phæd. p. 86 A. Rep. p. 420 C.

Obs. 5. As the indicative, when used as quoting the words of the person
speaking of something, gives to the sentence more of the appearance of
the *oratio recta*, it often happens that the construction is changed to the
oratio recta, instead of the *oratio obliqua*, the dependence of the sentences being wholly or partially done away: Plat. Symp. p. 175 A ἥκειν
ἀγγέλλοντα, ὅτι Σωκράτης οὗτος ἀναχωρήσας ἐν τῷ τῶν γειτόνων προθύρῳ ἕστηκε;
κἀμοῦ καλοῦντος οὐκ ἐθέλει εἰσιέναι: Xen. Cyr. I. 4, 28 ἐνταῦθα δὴ τὸν
Κῦρον γελάσαι τε ἐκ τῶν πρόσθεν δακρύων καὶ εἰπεῖν αὐτῷ ἀπιόντα θαρρεῖν, ὅτι
παρέσται αὐτοῖς ὀλίγου χρόνου· ὥστε ὁρᾶν σοι ἐξέσται κἂν βούλῃ ἀσκαρδαμυκτεί. Whence ὅτι is used even where the words of another, speaking in
the first or second person, of himself, or to some one else, are introduced;
as, Xen. Cyr. III. 1, 8 εἶπε δ᾽, ὅτι Εἰς καιρὸν ἥκεις, ἔφη: even before an imperative; as, Plat. Crit. p. 50 C ἢ ἐροῦμεν πρὸς αὐτούς, ὅτι Ἠδίκει γὰρ ἡμᾶς
ἡ πόλις καὶ οὐκ ὀρθῶς τὴν δίκην ἔκρινε;—immediately afterwards ἴσως ἂν
εἴποιεν (οἱ νόμοι), ὅτι, ὦ Σώκρατες, μὴ θαύμαζε τὰ λεγόμενα.

Optative and Indic. of historic tenses with ἄν.

§. 803. 1. Ἄν is used in these substantival clauses with the
opt. as in a simple sentence, to express that the supposition of the
verb depends on some condition either implied or expressed: Xen.
Anab. I. 6, 2 καταλλαγεὶς δὲ οὗτος Κύρῳ, εἶπεν, εἰ αὐτῷ δοίη
ἱππέας χιλίους, ὅτι τοὺς προκατακαίοντας ἱππέας ἢ κατακαίνοι
ἂν ἐνεδρεύσας, ἢ ζῶντας πολλοὺς αὐτῶν ἕλοι, καὶ κωλύσειε
τοῦ κάειν ἐπιόντας: Id. Cyr. I. 6, 3 μέμνημαι ἀκούσας ποτέ σου, ὅτι
εἰκότως ἂν καὶ παρὰ θεῶν πρακτικώτερος εἴη, ὥσπερ καὶ παρὰ ἀνθρώπων, ὅστις μή, ὁπότε ἐν ἀπόροις εἴη, τότε κολακεύοι, ἀλλ᾽ ὅτε τὰ
ἄριστα πράττοι, τότε μάλιστα τῶν θεῶν μεμνῷτο (the condition lies

---

[a] Matth. 529. 3. Stallb. Plat. Phæd. p. 95 C.　　[b] Stallb. Plat. Phæd. p. 86 A.

in ὅστις μή κ. τ. λ.): Demosth. p. 851, 22 οἶδα οὖν, ὅτι πάντες
ἂν ὁμολογήσαιτε.

2. Ἄν with ὅτι and the historic tenses of the indic. is used when
the verb of the dependent sentence is represented as depending
on a condition which is supposed not to take place: Demosth.
p. 830, 55 εἰ μὲν ὁ πατὴρ ἠπίστει τούτοις, δῆλον, ὅτι οὔτ' ἂν
τἆλλα ἐπέτρεπεν, οὔτ' ἂν ταῦθ' οὕτω καταλιπὼν αὐτοῖς ἔφραζεν.

Remarks.

§. 804. 1. In the passive and impersonal verbs the substantival clause
is the grammatical subject, though logically it is the object: λέγεται, ὅτι οἱ
πολέμιοι ἀποπεφεύγασιν—Δῆλόν ἐστιν, ὅτι ὁ ἄνθρωπος θνητός ἐστιν.

2. But these impersonal forms become personal, by making the subject
of the subst. clause the subject of the impersonal verb in the principal
clause, whereby the two clauses are more closely connected: Thuc. I. 93
καὶ δήλη ἡ οἰκοδομία ἔτι καὶ νῦν ἐστιν, ὅτι κατὰ σπουδὴν ἐγένετο:
Plat. Crit. p. 46 D νῦν δὲ κατάδηλος ἄρα ἐγένετο, ὅτι ἄλλως ἕνεκα λόγου
ἐλέγετο: Id. Phæd. p. 64 B καὶ σφᾶς γε οὐ λελήθασιν, ὅτι ἄξιοί εἰσι
τοῦτο πάσχειν ᵃ: Xen. Œcon. I. 19 ὅτι πονηρότατοί εἰσι, οὐδὲ σὲ λανθά-
νουσιν.

3. When ὅτι or ὡς is separated from the clause to which it belongs by
a parenthetical sentence, the conjunction is sometimes repeated, either
accidentally or for the sake of clearness: Hdt. III. 71 ἴστε, ὑμῖν ὅτι,
ἢν ὑπερπέσῃ ἡ νῦν ἡμέρη, ὡς οὐκ ἄλλος φθὰς ἐμεῦ κατήγορος ἔσται: Xen.
Anab. V. 6, 19 λέγουσιν, ὅτι, εἰ μὴ ἐκποριοῦσι τῇ στρατιᾷ μισθὸν, ὥστε ἔχειν
τὰ ἐπιτήδεια ἐκπλέοντας, ὅτι κινδυνεύσει μεῖναι τοσαύτη δύναμις ἐν τῷ Πόντῳ:
Id. Cyr. V. 3, 30 ἴσως κἀκεῖνο ἐννοεῖται, ὡς, εἰ—ὑφ' ἡμῶν ἀπολούνται, ὅτι
τάχα οὐδένα εἰκὸς σὺν αὐτῷ βούλεσθαι: Plat. Rep. p. 470 D σκόπει δή, εἶπον,
ὅτι ἐν τῇ νῦν ὁμολογουμένῃ στάσει, ὅπου ἄν τι τοιοῦτον γένηται καὶ διαστῇ
πόλις, ἐὰν ἑκάτεροι ἑκατέρων τέμνωσιν ἀγροὺς καὶ οἰκίας ἐμπιπρῶσιν, ὡς ἀλιτη-
ριώδης τε δοκεῖ ἡ στάσις εἶναι ᵇ.

4. Instead of this construction with ὅτι or ὡς, the infin. with acc. may
be used, or the participle; and the difference between these three constructions, whereby this relation of the object to the verb may be expressed, is so little material, that we find all three in the same author,
to express just the same idea; as, Hdt. VI. 63 ἐξαγγέλλει, ὥς οἱ παῖς
γέγονε: Ibid. 65 ὅτε οἱ ἐξήγγειλε ὁ οἰκέτης παῖδα γεγονέναι: Ibid.
69 ὅτε αὐτῷ σὺ ἠγγέλθης γεγενημένος.

5. Hence it sometimes happens that we find the substantival clause
and the infinitive after one and the same principal verb in the same
sentence: Hdt. III. 75 ἔλεγε, τὸν μὲν Κύρου Σμέρδιν ὡς αὐτὸς ὑπὸ Καμβύσεω ἀναγκαζόμενος ἀποκτείνειε, τοὺς μάγους δὲ βασιλεύειν:
Thuc. III. 3 ἐσηγγέλθη γὰρ αὐτοῖς, ὡς εἴη Ἀπόλλωνος Μαλόεντος ἔξω τῆς
πόλεως ἑορτή, ἐν ᾗ πανδημεὶ Μυτιληναῖοι ἑορτάζουσι, καὶ ἐλπίδα εἶναι
ἐπειχθέντας ἐπιπεσεῖν ἄφνω: Ibid. 25 καὶ ἔλεγε τοῖς προέδροις, ὅτι ἐσβολή
τε ἅμα ἐς τὴν Ἀττικὴν ἔσται καὶ αἱ τεσσαράκοντα νῆες παρέσονται, ἃς
ἔδει βοηθῆσαι αὐτοῖς· προαποπεμφθῆναί τε αὐτὸς τούτων ἕνεκα καὶ ἅμα
τῶν ἄλλων ἐπιμελησόμενος: Xen. Cyr. I. 3, 13 ἡ δὲ (Μανδάνη) ἀπεκρίνατο,

---

ᵃ Stallb. ad loc.   ᵇ Stallb. ad loc.

ὅτι βούλοιτο μὲν ἂν ἅπαντα τῷ πατρὶ χαρίζεσθαι, ἄκοντα μέντοι τὸν ταῦτα
χαλεπὸν νομίζειν (for νομίζοι) εἶναι καταλιπεῖν : Eur. Med. 777 sq. λέξω,
—ὥς καὶ δοκεῖ μοι ταῦτα, καὶ καλῶς ἔχειν γάμους τυράννων κ. τ. λ.

6. Hence also it happens that although ὅτι or ὡς has been used as if to introduce a substantival clause, the verb which should depend upon it follows
in the infinitive ; but this is only from the construction of the sentence
having been interrupted by a parenthesis intervening between ὅτι and
its verb : Xen. Cyr. I. 6, 18 λέγεις σύ, ἔφη, ὦ πάτερ, ὡς ἐμοὶ δοκεῖ, ὅτι,
ὥσπερ οὐδὲ γεωργοῦ ἀργοῦ οὐδὲν ὄφελος, οὕτως οὐδὲ στρατηγοῦ ἀργοῦ οὐδὲν
ὄφελος εἶναι : Id. Hell. II. 2, 2 εἶδες, ὅτι, ὅσῳ ἂν πλείους συλλέγωσιν ἐς
τὸ ἄστυ καὶ τὸν Πειραιᾶ, θᾶττον τῶν ἐπιτηδείων ἔνδειαν ἔσεσθαι : and also
the participle : Thuc. IV. 37 γνοὺς δὲ ὁ Κλέων καὶ ὁ Δημοσθένης, ὅτι, εἰ
καὶ ὁποσονοῦν μᾶλλον ἐνδώσουσιν, διαφθαρησομένους αὐτοὺς ὑπὸ τῆς
σφετέρας στρατιᾶς, ἔπαυσαν τὴν μάχην.

7. After the verbs μέμνημαι, οἶδα, ἀκούω, et similia, instead of
a substantival clause introduced by ὅτι or ὡς, there not unfrequently
follows an adverbial clause with ὅτε (poet. ἦμος, ἡνίκα). This appears to
arise from some ellipse, as τοῦ χρόνου, thus μέμνημαι (τοῦ χρόνου), ὅτι
ταῦτα ἔλεξας : Lysias in Poliuch. p. 151, 34 ἄξιον δὲ καὶ τούτους τοὺς συνδί-
κους εὔνους ἡμῖν εἶναι, ἐκείνου τοῦ χρόνου μνησθέντας, ὅτε—ἄνδρας ἀρίστους ἐνομίζετ' εἶναι : so we say, I remember when : Il. ξ, 71 ᾔδεα
μὲν γάρ, ὅτε πρόφρων Δαναοῖσιν ἄμυνεν : Il. ο, 18 ἦ οὐ μέμνῃ, ὅτε τ'
ἐκρέμω ὑψόθεν : Thuc. II. 21 μεμνημένοι καὶ Πλειστοάνακτα—ὅτε ἐσβαλὼν τῆς Ἀττικῆς ἐς Ἐλευσῖνα—ἀπεχώρησε πάλιν : Xen. Cyr. I. 6, 8 μέμνημαι καὶ τοῦτο, ὅτε, σοῦ λέγοντος, συνεδόκει καὶ ἐμοὶ ὑπερμέγεθες εἶναι ἔργον
τὸ καλῶς ἄρχειν : Plat. Menon. p. 79 D μέμνησαι ὅτ' ἐγώ σοι ἄρτι
ἀπεκρινάμην—: Id. Legg. p. 782 C τοὐναντίον ἀκούομεν ἐν ἄλλοις ὅτε
οὐδὲ βοὸς ἐτολμῶμεν γεύεσθαι : Soph. O. T. 1133 εὖ γὰρ οἶδ' ὅτι κάτοιδεν,
ἦμος τὸν Κιθαιρῶνος τόπον—ἐπλησίαζεν :—Eur. Troad. 70 οἶδ' ἡνίκ' Αἴας
εἷλκε Κασάνδραν βίᾳ : so in other combinations ; as, Il. ο, 207 ἐσθλὸν καὶ
τὸ τέτυκται, ὅτ' ἄγγελος αἴσιμα εἰδῇ (subject). So sometimes in Latin,
memini, quum darem ; vidi, quum prodiret ; audivi eum, quum
diceret.

8. And similarly the substantival clause after verbs which express some
mental emotion, as θαυμάζω, ἄχθεσθαι, ἀγανακτεῖν, αἰσχύνεσθαι, μέμφεσθαι, δεινὸν ποιεῖσθαι, δεινόν ἐστι, ἀγαπᾶν, φθονεῖν, αἰσχρόν ἐστι, &c., is introduced by εἰ, if, instead
of ὅτι, when the object of this mental emotion is to be represented not
as real, but as something possible, which the person can scarcely credit
to be real. The Attic politeness, which prefers indirect to direct assertion,
uses this idiom very frequently, even of a past and certain matter ; as,
Æsch. p. 337 (Reisk.) οὐκ ἀγαπᾷ, εἰ μὴ δίκην ἔδωκεν : Plat. Lach.
p. 194 A ἀγανακτῶ, εἰ οὑτωσὶ ἃ νοῶ μὴ οἷός τ' εἰμὶ εἰπεῖν : Id. Rep.
p. 343 E τόδε ἐθαύμασα, εἰ ἐν ἀρετῆς καὶ σοφίας τίθης μέρει τὴν ἀδικίαν,
τὴν δὲ δικαιοσύνην ἐν τοῖς ἐναντίοις [a] : Id. Phæd. p. 95 A ἐθαύμαζον εἴ τι
ἕξει τις χρήσασθαι τῷ λόγῳ αὐτοῦ : Demosth. p. 24, 23 οὐ δὴ θαυμαστόν
ἐστιν, εἰ στρατευόμενος καὶ πονῶν ἐκεῖνος (ὁ Φίλιππος) — ἡμῶν μελλόντων
(cunctantibus) — περιγίγνεται : Ibid. p. 25, 24 ἀλλ' ἐκεῖνο θαυμάζω,
εἰ Λακεδαιμονίοις μέν ποτε—ὑπὲρ τῶν Ἑλληνικῶν δικαίων ἀντήρατε (restitistis)
—, νυνὶ δ' ὀκνεῖτε ἐξιέναι καὶ μέλλετε (cunctamini) εἰσφέρειν ὑπὲρ τῶν ὑμετέρων
αὐτῶν κτημάτων : Id. p. 52, 43 θαυμάζω δ' ἔγωγε, εἰ μηδεὶς ὑμῶν μήτ'

a Stallb. ad loc.

ἐπθυμεῖται, μήτε ὀργίζεται, ὁρῶν—τὴν μὲν ἀρχὴν τοῦ πολέμου γεγενημένην περὶ τοῦ τιμωρήσασθαι Φίλιππον : Id. Mid. 29 οὐκ ἠσχύνθη, εἰ τοιοῦτο κακὸν ἐπάγει τῳ, that he, &c.

9. Frequently instead of ὅτι οὕτως, we find the relative ὡς, and for ὅτι τοιοῦτος, or ὅτι τόσος, the relatives οἷος, ὅσος : Plat. Crit. p. 43 B θαυμάζω αἰσθανόμενος, ὡς ἡδέως καθεύδεις[a] : Ibid. σὲ—εὐδαιμόνισα—, ὡς ῥᾳδίως αὐτὴν (τὴν ξυμφοράν) καὶ πράως φέρεις : Id. Phæd. p. 58 E εὐδαί-μων μοι ὁ ἀνὴρ ἐφαίνετο—ὡς ἀδεῶς καὶ γενναίως ἐτελεύτα : Il. ε, 757 Ζεῦ πάτερ, σὺ νεμεσίζῃ Ἄρει τάδε καρτερὰ ἔργα, ὁσσάτιόν τε καὶ οἷον ἀπώλεσε λαὸν Ἀχαιῶν for ὅτι τοσοῦτον καὶ τοιοῦτον : Hdt. I. 31 αἱ Ἀργεῖαι ἐμακάριζον τὴν μητέρα, οἵων τέκνων ἐκύρησε. So Homer : οἳ ἀγορεύεις, οἷά μ' ἔοργας, οἷον ἄκουσεν, pro iis, quæ dixisti etc : Il. ζ, 166 τὸν δὲ ἄνακτα χόλος λάβεν, οἷον ἄκουσεν : so Il. σ, 262 οἷος ἐκείνου θυμὸς ὑπέρβιος, οὐκ ἐθελήσει μίμνειν ἐν πεδίῳ for ὅτι τοιοῦτος—θυμός, as in Lat., *quæ ejus est atrocitas,* or *qud est atrocitate.*

Obs. For the constructions, such as ὡς λέγεται ὅτι σὺ ταῦτα ἐποίησας, instead of ὡς λέγεται, σὺ ταῦτα ἐποίησας, where the principal and the de-pendent clauses change places, see Index.

Final substantival clause introduced by ὡς, in order that, ὅπως, ἵνα, &c.

§. 805. 1. Substantival clauses of the second class signify the aim or end of the verb, which would usually stand in the equivalent acc., or more commonly with prepos. ἐπί, εἰς, or in the inf. ; and are introduced by ὡς, ὅπως, ἵνα (ὄφρα poet.), (μή), ὡς μή, ὅπως μή, ἵνα μή. Compare κελεύω σε τοῦτο—σε ποιεῖν τοῦτο —ἵνα ποιῇς τοῦτο. These relative conjunctions refer to a demon-strative in the principal sentence, either expressed or implied.

Moods.
Conjunctive and Optative.

2. The proper mood of the final sentence is the subjunctive, as the end or aim is something which either really resides in the will or imagination of the speaker or agent, or is supposed to do so. When the action of the verb depending on ἵνα, &c. relates to present or future time, the conjunctive is used, because the aim of a present action is immediately in the mind of the speaker ; but if the aim relates to the past, it requires an act of the imagination to recall it to the mind, and therefore the optative is used[b]. And hence the general rule is laid down, that when the principal verb is in the pres., pft., fut., or aorist with a present sense, the conjunctive is used ; but when the principal verb is in an his-

---

[a] Stallb. ad loc.   [b] Nitzsch Odyss. III. 76.

toric tense, the opt., (subj. of hist. tenses) is used ; if a past
action has for its object something yet to come, of course the
conjunctive is used, not the optative ; as, ταῦτα γράφω, γέγραφα,
γράψω, ἵν' ἔλθῃς, *ut venias*, that you may come : λέξον, ἵν'
εἰδῶ, *dic, ut sciam*, "that I may know :"—ταῦτα ἔγραφον, ἐγεγράφειν, ἔγραψα, ἵν' ἔλθοις, *ut venires :* but also μετεπεμψάμην,
"I sent for you," (past) ἵνα εἰδῶ, "that I may presently know :"
so we say, " I do this that you may"—" I did this that you might"
—" I did this that you may ;" so that generally speaking, where
in English we should use " may," the conj. is used where " might,"
the opt.: Il. λ. 289 sq. ἀλλ' ἰθὺς ἐλαύνετε μώνυχας ἵππους
ἰφθίμων Δαναῶν, ἵν' ὑπέρτερον εὖχος ἄρησθε, *ut gloriam vobis
paretis*; but Il. ε, princ. ἔνθ' αὖ Τυδεΐδῃ Διομήδεϊ Παλλὰς Ἀθήνη
δῶκε μένος καὶ θάρσος, ἵν' ἔκδηλος μετὰ πᾶσιν Ἀργείοισι γένοιτο,
ἰδὲ κλέος ἐσθλὸν ἄροιτο, *ut clarus fieret et gloriam sibi pa-
raret :* Il. τ, 347 ἀλλ' ἴθι οἱ νέκταρ τε καὶ ἀμβροσίην ἐρατεινὴν
στάξον (pres.) ἐνὶ στήθεσσ', ἵνα μή μιν λιμὸς ἵκηται, *ut ne fames
eum occupet :* but ibid. 351 ἡ δ' Ἀχιλῆϊ νέκταρ ἐνὶ στήθεσσι καὶ
ἀμβροσίην ἐρατεινὴν στάξ', ἵνα μή μιν λιμὸς ἀτερπὴς γούναθ' ἵκοιτο,
ut ne—occuparet : Od. a, 85 Ἑρμείαν—νῆσον ἐς Ὠγυγίην ὀτρύνομεν (for ὀτρύνωμεν), ὄφρα τάχιστα Νύμφῃ ἐϋπλοκάμῳ εἴπῃ νημερτέα βουλήν : v. 89 αὐτὰρ ἐγὼν Ἰθάκην ἐσελεύσομαι, ὄφρα οἱ
υἱὸν μᾶλλον ἐποτρύνω, καί οἱ μένος ἐν φρεσὶ θείω : Ibid. 174 καί
μοι τοῦτ' ἀγόρευσον ἐτήτυμον, ὄφρ' εὖ εἰδῶ : Il. a, 26 μή σε,
γέρον, κοίλῃσιν ἐγὼ παρὰ νηυσὶ κιχείω, μή νυ τοι οὐ χραίσμῃ
σκῆπτρον καὶ στέμμα θεοῖο : v. 32 ἀλλ' ἴθι, μή μ' ἐρέθιζε, σαώτερος
ὥς κε νέηαι ; but Plat. Rep. p. 393 E ὁ δὲ Ἀγαμέμνων ἠγρίαι-
νεν, ἐντελλόμενος νῦν τε ἀπιέναι καὶ αὖθις μὴ ἐλθεῖν, μὴ αὐτῷ τό τε
σκῆπτρον καὶ τὰ τοῦ θεοῦ στέμματα μὴ ἐπαρκέσοι — ἀπιέναι δὲ
ἐκέλευε καὶ μὴ ἐρεθίζειν, ἵνα σῶς οἴκαδε ἔλθοι : Od. ι, 355 sq.
δός μοι ἔτι πρόφρων, καί μοι τέον οὔνομα εἰπὲ αὐτίκα—νῦν, ἵνα τοι
δῶ ξείνιον, ᾧ κε σὺ χαίρῃς : Ibid. 154 sq. ὦρσαν δὲ Νύμφαι—
αἶγας ὀρεσκώους, ἵνα δειπνήσειαν ἑταῖροι : Xen. Cyr. I. 2, 3
(ἐκ τῆς τῶν Περσῶν ἐλευθέρας ἀγορᾶς καλουμένης) τὰ μὲν ὤνια καὶ
οἱ ἀγοραῖοι—ἀπελήλανται εἰς ἄλλον τόπον, ὡς μὴ μιγνύηται
ἡ τούτων τύρβη τῇ τῶν πεπαιδευμένων εὐκοσμίᾳ : Ibid. 15 ἵνα δὲ σαφέστερον δηλωθῇ πᾶσα ἡ Περσῶν πολιτεία, μικρὸν ἐπάνειμι
(*paucis repetam :*) Ibid. I. 4, 25 Καμβύσης—τὸν Κῦρον ἀπεκάλει,
ὅπως τὰ ἐν Πέρσαις ἐπιχώρια ἐπιτελοίη.

Obs. It might perhaps be more correct to state the general rule thus :
*When the dependent verb refers to present or future time, the conjunctive
is used ; when to past, the optative.*

Seeming exceptions.

§. 806. When an historic tense is used in the sense of a principal tense, the subjunctive of the principal tenses (conj.) is used.

When a principal tense is used in the sense of an historic tense, the subjunctive of the historic tenses (opt.) is used.

Conjunctive after the aorist, and other historic tenses.

1. When the aorist has the force of the perfect (§. 404.) the past action is considered as continuing and extending into present time, and the dependent verb refers to something present or future: Od. λ, 93 τίπτ᾽ αὖτ᾽, ὦ δύστηνε, λιπὼν φάος ἠελίοιο, ἤλυθες, ὄφρα ἴδῃ νέκυας καὶ ἀτερπέα χῶρον; here ἤλυθες = ἐλήλυθας, *advenisti*, *ades*, as, Il. a, 202 τίπτ᾽ αὖτ᾽, αἰγιόχοιο Διὸς τέκος, εἰλήλουθας; ἦ ἵνα ὕβριν ἴδῃ ᾿Αγαμέμνονος ᾿Ατρείδαο; Od. γ, 15 τοὕνεκα γὰρ καὶ πόντον ἐπέπλως, ὄφρα πύθηαι πατρός: Od. ν, 418 τίπτε τ᾽ ἄρ᾽ οὔ οἱ ἔειπες, ἐνὶ φρεσὶ πάντ᾽ εἰδυῖα; ἦ ἵνα που καὶ κεῖνος ἀλώμενος ἄλγεα πάσχῃ; Il. ε, 127 ἀχλὺν δ᾽ αὖ τοι ἀπ᾽ ὀφθαλμῶν ἕλον, ἤ πρὶν ἐπῆεν, ὄφρ᾽ εὖ γιγνώσκῃς ἠμὲν θεὸν ἠδὲ καὶ ἄνδρα: but Plat. Alcib. II. extr. ὥσπερ τῷ Διομήδει φησὶ τὴν ᾿Αθηνᾶν ῞Ομηρος ἀπὸ τῶν ὀφθαλμῶν ἀφελεῖν τὴν ἀχλύν, ὄφρ᾽ εὖ γιγνώσκοι ἠμὲν θεὸν ἠδὲ καὶ ἄνδρα: here ἀφελεῖν is aorist, but in Homer the aim of the verb is present, so that ἕλον is known to be used in a perfect sense: Eur. Med. 215 Κορίνθιαι γυναῖκες, ἐξῆλθον δόμων, μή μοι τι μέμφησθε: Id. Hecub. 27 κτείνει με χρυσοῦ—χάριν ξένος πατρῷος, καὶ κτανὼν ἐς οἶδμ᾽ ἁλὸς μεθῆχ᾽, ἵν᾽ αὐτὸς χρυσὸν ἐν δόμοις ἔχῃ: but Ibid. 697 Hec. ἐμὸς ξένος, Θρᾴκιος scil. ἔκτεινέ νιν: Chor. ὤμοι, τί λέξεις; χρυσὸν ὡς ἔχοι κτανών: here ἔκτεινε is the real aorist, and the aim of the verb is something past: Hdt. VII. 8, 1. extr. διὸ ὑμέας νῦν ἐγὼ συνέλεξα, ἵνα τὸ νοέω πρήσσειν ὑπερθέωμαι ὑμῖν: Plat. Legg. p. 653 sq. θεοὶ δὲ οἰκτείραντες τὸ τῶν ἀνθρώπων ἐπίπονον πεφυκὸς γένος—Μούσας ᾿Απόλλωνά τε μουσηγέτην καὶ Διόνυσον ξυνεορταστὰς ἔδοσαν, ἵν᾽ ἐπανορθῶνται τὰς γενομένας τροφὰς ἐν ταῖς ἑορταῖς μετὰ θεῶν: Demosth. p. 117, 26 τὰς πόλεις αὐτῶν παρῄρηται καὶ τετραρχίας κατέστησεν, ἵνα μὴ μόνον κατὰ πόλεις, ἀλλὰ καὶ κατ᾽ ἔθνη δουλεύωσιν.

2. In narrating past events as if they were present, the writer throws himself so completely into the past events which he is narrating, that they become to him as if they were present, and placing himself in the position of the subject of the past verb, he looks upon the aim thereof as he did, that is, as something

present or future: this poetic idiom (πρὸ ὀμμάτων ποιεῖν) is mostly used by the historians, especially Thucydides; but in other writers, both in prose and poetry, it is sometimes used also to mark the present continuance of a past action : Hdt. I. 29 Σόλων ἀπεδήμησε ἔτεα δέκα, ἵνα δὴ μή τινα τῶν νόμων ἀναγκασθῇ λῦσαι τῶν ἔθετο : Ibid. 9 ὁ μὲν δὴ λέγων ταῦτα ἀπεμάχετο ἀρρωδέων, μή τι οἱ ἐξ αὐτέων γένηται κακόν : Id. VII. 8. init. σύλλογον— Περσέων τῶν ἀρίστων ἐποιέετο, ἵνα γνώμας τε πύθηται σφέων καὶ αὐτὸς ἐν πᾶσι εἴπῃ τὰ θέλει : Cf. VI. 9. 100 : Thuc. II. 101 οἱ Ἕλληνες ἐβοήθησαν, μὴ καὶ ἐπὶ σφᾶς ὁ στρατὸς χωρήσῃ : Plat. Rep. p. 472 C παραδείγματος ἄρα ἕνεκα—ἐζητοῦμεν αὐτό τε δικαιοσύνην οἷόν ἐστι, καὶ ἄνδρα τὸν τελέως δίκαιον—καὶ ἀδικίαν αὖ καὶ τὸν ἀδικώτατον, ἵνα εἰς ἐκείνους ἀποβλέποντες, οἷοι ἂν ἡμῖν φαίνωνται εὐδαιμονίας τε πέρι καὶ τοῦ ἐναντίου, ἀναγκαζώμεθα καὶ περὶ ἡμῶν αὐτῶν ὁμολογεῖν κ. τ. λ. : Id. Protag. p. 320 A Περικλῆς δεδιὼς περὶ αὐτοῦ μὴ διαφθαρῇ δὴ ὑπὸ Ἀλκιβιάδου, ἀποσπάσας ἀπὸ τούτου καταθέμενος ἐν Ἀρίφρονος ἐπαίδευε : Id. Criton. p. 43 B καὶ ἐπίτηδές σε οὐκ ἤγειρον, ἵνα ὡς ἥδιστα διάγῃς [a] : Demosth. p. 25, 24 πολλὰ ἰδίᾳ πλεονεκτῆσαι—οὐκ ἠθελήσατε, ἀλλ᾿, ἵν᾿ οἱ ἄλλοι τύχωσι τῶν δικαίων, τὰ ὑμέτερ᾿ αὐτῶν ἀνηλίσκετε εἰσφέροντες καὶ προεκινδυνεύετε στρατευόμενοι : Id. p. 836. princ. εἴτε γὰρ, ὡς ὁ πάππος ὤφειλε τῷ δημοσίῳ καὶ διὰ ταῦθ᾿ ὁ πατὴρ οὐκ ἐβούλετο μισθωθῆναι τὸν οἶκον, ἵνα μὴ κινδυνεύσῃ, sc. ὁ οἶκος. This making past things appear present is very natural, when the writer or speaker is speaking of himself: Il. ι, 493 sq. ἀλλὰ σὲ παῖδα, θεοῖς ἐπιείκελ᾿ Ἀχιλλεῦ, ποιεύμην, ἵνα μοί ποτ᾿ ἀεικέα λοιγὸν ἀμύνῃς. So almost always in the Odyssey, when Ulysses is relating his own adventures : Od. ι, 102 αὐτὰρ τοὺς ἄλλους κελόμην—νηῶν ἐπιβαίνεμεν—, μήπως τις λωτοῖο φαγὼν νόστοιο λάθηται : Od. ι, 377 ἔπεσσί τε πάντας ἑταίρους θάρσυνον, μήτις μοι ὑποδείσας ἀναδύῃ.

Optative after a principal tense or aorist.

§. 807. A principal tense or (an aorist imper., conj., or opt.) in a present sense is followed by an optative.

a. When the historic present is used, this being equivalent to a past tense, and the aim of the verb being past : Eur. Hec. 10 πολὺν δὲ σὺν ἐμοὶ χρυσὸν ἐκπέμπει λάθρα πατήρ, ἵν᾿, εἴποτ᾿ Ἰλίου

---

[a] "*Ubi id quod propositum fuit nondum perfectum et transactum est, sed adhuc durare cogitatur.*" Stallb.

·εἴχη πέσοι, τοῖς ζῶσιν εἴη παισὶ μὴ σπάνις βίου: Ibid. 1149 μόνον ἰὲ σὺν τέκνοισί μ' ε ἰ σ ά γ ε ι δόμους, ἵν' ἄλλος μή τις εἰδείη τάδε.

β. When the writer or speaker introduces the aim of another person, not as existing in his own mind, but in the mind of that person, so that the sentence partakes of the character of the *oratio obliqua;* as, Il. η, 339 πύλας π ο ι ή σ ο μ ε ν (conj.) εὖ ἀραρυίας. ὄφρα δι' αὐτάων ἱππηλασίη ὁδὸς εἴη " *vult item a ceteris cogitari, quibus suum Nestor consilium suadet:*" Soph. Œ. C. 11 σ τ ῆ σ ό ν με κ ἀ ξ ί δ ρ υ σ ο ν, ὡς π υ θ ο ί μ ε θ α " *ita jubetur aliquis eâdem mente agere, quæ inest imperanti, optativus igitur non ad Œdipi, sed Antigonæ mentem spectat eam, quâ sedem jubetur eligere :*" Plat. Rep. p. 410 B ἆρ' οὖν, ἦν δ' ἐγώ, ὦ Γλαύκων, καὶ οἱ καθιστάντες μουσικῇ καὶ γυμναστικῇ παιδεύειν οὐχ οὗ ἕ ν ε κ ά τ ι ν ε ς ο ἴ ο ν τ α ι κ α θ ι σ τ ᾶ σ ι ν, ἵνα τῇ μὲν τὸ σῶμα θ ε ρ α π ε ύ ο ι ν τ ο, τῇ δὲ τὴν ψυχήν; " *Socrates non e suâ ipsius sententiâ rem affert; sed consilium, quod gymnastices conditores secuti sint, ex ipsorum mente indicat* [a]."

γ. When the mind of the writer or speaker at the moment when he is expressing the aim is dwelling on time past, and realising the intention which he had when he began the action he is now continuing: Arist. Ran. 24 αὐτὸς β α δ ί ζ ω καὶ π ο ν ῶ, τοῦτον δ' ὀ χ ῶ, ἵνα μὴ τ α λ α ι π ω ρ ο ῖ τ ο μηδ' ἄχθος φ έ ρ ο ι " *sentit enim jam Dionysus se frustra studuisse, ne laboraret famulus: nam qui irritum suum consilium ita pronuntiat, is non jam consilium a præsente rei contemplatione captum dicit, sed priorem cogitat consilii cogitationem* [b]."

Optative or Conjunctive after Optative.

§. **808.** When the principal verb is in the opt. with or without ἄν, the dependent verb is generally in the opt., if the aim proposed is merely a supposition, without any notion of its realisation; but if this notion does come in, the conjunctive is used; as, Soph. Aj. 1217 sq. γ ε ν ο ί μ α ν, ἵν' ὑλᾶεν ἔπεστι πόντου πρόβλημ' ἁλίκλυστον—, τὰς ἱερὰς ὅ π ω ς π ρ ο σ ε ί π ο ι μ ε ν 'Αθήνας: Demosth. p. 39, 3 ὡς δ' ἂ ν ἐ ξ ε τ α σ θ ε ί η μάλιστ' ἀκριβῶς, μ ὴ γ έ ν ο ι τ ο, ὦ πάντες θεοί[c]: but Plat. p. 28 D αὐτίκα—τ ε θ ν α ί η ν δίκην ἐπιθεὶς τῷ ἀδικοῦντι, ἵνα μὴ ἐνθάδε μ έ ν ω καταγέλαστος παρὰ νηυσὶ κορωνίσιν, ἄχθος ἀρούρης:—Eur. Troad. 698 παῖδα τόνδε παιδὸς ἐ κ θ ρ έ ψ α ι ς ἄ ν, Τρoίας μέγιστον ὠφέλημ', ἵν' οἵ ποτε ἐκ σοῦ γενόμενοι παῖδες 'Ίλιον πάλιν κ α τ ο ι κ ί σ ε ι α ν καὶ πόλις γ έ ν ο ι τ' ἔτι.

ᵃ Stallb. ad loc.   ᵇ Reisig. 169.   ᶜ Schäfer Appar. tom. I p. 456.

Interchange of Optative and Conjunctive.

§. 809. When two or more final clauses follow the same principal clause, it sometimes happens that the verb of one is in the conj., of the other in the opt., according to the proper force of these moods (§. 411. 1.). The former gives a notion of the realization of the proposed end, the latter has no such notion, but represents it as a mere possibility, or as a supposition existing only in the mind of some other person [a], frequently expressing the ulterior consequence of the conjunctive: Od. μ, 156 ἀλλ' ἐρέω μὲν ἐγὼν, ἵνα εἰδότες ἤ κε θάνωμεν, ἤ κεν ἀλευάμενοι θάνατον καὶ κῆρα φύγοιμεν, the second sentence is merely a wish, and a consequence which might follow if death were avoided: Il. ε, 567 περὶ γὰρ δίε ποιμένι λαῶν, μήτι πάθῃ, μέγα δέ σφεας ἀποσφήλειε πόνοιο, the first sentence expresses the immediate object of fear, the second the consequences resulting therefrom: Il. ο, 597 sq. Ἕκτορι γάρ οἱ θυμὸς ἐβούλετο κῦδος ὀρέξαι Πριαμίδῃ, ἵνα νηυσὶ κορωνίσι θεσπιδαὲς πῦρ ἐμβάλῃ ἀκάματον, Θέτιδος δ' ἐξαίσιον ἀρὴν πᾶσαν ἐπικρήνειε, the former sentence expresses the immediate result of the favour of Jove, the latter the consequences of that result: Hdt. IX. 51 ἐς τοῦτον δὴ τὸν χῶρον ἐβουλεύσαντο μεταστῆναι, ἵνα καὶ ὕδατι ἔχωσι χρᾶσθαι ἀφθόνῳ, καὶ οἱ ἱππέες σφέας μὴ συνοίατο (the primary, and secondary end). So Eur. El. 56 πηγὰς ποταμίας μετέρχομαι—, ὡς ὕβριν δείξωμεν Αἰγίσθου θεοῖς, γόους τ' ἀφείην: Id. Hec. 1138 ἔδεισα, μὴ σοὶ πολέμιος λειφθεὶς ὁ παῖς Τροίαν ἀθροίσῃ καὶ ξυνοικίσῃ πάλιν, γνόντες δ' Ἀχαιοὶ ζῶντα Πριαμιδῶν τινα Φρυγῶν ἐς αἶαν αὖθις ἄρειαν στόλον, κἄπειτα Θρήκης πεδία τρίβοιεν τάδε λεηλατοῦντες, γείτοσιν δ' εἴη κακὸν Τρώων, ἐν ᾧπερ νῦν—ἐκάμνομεν, "*alterum, Troja ut restitueretur, verebatur ne eveniret; de altero conjecturam faciebat, haud esse dissimile veri Achivos redituros* [b]."

Conjunctive and Optative with ἄν.

§. 810. To the final conjunctions ὡς, ὅπως, μή and ἵνα, the modal adverb ἄν is sometimes added, pointing to some (generally not expressed) condition: Od. ε, 167 f. πέμψω δέ τοι οὖρον ὄπισθεν, ὥς κε μάλ' ἀσκήθης σὴν πατρίδα γαῖαν ἵκηαι, αἴ κε θεοί γ' ἐθέλωσι: Od. β, 376 ἀλλ' ὄμοσον, μὴ μητρὶ φίλῃ τάδε μυθήσασθαι—, ὥς αν μὴ κλαίουσα κατὰ χρόα καλὸν ἰάπτῃ (so. ἐὰν ταῦτα ἀκούσῃ). Compare Od. μ, 156, §. 809. : Od. θ, 20 sq. καί μιν μακρότερον καὶ πάσσονα θῆκε ἰδέσθαι, ὥς κεν Φαιήκεσσι φίλος πάντεσσι γένοιτο,

sc. εἰ πρὸς τοὺς Φαίηκας ἀφίκοιτο: Od. β, 52 οἱ πατρὸς μὲν ἐς οἶκον
ἀπερρίγασι νέεσθαι Ἰκαρίου, ὡς κ' αὐτὸς ἐεδνώσαιτο θύγατρα,
δοίη δ' ᾧ κ' ἐθέλοι καί οἱ κεχαρισμένος ἔλθοι, that in that case, if they
were at his house, he might &c.[a] The opt. is used here after
the perf. according to §. 807. β.: Eur. Bacch. 509 sq. καθείρξατ'
αὐτὸν ἱππικαῖς πέλας φάτναισιν, ὡς ἂν σκότιον εἰσορᾷ κνέφας, sc.
ἐὰν καθειρχθῇ: Id. Hippol. 1304 f. δάκνει σε, Θησεῦ, μῦθος, ἀλλ'
ἔχ' ἥσυχος, τοὐνθένθ' ἀκούσας, ὡς ἂν οἰμώξῃς πλέον, ut, si quæ
sequuntur audieris (ἀκούσας), magis ingemiscere possis: Hdt. III.
44 ἐδεήθη, ὅκως ἂν καὶ παρ' ἑωυτὸν πέμψας ἐς Σάμον δέοιτο
στρατοῦ, ut, si opus esset, exercitum a se peteret: Xen. Cyr. V. 2, 21
διὰ τῆς σῆς χώρας ἄξεις ἡμᾶς, ὅπως ἂν εἰδῶμεν, ἅτε δεῖ φίλια
καὶ πολέμια νομίζειν. (The passages in which μὴ ἄν is used with
opt. are to be explained by §. 814. c. So Thuc. II. 93 ἦν προσ-
δοκία οὐδεμία, μὴ ἄν ποτε οἱ πολέμιοι ἐξαπιναίως οὕτως ἐπιπλεύ-
σειαν: Xen. Anab. VI. 1, 1 εἰ οὖν ταῦτα ἐγὼ ὁρῶν δοκοίην, ὅπου
δυναίμην, ἐνταῦθ' ἄκυρον ποιεῖν τὸ ἐκείνων ἀξίωμα, ἐκεῖνο ἐννοῶ, μὴ
λίαν ἂν ταχὺ σωφρονισθείην.)—In the following passage ὡς
and ὅπως are to be taken as modal adverbs, and ἄν seems to signify,
in some way or other : Id. Cyr. I. 2, 5 ἐπιμέλονται, ὡς ἂν βέλτιστοι εἶεν οἱ πολῖται, how the citizens may be best: Ibid. 10
βασιλεὺς ἡγεμὼν αὐτοῖς ἐστι, καὶ αὐτός τε θηρᾷ, καὶ τῶν ἄλλων ἐπι-
μελεῖται, ὅπως ἂν θηρῷεν: Ibid. II. 1, 4 βουλευσόμεθα, ὅπως
ἂν ἄριστα ἀγωνιζοίμεθα: Plat. Symp. p. 187 D πάλιν γὰρ ἥκει
ὁ αὐτὸς λόγος, ὅτι τοῖς μὲν κοσμίοις τῶν ἀνθρώπων, καὶ ὡς ἂν κοσμιώ-
τεροι γίγνοιντο οἱ μήπω ὄντες, δεῖ χαρίζεσθαι.)

Obs. 1. Hence the elliptic use of the opt. with ἄν to express a wish:
Il. ζ, 281 ὥς κε οἱ αὖθι γαῖα χάνοι! sc. εἰ τοῦτο δυνατὸν εἴη, utinam, si fieri
posset, terra devoraretur!

Obs. 2. The general rules and exceptions given above hold good for
the conj. and opt. with ἄν as well as without it.

Obs. 3. Ὡς ἄν with the opt. is far more rare in Attic than in Epic and
Ionic; ἵνα ἄν is very seldom found, see above (§. 809.): Od. μ, 156.
Soph. Œ. C. 189. Demosth. p. 780, 7 ἵνα μηδ' ἂν ἄκων αὐτῇ ποτε προσπέσῃ: ἵνα ἄν has generally the force of ubicunque or sicubi; ὄφρα ἄν (κε)
is only Epic: Od. μ, 51 ἐκ δ' αὐτοῦ πείρατ' ἀνήφθω, ὄφρα κε τερπόμενος ὄπ'
ἀκούῃς Σειρήνοιῑν: Il. μ, 25 sq. ὗε δ' ἄρα Ζεὺς συνεχές, ὄφρα κε θᾶσσον ἁλίπλοα
τείχεα θείη.

Ὅπως *and* ὡς *with Future Indicative.*—Ὅπως ἄν *with Future Indicative.*

§. 811. Verbs of *caring, considering, troubling oneself about, endeavouring, effecting,* and *inciting;* as, ἐπιμελεῖσθαι, φροντίζειν, δεδιέναι,

[a] See Nitzsch ad loc.

3 H 2

φυλάττειν, σκοπεῖν, σκέπτεσθαι, βουλεύεσθαι, ὁρᾶν, ποιεῖν, πράττειν, curare, μηχανᾶσθαι, παρακαλεῖν, παραγγέλλειν, προειπεῖν, αἰτεῖσθαι, ἀξιοῦν, ἄγε &c., are followed by ὅπως (ὅπως μή), and in Hdt. also by ὡς (on μή see §. 814.), with the fut. ind. instead of the conjunctive. The sense of this future is nearly allied to the conjunctive, and only differs therefrom in that it definitely expresses the possible realisation of the proposed end. After the verbs of *caring*, and *considering*, the original sense of ὅπως is clearly seen, as ὅτῳ τρόπῳ is used instead of it: Thuc. IV. 128 ἔπρασσεν, ὅτῳ τρόπῳ— ἀπαλλάξεται for ὅπως: Id. VI. 11 σκοπεῖν ὅτῳ τρόπῳ τὸ σφέτερον ἀπρεπὲς εὖ θήσονται: Xen. Cyr. I. 2, 3 οἱ Περσικοὶ νόμοι ἐπιμέλονται, ὅπως τὴν ἀρχὴν μὴ τοιοῦτοι ἔσονται οἱ πολῖται, οἷοι πονηροῦ ἢ αἰσχροῦ ἔργου ἐφίεσθαι: Ibid. II. 4, 31 Κῦρος, ὦ Ἀρμένιε, κελεύει οὕτω ποιεῖν σε, ὅπως ὡς τάχιστα ἔχων οἴσεις καὶ τὸν δασμὸν καὶ τὸ στράτευμα: Plat. Rep. p. 421 E παντὶ τρόπῳ φυλακτέον, ὅπως μήποτε αὐτοὺς λήσει εἰς τὴν πόλιν παραδόντα (sc. πενία καὶ πλοῦτος): Demosth. p. 21, 12 σκοπεῖσθε —τοῦτο, ὦ ἄνδρες Ἀθηναῖοι, ὅπως μὴ λόγους ἐροῦσι μόνον οἱ παρ' ἡμῶν πρέσβεις, ἀλλὰ καὶ ἔργον τι δεικνύειν ἕξουσιν: Id. p. 130, 75 δέδοικα, ὅπως μὴ πάνθ' ἅμα, ὅσα οὐ βουλόμεθα, ποιεῖν ἡμῖν ἀνάγκη γενήσεται. And ὅπως and ὡς are used with the ind. fut., even when the principal verb is in an historic tense, where we should expect the fut. opt., the *oratio obliqua* being changed into the *oratio recta*.

2. Sometimes ὅπως ἄν is used with fut. ind. to refer to a condition either expressed or understood: Hdt. III. 104 οἱ δὲ δὴ Ἰνδοὶ τρόπῳ τοιούτῳ καὶ ζεύξει χρεώμενοι ἐλαύνουσι ἐπὶ τὸν χρυσὸν λελογισμένως, ὅκως ἂν καυμάτων τῶν θερμοτάτων ἐόντων ἔσονται ἐν τῇ ἁρπαγῇ, i. e. ὅταν καύματα θερμότατα ᾖ.

Remarks on ὅπως.— Dawes's Canon.— Elliptical use of ὅπως and ὅπως μή.

§. 812. 1. Dawes laid down (Miscel. Crit. p. 227, 459.) that ὅπως is joined with the conj. of the pres., aor. I. pass., aor. II. act. midd. or pass., but never with conj. of aor. I. act. or midd., but in the place thereof the ind. fut. is used, and hence the ind. fut. and conjunctive are often interchanged; as, Plat. Tim. p. 18 E ὅπως οἱ κακοὶ χωρὶς οἵ τ' ἀγαθοὶ ταῖς ὁμοίαις ἑκάτεροι ξυλλέξονται, καὶ μή τις αὐτοῖς ἔχθρα διὰ ταῦτα γίγνηται. But as this canon rests on no grammatical or logical grounds, so it is shaken by the fact that in many passages, by the agreement of the MSS., ὅπως is joined with aor. I. conj. act.: a change of HI into EI, and Ω into O, being all that is required to make the aor. I. conj. into fut. ind., there were great opportunities opened to the inaccuracy of transcribers. The ancients no doubt regarded rather the difference of meaning in their use of one or the other, not the difference of form. There are many passages in Herod. and the Attic writers, prose and poetry, which contradict this rule ; as, Hdt. II. 120 extr. ὅκως ποιήσωσι ; Thuc. I. 73 ὅπως μὴ βουλεύσησθε : Ibid. IV. 66 ὅπως μὴ ἐπιβοηθήσωσιν : Lysias p. 138 extr. ὅπως μὴ ἐργάσησθε. In these examples all MSS. agree, and there are some cases, where the aorist conj., and fut. ind., have a different form ; as, ὅπως κλαύσω (F. κλαυσοῦμαι), ἐκπλεύσῃ (F. ἐκπλεύσεται), ἀνακομίσῃ (F. ἀνακομιεῖ), ἀπολαύσωμεν (F. ἀπολαυσόμεθα), ἀποφήνῃ (F. ἀποφανεῖ). In many passages the metre forbids any alteration[a]. The difference between these two forms doubtlessly is, that the fut. ind. represents the proposed end as something existing in future time ; the aor. conj. as something of which the future realisation is only conceived, but without any notion of its actually existing. See Æsch. Pers. 112 ταῦτά μοι μελαγχίτων φρὴν ἀμύσσεται φόβῳ,—μὴ πόλις πύθηται κένανδρον μέγ' ἄστυ Σουσίδος καὶ τὸ Κίσσινον πόλισμ' ἀντίδουπον ἔσσεται.

2. Ὅπως or ὅπως μή stands with the fut. ind. or with the conj. to express a desire or warning, ὅρα or ὁρᾶτε, *vide, videte*, being readily supplied by the mind : Xen. Anab. I. 7, 3 ὅπως οὖν ἔσεσθε ἄνδρες ἄξιοι τῆς ἐλευθερίας : Arist. Nub. 489 ἄγε νῦν, ὅπως, ὅταν τι προσβάλλωμαι σοφὸν περὶ τῶν μετεώρων, εὐθέως ὑφαρπάσει : Plat. Menon. p. 77 A ἀλλ' ὅπως μὴ οὐχ' οἷός τ' ἔσομαι πολλὰ τοιαῦτα λέγειν. So in the forms, δεῖ σ' (sc. σκοπεῖν) ὅπως in Attic poetry : Soph. Aj. 556 δεῖ σ' ὅπως πατρὸς δείξεις ἐν ἐχθροῖς, οἷος ἐξ οἵου 'τράφης. Conjunctive : Hdt. VI. 85 εἰ νῦν ὀργῇ χρεώμενοι ἔγνωσαν οὕτω Σπαρτιῆται, ὅκως ἐξ ὑστέρης μή τι ὑμῖν, ἢν ταῦτα πρήσσητε, πανώλεθρον κακὸν ἐς τὴν χώρην ἐσβάλωσι, *videte, ne—inferant.*

Ἵνα, ὡς, ὅπως (more rarely), with the Historic Indicative.

§. 813. Ἵνα, ὡς, ὅπως (more rarely) are joined with the historic tenses of the ind., to express an end proposed and wished for, but not attained, or not to be attained. The principal sentence expresses something which does not take place, so that the end proposed by, or which might have resulted therefrom, does not take place either. We may translate ὡς &c. by—*in which case I should* : Soph. Œ. R. 1389 οὐκ ἂν ἐσχόμην τὸ μὴ 'ποκλεῖσαι τοὐμὸν ἄθλιον δέμας, ἵν' ἦν τυφλός τε καὶ κλύων μηδέν, *ut essem cæcus* : Ibid. 1393 τί μ' οὐ λαβὼν ἔκτεινας εὐθύς, ὡς ἔδειξα μήποτε ἐμαυτὸν ἀνθρώποισιν, ἔνθεν ἦν γεγώς, *ut nunquam ostendissem* : Eur. Hippol. 640 sq. χρῆν δ' ἐς γυναῖκας πρόσπολον μὲν οὐ περᾶν, ἄφθογγα δ' αὐταῖς συγκατοικίζειν δάκη θηρῶν, ἵν' εἶχον μήτε προσφωνεῖν τινα, μήτ' ἐξ ἐκείνων φθέγμα δέξασθαι πάλιν, *ut possent* : Ibid. 925 (χρῆν) δισσάς τε φωνὰς πάντας ἀνθρώπους ἔχειν, τὴν μὲν δικαίαν, τὴν δ' ὅπως ἐτύγχανεν (i. e. *injustam*), ὡς ἡ φρονοῦσα τἄδικ' ἐξηλέγχετο πρὸς τῆς δικαίας, κοὐκ ἂν ἠπατώμεθα, *ut convinceretur* : Id.

---

[a] Dawes's error seems to have been one into which he, in common with other English scholars, too frequently fell : the laying down a rule from a number of instances too generally, and not caring to inquire whether there were any grammatical or logical grounds for it to rest upon, and then altering all the passages to suit his canon.

Phœn. 206 (Chorus) Τύριον οἶδμα λιποῦσ' ἔβαν —, Φοίβῳ δούλα μελάθρων ἵν' ὑπὸ δειράσι νιφοβόλοις Παρνασοῦ κατενάσθην, ἵνα depending on δούλα, *ut habitarem* (*at ibi habitare non potuit, quoniam, bello inter Polynicem et Eteoclem exorto, Thebis manere coacta erat*): Aristoph. Pac. 135 οὐκοῦν ἐχρῆν σε Πηγάσου ζεῦξαι πτερὸν, ὅπως ἐφαίνου τοῖς θεοῖς τραγικώτερος: Plat. Crit. p. 44 D εἰ γὰρ ὤφελον—οἷοί τε εἶναι οἱ πολλοὶ τὰ μέγιστα κακὰ ἐξεργάζεσθαι, ἵνα οἷοί τε ἦσαν αὖ καὶ ἀγαθὰ τὰ μέγιστα, καὶ καλῶς ἂν εἶχε, *quo efficere possent etiam bona maxima* (*at id non possunt*): Demosth. p. 837, 5 ἐχρῆν—παρασημήνασθαι κελεῦσαι τὰς διαθήκας, ἵν', εἴ τι ἐγίγνετο ἀμφισβητήσιμον, ἦν (*ut—liceret*) εἰς τὰ γράμματα ταῦτ' ἐπανελθεῖν καὶ τὴν ἀλήθειαν πάντων εὑρεῖν: Ibid. p. 849, 17 ἐζήτησεν ἄν με τὸν παῖδα τὸν γράφοντα τὰς μαρτυρίας, ἵν', εἰ μὴ παρεδίδουν, μηδὲν δίκαιον λέγειν ἐδόκουν: Id. p. 47, 27 οὐ γὰρ ἐχρῆν—ταξίαρχους παρ' ὑμῶν—ἄρχοντας οἰκείους εἶναι, ἵν' ἦν ὡς ἀληθῶς τῆς πόλεως ἡ δύναμις[a]; It is worthy of observation that ἄν is not used, in this construction, even where there is direct reference to a preceding hypothetical sentence containing the condition of the dependent clause.

Remarks on the construction of the seemingly final Conjunction μή.— Dawes's Canon.

§. 814. After verbs of *questioning, considering, reflecting, asking* and *inquiring*, and also verbs of *fear*, of *anxiety*, which imply reflection; as, σκοπεῖν, φροντίζειν, ὁρᾶν, ὑποπτεύειν, ἐννοεῖν, μετανοεῖν, ἀμφισβητεῖν, πυνθάνεσθαι, ἐξερευνᾶν, ὀκνεῖν, δεδιέναι, φοβεῖσθαι &c., the negative μή is used without any final conjunction, where in English we might use the word *that*, but more generally the word *lest*. Μή is a sort of interrogation (as in Lat. *ne*) which introduces an indirect question relating to the preceding object of anxiety, &c.; as, Demosth. p. 14, 18 ὀκνῶ μὴ μάταιος ἡμῖν ἡ στρατεία γένηται, I fear whether the expedition has not been undertaken in vain; that is, I fear that (or lest) it has. The construction of this sort of sentence is as manifold as that of the indirect question.

a. Hence we find the ind. of all the tenses, when the writer or speaker is inwardly persuaded that the object of his anxiety is really in existence; and hence especially of events which are either present or past to him: Od. ε, 300 δείδω, μὴ δὴ πάντα θεὰ νημέρτεα εἶπεν, I fear whether the goddess has not (=that she has) told us, &c.[b]: Eur. Ph. 92 ἐπίσχες, ὡς ἂν προεξερευνήσω στίβον, μή τις πολιτῶν ἐν τρίβῳ φαντάζεται, κἀμοὶ μὲν ἔλθῃ φαῦλος, whether there is not = I am afraid that, or lest: Thuc. III. 53 νῦν δὲ φοβούμεθα, μὴ ἀμφοτέρων ἡμαρτήκαμεν: Xen. Cyr. III. 1, 27 ὅρα, μὴ ἐκείνους αὖ δεήσει σε σωφρονίζειν ἔτι μᾶλλον, ἢ ἡμᾶς νῦν ἐδέησεν: Id. IV. 1, 18 ὅρα, μὴ πολλῶν ἑκάστῳ ἡμῶν χειρῶν δεήσει καὶ ὀφθαλμῶν: Plat. Lach. p. 187 B σκοπεῖν χρή, μὴ οὐ—ὑμῖν ὁ κίνδυνος κινδυνεύεται: Id. Rep. p. 451 A φοβερὸν —, μὴ σφαλεὶς τῆς ἀληθείας—κείσομαι[c]: Id.

---

[a] Schäfer ad loc.   [b] Nitzsch ad loc.   [c] Stallb. ad loc.

'hileb. p. 13 A φοβοῦμαι δὲ, μή τινας ἡδονὰς ἡδοναῖς εὑρήσομεν ἐναντίας:
d. Cratyl. p. 393 C φύλαττε, μή πη παρακρούσομαί σε[a].

b. The subjunct. of the principal tenses (conjunct.) after a principal,
nd of the historic tenses (opt.) after an historic tense. The subjunct.
s here deliberative. For examples see (§. 805. 2.) and Od. ε, 473 δείδω,
ι ἢ θήρεσσιν ἕλωρ καὶ κύρμα γίνωμαι: Xen. Cyr. I. 1, 3 ἐκ τούτου δὴ
ἰναγκαζόμεθα μετανοεῖν, μὴ οὔτε τῶν ἀδυνάτων οὔτε τῶν χαλεπῶν ἔργον ᾖ
for εἴη §. 806. 2.) τὸ ἀνθρώπων ἄρχειν: Id. M. S. IV. 2, 39 καὶ φροντίζω,
ι ἢ κράτιστον ᾖ μοι σιγᾶν: Plat. Phæd. p. 70 A τὰ δὲ περὶ τῆς ψυχῆς πολλὴν
ἱπιστίαν παρέχει τοῖς ἀνθρώποις, μὴ, ἐπειδὰν ἀπαλλαγῇ τοῦ σώματος,
ʼὐδαμοῦ ἔτι ᾖ: Eur. Med. 118 οἵ μοι, τέκνα, μή τι πάθηθ', ὡς ὑπερ-
ιλγῶ[b].

c. The opt. is also used in its secondary meaning to express a doubt as
to the realisation of the object, a suspicion only of its happening: Hdt.
VII. 103 ὅρα, μὴ μάτην κόμπος ὁ λόγος ὁ εἰρημένος εἴη, *vide, ne vana
jactatio fuerit hoc, quod a vobis dictum est.* Ἄν is added when the
suspicion is supposed to depend on a condition: Xen. Anab. VI. 1, 29
ἐκεῖνο ἐννοῶ, μὴ λίαν ἂν ταχὺ σωφρονισθείην: cf. the examples in
§. 810.

Obs. 1. After verbs of *looking into, inquiring, seeing,* such as ὁρᾶν, σκοπεῖν, μή with the ind. present expresses an inquiry whether something is
not: ὅρα μὴ ποιεῖ, see whether he is not doing it. With the conj., a fear
lest he should do it: ὅρα μὴ ποιῇ, see lest he do it. So the ind. in Eur.
Phœn. 92, given above in *a.*

Obs. 2. There is a difference also between the conj. pres. and aor., ὅρα
μὴ ποιῇ, lest he do it presently; μὴ ποιήσῃ, at some future, indefinite time.

Obs. 3. After verbs of *fear* or *anxiety,* εἰ (*whether, if*) is used instead of
μή, and μὴ οὔ, giving a more indefinite character to the feeling: Eur. Med.
187 (184) φόβος, εἰ πείσω δέσποιναν ἐμήν: " in voc. φόβος *inest notio
dubitandi; ac quum is, qui dubitat, sitne aliquid necne, etsi cogitatione plerumque in alterutram partem inclinat, id tamen non indicet, fit, ut ex cujus-
que loci conditione intelligendum sit, utrum εἰ valeat μὴ οὔ an* μή[c] :" so for μή
Androm. 60 καὶ νῦν φέρουσά σοι νέους ἥκω λόγους, φόβῳ μὲν εἰ τις δεσποτῶν
αἰσθήσεται.

Obs. 4. We also find the following constructions after verbs of *fear* and
anxiety: a. ὅπως, *quomodo,* Attic poetry: Eur. Heracl. 249 μὴ τρέσῃς,
ὅπως σέ τις σὺν παισὶ βωμοῦ τοῦδ' ἀποσπάσει βίᾳ: Id. Iph. T. 1002 τὴν θεὸν δ'
ὅπως λάθω, δέδοικα, *timore percussus delibero, quomodo—lateam.*—*b.* ὅπως
μή *quomodo non,* also Attic poetry: Soph. Œ. R. 1058 δέδοιχ', ὅπως μὴ
'κ τῆς σιωπῆς τῆσδ' ἀναρρήξει κακά.—*c.* ὅτι or ὡς, *that,* which signifies
merely the object of fear, without any notion of deliberation: Xen. Cyr.
V. 2, 12 μὴ φοβοῦ ὡς ἀπορήσεις[d]: cf. III. 1, 1. Demosth. p. 141 καὶ
τὸν φόβον ὡς οὐ στήσεται τοῦτο ἄνευ μεγάλου τινὸς κακοῦ.—*d.* Infinitive
with or without the article: φοβεῖσθαι τὸ ἀποθνήσκειν, δεῖσαι τὸ ζῆν.—
ὀρρωδῶ θανεῖν Eur.: Plat. Gorg. p. 457 E φοβοῦμαι διαλέγειν σε. See above
§. 664. 1. and §. 670. The omission of the article makes a great difference of sense: if the inf. has no article, the verb of *fearing* signifies *un-
willingness, hesitation;* if it has the article the verb takes its proper sense
of fear and the inf. with article signifies the object of fear.—*e.* ὥστε μή
with the inf. (rarely) where the object of the fear is expressed, as that
which is in consequence thereof avoided: Eur. Iph. T. 1391 φόβος δ' ἦν
ὥστε μὴ τέγγειν πόδα.

---

[a] Elmsl. Heracl. 483.   [b] Pflugk ad loc.   [c] Ibid.   [d] Bornemann ad loc.

ADJECTIVAL SENTENCE.

§. 815. 1. The adjectival sentence is the resolution of an adjective or participle, and therefore signifies the attribute of a substantive; as, οἱ πολέμιοι, οἱ ἀπέφυγον (= οἱ ἀποφυγόντες πολέμιοι)—τὰ πράγματα, ἃ ὁ 'Αλέξανδρος ἔπραξεν (= τὰ ὑπὸ τοῦ 'Αλεξάνδρου πραχθέντα πράγματα, or τὰ τοῦ 'Αλεξάνδρου πράγματα).—ἡ πόλις, ἐν ᾗ ὁ Πεισίστρατος τύραννος ἦν (= ἡ ὑπὸ τοῦ Πεισιστράτου τυραννευθεῖσα).

2. The inflexions of the relative pronoun which refers to the subst. in the principal clause, denote the gender and number, and frequently the case, which would be denoted by the inflexion of the simple adj. or participle.

3. A simple attribute such as Πεισίστρατος ὁ τύραννος, is, generally speaking, not resolved into an adjectival sentence such as ὃς τύραννος ἦν, except when particular emphasis is to be laid on that attribute ; but if the attribute is compounded of the adj. and certain dependents therefrom, the adjectival sentence is the most natural, and sometimes the only, way of expressing it.

Remarks on the Relative Pronoun.

§. 816. 1. Originally there was no distinct form for the relative pronoun in Greek, but the demonstrative performed the functions of the relative, being placed in both clauses ; in the first as a simple demonstrative, in the second as a retrospective demonstrative, as in German, *der Mann, der ;* in English, " the thing, that :" so Il. a, 125 ἀλλὰ τὰ μὲν πολίων ἐξεπράθομεν, τὰ δέδασται, *quæ ex urbibus diripuimus, ea distributa sunt :* (so Il. η, 481 οὐδέ τις ἔτλη πρὶν πιέειν πρὶν λεῖψαι ὑπερμενέϊ Κρονίωνι, nor did any one dare before to drink, before &c.: Pind. Nem. IV. 4 οὐδὲ μὲν ὕδωρ τόσον γε μαλθακὰ τέγγει γυῖα, τόσσον εὐλογία φόρμιγγι συνάορος.) The aspirated pronouns were demonstrative as well as those beginning with τ, till the necessities of language soon assigned to the latter the demonstrative, to the former the relative, function. There are many instances, as well in the other dialects as in the more perfect language of Attic, to prove that the relative pronouns were originally demonstrative ; as we find that the relative forms are used as demonstrative. (On the use of the demonstrative τοῦ, τῷ, τὸν for οὗ, ᾧ, ὅν, see §. 445 : so even in Attic, τέως for ἕως, τώς for ὡς.)

2. So Homer frequently uses, especially with γάρ, or καί, the relative ὅς as a demonstrative : Il. ζ, 59 μηδ' ὅντινα γαστέρι μήτηρ κοῦρον ἐόντα φέροι, μηδ' ὃς φύγοι, ne is quidem aufugiat : Il. φ, 198 ἀλλὰ καὶ ὃς δείδοικε Διὸς μεγάλοιο κεραυνόν : cf. Od. a, 286. Il. λ, 535. So οἵ—, οἵ, these—those, the one — the other : Il. φ, 353 τείροντ' ἐγχέλυές τε καὶ ἰχθύες, οἳ κατὰ δίνας, οἳ κατὰ καλὰ ῥέεθρα κυβίστων ἔνθα καὶ ἔνθα.—οἵ—οἵ τε : Il. ψ, 498 οἳ δεύτεροι, οἵ τε πάροιθεν.—οἵ for οὗτοι Hesiod. Theog. 22. So Pind. Pyth. III. 89. (B.)

3. In Attic (and Ionic prose) this use is confined to the following cases :

a. Καὶ ὅς, seldom καὶ ἥ, for καὶ οὗτος, καὶ αὕτη : Xen. Cyr. V. 4, 4 αἱ ὅς ἐξαπατηθεὶς διώκει ἀνὰ κράτος : Plat. Symp. p. 201 E καὶ ἥ, οὐκ 'φημήσεις ; ἔφη. In the oblique cases always the article, as καὶ τόν, *et* um.

b. Ὅς μέν—ὅς δέ Demosth. and later writers, but before them by Doric writers, not only in nom. but also in oblique cases sing. and plural : ἀrchyt. p. 676. ap. Gal. (238 Orell.) τῶν ἀγαθῶν ἃ μὲν ἐντὶ ἀνθρώπω, ἃ δὲ ὧν μερέων : Demosth. p. 248 πόλεις Ἑλληνίδας ἃς μὲν ἀναιρῶν, εἰς ἃς δὲ οὓς φυγάδας κατάγων. — ὁ μέν — ὅς δέ : Theogn. 207 ἀλλ' ὁ μὲν αὐτὸς τίσε κακὸν χρέος, ὃς δὲ φίλοισιν ἄτην ἐξοπίσω παισὶν ἐπεκρέμασεν (Bekker ὑδὲ φίλοισιν).

c. Ὅς καὶ ὅς, *this and that*, indefinite ; *such a one — any one*, very ʼare, only in nom. ; as, Hdt. IV. 68 τὰς βασιληίας ἱστίας ἐπιόρκηκε ὅς καὶ ὅς, in accus. τὸν καὶ τόν, τὸ καὶ τό, see §. 444. *b.*

d. In the phrase ἦ δ' ὅς, ἦ δ' ἥ, *said he, she*, mostly in Plato.

e. The following relative conjunctions are also used as demonst. : Il. o, 547 ὁ δ' ὄφρα (for τόφρα) μὲν εἰλίποδας βοῦς βόσκ' ἐν Περκώτῃ — αὐτὰρ ἐπεί κ. τ. λ.: εἷως for τέως Il. μ, 141 : ἵνα for ἐνταῦθα Il. κ, 127. So ὅτε μέν—ὅτε δέ even in Attic, and ὅτε μέν—ἄλλοτε δέ. So ὡς—ὡς, Il. ξ. 294 ὡς ἴδεν, ὥς μιν ἔρως πυκινὰς φρένας ἀμφεκάλυψεν. So Theocr. II. 82. So ἔνθα — ἔνθα, *ubi — ibi* Theocr. VIII. 48 ; ὅσον—ὅσον, *quantum — tantum* Id. IV. 39. Arist. Vesp. 213. (Hebr. X. 37.)

4. The relatives, compounded of a relative and indefinite pronoun, as ὅστις, ὁποῖος, ὁπόσος &c., express an indefinite, and hence a general notion, and therefore are frequently joined with the generalising adverbs δή, δήποτε, and are very commonly used in general propositions : Eur. Troad. 589 φεύγειν μὲν οὖν χρὴ πόλεμον ὅστις εὖ φρονεῖ. The indefinite notion is yet more strongly marked when these pronouns are applied to an object, as coming under some class, to denote its genus or essence, as is frequently the case with ὅστις, *such a one as*, in Attic and also in Epic : Od. β, 124 ὄφρα κε κείνη τοῦτον ἔχῃ νόον, ὅν τινά οἱ νῦν ἐν στήθεσσι τιθεῖσι θεοί : Xen. Anab. II. 6, 6 ταῦτα οὖν φιλοπολέμου δοκεῖ ἀνδρὸς ἔργον εἶναι, ὅστις — αἱρεῖται πολεμεῖν : Eur. Hipp. 918 δεινὸν σοφιστὴν εἶπας, ὅστις εὖ φρονεῖν τοὺς μὴ φρονοῦντας δυνατὸς ἔστ' ἀναγκάσαι.

5. Hence ὅστις is used in a definite force in adject. sentences to express an attribute belonging to the nature of the object, its real and peculiar property, while ὅς expresses merely an accidental property which may be assigned to other objects, as ἡ πόλις ἣ κτίζεται, but ἡ πόλις ἥτις ἐν Δελφοῖς κτίζεται, as early as Homer ; as, Il. ψ, 43 οὐ μὰ Ζῆν', ὅστις τε θεῶν ὕπατος καὶ ἄριστος : Hdt. II. 151 ἐν φρενὶ λαβόντες τὸ χρηστήριον, ὅτι ἐκέχρηστό σφι, i. e. *cujusmodi iis datum erat* : Ibid. 99, 7 πόλιν κτίσας ταύτην, ἥτις νῦν Μέμφις καλεῖται.

Obs. 1. On the use of these pronouns in indirect questions, being compounded of ὅς and τίς, interrog., see *Interrogative Sentences.*

Obs. 2. On ὅς τε, ὅστις τε, see §. 755. 3., ὅσπερ §. 734. 2. 3., ὅς γε, §. 735. 9.

Relation between the Principal and Dependent Sentences.

§.817. 1. The relation between the substantive and the adjectival clause is denoted by a demonstrative pronoun in the principal clause, pointing forwards to the relative pronoun in the dependent one, and this latter pointing backwards to the former; as, οὗτος ὁ ἀνήρ, ὃν εἶδες. The article ὁ, ἡ, τό, is to be reckoned as a demonstrative, as it originally had this sense (§. 444.); as, τὸ ῥόδον, ὁ θάλλει. Generally speaking it may be said, that whenever the article is used with a subst., it points to a relative clause either expressed or implied; as, τὸ ῥόδον καλόν ἐστι, that is ὃ ὁρᾷς or some such expression. But, as is obvious, this relative sentence need not be expressly stated when it is easily supplied, or the object is supposed to be sufficiently well known. Hence the name *Article*, ἄρθρον, that is, *a joint*, is very significant, as it expresses the connection or fitting in of the article and the relative in the two sentences, as it were the two parts of a joint: hence both the demonst. ὁ, ἡ, τό, and the relative ὅς, ἥ, ὅ, are termed not unfrequently, "*article*," the former *præpositivus*, the latter *postpositivus*.

2. When the object to which the relative refers is to be considered as indefinite, the article is omitted, and the relative refers directly to the subst.; as, ἀνήρ, ὃς καλός ἐστιν = ἀνὴρ καλός. When the relative refers to a personal pronoun, this supplies the place of the demonst.; as, ἐγώ, ὅς—σύ, ὅς &c. If no particular emphasis is to be laid on this pronoun it is omitted, and the relative refers to the person implied in the inflexion of the verb; as, καλῶς ἐποίησας, ὃς ταῦτα ἔπραξας: if the subst. to which the adject. clause refers is omitted, the adject. clause has the force of a substantive; as, ἦλθον οἱ ἄριστοι ἦσαν = ἦλθον οἱ ἄριστοι (sc. ἄνδρες).

Obs. 1. Substantives expressing *place*, *mode* or *manner*, &c. are sometimes followed by a local, modal or other relative adverb, according to the sense of the subst., instead of the relative pronoun; as, ὁ τόπος ὅθι ἔστη —ὁ τρόπος ὡς ἐβίωσε.

3. As to ὁ, ἡ, τό and the demonst. οὗτος, αὕτη, τοῦτο the relative ὅς, ἥ, ὅ answers, so the demonst. of quality or size, τοῖος, τοιοῦτος, τόσος, τοσοῦτος, have the proper relatives οἷος and ὅσος. But sometimes ὅς also is the relative to τοιοῦτος: Plat. Gorg. p. 473 E ὅταν τοιαῦτα λέγῃς, ἃ οὐδεὶς ἂν φήσειεν ἀνθρώπων, as in other relations ὅς often expresses quality: Plat. Theæt. p. 197 A οὐδένα τρόπον διαλέξομαι, ὧν γε ὅς εἰμι: Id. Phædr. p. 243 E τοῦτο μὲν πιστεύω, ἕωσπερ ἂν ᾖς ὃς εἶ: Id. Rep. p. 529 A οὐκ ἀγεννῶς μοι δοκεῖς τὴν—μάθησιν λαμβάνειν παρὰ σαυτῷ ἥ ἐστι. See *Interrog. Sentences*.

Omission of the Demonstrative before the Relative.

4. Not only is the demonst. omitted in the principal clause, when it is in the same case with the relative, but even when it is in a different case, where the pronoun can be easily supplied, and has no particular emphasis,—hence especially where the demonstr. would be quite indefinite ; and here the relative may be translated by *si qui*, and the demonst. is frequently omitted when an adjectival clause precedes, as we shall see farther on : Od. λ, 433 sq. ἡ (Clytæmnestra) δ᾽ ἔξοχα λύγρ᾽ εἰδυῖα οἷ τε κατ᾽ αἶσχος ἔχευε καὶ ἐσσομένῃσιν ὀπίσσω θηλυτέρῃσι γυναιξὶ καὶ (sc. ταύτῃ) ἥ κ᾽ εὐεργὸς ἔῃσιν : Soph. Phil. 139 καὶ γνώμᾳ (sc. ἐκείνου), παρ᾽ ὅτῳ τὸ θεῖον Διὸς σκῆπτρον ἀνάσσεται : Eur. Or. 591, 3 γάμοι δ᾽ ὅσοις μὲν εὖ πίπτουσιν (i. e. καλῶς ἔχουσι) βροτῶν, (τούτοις sc.) μακάριος αἰών· οἷς δὲ μὴ πίπτουσιν εὖ, (οὗτοι sc.) τά τ᾽ ἔνδον εἰσὶ τά τε θύραζε δυστυχεῖς : Thuc. II. 41 οὐδὲν προσδεόμενοι οὔτε Ὁμήρου ἐπαινέτου, οὔτε (τινὸς sc.) ὅστις ἔπεσι μὲν τὸ αὐτίκα τέρψει κ. τ. λ. : Lysias p. 152. 40 μὴ οὖν προκαταγινώσκετε ἀδικίαν τοῦ εἰς αὑτὸν μὲν μικρὰ δαπανῶντος —, ἀλλ᾽ ὅσοι (i. e. ἀλλὰ τούτων, ὅσοι) καὶ τὰ πατρῷα—εἰς τὰς αἰσχίστας ἡδονὰς εἰθισμένοι εἰσὶν ἀναλίσκειν : Plat. Rep. p. 373 B (ἡ πόλις) ὄγκου ἐμπλησταία καὶ πλήθους (sc. τούτων), ἃ οὐκέτι τοῦ ἀναγκαίου ἕνεκά ἐστιν ἐν ταῖς πόλεσιν[a]. So very often Lat. : Sallust. Cat. 58 *maximum est periculum* (sc. *iis*), *qui maxime timent.* So οὐκ ἔστιν, ὅς or ὅστις οὐ, ταῦτα ποιήσει.

5. There is a peculiar form in Greek, ἔστιν οἵ (λέγουσιν, *sunt qui dicunt*). This form was so firmly established in the language, that neither the number of the relative has any influence on the verb ἔστι, nor is the tense changed, though the time spoken of be past or future ; hence this form has assumed the character of the substantival pronoun ἔνιοι, and by means of the cases of the relative has a complete inflexion :—

Nom.—Ἔστιν οἵ = ἔνιοι : Xen. Cyr. II. 3, 18 οἱ μὲν ἔβαλλον ταῖς βώλοις, καὶ ἔστιν οἳ ἐτύγχανον καὶ θωράκων κ. τ. λ. ἔστιν ἅ = ἔνια. Ἔστιν ἃ ἦν χαλεπώτατα.

Gen.—Ἔστιν ὧν = ἐνίων : Thuc. III. 92 Λακεδαιμόνιοι τῶν ἄλλων Ἑλλήνων ἐκέλευον τὸν βουλόμενον ἔπεσθαι, πλὴν Ἰώνων καὶ Ἀχαιῶν καὶ ἔστιν ὧν ἄλλων ἐθνῶν.

Dat.—Ἔστιν οἷς = ἐνίοις. Ἔστιν οἷς οὐχ οὕτως ἔδοξεν.

Acc.—Ἔστιν οὕς = ἐνίους : Plat. Phæd. p. 111 D ἔστι δ᾽ οὕς καὶ βραχυτέρους τῷ βάθει τοῦ ἐνθάδε εἶναι καὶ πλατυτέρους.

<hr />

[a] Stallb. ad loc.

Ἔστιν ἅ = ἔνια: Thuc. II. 26 Κλεόπομπος τῆς παραθαλασσίου ἔστιν ἃ ἐδήωσε.

As a question — ἔστιν οἵτινες; Xen. M. S. I. 4, 6 ἔστιν οὕστινας ἀνθρώπων τεθαύμακας ἐπὶ σοφίᾳ; Also singular; as, Plat. Menon. p. 85 B ἔστιν ἥντινα δόξαν οὐχ αὑτοῦ οὗτος ἀπεκρίνατο;

Obs. 2. Sometimes, but rarely, we find the impft. ἦν: Xen. Hell. VII. 5, 17 τῶν πολεμίων ἦν οὓς ὑποσπόνδους ἀπέδοσαν: Id. Anab. I. 5, 7 ἦ δὲ τούτων τῶν σταθμῶν οὓς πάνυ μακροὺς ἤλαυνεν. With the singular of the relative: Id. Cyr. V. 3, 16 ἦν δὲ καὶ ὃ ἔλαβε χωρίον. Somewhat more frequently the plural εἰσίν: Thuc. VII. 44 οἱ ὕστερον ἥκοντες εἰσὶν οἱ διαμαρτόντες τῶν ὁδῶν κατὰ τὴν χώραν ἐπλανήθησαν: Plat. Legg. p. 934 D μαίνονται μὲν οὖν πολλοὶ πολλοὺς τρόπους, οὓς μὲν νῦν εἴπομεν, ὑπὸ νόσων, εἰσὶ δὲ οἳ διὰ θυμοῦ κακὴν φύσιν ἅμα καὶ τροφὴν γενομένην.

Obs. 3. Where the Latins said *sunt qui dicunt*, the Greeks would use the above form, ἔστιν οἱ λέγουσιν, or εἰσὶν οἱ λέγοντες, as Dem. p. 45, 18 εἰσὶν οἱ πάντ' ἐξαγγέλλοντες, *sunt qui omnia enunciunt*. But sometimes also we find εἰσὶν οἱ λέγουσιν, as Hdt. III. 45 εἰσὶ δὲ, οἳ λέγουσι, τοὺς ἀπ' Αἰγύπτου νικῆσαι Πολυκράτεα.

Obs. 4. Analogous to this formula is the use of ἔστιν with a relative adverb, the demonst. being omitted:—

Ἔστιν ὅτε = ἐνίοτε, *est quando*, i. e. *interdum*;
Ἔστιν ἵνα or ὅπου, *est ubi*, i. e. *aliquando*;
Ἔστιν οὗ or ἔνθα, *est ubi*, in many places;
Οὐκ ἔσθ' ὅπου, *nunquam*;
Ἔστιν ᾗ or ὅπη, *quodammodo*; or in many spots; οὐκ ἔστιν ὅπη, no whither;
Οὐκ ἔστιν ὅπως, *nullo modo*, οὐκ ἔστιν ὅπως οὐ, *certainly*.
Ἔστιν ὅπως; in the question, Is it possible that?

These expressions are especially Attic, both prose and poetry; as, Xen. Cyr. III. 1, 20 ὁ μὲν γὰρ ἰσχύϊ κρατηθεὶς ἔστιν ὅτε ᾠήθη τὸ σῶμα ἀσκήσας ἀναμαχεῖσθαι: Ibid. 24 δουλεύοντες ἔστιν ὅτε δύνανται καὶ μᾶλλον τῶν εὐδαιμόνων ἐσθίειν τε καὶ καθεύδειν.

Person of the Verb in the Adjectival Sentence.

§. 818. 1. The person of the dependent verb is determined by the substantive or demonstrative pronoun either expressed or to be supplied; as, ἐγὼ, ὃς γράφω, σὺ, ὃς γράφεις, ὁ ἀνήρ or ἐκεῖνος, ὃς γράφει — οἱ τῶν πολιτῶν ἄριστοι ἦσαν, τὴν πόλιν ἔσωσαν: Plat. Crit. p. 45 E ἀνανδρίᾳ τῇ ἡμετέρᾳ διαπεφευγέναι ἡμᾶς δοκεῖν, οἵτινές σε οὐ διεσώσαμεν.

2. Hence after the vocative, the second person is used; as, ἄνθρωπε, ὃς ἡμᾶς τοιαῦτα κακὰ ἐποίησας. Sometimes however the third person is used referring to a person speaking, or spoken to; as, Il. ρ, 248 ὦ φίλοι, Ἀργείων ἡγήτορες ἠδὲ μέδοντες, οἵτε παρ' Ἀτρείδης, Ἀγαμέμνονι καὶ Μενελάῳ, δήμια πίνουσιν καὶ σημαί-

ν ο υ σ ι ν, ἕκαστοι λαοῖς. Frequently there is a transition made from speaking of some one in the third person in the principal clause, to an emphatic apostrophe to him in the second in the relative clause: Od. δ, 686 ὕστατα καὶ πύματα νῦν ἐνθάδε δ ε ι π ν ή σ ε ι α ν· ο ἳ θάμ᾽ ἀγειρόμενοι βίοτον κ α τ α κ ε ί ρ ε τ ε πολλόν: Hdt. VIII. 142 ἄλλως τε, τουτέων ἁπάντων αἰτίους γενέσθαι δουλοσύνης τοῖσι ῞Ελ- λησι ᾽Α θ η ν α ί ο υ ς, οὐδαμῶς ἀνασχετόν· ο ἵ τ ι ν ε ς αἰεὶ καὶ τὸ πάλαι φ α ί ν ε σ θ ε πολλοὺς ἐλευθερώσαντες ἀνθρώπων — here Herodotus returns in the adject. sentence to the *oratio recta* which he had left. And even when the person of the verb in the relative clause does not refer to the subject of the principal verb, but to some other subst. in the principal clause, yet it often agrees, not with the subject itself, but with the person implied in that subject: Isocr. p. 141 ἐοίκατε γὰρ οὕτω δ ι α κ ε ι μ έ ν ο ι ς ἀ ν θ ρ ώ π ο ι ς, ο ἵ τ ι ν ε ς — τ ε θ ύ κ α μ ε ν — ἐ κ κ λ η σ ι ά ζ ο μ ε ν.

Agreement of the Relative Pronoun.

§. 819. The relative pronoun agrees in number and gender with the subst. to which it refers, as the attributive adjective with its subst., but its case depends on the verb in the relative clause; as, ὁ ἀνὴρ, ὃν εἶδες—ἡ ἀρετὴ, ἧς πάντες οἱ ἀγαθοὶ ἐπιθυμοῦσιν —οἱ στρατιῶται, οἷς μαχόμεθα &c.

But to this general rule there are many exceptions.

Exceptions in gender and number.

1. Constructio κ α τ ὰ σ ύ ν ε σ ι ν (§. 378.). In personal names this belongs rather to poetry than prose; as, Il. κ, 278 Διὸς τ έ κ ο ς, ἥ τ ε μοι αἰεί—παρίσταται: Il. χ, 87 φίλον θ ά λ ο ς, ὃ ν τέκον αὐτή: so in Homer always; βίη ῾Ηρακλείη, ὅσπερ: Soph. Philoct. 714 f ὦ μελέα ψ υ χ ὰ, ὃ ς μηδ᾽ οἰνοχύτου πόματος ἤσθη δεκέτη χρόνον: Eur. Suppl. 12 θανόντων ἑπτὰ γενναίων τ έ κ ν ω ν,— ο ὓ ς ποτ᾽ ᾽Αργείων ἄναξ ᾽Άδραστος ἤγαγε. In collective nouns or substantives used as such, this construction is used not unfre- quently in prose as well as poetry: Il. π, 368 λεῖπε λ α ὸ ν Τ ρ ω ϊ- κ ό ν, ο ὓ ς ἀέκοντας ὀρυκτὴ τάφρος ἔρυκε: Od. λ, 502 τῷ κε τ έ ῳ (τινὶ) στύξαιμι μένος καὶ χεῖρας ἀάπτους, οἳ κεῖνον βιόωνται: Hdt. VIII. 128 περιέδραμε ὅ μ ι λ ο ς—, οἳ αὐτίκα τὸ τόξευμα λαβόντες— ἔφερον ἐπὶ τοὺς στρατηγούς: Thuc. III. 4 τὸ τῶν ᾽Αθηναίων ν α υ- τ ι κ ὸ ν, οἳ ὥρμουν ἐν τῇ Μαλέᾳ: Eur. Or. 1127 sq. νῦν δ᾽ ὑπὲρ

ἀπάσης Ἑλλάδος δώσει δίκην, ὧν πατέρας ἔκτειν', ὧν τ' ἐτέλεσεν τέκνα: Plat. Phædr. p. 260 A πλήθει, οἵπερ δικάσουσι.

2. Here also belong the following cases:

a. Where the subst. is in the singular, but the relative in plural —the relative referring, in a general way, not to any definite individual, but to a class, and having the sense of οἷος; but this is more common in poetry than prose: Od. μ, 97 κῆτος, ἃ μυρία βόσκει ἀγάστονος Ἀμφιτρίτη: Il. ξ, 410 χερμαδίῳ, τά ῥα πολλὰ—παρ' ποσὶ μαρναμένων ἐκυλίνδετο: Eur. Or. 908 αὐτουργός, οἵπερ καὶ μόνοι σώζουσι γῆν[a]: Id. Helen. 448 Ἕλλην πεφυκώς, οἷσιν οὐκ ἐπιστροφαί: Id. Suppl. 870 φίλοις τ' ἀληθὴς ἦν φίλος, παροῦσί τε καὶ μὴ παροῦσιν ὧν ἀριθμὸς οὐ πολύς: Plat. Rep. p. 554 A αὐχμηρός γε τις—ὢν καὶ ἀπὸ παντὸς περιουσίαν ποιούμενος, θησαυροποιὸς ἀνήρ, οὓς δὴ (*cujusmodi homines*) καὶ ἐπαινεῖ τὸ πλῆθος[b]: Demosth. p. 328 (24) ἀνδρὶ καλῷ τε κἀγαθῷ, ἐν οἷς οὐδαμοῦ σὺ φανήσῃ γεγονώς. So also when the neuter plur. ἅ refers to an indefinite pronoun, or as adjective in neut. sing. used as a substantive, since in both of these a merely general notion is contained: Isocr. p. 67 E οὐδὲν τοιοῦτον κατασκευάζουσιν, ἐξ ὧν κ. τ. λ.: Thuc. III. 38 ἄλλο τι ἢ ἐν οἷς ζῶμεν. Cf. Plat. Alc. I. p. 129 C.

β. On the other hand a singular relative refers to a plur. subst. when the relative is used in an indefinite sense; as ὅστις, ὃς ἄν with conj. *quisquis, quicunque:* Il. λ, 367 νῦν αὖ τοὺς ἄλλους ἐπιείσομαι (*persequar*), ὅν κε κιχείω: Il. τ, 260 ἀνθρώπους τίννυνται, ὅτις κ' ἐπίορκον ὁμόσσῃ; Eur. Med. 220 δίκη γὰρ οὐκ ἔνεστ' ἐν ὀφθαλμοῖς βροτῶν, ὅστις πρὶν ἀνδρὸς σπλάγχνον ἐκμαθεῖν στυγεῖ δεδορκώς, οὐδὲν ἠδικημένος[c]: Id. Hec. 359 δεσποτῶν ὠμῶν φρένας τύχοιμ' ἄν, ὅστις ἀργύρου μ' ὠνήσεται.—So especially πάντες, ὅστις or ὃς ἄν with conj. (never πάντες οἵτινες, but always πάντες ὅσοι or ὅστις); as, Thuc. VII. 29 πάντας ἑξῆς, ὅτῳ ἐντύχοιεν, καὶ παῖδας καὶ γυναῖκας κτείνοντας: Plat. Rep. p. 566 D ἀσπάζεται πάντας, ᾧ ἂν περιτυγχάνῃ. So frequently the relative pronoun is placed first in the singular, while a substantive to which it belongs, generally a demonstr. pronoun, follows in the plur.: Soph. Antig. 707 ὅστις γὰρ αὐτὸς ἢ φρονεῖν μόνος δοκεῖ, ἢ γλῶσσαν, ἣν οὐκ ἄλλος, ἢ ψυχὴν ἔχειν, οὗτοι διαπτυχθέντες ὤφθησαν κενοί: Thuc. VI. 17 ὅ τι δὲ ἕκαστος ἢ ἐκ τοῦ λέγων πείθειν οἴεται, ἢ στασιάζων ἀπὸ τοῦ κοινοῦ λαβὼν ἄλλην γῆν, μὴ κατορθώσας, οἰκήσειν, ταῦτα ἑτοιμάζεται.

§. 820. 1. The relative sometimes agrees neither with the grammatical nor the natural gender of its subst., when it is in the neuter

---

[a] Porson. et Schäfer ad loc.   [b] Stallb. ad loc.   [c] Pflugk ad loc.

to signify that the substantival notion is to be taken not as particular, but general (§. 381.): Soph. Œ. T. 542 ἆρ' οὐχὶ μῶρόν ἐστι τοὔγχείρημά σου, ἄνευ τε πλήθους καὶ φίλων τυραννίδα θηρᾶν, ὃ πλήθει χρήμασίν θ' ἁλίσκεται. This may clearly be seen in the following examples: Xen. M. S. III. 9, 8 φθόνον δὲ σκοπῶν, ὅ τι εἴη, *quid sit invidia* (in what category it is to be classed), ὅστις εἴη, *qualis sit invidia*, the category is supposed to be fixed, and its properties alone inquired after. Cf. Plat. Gorg. p. 462 D τίς τέχνη ὀψοποιΐα;—Οὐδεμία, ὦ Πῶλε.—Ἀλλὰ τί, φάθι.—Φημὶ δὴ ἐμπειρία τις.

Obs. This neuter relative seems sometimes to refer to a masculine or feminine substantive, without the generalising sense as above; but in reality it refers to the whole sentence: Thuc. I. 59 τρέπονται ἐπὶ τὴν Μακεδονίαν, ἐφ' ὅπερ καὶ τὸ πρότερον ἐπέμποντο (where ἐφ' ὅπερ refers to τρέπονται ἐπὶ τ. Μακ.:) Id. III. 39 init. νῆσον δὲ οἵτινες ἔχοντες μετὰ τειχῶν καὶ κατὰ θάλασσαν μόνον φοβούμενοι τοὺς ἡμετέρους πολεμίους, ἐν ᾧ καὶ αὐτοὶ τριήρων παρασκευῇ οὐκ ἄφρακτοι ἦσαν πρὸς αὐτούς (where ἐν ᾧ refers to the sentence which is to be supplied after φοβούμενοι: μὴ ἐπέρχωνται.) So plur. Id. I. 69 καίτοι ἐλέγεσθε ἀσφαλεῖς εἶναι, ὧν (τοῦ ἀσφ. εἶναι) ἄρα ὁ λόγος τοῦ ἔργου ἐκράτει.

2. When the plural of the subst. (expressed or implied) is used for the singular, the relative may be in the singular; as, Eur. Iph. A. 991 sq. οἰκτρὰ γὰρ πεπόνθαμεν, ᾗ κενὴν κατέσχον ἐλπίδα.

§. 821. 1. When the relative refers to two or more objects, it is in the plural, and of the same gender with the substantives, if they are all of the same gender; but if the substantives express things inanimate, the relative is often in the neuter; as, Plat. Apol. p. 18 A ἐν ἐκείνῃ τῇ φωνῇ τε καὶ τῷ τρόπῳ ἔλεγον, ἐν οἷσπερ ἐτεθράμμην: Xen. Cyr. I. 3, 2 ὁρῶν αὐτὸν κεκοσμημένον καὶ ὀφθαλμῶν ὑπογραφῇ, καὶ χρώματος ἐντρίψει καὶ κόμαις προσθέτοις, ἃ δὴ νόμιμα ἦν ἐν Μήδοις: Isocr. p. 278 B ταῦτα δ' εἶπον, οὐ πρὸς τὴν εὐσέβειαν, οὐδὲ πρὸς τὴν δικαιοσύνην, οὐδὲ πρὸς τὴν φρόνησιν ἀποβλέψας, ἃ σὺ διῆλθες.

2. But if the substantives are of different genders, the relative pronoun, in personal names, agrees with the more worthy gender; in names of things it is generally neuter; as, Od. β, 284 θάνατον καὶ Κῆρα μέλαιναν, ὃς δή σφι σχεδόν ἐστι: Isocr. de Pac. p. 159 A ἥκομεν ἐκκλησιάζοντες περί τε πολέμου καὶ εἰρήνης, ἃ μεγίστην ἔχει δύναμιν ἐν τῷ τῶν ἀνθρώπων βίῳ τῷ. Sometimes it agrees with the last subst.: Isocr. p. 163 A ἢν δὲ τὴν εἰρήνην ποιησώμεθα—μετὰ πολλῆς ἀσφαλείας τὴν πόλιν οἰκήσομεν, ἀπαλλαγέντες πολέμων καὶ κινδύνων καὶ ταραχῆς, εἰς ἣν νῦν πρὸς ἀλλήλους κατέστημεν.

3. When there is in the adjectival sentence a substantive used as a predicate, the relative frequently, and indeed generally, does not agree with its own substantive, but suffers a sort of attraction

to the predicative subst.   The verb which with the subst. makes
up the predicate is generally one of *being*, or *calling*, or *being
called*: the reason of this is the importance of the predicative substantive: Hdt. II. 17 ἡ μὲν (ὁδὸς) πρὸς ἠῶ τρέπεται, τὸ καλέεται
Πηλούσιον στόμα: Id. V. 108 τὴν ἄκρην, αἱ καλεῦνται κληῖδες
τῆς Κύπρου: Id. VII. 54 Περσικὸν ξίφος, τὸν ἀκινάκην καλέουσι:
Plat. Phædr. p. 255 C ἡ τοῦ ῥεύματος ἐκείνου πηγή, ὃν ἵμερον
Ζεὺς Γανυμήδους ἐρῶν ὠνόμασε: Id. Phileb. p. 40 A λόγοι μὴ
εἰσιν ἐν ἑκάστοις ἡμῶν, ἅς ἐλπίδας ὀνομάζομεν: Demosth. p. 853. 31
ἔχει—Ἄφοβος—ὀγδοήκοντα μὲν μνᾶς, ἣν ἔλαβε προῖκα τῆς μητρός.
This is less frequent in Latin.

4. When the relative does not follow immediately on its subst.,
but on another substantive which forms part of the principal clause,
it agrees sometimes in number and case, not with its own, but with
this predicative substantive: Plat. Legg. p. 937 D καὶ δίκη ἐν
ἀνθρώποις πῶς οὐ καλόν, ὃ πάντα ἡμέρωκε τὰ ἀνθρώπινα; Id. Gorg.
p. 460 E οὐδέποτ᾽ ἂν εἴη ἡ ῥητορικὴ ἄδικον πρᾶγμα, ὅ γ᾽ ἀεὶ
περὶ δικαιοσύνης τοὺς λόγους ποιεῖται[a]: Ibid. p. 463 B ταύτης μοι δοκεῖ
τῆς ἐπιτηδεύσεως πολλὰ μὲν καὶ ἄλλα μόρια εἶναι, ἐν δὲ καὶ ἡ ὀψοποιϊκή,
ὃ δοκεῖ μὲν εἶναι τέχνη.

Exceptions to agreement in case.

§. 822. 1. As the adjectival sentence represents an attribute of its
subst., forming with it one whole notion, the Greek language endeavoured to make the adjectival sentence so coalesce with its substantive, that the unity of this whole notion should not be lost; they
effected this by placing the relative not in the case of the verb on
which it immediately depends, but in the case of its preceding
substantive.   This is called *attraction*, the relative being, as
it were, attracted to and acted upon by its substantive; as, Hdt. I.
23 Ἀρίονα διθύραμβον πρῶτον ἀνθρώπων τῶν (= ὧν) ἡμεῖς ἴδμεν.

2. This attraction, however, generally speaking, is confined to
those cases where the relative should stand in acc., but is attracted
by the gen. or dat. of the subst.   The unity of the subst. and adjectival sentence is very frequently yet more perfect, by the substant.
being transferred from the principal to the relative clause:
ἐπιθυμῶ ἧς ἔγραψας ἐπιστολῆς (=τῆς ὑπὸ σοῦ γραφθείσης ἐπιστολῆς)—χαίρω ᾗ ἔγραψας ἐπιστολῇ (=τῇ ὑπὸ σοῦ γραφθείσῃ ἐπιστολῇ); without a substantive (§. 817, 2.): μεμνημένος ὧν ἔπραξε or ὧν
ἔπραξε μεμν.—οἷς ἔχω χρῶμαι: even Homer Il. ε, 265 τῆς γάρ τοι

[a] Stallb. ad loc.

γενεῆς ἧς Τρωΐ περ εὐρύοπα Ζεὺς δῶκε: Il. ψ, 649 τιμῆς ἧστέ μ'
ἔοικε τετιμῆσθαι: Thuc. VII. 21 ἀγὼν ἀπὸ τῶν πόλεων ὧν ἔπεισε
(= τῶν πεισθεισῶν) στρατιάν: Arist. Thesm. 835 ἔν τε ταῖς ἄλλαις ἑορταῖς αἷσιν ἡμεῖς ἤγομεν: Soph. Œ. C. 334 ἦλθον ξὺν ᾧπερ εἶχον
οἰκετῶν πιστῷ μόνῳ: Xen. Cyr. III. 1, 33 σὺν τοῖς θησαυροῖς οἷς
ὁ πατὴρ κατέλιπεν (= τοῖς ὑπὸ τοῦ πατρὸς καταλειφθεῖσι): Ibid. II.
4, 17 ὁπότε δὲ σὺ προεληλυθοίης σὺν ᾗ ἔχοις δυνάμει: Ibid. III. 1,
34 ἐγὼ δὲ ὑπισχνοῦμαι, ἢν ὁ θεὸς εὖ διδῷ, ἀνθ' ὧν ἂν ἐμοὶ δανείσῃς,—
ἄλλα πλείονος ἄξια εὐεργετήσειν: Plat. Gorg. p. 519 A ὅταν τὰ
ἀρχαῖα προσαπολλύωσι πρὸς οἷς ἐκτήσαντο: so ἀνθ' ὧν for ἀντὶ τούτων, ἅ—ἐξ ὧν for ἐκ τούτων, ἅ; hence ἀνθ' ὧν for ὅτι, as, χάριν σοι
οἶδα, ἀνθ' ὧν ἦλθες, because that. The simplest form of attraction
is that which takes place with a subst. depending on a preposition,
and in the same case as is required by the verb of the relative:
Xen. M. S. II. 6, 34 ἐμοὶ ἐγγίγνεται εὔνοια πρὸς οὓς ἂν ὑπολάβω
εὐνοϊκῶς ἔχειν πρὸς ἐμέ for πρὸς τούτους, οὕς.

Obs. 1. But when the relative takes another preposition, or the same
used in another relation, the attraction is not admissible. The instances
which are adduced against this may be explained; as, Xen. Cyr. VIII. 2,
26 πολλὰ ἐμηχανᾶτο πρὸς τὸ πρωτεύειν *παρ' οἷς* ἐβούλετο ἑαυτὸν φιλεῖσθαι;
it would be correct to say, παρ' οἷς ἐβ. φιλεῖσθαι. The attraction is seldom
brought about by the repetition of a preposition with the relative; as in
Thuc. III. 64 ἀφ' ὧν ἐγένοντο ἀγαθοὶ, ἀπὸ τούτων ὠφελεῖσθαι: here either ἀπὸ
τούτων should have been omitted, or ἀφ' ὧν been merely ἅ, as the sense is,
to draw profit from those things wherein they have been brave: Lyc. c.
Leocr. c. 32 εἰς αὐτὸ τοῦτο τὴν τιμωρίαν τάξαντες, εἰς ὃ μάλιστα φοβούμενοι
τυγχάνουσι: Demosth. p. 95, 23 καὶ *περὶ ὧν* φασι μέλλειν αὐτὸν ποιεῖν,
καὶ *περὶ τούτων* προκατηγορούντων ἀκροᾶσθε for ἃ φασι etc.; Ibid. p. 96,
26 ἀφ' ὧν ἀγείρει καὶ προσαιτεῖ καὶ δανείζεται, ἀπὸ τούτων διάγει. There
is a very singular passage in Hdt. III. 31 οἱ δὲ βασιλήϊοι δικασταὶ κεκριμένοι
ἄνδρες γίνονται Περσέων, ἐς οὗ ἀποθάνωσι, ἢ σφι παρευρεθῇ τι ἄδικον, μέχρι
τούτου.

Obs. 2. When the attracted relative is followed by a predicative subst.
or adject., the attraction extends to them likewise; as, Demosth. p. 325,
10 ἐμὲ οὔτε καιρὸς—προσηγάγετο ὧν ἔκρινα δικαίων καὶ συμφερόντων
τῇ πατρίδι οὐδὲν προδοῦναι, for ἃ ἔκρινα δίκαια καὶ συμφέροντα.

Obs. 3. As the object of the attraction is to connect the relative immediately to its subst. as an attribute, it follows, of course, that properly it
can only take place when the real demonstrative attribute is omitted; as,
ἐλάττων ἐστὶ τούτου τοῦ ἀνδρός, ὃν εἶδες becomes ἐλάττων ἐστὶ τοῦ ἀνδρὸς οὗ
εἶδες or οὗ εἶδες ἀνδρός: or in an adjectiv. sentence used as a substantive, as,
Isocr. p. 46 B C ἡ πόλις ἡμῶν ὧν ἔλαβεν ἅπασι μετέδωκε, for μετέδωκεν ἐκείνων, ἃ ἔλαβεν: Xen. Anab. I. 9, 25 σὺν οἷς μάλιστα φιλεῖς for σὺν τούτοις, οὕς.
But when the demonst. is expressed in the principal clause (the article is
not meant here, as it is used not as a demonstrat., but merely as the
article) there are two distinct sentences connected together indeed, but
each in its whole and perfect form; so that the one form does not need the
other to complete it, nor properly can the relative clause be taken into the

principal clause as the attributive of the substantive, as there is an attribute there already; but the attraction had so powerful an influence on the language, that it also takes place when the demonstr. is expressed in the principal sentence, and even when the relative sentence is used as a substantive: Plat. Phæd. p. 70 A (ψυχὴ) ἀπηλλαγμένη τούτων τῶν κακῶν ὧν σὺ νῦν δὴ διῆλθες: Id. Rep. p. 556 B ἐλάττω φύσιν τῶν τοιούτων κακῶν οἴων νῦν δὴ εἴπομεν: Soph. Œ. R. 147 τῶνδε γὰρ χάριν καὶ δεῦρ' ἔβημεν, ὦν ὅδ' ἐξαγγέλλεται: Xen. Cyr. I. 6, 11 ἃ μὲν νῦν λέγονται λήψεσθαι οἱ στρατιῶται, οὐδεὶς αὐτῶν ἐμοὶ τούτων χάριν εἴσεται: Demosth. p. 843, 10 extr. μὴ γὰρ οἴεσθε αὐτὸν, ὑπὲρ ὦν ᾐρμηται μὴ λαβεῖν, ὑπὲρ τούτων ὑμῖν λειτουργεῖν ἐθελήσειν: Id. p. 70, 17 οἷς οὖν ὑμετέροις ἔχει (ὁ Φίλιππος), τούτοις πάντα τἆλλα ἀσφαλῶς κέκτηται. So sometimes, though but rarely, in Latin: Terent. Heaut. I. 1, 35 *hâc qui-dem caussâ, quâ dixi tibi.*

Obs. 4. The dative or nomin. of the relative seldom suffers attraction: Od. ω, 30 ὡς ὄφελες τιμῆς ἀπονήμενος ᾗσπερ ἄνασσες δήμῳ ἔνι Τρώων θάνατον καὶ πότμον ἐπισπεῖν (for ᾗπερ): Xen. Cyr. V. 4, 39 ἤγετο δὲ καὶ τῶν ἑαυτοῦ τῶν τε πιστῶν, οἷς ᾔδετο, καὶ ὧν (for ἐκείνων, οἷς) ἠπίστει πολλούς, i. e. *secum duxit multos suorum, et fidorum, quibus delectabatur, et eorum, quibus diffidebat :* Plat. Phæd. p. 69 A τοῦτο δ' ὁμοιόν ἐστιν ᾧ νῦν δὴ ἐλέγετο for τούτῳ ὅ: Xen. Hell. I. 2, 1 τῷ δ' ἄλλῳ ἔτει ᾧ ἦν Ὀλυμπιάς κ. τ. λ.: Hdt. I. 68 οὐδέν κω εἰδότες τῶν ἦν περὶ Σάρδις τε καὶ αὐτὸν Κροῖσον for τούτων ἃ ἦν [a]. The following are not to be classed here: Il. ψ, 649 τιμῇ ἧστί μ' ἔοικε τετιμῆσθαι; because we may say, τιμὴν τιμᾶσθαι; therefore ᾗστε may be for ᾗντε not ᾗτε: Arist. Plut. 1044 τάλαιν' ἐγὼ τῆς ὕβρεος ἧς ὑβρίζομαι; because ὕβριν ὑβρίζεσθαι: Thuc. VII. 70 πᾶς τέ τις, ἐν ᾧ προσετέτακτο, αὐτὸς ἕκαστος ἠπείγετο πρῶτος φαίνεσθαι; because προστάττομαί τι, i. e. τὴν φυλακήν.

Obs. 5. Sometimes, though but rarely, the attraction is not used by the Attics; as, Thuc. I. 50 τὰ σκάφη οὐχ εἷλκον ἀναδούμενοι τῶν νεῶν, ἃς καταδύσειαν: Eur. Med. 753 ὄμνυμι — ἐμμένειν ἅ σου κλύω for οἷς σου κλύω: Ibid. 758 τυχοῦσ' ἃ βούλομαι: Plat. Gorg. p. 520 B μέμφεσθαι τούτῳ τῷ πράγματι, ὃ αὐτοὶ παιδεύουσι (because of the demonst. :) Lysias p. 444 τῶν ἄλλων κακῶν, ἃ πεπόνθατε ὑπ' αὐτῶν, (seemingly because a genitive follows.)

Obs. 6. This attraction sometimes takes place in the local adverbs, so that the relative adverb appears in a form which expresses the direction of the demonstrative adverb, or of the substantive which precedes or is implied: Thuc. I. 89 διεκομίζοντο εὐθὺς (sc. ἐντεῦθεν) ὅθεν (for οὗ, *ubi*) ὑπεθεξίθεντο παῖδας: Soph. Trach. 701 ἐκ δὲ γῆς ὅθεν (*ubi*) προβλαστ' ἀναζέουσι θρομβώδεις ἀφροί: Id. Phil. 481 ἐμβάλου μ' ὅπη θέλεις ἄγων, ἐς ἀντλίαν, ἐς πρῷραν, ἐς πρύμνην ὅποι (for οὗ, *ubi*) ἥκιστα μέλλω τοὺς παρόντας ἀλγυνεῖν: Id. Ant. 228 τάλας, τί χωρεῖς (ἐκεῖσε) οἷ μολὼν δώσεις δίκην; (though here οἷ may be joined with μολών :) Eur. Iph. T. 118 χωρεῖν χρεὼν (ἐκεῖσε) ὅποι χθονὸς κρύψαντε λήσομεν δέμας: Id. Heracl. 19 πέμπων (ἐκεῖσε) ὅποι γῆς πυνθάνοιθ' ἱδρυμένους κήρυκας ἐξαιρεῖ.

---

[a] It is possible that the very difficult passage Thuc. V. 111. is a very unusual application of this principle of the attraction of the nomin., καὶ ἐνθυμεῖσθε ὅτι περὶ πατρίδος βουλεύεσθε, ἣν (sc. βουλὴν ἣ) μιᾶς περὶ, καὶ ἐς μίαν βουλὴν, τυχοῦσάν τε καὶ μὴ κατορθώσασαν, ἔσται, which deliberation will be for the only country you

have, and for the only (time of) deliberation which will be allowed you, whether it hits the right point (= is right) or fails (= is wrong.) This is thrown out only as a *possible* interpretation of a passage which is esteemed hopeless, (see Arnold, ad loc.) depending on an idiom of the language, though very anomalously applied.

Attraction of the Relatives, οἷος, ὅσος, ἡλίκος.

§. 823. The relatives, οἷος, ὅσος, ὁστισοῦν, ἡλίκος, suffer attraction, not only in the accus. but also in the nomin., when the verb εἶναι with an express subject stands in the relative sentence, as οἷος σὺ εἶ, οἷος ἐκεῖνος (or ὁ Σωκράτης) ἐστί; and this in a very peculiar manner, as the two following examples will shew : Xen. M. S. II. 9, 3 χαρίζομαι οἵῳ σοὶ ἀνδρί for χαρίζομαι ἀνδρὶ τοιούτῳ, οἷος σὺ εἶ, and in an adjectival sentence used as a subst., χαρίζομαι οἵῳ σοί, for χαρίζ. τῷ τοιούτῳ οἷος σὺ εἶ. This attraction consists in the omission of the demonstr., adject. or substantive, in gen., dat. or accus. ; as, τοιούτου ἀνδρός, τοιούτῳ ἀνδρί, τοιοῦτον ἄνδρα, or τοῦ τοιούτου, τῷ τοιούτῳ, τὸν τοιοῦτον, and then putting the relative by attraction in the case of the preceding substantive or of the demonstr. which is omitted ; as, ἀνδρὸς οἵου, ἀνδρὶ οἵῳ, ἄνδρα οἷον or οἵου, οἵῳ, οἷον : the verb of the relative sentence (εἶναι) is then also omitted, and the subject of the relative sentence agrees with the attracted relative. This attracted adjectival sentence assumes the character of an inflected adjective, and still greater connection and unity between the two sentences thus mixed up together is produced, by placing the substantive to which the relative refers in the adjectival sentence. So

Gen.	ἔραμαι οἷον σοῦ ἀνδρός.	ἔραμαι οἷον σοῦ.
Dat.	χαρίζομαι οἵῳ σοὶ ἀνδρί.	χαρίζομαι οἵῳ σοί.
Acc.	ἐπαινῶ οἷον σὲ ἄνδρα.	ἐπαινῶ οἷον σέ.
Gen.	ἔραμαι οἵων ὑμῶν ἀνδρῶν.	ἔραμαι οἵων ὑμῶν.
Dat.	χαρίζομαι οἵοις ὑμῖν ἀνδράσι.	χαρίζομαι οἵοις ὑμῖν.
Acc.	ἐπαινῶ οἵους ὑμᾶς ἄνδρας.	ἐπαινῶ οἵους ὑμᾶς.

Οἷος: Thuc. VII. 21 πρὸς ἄνδρας τολμηροὺς οἵους καὶ Ἀθηναίους, for οἷοι Ἀθηναῖοί εἰσιν : Lucian. Toxar. c. 11 οὐ φαῦλον τὸ ἔργον, ἀνδρὶ οἵῳ σοὶ πολεμιστῇ μονομαχῆσαι. So also Thuc. I. 70 δοκεῖτε οὐδ᾽ ἐκλογίσασθαι πώποτε, πρὸς οἵους ὑμῖν Ἀθηναίους ὄντας, καὶ ὅσον ὑμῶν καὶ ὡς πᾶν διαφέροντας, ὁ ἀγὼν ἔσται, *You do not seem to have considered what sort of people these Athenians are, and how much and how entirely they differ from you, against whom this contest will be ;* for οἷοί εἰσιν Ἀθηναῖοι πρὸς οὕς &c. So in an adject. sentence used for a substantive : Plat. Soph. p. 237 C οἵῳ γε ἐμοὶ παντάπασιν ἄπορον for τῷ τοιούτῳ, οἷός γε ἐγώ εἰμι, ἄπορόν ἐστιν. Here also belongs the attraction of οἷος with superl.; as, Plat. Symp. p. 220 B καί ποτε ὄντος τοῦ πάγου οἵου δεινοτάτου for τοιούτου, οἷός ἐστι δεινότατος. A curious construction is found in Plat. Apol. p. 39 C τιμωρίαν ὑμῖν ἥξειν εὐθὺς μετὰ τὸν ἐμὸν θάνατον πολὺ χαλεπωτέραν ἢ οἵαν ἐμὲ ἀπεκτόνατε, for ἢ αὔτη ἐστίν, οἴας ἐμὲ ἀπ. *quam quâ me affecistis.*—Ὅσος: Od. ι, 321 sq. τὸ μὲν (ῥόπαλον Κύκλωπος) ἄμμες ἐΐσκομεν εἰσορόωντες ὅσσον θ' ἱστὸν νηὸς ἐεικοσόροιο: Ibid. 325 τοῦ μὲν ὅσον τ' ὄργυιαν ἐγὼν ἀπέκοψα παραστὰς for τοσοῦτο ὅσον ἐστὶν ὄργυια: Od. κ, 113 τὴν δὲ γυναῖκα εὗρον ὅσην τ' ὄρεος κορυφήν, for τοσαύτην ὅση ἐστὶν ὄρεος κορυφή: Hdt. I. 160 ἐπὶ μισθῷ ὅσῳ δή, *mercede, quantulacunque est.* So also ὅσος in indefinite notions of magnitude: Id. I. 157 Μαζάρης τοῦ Κύρου στρατοῦ μοῖραν ὅσην δή κοτε ἔχων, *partem, quantulacunque erat.*—Ὁστισοῦν: Plat. Rep. p. 335 B ἔστιν ἄρα δικαίου ἀνδρὸς βλάπτειν καὶ ὁντινοῦν ἀνθρώπων for ἀνθρώπων καὶ ὁστισοῦν ἐστι.—Ἡλίκος: Arist. Ach. 703 εἰκὸς ἄνδρα κυφὸν ἡλίκον Θουκυδίδην ἐξολέσθαι.

Obs. 1. So Il. ι, 354 ἀλλ' ὅσον ἐς Σκαιάς τε πύλας καὶ φηγὸν ἵκανεν, i. e. ἐπὶ τοσοῦτον, ὅσον ἐστὶν ἐς Σκ., he only came as far as &c. Hence the forms ὅσον μόνον, *tantum non, almost,* ὅσον οὔ or ὁσονού. *prope,* &c.[a]

Obs. 2. We find τοῖον and τόσον similarly used in Homer, which is to be explained by the fact mentioned above (§. 816.) that the demonst. originally performed the functions of the relative: Il. ψ, 246 τύμβον δ' οὐ μάλα πολλὸν ἐγὼ πονέεσθαι ἄνωγα, ἀλλ' ἐπιεικέα τοῖον, i. e. τοῖον οἷον ἐπιεικές or τοῖον οἷος ἐπιεικής: Ibid. 454 ὃς τὸ μὲν ἄλλο τόσον φοίνιξ ἦν, ἐν δὲ μετώπῳ λευκὸν σῆμ' ἐτέτυκτο: Od. δ, 371 νήπιός εἰς, ὦ ξεῖνε, λίην τόσον, ἠὲ χαλίφρων.

Obs. 3. The attraction takes place even where οἷος stands for οἷός τε or ὥστε, and is joined with the infin. in the sense, *I am of such a nature, as,* (is sum, qui,) hence, *I can, I ought, I am prepared, I am able,* (so queo, *I am able,* from quis.) The relative οἷος points to a demonstr. τοιοῦτος which is sometimes expressed. The following are two instances of the idiom without attraction : Plat. Crit. p. 46 B ἐγὼ—τοιοῦτος οἷος τῶν ἐμῶν μηδενὶ ἄλλῳ πείθεσθαι ἢ τῷ λόγῳ: Id. Apol. p. 31 A ἐγὼ τυγχάνω ὢν τοιοῦτος, οἷος ὑπὸ τοῦ θεοῦ τῇ πόλει δεδόσθαι. With the attraction—the demonstr. sometimes precedes; as, Od. φ, 172 σὺ γάρ τοι σέ γε τοῖον ἐγείνατο πότνια μήτηρ, οἷόν τε ῥυτῆρα βιοῦ τ' ἔμεναι καὶ ὀϊστῶν: Plat. Rep. p. 415 E στρατοπεδευσάμενοι δὲ — εὐχὰς ποιησάσθων. — Οὐκοῦν τοιαύτας, οἵας χειμῶνός τε στέγειν καὶ θέρους ἱκανὰς εἶναι: Demosth p. 23, 19 (περὶ αὑτὸν ὁ Φίλιππος ἔχει) τοιούτους ἀνθρώπους οἵους μεθυσθῆναι ὀρχεῖσθαι τοιαῦτα, οἷα ἐγὼ νῦν ὀκνῶ πρὸς ὑμᾶς ὀνομάσαι: Lucian Hermot. c. 76 Στωϊκῷ τοιούτῳ—οἷῳ μήτε λυπεῖσθαι μήτ' ὀργίζεσθαι: but as a general rule the demonstr. is omitted: Xen. M. S. III. 11, 1 γυναικὸς καλῆς — καὶ οἵας συνεῖναι τῷ πείθοντι: Ibid. I. 4, 12 μόνην τὴν τῶν ἀνθρώπων (γλῶτταν) ἐποίησαν (οἱ θεοὶ) οἵαν ἀρθροῦν τε τὴν φωνήν κ.τ.λ.: Demosth. p. 23, 17 ἤκουον ἀνδρὸς οὐδαμῶς οἷόν τε ψεύδεσθαι.

Obs. 4. When τέ is attached to οἷος it refers more definitely to the demonstr., as it implies that something has preceded with which the word to which it is attached is connected; this of course must be the demonstrative of οἷος, as οἷος can refer to nothing else. See under τέ (§. 755. 3, 4.)

Obs. 5. When the adject. sentence is used as a substant. the article sometimes precedes the attracted οἷος, ἡλίκος, and the sentence takes the character of an inflected substantive :

[a] Passow Lex. v. ὅσος.

Nom.	ὁ οἷος σὺ ἀνήρ.
Gen.	τοῦ οἵου σοῦ ἀνδρός.
Dat.	τῷ οἵῳ σοὶ ἀνδρί.
Acc.	τὸν οἷον σὲ ἄνδρα.
Nom.	οἱ οἷοι ὑμεῖς ἄνδρες.
Gen.	τῶν οἵων ὑμῶν ἀνδρῶν.
Dat.	τοῖς οἵοις ὑμῖν ἀνδράσι.
Acc.	τοὺς οἵους ὑμᾶς ἄνδρας :

Xen. Cyr. VI. 2, 2 οἱ δὲ οἷοί περ ὑμεῖς ἄνδρες—καταμανθάνουσιν : Id. Hell. II. 3, 25 γνόντες μὲν τοῖς οἵοις ἡμῖν τε καὶ ὑμῖν χαλεπὴν πολιτείαν εἶναι δημοκρατίαν : Arist. Eccl. 465 ἐκεῖνο δεινὸν τοῖσιν ἡλίκοισι νῷν for τηλικούτοις, ἡλίκοι νὼ ἐσμεν.

Obs. 6. When the subject of the adject. sentence and the article are of different number, the subject is in the nomin. without partaking in the attraction ; this however is but seldom : Arist. Ach. 601 νεανίας δ᾽ οἷους σὺ διαδεδρακότας : Xen. Hell. I. 4, 16 οὐκ ἔφασαν δὲ τῶν οἵων περ αὐτὸς ὄντων : Æschin. F. Leg. p. 48 τρισμυρίους κιναίδους οἷουσπερ σύ : Demosth. p. 758 οἷοισπερ σὺ συμβούλοις.

Obs. 7. A similar attraction takes place in expressions such as, θαυμαστὸν ὅσον προὐχώρησε = θαυμαστόν ἐστιν ὅσον προὐχώρησε *mirum quantum processit* (for *mirum est, quantum processerit*). And even Plat. Rep. p. 350 D μετὰ ἰδρῶτος θαυμαστοῦ ὅσου for θαυμαστόν ἐστιν μεθ᾽ ὅσου : Id. Hipp. p. 282 C χρήματα ἔλαβε θαυμαστὰ ὅσα, for θαυμαστόν ἐστιν, ὅσα : Hdt. IV. 194 οἱ δέ (sc. πίθηκοι) σφι ἄφθονοι ὅσοι ἐν τοῖς οὔρεσι γίνονται : Id. I. 14 ὅσα πλεῖστα. So Lucian Toxar. c. 12 πολλοὺς καὶ ἄλλους εἶχε περὶ αὐτὸν—φιλίας πλεῖστον ὅσον ἀποδέοντας : Plat. Charm. p. 155 C ἀνέβλεψέ μοι τοῖς ὀφθαλμοῖς ἀμήχανόν τι οἷον. Also θαυμαστὴ ὅση ἡ προχώρησις αὐτοῦ. Lastly in adverbs, θαυμαστῶς ὡς, θαυμασίως ὡς : Plat. Rep. p. 331 A εὖ οὖν λέγει θαυμαστῶς ὡς σφόδρα for θαυμαστόν ἐστιν, ὡς.—So θαυμασίως ὡς ἄθλιος γέγονε for θαυμάσιόν ἐστιν, ὡς ἄθλιος γέγονε : Plat. Phæd. p. 66 A ὑπερφυῶς—ὡς ἀληθῆ λέγεις : Ibid. p. 96 C θαυμαστῶς ὡς : Id. Symp. p. 173 C ὑπερφυῶς ὡς χαίρω for ὑπερφυές ἐστιν, ὡς χαίρω : Demosth. p. 844, 1 θαυμαστῶς ἂν ὡς εὐλαβούμην.

Obs. 8. A peculiar method of making sentences coalesce is seen, when, after a verb of *asking* or *knowing*, &c. ὅστις or οἷος &c. stand in the sense of "*who*" (*what*) *he is*, with a demonstr., as the subject by inverse attraction (see below) of the verb εἶναι ; as, ἔρειο ὅστις οὗτός ἐστιν (for ἔρειο τοῦτον ὅστις ἐστιν), and on this a relative adjectiv. sentence follows, (such as ὃν ἄγει) referring to that demonstr., the full sentence being ἔρειο τοῦτον ὃν ἄγει ὅστις ἐστιν. The verb εἶναι and the second relative are omitted, and the first relative and the demonstr. to which the omitted relative refers are in the case of that relative ; as, Il. λ, 611 Νέστορ᾽ ἔρειο, ὅντινα τοῦτον ἄγει βεβλημένον ἐκ πολέμοιο, i. e. ὅστις οὗτός ἐστιν, ὃν ἄγει : Od. ι, 348 ὄφρ᾽ εἰδῇς, οἷόν τι ποτὸν τόδε νηῦς ἐκεκεύθει ἡμετέρη, i. e. οἷόν τι ποτὸν τόδε ἐστὶν, ὃ νηῦς ἐκ. But a more simple way of explaining this construction is, to translate the demonstr. " here"—whom brings he here.

Inverse Attraction.

§. 824. I. 1. Sometimes the relative does not stand in the case of its subst. in the principal clause, but this substant. in the case of the relative—this is called *Inverse Attraction*. It most frequently occurs when the subst. should be in the nom. or acc. ; as, Il. ξ. 371 ἀσπίδες ὅσσαι ἄρισται ἐνὶ στρατῷ ἠδὲ μέγισται, ἐσσάμενοι— ἴομεν: Il. κ, 416 φυλακὰς δ᾽ ἃς εἴρεαι, ἥρως, αὖτις κεκριμένη ῥύεται στρατόν: Soph. OE. C. 1150 λόγος δ᾽ ὃς ἐμπέπτωκεν ἀρτίως ἐμοὶ στείχοντι δεῦρο, (sc. τούτου,) συμβάλου γνώμην, *de eo tuam tecum reputa sententiam:* Id. Trach. 283 τάσδ᾽ ἅσπερ εἰσορᾷς, ἐξ ὀλβίων ἄζηλον εὑροῦσαι βίον, ἥκουσι πρός σε: Lysias p. 649 τὴν οὐσίαν ἣν κατέλιπε τῷ υἱεῖ, οὐ πλείονος ἀξία ἐστίν: Plat. Lys. p. 221 B οἷόν τε οὖν ἐστιν, ἐπιθυμοῦντα καὶ ἐρῶντα τούτου οὐ ἐπιθυμεῖ καὶ ἐρᾷ μὴ φιλεῖν; The dative is very seldom thus lost in attraction: Eur. Med. 11 (MSS.) Μήδεια ἁνδάνουσα μὲν φυγῇ πολιτῶν ὧν ἀφίκετο χθόνα, i. e. *placere studens civibus, in quorum terram fugā pervenit.* Sometimes a demonstrative is used in the principal clause to supply the case thus lost: Hom. Hymn. in Cerer. 66 κούρην τὴν ἔτεκον, γλυκερὸν θάλος, εἴδεϊ κυδρήν, τῆς ἁδινὴν ὄπ᾽ ἄκουσα: Arist. Plut. 200 τὴν δύναμιν ἣν ὑμεῖς φατὲ ἔχειν με, ταύτης δεσπότης γενήσομαι: Soph. OE. R. 449 τὸν ἄνδρα τοῦτον ὃν πάλαι ζητεῖς ἀπειλῶν κἀνακηρύσσων φόνον τὸν Λαΐειον, οὗτός ἐστιν ἐνθάδε: Eur. Or. 1604 sq. Ἑλένην μὲν ἣν σὺ διολέσαι πρόθυμος ὧν ἥμαρτες—, ἥ δ᾽ ἐστὶν, ἣν ὁρᾷτ᾽ ἐν αἰθέρος πτυχαῖς: Ibid. 580 sq. Ἀπόλλων ὃς μεσομφάλους ἕδρας νάων βροτοῖσι στόμα νέμει σαφέστατον, —τούτῳ πιθόμενος τὴν τεκοῦσαν ἔκτανον: Plat. Men. p. 96 A ὡμολογήκαμεν δέ γε, πράγματος οὗ μήτε διδάσκαλοι, μήτε μαθηταὶ εἶεν, τοῦτο διδακτὸν μὴ εἶναι. But this of course can only take place when the principal clause is placed after the relative one: Il. σ, 192 ἄλλου δ᾽ οὔ τευ οἶδα τεῦ ἂν κλυτὰ τεύχεα δύω, εἰ μὴ Αἴαντός γε σάκος Τελαμωνιάδαο: Soph. Trach. 151 τότ᾽ ἄν τις εἰσίδοιτο—κακοῖσιν οἷς ἐγὼ βαρύνομαι.

2. This inverse attraction is very common in οὐδεὶς ὅστις οὐ (or rarely ὅς, Plat. Alc. p. 103 B) the verb ἐστί being omitted: Plat. Protag. p. 317 C οὐδενὸς ὅτου οὐ πάντων ἂν ὑμῶν καθ᾽ ἡλικίαν πατὴρ εἴην: Id. Phæd. p. 117 D κλαίων καὶ ἀγανακτῶν οὐδένα ὅντινα οὐ κατέκλαυσε τῶν παρόντων.—Hence the formula, οὐδεὶς ὅστις οὐ, as a pronom. subst. (for πάντες, *nemo non*), which is inflected through all the cases ; as,

Nom.	οὐδεὶς	ὅστις	οὐκ ἂν ταῦτα ποιήσειεν.
Gen.	οὐδενὸς	ὅτου	οὐ κατεγέλασεν.
Dat.	οὐδενὶ	ὅτῳ	οὐκ ἀπεκρίνατο.
Acc.	οὐδένα	ὅντινα	οὐ κατέκλαυσε.

But sometimes this formula suffers the common attraction, the relative following the case of οὐδείς; as, Xen. Cyr. I. 4, 25 οὐδένα

ἔφασαν ὄντιν' οὐ δακρύοντ' ἀποστρέφεσθαι, for οὐδένα ἔφασαν
γενέσθαι ὅστις οὐ δακρύων ἀποστρέφοιτο : Plat. Protag. p. 323 C ὡς
ἀναγκαῖον οὐδένα ὄντιν' οὐχὶ ἀμωσγέπως μετέχειν αὐτῆς (τῆς
δικαιοσύνης).　So in questions with τίς : Thuc. III. 39 τίνα οἴεσθε
ὄντινα οὐ βραχείᾳ προφάσει ἀποστήσεσθαι ;

Obs. 1. To this inverse attraction belongs ὃς βούλει for ὃν βούλει :
so in Latin, *quivis* for *quemvis* : Plat. Gorg. p. 517 B ἔργα τοιαῦτα—,
οἷα τούτων ὃς βούλει εἴργασται : Id. Cratyl. p. 432 A τὰ δέκα ἢ ὅστις
βούλει ἄλλος ἀριθμός.

Obs. 2. The local adverbs also are thus attracted, in that the demonstr.
adverb assumes the form of the relative ; as, Soph. Œ. C. 1227 βῆναι
κεῖθεν ὅθεν περ ἥκει for κεῖσε, ὅθεν : Plat. Crit. p. 45 B πολλαχοῦ γὰρ
καὶ ἄλλοσε ὅποι ἂν ἀφίκῃ, ἀγαπήσουσί σε for ἀλλαχοῦ ὅποι.

Attraction by the transposition of the Substantive.

II. 1. There is also another sort of attraction, whereby the
connection between the two sentences is clearly marked ; by placing
the substantive, which logically should be joined to the demonstr.
in the principal clause, as οὗτός ἐστιν ὁ ἀνὴρ ὃν εἶδες, after and
in the same case with the relative or the dependent clause ; as, ὃν
εἶδες ἄνδρα, οὗτός ἐστιν.　The object of this collocation is to bring
prominently forward the adjectival sentence, on which in reality
the chief emphasis is laid, and to give it a substantival character ;
while the substantive on the contrary is little more than an adjective expressing some attribute of the adjectival sentence, and is in
the case of the verb thereof.—This is called *transposition*.

2. It is used in the following forms : *a.* Ὃν εἶδες ἄνδρα, οὗτός
ἐστιν. — *b.* Il. ρ, 640 εἴη δ' ὅστις ἑταῖρος ἀπαγγείλειε τάχιστα
Πηλείδῃ : Eur. Or. 1177 οἶδ' ἣν ἔθρεψεν Ἑρμιόνην μήτηρ ἐμή.—*c.* The
cases in the principal and dependent clause being different, as in
the form given in *a.* Nom. : Il. θ, 131 τὰς μέν οἱ δώσω, μετὰ δ' ἔσσεται, ἣν τότ' ἀπηύρων κούρην Βρισῆος : Soph. Aj. 1044 τίς δ'
ἐστιν, ὄντιν' ἄνδρα προσλεύσσεις στρατοῦ ; So Cicer. de Legg.
III. 5, 12 *hæc est enim,* q u a m *Scipio laudat in libris et* q u a m
maxime probat t e m p e r a t i o n e m *reipublicæ.*—Acc. : Xen. Anab.
I. 9, 19 εἴ τινα ὁρῴη κατασκευάζοντα, ἧς ἄρχοι χώρας : Eur. Bacch.
246 sq. ταῦτ' οὐχὶ δεινῆς ἀγχόνης ἐπάξια, ὕβρεις ὑβρίζειν, ὅστις
ἐστὶν ὁ ξένος : Id. Phœn. 955 ἐκ γένους δὲ δεῖ θανεῖν τοῦδ', ὃς
δράκοντος γέννος ἐκπέφυκε π α ῖ ς.　So Cicer. pro Sulla c. 33 q u æ
prima innocentis mihi d e f e n s i o *est oblata, suscepi.* — Dat. :
Thuc. VI. 30 τοῖς πλοίοις καὶ ὅση ἄλλη π α ρ α σ κ ε υ ὴ ξυνείπετο,
πρότερον εἴρητο κ. τ. λ. So Cicer. N. D. II. 48 q u i b u s b e s t i i s
erat is cibus, ut alius generis bestiis vescerentur, aut vires natura dedit

aut celeritatem. But generally when the subst. thus transposed would in the principal clause be in any other case than nom. or acc., a pronoun is used in the principal clause to supply its place: Il. φ, 441 οὐδέ νυ τῶνπερ μέμνηαι, ὅσα δὴ πάθομεν κακά: Eur. Or. 63 sq. ἦν γὰρ κατ' οἴκους Ἑλιφ', ὅτ' ἐς Τροίαν ἔπλει, ταρθένον,—ταύτῃ γέγηθε.

3. When attributive adjectives are joined to the substantive, either (*a*) the adjective and substantive are both transposed to the adjectival, while the demonstrative remains in the principal clause ; as, Il. ω, 167 τῶν μιμνησκόμενοι, οἵ δὴ πολέες καὶ ἐσθλοὶ — κέατο ψυχὰς ὀλέσαντες: Demosth. p. 1239 ταύτῃ ἥτις εἴη μεγίστη πίστις;—(*b*) or the subst. remains in the principal, and the adj. only is transposed to the relative clause: Od. δ, 11 υἱέϊ —, ὅς οἱ τηλύγετος γένετο κρατερὸς Μεγαπένθης: Eur. Or. 842 πότνι' Ἠλέκτρα, λόγους ἄκουσον, οἷς σοι δυστυχεῖς ἥκω φέρων;—(*c*) or the adjective remains in the principal, and the subst. is transposed to the relative clause: Eur. Herc. F. 1164 ἥκω ξὺν ἄλλοις, οἳ παρ' Ἀσώπου ῥοὰς μένουσιν ἔνοπλοι γῆς Ἀθηναίων κόροι: Arist. Ran. 916 ἕτεροι γὰρ εἰσιν οἷσιν εὔχομαι θεοῖς; — (*d*) or where there is more than one adjective, one of them remains with the subst. in the principal, the other is transposed to the relative clause ; as, Il. ν, 339 sq. ἔφριξεν δὲ μάχη φθισίμβροτος ἐγχείῃσιν μακρῇς, ἃς εἶχον ταμεσίχροας.

4. A word in apposition to the subst. to which the relative sentence refers is sometimes attracted to the relative clause: Od. a, 69 Κύκλωπος κεχόλωται, ὃν ὀφθαλμοῦ ἀλάωσεν ἀντίθεον Πολύφημον: Od. δ, 11. Il. γ, 122. η, 187. λ, 625. Plat. Hipp. M. p. 281 C τί ποτε τὸ αἴτιον, ὅτι οἱ παλαιοὶ ἐκεῖνοι, ὧν ὀνόματα μεγάλα λέγονται ἐπὶ σοφίᾳ, Πιττακοῦ καὶ Βίαντος—, φαίνονται ἀπεχόμενοι τῶν πολιτικῶν πράξεων[a] ; Plat. Apol. p. 41 A εὑρήσει τοὺς ὡς ἀληθῶς δικαστάς, οἵπερ καὶ λέγονται ἐκεῖ δικάζειν, Μίνως τε καὶ Ῥαδάμανθυς καὶ Αἰακός[b]: Eur. Hec. 771 πρὸς ἄνδρ', ὃς ἄρχει τῆσδε Πολυμήστωρ χθονός[c]: Ibid. 986 πρῶτον μὲν εἰπὲ παῖδ', ὃν ἐξ ἐμῆς χερὸς Πολύδωρον ἔκ τε πατρὸς ἐν δόμοις ἔχεις. So Arist. Poet. XI. ἔλεός τε καὶ φόβον οἵων πράξεων ἡ τραγῳδία μίμησίς ἐστιν, for πράξεις τοιαύτας οἵων κ. τ. λ. So frequently when in apposition to a demonstr.: Il. η, 186 ἀλλ' ὅτε δὴ τὸν ἵκανε—ὅς μιν ἐπιγράψας κυνέῃ βάλε φαίδιμος Αἴας: Eur. Hipp. 101 τήνδ', ἣ πύλαισι σαῖς ἐφέστηκεν Κύπρις. And

---

[a] Heindorf ad loc.   [b] Stallb. ad loc.   [c] Pflugk ad loc.

ometimes when the demonstr. is omitted; as, Plat. Rep. p. 402 C
ὑδὲ μουσικοὶ πρότερον ἐσόμεθα, οὔτε αὐτοὶ οὔτε οὖς φαμεν ἡμῖν παι-
ευτέον εἶναι, τοὺς φύλακας[a].

Obs. A substantive (mostly with the article) is often placed in the adject.
ientence, in the same case with the relative, to explain or define a notion
vhich has been signified in the former sentence by a periphrasis : Plat.
Theæt. p. 167 B ἕτερα τοιαῦτα, ἃ δή τινες τὰ φαντάσματα ὑπὸ ἀπειρίας
ἰληθῆ καλοῦσιν : Id. Rep. p. 477 C εἰ ἄρα μανθάνεις, ὃ βούλομαι λέγειν τὸ
ε ἶδος : Id. p. 583 E ὃ μεταξὺ ἄρα νῦν δὴ ἀμφοτέρων ἔφαμεν εἶναι τὴν ἡσυ-
χ ί α ν, τοῦτό ποτε ἀμφότερα ἔσται λυπή τε καὶ ἡδονή : Soph. Antig. 404 ταύτην
ἰδὼν θάπτουσαν ὃν σὺ τὸν νεκρὸν ἀπεῖπας—Without the article ; Thuc.
III. 12 ὃ τοῖς ἄλλοις μάλιστα, εὔνοια, πίστιν βεβαιοῖ, ἡμῖν τοῦτο (τὴν πίστιν)
ὁ φόβος ἐχυρὸν παρεῖχε.

An Adjectival clause with another clause depending on it.

§. 825. 1. When a relative clause is followed by another clause
depending on it, they often coalesce, the relative being in construction not with its own, but with the dependent clause, and in
the case required thereby ; while the adjectival clause is placed,
without any relative, after its dependent clause : Isocr. de Pace c.
16 ἀνθρώπους αἱρούμεθα τοὺς μὲν ἀπόλιδας, τοὺς δ' αὐτομόλους, οἷς
ὁ π ό τ α ν τ ι ς π λ ε ί ο ν α μ ι σ θ ὸ ν δ ι δ ῷ, μετ' ἐκείνων ἐφ' ἡμᾶς
ἀ κ ο λ ο υ θ ή σ ο υ σ ι ν for οἱ, ὁπόταν τις αὐτοῖς— διδῷ,—ἀκολου-
θήσουσιν : Id. Panath. c. 18 συνέβη κυρίαν ἑκατέραν γενέσθαι τῆς
ἀρχῆς τῆς κατὰ θάλατταν· ἣ ν ὁ π ό τ ε ρ ο ι ἂ ν κ α τ ά σ χ ω σ ι ν, ὑπηκόους ἔ χ ο υ σ ι τὰς πλείστας τῶν πόλεων : Plat. Rep. p. 466 A ὅτι
τοὺς φύλακας οὐκ εὐδαίμονας ποιοῦμεν, ο ἷ ς ἐ ξ ὸ ν π ά ν τ α ἔ χ ε ι ν τ ὰ
τ ῶ ν π ο λ ι τ ῶ ν, οὐδὲν ἔ χ ο ι ε ν; for οἱ, ἐξὸν αὐτοῖς—οὐδὲν ἔχοιεν[b] :
Id. Gorg. p. 492 B οἷς ἐξὸν ἀπολαύειν τῶν ἀγαθῶν—δεσπότην ἐπαγά-
γοντο κ. τ. λ.[c] : Demosth. p. 128, 68 πολλὰ ἂν εἰπεῖν ἔχοιεν Ὀλύνθιοι
νῦν, ἃ τότ' ε ἰ π ρ ο ε ί δ ο ν τ ο, οὐκ ἂν ἀπώλοντο, for οἱ, εἰ ταῦτα
τότε προεῖδ., οὐκ ἂν ἀπ. For an analogous construction, see γάρ
(§. 786. *Obs.* 5.).

Adverbial Relatives.

2. What is said of the construction of the pronouns ὅς, ὅστις
&c., holds good also of the adverbial relative pronouns ; as, οὗ, οἷ,
ὅθεν, ὅπως, ἵνα, ἔνθα, ἔνθεν &c. See the examples given under
the *Adverbial Sentences.*

a Stallb. ad loc.   b Ibid.   c Ibid.

The Moods in an Adjectival Sentence.

Indicative without ἄν.

§. 826. 1. The indic. is used when the attributive notion expressed in the adject. sentence is spoken of as something real or certain : ἡ πόλις, ἣ κτίζεται,—ἣ ἐκτίσθη,—ἣ κτισθήσεται.

2. The ind. fut. is used very frequently when something which will happen is spoken of: στρατηγοὺς αἱροῦνται, οἳ τῷ Φιλίππῳ πολεμήσουσιν. See §. 406.

3. After negatives also the ind. is used (where in Latin the conjunctive occurs,) when the truth or certainty thereof is to be expressed; as, Xen. Hell. VI. 1, 4 παρ' ἐμοὶ οὐδεὶς, ὅστις μὴ ἱκανός ἐστιν ἴσα ποιεῖν ἐμοί, *nemo, qui non possit.*

4. The Greek as well as the Latin uses the ind. in those adject. sentences which are introduced by the indefinite relative pronouns: as, ὅστις, *quisquis;* ὅστις δή, *quicunque;* ὅστις δή ποτε (Demosth. and the later writers, ὅστις δή ποτ' οὖν), ὅσος δή, ὅσος οὖν, *quantucunque;* ὁπόσος, ὁποσοσοῦν &c., expressing indefinite and general notions; because, though the particular nature of the object is unknown or indefinite, the event itself is considered as certain and real, while its indefiniteness is sufficiently marked by the indefinite pronouns : thus Hdt. VI. 12 δουληΐην ὑπομεῖναι, ἥτις ἔσται, *qualiscunque erit ;* I know it will be, though whether it will be intolerable or bearable I do not know: ἥτις εἴη, I am not certain whether it will be, nor do I know its nature : Id. VII. 16, 3 οὐ γὰρ δὴ ἐς τοιοῦτό γε εὐηθείης ἀνήκει τοῦτο, ὅ τι δή κοτέ ἐστι, τὸ ἐπιφαινόμενόν τοι ἐν τῷ ὕπνῳ, ὥστε δόξει, ἐμὲ ὁρῶν, σὲ εἶναι : Xen. Anab. VI. 5, 6 ἔθαπτον—, ὁπόσους ἐπελάμβανεν ἡ στρατιά: Eur. Or. 418 δουλεύουσιν θεοῖς, ὅ τι πότ' εἰσὶν οἱ θεοί. For ἤγγειλας οἷ' ἤγγειλας, *et simil.* (see §. 835. 1.)

5. The ind. is also used after these indefinite relatives when an object is spoken of in relation to its genus—in respect of its sort, or nature, where in Latin the indefinite conjunctive is used : Eur. Hipp. 918 δεινὸν σοφιστὴν εἶπας, ὅστις εὖ φρονεῖν τοὺς μὴ φρονοῦντας δυνατός ἐστ' ἀναγκάσαι : Aristoph. Vesp. 1168 κακοδαίμων ἐγὼ, ὅστις ἐπὶ γήρᾳ χίμετλον οὐδὲν λήψομαι, one of those who.

Indicative with ἄν (κέ).

§. 827. a. The ind. fut. with ἄν occurs (only, but very frequently, in Epic), when a future event is represented in the dependent clause, as certain under some particular condition : Il. ι, 155 ἐν δ' ἄνδρες;

ναίουσι πολύρρηνες, πολυβοῦται, οἵ κε ἐ δωτίνῃσι θεὸν ὡς τιμή-
σουσιν, if he comes to them, they will surely honour him : Il. μ,
226 πολλοὺς γὰρ Τρώων καταλείψομεν οὕς κεν Ἀχαιοὶ χαλκῷ
δῃώσουσιν, ἀμυνόμενοι περὶ νηῶν : Od. κ, 432 ἆ δειλοί, πόσ' ἴμεν;
τί κακῶν ἱμείρετε τούτων, Κίρκης ἐς μέγαρον καταβήμεναι; ἤ κεν
ἅπαντας ἢ σῦς ἠὲ λύκους ποιήσεται (sc. εἰ καταβησόμεθα).

Obs. 1. Homer sometimes uses the conjunc. instead of the future, with
this difference, that the future event is expressed with less certainty : Il. θ,
353 ὢ πόποι, αἰγιόχοιο Διὸς τέκος, οὐκέτι νῶϊ ὀλλυμένων Δαναῶν κεκαδησόμεθ',
ὑστάτιόν περ; οἵ κεν δὴ κακὸν οἶτον ἀναπλήσαντες ὄλωνται, who, if we
take no care for them, will probably perish.

Obs. 2. Where κέ is found with ind. pres. the reading is corrupt : Od.
α, 316 δῶρον δ', ὅττι κέ μοι δοῦναι φίλον ἦτορ ἀνώγει, where read either
with Hermann ἀνώγῃ, or with Nitzsch ὅττι τε.

b. The indic. of historic tenses, impft., plpft., aor., when it is to
be expressed that the notion of the adject. sentence would take
place, or have taken place under certain conditions, which conditions however do not, or have not happened (§. 424. a.) : Od. ε, 39
sq. πόλλ', ὅσ' ἂν οὐδέποτε Τροίης ἐξήρατ' Ὀδυσσεύς, εἴπερ
ἀπήμων ἦλθε, λαχὼν ἀπὸ ληΐδος αἶσαν : Od. ξ, 62 ἦ γὰρ τοῦγε θεοὶ
κατὰ νόστον ἔδησαν, ὅς κεν ἔμ' ἐνδυκέως ἐφίλει, sc. εἰ μὴ θεοὶ
ἔδησαν : Od. ι, 129 sq. (οὐδ' ἄνδρες νηῶν ἔνι τέκτονες)· οἷά τε πολλὰ
ἄνδρες ἐπ' ἀλλήλους νηυσὶν περόωσι θάλασσαν· οἵ κε σφιν καὶ νῆσον
ἐϋκτιμένην ἐκάμοντο : Soph. Œ. T. 1372 sq. ἐγὼ γὰρ οὐκ οἶδ',
ὄμμασιν ποίοις βλέπων πατέρα ποτ' ἂν προσεῖδον εἰς Ἅιδου
μολών : Eur. Med. 1339 οὐκ ἔστιν ἥτις τοῦτ' ἂν Ἑλληνὶς γυνὴ
ἔτλη, *quæ sustinuisset hoc* : Plat. Apol. p. 38 D οἷς ἂν (λόγοις)
ἔπεισα, εἰ ᾤμην δεῖν ἅπαντα ποιεῖν καὶ λέγειν.

c. There is also a passage in Od. σ, 260 where κέ is used in an
adjectival sentence in the sense of *frequency*, *being accustomed to do
so*; the condition being conceived in *animo loquentis*, as taking
place : καὶ γὰρ Τρῶάς φασι μαχητὰς ἔμμεναι ἄνδρας — οἵ κε τάχιστα
ἔκριναν μέγα νεῖκος ὁμοιΐου πολέμοιο [a].

Conjunctive.

§. 828. 1. If the attributive notion expressed by the adject.
sentence is not certain and real, but only supposed and possible,
the relative is followed by the conjunctive, if the verb of the principal clause is in one of the principal tenses (pres., pft., or fut.).
The adject. sentence can generally be taken as an expression of a
condition under which the verb of the principal clause will take

---

[a] Hermann de Part. ἄν p. 21, (whom
Kühner follows) would read οἵ τε. He
does not give any MSS. authority for it,
but says, " *poetam dedisse οἵ τε non dubium
esse puto.*"

effect; and the relative, with or without ἄν, can be resolved into ἐάν τις and the conjunctive : Od. α, 351 τὴν γὰρ ἀοιδὴν μᾶλλον ἐπικλείουσ᾿ ἄνθρωποι, ἥτις ἀκουόντεσσι νεωτάτη ἀμφιπέληται, men praise the song if it is very new. The attribute of the song is not expressed as any thing certain, as it would be by the indic., but as something supposed—something possible, (*if* it is new, ἐὰν νεωτάτη ᾖ.) Comp. Cicer. de Orat. II. 44, 185 *ut aut ad eos ipsi adducantur, si qui finitimi sunt et propinqui his ab talibus animi perturbationibus* [a] : Id. de Fin. III. 9, 31 *et iis, si quæ similia earum sunt :* Academ. II. 41, 128 *earum etiam rerum auctoritatem, si quæ illustriores videantur, amittere* (εἰ quæ i. q. *quæcunque*): Od. λ, 427 sq. ὡς οὐκ αἰνότερον καὶ κύντερον ἄλλο γυναικός, ἥτις δὴ τοιαῦτα μετὰ φρεσὶν ἔργα βάληται (ἐάν τις, sc. γυνή.—βάληται): Od. α, 415 οὔτε θεοπροπίης ἐμπάζομαι, ἥντινα μήτηρ, ἐς μέγαρον καλέσασα θεοπρόπον, ἐξερέηται (ἐάν τινα—ἐξερ.) : Il. ο, 491 sq. ῥεῖα δ᾿ ἀρίγνωτος Διὸς ἀνδράσι γίγνεται ἀλκή, ἠμὲν ὅτέοισιν κῦδος ὑπέρτερον ἐγγυαλίξῃ, ἠδ᾿ ὅτινας μινύθῃ τε καὶ οὐκ ἐθέλῃσιν ἀμύνειν (§. 816. 2.): Od. μ, 40 Σειρῆνας μὲν πρῶτον ἀφίξεαι, αἵ ῥα τε πάντας ἀνθρώπους θέλγουσιν, ὅτις σφέας εἰσαφίκηται· ὅστις ἀϊδρείῃ πελάσῃ, καὶ φθόγγον ἀκούσῃ Σειρήνων, τῷ οὔτι γυνὴ καὶ νήπια τέκνα οἴκαδε νοστήσαντι παρίσταται, οὐδὲ γάνυνται.

2. If ἄν is joined to the relative and the conjunctive, it belongs to the relative and not to the verb, and gives an indefiniteness to it, by annexing the notion, " be he who he may :" so ὃς ποιῇ, who will probably do it; ὃς ἄν ποιῇ, who, soever, will probably do it : Od. α, 158 ξεῖνε φίλ᾿, ἦ καί μοι νεμεσήσεαι, ὅττι κεν εἴπω; *si quid dixero :* Il. π, 386 sqq. ὅτε δή ῥ᾿ ἄνδρεσσι κοτεσσάμενος χαλεπήνῃ (Ζεύς), οἳ βίῃ εἰν ἀγορῇ σκολιὰς κρίνωσι θέμιστας, ἐκ δὲ δίκην ἐλάσωσι, θεῶν ὄπιν οὐκ ἀλέγοντες: Thuc. II. 62 καταφρόνησις δὲ (ἐγγίγνεται), ὃς ἂν καὶ γνώμῃ πιστεύῃ, τῶν ἐναντίων προέχειν : Xen. Hell. II. 3, 51 νομίζω προστάτου ἔργον εἶναι οἷον δεῖ, ὃς ἂν ὁρῶν τοὺς φίλους ἐξαπατωμένους μὴ ἐπιτρέπῃ: Id. Cyr. III. 1, 20 οὓς δ᾿ ἂν βελτίους τινὲς ἑαυτῶν ἡγήσωνται, τούτοις πολλάκις καὶ ἄνευ ἀνάγκης ἐθέλουσι πείθεσθαι: Ibid. I. 1, 2 ἄνθρωποι δὲ ἐπ᾿ οὐδένας μᾶλλον συνίστανται, ἢ ἐπὶ τούτους, οὓς ἂν αἴσθωνται ἄρχειν αὐτῶν ἐπιχειροῦντας: Plat. Rep. p. 402 D ὅτου ἂν ξυμπίπτῃ ἔν τε τῇ ψυχῇ καλὰ ἤθη ἐνόντα καὶ ἐν τῷ εἴδει ὁμολογοῦντα ἐκείνοις καὶ ξυμφωνοῦντα,—τοῦτ᾿ ἂν εἴη κάλλιστον θέαμα.

3. Hence the relative with ἄν is used to express indefinite properties, or the indefinite size of any thing; as, Hdt. VI. 139 ἡ

a O. M. Müller ad loc.

ɩ Πυθίη σφέας ἐκέλευε 'Αθηναίοισι δίκας διδόναι ταύτας, τ ὰ ς ἂ ν ὗτοὶ 'Αθηναῖοι δικάσωσι, *q u a s c u n q u e*—*constituissent.* The con-ɩnctive expresses that possibility and uncertainty which is implied ɩ an indefinite notion.

Obs. ɩ. On the conjunctive after an historic tense, see §. 806.   The ɔeaker identifies himself with the time past, so that he conceives of it as ɾesent.

Obs. 2. The indefinite notion expressed by the ind. with ὅστις, ὁπόσος :c. is different from that of the conjunctive, in that the former relates ɔ the indefinite nature of the event which does or is to happen, the latter ɔ the indefinite chances of the event happening ; when both these notions ɾe required, ὅστις ἂν is used with the conjunctive.

§. 829. Hence we may explain the conjunct. in the two follow-ɩng constructions, in which both the indefinite chance of the event ἐάν with conj.) happening, and the indefinite character of the event ʦelf is signified.

1. The conjunctive expresses an indefinite frequency, *as often as.* Ɫhe adjectival sentence contains a recurring condition under which ɦe principal verb has taken or will take place : Il. β, 391 ὃ ν ὃ ἐ ɪˑ ἐγὼ νἀπάνευθε μάχης ἐθέλοντα ν ο ή σ ω μιμνάζειν παρὰ νηυσὶ κορω-ɩˑίσιν, οὔ οἱ ἔπειτα ἄρκιον ἐσσεῖται φυγέειν κύνας ἠδ᾽ οἰωνούς, *as often* ʦ *I observe,* &c.   See the examples, §. 828. 1, 2.

2. The conjunct. is used when the adject. sentence forms part of ɩ comparison.   The attributive notion is considered as a condition ɔɾ assumption under which the comparison expressed in the prin-ːipal clause holds good.   If the comparison is considered abso-ute, and the adject. sentence expresses merely an attributive ɩotion of one of the objects of comparison, and not any such con-ɖition of it, the ind. is used.   As the comparison is always conceived ɔy the speaker as present, the conjunct. follows after an historic, ɩs well as after a principal tense : Il. ν, 63 αὐτὸς δ᾽, ὥ σ τ᾽ ἴρηξ ɔκύπτερος ὦρτο πετέσθαι, ὅ ς ῥα τ᾽ ἀπ᾽ αἰγίλιπος πέτρης περιμήκεος ɩρθείς, ὁ ρ μ ή σ η πεδίοιο διώκειν ὄρνεον ἄλλο, ὣ ς ἀπὸ τῶν ἤϊξε Πο-ɾειδάων ἐνοσίχθων (ἐ ὰ ν ὁρμήση) : Ibid. 179 ὁ δ᾽ αὖτ᾽ ἔπεσεν, μελίη ὅς, ἥ τ᾽ ὄρεος κορυφῇ—χαλκῷ ταμνομένη τέρενα χθονὶ φύλλα π ε-ɩάσσῃ : Il. ρ, 110 ὥστε λῖς ἠϋγένειος, ὅ ν ῥα κύνες τε καὶ ἄνδρες ɩπὸ σταθμοῖο δ ί ω ν τ α ι : Ibid. 134 ἑστήκει, ὥς τις τε λέων περὶ οἷσι ˑέκεσσιν, ᾧ ῥά τε νήπι᾽ ἄγοντι σ υ ν α ν τ ή σ ω ν τ α ι ἐν ὕλη ἄνδρες ɩπακτῆρες : Il. ο, 579 κύων ὥς, ὅ σ τ᾽ ἐπὶ νεβρῷ βλημένῳ ἀΐξη.

Remarks on the position, and the omission of ἂν *with the conjunctive.*

§. 830. 1. Ἂν is so closely connecteɖ with the relative that it forms ɔut one word with it, as in ὅταν, ἐπάν, ἐπειδάν, &c. (§. 428. *a.*) ; and hence

it cannot be separated from it, except by little words, such as δέ. This δ
is omitted in Homeric language very frequently, often in traged., sometimes in Hdt., rarely in Attic prose writers. For Homer see some of the
examples given above : Soph. El. 771 οὐδὲ γὰρ κακῶς πάσχοντι μῖσος ἐν
τέκῃ προσγίγνεται : Eur. Hec. 250 ὁρᾷς δ᾽ οὐδὲν ἡμᾶς εὖ, κακῶς δ᾽ ὅσον
δύνῃ : Id. Iph. T. 1064 καλόν τοι γλῶσσ᾽, ὅτῳ πίστις παρῇ : Id. Med. 515
ὦ Ζεῦ, τί δὴ χρυσοῦ μὲν ὃς κίβδηλος ᾖ τεκμήρι᾽ ἀνθρώποισιν ὤπασας σαφῆ : Id.
Alc. 76. 999 (ed. Wüst.) καὶ γὰρ Ζεύς, ὅ τι νεύσῃ, ξὺν σοὶ τοῦτο τελεῖνῃ :
Id. Hipp. 445 ὃν δ᾽ αὖ περισσὸν καὶ φρονοῦνθ᾽ εὕρῃ (sc. Κύπρις) μέγα, τοῦτον λαβοῦσα—καθύβρισεν : Id. Or. 793 ἀνήρ, ὅστις τρόποισι συντακῇ,
θυραῖος ὤν, μυρίων κρείσσων (ἐστὶν) ὁμαίμων—φίλος : Thuc. IV. 18 ὅσοι
νομίσωσι : Id. VII. 77 ἐν ᾧ ἀναγκασθῇ χωρίῳ μάχεσθαι is a doubtful reading,
as are most of the few passages in Attic prose, where the relative is found
without ἄν.

2. The omission of ἄν modifies the sense as follows :

Ὁ γενήσεται, which will be ; not supposition, but certainty.

Ὁ γένηται, which may or will probably be ; not certainty, but supposition.

Ὁ ἄν γένηται, whatsoever it may or will probably be. (See §. 828. 2.)

Optative without ἄν.

§. 831. 1. The relative without ἄν is joined with the opt. after
an historic, in the same sense as with the conj., after a principal
tense, expressing a possibility, and may be resolved into εἰ with opt.:
Il. κ, 20 ἥδε δέ οἱ κατὰ θυμὸν ἀρίστη φαίνετο βουλή, Νέστορ᾽ ἐπὶ
πρῶτον Νηλήϊον ἐλθέμεν ἀνδρῶν, εἴ τινά οἱ σὺν μῆτιν ἀμύμονα τεκτή-
ναιτο, ἥτις ἀλεξίκακος πᾶσιν Δαναοῖσι γένοιτο=εἴ τις—γένοιτο :
Plat. Rep. p. 455 B ἆρα οὕτως ἔλεγες, τὸν μὲν εὐφυῆ πρός τι
εἶναι, τὸν δὲ ἀφυῆ, ἐν ᾧ ὁ μὲν ῥᾳδίως τι μανθάνοι, ὁ δὲ χαλεπῶς.

2. Hence after an expression of indefiniteness (§. 826. 2.):
Soph. Trach. 905 sq. ἔκλαιε δ᾽ ὀργάνων ὅτου ψαύσειεν,
whatsoever : Thuc. VII. 29 πάντας ἑξῆς, ὅτῳ ἐντύχοιεν, καὶ
παῖδας καὶ γυναῖκας κτείνοντες.

3. Indefinite frequency. The principal verb is either in impft.
or frequentative aor., and expresses repetition or recurrence :
(§. 402. 1. 2.:) Il. κ, 489 sq. ὅντινα Τυδείδης ἄορι πλήξειε παραστάς, τὸν δ᾽ Ὀδυσεὺς μετόπισθε λαβὼν ποδὸς ἐξερύσασκεν : Il. β,
188 ὅντινα μὲν βασιλῆα καὶ ἔξοχον ἄνδρα κιχείη, τὸν δ᾽ ἀγανοῖς
ἐπέεσσιν ἐρητύσασκε παραστάς : v. 198 ὃν δ᾽ αὖ δήμου τ᾽ ἄνδρα
ἴδοι, βοόωντά τ᾽ ἐφεύροι, τὸν σκήπτρῳ ἐλάσασκε : Il. μ, 268
πάντοσε φοιτήτην, μένος ὀτρύνοντες Ἀχαιῶν· ἄλλον μειλιχίοις, ἄλλον
στερεοῖς ἐπέεσσιν νείκεον, ὅντινα πάγχυ μάχης μεθιέντα ἴδοιεν :
Il. ο, 743 ὅστις δὲ Τρώων κοίλης ἐπὶ νηυσὶ φέροιτο—, τὸν δ᾽
Αἴας οὔτασκε : Xen. Anab. I. 9, 20 φίλους γε μὴν ὅσους
ποιήσαιτο καὶ εὔνους γνοίη ὄντας, καὶ ἱκανοὺς κρίνειε συνερ-

γοὺς εἶναι, ὅ τι τυγχάνοι βουλόμενος κατεργάζεσθαι, ὁμολογεῖται πρὸς πάντων κράτιστος δὴ γενέσθαι θ ε ρ α π ε ύ ε ι ν.

4. Secondly, in its secondary and implied force (§. 418. 1. *a.*) of uncertainty, indefinite possibility, a supposition without any notion of its realization.

a. When the adjectival sentence expresses an uncertain, doubtful condition: Il. *v*, 344 μάλα κεν θρασυκάρδιος εἴη, ὃς τότε γ η - θ ή σ ε ι ε ν ἰδὼν πόνον, οὐδ' ἀκάχοιτο, i. e. εἰ γηθήσειεν: Il. *μ*, 228 ὧδέ χ' ὑ π ο κ ρ ί ν α ι τ ο θεοπρόπος, ὃς σάφα θυμῷ ε ἰ δ ε ί η τεράων, καί οἱ πειθοίατο λαοί, i. e. εἰ—εἰδείη: Od. *a*, 47 ὡς ἀπόλοιτο καὶ ἄλλος, ὅ τ ι ς τοιαῦτά γε ῥ έ ζ ο ι, i. e. εἴ τις ῥέζοι: Il. *γ*, 299 ὁ π π ό τ ε ρ ο ι πρότεροι ὑπὲρ ὅρκια π η μ ή ν ε ι α ν, ὧδέ σφ' ἐγκέφαλος χαμάδις ῥέοι, ὡς ὅδε οἶνος: Il. *ζ*, 521 οὐκ ἄν τις τοι ἀνήρ, ὃ ς ἐναίσιμος εἴη, ἔργον ἀ τ ι μ ή σ ε ι ε μάχης: Soph. Antig. 666 ἀλλ' ὃν πόλις στήσειε, τοῦδε χρὴ κλύειν (εἴ τινα στήσειε): Id. O. R. 706 ὡς αὐτὸν ἥξει μοῖρα πρὸς παιδὸς θανεῖν, ὅστις (εἴ τις) γένοιτ' ἐμοῦ τε κἀκείνου πάρα: Xen. Cyr. I. 6, 19 τοῦ μὲν αὐτὸν λέγειν, ἃ μὴ σαφῶς εἰδείη, φείδεσθαι δεῖ, when perhaps he does not know them for a certainty.

β. When the adjectival sentence forms part of an indefinite wish; as, Il. *ξ*, 107 νῦν δ' εἴη, ὃς τῆσδέ γ' ἀμείνονα μῆτιν ἐ ν ί - σ π ο ι: Il. *ρ*, 640 εἴη δ' ὅστις ἑταῖρος ἀ π α γ γ ε ί λ ε ι ε τάχιστα Πηλείδῃ: Soph. Trach. 953 εἴθ' ἀνεμόεσσά τις γ έ ν ο ι τ' ἔπουρος ἑστιῶτις αὔρα, ἥ τ ι ς μ' ἀ π ο ι κ ί σ ε ι ε ν ἐκ τόπων: Arist. Vesp. 1431 ἔ ρ δ ο ι τις, ἣν ἕκαστος ε ἰ δ ε ί η τέχνην. But the ind.: Eur. Med. 657 ἀχάριστος ὄ λ ο ι θ', ὅτῳ π ά ρ ε σ τ ι "*hic enim Chorus loquitur definite, quippe Jasonem cogitans,*" generally when the adjectiv. sentence is a member of a compound dependent clause, expressed as a wish.

Obs. Sometimes the opt. without ἄν is interchanged with the conjunct. with ἄν, but in different notions: Xen. Cyr. II. 4, 10 δοκεῖ γάρ μοι, ἔφη, πάντας μέν, ο ὓ ς ἄ ν τις β ο ύ λ η τ α ι ἀγαθοὺς συνεργοὺς ποιεῖσθαι ὁποιουτινοσοῦν πράγματος, ἥδιον εἶναι εὖ τε λέγοντα καὶ εὖ ποιοῦντα παρορμᾶν μᾶλλον, ἢ λυποῦντα καὶ ἀναγκάζοντα· ο ὓ ς δὲ δὴ τῶν εἰς τὸν πόλεμον ἔργων ποιήσασθαί τις β ο ύ λ ο ι τ ο συνεργοὺς προθύμους, τούτους παντάπασιν ἔμοιγε δοκεῖ ἀγαθοῖς θηρατέον εἶναι καὶ λόγοις καὶ ἔργοις: οὓς ἂν βούληται, *if a person wishes* (supposition, but with a notion of its really happening every day) *to make some others, be they who they may, I know not;* here ἄν belongs to the οὕς (*if there be any such*); οὓς δέ τις βούλοιτο, *but if a person should wish*... *I am not imagining that he does, but supposing he does* (without any notion of realisation) *wish to make certain others* &c. So that in the first clause the conjunctive expresses something which does really take place every day; but in the second clause it is not certain, or at least it is not represented as certain, whether Cyrus does really wish to do this; and therefore it is put in that indefinite form, οὕς τις βούλοιτο, instead of οὓς ἄν τις βούληται; so in the first case ποιεῖσθαι, to express the reality, in present

time, of the action; in the second, ποιήσασθαι, because it is not supposed
as present, nor yet future, but is a mere supposition, without any regard
to time, and therefore in aorist, (§. 401. 1.)

Optative with ἄν.

§. 832. The opt. is used in the adjectiv. sentence with ἄν, (εἰ)
when it expresses a supposition or assumption depending on certain conditions, hence a possibility; and the ἄν belongs not to the
relative, but to the verb: Il. o, 738 οὐ μέν τι σχεδόν ἐστι πόλις
πύργοις ἀραρυῖα, ἦ κ' ἀπαμυναίμεθα, sc. εἰ ἡμῖν εἴη τοιαύτη πόλις:
Od. ι, 126 οὐδ' ἄνδρες νηῶν ἔνι τέκτονες, οἵ κε κάμοιεν νῆας
ἐϋσσέλμους, αἵ κεν τελέοιεν ἕκαστα: Od. ε, 142 οὐ γάρ μοι
πάρα νῆες ἐπήρετμοι καὶ ἑταῖροι, οἵ κεν μιν πέμποιεν ἐπ' εὐρέα
νῶτα θαλάσσης: Od. ε, 165 f. αὐτὰρ ἐγὼ σῖτον καὶ ὕδωρ καὶ οἶνον
ἐρυθρὸν ἐνθήσω μενοεικέ, ἅ κεν τοι λιμὸν ἐρύκοι: Xen. M.S.
I. 2, 6 τοὺς δὲ λαμβάνοντας τῆς ὁμιλίας μισθὸν ἀνδραποδιστὰς ἑαυτὸν
ἀπεκάλει, διὰ τὸ ἀναγκαῖον αὐτοῖς εἶναι διαλέγεσθαι, παρ' ὧν ἂν
λάβοιεν τὸν μισθόν; Plat. Phæd. p. 89 D οὐκ ἔστιν ὅτι ἄν τις
μεῖζον τούτου κακὸν πάθοι.

Obs. We sometimes find the optative without ἄν, where we might
expect the optative with ἄν. In this case the event is represented as
indefinitely possible, without dependence or connection with any circumstances which might affect its realization. This is more common in poetry
than prose, as prose writers naturally paid more attention to the actual
circumstances of the case: Il. ε, 303 μέγα ἔργον, ὃ οὐ δύο γ' ἄνδρε φέροιεν.
A prose writer would have probably added ἄν to represent the condition, εἰ καὶ βούλοιτο: Plat. Euthyd. p. 292 E τίς ποτ' ἐστὶν ἡ
ἐπιστήμη ἐκείνη, ἣ ἡμᾶς εὐδαίμονας ποιήσειεν (but p. 293 A τίς ποτ' ἐστὶν ἡ
ἐπιστήμη, ἧς τυχόντες ἂν καλῶς τὸν ἐπίλοιπον βίον διέλθοιμεν). So
where a negative or a perfectly indefinite clause precedes; as, Æsch. P.V.
261 οὐκ ἔστιν ὅτῳ μείζονα μοῖραν νείμαιμ' ἢ σοί. It being previously stated
that there is no such person, makes it unnecessary to refer by ἄν to his
existence; as, οὐκ ἔστιν ὅτῳ ἄν &c., *there is no one, to whom if he existed,* (ἄν) &c.

Construction of several Adjectival Sentences together. — Change from the Relative to the Demonstrative Construction.

§. 833. When there are two or more adjectival clauses in succession, depending on the same verb, or on different verbs but in
the same government, the relative is generally used only once,
and thereby the two sentences are united into one; as, ἀνήρ, ὃς
πολλὰ μὲν ἀγαθὰ τοὺς φίλους, πολλὰ δὲ κακὰ τοὺς πολεμίους ἔπραξεν—
ἀνήρ, ὃς παρ' ἡμῖν ἦν καὶ (ὃς) ὑπὸ πάντων ἐφιλεῖτο — ἀνήρ, ὃν ἐθαυ-
μάζομεν καὶ (ὃν) πάντες ἐφίλουν. But if the verbs of the two
clauses require different cases, the relative should stand with each

in its proper case; as, ὁ ἀνὴρ, ὃ ς παρ' ἡμῖν ἦ ν καὶ ὃν πάντες ἐ φ ί λ ο υ ν. But the Greeks endeavoured to avoid this repetition either by omitting the second relative, or by using a demonstr. (mostly αὐτός) or a personal pronoun in the place of the relative, so that the dependent relative clause assumes the character of a demonstr. principal clause: *a.* Od. β, 114 ἄνωχθε δέ μιν γαμέεσθαι τῷ, ὅ τ ε ῷ τε πατὴρ κέλεται καὶ (sc. ὃ ς) ἀνδάνει αὐτῇ: Od. ι, 110 ἄμπελοι, α ἵ τ ε φέρουσιν οἶνον ἐριστάφυλον καί (sc. ἅς) σφιν (Κυκλώπεσσι) Διὸς ὄμβρος ἀέξει: Il. ν, 634 Τρωσίν, τ ῶ ν μένος αἰὲν ἀτάσθαλον, οὐδὲ δύνανται φυλόπιδος κορέσασθαι ὁμοίου πολέμοιο for καὶ οἳ οὐ δύνανται κ. τ. λ. : Il. γ, 235 οὕς κεν ἐῢ γνοίην καὶ (sc. ὧν) τοὔνομα μυθησαίμην. In prose where the clauses are opposed: Plat. Rep. p. 533 D ἃς ἐπιστήμας μὲν πολλάκις προσείπομεν διὰ τὸ ἔθος, δέονται δὲ ὀνόματος ἄλλου.—*b.* Il. α, 78 ἦ γὰρ ὀίομαι ἄνδρα χολωσέμεν, ὃ ς μέγα πάντων Ἀργείων κρατέει καί ο ἱ (for ᾧ) πείθονται Ἀχαιοί: Il. κ, 243 sqq. πῶς ἂν ἔπειτ' Ὀδυσῆος ἐγὼ θείοιο λαθοίμην, ο ὗ πέρι μὲν πρόφρων κραδίη καὶ θυμὸς ἀγήνωρ ἐν πάντεσσι πόνοισι, φιλεῖ δέ ἑ (for ὃν δὲ φιλεῖ) Παλλὰς Ἀθήιη ; Il. μ, 300 ὥστε λέων ὀρεσίτροφος, ὅ ς τ' ἐπιδευὴς δηρὸν ἔῃ κρειῶν, κέλεται δέ ἑ θυμὸς ἀγήνωρ: Od. α, 70 ἀντίθεον Πολύφημον, ὃ ο υ κράτος ἐστὶ μέγιστον πᾶσιν Κυκλώπεσσι, Θόωσα δέ μ ι ν τέκε Νύμφη : Od. ι, 20 ὃς πᾶσι δόλοισιν ἀνθρώποισι μέλω (*curæ sum*), καί μευ (for καὶ ο ὗ) κλέος οὐρανὸν ἵκει: Hdt. III. 34 Πρηξά-σπεα, τ ὸ ν ἐτίμα τε μάλιστα, καί οἱ τὰς ἀγγελίας ἔφερε ο ὗ τ ο ς : Plat. Rep. p. 395 D οὐ δὴ ἐπιτρέψομεν, ἣν δ' ἐγώ, ὧ ν φαμεν κήδεσθαι καὶ δεῖν α ὐ τ ο ὺ ς ἄνδρας γενέσθαι ἀγαθούς (for καὶ οὕς φαμεν δεῖν ἄνδρ. ἀγ. γεν.)[a]: Ibid. p. 505 E ὃ δὴ διώκει μὲν ἅπασα ψυχὴ καὶ τ ο ύ τ ο υ ἕνεκα πάντα πράττει: Id. Gorg. p. 452 D ὃ φῂς σὺ μέγιστον ἀγαθὸν εἶναι τοῖς ἀνθρώποις καί σε δημιουργὸν εἶναι α ὐ τ ο ῦ[b]: Id. Phileb. p. 12 B ἣν ὅδε Ἀφροδίτην μὲν λέγεσθαί φησι, τὸ δ' ἀληθέστατον α ὐ τ ῆ ς ὄνομα Ἡδονὴν εἶναι: Demosth. p. 122, 47 Λακεδαιμόνιοι, οἳ θαλάττης μὲν ἦρχον καὶ γῆς ἁπάσης, βασιλέα δὲ σύμμαχον εἶχον, ὑφίστατο δ' οὐδὲν α ὐ τ ο ύ ς, for οὓς οὐδὲν ὑφίστατο, *quibus nihil non cessit*: Id. p. 35, 24 ἐκεῖνοι τοίνυν, ο ἷ ς οὐκ ἐχαρίζονθ' οἱ λέγοντες οὐδ' ἐφίλουν α ὐ τ ο ύ ς[c]. So the Latin, Cic. de Orat. II. 74 *Themistocles, a d quem quidam doctus homo—accessisse dicitur, eique artem memoriæ—pollicitus esse se traditurum.*

Obs. 1. So also the relative adverbs are changed into demonstr. adverbs: Hdt. V. 49, 11 ἔ ν θ α βασιλεύς τε μέγας δίαιταν ποιέεται, καὶ τῶν χρημάτων οἱ θησαυροὶ ἐ ν θ α ῦ τ ά εἰσι.

Obs. 2. There are even some passages where, in the same sentence, we find both the relative and demonstr.: Hdt. IV. 44 Ἰνδὸν ποταμόν, ὃ ς κροκοδείλους δεύτερος ο ὗ τ ο ς ποταμῶν πάντων παρέχεται : Eur. Andr. 65ι

---

     [a] Stallb. ad loc.   [b] Ibid.   [c] Bremi ad loc.

(γυναῖκα βάρβαρον) ἣν χρῆν σ' ἐλαύνειν τήνδ' ὑπὲρ Νείλου ῥοάς. In such passages the demonstr. points to some thought to be supplied — which — and indeed that river is one of two, &c. — which — this I mean. But sometimes if the relative is separated from its verb by some other sentence, or if the adjectival sentence is very long, the demonstrative is used for the sake of clearness : Xen. R. Lac. X. 4 ὅς (Λυκοῦργος) ἐπειδὴ κατέμαθεν, ὅτι οἱ μὴ βουλόμενοι ἐπιμελεῖσθαι τῆς ἀρετῆς οὐχ ἱκανοί εἰσι τὰς πατρίδας αὔξειν, ἐκεῖνος ἐν τῇ Σπάρτῃ ἠνάγκασε κ. τ. λ.

Obs. 3. Sometimes a clause, which, although it is logically dependent, yet does not stand in the form of the relative construction, is joined to the preceding clause as grammatically a principal clause : Plat. Gorg. p. 483 E ἐπεὶ ποίῳ δικαίῳ χρώμενος Ξέρξης ἐπὶ τὴν Ἑλλάδα ἐστράτευσεν ; ἢ ὁ πατὴρ αὐτοῦ ἐπὶ τοὺς Σκύθας ; ἢ ἄλλα μυρία ἄν τις ἔχοι τοιαῦτα λέγειν (for ἢ τοιαῦτα ἄλλα μυρία ἃ ἄν τις ἔχοι λέγειν) : Id. Phæd. p. 41 B ἐπὶ πόσῳ δ' ἄν τις—δέξαιτο ἐξετάσαι—ἢ 'Οδυσσέα, ἢ Σίσυφον, ἢ ἄλλους μυρίους ἄν τις εἴποι καὶ ἄνδρας καὶ γυναῖκας : Ibid. p. 94 B λέγω δὲ τὸ τοιόνδε, ὡς εἰ καύματος ἐνόντος καὶ δίψους ἐπὶ τοὐναντίον ἕλκειν, ἐπὶ τὸ μὴ πίνειν· καὶ πείνης ἐνούσης ἐπὶ τὸ μὴ ἐσθίειν· καὶ ἄλλα μυρία που ὁρῶμεν ἐναντιουμένην τὴν ψυχὴν τοῖς κατὰ τὸ σῶμα : Id. Soph. p. 226 B καὶ πρός γε τούτοις ἔτι ξαίνειν καὶ κατάγειν (*deducere filum*) καὶ κερκίζειν καὶ μυρία ἐν ταῖς τέχναις ἄλλα τοιαῦτα ἐνόντα ἐπιστάμεθα.

Relative in the place of Demonstrative.

§. 834. 1. The relative pronoun is not only used to connect a dependent to a principal clause, but also sentences generally, between which there is no such relation, as it stands for a demonstrative which would point to a word in the preceding clause. This also is a very common Latin idiom, and used but seldom in Greek when compared with its very wide use in Latin — in Greek sentences very often begin, ταῦτα δὲ εἰπόντες, ταῦτα δὲ ἀκούσαντες, μετὰ δὲ ταῦτα, ἐκ τούτου δέ, ὡς δὲ ταῦτα ἐγένετο &c., where in Latin the relative *qui* &c. would be used.

2. We shall give some of the more unusual cases of this idiom :

a. In sentences which express the ground or reason, in place of the demonstr. with γάρ, both in poetry and prose ; as, Xen. M. S. III. 5, 15 sq. πότε γὰρ οὕτως Ἀθηναῖοι, ὥσπερ Λακεδαιμόνιοι, ἢ πρεσβυτέρους αἰδέσονται ; —οἱ ἀπὸ τῶν πατέρων ἄρχονται καταφρονεῖν τῶν πατέρων· — ἢ σωμασκήσουσιν οὕτως ; —οἱ οὐ μόνον αὐτοὶ εὐεξίας ἀμελοῦσιν, ἀλλὰ καὶ τῶν ἐπιμελουμένων καταγελῶσι κ. τ. λ. So Latin : Cicer. Phil. IV. 5 *virtus est una altissimis defixa radicibus :* qu æ (i. e. *hæc enim*) *nunquam ullâ vi labefactari potest, nunquam demoveri loco.*

b. When the whole sentence is interrupted by one or more parentheses : generally there is joined to the relative some conjunction, as ἄρα, igitur, which denotes that the interrupted sentence is taken up again : Il. λ, 221 (τίς δὴ πρῶτος Ἀγαμέμνονος ἀντίος ἦλθεν ;) 'Ιφιδάμας Ἀντηνορίδης, ἠΰς τε μέγας τε, ὃς τράφη ἐν Θρήκῃ κ. τ. λ. : Vers. 230 ὅς ῥα τότ' Ἀτρεΐδεω Ἀγαμέμνονος ἀντίος ἦλθεν. So also in prose.

c. In addresses, questions, commands, but only in poetry : Soph. Œ. C. 1354 νῦν δ' ἀξιωθεὶς εἶσι κἀκούσας γ' ἐμοῦ τοιαῦθ', ἃ μὴ τοῦδ' οὔποτ' εὐφρανεῖ βίον· ὅς γ', ὦ κάκιστε, σκῆπτρα καὶ θρόνους ἔχων, — τὸν αὐτὸς αὐτοῦ πατέρα τόνδ' ἀπήλασας, for σύ γ', ὦ κάκιστε : Eur. Or. 746 Or. ψῆφον ἀμφ' ἡμῶν πολίτας ἐπὶ φόνῳ θέσθαι χρεών· — Pyl. ἣ κρινεῖ τί χρῆμα ; for αὕτη δὲ τί χρῆμα κρινεῖ : Soph. Œ. T. 723 τοιαῦτα φῆμαι μαντικαὶ διώρισαν· ὧν ἐντρέπου σὺ μηδέν for τούτων δὲ ἐντρέπου σὺ μηδέν.

Especial peculiarities.—Relative with the principal Verb repeated.—Relative joined to an explanatory Infinitive or whole Sentence.

§. 835. 1. Sometimes the relative pronouns are joined in poetry with the principal verb repeated, to avoid by an indefinite expression the direct assertion of something disagreeable : Eur. Med. 894 ἀλλ' ἐσμὲν, οἶον ἐσμὲν, οὐκ ἐρῶ κακόν, γυναῖκες : Ibid. 1018 ἤγγειλας οἷ' ἤγγειλας, οὗ σε μέμφομαι. So with relative adverbs : Soph. Œ. C. 273 ἱκόμην ὦ' ἱκόμην : so ὅπη Æsch. Ag. 67 ἔστι δ' ὅπη νῦν ἐστί : especially ὡς and ὅπως Eur. Or. 78 sq. ἐπεὶ πρὸς Ἴλιον ἔπλευσ' ὅπως ἔπλευσα θεομανεῖ πότμῳ : Id. Hec. 873 πάσχοντος ἀνδρὸς Θρηκὸς οἷα πείσεται : *Ita loquuntur, qui rei gravis aut male ominatæ mentionem declinent* [a].

2. As a substant. is taken into an adjectiv. sentence as an explanation or illustration of the notion signified by it (§. 824. *Obs.*), so the relative is sometimes explained in an analogous manner by an infinitive, or a whole sentence, which repeats as it were, but in a more definite way, that to which the relative refers : Thuc. V. 6 ὥστε οὐκ ἂν ἔλαθεν αὐτόθεν ὁρμώμενος ὁ Κλέων τῷ στρατῷ· ὅπερ προσεδέχετο ποιήσειν αὐτὸν, ἐπὶ τὴν Ἀμφίπολιν, ὑπεριδόντα σφῶν τὸ πλῆθος, ἀναβήσεσθαι. So Cicero de Offic. III. 31, 112 *criminabatur etiam, quod Titum filium ab hominibus relegasset, et ruri habitare jussisset. Quod cum audivisset adolescens filius, n e g o t i u m e x h i b e r i p a t r i, accurrisse Romam—dicitur.* So Xen. Hier. VI. 12 ὁ δ' ἐζήλωσας ἡμᾶς, ὡς τοὺς μὲν φίλους μάλιστα εὖ ποιεῖν δυνάμεθα, τοὺς δ' ἐχθροὺς πάντων μάλιστα χειρούμεθα, οὐδὲ ταῦτ' οὕτως ἔχει, as in Latin, *q u o d* for *quod attinet ad id, quod.* Sometimes in plur. : Xen. Hell. II. 3, 45 ἁ δ' αὖ εἶπεν, ὡς ἐγώ εἰμι οἷος ἀεί ποτε μεταβάλλεσθαι, κατανοήσατε καὶ ταῦτα : Eur. Or. 584 ἐφ' οἷς δ' ἀπειλεῖς, ὡς πετρωθῆναί με δεῖ, ἄκουσον.

The Adjectival Sentence used for the other Dependent Sentences.

§. 836. 1. Adjectival sentences have the force of substantival sentences, when they represent an adj. or part. used as a substantive ; as, ἦλθον οἱ ἄριστοι ἦσαν, for ἦλθον οἱ ἄριστοι (sc. ἄνδρες). These we call Substantival Adjective Sentences. The relative which introduces such adject. sentences is not an adjectival, but a substantival pronoun. In English we use the demonstrative, " they who were the bravest came." This use of the adj. sentence is mostly Epic.—See examples above. So Il. η, 50 αὐτὸς δὲ προκάλεσσαι Ἀχαιῶν ὅστις ἄριστος (= Ἀχαιῶν τὸν ἄριστον) : Plat. Rep. p. 466 E ἄξουσι τῶν παίδων εἰς τὸν πόλεμον ὅσοι ἁδροί, *ex liberis quotquot adoleverunt* (= *omnes adolescentes*) : Demosth. p. 231, 4 οἷς γὰρ εὐτυχήκεσαν ἐν Λεύκτροις, οὐ μετρίως ἐκέχρηντο (= τοῖς εὐτυχήμασιν.

2. The relative clause which refers not to a single subst., but to the substantival notion expressed by the whole sentence, is also to be looked upon as a substantival adjective sentence : Plat. Symp. p. 193 B φίλοι γὰρ γενόμενοι καὶ διαλλαγέντες τῷ θεῷ ἐξευρήσομέν τε καὶ ἐντευξόμεθα τοῖς παιδικοῖς τοῖς ἡμετέροις αὐτῶν, ὃ τῶν νῦν ὀλίγοι ποιοῦσι. In Latin we generally find "*i d q u o d.*" So sometimes in Greek, especially in Plato : Theæt. p. 172

---

[a] Pflugk ad loc.

D : Gorg. p. 461 C ἐκ ταύτης ἴσως τῆς ὁμολογίας ἐναντίον τι συνέβη ἐν τοῖς λόγοις, τοῦθ᾽ ὃ δὴ ἀγαπᾷς, αὐτὸς ἄγων ἐπὶ τοιαῦτα ἐρωτήματα. Here also an attraction occurs, as we have seen above (§. 821.) : Demosth. p. 205, 13 προσήκει δήπου πλείω χάριν αὐτοὺς ἔχειν ὧν ἐσώθησαν ὑφ᾽ ἡμῶν, — ἢ ἃ ν ἀδικεῖν κωλύονται νῦν ὀργίζεσθαι, for ἐκείνων, ὅτι. Even a real substantival sentence introduced by ὅτι assumes sometimes the form of a (substantival) adjective sentence, as from ἀντὶ τούτου, ὅτι comes ἀντὶ τούτου οὗ or ἀνθ᾽ ὅτου.

Obs. 1. On οἷος, ὅσος &c., for ὅτι τοιοῦτος, τόσος &c., see §. 804. 9.

3. The adjectival sentence frequently supplies the place of an adverbial sentence introduced by ὅτι, *because :* Hdt. I. 33 (Κροῖσος Σόλωνα) ἀποπέμπεται, κάρτα δόξας ἀμαθέα εἶναι, ὅς, τὰ παρεόντα ἀγαθὰ μετεὶς, τὴν τελευτὴν παντὸς χρήματος ὁρᾶν ἐκέλευε (=κελεύσαντα) : Xen. M. S. II. 7, 13 θαυμαστὸν ποιεῖς, ὃς ἡμῖν μὲν οὐδὲν δίδως (=θ. π. ἡμῖν—διδούς).

4. The adjectiv. sentence can also be used for a substant. final sentence. The relative is then followed by an ind. fut. or a conjunct. (with κέ in Epic) if the verb on which it depends is a principal tense, or with the opt. when the verb is an historic tense ; the conj. however is often used after an historic tense : Eur. Iph. T. 1217 καὶ πόλει πέμψον τίν᾽, ὅστις σημανεῖ : Xen. M. S. II. 1, 14 ὅπλα κτῶνται, οἷς ἀμυνοῦνται τοὺς ἀδικοῦντας : Plat. Men. p. 89 E εἰς καλὸν ἡμῖν αὐτὸς ὅδε παρεκαθίζετο, ᾧ μεταδῶμεν τῆς σκέψεως, *quem (ut eum) participem facere possimus :* Thuc. VII. 25 καὶ τῶν νεῶν μὲ εἰς Πελοπόννησον ᾤχετο, πρέσβεις ἄγουσα, οἵπερ τὰ σφέτερα φράζωσι : Il. ι, 165 κλητοὺς ὀτρύνομεν, οἵ κε ἔλθωσ᾽ ἐς κλισίην Πηληϊάδεω Ἀχιλῆος : Od. ο, 457 καὶ τότ᾽ ἄρ᾽ ἄγγελον ἧκαν, ὃς ἀγγείλειε γυναικί.

5. The adject. sentence is very often used for an adverb. sentence introduced by ὥστε :

a. After οὕτως or ὧδε : Soph. Antig. 220 οὐκ ἔστιν οὕτω μῶρος, ὃς θανεῖν ἐρᾷ : Demosth. p. 13, 15 τίς οὕτως εὐήθης ἐστὶν ὑμῶν, ὅστις ἀγνοεῖ τὸν ἐκεῖθεν πόλεμον δεῦρο ἥξοντα [a] : Id. p. 100, 44 οὐ γὰρ οὕτω γ᾽ εὐήθης ἐστὶν ὑμῶν οὐδείς, ὃς ὑπολαμβάνει.

b. After τοιοῦτος, τηλικοῦτος, τοσοῦτος : Isocr. Epist. p. 408 D χρὴ ἐπιθυμεῖν δόξης — τηλικαύτης τὸ μέγεθος, ἣ ν μόνος ἂν σὺ τῶν νῦν ὄντων κτήσασθαι δυνηθείης. Generally the demonstratives are followed by their proper relatives, οἷος, ὅσος : Eur. Heracl. 745 σύμμαχος γενοίμην μοι τοιοῦτος, οἷος ἂν τροπὴν Εὐρυσθέως θείην. And generally the verb is in the infin. as after ὥστε, as the adjectiv. sentence expresses the consequence or result of the principal clause : Plat. Symp. p. 211 B τὰ δὲ ἄλλα πάντα καλὰ ἐκείνου μετέχοντα τρόπον τινὰ τοιοῦτον, οἷον — μήτε τι πλέον μήτε ἔλαττον γίγνεσθαι μηδὲ πάσχειν μηδέν : Id. Apol. c. 18 ἐγὼ τυγχάνω ὢν τοιοῦτος, οἷος ὑπὸ τοῦ θεοῦ τῇ πόλει δεδόσθαι : Soph. Œ. T. 1295 θέαμα δ᾽ εἰσόψει τάχα τοιοῦτον, οἷον καὶ στυγοῦντ᾽ ἐποικτίσαι : Xen. Anab. IV. 8, 12 δοκεῖ — τοσοῦτον χωρίον κατασχεῖν διαλιπόντας τοὺς λόχους, ὅσον ἔξω τοὺς ἐσχάτους λόχους γενέσθαι τῶν πολεμίων κεράτων. This illustrates the derivation of ὡς from ὅς.

Obs. 2. So the phrases ὅσον γ᾽ ἔμ᾽ εἰδέναι, *quantum equidem sciam*, must be explained, *in so far as* (or *that*) *I can know.* Also οὐδὲν οἷον with infin. (*il n'y a rien de tel*) ; as, οὐδὲν οἷον ἀκοῦσαι τῶν λόγων αὐτοῦ, properly "nothing is of such a nature as — nothing is better than to hear his words=it is best" &c.

Obs. 3. When οὕτως or ὧδε is followed by the relative ὅς, ὅστις for ὥστε, there is something contrary to the general character of the

---

[a] Bremi ad. loc.

Greek construction, which aims at connecting the principal and dependent clauses together by the use of the forms corresponding to each
other ; as, ὁ or οὗτος—ὅς ; τοσοῦτος—ὅσος ; τοιοῦτος—οἷος ; οὕτως—ὥστε.
On the contrary, the construction in which τοιοῦτος, τοσοῦτος, is
followed by οἷος, ὅσος instead of ὥστε, is in harmony with this
general principle of the language.

c. This takes place in the forms ἐπὶ τούτῳ, ἐπὶ τοῖσδε—ἐφ' ᾧτε, or (the
demonstrative being merged in the relative) ἐφ' ᾧτε alone, *on condition that*,
with the ind. fut., or usually with the infin., for ἐπὶ τούτῳ, ἐπὶ τοῖσδε, ὥστε,
as often in Thuc.; as, III. 114 σπονδὰς καὶ ξυμμαχίαν ἐποιήσαντο — ἐπὶ
τοῖσδε, ὥστε μήτε Ἀμπρακιώτας — στρατεύειν ἐπὶ Πελοποννησίους, μήτε
κ. τ. λ.

6. On ὅς, ὃς ἄν, ὅστις ἄν, with conjunct. for an hypothetical adverb.
sentence with ἐάν, see §. 828. 1. So after general sentences or affirmations
which are true under certain circumstances or conditions, to explain and
give these circumstances ; as, βέλτερον, ὅς, it is better for one, if he &c. :
Il. ξ, 81 βέλτερον ὃς φεύγων προφύγῃ κακὸν ἠὲ ἁλώῃ : Hesiod. Oper. 327 ἴσον
δ' ὅς θ' ἱκέτην ὅστε ξεῖνον κακὸν ἔρξῃ, ὅς τε κασιγνήτοιο ἑοῦ ἀνὰ δέμνια βαίνῃ —,
ὅς τε τευ ἀφραδίῃς ἀλιταίνεται ὀρφανὰ τέκνα, ὅς τε γονῆα γέροντα — νεικείῃ· τῷ δ'
ἤτοι Ζεὺς αὐτὸς ἀγαίεται : Eur. Fragm. inc. 49 συμφορὰ δ', ὃς ἂν τύχῃ κακῆς
γυναικός : Thuc. VI. 16 οὐκ ἄχρηστος ἥδ' ἡ ἄνοια, ὃς ἂν — τὴν πόλιν ὠφελῇ :
Id. II. 44 τὸ δ' εὐτυχὲς, οἳ ἂν τῆς εὐπρεπεστάτης λάχωσιν, ὥσπερ οἵδε νῦν
τελευτῆς, ὑμεῖς δὲ λύπης : Xen. Hell. II. 3, 51 νομίζω, προστάτου ἔργον εἶναι
οἵου δεῖ, ὃς ἂν ὁρῶν τοὺς φίλους ἐξαπατωμένους μὴ ἐπιτρέπῃ : Id. Anab. II. 6, 6
ταῦτα οὖν φιλοπολέμου δοκεῖ ἀνδρὸς ἔργα εἶναι, ὅστις, ἐξὸν — εἰρήνην ἄγειν ἄνευ
αἰσχύνης καὶ βλάβης, αἱρεῖται πολεμεῖν.

ADVERBIAL SENTENCES.

§. 837. An adverbial sentence is the resolution of an adverb or
gerund, and expresses therefore the accidents, or circumstances
attending on the action of the verb ; as, ὅτε τὸ ἔαρ ἦλθε, τὰ
ἄνθη θάλλει (= τοῦ ἔαρος ἐλθόντος). The adverbial is joined to the
principal clause by the relative adverbs, such as οὗ, ὅθι, ὡς, ὅτε &c.
The relatives refer back to a demonstr. adverb (expressed or supplied) in the principal clause, whereby the two clauses are joined
into one (§. 795. 3.); as, ὅτε τὸ ἔαρ ἦλθε, τότε τὰ ἄνθη θάλλει—
ὡς ἔλεξας, οὕτως ἔπραξας. The demonstrative adverbs (local,
temporal, &c.) signify the notion (local, temporal, &c.) which the
adverbial clause represents.—Local ; as, ἐνταῦθα, ἐκεῖ.—Temporal ;
as, τότε.—Mode and Manner ; as, οὕτως.—Causality ; as, ἐκ τούτου,
ἐπὶ τούτῳ.—Comparison ; as, οὕτως, τοσοῦτον, τοσούτῳ. As one or
other of these demonstr. adverbs stands in the principal clause,
the adverbial sentence is local, temporal, &c.

Local Adverbial Sentences.

§. 838. A local adverb. sentence is the resolution of a local
adverb, or of the case of a subst. which, either with or without a

preposition, expresses an adverbial notion of *place*. These sentences are introduced by the relative local adverbs, οὗ, ᾗ, ὅπῃ, ὅπου,
ἔνθα, ἵνα—*ubi*—; ὅθεν, ἔνθεν—*unde*—; οἷ, ὅποι, ᾗ, ὅπῃ—*quo*—and
like the local adverbs express either *where, whence, whither*. The
principal clause contains a corresponding demonstrative adverb,
either expressed or implied; as, ἐνταῦθα, ἐκεῖ, ἐκεῖσε, ταύτῃ &c.
The use of the moods in the adverbial is exactly the same as in the
adject. sentence: Il. μ, 48 ὅππῃ τ' ἰθύσῃ, τῇ τ' εἴκουσι στίχες
ἀνδρῶν. *quocunque—ibi*: Hesiod. Opp. 206 τῇ δ' εἶς, ᾗ σ' ἂν ἐγώ
περ ἄγω, εο—*quocunque*: Hdt. I. 11 ἐκ τοῦ αὐτοῦ μὲν χωρίου ἡ
ὁρμὴ ἔσται, ὅθενπερ καὶ ἐκεῖνος ἐμὲ ἐπεδέξατο γυμνήν: Id. III. 39
ὅκου γὰρ ἰθύσειε στρατεύεσθαι, πάντα οἱ ἐχώρεε εὐτυχέως (*indefinite
frequency*): Thuc. II. 11 ἔπεσθε (ἐκεῖσε), ὅποι ἂν τις ἡγῆται:
Xen. Anab. IV. 2, 24 μαχόμενοι δὲ οἱ πολέμιοι καὶ ὅπῃ εἴη στενὸν
χωρίον προκαταλαμβάνοντες ἐκώλυον τὰς παρόδους (optative on account
of the historic tense, ἐκώλυον): Id. Cyr. III. 3, 5 ἐθήρα ὅποντερ
ἐπιτυγχάνοιεν θηρίοις, *anywhere where*: Plat. Apol. p. 28 D οὗ ἂν
τις ἑαυτὸν τάξῃ—ἐνταῦθα δεῖ—μένοντα κινδυνεύειν.

Obs. On the attraction of local adverbs, see §. 822. *Obs.* 6. §. 824.
Obs. 2; on their pregnant construction §. 716. *Obs.* 1; and change of
relative into demonstrat. construction, §. 833. *Obs.* 1.

Temporal Adverbial Sentences.

839. 1. A temporal adverb. sentence is the resolution of a temporal adverb or gerund, or the case of a subst. with or without a
preposition, expressing a notion of *time*. Thus the sentence ὅτε ἡ
νὺξ ἐγένετο may be a resolution either of νύκτωρ, or a gerund
(§. 696.), νυκτὸς γενομένης; or a subst. with a preposition, ἐν τῇ
νυκτί; or the dative alone, τῇ νυκτί; or the genit. alone, τῆς νυκτός.
The adverbial sentence is less used in Greek than in modern languages in consequence of the powers of the participle; as, *when he
had done this he went away*, ταῦτα ποιήσας, ἀπέβη (§. 696.).

2. The time in which the dependent verb stands in relation to
the principal verb is either coincident, ἐν ᾧ σὺ γράφεις, ὁ ἑταῖρος
ἐπιγίνεταί—ὅτε σὺ ἔγραφες, ὁ ἑταῖρος ἐπεγίγνετο &c.; or antecedent,
ἐπειδὴ ὁ Κῦρος ἐπεληλύθει (ἐπῆλθεν), οἱ πολέμιοι ἀπέφευγον; or consequent, πρὶν ὁ Κῦρος ἐπῆλθεν, οἱ πολέμιοι ἀπέφυγον.

3. The conjunctions whereby these adverb. sentences are introduced are,

 a. For adverbial sentences—coincident in time with the principal
clause, ὅτε, (εὖτε Epic, formed by a resolution of the aspirate

ɔrm ὅτε,) ὁπότε, ὡς (ὥσπερ Hdt.; ὅπως in Attic poetry, ὅκως
Hdt.), ἡνίκα, which expresses a point, and ἐν ᾧ, ἕως, *while*, (ὄφρα,
ɪs *long as*,) which express a space of time.

b. Antecedent to the principal clause, ἐπεί (ἐπειή poet.; ἐπεί τε
Hdt.), ἐπειδή, *postquam*; ἐξ οὗ, ἐξ ὅτου, also ἐξ ὧν, *ex quo*; and ἀφ'
ɔῦ, since.

c. Consequent, πρίν, πρὶν ἤ, *priusquam*; ἕως, ἕως οὗ (τέως in Post-
Homeric Epic writers, and even now and then in Attic prose), εἰς
ὅ, ἔστε, μέχρις or ἄχρις οὗ, μέχρις ὅτου, μέχρι, (ἄχρι poet.) (ὄφρα
poet.).

Obs. Ὅτε, ὁπότε, ὡς, ἐπεί, ἐπειδή, have also very often a causal force—
since.

4. These relative adverbs refer to a demonstr. adverb, either expressed or implied in the principal clause; as, ὅτε — τότε; ἕως —
τέως (poet.); ἦμος—τῆμος poet.; ὄφρα—τόφρα poet.; ἡνίκα—τηνίκα
(poet.); πρίν (sc. τούτου), *prius*, — ἤ, *quam*; ὡς — ὥς; and frequently, especially in Hdt., ὡς, ὅτε — ἐνταῦθα; οὕτω δή, often
stands in the principal clause when it is placed after the subordinate clause, as the result thereof.

Use of the Moods in Temporal Adverbial Sentences.

Indicative.

§. **840.** The indic. is used when what is said is to be represented as something real—as a fact: Il. δ, 221 ὄφρα τοι ἀμφε-
πένοντο βοὴν ἀγαθὸν Μενέλαον, τόφρα δ' ἐπὶ Τρώων στίχες
ἤλυθον: Il. λ, 90 ἦμος δὲ δρυτόμος περ ἀνὴρ ὡπλίσσατο δόρπον,
—τῆμος σφῇ ἀρετῇ Δαναοὶ ῥήξαντο φάλαγγας: Il. ω, 31 ἀλλ'
ὅτε δὴ ῥ' ἐκ τοῖο δυωδεκάτη γένετ' ἠώς, καὶ τότ' ἄρ' ἀθανάτοισι
μετηύδα Φοῖβος Ἀπόλλων: Il. α, 432 οἱ δ' ὅτε δὴ λιμένος πολυ-
βενθέος ἐντὸς ἵκοντο, ἱστία μὲν στείλαντο, θέσαν δ' ἐν νηὶ μελαίνῃ:
Od. ι, 233 μένομέν τε μιν ἔνδον ἥμενοι, ἕως ἐπῆλθε νέμων: Il. ν,
495 Αἰνείᾳ θυμὸς ἐνὶ στήθεσσι γεγήθει, ὡς ἴδε λαῶν ἔθνος ἐπισπό-
μενον ἑοῖ αὐτῷ: Od. α, 363 κλαῖεν ἔπειτ' Ὀδυσῆα, φίλον πόσιν,
ὄφρα οἱ ὕπνον ἡδὺν ἐπὶ βλεφάροισι βάλε γλαυκῶπις Ἀθήνη: Hdt.
VI. 41 καὶ ὥσπερ ὡρμήθη ἐκ Καρδίης πόλιος, ἔπλεε διὰ τοῦ Μέλανος κόλπου: Ibid. 83 οἱ δοῦλοι—ἔσχον πάντα τὰ πρήγματα—, ἐς
ὃ ἐπήβησαν οἱ τῶν ἀπολομένων παῖδες: Id. VII. 7 ὡς δὲ
ἀνεγνώσθη Ξέρξης στρατεύεσθαι ἐπὶ τὴν Ἑλλάδα, ἐνθαῦτα—
στρατηίην ποιέεται: Id. IX. 6 ἐπεὶ δὲ—σχολαίτερα ἐποίεον—,
οὕτω δὴ ὑπεξεκομίσαντο—πάντα: Id. I. 11 ὡς δὲ ἡμέρη τάχιστα

ἐγεγόνεε (ὡς τάχιστα, *quum primum, as soon as*) : Thuc. I. 8
οἱ γὰρ ἐκ τῶν νήσων κακοῦργοι ἀνέστησαν ὑπ' αὐτοῦ, ὅτε περ (*just*
when) καὶ τὰς πολλὰς αὐτῶν κατῴκιζε : Isocr. p. 348 B οὐ πρότερον ἐπαύσαντο, πρὶν τόν τε πατέρα ἐκ τοῦ στρατοπέδου μετε-
πέμψαντο, καὶ τῶν φίλων αὐτοῦ τοὺς μὲν ἀπέκτειναν, τοὺς δ' ἐκ τῆ
πόλεως ἐξέβαλον : Xen. Hell. I. 1, 3 ἐμάχοντο, μέχρις οἱ
Ἀθηναῖοι ἀνέπλευσαν : Xen. Cyr. VII. 5, 39 ὁ δὲ ὄχλος πλείω
καὶ πλείων ἐπέρρει, ἕωσπερ ἔφθασεν ἑσπέρα γενομένη, *until*
this : Ibid. VIII. 8, 9 ἀρχόμενοι δὲ τοῦ σίτου ἡνίκα περ οἱ πρώ-
αίτατα ἀριστῶντες, μέχρι τούτου ἐσθίοντες καὶ πίνοντες διάγουσιν,
ἔστε περ οἱ ὀψιαίτατα κοιμώμενοι, *until that.*

Obs. The perfect coincidence of two clauses is also signified by making
the logically dependent a grammatically independent clause, and joining
it with the other clause by καί, or generally τέ — καί, also δέ. Compare
the examples given (§. 754.), and the following : Il. τ, 241 αὐτίκ' ἔπει'
ἅμα μῦθος ἔην, τετέλεστο δὲ ἔργον : Hdt. III. 135 καὶ ἅμα ἔπος τε (ἔφατε)
καὶ ἔργον ἐποίεε. Hence the proverbial phrases, ἅμ' ἔπος καὶ ἅμ' ἔργον, ἅ'
ἔπος τε καὶ ἔργον, *dictum factum, no sooner said than done* : Demosth. l.
p. 50, 36 τοιγαροῦν ἅμα ἀκηκόαμέν τε καὶ τριηράρχους καθίσταμεν.

Conjunctive.

§. 841. 1. The conjunctive is used after temporal relative adverbs or conjunctions, when what is said is not considered as an
actual fact, but only as something imagined or thought of, and
the verb of the principal clause is in a principal tense.　These conjunctions frequently take the particle ἄν,—ὅταν, ὅτανπερ, (εὖτ' ἄν
epic), ὁπόταν, ἡνίκ' ἄν, ἐπάν (ἐπήν), ἐπειδάν, πρὶν ἄν, ἕως ἄν, μέχρις
ἄν (ἄχρις ἄν poet.), ἔστ' ἄν (εἰσόκε epic, ὄφρ' ἄν poet.),—which ἄν
points to certain circumstances on which the time of the conjunction, or action of the conjunctive depends.

2. With those relative conjunctions which express a *point of*
time, such as those from ὅταν down to ἐπειδάν, the ἄν belongs to
the time of the conjunction, and consequently of the verb, and
gives an indefinite and uncertain sense to the conjunction, by
shewing that it depends on certain conditions—that it is uncertain
and future [a] : thus while ὅτε would express *when*, ὅταν &c. signify
whensoever : hence as the conjunctive is the proper expression of
future uncertainty, these conjunctions compounded or joined with
ἄν, take the conjunctive, except sometimes in the *oratio obliqua.*
And thus they frequently mark that the principal clause depends
on an action taking place at some uncertain indefinite time,—and

[a] Ellendt. Lex. Soph. ad voc. ὅταν et ἡνίκα.

which it represents as the condition, cause, or reason of the principal clause; *then, when, or if, soever you do what is right:* τότε δὴ,
ὅταν, ἃ χρὴ, ποιῇς, εὐτυχεῖς, or εὐτυχήσεις. The aorist conjunctive
expresses something which it is conceived will be complete at some
future time, and is translated into Latin by the *fut. exactum :*
as, τότε δὴ, ὅταν, ἃ χρὴ, ποιήσῃς, εὐτυχήσεις, *tum demum, quum
officia tua expleveris, felix eris.* Thus also πρὶν ἄν introduces
the condition of the principal verb, so that the dependent verb
taking effect is the condition of the principal action; but with the
other conjunctions coming after πρὶν ἄν in the above list, expressing a space of time, *until, whilst,* the conjunctive expresses some
future uncertain event up to or during which the principal action
continues; and thus often represents the final cause, the aim or
intent of the principal verb, so that these conjunctions come very
near to the final conjunctions, and indeed ὄφρα is often used as
such in poetry: ἄν, if used, generally adds to the uncertainty of
the point or duration of time, thus making the conjunction less
definite: Od. η, 202 θεοὶ φαίνονται ἐναργεῖς ἡμῖν, εὖτ' ἔρδωμεν
ἀγακλειτὰς ἑκατόμβας: Od. ζ, 183 οὐ μὲν γὰρ τοῦγε κρεῖσσον καὶ
ἄρειον, ἢ ὅθ' ὁμοφρονέοντε νοήμασιν οἶκον ἔχητον ἀνὴρ ἠδὲ γυνή:
Od. θ, 444 μήτίς τοι καθ' ὁδὸν δηλήσεται, ὁππότ' ἄν αὖτε εὕδῃσθα
γλυκὺν ὕπνον: Od. α, 41 ἐκ γὰρ Ὀρέσταο τίσις ἔσσεται Ἀτρεΐδαο,
ὁππότ' ἄν ἡβήσῃ τε καὶ ἧς ἱμείρεται (for ἱμείρηται) αἴης: Il. ο, 232
τόφρα γὰρ οὖν οἱ ἔγειρε μένος μέγα, ὄφρ' ἄν Ἀχαιοὶ φεύγοντες νῆάς
τε καὶ Ἑλλήσποντον ἵκωνται: Il. α, 509 τόφρα δ' ἐπὶ Τρώεσσι τίθει
κράτος, ὄφρ' ἄν Ἀχαιοὶ υἱὸν ἐμὸν τίσωσιν: Plat. Prot. p. 335 B
ἐπειδὰν σὺ βούλῃ διαλέγεσθαι, ὡς ἐγὼ δύναμαι ἕπεσθαι, τότε σοι
διαλέξομαι; Il. ι, 702 μαχήσεται, ὁππότε κέν μιν θυμὸς ἐνὶ στήθεσσιν ἀνώγῃ καὶ θεὸς ὄρσῃ: Od. ι, 138 ἀλλ' ἐπικέλσαντας μεῖναι
χρόνον, εἰσόκε ναυτέων θυμὸς ἐποτρύνῃ καὶ ἐπιπνεύσωσιν ἀῆται:
Hdt. VII. 8, 2 οὐ πρότερον παύσομαι, πρὶν ἢ ἕλω τε καὶ πυρώσω
τὰς Ἀθήνας: Eur. Med. 278 sq. οὐκ ἄπειμι πρὸς δόμον, πρὶν ἄν
σε γαίας τερμόνων ἔξω βάλω: Demosth. p. 128, 69 ἕως ἄν σώζηται
τὸ σκάφος—, τότε χρὴ καὶ ναύτην καὶ κυβερνήτην—προθύμους εἶναι
(*dum servari possit* [a]).

3. Hence the conjunct. expresses an indefinite frequency. The
principal clause expresses an action repeated at different times,
or places, or by different persons; the adverbial clause gives the
time in which, and at the same time the condition under which
the action of the principal verb is thus repeated: Od. α, 192

---

[a] Bremi ad loc.

(Λαέρτη) βρῶσίν τε πόσιν τε παρτιθεῖ, εὖτ' ἄν μιν κάματος κατὰ γυῖα
λάβῃσιν: Xen. Cyr. III. 3, 26 ὅπερ καὶ νῦν ἔτι ποιοῦσιν οἱ βάρβαροι
βασιλεῖς· ὁπόταν στρατοπεδεύωνται, τάφρον περιβάλλονται εὐπετῶς διὰ
τὴν πολυχειρίαν: seldom ὡς: Hdt. IV. 172 τῶν δὲ ὡς ἕκαστός οἱ
μιχθῇ, διδοῖ δῶρον, τὸ ἂν ἔχῃ φερόμενος ἐξ οἴκου.

4. Hence also in Epic, when the adverbial clause forms part of
a simile, expressing the condition under which the simile holds
good, as this is not an actual fact, but only something imagined:
Il. ν, 334 ὡς δ' (ἔστιν) ὅθ' ὑπὸ λιγέων ἀνέμων σπέρχωσιν ἄελλαι ἤματι
τῷ, ὅτε τε πλείστη κόνις ἀμφὶ κελεύθους —· ὡς ἄρα τῶν ὁμόσ' ἦλθε
μάχη: ("Εστι, as it actually takes place; ὅτε σπέρχωσιν, supposing
that at some time &c.:) Il. ξ, 16 ὡς δ' ὅτε πορφύρῃ πέλαγος — ὡς
ὁ γέρων ὥρμαινε: Il. ο, 80 ὡς δ' ὅτ' ἂν ἀΐξῃ νόος ἀνέρος — ὡς κ. τ. λ.:
Ibid. 605. 624 ἐν δ' ἔπεσ', ὡς ὅτε κῦμα θοῇ ἐν νηὶ πέσῃσιν: Il. σ,
212. 297. Od. ι, 392 ὡς δ' ὅτ' ἀνὴρ χαλκεὺς πέλεκυν μέγαν ἠὲ σκέ-
παρνον εἰν ὕδατι ψυχρῷ βάπτῃ μεγάλα ἰάχοντα, φαρμάσσων· — ὡς τοῦ
(Κύκλωπος) σίζ' ὀφθαλμὸς ἐλαϊνέῳ περὶ μοχλῷ: Eur. Hec. 1025, we
must read ἐκπεσεῖ for ἐκπέσῃ.

Remarks on the Conjunctive Construction.

§. 842. 1. When an historic tense in the principal clause is followed by
a conjunctive in the dependent clause, this is a change from the *oratio
obliqua* to the *recta*.

2. We find some of these conjunctions with the conj.; without ἄν in
the more definite sense of *when*, as distinguished from *whensoever*, frequently in Epic, sometimes in Ionic prose, as, ὡς, Hdt. V. 172: ἐς οἷ,
Id. III. 31 οἱ δὲ βασιλήϊοι δικασταὶ κεκριμένοι ἄνδρες γίνονται Περσέων, ἐς οἱ
ἀποθάνωσι, ἢ σφι παρευρεθῇ τι ἄδικον, μέχρι τούτου: πρίν, Id. VI. 82 πρὶν γε
δὴ ἱροῖσι χρήσηται καὶ μάθῃ: πρὶν ἤ, Id. I. 19. IV. 196: μέχρι, IV. 119
μέχρι δὲ τοῦτο ἴδωμεν, μενέομεν παρ' ἡμῖν, &c. Some are thus used, though
but seldom, in Attic; as, ἡνίκα, πρίν in Attic poets and prose writers;
as, Eur. Or. 1343 πρὶν ἐτύμως ἴδω τὸν Ἑλένας φόνον: Thuc. VIII. 9 οἱ δὲ
Κορίνθιοι — οὐ προεθυμήθησαν ξυμπλεῖν, πρὶν τὰ Ἴσθμια — διεορτάσωσιν: Ibid.
οὐ βουλόμενοί πω πολέμιον ἔχειν, πρίν τι καὶ ἰσχυρὸν λάβωσι: Plat. Tim. p. 57
B λυόμενα οὐ παύεται, πρὶν ἤ — διαλυτὰ ὄντα ἐκφύγῃ — ἢ νικηθέντα — μείνῃ: Id.
Legg. p. 873 A. Æschin. §. 60. ed. Bremi μήτ' ἀπογνώτω μηδὲν μήτε κατα-
γνώτω, πρὶν ἀκούσῃ: Antiphon. ad Pharm. p. 619 πρὶν ἐν αὐτῷ ὦσι τῷ καιρῷ
γ' ἤδη καὶ γιγνώσκωσι τὸν ὄλεθρον, ἐν ᾧ εἰσι: μέχρι, ἄχρι, ἕως in poetry;
Soph. Aj. 571 μέχρις μυχοὺς κίχωσι νερτέρου θεοῦ. — μέχρις οὗ often
Thucyd.: ἐπεί Soph. Œ. C. 1226. Ant. 1025.

3. Homer joins ὅτε κε, εἰσόκε sometimes with ind. fut.: Il. ν, 335
ἀλλ' ἀναχωρῆσαι, ὅτε κεν ξυμβλήσεαι αὐτῷ: Od. θ, 317 ἀλλά σφωε δόλος καὶ
δεσμὸς ἐρύξει, εἰσόκε μοι μάλα πάντα πατὴρ ἀποδώσει ἔεδνα. This may be
accounted for by the near affinity of the conjunct. to the fut. (§. 415. 2.)

Optative.

§. 843. The opt. is used after historic tenses with the same :onstructions as the conjunctive after principal tenses (§. 414.).

a. (§. 841. 2.): Od. ε, 385 ὦρσε δ' ἐπὶ κραιπνὸν Βορέην, πρὸ)ὲ κύματ' ἔαξεν, ἕως ὅγε Φαιήκεσσι φιληρέτμοισι μιγείη (but ὄρνυσι Βορέην καὶ ἄγνυσι κύματα, ἕως—μιγῇ): Il. φ, 580 Ἀγήνωρ οὐκ ἔθελεν φεύγειν, πρὶν πειρήσαιτ' Ἀχιλῆος.

b. Very frequently to express *indefinite frequency* (§. 841. 3.). After the impft. or frequentative aorist, in the principal clause: Od. θ, 69 sq. πὰρ δ' ἐτίθει κάνεον καλήν τε τράπεζαν, πὰρ δὲ δέπας οἴνοιο, πιεῖν, ὅτε θυμὸς ἀνώγοι, when, or as often as he might have a mind: Il. κ, 14 αὐτὰρ ὅτ' ἐς νῆάς τε ἴδοι καὶ λαὸν Ἀχαιῶν, πολλὰς ἐκ κεφαλῆς προθελύμνους ἕλκετο χαίτας: Od. η, 136 εὗρε δὲ Φαιήκων ἡγήτορας ἠδὲ μέδοντας σπενδόντας δεπάεσσιν ἐϋσκόπῳ Ἀργειφόντῃ, ᾧ πυμάτῳ σπένδεσκον, ὅτε μνησαίατο κοίτου: Od. λ, 510 sqq. ἤτοι ὅτ' ἀμφὶ πόλιν Τροίην φραζοίμεθα βουλάς, αἰεὶ πρῶτος ἔβαζε καὶ οὐχ ἡμάρτανε μύθων· — αὐτὰρ ὅτ' ἐν πεδίῳ Τρώων μαρνοίμεθα χαλκῷ, οὔποτ' ἐνὶ πληθυῖ μένεν ἀν- δρῶν, — ἀλλὰ πολὺ προθέεσκε: Il. ν, 711 λαοὶ ἕπονθ' ἕταροι, οἳ οἱ σάκος ἐξεδέχοντο, ὁππότε μιν κάματός τε καὶ ἱδρὼς γούναθ' ἵκοιτο: Hdt. VI. 61 ὅκως δὲ ἐνείκειε ἡ τροφὸς (τὸ παιδίον), πρός τε τὤγαλμα ἵστα καὶ ἐλίσσετο τὴν θεὸν ἀπαλλάξαι τῆς δυσ- μορφίης τὸ παιδίον: Ibid. 75 ὅκως γάρ τεῳ ἐντύχοι Σπαρτιη- τέων, ἐνέχραυε ἐς τὸ πρόσωπον τὸ σκῆπτρον: Id. VII. 119 ὅκως δὲ ἀπίκοιτο ἡ στρατιή, σκηνὴ μὲν ἔσκε πεπηγυῖα ἑτοίμη, ἐς τὴν αὐτὸς σταθμὸν ποιεέσκετο Ξέρξης· ἡ δὲ ἄλλη στρατιὴ ἔσκε ὑπαίθριος· ὡς δὲ δείπνου γένοιτο ὥρη, οἱ μὲν δεκόμενοι ἔχεσκον πόνον· οἱ δὲ, ὅκως πλησθέντες νύκτα αὐτοῦ ἀγάγοιεν (*transegissent*), τῇ ὑστεραίῃ τήν τε σκηνὴν ἀνασπάσαντες καὶ τὰ ἔπιπλα πάντα λαβόντες, οὕτω ἀπελαύνεσκον: Id. I. 17 ὡς δὲ ἐς τὴν Μιλησίην ἀπί- κοιτο, so often: Plat. Phæd. p. 59 D ἀεὶ γὰρ δὴ καὶ τὰς πρόσθεν ἡμέρας εἰώθειμεν φοιτᾶν—πρὸς τὸν Σωκράτη· —περιεμένομεν οὖν ἕκαστοτε, ἕως ἀνοιχθείη τὸ δεσμωτήριον· —ἐπειδὴ δὲ ἀνοι- χθείη, ᾔειμεν παρὰ τὸν Σωκράτη.

Obs. Sometimes in this construction ἄν is joined to the impft. (seldom the aorist) in the principal clause (§. 424. β.): Hdt. III. 51 ὁ δὲ, ὅκως ἀπελαυνόμενος ἔλθοι ἐς ἄλλην οἰκίην, ἀπελαύνετ' ἄν καὶ ἀπὸ ταύτης—, ἀπελαυνόμενος δ' ἄν ἦιε ἐπ' ἑτέρην τῶν ἑταίρων: Xen. Cyr. VII. 1, 10 ὁπότε προσβλέψειέ τινας τῶν ἐν ταῖς τάξεσι, τότε μὲν εἶπεν ἄν κ.τ.λ.: Id. Anab. I. 5, 2 οἱ μὲν ὄνοι, ἐπεί τις διώκοι, προδραμόντες ἄν εἱστήκεσαν (the plpft. has the force of impft). See *Hypothetical Sen- tences.*

§. 844. Secondly, the opt. is used in its secondary force (§. 418.) of an *indefinite possibility—uncertainty.*

a. When the adverbial clause contains an uncertain doubtful condition, or circumstances under which the verb of the principal clause would take effect : Od. β, 31 ἠέ τιυ' ἀγγελίην στρατοῦ ἔκλυε ἐρχομένοιο, ἥν χ' ἡμῖν σάφα εἴποι, ὅτε πρότερός γε πύθοιτο ; if perhaps he has heard it : Xen. M. S. II. 1, 18 ὁ μὲν ἑκὼν πεινῶν φάγοι ἄν. ὁπότε βούλοιτο (but directly afterwards, τῷ δ' ἐξ ἀνάγκης ταῦτα τι σχοντι οὐκ ἔξεστιν, ὁπόταν βούληται, παύεσθαι) : Plat. Amat. p. 133 A ὁπότε γάρ τοι τὸ φιλοσοφεῖν αἰσχρὸν ἡγησαίμην εἶναι, οὐδ' ἂν ἄνθρω- πον νομίσαιμι ἐμαυτὸν εἶναι. So also ὅτε μή, **nisi ;** often in Homer with opt. : also π ρ ὶ ν ἄ ν with opt. instead of εἰ μή (see remarks on πρίν below) : Xen. Hell. II. 3, 48 ἐγὼ δὲ κείνοις μὲν ἀεί τοτι πολεμῶ τοῖς οὐ πρόσθεν οἰομένοις καλὴν ἂν δημοκρατίαν εἶναι, π ρ ὶ ν ἄ ν καὶ οἱ δοῦλοι καὶ οἱ δι' ἀπορίαν δραχμῆς ἂν ἀποδόμενοι τὴν πόλιν δραχμῆς μ ε τ έ χ ο ι ε ν, καὶ τοῖσδέ γ' αὖ ἀεὶ ἐναντίος εἰμί, οἳ οὐκ οἴονται καλὴν ἂν ἐγγενέσθαι ὀλιγαρχίαν, π ρ ὶ ν ἄ ν ἐς τὸ ὑπ' ὀλίγων τυραν- νεῖσθαι τὴν πόλιν κ α τ α σ τ ή σ ε ι α ν.

b. When the adverbial clause forms part of a wish : Il. φ, 429 τοιοῦτοι νῦν πάντες ὅσοι Τρώεσσιν ἀρωγοί, — εἶεν, ὅτ' Ἀργείοισι μαχοί- ατο θωρηκτῇσιν : Il. σ, 465 αἲ γάρ μιν θανάτοιο δυσηχέος ὧδε δυναίμην ἀποκρύψαι, ὅτε μιν μόρος αἰνὸς ἱκάνοι.

c. When the dependent clause is a continuation of an optative construction ; as, Soph. Œ. C. 776 ὥσπερ τις εἰ σοι λιπαροῦντι μὲν τυχεῖν μηδὲν διδοίη μηδ' ἐπαρκέσαι θέλοι, πλήρη δ' ἔχοντι θυμὸν ὧν χρή- ζοις, τότε δωροῖθ', ὅ τ' οὐδὲν ἡ χάρις χάριν φ έ ρ ο ι.

Obs. Sometimes instead of the simple conjunctions ὅτε, ἐπεί &c. the forms compounded with ἄ ν, ὅ τ α ν, ἐ π ά ν, are used with the opt. both in its primary and secondary force. In prose this seems only to happen, either when the idea is borrowed from another person and not the original creation of the speaker's own mind, or when the principal verb is in the opt. with or without ἄν [a] : Od. β, 105 ἔνθα καὶ ἡματίη μὲν ὑφαίνεσκεν μέγα ἱστόν, νύκτας δ' ἀλλύεσκεν, ἐπὴν δαΐδας παραθεῖτο (indefinite frequency) : Il. ω, 226 αὐτίκα γάρ με κατακτείνειν Ἀχιλλεύς—, ἐπὴν γόου ἐξ ἔρον εἵην (con- tinuation of a wish) : Il. τ, 205 sqq. ἦ τ' ἂν ἔγωγε νῦν μὲν ἀνώγοιμι πτολεμί- ζειν υἷας Ἀχαιῶν— ἅμα δ' ἠελίῳ καταδύντι τεύξεσθαι μέγα δόρπον, ἐπὴν τισαί- μεθα λώβην (oratio obliqua) : Æsch. Pers. 448 ἐνταῦθα πέμπει (Præs. histor.) τούσδ', ὅπως, ὅ τ α ν νεῶν φθαρέντες ἐχθροὶ νῆσον ἐ κ σ ω ζ ο ί α τ ο, κτείνειαν εὐχείρωτον Ἑλλήνων στρατόν (oratio obliqua) : Xen. Cyr. I. 3, 11 ἐπειδὰν δὲ πάνυ σπουδάζοι φαγεῖν, εἴποιμ' ἄν, ὅτι παρὰ ταῖς γυναιξίν ἐστιν : Demosth. p. 865, 6 οὐκ ἔσθ' ὅστις οὐχ ἡγεῖτο τῶν εἰδότων δίκην με λήψεσθαι παρ' αὐτῶν, ἐπειδὰν τάχιστα ἀνὴρ εἶναι δ ο κ ι μ α σ θ ε ί η ν. In many passages the reading varies [b].

---

[a] Stallb. Plat. Phæd. p. 101 D.　　　　[b] Bernhardy, Synt. p. 413.

Optative with ἄν (κ έ).

§. 845. The opt. is used with ἄν when the adverbial sentence expresses an assumption, supposition, conjecture, of something happening at some time or season, depending on some condition to be supposed or expressed (§. 419. 1.) : Demosth. p. 48, 31 φυλάξας (Φίλιππος) τοὺς ἐτησίας ἢ τὸν χειμῶνα ἐπιχειρεῖ (ἡμῖν), ἡνίκ' ἂν ἡμεῖς μὴ δυναίμεθα ἐκεῖσε (εἰς τὴν τοῦ Φιλίππου χώραν) ἀφικέσθαι, when though we wished it ever so much, at any rate, we could not come.

Remarks on the use of ἕως.

§. 846. Ἕως, *until*, expresses a point of time up to which the principal action did or is to continue, or up to which it did or will not take place ; so that the dependent clause frequently denotes the aim or intent of the principal verb.   When this point of time is past, the indicative is used ; when present or future, the conjunctive.

1. With the historic tenses of the indicative, after an historic tense in the principal clause : Od. η, 280 νήχον πάλιν ἕως ἐπῆλθον ἐς ποταμόν : Æsch. Pers. 426 οἰμωγὴ κατείχεν ἅλα, ἕως κελαινῆς νυκτὸς ὄμμ' ἀφείλετο.   Or where it is said in the principal clause, "that an action might continue, or have continued, until another action took place :" Plat. Gorg. p. 506 B ἡδέως ἂν διελεγόμην ἕως τὴν τοῦ Ἀμφίονος ἀπέδωκα ῥῆσιν.

Obs. Sometimes we find ἕως with an historic tense after the historic present : Eur. Alc. 757 πίνει ἕως ἐθέρμην' αὐτὸν ἀμφιβᾶσα φλόξ.

2. With the conjunctive, of a present or future point of time—expressing the event which determines the action (whether positive or negative) of the principal clause as something future and possible, not as a fact.   It is used both with ἄν and without, but in prose writers it generally takes it [a].   Ἄν adds to the uncertainty of the event by making the conjunction more indefinite — *until whenever it may* : Soph. Phil. 753 ἕως ἀνῇ τὸ πῆμα, σῷζ' αὐτά : Id. Œ. R. 834 ἕως δ' ἂν ἐκμάθῃς, ἔχ' ἐλπίδα.   Without ἄν in prose : Xen. Cyr. VII. 5, 39 περιμένετε ἕως τὸν ὄχλον διωσώμεθα.   Both with and without ἄν it frequently denotes the aim of the principal clause, as being that on the gaining of which the action will cease : Soph. Œ. C. 77 σιγήσομαι—ἕως ἂν ἐκμάθω.

3. With the optative (*a*) in the same sense as the conjunctive, but depending on an historic tense : Od. ε, 385 ὦρσε δ' ἐπὶ κραιπνὸν Βορέην, πρὸ δὲ κύματ' ἔαξεν, ἕως ὅγε Φαιήκεσσι φιληρέτμοισι μιγείη.   So in the *oratio obliqua* : Soph. Trach. 684 σῴζειν (ἐκέλευε) ἕως ἂν ἀρτίχριστον ἁρμόσαιμί που : cf. Arist. Eq. 133.   In this construction ἄν is generally omitted [b] ; if it is used, it has the same force as with the conjunctive.   So after a clause expressing an indefinitely repeated past action : Plat. Phæd. p. 59 D περιεμένομεν ἑκάστοτε ἕως ἀνοιχθείη τὸ δεσμωτήριον.   (*b*) When the adverbial clause is a continuation of a principal clause, expressed by the opt., as of a *wish*, &c. : Plat. Rep. p. 501 C καὶ τὸ μὲν ἄν, οἶμαι, ἐξαλείφοιεν, τὸ δὲ ἐγγράφοιεν ἕως ὅτι μάλιστα ποιήσειαν κ. τ. λ. : Id. Phæd. p. 101 D οὐκ ἀποκρίναιο ἕως ἂν τὰ ἀπ' ἐκείνης ὁρμηθέντα σκέψαιο.

---

[a] Elms. Heracl. 959.   [b] Elms. Heracl. 959.   Stallb. Rep. p. 501 C.

§. 847. Ἕως, *as long as—whilst*, denotes a space of time during which some action did, does, or will continue.

1. With the historic tenses of the indicative, when a past action is spoken of : Od. ν, 314 πάρος ἠπίη ἦσθα, ἕως ἐνὶ Τροίῃ πολεμίζομεν.

2. With the pres. ind., when a present space of time is spoken of, in which something is doing or to be done — *whilst :* Plat. Apol. Socr. p. 39 οὐδὲν γὰρ κωλύει διαμυθολογῆσαι—ἕως ἔξεστι.

3. With the conjunctive, when a present action is conceived as possibly continuing during another action, over an indefinite space of time, *as long as.* In this construction the conjunctive always takes ἄν, which seems to increase the notion of duration by making it indefinite—*as long as*, however long it may be : Æsch. Ag. 1434 ἕως ἂν αἴθῃ πῦρ ἐπ' ἐσχάρης ἐμῆς Αἴγισθος. In the *oratio obliqua* it is used with the opt. : Plat. Theæt. p. 155 A φήσομεν μηδὲν ἂν μεῖζον μήτε ἔλαττον γενέσθαι ἕως ἴσον εἴη αὐτὸ ἑαυτῷ.

Obs. The difference between the ind. and conj. with ἕως in this sense is, that the conjunctive implies that the principal action is to continue to the end of the dependent action ; the indic., that the principal action is to be done, while the other is taking place, but not that it is necessarily to be coextensive with it : Arist. Eq. 110 χρησμοὺς ἔνεγκε ἕως καθεύδει, do it while he is sleeping ; ἕως ἂν καθεύδῃ would be, continue to do so *as long as he sleeps.*

Remarks on the use of πρίν.

§. 848. 1. Πρίν, *before, before that, until ;* is used with the indic., conjunctive, optat. and infinitive. The clause to which it is attached defines and limits the preceding clause, by giving the event whereupon it will begin, or whereupon it will end, or up to which it did or will continue, or before which it did or will happen.

2. It is used with conjunctive and opt. only when a negative clause precedes ; with the indic. and infin. after both negative and affirmative clauses.

3. Indicative, *until ;* when the action which is defined, and the event which limits it are both past, and are represented as past facts. Hence in narrations ; as, Æsch. P. V. 479 οὐκ ἦν ἀλέξημ' οὐδέν——πρὶν ἐγὼ σφίσιν ἔδειξα κράσεις.

Obs. 1. The ind. fut. is sometimes used seemingly in expressions of future events, after negative clauses ; as, Il. α, 29 τὴν δ' ἐγὼ οὐ λύσω—πρίν μιν καὶ γῆρας ἱκάνει—but πρίν is in these passages to be translated *sooner.*

4. Conjunctive [a]—only after negative clauses, and of something future, after principal tenses. The reason of this is founded on the logical relations of the two sentences : the dependent clause expresses by πρὶν ἄν and conjunct. the event or condition on which the principal clause takes effect : so that if the principal clause has taken effect, (that is, if the principal verb is affirmative) it implies that the condition has taken place too ; so that if we said ποιήσω πρὶν ἂν ἔλθῃ, it would imply that the person had come before the action took place, whereas the action is to take place before the person comes, and he may never come at all : so that πρὶν ἄν after an affirmative sentence would express a degree of connection between the two clauses which does not exist ; but οὐ ποιήσω πρὶν ἂν ἔλθῃ

---

[a] Elmsley Med. 215. Herm. on Elmsley Med.

:ontains no such contradiction, as if the action is done, the person must
1ave come, for the action was not to be done unless or until he came; so
.hat πρὶν ἄν with conjunct.=ἐὰν μή, and may be translated *until:* ἄν is
:ometimes omitted[a]; with ἄν, Soph. Œ. C. 1040 οὐχὶ παύσομαι πρὶν ἄν
γε τῶν σῶν κύριον στήσω τέκνων: without ἄν, Id. Philoct. 917 μὴ στέναζε
πρὶν μάθῃς: Hdt. I. 136.

5. *a.* The optative is used in the same sense, but not so frequently as the
subjunctive, in the *oratio obliqua*, after historic tenses, or an opt. preceding,
and only after negative clauses, for the same reason as given above;
where the event on which the principal clause depends as its condition is
quoted from the original assertion of another person, and adopted by the
writer into his own sentence (§. 802. 3. *b.*): Soph. Phil. 199 τοῦ μὴ πρότερον
τόνδ' ἐπὶ Τροίᾳ τεῖναι τὰ θεῶν ἀμάχητα βέλη, πρὶν ὅδ' ἐξήκοι χρόνος: πρὶν ὅδ'
ἐξήκοι χρόνος is a quotation from the supposed original decree of the gods,
in which it would have been ἐξήκῃ: so Xen. Cyr. I. 4, 14 ἀπηγόρευε
μηδένα βάλλειν πρὶν Κῦρος ἐμπλησθείη: Isocr. Evag. p. 201 D εἰθισμένων—μὴ
διαλλάττεσθαι τοῖς ἀποστᾶσι πρὶν κύριοι γένοιντο τῶν σωμάτων: Xen. Anab.
VII. 7. 57 ἐδέοντο μὴ ἀπελθεῖν πρὶν ἄν ἀπάγαγοι, the original words of entreaty, adopted by the writer.

β. After an optative or some word introducing some past opinion,
mental determination, &c., which either is or might be in the optative
and of which the condition expressed by the optative is a continuation;
so Soph. Trach. 551 ἔδοξέ μοι μὴ σῖγα πρὶν φράσαιμί σοι τὸν πλοῦν ποιεῖσθαι:
wish, Soph. Phil. 961 ὄλοιο μή πω, πρὶν μάθοιμ' εἰ καὶ κ. τ. λ.: after κατα-
φαίην, Œ. R. 505: ἔθελε, Il. φ, 586: ἡγοῦντο, Isocr. p. 347 E: νομίσαντες,
Thuc. IV. 117: οἴεσθαι, Xen. Hell. II. 3, 48; or when the opinion is
implied in the context: so Plat. Rep. p. 402 B προθυμούμεθα διαγιγνώσκειν ὡς
οὐ πρότερον ἐσόμενοι γραμματικοὶ (as we thought we should not) πρὶν οὕτως
ἔχοιμεν.

Obs. 2. There are some passages where an affirmative clause seems
to precede the conjunct., but in reality the negative is implied in some
part of the principal clause[b]; as, Soph. Ant. 175 ἀμήχανον=οὐκ ἄν μάθοις:
Eur. Or. 1218 φύλασσε δ' ἥν τις=μή τις: so τίς interrog. Id. Her. 180
=οὐδείς.

Obs. 3. There are passages where the optative seems to follow a principal tense, and a conjunct. an historic tense; as, Soph. Aj. 740 τὸν ἄνδρ'
ἀπηύδα—μὴ 'ξωπαρήκειν, πρὶν παρὼν αὐτὸς τύχῃ[c]: but when an infin. pres. or
fut. depends on the past verb, the conjunct. depends upon that. In Soph.
Phil. 199 οὐκ ἔσθ' ὡς οὐ θεῶν του μελέτῃ=οὐκ ἔσθ' ὅπως οὐ Θεός τις
ἐμελέτησε[d]: and Id. Trach. 2 λόγος μὲν ἔστ' ἀρχαῖος=ἦν λόγος.

6. When the action of the principal verb, whether positive, (I will,)
or negative, (I will not,) is to be represented as continuing up to a certain event, or happening before it, and thus the dependent verb is not
to be considered the condition, but the consequence of, and something
posterior in point of time to, the principal verb, πρὶν is used with the
infin. after the analogy of ὥστε with infin. which expresses the result:
(§. 665. *Obs.*) Il. ι, 387 οὐδέ κεν ὡς ἔτι θυμὸν ἐμὸν πείσει Ἀγαμέμνων, π ρ ὶ ν
γ' ἀπὸ πᾶσαν ἐμοὶ δ ό μ ε ν α ι θυμαλγέα λώβην = I will continue unper-
suaded by Agamemnon till in consequence hereof; οὐ πείσει is prior
and continues till δόμεναι: Od. κ, 385 τίς γάρ κεν ἀνὴρ πρὶν τλαίη πάσ-

---

[a] R. P. Med. 222. [b] Elmsley Med. 215. Ellendt Lex. Soph. πρίν.
[c] τύχοι Dindorf. Herm. ad loc. " Omnes libri τύχῃ." [d] Ellendt Lex. Soph. πρίν.

σασθαι ἰδητύος ἠδὲ ποτῆτος, π ρ ὶ ν λ ύ σ α σ θ ἑτάρους : Il. a, 98 εἰδ᾽ ἐγ πρὶν λοίμοιο βαρείας Κῆρας ἀφέξει, π ρ ί ν γ᾽ ἀπὸ πατρὶ φίλῳ δ ό μ ε ν α ι (sc. Ἀγαμέμνονα) ἑλικώπιδα κούρην ἀπριάτην, ἀνάποινον, ἄ γ ε ι ν δ᾽ ἱερὴν ἑκατόμβην. Hdt. VI. 119 Δαρεῖος, π ρ ὶ ν μ ὲ ν αἰχμαλώτους γ ε ν έ σ θ α ι τ ο ὺ ς Ἐρετριέας, ἐνεῖχέ σφι δεινὸν χόλον—ἐνεῖχε χόλον is prior, and continues till αἰχμαλώτους γενέσθαι τοὺς Ἐρετριέας : Id. VII. 2 ἴσαν γὰρ Δαρείῳ, καὶ π ρ ό τ ε ρ ο ν ἢ β α σ ι λ ε ῦ σ α ι, γεγονότες τρεῖς παῖδες : Eur. Med. 78 ἀπωλόμεσθ᾽ ἄρ᾽, ε κακὸν προσοίσομεν νέον παλαιῷ, π ρ ὶ ν τόδ᾽ ἐ ξ η ν τ λ η κ έ ν α ι.

Obs. 4. Πρὶν with the inf. pres. expresses that something happened up to the beginning of an action; perfect inf. up to the time following it: aor. infin. up to the perfection or end : so πρὶν δειπνεῖν, *priusquam cænem* [a], or *cænatum eo* [b] : δειπνῆσαι, *priusquam cænavero* ; δεδειπνηκέναι, *priusquam a cænd surrexero.*

Obs. 5. When the principal and dependent clauses have a common subject, it is not repeated in the latter : when the subject is different, it stands in the dependent clause in acc. before the infin., but sometimes it is wanting, as in Il. a, 98 given above; but Il. ζ, 82 στῆτ᾽ αὐτοῦ,—πρὶν αὖτ᾽ ὁ χερσὶ γυναικῶν φεύγοντας πεσέειν, δηΐοισι δὲ χάρμα γενέσθαι—φεύγοντας refers to λαόν in the former part of the sentence.

Obs. 6. The Homeric πάρος, when it is used as a conjunction, as πρό, always has the infinitive; as, Il. σ, 245 ἐς δ᾽ ἀγορὴν ἀγέροντο, πάρος δόρπω μέδεσθαι : Il. ψ, 764 αὐτὰρ ὄπισθεν ἴχνια τύπτε πόδεσσι, πάρος κόνιν ἀμφιχυθῆναι.

Obs. 7. In some passages we find the infin. and conjunctive, or opt. construction, with πρίν in successive sentences, joined together by ἤ, or : Il. ρ, 504 οὐ γὰρ ἔγωγε Ἕκτορα Πριαμίδην μένεος σχήσεσθαι ὀΐω, πρίν γ᾽ ἐπ᾽ Ἀχιλλῆος καλλίτριχε β ή μ ε ν α ι ἵππω, νῶϊ κατακτείναντα, φ ο β ῆ σ α ί τε στίχας ἀνδρῶν Ἀργείων, ἤ κ᾽ αὐτὸς ἐνὶ πρώτοισιν ἁ λ ῴ η.

Obs. 8. Πρίν is very seldom indeed found with the conjunct. after an affirmative clause : Simonid. in Brunck. Gnom. n. 4. v. 11. Gaisf. poet. Gr. min. n. 231 φθάνει δὲ τὸν μὲν γῆρας ἄζηλον λαβὸν, πρὶν τέρμ᾽ ἵκηται.

Causal Adverbial Sentences.

§. 849. A causal adverbial sentence is a resolution of a gerund; as, ἐπεὶ ταῦτα λέγεις, ἁμαρτάνεις (ταῦτα λ έ γ ω ν ἁμαρτάνεις), or a substantive, or infin. used as a substantive, joined with a causal preposition, or subst. in the local dat.; as, διὰ τοῦτο, ὅτι πολλά τε καὶ καλὰ ἔργα ἀπεδείξατο, μεγάλην δόξαν ἐκτήσατο (διὰ τὴν πολλῶν τε καὶ καλῶν ἔργων ἀπόδειξιν or πολλά τε καὶ καλὰ ἔργα ἀποδειξάμενος μεγάλην δόξαν ἐκτήσατο.) The substantive is considered as an adverb, as defining merely the accidents or circumstances of the verb; so σὺν σπουδῇ (= σπουδαίως) ἀπῆλθεν.

Adverbial sentences expressing the reason of the principal clause.

1. The reason or cause of what is said in the principal clause is expressed by a temporal adverb. sentence introduced by the

---

[a] Herm. Med. 78.　　　　　　　　[b] Elm. Med. 78.

:emporal conjunctions ὅτε, ὁπότε, ὡς, ἐπεί, *since*, (perhaps :onnected with ἕπομαι, *sequor*,) (ἐπεί τε Hdt., ἐπειή epic,) *quoniam*, ̦uisque, ἐπειδή, *quoniam*, ἐπεί, ἐπείπερ, ἐπειδήπερ, and by the con- unctions of place, applied to notions of time; as, ὅπου, *quando-* ̧uidem. The reason is conceived as coincident with the principal ̦erb (ὅτε, ὁπότε, ὡς) or antecedent to it, (ἐπεί, ἐπειδή.)

2. In these sentences the ind. is the most usual mood, but some- times, as in the temporal dependent clauses, (§. 845.) the opt. with ἄν, and also the ind. of historic tenses with ἄν, when it is to be signified that the event of the adverbial sentence (that is, the reason) would have taken or would take place, under certain con- ditions—the possibility of its happening being conceived of as the reason of the principal clause: *a.* Ind.: Il. φ, 95 μή με κτεῖν᾽, ἐπεὶ οὐχ ὁμογάστριος Ἕκτορός εἰμι, *quoniam—sum*: Hdt. I. 68 ἦ κου ἄν, ὦ ξεῖνε Λάκων, εἴπερ εἶδες, τόπερ ἐγώ, κάρτα ἂν ἐθωΰμαζες, ὅκου νῦν οὕτω τυγχάνεις θώϋμα ποιεύμενος: Æsch. Ag. 827 νίκη δ᾽, ἐπείπερ ἕσπερ᾽, ἐμπέδως μένοι! Demosth. p. 9, 4 ὅτε τοίνυν ταῦθ᾽ οὕτως ἔχει, προσήκει προθύμως ἐθέλειν ἀκούειν.—*b.* Opt. with ἄν: Il. ι, 304 νῦν γάρ χ᾽ Ἕκτορ᾽ ἕλοις, ἐπεὶ ἂν μάλα τοι σχε- δὸν ἔλθοι, *since he might come near enough to you*: Plat. Prot. p. 335 D δέομαι οὖν σου παραμεῖναι ἡμῖν, ὡς ἐγὼ οὐδ᾽ ἂν ἑνὸς ἥδιον ἀκούσαιμι ἢ σοῦ. — *c.* Ind. of historic tenses with ἄν.— (Some such clause as *if he had not*, must be supplied:) Il. ο, 228 ὑπόειξεν χεῖρας ἐμάς, ἐπεὶ οὔ κεν ἀνιδρωτί γ᾽ ἐτελέσθη, *he retreated, since, if he had not, it* &c.

Obs. 1. The clause of which the reason is so given must sometimes be supplied from the context, when ὡς (and also γάρ) is used: so in an answer: Soph. Aj. 38 ἦ καί, φίλη δέσποινα, πρὸς καιρὸν πονῶ; Minerva: ὡς ἔστιν ἀνδρὸς τοῦδε τἄργα ταῦτά σοι: *yes, since* &c. So often in the dia- logues of tragedy.

Obs. 2. Ἐπεί introduces questions and commands, where it must be translated "*then*." See below under ὥστε.

3. The reason or cause may be expressed by a subst. sentence, in- troduced by ὅτι, διότι (formed from διὰ τοῦτο, ὅτι), διόπερ, διότι περ, *from exactly the same reason that*, and the two poetic words οὕνεκα (τούτου ἕνεκα, ὅ) or ὁθούνεκα (ὅτου ἕνεκα, as οὕνεκα for οὗ ἕνεκα.) The relative ὅτι, *quod*, refers to a demonstr. in the principal clause, expressed or supplied; as, τούτῳ, διὰ τοῦτο, ἐκ τούτου &c.

4. Here also when there is no condition to be expressed, the ind. is the prevailing mood: Od. ψ, 224 αὐτὰρ μή νυν μοι τόδε (i. e. ἕνεκα τούτου) χώεο, μηδὲ νεμέσσα, οὕνεκά σ᾽ οὐ τὸ πρῶτον, ἐπεὶ ἴδον, ὧδ᾽ ἀγάπησα: Plat. Euthyphr. p. 9 sq. ἆρα τὸ ὅσιον,

ὅτι ὅσιόν ἐστι, φιλεῖται ὑπὸ τῶν θεῶν, ἤ, ὅτι φιλεῖται, ὅσιώ
ἐστι; Soph. Aj. 123 ἐποικτείρω δέ νιν—, ὁθούνεκ' ἄτῃ συγκατά-
ζευκται κακῇ.

Conditional Adverbial Sentences.

§. 850. 1. A conditional or hypothetical sentence expresses a
condition, and is introduced by the hypothetical conjunctions εἰ
and ἐάν (ἤν, ἄν). It is a resolution of an adverb, as εἰ οὖτω
ποιοίης, ἁμαρτάνοις ἄν (=οὖτω γ' ἄν ἁμαρτάνοις): or a gerund, as
εἰ ταῦτα λέξειας, ἁμάρτοις ἄν (=ταῦτα λέξας ἁμάρτοις ἄν): or
a substantive, (or infin. used as a subst.,) with a preposition, ἐπί
with dat., ἄνευ with gen.; εἰ τὰ πράγματα οὕτως ἔχει (=ἐπὶ τῷ
τὰ πράγματα οὕτως ἔχειν)—εἰ μὴ τοῦτο ἐγένετο, καὶ ἐκεῖνο οὐκ ἂν
ἐγένετο (=ἄνευ τούτου καὶ ἐκεῖνο οὐκ ἂν ἐγένετο). See below.
The conjunction εἰ (ἐάν) refers to a demonst. in the principal
clause, generally supplied, but sometimes expressed, τότε, τότε
δή, οὕτως: Xen. Cyr. VIII. 1, 3 εἰ τοίνυν μέγιστον ἀγαθὸν τὸ σω-
θαρχεῖν φαίνεται εἰς τὸ καταπράττειν τὰ ἀγαθά, οὕτως ἴστε, ὅτι
κ. τ. λ. The principal clause expresses something which depends
on the other clause as its condition, or as some consequence or
effect resulting from it: as the condition precedes that to which it
is the condition, the cause the effect, the dependent is termed
protasis, the principal clause *apodosis*.

2. The conditional construction appears, in the Greek language,
in a variety of different forms, whereby the nicest relations between the protasis and apodosis are accurately distinguished; and
therefore it will be advisable to treat separately of the different
forms of protasis and apodosis.

Obs. Εἰ is both in form and meaning the same as the Lat. *si*; *ei, si,
si* French, *if* Engl., *ob* German, are used as expressions of deliberation,
as well as of condition. See below, *Interr. Sentences.*

Different forms of the Protasis.

§. 851. 1. The condition stands to that whereof it is the condition, as the cause to the effect. The condition is an assumed
or supposed cause. When therefore the speaker states the condition, he does not know whether it will be viewed by others as
really the cause of the apodosis, or not. Wherefore as it is merely
a possibility or supposition, we might expect that the subjunctive
moods would be used—but the notion of its only being a possibility
is given in this construction, not by the moods of the verb, but by

ə conjunctions ϵἰ, ἐάν; and the view which others might take
it is not regarded, but only the degree of persuasion in the
ɛaker's mind, as to the existence or non-existence of the con-
ʒion.

2. This conviction is threefold.

I. The condition is regarded by the speaker as something cer-
ɪn and real, of which he has such a persuasion, that he has no
ɔubt of it, but still he does not express it as an actual fact;
which case ϵἰ with any tense of the indic. is used; as, ϵἰ τοῦτο
'γεις—ϵἰ τοῦτο ἔλεγες—ϵἰ τοῦτο πεποίηκας—ϵἰ τοῦτο ἐπεποιήκεις
ποίησας)—ϵἰ τοῦτο λέξεις.

II. The condition is not a conviction, but only a supposition—
may happen, but he does not know or feel convinced that it will;
ɪ this case either the conjunct. with ἐάν is used, as ἐὰν τοῦτο
ἔ γ η s, or the opt. with ϵἰ, as ϵἰ τοῦτο λ έ γ ο ι s.

a. Conjunctive in its secondary sense (§.411. 1.), with ἐάν:—when
ɦe speaker regards the condition as a supposition of which he is not
ɛrtain, but yet has some expectation that it will be realised; as,
ἀν τοῦτο λέγῃς, I know not whether you will say it, I only *suppose*
ɔu may, but from the present posture of affairs, I rather expect
ɔu will.

b. Optative in its secondary sense (§. 411. 1.), with ϵἰ : — when
ɦe speaker regards the condition as a mere supposition, without
ɪny notion of its realization, so that the notion of doubt, un-
ɛertainty, indefiniteness is implied thereby; as, ϵἰ τοῦτο λέγοις.

Obs. ɪ. The Latin generally uses the present conjunct. for both these
'orms, *si hoc dicas* = ἐὰν τοῦτο λέγῃς and ϵἰ τοῦτο λέγοις; but sometimes the
ɔptative, as in Greek; as, *si hoc diceretur, vere diceretur.*

III. The condition is regarded by the speaker as something, of
ʈhe non-existence or impossibility of which he has a conviction.
In this case the indic. of the historic tenses is used; as, ϵἰ τοῦτο
ἔ λ ϵ γ ϵ s, *si hoc diceres, if you said this;* ϵἰ τοῦτο ἔ λ ϵ ξ α s, *si hoc
dixisses, if you had said this,* but I know you did not. In French
the indic. is used as in Greek; as, *s'il a v a i t, il donnerait.*

Obs. 2. The forms of the hypothetical conjunction ἤν, ἄν, come from
ἐάν, but the shortened form ἄν is not used in tragedy. The Æolic and
Doric used αἰ for ϵἰ, which is also found in Epic, but only in combinations
with γάρ and θε, αἰ γάρ — αἴθε for the Attic ϵἰ γάρ, εἴθε, in wishes or addresses; and with κε (αἰ κε for the Attic ἐάν) both in indirect questions,
after verbs of seeking, trying, and in real hypothetical sentences, when the
expectation implies a hope, or wish, or anxiety for.

Different Forms of the Apodosis.

§. 852. 1. The relation between that which depends on the condition, and the condition itself, is also threefold : — *a.* It is either a necessary, certain, undoubted result from the protasis; in which case the indic. is used; as, εἰ τοῦτο λέγεις, ἁμαρτάνεις — εἴ τι ἔχει, καὶ δίδωσιν — εἰ εἰσὶ βωμοί, εἰσὶ καὶ θεοί — ἐὰν τοῦτο λέγῃς, ἁμαρτάνεις; — *b.* or only a supposed, uncertain, indefinite, possible result; in this case the opt. is used with ἄν; as, εἰ τοῦτο λέγοις, ἁμαρτάνοις ἄν, *erraveris,* εἴ τι ἔχοι, δοίη ἄν; — *c.* or it depends on a condition which is conceived not to take place (§. 424. 3. *a.*), and therefore is itself certain not to take place; in which case the indic. of historic tenses is used with ἄν; as, εἰ τοῦτο ἔλεγες, ἡμάρτανες ἄν, *si hoc diceres, errares (at, ut scio, hoc non dicis; ergo non erras)*; εἴ τι εἶχεν, ἐδίδου ἄν, *si quid haberet, daret, s'il avait quelque chose, il donnerait;* εἰ τοῦτο ἔλεξας, ἥμαρτες ἄν, *si hoc dixisses, errasses (at, ut scio, hoc non dixisti ; ergo non errasti)*; εἴ τι ἔσχεν, ἔδωκεν ἄν, *si quid habuisset, dedisset.*

Obs. The protasis in which the conj. with ἄν is used has no corresponding conjunct. for the apodosis in the common dialects, as for it the fut. ind. is used; the supposed certainty and reality of the conjunct. being expressed in the form of an actual certainty and reality by the fut. But in Homer we find a good many passages when the conjunct. with ἄν, with or without κέ, stands in the apodosis; as, Il. a, 137 εἰ δέ κε μὴ δώωσιν, ἐγὼ δέ κεν αὐτὸς ἕλωμαι. See §. 855. Obs. 3.

2. The character of the protasis generally determines that of the apodosis as in the above instances. A condition which is known to be certain (εἰ with ind.) admits of the result being expressed with certainty; as, εἰ τοῦτο λέγεις, ἁμαρτάνεις. So a condition which, though only supposed, yet conveys a notion of its realisation (conj. with ἐάν); as, ἐὰν τοῦτο λέγῃς (λέξῃς), ἁμαρτήσῃ, *errabis,* or ἁμαρτάνεις, *erras.* A condition which is a mere supposition — possibility (εἰ with opt.), of course admits of no result more certain than itself — a mere supposition or possibility; as, εἰ τοῦτο λέγοις, ἁμαρτάνοις ἄν. And when the speaker has determined on the non-existence or impossibility of the condition (εἰ with ind.), the result which would have followed therefrom is also denied and impossible; as, εἰ τοῦτο ἔλεγες, ἡμάρτανες ἄν.

3. But in Greek this general principle is deviated from, and the apodosis is expressed in a form which does not correspond with the protasis; as, εἰ τοῦτο λέγεις, ἁμαρτάνοις ἄν. And with most of the forms of the protasis, each of the three forms (ind. conj. and opt.) of apodosis is used.

Forms of the Protasis and Apodosis [a].

Εἰ with Indicative.

§. 853. Εἰ with any tense of the indic. When the speaker regards the condition as certain, the result thereof is expressed in the apodosis,

a. Generally by a corresponding tense of the indic. (or by the imperative), as something certain, undoubted, necessary ; as, εἰ τοῦτο λέγεις, ἁμαρτάνεις—εἰ θεὸς ἔστι, σοφός ἐστι: Plat. Rep. p. 408 C εἰ μὲν (ὁ Ἀσκληπιὸς) θεοῦ (sc. τοῦ Ἀπόλλωνος υἱὸς) ἦν, οὐκ ἦν, φήσομεν, αἰσχροκερδής· εἰ δ᾽ αἰσχροκερδής, οὐκ ἦν θεοῦ, *si Apollinis filius erat, non erat sordidi lucri cupidus.* — Εἰ ἐβρόντησε, καὶ ἤστραψεν. — Εἰ τοῦτο λέξεις, ἁμαρτήσῃ: Plat. Protag. p. 319 A ἦ καλόν, ἦν δ᾽ ἐγώ, τέχνημα ἄρα κέκτησαι, εἴπερ κέκτησαι, if you really possess it, you possess a fine contrivance.

b. Very often by an opt. with ἄν, when the result is to be represented as uncertain, as only possible, not decided upon in the speaker's mind, and hence this is a less decided, more polite way of expressing the notion of the fut. indic., ἄν referring to the condition of the former sentence : Εἰ τοῦτο λ έ γ ε ι ς, ἁ μ α ρ τ ά ν ο ι ς ἄ ν: Od. ι, 277 οὐδ᾽ ἂν ἐγὼ Διὸς ἔχθος ἀλευάμενος πεφιδοίμην οὔτε σεῦ οὔθ᾽ ἑτάρων, ε ἰ μ ὴ θυμός με κ ε λ ε ύ ε ι: Il. ζ, 128 sq. εἰ δέ τις ἀθανάτων γε κατ᾽ οὐρανοῦ ε ἰ λ ή λ ο υ θ α ς, οὐκ ἂν ἐγώ γε θεοῖσιν ἐπουρανίοισι μ α χ ο ί μ η ν : Il. α, 293 sq. ἦ γάρ κ ε ν δειλός τε καὶ οὐτιδανὸς κ α λ ε ο ί μ η ν, ε ἰ δὴ σοὶ πᾶν ἔργον ὑ π ε ί ξ ο μ α ι, ὅττι κεν εἴπῃς: Eur. Hipp. 471 ἀλλ᾽ εἰ τὰ πλείω χρηστὰ τῶν κακῶν ἔχεις, ἄνθρωπος οὖσα, κάρτα γ᾽ εὖ π ρ ά ξ ε ι α ς ἄ ν, "*ubi enuntiatum conditionale rem continet, quæ pro verâ ponitur, indicativus adjungi solet, quamvis sequatur optativus, quippe de re, quæ probabili conjectura inde efficitur:*" Plat. Apol. p. 25 B πολλὴ γὰρ ἄν τις εὐδαιμονία ε ἴ η περὶ τοὺς νέους, ε ἰ εἷς μὲν μόνος αὐτοὺς δ ι α φ θ ε ί ρ ε ι, οἱ δ᾽ ἄλλοι ὠφελοῦσιν, "*loquitur Socrates ita, ut verum esse ponat, quod Melitus antea affirmaverat,*" great would be the good fortune of the young, if one only, as you say : Ibid. p. 37 D πολλὴ μέντ᾽ ἄν με φιλοψυχία ἔ χ ο ι, — ε ἰ οὕτως ἀλόγιστός ε ἰ μ ι, ἄν in that case : Ibid. p. 30 B ε ἰ μὲν οὖν ταῦτα λέγων δ ι α φ θ ε ί ρ ω τοὺς νέους, ταῦτ᾽ ἂν ε ἴ η βλαβερά: Id. Theæt. p. 171 B οὐκοῦν τὴν αὑτοῦ (οἴησιν) ἂν ψευδῆ ξ υ γχ ω ρ ο ῖ, ε ἰ τὴν τῶν ἡγουμένων αὐτὸν ψεύδεσθαι ὁ μ ο λ ο γ ε ῖ ἀληθῆ εἶναι: Demosth. p. 52, 42 νῦν δ᾽ ἴσως ἂν ἐ κ κ α λ έ σ α ι θ᾽ ὑμᾶς (ὁ Φίλιππος), ε ἴ π ε ρ μὴ παντάπασιν ἀ π ε γ ν ώ κ α τ ε.

---

a Dissen Kleine Schrift. p. 47–92 sqq.

Obs. When ἄν is wanting in the apodosis, a wish is expressed, or the possibility is represented as nearly approaching to a wish, without any notion at all of realisation; something which might possibly happen without any notion of circumstances which might make it more or less possible : Eur. Phœn. 1207 εἰ δ' ἀμείνον' οἱ θεοὶ γνώμην ἔχουσιν, εὐτυχὴς εἴην ἐγώ, happy should I be! Cf. §. 855. *Obs.* 6.

c. Sometimes by the indic. of historic tenses, when the result is considered by the speaker as something which does not or will not happen—*It would be thus, if this were so ; but this is not so,* and therefore the condition is denied also, either directly or by implication : Eur. Or. 555 sq. εἰ γὰρ γυναῖκες ἐς τόδ' ἥξουσιν θράσους, ἄνδρας φονεύειν, καταφυγὰς ποιούμεναι ἐς τέκνα, — παρ' οὐδὲν αὐταῖς ἦν ἂν ὀλλύναι πόσεις. (So χρῆν without ἄν, *oportebat* : Eur. Hipp. 459 sqq. χρῆν σ' ἐπὶ ῥητοῖς ἄρα πατέρα φυτεύειν ἢ ἐπὶ δεσπόταις θεοῖς ἄλλοισιν, εἰ μὴ τούσδε γε στέρξεις νόμους : Ibid. 506 εἴ τοι δοκεῖ σοι, χρῆν μὲν οὔ σ' ἁμαρτάνειν :) Demosth. p. 833, 63 εἰ γὰρ ἐκεῖνα ἀνήλωται ὀρθῶς, οὐδὲν ἂν τῶν νῦν παραδοθέντων ἐξήρκεσεν εἰς ἕκτον ἔτος, ἀλλ' ἢ παρ' αὐτῶν ἄν με ἔτρεφον, ἢ τῷ λιμῷ περιεῖδον ἀπολόμενον.

Ἐάν (ἤν, ἄν ; Epic, εἴ κε, αἴ κε, also εἰ *alone*) *with Conjunctive.*

§. 854. 1. The conj. with ἐάν is used when the speaker regards the condition, as a supposition, something not actually known, but of the realisation of which he has some expectation.

Obs. 1. Εἰ is also sometimes in Epic (especially in the combinations, εἴπερ, εἰ γοῦν, εἰ δή and καὶ εἰ), and very usually in Doric and Attic poets, as regularly for instance in Pindar, used with the conjunct. : cf. Od. μ, 96. ξ, 373. a, 204. Il. μ, 223, &c. In Hdt. (II. 13 εἰ μὴ—ἀναβῇ : VIII. 49 εἰ νικηθέωσι : Ibid. 118 εἰ μὴ—γένηται) MSS. vary. In traged. some single instances are found[a]: Soph. Œ. R. 198 εἴ τι νὺξ ἀφῇ : Id. Œ. C. 1442 εἰ σου στερηθῶ. In Attic prose writers the MSS. are very doubtful. Otherwise a nice distinction is preserved between εἰ with conj. and ἐάν with conj. Εἰ τοῦτο γένηται comes nearer to fut. ind. (εἰ—γενήσεται) than ἐὰν τοῦτο γένηται ; as the ἄν in ἐάν points to certain conditions. Cf. §. 830. 2. §. 845. In later writers the use of εἰ for ἐάν however returns, and they even use ἐάν with ind., which is also found in Hdt. (II.13. III. 69. I. 206) though the readings are most probably corrupt : in Homer ἐάν can be resolved into εἰ ἄν by the interposition of a small word ; as, εἴπερ ἄν, εἰ δ' ἄν.

Obs. 2. The Æolic or Doric writers regularly join αἰ (without κά) to the conjunct. ; and on the other hand αἴ κα (= ἐάν), and also ὄκκα (= ὅταν), ἐπεί κα (= ἐπάν) to the indicative.

2. The consequent is expressed in the apodosis :

a. Generally by a principal tense of the indic., most usually the fut. (or the imperative) ; as, ἢν τοῦτο λέγῃς, ἁμαρτάνεις. —'Εάν τι

a Herm. Aj. 491.

ἔχῃς, δώσεις: Od. μ, 53 αἰ δέ κε λίσσηαι ἑτάρους, λῦσαί τε κελεύῃς, οἱ δέ σ' ἔτι πλεόνεσσι τότ' ἐν δεσμοῖσι δεόντων, (αἴ κε expresses the anxiety, and wish of Circe, §. 851. *Obs.* 2.:) Plat. Rep. p. 473 D ἐὰν μὴ—ἢ οἱ φιλόσοφοι βασιλεύσωσιν ἐν ταῖς πόλεσιν, ἢ οἱ βασιλῆς τε νῦν λεγόμενοι καὶ δυνάσται φιλοσοφήσωσι γνησίως τε καὶ ἱκανῶς, καὶ τοῦτο εἰς ταὐτὸν ξυμπέσῃ, δύναμίς τε πολιτικὴ καὶ φιλοσοφία —, οὐκ ἔστι κακῶν παῦλα—ταῖς πόλεσι.

Obs. 3. Ἄν is sometimes added to the fut. ind.[a]: Xen. Cyr. IV. 5. 49 κἂν μὲν δοκῶμεν ὠφελεῖν πλέον ἐπ' αὐτῶν συναγωνιζόμενοι, οὕτω προθυμίας οὐδὲν ἂν ἐλλείψομεν: and similarly Ibid. VII. 5, 21 ὅταν δὲ καὶ αἴσθωνται ἡμᾶς ἔνδον ὄντας, πολὺ ἂν μᾶλλον ἢ νῦν ἀχρεῖοι ἔσονται ὑπὸ τοῦ ἐκπεπλῆχθαι. Cf. §. 424. δ.

Obs. 4. Analogously to this fut. ind., Homer uses the aor. or pres. conj. with ἄν, but sometimes also without it.

b. Sometimes by optative with ἄν (as §. 853. b.): Il. δ, 97 τοῦ κεν δὴ παμπρῶτα παρ' ἀγλαὰ δῶρα φέροιο, αἴ κεν ἴδῃ Μενέλαον— πυρῆς ἐπιβάντ' ἀλεγεινῆς: Xen. Apol. 6 ἢν δὲ αἰσθάνωμαι χείρων γιγνόμενος καὶ καταμέμφωμαι ἐμαυτόν, πῶς ἂν ἐγὼ ἂν ἡδέως βιοτεύοιμι ; Plat. Phæd. p. 93 B οὐχί,—ἐὰν μὲν μᾶλλον ἁρμοσθῇ (ἁρμονία)—, μᾶλλον—ἂν ἁρμονία εἴη καὶ πλείων.

Obs. 5. Ἐάν with conjunct. differs very little from εἰ with ind. fut., hence we find both forms in the same paragraph: Hdt. III. 36 οἱ δὲ θεράποντες, ἐπιστάμενοι τὸν τρόπον αὐτοῦ (τοῦ Καμβύσεω), κατακρύπτουσι τὸν Κροῖσον, ἐπὶ τῷδε τῷ λόγῳ, ὥστε, εἰ μὲν μεταμελήσει τῷ Καμβύσῃ, καὶ ἐπιζητήσει τὸν Κροῖσον, οἱ δὲ, ἐκφήναντες αὐτὸν, δῶρα λάμψονται ζωάγρια Κροίσου, ἢν δὲ μὴ μεταμέληται μηδὲ ποθῇ μιν, τότε καταχρῆσθαι (*interfecturos esse Cræsum*).

Εἰ *with Optative.*

§. 855. The optative with εἰ is used when the antecedent is regarded by the speaker as a mere supposition, without any notion of its realisation, and is to be represented as uncertain, only just possible, ἄν making the result from the antecedent still more indefinite. The consequent is then expressed:

a. Most generally by the opt. with ἄν, whereby both antecedent and consequent are represented as mere suppositions. This is a peculiar idiom of the Attic dialect, which loved to modify disagreeable facts or assertions into polite possibilities or suppositions.—Εἴ τι ἔχοι, δοίη ἄν.—Εἰ ταῦτα λέγοις, ἁμαρτάνοις ἄν: Od. ε, 177 sq. οὐδ' ἂν ἐγὼν ἀέκητι σέθεν σχεδίης ἐπιβαίην, εἰ μή μοι τλαίης γε, θεά, μέγαν ὅρκον ὀμόσσαι, μήτι μοι αὐτῷ πῆμα κακὸν βουλευσέμεν ἄλλο.

---

[a] Dissen Kleine Schrift. pp. 101, 113.

Obs. 1. On the omission of ἄν in apodosis see §. 853. *Obs.*: Il. ε, 214 αὐτίκ᾽ ἔπειτ᾽ ἀπ᾽ ἐμεῖο κάρη τάμοι ἀλλότριος φώς, εἰ μὴ ἐγὼ τάδε τόξα φαεινῷ ἐν πυρὶ θείην, let him cut off : Xen. Cyr. IV. 1, 21 ἀλλ᾽ εἴ γε μέντοι ἐθέλων τις ἔποιτο, καὶ χάριν ἔγωγέ σοι εἰδείην.

Obs. 2. The protasis is sometimes not directly expressed as such, but contained in a relative sentence, or in the general sense of the context ; but it sometimes is altogether wanting, being supposed to be known to the person spoken to : so the protases—*If one wished—if I might—if this were the case* &c., are generally omitted as easily supplied ; as, ἡδέως ἂν ἀκούσαιμι ; and the consequent sometimes must be repeated in the place of a regular antecedent, as it actually is in Æsch. Ag. 1016 πείθοι᾽ ἄν, εἰ πείθοι᾽· ἀπειθοίης δ᾽ ἴσως : Hdt. IX. 71 ἀλλὰ ταῦτα μὲν καὶ φθόνῳ ἂν εἴποιεν (§. 425. c.) ; ἄν here marks that there is some antecedent to be supplied (sc. εἰ εἴποιεν). Sometimes the antecedent is contained in a participle such as ἐλθὼν (= εἰ ἔλθοις) λάβοις ἄν. Hence also the use of the opt. with ἄν for the imper. λέγοις ἄν, would you say, if you please. These elliptic forms are used, especially in Attic, as more moderate expressions of the notion of indic. (§. 425. a., b.) On κέ or ἄν in protasis see §. 860. 1.

b. Sometimes by the indic., when the consequent is spoken of as certain.—Εἰ τοῦτο λέγοις, ἁμαρτάνεις.—Εἰ τοῦτο γένοιτο, ἔσται καὶ ἐκεῖνο : Il. κ, 222 sq. εἴ τίς μοι ἀνὴρ ἅμ᾽ ἕποιτο καὶ ἄλλος, μᾶλλον θαλπωρὴ καὶ θαρσαλεώτερον ἔσται : Hdt. I. 32 οὐ γάρ τοι ὁ μέγα πλούσιος μᾶλλον τοῦ ἐπ᾽ ἡμέρην ἔχοντος ὀλβιώτερός ἐ σ τ ι, εἰ μή οἱ τύχη ἐπίσποιτο, πάντα καλὰ ἔχοντα τελευτῆσαι εὖ τὸν βίον : Thuc. II. 39 extr. εἰ ῥαθυμίᾳ μᾶλλον ἢ πόνων μελέτῃ, καὶ μὴ μετὰ νόμων τὸ πλεῖον ἢ τρόπων ἀνδρείας ἐ θ έ λ ο ι μ ε ν κινδυνεύειν, π ε ρ ι γ ί γ ν ε τ α ι ἡμῖν τοῖς μέλλουσιν ἀλγεινοῖς μὴ προκάμνειν.

Obs. 3. Homer uses the conj. with ἄν instead of ind. fut. in the apodosis : Il. λ, 386 ε ἰ μὲν δὴ ἀντίβιον σὺν τεύχεσι π ε ι ρ η θ ε ί η ς, οὐκ ἄν τι χ ρ α ί σ μ ῃ σ ι βιός. See §. 852. *Obs.*

Obs. 4. Sometimes the opt. and indic. are used in different parts of the same protasis : Lysias p. 179, 32 δεινὸν ἂν εἴη, εἰ νῦν μὲν — συγγνώμην ἔ χ ο ι τ ε, ἐν δὲ τῷ τέως χρόνῳ — θανάτῳ ἐ κ ο λ ά ζ ε τ ε, *if you were* (uncertain) *and yet did* — certain past fact : Eur. Orest. 497 sqq. εἰ τόν δ᾽ (ἄνδρα) ἀ π ο κ τ ε ί ν ε ι ε ν ὁμόλεκτρος γυνή, χὼ τοῦδε παῖς αὖ μητέρ᾽ ἀ ν τ α π ο κ τ ε ν ε ῖ, κἄπειθ᾽ ὁ κείνου γενόμενος φόνῳ φόνον λ ύ σ ε ι, πέρας δὴ ποῖ κακῶν προβήσεται.

Obs. 5. Sometimes ἄν (κέ) is used with fut. ind. in apodosis. (See §. 854. *Obs.* 3.) : Od. μ, 345 f. εἰ δέ κεν εἰς Ἰθάκην ἀφικοίμεθα πατρίδα γαῖαν, αἶψά κεν Ἠελίῳ Ὑπερίονι πίονα νηὸν τ ε ύ ξ ο μ ε ν : Od. ρ, 540 εἰ δ᾽ Ὀδυσεὺς ἔλθοι, καὶ ἵκοιτ᾽ ἐς πατρίδα γαῖαν, αἶψά κε σὺν τῷ παιδὶ βίας ἀποτίσεται ἀνδρῶν.

c. By the indic. of historic tenses with ἄ ν.

a. But seldom, and only when the antecedent is denied : Plat. Alc. p. 111 E εἰ βουληθεῖμεν εἰδέναι μὴ μόνον ποῖοι ἄνθρωποί εἰσιν, ἀλλ᾽ ὁποῖοι ὑγιεινοὶ ἢ νοσώδεις, ἆρα ἱκανοὶ ἂ ν ἡμῖν ἦ σ α ν διδάσκαλοι οἱ πολλοί ; Xen. Venat. XII. 22 εἰ οὖν εἰδεῖεν τοῦτο, ὅτι θεᾶται αὐτοὺς (ἡ Ἀρετή), ἵεντο ἂν ἐπὶ τοὺς πόνους καὶ τὰς παιδεύσεις: Id. Cyr. II. 1, 9 ἐγὼ μὲν ἄν, ἔφη ὁ Κῦρος, εἰ ἔχοιμι, ὡς τάχιστ' ἂν ὅπλα ἐποιούμην (so vulg.) πᾶσι Πέρσαις κ. τ. λ.: Eur. Or. 1125 sq. εἰ μὲν γὰρ εἰς γυναῖκα σωφρονεστέραν ξίφος μεθεῖμεν, δυσκλεὴς ἂν ἦν φόνος.

β. Very commonly to express the frequency of a past action, as with the temporal conjunctions, ὅτε, ὁπότε &c. The opt. is here used in its proper force, as the subjunctive of an historic tense in the principal clause. Ἄν, in its affirmative force, expresses the condition, on the recurrence of which the action takes place. It would seem that this construction was not used by Homer, at least there are very few instances of it, where the reading is not doubtful: Xen. Anab. II. 3, 11 καὶ εἴ τις αὐτῷ δοκοίη τῶν πρὸς τοῦτο τεταγμένων βλακεύειν, ἐκλεγόμενος τὸν ἐπιτήδειον ἔπαιεν ἄν: Ibid. I. 9, 19 εἰ δέ τινα ὁρῴη ὄντα οἰκονόμον, ἐκ τοῦ δικαίου [καὶ] κατασκευάζοντά τε ἧς ἄρχοι χώρας, καὶ προσόδους ποιοῦντα, οὐδένα ἂν πώποτε ἀφείλετο, ἀλλὰ καὶ πλείω προσεδίδου: Id. M. S. IV. 6, 13 εἰ δέ τις αὐτῷ περὶ του ἀντιλέγοι,—ἐπὶ τὴν ὑπόθεσιν ἐπανῆγεν ἂν πάντα τὸν λόγον. In Lat. the imperf. conjunct. is used both in protasis and apodosis: Horat. Sat. I. 3, 4 *Caesar, qui cogere posset, si peteret per amicitiam patris atque suam, non quidquam proficeret.* See §. 424. β.

Obs. 6. From this usage of εἰ with opt. in the conditional sentence, is derived the common form for expressing a wish; the apodosis, which forms part of the wish in the speaker's mind being suppressed: as, εἰ τοῦτο γένοιτο, scil. εὐτυχὴς ἂν εἴην: Il. π, 559 ἀλλ' εἴ μιν ἀεικισσαίμεθ' ἐλόντες, τεύχεά τ' ὤμοιϊν ἀφελοίμεθα, καί τιν' ἑταίρων αὐτοῦ ἀμυνομένων δαμασαίμεθα νηλέϊ χαλκῷ! So in Latin, *O si.*

Εἰ *with Indicative of Historic Tenses.*

§. 856. Εἰ is used with indic. of historic tenses, when the truth of the antecedent is denied. The consequent is then expressed,

α. Generally by a corresponding tense of the indic. with ἄν, whereby the truth of the consequent also is (illogically) denied; as, εἰ τοῦτο ἔλεγες, ἡμάρτανες ἄν, *si hoc diceres, errares; at hoc non dicis: ergo non erras:* Il. λ, 750 sqq. καὶ νυ κεν Ἀκτορίωνε Μολίονε παῖδ' ἀλάπαξα (*evertissem*), εἰ μή σφωε πατὴρ εὐρυκρείων Ἐνοσίχθων ἐκ πολέμου ἐσάωσε (*servasset*): Thuc. I. 9 οὐκ ἂν οὖν νήσων ἐκράτει (ὁ Ἀγαμέμνων), εἰ μή τι καὶ ναυτικὸν εἶχεν: Plat. Gorg. p. 516 E εἰ ἦσαν (*essent*) ἄνδρες ἀγαθοί, οὐκ ἄν ποτε ταῦτα ἐπάσχον (*paterentur*): Id. Phaed. p. 73 A εἰ μὴ ἐτύγχανεν αὐτοῖς ἐπιστήμη

ἐνοῦσα καὶ ὀρθὸς λόγος, οὐκ ἂν οἷοί τ' ἦσαν τοῦτο ποιεῖν : Id. Apol. p. 31 D εἰ ἐγὼ πάλαι ἐπεχείρησα πράττειν τὰ πολιτικὰ πράγματα, πάλαι ἂν ἀπολώλη καὶ οὔτ' ἂν ὑμᾶς ὠφελήκη οὐδὲν οὔτ' ἂν ἐμαυτόν : Id. Euthyd. p. 12 D εἰ μὲν οὖν σύ με ἠρώτας, εἶπον ἂν (*interrogaret, dicerem*) : Id. Rep. p. 329 B εἰ γὰρ ἦν (*esset*) τοῦτ' αἴτιον, κἂν ἐγὼ τὰ αὐτὰ ταῦτα ἐπεπόνθη (*eadem mihi evenissent*, with the notion of the continuance of the consequent) : Xen. Cyr. I. 2, 16 ταῦτα δὲ οὐκ ἂν· ἐδύναντο (*possent*) ποιεῖν, εἰ μὴ καὶ διαίτῃ μετρίᾳ ἐχρῶντο (*uterentur*) : Demosth. p. 830, 55 εἰ δ' ἐπίστευεν (αὐτοῖς) (*fidem haberet*), οὐκ ἂν δήπου τὰ μὲν πλεῖστ' αὐτοῖς τῶν χρημάτων ἐνεχείρισε (*tradidisset*).

Obs. 1. The tenses are used as follows : Impft.—to express a continued action, either extending from past time to present or future, or continuing in past time. In Latin also generally the impft. is used, as the speaker places himself in past time: εἰ ἐπείσθην, οὐκ ἂν ἠρρώστουν, *si obediisses. (nunc) non ægrotarem*, I should not *now* be sick, or have been sick ; εἰ ταῦτα εἶδες, κάρτ' ἂν ἐθαύμαζες, *mirareris*, you would wonder — you had wondered : Xen. M. S. I. 1, 5 δῆλον οὖν, ὅτι οὐκ ἂν προέλεγεν (ὁ Σωκράτης), εἰ μὴ ἐπίστευεν ἀληθεύσειν, implying the custom of Socrates as long as he lived. Plpft.—to express the notion of the continued duration of the consequent (§. 400. 2.). The Aorist has the force of the impft. both with regard to past and present time, but with the notion of the action being momentary — or of the plpft. without the notion of the consequent continuing in its effects : Plat. Gorg. p. 447 E εἰ ἐτύγχανεν ἂν ὑποδημάτων δημιουργὸς, ἀπεκρίνατο ἂν δήπου σοι.

Obs. 2. From this form of the hypothetical sentence is derived the form of expressing a wish which cannot be realised, by ind. of historic tenses (the apodosis being suppressed) ; as, εἰ τοῦτο ἐγένετο, sc. εὐτυχὴς ἂν ἦν or ἐγενόμην : Xen. M. S. I. 2, 46 εἴθε σοι συνεγενόμην ! *utinam tecum fuissem !* Eur. El. 1068 εἴθ' εἶχες, ὦ τεκοῦσα, βελτίους φρένας ! *utinam haberes !* The optative on the contrary expresses a wish without any notion whether it be possible or impossible : Il. λ, 670. The forms of expressing an useless wish, εἰ γάρ or εἴθ, ὡς ὤφελον, -ες, -ε (ὄφελον not Attic), are remarkable ; they are used especially in poetry joined with the infin. pres. when the action is present, with the inf. aorist when it is past : Il. a, 415 αἴθ' ὄφελες παρὰ νηυσὶν ἀδάκρυτος καὶ ἀπήμων ἧσθαι ! O that you were sitting (you ought to be sitting) ! Il. φ, 269 ὡς μ' ὄφελ' Ἕκτωρ κτεῖναι ! *utinam me interfecisset !* Sometimes ὤφελε without εἴθε &c. : Eur. Or. 867 ὁρῶ δ' ἄελπτον φάσμ', ὃ μήποτ' ὤφελον : Demosth. p. 783, 23 ὤφελε γὰρ μηδεὶς ἄλλος Ἀριστογείτονι χαίρειν. Here also belongs the Homeric formula. εἴ ποτ' ἔην γε ! if he were yet in existence, but he is not ! Il. ω, 426. Od. ω, 289. Il. γ, 180. λ, 762. Od. o, 268. τ, 315.

Obs. 3. Without the protasis.—The ellipse of εἰ παρῆσθα, εἰ μὴ εἶδες, εἰ τις ἔλεγε, εἰ ἐδυνάμην &c., is very common : Xen. Anab. I. 5, 8 εὐθὺς δὲ σὺν τούτοις εἰσπηδήσαντες εἰς τὸν πηλὸν, θᾶττον ἢ ὥς τις ἂν ᾤετο, μετεώρους ἐξεκόμισαν τὰς ἁμάξας, as in Latin, *putares, crederes, diceres, cerneres, videres*, you would think &c. : Plat. Theat. p. 144 A ἐγὼ μὲν οὔ τ' ἂν ᾠόμην γενέσθαι, if any one had said it to me : Eur. Iph. A. 1591 πληγῆς κτύπου γὰρ πᾶς τις ᾔσθετ' ἂν σαφῶς, scil. εἰ παρῆν· Xen. Cyr. VII, 1, 38

νθα δὴ ἔγνω ἄν τις, ὅσον ἄξιον εἴη τὸ φιλεῖσθαι ἄρχοντα ὑπὸ τῶν ἀρχομένων.—
Ἐβουλόμην ἄν (sc. εἰ ἐδυνάμην), *vellem* (*si possem*; *at non possum*);
ut βουλοίμην ἄν, *velim*, is often a polite way of saying, βούλομαι, *volo.*—
Ἐβουλήθην ἄν, *voluissem,*—ἥκιστ' ἄν ἠθέλησα, *minime voluissem*: Plat. Phædr.
ι. 228 A καίτοι ἐβουλόμην γ' ἄν μᾶλλον (ἀπομνημονεύειν τὰ Λυσίου), ἤ μοι πολὺ
ρυσίον γενέσθαι. In these cases ἄν refers to the suppressed antecedent.

b. Not unfrequently by the opt. with ἄν. The antecedent being
lenied, and the consequent not being actually denied, but signified
;o have been a possible consequence of the antecedent being true :
Il. β, 80 εἰ μέν τις τὸν ὄνειρον Ἀχαιῶν ἄλλος ἔνισπεν, ψεῦδός κεν
φαῖμεν καὶ νοσφιζοίμεθα μᾶλλον : Thuc. II. 60 εἴ μοι καὶ μέσως
ἡγούμενοι μᾶλλον ἑτέρων προσεῖναι αὐτὰ πολεμεῖν ἐπείσθητε, οὐκ
ἄν εἰκότως νῦν γε τοῦ ἀδικεῖν αἰτίαν φεροίμην, *if you had been
persuaded* &c., *it would have followed that* &c. In Epic the apodosis
is frequently placed first as a possible event, but is afterwards
denied, at least as far as it is a result of the antecedent, by the
use of the negative form of the protasis, and thus a feeling of surprise is awakened by disappointing the expectations raised by the
apodosis : Il. ε, 311 καί νυ κεν ἔνθ' ἀπόλοιτο ἄναξ ἀνδρῶν
Αἰνείας, εἰ μὴ ἄρ' ὀξὺ νόησε Διὸς θυγάτηρ Ἀφροδίτη, *and now
might have perished*, cf. 388 : Il. ρ, 70 ἔνθα κε ῥεῖα φέροι κλυτὰ
τεύχεα Πανθοΐδαο Ἀτρεΐδης, εἰ μή οἱ ἀγάσσατο Φοῖβος Ἀπόλλων.
So also the opt. is found when an historic tense is used, not in its
conditional, but in its proper, force to express a past action : Thuc.
VI. 92 εἰ πολέμιός γε ὢν σφόδρα ἔβλαπτον (*since* or *although I did
you great injury*—*nocebam*, not *nocerem*), καὶ ἄν φίλος ὢν
ἱκανῶς ὠφελοίην, *as the result of the former clause* : Soph. El.
797 πολλῶν ἄν ἥκοις, ὦ ξέν', ἄξιος τυχεῖν, εἰ τήνδ' ἔπαυσας
τῆς πολυγλώσσου βοῆς, *si hanc avocaveras*, not *avocasses.*

Imperative in the Apodosis.

c. When a command is given conditionally on some other event
happening, the imperative is used in the apodosis ; and when the
protasis is of such a nature as to render necessary a more limited
command than would otherwise have been given, an adverb is often
used with the imper. to express—*at least, nevertheless,* &c. : Il. μ,
348 εἰ δέ σφιν καὶ κεῖθι πόνος καὶ νεῖκος ὄρωρεν, ἀλλά περ οἶος
ἴτω κ. τ. λ.

§. 857. *The most usual forms of the Protasis and Apodosis.*

1. *Condition—actual.*

PROTASIS.	APODOSIS.
εἰ τοῦτο ποιεῖς,	ἁμαρτάνεις, result certain.
———— ἐποίεις,	ἁμαρτάνοις ἄν, result uncertain.
———— πεποίηκας,	ἡμάρτανες ἄν, result denied.
———— ἐποίησας.	
———— ἐπεποιήκεις.	
———— ποιήσεις.	

2. *Condition supposed without any definite notion of its realisation.*

εἰ τοῦτο ποίοις,　　　　ἁμαρτάνοις ἄν, result uncertain.
　　　　　　　　　　　ἁμαρτάνεις, result certain.
　　　　　　　　　　　ἡμάρτανες ἄν (rarely), result denied.
　　　　　　　　　　　———— frequency.

3. *Condition supposed with notion of realisation.*

ἐὰν τοῦτο ποιῇς,　　　　ἁμαρτάνεις, result certain.
　　　　　　　　　　　ἁμαρτάνοις ἄν, result uncertain.
　　　　　　　　　　　ἁμάρτανε, result a command.

4. *Condition conceived as not existing nor possible.*

εἰ τοῦτο ἐποίεις,　　　　ἡμάρτανες ἄν, result certain.
———— ἐποίησας,　　　　ἁμαρτάνοις ἄν, result probable.

Remarks on the Ellipse of ἄν *in the Apodosis with Indicative.*

§. 858. 1. On the opt. without ἄν, see §. 853. *Obs.*; but ἄν is omitted with the ind., when the speaker puts out of sight for the time the conditions and circumstances stated in the protasis on which the consequent depends, and thus represents the action of the apodosis, independently of any such restrictions, as if it had actually happened; while the condition in the protasis guards sufficiently against the supposing from this form of expression that it is meant to speak of the thing as having really happened. This mode of putting the actual in the place of the conditional realisation is emphatic, and gives a notion of the certainty of the consequent, if the restriction contained in the apodosis had not intervened. Compare Liv. XXXIV. 29 *et difficilior facta e r a t oppugnatio, ni T. Quinctius—s u p e r- v e n i s s e t:* Hor. Od. II. 17, 27 *me truncus illapsus cerebro s u s t u- l e r a t, nisi Faunus ictum dextrâ l e v a s s e t:* Soph. Œ. R. 1326 ἀλλ' εἰ τῆς ἀκυνούσης ἔτ' ἦν πηγῆς δι' ὤτων φραγμός, οὐκ ἂν ἐσχόμην τὸ μὴ 'ποκλεῖ- σαι τοὐμὸν ἄθλιον δέμας: Eur. Hec. 1111 εἰ δὲ μὴ Φρυγῶν πύργους πεσόντας

ἦσμεν Ἑλλήνων δορί, φόβον π α ρ έ σ χ ε ν οὐ μέσως ὅδε κτύπος: Ibid. 779
τύμβου δ', εἰ κτανεῖν ἐβούλετο, οὐκ ἠξίωσεν, ἀλλ' ἀφῆκε πόντιον: Lycurg.
Leocr. p. 154 εἰ μὲν οὖν ζῶν ἐτύγχανεν ὁ Ἀμύντας, ἐκεῖνον αὐτὸν π α ρ ε ι χ ό-
μ η ν· νῦν δὲ ὑμῖν καλῶ τοὺς συνειδότας: Plat. Gorg. p. 514 C εἰ δὲ μήτε
διδάσκαλον εἴχομεν—, οὕτω δὴ ἀνόητον ἦν δήπου ἐπιχειρεῖν τοῖς δημοσίοις
ἔργοις [a]: so in English—I *had* done so; or the opt. with *εἰ* may stand in
the protasis : Il. γ, 453 οὐ μὲν γὰρ φιλότητί γ' ἐκεύθανον, εἴ τις ἴδοιτο:
Xen. Cyr. V. 5, 22 οὐκοῦν τούτου τυχὼν παρὰ σοῦ οὐδὲν ἧνυον, εἰ μὴ τούτους
πείσαιμι.

2. Hence the indic. of the historic tenses without ἄν is ironical—*without doubt* : Arist. Nub. 1338 ἐ δ ι δ α ξ ά μ η ν μέντοι σε νὴ Δί', ὦ μέλε, τοῖσιν δικαίοις ἀντιλέγειν, εἰ ταῦτά γε μέλλεις μ' ἀναπείσειν, ὡς δίκαιον καὶ καλὸν
τὸν πατέρα τύπτεσθ' ἐστὶν ὑπὸ τῶν υἱέων, I had to be sure sent you to
school; (but without irony, οὐκ ἄν ἐδιδαξάμην σε, *te in disciplinam non
tradidissem.*)

Obs. 1. The protasis is sometimes wanting, and is supplied by the context to the mind of the reader, which is thus secured from any danger of
taking the ind. assertion to be really unconditional : Plat. Symp. p. 190 C
οὔτε γὰρ ὅπως ἀποκτείναιεν εἶχον καὶ ὥσπερ τοὺς γίγαντας κεραυνώσαντες τὸ γένος
ἀφανίσαιεν—αἱ τιμαὶ γὰρ αὐτοῖς καὶ τὰ ἱερὰ τὰ παρὰ τῶν ἀνθρώπων ἠφανίζετο.

3. This ellipse of ἄν is most usual in expressions of *necessity, duty, pro-
priety, possibility, liberty, inclination,* &c. ; as, χρῆν, ἔδει, ὄφελον, verbal adj.
ending in τ έ ο ς, προσῆκε, καιρὸς ἦν, εἰκὸς ἦν, καλὸν—, αἰσχρὸν ἦν, καλῶς εἶχε,
ἐξῆν, ἐνῆν, ἦν, ὑπῆρχε, ἔμελλες, ἐβουλόμην, as it accorded with the genius of the
Greeks as well as Latins, to represent that which was necessary &c., as uncon-
ditionally true, its not happening partially being kept out of sight : Hdt.
I. 39 εἰ μὲν γὰρ ὑπὸ ὀδόντος τοι εἶπε τελευτήσειν με—, χ ρ ῆ ν δή σε π ο ι ε ῖ ν,
o p o r t e b a t te hoc facere, you ought—but now it said not thus, therefore
you ought not, &c.: Soph. Œ. R. 255 οὐδ' εἰ γὰρ ἦν τὸ πρᾶγμα μὴ θεήλατον,
ἀκάθαρτον ὑμᾶς ε ἰ κ ὸ ς ἦ ν οὕτως ἐᾶν, *d e c e b a t,* it was fitting : Xen. M. S.
II. 7, 10 εἰ μὲν τοίνυν αἰσχρόν τι ἔμελλον ἐργάσασθαι, θάνατον ἀντ' αὐτοῦ
π ρ ο α ι ρ ε τ έ ο ν ἦ ν· νῦν δ' ἃ μὲν δοκεῖ κάλλιστα καὶ πρεπωδέστατα γυναιξὶν
εἶναι ἐπίστανται, ὡς ἔοικε κ. τ. λ., *mors præferenda erat.* So also with infin. :
Ibid. I. 3, 3 οὔτε γὰρ θεοῖς ἔφη κ α λ ῶ ς ἔ χ ε ι ν, εἰ ταῖς μεγάλαις θυσίαις
μᾶλλον ἢ ταῖς σμικραῖς ἔχαιρον: Demosth. p. 112, 6 εἰ μὲν οὖν ἅπαντες ὡμολογοῦμεν, Φίλιππον τῇ πόλει πολεμεῖν—, οὐδὲν ἄλλο ἔ δ ε ι (*o p o r t e b a t*) τὸν
παριόντα (*oratorem*) λέγειν καὶ συμβουλεύειν, ἢ ὅπως ἀσφαλέστατα—αὐτὸν ἀμυ-
νούμεθα.

Obs. 2. Very often without any expressed protasis : Xen. Anab. VII. 7,
40 α ἰ σ χ ρ ὸ ν ἦ ν τὰ μὲν ἐμὰ διαπεπρᾶχθαι, *t u r p e e r a t* : Id. Hell. II. 3,
41 ἐ ξ ῆ ν ταῦτα ποιεῖν, *l i c e b a t* : Plat. Rep. p. 450 D κ α λ ῶ ς ε ἶ χ ε ἡ
παραμυθία : Id. Euthyd. p. 304 D καὶ μήν, ἔφη, ἄ ξ ι ό ν γ' ἦν ἀκοῦσαι : Id.
Charmid. p. 171 E ὅτι πράττοντες ὀρθῶς ἔ μ ε λ λ ο ν πράξειν, *f a c t u r i
e r a n t* : Æschin. p. 455, 2 ἐ β ο υ λ ό μ η ν μὲν οὖν κ.τ.λ.: Demosth. p. 838,
10 τὴν μὲν διαθήκην ἠφανίκατε, ἐξ ἧς ἦν (*licebat*) εἰδέναι περὶ πάντων τὴν ἀλήθειαν.

Obs. 3. But ἄν is sometimes used with all the expressions given above (3.),
as in Latin the conjunctive is sometimes used for indic. ; as, Sall. Cat. 7
memorare p o s s e m for the more usual *p o t e r a m* : Demosth. p. 40, 1
εἰ γὰρ ἐκ τοῦ προεληλυθότος χρόνου τὰ δέοντα οὗτοι συνεβούλευσαν, οὐδὲν ἄ ν
ὑμᾶς νῦν ἔ δ ε ι βουλεύεσθαι : Id. I. princ. εἰ μὲν ἐβούλετο Ἄφοβος—τὰ δίκαια
ποιεῖν—, οὐδὲν ἄ ν ἔ δ ε ι δικῶν οὐδὲ πραγμάτων ἀ π έ χ ρ η γὰρ ἂν τοῖς ὑπ' ἐκεί-

---

a Stallb. ad loc.

νων γνωσθεῖσιν ἐμμένειν. When an antithesis between the action, if it had taken place, and its not taking place, is to be emphatically brought forward, ἄν is naturally added, as it brings the counteracting circumstances clearly before the mind—*in that case :* Plat. Rep. p. 328 C ὦ Σώκρατες, οὐδὲ θαμίζεις ἡμῖν καταβαίνων εἰς τὸν Πειραιᾶ· χρῆν μέντοι· εἰ μὲν γὰρ ἐγὼ ἔτι ἐν δυνάμει ἦν τοῦ ῥᾳδίως πορεύεσθαι πρὸς τὸ ἄστυ, οὐδὲν ἂν σε ἔδει ἰέναι, ἀλλ' ἡμεῖς ἂν παρὰ σὲ ᾖμεν. νῦν δὲ σὲ χρὴ πυκνότερον δεῦρο ἰέναι: Xen. Anab. V. 1, 10 εἰ μὲν ἠπιστάμεθα σαφῶς —, οὐδὲν ἂν ἔδει ὧν μέλλω λέγειν· νῦν δέ, ἐπεὶ τοῦτ' ἄδηλον, δοκεῖ μοι: Demosth. p. 861, 58 καὶ εἰ μὲν μὴ καὶ παρὰ τοῖς αὐτοῦ φίλοις καὶ παρὰ τῷ διαιτητῇ προεγνωσμένοις ἀδικεῖν τούτους ἐποιεῖτο τοὺς λόγους, ἧττον ἂν ἦν ἄξιον θαυμάζειν· νῦν δέ κ. τ. λ.: Id. p. 525, 15 εἰ τοίνυν ἀπέχρη τοὺς τοῖς Διονυσίοις τι ποιοῦντας κατὰ τούτους τοὺς νόμους δίκην διδόναι, οὐδὲν ἂν προσέδει τοῦδε τοῦ νόμου· ἀλλ' οὐκ ἀπέχρη.

Obs. 4. The present forms, χρή, δεῖ, προσήκει, καλῶς ἔχει &c., are used of things which may yet happen—the impft. of things which cannot happen.

§. 859. The omission of ἄν becomes almost necessary, if in the apodosis there is an historic tense of the verb κινδυνεύειν, *to be in danger, to seem*, with an infin., as this verb itself denies the actual existence of that which only threatens, is near being, or seems to be in existence : Thuc. III. 74 ἡ πόλις ἐκινδύνευσε πᾶσα διαφθαρῆναι, εἰ ἄνεμος ἐπεγένετο τῇ φλογὶ ἐπίφορος ἐς αὐτήν : Æsch. p. 515 R εἰ μὴ δρόμῳ μόλις ἐξεφύγομεν εἰς Δελφούς, ἐκινδυνεύσαμεν ἀπολέσθαι. So *cœpisse* in Latin : Tacit. Agr. 37 *Britanni circumire terga vincentium cœperant, ni Agricola quatuor militum alas—venientibus opposuisset.* So, for the same reason, when ὀλίγου, μικροῦ, τάχα, *nearly—almost*, are added to the ind. of historic tenses in the apodosis : Plat. Symp. p. 198 C ἔγωγε ἐνθυμούμενος, ὅτι αὐτὸς οὐχ οἷός τ' ἔσομαι οὐδ' ἐγγὺς τούτων οὐδὲν καλὸν εἰπεῖν, ὑπ' αἰσχύνης ὀλίγου ἀποδρὰς ᾠχόμην, εἴ πῃ εἶχον. Without any protasis : Id. Apol. princ. ὅτι μὲν ὑμεῖς, ὦ ἄνδρες Ἀθηναῖοι, πεπόνθατε ὑπὸ τῶν ἐμῶν κατηγόρων, οὐκ οἶδα· ἐγὼ δ' οὖν καὶ αὐτὸς ὑπ' αὐτῶν ὀλίγου ἐμαυτοῦ ἐπελαθόμην οὕτω πιθανῶς ἔλεγον: Xen. Cyr. I. 4, 8 καί πως διαπηδῶν αὐτῷ ὁ ἵππος πίπτει εἰς γόνατα, καὶ μικροῦ κἀκεῖνον ἐξετραχήλισεν: Bion. V. 5 sqq. εἰ μὲν γὰρ βιότῳ διπλόον χρόνον ἄμιν ἔδωκεν ἢ Κρονίδας, ἢ Μοῖρα πολύτροπος, ὥστ' ἀνύεσθαι τὸν μὲν ἐν εὐφροσύνᾳ καὶ χάρματι, τὸν δ' ἐνὶ μόχθῳ, ἦν τάχα μοχθήσαντι τοῦ ὕστερον ἐσθλὰ δέχεσθαι. So *prope* and *pæne* in Latin : Tacit. Hist. I. 64 *prope in prælium exarsere, ni Valens animadversione paucorum oblitos jam Batavos imperii admonuisset.*

Remarks on some peculiarities of the conditional construction.

1. Ἄν (κέ) in the protasis.—2. Ellipse of the protasis.—3. Ellipse of the apodosis.—4. Εἰ δ' ἄγε, εἰ δέ elliptic.—5. Εἰ δέ, or ἐὰν δέ, for εἰ δὲ μή, ἐὰν δὲ μή.—Εἰ δὲ μή for εἰ δέ.—6. Εἰ μή, or εἰ μὴ ἄρα, ironic.—7. Εἰ μή, except, εἰ μὴ εἰ, *nisi si* ;—πλὴν εἰ, or πλὴν εἰ μή.—8. Protasis without εἰ, as a principal sentence. 9. Double protasis.

§. 860. 1. Ἄν (κέ) in the protasis. This is used when the condition in the protasis itself depends on some condition, generally not expressed, but supplied ;—so for instance, εἰ ταῦτα λέγοις ἄν, *if you were under such and such circumstances—were an opportunity given you—if perhaps*—Od. θ, 352 sq. πῶς ἂν ἐγώ σε δέοιμι μετ' ἀθανάτοισι θεοῖσιν, εἴ κεν Ἄρης οἴχοιτο,

ρέος καὶ δεσμὸν ἀλύξας.   Here the protasis depends on ἀλύξας, *should Mars
'epart, in case, if he could escape, &c.* : Il. ι, 444 sqq. ὡς ἂν ἔπειτ' ἀπὸ σεῖο,
βίλον τέκος, οὐκ ἐθέλοιμι λείπεσθ', οὐδ' εἴ κεν μοι ὑποσταίη θεὸς αὐτός,
ἥρας ἀποξύσας, θήσειν νέον ἡβώοντα, *not even if a god, (supposing it to be
)ossible,* κέν) *should promise* : Il. κ, 380 τῶν (sc. χαλκοῦ τε χρυσοῦ τε) κ'
ἴμμιν χαρίσαιτο πατὴρ ἀπερείσι' ἄποινα, εἴ κεν ἐμὲ πεπύθοιτ' ἐπὶ
ἤηυσὶν Ἀχαιῶν : Od. ν, 389 αἴ κε μοι ὡς μεμανῖα παρασταίης—, καί κε
·ριηκοσίοισιν ἐγὼν ἄνδρεσσι μαχοίμην : Od. μ, 345 εἰ δέ κεν εἰς Ἰθάκην
ἱφικοίμεθα—, αἶψά κεν Ἡελίῳ—πίονα νηὸν τεύξομεν : Od. ξ, 120 Ζεὺς
γάρ που τόγε—οἶδε—, εἴ κε μιν ἀγγείλαιμι ἰδών (i. e. εἰ ἴδοιμι) :
Il. ζ, 50 τῶν κέν τοι χαρίσαιτο πατὴρ ἀπερείσι' ἄποινα, εἴ κεν ἐμὲ ζωὸν
τεπύθοιτ' ἐπὶ νηυσὶν Ἀχαιοῖ : Il. χ, 219 οὗ οἱ νῦν ἔτι γ' ἔστι πεφυγμένον
ἴμμε γενέσθαι, οὐδ' εἴ κεν μάλα πολλὰ πάθοι ἑκάεργος Ἀπόλλων, *not even,
if it were possible* : Xen. Cyr. III. 3, 55 τοὺς δ' ἀπαιδεύτους παντάπασιν ἀρετῆς θαυμάζοιμ' ἄν—, εἴ τι πλέον ἂν ὠφελήσειε λόγος καλῶς ῥηθεὶς εἰς
ἀνδραγαθίαν, ἢ τοὺς ἀπαιδεύτους μουσικῆς ἆσμα μαλὰ καλῶς ἀσθὲν εἰς μουσικήν :
Id. Vectig. VI. 2 εἰ λῷον καὶ ἄμεινον εἴη ἂν τῇ πόλει οὕτω κατασκευα-
ζομένῃ i. e. εἰ οὕτω κατασκευάζοιτο : Plat. Protag. p. 329 B ἐγὼ εἴπερ
ἄλλῳ τῳ ἀνθρώπων πειθοίμην ἄν, καὶ σοὶ πείθομαι, *si ulli alii, si id
mihi affirmet, fidem habeam* [a] : Demosth. p. 44 extr. οὗτοι παντελῶς
οὐδ' εἰ μὴ ποιήσαιτ' ἂν τοῦτο,—εὐκαταφρόνητόν ἐστιν : Id. p. 1201, 8
εἰ τοίνυν τοῦτο ἰσχυρὸν ἂν ἦν τούτῳ πρὸς ὑμᾶς τεκμήριον—, κἀμοὶ γενέσθω
τεκμήριον κ. τ. λ.)

2. **Ellipse of the protasis.** The antecedent which should properly be
expressed in the protasis is sometimes contained in a relative dependent
clause, (§. 836. 1.) or some word of the sentence : Il. ζ, 521 οὐκ ἄν τις ἀνὴρ
ὃς ἐναίσιμος εἴη, ἔργον ἀτιμήσειε : Hdt. VII. 3 δοκέει δέ μοι, καὶ ἄνευ
ταύτης τῆς ὑποθήκης βασιλεῦσαι ἂν Ξέρξης, i. e. εἰ μὴ εἴη αὔτη ἡ
ὑπ. : Thuc. III. 19 ἄνευ σεισμοῦ οὐκ ἄν μοι δοκέει τὸ τοιοῦτο ξυμβῆναι,
i. e. εἰ μὴ ἐγένετο σεισμός : Plat. Phæd. p. 99 A ἄνευ τοῦ τὰ τοιαῦτα
ἔχειν οὐκ ἂν οἶός τ' ἦν, i. e. εἰ μὴ—εἶχεν. — Οὕτω γ' ἂν ἁμαρτάνοις,
i. e. εἰ οὕτω ποιοίης.   Very often in a gerundial participle ; see above
(§. 850. 1.) : Xen. M. S. I. 4, 14 οὔτε γὰρ βοὸς ἂν ἔχων σῶμα, ἀνθρώπου
δὲ γνώμην, ἠδύνατ' ἂν πράττειν ἃ ἐβούλετο. — When the apodosis states a
supposed consequent which is denied, (ind. of hist. tenses with ἄν)
(§. 852. 1.) it frequently happens that the protasis which also denies the
fact of the supposed antecedent, takes the form of a principal clause,
introduced by ἀλλά : Od. η, 277 ff. ἔνθα κέ μ' ἐκβαίνοντα βιήσατο κῦμ' ἐπὶ
χέρσου—ἀλλ' ἀναχασσάμενος νῆχον πάλιν for εἰ μὴ ἔνηχον.

3. **Ellipse of apodosis.**

a. In the expression of a wish : εἴθε τοῦτο γένοιτο, εἴθε τοῦτο ἐγένετο
(§. 855. Obs. 6. §. 856. Obs. 2.).

b. In expressions of emotion, feeling, &c., (ἀποσιώπησις) : Il. α, 340 ff.
εἴποτε δ' αὖτε χρειὼ ἐμεῖο γένηται ἀεικέα λοιγὸν ἀμῦναι τοῖς ἄλλοις—.

c. When it can be readily supplied from the context; as in Homer in
the combination εἰ δ' ἐθέλεις, with or without inf. : Il. φ, 487 εἰ δ'
ἐθέλεις πολέμοιο δαήμεναι (sc. ἄγε, μάχου ἐμοί)· ὄφρ' εὖ εἰδῇς.—And especially in Attic, when two conditional sentences are opposed by εἰ (ἐὰν)
μέν—εἰ (ἐὰν) δὲ μή, the first has no apodosis, as it is easily supplied,
and the mind hastens on to the following opposed thought.   Even in
Homer: Il. α, 136 ἀλλ' εἰ μὲν δώσουσι γέρας — (sc. καλῶς ἥξει)· εἰ δέ κε
μὴ δώωσιν, ἐγὼ δέ κεν αὐτὸς ἕλωμαι : Plat. Rep. p. 575 D ἐὰν μὲν ἑκόντες

ὑπείκωσιν (sc. καλῶς ἔχει)· ἐὰν δὲ μὴ ἐπιτρέπῃ ἡ πόλις,—τὴν πατρίδα—κολάπ-
ται [a]: Id. Protag. p. 325 D καὶ ἐὰν μὲν ἑκὼν πείθηται (sc. καλῶς ἔχει)· εἰ δὲ
μή,—εὐθύνουσιν ἀπειλαῖς καὶ πληγαῖς.

4. A practical ellipse of the protasis takes place in the Homeric ex.
pressions, εἰ δ' ἄγε, i. e. εἰ βούλει, ἄγε : Il. α, 524 εἰ δ' ἄγε τοι κεφαλῇ
κατανεύσομαι : also εἰ δὲ or εἰ δ' ἄγε is used in an antithesis, to which
a verb must be supplied from the context : Il. α, 302. ι, 46 ἀλλ' ἄλλα
μένουσι καρηκομόωντες Ἀχαιοί, εἰσόκε περ Τροίην διαπέρσομεν· εἰ δὲ καὶ αὐτὰ
(sc. οὐ μενέουσι), φευγόντων σὺν νηυσὶ φίλην ἐς πατρίδα γαῖαν.

5. Εἰ δέ for εἰ δὲ μή and εἰ δὲ μή for εἰ δέ. When two conditional
sentences are opposed as alternatives, εἰ δέ is often used for εἰ δὲ μή.
as the first clause is already negatived by means of the opposed sentence :
Plat. Protag. p. 348 A κἂν μὲν βούλῃ ἔτι ἐρωτᾶν, ἕτοιμός εἰμί σοι παρέχειν
(sc. ἐμέ) ἀποκρινόμενος· ἐὰν δὲ βούλῃ, σὺ ἐμοὶ πάρασχε, but if you wish
to take the other course=if you do not wish to do this. And on the other
hand, a negative sentence is often followed by εἰ δὲ μή for εἰ δέ, this
form being commonly used to express the contrary of the former conditional sentence : Cf. Hdt. VI. 56 : Thuc. II. 5 : Plat. Hipp. M. p. 285 E
Λακεδαιμόνιοι οὐ χαίρουσιν, ἄν τις αὐτοῖς ἀπὸ Σόλωνος τοὺς ἄρχοντας τοὺς ἡμετέρους καταλέγῃ· εἰ δὲ μή (otherwise) πράγματ' ἂν εἶχες μανθάνων [b] : Id. Rep.
p. 521 B : Xen. Cyr. III. 1, 35 πρὸς τῶν θεῶν, μὴ οὕτω λέγε· εἰ δὲ μή
(otherwise) οὐ θαρροῦντά με ἕξεις.

6. Εἰ μή or εἰ μὴ ἄρα is often used ironically as *nisi forte*,
it must be, since its not being supposes an absurdity ; Plato frequently in
answers : Plat. Rep. p. 430 E ἀλλὰ μέντοι, ἦν δ' ἐγώ, βούλομαί γε, εἰ μή
ἀδικῶ : Ibid. p. 608 E σὺ δὲ τοῦτ' ἔχεις λέγειν ; Εἰ μὴ ἀδικῶ γ', ἔφην.

7. When εἰ μή means *except*, a second εἰ is sometimes added ; as,
εἰ μή εἰ, except if, the real predicate of εἰ μή being suppressed :
Plat. Gorg. p. 480 B οὐ χρήσιμος οὐδὲν ἡ ῥητορικὴ ἡμῖν, ὦ Πῶλε, εἰ μὴ εἰ
τίς ὑπολάβοι κ. τ. λ. [c], except (it were) supposing that, &c. : Id. Symp.
p. 205 E οὐ γὰρ τὸ ἑαυτῶν, οἶμαι, ἕκαστοι ἀσπάζονται, εἰ μή εἴ τις τὸ μὲν
ἀγαθὸν οἰκεῖον καλεῖ : Cf. Thuc. I. 17. So also in the same sense, πλὴν εἰ
or πλὴν εἰ μή, but with the following distinction between them :
" *Si dicimus* πλὴν εἰ, *continet τὸ* πλὴν *conditionem exceptam, nec indiget τῷ*
μή ; *sin* πλὴν εἰ μή, *in ipsâ conditione negativâ comprehenditur* [d] : Lucian. Dial.
Mort. XXIV. 2 Σὺ δέ, ὦ βέλτιστε, οὐχ ὁρῶ ὅ τι ἀπολαύεις αὐτοῦ, πλὴν εἰ μὴ
τοῦτο φῄς κ. τ. λ. "*non video, quem fructum capias ex isto (monumento),*
nisi excipiens dicas, magis te premi, quam nos, tantorum lapidum pondere."
This εἰ μή is often used after τί (=τί ἄλλο)— ; and οὐδεὶς ἄλλος : Hom.
hymn. Cer. 78 οὐδέ τις ἄλλος αἴτιος ἀθανάτοισιν, εἰ μὴ νεφεληγερέτα
Ζεύς : Arist. Eqq. 1106 μηδὲν ἄλλ', εἰ μὴ ἔσθιε : Xen. Œc. IX. 1 τί
δέ, εἰ μὴ ὑπισχνεῖτό γε ἐπιμελήσεσθαι : Cf. Cyr. I. 4, 13.

8. The conditional protasis sometimes stands in the indic. without εἰ, as
a principal clause, for the sake of emphasis—generally with the particles
καὶ δή, *et vero*, to signify some assumption, (*fac ita esse.*) Sometimes εἶεν also precedes : Æsch. Eum. 883 καὶ δὴ δέδεγμαι· τίς δὲ
μοι τιμὴ μένει; *fac, me accipere : quis mihi honor conceditur :* Eur. Med.
390 sq. εἶεν· καὶ δὴ τεθνᾶσι· τίς με δέξεται πόλις ; Id. Androm. 335
τέθνηκα τῇ σῇ θυγατρὶ καί μ' ἀπώλεσε· μιαιφόνον μὲν οὐκ ἔτ' ἂν φύγοι
μύσος, *fac, me interfectum esse a tuâ filiâ :* Id. Or. 646 ἀδικῶ· λαβεῖν χρή μ'
ἀντὶ τοῦδε τοῦ κακοῦ ἀδικόν τι παρὰ σοῦ : Xenoph. Anab. V. 7, 9 τοὺς δ'
ὑμᾶς ἐξαπατηθέντας—ὑπ' ἐμοῦ ἥκειν εἰς Φᾶσιν· καὶ δὴ καὶ ἀποβαίνομεν

---

[a] Stallb. ad loc.   [b] Heindorf. ad loc.   [c] Stallb. ad loc.   [d] Hoog. Gr. Part. 532.

· τὴν χώραν (*fac etiam nos descendere*). In the same way καὶ δή is
ined to a participle: Xen. Cyr. IV. 3, 5. So in Latin.

9. Sometimes a protasis is followed by another protasis, to explain and
:fine more accurately the force of the former : Plat. Phæd. p. 67 E
γὰρ διαβέβληνται μὲν πανταχῆ τῷ σώματι, αὐτὴν δὲ καθ' αὑτὴν ἐπιθυμοῦσι τὴν
υχὴν ἔχειν, τούτου δὲ γιγνομένου εἰ φοβοῖντο καὶ ἀγανακτοῖεν,
, πολλὴ ἂν ἀλογία εἴη, εἰ μὴ ἄσμενοι ἐκεῖσε ἴοιεν. So often in
atin.

Concessive Adverbial Sentences.—*Remarks on* εἰ (*ἐὰν*) *καί and* καὶ εἰ (*ἐάν*).

§. 861. 1. Καί is added to εἰ or ἐάν when the protasis has a
oncessive force, that is, when it grants or allows some antecedent ;
.nd the apodosis has an adversative force, that is, when it denies
he consequent which might be expected to follow. The proper sign
)f this adversative force of the apodosis is ὅμως, either expressed
)r supplied.

2. There is a difference between εἰ καί and καὶ εἰ—in εἰ καί,
although, καί belongs to the sentence, and allows something which
loes or will really exist, or has existed ; .as, εἰ καὶ θνητός εἰμι,
(*if indeed*) *although I am mortal*—in καὶ εἰ, *even if*, καί belongs to εἰ
ﬡnd not to the sentence ; allowing a supposed case which does not
ⴰxist, and in many cases is impossible ; as, καὶ εἰ ἀθάνατος ἦν,
ⴰven *if I were immortal* : Soph. Œ. R. 302 πόλιν μέν, εἰ καὶ μὴ
βλέπεις, φρονεῖς δ' ὅμως, οἵᾳ νόσῳ ξύνεστιν, *etsi* (*quamquam*) *cæcus es,
vides tamen, quo in malo versetur civitas :* Æsch. Choeph. 296 κεἰ
μὴ πέποιθα, τοὔργον ἔστ' ἐργαστέον, *etiamsi non fido, perpetrandum
facinus est.*

Obs. 1. The construction is the same as in the simple conditional sentences. Sometimes in εἰ καί the καί does not belong to the whole
sentence, but to the next word ; as, Eur. Androm. 1080 ἄκουσον, εἰ καὶ
σοῖς φίλοις ἀμυναθεῖν χρῄζεις, τὸ πραχθέν. Cf. Xen. M. S. I. 6, 12.

Obs. 2. Very frequently εἰ stands alone in a concessive sentence ; sometimes also εἴπερ, *although in truth*, especially when the apodosis is
negative : Il. κ, 225 μοῦνος δ' εἴπερ τε νοήσῃ, ἀλλά τε οἱ βράσσων
τε νόος, λεπτὴ δέ τε μῆτις : Il. λ, 116 ἥ δ', εἴπερ τε τύχῃσι μάλα σχεδόν, οὐ δύναταί σφιν χραισμεῖν : Il. μ, 233 ὡς ἡμεῖς, εἴπερ τε πύλας καὶ
τεῖχος Ἀχαιῶν ῥηξόμεθα (conj.) σθένεΐ μεγάλῳ, εἴξωσι δ' Ἀχαιοί, οὐ κόσμῳ
παρὰ ναῦφιν ἐλευσόμεθ' αὐτὰ κέλευθα : Od. α, 167 οὐδέ τις ἡμιν θαλπωρή,
εἴπερ τις ἐπιχθονίων ἀνθρώπων φησὶν ἐλεύσεσθαι : so also εἴπερ καί,
Odyss. ι, 35.

Obs. 3. The place of a concessive sentence is most frequently supplied
by a gerundial participle, either alone or with καί, καίπερ, &c. See above,
(§. 697. c.)

Adverbial sentence expressing the result or effect.

§. 862. This adverbial sentence is a resolution of an adverb of mode and manner, and is introduced by the conjunctions ὥστε and (rarely) ὡς, which refer to the demonstrative οὕτως, either expressed or supplied in the principal clause: οὕτω καλός ἐστιν, ὥστε θαυμάζεσθαι (=θαυμασίως καλός ἐστιν)—τίς οὕτως ἄπραστος ἦν, ὥστε (ὡς) ἀποκτεῖναι τὸ καλὸν ἐκεῖνο μειράκιον; but these dependent clauses not only express the notion of the modal adverb, but also that of the acc. or infin. used as a substantive expressing the effect, and then they must be treated as substantival sentences (§. 796); in this case ὥστε refers to a subst. demonstr., such as τοῦτο expressed or supplied; as, ἀνέπεισε Ξέρξη τοῦτο, ὥστε ποιέειν ταῦτα (Hdt.).

Construction.

I. *Indicative and Infinitive.*

§. 863. 1. The indic. is used when the result or effect is to be represented as a fact — something really following from the principal verb, but not immediately or of necessity; hence ὥστε may frequently be translated *itaque*: Hdt. VI. 83 Ἄργος δὲ ἀνδρῶν ἐχηρώθη οὕτω, ὥστε οἱ δοῦλοι αὐτέων ἔσχον πάντα τὰ πρήγματα: Xen. Cyr. I. 4, 5 ταχὺ δὲ καὶ τὰ ἐν τῷ παραδείσῳ θηρία ἀνήλωκε—, ὥστε ὁ Ἀστυάγης οὐκέτ᾽ εἶχεν αὐτῷ συλλέγειν θηρία: Ibid. §. 15 καὶ τολοιπὸν οὕτως ἥσθη τῇ τότε θήρᾳ (ὁ Ἀστυάγης), ὥστε ἀεί, ὁπότε οἷόν τε εἴη, συνεξῄει τῷ Κύρῳ, καὶ ἄλλους τε πολλοὺς παρελάμβανε: Demosth. p. 95, 23 εἰ γὰρ ἤδη τοσαύτην ἐξουσίαν τοῖς αἰτιᾶσθαι καὶ διαβάλλειν βουλομένοις δίδοτε, ὥστε καὶ περὶ ὧν φασι μέλλειν αὐτὸν ποιεῖν, καὶ περὶ τούτων προκατηγορούντων ἀκροᾶσθε, τί ἂν τις λέγοι; Id. p. 118, 28 οὕτω δὲ κακῶς διακείμεθα—, ὥστ᾽ ἄχρι τῆς τήμερον ἡμέρας οὐδὲν—πρᾶξαι δυνάμεθα.

2. The infin. is used when the result or effect is to be represented, not as an actual fact, but as *supposed* to follow from the principal clause, directly and of necessity, so that logically the two clauses are very closely connected; hence it is used in the following cases:

a. When the result or effect follows from, and is, as it were, implied in the nature of some thing. The ind. is sometimes though rarely used in this case, when the result is to be conceived, not in its close connection with the thing, but as a fact existing externally to it: Xen. M. S. I. 2, 1 ἔτι δὲ πρὸς τὸ μετρίων δεῖσθαι πεπαιδευ-

)s (ὁ Σωκράτης) οὔτως, ὥστε πάνυ μικρὰ κεκτημένος πάνυ ῥᾳδίως
ειν ἀρκοῦντα: Plat. Apol. p. 37 C εἰ οὔτως ἀλόγιστός εἰμι, ὥστε
δύνασθαι λογίζεσθαι, ὅτι ὑμεῖς—οὐχ οἷοί τε ἐγένεσθε ἐνεγκεῖν
ἐμὰς διατριβάς.

. When the result or effect includes the notion of an aim or
pose: Thuc. IV. 23. extr. Πελοποννήσιοι δὲ ἐν τῇ ἠπείρῳ στρα-
εδευσάμενοι, καὶ προσβολὰς ποιούμενοι τῷ τείχει, σκοποῦντες καιρόν,
ις παραπέσοι, ὥστε τοὺς ἄνδρας σῶσαι, i. e. *observantes, si qua forte*
rretur occasio, ut cives suos servarent.

. When ὥστε implies the notion of *on that condition that,* e á
nditione ut: Demosth. p. 68, 11 ἀκούει τοὺς μὲν ὑμετέρους
ιγόνους, ἐξὸν αὐτοῖς τῶν λοιπῶν ἄρχειν Ἑλλήνων, ὥστ' αὐτοὺς
ακούειν βασιλεῖ, οὐ μόνον οὐκ ἀνασχομένους τὸν λόγον τοῦτον
τ. λ., *quum possent ceteris Græcis ita imperitare, ut ipsi dicto*
dientes essent regi [a].

d. Usually, when a demonst., such as οὔτως, stands in the prin-
al clause, to introduce the dependent clause.

e. When the notion of the principal verb is compared with some
sult or effect. If this is equal to the result or effect, the predi-
te of the principal clause is in the positive degree; and this case
the same as that given under *a*. If it is unequal, it is in the
mparative, and the dependent clause is introduced by ἢ ὥστε;
, Hdt. III. 14 ὦ παῖ Κύρου, τὰ μὲν οἰκήϊα ἦν μέζω κακά, ἢ ὥστε
ακλαίειν [b].

Obs. 1. Sometimes instead of compar. we find the positive, but in a
mparative sense, and ἤ, and sometimes ὥστε, is omitted; as, Hdt. VI. 109
ιίγους γὰρ εἶναι στρατιῇ τῇ Μήδων συμβαλέειν, *pauci sunt ad*: Xen. Cyr. IV.
. 15 ὀλίγοι ἐσμέν, ὥστε ἐγκρατεῖς εἶναι: Ibid. I. 5, 11 ἴωμεν ἐπὶ τοὺς πολε-
ίους, οὓς ἐγὼ σαφῶς ἐπίσταμαι — ἰδιώτας ὄντας, ὡς πρὸς ἡμᾶς ἀγωνίζεσθαι, im-
ritiores esse, quam ut nobiscum decertent. " Quum Græci nullum habeant
ιcabulum, quo nimis significent, præter περισσῶς, quod vero in compara-
one adhibent, nunc comparativo ad id indicandum, nunc positivo, pronuncia-
onis vi aucto, utuntur [c]:" Xen. M. S. III. 13, 3 ψυχρόν, ὥστε λούσασθαι,
ττίν.

Obs. 2. When ὥστε is omitted, the infinitive of itself expresses the
esult: Soph. Œ. R. 1293 τὸ γὰρ νόσημα μεῖζον ἢ φέρειν: Eur. Hec. 1107
ὐγγνωσθ', ὅταν τις κρεῖσσον' ἢ φέρειν κακὰ πάθῃ, ταλαίνης ἐξαπαλλάξαι ζόης :
Thuc. II. 61 ταπεινὴ ὑμῶν ἡ διάνοια ἐγκαρτερεῖν, ἃ ἔγνωστε.

Obs. 3. In Homer ὥστε is found only with infin., and that in two places
nly: Il. ι, 42 εἰ δέ τοι αὐτῷ θυμὸς ἐπέσσυται, ὥστε νέεσθαι, ἔρχεο : Od. ρ,
ι οὐ γὰρ ἐπὶ σταθμοῖσι μένειν ἔτι τηλίκος εἰμί, ὥστ' ἐπιτειλαμένῳ σημάντορι
άντα πιθέσθαι. Homer used the infin. without ὥστε : Il. λ, 20 τόν (θώρηκα)
οτέ οἱ Κινύρης δῶκε, ξεινήϊον εἶναι. In Hesiod also ὥστε is only found,
)pp. 44.

Obs. 4. Sometimes the dependent clause with ὥστε is only an explana-

a Bremi ad loc.   b Valcken. ad loc.   c Bornemann ad loc.   Hermann
d Viger. p. 885.

tion of a subst. in the principal clause, the explanation being regarded as the result of the notion of the substantive: Soph. Œ. C. 969 διδαξω, εἰ τι θέσφατον πατρὶ χρησμοῖσιν ἱκνεῖθ', ὥστε πρὸς παίδων θανεῖν: Eur. Or. 52 ἐλπίδα δὲ δή τιν' ἔχομεν, ὥστε μὴ θανεῖν.

Obs. 5. In adverb. sentences, introduced by ὥστε, the same attraction takes place as we have seen above with infin. (§. 673. 2.) ; as, Xen. Cyr. Il. 1, 19 οἱ Πέρσαι ἐνόμισαν, εἰ παρακαλούμενοι, ὥστε τὰ ὁμοῖα ποιοῦντες τῶν αὐτῶν τυγχάνειν, μὴ ἐθελήσουσι ταῦτα ποιεῖν, δικαίως ἂν—ἀμηχανοῦντες βιοτεύειν: Eur. Phœn. 488 ἐξῆλθον ἔξω τῆσδ' ἑκὼν αὐτὸς χθονός, — ὥστ' αὐτὸς ἄρχειν αὖθις ἀνὰ μέρος λαβών. And this attraction may be omitted under the same circumstances as with the infin. (§. 674.)

Obs. 6. If the subordinate sentence is negative, with the ind. οὐ is used, with infin. μή, or when the principal sentence is negative also, μή οὐ. See §. 744. 2.

Remarks on ὡς, ὥστε (ὅσον, ὅσα, ὅ, τι) *with Infinitive, in a seemingly independent parenthesis.*

§. 864. 1. We frequently find a seemingly independent parenthesis introduced by ὡς (very rarely and only in suspected passages ὥστε) with the infin. The force of such a sentence is very often restrictive. The principal clause, the result or effect of which it expresses, must be supplied: Hdt. II. 10 ὥστε (al. leg. ὡς) εἶναι (i. e. ἐξεῖναι) σμικρὰ ταῦτα μεγάλοισι συμβαλέειν, i. e., *ita, ut liceat comparare.* So Thuc. IV. 36 ὡς μικρὸν μεγάλῳ εἰκάσαι : Hdt. VII. 24 ὡς μὲν ἐμὲ συμβαλλεόμενον εὑρίσκειν, μεγαλοφροσύνης εἵνεκα αὐτὸ Ξέρξης ὀρύσσειν ἐκέλευε, *ut ego quidem hanc rem considerans reperio.* So very usually, ὡς ἔπος εἰπεῖν, *ut ita dicam, propemodum dixerim* : Id. II. 25 ὡς ἐν πλέονι λόγῳ δηλῶσαι : Xen. M. S. III. 8, 10 ὡς δὲ συνελόντι εἰπεῖν, *ut paucis absolvam* : Plat. Rep. p. 414 A ὡς ἐν τύπῳ, μὴ δι' ἀκριβείας, εἰρῆσθαι, *ut summatim dicamus, neque rem diligenter persequamur*—ὡς γέ μοι δοκεῖν, *ut mihi quidem videtur*, properly *tali modo ut mihi videatur* : Hdt. II. 125 ὡς ἐμὶ εὖ μεμνῆσθαι. Very often these sentences are expressed shortly without ὡς; as, οὐ πολλῷ λόγῳ εἰπεῖν, especially ὀλίγου, μικροῦ, πολλοῦ δεῖν, *ita ut paulum, multum absit*; and still shorter, ὀλίγου, *prope, pæne.* So Demosth. p. 42, 7 συνελόντι δ' ἁπλῶς (scil. εἰπεῖν): Hdt. VI. 30 ὁ δὲ οὔτ' ἂν ἔπαθε κακὸν οὐδὲν, δοκέειν ἐμοί. So must be explained Eur. Med. 228 ἐν ᾧ γὰρ ἦν μοι πάντα, γιγνώσκειν καλῶς (as was well known), κάκιστος ἀνδρῶν ἐκβέβηχ' οὑμὸς πόσις.

2. A very singular use of ὡς, *as*, with infin. is found in Herod. in restrictive sentences : II. 8 τὸ ὦν δὴ ἀπὸ Ἡλιουπόλιος οὐκέτι πολλὸν χωρίον ὡς εἶναι Αἰγύπτου, for Egypt, *ut in Ægypto* : Id. II. 135 ἡ Ῥοδῶπις— μεγάλα ἐκτήσατο χρήματα, ὡς ἂν εἶναι Ῥοδώπιος, ἀτὰρ οὐκ ὡς γε ἐς πυραμίδα τοσαύτην ἐξικέσθαι, looked at as the property of a private lady like Rhodopis, but still not so large &c.

3. After the same analogy we find ὅσον, ὅσα, ὅτι joined with infin. instead of ὡς : ὅσον γέ μ' εἰδέναι, *quantum sciam* (properly *pro tanto, quantum scire possim*), ὅτι μ' εἰδέναι.

II. Ὥστε *with Optative, with or without* ἄν.

§. 865. The opt. is used after ὥστε (a) without ἄν when the principal verb is in the opt., so that both the principal notion and ĩ ts result are represented as suppositions only, but generally (*b*) with ἄν when the result is to be represented as a supposition or possibility depending on conditions: Xen. Œc. I. 13 εἴ τις χρῷτο τῷ ἀργυρίῳ, ὥστε — κάκιον τὸ σῶμα ἔχοι, — πῶς ἂν ἔτι τὸ ἀργύριον αὐτῷ ὠφέλιμον εἴη; Plat. Apol. p. 24 A ὥστε — θαυμάζοιμ᾽ ἄν, εἰ οἷός τ᾽ εἴην ἐγὼ ὑμῶν ταύτην τὴν διαβολὴν ἐξελέσθαι: Id. Symp. p. 197 A τοξικήν γε μὴν καὶ ἰατρικὴν καὶ μαντικὴν Ἀπόλλων ἀνεῦρεν, ἐπιθυμίας καὶ ἔρωτος ἡγεμονεύσαντος, ὥστε καὶ οὗτος Ἔρωτος ἂν εἴη μαθητής: Demosth. p. 845, 3 (ταῦτα πεποίηκεν) ὥστε πολὺ ἂν δικαιότερον διὰ ταῦτα τὰ ἔργα τοῦτον μισήσαιτε, ἢ ἐμοῦ τινα ἀνεπιείκειαν καταγνοίητε: Ibid. p. 851, 23 Φίλιππος δ᾽ οὔτε φίλος οὔτ᾽ ἐχθρός (ἐστιν), ὥστ᾽ οὐδὲ ταύτην ἄν τις ἐπενέγκοι δικαίως τὴν αἰτίαν: Arist. Ach. 941 (of a vessel) ἰσχυρόν ἐστιν, ὥστ᾽ οὐκ ἂν καταγείη, *ut non facile frangatur (frangi possit)*, scil. *etiamsi magnâ vi utare.*

III. *Indicative of Historic Tenses with ἄν.—Infinitive with ἄν.*

§. 866. 1. The ind. of historic tenses with ἄν is used with ὥστε, when the result is represented as taking place, or having taken place only under certain conditions: Xen. Cyr. I. 4, 3 οὕτω καὶ Κύρου ἐκ τῆς πολυλογίας οὐ θράσος διεφαίνετο, ἀλλ᾽ ἁπλότης τις καὶ φιλοστοργία, ὥστ᾽ ἐπεθύμει ἄν τις πλείω ἀκούειν αὐτοῦ, ἢ σιωπῶντι παρεῖναι (sc. εἰ δυνατὸν ἦν).

2. In the place of the ind. of historic tenses with ἄν, the infin. with ἄν may be used: Thuc. II. 49 τὰ ἐντὸς οὕτως ἐκαίετο, ὥστε — ἥδιστα ἂν εἰς ὕδωρ ψυχρὸν σφᾶς αὐτοὺς ῥίπτειν, i. e. ὥστε — ἔρριπτον ἄν, scil. εἰ ἠδύναντο.

Remarks.

Ὥστε with Imperative, or in an Interrogative Sentence.

§. 867. 1. Lastly, ὥστε is also joined with the imperative; not that the imper. depends upon it, or is construed with it, but it arises from a sudden and emphatic change from the *oratio obliqua* to the *oratio recta*: Soph. El. 1175 θνητοῦ πέφυκας πατρός, Ἠλέκτρα, φρόνει, θνητὸς δ᾽ Ὀρέστης, ὥστε μὴ λίαν στένε, for ὥστε μὴ — στένειν: Demosth. p. 129, 70 γράφω δέ, ὥστε, ἂν βούλησθε, χειροτονήσατε [a] : Lucian. Dial. Mort. II. princ. οὐ φέρομεν, ὦ Πλούτων, Μένιππον τουτονὶ τὸν κύνα παροικοῦντα, ὥστε ἢ ἐκείνόν ποι κατάστησον, ἢ ἡμεῖς μετοικήσομεν εἰς ἕτερον τόπον. So also ὥστε is used in a question: Demosth. p. 858, 47 εἰ — ὁ πατὴρ ἠπίστει τούτοις, δῆλον ὅτι οὔτ᾽ ἂν τἆλλα ἐπέτρεπεν, οὔτ᾽ ἂν ἐκείν᾽ οὕτω καταλιπὼν αὐτοῖς ἔφραζεν, ὥστε πόθεν ἴσασιν; (*ergo unde scierunt ?*) See *Interrogative Sentences.*

---

[a] Bremi ad loc.

Construction of ἐφ' ᾧ or ἐφ' ᾧτε.

2. For ὥστε, *ed conditione*, ut; *ita*, ut; the Post-Homeric
language uses ἐφ' ᾧ, or more usually, ἐφ' ᾧτε, which refers to the
demonstrative, either expressed or implied in the principal clause, ἐπὶ
τούτῳ (or ἐπὶ τοῖσδε in Hdt. and Thuc.). Ἐφ' ᾧ or ἐφ' ᾧτε is used
either with ind. fut. or infin. ; as, Hdt. III. 83 ἐπὶ τούτῳ δὲ ὑπεξίσταμαι
τῆς ἀρχῆς, ἐπ' ᾧτε ὑπ' οὐδενὸς ὑμέων ἄρξομαι: Id. VI. 65 Κλεομένης
συντίθεται Λευτυχίδῃ—, ἐπ' ᾧτε, ἢν αὐτὸν καταστήσῃ βασιλῆα ἀντὶ Δημαρήτου,
ἕψεταί οἱ ἐπ' Αἰγινήτας: Id. VII. 153 τούτοισι δ' ἂν πίσυνος ἐὼν κατήγαγε,
ἐπ' ᾧτε οἱ ἀπόγονοι αὐτοῦ ἱροφάνται τῶν θεῶν ἔσονται: Ibid. 154 ἐρρύ-
σαντο δὲ οὗτοι ἐπὶ τοῖσδε καταλλάξαντες, ἐπ' ᾧτε Ἱπποκρατέϊ Καμάρινα
Συρακουσίους ἀποδοῦναι: Id. I. 22 διαλλαγὴ δέ σφιν ἐγένετο ἐπ' ᾧτε
ξείνους ἀλλήλοισι εἶναι καὶ ξυμμάχους: Plat. Apol. p. 29 C ἀφίεμέν σε,
ἐπὶ τούτῳ μέντοι, ἐφ' ᾧτε μηκέτι ἐν ταύτῃ τῇ ζητήσει διατρίβειν
μηδὲ φιλοσοφεῖν: Xen. Hell. II. 2, 20 ἐποιοῦντο εἰρήνην, ἐφ' ᾧ τά τε
μακρὰ τείχη καὶ τὸν Πειραιᾶ καθελόντας—Λακεδαιμονίοις ἕπεσθαι.

Obs. So also Hdt. III. 36 οἱ δὲ θεράποντες — κατακρύπτουσι τὸν Κροῖσον
ἐπὶ τῷδε τῷ λόγῳ, ὥστε, εἰ μὲν μεταμελήσει τῷ Καμβύσῃ, καὶ ἐπιζητήσει τὸν Κροῖσον, οἱ δὲ ἐκφήναντες αὐτὸν δῶρα λάμψονται ζωάγρια Κροίσου,
ἢν δὲ μὴ μεταμέληται, μηδὲ ποθῇ μιν, τότε καταχρῆσθαι (*interfecturos esse
Croesum*).

Comparative Adverbial Sentences.

§. 868. 1. The comparison expressed by adverbial sentences is
of two kinds—a comparison in respect of quality, or in respect of
quantity, either in external size or internal power ; as, λέγεις οὕτως,
ὡς φρονεῖς—ὅσῳ (ὅσον) σοφώτερός τις ἐστί, τοσούτῳ (τοσοῦτο) σωφρονέστερός ἐστιν.

Comparative Adverbial Sentences of Quality

2. Are introduced by the relative adverbs, ὥς, ὥστε, ὥσπερ,
ὅπως (Epic ἠύτε, seldom εὖτε) which refer to a demonstr. adverb,
either expressed or supplied in the principal clause, οὕτως, ὧδε,
also ὥς (poet., rarely in prose, ὡς — ὥς Plat. Rep. p. 530 D).
They are to be regarded as resolutions of an adverb or of an instrumental dative used adverbially (§. 837.).

The Construction

3. Is the same as that of the adject. sentence (§. 826. ff.) : as,
Ζεὺς δίδωσιν, ὅπως ἐθέλει, or ὅπως ἂν ἐθέλῃ, ἑκάστῳ: and in Epic the
conj. without ἄν occurs ; as, Od. a, 349 Ζεὺς — δίδωσιν ἀνδράσιν
ἀλφηστῇσιν, ὅπως ἐθέλῃσιν, ἑκάστῳ: this conj. expresses indefinite frequency. Ὥς ἄν or ὥσπερ ἄν is very common with the
opt., when the verb of the comparative clause is to be represented

a supposition depending on some condition, a mere possibility
. 425.) : Plat. Phædr. p. 230 B ἀκμὴν ἔχει τῆς ἄνθης, ὧ s ἂν
ὡδέστατον παρέχοι τὸν τόπον : Id. Phæd. p. 87 B ἐμοὶ γὰρ
ꞏκεῖ ὁμοίως λέγεσθαι ταῦτα, ὥσπερ ἂν τις περὶ ἀνθρώπου ὑφάντου
ꞇεσβύτου ἀποθανόντος λέγοι τοῦτον τὸν λόγον.

4. In comparisons either the present is used, the object of com-
arison being considered as something present, or the aorist
}. 402. 3.), as the comparison serves to explain something else, and
ιerefore results from the experience of time past ; or the future, as
ιe similitude deduced from past experience expresses an occurrence
ꞏhich will happen in future.   In Homer the comparative adverbs,
ꞏs, ὥστε, ἠΰτε, are used with a. Indic. pres. or aor., when the
bject of comparison is to be expressed as a real fact.   b. Ind.
ut., when a fact is to be expressed as actually happening in future
ime.   c. Conjunctive pres. or more usually the aorist, used much
ιs the ind. fut. (§. 415.), as commonly in Homer when the reali-
ιation of the fact in fut. time is only expected.—Indic. Il. ι, 4 ὡ s
ꞇ´ ἄνεμοι δύο πόντον ὀρίνετον—, ὡς ἐδαΐζετο θυμὸς ἐνὶ στήθεσσιν
Αχαιῶν : Il. μ, 421 ἀλλ᾽ ὥστ᾽ ἀμφ᾽ οὔροισι δύ᾽ ἀνέρε δηριάασθον—,
ᾑς ἄρα τοὺς διέεργον ἐπάλξεις : cf. Il. ν, 703. ο, 691. ρ, 755 : Il. κ,
183 ὡ s δὲ κύνες περὶ μῆλα δυσωρήσονται ἐν αὐλῇ—, ὡς τῶν νήδυμος
ὕπνος ἀπὸ βλεφάροιϊν ὀλώλει : Il. ο, 381 ὥστε μέγα κῦμα—νηὸς
ὑπὲρ τοίχων καταβήσεται—, ὥς : Il. ρ, 434 ὥστε στήλη μένει
ἔμπεδον, ἥτ᾽ ἐπὶ τύμβῳ ἀνέρος ἑστήκει.—Conj. Il. β, 474 τοὺς δ᾽,
ὥστ᾽ αἰπόλια πλατέ᾽ αἰγῶν αἰπόλοι ἄνδρες ῥεῖα διακρίνωσιν, ἐπεί
κε νομῷ μιγέωσιν, ὡς τοὺς ἡγεμόνες διεκόσμεον ἔνθα καὶ ἔνθα, as the
goatherds *might*—not *will* : Il. κ, 485 sq. ὡ s δὲ λέων μήλοισιν
ἀσημάντοισιν ἐπελθὼν αἴγεσιν ἢ ὄϊεσσι κακὰ φρονέων ἐνορούσῃ· ὡ s
μὲν Θρῇκας ἄνδρας ἐπῴχετο Τυδέος υἱός : Il. π, 428 οἱ δ᾽, ὥστ᾽ αἰγυ-
πιοὶ—μάχωνται, ὡ s οἱ—ἐπ᾽ ἀλλήλοισιν ὄρουσαν : Il. ε, 161 ὡ s
δὲ λέων ἐν βουσὶ θορὼν ἐξ αὐχένα ἄξῃ πόρτιος ἠὲ βοός—, ὡς τοὺς
ἀμφοτέρους ἐξ ἵππων Τυδέος υἱὸς βῆσε : cf. Il. ρ, 168. Od. χ, 302,
where the aorist conj. is used.

Remarks on the Comparative Sentences.

1. Οὕτως (ὧς)—ὡ s in wishes or protestations.—2. Comparative adv. sentence for an adject. sentence—ὁ αὐτός, ἴσος, ὥσπερ.—3. Attraction of
the case.—4. A comparative clause shortened and coalescing with
principal clause.—5. Ὡς, after definitions of degree, &c.—6. Ὡς ἔοικε
&c. used personally.

§. 869. 1. Οὕτως (ὧς)—ὡ s is used in wishes followed by protestations, so that the comparative sentence introduced by ὡ s expresses

the subject matter of the protestation.   So in Latin, *ita me dii ament,*
ut ego nunc—lætor Terent. Heaut. IV. 3, 8 : Il. *ν*, 825 εἰ γὰρ ἐγὼν οὕτω
γε Διὸς παῖς αἰγιόχοιο εἴην ἤματα πάντα—, ὥς νῦν ἡμέρη ἥδε κακὸν φέρει Ἀργείοισι πᾶσι μάλα : Il. *θ*, 538 εἰ γὰρ ἐγὼν ὥς εἴην ἀθάνατος καὶ ἀγήρως ἤματα
πάντα, τιοίμην δ', ὡς τίετ' Ἀθηναίη καὶ Ἀπόλλων, ὡς νῦν ἡμέρη ἥδε κακὸν φέρει
Ἀργείοισιν : Arist. Nub. 516 οὕτω νικήσαιμί γ' ἐγὼ καὶ νομιζοίμην σοφός,
ὡς ὑμᾶς ἡγούμενος εἶναι θεατὰς δεξιούς,—πρώτους ἠξίωσ' ἀναγεῦσ' ὑμᾶς : Lucian.
Philops. §. 27 οὕτως ὀναίμην, ἔφη, τούτων, ὡς ἀληθῆ — πρὸς σὲ ἐρῶ.   But
sometimes the relative clause with ὡς is omitted : Eur. Med. 714 οὕτως
ἔρως σοι πρὸς θεῶν τελεσφόρος γένοιτο παίδων, καὐτὸς ὄλβιος θάνοις, where the
context will supply ὡς ἀντομαί σε — ἱκεσία τε γίγνομαι, οἴκτειρον, οἴκτειρόν με
τὴν δυσδαίμονα.

2. A comparative adv. sentence stands for an adject. sentence, especially
with ὥσπερ after ὁ αὐτός, ἴσος &c.: Xen. Anab. I. 10, 10 βασιλεὺς
—εἰς τὸ αὐτὸ σχῆμα κατέστησεν ἐναντίαν τὴν φάλαγγα, ὥσπερ τὸ πρῶτον μαχού-
μενος συνήει : Plat. Phæd. p. 86 A εἴ τις διισχυρίζοιτο τῷ αὐτῷ λόγῳ ὥσπερ
σύ[a] : Plat. Legg. p. 671 C τοῦτον δὲ εἶναι τὸν πλάστην τὸν αὐτὸν ὥσπερ
τότε.

Obs. Homer and other poets often use ὡς ὅτε, *as when*, in comparisons, (properly ὡς ἔστι τότε, ὅτε, (§. 841. 4.)   Very frequently we find in
comparisons ὡς εἰ, ὡς ἂν εἰ, *quasi*.

3. In sentences introduced by ὡς, ὥσπερ, ὥστε, an attraction takes place
sometimes, especially of the acc. ; this however is but seldom : Lys. p. 492,
72 οὐδαμοῦ γὰρ ἔστιν Ἀγόρατον Ἀθηναῖον εἶναι ὥσπερ Θρασύβουλον.
Frequently the nomin. stands alone, to which a verb must be supplied from
the context : Arist. Ran. 303 ἔξεστι δ', ὥσπερ Ἡγέλοχος, ἡμῖν λέγειν :
Plat. Phæd. p. 111 A ζῷα δ' ἐπ' αὐτῆς εἶναι ἄλλα τε πολλὰ καὶ ἀνθρώπους, τοὺς
μὲν ἐν μεσογείᾳ οἰκοῦντας, τοὺς δὲ περὶ τὸν ἀέρα, ὥσπερ ἡμεῖς .(sc. οἰκοῦμεν)
περὶ τὴν θάλατταν κ. τ. λ.[b] : Demosth. p. 37 Spald. ἐχρῆν αὐτὸν — τὰ ὅπλα
ἀναλίσκοντα, ὥσπερ ἐγὼ, οὕτω μὲν ἀφαιρεῖσθαι τὴν νίκην.

4. The comparative clause is shortened and coalesces with the principal
clause in various ways : Plat. Phileb. p. 61 C καθάπερ ἡμῖν οἰνοχόοις τισίν,
for ἡμῖν, καθάπ. οἰν. : Id. Protag. p. 352 B οὐδὲ ὡς περὶ τοιούτου αὐτοῦ ὄντος
διανοοῦνται, i. e. οὐδὲ περὶ αὐτοῦ διαν., ὡς τοιούτου ὄντος : Id. Legg. p. 694
οὐδεὶς ἂν στόλος ὥρμησε καταφρονήσας ὡς ὄντων ἡμῶν βραχέος ἀξίων, for καταφρ.
ἡμῶν ὡς ὄντων βρ. ἀξ.

5. Ὡς, with a subst., is frequently used like *ut* in Latin, after definitions of the measure or degree of any quality of a person, in the sense of
—*as might be expected—as is possible—as is proper.*   This ὡς expresses a
notion of coincidence and equality between the two objects, *as ;* or of a
qualification of the expression, by stating that the degree was not to be
taken in its full force, but only when compared with the nature of the
person or of the case, *for ;* in the former case, the verb which is suppressed
after ὡς would agree with, in the latter it would contradict the quality
spoken of ; as, Soph. Œ. R. 1118 Λαΐου γὰρ ἦν, εἴπερ τις ἄλλος, πιστός,
ὡς νομεὺς ἀνήρ, *ut pastor est fidus,* as a shepherd is :   Thuc.
IV. 84 ἦν δὲ οὐδὲ ἀδύνατος, ὡς Λακεδαιμόνιος, εἰπεῖν, *ut Lacedæmonius,*
for a Lacedæmonian ; it being well known that the Lac. were not orators.
So ὡς ἐκ τῶν δυνατῶν, ὡς ἐκ τῶν ὑπαρχόντων Thuc., as they were able, as
they were situated : Xen. Anab. IV. 3, 31 καὶ γὰρ ἦσαν ὡπλισμένοι, ὡς ὁ
τοῖς ὄρεσιν : Thuc. III. 113 ἄπιστον τὸ πλῆθος λέγεται ἀπολέσθαι, ὡς πρὸς τὸ
μέγεθος τῆς πόλεως, for the size of the city.

[a] Stallb. et Heindorf ad loc.   [b] Heindorf ad loc.

6. The impersonal form ὡς ἔοικε is, in a parenthesis, frequently used :rsonally, as it is referred to the subject of the principal clause, and ;rees in person with that subject: Hdt. III. 143 οὐ γὰρ δή, ὡς οἴκασι, ἰουλέατο εἶναι ἐλεύθεροι: Xen. Con. IV. 53 σὺ δ', ὡς ἔοικας, εἰ τοῦτο ῖνοιτο, νομίζεις ἂν διαφθαρῆναι αὐτόν: Plat. Rep. p. 372 C ἄνευ ὄψου, ἔφη, ς ἔοικας, ποιεῖς τοὺς ἄνδρας ἑστιωμένους: Ibid. p. 404 D Σικελικὴν ποικιλίαν ἰῶν, ὡς ἔοικας, οὐκ αἰνεῖς: Ibid. p. 426 B οὐκ ἐπαινέτης εἶ, ἔφην ἐγώ, ὡς ικας, τῶν τοιούτων ἀνδρῶν. So also in Attic poets: Soph. El. 516 ἀνειμένη ἰν, ὡς ἔοικας, αὖ στρέφει: Eur. Med. 337 ὄχλον παρέξεις, ὡς ἔοικας, ὦ γύναι. ο also sometimes *videri* in Latin; as, *ut videris, non recte judicas.*

Comparative Adverbial Sentences of Quantity or Degree.

§. 870. In these sentences, the quantity or degree of the prin-ipal verb is said to be equal with that of the dependent verb; hey are resolutions of an instrumental dative, used as an adverb §. 609. 1.), or an accus. of quantity (§. 578.).

The adverbial sentence is introduced

a. By the relatives, ὅσω (ὅσον), referring to a demonstrat. in he principal clause, τοσούτω (τοσοῦτον): Xen. Cyr. VIII. ', 4 τοσοῦτον διαφέρειν ἡμᾶς δεῖ τῶν δούλων, ὅσον οἱ μὲν δοῦλοι ἄκοντες ῖοῖς δεσπόταις ὑπηρετοῦσιν.

b. By ὅσω, ὅσον, referring to the demonstr. τόσω, τόσον, ῖοσούτω, τοσοῦτον; but both the predicates are either in the ɔomparat. or superl.; as, ὅσω (ὅσον) σοφώτερός τις ἐστιν, τοσούτω ῖτοσοῦτον) σωφρονέστερός ἐστιν — ὅσω (ὅσον) σοφώτατός τις ἐστί, ῖοσούτω (τοσοῦτον) σωφρονέστατός ἐστιν: Thuc. VIII. 84 ὅσω μά-λιστα καὶ ἐλεύθεροι ἦσαν ναῦται, τοσούτω καὶ θρασύτατα προσπεσόντες ῖὸν μισθὸν ἀπήτουν. Also a superlat. stands in the former, a com-parat. in the latter clause: Demosth. p. 21, 12 ὅσω γὰρ ἑτοι-μότατ' αὐτῷ (τῷ λόγῳ) δοκοῦμεν χρῆσθαι, τοσούτω μᾶλλον ἀπι-στοῦσι πάντες αὐτῷ.

Obs. 1. Sometimes τοσούτω is suppressed, especially when the rela-tive clause of the comparison stands last: Thuc. II. 47 αὐτοὶ μάλιστα ἔθνησκον, ὅσω καὶ μάλιστα προσῇεσαν: Plat. Gorg. p. 458 A μεῖζον γὰρ αὐτὸ ἀγαθὸν ἡγοῦμαι, ὅσωπερ μεῖζον ἀγαθόν ἐστιν αὐτὸν ἀπαλλαγῆναι κακοῦ τοῦ μεγί-στου ἢ ἄλλον ἀπαλλάξαι: Id. de Rep. p. 472 A ὅσω ἄν, ἔφη, τοιαῦτα πλείω λέγῃς, ἧττον ἀφεθήσει ὑφ' ἡμῶν: Id. Apol. p. 39 D καὶ χαλεπώτεροι ἔσονται, ὅσω νεώτεροί εἰσι. So Latin: Ovid. Epist. IV. 19 *Venit Amor gravius, quo serius.*

Obs. 2. When ὅσω—τοσούτω are both suppressed, the two clauses may coalesce into one sentence: Xen. M. S. IV. 1, 3 αἱ ἄρισται δοκοῦσαι εἶναι φύσεις μάλιστα παιδείας δέονται.

Obs. 3. If the one predicate differs from the other in degree, they stand as ɔoordinates with the disjunctive particle ἤ (§. 779.).

Obs. 4. Frequently a comparative clause introduced by ὡς, ὅπως, ᾗ, or ὅσον, and expressing a possibility, serves to strengthen a superlative, or a comparative: Hdt. VI. 44 ἐν νόῳ ἔχοντες ὅσας ἂν πλείστας δύναιυτο καταστρέφεσθαι τῶν Ἑλληνίδων πολίων: Thuc. VII. 21 ἄγων ἀπὸ τῶν πόλεων ὧν ἔπεισε στρατιὰν, ὅσην ἑκασταχόθεν πλείστην ἐδύνατο: Ibid. πληροῦν ναῦς ὡς δύνανται πλείστας: Xen. M. S. II. 2, 6 ἐπιμελοῦνται οἱ γονεῖς πάντα ποιοῦντες, ὅπως οἱ παῖδες αὐτοῖς γένωνται ὡς δυνατὸν βέλτιστοι: Id. Cyr. VII. 1, 9 ᾗ ἂν δύνωμαι τάχιστα: Ibid. I. 4, 14 διαγωνίζεσθαι ὅπως ἕκαστος τὰ κράτιστα δύναιτο: Demosth. p. 108, 75 εἶπε ὡς οἱόν τε τὰ ἄριστα. So also ὡς ἂν with the opt. of another verb, expressing that whereto the superl. notion applies, frequently in Xen., Plat. and others; as, Xen. Œcon. XX. 7 οὕτως ὡς ἂν ἄριστα μάχοιντο: Demosth. p. 15, 21 ὡς ἂν κάλλιστ' αὐτῷ τὰ παρόντ' ἔχοι. For the same purpose οἷος, ὅτι, with εἶναι are used: Soph. Œ. R. 344 δι' ὀργῆς ἥτις ἀγριωτάτη (sc. ἐστίν): Xen. M. S. IV. 8 extr. ἐδόκει τοιοῦτος εἶναι, οἷος ἂν εἴη ἄριστός γε ἀνὴρ καὶ εὐδαιμονέστατος. But generally the verb is suppressed with these relatives, and hence the elliptic forms ὡς, ὅπως ἄριστα, οἷον χαλεπώτατον &c.: Demosth. p. 23, 18 ἀνήρ ἐστιν ἐν αὐτοῖς οἷος ἔμπειρος πολέμου &c. τοιοῦτος, οἷος δύναται εἶναι ἔμπειρος πολέμου. So the expressions ὡς ἀληθῶς, really; ὡς ἀτεχνῶς, straightway; ὡς τάχι, μάλα, ὡς ἐπὶ τὸ πολύ, *plerumque,* are to be explained; and ὡς ἕκαστοι that is ἕκαστοι, ὡς ἕκαστοι ἦσαν. On θαυμαστῶς ὡς &c. see §. 823. *Obs.* 7.

INTERROGATIVE SENTENCES.

§. 871. 1. Sentences in general express a judgment—the agreement or disagreement of a subject with the predicate. The interrogative sentence expresses ignorance or a doubt as to this agreement or disagreement—"This is so?"—"This is not so?" They either do not depend on another verb (direct); as, "*Is my friend come?*" or they do depend on another verb (indirect), "*Do you know whether my friend is come?*" Each of these is either contained in a single clause (simple) as above, or contains two clauses (compound), "*Do you know whether he is come or not?*" and as the question relates to an object (person or thing), or the verb of the sentence, they are either nominal or verbal. The nominal interrog. sentence is introduced by a substantival or adjectival pronoun; the verbal interrog. sentence by an adverbial interrog. pronoun, or an interrogative particle; as, τίς ταῦτα ἐποίησεν; — ἆρα ταῦτα ἐποίησας;

2. An interrogative sentence is generally known only by the position of the words and the mode of pronunciation; the word on which, as containing the question, the emphasis is to be placed, being usually placed first in the sentence. The note of interrogation in Greek is an English semicolon; as, Od. ε, 204 οὕτω δὴ οἰκόνδε φίλην ἐς πατρίδα γαῖαν αὐτίκα νῦν ἐθέλεις ἰέναι; So especially in negations; as, οὐκ ἐθέλεις ἰέναι;

Obs. Those sentences which imply an expectation that the fact is so,

ıd therefore have affirmative answers, are called *affirmative questions*.
hose which imply an expectation that it is not so, and have negative
ıswers, are called *negative questions*.

Simple Direct Questions

§. 872. 1. are introduced by the interrog. pronouns, τίς, τί (Epic
ίη), ποῖος, πόσος &c., πῶς, πῇ, ποῦ, πόθι, πόθεν, πόσε &c.; as, τίς
λθεν; τί ποιεῖς; ποῖόν σε ἔπος φύγεν ἔρκος ὀδόντων; πῶς λέγεις;
l. φ, 422 πόσε φεύγετε;

Obs. 1. The interrog. words are not always in the beginning of the
entence, and even sometimes stand last, so that there is a sudden and
ınexpected change at the end of an *oratio recta* to the interrogative form:
Ξur. Phœn. 716 λέγει δὲ δὴ τί τῶν ἐκεῖ νεώτερον; Id. Hipp. 524 δειμαίνεις δὲ
·ί; Id. Ion. 1012 τί τῷδε χρῆσθε; δύνασιν ἐκφέρει τίνα; Id. Or. 401 ἦρξω
ἱὲ λύσσης πότε;

Τίς, τί, ποῖος &c. πῶς &c. *with other Particles.*—Γάρ.

2. These interrog., especially τίς, are frequently joined with
ɔther particles:

a. Τίς ποτε, *quis tandem?* τί ποτε (for which Hom. τίπτε),
quid tandem?

b. Τίς τε, *who then?* τίς τ' ἄρ' (ἄρα §. 788.), *lo, who then?*
(τέ see §. 755.); τίς νυ, *quisnam* (§. 732.): Od. α, 62 τί νύ οἱ
τόσον ὠδύσαο, Ζεῦ; (Expostulation—*why therefore?*) These three
combinations are only Epic.

c. Τίς ἄρα, τί ἄρα, so also ποῖος ἄρα, πότερος ἄρα,
πῶς ἄρα &c., where ἄρα signifies the embarrassment of the person who asks the question, or a doubt as to its decision, or his
expectation of some surprising answer: Æsch. Sept. 91 τίς ἄρα
ῥύσεται, τίς ἄρ' ἐπαρκέσει θεῶν ἢ θεᾶν; Eur. Iph. T. 478 πότερος
ἄρ' ὑμῶν ἐνθάδ' ὠνομασμένος Πυλάδης κέκληται; In Homer ἦ is
always before this ἄρα in interrog. In Attic poetry ἄρα is lengthened into ἆρα for the metre (see §. 789. *Obs.*): Eur. Iph. T. 458
τίς ἆρα μήτηρ ἡ τεκοῦσ' ὑμᾶς ποτε;

d. Τί δή (but also πῶς δή, ποῦ δή &c.), *quidum*, frequently to express the impatience, reluctance, surprise of the person who asks the question; τί δή ποτε, *quid tandem:* Eur.
Med. 1001 τί δὴ κατηφεῖς ὄμμα καὶ δακρυρροεῖς; Cf. §. 723. 2.
For τί δαί see §. 727. Also τίς δὴ οὖν, τί δὴ οὖν, *who,
what then? out with it;* but in τί οὖν δή and πῶς οὖν δή, δή
is only connective (§. 723. 2.).

e. Τί οὖν (but also τί alone) with a negative is used in ani-

mated expressions of exhortation or encouragement, as Lat. quin:
Plat. Protag. p. 310 A τί οὖν οὐ διηγήσω ἡμῖν τὴν ξυνουσίαν;

f. Τί μήν like πῶς μήν, *quid quæso?* *quid vero?* (§. 723.)

g. Τί δέ; To give emphasis to the subject matter of the
question in an antithesis, or a change of the form of the sentence.
The words which express this subject matter are frequently separated from their sentence and placed first with τί δέ, and then the
predicate of the real interrog. sentence with a second interrog.
word: Plat. Rep. p. 332 E τίς δὲ πλέοντας πρὸς τὸν τῆς θαλάττης
κίνδυνον (sc. εὖ ποιεῖ);—Κυβερνήτης.—Τί δὲ ὁ δίκαιος; ἐν τίνι
πράξει καὶ πρὸς τί ἔργον δυνατώτατος φίλους ὠφελεῖν καὶ ἐχθροὺς βλάπτειν [a]; Ibid. p. 341 D τί δὲ κυβερνήτης; ὁ ὀρθῶς κυβερνήτης ναυτῶν
ἄρχων ἐστὶν ἢ ναύτης; Id. Gorg. p. 502 A τί δὲ ὁ πατὴρ αὐτοῦ Μέλης;
ἢ πρὸς τὸ βέλτιστον βλέπων ἐδόκει σοι κιθαρῳδεῖν;—Τί δ' οὔ; But
why not?=Surely.

h. On τί καί, ποῖος καί, πῶς καί &c. &c., see §. 760. 2.

i. Very often γάρ is added to the interrog., as πῶς γάρ, τίς γάρ
&c., having an inferential force (§. 786. 2.), with an expression of
surprise: Il. a, 123 πῶς γάρ τοι δώσουσι γέρας μεγάθυμοι Ἀχαιοί;
σ, 182 Ἶρι θεά, τίς γάρ σε θεῶν ἐμοὶ ἄγγελον ἧκεν;— Τί γάρ;
quid ergo? expresses feeling, but it is also used to denote a
new thought; as, καὶ τί γάρ; and what now? But γάρ also has
its logical force in this formula, τί γάρ; *quid enim?* or *quidni
enim?* (= surely—naturally.) Observe especially the Attic, πῶς
γάρ; as an expressive form of a negative answer (= in no wise).
So in the same sense in Attic, πόθεν; πόθεν γάρ; On the other
hand, πῶς γάρ οὔ; πόθεν δὲ οὔ; has an affirmative force—
why not? (=*utique, sane*) as an answer: Xen. M. S. IV. 4, 13
οὐκοῦν ὁ μὲν τὰ δίκαια πράττων δίκαιος, ὁ δὲ τὰ ἄδικα ἄδικος; Πῶς
γάρ οὔ; But γάρ is not unfrequently used also without an
interrog. word in the above meaning: Demosth. p. 43, 10 γένοιτο
γὰρ ἄν τι καινότερον, ἢ Μακεδὼν ἀνὴρ Ἀθηναίους καταπολεμῶν καὶ
τὰ τῶν Ἑλλήνων διοικῶν [b]; Ibid. p. 47, 27 οὐ γὰρ ἐχρῆν—ταξιάρ-
χους παρ' ὑμῶν—εἶναι, ἵν' ἦν ὡς ἀληθῶς τῆς πόλεως ἡ δύναμις;

Obs. 2. Πώμαλα is used in Doric and Attic in the sense of πῶς γάρ;
(=*minime*,) which clearly was originally interrogative, πῶς μάλα; How in
the world?

k. Τί μαθών, τί παθών, *cur, why?* always used in a bad
sense. The former signifies an intentionally, the latter an accidentally, wrong action; as, τί μαθὼν τοῦτο ἐποίησας; What is
your intention, with what aim did you this? τί παθὼν τοῦτο ἐποίη-

---

[a] Stallb. ad loc.   [b] Bremi ad loc.

·as; *quid expertus, hoc fecisti?* What, has come to you that you
lid this? The latter as early as Homer: Il. λ, 313 τί παθόντε
.ελάσμεθα θούριδος ἀλκῆς; Arist. Nub. 339 τί παθοῦσαι —
'νηταῖς εἴξασι γυναιξίν; Ibid. 1510 τί γὰρ μαθόντ' ἐς θεοὺς ὑβρί-
ετον;

Obs. 3. So also ὅ τι μαθών occurs in indirect questions: Plat. Apol.
ι. 36 B τί ἄξιός εἰμι μαθεῖν ἢ ἀποτῖσαι, ὅ τι μαθὼν ἐν τῷ βίῳ οὐχ ἡσυχίαν ἦγον[a],
'roptereα quod: Id. Euthyd. p. 299 A πολὺ μέντοι, ἔφη, δικαιότερον τὸν ὑμέ-
·ερον πατέρα τύπτοιμι, ὅ τι μαθὼν σοφοὺς υἱεῖς οὕτως ἔφυσεν, what he meant
ιy begetting—because he has begotten.

Ἦ; ἆρα; ἆρ' οὐκ, ἆρα μή; μή; μῶν; μῶν οὖν; μῶν μή, μῶν οὔ;

§. 873. 1. Ἦ, generally with other particles, implies an assevera-
:ion, as it supposes the subject matter of the question as really
ιxisting. Homer, ἦ ῥα (for which Attic ἆρα), ἦ ἄρα δή, ἦ ῥά
ιυ, ἦ νυ, ἦ νύ που; Ἦ occurs in Homer without a particle,
when a question is answered by a conjecture in another question
:mmediately following: Od. ι, 405 τίπτε τόσον — ἐβόησας — ; ἦ
μήτις σευ μῆλα—ἐλαύνει; ἦ μήτις σ' αὐτὸν κτείνῃ; In Attic, ἦ που,
ιum forte, *whether perchance*, when a negative answer is expected: Eur. Med. 695 ἦ που τετόλμηκ' ἔργον αἴσχιστον τόδε;—
ἦ γάρ, *is it not so?* Plat. Hipp. p. 363 C ἦ γάρ, ὦ Ἱππία, ἐάν
τι ἐρωτᾷ σε Σωκράτης, ἀποκρινεῖ;

2. Ἆρα is a lengthened form of ἄρα, first used in the Post-
Homeric dialect, and especially in Attic. Originally, ἄρα was
placed after the interrog., but it afterwards assumed an interrog.
force, and was therefore lengthened into ἆρα, and stood as other
interrogatives at the beginning of the sentence, though in poetry
it was allowable to place ἆρα as well as ἄρα in the middle. It
expresses like ἄρα in τίς ἄρα &c. (§. 872. *c.*), embarrassment,
doubt; hence surprise, incredulity. The Attic politeness used
this particle with a marked emphasis of tone in very pointed and
decided questions; hence ironically, as the speaker pretended to be
embarrassed or in doubt. As ἆρα generally implies doubt and surprise, it generally prepares one for a negative answer: Eur. Alc.
495 Ἄδμητον ἐν δόμοισιν ἆρα κιγχάνω; Here uncertainty only
is expressed, from which he desires to be freed: Soph. Phil. 976
οἴμοι, τίς ἀνήρ; ἆρ' Ὀδυσσέως κλύω; (astonishment:) Xen. Cyr.
VII. 5, 40 ἆρα, ἔφη, ὦ ἄνδρες, νῦν μὲν καιρὸς διαλυθῆναι; (Ironical
= I should think it was time to go.) Ἆρα has also the power of
expressing a positive consequence or result: Eur. Alc. 351 ἆρά
μοι στένειν πάρα; Is it not then my lot to mourn?

[a] Stallb. ad loc.

3. Οὐ or μή is attached to ἆρα, according as the person who asks the question expects an affirmative or negative answer to his question: ἆρ' οὐκ ἔστιν ἀσθενής; *nonne ægrotat? Ægrotat :* ἆρα μή ἔστιν ἀσθενής; *numnam ægrotat?* (He is not perhaps sick? *Non ægrotat :* Plat. Phæd. p. 64 C ἆρα μὴ ἄλλο τι ᾖ ὁ θάνατος; Cf. Id. Rep. p. 405 A. Xen. Œcon. IV. 4 ἆρα—μὴ αἰσχυν θῶμεν τὸν Περσῶν βασιλέα μιμήσασθαι; We shall not be ashamed &c.? On the construction of ἄρα μή see *Obs.* 2.

4. Μή; *not perhaps?* = *whether perhaps*, expresses anxiety, and hence prepares one for a negative answer: Xen. M. S. IV. 2, 1: ἀλλὰ μὴ ἀρχιτέκτων βούλει γενέσθαι;—Οὐκ οὖν ἔγωγ', ἔφη. *Minime gentium.* Ἀλλὰ μὴ γεωμέτρης ἐπιθυμεῖς, ἔφη, γενέσθαι ἀγαθός; —Οὐδὲ γεωμέτρης, ἔφη, κ. τ. λ.: Ibid. IV. 2, 12 μὴ οὖν, ἔφη, Εὐθύδημος, οὐ δύνωμαι ἐγὼ τὰ τῆς δικαιοσύνης ἔργα ἐξηγήσασθαι; Shall I not perhaps be unable? Whether shall I be able? When οὐ stands in a sentence introduced by μή, it belongs to some single word, not to the whole sentence. Μή is distinguished from ἆρα μ only in that the question is less pointed and emphatic. — Μή τι *num forte :* Plat. Rep. p. 466 A Τί οὖν; νῦν ἡμῖν ὁ τῶν ἐπικούρων βίος, ὥσπερ τοῦ γε τῶν ὀλυμπιονικῶν πολύ γε καὶ καλλίων και ἀμείνων φαίνεται, μή πη κατὰ τὸν τῶν σκυτοτόμων φαίνεται βίον ἢ τινῶν ἄλλων δημιουργῶν ἢ τὸν τῶν γεωργῶν; Οὔ μοι δοκεῖ, ἔφη: Ibid. p. 486 E Τί οὖν; μή πη δοκοῦμέν σοι οὐκ ἀναγκαῖα ἕκαστα διεληλυθέναι—; Ἀναγκαιότατα μὲν οὖν, ἔφη.

Obs. 1. When an affirmative answer follows a question introduced by μ or ἆρα μή, it always seems contrary to the expectation of the speaker Æsch. Suppl. 309 μὴ καὶ λόγος τις Ζῆνα μιχθῆναι βροτῷ; there is surely not a report? The chorus answers, καὶ κρυπτά γ' Ἥρας ταῦτα τῶν παλλαγμάτων *immo non modo amat, sed clam conjuge amat :* Plat. Crit. p. 44 E ἆρά γε μ ἐμοῦ προμηθεῖ;—εἰ γάρ τι τοιοῦτον φοβεῖ, ἔασον αὐτὸ χαίρειν; *numne de s sollicitus es?* you are not anxious about me? Socr. καὶ ταῦτα προμηθοῦμαι, ὦ Κρίτων, καὶ ἄλλα πολλά.

5. Μῶν (from the interrog. μή and οὖν) answers exactly to the Latin *num, It is not then? whether?* and hence always prepares one for a negative answer: Eur. Hec. 754 τί χρῆμα μαστεύουσα; μῶν ἐλεύθερον αἰῶνα θέσθαι; ῥᾴδιον γάρ ἐστι σοι. Hec. answers, Οὐ δῆτα τοὺς κακοὺς δὲ τιμωρουμένη αἰῶνα τὸν ξύμπαντα δουλεῦσαι θέλω. In the passages wherein a not unwelcome surprise is mingled with the doubt, and hence the speaker rather wishes than fears the subject-matter of his question, μῶν seems to introduce a question to which there is an affirmative answer: Plat. Protag. p. 310 D τί οὖν σοι, ἦν δ' ἐγώ, τοῦτο; μῶν τί σε ἀδικεῖ Πρωταγόρας; Καὶ ὃς γελάσας Νὴ τοὺς θεούς, ἔφη, ὦ Σώκρατες, ὅτι γε μόνος ἐστὶ σοφός, ἐμὲ δὲ οὐ

ⁿοιεῖ. Whether does Protag. wrong you? From the frequent use of this word, the elements μή and οὖν which composed it were so little recognised therein, that they are joined with it, μ ῶ ν ο ὖ ν, μ ῶ ν ᴜ ή : Æsch. Choeph. 171 μ ῶ ν ο ὖ ν 'Ορέστου κρύβδα δῶρον ᾖ τόδε ; Eur. Andr. 81 μ ῶ ν ο ὖ ν δοκεῖς σου φροντίσαι τίν' ἀγγέλων : Plat. Phæd. p. 84 C τί, ἔφη, ὑμῖν τὰ λεχθέντα ; μ ῶ ν μ ὴ δοκεῖ ἐνδεῶς λέγεσθαι : but when μῶν is followed by οὐ the answer is affirmative, (*nonne :*) Soph. Œ. C. 1727 ἐν οἷς τί χρῆν ποιεῖν ἐμέ ; μ ῶ ν ᴏ ὐ χ ὅπερ ἐποίουν ; *nonne, quod faciebam ?*

Obs. 2. The use of the moods after μή, ἆρα μή, μῶν μή in direct questions, is the same as that of indirect questions after μή (§. 814.).

Οὐ ; οὐκοῦν, οὐ μέντοι ; οὐ δή ; οὐ δή που ; οὔτι που ;—ἀλλά ; ἀλλ' ἤ ;—δέ ;—εἶτα, ἔπειτα.

§. 874. 1. Οὐ; *non, nonne ?* and with the notion of a result from what goes before, ο ὐ κ ο ῦ ν (§. 791. *Obs.*) *non* or *nonne ergo ?* are always affirmative: Soph. Aj. 79 ο ὐ κ ο ῦ ν γέλως ἥδιστος εἰς ἐχθροὺς γελᾶν ;

2. Ο ὐ μ έ ν τ ο ι, *not in truth ?* is used when the speaker seems to deny the subject-matter, while it is affirmed in the answer with the more certainty : Plat. Phædr. p. 229 B εἰπέ μοι, ὦ Σώκρατες, ο ὐ κ ἐνθένδε μ έ ν τ ο ι ποθὲν ἀπὸ τοῦ Ἰλισσοῦ λέγεται ὁ Βορέας τὴν Ὠρείθυιαν ἁρπάσαι ; Socrates answers, Λέγεται γάρ : Ibid. p. 261 C σὺ δ' εἰπὲ ἐν δικαστηρίοις οἱ ἀντίδικοι τί δρῶσιν ; ο ὐ κ ἀντιλέγουσι μ έ ν τ ο ι ; ἢ τί φήσομεν ; Τοῦτ' αὐτό, is Phædrus's answer.

3. Ο ὐ δ ή, generally ο ὐ δ ή π ο υ, also ο ὔ τ ι π ο υ, in Attic, is used ironically, to express a question to which a denial is confidently expected : Plat. Theæt. p. 146 A ο ὔ τ ι π ο υ ἐγὼ ὑπὸ φιλολογίας ἀγροικίζομαι ; I am not ! am I not ?

4. Very frequently questions are introduced by ἀ λ λ ά, when the question is opposed to some thought in the speaker's mind, or when an application or remonstrance is made, in the shape of a question : Eur. Med. 330 λόγους ἀναλοῖς· οὐ γὰρ ἂν πείσαις ποτέ ! 'Αλλ' ἐξελᾷς με, κοὐδὲν αἰδέσει λιτάς ; in this sense we often find ἀλλ' ἤ = *an* (§. 774) : Xen. Symp. I. 15 ἀλλ' ἤ ὀδύνη σε εἴληφε ; Soph. El. 879 XP. πάρεστ' 'Ορέστης ἡμῖν—ΗΛ. ἀ λ λ ' ἤ μέμηνας—κἀπὶ τοῖς ἐμοῖς γελᾷς ; (no, he is not come) but are you not mad ?

5. Also δέ is sometimes used in animated questions, referring to some suppressed thought : Hdt. I. 32 Κροῖσος δὲ σπερχθεὶς εἶπε· Ὦ ξεῖνε 'Αθηναῖε, ἡ δὲ ἡμετέρη εὐδαιμονίη οὕτω τοι ἀπέρριπται ἐς τὸ μηδέν, ὥστε οὐδὲ ἰδιωτέων ἀνδρῶν ἀξίους ὑμέας ἐποίησας ; i. e. ἰδιώτας

μὲν εὐδαίμονας νομίζεις, ἡ δέ κ. τ. λ.: Demosth. p. 107, 70 εἰπέ μοι, σὺ δὲ δὴ τί τὴν πόλιν ἡμῖν ἀγαθὸν πεποίηκας;

6. Εἶτα and ἔπειτα in questions implying reluctance, irony astonishment, express an antithesis—that is, that something result‹ from what has gone before, which is not expected: Plat. Crit. p. 43 B εἶτα πῶς οὐκ εὐθὺς ἐπήγειράς με; Id. Apol. p. 28 B ἴσως δ᾽ ἂν οὖν εἴποι τις· Εἶτ᾽ οὐκ αἰσχύνει, ὦ Σώκρατες, τοιοῦτον ἐπιτήδευμα ἐπιτηδεύσας, ἐξ οὗ κινδυνεύεις νυνὶ ἀποθανεῖν: Xen. M. S. I. 4, 11 ἔπειτ᾽ οὐκ οἴει φροντίζειν (θεοὺς ἀνθρώπων): Demosth. p. 71 extr. εἰ οὐχ ὁρᾶτε Φίλιππον ἀλλοτριωτάτας ταύτῃ (τῇ ἐλευθερίᾳ) καὶ τὰς προση-γορίας ἔχοντα;

Direct Double Questions

§. 875. *a.* In Homeric, sometimes in Attic poetry, are introduced by ἤ—ἤ *either—or, utrum—an :* Od. ζ, 120 ἤ ῥ᾽ οἵγ᾽ ὑβρισταί τε καὶ ἄγριοι οὐδὲ δίκαιοι, ἠὲ φιλόξεινοι καί σφιν νόος ἐστὶ θεουδής;

b. In post-Homeric, especially in Attic, by πότερον (πότερα) —ἤ; as, πότερον οὗτοι ὑβρισταί εἰσιν ἢ φιλόξεινοι. When both the clauses have the same verb it is sometimes placed first, with πότε-ρον: Xen. Cyr. III. 1, 15 πότερα δ᾽ ἡγῇ, ὦ Κῦρε, ἄμεινον εἶναι, σὺν τῷ ἀγαθῷ τὰς τιμωρίας ποιεῖσθαι, ἢ σὺν τῇ σῇ ζημίᾳ; Also more than one clause may be opposed to the one introduced by πότερα: Hdt. III. 82 κόθεν ἡμῖν ἡ ἐλευθερίη ἐγένετο καὶ τεῦ δόντος; κότερα παρὰ δήμου, ἢ ὀλιγαρχίης, ἢ μουνάρχου;

Obs. 1. The ἤ or the πότερον in the first clause is sometimes omitted; as, Od. a, 226 εἰλαπίνη ἠὲ γάμος; Cf. Il. κ, 62: Eur. Or. 1532 sq. τί δρῶμεν· ἀγγέλλωμεν ἐς πόλιν τάδε, ἢ σῖγ᾽ ἔχωμεν; Xen. Cyr. III. 1, 12 τί δέ, ἢν χρή-ματα πολλὰ ἔχῃ, ἐᾷς πλουτεῖν, ἢ πένητα ποιεῖς;

Obs. 2. When a general or indefinite question has preceded, the one following thereon is introduced by ἤ, *an,* referring back to the preceding one, to correct or qualify it. The first question expresses the uncer-tainty of the speaker—the one which follows with ἤ, *an,* signifies the only thing which the speaker can suppose, in case the person of whom the question is asked, does not choose to inform him better: Il. a, 203 τάχ᾽ ἄν ποτ᾽ αἰγιόχοιο Διὸς τέκος εἰλήλουθας; ἦ ἵνα ὕβριν ἴδῃ 'Αγαμέμνονος 'Ατρείδαο (=*quamquam quid quæro? certe venisti, ut—?*) Plat. Symp. p. 173 A ἀλλὰ τίς σοι διηγεῖτο; ἢ αὐτὸς Σωκράτης [a]; Id. Parm. p. 173 B πόθεν οὖν δὴ ἀρξόμεθα καὶ τί πρῶτον ὑποθησόμεθα; ἢ βούλεσθε ἀπ᾽ ἐμοῦ ἄρξωμαι; Id. Menon. p. 71 B ὃ δὲ μὴ οἶδα τί ἐστι, πῶς ἂν, ὁποῖόν γε τι, εἰδείην; ἢ δοκεῖ σοι οἷόν τε εἶναι—;

c. 'Αρα—ἤ, *num—an :* Plat. Euthyphr. p. 9 extr. ἆρα τὸ ὅσιον, ὅτι ὅσιόν ἐστι, φιλεῖται ὑπὸ τῶν θεῶν, ἤ, ὅτι φιλεῖται, ὅσιόν ἐστιν.

d. Μῶν—ἤ, seldom: Eur. El. 500 τί δ᾽, ὦ γεραιέ, διάβροχον τόδ᾽

---

[a] Stallb. ad loc.

ὄμμ' ἔχεις; μῶν τἀμὰ διὰ χρόνου σ' ἀνέμνησαν κακά; τὰς Ὀρέστου τλήμονας φυγὰς στένεις; Μή—ἤ, *whether*—*or:* Plat. Phæd. p. 78 D αὐτὴ ἡ οὐσία—πότερον ὡσαύτως ἀεὶ ἔχει κατὰ ταὐτὰ ἢ ἄλλοτ' ἄλλως; αὐτὸ τὸ ἴσον, αὐτὸ τὸ καλόν, αὐτὸ ἔκαστον, ὃ ἔστι, τὸ ὄν, μή ποτε μεταβολὴν—ἐνδέχεται; ἢ ἀεὶ αὐτῶν ἔκαστον, ὃ ἔστι, μονοειδὲς ὄν, αὐτὸ καθ' αὑτό, ὡσαύτως καὶ κατὰ ταὐτὰ ἔχει καὶ οὐδέποτε —ἀλλοίωσιν—ἐνδέχεται; Id. Rep. p. 479 B καὶ μεγάλα δὴ καὶ σμικρὰ καὶ κοῦφα καὶ βαρέα μή τι μᾶλλον, ἃ ἂν φήσωμεν, ταῦτα προσρηθήσεται ἢ τἀναντία; Οὐκ, ἀλλ' ἀεί, ἔφη, ἔκαστον ἀμφοτέρων ἔξεται.

Obs. 3. If the second clause is negative, either ἢ οὐ is used, or ἢ μή, the former when the predicate, the latter when only some particular part of the sentence is denied: Plat. Rep. p. 473 A ἀλλὰ σὺ πότερον ὁμολογεῖς οὕτως, ἢ οὔ (for ἢ οὐχ ὁμολ.); Id. Phædr. p. 263 C τὸν Ἔρωτα πότερον φῶμεν τῶν ἀμφισβητησίμων, ἢ τῶν μὴ (sc. ἀμφισβ.);

e. Ἄλλο τι ἤ, an elliptic compound question for ἄλλο τι γένοιτ' ἄν, ἤ (post Homeric), is used in the sense of *nonne:* from its frequent use, this expression became a mere adverb; Hdt. I. 109 ἄλλο τι ἢ λείπεται τὸ ἐνθεῦτεν ἐμοὶ κινδύνων ὁ μέγιστος; *nonne relinquitur mihi—?* Xen. Cyr. III. 2, 18 ἄλλο τι οὖν, ἔφη, ἢ διὰ τὸ γῆς σπανίζειν ἀγαθῆς νῦν πένητες νομίζετ' εἶναι; Id. Anab. IV. 7, 5 ἄλλο τι ἢ οὐδὲν κωλύει παριέναι; Plat. Phæd. p. 70 A B φέρε δή, ἦ δ' ὅς, ἄλλο τι ἡμῶν αὐτῶν ἢ τὸ μὲν σῶμά ἐστι, τὸ δὲ ψυχή; Οὐδὲν ἄλλο, ἔφη: Id. Euthyphr. p. 15 C we find τοῦτο δ' ἄλλο τι ἢ θεοφιλὲς γίγνεται; ἢ οὔ; (*annon:*) and sometimes ἤ was dropped, and the two sentences coalesced; and then perhaps it should be written ἄλλοτι: Plat. Hipparch. p. 226 E ἄλλοτι οὖν οἵγε φιλοκερδεῖς φιλοῦσι τὸ κέρδος; Id. Men. p. 82 C εἰ ἦν ταύτῃ δυοῖν ποδοῖν, ταύτῃ δὲ ἑνὸς ποδὸς μόνον, ἄλλο τι ἅπαξ ἂν ἦν δυοῖν ποδοῖν τὸ χωρίον; Ibid. p. 84 D ἄλλο τι οὖν γένοιτ' ἂν τέτταρα ἴσα χωρία τάδε; for ἄλλο τι γένοιτ' ἂν ἢ οἵγε φιλοκερδεῖς &c.

Obs. 4. Sometimes ἄλλο τι ἤ is not used as a mere interrog. particle or as an elliptic question. The question is then introduced by some other interrog. particle, and ἄλλο τι is the subject or object of the verb: Plat. Phæd. p. 64 C ἡγούμεθά τι τὸν θάνατον εἶναι; πάνυ γε.—Ἆρα μὴ ἄλλο τι ἢ τὴν τῆς ψυχῆς ἀπὸ τοῦ σώματος ἀπαλλαγήν; Ibid. p. 258 A ἤ σοι ἄλλο τι φαίνεται τὸ τοιοῦτον ἢ λόγος συγγεγραμμένος; It is also used without any interrog. particle where ἄλλο τι is the predicate, and between ἄλλο τι and ἤ the subject is placed: Plat. Phæd. p. 106 E ἄλλο τι ψυχὴ, ἤ, εἰ ἀθάνατος τυγχάνει οὖσα, καὶ ἀνώλεθρος ἂν εἴη;

Obs. 5. As ἄλλος, ἄλλο is often used instead of ἄλλος τις, ἄλλο τι (Xen. Cyr. IV. 4, 8 εἰ δ' ἄλλο τις ὁρᾷ ἄμεινον, λεγέτω), so is ἄλλο as interrog. instead of ἄλλο τι: Xen. M. S. I. 17 ἄλλο γε ἢ ἀφροσύνη πρόσεστι τῷ θέλοντι τὰ λυπηρὰ ὑπομένειν.

Indirect Questions,

§. 876. Although they are in form adverb. sentences, yet are to be regarded as substant. sentences, and then may stand as the object or subject of the verb; as, εἰ τοῦτο ποιήσεις, οὐκ οἶδα—εἰ τοῦτο ποιήσεις, οὐ δῆλόν ἐστι.

Simple Indirect Questions

§. 877. Are introduced by

a. The interrog. pronouns ὅστις, ὁποῖος, ὁπόσος, ὁπότερος,—ὅπως, ὅπου, ὅπη, ὁπότε, &c. as, οὐκ οἶδα, ὅστις ἐστί—ὅπως τὸ πρᾶγμα ἔπραξεν.

Obs. 1. If the question is repeated by the person to whom it is addressed before he answers it, the pronouns compounded with ὅς are used instead of the simple pronoun; as, ὅστις for τίς, ὅπως for πῶς; this second question is considered as dependent upon, *"do you ask :"* Arist. Ran. 198 οὗτος τί ποιεῖς; Dion. ὅτι ποιῶ; Id. Ach. 594 ἀλλὰ τίς γὰρ εἶ; Δ. Ὅστις; πολίτης χρηστός: Plat. Euthyphr. p. 2. B ἀλλὰ δὴ τίνα γραφήν σε γέγραπται; Σ. Ἥντινα; οὐκ ἀγεννῆ, ἔμοιγε δοκεῖ: Id. Hipp. M. p. 292 C πῶς δή, φράσω ἐγώ. Ὅπως; φήσει, οὐχ οἶόστ' εἰ μεμνῆσθαι: Id. Legg. p. 662 A καὶ τὰ ἂν ταῦτά γ' ἔτι ξυγχωροῖμεν; Ἀθ. Ὅπως; εἰ θεὸς ἡμῖν—δοίη τις συμφωνίαν.

Obs. 2. As the pronouns τίς, τί, ποῖος, πῶς, &c. are the proper forms for the direct question, so those compounded with the relat. ὅς, as ὅστις, ὁποῖος, &c., belong to the indirect question, the relative part of the compound ὁ in ὁποῖος signifying the dependence of the interrog. sentence. Sometimes, however, the simple forms are used, the indirect question assuming the character of the direct. Sometimes we even find τίς, ποῖος, πῶς, and τίς, ὅστις, ποῖος, ὁποῖος, in the same passage: Plat. Crit. p. 48 A οὐκ ἆρα—ἡμῖν οὕτω φροντιστέον, τί ἐροῦσιν οἱ πολλοὶ ἡμᾶς, ἀλλ' ὅτι ὁ ἐπαΐων τις τῶν δικαίων καὶ ἀδίκων [a]: Id. Phileb. p. 17 B ἀλλ' ὅτι (ἔσμεν) πόσα τέ ἐστι καὶ ὁποῖα: Id. Gorg. p 500 A ἆρ' οὖν παντὸς ἀνδρός ἐστιν ἐκλέξασθαι ποῖα ἀγαθὰ τῶν ἡδέων ἐστὶ καὶ ὁποῖα κακά; Ibid. p. 448 E ἀλλ' οὐδεὶς ἐρωτᾷ, ποῖα τις εἴη ἡ Γοργίου τέχνη, ἀλλὰ τίς καὶ ὅντινα δέοι καλεῖν τὸν Γοργίαν.— Sometimes, but less frequently, the relative form is placed first; as, Id. Rep. p. 414 D οὐκ οἶδα, ὁποίᾳ τόλμῃ ἢ ποίοις λόγοις χρώμενος ἐρῶ. Ὁποῖος, &c., on the other hand are not used for ποῖος in the direct question, in good authors [b], or they only seem to be so used, as they really depend on a principal clause suppressed.

Obs. 3. Sometimes the indirect questions are introduced by ὅς, ὡς, οἷος, ὅσος, for ὅστις, ὅπως, ὁποῖος, ὁπόσος. But this is rare, and could not have obtained till the origin of the relative ὅς from the demonst. was no longer perceived: Æschin. Ctes. §. 94 ὃν δὲ τρόπον, καὶ δι' οἵων κακουργημάτων, ταῦτ' ἤδη ἄξιόν ἐστιν ἀκοῦσαι: Plat. Rep. p. 327 E ὁρᾷς οὖν ἡμᾶς, ἔφη, ὅσοι ἐσμέν; Id. Men. p. 80 C καὶ νῦν περὶ ἀρετῆς, ὃ ἐστιν, ἐγὼ μὲν οὐκ οἶδα: Soph. O. C. 1171 ἔξοιδ' ἀκούων τῶνδ', ὃς ἔσθ' ὁ προστάτης.

Obs. 4. The same distinction seems to be preserved in the use of ὅς for ὅστις, (which latter is in the indirect question, what τίς is in the direct,) as in Latin between *qui* and *quis*, ὅστις being used when some question is asked as to the person or thing, *who is he ?* ὅς, when it is

[a] Stallb. ad loc.   [b] R. P. Phœn. 892.

asked as to the quality thereof, *what is he ?* the person or thing being supposed to be known.

b. Ε ἰ (*si*), *whether*, (§. 850. *Obs.*) can properly be used like ἤ only in compound questions; it signifies an alternative—a hesitation between two possible things; but very frequently one clause only is expressed, the other being implied therein, and existing in the speaker's mind; so after verbs of *reflection, consideration, inquiring, asking, trying, knowing, saying*, &c.: ὁρᾶν, σκοπεῖν, εἰδέναι, σκέπτεσθαι, φοβεῖσθαι, &c.—πειρᾶσθαι, ἐπινοεῖν, ἐρωτᾶν—λέγειν, φράζειν, &c.: Il. ε, 183 σάφα δ' οὐκ οἶδ', εἰ θεός ἐστι: Il. a, 83 φράσαι, εἴ με σαώσεις: Xen. Anab. VII. 3, 37 σκέψαι, εἰ ὁ Ἑλλήνων νόμος κάλλιον ἔχει: Id. M. S. II. 2, 2 ἤδη δέ ποτε ἐσκέψω, εἰ ἄρα—τὸ ἀχαριστεῖν πρὸς μὲν τοὺς φίλους ἄδικόν ἐστι: Id. Cyr. VIII. 4, 16 τὰ δὲ ἐκπώματα οὐκ οἶδ' εἰ Χρυσάντᾳ τούτῳ δῶ. Ἐάν also with conj. is used when something expected, but as yet untried, is spoken of: Il. o, 32 ὄφρα ἴδῃ, ἤν τοι χραίσμῃ: Xen. M. S. IV. 4, 12 σκέψαι ἐὰν τόδε σοὶ μᾶλλον ἀρέσκῃ.

Obs. 5. Very frequently, esp. in Homer, this deliberative (ἐάν, ep. εἴ κε, αἴ κε) is joined with verbs expressing any action whatever, there being implied therein the notion of σκοπεῖν or πειρᾶσθαι. In such sentences the conjunctive or opt. is used, as the principal verb is in a principal or historic tense, with the exceptions given above (§. 806 sqq.): Il. λ, 796 sqq. ἀλλὰ σέ περ προέτω, ἅμα δ' ἄλλος λαὸς ἑπέσθω Μυρμιδόνων, αἴ κεν τι φόως Δαναοῖσι γένηαι· καί τοι τεύχεα καλὰ δότω πόλεμόνδε φέρεσθαι, αἴ κε σε τῷ ἴσκοντες ἀπόσχωνται πολέμοιο Τρῶες, ἀναπνεύσωσι δ' Ἀρήϊοι υἷες Ἀχαιῶν τειρόμενοι: Il. κ, 55 f. ἐγὼ δ' ἐπὶ Νέστορι δῖον εἰμι καὶ ὀτρυνέω ἀναστήμεναι (πειρώμενος), αἴ κ' ἐθέλῃσιν ἐλθεῖν: Il. ν, 172 γλαυκιόων δ' ἰθὺς φέρεται μένει, ἤν τινα πέφνῃ ἀνδρῶν: Od. a, 379 ἐγὼ δὲ θεοὺς ἐπιβώσομαι αἰὲν ἐόντας, αἴ κε ποθὶ Ζεὺς δῷσι παλίντιτα ἔργα γενέσθαι: Hdt. I. 75 ἴς τε τὰ χρηστήρια ἔπεμπε, εἰ στρατεύηται ἐπὶ Πέρσας for στρατεύοιτο, see below, *Oratio obliqua.* Thuc. I. 58 Ποτιδαιᾶται δὲ πέμψαντες μὲν καὶ παρ' Ἀθηναίους πρέσβεις, εἴ πως πείσειαν.

Obs. 6. Ἤ, *an*, is also used sometimes in the Epic writers, for a simple question, the other clause being suppressed: Od. π, 138 ἀλλ' ἄγε μοι τόδε εἰπὲ, καὶ ἀτρεκέως κατάλεξον, ἤ καὶ Λαέρτῃ αὐτὴν ὁδὸν ἄγγελος ἔλθω.

c. Μ ή, (as in the direct question) *whether, not whether*, is used in Homer only with conjunctive after principal, opt. after historic, tenses, but in Attic with ind.: Il. κ, 97 καταβήομεν, ὄφρα ἴδωμεν, μὴ τοὶ μὲν καμάτῳ ἀδδηκότες ἠδὲ καὶ ὕπνῳ κοιμήσωνται, *whether they are not*, &c.: Od. φ, 394 ὁ δ' ἤδη τόξον ἐνώμα, πάντη ἀναστρωφῶν, πειρώμενος ἔνθα καὶ ἔνθα, μὴ κέρα ἶπες ἔδοιεν, ἀποιχομένοιο ἄνακτος. See above (§. 814.).

Obs. 7. The difference between μή with ind. and conj. in Attic Greek, is, that the ind. asks whether he is doing it now, μὴ ποιεῖ, the conjunct. whether he may not do it presently, μὴ ποιῇ—but μή, with conjunctive, often signifies *lest*. See §. 814.

3 8 2

Indirect Compound Questions

§. 878. Are introduced by

a. Ἤ—ἤ Homer, rarely Attic poets (cf. §. 875. *a.*): Od. *a*, 175 ἀγόρευσον—, ἠὲ νέον μεθέπεις, ἢ καὶ πατρώϊός ἐσσι ξεῖνος: Od. ζ, 141 μερμήριξεν Ὀδυσσεύς, ἢ γούνων λίσσοιτο—, ἢ αὔτως λίσσοιτ', εἰ δείξει πόλιν καὶ εἵματα δοίη: Od. γ, 214 εἰπέ μοι, ἠὲ ἑκὼν ὑποδάμρασαι, ἢ σέ γε λαοὶ ἐχθαίρουσιν: Soph. Œ. R. 80 οἶδε γὰρ κρινοῦσί γε, ἢ χρ' σε μίμνειν ἢ πορεύεσθαι πάλιν: Eur. Med. 480 οὐδ' ἔχω μαθεῖν, ἢ θεοὺς νομίζεις τοὺς τότ' οὐκ ἄρχειν ἔτι, ἢ καινὰ κεῖσθαι θέσμ' ἐν ἀνθρώποις τανῦν.

b. Π ό τ ε ρ ο ν (πότερα)—ἤ post-Homeric, (see §. 875. *b.*) i. e. οὐκ οἶδα, πότερον ζῆ ἢ τέθνηκεν.

Obs. Πότερον or ἤ may be suppressed in the first clause : Od. δ, 110 οὐδέ τι ἴδμεν, ζώει ὅγ' ἢ τέθνηκεν. Cf. §. 875. *Obs.* 1.

c. Ε ἰ—ἤ, like πότερον—ἤ, but with this difference, that εἰ–ἤ expresses uncertainty, and a determination to see the result: Il. χ, 246 ἵνα εἴδομεν, εἴ κεν Ἀχιλλεὺς—ἔναρα βροτόεντα φέρηται—, ἤ κεν σῷ δουρὶ δαμείη: Il. θ, 533 εἴσομαι, εἴ κε μ' ὁ Τυδεΐδης κρατερὸς Διομήδης πὰρ νηῶν πρὸς τεῖχος ἀπώσεται, ἢ καὶ ἐγὼ τὸν χαλκῷ δηώσας ἔναρα βροτόεντα φέρωμαι: Plat. Apol. p. 18 A τούτῳ τὸν νοῦν προσέχειν, εἰ δίκαια λέγω, ἢ μή.

d. Ε ἴ τ ε—ε ἴ τ ε, in the same sense as εἰ—ἤ, except that εἴτε– εἴτε expresses that the two clauses stand in the same relation to the principal verb: Il. μ, 239 τῶν (οἰωνῶν) οὔτι μετατρέπομ' οὐδ' ἀλεγίζω, εἴτ' ἐπὶ δεξί' ἴωσι πρὸς Ἠῶ τ' Ἠέλιόν τε, εἴτ' ἐπ' ἀριστερὰ τοίγε ποτὶ ζόφον ἠερόεντα: Soph. Antig. 38 καὶ δείξεις τάχα, εἴτ' εὐγενὴς πέφυκας, εἴτ' ἐσθλῶν κακή. Often in prose, as Plat. Rep. p. 484 C. In poetry the following forms also occur ; εἴτε—ἤ. Il. β, 349 πρὶν δ' Ἄργος δ' ἰέναι, πρὶν καὶ Διὸς αἰγιόχοιο γνώμεναι εἴτε ψεῦδος ὑπόσχεσις, ἠὲ καὶ οὐκί; or the reverse, ἤ—εἴτε, as Soph. Œ. R. 1115: also εἰ—εἴτε Eur. Alc. 140. And in poetry the first εἴτε is sometimes suppressed: Soph. Trach. 236 ποί γῆς; πατρῴας, εἴτε βαρβάρου λέγε. Cf. §. 778. *Obs.*

Moods in the Interrogative Sentence

§. 879. Are used in the same constructions, except some few peculiarities, as in the simple sentence. The ind. is used in *both* direct and indirect questions, as in other languages, to inquire whether a fact really is or not. On conjunct. and opt. see §. 417 and

.8. *θ.* : on the pres. or fut. ind. after a past tense, see *Oratio obliqua.*
he conjunct. after principal, opt. after historic tenses, has a de-
)erative force (§. 417.). The ind. of historic tenses, and the opt. is
ied with ἄν (§. 424. *a*, *β*. 425. 1.) :   Xen. M. S. IV. 2, 30 τοῦτο
)ὸς σὲ ἀποβλέπω, εἴ μοι ἐθελήσαις ἂν ἐξηγήσασθαι, sc. εἰ βού-
)ιο :   Id. Cyr. IV. 32, 4 σκοπῶν, ὅπως ἂν κάλλιστα καὶ τάχιστα
ιῦτα γένοιτο (sc. εἰ γένοιτο).—Πῶς with ind. and κέ: Il. χ,
)2.   On εἰ with ἄν, see above (§. 877. *Obs.* 5.).

Obs. 1. The opt. without ἄν is used also after a principal tense, when
ιe notion of uncertainty or doubt is to be conveyed by the question ;
:f. §. 814. *c.*) as, Plat. Hipp. p. 297 E ὅρα γάρ, εἰ—τοῦτο φαῖμεν εἶναι
ιλόν.

Obs. 2. Κέν is often added by Homer to the conjunct. or opt. of an
ιdirect question ; as, Il. ι, 619 φρασσόμεθ᾽, ἤ κε νεώμεθ᾽ ἐφ᾽ ἡμέτερ᾽ ἤ
ε μένωμεν :   Od. α, 268 θεῶν ἐν γούνασι κεῖται, ἤ κεν νοστήσας ἀπο-
ίσεται (i. e. ἀποτίσηται), ἠὲ καὶ οὐκί :   Od. ο, 299 ὁρμαίνων, ἤ κεν
᾽άνατον φύγοι, ἤ κεν ἁλῴη.

Obs. 3. On the conjunctive after a past tense, see *Oratio obliqua.*

Obs. 4. When an opt. is used in the second clause after a conjunct.
n the first clause of a compound indirect question, the opt. expresses, as in
ι final sentence, the less immediate thought (§. 809.) :   Il. π, 650 f.
βράζετο θυμῷ—μερμηρίζων, ἤ ἤδη καὶ κεῖνον ἐνὶ κρατερῇ ὑσμίνῃ—Ἕκτωρ χαλκῷ
᾽ η ώ σ ῃ, ἀπό τ᾽ ὤμων τεύχε᾽ ἕληται, ἤ ἔτι καὶ πλεόνεσσιν ὀφέλλειεν πόνον
ιλπύν.

The answer to a question

§. 880. Is expressed

a. By repeating the word which expresses the subject matter of the
question : Eur. Hipp. 1385 sq. ὁρᾷς με, δέσποιν᾽, ὡς ἔχω, τὸν ἄθλιον ;—
Ὁρῶ. If the answer is negative a negative is prefixed ; as, Ibid. 90 sq.
υἶσθ᾽ οὖν, βροτοῖσιν ὃς καθέστηκεν νόμος ;—Οὐκ οἶδα.

b. By φημί, φήμ᾽ ἐγώ, ἔγωγε—or negat. οὐ φημί, οὐκ ἔγωγε,
οὔ : Demosth. p. 14, 20 τί οὖν ;—σὺ γράφεις ταῦτ᾽ εἶναι στρατιωτικά ; Μὰ Δί᾽,
οὐκ ἔγωγε.

c. Very frequently by an explanatory γέ, which marks the connection
between the answer and question ; *yes, surely, at least.* It has a double
force. *a.* It assents to the subject-matter of the question by introducing a
statement which *a fortiori,* proves the other true, and therefore it is used
to give assent, and add something more to the question [a] ; and this is its
more usual force (cf. §. 735. 8.) : Eur. Hipp. 94 sq. ἐν δ᾽ εὐπροσηγό-
ροισιν ἔστι τις χάρις ; Hipp. Πλείστη γε καὶ κέρδος γε σὺν μόχθῳ βραχεῖ.
β. It asserts the subject matter, by introducing a sentence stating certain
circumstances under which it is true ; as, Eur. Phœn. 1616 τίς ἡγεμών μοι
ποδὸς ὁμαρτήσει τυφλοῦ ; ἥδ᾽ ἡ θανοῦσα ; ζῶσά γ᾽ ἂν σάφ᾽ οἶδ᾽ ὅτι : Id. Iph.
Taur. 484 πότερον ἀδελφὼ μητρός ἐστον ἐκ μιᾶς ; φιλότητί γ᾽, ἔσμεν δ᾽ οὐ κασι-
γνήτω, γυναί. This γέ is also added to a negative answer ; as, Eur. Iph. A.
1117 εἰφ᾽, ἂν ἐρωτήσω σε, γενναίως, πόσι.—Οὐδὲν κελευσμοῦ δεῖ γ᾽, ἐρωτᾶσθαι
θέλω—and a strong affirmation can precede it, such as ναί, νὴ Δία.

---

[a] Elmsl. Iph. Taur. 806.

d. By γάρ, (§.786.) as a stronger explanation than γέ, which removes the doubt expressed in the question, by giving the grounds for it: Eur. Hipp. 279 sq. ὁ δ' ἐς πρόσωπον οὐ τεκμαίρεται βλέπων; Tr. ἔκδημος ἁ γὰρ τῆσδε τυγχάνει χθονός: Ibid. 329 sq. Tr. κἄπειτα κρύπτεις χρῆσθ' ἱσσωμένης ἐμοῦ; Ph. ἐκ τῶν γὰρ αἰσχρῶν ἐσθλὰ μηχανώμεθα.

e. By ναί, νὴ τὸν Δία—πάνυ, κάρτα, &c.; often found with γέ, as πάνυ γε—also εὖ γε, καλῶς γε, &c.: Plat. Apol. p. 25 B ἔστι τις, ἔφην ἐγώ, ἢ οὔ.—Πάνυ γε, ἦ δ' ὅς.

f. By τοί (§. 736.), μέντοι (§. 730. a.), οὖν (§. 737.), which assent to it in the same way as γέ, by introducing something which implies it: Plat. Gorg. p. 447 B τί δέ, ὦ Χαιρεφῶν; ἐπιθυμεῖ Σωκράτης ἀκοῦσαι Γοργίου; Chœr. ἐπ' αὐτό γε τοι τοῦτο πάρεσμεν: Plat. Phæd. p. 65 D φαμέν τι εἶναι—δίκαιον αὐτὸ ἢ οὐδέν; Φαμὲν μέντοι νὴ Δία [a]: Ibid. p. 68 B αἱ πολλὴ ἂν ἀλογία εἴη; Πολλὴ μέντοι νὴ Δία: Ibid. p. 73 D ἀλλὰ του μυρια τοιαῦτ' ἂν εἴη. Μυρία μέντοι νὴ Δι', ἔφη ὁ Σιμμίας: Ibid. p. 82 C οὐ γὰρ ἂν πρέποι, ἔφη, ὦ Σώκρατες, ὁ Κέβης· Οὐ μέντοι μὰ Δι', ἦ δ' ὅς: Id. Phædr. p. 262 D οὐκοῦν δῆλον, ὡς τὸ πάθος τοῦτο δι' ὁμοιοτήτων τινῶν εἰσερρύη; γίγνεται οὖν οὕτω.

g. By μενοῦν (§. 730. b.), introducing something which implies it, and thus assenting to it, (*utique*), *yea rather*, or something which states it more correctly, and thus partially denying it, (*immo*) *nay rather*: Plat. Phædr. p. 230 A B ἆρ' οὐ τόδε ἦν τὸ δένδρον, ἐφ' ὅπερ ἦγες ἡμᾶς;—Τοῦτο μενοῖ αὐτό: Id. Protag. p. 309 C 'Αλλ' ἢ σοφῷ τινι ἡμῖν, ὦ Σώκρατες, ἐντυχὼν πάρει; Socr. Σοφωτάτῳ μὲν οὖν δήπου τῶν γε νῦν, εἴ σοι δοκεῖ σοφώτατος εἶναι Πρωταγόρας [b]: Id. Gorg. p. 466 A τί οὖν φῄς; κολακεία δοκεῖ σοι εἶναι ἡ ῥητορική; —Κολακείας μενοῦν ἔγωγε εἶπον μόριον [c]: often οὖ μενοῦν, *no, truly not*.

h. By οὐ γὰρ οὖν, κομιδῆ μὲν οὖν, *neutiquam*.

i. Sometimes the answer begins with καί, the reply being then a continuation of the subject matter of the question, and implying the truth of the doubt which suggested the question to him who asked it, and whence we must collect whether the answer is affirmative or negative; as, Eur. Ph. 433 ἐνταῦθα Ταλαοῦ παῖς ξυνῆκε θέσφατα; P. Κάδωκεν ἡμῖν δύο δυοῖν νεάνιδας: Καὶ in καὶ τοῦτο, καὶ ταῦτα, *et quidem*, like γέ, does more than affirm the question, while τοῦτο, ταῦτα, alone, only affirm it: Arist. Pac. 374 Π. Οὐκοῦν ἕτερόν γ' ἔτ' ἐκ Λακεδαίμονος μέτει ἀνύσας τι; K. Ταῦτ', ὦ δέσποθ': Plat. Rep. p. 456 E τί δέ; αἱ γυναῖκες τῶν γυναικῶν οὐχ αὗται ἔσονται βέλτισται; Καὶ τοῦτο, ἔφη, πολύ (sc. βέλτισται ἔσονται).

Obs. 1. When there is a rapid interchange of question and answer, the question is often interrupted, so that the answer separates the question into two parts. See Eur. Hec. 1258 sqq. 1270 sqq. When several questions are asked in succession, of course they are answered in the same order. The answer to a compound question belongs to the latter clause; as, Eur. Or. 1533 Τί δρῶμεν; ἀγγέλλωμεν εἰς πόλιν τόδε; ἢ σῖγ' ἔχωμεν;—'Ασφαλέστερον, φίλαι (sc. σῖγα ἔχειν).

Obs. 2. The answer often assumes the form of a question, especially in certain formulas; as, τί δ' οὐ μέλλει; τί δ' οὐκ ἔμελλε; *why should it not=certainly*; and the negative is omitted in this formula, τί μέλλει; ἀλλὰ τί μέλλει; ἀλλὰ τί γὰρ μέλλει; *what will he do, if not?* *quidni?=certainly*: Plat. Hipp. Maj. p. 287 [d]: Id. Hipp. Min. p. 373 D. Σ. δρόμῳ μὲν ἄρα καὶ τῷ θεῖν τάχος μὲν ἀγαθόν, βραδυτὴς δὲ κακόν; Ἱπ. 'Αλλὰ τί μέλλει; So also ἀλλὰ τί οἴει; Id. Rep. p. 332 C and ἀλλὰ τί; *quidni?*

---

a Stallb. ad loc.   b Stallb. ad loc.   c Stallb. ad loc.   d Heindorf. ad loc.

d. Phæd. p. 89 B οὐκ, ἂν γε ἐμοὶ πείθῃ—. ᾽Αλλὰ τί [a]; also ἄληθες; accent thrown back) in ironical replies, *really? who would think it? ἔ ἐανε?* so πώμαλα originally a question, *πῶς μάλα; how then?* in Doric ᴑriginally, then Attic, for οὐδαμῶς: see §. 872. *Obs.* 2.

Remarks on the Interrogative Sentence.

A relative Sentence coalescing with a Question.

§. 881. 1. When the interrog. sentence is composed of an adject. interrogative pronoun, εἶναι, and a substant., and followed by a relative sentence referring to it, as ποῖός ἐστιν ὁ μῦθος, ὃν εἶπες, the verb εἶναι and the relative are omitted, and the verb of the relative sentence becomes the governing verb of the interrog. sentence: Il. π, 440 ποῖον τὸν μῦθον ἔειπες; Il. κ, 82 τίς δ' οὗτος κατὰ νῆας ἀνὰ στρατὸν ἔρχεται οἶος; Il. λ, 612 ἀλλ' ἴθι νῦν—Νέστορ' ἔρειο, ὅντινα τοῦτον ἄγει βεβλημένον ἐκ πολέμοιο: Hdt. VII. 48 δαιμόνιε ἀνδρῶν, κοῖα ταῦτα λέγεις εἶναι δύο μοι πολεμιώτατα; Soph. Aj. 46 ποιαῖσι τόλμαις ταῖσδε καὶ φρένων θράσει; Eur. Hec. 188 τί τόδ' ἀγγέλλεις; Ibid. 501 τίς οὗτος σῶμα τοὐμὸν οὐκ ἐᾷς κεῖσθαι; Plat. Phæd. p. 79 B ποτέρῳ οὖν ὁμοιότερον τῷ εἴδει φαῖμεν ἂν εἶναι—τὸ σῶμα; Id. Gorg. p. 520 extr. ἐπὶ ποτέραν οὖν με παρακαλεῖς τὴν θεραπείαν;

2. We must distinguish from this the case where the article precedes the interrog. pronoun, whereby it is signified that the subject matter of the question is well known, or already spoken of: Plat. Rep. p. 421 extr. Ἕτερα δὴ—τοῖς φύλαξιν εὑρήκαμεν, ἃ παντὶ τρόπῳ φυλακτέον, ὅπως μήποτε αὐτοὺς λήσει εἰς τὴν πόλιν παραδύντα. Τὰ ποῖα ταῦτα; i. e. ποῖά ἐστι ταῦτα, ἃ λέγεις [b]; Arist. Pac. 696 εὐδαιμονεῖ· πάσχει δὲ θαυμαστόν· ᾽ΕΡΜ. τὸ τί; Ibid. 693 οἷά μ' ἐκέλευσεν ἀναπυθέσθαι σου. ΤΡΥΓ. τὰ τί; (referring to οἷα :) Id. Nub. 776 ἄγε δὴ ταχέως τουτὶ ξυνάρπασον. ΣΤΡΕΨ. τὸ τί; Id. Av. 1039 νόμους νέους ἥκω παρ' ὑμᾶς δεῦρο πωλήσων. ΠΕΙ. τὸ τί;

Rhetorical change of a Dependent into a direct Interrog. Sentence.

§. 882. 1. In many writers a dependent sentence introduced by a conjunction assumes the form of an interrog. sentence, the conjunction being still retained. This frequently gives a rhetorical force of expression to the construction: Xen. M. S. I. 4, 14 ὅταν τί ποιήσωσι, νομιεῖς αὐτοὺς σοῦ φροντίζειν; Plat. Gorg. p. 448 C νῦν δ' ἐπειδὴ τίνος τέχνης ἐπιστήμων ἐστί, τίνα ἂν καλοῦντες αὐτὸν ὀρθῶς καλοῖμεν; Soph. Aj. 106 θανεῖν γὰρ αὐτὸν οὔ τι πω θέλω. Min. Πρὶν ἂν τί δράσῃς, ἢ τί κερδάνῃς πλέον; Aj. Πρὶν ἂν—νῶτα φοινιχθεὶς θάνῃ: Demosth. p. 43, 10 πότε ἃ χρὴ πράξετε; ἐπειδὰν τί γένηται; Hence the elliptic expressions, ἵνα τί; ὡς τί; (sc. γένηται,) with what intent? ὅτι τί; (sc. γίγνεται) on what grounds? Plat. Apol. p. 26 D ἵνα τί ταῦτα λέγεις; Eur. Or. 756 ὡς τί δὴ τόδε; Or. ὡς νιν ἱκετεύσω με σῶσαι: Plat. Charmid. p. 161 C ὅτι δὴ τί γε; ἔφη.

2. So the interrog. pronoun τί followed by a negation=οὐδὲν οὔ, *nihil non,* and is inserted in a sentence without any change of the construction:

---

[a] See Heindorf.　　　　[b] Stallb. ad loc.

Demosth. p. 241, 29 ἐλαυνομένων καὶ ὑβριζομένων καὶ τί κακὸν οὐχὶ ἐσχόντων πᾶσα ἡ οἰκουμένη μεστὴ γέγονε προδοτῶν for οὐδὲν κακὸν οὐ πασχ.

Two or more Interrog. Sentences in one.

§. 883. 1. Two or even more interrog. words may be attached to the same verb, so that two or more questions on different points are expressed in one sentence; Soph. Aj. 1164 τίς ἄρα νέατος ἐς πότε λήξει πολυπλάγκτων ἐτέων ἀριθμός [a]; Eur. Hel. 1559 ὦ τλήμονες, πῶς ἐκ τίνος νεὼς ποτε Ἀχαΐδος θραύσαντες ἥκετε σκάφος; Id. Iph. T. 1322 οὐδ᾽ ἔχω, ὅπα πρὸς πότερον εἴπω: Id. Ph. 1295 πότερος ἄρα πότερον αἱμάξει; Plat. Ion. p. 530 A πῶς τί ἠγωνίσω; Plat. Hipp. M. p. 297 extr. πῶς τί ἄρ᾽ ὁ ἀγωνιζοίμεθα [b]: Id. Th. p. 208 E πῶς τί τοῦτο; Id. Soph. p. 261 E: Id. Rep. p. 400 A ποῖα δ᾽ ὁποίου βίου μιμήματα, οὐκ ἔχω λέγειν [c]: Demosth. p. 429, 8 ἐξετάζεσθαι, τίς τίνος αἴτιός ἐστι. So with the relative; as, Soph. Ant. 942 οἷα πρὸς οἵων ἀνδρῶν πάσχω; Often in a construction with a participle: Eur. Alc. 145 ὦ τλήμων, οἵας οἷος ὢν ἁμαρτάνεις: Plat. Symp. p. 195 A οἷος οἵων αἴτιος ὢν τυγχάνει.

2. By a remarkable brevity of expression we find fresh questions inserted between a substantive in an interrog. sentence, and its article, by the answer to which the nature of the subst. is more clearly defined. Plat. Rep. p. 332 C Ὦ Σιμωνίδη, ἡ τίσιν οὖν τί ἀποδιδοῦσα ὀφειλόμενα καὶ προσῆκον τέχνη ἰατρικὴ καλεῖται; *to whom does it give its gifts? what are they?* All these points are answered together in Ἡ σώμασι φάρμακά τε καὶ σιτία καὶ ποτά.

Of the Oratio obliqua, or indirect construction.

§. 884. 1. The words or thoughts of any one, whether of a third person spoken of, or of a person spoken to, or of a person himself speaking, may be looked at by the speaker in two ways: either they are given in the very way and form in which the person expressed them, and in this case, in their relation to the person whose words they are, they are considered as not depending on a mere supposition in the mind of that person, but as a fact which he stated as a fact; and this is called the *oratio recta*; as, I thought " all men are mortal;" he told me, " the peace is concluded:"—or without any verb preceding—all men are mortal.

2. Or they are referred to the mind of the speaker, or some other person, and looked at in the relation in which they stand to the writer or speaker—not as a statement of a fact, but as a supposition which he forms from the mind and knowledge of the person spoken of: or when the writer is speaking of himself, he views it as an act in his own mind, not as a fact out of it; and thus they are made dependent on a verb of perceiving or of com-

---

a Hermann. ad loc. b Heindorf. ad loc. c Stallb. ad loc.

municating something: this is called the *oratio obliqua*; as, "he said the peace was concluded."

There are two sorts of *oratio obliqua*.

1. Where a single clause is stated as depending on what another person said or thought; as, ἔλεγον ὅτι οὗτος ἔλθοι.

2. Where the sentence is composed of a principal and dependent clause or clauses, all of which are referred to what another person says or thinks; as, ἔλεγον ὅτι οὗτος ἔλθοι ὃς ταῦτα ποιήσειε.

Obs. 1. We must not confound with the simple *oratio obliqua* or consider as exceptions to it, those dependent sentences which are introduced by the writer after a verb of saying or thinking, not as part of what was said or thought, but as a quality or accident belonging to something said; as, Demosth. p. 127 ἐφ' οἷς ἤδη χαριοῦνται ταῦτα ἔλεγον—where ἐφ' οἷς ἤδη χαριοῦνται does not represent what they said, " ἐπὶ τούτοις ἤδη χαριούμεθα," but they said, ταῦτα, (and this might be resolved into a clause in the *oratio obliqua*,) of which Demosthenes observes, ἤδη χαριοῦνται: nor with the compound *oratio obliqua*, those which are introduced in the same way after a really dependent clause (with acc. and infin.), as, Plat. Gorg. p. 513 A εἰ δέ σοι οἴει ὁντινοῦν ἀνθρώπων παραδώσειν τέχνην τινὰ τοιαύτην, ἥτις σε ποιήσει μέγα δύνασθαι κ.τ.λ. If the opt. is used in the *oratio obliqua*, of course the opt. will also be generally used in the sentence depending on that opt.; this however, is regulated not by the rules of the *oratio obliqua*, but by the simple use of the opt. in dependent sentences. See §. 802 ff.

3. The statement which in the *oratio recta* stands in the words of the person who made it, is expressed in the *oratio obliqua* by the acc. and infin. (§. 664, 665.), by ὅτι or ὡς and the *verbum finitum* (§. 801.), or by a participle; as, ἐπήγγειλε τοὺς πολεμίους ἀποφυγεῖν— ὅτι οἱ πολέμιοι ἀποφύγοιεν or ἀπέφυγον—τοὺς πολεμίους ἀποφυγόντας. To these must be added the logically dependent sentences introduced by γὰρ, οὖν, μέντοι, &c., which imply a person stating them as proofs or inferences. A wish, command, or desire is expressed in the *oratio obliqua* by the infin. (§. 663. *b*.); as, ἔλεξε τοῖς στρατιώταις ἐπιθέσθαι τοῖς πολεμίοις (*or. recta*, ἐπίθεσθε).

4. A statement which would have been expressed in a dependent sentence in the *oratio recta*, does not change its form in the *oratio obliqua*, except that in the place of the indic. (if this was the mood in the *or. recta*) the conj. and opt. are used.

Obs. 2. An acc. and inf. sometimes depend on a verb of perceiving or communicating which is suppressed, though implied in the context, so that they seem to be independent: Hdt. VII. 220 λέγεται δὲ, ὡς αὐτός σφεας ἀπέπεμψε Λεωνίδης, μὴ ἀπόλωνται κηδόμενος· αὐτῷ δὲ καὶ Σπαρτιητέων τοῖσι παρεοῦσι οὐκ ἔχειν εὐπρεπέως ἐκλιπεῖν τὴν τάξιν. This is very common in Herodotus.

Obs. 3. Parentheses, and especially those which γάρ connects with the context, although they grammatically are independent sentences, yet frequently assume the form of the *oratio obliqua* in the opt., generally when a sentence introduced by ὅτι or ὡς precedes, of which the parenthesis

seems to be a continuation.　This is first found in Hdt. and in Attic prose
more frequently than in poetry : Æsch. Ag. 615 ταῦτ' ἀπάγγειλον πόσει,
ἥκειν ὅπως τάχιστ' ἐράσμιον πόλει· γυναῖκα πιστὴν δ' ἐν δόμοις εὕροι μολών,
οἵαν περ οὖν ἔλειπε : Hdt. VII. 3 ἔλεγε—, ὡς αὐτὸς μὲν γένοιτο Δαρείῳ ἔτι
βασιλεύοντι—, 'Αρταβαζάνης δὲ ἔτι ἰδιώτῃ ἐόντι Δαρείῳ· οὔκων οὔτ' εἰκὸς εἴη
οὔτε δίκαιον, ἄλλον τινὰ τὸ γέρας ἔχειν πρὸ ἑωυτοῦ : Xen. Anab. VII. 3, 13
ἔλεγον πολλοὶ κατὰ ταὐτά, ὅτι παντὸς ἄξια λέγοι Σεύθης· χειμὼν γὰρ εἴη, καὶ
οὔτε οἴκαδε ἀποπλεῖν τῷ βουλομένῳ δυνατὸν εἴη κ. τ. λ. : Id. Hell. III. 2, 23
ἀποκριναμένων δὲ τῶν 'Ηλείων, ὅτι οὐ ποιήσειαν ταῦτα· ἐπιληΐδας γὰρ ἔχοιεν
τὰς πόλεις· φρουρὰν ἔφηναν οἱ ἔφοροι : Plat. Rep. p. 420 C ὥσπερ οὖν ἂν εἰ
ἡμᾶς ἀνδριάντας γράφοντας προσελθών τις ἔψεγε λέγων, ὅτι οὐ τοῖς καλλίστοις
τοῦ ζῴου τὰ κάλλιστα φάρμακα προστίθεμεν — οἱ γὰρ ὀφθαλμοί, κάλλιστον ὄν,
οὐκ ὀστρείῳ ἐναληλιμμένοι εἶεν, ἀλλὰ μέλανι —, μετρίως ἂν ἐδοκοῦμεν πρὸς αὐτὸν
ἀπολογεῖσθαι λέγοντες κ. τ. λ.[a]　So also opt. with ἄν : Ibid. p. 458 extr.
δῆλον δή, ὅτι γάμους τὸ μετὰ τοῦτο ποιήσομεν ἱεροὺς εἰς δύναμιν ὅτι μάλιστ'
εἶεν δ' ἂν ἱεροὶ οἱ ὠφελιμώτατοι.

Use of the Moods in the Oratio Obliqua.

I. *Optative.*

§. 885. 1. Since the *oratio obliqua* represents any statement or judgment as depending on a supposition, of course the two subjunctive
moods, being the proper expressions of supposition, are the proper
forms of the *oratio obliqua.*　But in Greek the conjunctive is never
used in the principal clauses of the *oratio obliqua*, and in the dependent clauses introduced by ὅς ἄν, ὅταν, πρὶν ἄν &c., only when it
would have been used in the *oratio recta.*　So it is not correct to say,
λέγει, ὅτι ὁ ἄνθρωπος θνητὸς ᾖ ; and in φημὶ αὐτὸν, ἐὰν τοῦτο λέξῃ,
ἁμαρτάνειν, the conjunct. λέξῃ is not used on account of the *oratio
obliqua*, but because it would have been used in the *oratio recta*;
as, ἐὰν τοῦτο λέξῃ, ἁμαρτάνει.　When the verb of the principal
clause is in time present to the speaker, the mood of the *oratio
recta* is retained ; as, λέγει, ὅτι ὁ ἄνθρωπος θνητός ἐστιν — φημί, ὅτι
αὐτός, ἐὰν τοῦτο λέξῃ, ἁμαρτάνει : or the accus. and infin. is used ;
as, λέγει, τὸν ἄνθρωπον θνητὸν εἶναι — φημί, αὐτὸν, ἐὰν τοῦτο λέξῃ,
ἁμαρτάνειν.　See construction of ὅτι and ὡς, §. 802. 3.　The reason why the conjunctive is not used in the *oratio obliqua* is, that
the conjunct. expresses something yet to come—while that which
is conceived in one's own mind, or drawn from the mind of another
person, must be, as far as it is only a mental act, already past.

2. But when the verb of the principal clause is in an historic
tense, the opt. is necessarily used in the *oratio obliqua*, and the
opt. is thus used either for the ind. or conjunct.　In the former
case it expresses that the thing spoken of in the indic. as a
reality, is to be regarded only as another person's mode of view-

a Stallb. ad loc.

ing it—another person's assertion. In the latter case it expresses that the thing which the conjunctive spoke of in the *oratio recta*, as a supposition or possibility, is to be considered as only conceived of by another person in the light of a supposed possibility. So ἐὰν τοῦτο λέγῃς, ἁμαρτήσῃ—ἔλεξέ, σε, εἰ τοῦτο λέγοις, ἁμαρτήσεσθαι: Hdt. III. 75 τελευτῶν ἔλεγε, ὅσα ἀγαθὰ Κῦρος Πέρσας πεποιήκοι (*fecisset*): Xen. Ages. I. 10 Τισσαφέρνης μὲν ὤμοσεν Ἀγησιλάῳ, εἰ σπείσαιτο, ἕως ἔλθοιεν, οὓς πέμψειε πρὸς βασιλέα ἀγγέλους, διαπράξεσθαι αὐτῷ ἀφεθῆναι αὐτονόμους τὰς ἐν τῇ Ἀσίᾳ πόλεις Ἑλληνίδας. We must not confuse this construction with those cases where the opt. is used to express *uncertainty*, as opposed to the certainty of the ind., for in these cases the opt. does not arise from the *oratio obliqua*, but would have been used in the *oratio recta*. Cf. §. 802. 3. and §. 888.

Obs. Sometimes the *oratio obliqua* is used in the dependent clauses of an *oratio recta*, when it is to be marked that a statement is made, not as by the speaker himself, but as passing in another person's mind: Hdt. VII. 2 ἐστασίαζον (οἱ παῖδες), ὁ μὲν Ἀρταβαζάνης, κατότι πρεσβύτατός τε εἴη παντὸς τοῦ γόνου, καὶ ὅτι νομιζόμενα εἴη — πρὸς πάντων ἀνθρώπων, τὸν πρεσβύτατον τὴν ἀρχὴν ἔχειν Ξέρξης δὲ, ὡς Ἀτόσσης τε παῖς εἴη —, καὶ ὅτι Κῦρος εἴη ὁ κτησάμενος τοῖσι Πέρσῃσι τὴν ἐλευθερίην: Thuc. II. 21 οἱ Ἀχαρνῆς ἐκάκιζον τὸν Περικλέα, ὅτι στρατηγὸς ὢν οὐκ ἐπεξάγοι, *quod (quia) exercitum non educeret* (*e mente Acharnensium*): Soph. Trach. 903 κρύψασ᾽ ἐμαυτὴν, ἔνθα μή τις εἰσίδοι, *ubi se a nullo visum iri credebat.* (But Id. Aj. 658 κρύψω τόδ᾽ ἔγχος τοὐμόν — γαίας ὀρύξας, ἔνθα μήτις ὄψεται, *oratio recta.*) So Latin, Liv. XL. 18 *in Hispaniâ prorogatum veteribus est imperium cum exercitibus, quos haberent.*

3. If the opt. in the *oratio obliqua* stands for the conjunct. in *oratio recta*, ἄν may be joined to the conjunction by which it is introduced; see §. 844. *Obs.*: Il. η, 387 ἠνώγει Πρίαμος — εἰπεῖν, αἴ κε περ ὔμμι φίλον καὶ ἡδὺ γένοιτο, μῦθον Ἀλεξάνδροιο (*e mente Priami, non referentis*): Il. β, 597 στεῦτο γὰρ εὐχόμενος νικησέμεν, εἴπερ ἂν αὐταὶ Μοῦσαι ἀείδοιεν: Thuc. VIII. 54 καὶ ἐψηφίσαντο πλεύσαντα τὸν Πείσανδρον καὶ δέκα ἄνδρας μετ᾽ αὐτοῦ πράσσειν, ὅπῃ ἂν αὐτοῖς δοκοίη ἄριστα ἕξειν: cf. VIII. 68. Antiphon. p. 722 (59, §. 34. Bekk.) οὗτοι δὲ θάνατον τῷ μηνυτῇ τὴν δορεὰν ἀπέδοσαν, ἀπαγορευόντων τῶν φίλων τῶν ἐμῶν μὴ ἀποκτείνειν τὸν ἄνδρα, πρὶν ἂν ἐγὼ θέλοιμι.

II. *Indicative.*

§. 886. Though the nature of the *oratio obliqua* would seem to require the optative as the proper expression of a supposition, yet it is not always used, and the indic. is used far more frequently; so that objects are brought before the mind not as mere conceptions but as facts, which gives great power of representation to the language. In the use of the indic. we must distinguish two cases:

1. Where the statement, though it depend upon another person's conception, is to be marked as something real, in opposition to a mere supposition or possibility ; the fact being stated in the form which the person originally used when he stated it as a fact : Hdt. VI. 132. below, *b*.

2. Where the *oratio obliqua* assumes the character of *orat. rect.* This frequently happens in stating something which holds an important place in the events detailed in the sentence, which is as it were the essence of it, such as the argument whereby some person was influenced (thus after verbs of persuading), the especial reason, ground, end, aim, essence of the mental determination, reflection, &c.—the terms or conditions on which any thing is granted, which give a character to the whole action ; or some remarkable declaration, to draw attention to the importance of which in the order of thought, it is stated, as nearly as possible, in the form in which the person originally stated it : inasmuch as this clause is logically the principal clause (on which frequently the other depends), it is not in form made dependent on it, while its grammatical subordinate relation is preserved, so as not to be wholly lost, by retaining the conjunction by which it is introduced.

3. Hence we often find a curious mixture of the *oratio obliqua* and *recta*. The infin. and acc. follows the verb in the *oratio obliqua*, and then follows a dependent clause in which the verb stands in the *oratio recta*, marking the most important words of the sentence by giving them in the mood in which they would originally have been uttered ; as, Hdt. I. 136 ἐκέλευε τῆς ἑαυτοῦ χώρης οἰκεῖν ὅκου βούλονται (originally ὅκου βούλεσθε).

a. Substant. sentences (see §. 802.) : Hdt. III. 61 τοῦτον τὸν ἄνδρα ἀναγνώσας (*persuadere*) ὁ Μάγος Πατιζείθης, ὥς οἱ αὐτὸς διαπρήξει (argument whereby he persuaded), εἷσε ἄγων ἐς τὸν βασιλήϊον θρόνον : Ibid. 84 οἱ δὲ λοιποὶ τῶν ἑπτὰ ἐβουλεύοντο, ὡς βασιλέα δικαιότατα στήσονται (end of the deliberation) : Id.VII. 8, 1 τοῦτο ἐφρόντιζον, ὅκως μὴ λείψομαι τῶν προτερῶν γενομένων ἐν τιμῇ τῇδε (*ne inferior essem*), μηδὲ ἐλάσσω προσκτήσομαι δύναμιν Πέρσῃσι (end of the thought) : Xen. Cyr. II. 2, 1 ἀεὶ μὲν οὖν ἐπεμελεῖτο ὁ Κῦρος, ὁπότε συσκηναῖεν, ὅπως εὐχαριστότατοι —λόγοι ἐμβληθήσονται (object or essence of the care).

b. Adject. sentences : Hdt. VII. 54 Ξέρξης — εὔχετο πρὸς τὸν ἥλιον, μηδεμίην οἱ συντυχίην τοιαύτην γενέσθαι, ἥ μιν παύσει καταστρέψασθαι τὴν Εὐρώπην πρότερον ἢ ἐπὶ τέρμασι τοῖσι ἐκείνης γένηται

the clause beginning with ἡ μιν παύσει expressing the especial aim
)f the prayer): Id. VI. 132 (Μιλτιάδης) αἰτήσας νέας ἑβδομήκοντα,
:αὶ στρατιήν τε καὶ χρήματα τοὺς Ἀθηναίους, οὐ φράσας σφι, ἐπ'
)ν ἐπιστρατεύεται (he is *really* marching) χώρην, ἀλλὰ φὰς
ιὑτοὺς καταπλουτιεῖν, ἥν οἱ ἕπωνται· (§. 887.) ἐπὶ γὰρ χώρην
·οιαύτην δή τινα ἄξειν, ὅθεν χρυσὸν εὐπετέως ἄφθονον οἴσονται·
(will certainly gain) λέγων δὲ τοιαῦτα αἴτεε τὰς νέας: Xen. Hell.
[I. 3, 2 ἔδοξε τῷ δήμῳ τριάκοντα ἑλέσθαι, οἳ τοὺς πατρίους νόμους
:υγγράψουσι, καθ' οὓς πολιτεύσουσι (essence and especial aim of the decree).

c. Adverb. sentences: Xen. Anab. III. 5, 13 ὅμοιοι ἦσαν θαυμάζοντες, ὅποι ποτὲ τρέψοιτο οἱ Ἕλληνες (essence of the θαῦμα)
καὶ τί ἐν νῷ ἔχοιεν: Ibid. I. 3, 14 εἷς δὲ δὴ εἶπε — στρατηγοὺς
μὲν ἑλέσθαι ἄλλους ὡς τάχιστα, εἰ μὴ βούλεται (condition or
terms) Κλέαρχος ἀπάγειν — ἐλθόντας δὲ Κῦρον αἰτεῖν πλοῖα, ὡς ἀπο-
πλέοιεν· ἐὰν δὲ μὴ διδῷ ταῦτα (§. 887.), ἡγεμόνα αἰτεῖν Κῦρον,
ὅστις [ὡς] διὰ φιλίας τῆς χώρας ἀπάξει (especial point of the
request) — πέμψαι δὲ καὶ προκαταληψομένους τὰ ἄκρα, ὅπως μὴ
φθάσουσιν (especial aim) ὁ Κῦρος μήτε οἱ Κίλικες καταλαβόντες,
ὧν πολλοὺς καὶ πολλὰ χρήματα ἔχομεν ἡρπακότες (argument on
which the request was grounded). So also when the conjunctive
would have been the form of any part of the original statement, it
is used in the same way and for the same purposes as the ind.:
Plat. Legg. p. 683 εἰ γοῦν — τις ἡμῖν ὑπόσχοιτο θεὸς ὡς, ἐὰν ἐπιχει-
ρήσωμεν,—οὐ χείρους ἀκουσόμεθα. So in Latin, *Jugurtham maxime
vivum, sin id parum procedat, necatum sibi traderet.* — (See
below, §. 887.)

d. Indirect interrog. sentences.—The indic. is generally used in
these sentences, attention being drawn to the question by stating it
in the form in which it was originally stated. The indic. of past tenses
very often followed the same tenses in principal sentences: Od. ρ,
120 εἴρετο δ' αὐτίκ' ἔπειτα βοὴν ἀγαθὸς Μενέλαος, ὅττευ χρηΐζων
ἱκόμην Λακεδαίμονα δῖαν: Hdt. III. 78 εἴρετο, ὅ τι οὐ χρᾶται
τῇ χερί: Isocr. Paneg. p. 56 D τὰς στάσεις ἐποιοῦντο πρὸς ἀλλήλους οὐχ ὁπότεροι τῶν λοιπῶν ἄρξουσιν, ἀλλ' ὁπότεροι
φθήσονται τὴν πόλιν ἀγαθόν τι ποιήσαντες: Thuc. II. 4 οἱ Πλα-
ταιῆς ἐβουλεύοντο, εἴτε κατακαύσουσιν, ὥσπερ ἔχουσιν,
ἐμπρήσαντες τὸ οἴκημα, εἴτε τι ἄλλο χρήσονται: Xen. Cyr. IV.
2, 3 ἐννοηθέντες δὲ, οἷά τε πάσχουσιν ὑπὸ τῶν Ἀσσυρίων, καὶ
ὅτι νῦν τεθναίη μὲν ὁ ἄρχων αὐτῶν, ἔδοξεν αὐτοῖς — ἀποστῆναι: Plat.
Apol. p. 21 B πολὺν μὲν χρόνον ἠπόρουν, τί ποτε λέγει, for ὅ τι
λέγοι.

III. *Conjunctive.*

§. 887. Analogously to the use of the ind. of hĭstoric tenses in dependent clauses after an historic tense, so after a past verb of perceiving or communicating, followed by the *oratio obliqua*, we find a dependent clause in the conjunctive, to mark the point on which the rest of the sentence turns—that being the mood proper to the expression at the time when it was used, as of a future event, and the parties being introduced as speaking or perceiving, as they originally spoke or perceived; hence part of the sentence seems to be in the *oratio obliqua* and part in the *oratio recta*: Hdt. I. 29 ὁρκίοισι μεγάλοισι κατείχοντο Ἀθηναῖοι, δέκα ἔτεα χρήσεσθαι νόμοισι, τοὺς ἂν σφι Σόλων θῆται : (the oath was δέκα ἔτεα χρησόμεθα, the proper form thereupon being τοὺς ἄν, &c.:) Thuc. II. 13 (ὁ Περικλῆς) προηγόρευε τοῖς Ἀθηναίοις, ὅτι—τοὺς ἀγροὺς τοὺς ἑαυτοῦ καὶ τὰς οἰκίας, ἢν ἄρα μὴ δῃώσωσιν οἱ πολέμιοι—ἀφίησιν αὐτὰ δημόσια εἶναι : Xen. Cyr. IV. 5, 36 τοὺς ἱππέας ἐκέλευσε φυλάττειν τοὺς ἀγαγόντας, ἕως ἄν τις σημάνῃ : Id. Hell. II. 1, 24 Λύσανδρος δὲ τὰς ταχίστας τῶν νεῶν ἐκέλευσεν ἕπεσθαι τοῖς Ἀθηναίοις· ἐπειδὰν δὲ ἐκβῶσι, κατιδόντας ὅ τι ποιοῦσιν, ἀποπλεῖν : Id. Anab. II. 3, 6 ἔλεγον δὲ οἱ ἄγγελοι, ὅτι εἰκότα δοκοῖεν λέγειν βασιλεῖ, καὶ ἥκοιεν ἡγεμόνας ἔχοντες, οἳ αὐτούς, ἐὰν σπονδαὶ γένωνται, ἄξουσιν, ἔνθεν ἕξουσι τὰ ἐπιτήδεια : Plat. Apol. init. ἔλεγον, ὡς χρῆν ὑμᾶς εὐλαβεῖσθαι, μὴ ὑπ᾽ ἐμοῦ ἐξαπατηθῆτε.

Interchange of Conjunctive, Optative, and Indicative.

§. 888. The conj. and ind. are sometimes found in the *oratio obliqua* to express reality and certainty, as opposed to a mere supposition and possibility expressed by the opt. in another part of the sentence : Hdt. VIII. 70 ἀρρώδεον, ὅτι αὐτοὶ μὲν, ἐν Σαλαμῖνι κατήμενοι, ὑπὲρ γῆς τῆς Ἀθηναίων ναυμαχέειν μέλλοιεν, νικηθέντες δὲ ἐν νήσῳ ἀπολαμφθέντες πολιορκήσονται : Xen. Anab. III. 5, 19 ὅμοιοι ἦσαν θαυμάζοντες, ὅποι ποτὲ τρέψονται οἱ Ἕλληνες καὶ τί ἐν νῷ ἔχοιεν : Id. Hell. V. 2, 38 διδάσκων, ὅτι οἱ Ὀλύνθιοι κατεστραμμένοι τὴν μείζω δύναμιν Μακεδονίας εἶεν καὶ οὐκ ἀνήσουσι τὴν ἐλάττω.

IV. *Accusative with Infinitive, instead of Verbum finitum.*

§. 889. In Greek any dependent clause in an *oratio obliqua* may stand in the accus. and infin. depending on a verb of saying, &c. expressed or implied, instead of the *verbum finitum*; in Latin this

is restricted to such clauses of the *oratio obliqua*, as are introduced
by relative pronouns or relative conjunctions, and are in reality
the principal clause.

a. Adject. sentences: Hdt. VI. 117 ἄνδρα οἱ δοκέειν ὁπλίτην
ἀντιστῆναι μέγαν, τοῦ (for οὗ) τὸ γένειον τὴν ἀσπίδα πᾶσαν
σκιάζειν: Thuc. I. 91 (ἔφασαν) ὅσα αὖ μετ' ἐκείνων βουλεύεσθαι,
οὐδενὸς ὕστεροι γνώμῃ φανῆναι: i. e. *de quibus rebus* c o n s u l t a v i s-
s e n t (not *de q. r. se consultavisse*). Cf. Corn. Nep. Them. VII.
*illorum urbem ut propugnaculum oppositum esse barbaris, apud q u a m
jam bis c l a s s e s r e g i a s f e c i s s e naufragium,* (i. e. *apud hanc
enim etc.* as properly a principal clause.)

b. Adverb. sentences.—*a.* Local, temporal, causal, comparative:
Plat. Rep. p. 408 C οἱ τραγῳδοποιοὶ—᾿Απόλλωνος μέν φασιν ᾿Ασκλη-
πιὸν εἶναι, ὑπὸ δὲ χρυσοῦ πεισθῆναι πλούσιον ἄνδρα θανάσιμον ἤδη
ὄντα ἰάσασθαι, ὅ θ ε ν δὴ καὶ κ ε ρ α υ ν ω θ ῆ ν α ι αὐτόν: Latin,
u n d e *fulmine e u m p e r c u s s u m esse,* i. e. *et i n d e* (as logically
a principal sentence): Hdt. III. 26 λέγεται —, ἐ π ε ι δ ὴ ἐκ τῆς
᾿Οάσιος ταύτης ἰ έ ν α ι—, ἐπιπνεῦσαι νότον μέγαν: Ibid. 35 ὡ ς δ ὲ
(*quum*) ἐν τῇ καρδίῃ ε ὑ ρ ε θ ῆ ν α ι ἐνεόντα τὸν δϊστὸν, εἰπεῖν πρὸς
τὸν πατέρα κ. τ. λ.: Id. VI. 84 Σκύθας γὰρ (sc. φασί) τοὺς νομάδας,
ἐ π ε ί τ ε σφι Δαρεῖον ἐ σ β α λ ε ῖ ν ἐς τὴν χώρην, μετὰ ταῦτα μεμο-
νέναι μιν τίσασθαι, i. e. *postquam invasisset:* Id. VII. 148 μετὰ δὲ,
ὡ ς ἐ λ θ ε ῖ ν τ ο ὺ ς ἀ γ γ έ λ ο υ ς ἐς δὴ τὸ ῎Αργος, ἐπελθεῖν ἐπὶ τὸ
βουλευτήριον: Ibid. 150 extr. ἐ π ε ὶ δ έ σ φ ε α ς π α ρ α λ α μ β ά ν ε ι ν
τοὺς ῞Ελληνας, οὕτω δὴ, ἐπισταμένους ὅτι οὐ μεταδώσουσι τῆς ἀρχῆς
Λακεδαιμόνιοι, μεταιτέειν κ. τ. λ. (the finite verb being used in the
sentence depending on ἐπισταμένους, and the infin. in the sentence
depending on the preceding verb λέγεται): Hdt. II. 121. §. 2 ὡ ς δ ὲ
τ υ χ ε ῖ ν τ ὸ ν β α σ ι λ ῆ α ἀνοίξαντα τὸ οἴκημα, θωῦμάσαι κ. τ. λ. ὡ ς
δ ὲ ἀεὶ ἐλάσσω φ α ί ν ε σ θ α ι τὰ χρήματα—, ποιῆσαί μιν τάδε. This
construction is very common in Herodotus. Thuc. II. 102 λέγεται δὲ
καὶ ᾿Αλκμαίωνι τῷ ᾿Αμφιάρεω, ὅτε δὴ ἀ λ ᾶ σ θ α ι α ὐ τ ὸ ν μετὰ τὸν
φόνον τῆς μητρὸς, τὸν ᾿Απόλλω ταύτην τὴν γῆν χρῆσαι οἰκεῖν: Xen.
Cyr. V. 2, 4 ἀπήγγελλον τῷ Κύρῳ, ὅτι τοσαῦτα εἴη ἔνδον ἀγαθά, ὅσα
ἐπ' ἀνθρώπων γενεάν, ὡ ς σφίσι δ ο κ ε ῖ ν (i. e. *ut sibi videretur*),
μὴ ἂν ἐπιλιπεῖν τοὺς ἔνδον ὄντας: Plat. Rep. p. 614 B ἔφη δὲ,
ἐ π ε ι δ ὴ οὗ ἐ κ β ῆ ν α ι τὴν ψυχὴν, πορεύεσθαι μετὰ πολλῶν καὶ
ἀφικνεῖσθαι σφᾶς εἰς τόπον τινὰ δαιμόνιον, ἐν ᾧ—δ ύ' ε ἶ ν α ι χάσματε
κ. τ. λ.: Id. Rep. p. 359 D ἰδεῖν—νεκρόν, ὡ ς φ α ί ν ε σ θ α ι, μείζω
ἢ κατ' ἄνθρωπον.

β. Conditional: Hdt. III. 108 λέγουσι δὲ καὶ τόδε ᾿Αράβιοι, ὡς
πᾶσα ἂν γῆ ἐπίμπλατο τῶν ὀφίων τούτων, ε ἰ μ ὴ γ ί ν ε σ θ α ι κατ'

αὐτοὺς οἶόν τι κατὰ ἐχῖδνας ἠπιστάμην γίνεσθαι : Thuc. IV. 98 ἁ
'Αθηναῖοι ἔφασαν, εἰ μὲν ἐπιπλέον δυνηθῆναι τῆς ἐκείνων κρατῆσαι, τοῦτ' ἂν ἔχειν, i. e. *si ampliorem illorum agri partem in suam
potestatem redigere possent, se eam retenturos.*

c. Mixed sentences : Hdt. VI. 137 ἐπεί τε γὰρ ἰδεῖν τοὺς
'Αθηναίους τὴν χώρην, τήν σφισι ὑπὸ τὸν 'Υμησσὸν ἐοῦσαν ἔδοσαι
οἰκῆσαι μισθὸν τοῦ τείχεος τοῦ περὶ τὴν ἀκρόπολίν κοτε ἐληλαμένον
ταύτην ὡς ἰδεῖν τοὺς 'Αθηναίους ἐξεργασμένην εὖ, τὴν (i. e. ἣν)
πρότερον εἶναι κακήν τε καὶ τοῦ μηδενὸς ἀξίην, λαβεῖν φθόνον κ. τ. λ.:
Id. III. 105 εἶναι δὲ (λέγεται) ταχύτητα οὐδενὶ ἑτέρῳ ὁμοίαν, οὔτε
ὥστε, εἰ μὴ προλαμβάνειν τῆς ὁδοῦ τοὺς 'Ινδούς, ἐν ᾧ τοὺς
μύρμηκας συλλέγεσθαι, οὐδένα ἂν σφεων ἀποσώζεσθαι.

Change from the Oratio Obliqua to the Recta, and from the Recta to the Obliqua.—Change of person.

§. 890. It being the genius of the Greek language to bring
things before the eyes of the reader as much as possible, the *oratio
obliqua* is sometimes, and especially in Attic prose, changed suddenly to the *oratio recta ;* the person spoken of in the *oratio obliqua*
as saying something, being suddenly introduced in the *oratio recta*
as speaking of himself in the first person, or to some one else in the
second person : and on the other hand, the *oratio recta* is with
equal facility changed into the *oratio obliqua.* See ind. with *oratio
obliqua* above §. 886 : Lysias p. 897 καλέσας αὐτοὺς εἶπε Διογείτων,
ὅτι καταλίποι αὐτοῖς ὁ πατὴρ εἴκοσι μνᾶς ἀργυρίου καὶ τριάκοντα στατῆ-
ρας. Ἐγὼ οὖν πολλὰ τῶν ἐμαυτοῦ δεδαπάνηκα εἰς τὴν
ὑμετέραν τροπήν κ. τ. λ. : Xen. Cyr. I. 4 extr. ἐνταῦθα δὴ τὸν Κῦρον
γελάσαι τε ἐκ τῶν πρόσθεν δακρύων καὶ εἰπεῖν αὐτῷ ἀπιόντα θαρρεῖν,
ὅτι παρέσται αὖθις ὀλίγον χρόνον· ὥστε ὁρᾶν σοι ἐξέσται, κᾶν
βούλῃ, ἀσκαρδαμυκτεί : Id. Hell. I. 1, 27 ἑλέσθαι δὲ ἐκέλευον ἄρχοντας —, μεμνημένους ὅσας τε ναυμαχίας — νενικήκατε καὶ ναῦς
εἰλήφατε — ἡμῶν ἡγουμένων : Ibid. II. 1, 25 ('Αλκιβιάδης)
οὐκ ἐν καλῷ ἔφη αὐτοὺς ὁρμεῖν, ἀλλὰ μεθορμίσαι ἐς Σηστὸν παρῄνει—·
οὗ ὄντες ναυμαχήσετε, ἔφη, ὅταν βούλησθε : Plat. Protag.
p. 302 C ἐρωτᾷ οὖν Ἑρμῆς Δία, τίνα οὖν τρόπον δοίη δίκην καὶ αἰδῶ
ἀνθρώποις. Πότερον ὡς αἱ τέχναι νενέμηνται, οὕτω καὶ ταύτας νείμω;
On the other hand : Xen. Anab. VII. 1, 39 ἐλθὼν δὲ Κλέανδρος
Μάλα μόλις, ἔφη, διαπραξάμενος ἥκω· λέγειν γὰρ 'Αναξίβιον, ὅτι οὐκ
ἐπιτήδειον εἴη κ. τ. λ.

CHAP. V.

Especial peculiarities in the Construction of Words and Sentences.

I. *Ellipse.*

§. 891. 1. Ellipse is the suppression of a sentence or part of a sentence, which is logically of minor importance, but which grammatically is required to express a notion or thought, and must be supplied. The use of ellipse arises from an endeavour to mark the unity and connectedness of the parts of a simple or compound thought by the form of the sentence, and to give brevity and power to the expression.

2. The notion of the suppressed word must of course be general and indefinite, and implied in the word which would define it were it not suppressed, as οἱ θνητοί (sc. ἄνθρωποι), ἡ αὔριον (sc. ἡμέρα), or supplied from the context or common use, as εἰς διδασκάλου ἰέναι. So, if a sentence is suppressed, it must be of a general nature and easily supplied.

Obs. 1. The principle of ellipse has been often confounded with brachylogy; and, it is needless to say, it has been much abused by its application to cases where it does not apply. The legitimate use of ellipse and brachylogy seems to be mostly confined to two cases: —1. Where the context, or some word in it, suggests to the mind the suppressed notion. —2. (More rare) where the every day usages of speech had created and familiarised a shortened form of expression. Within these limitations it is a true principle of the Greek language — beyond them it creates confusion and conceals other grammatical principles.

a. *Ellipse of a simple Sentence.*

3. On the ellipse of the subject see §. 373, and of εἶναι see §. 376; on the ellipse of a substantive defined by an attributive, adj., part., or gen. (as οἱ θνητοί, τὸ καλόν, οἱ ἔχοντες, εἰς ᾅδου ἀφικέσθαι, ὁ Σωφρονίσκου) see §. 436.

Obs. 2. In many phrases the subst. suppressed after the adj. is implied in the verb. So that this is brachylogy rather than ellipse, see §. 823. *d.*: Lucian. D. mar. 2 ὡς βαθὺν ἐκοιμήθης (sc. ὕπνον): Eur. Herc. F. 178 τὸν καλλίνικον ἐκώμασε (sc. κῶμον): Id. El. 804 ὅπως πευστηρίαν θοινασόμεσθα (sc. θοίνην): Plat. Lach. p. 184 D τὴν ἐναντίαν γὰρ Λάχης Νικίᾳ ἔθετο (sc. ψῆφον, according to the usual form θέσθαι ψῆφον).

4. The object of a verb sometimes stands without that verb, especially in prayers, curses, &c.; the verb can generally be readily supplied from common use: ἐς κόρακας, ἐς φθόρον, εἰς ὄλεθρον (sc. ἄπιθι or ἔρρε)—πρὸς σὲ γονάτων (sc. ἱκετεύω).

Obs. 3. The notion which is required to define another, as an attributive defines a substantive, the object the verb, &c. can never be supplied. Some verbs however have a pregnant force, so that the notion defined implies the notion defining it; as φυλάσσειν in Homer = φυλάσσειν νύκτα, to watch through the night—to keep the night watch.

b. Ellipse in a compound Sentence.

5. *a.* A substantive to which an attributive relative sentence refers may be suppressed; as, εἴη, ὅστις ἀπαγγείλειε τάχιστα Πηλείδῃ: Thuc. II. 11 ἕπεσθε, ὅποι ἄν τις ἡγῆται i. e. εἰς τοῦτον τὸν τόπον, ὅποι (§. 836. 1.).

b. A whole sentence may be suppressed which a following sentence defines; so in the combinations, οὐχ ὅτι, μὴ ὅτι—, ἀλλά §. 762. 2.; so also, οὐχ ὅτι in the sense of *quamquam, although*; (ἀλλά does not follow this phrase as an antithesis :) Plat. Protag. p. 336 D Σωκράτει γε ἐγὼ ἐγγυῶμαι μὴ ἐπιλήσεσθαι, οὐχ ὅτι παίζει καί φησιν ἐπιλήσμων εἶναι. Also in final or interrog. clauses introduced by ὅπως μή and μή, and in hypothetical clauses, either where a wish is expressed, as εἴθε τοῦτο γένοιτο (§. 856. *Obs.* 2.), or where two hypothetical clauses are opposed, whereof the principal one is generally suppressed. See §. 860. *c.*

6. Another case of ellipse is, where a conditional protasis is omitted, but signified by attaching to the verb of the apodosis the conditional particle ἄν, which suggests to the mind the suppressed sentence; as, ἡδέως ἂν ἀκούσαιμι, ἡδέως ἂν ἤκουσα (§. 860. 2.).

II. *Brevity of Expression or Brachylogy.*

§. 892. 1. There is a wide distinction to be drawn between ellipse and brachylogy. In ellipse some element of the notion or thought is actually suppressed; in brachylogy it only seems to be suppressed, but in reality is in some way expressed or involved either in the whole sentence or some member thereof. The use of ellipse, as it depends partly on perception and common usage, and partly on the nature of the language, may be reduced to certain rules; but brachylogy depends solely on the pleasure of the speaker, so that he may use it whenever he thinks that his brevity of expression is sufficiently cleared up by the context or other circumstances.

2. The readiness of apprehension which is so especially the

haracteristic of the Greek mind, naturally gave greater scope to
his figure in the Greek than in any other language; and it is a
'ant of this rapidity and readiness which makes the Greek language
o difficult to master, and yet so profitable a mental exercise to
he moderns. Many instances of it have already occurred in ex-
ιlaining the different forms of construction, as οἱ ἐκ τῆς ἀγορᾶς
:νθρωποι ἀπέφυγον, and some will be found below. We can only
reat of some of those instances of brachylogy which from their
'requent use may be laid down as principles of interpretation for
;he language.

The notion of a Substantive or Adjective involved in the context or part thereof.

§. 893. *a.* The subject of one sentence is supplied from the object
of the last—Attic prose, except orators, and sometimes poetry:
Hes. Opp. 513 καί τε διὰ ῥινοῦ βοὸς ἔρχεται, οὐδέ μιν ἴσχει
(sc. ῥινός): Thuc. VIII. 44 ἐξεφόβησαν μὲν τοὺς πολλοὺς, οὐκ
εἰδότας τὰ πρασσόμενα, καὶ ἔφευγον (οἱ πολλοί).

b. The substantive of the latter of two coordinate sentences is
generally supplied from the former, in which it already stands;
the article which would be joined to the substantive in the second
clause standing alone; as, Plat. Epist. p. 354 E μετρία ἡ θεῷ δουλεία, ἄμετρος δὲ ἡ τοῖς ἀνθρώποις.

c. A subject is supplied from the predicate, or a predicate
from the subject, when the same word would be both subject and
predicate; as, Hdt. VIII. 80 ἴσθι γὰρ ἐξ ἐμεῖο (sc. ποιεύμενα) τὰ
ποιεύμενα ὑπὸ Μήδων: Ibid. 142 τούτων ἁπάντων αἰτίους γενέσθαι (sc. αἰτίους) τῆς δουλοσύνης τοῖς Ἕλλησι Ἀθηναίους.

d. A substantive cognate to some word in the sentence, is supplied
from that word (παρώνυμα). So Homer, (θεοί) δωτῆρες ἐάων
sc. δόσεων. So also Il. ω, 528 δώρων οἷα δίδωσι κακῶν, ἕτερος δὲ
ἐάων: Il. υ, 99 καὶ δ' ἄλλως (sc. βληθέν) τοῦ γ' ἰθὺ βέλος πέτετ' οὐδ'
ἀπολήγει. So cognate notion of verb (see acc. §. 548.): δεινόν,
δεινὰ βοᾶν sc. βόημα, βοήματα.—τρεῖς πλήσσεσθαι sc. πληγάς: Soph.
El. 1075 Ἠλέκτρα τὸν ἀεὶ πατρὸς (sc. στόνον) δειλαία στενάχουσα:
Eur. Ph. 325 δακρυόεσσαν (sc. ἰάν) ἱεῖσα. Also Hdt. VIII. 114
ὡς εἰπεῖν sc. ἔπος, and thence in old Attic (tragedy, ὡς εἰπεῖν ἔπος,
and so commonly Plato and Demosth.).

e. The affirmative εἷς, ἕκαστος, is supplied from οὐδείς; as, Plat.
Symp. p. 192 E ταῦτα ἀκούσας οὐδ' ἂν εἷς ἐξαρνηθείη—, ἀλλ' ἀτεχνῶς οἴοιτ' ἂν ἀκηκοέναι κ. τ. λ.ᵃ: Id. Rep. p. 366 D. Demosth.

ᵃ Stallb. ad loc.

Midian. §. 18 οὐκοῦν δεινὸν — μηδένα τολμῆσαι πώποτε μηδ' ὡς οἱ νόμοι διδόασιν ἅψασθαι, ἀλλ' οὕτως εὐλαβῶς—διακεῖσθαι.

Where a Pronoun is supplied from the context or part thereof.

§. 894. *a.* Where a person has been already mentioned, the pronoun as the object of the verb is supplied therefrom, except where especial emphasis is required : Xen. Hell. III. 4, 3 ἐπαγγειλαμένου τοῦ Ἀγησιλάου τὴν στρατείαν, διδόασιν οἱ Λακεδαιμόνιοι (sc. αὐτῷ ταῦτα).

δ. So also the pronoun is supplied to a genitive absolute from the foregoing sentence : Hdt. I. 3 τοὺς δὲ (Asiatics), προισχομένων (ἐκείνων Greeks) ταῦτα, προφέρειν σφι Μηδείης τὴν ἁρπαγὴν ὡς οὐ δόντες αὐτοὶ δίκας, οὐδὲ ἐκδόντες ἀπαιτεόντων (σφῶν Asiatics).

c. Very frequently the reflexive pronoun ἑαυτοῦ is supplied from the pronoun αὐτός : Il. *a*, 355 ἑλὼν γὰρ ἔχει γέρας, αὐτὸς (sc. ἑαυτῷ) ἀπούρας : Soph. Phil. 691 ἵν' αὐτὸς (sc. ἑαυτῷ) ἦν πρόσουρος. Even in antithesis : Il. ψ, 647 χαίρει δέ μοι ἦτορ, ὥς μευ ἀεὶ μέμνησαι ἐνηέος for ἐνηὴς ἐνηέος : Od. θ, 167 οὕτως οὐ πάντεσσι θεοὶ (sc. πάντα) χαρίεντα διδοῦσιν ἀνδράσιν, οὔτε φυήν, οὔτ' ἂρ φρένας, οὔτ' ἀγορητύν.

Where a verbal notion is supplied from a preceding verb, or verbal notion.

§. 895. 1. *a.* After δῆλον ὅτι, οἶδ' ὅτι, εὖ οἶδ' ὅτι, ἴσθ' ὅτι, the verb is very often supplied from the predicate or preceding sentence ; as Plat. Gorg. p. 475 C. Socr. Οὐκοῦν κακῷ ὑπερβάλλον τὸ ἀδικεῖν κάκιον ἂν εἴη τοῦ ἀδικεῖσθαι : Po. Δῆλον δὴ ὅτι sc. κάκιον ἂν εἴη. Hence the affirm. adverb, δηλονότι, *certainly, clearly.*

b. One verbal form is supplied from another in the context. So pass. from active : Thuc. VI. 79 καὶ τοῖς γε Ἀθηναίοις βοηθεῖν, ὅπως ὑπ' ἄλλων (sc. ἀδικῶνται) καὶ μὴ—τοὺς ἄλλους ἀδικῶσιν : Soph. Œ. C. 1102 τῷ τεκόντι πᾶν (sc. τεχθέν) φίλον. : Æsch. Eum. 140 ἔγειρε καὶ σὺ τήνδ', ἐγὼ δέ σε. So the participle, from the verbum finitum or infin. : Thuc. II. 11 τὴν τῶν πέλας δῃοῦν ἢ τὴν ἑαυτῶν ὁρᾶν sc. δῃουμένην : Æsch. Ag. 364 καὶ τὸν μὲν ἥκειν (sc. πῆμα φέροντα). τὸν δ' ἐπεισφέρειν κακοῦ κάκιον ἄλλο πῆμα, λάσκοντας δόμοις : Od. ο, 152 χαίρετον, ὦ κούρω, καὶ Νέστορι ποιμένι λαῶν εἰπεῖν sc. χαίρειν. This frequently happens when, after οἶμαι δὲ καί, an infin. should follow : Plat. Apol. p. 25 extr. ταῦτα ἐγώ σοι οὐ πείθομαι, ὦ Μέλητε, οἶμαι δὲ οὐδὲ ἄλλον ἀνθρώπων οὐδένα sc. πείσεσθαί σοι [a] : Id. Rep. p. 608 ξύμφημί σοι —, οἶμαι δὲ καὶ ἄλλον ὁντινοῦν

a Stallb. ad loc.

(sc. ξυμφήσειν).—Very commonly, especially in Attic, an infin. of a preceding verb is supplied after μέλλω, in its future sense; as, Eur. Hipp. 441 τοῖς ἐρῶσι—ὅσοι τε μέλλουσ᾽ (ἐρᾶν sc.).: Thuc. III. 55 οὔτε ἐπάθετε οὔτε ἐμελλήσατε (παθεῖν): Isocr. p. 213 B τὰς μὲν ἐπόρθουν, τὰς δὲ ἔμελλον (πορθεῖν), ταῖς δὲ ἠπείλουν τῶν πόλεων (πορθεῖν). In dialogue, especially Plato, τί δ᾽ (πῶς γὰρ) οὐ μέλλει; *How should it not?* From a participle in the principal clause is supplied the finite verb of the dependent: Soph. El. 1433 νῦν (βᾶτε) τὰ πρὶν εὖ θέμενοι τάδ᾽ ὡς πάλιν sc. εὖ θῆσθε.

2. The effect of the verb being thus used only once is to give an appearance of unity to the two clauses.—Hence it is very usual to omit the verb in dependent clauses introduced by ὅσπερ, ὥσπερ: Eur. Med. 1162 φίλους νομίζουσ᾽ οὔσπερ ἂν πόσις σέθεν, sc. νομίζῃ: Plat. Legg. p. 710 D πάντα σχεδὸν ἀπείργασται τῷ θεῷ, ὅπερ (sc. ἀπεργάζεται) ὅταν βουληθῇ διαφερόντως εὖ πρᾶξαί τινα πόλιν: Od. λ, 411 ἑταῖρον νωλεμέως κτείνοντο σύες ὡς ἀργιόδοντες, οἵ ῥα τ᾽ ἐν ἀφνειοῦ ἀνδρὸς μέγα δυναμένοιο ἢ γάμῳ ἢ ἐράνῳ ἢ εἰλαπίνῃ, sc. κτείνονται, where the former verb is supplied from the latter. This is also very usual in those hypothetical sentences, which only express that what is in the principal clause belongs especially to the person spoken of in the conditional clause. The protasis consists of εἰ, or εἴπερ τις, or ἄλλος τις, or εἴπερ που, εἴπερ ποτέ &c. Compare the full expression in Demosth. p. 701, 7 ἐγὼ δ᾽, εἴπερ τινὶ τοῦτο καὶ ἄλλῳ προσηκόντως εἴρηται, νομίζω κἀμοὶ νῦν ἁρμόττειν εἰπεῖν, with the shortened one, Hdt. IX. 27 ἡμῖν ἐστι πολλά τε καὶ εὖ ἔχοντα, εἰ τέοισι καὶ ἄλλοισι Ἑλλήνων. Εἴπερ alone: Plat. Rep. p. 497 E οὐ τὸ μὴ βούλεσθαι, ἀλλ᾽, εἴπερ (sc. τὶ διακωλύσει), τὸ μὴ δύνασθαι διακωλύσει[a]: so ὡς οὔτις, ὡς οὐδεὶς ἄλλος. In the same sense: Plat. Apol. p. 28 E τότε μὲν, οὗ ἐκεῖνοι ἔταττον, ἔμενον, ὥσπερ καὶ ἄλλος τις.

3. There are some instances in which this brachylogy produces some difficulty in the construction, and which therefore require to be specially observed. The verb is placed in the dependent and not in the principal clause, and agrees with the subject thereof, and therefore must be supplied to the principal clause in the number and person required by its subject. This also commonly occurs in dependent clauses introduced by ὥσπερ, ὥσπερ ἂν εἰ, ὅσπερ, *et sim.* and the effect of it is to mark strongly the unity of the two clauses: Il. ι, 46 εἰ δὲ καὶ αὐτοὶ (sc. φεύξονται), φευγόντων σὺν νηυσί: Thuc. I. 82 ἀνεπίφθονον, ὅσοι(,) ὥσπερ καὶ ἡμεῖς

---

[a] Stallb. ad loc.

ὑπ' Ἀθηναίων ἐπιβουλευόμεθα, μὴ Ἕλληνας μόνον, ἀλλὰ καὶ
βαρβάρους προσλαβόντας διασωθῆναι (for ὅσοι ἐπιβουλεύονται, ὥσπερ
καὶ ἡμεῖς ἐπιβουλευόμεθα) : Id. III. 67 ἦν οἱ ἡγεμόνες, ὥστε
νῦν ὑμεῖς κεφαλαιώσαντες πρὸς τοὺς ξύμπαντας διαγνώμας ποιήσεσθε.
ἧσσόν τις ἐπ' ἀδίκοις ἔργοις λόγους καλοὺς ζητήσει : Xen. Cyr. IV. 1, 3
αὐτὸς οἶδα οἷος ἦν· τὰ μὲν γὰρ ἄλλα, ὅσαπερ, οἶμαι, καὶ πάντες ὑμεῖς
ἐποιεῖτε (ἐποίει). So often in Latin comparative sentences, *si
cariora semper omnia quam decus atque pudicitia fuit.* It occurs
less frequently in other dependent sentences ; as, Eur. Or. 1043
σὺ νῦν μ', ἀδελφέ, (sc. κτεῖνε) μή τις Ἀργείων κτάνῃ.

c. A verb of a general meaning is supplied from a following verb
of special meaning, as every particular verb implies the general verbal
notion of action, or state : so ποιεῖν, ἐργάζεσθαι, γίγνεσθαι, εἶναι, συμβαίνειν, &c. thus τί ἄλλο ἤ,—οὐδὲν ἄλλο ἤ—ἄλλο τι ἤ for τί
ἄλλο ποιεῖ or ἔστιν or such like, ἢ ὅτι (cf. Lucian. Dial. Deor. V. 5
λυπεῖς, ὦ Ἥρα, σεαυτήν, οὐδὲν ἄλλο, κἀμοὶ ἐπιτείνεις τὸν ἔρωτα
ζηλοτυποῦσα) : Thuc. III. 39 τί ἄλλο οὗτοι, ἢ ἐπεβούλευσαν ; IV.
14 οἱ Λακεδαιμόνιοι—ἄλλο οὐδὲν ἢ ἐκ γῆς ἐναυμάχουν : Xen.
M. S. II. 3, 17 τί γὰρ ἄλλο ἢ κινδυνεύσεις ; = οὐδὲν ἄλλο (sc.
ποιεῖς), ἢ ὅτι κινδ : Id. Cyr. I. 4, 24 μόνος ἐκεῖνος οὐδὲν ἄλλο
(sc. ἐποίει) ἢ τοὺς πεπτωκότας περιελαύνων ἐθεᾶτο : Plat. Euth. p.
277 D καὶ νῦν τούτω οὐδὲν ἄλλο ἢ χορεύετον περὶ σέ : Id. Phæd.
p. 63 D τί δέ, ὦ Σώκρατες, ἔφη ὁ Κρίτων, ἄλλο γε ἢ πάλαι μοι λέγει
ὁ μέλλων σοι δώσειν τὸ φάρμακον[a]. (In full : Plat. Rep. p. 424 D
οὐδὲ γὰρ ἐργάζεται ἄλλο γε (sc. ἡ παρανομία), ἢ κατὰ σμικρὸν
εἰσοικισαμένη ἠρέμα ὑπορρεῖ πρὸς τὰ ἔθνη.) From frequent usage
the original construction of the phrase was lost, and it was applied,
where grammatically it was inapplicable, as a mere adverb : Thuc.
VII. 75 οὐδὲν γὰρ ἄλλο ἢ πόλει ἐκπεπολιορκημένῃ ἐῴκεσαν ὑποφευ-
γούσῃ. So often in Latin, *nihil aliud, amplius quam* is
used as an adverb : Liv. XXII. 60 *quid aliud quam admo-
nendi essetis :* XXXVII. 21 *classis ad insulam se recepit, nihil
aliud quam depopulato hostium agro :* Suet. Calig. 44 *nihil
amplius quam Adminio — in deditionem recepto magnificas
Romam litteras misit.* The same may be said of the interrog. forms,
ἄλλο τι ἤ, or ἄλλο τι, *nonne ?* where, after the phrase became a
mere interrog. form, the ἤ was dropped. See §. 875. e.

d. An important use of brachylogy is where several objects
depend on one verb, which strictly can be applied to only one of
them ; but the notion of the verb is such as admits of a more

---

[a] Heindorf ad loc.

general, or more particular application. This sort of brachylogy is
called *Zeugma :* Il. γ, 326 ἧχι ἑκάστῳ ἵπποι ἀερσίποδες καὶ ποίκιλα
τεύχε' ἔκειτο (containing the particular notion of "lying," as the
general notion of being in store, ready): Hdt. IV. 106 ἐσθῆτα δὲ
φορέουσι τῇ Σκυθικῇ ὁμοίην, γλῶσσαν δὲ ἰδίην : Pind. Ol. I. 88 (B)
ἔλεν δ' Οἰνομάου βίαν πάρθενόν τε σύνευνον, *vicit Œnomaum, obtinuit
virginem* [a] : Id. Nem. X. 25 ἐκράτησε δὲ καί ποθ' Ἕλληνα στρατὸν,
τύχᾳ τε μολὼν καὶ τὸν Ἰσθμοῖ καὶ τὸν Νεμέᾳ στέφανον : Soph. Trach.
356. cf. 364 ὡς τῆς κόρης ταύτης ἕκατι κεῖνος Εὔρυτόν θ' ἕλοι, τήν θ'
ὑψίπυργον Οἰχαλίαν.

Obs. 1. It is one of the great properties of the Greek language, that the
Greek mind from its quickness of apprehension, and exactness in the application of notions, seems to have been able thus to deduce a general notion
implied in some particular verb, and then to apply to it a new substant. in
a particular sense suitable to the new object, and implied in that general
notion. So Æsch. Choeph. 360 βασιλεὺς γὰρ ἦς, ὄφρ' ἔζης, μόριμον λάχος πιμπλάντων χεροῖν πεισίβροτόν τε βάκτρον. In μόριμον λάχος χεροῖν πιμπλάντων
is implied the general notion of *governing* — this implies the notion of
wielding the sceptre, in which sense it is carried on and applied to βάκτρον.

e. So a verb of perception or communication is supplied from a
foregoing verb of cognate meaning : Xen. Hell. II. 2, 17 ἀπήγγειλεν, ὅτι αὐτὸν Λύσανδρος κελεύει ἐς Λακεδαίμονα ἰέναι· οὐ γὰρ
(sc. ἔλεγεν) εἶναι κύριος ὧν ἐρωτῷτο ὑπ' αὐτοῦ, ἀλλὰ τοὺς Ἐφόρους
See §. 884. *Obs.* 1.

f. A simple verb is supplied from the compound verb, in as much
as this latter contains the notion of the former : Plat. Gorg. p.
493 C ἀλλὰ πρότερον πείθω τί σε καὶ μετατίθεσαι, εὐδαιμονεστέ-
ρους εἶναι τοὺς κοσμίους τῶν ἀκολάστων; i. e. *persuadeone tibi mutatá-
que sententiâ putas, feliciores esse temperantes libidinosis?* Thuc. I.
44 οἱ Ἀθηναῖοι μετέγνωσαν Κερκυραίοις ξυμμαχίαν μὴ ποιήσασθαι
for μετέγνωσαν καὶ ἔγνωσαν : Xen. Cyr. I. 1, 3 ἐκ τούτου δὴ ἠναγκα-
ζόμεθα μετανοεῖν (i. e. μετανοεῖν καὶ νοεῖν), μὴ οὔτε τῶν ἀδυνάτων
οὔτε τῶν χαλεπῶν ἔργων ᾖ τὸ ἀνθρώπων ἄρχειν. So also with other
verbs which imply a change from one opinion to another, so that
the new opinion is supplied from relinquishing the old one : Plat.
Lys. p. 222 B οὐ ῥάδιον ἀποβαλεῖν τὸν πρόσθεν λόγον, ὡς οὐ τὸ ὅμοιον
τῷ ὁμοίῳ κατὰ τὴν ὁμοιότητα ἄχρηστον, i. e. *non est facile priorem reji-
cere rationem, ut non putemus, simile simili, quatenus simile est, inutile
esse ;* hence also οὐ which at first seems not wanted — ἀποβαλεῖν
τὸν λόγον = *rejectâ priore ratione sententiam ita mutare, ut putemus
cett.*

Obs. 2. In the two former examples the second clause may depend on the

---

[a] Dissen ad loc.

compound verb as representing an accus., which is the proper expression of that *to* which a change takes place.

g. A compound verb in one clause is supplied from the same verb in the former, the preposition with which it is compounded being placed alone in the second clause. See §. 643. *Obs.* 1.

h. An affirmative verb is supplied from a negative; this is most commonly the case in an antithesis introduced by an adversative conjunction: Il. ε, 819 οὔ μ' εἴας μακαρέσσι θεοῖς ἀντικρὺ μάχεσθα τοῖς ἄλλοις· ἀτὰρ, εἴ κε Διὸς θυγάτηρ 'Αφροδίτη ἔλθησ' εἰς πόλεμον, τήν γ' οὐτάμεν ὀξέϊ χαλκῷ (sc. ἐκέλευες, in εἴας) : Soph. O. R. 236 τὸν ἀνδρ' ἀπαυδῶ τοῦτον—μήτ' εἰσδέχεσθαι, μήτε προσφωνεῖν τινα. ὠθεῖν δ' ἀπ' οἴκων πάντας : Id. El. 71 καὶ μή μ' ἄτιμον τῆσδ' ἀποστείλητε γῆς, ἀλλ' ἀρχέπλουτον καὶ καταστάτην δόμων (i. e. στέλλετε = ποιεῖτε) : Hdt. VII. 104 ὁ νόμος—ἀνώγει τὠυτὸ ἀεί, οὐκ ἐᾷ φεύγειν οὐδὲν πλῆθος ἀνθρώπων ἐκ μάχης, ἀλλὰ μένοντας ἐν τῇ τάξ ἐπικρατέειν ἢ ἀπόλλυσθαι : Id. IX. 2 οὐδὲ ἔων ἰέναι ἑκαστέρω, ἀλλ' αὐτοῦ ἱζόμενον ποιέειν : Plat. Apol. p. 36 B ἀμελήσας, ὡς οἱ πολλοί (sc. ἐπιμελοῦνται[a]) : compare Latin, Cic. N. D. I. 7, 17 *tu autem* n o l o *existimes, me adjutorem huic venisse,* s e d *auditorem.*

Where a sentence is supplied either wholly or partially.

§. 896. In an antithesis one clause frequently requires to be supplied from the other : Il. χ, 265 ὡς οὐκ ἔστ' ἐμὲ καὶ σὲ φιλήμεναι, for ἐμὲ σὲ καὶ σὲ ἐμέ : Hes. Opp. 182 οὐδὲ πατὴρ παίδεσσιν ὁμοίιος. οὐδέ τι παῖδες (sc. πατρί), οὐδὲ ξεῖνοι ξεινοδόκῳ καὶ ἑταῖρος ἑταίρῳ : Soph. Œ. T. 489 τί γὰρ ἢ Λαβδακίδαις (sc. πρὸς τὸν Πόλυβον) ἢ τῷ Πολύβῳ (sc. πρὸς τοὺς Λαβδακίδας) νεῖκος ἔκειτο ; Eur. Or. 742 οὐκ ἐκεῖνος (sc. ἐκείνην), ἀλλ' ἐκείνη κεῖνον ἐνθάδ' ἤγαγεν : Thuc. I. 73 οἱ γὰρ παρὰ δικασταῖς οὔτε ἡμῶν (sc. πρὸς τούτους), οὔτε τούτων (sc. πρὸς ἡμᾶς) οἱ λόγοι ἂν γίγνοιντο : Demosth. p. 30, 17 ἐπράξαμεν ἡμεῖς (sc. πρὸς ἐκείνους) καὶ ἐκεῖνοι πρὸς ἡμᾶς εἰρήνην. Sometimes the sentence is wholly omitted, when it is implied necessarily in the notion which it expresses, as Od. κ, 35 νυκτὶ δ' ὁμῶς πλέει. which implies καὶ ἤματι.

Obs. Very often where in two coordinate sentences the same predicate would be used in the sing. to each of them, the predicate is used once in the plural, the two being considered as making up one plural notion; as, ὁ Σωκράτης καὶ ὁ Πλάτων ἦσαν σοφοί, for ὁ Σ. ἦν σοφός, καὶ ὁ Π. ἦν σοφός.

---

[a] Stallb. ad loc.

Aposiopesis.

§. 897. This figure of rhetoric consists in the sentence being suddenly broken off, at the will of the speaker. In animated and excited passages, the verb is often suppressed after μή; as in tragedy for instance, μὴ δῆτα, and μή alone: Soph. Ant. 577 μὴ τριβὰς ἔτι, ἀλλά νιν κομίζετ᾽ εἴσω: Eur. Ion 1225 μὴ ταῦτα: Id. Med. 769 μή μοι σύ sc. ταῦτα εἴπῃς: Arist. Vesp. 1179 μή μοι γε μύθους. Μ ὴ σ ύ γ ε is very common as an earnest dissuasive: Soph. Œ. C. 1441 Pol. εἰ χρή, θανοῦμαι: Antig. μὴ σύ γ᾽ (sc. ταῦτ᾽ εἴπῃς), ἀλλ᾽ ἐμοὶ πιθοῦ. So in dissuasive wishes μ ὴ γ ά ρ, *absit, ut:* Demosth. p. 295, 8 τίς οὐχὶ κατέπτυσεν ἂν σοῦ; μὴ γὰρ τῆς πόλεώς γε, μηδ᾽ ἐμοῦ sc. καταπτύσειεν: Plat. Prot. p. 318 B ἀλλὰ μὴ οὕτως: Id. Rep. p. 381 E μ ὴ γ ά ρ, ἔφη (sc. τοιαῦτα λεγόντων): Eur. Troad. 212 μ ὴ γ ὰ ρ δ ὴ δίναν γ᾽ Εὐρώτα sc. ἔλθοιμεν: so μ ή τ ο ι γ ε Xen. Cyr. II. 3, 24. Demosth. p. 45, 19 μή μοι μυρίους μηδὲ δισμυρίους ξένους μηδὲ τὰς ἐπιστολιμαίους ταύτας δυνάμεις (sc. ψηφίσησθε), ἀλλ᾽ ἢ τῆς πόλεως ἔσται sc. ἡ δύναμις. Sometimes the apodosis is wholly suppressed when the speaker is excited. See above (§. 860. 3. *b.*).

Contraction of Sentences.

§. 898. There are some other forms, besides those mentioned under their respective heads, whereby the close connection of two sentences, or two clauses of the same sentence, is represented in language, which remain yet to be noticed.

1. When an infin. or part. stands in the same sentence with some other verbum finitum, the subst. which properly depends on the infin. or part. is frequently made to depend on the verbum finitum, so that it is in the case required thereby.

a. Participle: Soph. El. 47 ἄγγελλε δ᾽ ὅρκῳ προστιθείς, for ἄγγ. προστιθεὶς ὅρκον: Id. Ant. 23 Ἐ τ ε ο κ λ έ α μὲν, ὡς λέγουσι, σὺν δίκῃ χ ρ η σ θ ε ὶ ς δικαίᾳ καὶ νόμῳ κατὰ χθονὸς ἔ κ ρ υ ψ ε: Id. Phil. 54 λόγοισιν ἐκκλέψας λέγων: Thuc. III. 59 (δεόμεθα ὑμῶν) φείσασθαι δὲ καὶ ἐπικλασθῆναι τῇ γνώμῃ ο ἴ κ τ ῳ σ ώ φ ρ ο ν ι λαβόντας (where another reading is οἶκτον σώφρονα): Xen. Cyr. VII. 1, 40 οὗτοι δὲ ἐπειδὴ ἠπόρουντο, κ ύ κ λ ῳ πάντοθεν ποιησάμενοι, ὥστε ὁρᾶσθαι τὰ ὅπλα, ὑπὸ ταῖς ἀσπίσιν ἐκάθηντο, for κύκλον ποιησάμενοι ἐκάθηντο: Ibid. I. 6, 33 ὅπως σ ὺ ν τ ο ι ο ύ τ ῳ ἔ θ ε ι ἐθισθέντες πρᾳότεροι πολῖται γένοιντᾳ: Ibid. II. 3, 17 τοῖς δ᾽ ἑτέροις εἶπεν, ὅτι βάλλειν δεήσοι ἀναιρουμένους ταῖς βώλοις: cf. VIII. 3, 27.

β. Infinitive: Il. σ, 585 οἱ (κύνες) δ᾽ ἤτοι δ α κ έ ε ι ν μὲν ἀπετρα-
πῶντο λ ε ό ν τ ω ν: Il. η, 409 οὐ γάρ τις φειδὼ ν ε κ ύ ω ν κατατεθνηώ-
των γίγνετ᾽ — πυρὸς μ ε ι λ ι σ σ έ μ ε ν ὦκα (for νέκυας μειλίσσεις):
Hom. Hymn. Cer. 281 sq. οὐδέ τι π α ι δ ὸ ς μνήσατο τηλυγέτοιο ἀπὸ
δαπέδου ἀ ν ε λ έ σ θ α ι: Soph. El. 1269 (1277) μή μ᾽ ἀποστερήσῃς
τῶν σῶν προσώπων ἡ δ ο ν ὰ ν μ ε θ έ σ θ α ι (ἀποστερεῖν τινά τι and
μεθέσθαι τινός), but see §. 362. 5.: Id. Phil. 62 οὐκ ἠξίωσαν τ ὸ ν
Ἀ χ ι λ λ ε ί ω ν ὅ π λ ω ν ἐλθόντι δ ο ῦ ν α ι: Id. Antig. 490 κείσηι—
ἐπαιτιῶμαι τοῦδε β ο υ λ ε ῦ σ α ι τ ά φ ο υ, for βουλεῦσαι τόνδε τάφον:
Eur. Hipp. 1391 λ ό γ χ α ς ἔραμαι διαμοιρᾶσαι, for ἔρ. διαμ. με
λόγχῃ: Id. Hell. 683 τίνων χρήζουσα π ρ ο σ θ ε ῖ ν α ι π ό ν ω ν, for
τίνας πόνους προσθ. χρήζ.: Thuc. I. 138 τοῦ Ἑ λ λ η ν ι κ ο ῦ ἐλπίδα
ἣν ὑπετίθει αὐτῷ δ ο υ λ ώ σ ε ι ν: Id. III. 6 τῆς μὲν θ α λ ά σ σ η ς
εἷργον μὴ χ ρ ῆ σ θ α ι τοὺς Μιτυληναίους: Id. V. 15 ἐπιθυμία τ ῶ ν
ἀ ν δ ρ ῶ ν τῶν ἐκ τῆς νήσου κ ο μ ί σ α σ θ α ι: Xen. Anab. V. 4. 9 τί
ἡ μ ῶ ν δεήσεσθε χ ρ ή σ α σ θ α ι; Plat. Crit. p. 52 B οὐδ᾽ ἐπιθυμία
σε ἄλλης π ό λ ε ω ς, οὐδ᾽ ἄλλων νόμων ἔλαβεν — ε ἰ δ έ ν α ι: Id.
Legg. p. 626 D δοκεῖς γάρ μοι τῆς θεοῦ ἐ π ω ν υ μ ί α ς ἄξιος εἶναι
μᾶλλον ἐ π ο ν ο μ ά ζ ε σ θ α ι: Id. Rep. p. 459 B σφόδρα ἡμῖν δεῖ ἄκρων
ε ἶ ν α ι τ ῶ ν ἀ ρ χ ό ν τ ω ν: Ibid. p. 437 B τὸ ἐφίεσθαί τινος λαβεῖν.
So also with the article: Demosth. p. 19, 4 τ ο ύ τ ω ν οὐχὶ νῦν ὁρῶ
τὸν καιρὸν τοῦ λ έ γ ε ι ν, for οὐχ ὁρῶ τὸν καιρὸν τοῦ ταῦτα λέγειν.
Compare the Latin, *h o r u m non ideo opportunitatem d i c e n d i.*

Obs. 1. This construction is sometimes explained by supplying a pronoun,
such as ἄγγελλε ὅρκῳ προστιθεὶς αὐτόν: but it is evident that this is absurd,
and moreover keeps out of view that unity of the sentence, which was intended to be marked by this form.

2. Analogous to this there is a sort of attraction which takes
place in almost all dependent clauses, the subject of the dependent being transferred to the principal clause, in which it stands as
the object. In this construction the unity of the clauses is visibly
signified; and the subject of the principal clause, which is the
leading notion of the whole sentence, is brought prominently forward. In Latin this idiom is found, but far less frequently than
in Greek: *nosti M a r c e l l u m, q u a m t a r d u s s i t,* for *quam
tardus sit Marcellus:* Il. β, 409 ᾔδει γὰρ κατὰ θυμὸν ἀ δ ε λ φ ε ὸ ν
ὡς ἐπονεῖτο: Hdt. III. 68 οὗτος—πρῶτος ὑ π ό π τ ε υ σ ε τ ὸ ν Μάγον ὡς οὐκ εἴη ὁ Κύρου Σμέρδις: Id. III. 80 εἴδετε μὲν γὰρ τ ὴ ν
Καμβύσεω ὕ β ρ ι ν ἐπ᾽ ὅσον ἐπεξῆλθε: Thuc. VI. 76 τοὺς μέλλοντας
ἀπ᾽ αὐτῶν λόγους (δείσαντες) μὴ ὑμᾶς πείσωσιν: Id. III. 51 τούς
τε Πελοποννησίους (ἐφυλάττετο ὁ Νικίας) ὅπως μὴ ποιῶνται ἔκπλους
αὐτόθεν: Id. I. 72 τὴν σφετέραν πόλιν ἐβούλοντο σημαίνειν ὅση εἴη
δύναμιν: Eur. Med. 37 δέδοικα δ᾽ αὐτὴν μή τι βουλεύσῃ: Ibid. 39

δειμαίνω τέ νιν (αὐτὴν) μὴ θηκτὸν ὥσῃ φάσγανον δι' ἥπατος : cf. 252.
283. 248 (ἄνδρες) λέγουσι δ' ἡμᾶς (γυναῖκας) ὡς ἀκίνδυνον βίον ζῶμεν
κατ' οἴκους : Plat. Rep. p. 327 princ. κατέβην χθὲς εἰς Πειραιᾶ —
προσευξόμενός τε τῇ θεῷ καὶ ἅμα τὴν ἑορτὴν βουλόμενος θεάσασθαι
τίνα τρόπον ποιήσουσιν : Ibid. p. 372 E σκοποῦντες γὰρ καὶ τοιαύτην
τάχ' ἂν κατίδοιμεν τήν τε δικαιοσύνην καὶ ἀδικίαν ὅπῃ ποτὲ ταῖς πόλεσιν
ἐμφύονται : Ibid. p. 472 C ἐζητοῦμεν αὐτό τε δικαιοσύνην οἷόν ἐστι,
καὶ ἄνδρα τὸν τελέως δίκαιον : Id. Theæt. p. 146 E γνῶναι ἐπιστήμην
αὐτὸ ὅ τι ποτ' ἐστιν : Demosth. p. 831, 57 οὐσίαν, ἣν καὶ ὑμῶν οἱ
πολλοὶ συνῄδεσαν ὅτι κατελείφθη, — αἰσχρῶς διήρπασεν : Ibid. p. 847,
10 βούλομαι δὲ ταύτην (ἀπόκρισιν) ὡς ἐστιν ἀληθὴς ἐπιδεῖξαι :
Ibid. p. 838 in. δείξατε γὰρ ταύτην τὴν οὐσίαν τίς ἦν, καὶ ποῦ παρέδοτέ
μοι καὶ τίνος ἐναντίον : Ibid. p. 126, 61 τὸν Εὐφραῖον οἷα ἔπαθε
μεμνημένος. With Gen. : Hdt. VI. 48 ἀπεπειρᾶτο τῶν Ἑλλήνων ὅ τι
ἐν νῷ ἔχοιεν : Xen. Cyr. V. 3, 40 οἱ ἄρχοντες αὐτῶν ἐπιμελεῖ-
σθων ὅπως συσκευασμένοι ὦσι πάντα : Id. M. S. I. 4, 13 τίνος γὰρ
ἄλλου ζῴον ψυχὴ πρῶτα μὲν θεῶν — ἤσθηται ὅτι εἰσί; Plat. Rep.
p. 407 A Φωκυλίδου — οὐκ ἀκούεις πῶς φησι, δεῖν, ὅταν τῷ ἤδη βίος
ᾖ, ἀρετὴν ἀσκεῖν. We rarely find such constructions as, Arist. Av.
1269 δεινόν γε τὸν κήρυκα, τὸν παρὰ τοὺς βρότους οἰχόμενον,
εἰ μηδέποτε νοστήσει πάλιν : so Senec. de Benef. IV. 32 *Deos
verisimile est ut alios indulgentius tractent.* And yet more
remarkable is Xen. Cyr. II. 1, 5 τοὺς μέντοι Ἕλληνας, τοὺς
ἐν τῇ Ἀσίᾳ οἰκοῦντας, οὐδέν πω σαφὲς λέγεται εἰ ἕπονται. So
in a subst. sentence : Arrian. I. 27 ἠγγέλθη — τοὺς Ἀσπενδίους
ὅτι οὐδὲν τῶν συγκειμένων πρᾶξαι ἐθέλοιεν.

Obs. 2. Here also belongs a remarkable construction of δεῖ : Soph.
Aj. 553 ὅταν δ' ἵκῃ πρὸς τοῦτο, δεῖ σ' ὅπως πατρὸς δείξεις ἐν ἐχθροῖς,
οἷος ἐξ οἵου 'τράφης : Id. Phil. 54 τὴν Φιλοκτήτου σε δεῖ ψυχὴν ὅπως
λόγοισιν ἐκκλέψεις λέγων : Cratin. ap. Athen. IX. p. 373 δεῖ σ' ὅπως
Ἀλεκτρυόνος μηδὲν διοίσεις τοὺς τρόπους. And perhaps analogously,
Thuc. II. 7 Λακεδαιμονίοις — τοῖς τὰ ἐκείνων ἑλομένοις — ναῦς ἐπετάχθησαν ποιεῖσθαι, for νῆες ἐπετάχθησαν ποιεῖσθαι.

Obs. 3. And not only the subject, but sometimes also the predicative
nominative of the dependent clause, stands in the principal clause in accus.:
Æsch. Sept. 17 ἡ γὰρ νέους ἕρποντας εὐμενεῖ πέδῳ, ἅπαντα πανδοκοῦσα παιδείας
ὅπλον, ἐθρέψατ' οἰκιστῆρας ἀσπιδηφόρους πιστοὺς ὅπως γένοισθε πρὸς
χρέος τόδε, i. e. ἐθρέψατο, ὅπως γένοισθε πιστοὶ οἰκιστῆρες ἀσπιδηφόροι. So
often Plautus : Pœn. II. v. 5 *nec potui tamen propitiam Venerem
facere uti esset mihi.*

3. So also when the clause depends on a verbal notion expressed by a substantive in the principal clause, the subject
(or object) thereof is attracted into the principal clause, and
placed in the genitive as the object of the subst.: Thuc. I. 61

ἦλθε δὲ καὶ τοῖς Ἀθηναίοις εὐθὺς ἡ ἀγγελία τῶν πόλεων ἐπ: ἀφεστᾶσι: Ibid. 97 ἅμα δὲ καὶ τῆς ἀρχῆς ἀπόδειξιν ἔχει τῆς τῶν Ἀθηναίων ἐν οἵῳ τρόπῳ κατέστη: Id. II. 42 οὔτε (τις) πενίας ἐλπίδι ὡς κἂν ἔτι διαφυγὼν αὐτὴν πλουτήσειεν, ἀναβολὴν τοῦ δεινοῦ ἐποιήσατο, i. e. ἐλπίδι, ὡς κἂν διαφυγὼν τὴν πενίαν πλουτήσειεν—: πενίας ἐλπίδι, *hope in relation to his poverty.* The dependent clause expresses more accurately the exact object of the hope, πενία being the object of the dependent clause ; hence αὐτήν is used.

Obs. 4. There are some remarkable passages where an attributive, which should stand with its subst. in the dependent clause, is transferred to the principal clause, while the subst. remains where it was : Eur. H. F. 842 ὡς—γνῷ μὲν τὸν Ἥρας οἷός ἐστ' αὐτῷ χόλος: Stob. II. p. 197. ed. Grot. (353. 22. Gesn.) ὁρᾷς τὸν εὐτράπεζον ὡς ἡδὺς βίος; in Soph. Trach. 97 ἅλιον αἰτῶ τοῦτο, καρῦξαι τὸν Ἀλκμήνας πόθι μοι πόθι παῖς ναίει, τοῦτο only prepares the way for the whole dependent clause. For an analogous idiom, see §. 824. 1.

4. Where two clauses are of such a nature that either of them might stand as the principal clause, and the other made to depend upon it, as ἤκουσα ὅτι μέλλει ἥξειν, or μέλλει ἥξειν ὡς ἤκουσα, this relation and the close connection between them is signified by their both assuming the form of a dependent clause ; that which logically speaking is the principal clause standing as a subst. sentence with ὅτι or ὡς, *that,* or in the acc. with infin. This is most usual in Hdt., rarely in Attic prose, and very seldom if ever in the orators: Xen. Anab. VI. 4, 18 ὡς γὰρ ἐγὼ—ἤκουσά τινος, ὅτι Κλέανδρος ἐκ Βυζαντίου ἁρμοστὴς μέλλει ἥξειν: Hdt. I. 65 ὡς δ' αὐτοὶ Λακεδαιμόνιοι λέγουσι Λυκοῦργον ἐπιτροπεύσαντα — ἐκ Κρήτης ἀγαγέσθαι ταῦτα: Id. I. 191 ὑπὸ μεγάθεος τῆς πόλιος, ὡς λέγεται—τῶν περὶ τὰ ἔσχατα τῆς πόλιος ἑαλωκότων τοὺς τὸ μέσον οἰκέοντας τῶν Βαβυλωνίων οὐ μανθάνειν ἑαλωκότας: Id. III. 14 ὡς δὲ λέγεται ὑπ' Αἰγυπτίων, δακρύειν μὲν Κροῖσον: Id. IV. 5 ὡς δὲ Σκύθαι λέγουσι, νεώτατον ἁπάντων ἐθνέων εἶναι τὸ σφέτερον: Ibid. 95 ὡς δὲ ἐγὼ πυνθάνομαι τῶν τὸν Ἑλλήσποντον οἰκεόντων Ἑλλήνων καὶ Πόντον, τὸν Ζάλμοξιν τοῦτον, ἐόντα ἄνθρωπον, δουλεῦσαι ἐν Σάμῳ: Plat. Rep. p. 347 A οὗ δὴ ἕνεκα, ὡς ἔοικε, μισθὸν δεῖν ὑπάρχειν τοῖς μέλλουσιν ἐθελήσειν ἄρχειν[a]: Id. Phil. p. 20 C τόδε γε μήν, ὡς οἶμαι, περὶ αὑτοῦ ἀναγκαιότατον εἶναι λέγειν: Id. Soph. p. 263 D παντάπασιν, ὡς ἔοικεν, ἡ τοιαύτη σύνθεσις— γίγνεσθαι λόγος ψευδής. So also in poetry ; as, Æsch. Pers. 570 τυτθὸν ἐκφυγεῖν ἄνακτ' αὐτόν, ὡς ἀκούομεν: Ibid. 185 τούτων στάσιν τιν', ὡς ἐγὼ 'δόκουν ὁρᾶν, τεύχειν ἐν ἀλλήλῃσι: Soph. Trach.

---

[a] Stallb. ad loc.

1228 ἀνὴρ ὅδ' ὡς ἔοικεν οὐ νέμειν ἐμοὶ φθίνοντι μοῖραν: Id.
Antig. 736 ὅδ' ὡς ἔοικε τῇ γυναικὶ ξυμμαχεῖν[k]. So also, but
not nearly so frequent, in Latin: Cicer. de Offic. I. 7, 22 *atque ut
p l a c e t Stoicis, quæ in terrâ gignuntur, ad usum hominis o m n i a
c r e a r i, h o m i n e s autem hominum causâ e s s e g e n e r a t o s:* Id.
N. D. I. 37, 94 *isti autem quemadmodum asseverant, ex corpusculis—
concurrentibus temere atque casu m u n d u m e s s e p e r f e c t u m* (for
mundus est perfectus).

Pleonasm.

§. 899. Pleonasm is the using a word the notion whereof has
occurred already in some other part of the sentence; as, πάλιν αὖθις.
But it must not be forgotten that by this repetition of the notion
it is generally defined, explained, or enforced. There is, properly
speaking, no such thing as pleonasm either in a logical or grammatical point of view; and many expressions only seem pleonastic
from our own forms of language. In poetry of course, as using
forcible and striking expressions, this supposed pleonasm most
frequently occurs.

The most remarkable cases of seeming pleonasm are,

1. The attaching to a word another word of the same root to
heighten the notion thereof.—*a.* A neuter verb with its cognate
notion, (which being very generally omitted seems, when expressed,
to be pleonastic,) in the acc.; as, μάχην μάχεσθαι, πόλεμον πολεμεῖν
(§. 548. *a.*), and in instrumental dat.: Plat. Symp. p. 195 B φεύγων φυγῇ, so φύσει πεφυκώς Xen. and others (§. 548. *Obs.* 6.).—*b.*
A verb with its participle; as, φεύγων ἔφυγε (§. 715. 3.).—*c.* An
adjective with its abstract subst. or instrumental dat.; as, Soph.
Œ. R. 1469 ἴθ' ὦναξ, ἴθ' ὦ γονῇ γενναῖε: Plat. Soph. p. 231
B ἡ γένει γενναία σοφιστική[b]: μεγέθει μέγας, πλήθει πολλοί Hdt.
and Plat.—*d.* An adject. or adv. with an adverb (mostly poet.),
Homer: οἰόθεν οἶος, *quite alone*; αἰνόθεν αἰνῶς, *terribly violent*; κεῖτο
μέγας μεγαλωστί, *far extended.* So also Plat. Lach. p. 183 D ἐν τῇ
ἀληθείᾳ ὡς ἀληθῶς. These pleonastic adverbs must be translated
by some word which heightens the original notion.

2. Synonymous adverbs or adverbial expressions are frequently
combined: Plat. Phæd. p. 66 C ὡς ἀληθῶς τῷ ὄντι: Demosth. p. 849, 15 εὐθὺς παραχρῆμα (*statim in ipso facinore*) —αὐτίκα
ἄφνως, ἐξαίφνης εὐθύς—πάλιν αὖθις—εἶτ' αὖθις—τάχα ἴσως—ἀεὶ συνεχῶς—ὡς οἷον, *as for instance*—ἔπειτα μετὰ ταῦτα—εὖ μάλα, εὖ σφόδρα

    ᵃ Erfurdt ad loc.   ᵇ Heindorf ad loc.

—πάντάπασι καὶ πάντως—οὕτω τε καὶ ταύτῃ—. Most of these combinations serve to strengthen or generalise the adverbial notion; and in poetry, if particular attention is to be called to any notion, two, or even three, synonymous words are used for that purpose; as, Soph. Aj. 310 κόμην ἀ π ρ ὶ ξ ὄ ν υ ξ ι συλλαβεῖν χ ε ρ ί; in some of these forms which seem to have crept into the written from the common language, it must be allowed that this repetition is somewhat redundant.

3. The verbum finitum is joined frequently, in prose, with a participle of the same or a cognate verb; as, βλέποντα ὁρᾶν—ἔφη λέγων—ἔλεγε φάς—εἶπον λέγων—ἦ δ' ὅς λέγων Arist. Vesp. 795.—ἔφασκε λέγων.

4. Very frequently in poetry a concrete notion is expressed by a periphrasis with the abstract. So σχῆμα δόμων, for δόμοι. So Eur. Hec. 718 ἀλλ' εἰσορῶ γὰρ τ ο ῦ δ ε δ ε σ π ό τ ο υ δ έ μ α ς 'Αγαμέμνονος.—βίη Ἡρακλῆος—σθένος Ἕκτορος. See §. 442. d.

5. Very often the part is joined to the whole by καί, τέ when the part is to be especially distinguished: Homer Ἕκτορι μὲν καὶ Τρωσί: Æsch. Cho. 145 ξὺν θεοῖσι καὶ Γῆ καὶ Δίκῃ. Very often ὦ Ζεῦ καὶ θεοί. So in prose; as, 'Αθηναῖοι καὶ 'Ιφικράτης—Αἴγυπτος καὶ 'Αλεξάνδρεια. In Latin frequently: Cic. de Divin. I. 53 *fore, ut armis Darius et Persæ ab Alexandro et Macedonibus vincerentur.*

6. To call particular attention to a leading notion or thought, the Greeks frequently express it twice—once positively, and then negatively, or *vice versa;* (Parallelismus antitheticus :) Od. ρ, 415 οὐ γάρ μοι δοκέεις ὁ κάκιστος 'Αχαιῶν ἔμμεναι, ἀλλ' ὥριστος : Hdt. II. 43 οὐχ ἥκιστα, ἀλλὰ μάλιστα : Thuc. VII. 44 μέγιστον δὲ καὶ οὐχ ἥκιστα ἔβλαψεν ὁ παιωνισμός : Demosth. p. 108, 73 λέξω πρὸς ὑμᾶς καὶ οὐκ ἀποκρύψομαι.

7. The notion of a single word is sometimes repeated in a whole sentence: Od. α, init. ἄνδρα μοι ἔννεπε, Μοῦσα, π ο λ ύ τ ρ ο π ο ν, ὃς μ ά λ α π ο λ λ ὰ π λ ά γ χ θ η : Hdt. I. 79 ὥς οἱ π α ρ ὰ δ ό ξ α ν ἔσχε τὰ πρήγματα, ἦ ὡ ς α ὐ τ ὸ ς κ α τ ε δ ό κ ε ε.

8. Partly for clearness, partly for emphasis' sake, a word is repeated by a demonstr. pronoun: Thuc. IV. 69 αἱ ο ἰ κ ί α ι τοῦ προαστείου ἐπάλξεις λαμβάνουσαι α ὗ τ α ι ὑπῆρχον ἔρυμα : Xen. Cyr. VI. 1, 17 ὑμεῖς δὲ τὰ π ρ ό σ ο ρ α ὑμῖν αὐτοῖς τῆς 'Ασσυρίας ἐ κ ε ῖ ν α κτᾶσθε καὶ ἐργάζεσθε : Isocr. p. 241 C τ ὰ ς Κυκλάδας νήσους, περὶ ἃς ἐγένοντο πολλαὶ πραγματεῖαι κατὰ τὴν Μίνω τοῦ Κρητὸς δυναστείαν, τ α ύ τ α ς τὸ τελευταῖον ὑπὸ Καρῶν κατεχομένας, ἐκβαλόντες ἐκείνους οὐκ ἐξιδιώσασθαι τὰς χώρας ἐτόλμησαν : Eur. Phœn. 507 ἐ μ ο ὶ μὲν,

εἰ καὶ μὴ καθ᾽ Ἑλλήνων χθόνα τεθράμμεθ᾽, ἀλλ᾽ οὖν ξυνετά μοι δοκεῖς λέγειν.

9. The accidents both of time and place of an action, which are contained in the context, and therefore in most languages not actually expressed, the Greeks, especially their poets, loved to signify expressly by participles, such as ἰών, μολών, ἐλθών, παρών &c., ἔχων, ἄγων, φέρων (§. 696. *Obs.* 2. §. 698. *Obs.* 2.).

Anacolouthon.

§. 900. 1. Anacolouthon is the grammatical term for a construction where one part does not follow from the other—where the construction with which a sentence begins is not continued throughout, as the rules of grammar would require, though the sense is the same, or nearly so, as if it were. The source hereof is the rapidity with which in the Greek mind one thought followed on another; and the endeavour to express each part of a thought in its most accurate, elegant, and forcible form—that which should most fully correspond to the idea in the speaker's mind, and would most forcibly convey it to the hearer, whose own powers of mind would enable him to recognise its meaning in spite of its grammatical inaccuracy. The Greek language being so much a transcript of their actual thoughts, and their written language being formed so much from the expression of those thoughts in every day life, it is not to be wondered at that these constructions occur frequently in the best authors.

2. There are three sorts of anacolouthon: — *a.* Grammatical. — *b.* Those which seem to proceed from mere carelessness. — *c.* Rhetorical.

3. The authors who use it most may be divided into

a. Those whose general style is careless and loose, with whom anacolouthon is very common. Among these we must place Herodotus, who not always troubling himself about the rules and accuracies of grammar, told the stories of old days in a simple, easy, quaint style, such as we might expect in the old chronicles and legends from which he drew much of the materials of his histories. The irregular constructions of Herodotus have a peculiar charm, as arising from and not unsuitable to the spirit of his history, and his simple, childlike style of narrative.

β. To the second class belong those who, engrossed with the subject, were overpowered by their flow of thought, and endeavouring to concentrate these ideas in all their fulness in as few words as possible, passed from thought to thought, without taking

much care that the several parts of the whole sentence should be
connected together with strict grammatical accuracy ; but engrossed
with a new sentence before they had scarcely written down the
last, passed from one construction into another, as the thought
clothed itself more naturally in one form or the other, without
taking the pains to connect them grammatically, or perhaps being
unable to do so without weakening the expression.   To this class
belongs Thucydides, whose constructions, in spite of, or perhaps
because of, their grammatical inaccuracy, have a power and depth
of expression which perhaps no other prose writer ever attained.
The same may be said of some of the constructions in Pindar and
Æschylus.

γ. To the third class belong those who aimed at giving their
writings the easy off hand style of common life, which every one
could follow and sympathise with.   This is of course the proper
character for the dialogues, which having a dramatic character,
aim to place the reader in the midst of the characters introduced,
and to which therefore an inartificial easy style is indispensable,
not avoiding those inaccuracies of language which abound in common life, and without which the dialogue would lose much of its
reality.   Plato of course is at the head of this school of writers;
whose grammatical inaccuracies do not arise from ignorance of the
grammar of the language or carelessness, but from the instincts of
that pure taste which led him to those forms of language which
would best suit the style of his writings and the temper of his
hearers.   Most of his anacoloutha arise from some sort of attraction which most naturally affects the language of common life.
the case of a substantive being not that required by its own verb,
but some other near which it happens to stand, or the latter part
of a sentence following the construction of a parenthesis, instead
of the sentence with which it is grammatically connected.

4. Of the anacoloutha arising from accidental carelessness it is
impossible to treat ; some are noticed under the constructions which
they violate.

5. Of the rhetorical anacolouthon there are two sorts to be
especially mentioned :—

a. When the notion which gives rise to the train of thought is
placed at the beginning thereof as the logical subject, it frequently
happens that after a break in the sentence this same notion stands
as the grammatical object to the verb : Xen. Hier. IV. 6 ὥσπερ οἱ
ἀθληταὶ οὐχ, ὅταν ἰδιωτῶν γένωνται κρείττους, τοῦτο αὐτοὺς εὐφραίνει,
ἀλλ' ὅταν τῶν ἀνταγωνιστῶν ἥττους, τοῦτ' αὐτοὺς ἀνιᾷ, for τούτῳ εὐφραί-
νονται—ἀνιῶνται.

β. To place the opposition between two notions in as strong a light as possible, they stand each at the beginning of its own sentence in the same form, though the form required by the construction of each is different : Plat. Phædr. p. 233 B τοιαῦτα γὰρ ὁ ἔρως ἐπιδείκνυται· δυστυχοῦντας μὲν, ἃ μὴ λύπην τοῖς ἄλλοις παρέχει, ἀνιαρὰ ποιεῖ νομίζειν, εὐτυχοῦντας δὲ καὶ τὰ μὴ ἡδονῆς ἄξια παρ' ἐκείνων ἐπαίνου ἀναγκάζει τυγχάνειν, for παρ' εὐτυχούντων δὲ καὶ τὰ μὴ ἡδονῆς ἄξια ἐπαίνου ἀναγκ. τυγχάνειν. A very remarkable instance of this anacol. is to be found in Xen. Cyr. IV. 6, 3 and 4.

Position of words in a Sentence.

§. 901. The position of words in a sentence is twofold :—*a.* Usual. —*b.* Inverted.

Usual Position.—Simple Sentence.

1. The subject stands first, the predicate (verb or adjective with εἶναι) last. The object is placed before the predicate, the attribute after its substantive ; as, Κῦρος, ὁ βασιλεὺς, καλῶς ἀπέθανεν—Κύπριοι πάνυ προθύμως αὐτῷ συνεστράτευσαν Xen. Cyr. VII. 4, 1 : Παῖς μέγας —ἀνὴρ ἀγαθός—ὁ παῖς ὁ μέγας—ὁ ἀνὴρ ὁ ἀγαθός—ὁ παῖς ὁ τοῦ Κύρου —ὁ πόλεμος ὁ πρὸς τοὺς Πέρσας.

2. When several objects belong to the same predicate, the most important one is generally placed next before the predicate, and the rest placed before it in the order in which each is supposed to have been added to the first object, those that entered the mind first being placed nearest to it : οἱ Ἕλληνες τοὺς Πέρσας ἐνίκησαν —οἱ Ἕ. ἐν Μαραθῶνι τοὺς Π. ἐνίκησαν—οἱ Ἕλληνες ταύτῃ τῇ ἡμέρᾳ ἐν Μαραθῶνι τοὺς Πέρσας ἐνίκησαν. In this way the local and temporal adverbs generally precede the direct object (τότε or ταύτῃ τῇ ἡμέρᾳ τοὺς Π. ἐνίκησαν),—an object of a person in the dative and accus. precedes an object of a thing (τὸν παῖδα τὴν γραμματικὴν διδάσκω—τῷ παιδὶ βιβλίον δίδωμι),—the adverb of time an adverb of place (τότε or ταύτῃ τῇ ἡμέρᾳ ἐν Μαραθῶνι τοὺς Π. ἐνίκησαν). The modal adverb is generally placed next the predicate, as being immediately connected with it and modifying its sense ; as, οἱ Ἕλληνες ταύτῃ τῇ ἡμέρᾳ ἐν Μαραθῶνι τοὺς Πέρσας καλῶς ἐνίκησαν.

Compound Sentence.

3. The position of the dependent sentence corresponds to that of the word, of which it is a resolution ; Plat. Phæd. p. 59 E ὁ θυρωρός, ὅσπερ εἰώθει ὑπακούειν, εἶπε περιμένειν : Xen. Cyr. III. 2, 3 ὁ δὲ Κῦρος, ἐν ᾧ συνελέγοντο, ἐθύετο· ἐπεὶ

δὲ καλὰ ἦν τὰ ἱερὰ αὐτῷ, συνεκάλεσε τούς τε τῶν Περσῶν ἡγεμόνας καὶ τοὺς τῶν Μήδων. Ἐπεὶ δὲ ὁμοῦ ἦσαν, ἔλεξε τοιάδε. But a substant. sentence, (even when it expresses the grammatical subject,) stands after the verb; as, Xen. Cyr. I. 4, 7 οἱ δ' ἔλεγον, ὅτι ἄρκτοι—πολλοὺς ἤδη πλησιάσαντας διέφθειραν, or λέγεται ὅτι κ. τ. λ.

Inverted Position.

§. 902. 1. When the predicate is put before the subject, the attributive before its subst., or the objective words, especially the adverb, after the verb, the position is called *inverted*; as, οὐκ ἀγαθὸν πολυκοιρανίη· εἷς κοίρανος ἔστω: Xen. Cyr. III. 2, 25 καὶ γὰρ, ἔφασαν, πολύχρυσος ὁ ἀνήρ: Ibid. 7 εἶχον δὲ Χαλδαῖοι γέρρα—· καὶ πολεμικώτατοι δὲ λέγονται οὗτοι τῶν περὶ ἐκείνην τὴν χώραν εἶναι: Demosth. p. 112, 5 οὐδ' ἂν ἐλπὶς ἦν αὐτὰ γενέσθαι βελτίω—ἀγαθὸς ὁ ἀνήρ —τὸ τῆς ἀρετῆς κάλλος—or yet more strongly, τῆς ἀρετῆς τὸ κάλλος: Plat. Prot. p. 343 B οὗτος ὁ τρόπος ἦν τῶν παλαιῶν τῆς φιλοσοφίας, *veterum sapientiæ.*—μέγας παῖς—ὁ βασιλεὺς Κῦρος—ὁ πρὸς τοὺς Πέρσας πόλεμος: Hdt. VII. 53 τῶνδε δὲ εἵνεκα προαγορεύω ἀντέχεσθαι τοῦ πολέμου ἐντεταμένως: Plat. Phæd. p. 58 D ἀλλὰ πειρῶ ὡς ἂν δύνῃ ἀκριβέστατα διελθεῖν πάντα: Demosth. p. 112, 7 ἀνάγκη φυλάττεσθαι καὶ διορθοῦσθαι περὶ τούτου: Ibid. p. 111, 3 αἱ δὲ τοιαῦται πολιτεῖαι συνήθεις μέν εἰσιν ὑμῖν, αἴτιαι δὲ τῆς ταραχῆς καὶ τῶν ἁμαρτημάτων.

2. If particular emphasis is to be laid on the subject, it is placed last in the sentence; and if two words are to be thus distinguished, one is placed first, the other last: Xen. Cyr. III. 2, 9 οὕτω δὴ ἡγοῦντο μὲν οἱ Ἀρμένιοι· τῶν δὲ Χαλδαίων οἱ παρόντες, ὡς ἐπλησίαζον οἱ Ἀρμένιοι, ταχὺ ἀλαλάξαντες ἔθεον.— Πασῶν ἀρετῶν ἡγεμών ἐστιν ἡ εὐσέβεια: Plat. Phæd. p. 58 E εὐδαίμων γάρ μοι ἀνὴρ ἐφαίνετο, ὦ Ἐχέκρατες, καὶ τοῦ τρόπου καὶ τῶν λόγων.

3. When any part of a sentence is placed out of its proper position, either first or last, it is to be considered as done for emphasis' sake: Plat. Apol. p. 18 C ἔπειτά εἰσιν οὗτοι οἱ κατήγοροι —ἀτεχνῶς ἐρήμην κατηγοροῦντες (*reum absentem accusantes*), ἀπολογουμένου οὐδενός. If the writer first expresses a thought generally, and then applies it to some particular object or case, so that emphasis is to be laid thereon, the end of the sentence is its proper place, to produce a permanent impression on the mind: Plat. Rep. p. 572 B δεινόν τι καὶ ἄγριον καὶ ἄνομον ἐπιθυμιῶν εἶδος ἑκάστῳ ἔνεστι, καὶ πάνυ δοκοῦσιν ἡμῶν ἐνίοις μετρίοις

εἶναι, *etiam in nonnullis nostrum, qui admodum videantur moderati esse* [a] : Demosth. p. 42, 8 ἀλλὰ καὶ μισεῖ τις ἐκεῖνον, ὦ ἄνδρες Ἀθηναῖοι, καὶ δέδιεν καὶ φθονεῖ, καὶ τῶν πάνυ νῦν δοκούντων οἰκείως ἔχειν αὐτῷ.

Obs. The proper position of the several parts of speech, is given under the respective heads ; see *Index*.

Compound Sentences.

§. 903. 1. In dependent sentences the inverted position is more usual than in the words which they represent, and is used as the sense and rhythm of the sentence may require.

2. A subst. sentence introduced by ὅτι, ὡς, *that,* is placed before the principal verb, when that which it expresses is to be brought more directly forward : Demosth. p. 116, 21 ὅτι μὲν δὴ μέγας ἐκ μικροῦ—ὁ Φίλιππος ηὔξηται —, παραλείψω. The same is true of the final subst. sentence ; as, Xen. Cyr. I. 2, 15 ἵνα δὲ σαφέστερον δηλωθῇ πᾶσα ἡ Περσῶν πολιτεία, μικρὸν ἐπάνειμι. For the inverted position of an adj. sentence (ὃν εἶδες ἄνδρα, οὗτός ἐστιν) see §. 824. II. It also occurs in local adverb. sentences, introduced by relative adverbs of place, οὗ, ᾗ, ἵνα &c.; as, Il. μ, 48 ὅππῃ τ᾽ ἰθύνῃ, τῇ τ᾽ εἴκουσι στίχες ἀνδρῶν : see §. 824. II. In temporal and conditional adverb. sentences there is no change of this sort, as their proper place is before the verb.

3. If in a dependent sentence (especially an adject. sentence) any word is to be especially brought forward, it is placed sometimes before the conjunction ; as, Plat. Apol. p. 19 D τοιαῦτ᾽ ἐστὶ καὶ τἄλλα, περὶ ἐμοῦ ἃ οἱ πολλοὶ λέγουσιν. Cf. Hdt. VI. 11 ὑμέες ἤν. Compare Latin : Cic. de Divin. I. 40 *deus ut haberetur.*

4. If in a number of clauses the attention is to be particularly called to any one word, as the leading notion of the whole sentence, it is placed either at the beginning or end of the whole sentence. See §. 902. 3 : Xen. Cyr. V. 2, 11 τούτων ἐγώ σοι, εὖ ἴσθι, ἕως ἂν ἀνὴρ δίκαιος ὦ,—οὔποτ᾽ ἐπιλήσομαι : Plat. Phæd. p. 59 D E τῇ γὰρ προτεραίᾳ ἡμέρᾳ ἐπειδὴ ἐξήλθομεν ἐκ τοῦ δεσμωτηρίου ἑσπέρας, ἐπυθόμεθα, ὅτι τὸ πλοῖον ἐκ Δήλου ἀφιγμένον εἴη. Very frequently a subject common to both the principal and subordinate clause is placed first ; as, Xen. Cyr. V. 4, 26 οἱ δὲ Ἀσσύριοι ὡς ἤκουσαν ταῦτα, πάντα ἐποίουν.

5. In a sentence which stands with others in a paragraph, that word is most properly placed first which is most connected with

---

[a] Stallb. ad loc.

the preceding sentence; as, Hdt. VII. 104 ποιεῦσι — τὰ ἂν ἐκεῖνος ἀνώγῃ· ἀνώγει δὲ τωὐτὸ αἰεί: Plat. Phæd. p. 60 A καὶ ὁ Σωκράτης βλέψας εἰς τὸν Κρίτωνα· ᾿Ω Κρίτων, ἔφη, ἀπαγαγέτω τις ταύτην οἴκαδε. Καὶ ταύτην μὲν ἀπῆγόν τινες τῶν τοῦ Κρίτωνος βοῶσάν τε καὶ κοπτομένην.

Hyperbaton.

§. 904. 1. An especial method of bringing a word or words prominently forward is by separating those which, as making up one notion, would naturally be joined together. Hereby generally only one is marked as important, but sometimes two, especially when they stand at the beginning and end of the sentence (§. 902. 3.): Il. β, 483 ἐκπρεπέ ἐν πολλοῖσι καὶ ἔξοχον ἡρώεσσιν: Od. α, 4 πολλὰ δ᾽ ὅγ᾽ ἐν πόντῳ πάθεν ἄλγεα ὃν κατὰ θυμόν: Hdt. III. 135 ἐξηγησάμενος πᾶσαν καὶ ἐπιδέξας τὴν Ἑλλάδα: Soph. Aj. 187 ἀλλ᾽ ἀπερύκοι καὶ Ζεὺς κακὰν καὶ Φοῖβος Ἀργείων φάτιν: Plat. Rep. p. 401 B ἆρ᾽ οὖν τοῖς ποιηταῖς ἡμῖν ἐπιστατητέον καὶ προσαναγκαστέον τὴν τοῦ ἀγαθοῦ εἰκόνα ἤθους ἐμποιεῖν τοῖς ποιήμασιν, for τὴν τοῦ ἀγαθ. ἤθους εἰκ.: Lysias de inval. §. 21 πρὸς ἓν ἕκαστον ὑμῖν τῶν εἰρημένων[a]: Demosth. p. 110, 1 πολλῶν, ὦ ἄνδρες Ἀθηναῖοι, λόγων γιγνομένων: Ibid. p. 111, 3 ἀξιῶ — μηδεμίαν μοι διὰ τοῦτο παρ᾽ ὑμῶν ὀργὴν γενέσθαι. So the comparative is often separated from the words used to strengthen it; as, πολύ, πολλῷ: Xen. Cyr. VI. 4, 8 ἥξειν αὐτῷ σὲ πολὺ Ἀράσπου ἄνδρα καὶ πιστότερον καὶ ἀμείνονα, for σὲ πολὺ πιστ. κ. ἀμ. ἄνδρα Ἀράσπου (i. e. ἢ τὸν Ἀ.): Demosth. Mid. 49 οἱ δὲ ἠτιμωμένοι διὰ πολλῷ τούτων εἰσὶν ἐλάττω πράγματα, for ἠτιμ. εἰσὶ διὰ πράγματα πολλῷ ἐλάττω τούτων. So in Lat. as Cic. de Orat. II. 46, 192 *sed alia sunt majora multo.*

Obs. 1. The old grammatical term for this is hyberbaton, ὑπερβατόν, Latin, *verbi trangressio.* See Quintil. VIII. 6, 62.

Obs. 2. This figure however frequently makes the sentence obscure, an example which it is not expedient to follow: Plat. Rep. p. 358 E περὶ γὰρ τίνος ἂν μᾶλλον πολλάκις τις νοῦν ἔχων χαίροι λέγων καὶ ἀκούων; where πολλάκις belongs to λέγων καὶ ἀκούων: Ibid. p. 523 D ἐν πᾶσι γὰρ τούτοις οὐκ ἀναγκάζεται τῶν πολλῶν ἡ ψυχὴ τὴν νόησιν ἐπερέσθαι, τί ποτ᾽ ἐστι δάκτυλος, for τί ποτε τῶν πολλῶν ἐστι δάκτυλος, quid tandem sit e multis rebus digitus: Id. Crit. p. 50 extr. πρὸς μὲν ἄρα σοι τὸν πατέρα οὐκ ἐξ ἴσου ἦν τὸ δίκαιον καὶ πρὸς τὸν δεσπότην, for ἐξ ἴσου σοὶ ἦν: Lysias de cæd. Eratosth. §. 16 προσελθοῦσα οὖν μοι ἐγγὺς ἡ ἄνθρωπος τῆς οἰκίας τῆς ἐμῆς, for ἐγγὺς τῆς οἰκ. τ. ἐμῆς: Id. c. Agor. p. 463 R. §. 22 καὶ αὐτὸ τὸ ψήφισμα σοῦ τὸ τῆς βουλῆς καταμαρτυρήσει, for σοῦ καταμαρτ.

Obs. 3. When a negative is prefixed to an article or a relative, a conjunction or a preposition, it may not be separated therefrom, for it is attached to

---

[a] Bremi ad loc.

it, for the purpose of marking or suggesting an antithetical clause to be supplied by the mind : Lysias de cæd. Eratosth. §. 28 οἱ μὴ τὰ δίκαια πράττοντες = οἱ μὴ τὰ δίκ., ἀλλὰ τὰ ἄδικα πρ. : Plat. Crit. p. 47 D πειθόμενοι μὴ τῇ τῶν ἐπαϊόντων δόξῃ [a] : Id. Phæd. p. 77 E μᾶλλον δὲ μὴ ὡς ἡμῶν δεδιότων (in opposition to what precedes ὡς δεδιότων) : Xen. M. S. III. 9, 6 τὸ δὲ ἀγνοεῖν ἑαυτὸν καὶ μὴ ἃ οἶδε δοξάζειν τε καὶ οἴεσθαι γιγνώσκειν, ἐγγυτάτω μανίας ἐλογίζετο εἶναι : Thuc. III. 57 εἰ δὲ περὶ ἡμῶν γνώσεσθε μὴ τὰ εἰκότα : Id. I. 141 πολεμεῖν δὲ μὴ πρὸς ὁμοίαν ἀντιπαρασκευὴν ἀδύνατοι.

Obs. 4. In poetry an attributive genitive, or an object which belongs to two clauses, is placed in the second only : Æsch. Prom. 21 οὔτε φωνὴν οὔτε του μορφὴν βροτῶν ὄψει : Eur. Troad. 1209 ὦ τέκνον, οὐχ ἵπποισι νικήσαντά σε, οὐδ᾽ ἥλικας τόξοισι.

2. The relation between the same or cognate notions, especially if they are contraries, is signified by their being put beside one another : (*Opposita juxta se posita magis exsplendescunt :*) Od. ε, 155 παρ᾽ οὐκ ἐθέλων ἐθελούσῃ : so αὐτὸς αὐτοῦ &c. : Demosth. p. 111, 2 ἡ μὲν πόλις αὐτὴ παρ᾽ αὑτῆς δίκην λήψεται : Plat. Phædr. p. 277 C ποικίλῃ μὲν ποικίλους ψυχῇ καὶ παναρμονίους διδοὺς λόγους, ἁπλοῦς δὲ ἁπλῇ : Xen. Anab. V. 6, 2 ἠξίουν Ἕλληνας ὄντας Ἕλλησι κ. τ. λ. Hence ἄλλος ἄλλο, *alius aliud* ; ἄλλος ἄλλοθι, *alius alibi* ; ἄλλος ἄλλοσε, *alius alio* ; ἄλλος ἄλλοθεν, *alius aliunde* ; ἄλλος ἄλλῃ, *alius aliâ* (sc. *viâ*), &c. ; *one did this, the other that,* &c. : Plat. Apol. p. 37 D καλὸς οὖν ἄν μοι ὁ βίος εἴη — ἄλλην ἐξ ἄλλης πόλιν πόλεως ἀμειβομένῳ.

3. When in a sentence, or two coordinate sentences, there are two words joined together, which are opposed to two other words likewise joined together, the words which correspond to each other, correspond to each other in their position ; the arrangement of the words of the one pair being exactly the contrary to that of the other pair of words. So subst. adj., adj. subst. This figure is called *Chiasma* from its analogy to a X ; as, πολλάκις ἡδονὴ βραχεῖα μακρὰν τίκτει λύπην : Plat. Phæd. p. 60 A ὕστατον δὴ σὲ προσεροῦσι νῦν οἱ ἐπιτήδειοι καὶ σὺ τούτους : Demosth. c. Onetor. §. 25 μάρτυρας δὲ τῶν μὲν ὑμῖν παρέξομαι, τῶν δ᾽ ἐπιδείξω μεγάλα τεκμήρια : Theocr. VIII. 1, 2 Δάφνιδι τῷ χαρίεντι συνήντετο βωκολέοντι μᾶλα νέμων, ὡς φαντί, κατ᾽ ὤρεα μακρὰ Μενάλκας. The Latins also were very fond of this figure, i. e. Cic. Tusc. II. 4, 11 *philosophia medetur animis, inanes sollicitudines detrahit, cupiditatibus liberat, pellit timores* [b].

4. Sometimes the predicates of two coordinate sentences are placed contrary to their natural order ; the one whose sense requires that it should follow the other being placed before it (ὕστερον

---

[a] Stallb. ad loc.   [b] Adnot. ad loc.

πρότερον). This latter takes place, when the notion which should stand second, is to be brought forward as the more important notion or thought of the two : Od. μ, 134 τὰς μὲν ἄρα (sc. Νύμφας) θρέψασα τεκοῦσά τε πότνια μήτηρ Θρινακίην ἐς νῆσον ἀπῴκισε τηλόθι ναίειν.

5. Another powerful method of calling attention to a word or the notion whereon emphasis is to be laid, is the placing immediately after it some particle, as πέρ, δή, γέ (§. 720. §. 734. ff.), or ἄν (§. 432. b.), or a parenthetical word such as οἶμαι &c., and in a speech, ὦ ἄνδρες Ἀθηναῖοι : Demosth. p. 40, 2 τί οὖν ἐστι τοῦτο; ὅτι οὐδέν, ὦ ἄνδρες Ἀθηναῖοι, τῶν δεόντων ποιούντων ὑμῶν κακῶς τὰ πράγματ' ἔχει : Ibid. p. 43, 10 πότ' οὖν, ὦ ἄνδρ. Ἀθ., πότε ἃ χρὴ πράξετε; Ibid. p. 53, 44 εὑρήσει τὰ σαθρά, ὦ ἄνδρ. Ἀθ., τῶν ἐκείνου πραγμάτων αὐτὸς ὁ πόλεμος.

TABLE

OF

CORRESPONDING PARAGRAPHS.

———————

Kühner.		Kühner.		Kühner.		Kühner.	
§. 385	§. 350	§. 419	§. 379	§. 452	§. 411 2.		{ §. 448
389	351	420	380	454	424	§. 485	{ 449
390	357	421	381	455	429		(450
391	358	422	382	456	430	486	451
392	359	423	383	457	431	487	452
392 a.	360	424	384	458	432	488	453
393	361	— a.	385	459	412	489	454
394)		425	386	460	413	490	455
395 }	362	426	387	461	414	491	456
396 }		427	388	462	415	492	457
397)		429	389	463	416	493	{ 458
398	363	430	390	464	417		{ 459
399	364	431	391	465	419	494	460
400	365	432	392	466 }	418	495	461
401	366	433	393	467 }		496	462
402	367	434	394	469	420	497	463
403	368	435	395	470	421		{ 464
404	369	436	396	471	433	498	{ 465
405	352	437	397	472	434		(466
406	353	438	398	473	435	499	467
407	354	439	399	474	436	500	580
408	355	440	400	475	437	501	468
409	356	441	401	476	438	502	{ 469
410	—	442	402	477 {	439 / 440		{ 470
411	370	443	403	478	441	503	471
412	371	444	404	479	442	504	472
413	372	445	405	480	443	505	473
414	373	446	406	481	444	506	{ 474
415	374	447	407	482	445		{ 475
416	375	448	408	483	446	507	476
417	376	449	410	484 ·	447	508	477
418	377	450	411			509	478
418 1.	378	451	422			510 ª	479

ª The cases having been entirely remodelled from §. 510. to §. 591. it has been thought better not to draw out a table of corresponding paragraphs, which in many places would mislead those who referred to them. The Indices will remedy any inconvenience which may arise from this omission.

Kühner. §.592	§.614	Kühner. §.637	§.664	Kühner. §.682	§.711	Kühner. §.727	§.759
592	614	637	664	682	711	727	759
593	615	638	665	683	712	728	760
594	616	639	666	684	713	729	761
595	617	640	667	685	714	730	761
596	618	641	668	686	715	731	763
597	619	642	669	687	716	732	764
598	620	643	670	688	717	733	765
599	621	644	671	689	718	734	766
600	622	645	672	690	719	735	767
601	623	646	673		720	736	768
602	624	647	674		721	737	769
603	625	648	675	691 }	722	738	770
604	626	649	676	692 }	723	739	771
605	627	650	677		724	740	772
606	628	651	678	693	725	741	773
607	629	652	679	694	726	742	774
608	630	653	680	695	727	743	775
609	631	654 }	681	696	728	744	776
610	632	655 }		697	729	745	777
611	633	656	682	698	730	746	778
612	634	657	683	699	731	747	779
613	635	658	684	700	732	748	780
614	636	659 {	685	701	733	749	781
615	637		686	702	734	750	782
616	638	660 {	687	703 }		751	783
617	639		688	704 }	735	752	784
618	640	661 {	689	705	736	753	785
618 4.	621 Obs.2.		690	706	737	754	786
619	643	662	691	707	738	755	787
620	644	663 {	692	708	739	756	788
621	645		693	709	740	757	789
622	646	664	694	710	741	758	790
623	647	665	695	711	742	759	791
624 {	648	666	696	712	743	760	792
	649	667	697	713	744	761	793
625	650	668	698	714	745	762	794
626	651	669	699	715	746	763	795
627	652	670	700	716	747	763 Obs.2.	816 c.
628 {	653	671	701	717 {	748	764	796
	654	672	702		749	765	797
629	655	673	703	718	750	766	798
630	656	674	704	719	751	767	799
631	657	675	705	720	752	768 {	800
632	658	676	706	721	753		801
633 {	659	677	707	722	754	769	802
	660	678 }	708	723	755	770	803
634	661	679 }		724	756	771	804
635	662	680	709	725	757	772	805
636	663	681	710	726	758		

hner.		Kühner.		Kühner.		Kühner.	
'73 {	§. 806	§. 796	§. 830	§. 822	§. 859	§. 845	§. 885
	807	797	831	823	860	846	886
	808	798	832	824	861	847	887
'74	809	799	833	825 1.	862	848	888
'75	810	800	834	825 2.	863	849	889
'76	811	801	835	826	864	850	890
'77	812	802	836	827 1.	865	851	891
'78	813	803	837	827 2.	866	852	892
'79 {	814	804	838	828	867	852 *a. c. i. k.*	893
	748	805	839	829	868	852 *b. f.*	894
780	815	806	840	830	869	852 *d.g.k.l.m.*	895
781	816	807	841	831	870	852 *h.*	896
782	817	808	842	832	871	853 1.	895 *d.*
783	818	809	843	833	872	853 2.	895 *f.*
784	819	810	844	834	873	854	897
785	820	811	845	835	874	855	895 2.
786	821	812	848	836	875	856	898
787	822	813	849	837 1.	876	857	898 2. 3. 4.
788	823	814	850	837 2.	877	858	899
789 }	824	815	851	838	878	859	900
790 }		816	852	839	879	862 3.	901
791	825	817	853	840	880	863	902
792	826	818	854	841	881	864	903
793	827	819	855	842	882	865	904
794	828	820	856	843	883		
795	829	821	858	844	884		

INDEX OF MATTERS.

The first figures refer to the §., the others to the paragraphs.

Abstract, use of for the concrete, 353. 1.
Abstract notions, expressed by neuter adjectives, 436.
Accusative, notion of, 471. 4. 2.
———— division of the notions expressed by, 548. 2.
———— rules for the use of, 546.
———— absolute, 581. 700.
———— adverbial (ἡδὺ γελᾶν), 548. f.
———— adverbial, use of with various verbs, 549. d. 551. f. 552. f. 553. e. 554. d. 555. d. 556. e.
———— cognate, after verbs of motion, 559. Obs. 2.
———— cognate to a notion implied in the verb (σιγᾶ = οὐ λέγει λόγους), 548. d.
———— cognate to a notion implied in the verb, use of with various verbs, 551. d. 552. d. 554. c. 556. d. 566. 1.
———— double, joined with verbs implying two coincident notions, 546. 2.
———— double, of cognate notion and patient (διδάσκω σε διδάγματα), joined with what verbs, 547. B.
———— double, list of verbs followed by, 583.
———— elliptic (μέγα sc. χάρμα χαίρειν), 548. e. 551. e. 552. e. 553. d.
———— neuter, adverbial use of, 579. 4.
———— participle, for nom. part., 682. 1.
———— participle, used absolutely, 700.
———— participle, for other cases, 711.
———— in apposition, 580.
———— of cognate notion (κοιμᾶσθαι ὕπνον), 548. b.
———— of cognate notion, joined with what verbs, 547. A.

Accusative of cognate notion, use of with various verbs, 549. b. 551. b. 552. b. 553. b. 554. a. 555. b. 556. b.
———— of cognate substantive (βουλὴν βουλεύω), 548. a.
———— of cognate substantive, use of with various verbs, 549. a. 550. a. 551. a. 552. a. 553. a. 555. a. 556. a.
———— of duration in time and space, 548. g.
———— of equivalent notion (ἀποκατθανεῖν δίκην = θάνατον), 548. c.
———— of equivalent notion, use of with various verbs, 549. c. 550. b. 551. c. and 2. 552. c. 553. c. 554. b. 555. c. 556. c.
———— of the patient, 582. 1, 2.
———— of the patient, with neuter verbs, 545. Obs. 2.
———— of the part (τύπτω σε α- φαλήν), 545. 5.
———— of quantity (δύο σταδίους), 578.
———— of quantity, in an adverbial form (πολλά, sæpe), 578. Obs. 1.
———— of time (τοῦτον τὸν χρόνον), 577.
———— of time, in an adverbial form (ἐννῆμαρ, νύκτωρ &c.), 577. Obs. 1.
———— with adjectives expressing quality (καλὸς τὰ ὄμματα), 579. 2.
———— with εἰμί (εὖρος, μέγεθος, γένος, πρόφασιν &c.), 579. 3.
———— with infinitive, 672.
———— with inf. in exclamations, 679.
———— with inf. in an oratio obliqua, instead of verbum finitum, 889.
———— with inf. in independent clauses of the oratio obliqua, 889.
———— with inf., for nom. with infin. (νομίζω ἐμαυτὸν ταῦτα εἰπεῖν), 673. 1.
———— with inf., for gen. and dat. with inf., 674, 675.

Accusative with inf., instead of the construction with ὅτι or ὡς, 804. 4.
———— with inf. in one of two clauses contracted together, 898. 4.
———— with inf., use of as subject of a sentence (λέγεται, δοκεῖ, καλόν ἐστιν &c.), 676.
———— with participle, 681, 682.
———— with verbs transitive, notions expressed by, 545. 1.
———— with verbs neuter, notion expressed by, 545. 2.
———— with verbs passive, notion expressed by, 545. 3.
———— with verbs transmissive, notion expressed by, 545. 4.
———— used in a pure adverbial sense (τοὐναντίον, τἄλλα, λοιπόν, ἀμφότερον &c.), 579. 4.
———— use of, as object of the verb, 544.
———— use of, to define the verbal notion (ἀλγεῖ τὴν κεφαλήν), 579. 1.
———— with verbals in -τέος, for the dative, 613. Obs. 5.
———— after prepositions, 624—639.
———— after verbs of hearing, 487. 3. 485. Obs.
———— after verbs of sorrow for, 489. Obs. 2.
———— after verbs of desire, 498. Obs. 2.
———— after verbs which exchange their neuter for a corresponding transitive sense (ἐκπλεῖν πολεμίους), 548. Obs. 1.
———— after verbs of motion, 557—559.
———— after verbs of moving along, 558.
———— after verbs of motion to, 559.
———— after verbs of doing, accomplishing, furnishing, &c. 560.
———— after verbs of learning, studying, practising, &c. 561.
———— after verbs of eating, drinking, &c. 562.
———— after verbs of labouring, undertaking, playing, &c. 563.
———— after verbs of fighting, contending, conquering, &c. 564.
———— after verbs of being wrong, impious, pious, &c. 565.
———— after verbs of saying, telling, proclaiming, &c. 566. 1.
———— after verbs of praying, vowing, swearing, &c. 566. 2.
———— after verbs of singing, shouting, sounding, &c. 566. 3.
———— after verbs of crying, mourning, lamentation, &c. 566. 4.

Accusative after verbs of confessing, admitting, denying, &c. 567.
———— after verbs of prosecuting, defending, decreeing, blaming, &c. 568.
———— after verbs of making, building, contriving, &c. 569. 1.
———— after verbs of creating, bringing forth, &c. 569. 2.
———— after verbs of writing, painting, spinning, &c. 569. 3.
———— after verbs of pouring, scattering, &c. 570.
———— after verbs of heaping up, digging, &c. 571.
———— after verbs of preparing meat, drink, &c. 572.
———— after verbs of giving, paying, selling, &c. 573.
———— after verbs of receiving, 574.
———— after verbs of seeing, hearing, &c. 575.
———— after verbs of possessing, finding, wearing, &c. 576. 1.
———— after verbs of obtaining, choosing, gathering, &c. 576. 2.
Accusatival relation of self to the middle verb, 362. 3.
Active form of verbs, 357. 358.
———— form of verbs used for the middle, 363. 4.
———— and middle sense of verbs, dissimilarity of, in certain cases, 363. 6.
Adjective, notion of, 356. 1.
———— original force of, 356. 2.
———— attributive, 438. ff.
———— attributive, proleptic usage of, 439. 2.
———— after article and substantive, as predicate, 458. Obs. 2.
———— agreement of, with one of several subjects, 391. Obs.
———— agreement of, with a substantive in construction with another substantive (ἐμὰ κήδεα θυροῦ), 440.
———— construction of the predicative, with several subjects of the same gender, 391. 1.
———— construction of the predicative, with several subjects of different genders, 391. 2.
———— followed by its substantive in the genitive, and in the same gender therewith (ἡ πολλὴ τῆς γῆς, for τὸ πολὺ τῆς γῆς), 442. e.
———— not agreeing with its subst. in gender and number, 378. b.
———— not agreeing with its immediate attributive, 379. a.
———— position of, as predicate, 459. 1.
———— use of, for the attributive genitive, 435. a.

Adjective, use of, for the substantive in apposition, 435. *b.*

―――― use of, instead of adverbs (χθιζὸς ἦλθεν for χθές), 714.

―――― use of οὐκ and μή with, 746.

―――― used without its substantive, 436.

―――― in the masc. used with a substantive in the fem., 390. *c.*

―――― neuter used to signify abstract notions, 436. γ.

―――― neuter with a gen. of the subst. (τὸ πολὺ τοῦ βίου), 442. *b.*

―――― in the neut. sing. with a masc. or fem. subject, 381.

―――― in the neut. plural with a genitive substantive, 442. *Obs.*

―――― predicative attracted by vocative, 479. 4.

―――― two together (τὰ ψευδῆ καλά), of which the latter is substantive, 458. *Obs.* 1.

―――― verbal, 613.

―――― verbal in τός, transitive force of, 356. *Obs.*

―――― with ἄν, 430.

Adjectival clause, for a substantival, 798. *c.*

―――― clause with another clause depending on it, 825. 1.

―――― clauses in succession, construction of, 833.

―――― clauses, demonstrative construction of, 833.

―――― relation of self to the middle verb, 362. 4.

―――― sentence, 815.

―――― sentence, use of, for the other dependent sentences, 836.

―――― sentence, use of the moods in, 826.

Adverbs, notion of, 713.

―――― confirmative, μήν, μάν 728. — μέν. 729. — μέντοι, μενοῦν, μενδή 730. — ἦ, ἦτοι 731. — νύ 732. — νή, ναί, μά 733.

―――― compounded with prepositions, 644.

―――― in ον, as οὖ, πού 522. *Obs.* 1.

―――― in θεν, as ἐνδόθεν 522. *Obs.* 1.

―――― incressive or emphatic, 762.

―――― intensive, πέρ 734. — γέ 735.

―――― local (ἐνταῦθα, οὗ, ἐγγύθεν &c.), 715.

―――― local, attraction of, 822. *Obs.* 6.

―――― local, pregnant construction of (ὅποι γῆς ἐσμέν), 646. *Obs.*

―――― local (ἐκεῖθεν, ἐνθένδε), with the article, pregnant construction of (ὁ ἐκεῖθεν πόλεμος for ὁ ἐκεῖ. π.), 647. *Obs.*

―――― modal, 718.

―――― modal, δή 720—724. — δῆτα 725. — θήν, δῆθεν, δήπουθεν 726.—ὧν 727.

Adverbs, modal, with article, 456. 2. *c.*

―――― of mode and manner, 717.

―――― negative (οὐκ, μή), 738—750.

―――― of place and time, article with, 456.

―――― relative, changed into demonstrative, 833. *Obs.* 1.

―――― with the principal verb repeated (ἔπλευσ᾽ ὅπως ἔπλευσα), 835. 1.

―――― restrictive, τοί 736.—οὖν 737.

―――― temporal, 716. — νῦν, νύν 719. —ἤδη 720.

―――― use of as attributive adjectives, 436. *c.*

―――― with article and prepos. and case, 456.

―――― with attributive gen. and article, 456.

―――― with gen. 509. 2.

Adverbial acc., 548. *f.* 549. *d.* 551. *f.* 552. *f.* 553. *e.* 554. *d.* 555. *d.* 556. *e.*

―――― clause for a substantival, 798. *b.*

―――― force of prepositions, 640.

―――― notions, expressed by the participle, 695. 3.

―――― relatives, 825. 2.

―――― sentences, 837.

―――― sentences, causal, 849.

―――― sentences, comparative, 868. 1.

―――― sentences, comparative, of quality, 868. 2.

―――― sentences, comparative, of quality, use of the moods and tenses in, 869. 3, 4.

―――― sentences, comparative, of quantity or degree, 870.

―――― sentences, concessive, use of εἰ καί and καὶ εἰ in, 861.

―――― sentences, conditional, 850.

―――― sentences, conditional, different forms of the protasis in, 851.

―――― sentences, conditional, different forms of the apodosis in, 852.

―――― sentences, conditional, different forms of protasis and apodosis in, 853.

―――― sentences, conditional, double protasis in, 860. 9.

―――― sentences, conditional, ellipse of the protasis in, 860. 2.

―――― sentences, conditional, ellipse of the apodosis in, 860. 3.

―――― sentences, conditional, table of the most usual forms of the protasis and apodosis in, 857.

―――― sentences expressing the reason of the principal clause, 849. 1.

―――― sentence expressing result or effect, 862.

Adverbial sentence, expressing result or effect, use of indicative and infinitive in, 863.

———— sentence, expressing result or effect, use of opt. with or without ἄν in, 865.

———— sentence, expressing result or effect, use of indicative and infinitive with ἄν in, 866.

———— sentence, expressing result or effect, use of ὥστε with imperative in, 867. 1.

———— sentence, expressing result or effect, use of ἐφ' ᾧ or ᾧτε in, 867. 2.

———— sentences, local, 838.

———— sentences, temporal, 839.

———— sentences, temporal, use of ind. mood in, 840.

———— sentences, temporal, use of conj. mood in, 841, 842.

———— sentences, temporal, use of opt. mood in, 843, 844.

———— sentences, temporal, use of opt. with ἄν in, 845.

———— sentences, temporal, use of ἕως in, 846, 847.

———— sentences, temporal, use of πρίν in, 848.

Adversative clauses, when coordinate, 763. 1.

Affirmative verb to be supplied from a negative, 895. h.

Agreement of the copula with the predicate, 389.

———— of demonstr. pronoun with its subject, 381. Obs. 1, 2.

———— of οὐδείς and μηδείς with the subject, 381. Obs. 3.

———— of the predicate with its subject, 377.

———— of the predicate, with a subject expressed by τό or τά, with the gen. plur. of a subst., 380. 1.

Anacolouthon, 477.

———— meaning and origin of, 900. 1.

———— sorts of, 900. 2.

———— in the participial construction, 707.

———— participle in nom. for the other cases, 707, 708.

———— participle in nom. without any verbum finitum, 709.

———— participle in gen. for some other case, 710.

———— participle in accus. for some other case, 711.

———— participle in dative for some other case, 712.

———— very common in Herodotus, 900. a.

Anacolouthon, use of, in Thucydides, 900. β.

———— use of, in Plato, 900. γ.

Anomalies, grammatical, how to be accounted for, 378.

Antecedent, coincident, consequent notions, 471. 3.

———— notion, 480. 2.

Antithesis, omission of one clause of, 896.

Aorist, proper sense of, 401. 1.

———— interchange of, with the perfect, 401. 6.

———— use of, as a narrative tense, 401. 3.

———— use of, as an instantaneous future, 403. 2.

———— use of, in comparisons or similes, 402. 3.

———— use of, in the conjunctive, opt., and inf. moods, 405.

———— use of, to express an attempt already taken place, 403. Obs.

———— use of, to express determination, 403. 1.

———— use of, to express frequency, 402. 1, 2.

———— use of, to express induction, 402. 1, 2.

———— use of to represent a momentary action, 401. 2, 4, 5.

———— use of, for impft., perf., and plupft., 404.

———— use of, with τί οὖν, to express a command, 403. 3.

———— I. middle, seeming passive force of, 364. b.

———— I. passive, and aor. II. passive, difference between, 367. 1.

———— I. and II. passive, used to express reflexive and intransitive notions, 367. 2.

———— II. middle, distinguished from aor. I. middle, 365. 1.

———— II. middle, seeming passive force of, 365. 2.

———— conjunctive, used to express the futurum exactum in Latin, 407. Obs. 2.

———— conjunctive, use of in negative or prohibitory forms with μή, 420, 3.

———— indicative, use of with ἄν, 424. β.

———— iterative, form of in σκον, 402. Obs. 3.

Apodosis, ellipse of, 860. 3.

———— forms of, in conditional sentences, 852, 853.

Aposiopesis, 807.

Apposition, 467.

———— accus. in, 580.

———— of adject. with names of persons, 467, 4.

Apposition of adject. with possessive pronouns (ἐμὸς τοῦ ἀθλίου βίος), 467. 4.
———— nomin. in, used for attributive gen. 435. e.
———— with a substantive, 467. 1.
———— with a substantival pronoun, 467. 3.
———— with ὡς prefixed, 467. Obs. 3.
———— used to limit former expression, 467. Obs. 2.
Article, use and meaning of, 446.
———— before a single word or sentence, 457. 1.
———— omission of, before adverb and subst., &c. 456. Obs.
———— omission of, before latter of two attributive gen. 459. 8.
———— omission of, with collective nouns, 447. Obs.
———— peculiar collocations of, 459.
———— position of, 458.
———— praepositive and postpositive, 817. 1.
———— repeated before each of several subst. 459. 9.
———— separated from its subst. 459. 4.
———— separated from its subst. by particles, μέν, &c. 459. 7.
———— use of, as a demonstrative, 444.
———— use of, as a relative pronoun, 445.
———— use of, for the relative pronoun, accounted for, 445. 1.
———— use of, in Post-Homeric writers, 462.
———— with adjectives used as substantives, 451. 1.
———— with adverbs of place and time, 456. a. b.
———— with modal adverbs, 456. c.
———— and attributive gen. with adverb, 456.
———— with two attributives of same subst. 459. 5.
———— with personal nouns, 450.
———— with abstract nouns, 448.
———— with collective nouns, 447.
———— with material nouns, 449.
———— with numerals, 454, 455.
———— with participles used as subst. 451. 2.
———— with predicate, 460.
———— with personal pronouns, 452.
———— with demonstrative pronouns, 453.
———— with indefinite pronouns, 454.
———— with the subject, 460.
———— with subst. and attrib. gen. 461.
———— use of, in οἱ ἀμφί, περί τινα &c. 456. 1.
———— with ἄλλοι 454. 3.

Article with ἄμφω, ἀμφότεροι 455.
———— with ἕκαστος 454. 2.
———— with ἕτερος 454. 3.
———— with πάντες 454.
———— with πλείους 454. Obs. 3.
———— with ταὐτὸν θάτερον 459. 6.
Asyndeton, figure explained, 792.
———— in the participial construction, 706.
———— in negative clauses, 775. Obs. 2.
Attraction, constructions by, 389.
———— of local adverbs, 647. Obs. 822. Obs. 6.
———— of causal gen. 501. Obs. 4.
———— of the infin. 672. 3. 673. 2. 675. Obs.
———— of the infin. with ὥστε 863. Obs. 5.
———— of participle, 682.
———— of prepos. with the article, 647.
———— of the vocative, 479. 4.
———— of relatives, where admissible, 822.
———— of relatives, the object and use of, 822. Obs. 3.
———— of relatives (οἷος, ὅσος, ἡλίκος), 823.
———— Inverse, nature of, 324. 1.
———— inverse of οὐδεὶς ὅστις οὐ, 824. I. 2.
———— inverse of ὃς βούλει, quivis, 824. I. Obs. 1.
———— by transposition of the subst. 824. II. 1.
———— of the case in comparative sentences introduced by ὡς, ὥσπερ, ὥστε 869. 3.
———— of the copula to the predicate (ἡ περίοδός εἰσι στάδιοι ἕξ), 389.
Attributive construction, 433.
———— forms, origin of, 434.
———— forms, interchange of, 435.
———— adjective, 438.
———— adjectives, proleptic usage of (εὔφημον κοίμησον στόμα, for ὥστε εὔφημον εἶναι), 439. 2.
———— genitive, 463, 534.
———— gen., forces of, 466. Obs. 2.
———— gen., proper case of verb used instead of, 466. Obs. 3.
———— gen. with article, 461.
———— gen. and article with adverb, 456.
———— gen., causal, 499. Obs. 2.
———— gen., collocation of, 459. 2.
———— gen., objective, 464.
———— gen., subjective, 464.
———— gen., passive, 466.
———— gen. of procession, 483. Obs. 2.

Attributive gen., use of prepos. with, 464. *Obs.*
———— sentence, inversion of the members of, 442.
Attributives, two with the same subst., use of Article with, 459. 5.

Brachylogy, 892.

Canon, Dawes's, 812. 1. 814. 748. *Obs.* 3.
Cases, notions of the, 471. 4.
—— principles of the, 471. 3.
—— properly only three, 471. 4.
—— as object of verb, 471.
—— Greek, general observations on, 473.
—— modern and Greek, contrast between, 473.
—— difference between the, in expressing relations of time, 606. *Obs.* 1.
—— use of, with the infin. 672, 673.
—— absolute, accusative, 700.
—— absolute, dative, 699.
—— absolute, genitive, 695. 2.
—— dependent, 480.
Cause, antecedent notion of, in gen. 480. 2. 1.
Causal genitive, 481.
———— gen., attraction of, 501. *Obs.* 4.
———— attributive gen. 499. *Obs.* 2.
———— gen. after all verbs, 481. 1.
———— notion, expressed by the participle, 697.
———— notion, expressed by the preposition, 616. — See also under each preposition.
———— objective relation, expressions of, 468. *c.*
———— relation, expressed by adjectives, 714. *c.*
Causative verb, 357. 3.
Chiasma, meaning and use of the figure, 901, 3.
Cognate notion, acc. of, 548. *b.* 549. *b.* 551. *b.* 552. *b.* 553. *b.* 554. *a.* 555. *b.* 556. *b.*
———— notion of the verb, in what cases expressed, 544. 3, 4.
———— notions, juxta-position of, 904. 2.
———— substantive, acc. of, 548. *a.* *Obs.* 5. 549. *a.* 550. *a.* 551. *a.* 552. *a.* 553. *a.* 555. *a.*
Collocation of prepositions, 651.
Combination of two synonymous adverbs, 899. 2.
Comparatio compendiaria, laws for the use of, 781. *d.*
Comparatives, gen. with, 502. 2.
Comparative, followed by ἤ ὥστε, with inf. 863. *e.*

Comparative, followed by ἤ with inf. 863. *Obs.* 2.
———— use of ἤ and the gen. with, 780.
———— use of, for the positive, 784.
———— without second clause of comparison, 784.
———— ἤ, 779.
———— clause, coalescing with principal clause, 869. 4.
———— particles ὡς, ὥστε, οἷον &c., with the participle and absolute cases, 701—704.
———— sentences, use and construction of, 868. 2—4.
———— adv. sentence for an adject. sentence, 869. 2.
———— adv. sentences of quantity or degree, 870.
Comparison, two sorts of, in adverbial sentences, 868. 1.
Complex attributive sentences, 437.
———— objective sentence, 469.
Compound adj., used for the attributive gen. 435. *Obs.*
———— sentences, 751.
———— verbs, use of tmesis in, 643.
Concrete notion expressed by a periphrasis with the abstract, 899. 4.
Conditions, notion of the, expressed by the participle, 697. *b.*
Conditionals, use of the moods as, 422.
Conditional protasis, use of, without εἰ, as a principal clause, 860. 8.
———— sentences, forms of protasis in, 851. 1. 853.
———— sentences, forms of apodosis in, 852, 853. 857.
Confirmative adverbs, 728—733.
Conjunctions, origin of, 751. 2.
———— coordinate or copulative, 751. 3.
———— disjunctive, tragic and epic use of, 777. *Obs.* 4.
———— hypothetical, use of, 778.
———— introducing depending sentences, 795. 3.
———— subordinate (ὅτε &c.), 751. 3.
Conjunctive mood, notion of the, 414.
———— mood, secondary meaning of, 411. 1.
———— mood—the subjunctive of the principal tenses, 410. *b.*
———— mood, general rule for use of, in the final sentence, 805. 2.
———— after historic tenses, 806.
———— after an optative, 808.
———— after μή 805. 810. 814. *b.*
———— after ὡς, ὅπως, ἵνα &c. 805. 2. 810.

Conjunctive, use of, for the indicative future, 415.
———— use of, in adjectival sentences, 828, 829.
———— use of, in comparisons, 419. 2.
———— use of, in compound sentences, 419.
———— use of, in dependent sentences, to express frequency, 419. 1.
———— use of, in dependent clauses of the oratio obliqua, 885. 1.
———— use of, in oratio obliqua, 887.
———— with ἄν, 830.
———— with ἐάν, 854.
———— with ὅς, ὅστις &c., or ὅς ἄν, 828, 829.
———— with ὅταν, ὁπόταν, ἡνίκ' ἄν, ἐπάν, ἕως ἄν &c. 841, 842.
———— aor. for the present, 405.
———— aor. for the Latin futurum exactum, 407. Obs. 2.
———— aor. with μή, for the imperative, 420. 3.
Conjunctivus adhortativus, 416.
———— deliberativus, 417.
Construction, attributive, 433.
———— by attraction, 389.
———— indirect, or oratio obliqua, 884.
———— κατὰ σύνεσιν, 378—380.
———— objective, 468.
———— of prepositions with different cases, 648.
———— of sentences, 898.
———— of νομίζειν with the dative, 591. Obs.
———— of τίσασθαι, 585.
Coordinate attributive construction, 441.
———— or copulative conjunctions, 751. 3.
———— sentences, 751. 3.
———— sentence, copulative and connexive forms of the, 753. 2, 3.
———— sentences expressing subordinate thoughts, 752.
Coordination of sentences logically subordinate, 785.
Copula, agreement of the, with the predicate, 389.
———— εἶναι, ellipse of the, 376.
———— εἶναι and predicative adjective, 375.
Copulative conjunctions (τέ, καί), 754.

Dative, notion of the, 471. 4, 3. 586.
———— heads of, 586. 3.
———— absolute, 699.
———— circumstantial or modal, 603, 604.
———— instrumental, 607—611.

Dative, instrumental, instead of cognate or equivalent acc. 548. Obs. 6.
———— local, 605.
———— expressing reference to, 599, 600.
———— temporal, 606.
———— transmissive, 587—594.
———— after prepositions, 622, 623. 631—639.
———— after verbs, adjectives, and adverbs of coincidence, equality, similarity, &c. 594.
———— after verbal adjectives in τέος, 613. 5.
———— after ἀντίος, ἐχθρός, διάφορος &c. 601. 2.
———— after φίλος, κοινός, συγγενής &c. 590.
———— after verbs expressing the above notions, 590.
———— after πέλας, ἐγγύς, ἀγχοῦ, 592. 2.
———— after verbs expressing the above notions, 592. 1.
———— after ἀκόλουθος, διάδοχος, ἑξῆς &c. 593. 2.
———— after δεῖ and χρή, 594. 3.
———— after φίλος, εὔνους, ὠφέλιμος, 596. 3.
———— after verbs of governing, 518. Obs. 3.
———— after verbs of transmission or communication of any thing, 581. 1.
———— after verbs of granting, offering, paying, &c. 588. 1.
———— after words denoting what is allotted or decreed, 588. 2.
———— after verbs of sharing with, selling to, &c. 588. 3.
———— after verbs of speaking, praying, swearing, to, &c. 589. 1.
———— after verbs of counselling, praising, reproaching, &c. 589. 3.
———— after verbs and adjectives of uniting oneself to, or associating, 590.
———— after verbs of adopting, or applying oneself to, 591.
———— after verbs of meeting, sending, pouring, &c. 592. 1.
———— after verbs, adjectives, &c. of obeying, trusting, &c. 593. 1, 2.
———— after verbs of agreeing with, &c. 594. 1.
———— after verbs, adject., and adv. of equality and agreement, 594. 2.
———— after verbs of being suitable for, &c. 594. 3.
———— after verbs of pleasing, 594. 4.
———— after verbs of helping, favouring, &c. 596. 1.
———— after verbs of serving as a slave, 596. 2.

Dative after verbs and adject. of hostility, contention, &c. 601. 1.
—— after verbs of taking away, 602. 1.
—— after verbs of coming, going, 604. 2.
—— after a verb to define a place, ('Ελλάδι ναίων), 605. 1.
—— after verbs of governing, Homeric use of, 605. 3.
—— after verbs of joy, sorrow, &c. 607.
—— after verbs of action, 607.
—— after verbs of measuring, deciding, &c. 609. 3.
—— in notions of price and value, 609. 2.
—— in the σχῆμα καθ᾽ ὅλον καὶ μέρος, 597. Obs. 3.
—— of the accessories of any thing (αὐτοῖς τοῖς ἵπποις), 604. 1.
—— of the accessories of any thing (στρατῷ, στόλῳ, πλήθει, ναυσί &c.), 604. 2.
—— of the circumstances under which any thing takes place (κακῇ αἴσῃ), 603. 1.
—— of the instrument or means, 607, 608.
—— of the material, 610.
—— of the mode or manner, 603. 2.
—— of the participle for another case, 712.
—— of certain participles (βουλομένῳ, ἡδομένῳ &c.) with εἶναι and γίγνεσθαι, 599. 3.
—— of the personal pronouns, seemingly redundant, 600. 2.
—— of point of superiority, 504. Obs. 1.
—— of substantives and adjectives after εἶναι and γίγνεσθαι, 507.
—— of time (τρίτῃ ἡμέρᾳ), 606.
—— with comparatives, &c. 609. 1.
—— with the infinitive, 672.
—— with the participle, 682, 683.
—— with passive verbs, sense of, 611.
—— with κελεύειν, ' to admonish,' Attic use of, doubtful, 589. Obs. 3.
—— with νομίζειν explained, 591.Obs.
—— with οἶος, τοιοῦτος, apparent use of, 594. Obs. 2.
Datival relation of self to the middle verb, 362. 2. 2.
Dativus commodi et incommodi, 595.
—— commodi, 596, 597, 598.
—— incommodi, 601, 602.
Demonstrative, omission of the, 817. 4.
—— pronoun, 655.
—— pronoun, agreement of, with its subject, 381. Obs. 1, 2.
—— pronoun αὐτός, 656.

Demonstrative pronoun, referring to a substantival notion implied in a preceding word, 373. Obs.
Dependent cases, 480.
—— sentence changed into an interrog. 882.
—— sentences, use of οὐκ and μή in, 742—744.
Deponent verb, 357. 5. 362. 9. 368.
Difference, notion of with gen. 503.
—— between οὐ and μή, 739.
Double accusative, list of verbs followed by, 583.
—— accusative, use of, 582. 3.
—— genitive, 543.
Dual, proper use of the, 387. 1.
—— adjective with plural subst. 388. a.
—— subject with a plural verb, 387. 2.
—— substantive, fem., with masc. attributive (τούτω τὰ τέχνα), 388. b.
—— verb, used with a plural subject, 388.

Elements of a simple sentence, 371.
Ellipse, meaning and use of, 891. 1, 2.
—— and brachylogy, difference between, 892. 1.
—— of ἄν in apodosis with indic. 858.
—— of the apodosis, 860. 3.
—— of the copula εἶναι, 376.
—— of γάρ, 786. Obs. 2.
—— of indefinite pronoun τὶς, 373. 5.
—— of the protasis, 860. 2.
—— in a simple sentence, 891. 3, 4.
—— in a compound sentence, 891. 5, 6.
—— of the subject, 373.
—— of the substantive before an attributive adj. 436.
Elliptic accus. 548. e. 551. e. 552. e. 553. d.
—— expressions, 860. 4—7.
Elliptical use of infinitive in commands and wishes, 671.
—— use of γάρ, 786. Obs. 7.
Equivalent notion, 545. 5.
—— notion, acc. of, 548. c. 549. c. 550. b. 551. c. 551. 2. 552. c. 553. c. 554. b. 555. c. 556. c.
—— acc., particular uses of, 579.
Essential words, 351.
Etymology of ἄν, 423.
Exchange of cases in the participial construction, 708.
Examples and explanation of relative tenses, 394. 8.

Feminine adjective with neuter subst. (τὸ γυναικίόν ἐστι καλή), 378. b. 379.
—— plural with verb singular, 386.

Feminine plur. with neuter sing. (αἱ μεταβολαὶ λυπηρόν), 381.

——— dual with masc. adjective (τούτω τὰ τεχνά), 388. b.

Formal words, 351.

Frequency, expressed by the impft. ind. with ἄν, 424. β.

Future, proper sense of, 406. 1.

——— expressed by a periphrasis with μέλλω, 408.

——— use of, for present, 406. 4.

——— ind., difference of, from opt. with ἄν, 426. 2.

——— ind., use of, to express probable repetition in fut. time, 406. 2.

——— ind., use of, to express comparison, 406. 2.

——— ind., use of, to express necessity, 406. 3.

——— ind., use of, to express intention, 406. 5.

——— ind., use of, to express a desire, 413. 1.

——— ind., use of, interrogatively, to express a strong command, 413. 2.

——— ind., use of, with ἄν, 424. δ.

——— middle, seeming passive force of, 364. a.

Futurum exactum (iii.), proper sense of, 407. 1.

——— exactum (iii.), use of, to express continuance in future time, 407. 1.

——— exactum (iii.), for simple future, 407. 2.

Gender, especial peculiarities of, 390.

——— of adjectives, &c. in the constructio κατὰ σύνεσιν, 378. b. 379, 380. 2.

——— of adjectives, &c. in sayings, proverbs, &c. (αἱ μεταβολαὶ λυπηρόν), 381.

——— of the predicative adjective with substantives of different genders, 391.

——— of the predicative substantive, 382.

——— of relative pronouns, 819, 821.

Genitive, notion of, 471. 4. 1.

——— antecedent notion expressed by, 480. 1.

——— power of, 480.

——— absolute, 541, 695. 2.

——— absolute for some other case, 710.

——— attributive, 463, 534.

——— attributive of procession, 483. Obs. 2. 4.

——— attributive, use of article with, 461.

——— attributive, used for material adjective, 435. b.

Genitive, attributive, used for nominative in apposition, 435. d.

——— attributive, used without its substantive, 436. b.

——— causal attributive, 499. Obs. 2.

——— double attributive, 465, 466. Obs. 1.

——— elliptic attributive (ὁ τοῦ βασιλέως υἱός), explanation of, 483. Obs. 2.

——— causal, 481.

——— causal, after substantives (φόβοι πολεμίων, metus ab hostibus), 499. Obs. 2.

——— causal, after all verbs, 481. 1.

——— double, 543.

——— material, 480. 6. 538—540.

——— partitive, 533. ff.

——— (partitive) after εἶναι and γίγνεσθαι, 533. 1.

——— privative, 529.

——— relative, notion of, 502.

——— separative, 530, 531.

——— the latter of two substantives in, 542. 1.

——— of the article with an infinitive to express the aim or intent of an action, 492.

——— of cause, 480. 1.

——— of partition, 480. 4.

——— of place, 522.

——— of place, after verbs of motion, 522. 2.

——— of position, 480. 3. 524 ff.

——— of personal pronouns (μοῦ, σοῦ &c.), for the possessive pronouns (ἐμός &c.), 652. 3.

——— of personal pronouns, for the dat. comm. 652. Obs. 4.

——— of price, 515.

——— of privation, 480. 6.

——— of property or possession, 521. 1.

——— of quality (ἀνδρός ἐστιν ἀγαθοῦ εὖ ποιεῖν κ.τ.λ.), 521. 2.

——— of relation, 480. 2.

——— of separation, 480. 5.

——— of temporal separation (δευτέρῳ ἔτει τούτων), 532.

——— of a point of time (θέρους, ἡμέρας, νυκτός), 523.

——— of a space of time (δέκα ἡμερῶν), 523.

——— with the infinitive, 672.

——— with the participle, 681.

——— after adjectives compounded with α privative, 529. Obs. 2.

——— after adjectives and adverbs expressing connection or dependence, 520.

——— after adjectives expressing fulness, 539. 2.

Genitive after adjectives of misery (τάλαινα τῶν ἀλγέων), 489.
————— after adjectives expressing opposition, proximity, &c. 525.
————— after verbal adjectives in ικός, 494.
————— after verbal adj. expressing a transitive action, 494.
————— after adverbs expressing proximity to, or distance from, 526.
————— after comparatives, 502. 2.
————— after interjections (οἴμοι κακῶν!), 489.
————— after numerals in -άσιος (διπλάσιος), 502. 3.
————— after numerals in -πλοῦς (διπλοῦς), 502. 2.
————— after prepositions, 618—621. 627—639.
————— after substantives, used as prepositions, 621. Obs. 2.
————— after superlative adjectives, 502. 2.
————— after passive and intransitive verbs (ἀλόχου σφαγείς), 483. Obs. 3.
————— after verbs of smell (ὄζειν ἴων), 484.
————— after verbs of examining, inquiring, saying, 486.
————— after verbs of hearing, in the sense of to 'obey,' 487. 4.
————— after verbs of grief, sympathy, &c. 488.
————— after verbs of anger and annoyance, 490.
————— after verbs of benefit, advantage, enjoyment, 491.
————— after verbs of wondering, praising, &c. with an acc. of patient (ζηλῶ σε τῆς εὐτυχίας), 495.
————— after verbs of caring for, thinking much of, 496.
————— after verbs of 'drinking in honour of,' 497.
————— after verbs of desire or longing for, 498.
————— of thing, after verbs of grudging, with dative of person (φθονεῖν τινι τῆς σοφίας), 499.
————— of thing, after verbs of requital and revenge, with acc. of person (τιμωρεῖσθαί τινα φόνου), 500.
————— of thing, after verbs of prosecution and sentencing (ἐπαιτιᾶσθαί τινα φόνου), 501.
————— after recipient verbs, 501. Obs. 3.
————— after verbs of superiority, &c. 504.
————— after verbs of inferiority, 505.
————— after verbs of aiming at a mark, 505.

Genitive after verbs of striving after, 507.
————— after verbs of catching, reaching after, 508.
————— after verbs of obtaining, &c. 509. 1.
————— after verbs of meeting with or approaching, 510.
————— after verbs of failing in, missing, &c. 511.
————— after verbs of remembering and forgetting, 512.
————— after verbs of beginning, 513.
————— after verbs of ceasing, stopping, 514.
————— after verbs of buying and selling, 515. 2.
————— after verbs of exchange and barter, 516.
————— after verbs of valuing, 517.
————— after verbs of governing, being superior to, 518.
————— after verbs expressing privation, 529. 1.
————— after verbs of removal, separation, departure, &c. 530. 1.
————— after verbs of beginning, 530. 2.
————— after verbs of leaving off, ceasing, &c. 531.
————— after verbs of driving away from, delivering from, 531.
————— after verbs of participation, communication, &c. 535.
————— after verbs of contact, 536.
————— after verbs of praying or vowing, 536. Obs. 6.
————— after verbs of eating and drinking, 537.
————— after verbs of making, forming, &c. 538.
————— after verbs of being full and filling, 539. 1.
————— after ἔμπειρος, ἐπιστήμων, τρίβων, ἀδαής, ἀπαίδευτος, ἰδιώτης &c. 493.
————— after ἄλλος, ἕτερος, διάφορος, ἐναντίος &c. 503.
————— after ἄξιος, ἀνάξιος, ἀντάξιος, 517.
————— after κοινός, ἴσος, ὅμοιος, συνεργός, συγγενής &c. 519.
————— after φίλος, ἐχθρός, διάδοχος, ἀκόλουθος &c. 520.
————— after ἴδιος, οἰκεῖος, κύριος, πρέπων, 521. 3.
————— after ἀντίος, μέσος, παραπλήσιος, 525.
————— after ἐλεύθερος, μόνος, κενός, γυμνός &c. 529. 1.
————— after ἄτερ, νόσφιν, χωρίς, πλήν, 529. 2.

Genitive, after πλέος, πλήρης, πλούσιος, δασύς &c. 539. 2.

———— after the adverbs εὐθύ, ἰθύς, ἄχρι, μέχρι, 509. 2.

———— after adverbs of position, proximity to, distance from (ἄντα, ἐνώπιον, πρόσθεν, ἐγγύς), 526.

———— after ἑξῆς, ἐφεξῆς, &c. 520.

———— after ποῦ, πῇ, πόθεν, οὐδαμοῦ, πανταχῇ &c. 527.

———— after εὖ, καλῶς, μετρίως, ὡς, with εἶναι, κεῖσθαι, ἔχειν, ἥκειν &c. (εὖ ποδῶν εἶχεν), 528.

———— after ἀκούειν &c., πυνθάνεσθαι &c., μανθάνειν, ἐπίστασθαι, ἐνθυμεῖσθαι &c. 485.

———— after μελετᾶν, in sense of 'to care for,' 496.

———— after κρατεῖν, 519. Obs. 1.

———— after εἶναι, γίγνεσθαι, 483. 521. a.

———— after δεῖσθαι, to request, 529. Obs. 1.

———— after ὑπηρετεῖν, 596. Obs. 3.

Genitival form of local adverbs, οὗ, ποῦ, ἀγχοῦ, ὁμοῦ, 522. Obs. 1.

———— relation of self to the middle verb, 362. 2. 1.

Gerund, proper expression for, in Greek, 695.

Greek and modern cases, contrast between, 473.

Herodotus, style of, 900. a.

Historic tenses, difference in the signification of, 394. 6.

Hyperbaton, meaning and use of, 904.1.

Hypothetical sentences, see Adverbial hypothetical sentences.

Imperative, proper sense of, 410. d. 420. 1.

———— sense of, in the different tenses, 420. 2.

———— aorist for the present, 405.

———— use of in negative or prohibitory forms, 420. 3.

———— use of certain (εἰπέ, ἄγε, φέρε, ἴδε), in the singular, with a substantive in plural, 390. a.

———— in apodosis of conditional sentences, 856. c.

———— of ii. pers. with τὶς or πᾶς τις, 390. γ.

———— of iii. pers. sing., perf., mid., or pass. (λελείφθω, reliquum esto), 399. Obs. 1.

———— with ἄν, incorrect, 424. ε.

———— with ὥστε, 867. 1.

Imperfect, proper sense of, 398. 1.

———— indicative, use of, with ἄν, 424. β.

Imperfect, use of, to signify an attempt, 398. 2.

———— use of, as conditional, 398. 3.

———— use of, for present, 398. 4.

———— use of, to express continuance, 401. 4.

———— use of, to express frequency, 402. 2.

———— use of as a descriptive tense, 401. 2.

———— iterative form of in σκον, 402. Obs. 3.

Impersonal form ὡς ἔοικε in parentheses, used personally, 869. 6.

Indefinite article, 446.—Remarks.

———— pronoun, 659.

———— pronoun, ellipse of, 373. 5.

Independent sentences, use of οὐκ and μή in, 740, 741.

Indicative, notion of the, 410. 1, 2. a. and Obs. 412.

———— future, use of, to express a desire, 413. 1.

———— future, for conj. adhortativus, 413. 3.

———— future with οὐ for imperative (οὐ παύσῃ λέγων; for παύου λέγων), 413. 2.

———— future with ἄν, 424. δ.

———— future with ἄν, in the apodosis of hypothetical sentences, 854. Obs. 3. 855. Obs. 5.

———— future with ἄν joined to a relative, 827. a.

———— future with ὅπως, ὡς εἰ, 811.

———— future with ὅπως ἄν, 811. 2.

———— future with οὐ μή, 748.

———— imp., aorist, and plup. with ἄν, difference between, 456. Obs. 1.

———— present and perfect not used with ἄν, 424. γ.

———— in apodosis, 852. 1. 853. e. 854. a. 855. b.

———— in oratio obliqua, 886.

———— in adverbial sentences, 840. 863.

———— in dependent sentences with ὅτι and ὡς, that, 802.

———— in dependent sentences with μή, 814.

———— in dependent sentences with relatives, 826, 827.

———— in dependent sentences with temporal conjunctions, ὅτε, ἐπεί, μέχρι &c. 840.

———— in dependent sentences with temporal conjunctions, ὅτε, ὁπότε, ὡς, since; ἐπεί, ἐπειδή, ὅπου, 849. 2.

———— in dependent sentences with ὅτι, διότι, οὕνεκα, ὁθούνεκα, 849. 3.

———— in dependent sentences with εἰ, 851. 2. I. and 853.

Indicative of historic tenses, to express a condition, 422.
———— of historic tenses used in wishes, 418. *Obs.* 1.
———— of historic tenses, use of, with ἵνα, ὡς, ὅπως, 813.
———— of historic tenses with ἕως, 846. 1.
———— of historic tenses with ἄν after ὅτι, ὡς, that, 803. 2.
———— of historic tenses with relatives, 827. *b.*
———— of historic tenses with temporal conj. ὅτε &c. 849. 2.
———— of historic tenses with εἰ, 851. III. 856.
———— of historic tenses with ἄν after ὥστε, 860.
———— with ἄν, 424. β. Cf. 827. 852. 1. 853. *c.* 855. *c.* 856. *a.*
———— with ὥστε, ὡς, 863. 1.
Infinitive mood, notion expressed by the, 662.
———— aor. for passive (ἄξιος θαυμάσαι), 667. *Obs.* 3. 669. *Obs.* 2.
———— aor. for present, 405.
———— aor., pres., and future, difference between, 405. *Obs.* 2.
———— elliptical use of, in commands and wishes, 671.
———— pres. for aor. in an oratio obliqua, 395. *Obs.* 2.
———— perf. mid. or pass. in an oratio obliqua, for imperative perf. mid. or passive, 399. *Obs.* 1.
———— after πρίν, 848. 6.
———— after ὥστε, 863. 2.
———— after οἷος, ὅσος, 823. *Obs.* 3.
———— after ὡς and ὥστε, as; ὅσον, ὅσα, ὅτι, 864.
———— as explanation of the relative in adjectival sentences, 835. 2.
———— change of impersonal construction with, into the personal, 677.
———— for ὥστε with inf. 863. *Obs.* 2.
———— for ὡς with inf. (οὐ πολλῷ λόγῳ εἰπεῖν, ὀλίγου δεῖν), 863. *Obs.* 2.
———— instead of part. after δεικνύναι, ἀγγέλλειν, φαίνεσθαι, ποιεῖν, 684. *Obs.* 2.
———— instead of part. after verbs of mental feeling, 685. *Obs.*
———— instead of part. after ἀνέχεσθαι, ὑπομένειν, τλῆναι, τολμᾶν, περιορᾶν, ἐπιτρέπειν, ἀποκάμνειν, 687. *Obs.*
———— instead of part. after ἄρχεσθαι, παύειν, 688. *Obs.*
———— instead of part. after παντοῖος ἐγένετο, πειρᾶσθαι, παρασκευάζεσθαι, ἐπείγεσθαι, 690. *Obs.* 1.
———— instead of part. after certain

impersonal expressions (πρέπει, λυσιτελεῖ, φίλον ἐστίν &c.), 691.
Infinitive, instead of part. after ἔχειν, 692. *Obs.*
———— instead of part. after φθάνειν, 694. *Obs.* 4.
———— use of, as a general expression of necessity for δεῖ or χρή, 671. *c.*
———— use of, in questions expressing reluctance, 671. *d.*
———— use of, with αἱ γάρ, εἴθε, 671. *e.*
———— use of, in adverbial sentences, 863.
———— use of οὐκ and μή with, 745.
———— use of, with nom., gen., dat., and acc. 672, 673.
———— use of ὡς, ὥστε with, in seemingly independent parentheses, 864.
———— or inf. with acc. after a suppressed verb of perceiving or communicating, 884. *Obs.* 2.
———— with acc. instead of the construction with ὅτι or ὡς, 804. 4.
———— with adjectives, as acc., in Homer (θείειν ἄριστος), 667. *Obs.* 1.
———— with ἄν, 429.
———— with ἄν after ὥστε, 866.
———— with ὥστε, 664. *Obs.* 3.
———— with the article, use of, for inf. without art. 670.
———— with the article, use of, as a substantive, 678.
———— with the article, use of, in exclamations and questions, 679. 1.
———— with the article, use of, in adverbial expressions (τὸ νῦν εἶναι), 679. 2.
———— as object after verbs denoting a motion of the will, 664.
———— as object after verbs of thinking, or saying, &c. 665.
———— as object after verbs of ability, efficacy, causing, &c. 666.
———— after adjectives and substantives to define the notion thereof (ἄξιος θαυμάζεσθαι), 667.
———— after εἶναι and γίγνεσθαι with a substantive, 668.
———— after συμβαίνει, δεῖ, χρή &c. 669. *a.*
———— after adjectives and subst. 669. β. γ.
———— after verbs of giving, taking, going, like Latin supine (ἥκω μανθάνειν), 669. *e.*
Intensive particles, 734—737.
Interchange of oratio obliqua with oratio recta, 890.
———— of prepositions, 649.
Interjections with gen. 489.
Interrogative particles, use and senses of, 872. 2.

Interrogative pronoun, preceded by article, 881. 2.
————— sentences, use and forms of, 371. 3. 871.
————— sentences containing simple direct questions, 872—874.
————— sentences containing direct double questions, 875.
————— sentences containing simple indirect questions, 877.
————— sentences containing indirect compound questions, 878.
————— sentences, moods in the, 879.
————— sentences, answer to the question of, 880.
————— sentences, coalition of a relative sentence with (ποῖον τὸν μῦθον ἔειπες; for ποῖός ἐστιν ὁ μῦθος, ὃν εἶπες;), 881. 1.
————— sentences substituted for dependent sentences (ὅταν τί ποιήσωσι;), 882.
————— sentences, two or more in one (τίς τίνος αἴτιός ἐστι;), 883.
Intransitive verb, 357. 2, 4.
————— verb used as transitive, 359. 2.
————— verb used as passive (ἐκπίπτειν ὑπό τινος), 359. 3.
————— verb with gen. 483. Obs. 3.
Inversion of the members of the attributive sentence, 442.
Inverted position in a simple sentence, 902.
————— position in a compound sentence, 903.

Language, 350. 1.
Limitation, notion of, expressed by the participle, 697. c.
————— and denial, modes of expressing, 773.
Local forms in ι, οι, ω, ησι, ασι, 605. Obs. 1.
————— objective relation, 468. a.

Masculine adjective, used with a fem. substantive, 390. c.
————— adjective with neut. subst. (μειράκιόν ἐστι καλός), 378. b. 379.
————— or fem. plur. noun, used with a verb sing. 386.
————— in plur. with adj. in neuter (οἱ πολλοὶ δεινόν), 381.
Material genitive, 538—540.
—————, antecedent notion of, in gen. 480. 2. 7.
Means, notion of the, expressed by the participle, 697. d.
Metonymy, 353.
Middle voice, twofold function of, 362.

Middle verb, 357. 5.
————— and active sense of verbs, difference between, 363. 6.
————— verb, passive force of, 364. 2, 3, 4.
————— verb, reciprocal force of, 364. 1.
————— verb, reflexive notion of, 362. 1.
————— verb, remarks on the reflexive force of, 363.
————— verb followed by the personal pronoun, 363. 2.
————— verb for the active, 363. 3, 4.
————— verb with 'self' in the genitival relation (ἀποπέμπεσθαι, to send away from oneself), 362. 1.
————— verb with 'self' in the datival relation (ἄγεσθαι γυναῖκα, ducere sibi uxorem, to marry), 362. 2.
————— verb with 'self' in the accusatival relation (λούεσθαι, to wash oneself = to bathe), 362. 3.
————— verb with 'self' in the adjectival relation (νίπτεσθαι τοὺς πόδας, to wash one's own feet), 362. 4.
————— verb with 'self' in more than one relation, 362. 5.
————— forms, use of to signify the passive notion, 366.
Modal objective relations, expressions of, 468. d.
Mood, meaning of the term, 410. 1.
Moods, division of, 410. 2.
————— the general power of the, 411. 2.
————— use of, as conditionals, 422.
————— use of, in dependent sentences, 797.
————— use of different, in sentences connected by καί, 759. Obs. 4.
————— in temporal adverbial sentences, 840.
————— in the interrogative sentence, 879.
————— in oratio obliqua, 885.
————— in oratio obliqua, interchange of, 888.

Negative particles, 738—750.
————— repetition of the, 747.
————— seeming pleonasm of, 748—750.
————— clauses, connection and opposition of, 775.
————— and positive clause, connection of, 775. 3. a. β.
Neuter adj. with masc. or fem. subst. (γυνὴ θῆλύ ἐστιν), 381.
————— plural, joined with a verb singular, 384.
————— plural, with a verb singular, principle of the construction of, 384. Obs. 2.

Neuter plural, used with a verb plural, 385.

——— plural, use of a predicative adj. in the, for the neuter singular, 383.

——— subst. with masc. or fem. adj. (φίλε τέκνον), 379.

Nominative, not strictly a case, 474.

Nominative, force of, 476.

——— peculiarities in the use of, 477, 478.

——— as expression of object, after εἶναι &c. 476. 2.

——— emphatic at beginning of a sentence, 477. I.

——— at the beginning of a sentence, in seeming apposition to a subst. of a preceding sentence in an oblique case, 477. 2.

——— of a thing or person in the phrases ὄνομά ἐστί μοι, ὄνομα ἔχω, 475. Obs. I.

——— in the σχῆμα καθ᾽ ὅλον καὶ μέρος, 478.

——— instead of oblique case, 476. Obs. 2.

——— use of, to express the subject of the sentence, 475. I.

——— use of, to express the object of the verbal notion, 475. 2.

——— use of, for the vocative, 476.

——— with infinitive, 672.

——— with inf. for the acc. with inf. 673. 2. and Obs.

——— with participle, 681.

——— partic. for the other cases, 707, 708.

——— partic. without any verbum finitum, 709.

——— of verb in passive voice, the object of verb in active, as ἐγὼ πιστεύομαι—πιστεύειν τινί, 372.

Notions, antecedent, coincident, consequent, 471. 3.

——— implied in a transitive verb, 545. I.

——— implied in a neuter verb, 545. 2.

——— implied in a passive and middle verb, 545. 3.

——— implied in a transmissive verb, 544. 4.

Nouns, substantive, 352.

Noun, different meanings of the same, 352. 5.

Number, 354, 355.

——— especial peculiarities of, 390.

——— in the constructio κατὰ σύνεσιν, 378—380.

——— of adjective, participle, &c. different from that of the substantive, 378. b.

——— of the predicative substantive, 382.

——— of the relative pronoun, 819 —821.

——— of the verbal adjectives in τός and τέος, 383.

——— of the verb, which has several subjects disjunctively united by ἤ—ἤ, οὔτε—οὔτε, 393. 8.

Numerals with article, 455. I.

——— ordinal with article, 455. 3.

Objective construction, 468.

——— relations of place and time, expression of, 468.

——— sentence, complex, 469.

Object of the verb expressed by the cases, 471.

Omission of prepositions, 650.

——— of one of the clauses of an antithesis, 896.

——— of a subst. or adj. the notion of which is involved in the context, 893.

——— of the verb in dependent clauses, 895. 2.

——— of a verbal form to be supplied from a preceding verb, 895. a. b.

Optative, notion of the, 414.

——— mood, secondary meaning of, 411. I.

——— use of, to express a supposition, 418. a.

——— use of, to express a wish, 418. b.

——— use of, to express a command, 418. c.

——— use of, to express desire, willingness, &c. 418. d.

——— use of, in direct questions, 418. e.

——— use of, in negative questions, 418. f.

——— use of, in compound sentences, 419.

——— aorist for present, 405.

——— instead of an imperative, 420. Obs. I.

——— and conjunctive, interchange of, 809.

——— and conj. with ἄν, interchange of, 831. Obs.

——— after a principal tense or aor. 807.

——— or conj. after optative, 808.

——— without ἄν, in independent sentences, 426. I.

——— without ἄν, with negatives, 426. Obs. I.

——— in dependent sentences; after ὅτι, ὡς, that, 802.

Optative in dependent sentences, after ὡς, ὅπως, ἵνα &c. 805. 2. 807, 808.

———— in dependent sentences, after μή, 814. b. c.

———— in dependent sentences, after οὐ μή, 748.

———— after the temporal conjunctions, ὅτε, ὡς, ἕως &c. 843. 844.

———— after the hypothetical conj. εἰ, 851. b. 855.

———— after ὥστε, 865.

———— after a relative, 831.

———— with ἄν, 425. cf. 852. 1. 853. b. 854. b. 855. a. 856. b.

———— with ἄν in dependent sentences, after ὅτι, ὡς, that, 803. 1.

———— with ἄν in dependent sentences, after a relative, 832.

———— with ἄν in dependent sentences, after the temporal conjunctions, ὅτε, ὡς, ἕως &c. 845.

———— with ἄν in dependent sentences, after ὥστε, 865.

———— with ἄν in dependent sentences, after the causal conjunctions, ὅτε, ὡς, ἐπεί, quoniam, &c. 849. 2.

———— with ἄν after ὡς, ὅπως, ἵνα &c. 810.

———— with ἄν after μή, 810, 814. c.

———— in oratio obliqua, use of, 885.

Oratio obliqua, laws of the, 884.

———— use of the moods in, 885 —888.

———— use of the optative in, 885.

———— use of the indicative in, 886.

———— use of the conjunctive in, 887.

———— interchange of conj., opt., and ind. in, 888.

———— acc. with inf. instead of verbum finitum in, 889.

———— and recta, mixture of, 886. 3.—in subst. sentences, a.—in adject. sentences, b.—in adverb. sentences, c.—in indirect interrog. sentences, d.

———— changed into recta, 842. 1.

———— interchange of, with oratio recta, 890.

Origin of prepositions, 472.

Original forms of verbs, 358.

Parallelismus antitheticus, 899. 6.

Parenthesis, use of, 798. 2.

Participle, notion expressed by the, 662.

———— use and force of the, 680.

———— construction of the, 681. 1, 2. 682.

———— certain peculiar constructions of, 705.

Participle, attributive, agreement of with the substantival notion expressed by a periphrasis, 380. 2.

———— in the nom. by attraction, with what verbs constructed, 683—694.

———— in the nom., and acc. with inf., difference between, 683. Obs. 687. Obs. 688. Obs.

———— for the verbum finitum, 705. 2. 4.

———— for the verbum finitum, in one of two sentences connected by καί, τέ—καί, μέν—δέ, 759. Obs. 4. 765. 2.

———— not agreeing with its immediate attributive, 379. a.

———— not agreeing with its subst. in gend. and number, 378. b.

———— nominative, use of the, without any verbum finitum, 709.

———— genitive, use of the for some other case, 710.

———— accusative, use of for some other case, 711.

———— dative, use of for some other case, 712.

———— of the same root and meaning attached to the verb of the sentence (ὑπακούων ὑπακούει), 705. 3.

———— used as a subst. (οἱ ἥβωντες for ἔφηβοι), 436. a.

———— common use of certain, as adverbial expressions, 696. Obs. 1.

———— use of, as the completion of the verbal notion, 681.

———— use of certain, to express the English 'with,' 697. Obs. 2.

———— use of the, in the dat. absolute, 699.

———— use of the, in the acc. absolute, 700.

———— use of, to define a demonstr. used with a preceding verb, 693.

———— use of, as the Latin gerund, 695—698.

———— use of, as gerund, to express temporal, causal, and adverbial notions, 695.

———— use of, to express the time of any notion, 696.

———— use of, to express the cause or reason, 697. a.

———— use of, to express the conditions, 697. b.

———— use of, to express limitation, 697. c.

———— use of, to express the means, 698. d.

———— use of, to express mode and manner, 698. e.

———— use of, in the gen. without a subject, 696. Obs. 3.

Participle, use of, in the gen. with ἐπί, 696. *Obs.* 4. 700. *Obs.* 2.

—————— use of the, with comparative particles, ὡς, ὥστε, ἅτε, οἷον, οἷα, 701 —704.

—————— use of οὐκ and μή with, 746.

—————— with dat. of reference, use of, 599. 2. 3.

—————— after verbs of sensual and mental perception, 683.

—————— after verbs of shewing, proving, appearing, &c. 684.

—————— after verbs of mental feelings and affections, 685.

—————— after verbs of satisfying oneself, enjoying the possession of, being full of anything, 686.

—————— after verbs of permitting, tolerating, persevering, &c. 687.

—————— after verbs of beginning and ceasing, 688.

—————— after verbs of being in luck, in error, deficient, 689.

—————— after πειρᾶσθαι, παρασκευάζεσθαι, ἐπείγεσθαι, 690.

—————— after πολλός, παντοῖός ἐστι, 690.

—————— after certain impersonal expressions, 'it is good, fitting, profitable, to my mind,' &c. 691.

—————— after ἔχειν, as ἔχω κτησάμενος, 692.

—————— after τυγχάνω, κυρῶ, λανθάνω, διατελῶ, διαγίγνομαι, διάγω, φθάνω, οἴχομαι, 694.

—————— with εἶναι for the verbal form (δεδορκὼς ἦν), 375. 4.

—————— of εἶναι omitted after verbs of declaring, 682. 3.

—————— of εἶναι omitted after τυγχάνειν and κυρεῖν, 694. *Obs.* 1.

—————— of εἶναι omitted after an adj. or subst. following a part. (λύτρα φέρων καὶ ἱκέτης), 705. 6.

—————— with ἄν, 429.

Participial construction, asyndeton in the, 706.

—————— construction, anacoluthon in the, 707.

—————— construction, exchange of cases in the, 708.

Particles.—See Adverbs and Conjunctions.

—————— intensive, 734—737.

—————— negative, 738—750.

—————— (μὲν &c.), after a vocative, 479. 5.

Partition, antecedent notion of, in gen. 480. 2, 4.

Partitive genitive, 533. *ff.*

—————— notion, expressed by μέρος, 535. *Obs.* 1.

Passive voice, 367.

—————— force of middle, 364. 2.

—————— verbs with gen. 483. *Obs.* 3.

Perfect, proper sense of, 399. 1.

—————— use of, to connect a completed action with present time, 399. *a.*

—————— use of, to represent an action, continuing in its effects, 399. *b.*

—————— use of, in imperative, to express strong exhortation, 399. *Obs.* 1.

—————— use of, as a present perfect, 399. *Obs.* 2.

—————— use of, to express frequency, 399. *Obs.* 3.

—————— use of, for a future, 399. 2.

Periphrasis for a personal name ('Ορφεία γῆρυς), 442. *d.*

—————— with μέλλω for the future, 408.

Person, especial peculiarities of, 390.

—————— of the verb with several subjects, 392.

—————— of the verb in the adjectival sentence, 818.

Personal construction for impersonal with inf. (δίκαιός εἰμι τοῦτο πράττειν), 677.

—————— construction for impers. with the participle, 684. *Obs.* 1.

—————— construction for impers. with ὅτι, ὡς, 804. 2.

—————— name, expressed by a periphrasis, 442. *d.*

Place, notion of, expressed by the cases, 522, 577, 605.

—————— notion of, expressed by prepositions, 614. 3.

—————— notion of, expressed by adv. 715.

—————— notion of, expressed by adjectives, 714. *a.*

—————— expression of objective relations of, 468. *a.*

Plato, style of, 900. γ.

Pleonasm, 899.

—————— apparent, of μή, οὐ—οὐ μή— μὴ οὐ, 748—750.

Pleonastic use of two words of the same root, 899. 1.

Pluperfect, proper sense of, 400. 1.

—————— use of, to express a past action continuing in its effects, 400. 2.

—————— use of, as an impft. of present pft. 400. 2.

Plural number, 355.

—————— of proper, material, and abstract nouns, 355.

—————— forms of pronouns, joined to a singular, 383. *Obs.*

—————— gen. of a subst. with τό or τά (τὰ τῶν διακόνων κ. τ. λ.), 380. 1.

—————— masc. or fem. joined to a verb singular (σχῆμα Βοιωτικόν), 386.

Plural neuter, joined to a verb singular, 384.
—— neuter, joined to a verb plural, 385.
—— for the singular, 355. *Obs.* 1, 2.
—— of the first person instead of the singular, 390. *d.*
—— neuter of the predicate for the singular, 383.
—— predicate, joined with vocative singular, in addresses, 390. β.
—— subject joined with a singular verb, 390. *b. d.*
—— subject joined with a dual verb, 388.
—— verb, agreement of a, with a singular subject, 378. *a.*
—— (or dual) verb, used with a singular noun, 393. 5.
—— verb, used with a dual subject, 387. 2.
—— verb with a subst. in singular and μετά, *cum,* 380. *Obs.* 1.
Position, antecedent notion of, in gen. 480. 2, 3.
—— (usual) of words in a simple sentence, 901. 1, 2.
—— (usual) of words in a compound sentence, 901. 3.
—— (inverted) of words in a simple sentence, 902.
—— (inverted) of words in a compound sentence, 903.
—— of ἄν, 431.
—— of the article, ὁ, ἡ, τό, 458.
—— of prepositions, 651.
—— of the pronouns, 452—454.
—— of gen. of personal pron. μοῦ, σοῦ &c. 652. 3. and *Obs.* 3, and 4.
—— of αὐτοῦ, -ῶν, 652. *Obs.* 3.
—— of reflexive pronouns, ἑαυτοῦ &c. 652. 3. and *Obs.* 3.
—— of αὐτός with ἕκαστος, 656.
—— of αὐτός with reflexive pron. and preposition (ἐν αὐτὸς αὐτῷ), 656. *Obs.* 4.
—— of τὶς, 446, *Remarks.* 660.
—— of τέ, 756.
—— of μέν and δέ, 765. 1.
—— of γέ, 735. *Obs.* 2.
—— of οὐ and μή, 738. *Obs.* 1.
—— of ὦ with the vocative, 479. 3.
—— of interrog. words, 872. *Obs.* 1.
Positive adjectives with comparative force, with gen. 502. 3.
—— for comparative with ὥστε, 863. *Obs.* 1.
Potential optative, 426. 1.
Predicate of a sentence, 371, 374.
—— agreement of the, with a subject expressed by τό or τά with the gen. plur. of a subst. 380. 1.

Predicate with more than one subject, 391, 392.
—— with article, 460.
—— temporal relations of, 394.
Predicative adject., and the copula εἶν. 375.
—— adject. in the neuter plur. instead of neuter sing. 383.
—— substantive, joined with a subject of different gender or number, 382.
—— subst. with εἶναι, 375. 2.
Prepositions, origin and power of, 472.
—— use of, in language, 614. 1.
—— original force of, 614. 2 3. 4.
—— original adverbial force of, 640.
—— secondary force of, 646.
—— posterior to cases, 472. 2
—— ellipse of, absurd. 472. 2
—— attraction of with the ar (οἱ ἐκ τῆς ἀγορᾶς ἄνθρωποι ἀπέφυγ? for οἱ ἐν τῇ ἀγ.), 647.
—— collocation of, 651.
—— in composition, 641, 642
—— joined or compounded wi adverbs, 644.
—— use of, with the cases, 614
—— construction of, with different cases, 648.
—— used with attrib. gen. 474 *Obs.*
—— constructed with a gen. only, 618—621. — (ἀντί 618. — περί 619. — ἀπό 620. — ἐκ 621.)
—— constructed with a dative 622, 623. — (ἐν 622. — σύν 623.)
—— constructed with an accus 624—626. — (ἀνά 624. — εἰς 625. — ὡς 626.)
—— constructed with gen. and acc. 627—630. — (διά 627. — κατά 628. 629. — ὑπέρ 630.)
—— constructed with gen., dat., and acc. 631—639. — (ἀμφί 631. — περί 632. — ἐπί 633, 634, 635. — μετά 636. — παρά 637. — πρός 638. — ὑπό 639.)
—— pregnant construction of (πίπτειν ἐν γούνασι, κεῖσθαι εἰς π. 645, 646.
—— difference of, from adverbs of place, 617. *Obs.* 1.
—— division of, as to meaning, 615.
—— interchange of (ἀνὰ πᾶσαν τὴν Ἑλλάδα καὶ περὶ Ἰωνίην ἦν λόγος), 649.
—— repetition and omission of, 650.
Present absolute, use of, 395. 1, 2.

Present historic, use of, 395. 2. 806. 2.
———— in the sense of perfect and aor. 396.
———— use of, for future, 397.
———— use of, in comparisons, 868. 4.
———— use of, to signify an attempt, 398. 2.
———— use of, to express frequency, 395. 1.
Pretii genitivus, 515.
Privation, antecedent notion of, in gen. 480. 2. b.
Privative genitive, 529.
Proleptic usage of attributive adjectives (εὔφημον κοίμησον στόμα, i. e. ὥστε εὔφημον εἶναι), 439. 2.
Pronouns, use of, 652.
Pronoun demonstrative, 655.
———— demonstr. αὐτός, 656.
———— demonstr., prospective use of the, 657.
———— demon., retrospective power of, 658.
———— demon., omission of before the relative, 817. 4, 5.
———— demonstr. and relative in the same sentence, 833. Obs. 2.
———— indefinite (τὶς, τὶ), 659.
———— indefinite, position of, 666.
———— indef. (ὅστις, ὁποῖος, ὁπόσος &c.) notion and use of, 816. 4.
———— interrog.— See Interrogative sentences.
———— interrog., preceded by article, 881. 2.
———— personal of the third person, prospective use of, 657.
———— personal, retrospective power of, 658.
———— reflexive (ἐμαυτοῦ &c.), 653.
———— reflexive, used instead of reciprocal, 654. 2.
———— reflexive of third person (οὗ, σφίσιν, ἑαυτοῦ, ἕος, σφέτερος &c.), used for that of first and second person, 654. 1.
———— reflexive, use of with comparatives, 782. g.
———— relative.—See Relative.
———— not agreeing with its immediate attributive, 379. b.
———— plural forms of, joined to a singular, 383. Obs.
Protasis, forms of, in conditional sentences, 851. 1. 853, 857.—See Adverbial conditional sentences.

Quantity, accus. of, 578.
———— adverbial acc. of, 578. Obs. 2.
Questions, affirmative and negative, 871. Obs.

Questions, simple direct, 872. 1.
———— simple direct, formulæ in, 872. 2.
———— simple direct, moods used in, 873. Obs. 2.
———— direct double, forms used in, 875.
———— indirect, form of, 876.
———— simple indirect, proper forms for, 877.
———— indirect compound, 878.
———— forms used in answering, 880.
———— coalescing with a relative sentence, 881. 1.

Reciprocal force of middle, 364. 1.
Reflexive force of middle verb, remarks on, 363.
———— pronoun.—See Pronoun reflexive.
———— verb, 357. 5.
Relation, antecedent notion of, in gen. 480. 2. 2.
Relative adverbs for ὅς, ἥ, ὅ, 817. Obs. 1.
———— adverbs changed into demonstrative, 833. Obs. 1.
———— adverbial, 825. 2.
———— construction changed into the demonstrative, 833.
———— genitive, 502.
———— pronoun, use of, 816.
———— pronoun, rule for use of, 818.
———— pronoun, compounds of, 816. 4.
———— pronouns of quality and size, 817. 3.
———— pronoun, use of with ἔστιν, 818. 5. Obs. 1—4.
———— pronoun, in the constructio κατὰ σύνεσιν, 819. 1.
———— in place of demonstrative (ὅς for οὗτος) in adjectival clauses, 834. 1.
———— pronoun, use of, demonstratively, 816, 823. Obs. 2.
———— pronoun, exceptions to usual agreement of, in gender and number, 819—821.
———— attraction of, 822.
———— (οἷος, ὅσος, ἡλίκος), attraction of, 823.
———— inverse attraction of, 824. I.
———— (οὐδεὶς ὅστις οὐ), inverse attraction of, 824. I. 2.
———— (ὃς βούλει) inverse attraction of, 824. I. Obs. 1.
———— attraction of by transposition of subst. 824. II.
———— construction of, 826—832.
———— changed into demonstrative or personal pronoun, 833.
———— in the same sentence with a

demonstr. (ὃς οὗτος ποταμός), 833. *Obs.* 2.

Relative, with the principal verb repeated (ἤγγειλας οἳ ἤγγειλας), 835. 1.

—— joined to an explanatory inf., or whole sentence, 835. 2.

—— sentences.—See Adjectival sentences.

—— sentence, coalescing with a question, 881. 1.

Repetition of the negative, 747.

—— of prepositions, 650.

—— of substantive by the use of a demonstrative pronoun, 899. 8.

Retrospective power of the demonstr. and personal pronoun, 658.

Rhetorical anacolouthon, 900. 5.

Schema.—See σχῆμα.

Self, relations of, to the middle verb, 362. 2.

Sentence, elements of a simple, 371.

—— unity of a, 370.

Sentences, adjectival, 795. β. 815.

—— adjectival, person of verb in, 818.

—— adjectival, use of the moods in, 826.

—— adverbial, 795. γ. 837.

—— complex objective, 469.

—— compound, 751. 1. 794. 1.

—— coordinate, 751. 3.

—— contraction of, 898.

—— dependent, 794. 1.

—— dependent interrog. 795. *a.*

—— dependent, tests of, 796.

—— dependent, moods and tenses in, 797.

—— dependent, interchange of clauses in, 798.

—— interrogative, 871. 1.

—— interrogative, use of ὥστε in, 867. 1.

—— principal, 794. 1.

—— relation between principal and dependent, 817.

—— simple, 794. 1.

—— subordinate, 751. 3.

—— subordinate, construction of, 793.

—— substantival, 795. *a.* 799.

—— with article, used as substantives, 457. 3.

Separative genitive, 530, 531.

Simple verb to be supplied from a compound verb, 895. *f.*

Singular number, 354.

—— interchange of, with the plural, 390. *a. d.*

—— of imperatives, as εἰπέ, used with a plural subst. 390. *a.*

—— subst. for a plural, 354. *Obs.*

Singular verb, use of, after a plur. subject implied in some part of the sentence, 390. *b.*

—— verb with a masc. or fem. noun in the plural, 386.

—— verb with a neuter plural, 384.

—— verb with several nouns in plur. 393. 7.

Subject of a sentence, 371, 372.

—— of the passive verb, the object of the active verb, (πιστεύομαι — πιστεύειν τινι), 372. 4.

—— ellipse of the, 373.

—— elliptically expressed by a preposition, and the case of the numeral (εἰς δέκα ἄνδρας ἦλθον), 372. *Obs.* 2.

—— implied in the predicate, 373. 2.

—— indefinite, 373. 1.

—— to be supplied from the context, 373. 3.

—— to be supplied from some word in the sentence, 373. 4.

—— of the dependent standing as the object of the principal clause, 898. 2.

—— masc. or fem. with an adj. in the neuter, 381.

—— in the neut. plur., joined to a verb sing. 384.

Subordinate attributive construction, 441.

—— conjunctions, 751. 3.

—— sentences, 751. 3. 793.

Substantive, notion of the, 352.

—— number of the, 354.

—— abstract for concrete, 353.

—— and attribut. gen. with article, 461.

—— attribut. use of, with a preposition, 436. *d.*

—— used as attribut. adjective, 439. 1.

—— ellipse of, before an attributive genitive, 436. *b.*

—— mostly with the article in a relative sentence to explain or define a preceding notion, 824. *Obs.*

Substantives usually omitted before an adj., list of, 436. β.

Substantival clauses, use and construction of, 799—801.

—— sentences with ὅτι, ὡς, 800.

—— sentences with ὅτι, ὡς, construction of, 801.

—— sentences with ὅτι, ὡς, use of the moods in, 802. *ff.*

—— sentences with ὅτι, ὡς, personal construction of, for the impersonal, 804. 2.

—— sentences with ὅτι, ὡς, change of into the acc. with inf. or the participle, 804. 4.

Substantival clause with ὅτι or ὡς, and the infin. with accus. after the same verb, 804. 5.
——————— clause introduced by ὅτε instead of ὅτι, 804. 7.
——————— clause introduced by εἰ instead of ὅτι, 804. 8.
——————— adjective sentences, 836. 1.
——————— final sentence introduced by ὡς, ὅπως, ἵνα, &c. 805. 1.
——————— final sentence, use of conj. and opt. in, 805. 2. 808.
——————— final sentence, interchange of conj. and opt. in, 809.
——————— final sentence, conj. and opt. with ἄν in, 810.
——————— final sentence, ὅπως and ὡς with fut. ind. in, 811.
——————— final sentence, future ind. with ἄν in 811.
——————— final sentence, introduced by ὡς, ὅπως, ἵνα &c., elliptical use of ὅπως and ὅπως μή in, 812.
——————— final sentence, ind. of historic tenses in, 813.
——————— final sentence, construction of μή in, 814. a. b. c.
——————— final sentence, construction of εἰ, ὅπως μή, ὅπως, ὅτι or ὡς, that, inf. with or without art., and ὥστε μή, after verbs of fear in, 814. Obs. 4.
Superlative with gen. 502. 3.
——————— strengthened by a comparative clause, 870. Obs. 4.
Syntax, province of the, 350. 2.

Temporal objective relation, 468. b.
——————— relations of the predicate, 394.
Tenses absolute, 394. 1.
——————— primary and secondary, 361.
——————— principal and historic, 394. 5.
——————— relative, 394. 2, 3:
——————— difference between absolute and relative, 394. 4.
——————— table of the absolute and relative, 394. 7.
——————— table of the powers of, 409.
——————— in the dependent sentences, 797.
Thought verbal, notions contained in, 471. 3.
Thucydides, style of, 900. β.
Time, notion of, expressed by adjectives, 714. b.
——————— notion of, expressed by the cases, 523, 577, 606.
——————— notion of expressed by the participle, 696.
——————— notion of expressed by the preposition, 615. 2. — See also under each preposition.
——————— accus. of, 577.

Time, difference between gen. and acc. of, 577. Obs. 1.
——————— adverbial expression of, 577. Obs. 2.
——————— expression of objective relations of, 468.
Tmesis in compound verbs, 643.
Transitive verb, 357, 2, 3.
——————— verbs, used as intransitive or reflexive (τρέπω for τρέπομαι), 360.
Transmissive dative, 587—594.
——————— verb, 357. II. 1.
Transposition, 824. II. 1.
Two clauses both assuming the form of dependent clauses, 898. 4.

Unity of a sentence, 370.

Verb, different sorts of, 357.
——————— causative, 357. 3.
——————— deponent, 362. 9. 368.
——————— intransitive, used as transitive and passive, 359.
——————— passive and intrans. with gen. 483. Obs. 3.
——————— reciprocal, 357. 6.
——————— reflexive, 357. 5.
——————— transitive, used as intransitive, 360.
——————— agreement of the, with the predicate (ἡ περίοδός εἰσι στάδιοι ἕξ), 389.
——————— construction of, with several subjects, 393.
——————— construction of, with several subjects of different persons, 392.
——————— agreement of, with one of several subjects, 393, 1, 2.
——————— construction of, with several subjects, united by disjunctives, 393. 8.
——————— of general meaning supplied from a verb of special meaning, 895. c.
Verbs of action, acc. with, 559—568.
——————— of motion, twofold sense of, 557. 1.
——————— of motion, use of acc. with, 557, 558, 559.
——————— of perception, acc. with, 575.
——————— of possession, acc. with, 576.
——————— of production, or effect, acc. with, 569—572.
——————— of reception, acc. with, 574.
——————— of transmission, acc. with, 573.
——————— with one acc. case, 548. 1.
——————— with a double acc., list of, 583.
Verbum finitum and infinitum, 369.
——————— finitum, replaced by acc. with infin. in an oratio obliqua, 889.
——————— finitum in one, and participle in the other of two coordinate sentences, united by καί, τέ—καί, μέν—δέ, 759. Obs. 4. 765. 2.

Verbal form of the predicate, resolution of, into the participle and εἶναι (νῆσός ἐστιν ἀπέχουσα), 375. 4.

―――― adjectives in τέος and τός in plural instead of singular, 383.

―――― adjectives, construction of, 613.

―――― thought, notions contained in, 471. 3.

Vocative, force of, 479.

―――― not objective, 473.

―――― not strictly a case, 474.

―――― notion and use of the, 479.

―――― attraction with the, 479. 4.

―――― followed by a particle, 479. 5.

Voice, active, middle, and passive, 357. 8. 358.

Wish, expressed by opt. with εἰ (εἰ γένοιτο), 855. Obs. 6.

―――― expressed by indic. of historic tenses, 856. Obs. 2.

―――― expressed by οὕτως (ὥς)—ὥς, 869. 1.

―――― expressed by γάρ, 786. 2.

Words, essential and formal, 351.

―――― between article and its subst. 459. 4.

Zeugma, 895. d.

INDEX OF WORDS.

The first figures refer to the §., the others to the paragraphs.

Those words which have asterisks prefixed are not actually mentioned in this volume, but their construction is explained by that of analogous words in the section to which the reference is made.

a privat., compounds with, 529. 1. and *Obs*. 2, and 3.
ἀγαθός τι 579. 2.—with dat. comm. 602. 3.
ἀγάλλεσθαι with dat. 607.
ἀγανακτεῖν with acc. 549. *c*. —with dat. 607. — with part. 685.
ἀγανακτεῖν εἰ for ὅτι 804. 8.
ἀγαπᾶν with acc. 549. *c*.— with dat. 607. — with partic. 685. —ἀγαπᾶν εἰ for ὅτι 804. 8.
ἀγάσασθαι and ἀγασθῆναι 367..3.
ἄγασθαι with gen. and acc. 495. and *Obs*. 3.—with double gen. ib. — with dat. 607.
ἀγγελία τινός, *de aliquo*, 486. *Obs*. 2.
ἀγγελίης ἐλθεῖν 481. 1.
ἀγγέλλειν with infin. 665.— with part. 684. Difference between inf. and part. ib. *Obs*. 2. *b*.—with acc. 566. 1.
ἀγγέλλεται with acc. with inf. 676. 2. *a*.
ἄγε with plural, 390. 2.
ἄγε with conjunctive, 416.
ἄγε δή 721. 2.—ἄγε μήν 728. 1.
ἄγειν and compos. intrans. 360.
ἄγειν with gen. 530.—with acc. (γελωτα &c.) 552.
ἀγεμόνευμα for ἡγεμόν 353. 1.
ἄγκαθεν λαβεῖν τι 646. *Obs*.

ἀγνοεῖν with gen.485.—with part. 683.
ἀγοράζειν with gen. 515. 2.
ἀγοραῖος for ἐν ἀγορᾷ 714. *a*.
ἀγχιστῖνος for ἄγχι ἀλλήλων 714. *a*.
ἄγχι, ἄγχοῦ with gen. 526. —ἀγχοῦ with dat. 592. 2.
ἄγων, *with*, 698. *Obs*. 2.
ἀγωνίζεσθαι with acc. 563. —with dat. 601. 1.
ἀδαής with gen. 493.
ἀδελφός omitted, 436. β.— with. gen. 519. — with dat. 594. 2.
*ἄδην with gen. 540.
ἄδην 578. *Obs*. 2.
ἀδικεῖν with single and double acc. 583.2.—with part. 689.
ἀδικήσεσθαι seemingly pass. 364. *Obs*.
*ἄδικος ἀδικίαν 548.2.*Obs*.2.
ἀδύνατον ὄν acc. abs. 700. 2. *a*.
ἀδύνατός εἰμι with inf. 666. —with ὥστε ib. *Obs*.
ἄδωρος with gen. 529. *Obs*. 2.
ἀείδειν with dat. 601.
ἄειρε with gen. 530.
ἄζυξ with gen. 529. *Obs*. 2.
ἀηδές ἐστι with part. 691.
ἀθέατος with gen. 529. *Obs*. 2.
Ἀθήνησιν 605. *Obs*. 1.
ἄθικτος with gen. 529. *Obs*. 3.
ἀθρόος for adverb, 714. *c*.
ἀθύρων with acc. 563.
ἀθῷος with gen. 529. *Obs*. 3.
αἰ for εἰ,—αἰ γάρ, αἴθε for εἰ γάρ, εἴθε 851. *Obs*. 2.

αἰ with conj. 854. *Obs*. 2.
αἰαῖ with gen. 489.
αἰ γάρ with inf. 671. *e*.
αἰδεῖσθαι with acc. 550.— with τό and inf. 670.— with part. 685. — with inf. ib. *Obs*.
ἆδρις with gen. 493.
αἰδώς of person, 355. 1.— τινός 496. *Obs*. 4.
δίειν with gen. 485.—with acc. 575.
αἴκα (= ἐάν) with ind. 854, *Obs*. 2.
αἴ κε 854. 2. *a*.
(αἰκίζεσθαι) αἰκίσασθαι and αἰκισθῆναι 368. 3. *b*.
αἵματα 355. *b*.
αἰνεῖν τινά τινος 495.—αἰνεῖν αἶνον with acc. 583.5.
αἰνίσσεσθαι with acc. 566.
αἰνόθεν αἰνῶς 899. 1.
(αἴρειν) ἀπ—, ἀνταίρ. intrans. 360.
αἴρειν, αἴρεσθαί τι 362. 2.— αἴρεσθαι with acc. 576.2. —αἴρεσθαί τι τινί, dat. incom. 601. 1.
αἴρεσθαι πόνον 563.
αἱρεῖν, *to prosecute*, with gen. 501.—with double acc. 583.6.—*to take*, with acc. 576. 2.
αἱρεῖσθαι with acc. 553.
αἰσθάνομαι for the perf. 396.
αἰσθάνεσθαι with gen. 485. —with acc. 575.—with part. 683. Difference between inf. and part. with, ib. *Obs*.

*ἀίσσειν with acc. 558. 2.
αἰσυμνᾶν with gen. 518.
αἰσχρὸν ὄν, acc. abs. 700.
2. a.—with dat. incom.
602. 3.—αἰσχρόν ἐστιν εἰ
for ὅτι 804. 8.
αἰσχύνεσθαι with acc.550.—
with dat. 607.—with inf.
664.—with τό and inf.
670.—with part. 685.—
with inf. ib. Obs.
αἰσχύνεσθαι εἰ for ὅτι 804.8.
αἰτεῖν, -εῖσθαι with double
acc. 583. 8.—τινός τι,
παρά τινός τι ib. Obs.
(αἰτιᾶσθαι) inf. ᾐτιᾶσθαι
passiv. 368. 3. a.
αἰτιᾶσθαι with gen. 501.
αἴτιον δέ, τοῦτο omitted with,
655. Obs. 4.
αἴτιός εἰμί τινι 600. 1.—with
inf. 666. — with τό and
inf. 670.
αἰφνίδιος for adverb. 714. c.
(ἀκεῖσθαι) ἀκέσασθαι and
ἀκεσθῆναι 368. 3. b.
ἀκήρατος with gen. 529.
Obs. 3.
ἄκλαυστος with gen. 529.
Obs. 3.
ἀκμήν, accus. 577. Obs. 2.
ἀκόλουθος with gen. 520.—,
-εῖν, -ως, -ητικος with
dat. 593. 1, 2.
ἀκοντίζειν with gen. 506.
ἀκούειν, to be called, 475. 2.
ἀκούειν, audivisse, 396.
ἀκούειν with gen. and acc.
487. 1. and 3.—with acc.
575.
ἀκούειν, to obey, with gen.
and dat. ibid. 487. 4.—
ἀκούειν with part. 683.
Difference between inf.
and part. with, ibid. Obs.
ἀκούεσθαι for ἀκούειν 363.
5.
ἀκούω ὅτε for ὅτι 804. 7.
ἄκρα applied to persons,
382. 1.
*ἀκρατής with gen. 505.
ἀκροᾶσθαι with gen. 485.
ἄκρος for adverb, 714. a.
ἀκτίς for ἷνες 354. 2.
ἄκων for adverb, 714. c.
ἀλαλάξαι with acc. 566. 1.
ἀλαλκεῖν with gen. 531.—
with dat. 596.
*ἀλαοῦν with gen. 529. 1.
ἀλᾶσθαι with acc. viæ, 558.
ἀλγεῖν with gen. 488.—with
acc. 549. — τὴν κεφαλήν

&c. 579. 1. a.—with dat.
607.
ἄλγος τινός, pro aliquo, 488.
Obs. 1.
ἀλέγειν and -ίζειν with gen.
and acc. 496. and Obs. 1.
ἀλέξειν with dat. 596.
*ἀληθές in answers, 880.
Obs. 2.—acc. 579. 4.
ἀληθεύειν with acc. 565. 1.
ἄλημα of person, 353. 1.
ἁλίσκεσθαι with gen. 501.
—with part. 684.
*ἀλιτέσθαι with acc. 548.
Obs.1.—*ἀλιτεῖν τινι 602.
ἀλλά expression of limitation and denial, 773.—
οὐ μᾶλλον, οὐ τὸ πλέον,
ἀλλά 773. Obs. 5. — οὐ
μὴν ἀλλά; οὐ μέντοι ἀλλά;
οὐ γὰρ ἀλλά 773. 6.—
ἀλλά to mark a transi-
tion to different or con-
trary thoughts, 774.—
ἀλλά after εἰ, ἐπεί ibid.
Obs. 1.—ἀλλ' οὖν ibid.—
ἀλλά, certe, in the middle
of a sentence, ibid. —
ἀλλά at the beginning of
a sentence, ibid. Obs. 2.
ἀλλά in a question, 874. 4.
ἀλλά after the vocat. 479.5.
ἄλλα, ἄλλοι, οἱ ἄλλοι, asyndeton with, 792. 2. h.
ἀλλ' ἄρα 787. c.
ἀλλά γε 735. 9.
ἀλλὰ δή 721. 3.—ἀλλὰ δῆτα
725. 2. f.
ἀλλ' ἥ in a question. ibid. b.
ἀλλ' ἥ 731. Obs.—ἀλλ' ἤτοι,
ἀλλ' ἤτοι μέν 731. 2, 3.
ἀλλ' ἥ (οὐκ, οὐδὲν ἀλλ' ἤ;
οὐδὲν ἄλλο, ἀλλ' ἤ; οὐδὲν
ἕτερον, ἀλλ' ἤ; τί ἄλλο,
ἀλλ' ἤ; ἄλλο τι, ἀλλ' ἤ)
773. 5.
ἀλλὰ μέν δή 730. c.
ἀλλὰ μήν 728. d.
ἀλλ' οὐ γάρ, ἀλλὰ γάρ 786.
Obs. 6.
ἀλλ' οὐ μὰν οὐδέ.—ἀλλ' οὐ
μάν 728. b. — ἀλλὰ μέν
729. 3. e. — ἀλλὰ μέντοι
730. a.
ἀλλὰ τί μέλλει; ἀλλὰ τί ;
ἀλλὰ τί γὰρ μέλλει ; ἀλλὰ
τί οἴει; in an answer,
880. Obs. 2.
ἀλλά τοι 736. 4.
ἀλλάττειν, -εσθαι with. gen.
516. 2.—with acc. 573,
574.

ἄλλεσθαι with acc. 556.
ἄλλη, alio, 605. Obs. 5.—
alio modo, 603. 2.
ἀλλήλων &c. not used for
ἑαυτῶν &c. 654. 2.
ἄλλην καὶ ἄλλην 558. 1.
ἄλλο ἤ or ἄλλο τι ἤ 895. c.
ἄλλοθι with gen. 527.
ἀλλοῖος with gen. 503.
ἀλλόκοτος with gen. 503.
ἄλλος ἄλλο for ἄλλος τις
ἄλλο τι 875. e.
ἄλλος ἄλλοι, (ἄλλος ἄλλο-
θεν) in apposition with
another nom. 478.
ἄλλος ἄλλοθεν, ἄλλος ἀλ-
λόσε, ἄλλος ἄλλῃ &c.
899. 1.
ἄλλος with gen. 503.—ἤ
ib. Obs. 2.
ἄλλος, on the other side,
714. Obs 2.
ἄλλο τι ἤ and ἄλλο τι in a
question, nonne, 875. e.
and Obs.
ἄλλοσε ὅποι for ἄλλοσε
ὅποι by attract. 824. Obs.
2.
ἀλλότριος with gen. 503.
ἀλύειν with acc. 549. d.
ἄλυπος with gen. 529. Obs. 3
ἀλύσκειν with gen. 530.
ἀλῶναι with gen. 501.
ἀλώπηξ, fox-skin, 353. 2.
ἅμα with dat. 594. 2.—Dative
603. 2. — in partic. 696.
Obs. 5.—with dat. and
part. 699.—ἅμα—καί for
ὅτε 752.
*ἀμαθὴς ἀμαθίαν 548. Obs.
2.—with acc. 579. 2.
ἀμαξεύειν with acc. 558.
ἁμαρτάνειν with gen. and
acc. 511.—with acc. 565.
—with part. 656.
ἀμείβειν, -εσθαι, double
sense of, 548. Obs. 1.—
with gen. 516.—with acc.
558.
ἀμεινόν ἐστι with part. 691.
ἀμελεῖν with gen. and acc.
496. and Obs. 1. — with
infin. 664.
ἀμέλξεται seemingly pass.
364.
ἀμελοῦμαι 372.
ἀμεμφία with dat. 589. Obs.4.
ἀμηχανεῖν with acc. 551. 2.
*ἀμήχανός εἰμι with τό and
infin. 670.—with inf. for
ἀμήχανόν ἐστι with acc.
with inf. 677.

ιλλᾶσθαι with acc. 563.
—with dat. 601.
ινημονεῖν with acc. 551.2.
ιοιρος with gen. 529.
ιολγῷ νυκτός 606.
ιπελος for οι 354.
ιπλακεῖν with. acc. 565.
ιύειν with gen. 531.—
with dat. 531. Obs. 3.
596.
ιφί, prepos. with gen., dat.
and acc. 631.—as adv.
640.—with dat. in preg-
nant constr. for acc. 645.
b.—with dat. and acc.
in same passage, 648.
ιφὶ περί 640. 3.
ιφὶ ἕνεκα 621. Obs. 2.
ιφιεννύναι with double acc.
583. 81. Obs.
ιφίς with gen. 526.
ιφισβητεῖν with acc. 551.
1. e.—with dat. 601.
ιφότερον, ἀμφότερα, acc.
579. 4.
ιφω λέγεται 384. Obs. 1.
ν, modal adverb, 423.—
Nature and use of, 424.
ν with ind. fut. 424. δ.
ν seemingly with indic.
pres. and perf. 424. γ.
ν not used with imperat.
424. e.
ιν with indic. impf., plperf.
and aor. 424.a.—omitted,
858, 859.
ιν with conjunc. in Homer
424. ζ.—with conj. deli-
berativus, ibid. η.—with
conjunctions, as ἐάν, ἐπάν,
ὅταν, πρὶν ἄν, ὃς ἄν 428.
ιν with opt. 425. d.—omitted, 426.
ιν with infin. and partic.
429.
ιν without verb, 430.
ιν with adjec. and adverbs
430.
ιν, position of, 431.
ἰν φαίη (εἴποι) 431. Obs. 3.
ιν repeated 432.
ιν used once with two verbs,
432. Obs. 2.
ἰν κε 432. Obs. 5.
ιν in protasis 860. 1.
ιν in relative sentence omitted before conjunct. 830.
ιν in relative sentence omitted before opt. 832. Obs.
ινά, prep. with dat. and
acc. 624. — as adverb,
640. 2.
GR. GR. VOL. 11.

ἀνά and περί with acc. in
same sentence, 649.
ἀνα- in compos. 624. Obs.
ἀναβάλλεσθαι with infin.
664.—with τό and infin.
670.
ἀναβλέπειν with acc. 554.—
ἀναβλέπειν τινί 589. 2.
ἀνάγειν with acc. νίᾳ, 558.
ἀναγιγνώσκειν with infin.
664.
ἀναγκάζειν τινά τι 583. 14.
—ἀναγκάζομαί τι ibid.
ἀναγκαῖον and ἀναγκ. ὄν,
acc. absol. 700.
ἀνάγκη ἐστί with inf. 669. a.
ἀναδῦναι with gen. 530.
*ἀναίνεσθαι with part. 684.
ἀνακαλεῖν ὄνομά τινα 583.89.
*ἀνακεράννυσθαι φιλίαν 572.
*ἀνακουφίζω with gen. 531.
ἀνακῶς ἔχειν with gen. 496.
ἀναρμάρτητος with gen. 529.
ἀναμιμνήσκειν with gen. and
acc. 512. Obs. — with
double acc. 583. 15.
ἄναντα 558. 1.
ἄναξ with local dat. 605.
Obs. 4.
ἀνάξιος with gen. 517.
ἀναπείθειν with ὥστε 664.
*ἀναπνεῖν with gen. 531.
ἀνάριθμος with gen. 529.
Obs. 2.
ἀνάσσειν with. gen. 518.—
with dat. 605. 3.
ἀναχάζεσθαι with gen. 530.
ἀνδάνειν with dat. 594. 4.
ἀνδρίαι 355. γ.
ἄνειν, ἀνύειν, ἀνύτειν with
acc. 560. 2.
ἀνέλκειν with gen. 530.
*ἀνεπιστήμων with gen. 493.
ἄνευθε with gen. 526.529.2.
ἀνέχειν χεῖράς τινι 589. 2.
ἀνέχεσθαι with gen. 504.—
with inf. 664. 1. 687. Obs.
1.—with partic. 687.
ἀνήκοος with gen. 529. Obs.
2.—with acc. 579. 2.
ἀνηκουστεῖν with gen. 487.
4.—with dat. 593. 1.
ἀνήνεμος with gen. 529.
Obs. 2.
ἀνήρ, ἄνδρες omitted, 436.
ἀνθάπτεσθαι with gen. 536.
ἀνθεῖν with gen. 539. 1.
*ἄνθος of person, 353.
ἄνθρωπος, ἄνθρωποι omitted,
436.
ἀνθρώποις, inter homines,
605. 2.

ἀνιέναι with gen. 531.
ἀνιστορεῖν with double acc.
583. 86.
ἀνορέαι 355.
ἀνοτοτύξειν with acc. 566.3.
ἄντα, ἄντην, ἀντία, ἀντίον
with gen. 526.
ἀνταίρειν intrans. 360.
ἀντάλλαγμα, ἀνταλλάττειν,
ἀνταλλάττεσθαι with gen.
and dat. 516. and Obs. 1,
2.
*ἀνταμείβεσθαι with acc.
583. 12.
ἀντᾶν with gen. 510. 1, 2.—
with dat. 592.
ἀντάξιος with gen. 517.
ἀνταυγεῖν with acc. 555. c.
ἀντέχεσθαι with gen. 536.
ἄντην 558.
ἄντην ἔρχεσθαι 558. 1.
ἀντί, prep. with gen. 618.—
as adverb, 640. — ἀντί
with inf. for ἀντὶ τοῦ with
inf. 678. Obs. 1.
ἀντι- in compos. 618. Obs.
ἀντιάζειν with dat. 592.
ἀντιᾶν with gen., dat. and
acc. 510. 1, 2.—with dat.
592.
ἀντιβίην ἐλθεῖν 558.—ἀντιβίην ibid.
ἀντιβολῆσαι with gen. 510.
1.
ἀντικρύς with gen. 526.
ἀντιλαμβάνεσθαι with gen.
536.
ἀντιλέγειν with τό and inf.
670.
ἀντίον, accus. 558. 1.
ἀντίος with gen. 525.
ἀντίπαλος with gen. 519.
ἀντιποιεῖσθαι with gen. 536.
Obs. 1.
ἀντίστροφος with gen. 525.
ἀντίφθογγος with gen. 519.
ἀνύσας, quickly, straightway, 696. Obs. 1.
ἄνω with gen. 526.—with
dat. 605. Obs. 5.
ἄξιός εἰμι with inf. 667.—
for ἄξιόν ἐστι with acc.
with inf. 677.
ἄξιος, ἀξίως, ἀξιοῦν, -οῦσθαι
with gen. 517. — ἄξιός
τινός εἰμί τινι 600. 1.
ἄοκνος for adverb, 714. c.
*ἀπαγορεύειν εὖ, κακῶς with
acc. 583. 102.—with inf.
664.
ἀπάθης with gen. 529. Obs.
2.

ἀπαίδευτος with gen. 493. 529.

ἀπαίρειν intrans. 360.—with acc. 558.

ἄπαις with gen. 529. Obs. 2.

ἀπαιτεῖν with double acc. 583. 8.

ἀπαλλακτέον ἐστί τινα and τινος 613. Obs. 2.

ἀλλάττειν, neuter, 360.

ἀπαλλάττειν with gen. 531. — -εσθαι with acc. 559. Obs. 2.—with partic. 688.

ἀπάνευθε with gen. 526.

ἄπαντα εἶναί τινι 382.

ἀπαντᾶν with gen. and acc. 510.—with dat. 592.

ἀπαντικρύ with gen. 526.

ἀπαξιοῦν with 517.

ἀπατᾶν with double accus. 583. 17.

ἀπάτωρ with gen. 529. Obs. 2.

ἀπαυρᾶν with gen. 491.— *τινί τι 602.

ἀπέβη sc. τὰ πράγματα 373. 3.

ἀπειθεῖν with gen. 487. 4.— with dat. 593.

ἀπειλεῖν with acc. 566. 2.

ἄπειρος, -ως with gen. 493.

ἀπεντεῦθεν 644.

ἄπεπλος with gen. 529. Obs. 2.

ἀπεύχεσθαι with dat. 589.

ἀπέχειν with gen. 530.— ἀπέχεσθαι with gen. 531. —with τό and inf. 670.

ἀπέχρη and ἀπέχρη ἄν 858. Obs. 3.

ἀπιέναι with gen. 530.

ἀπιστεῖν with inf. 665.

ἀπιστοῦμαι ὑπό τινος, mihi non creditur ab aliq. 372.

ἀπό, prep. with gen. 620.— as adverb, 640.—in pregnant sense, for ἐν with dat. 646. c. — ἀπό with the artic. for ἐν (οἱ ἀπὸ τῆς ἀγορᾶς ἄνθρωποι ἀπέφυγον) 647.

ἀπὸ πρώτης, ἀπὸ τοῦ εὐθέος, ἀπὸ τοῦ προφανοῦς 640.

ἀπὸ γλώσσης, ἀπὸ στόματος, ἀπὸ μνήμης, ἀπ' ὀμμάτων, ἀπὸ σπουδῆς. ἀπὸ γνώμης, ἀπὸ χειρός, ἀπὸ φωνῆς &c. 640.

ὑπὸ— ἕνεκα 621. Obs. 2.

ἀπο- in compos. 620. Obs.

ἀπ' οὐρανόθεν 530. Obs. 3.

ἀπογεύεσθαι with gen. 537.

ἀποδεικνύναι with εἶναι 666.

ἀποδέχεσθαι with gen. 485.

ἀποδίδοσθαι with gen. of price, 515. 2.

ἀποδιδράσκειν with acc. 548. Obs. 1.

ἀπόδοσις with dat. 588. Obs.

ἀποζευγνύναι with acc. 558. 2.

ἀποθνήσκειν with acc. 552. a.

ἀποικεῖν with acc. 548. Obs. 1.

ἀποκάμνειν with inf. and part. 687. Obs.

ἀποκλαίειν with acc. 566. 4.

*ἀποκρίνεσθαι τὸ ἐρωτώμενον 566. 1.

ἀπολαύειν with gen. 491.— *with acc. 576. 2.

ἀπολυεῖσθαι with dat. 596.

Ἄπολλον as interject. with gen. 489.

ἀπολωλέναι κακὸν μόρον 552. b.

ἀπομιμνήσκεσθαι with gen. and acc. 512. Obs.

ἀπονέμειν with dat. 588. 3.

ἀποπειρᾶσθαι with gen. 493.

ἀπόπρο 640. 3.

ἀπόπροθεν, -θι with gen. 526.

ἀπορραίειν with double acc. 583. 144.

ἀπορεῖν, -ία with gen. 529. —with acc. 551. 2.

ἀπορροφεῖν with gen. 537.

ἀποσυλᾶσθαί τι 583, 146.

ἀποστερεῖν with gen. 529. —with double acc. 583. 144. — ἀποστερούμαί τι ibid.

*ἀποστίλβειν with gen. 483.

ἀποστρέφεσθαι with acc. 548. Obs. 1.

ἀποσφαλεὶς φρενῶν 529. 1.

ἀποταυροῦσθαι with acc. 554. c. see add.

ἀπούρασθαι, seemingly pass. 364. b.

ἀποφεύγειν with acc. 548. Obs. 1.—with dat. 598.

ἀποχωρεῖν with acc. 548. Obs. 1.

ἀπρεπῶς with dat. 594. 3.

(ἅπτειν) συνάπτ. intran. 360.

ἅπτεσθαι with gen. and dat. 536. and Obs. 4.

ἀπύειν with acc. 566. 1.

ἀπωθεῖσθαι with double acc. 583. 24.

ἀπωλλύμην εἰδότων 483. Obs. 3.

ἄρα 787.—of continued action 788.—rapidity ibid. 2 and 3. — unexpected ibid. 4 and 5.—explicative 789. — conclusive ibid. b.—ἄρα omitted 792. c. — ἄρα in a question 872. 2.

ἄρα for ἄρα 789. b.

ἆρα, interrog. 873.—ἆρ' α. ἆρα μή ib. 3. and Obs. 1. ἆρα—ἤ 875. c.

ἆρα δῆτα 725. 2.

ἀρᾶσθαι with acc. 566. 2.— with dat. 589. 3.

ἀρείν, to suit, please, with dat. 594. 4.

ἀρέσκειν τινά, τινί τι 594. Obs. 2.

*ἀρέσκεσθαι with gen. 494 —with dat. 594. 4. 607.

ἀρεστῶς with dat. 594. 4.

ἀρήγειν with dat. 596.

ἄρ' ἦν 398. 4.

ἀριθμεῖσθαι with gen. 533. 2.

ἀριθμῶν 579. 3.

ἀριθμῷ, certo numero, 600. 1.

ἀριστερᾶς (χειρός) 530. Obs. 1.

ἀριστεύειν with gen. 504.— with acc. 553.

ἀρκεῖν with acc. 573. Obs. 2.

ἀρκεῖσθαι with dat. 607.

ἁρμόττειν with dat. 594. 3.

ἀρκεῖσθαι with acc. 567.— with inf. 665.

ἄρνησίς ἐστιν with τό and inf. 670.

ἀρνύσθαι with acc. 576. 2.

ἁρπάζειν with acc. 576. 2.

ἀρτύειν, ἀρτύνειν with acc. 569.

ἀρξάμενος ἀπό τινος 696. Obs. 1.

ἄρξεται, parebit 364.

ἀρτιμαθής with gen. 493.

ἀρύειν with gen. 537.—with acc. 570.

ἄρχειν with gen. 518.—with dat. ib. 3. and 605. 3.— with acc. 553.

ἄρχειν, -εσθαι with gen. 513. 530. 2.

ἄρχεσθαι with partic. 688.— with inf. ibid. Obs.

ἀρχεύειν with gen. 518.— with dat. 605. 3.

ἀρχήν, accus. 580. 1.

ἀρχῆς, at the beginning, 523. and Obs.

ἄρχομαι ὑπό τινος, mihi imperatur ab aliq. 372. 4.

ιχόμενος, at the beginning, 696. Obs. 1.
ιχων with loc. dat. 605. Obs. 4.
ται, ᾶσασθαι with gen. 540.
τεβεῖν with accus. 565.— εἷς, περί τινα ib. Obs.
τθενεῖν with acc. 552. b.
τκεῖν with acc. 561.
τκεῖσθαι with dat. 610.
τκενος with gen. 529. Obs. 2.
σμενος for adverb 714. c.
σπίς = ὁπλῖται 354.
σπονδος for adverb 714. c.
σσον with gen. 526.
στράπτει scil. ὁ θεός 373. 2.
στράπτειν with acc. 570.
σχαλᾶν with dat. 607.— with partic. 685.
τάρ 771. 3.—ἀτὰρ μέν 729. e.—ἀτάρ after the voc. 479. 5.
τε with partic. and absol. cases 704.—ἅτε δή 721. 3.
τερ, ἄτερθε with gen. 529. 2.
τη of person 353.
τιμάζειν with double acc. 583. 27.
ἔτιμος with gen. 529. Obs. 3.
ἔτος with gen. 539. 2.
ἰτύξεσθαι πεδίοιο 522. 2.
ἰῦ, contra 771.
ἰυδᾶν with acc. 566.
ἰυλᾶσθαι for αὐδᾶν 363. 5.
ἰῦθις 771.
ἰῦξεσθαι with gen. 483.
ἰῦριον, accus. 577. Obs. 2.
αἰτάρ 771.—Etymology of, 788. 2.—ἀτάρ τοι 736. 4.
ἀῦτε 771.
ἰύτειν with acc. 566. 3.
αὔτη, heus tu, 476.
αὐτίκα, asyndet. 792. a.
αὐτίκα with gen. 527. with partic. 696. Obs. 5.
αὖτις 771.
αὐτόδιον 558.
αὐτός in αὐτοῖς ἵπποις 604.1.
αὐτός, pers. pron., use of 6;2.—Difference of from reflexive ἑαυτοῦ 653.— Meaning of αὐτός, ipse, αὐτὸ τοῦτο, τοῦτ' αὐτό 656. —Referring to a personal pronoun in the verb 656. Obs. 1.—αὐτός for the reflexive pron. 656. Obs. 4. —αὐτοὶ κατ' αὐτῶν, αὐτὸς πρὸς αὐτόν &c. 656. Obs. 1.—αὐτός in abstract notion (αὐτὸ τὸ καλόν) ibid.

Obs. 2.—αὐτά in abst. notions ibid.—αὐτός, solus, (αὐτοί ἐσμεν) ibid. Obs. 3. —Other various uses of 656. — αὐτός, retrospective force of 658.
αὐτός for αὐτὸς ἑαυτοῦ, αὐτὸς ἑαυτῷ κ. τ. λ. 894. c.
αὐτὸς αὐτοῦ, αὐτὸς αὐτῷ &c. 904. 2.
αὐτοῦ (αὐτῷ), ταύτη, τῇδε 605. Obs. 1.—αὐτοῦ τῇδε 655. 5.
αὐτοῦ, ἧς, ὧν for σφέτερος 652. 3.
αὐτοῦ, reflexive pron. use of, 656. Obs. 1.
αὐτῷ, αὐτῇ, dat. of reference 600. 2.
ἀφαιρεῖσθαι, double accus. 583. 28.—τινί τι, ἀφαιρεῖν τινί τι 602. 1.—ἀφαιρεῖσθαι pass. with acc. 583. 28.
ἄφαρ, etymology of, 788. 2.
ἀφιλλεσθαι with acc. 556.
ἄφθονος ὅσος 823. Obs. 7.
ἀφιέναι, -ίεσθαι with gen. 531.
ἀφίκετο with inf. 669. a.
ἀφικνεῖσθαι with acc. 559.
ἄφιλος with gen. 529. Obs. 2.
ἀφίστασθαι with acc. 553.
ἀφνειός with gen. 539. 2.
ἀφορμᾶσθαι with acc. 558.
ἀφ' οὗ, since, 839. b.
ἄφωνος with gen. 529. Obs.
ἄχος τινός 488. Obs. 1.
ἄχθεσθαι with gen. 490.— with dat. 607. — with acc. 549.—with partic. 685.—ἄχθεσθαι εἰ for ὅτι 804. 8.
ἄχρις with gen. 509. 2.
ἄχρις, ἄχρις οὗ 839. c. see ἕως.—ἄχρις ἄν with conj. see ἕως ἄν under ἕως.—
ἄχρις without ἄν with conj. 842. 2.
ἄψορρος for adverb 714. a.
ἀψόφητος with gen. 529. Obs. 2.
ἀωρί with gen. 527.
ἀωρίαν with gen. 577. Obs.1.
ἀωτεῖν with acc. 556.

βάζειν with acc. 566.—with double acc. 583. 31.
βάθος, accus. 579. 3.
βαίνειν with gen. 530.— with acc. 558. 1. 2.

βάλλειν and comp. intrans. 360.
βάλλειν with gen. 504. 506. with gen. and acc. ibid. Obs.
βάλλειν with double acc. 583. 32.
βάραθρον, of a person 353.1.
βασιλεύειν with gen. 518.— with dat. 605.
βασιλεύεσθαι with acc. 553.
βασκαίνειν with dat. 601.
βαΰζειν with acc. 566. 3.
βία, periphrasis with, 442. 2.
βιάζειν and -εσθαι 368.—
βιάζεσθαι, βεβιάσθαι, βιασθῆναι pass. 368.
βιβρώσκειν with acc. 562.
βίος, subsistence, 353.
βλακεύειν and -εσθαι 363. 6.
βλάπτειν with gen. 531.— with double acc. 583. add.—with dat. 602. 2.
*βλάπτεσθαί τινι 611.
βλαστάνειν with acc. 555. add.
βλασφημεῖν βλασφημίαν &c. 566. 2.
βλάψεσθαι, seemingly pass. 364. a.
βλέπειν with acc. 554.
βοᾶν with acc. 566. 3.
βοηθεῖν with acc. 573. Obs. 2. —βοήθεια with dat. 596. and Obs. 2.
βόσκημα of a person 353.
βούλεσθαι with acc. 551. 1.
βουλήσομαι, volo, sc. si licet 406. 4.—with inf. 664.
βουλεύειν with acc. 551. 1.
βουλεύεσθαι with inf. 664. —with ὅπως and conj. ib. Obs. 3.
βοῦς, oxhide, 353. 3.
βραδύς for βραδέως 714. c.
βρέμειν with acc. 566. 3.
βριάειν intrans. and trans. 360. Obs. 2.
βρίθειν with gen. 539. 1.
βροντᾶ sc. ὁ θεός 373. 2.
βρύειν with acc. 555.—with dat. 610.

γάλα omitted 436. β.
γάλαξι 355. b.
γαμεῖν with gen. 533. 3.— with double acc. 583. 36.
γάμοι, nuptiæ, 355. Obs. 1.
γανοῦν with acc. 549. d.
γάρ, various uses of, 786.—
καὶ γάρ ib. Obs. 3.—γὰρ δή 721. 3.—γὰρ δῆτα 725.

—γάρ θην 726.—γάρ ῥα 787. c, 788. — γάρ ἄρα 789.—γάρ τοι 790.—γάρ omitted 792, 786. Obs. 2. —γάρ in question 872. i. —in answer 880. d.

γάρ after vocat. 479. 5.

γέ 735.—γέ μέν 729. d.—γέ μέν — δή 730. c.—γέ μήν 735. 10.—γέ τοι 736. 1. Cf. 790. Obs.

γέ, in answers, 880. c.

γεγωνεῖν with acc. 566.

γελᾶν with acc. 549.—with double acc. 583. 37.— with dat. 607.

γέλως, homo ridiculus, 353.

γέμειν with gen. 539. 1.

γενεή, γένος, γόνος for υἱός 353.

γενναῖος γένει or γονῇ 899. 1.

γεννᾶν with acc. 569. 2. parentem esse, 396.

γένος, accus. 579. 3.

γέρων εἰμί with inf. 666.

γεύειν with double acc. 583. 38.

γεύεσθαι with gen. 537.

γῆ omitted 436. β.

γηθεῖν with acc. 549.—with partic. 685.

γηραίνειν with acc. 553. c.

γῆρας, periphrasis with, 442. d.

γηρύεσθαι and -ειν 363.— with acc. 566.

γίγνεσθαι seemingly as copula 375.—with an adverb, ibid.

γίγνεσθαι with gen. origin. 483.—with gen. possess. 521.—with gen. partit. 533. 1.—with dat. comm. 597.—and an abstract subst. with inf. 668. c.

γίγνεται, at the beginning of a sentence, with a plural verb following, 386.

γίγνεταί μοι τι βουλομένῳ, ἡδομένῳ, ἀσμένῳ, ἐλπομένῳ 599. 3. — γίγνεται ὥστε 669.

γιγνώσκειν with gen. 485.— with acc. 551. 1, 2.—τί τινι 609. 3.—with infin. 665.—with part. 683.— inf. with part. ib. Obs. 2.

γιγνώσκειν καλῶς, as is well known, 864.

γιγνώσκω for ἔγνωκα 396.

γλίχεσθαι with gen. and

acc. 536. and Obs. 4.— περί τινος ibid. Obs. 5.— with ὡς and indic. fut. 664. Obs. 3.

γνώμη omitted 436. β.

γνώμην ἐμήν 579. 3.

γοᾶσθαι and γοᾶν 363.— with acc. 566. 4.—with double acc. 583. 39.

γοῦν 735. 4.

γουνάζεσθαι with gen. 536. Obs. 6.

γράφειν with acc. 569. 3.

γράφειν and γράφεσθαι νόμους 362. 2.

γράφεσθαι with gen. 501.— ἕνεκά τινος, ἐπ' αἰτία τινός ib. Obs. 2.—with double acc. 583. 40.

γυμνάζειν with double acc. 583. 41.

γυμνός with gen. 529. 1.

γυνή omitted 436. β.

δαί 727.

δαίεσθαι with double acc. 583. 43.

δαιμόνιε ξείνων 534. Obs. 2.

δαίνυσθαι with acc. 562.

δαίρω with double acc. 583. 42.

δακρύειν with acc. 566. 4.

δάκρυον for δάκρυα 354.

δαμῆναι, δμηθῆναι 367. Obs. 2.

δ' ἄρ' 788.

δασύς with gen. and dat. 539. 2. and Obs.

δέ, adversative copula, 763. —μέν—δέ 764.—position of 765.—various uses of 765-767.— δέ for γάρ, οὖν, δέ in questions and answers 768. — καί δέ 769.—δέ in apodosis 770. —after a participle 770. Obs.

δέ after a vocat. 479. 5.

δέ in questions 874. 5.

δε accusatival suffix 559. Obs. 1.

δέ ἄρα 789. b.

δέ γε 735. 10.

δέ δή 721. 1.

δεδιέναι with acc. 550. a, b.

δεδογμένον, acc. absol. 700.

δεδοικέναι with inf. 664.

δεδράμηκα for -ηκα 363. 5.

δεῖ with gen. 529. 1.—with dat. 594. 3.—with inf. 669. a.—with dat. and acc. with inf. 674.

δεῖ different from ἰδέα 857. Obs. 4.

δεῖ σ' ὅπως for δεῖ σε σκοπεῖν ὅπως 812. 2.

δεικνύναι with partic. 684. —Difference between its use with inf. and partic. ibid. Obs. 3.

(δεικνύναι) διαδ. intran. 366. —with acc. 569. 2.

δειμαίνειν with acc. 550. a. b.

δεῖν, egere with gen. 529. 1 —arcere with gen. 531.

δεῖν (to bind) with double acc. 585. 47.

δεινόν ἐστιν εἰ for ὅτι 804. 8.

δεινὸν ποιεῖσθαι εἰ for ὅτι 804. 8.

δεινός τι 579. 2.—δεινός εἰμι with inf. 666.

δειπνεῖν with acc. 562.

δεῖσθαι with gen. and acc. 529. 1. and Obs. 1.—with inf. 664.—with ὅπως and conj. ibid. Obs. 3.

δεῖσθαι (to ask) with double acc. 583. 45.

δεῖσθαι, δεθῆναι δεσμόν 583. 47.

δέκα ἡμερῶν, ἐτῶν, genitive of space of time, 523.

δελεάζειν with acc. 576. 2.

δέμας in periphrasis 442. d.

δέμας 580. 1.

δέμειν with acc. 569.

δεννάζειν with acc. 566. 2.

δεξιᾶς (χειρός) 530. Obs. 1.

δέον acc. absol. 700.

δέος (τὸ) with acc. 360. Obs. 3. add.

δέος ἐστί with τό and inf. 668. Obs.

δέρκεσθαι with acc. 554.

(δέρκομαι) δερχθῆναι pass. 368. b.

δεσπόζειν with gen. and acc. 518. and Obs. 3.

δεύειν with acc. 570.

δεύεσθαι with gen. 529. 1.

δεῦρο with conjunct. 416.— with gen. 527.

δευτεραῖος, on the second day, 714. b.

δεύτερος with gen. 502. 3.

δεχήμερος, adverbial, 714.b.

δέχεσθαι with gen. 530. 1. c. 501. Obs. 3.—with gen. of price 516.—with acc. 567-574. — with double acc. 583. 46. — τινί τι 598.

(δέχομαι) δέξασθαι and διθῆναι 368. — ἐδεχόμην, ass. ibid.

uses of, 720, 721, 722, 23.—δὴ τότε, δὴ γάρ ib. ἦ αὖτε ib. Obs.—δὴ ῥα ὅτε 788. 3.

ἐν 726.

τήριος with gen. 542. 2.

ἐῖσθαι with double acc. 583. add.

ἡμων with gen. 494.

ιον εἶναι, ποιεῖν with part. 584.—δῆλός εἰμι ποιῶν τι ibid. Obs. 2.

ιον and δῆλον ὄν, acc. absol. 700. a.—δῆλον ὅτι without verb 895. a.

λός εἰμι ὅτι for δῆλόν ἐστιν ὅτι 804. 2.

λοῦν intrans. 360.—ἐδή-λωσε, apparebat, 373. 1.

λοῦν with gen. and acc. 486, 487. 1. — with part. 684.

ιμηγορεῖν with acc. 566.1.

ἦμος omitted 436. b.

ἡμοσίᾳ 603. 2.

ἦ που 724. 2.

ἥπουθεν 726.

ἡρόν, δηρὸν χρόνον 577. Obs. 2.

ἡρός for adverb 714. b.

ἦτα 725.

ἱα θεάων 534. Obs. 2.

ιά (διαί), prep. with gen. and acc. 627. — as adverb 640.

ιια- in compos. 627. Obs.

ιὰ πρό 640. 3.

ιαβάλλειν with acc. 568.—-εσθαι with dative 601. Obs. 3.

διάγειν with part. 694.

διαγίγνεσθαι with part. 694.

διαδέχεσθαι, διάδοχος, διαδοχή with dat. 593. 1. 2.

διαδιδόναι with gen. 535.

διάδοχος with gen. 520. Cf. διαδέχεσθαι.

διαειδειν with dat. 601.

διαθεᾶσθαι with gen. 485.

διακεῖσθαι τὴν γνώμην with ὡς and gen. abs. 702.

διακελεύεσθαι with ὅπως with ind. fut. 664. Obs. 1.

διακωλύειν with inf. 664. 1.

διαλέγεσθαι with dat. 589.

διαλιπὼν χρόνον 696. Obs. 1.

διαλλάττεσθαι with dat. 590.—ειν with part. 688.

διαμνημονεύειν with genitive 512.

* διανεμεῖσθαί τι 545. 3.

διανοεῖσθαι with gen. 485. ὅπως with ind. fut. 664. Obs. 4.—with inf. 665.—with ὡς and gen. abs. 702.

διαπειρᾶσθαι with gen. 493.

διαπράττεσθαι with inf. 666.

διαπρήσσειν πεδίοιο 522. 2.

διακοπεῖν with gen. 485.

διὰ τάχους 627. 3. f.

διατελεῖν with part. 694.—without part. ib. Obs. 1.

διατρίβειν with acc. 552.—with double acc. 583. 48.

διαφέρειν with gen. 503, 504. — ἤ 503. Obs. 2.—with acc. 579. 1.—τινός τινι 585. 1.

* διαφέρειν τι and εἴς τι and τινί 504. Obs. 1.

*διαφθείρεσθαι with acc. 552.

διάφορος with gen. 503. 504. γ.—with dat. 594. 601.2.

διάφωνος with dat. 594.

διαψεύδεσθαι with gen. 511.

διδακτός τινος 483. Obs. 3.

διδασκαλικός with gen. 494.

διδάσκειν with double acc. 583. 49.—with inf. 665.

* διδάσκεσθαί τι 545. 3.

διδάσκεσθαι, meaning of, 363. 6, 362. 6.

* διδασκόμενος with gen. 493.

(διδόναι) ἐκδ. intrans. 360.

διδόναι with part. gen. 535.—with gen. pret. 515. 2.—with acc. 573.—with dat. 588.—with inf. 669. e.

διειναι with part. 694.

διεξελθεῖν with acc. 558.

διευλαβεῖσθαι with gen. 496.

διέχειν with gen. 530. 1.

δικάζειν with gen. 501.—with acc. 568. — with double acc. 585. 50.—δικάζεσθαι with dat. 601, 598. Obs. 3.

δίκαιός τι 579. 2.—δίκαιός εἰμι with inf. 667.—δίκαιόν ἐστι with inf. 669.—δίκαιός εἰμι pers. for δίκαιόν ἐστι with acc. with inf. 677.

δικαιοῦν with inf. 664. 1.—with ὥστε ib. Obs. 4.

δίκῃ 603. 2.

δίκην 580.

δίμηνος, adverbial, 714. b.

διοικεῖν and -εῖσθαι 363.

διοικεῖν with double acc. 583. 51.

διορίζειν with gen. 530. 1.

διπλάσιος with gen. 502. 3. —ἤ 503. Obs. 2.

διπλοῦς with gen. 502. 3. 503. Obs. 2.

δισκεῖν with dat. 601.

δὶς τόσος with gen. 502. 3.

διφρηλατεῖν with acc. 558.

δίχα with gen. 529. 2.

διχῇ 603. 2.

διχὴν with gen. 498.

διώκειν with gen. and περί, ἕνεκά τινος 501. and Obs. 2.—with acc. 558. — to prosecute, with acc. 568. —with double acc. 583. 52.

διώκειν πεδίοιο 522. 2.

δοία, in two ways, 579. 4.

δοκεῖ with acc. with inf. 676.

δοκεῖν with acc. 551. 1.—with dat. 600. — videri, personal 676. Obs.

δόκησις προσγίγνεται with τό and inf. 668. Obs.

δοκοῦν. acc. abs. 700.

δοκῶ for δοκῶ ὅτι 798.—parenthet. ibid. 3.

δοξάζειν with acc. 551. 1.

δόξαν, acc. abs. 700.

δόξαν ταῦτα and δόξαντα ταῦτα 384. Obs. 1.

*δορυφορεῖν with dat. 596. 1.

δόσις with dat. 588. Obs.

δουλεύειν with acc. 553.—with dat. 596. 2.

δοῦλος with gen. 520.

δοῦλος δουλείας 548. 2. Obs. 2.

δούρε ἄλκιμα 384. Obs. 1.

δόχμια 558. 1.

δρᾶν with double acc. 583. 53.—*καλά, κακά etc. with acc. and dat. 596. add. 1.

*δραπετεύειν with acc. 548. 1.

δράττεσθαι with gen. 536.—with acc. 576. 2.

δρέπειν with acc. 576. 2.

δύνασθαι with nom. 475. 2.—with acc. quantit. 578.—with inf. 666. — with ὥστε ibid. Obs.

δυνατός εἰμι with inf. 666.—pers. for δυνατόν ἐστι with acc. with inf. 677.—δυνατὸν ὄν, acc. abs. 700.

δύο, δύω, δυοῖν with the plur. (δύο σκόπελοι) 388.

δυστάλας with gen. 489.

δυστομεῖν with double acc. 583. 54.

δυσφορεῖν with dat. 607.

δυσχεραίνειν with acc. 549. c.—with dat. 607.

δώματα for δῶμα 355.

δωρεάν, *gratis*, 580. 1.

δωρεῖν and -εῖσθαι 368.— with acc. 573.

δωρεῖσθαί τινί τι 588. — τινά τινι ibid. Obs. add.

δωρηθῆναι pass. 368. 4.

δώρημα with dat. 588. Obs.

δωτίνην, *gratis* 580. 1.

ἴα with conjunct. 416.

ἐάν with inf. 664.

ἐάν 850. 1.—ἐάν, ἤν, ἄν, different forms of, 851. Obs. 2. — construct. with the conj. 851. 2. 11. and 854. —in apodosis, ind., (ind. fut.) with ἄν, Conj. with or without ἄν, Opt. with ἄν 854.—ἐάν with conj. interchanged with εἰ with ind. fut. ib. Obs.

ἐάν, an, 877. Obs. 5.

ἐάν δέ for ἐάν δὲ μή 860. 5.

ἐάν καί, if even, 861.

*ἐάν for ὅτι 798.

ἐάνπερ 734. 4.

ἐάν τε (ἤν τε, ἄν τε)—ἐάν τε (ἤν τε, ἄν τε) 778. b. —ἐάν — καί for ἐάντε— ἐάντε ibid.

ἐαρινός, adverbial, 714. b.

ἑαυτοῦ, use of 653.—for ἐμαυτοῦ, σαυτοῦ 654. b. —ἑαυτῶν, οἷς, οὕς for ἀλλήλων &c. 654. 2.

ἐάων (sc. δόσεων) δωτῆρες 893. d.

ἐβουλόμην and ἐβ. ἄν 858. 3. and Obs. 3.

ἐγγίζειν with gen. 510.— with dat. 592.

ἐγγλύφειν with acc. 569. 3.

ἐγγύς, ἐγγύθι, ἐγγύτατα, -ω with gen. 526.—with dat. 592. 2.

ἐγκαλεῖν with gen. 501.— with dat. 589. 3.

ἐγκανάζω with acc. 570.

ἐγκλίνειν with acc. 548. Obs. 1.

ἐγκολάπτειν with acc. 569. 3.

ἐγκρατής with gen. 518. Obs. 2.

ἐγκωμιάζειν with double acc. 583. 55.

...μιον with dat. 598. Obs.

ἐγώ, use of, 652.

ἔδει for ἔδει ἄν 858. 3. and Obs. 3.

ἔδειν with gen. and acc. 537. and Obs.—with acc. 562.

ἔζειν with acc. 556.

ἐθέλειν, cf. θέλειν.—ἐθελήσω, *volo*, sc. *si licet* 406. 4.

ἐθελοντής, adverbial, 714. c.

ἐθίζειν with double acc. 583. 56.

ἐθίζεσθαι with acc. ibid.

εἰ 850.—Etym. of ib. Obs.

εἰ with indic. 851. 2. 1, 853. in apod., ind., opt. with ἄν, opt. without ἄν, ind. of historic tenses 852.

εἰ with indic. of historic tenses 851. 2. III. 856.— in apod.: ind. of historic tenses with ἄν, opt. with ἄν 856. — Difference between imperf. aor. and plpf. with ἄν in the apod. 856. Obs. 1.—εἰ with indic. of historic tenses as an expression of a wish 856. Obs. 2.—Ind. of historic tenses without ἄν in apod. 858.

εἰ with conj. 854. Obs. 1.

εἰ with opt. 852, 855.—in apod.: opt. with ἄν, opt. without ἄν, indic., indic. fut. with ἄν, ind. of historic tenses, conj. with ἄν 855. — εἰ with opt. interchanged with εἰ with ind. ib. Obs. 5.—εἰ with opt., as expression of wish 855. Obs. 6.

εἰ, concessive, 861.

εἰ, in wishes, 418. d.

εἰ—εἴτε and εἴτε—εἰ δέ 778.

εἰ for ὅτι 798, 804. 8.

εἰ for μή, after a verb of fear, 814. Obs. 3.

εἰ, an, 877. b.—εἰ—ἤ 878. c. —εἰ — εἴτε ibid. b.

εἰ ἄρα for εἰ ἄρα 789. Obs.

εἰ ἄρα, *si forte*, 788. 5.

εἰ γάρ, in wishes, 418. 786. 2, 856. Obs. 2.

εἰ γε 735. 1.

εἰγοῦν with conj. 854. Obs. 1.

εἰ δ' ἄγε 860. 4.

εἰ δέ ellipt. 864. 4.—εἰ δέ for εἰ δὲ μή 864. 5.—εἰ δὲ μή for εἰ δέ 865. 6.

εἰ δή, if then, 721.—εἰ δή ῥα 787. c.

εἰ δή with conj. 854. Obs. 1.

εἰ καί, if even, 861. 2.

εἰ μὲν δή 729. 9.

εἰ μή, ironic. 860. 6—εἰ μή except, 865. 7.—εἰ μή εἰ nisi si, 865. 7.

εἰ μή γε 735. 9.—εἰ μὴ ἄρα 787.—nisi forte 788. 5.

εἰ ποτ' ἔην γε 856. Obs. 2.

εἰ τις or εἰ ἄλλος τις ellipt. 895. 2.

εἰδεῖν, to see, with gen. 45? 2.—with acc. 575.—wit double acc. 583. 57.

εἰδέναι with gen. 4?5.— (*εἰδώς with gen. 493.— with inf. 665.—with part. 683. — Difference between εἰδέναι with inf. and partic. ib. Obs. 2.— with ὡς and gen. ibs. 702.—εἰδέναι ὅτι for ὅτι 804. 6.

εἴδεσθαι with dat. 594. 2.

εἴεν, *fac ita esse*, 860. 8.

εἶθαρ, etymology of, 788. 2.

εἶθε, form of, 726. — in wishes 418. b.; and Obs. 1. and 856. Obs. 2.

εἶθε with inf. 671. e.

εἶθε γάρ 786. 2.

εἰκάζειν τί τινι 609. 3.

εἴκειν with gen. 530.—with acc. 567-573.—*with dat. 593.

εἰκῆ, *frustra*, 603. 2.

εἰκός, εἰκότως with dat. 594. 3.

εἰκὸς ἦν 858. 3.

εἰνάετες, accus. 577. Obs. 2.

εἶναι as copula 374. b. 375. 2, 3.—εἶναι as substantive verb 375. 3.—εἶναι with an adv. ibid.—εἶναι with a partic. (ἐπιστάμενός εἰμι) for the simple verb 375. 4.—εἶναι as copula omitted 376.

(εἶναι) ἦν ἐγγὺς ἡλίου δυσμῶν sc. ἡ ἡμέρα 373. 3.

(εἶναι) ἔστιν and ἦν at the beginning of sentence followed by plural (σχῆμα Πινδαρικόν) 386. 2.—ἔστω οἱ for εἰσὶν οἱ 386. Obs. 2.

(εἶναι) ἦν ἄρα seemingly for ἔστιν 398. 4.

εἶναι, seemingly redundant, in ὀνομάζειν, -εσθαι 474. Obs. 3.

εἶναι with gen. origin. 483. —with gen. possess. 521.

αι with gen. partitive 533. 1.
αι with adv. and gen. 528.
—with acc. of quality &c. 579. 3—with dat. possess. 597.
᾽αι and a subst. with inf. 668. 6.—εἶναι and an abstract subst. with inf. 668. c.
ἶναι) the partic. of εἶναι omitted with adj. and subst. after verbs of declaring 682. 3. — after τυγχάνειν, κυρεῖν 683. Obs. 1.—with an adj. or subst. after a partic.; as, λύτρα φέρων κ. ἱκέτης sc. ὤν 705. 6.
ἰνάνυχες, acc. 577. Obs. 2.
ἶο for ἐμοῦ 654. 1.
ἰπέ, applied to many objects 390. 2. a.
ἰπεῖν with gen. 486.
ἰπεῖν with acc. 566. 1.— with double acc. 583. 68.
:ἰπεῖν with dat. 589.—with dat. and acc. with inf. 674.
ἴπερ 734. 4.—with conj. 854. Obs. 1.—εἴπερ concessive 861. Obs. 2.—εἴπερ or εἴπερ τις, or εἴπερ ἄλλος τις, εἴπερ που, εἴπερ ποτέ elliptic 895. 2.
εἴργειν, -εσθαι with gen. 531. —with double acc. 583. 58.—τινί τι 596. Obs. 1. —with inf. 664. — with τό and inf. 670.
εἰρημένον, acc. abs. 700.
εἰρήνη with gen. 529.
εἰς (ἐς) prep. with acc. 625. as adv. 640.—in pregnant force for ἐν with dat. 646. a.—with the article for ἐν (ἡ λίμνη ἐκδιδοῖ ἐς τὴν Σύρτιν τὴν ἐς Λιβύην) 647.
εἰς τότε, τῆμος, εἰς νῦν, εἰς ὅτε, ἐς οὗ, ἐς αὐτίκα, εἰς πρόσθεν, εἰς τὸ πρόσθεν 644.
εἰς-, ἐς- in compos. 625. Obs.
εἰς ὁ 839. c. See ἕως.
εἰς with dat. 594. 2.
εἰσάγειν with gen. 501.— εἰσάγειν γυναῖκα for εἰσάγεσθαι 363. 3.
εἰσάπαξ 644.
εἴσατο ἰδεῖν, ἀκοῦσαι 667. Obs. 2.
εἰσέτι with acc. 644. Obs.

εἰσὶν οἱ λέγοντες for οἱ λέγουσιν 451. 2,817. Obs. 3.
εἰσὶν οἵ 817. Obs. 2.
εἰσοπίσω, ἐσοπ. 644.
εἰσόκε, see ἕως ἄν under ἕως. with indic. fut. 842. 3.
εἰσορᾶν with gen. 485.— with verbs of appearing &c. 667. Obs. 2.—* with partic. 683.
εἰσοψέ 644.
* εἰσπλεῖν ὑμέναιον 558. 1.
εἰσπράττειν with double acc. 583. 135.
εἰσφέρειν with acc. 573. with acc. 573.
εἶτα = ὅμως 772. 4.—with partic. 697. c. — εἶτα in questions 874. 6. — εἶτα δῆτα 725. 2.
εἶτε—εἶτε 778.—εἴτ᾽ οὖν— εἴτ᾽ οὖν ibid.—εἴτε—ἤ or ἤ — εἴτε ibid. Obs.—εἴτε omitted ibid.—εἰ — εἴτε ibid. — εἴτε — δέ ibid. — εἴτε δή 721.—εἶτ᾽ ἄρα for εἶτ᾽ ἄρα 789. Obs.
εἴτε—εἴτε; εἴτε—ἤ in the indirect question 878. d.
εἶχε καλῶς for εἶχεν ἄν 858. 3.
εἰωθέναι with inf. 664.
ἐκ, ἐξ, prep. with gen. 621. —as adv. 640.—in pregnant force with verbs of standing &c. for ἐν with dat. 646. c.—ἐκ with the article for ἐν (οἱ ἐκ τῆς ἀγορᾶς ἄνθρωποι ἀπέφυγον) 647. a.
ἐκ- in compos. 621. Obs. 1.
ἐκ τοῦ ἐμφανοῦς, ἐκ χειρός, ἐκ ποδός 523. Obs. add.
ἐκ προσηκόντων, ἐκ τοῦ εὐπρεποῦς, ἐκ παντὸς τρόπου, ἐκ βίας 523. Obs. add.
ἐκ τότε 640.
ἕκαστος ὡς ἕκ. adverbial, singly, 714. Obs. 2.
ἕκαστος with another nominat. 478.
ἑκάτερος with another nominat. 478.
* ἐκβαίνειν with acc. 558.
* ἐκδιδάσκεσθαι with double acc. 583. 49.
ἐκδύειν with double accus. 583. 59.—ἐκδύομαί τι ib.
ἐκεῖ illuc and illic, 605. Obs. 5.
ἐκεῖθεν with article for ἐκεῖ (ὁ ἐκεῖθεν πόλεμος δεῦρο ἥξει) 647. Obs.

ἐκεῖνα joined with a singular noun 383. Obs.
ἐκεῖνος, η, o local demonstrative 655. 1. — used twice ib. Obs. 3. — opposed to οὗτος ib. 7.— ἐκεῖνος used of well-known things ib. 8. — ἐκεῖνος prospective 657.—retrospective 658.
ἐκεῖσε in pregnant force for ἐκεῖ 646. d.
ἕκητι with gen. 621. Obs. 2.
* ἐκκάμνειν with acc. 549.
ἐκλέγειν with double acc. 583. 60.
ἐκλείπειν with part. 688.
ἐκπαγλεῖσθαι with accus. 550. b.
* ἐκπίνω with acc. 537. Obs.
* ἐκπλήττεσθαι with acc. 550.
ἐκστῆναι with accus. 548. Obs. 1.
ἐκτίνειν with acc. 573.
ἐκτός with gen. 526.
ἐκτόσθεν 644.
ἐκτρέπεσθαι with acc. 548. Obs. 1.
ἑκών, adverbial, 714. c.
ἑκὼν εἶναι 667. Obs. 1.
ἔλαιον, of a place, 353.
ἐλᾶν (to strike) with double acc. 583. 61.
ἔλαττον without ἤ with a numeral, 780. Obs. 1.— as an adverb, ibid.
ἐλαττοῦσθαι with gen. 505.
ἐλαύνειν with acc. 558.—to forge, with acc. 569. — with double acc. 583. add.
ἐλαύνειν in compos. intrans. 360.
ἐλαύνεσθαι with acc. 558.
* ἐλαχίστου ἡγεῖσθαι 517.
ἤλδεσθαι with gen. and acc. 498. and Obs. 2.
ἐλέγχεα, of person, 353.
ἐλέγχειν with double acc. 583. 62. — with part. 684.
* ἐλεεῖν with acc. 549.
ἐλευθερία, ἐλεύθερος, ἐλευθεροῦν with gen. 529–531.
Ἐλευσῖνι 605. Obs. 1.
ἐλθεῖν ἀγγελίης 481. 1.
ἐλθεῖν ἀγγελίην, ἐξεσίην &c. 558.
ἐλίσσειν, saltando celebrare, with acc. 359. 2. add.
ἕλκειν with acc. 552.—to

weigh, with acc. 578.—with dat. 589. 2.
ἑλκεμέναι νειοῖο 522. 2.
ἑλκύειν κόρδαχα &c. 556.
Ἑλλάς, Ἕλλην adject. 439.1.
ἐλλείπεσθαι with gen. 529.—with part. 688.
ἕλπεσθαι with acc. 550.—with inf. 665.—with ὥστε ibid. Obs.
ἐλπίζειν with acc. 550.—with dat. 607.—with inf. 665. — with ὥστε ibid. Obs.
ἐμαυτοῦ, supplied by ἑαυτοῦ, 654.
ἐμβαίνειν, ἐμβατεύειν with acc. 558.
ἔμελλες for ἔμ. ἄν 858.
ἐμμένει with part. 691.
ἐμός for μου 652. Obs. 6.
ἐμοῦ for ἐμαυτοῦ 652. Obs.5.
ἐμπάζεσθαι with gen. 496.
ἔμπαλιν with gen. 503.—ἤ ibid. Obs. 2.
ἐμπάσσειν with gen. 540. Obs.
ἔμπειρος with gen. 493.
ἐμπελάζεσθαι with genitive 510. 1.—with dat. 592.
ἔμπης with partic. 697. c.
ἐμπίπλασθαι with part. 686.
ἔμπλεος with gen. 539.
ἐμπόδων with dat. 601. 2.
ἐμπολᾶν with acc. 576. 2.
ἐμπρήθειν with gen. 540. Obs.
ἔμπροσθεν with gen. 526.—inante 644.
ἐμφερής with dat. 594. 2.
ἐν, ἐνί, εἰν, εἰνί, prep. with dat. 622.—as adv. 640. 2.
ἐν- in compos. 622. Obs.—in pregnant force for εἰς 645. a.
ἐν τοῖς, ἐν ταῖς with superlat. (as πρῶτοι) 444. 5. a.
ἐν ᾧ, whilst, 839. See ἕως.
ἔναγχος, accus. 577. Obs.2.
ἐναντίον, -ίον with gen. 503, 525,526.—with dat. 601. 3.—ἤ ibid. Obs. 3.
ἐναρίζειν with double acc. 583. 63.
ἐνγεταυθί 644. Obs.
ἔνδεια with gen. 529.
ἔνδηλός εἰμι, γίγνομαι, ποιῶν τι 684. Obs. 1.
ἔνδοθεν with the article for ἔνδον (τὴν ἔνδοθεν τράπεζαν φέρε) 647. Obs.
*ἔνδοξός τι 579. 2.

*ἐνδύειν, ἐνδύεσθαι with acc. 583. 81. Obs.
ἕνεκα, accus. 580. 1.
ἕνεκα, ἕνεκεν, εἵνεκα, εἵνεκεν, οὕνεκα with gen. 621. Obs. 2. supposed ellipse of, 488.
ἔνεστιν with inf. 666.
ἐνῆν and ἐνῆν ἄν 858. 3. and Obs. 3.
ἔνθα, ubi 838.
ἔνθα—ἔνθα, ubi—ibi 816. e.
ἔνθα, ἐνθάδε, force of, 605. Obs. 5.
ἔνθα περ 734. 3.
ἔνθεν, unde 838.
ἔνθεν, unde for οὗ, cujus, 530. Obs. 3.
ἔνθενθε with the article for ἔνθα (ὁ ἔνθενθε πόλεμος ἐκεῖσε τρέψεται) 647.Obs.
ἔνθεος with gen. 519.
(ἐνθυμεῖσθαι) ἐντεθυμῆσθαι passive, 368. a.
ἐνθυμεῖσθαι with gen. 485.—with acc. 551.—with part. 683.
ἐνιαύσιος, adverbial, 714. b.
ἐνμεντευθενί 644. Obs.
*ἐννέπειν with acc. 583. 68.—with dat. and acc. with inf. 674. — with partic. 684. Obs. 2. b.
ἐννῆμαρ, accus. 578. Obs. 2.
ἐννοεῖν with gen. 485.—with partic. 683.
ἔννομος with gen. 519.
*ἐνοχλεῖν with acc. 582. 1.—with dat. 601.
ἔνοχος with gen. 501.
ἐνταῦθα with gen. 527.—ἐνταῦθα, force of, 605. Obs. 5.—with partic. 696. Obs. 6.—ἐνταῦθ ἤδη 719. 4. b.—ἐνταῦθα δή 721.
ἐνταυθοί, huc and hic, 605. Obs. 5.
*ἐντέλλεσθαι with acc. 566.—with dat. 589. 3.
ἐντέμνειν with acc. 569. 3.
ἐντρέπεσθαι with gen. 507.
ἔντροφος with gen. 519.
ἐντυγχάνειν with gen. 509.
ἐνώπιον with gen. 526.
ἐξ ἀγχιμόλοιο, ἐξ ἀπροσδοκήτου, ἐξ ἑτοίμου, ἐξ ἀέλπτου 523. Obs. add.
ἐξ ὁμόθεν 644.
ἐξ οὗ, ὅτου, ὧν, since, 839. b. See ὅτε.
ἐξαιρεῖσθαι, pass. with acc. 583. 28.

ἐξαίφνης 523. Obs. add.—with partic. 696. Obs. 3.
ἐξαναζεῖν with acc. 555. c.
ἐξαναχωρεῖν with acc. 548. Obs. 1.
ἐξανέχεσθαι with part. 685.
ἐξαπίνης 523. Obs. add.
ἐξαρέσκεσθαι with dat. 594. 4.
ἔξαρνος with acc. 581. Obs.
ἐξάρχειν with gen. and acc. 513. and Obs.
*ἐξειρεῖν τί τινι, apud aliquem 605. 2.
ἐξελέγχειν with part. 684.
ἐξερέσθαι with gen. 486.
ἔξεστιν with dat. 588. 2.—with inf. 666. d.
ἐξετάζειν with gen. 486.—with double acc. 583.64.
ἐξέτι with gen. 644. Obs.
ἐξηγεῖσθαι with gen. and acc. 518. Obs. 3.
ἐξῆν and ἐξῆν ἄν 858. 3.
ἑξῆς with gen. 520.—ἑξῆς 523. Obs. add.—with dat. 593. 2.
ἐξίστασθαι with gen. 530.—ἐξίσταμαι καρδίας τὸ δρᾶν 670.
ἐξόθεν, exinde, 644.
ἐξόν, accus. absolute, 700.
ἐξοπίσω 644.
ἐξορκοῦν with acc. 566. 2.—with double acc. 583. add.
ἔξω with gen. 526.
ἐοικέναι with acc. 579. 1.—εἴς τι ib. Obs. 1.—with dat. 594. 2.—with part. 682. 2, 684.
ἑός for ἐμός, σός 654. c.
ἐπαινεῖν with gen. 495.—with double acc. 583. 65.—with dat. and acc. 594. and Obs.
ἐπαίρεσθαί τι τινί, dat. incom. 601. 1.—with dat. instr. 607.
ἐπαίσσειν with gen. 507.—with acc. 558. 2.
ἐπαιτιᾶσθαι with gen. 501.
ἐπάν, see ὅταν under ὅτε.—ἐπάν with opt. for ἐπεί 844. Obs.
ἐπανάστασις with dat. 601. Obs. 2.
ἐπαρκεῖν with gen. 535.—with dat. 596.
ἐπαυρέσθαι with gen. 491.
ἐπεί, since, 839.—ἐπεί with conj. for ἐπάν 842. 2.

ἐπεί after a vocat. 479. 5.
ἐπεί θην 726. 1.—ἐπεὶ οὐ μέν 729. b. — ἐπεί νυ 732.
ἐπεί γε 735. 9. — ἐπεί τε, postquam, quoniam, 755. 4. (See ἐπεί.)—ἐπεί ρα 788. 3. — ἐπεί τοι 790. Obs.—ἐπεὶ οὖν 791. 1.
πείγειν, intrans. 360.
πείγεσθαι with gen. 507. —with acc. 558.—with partic. and inf. 690. Obs. 1.
πειδάν for ὅταν, see under ὅτε.—with opt. for ἐπειδή 844.
πειδή, postquam 839. See ὅτε. — in questions and commands, 849. Obs. 2.
πειδή, quoniam 720. (See ὅτε.)
ἐπειή 849. 1. See ἐπεί.
ἔπειτα=ὅμως 772.3.—ἔπειτα in questions, 874. 6.—ἐπ. δῆτα 725. 2.
ἔπειτα with partic. 697. c.
ἐπεμπίπτειν βάσιν 558. 2.
ἐπεξιέναι with gen. 501.
ἐπέοικε with acc. with inf. 676. b.—with part. 691.
ἕπεσθαι with gen. 536.— with acc. 559.—with dat. 593.—with dat., with acc., with prep. 593. Obs.
ἐπεσσύσθαι with ὥστε 664. Obs. 3.
ἐπευφημεῖν with double acc. 583. 70.
ἐπήν see ἐπάν.
ἐπί, prep. with gen. 633.— —with dat. 634.—with acc.635.—as adverb,640. —with dat. in pregnant force for acc. 645. ibid. Obs.3.—with acc. inter-changed with εἰς and acc. 649.— ἐπί with gen. in-terchanged with ἐν and dat. ibid.—with gen. and partic. pres. (ἐπὶ Κύρου βασιλεύοντος) 696. Obs. 4.—with dat. and part. 699. Obs. 2.
ἐπί- in compos. 635. Obs.
ἐπὶ μᾶλλον 644.
ἐπὶ τούτῳ, ἐπὶ τοῖσδε, ἐφ' ᾧτε (ὥστε) with ind. fut. or inf. 836. c.
ἐπιβαίνειν with acc. 558.
ἐπιβάλλεσθαι with gen. 507.
ἐπιβατεύειν with gen. 507.

ἐπιβουλεύομαι ὑπό τινος 372. 4.
ἐπίδοξός εἰμι for ἐπίδοξόν ἐστι with acc. with inf. 677.
ἐπιθυμεῖν with gen. 498.— with inf. 664.
ἐπικαλεῖν with dat. 589. 3.
ἐπικέσθαι with double acc. 583. 67.
ἐπικουρεῖν with dat. 596.
ἐπιλαμβάνεσθαι with gen. 536.
ἐπιλανθάνεσθαι with gen. and acc. 512. and Obs. with part. 683.
ἐπιλείπειν with part. 688.
ἐπιλείπεσθαι with gen. 529.
ἐπιλύεσθαι with τό and inf. 670.
ἐπιμαίεσθαι with gen. and acc. 508. and Obs.
ἐπιμελείᾳ 603. 2.
ἐπιμέλεσθαι, -εῖσθαι with gen. and acc. and περί τινος 496. Obs. 1.—with acc. 551. 1.—with τό and inf. 670.
ἐπιμελής with gen. 496. Obs. 4.
ἐπιμιμνήσκεσθαι with gen. and acc. 512. Obs.
ἐπινάσσειν with gen. 539.
ἐπίπαγχυ 644.
ἐπιπλήσσειν with dat. 589. 3.
ἐπιπολαῖος for adverb, 714. a.
ἐπιπολῆς 523. Obs. add.
ἐπίπροσθεν, ἐπιπρόσω 644.
ἐπισκήπτεσθαι with gen.501.
ἐπιστάμενος with gen. 493. —* dat. 608. Obs. 1.
ἐπίστασθαι with gen. 485.— with part.683. Difference between inf. and part. ibid. Obs.—with ὡς and gen. absol. 702.
ἐπιστατεῖν with gen. 518. with dat. ib. Obs. and 605. 3.
ἐπιστέλλομαί τι with dat. 589. 3.
ἐπιστέφεσθαι with gen. 507.
ἐπιστρεφής with gen. 539. 2.
ἐπιστήμων with gen. 493. with acc. 579. 2.
ἐπιστρέφεσθαι with gen. 507.
ἐπίστροφος with gen. 493.
ἐπισχὼν χρόνον 696. Obs.1.
ἐπιτάττειν with gen. 518.

ἐπιτέλλεσθαι with dat. 589. 3.— -ειν with inf. 664. 1.
ἐπιτηδές, consulto, 580. 1.
ἐπιτηδειός εἰμι with inf. 666.
ἐπιτηδεύειν with acc. 561.
ἐπιτιμᾶν with dat. 589. 3.
*ἐπιτρέπομαί τι 545. 3.— -ειν with inf. 664, 687. Obs.—with part. 687.
ἐπιτρέφεσθαι with gen. 496.
ἐπίτριμμα of person, 353. 1.
*ἐπιτροπεύειν with gen.518. —with acc.359. Obs. add.
ἐπιτύφεσθαι with gen. 498.
ἐπιφθόνως διακεῖσθαι with gen. 499.
ἐπιχαίρειν with acc. 549.
ἐπιχειροῦμαι 372. 4.— -ειν with inf. 664.
ἐπιχεῖσθαι with gen. 497.
ἐπιχώριος with gen. 520.
ἐπιψηφίζειν with dat. 588.
ἑπόμενος with dat. 593.
*ἐπώνυμός τινος 519.
ἐρᾶν, ἔρασθαι, ἐρατίζειν with gen. 498.
ἐρᾶν with acc. 549.
ἐράσασθαι and ἐρασθῆναι 367. 3.
(ἐργάζεσθαι) εἰργάσθαι, ἐργασθῆναι, ἐργασθήσεσθαι passive, 368.
ἐργάζεσθαι with acc. 560. —with double acc. 583. 69.
ἔργον, ἔργα omitted, 436.
ἔρδειν with double acc. 583. 71.
ἐρεῖν with double acc. 583. 73.
ἐρέσθαι with double acc. 583. 72.
*ἐρείνειν with double acc. 583. 74.
*ἐρείδεσθαι with gen. 536.
ἔρημος, ἐρημοῦν with gen. 529.
ἐρητύειν with gen. 531.
ἐρίζεσθαι with acc. 564.— ἐρίζειν, ἔρις with dat. 601. and Obs. 2.
ἔρις of persons, 353.
ἔρπειν with acc. viæ 558.
ἔρχεσθαι with acc. 559.— ὁδόν 558.—τινί for πρός τινα 592.—with part. fut. 690. Obs. 2.
ἔρχονται πεδίοιο 522. 2.
*ἐρωεῖν with gen. 531.
ἐρωτᾶν with double acc. 583. 74.

ἐρώτησίς τινος, de aliquo, 486. Obs. 2.
ἐς see εἰς.
ἐσηκούειν with dat. 593.
ἐσθής for ἐσθῆτες 354.
ἐσθίειν with gen. and acc. 537. Obs.—with acc. 562.
ἐσιόντι 599.
ἐσπλέοντι 599.
ἐσσύμενος with gen. 507.
ἴστ' ἄν, see ἕως ἄν under ἕως.
ἴστε 839. c. See ἕως.
*ἴστε περ 734. 2. 3.
ἴστι τῶν αἰσχρῶν, ἀτόπων &c. 521. 2.
ἴστι μοί τι βουλομένῳ, ἡδομένῳ, ἀσμένῳ, ἐλπομένῳ 599. 3.
ἴστι, (licet) with dat. 588. 2. —with inf. 666.—ὥστε ibid. Obs. 2.
ἴστι (accidit) with inf. 669. —with ὥστε ib. Obs. 1.
ἴστι with partic. 691.
ἴστιν οἵ = τινοί, ἴστιν ὧν = ἐνίων &c. 817. 5.
ἴστιν ὅτε 817. Obs. 4.
ἴστιν ὅπου, ὅπη, ὅπως, — ἴστιν οὗ, ἵνα, ἔνθα, ᾗ 817. Obs. 4.
ἐστιᾶν with gen. 537.
ἐστιᾶν γάμους 583. 75.— double acc. ibid.
ἴσω with gen. 526.
ἴσωθεν gen. 522. Obs. 1.
ἕτερος, ἑτέρωθι with gen. 503.
ἐτέων gen. temp. 523.
ἔτι τοίνυν 790.
ἑτοιμάζειν with acc. 569.
ἔτος εἰς ἔτος 577. Obs. 2.
εὖ λέγειν &c. with acc. 583. 102.
εὖ ἔχειν, ἥκειν with gen. 528.
εὖ ποιεῖν with part. 689.
εὖ πράττειν τινός 483. Obs. 3.
εὐδαιμονίζειν, εὐδαίμων with gen. 495. — with acc. 552.
εὕδειν with acc. 556.
εὐδοκιμεῖν and -εῖσθαι 363. 5.
εὐεργετεῖν with double acc. 583. 76.
εὐθύ with gen. 509. 2.—with the partic. 696. Obs. 5.
εὐλογεῖν with double acc. 583. 77.
εὔνοιαι, marks of favour, 355. γ.
εὔνους with dat. 596. 3.
εὐορκεῖν with acc. 566. 2.
εὐπορεῖν with gen. 439.

εὗρεν asyndet. 792.
εὑρίσκειν with acc. 569. 1. 576. 2.— -εῖσθαι with part. 684.
εὖρος, accus. 579. 3.
εὐσεβεῖν with acc. 565.— εἰς, περί, πρός τινα ibid. Obs.
εὖτ' ἄν, see ὅταν under ὅτε.
εὖτε for ὅτε, see ὅτε.
εὐτυχεῖν with acc. 552.— with part. 689.
εὐφημεῖν with dat. 589. 3.
εὐφραίνειν with double acc. 583. 78.
εὔχεσθαι with acc. 566. 2. —with inf. 665.
εὐχετᾶν with acc. 566. 2.
εὐωχεῖν, -εῖσθαι with gen. and acc. 537. and Obs.
εὐωχεῖν with double acc. 583. 79.
ἐφ' ἅπαξ 644.
ἐφάπτεσθαι with gen. and acc. 536. Obs. 4.
ἐφεξῆς with gen. 520.— with dat. 593. 2.
ἐφέστιος for adverb, 714. a.
ἐφίεσθαι with gen. and acc. 507. and Obs.
ἐφορεύειν with gen. 518.
*ἐφυβρίζειν θυμῷ 549.
ἐφυμνεῖν with acc. 566. 3.
ἐφ' ᾧ, ἐφ' ᾧτε with ind. fut. or inf. 836, 867.
ἔχειν and compos. intrans. 360. — with gen. 514, 531. — with acc. 576. —with inf. 664.—with τό and inf. 670.—with part. ποιήσας ἔχω 692. — with inf. ib. Obs.
ἔχειν εὖ, καλῶς &c. with gen. 528.—πενθικῶς &c. with gen. 489.
ἔχειν γνώμην with ὡς and gen. absol. 702.
ἔχεσθαι with gen. 536.
ἐχθαίρω with double acc. 583. 80.
ἐχθρός with gen. 520.—with dat. 601. 3.
ἔχω, possum, with inf. 666. —with ὥστε ibid. Obs. 2.
ἔχων ληρεῖς, φλυαρεῖς, κυπτάζεις ἔχων 698.—ἔχων, with, ib. Obs. 2.—pleonast. ib. Obs. 2.
ἑώθινός adverbial, 714. b.
ἕως, whilst and until, 846. —with ind. 840.—with ind. of hist. tenses, 840.

—ἕως ἄν with conj. 84.
—ἕως without ἄν wit conj. 842. 2.—ἕως wit opt. 843, 844.—ἕως wit opt. and ἄν 843.
ἕως for τέως 816. e.
ἕως οὗ, until, 839. e.

ζεῖν with gen. 540. Obs.
ζηλοῦν with gen. 495.
ζηλώματα of person, 353. 1.
ζημιοῦν with double acc. 583. 82.
ζημιώσεσθαι seemingly passive, 364.
ζωγρεῖν with acc. 576. 2.
ζώειν, ζῆν with acc. 552.
ζωννύναι with double acc. 583. 81.

ἤ, alternative, aut.—ἤ-ἤ 777. 3.—in direct questions, 875.— in indirect questions, 877.—ἤ-ἤτα or ἤτοι—ἤ 777. 5.—ἤ alias, alioquis, 777. Obs. 3. in questions, an 875. Obs. 2. 876. Obs. 6.—ἤ and ἤ μή in questions 875. Obs. 3. and 4.—ἤ εἴτε 778. — in indirect questions, 878.—
ἤ comparative, 779.—τίς, τί—ἤ ib. Obs. 1.—ἤ ib.—ἤ with comparative, 780, 783. Obs.—ἤ without μᾶλλον or after a positive adjec. 779. Obs. 3. — with πλέον, πλεῖν, ἔλαττον and a numeral omitted, 780. Obs. 1.—ἤ with genitive after a comparative, 780. Obs. 2.
ἤ κατά with acc. or ἤ πρός with acc. after a compar. 783.
ἤ ὡς, than as, after a compar. 779. Obs. 2.—ἤ ὡς with the optat. and ἄν 783. Obs.
ἤ ὥστε with inf. 863. e.
ἤ ὥστε with inf. after a compar. 783. Obs. 2.
ἤ 731. 1.
ἤ δή, ἤ μάλα δή 724. 2.
ἤ δῆτα 725. 2.
ἤ μήν 729, 731.
ἤ μήν—γε 735. 10.
ἤ μέν 729. a.
ἤ οὐ after μᾶλλον 749. 3.
ἤ που, ἤ τοι, ἤ γε 731. 1.—
ἤ τοι 790. Obs.

ρά νυ 732.
with gen. 527.—ἦ, ubi, quo 838.
with superlative, 870. Obs. 4.
ἔχειν, ἥκειν with gen. 528.
δ᾿ ὅς, ἦ δ᾿ ἦ 816. d.
τις ἦ οὐδείς 659. Obs. 2.
, interrog., ἦ ἄρα δή, ἦ ρά νυ, ἦ νυ, ἦ νύ που, ἦ που, ἦ γάρ 873. 1.
ꞮΒᾶν with acc. 553.
ἡγεῖσθαι), ἡγῆσθαι passive, 367. a.
ἡγεῖσθαι with gen. 533. 2.
with gen., dat., acc. 518. and Obs. 3.—with acc. 551.2.—with dat. 596.2. with inf. 665.
ἡγεμονεύειν with gen. and dat. 518. and Obs. 3.— with dat. 596. 2.
ἡγεμονεύομαι 372. 4.
ἠδέ, and, 777. Obs. 4.
ἥδεσθαι with acc. 549. — with dat. 607. — with partic. 686.
ἤδη, force of, 719. 4.—νῦν ἤδη, ἤδη νῦν, ἤδη οὐκ, ἤδη ποτέ, οὗτος ἤδη, οὗτως ἤδη, τότ᾿ ἤδη, ἐνταῦθ᾿ ἤδη, καὶ ἤδη 719. 4. b.
ἡδονή τινος, de aliquo, 489.
ἠέριος, adverbial, 714. b.
ἥκειν εὖ, καλῶς &c. with gen. 528.
ἥκω, veni, 396.
ἦλθε with inf. 669.
ἡλίκος attracted, 823. Obs. 5.
ἥλιοι, soles, 355. b.
*ἡμάτιος, adverbial, 714.
ἤματι, ἡμέρᾳ 606.
ἡμέν—ἠδέ 777. Obs. 4.
ἡμέρα omitted 436.
ἡμέραν, acc. of time, 577.
ἡμέρας gen. of time, 523.
ἡμερεύειν κελεύθου 522. 2.
ἡμερήσιος, adverbial, 714. b.
ἡμῖν, dat. of reference, 599, 600.
ἡμιόλιος with gen. 502.— ἦ ibid. Obs. 3.
ἥμισυς (ὁ) τοῦ χρόνου, — ἡ ἡμίσεια τῆς γῆς 442. c.
ἥμισυς ἦ 503. Obs. 2.
ἦμος, accus. 577. Obs. 2.— ἦμος for ὅτε 804. 7.
ἡμῶν for ἡμέτερος 652. 3.
ἡμῶν &c. for ἀλλήλων &c. 654. 2. Obs.
ἦν, see ἐάν.
ἦν and ἦν ἄν 858. 3. Obs. 3.

ἡνίκα, when, 839. a. See ὅτε.
—ἡνίκ᾿ ἄν see ὅταν under ὅτε. — ἡνίκα without ἄν with conj. 842. 2.
ἡνίκα περ 734. 3.—ἡνίκα for ὅτε 804. 7.
ἠοῦς 523.
ἠπατημένος τινός 483. Obs. 3.
ἥπερ 779. Obs. 4.
ἤσθαι with acc. 556.
ἡσθῆναι with. acc. 488.
ἡσσητέον τινός 613. 3.
ἥσσων εἰμί with inf. 666.
ἡσυχῇ, quietly, dat. 613. 2.
ἡσυχία with gen. 529.
ἥσυχος, adverbial, 714. c.
ἦτε—ἦτε 777. Obs. 1.
ἦτοι, confirmative partic. 731. 2, 3, 4. — ἦτοι — ἦ, aut — aut 777. 5. — ἦτοι μέν 731. 2, 3.
ἡττᾶσθαι with gen. and ὑπό τινος 505. and Obs.
ἡττήσεσθαι, seemingly pass. 364.
ηὖκται, pass. 368.
ηὖτε, as, so as, in comparative adverbial sentences, 868.
ἠχεῖν with acc. 566. 3.

θακεῖν with acc. 556.
θαλάσσιος for adverb, 714.a.
θαλέθειν, θάλλειν with acc. 555. c.
θάλπῃ 355.
*θάμβειν with acc. 550. b.
θάνατοι 355. b.
θαρρεῖν with acc. 550.— *τινι 607.
θάσσειν with acc. 556.
θάτερα, accus. 579. 4.
θαῦμα with inf. 667.
θαυμάζειν with gen. and acc. 495. and Obs. 2.—with acc. 550.—with dat. 607. —θαυμάζω εἰ for ὅτι 804. 7.
θαυμάσιος with gen. 495.
θαυμασίως, θαυμαστῶς ὡς 823. Obs. 7.
θαυμαστὸν ὅσον 823. Obs. 7.
θεᾶσθαι with gen. 485.
(θεᾶσθαι) θεάσασθαι and θεαθῆναι 368.
θέατρον for θέαται 353. 2.
θέειν πεδίοιο 522. 2.
θέλειν with acc. 551. 1.— with inf. 664.—with ἄστε ibid. Obs. 4. — with τό and inf. 670. — θέλειν, solere 402. Obs. 1.

θεμιστεύειν with gen. 518.
θεν, suffix for the gen. 530. Obs. 3.—θεν suffix 726. 1.
θεραπεύειν with double acc. 583. 83.
θεραπεύεσθαι θεραπείαν 583. 83.
θεραπεύσεσθαι, seemingly passive, 364. a.
θέρεσθαι with gen. 540. Obs.
θερινός for adverb 714. b.
θέρους 523.
θεωρεῖν with gen. 485.
θήν 726.
θητεύειν with dat. 596. 2.
θιγγάνειν with gen. and dat. 536. and Obs. 4.
θνήσκειν with acc. 552.— mortuum esse 396.
θνητοῖς, inter mort. 605. 2.
θοάζειν with acc. 556.
θοινίζειν, with double acc. 583. 84.
θρέεισθαι with acc. 566. 4.
θρέμμα, of a person, 382. 1.
θρέψεσθαι, seemingly pass. 364.
θρηνεῖν with acc. 566. 4.
θροεῖν with acc. 566. 3.
θρώσκειν with acc. 556, 558.
θυγάτηρ, omitted, 436.
θύει sc. ὁ θυτήρ 373. 2.
θύειν and -εσθαι 363. 6.
θύειν ἐπινίκια, εὐαγγέλια, διαβατήρια, γενέθλια, Λύκαια, γάμους 560. 3.
θυμοβόρος with acc. 581. Obs. 1.
θυμοί 355.
θυμοῦσθαι with gen. 490.— with dat. 601.
θυραῖος for adverb 714. a.
θῶκος, marketplace, 353. 2.
θωΰσσειν with acc. 566. 3.

(ἰᾶσθαι) ἰάσασθαι and ἰαθῆναι 368.
ἰαύειν with acc. 556.
ἰάχειν with acc. 566. 3.
ἰδέ, applied to plural, 390. 2. a.
ἰδεῖν with gen. 485.—with acc. 554.
ἰδεῖν, ἰδέσθαι, with verbs of appearing &c. 667. Obs. 2.
ἰδίᾳ 603. 2.
ἴδιος with gen. 521. 3.
ἰδιωτεύειν, ἰδιώτης with gen. 493.
ἰδροῦν with acc. 555.
ἱέναι and compos. intrans. 360.—with gen. 531.

ἰέναι with gen. 506, 522. 2.
—with dat. 592.

ἰέναι, εἶμι with fut. sense,
397. a.

*ἰέναι with acc. 559.—with
acc. viæ 558.

ἰέναι with part. fut. and
pres. 690. Obs. 2.

ἱεράσθαι with acc. 553.

ἱερός with gen. 521. 3.

ἵζω with acc. 556.

ἰθέως with partic. 696. Obs. 5.

ἴθι δή 721. 2.

ἰθύνειν with acc. 559.

ἰθύ(ς) with gen. 509. 2.

ἱκανός εἰμι with inf. 666.—
with ὥστε ibid. Obs. 2.

ἰκάνω ἡδομένῳ τινί &c. 599.

ἴκελός τι 579. 2.

ἱκετεύειν with gen. 536. Obs.
6.—with acc. 566. 2.—
with double acc. 583. 85.
—with inf. 664.

ἰκνεῖσθαι with gen. 536.
Obs. 6.—with acc. 559.
—τινι ad aliq. 592.

ἱμείρειν, -εσθαι with gen.
and acc. 498. and Obs. 2.

ἵνα, final conj. that, 805.
— with conj. and opt.
805. sqq.

ἵ a ἄν with conj. and opt.
810. and Obs. 3.—with
indic. of historic tenses,
813.

ἵνα δή 721. 3.—ἵνα περ 734. 3.

ἵνα μή see ἵνα.

ἵνα τί; 882. 1.

ἵνα with gen. 527, 838.

ἵνα for ἐνταῦθα 816. e.

ἵπποις cum eq. 604.

ἵππος for ἵπποι 354.

ἴς in periphrasis 442. d.

ἴσθ ὅτι without verb 889.

ἰσόμοιρος, ἰσόρροπος, ἴσος
with gen. 519.

ἴσον, accus. quantit. 578.
Obs. 2.

ἰσόρροπος with gen. 519.

ἴσος, ἴσως with dat. 594.

ἵστασθαι with acc. 556.

ἱστορεῖν with double acc.
583. 86.

ἰσχανᾶν with gen. 536.

ἰσχύειν with dat. 609. 1.

ἰύζειν with acc. 566. 3.

*ἰχθύες, fish-market, 353. 3.

κάθαρμα, of person, 353. 1.

καθαρός with gen. 529.

καθαίρειν with double acc.
583. 87.

καθίζειν with acc. 556.

καθίστασθαι καλῶς with gen.
528.

*καθορᾶν with partic. 688.

καθύπερθε with gen. 526.

καί, omitted with ἄλλοι,
ἄλλα, οἱ ἄλλοι, τὰ τοιαῦτα
792. 2. k.

καί—καί 757.—τέ—καί 758.

καί alone, atque, ac 759.
at the beginning of an
interrog. sentence ib. 2.
— adversative ib. 3.—
increasive ib. 4.—for τέ
—καί ib. Obs. 1.—with
πολύς ib. Obs. 2.—in apo-
dosis ib. Obs. 3.—καί,
etiam, 760.—καί, etiam,
referring to a καί in an-
other clause 761.—καί
for ὅτε 752. 2.—καί with
ὅμοιος, ἴσος, ὁ αὐτός 594.
Obs. 4.—καί after a par-
tic. 696. Obs. 6.

καί with partic. 697. c.

καί in an answer 880. i.

καὶ γάρ 786. Obs. 7.

καί—γέ 735. 10.

καὶ δὴ καί 724.

καὶ δῆτα 725.

καὶ ἐάν, καὶ εἰ, even if, 861. 2.

καὶ ἤδη 719. 4. b. — καὶ
δή, 724. 2.— καί δή, fac
ita esse 820. 8. with a
partic. ibid.

καὶ μέν 729. c.

καὶ μὲν δή 730. c.

καὶ μέντοι 730. a.—καὶ μέντοι καί ib.

καὶ μήν 728. c.—καὶ μὴν καί,
καὶ μὴν οὐδέ ib.

καί — μήν — γέ 735. 6.

καί νυ κε 732.

καὶ ὅς, καὶ ἥ for καὶ οὗτος,
καὶ αὕτη 816. c.

καί ῥα 788.

καὶ ταῦτα with partic. 697. c.
—καὶ ταῦτα or καὶ τοῦτο
in an answer 880. i.

καὶ τοίνυν 790. 1.

καίεσθαι with gen. 498.

καινοτομεῖν τι 560. 2.

καίνυσθαί τινα with inf. 667.
Obs. 1.

καίπερ with partic. 697. c.

καιρόν, ad tempus, 577. Obs.
1. and 2.

καίτοι 736. 4. 790. Obs.—
—with partic. 697.

καίτοι γε 735. 6.

*κακολογεῖν, κακοποιεῖν with
acc. 582. 3. 1.

κακός τι 579. 2.—with dat.
601. 3. — πόσων κακο
548. Obs. 2.

κακός εἰμι with inf. 666.

*κακουργεῖν with acc. 572.
1.—with double acc. 583.
88.

κακῶς λέγειν, ποιεῖν with
acc. 583. 102.

καλεῖν ὄνομά τι 588.

καλεῖν with double accu.
583. 89.

καλεῖσθαι, κεκλῆσθαί τινα
483.

καλεῖσθαι βουλήν 559.

καλλιερῶ, -οῦμαι 363. 5.

καλλιστεύειν with gen. 504.
—with acc. 579. 2.

καλός τι 579. 2.—with dat.
601. 3.

καλούμενος, so called, 438.

καλῶς ἔχειν, ἥκειν with gen.
528.

καλῶς λέγειν with acc. 583.
102.

κάμνειν with partic. 687.

κάμνειν with accus. 552.—
τοὺς ὀφθαλμούς 552. c.

κἂν with the imperat. 424. c.

κἂν εἰ, at least, 430.

κάρα, in periphrases, 442. d.

κάρηνα for the sing. 355.
Obs. 1.

καρποῦσθαι with acc. 576.
1. 2.

καρτερεῖν with acc. 563.—
with partic. 687.

κατά, prep. with gen. 628.
with acc. 629.—as adv.
640.—κατα- in compos.
629. Obs.

κᾆτα with partic. 697.

καταβαίνειν, -εσθαι with acc.
557. Obs. 558.

καταγελᾶν with dat. 589. 3.

καταγιγνώσκειν with accus.
551. 2.

καταδηλός εἰμι. γίγνομαί ποιῶν τι 684. Obs. 2.

κατακλείειν with gen. 531.

κατακούειν with gen. 487. 4.
—with dat. 593.

καταλλάττεσθαι with dat.
590.

καταλύειν with dat. 590.

*καταμανθάνειν with gen.
485.

κάταντα 558.

καταντίον with gen. 526.

καταπάσσειν with gen. 540.
Obs.

κατάπαυμα, of person, 353.

καταπλήττεσθαι with acc. 550.

αταπροΐξεσθαι with partic. 689.

αταρᾶσθαι with dat. 589.

:αταρνεῖσθαι with inf. 665.

:ατάρχειν, -εσθαι with gen. and acc. 513. and Obs.

:ατασβεννύναι with double acc. 583. 90.

:ατατιθέναι with gen. pret. 516.

:ατατήκομαι with acc. 549.c.

καταυτόθι 644.

καταφείη, of a person, 353.

καταφρονεῖν with gen. 496. —with acc. 551. 1.

κατεάγη τῆς κεφαλῆς 522. Obs. 3.

κατέλαβε with inf. 669.

κατεργάζεσθαι with inf. 666.

κατεύχεσθαι with dat. 589.1.

κατέχειν with. inf. 664.

κατηγορεῖν with acc. 568.

κατήκοος with gen. 487. 4.

κατιδεῖν, see καθορᾶν.

κατομνύναι with acc. 566. 2.

κατόπισθεν 644.

κάτω with gen. 526.

κέ, κέν, (see ἄν,) position of, 431.

κεῖθεν, see ἐκεῖθεν — κεῖθεν ὅθεν for κεῖσε ὅθεν by attract. 824. Obs. 2.

κεῖθι, illic and illuc 605. and Obs. 5.

κείρειν with double acc. 583. 91.—φόνον 576. 2.

(κεῖσθαι) (δια-, προσ-) ὑπό τινος 359. 3.

κεῖσθαι with gen. separat. 530. 1.—with acc. 556.

κεῖσθαι καλῶς with gen. 528.

κεκομμένος φρενῶν 529.

κέκρανται as III. pers. perf. 386. Obs. 1.

κεκτῆσθαι with acc. 576. 1.

κελαδεῖν with acc. 566. 3.

κελεύειν with acc. 566. 2.— with double acc. 583. 92. —with dat. and acc. 589. 3. and Obs. 3.—with inf. 664.—with dat. and acc. with inf. 674.

*κέλευθός τινος, to a place, 509.

κενός with gen. 529.

κέραμος, prison, 353. 2.— for κέραμοι 354.

κεραννύναι with acc. 572.

κερδαίνειν with acc. 576. 2.

κερκίς, the weaving, 353. 2.

κερτομέω with double acc. 583. 93.

κεύθειν, intransit. 360.

κεφάλαιον δέ 655. Obs. 4.

κήδεσθαι with gen. and acc. 496. and Obs. 1.

κήδευμα, applied to a person, 382. 1.

κῆδός τινος 496. Obs. 4.

κῆρ, in periphrases, 442. d.

κηρύσσει sc. ὁ κῆρυξ 373. 2.

κηρύσσειν with acc. 566.

κηρύσσομαί τι 545. 3.

*κικλήσκειν with double acc. 583. 89.

κιθαρίζειν with acc. 566. 3.

κινδυνεύειν with gen. 496. —with acc. 552.—with inf. 665.

κινδυνεύειν does not take ἄν 859.

κινεῖν with double acc. 583. 94.

κιττᾶν with gen. 498.

κλάζειν with acc. 566. 3.

(κλαίειν) κεκλαυμένος 363. 5.

κληρονομεῖν, κληροῦσθαι with gen. 519.

κλίμακες for the sing. 355. Obs. 1.

κλίνειν and compos. intrans. 360.

κλίνεσθαί τινι 592.

κλύειν, audire, 475.2.—with gen. 485. — with acc. 575.—with dat. 598.— with partic. 683.

κλύω, audivi, 396.

(κνῆν) κνάσασθαι, seemingly passive, 364. b.

κνίζεσθαι with gen. 498.

κοιμᾶσθαι ὕπνον 556.

κοινῇ 603. 2.

κοινός with gen. 519.—with partitive gen. 535.

κοινός, κοινωνία with dat. 590.

κοινοῦν, -οῦσθαι with gen. 535.—with acc. 573.— with dat. 588. 3.

κοινωνεῖν with gen. 535.— with dat. 588. 3.

κοιρανεῖν with gen. 518.

κολάζειν with double acc. 583. 95.

κολάζεσθαι for κολάζειν 363. 3.

κομιδῇ 603. 2.

κομπεῖν with acc. 566.

κονίαι and κονίη 355. b.

κονίειν πεδίοιο 522. 2.

κόπτεσθαί τινα 566. Obs.

κορέννυσθαι with gen. 540.

κοτεῖν with gen. 490. —*with acc. 549.—with dat. 601.

κότος τινός, de aliquo, 490. Obs.

κράζειν with acc. 566. 3.

κραίνειν with gen., dat. and acc. 518. and Obs. 3.

κρατεῖν with gen., dat. and acc. 518. and Obs. 1. 3. —with double acc. 583. 96.—with dat. 605. 3.

κρατεῖσθαι with gen. 505.

κρατιστεύειν with gen. 504.

κράτος in periphrases, 442. d.—with acc. 579. 5.

κρατοῦμαι ὑπό τινος 372. 4.

κρείσσων with gen. 502. 2.

κρηναῖος for ἐν κρήνῃ 714.

κριθαί 355. b.

κρίνασθαι, seemingly pass. 364.

κρίνειν with gen. 486, 520. b. —with acc. 568. — with double acc. 583.97.—and -εσθαι with gen. and περί τινος 501. and Obs. 2.— κρίνειν τί τινι 609.

(κρίνειν) ἀποκεκρίσθαι pass. 368. a. — ἀποκρίνασθαι and -θῆναι 368. b.

κροταλίζειν, κροτεῖν with acc. 548. Obs. 1.

κρότημα, of a person, 353.

κρύπτειν, -εσθαι with acc. 582. 5.—with double acc. 583. 98.—with dat. and acc. 582. Obs. 3.

κρύπτομαί τι, celor aliquid, 583. 98.

κτᾶσθαι with gen. 515. 2.— with acc. 576. 2.

(κτᾶσθαι) κεκτῆσθαι passive 368. a.—κτήσασθαι and -θῆναι 368. b.

κτῆμα with an adjective for the simple neuter of adjective 381. Obs. 4.

κτίζειν with acc. 569.

κτυπεῖν with acc. 566. 3.

κῦμα for κύματα 354.

κυναγετεῖν διωγμόν 559. Obs. 2.

κυπτάζεις ἔχων 698. Obs. 1.

(κύπτειν) ὑποκ., succumbere, 360.

κυρεῖν, seemingly as copula, 375. 3.—with gen. and acc. 509. and Obs.—with acc. 576. 2.—with partic. 694.—without partic. ib. Obs. 1.

κυριεύειν with gen. 518.
κύριος with gen. 521. 3.
κωκύειν with acc. 566. 4.
κώκυμα, of a person, 353.
κωλύειν with gen. 531. —with inf. 664.—with τό and inf. 670.
*κωμῳδεῖν with acc. 566.1.

λαβών, with, 698. Obs. 2.—pleonast. ibid.
λαγχάνειν with gen. and acc. 509. and Obs.—δίκην with dat. 601.1.
λάζυσθαι with gen. and acc. 536. and Obs. 4.
λαθών, secretly, 698.
λαιᾶς (χειρός) 530. Obs.1.
λαλεῖν with dat. 589. 3.
(λαμβάνειν) ἀναλ., ὑπολ. intransit. 360.
λαμβάνειν with acc. 574.—-εσθαι with gen. 536. and Obs. 3.
λάμπειν with acc. 555.
λάμπεσθαι for λάμπειν 363.
λανθάνειν with double acc. 583. 101.
λανθάνεσθαι with gen. 512.
λανθάνω with partic. 694.—in part. with finite verb, ibid. and Obs. 3.
λανθάνω, ὅτι ταῦτα ποιῶ for λανθάνει, ὅτι κ. τ. λ. 804.
λατρεύειν with acc. 553.c.—with dat. 596. 2.
λάχανα, of a place, 353. 2.
λέγειν with gen. and acc. 486,487.—λόγους,ῥήματα &c. 566.1.—with double acc. 583. 102.—with dat. 589.—with inf. 664,665.
*λέγειν with τό and inf. 670.—with dat. and acc. with inf. 674.
λέγειν, -εσθαι with partic. 684. Obs. 2. b.
λέγειν with ὡς and genit. absol. 702.
λέγειν εὖ, κακῶς with acc. 583. 102.
(λέγειν) λέξομαι seemingly passive, 364.
λέγεται with acc. with inf. 676. a.
λεγόμενος, so called, 438. Obs.
λείπειν, -εσθαι with gen. 529.
(λείπειν) ἐλλ., ἐπιλ., ἀπολ. intrans. 360.—λείπεσθαι seemingly passive, 364.

—λιπῆναι different from λειφθῆναι 367. Obs. 2.
λείπεσθαι with partic. 688.
λειτουργεῖν with acc. 553.
λέκτρα for λέκτρον 355.
λεύσειν with acc. 554. 515.
λέων, lion-skin, 353. 2.
λήγειν with gen. 514.—with partic. 687.
λήθειν, ληθάνειν with gen. 512.
λήκειν with acc. 566. 3.
ληρεῖν with dat. 589.
ληρεῖς ἔχων 698. Obs. 1.
λῆρος, nugator, 353. 1.
λίθος for λίθοι 354.
λιλαίεσθαι with gen. 498.
λιπαρεῖν with partic. 687.
λίσσεσθαι with gen. 536. Obs. 6.—with acc. 566. 2.—with double acc. 583. 103.—with inf. 664. 1.—with ὅπως and conj. ibid. Obs. 3.
(λογίζεσθαι)λογίσασθαι and λογισθῆναι 368. b.—with acc.551.1.—with inf.665.
λόγος τινός, de aliquo, 486. Obs. 2.
λοιδορεῖν with acc. 566. 2.—with dat. 589. 3.
λοιδορεῖσθαί τινι 589. 3.
λοιπόν 579. 4.
λούειν with double acc. 583. 104.
λούεσθαι with gen. 540. Obs.
λοχεύειν with double acc. 583. 105.
λύειν and λύεσθαί τι 362. Obs. 1.—λύσεσθαι seemingly passive, 364. a.
λύειν with gen. 531.—with gen. pretii, 516.
λύει τέλη with partic. 691.
λυμαίνεσθαι with double acc. 583. 106.—with dat.602. 2.
λυπεῖσθαι with dat. 607.
λύσις with gen. 529. 1.
λυσιτελεῖν (λύειν τέλη) with dat. 596.—with part. 691.
(λωβᾶσθαι) λωβηθῆναι passive, 368. b.
λωβᾶσθαι with double acc. 583. 108.—with dat. 602. 2.
λωφᾶν with gen. 514.

μά 733.—μὰ Δία 566. 2.
μαίνεσθαι with acc. 549.

*μακάριός τι and εἴς τι 579. 2. and Obs.
μακρά, accus. 578. Obs. 2.—μακράν 558.1.—μακρά for adverb, 714. b.
μάλιστα with gen. 502. 3.
μᾶλλον with gen. 502. 2.—μᾶλλον ἀλλ᾽ οὐ 779. Obs. 2.—μᾶλλον ἢ οὐ 749. 3.
μάν 728.
μανθάνειν for μεμαθηκέναι 396.
μανθάνειν with gen., with gen. and acc. 485.—with acc. 561.—with inf. 665.—with partic. 683.—Difference between inf. and partic. ibid. Obs.
μανίαι 355.
μαντεύεσθαι with acc. 566.
μάρνασθαι with dat. 601.
μαρτυρεῖν with acc. 566.—with partic. 683.
(μάσσειν) μάξασθαι seemingly passive, 364. b.—with acc. 572.
μαστιγοῦσθαι, μαστιγώσεσθαι seemingly passive, 364. a.
μάχην μάχεσθαι 564.
μάχεσθαι with dat. 601.
μέγα, μέγιστα, accus. 578. Obs. 2.
μεγαίρειν with gen. 499.—with dat. and acc. with inf. 674.
μέγαρα for μέγαρον 355. Obs. 1.
μέγεθος, mirum in modum, accus. 579. 5.
μέγιστον δέ 580. Obs.2. 655. Obs. 4.
μεθιέναι, -εσθαι with gen. 531. — μεθιέναι, -εσθαι with partic. 688.
μεθυσθῆναι with gen. 483. Obs. 3.
μεῖζον with gen. 502. 2.
μεῖον with the plur. 581. Obs. 3.—μεῖον without ἢ with numerals 780. Obs. 1.—as adverb with numerals, ibid.
μειονεκτεῖν with gen. 505.
μειοῦσθαι with gen. 505.
μελέδημά τινος with gen. 496. Obs. 4.
μέλει μοί τινος and τι 496 and Obs. 2.
μέλεος with gen. 489.
μέλεσθαι with gen., μέλεταί τι 496. and Obs. 2.

μελετᾶν with gen. and acc. 496.—with acc. 561.

μέλημα of a person, 353.—with dat. 598. *Obs.*

μελίσσειν with gen. 540. *Obs.*

μέλλειν with inf. 664.

(μέλλειν) μέλλω γράφειν, scripturus sum, 408.

μέλπειν with acc. 566. 3.

μεμαέναι with gen. 508.

μέμνημαι ὅτε for ὅτι 804. 7.

μέμονα with inf. 664. 1.

μεμπτός transit. 356. *Obs.*

μέμφεσθαι with gen. 495.—with acc. 568.

μέμφεσθαι εἰ for ὅτι 804. 8.

μέμφεσθαι, μεμφθῆναι and μέμψασθαι 368.

μέμφεσθαι with gen. and acc. 495. and *Obs.* 3.—with dat. and acc. 589. 3. and *Obs.* 2.

μέμψιν with dat. 589.*Obs.*4.

μέν after the vocat. 479. 5.

μέν for μήν 729.

μέν – δέ 764. Position of, 765, 766. — μέν alone, 766.—μέν–δέ, δέ–δέ 770.

μέν γε 735.

μέν δή 720, 730.

μέν ῥα 788. 1.

μὲν τοίνυν 790. 2.

μεναίνειν with dat. 601.

μένειν 601.

μενοινᾶν with acc. 551. 1.

μενοῦν 730.—in answers, 880. g.

μένος in periphrases,442.d.

μέντοι 730, 736. 3.—in answers, 880.f.

μεριμνᾶν with acc. 551. 1.

μερμηρίζειν with acc. 551. 1.

μέρος, accus. 579. 3.

μεσονύκτιος for adverb, 714. b.

μέσος, with gen. 525.

μέσος for adverb, 714. a.

*μεσσηγύ with gen. 526.

μεστὸν εἶναι with part. 686.

μεστός, μεστοῦν with gen. 539. 1, 2.

μετά, prep. with gen., dat. and acc. 636.—as adverb, 640. — μετα- in compos. 636.*Obs.*—μετά with acc. and part. μετὰ ταῦτα γενόμενα) 696. *Obs.* 4.

μεταβάλλειν with acc. 553.

μεταδιδόναι with gen. 535.

—τι ibid. *Obs.*—with dat. 588. 3.

*μεταίτιος with dat. 596.

μεταλαγχάνειν μέρος 535. *Obs.* 1.

μεταλαμβάνειν with gen.535.

μεταμέλει μοί τινος and τι 496. and *Obs.* 2.

μεταμελεῖν with partic. 685.

μεταξύ with partic. 696.*Obs.* 5.

*μεταξύ with gen. 526.

μεταστρέφεσθαι with gen. 507.

μετέρχεσθαι with gen. 536. *Obs.* 6.

μέτεστί μοί τινος and τι 535. and *Obs.*

μετέχειν with gen. and acc. 535. and *Obs.*—with dat. 588. 3.

μετέωρος for adverb, 714. a.

*μετόπισθε with gen. 526.

μετρίως ἔχειν, ἥκειν with gen. 528.

μέχρις with gen. 509. 2. — —μέχρις, μέχρις ὅτου 839. c. See ἕως. — μέχρις ἄν with conj. see ἕως ἄν under ἕως. — μέχρις, μέχρις οὗ without ἄν with conj. 842. 2.

μέχρι τότε 644.

μή force of, 738. — difference from οὐ 739. — in principal clauses, 741.— μή in direct interrog. sentences, 873. 3. 4.—in indirect interrog. sent. 877. c.—μή in depend. clauses, 742.—in relative, 743.— in final and conditional, in consequential sent. with ὥστε, in indirect questions, 744. — in infinitive and infinitival sent. 745.—with abstract substan. 745. *Obs.* 3.— μή with participles and adjectives,746.—μή pleonastic, after expressions of *fear, doubt, &c.* 749.

μή with II. person conj. for the imperative, 420. 3.

μή with II. person imper. aor. for the conj. 420. *Obs.* 5.

μή, interrog. 805. 2. 814. — with conj. and opt. 805, 809, 814. b.—μὴ ἄν with conj. and opt. 810. —with indic. 811. 814.

μή, μὴ δῆτα, μὴ σύ γε, μὴ γάρ without a verb, 897.

μὴ δή, ne jam, 720. 2.—μὴ δή with imperat. (only) 721. 2.

μὴ δῆτα 725. 2.

μὴ μέν 729. b.—μὴ μὲν δή ibid.

μὴ μενοῦν 730. b.

μὴ μήν 728. b.

μὴ νυ τοι 732.

μὴ ὅτι, μὴ ὅπως — ἀλλά καί (ἀλλά) 762. 2, and 3.

μὴ οὐ 749, 750.

μὴ τοίνυν 790. 2.

μηδαμοῦ διελθεῖν 646. *Obs.*

μηδέ see οὐδέ.

μηδέ–γε 735. 10.

μηδὲ δή 721.

μήδεσθαι with acc. 551. 1.

μηδείς and μηδέν εἰμι 381. *Obs.* 3.

μηδέν, in no respect, 579.4.

μηκᾶσθαι with acc. 566. 3.

μῆκος, accus. 579. 3. and 5.

μήν (μάν) 728.

μηνιαῖος for adverb, 714.b.

μηνίειν with gen. 490.

μήνιμα of a person, 353. 1.

μῆνις of a person, 353. 1.

μήτε—μήτε, see οὔτε—οὔτε.

μήτηρ omitted, 436.

μῆτι, μήτοι, nedum, 762.*Obs.*

μητίεσθαι with acc. 551. 1.

μήτι γε δή, μήτι δή, nedum, 721. 1.

μήτοι γε δή, nedum, 721. 1.

μήτοι, see οὔτοι. — μήτοι γε without verb, 897.

μηχανᾶσθαι with acc. 569.1. —as passive, 368. 3.

μηχανᾶσθαι with ὅπως and ind. fut. 664. *Obs.* 3.

μία with dat. 594. 2.

μίγδα with dat. 590.

μιγνύναι and compos. intrans. 360.

μίγνυσθαι with dat. 590.

μικρόν, μικρά, accus. 578. *Obs.* 2.

μικροῦ sc. δεῖν 864.

μικροῦ δεῖν 864.

(μιμεῖσθαι) μεμιμῆσθαι passive, 368. a.

*μιμεῖσθαι τἆλλα with acc. 561.

μίμνειν with dat. 588. 2.

μιμνήσκειν, -εσθαι with gen. and acc. 512. and *Obs.*

μιμνήσκεσθαι with partic. 683. Difference between inf. and partic. ib. *Obs.*

μίσγειν and compos. in-
trans. 360.
μῖσος τινος 499. Obs. 2.
μνᾶσθαι with gen., with
gen. and acc. 512. and
Obs.
μνημονεύειν with gen. and
acc. 512. and Obs.
μογεῖν with acc. 563.
μοί dat. comm. 598. — dat.
of interest, 600. 2.
μοῖρα omitted, 436.
μολεῖν with acc. 558.
μόνος for adverb, 714.—
μόνος and μόνον, differ-
ence between, ib. Obs. 3.
μόνος, μονοῦν with gen. 529.
μοῦ, μοί, μέ used retrospec-
tively, 658.
μοῦ, μοί, μέ, for ἐμοῦ, ἐμοί,
ἐμέ 652. Obs. 2.—μοῦ for
ἐμός (μοῦ ὁ πάτηρ for
ἐμός) 652. 3.—μοῦ before
its substantive for μοί
652. Obs. 4.
μοχθεῖν with acc. 563.
μυθεῖσθαι with acc. 566. 1.
μύζειν with acc. 566. 1, 3.
μυσάττεσθαι with acc. 549.
μυχοίτατος for ἐν μυχοιτάτῳ
714. a.
μυχῷ, local dat. 605. 1.
μῶν 873. 5.—μῶν δῆτα 725.
—μῶν οὖν, μῶν μὴ 873. 5.
—μῶν—ἦ 875. d.

ναί 733.—ναὶ μὰ Δία 566. 2.
ναίειν, ναιετάειν with acc.
. 576. 1.
νάσσειν with gen. 539. 1.
ναῦσιν, cum ναυ. 604.
νέμειν with acc. 573, 576.1.
νεμεσᾶν with dat. 601.
νέον, accus. 577. Obs. 2.
νέρθε with gen. 526.
νή 733.—νὴ Δία 566. 2.
νήειν with acc. 571.
νηκουστεῖν with gen. 487. 4.
νηνεμίης 523.
νίζεσθαι with double acc.
583. 116.
νικᾶν intransit. 360. — πυγ-
μήν, Ὀλύμπια, γνώμην,
ἀρετήν 564.
νικᾶσθαι with gen. 505.—
with dat. ib. Obs.
νίπτεσθαι with gen. 540.
Obs.
νίφει sc. ὁ θεός 373. 2.
νοεῖν with acc. 551. 1.—
with partic. 683.
νομίζειν with acc. 551. 2.

561.—with dat. 588.(uti)
591. Obs.—with inf. 665.
νομοθετεῖν with acc. 568.
νοσεῖν with acc. 552.
νόσος of a person, 353. 1.
νόστος τινός, reditus in locum, 519. Obs. 3.
νοσφίζειν with gen. 530. 1.
νόσφιν with gen. 529. 2.
νουθετεῖν with inf. 664.
νύ, partic. confirmative, 732.
νύκτα, νύκτας acc. of time,
577.
νύκτες, horae nocturnae, 355.
Obs. 1.
νύκτωρ, accus. 577. Obs. 2.
νύμφευμα for νυμφή 353. 1.
νῦν, νύν, νυνί 719.—νῦν δέ,
but now, ib. 2.—νῦν ἤδη
719.4.—νῦν δέ—γάρ 786.
—νῦν δὴ 720. 2.—νῦν μὲν
δὴ 729. f.
νύχιος for adverb, 714. b.
νοτίζειν with acc. 558. 1.

ξέειν, ξύειν with acc. 569. 1.
ξενοῦσθαι with dat. 590.
ξίνως ἔχειν with gen. 493.
ξυναλλάττεσθαι with dat.
590.
ξυνιέναι ξυνόδους 559. Obs.
2.
ξυνῳδός with dat. 594. 2.
ξυρεῖν with double acc. 583.
119.

ὁ- in the pron. ὁποῖος, ὁπόσος &c. 816, 877.
ὁ αὐτός, idem, 454. 3.—ὁ βουλόμενος, ὁ τυχών &c. 451.
—ὁ αὐτός with dat. 594.
2. 605. 4.
ὁ, ἡ, τό as a demonst. pron.
443, 444.
ὁ, ἡ, τό as relative pron.
445.
ὁ, ἡ, τό as article. See
under Article.
ὁ, ἡ, τό with ἀπό and ἐκ for
ἐν and with εἰς for ἐν, as
οἱ ἐκ τῆς ἀγορᾶς ἄν-
θρωποι ἀπέφυγον–ἡ λίμνη
ἐκδιδοῖ ἐς τὴν Σύρτιν τὴν
ἐς Λιβύην 645.
ὁ, ἡ, τό, demonst. pron.,
prospective use of, 657.
ὁ, ἡ, τό, retrospective, 658.
ὅ for ὅτι, that, 800.
ὁ ἡλίκος attracted, 823. Obs.
4.
ὁ μέν–ὃς δέ 816. 3.
ὁ οἷος attracted, 823. Obs. 4.

ὅγε, ἥγε, τόγε local de-
monstrative, 655.— re-
peats a subject, 655. 2.
ὀγμεύειν with acc. 55..
ὅδε, ἥδε, τόδε of local demonstrative, 655.—
ἐμός 655. 2.—ὅδε for ἐγώ
σύ 655. 4.—ὅδε general
prospective, 655. 6. —
ὅδε prospective use of
657. 2.—ὅδε, ἥδε, τόδε
retrospective, 658.
ὁ μέν,—ὁ δέ; τὸ μέν,—τὸ
δέ; τὰ μέν,—τὰ δέ; ι
μέν τις,—ὁ δέ τις &c. 444
d.
ὁ μέν — ὁ δέ, οἱ μέν — οἱ δ
without another nom
478.
ὁ δέ in narrations (idemque
655. Obs. 2.
ὁδοποιεῖν with acc. 569.
ὁδός omitted, 436.
*ὁδός τινος, to a place, 509.
2.
ὁδοῦ gen. loci, 522. 2.
ὀδυνᾶσθαι, with acc. 549.
ὀδύρεσθαι with gen. 488.—
with acc. ib. Obs. 2. and
566. 4.—with double acc.
583. 119.
ὄζειν with gen. and ἀπό 484
—with acc. 555.
ὅθεν 838.
ὅθενπερ 734. 3.
ὅθεσθαι with gen. 496.
ὁθούνεκα, see ὅτι.
οἱ ἄλλοι and ἄλλοι, οἱ πολλοί and πολλοί, οἱ πλείος
and πλείους, οἱ ὀλίγοι and
ὀλίγοι 454. 3.
οἱ ἀμφί (περί) τινα 436. d.
οἵ, quo, with gen. 527.
οἵ, quo, 605. Obs. 3. 878.
οἵ, quo, pregnant force of
for οὗ 646. d.
οἵ περ 734. 4.
οἷα with partic. and gen.
abs. 704.
οἷα δὴ 721. 3.
οἶδα with acc. 551. 2.
οἶδα for οἶδα ὅτι 798.—parenthet., ibid. 2.
οἶδα ὅτε for ὅτι 804. 6.
οἶδ' ὅτι without a verb, 892.
οἰκεῖν with acc. 576. 1.—intrans. 360.
(οἰκεῖσθαι) ᾠκῆσθαι passive,
368.
οἰκεῖος with gen. 521. 3.
οἰκία, οἶκος omitted, 436.
οἰκίζειν with acc. 569. 1.

ἰκτείρειν with gen. 488.—
—with acc. ib. *Obs.* 1.—
—with acc. 549.
ἰκτός τινος, *pro aliquo*, 488.
Obs. 1.
ἰικτροχέειν with acc. 566. 4.
ἰ̓μαι for οἶμαι ὅτι 798. 1.—
parenthet., ibid. 2.
οἶμοι τινός 489.
οἰμώζειν with acc. 566. 4.
οἰνίζεσθαι with dat. for the
gen. pretii, 516. *Obs.* 2.
οἶνος, *wine-shop*, 353. 2.
οἰνοχοεύει scil. οἰνοχόος 373.
2.
οἰόθεν οἶος 899. 1.
οἶον, *how*, 579. 4.—οἶόν τε
ὄν acc. absol. 700.—οἶον
with partic. and gen.
absol. 704.
οἶος seemingly with dat. 594.
Obs. 2.—οἶος with superlative, 870. *Obs.* 4.—οἶος,
οἶόστ' εἰμί with inf. 666.
οἶος for ὅτι τοιοῦτος 804. 9.
—οἶος ἐκείνου θυμὸς ὑπέρ-
βιος, *quæ ejus est atro-
citas*, ibid.
οἶος 817. 3.—attracted, 823.
and *Obs.* 5.
οἶος with a verb repeated
(ἤγγειλας, οἳ ἤγγειλας),
835.
οἶος in indirect questions,
for ὁποῖος 877. *Obs.* 2.
οἶος, οἶόστε with inf. attracted, 823. *Obs.* 3.
οἴσεται seemingly passive,
364. a.
οἶσθ' ὁ δρᾶσον, οἶσθ' ὥς ποίησον, οἶσθα ἃ γενέσθω;
421.
* ὀιστεύειν with gen. 506.
οἰχνεῖν ἀγγελίης 481. 1.
οἴχομαι, *abii*, 396. — with
acc. 548. *Obs.* 1.
οἴχομαι with partic. 694.
ὀκνεῖν with inf. 664.
ὀλέθριος with gen. 542. 2.
ὄλεθρος of a person, 353.
ὄλεθρος, adjective, 430.
ὀλίγον, accus. 578. *Obs.* 2.
ὀλίγου δεῖν or ὀλίγου 864.
—ὀλίγου ἡγεῖσθαι 517.—
ὀλίγῳ, dat. of quantity,
609. 1.—ὀλίγοι εἰσίν with
inf. 666.
ὀλιγωρεῖν with gen. 496.
(ὀλοφύρεσθαι) ὀλοφύρασθαι
and ὀλοφυρθῆναι 368. b.
ὀλοφύρεσθαι with gen. 488.
—with acc. 566. 4.

ὁμαρτεῖν with dat. 593.—
ὁμαρτεῖσθαι with acc. ib.
Obs.
ὁμέστιος with gen. 519.
ὁμηλικία with dat. 594. *Obs.*
I.
Ὁμήρῳ, *apud Hom.* 605. 2.
ὁμιλεῖν with dat. 590.
* ὁμιλία with dat. 590.
ὁμοῖα in periphrases, 442. d.
ὀμνύναι with acc. 566. 2.
ὅμοια 580. 1.
ὅμοιον εἶναι with partic.
construction of, 682. 2,
684.
ὅμοιος with gen. 519.
ὅμοιος, -ως, ὁμῶς, ὁμόγλωσσος, ὁμώνυμος with dat.
594.
ὁμοιότης, ὁμοίωσις with dat.
594. *Obs.*
ὁμοιοῦν with dat. 594.
ὁμολογεῖν with acc. 567.—
with dat. 594. — with
partic. 684.
ὁμολογεῖσθαι with partic.
684. *Obs.* 2. b.
ὁμολογεῖται with acc. with
inf. 676. 2. a.
ὁμόστολος with gen. 519.
ὁμώνυμος with gen. 519.
ὁμῶς 772.—with partic. 697.
ὄναρ κ. ὕπαρ, accus., 577.
Obs. 2.
ὀνειδίζειν with gen. 495.—
with acc. 566. 2.—with
double acc. 583. 120.—
with dat. 589. 3.
ὀνειροπολεῖν with acc. 552.
d.
ὀνίνασθαι with gen. and τι
ἔκ τινος 491. and *Obs.* 2.
—with double acc. 583.
121.
ὄνομα in periphrases, 442. d.
—acc. 579. 3. 580. 1.
ὀνομάζειν, -εσθαι with εἶναι
475. *Obs.* 3. 666.
ὀνομάζειν with double acc.
583. 122.
ὀνομάζεσθαί τινα 362. 4.
ὀξύς adverbial, 714. c.
ὀπάζειν with acc. 573.—with
dat. 588.
ὅπη, ὅπως ἔχειν, ἥκειν with
gen. 528.
ὅπη, ὅποι, *quo*, 605. *Obs.* 3.
—ὅπη, ὅπου, ὅποι 838.
ὀπηδεῖν with dat. 593.
ὄπισθεν, ὀπίσσω with gen.
526.
ὁπλίζειν with acc. 569. 572.

ὅποι pregnant, for ὅπου 646.
Obs. 2.
ὁπόσος, ὁπόσος οὖν, *quantuscunque*, with indic.
826. 4.—with conj. 828.
Obs. 2. See ὅς, ἥ, ὅ.
ὁπόταν, see ὅταν under ὅτε.
ὁπότε, *when*, 839. See ὅτε.
ὁπότε, *since*. See ὅτε.
ὅπου with gen. 527.
ὅπου pregnant, for ὅποι 646.
Obs. 2.—ὅπου, *quando-
quidem*. See ὅτε.
ὅπου περ 734. 3.
ὅπως with gen. 528.
ὅπως (interrog.) when used
for πῶς 877. *Obs.* 2.
ὅπως with superlat. 870.
Obs. 4.
ὅπως, *that*. See ὅτι.
ὅπως final conj. 805.—with
conj. and opt. 805. sqq.
ὅπως ἄν with conj. and
opt. 810.—ὅπως (ὅπως
ἄν) with indic. fut. 811. 2.
—ὅπως, ὅπως μή with conj.
pres., aor. I. pass. and
aor. II. midd. 812.—ὅπως
and ὅπως μή with II. pers.
indic. fut. or conj. ellipt.
812. 2.—ὅπως with indic.
of historic tenses 813.—
ὅπως, *as*, and ὅπως μή
after verbs of fear &c.
814.
ὅπως, temporal conj. 839.
See ὅτε.
ὅπως (ἔπλευσ' ὅπως ἔπλευσα)
835.
ὅπως, in comparative adverbial sentences, 868.
ὅπως μή, see ὅπως.
ὁρᾶν with gen. loci, 522.—
with acc. 554.--after verbs
of appearing, &c. 667.
Obs. 2.—with part. 683.
ὁρᾷς, ὁρᾶτε for ὁρ., ὅτι 798.
1.—parenthet., ibid. 3.
ὁρᾶσθαι for ὁρᾶν 363. 5.
ὀρέγεσθαι with gen. 508.
ὄρειος adverbial, 714. a.
(ὀρθοῦν) κατορθ. intrans.
360.
ὁρίζειν and -εσθαι 363. 5.
ὅρκιος adverbial, 714. c.
ὁρκοῦν with double acc.
583. 123.
ὀρκωμοτεῖν with τό and inf.
670.
ὁρμαίνειν with acc. 551. 1.
ὁρμᾶν, -ᾶσθαι with gen. 507.
—with acc. 556.

ἀρρωδεῖν with inf. 664.
ὀρύσσειν with acc. 571.
ὀρφανός with gen. 529.
ὀρχεῖσθαι σχημάτια &c. 556.
ὀρχεῖσθαι with dat. 598.
ὅς, ἥ, ὅ, qui, quae, quod, use of, 817.—for οἷος 817. 3.
—agreement of, 819.—attraction of, 822, 825.—inverse attraction 824.—attraction in position, 825.—ὅς, ἥ, ὅ with indic. 826.—with indic. and ἄν 827.—with conj. 828, 829.—with conj. and ἄν omitted, 830.—with opt. 831.—with conj. and opt. interchanged, ib. Obs.—with opt. and ἄν 832.—ὅς, ἥ, ὅ changed into the demonstr. constr. 833.—ὅς with the demonstr. 833. Obs. 2.—ὅς for the demonstr. (qui for is) 834.—ὅς for οὗτος γάρ 834.—ὅς ἄρα, is igitur, 834.—ὅς for οὗτος in addresses &c. 834.—ὅς with the epexegetic subst. 835. 2.—ὅς for ὅτι, 836. 3.—ὅς with ind. fut. or conj. or opt. for ἵνα, ut, ib. 4.—ὅς (after οὕτως, ὧδε, τοιοῦτος, τηλικοῦτος, τοσοῦτος) for ὥστε 836. 5. Obs. 2, and 3.—in the form, ἐπὶ τούτῳ, ἐπὶ τοῖσδε, ἐφ᾽ ὧτε with ind. fut. or inf. 836. 5. c.—ὅς, ὃς ἄν, ὅστις ἄν with conj. for ἐάν or εἰ 828. 1, 836. 6.
ὅς in indirect questions, for ὅστις 877. Obs. 3, and 4.
ὅς, ἥ, ὅ, demonstrative, 816.—ὃς μέν—ὃς δέ ib. 3. b.—ὃς καὶ ὃς ib. c.
ὃς βούλει for ὃν βούλ. 824. Obs. 1.
ὅσγε 735. 9.
ὃς δ᾽ ἤτοι 731. 4.
ὅσα πλεῖστα 823. Obs. 7.
ὅσον—ὅσον, tantum—quantum, 795. 3. e.
ὅσον—τοσοῦτο 870.
ὅσον, accus. of quantity, 578. Obs. 2.—ὅσον, ὅσῳ with compar. and superl. 870.—ὅσον, only; ὅσον μόνον, tantum non, almost, ὅσον οὐ or ὁσονού, prope 823. Obs. 1.—ὅσον, ὅσα with inf.; as, ὅσον γ᾽ ἐμ᾽ εἰδέναι 836. Obs. 2. 864. 3, 4.
ὅσος for ὅτι τόσος 804. 9.
ὅσος 817. 3.—attracted 823.
ὅσος in indirect questions, for ὁπόσος 877. Obs. 3.
ὅσος δή, ὅσον οὖν, quantuscunque with indic. 826. 4.—with conj. 828. Obs. 2. Cf. ὅς, ἥ, ὅ.
ὅσπερ, ὅσοσπερ &c. 734. 3.
ὁσάτιος for ὅτι τόσος 804.9.
ὅσσε δαίεται,—ὅσσε φαεινά &c. 384. Obs. 1.
ὅσσε 755. 3.
ὅστις force of, 816. 4.—seemingly for τίς 871. Obs. 1.
ὅστις with the demonstr. (ὅντινα τοῦτον ἄγει) 823. Obs. 8.
ὅστις, ὅστις δή, quicunque, with indic. 826. 4. 5.—with conj. 828. Obs. 2. Cf. ὅς, ἥ, ὅ.
ὅστις τε 755. 3.
ὀσφραίνεσθαι with gen. and acc. 485. and 487.
ὅσῳ—τοσούτῳ 870.
ὅταν see ὅτε.
ὅτε 839.—with indic. 840.—ὅταν with conj. 841.—ὅτε with conj. for ὅταν 842. 2.—ὅτέ κε with ind. fut. ib. 3.—ὅτε with opt. 843, 844.—ὅταν with opt. 844. Obs.—ὅτε with opt. and ἄν 845.—ὅτε, since, with ind. 847. 2.—with opt. and ἄν ibid.—with ind. of hist. tenses and ἄν ibid.
ὅτε for ὅτι 804. 7.
ὅτε γε 735.
ὅτε δῆτα 725.
ὅτε μέν—ὅτε δέ for τότε μέν—τότε δέ 816. 3. e.
ὅτε ῥα, ὅτε δή ῥα 788. 3.
ὅτι, quod, with inf., as ὅτι μ᾽ εἰδέναι 864. 2. 3.
ὅτι with superlat. 870. Obs. 4.
ὅτι, that, with indic. and opt. 801., 802.—with opt. and ἄν 803.—with ind. of historic tenses and ἄν 803. 2.—ὅτι repeated after a parenthesis, 804. 3.—ὅτι acc. with inf. and part. 804.4.—ὅτι interchanged with inf. (acc. with inf.) 804. 5.—ὅτι after a verb of fear, 814. Obs. 4.—in quotations, 802. Obs.
ὅτι, because, constr. 849. 4
ὅτι τί 882. 1.
ὅτι μαθών 872. Obs. 3.
ὀτοβεῖν with acc. 566. 3.
ὀτρύνειν with dat. 589. Obs. 1.
οὐ 738. sqq.
οὐ γὰρ ἀλλά, surely, 773.—οὐ μὴν ἀλλά and μέντοι ἀλλά, verumtamen ibid.
οὐ—οὔτε 775. 2. a.
οὐ with II. person indic. future, interrogative for the imperative (οὐ λέξεις =λέγε), 413. 2.
οὐ in questions, 874.
οὐ with I. person indic. future, interrogative for the conj. adhortativus. 413. 3.
οὐ δή 724. 2. 874. 3.—οὐ δή που ibid.
οὐ δῆτα 725.
οὐ μέν θην—γέ 726. 1.—οὐ μὲν δή 729 b. 730.
οὐ μέν 729.—οὐ μὲν γάρ ib.—οὐ μέντοι ibid.—οὐ μέντοι in questions, 874. 2.
οὐ μενοῦν 730. b.
οὐ μή const. 748.—Dawes's canon, ib. Obs. 3.
οὐ μή with II. person indic. future, interrogative (οὐ μὴ φλυαρήσεις; = μὴ φλυάρει), 413. 748.
οὐ μήν 728. b.
οὐ μόνον—ἀλλὰ καί or ἀλλά;—οὐ μόνον, ὅτι—ἀλλὰ καί 762. 1. 2.
οὐ τάδ᾽ ἐστίν, εἰσίν 655. 3.
οὔτι που in questions 874.3.
οὔ τοι 790. Obs.
οὐ τοίνυν 790. 2.
οὐ φθάνειν with partic. and καί; καὶ εὐθύς 694. Obs. 2.
οὐ with gen. 527.—ubi 838.
οὗ, οἷ, ἕ &c. reflexive pron. for ἐμοῦ, σοῦ, ἐμοί, σοί &c. 654.
οὗ, οἷ, ἕ, μίν, personal pron., prospective use of, 657.1.
οὐδ᾽ ἄρα 787. c. 788. 1.
οὐδαμῇ, οὐδαμοῦ with gen. 527.
οὐδέ 776.—οὐδέ—οὐδέ ibid. Difference between οὐδέ and καὶ οὐ ibid. Obs. 2.
οὐδέ—οὔτε 775.—οὔτε—

οὐδέ 775. d. and Obs. 4.—
οὐδέ—οὔτε—οὔτε—οὐδέ
776. 3.—τέ—οὐδέ; οὐδέ
—τέ or καί ibid. 4.—οὐδέ,
ne—quidem, ibid. 5.
οὐδὲ δή 724. 1. — οὐδὲ μέν
729. b.—οὐδέ—γέ 735. 10.
οὐδὲ πολλοῦ δεῖ, minime
gentium, 747. Obs.
οὐδείς and οὐδέν εἰμι 381.
Obs. 3.
οὐδεὶς ὅστις οὐ, nemo non,
attracted, 824. 2.
οὐδὲ μή with conjunct. 415.
οὐδὲν ἄλλο ἤ 895. c.
οὐδὲν οἷον with inf. 836.
Obs. 2.
οὐδέν, in no respect, 579. 4.
οὐδέπερ with partic. 617. c.
οὐδέτερα accus. 579. Obs. 4.
οὐκ ἂν οἶδ' εἰ δυναίμην 431.
Obs. 2.
οὐκ ἂν φθάνοις λέγων 694.
and Obs. 2.
οὐκ ἔστιν ὅπου, ὅπη, ὅπως,
ὅπως οὐ 817. Obs. 4.
οὐκ οἶδ' ἂν εἰ πείσαιμι 431.
Obs. 2.
οὐκοῦν δῆτα 725.
οὔκων, οὐκ ὤν, use of, in
Herod. 752. 3.
οὐκοῦν and οὔκουν 791. Obs.
οὖν 737.— γάρ 786. Obs. 4.
—οὖν consequential, 791.
—οὖν in answers, 880. h.
οὕνεκα with gen. 621. Obs.
2. — οὕνεκα, that. See
ὅτι.
οὐράνιος adverbial, 714. a.
οὔτ' ἄρα—οὔτε 787. c. 788. 1.
οὐτάζειν with double acc.
583. 124.
οὔτε—οὔτε 775. 1.—οὔτε—
τε οὐ for οὔτε ib. Obs. 1.
—οὐ — οὔτε ibid. a. —
οὐδέ — οὔτε ibid. b. —
οὔτε — οὐ ib. c. — οὔτε
omitted in first clause ib.
Obs. 3.—οὔτε—οὐδέ ib. d.
and Obs. 4.—οὔτε—τέ or
καί ib. a.—οὔτε—δέ ib. β.
οὔτε γε 735. 10.
οὗτος, αὕτη, τοῦτο, local demonstrative and various
uses of, 655.—prospec-
tive 657.— retrospective
658.
οὗτος, heus ! 476. a.
οὗτος, οὕτως ἤδη 719. 4. b.—
οὕτως δή 721.
οὕτω δή in a principal clause,
839.

οὕτως, ὡς in wishes, 418. b.
—οὕτω 697. Obs. 869.
οὕτως differs from ὧδε 655.
6.
οὕτως with particip. 696.
Obs. 6.
οὕτως ἔχειν, ἥκειν with gen.
528.
οὐχ, ὅπως οὐχ ὅτι,—ἀλλὰ
καί (ἀλλά) 762. 2.—οὐχ
οἷον—ἀλλὰ ib.
οὐχ ὅτι, quamquam, 891. 5. b.
οὐχί 738. 2.
ὄφελος, of a person, 353.
ὀφλεῖν, ὑπό τινος 359. 3.
ὀφλισκάνειν with acc. 552. b.
ὄφρα, final conj. 805.—with
conj. and opt. 805. 2,
809.—ὄφρ' ἄν 810. Obs. 3.
ὄφρα for τόφρα 816. a.
ὄφρα, until, 839. 4. See ἕως.
ὄφρ' ἤτοι 731. 4.
ὀψέ with gen. 527.
ὀψείειν with gen. 498.
ὄψιος adverbial, 714. b.
ὄψον, of a place, 353. 2.

παιδεύειν with double acc.
583, 125.
παίδευμα, of a person, 382.
παιδεύματα, of a person,
355. Obs. 2, 382. 2.
παιδεύεσθαι, seemingly
passive, 364.
παίειν and comp. intransitive, 360. 8.
παίειν with double acc. 583.
126.
παίζειν with acc. 563.
παιπάλημα, of a person, 353.
παῖς omitted 436.
παλαίειν with acc. 563.
πανημέριος adverbial, 714. b.
πάννυχα, acc. 577. Obs. 2.
πάντα and τὰ πάντα, applied
to a person, 382.
πάντα acc. quantit. 578.
Obs. 2. — πάντα, at all
events, 579. 4.
πάντα ποιεῖν and λέγειν with
partic. 690.
πανταχῇ, -οῦ with gen. 527.
παντῆμαρ, acc. 577. Obs. 2.
παντοῖον εἶναι, γίγνεσθαι
with partic. and inf. 690.
παρά, prep. with gen. dat.
and acc. 637.—as adverb
640.—pregnant force of
with dat. 645. e.—with
acc. 646. b
παρα- in compos. 637. Obs.
παράθυρος adverbial, 714. a.

παραινεῖν with dat. 589. 3.
—with inf. 664.
παρακελεύεσθαι with ὅπως
with ind. fut. 664. Obs.
4.
παρακέλευσις with dat. 589.
Obs. 4.
παρακρούεσθαί, with double
acc. 583. 127.
παραλαμβάνειν with gen.
515. 2.
παραλιπόντι 599.
παραμελεῖν with gen. and
acc. 496. Obs. 1.
πάραντα 558.
παραπλήσιος with gen. 525.
—with dat. 594. 2.
παρασκευάζεσθαι with inf.
664. 1.—with ὅπως with
ind. fut. 664. Obs. 3.—
with partic. and inf. 690.
and Obs. 2.—with ὡς and
partic. ibid. Obs. 2.
παρασκευαστικός with gen.
494.
παρατυχόν, acc. abs. 700.
παραυτίκα, παραυτόθεν, παρ'
αὐτόθι 642.
παραχωρεῖν with gen. 530.
—*with dat. 593. 1.
παρεγγυᾶν with dat. 589. 3.
παρεῖναι with dat. 592.
παρέκ 640. 3.
παρεστιν with inf. 666.—
with ὥστε ib. Obs.
παρέχει sc. ὁ θεός 373. 3.
παρέχειν with dat. 588.—
ἀσχολίαν, πράγματα, ὄ-
χλον with inf. 668. c.—
παρέχον, acc. absol. 700.
παριέναι with gen. 531.
παρόν, acc. absol. 700.
παροξύνειν with inf. 664.
πάρος 848. Obs. 6.
πᾶς with another nom. 478.
πᾶς, adverbial, 714.
πᾶς τις with the II. pers.
imperat. 390. γ.
πάσσειν with gen. 540. Obs.
πάσχειν with acc. 552.
πατεῖν with acc. 558.
πατεῖσθαι, to eat, with acc.
562.
πατήρ omitted 436.
παύειν and compos. for παύεσθαι 360.
παύειν with double acc.
583. 128. — -εσθαι with
gen. 514.—with partic.
688. — παύειν with inf.
ibid. Obs.
πεδᾶν with gen. 531.

πεδοῖ, humi, humum 605. Obs. 5.

πέζῃ 603. 2.

πείθειν with double acc. 583. 129.—with inf. 664, 665.—with ὡς 664. Obs. 3.—with ὥστε ib.—with τό and inf. 670.

πείθεσθαι with gen. 487. 4.—with dat. 593.

πεινῆν with gen. 498.

πειρᾶν and -ᾶσθαι 363. 6.—with gen. 493. — *with acc. 560. 2.—*with dat. 601. Obs. 3.—with inf. 664.—with part. and inf. 690.

πειστέον ἐστίν τινα and τινι 613. Obs. 2.

πελάζειν, πέλας, with gen. 510. 1, 2. cf. 526.—with dat. 592. 1, 2.

πέμπειν ἑορτήν, Παναθήναια 569.—with dat. 592.

πένεσθαι with gen. 529.

πένης with gen. 529.

πενθικῶς ἔχειν with gen. 488.

πέπαλται with part. 691.

πεποιδέναι with dat. 593.

πέπρωται with acc. with inf. 676. b.

πέρ 734.—with part. 697. c.

πέρα with gen. 526.

περαίνειν with acc. 560. 2.—with double acc. 583. 130.

περᾶν with acc. viæ 558.—to accomplish, with accus. 560. 2.

περί, prep. with gen., dat. and acc. 632.—as adverb 640. 2.

περί with acc. in pregnant force for the dat. 645. b.

περί with gen. and ὑπέρ with gen. interchanged 646.

περιαμπετίξ 640. 3.

*περιβαίνειν with dat. 596.

περιγίγνεσθαι with gen. 504.

περιδίδοσθαι with gen. 515. 2.

περιεῖναι with gen. 504.

περιέχεσθαι with gen. 536.

περιιδεῖν, see περιορᾶν.

*περιμένειν with inf. 664.

περίοδον (τήν) 579. 3.

περιορᾶν with inf. 664.—with part. 687.—with inf. ibid. Obs.

περὶ πρό 640. 3.

περισσός with gen. 502. 3.

περιστεφής with gen. 539. 2.

περιτεθεῖσθαί τι 545. 3.

*περί τινος ἕνεκα 621. Obs. 2.

περίτριμμα, of a person, 353.

περιχορεύειν with acc. 556. c.

πέσσειν with acc. 572.

πεφυγμένον εἶναι for πεφευγέναι 363. 5.

πεφυκέναι (εὖ) τι 579. 1.—πεφυκέναι and a subst. with inf. (ad) 668.

πή with gen. 527.

πηδᾶν with acc. 556. e.

πῆμα, of a person, 353.

πημαίνειν with double acc. 583. 131.

πίμπλημι with gen. 539.

πίνειν with gen. and acc. 537. and Obs.—with acc. 562.

πιπίσκειν with double acc. 583. 132.

πίπτειν ὑπό τινος 359.—with acc. 556.—πίπτειν τινί for εἴς τι 592.

πίστεις, testimonia, 355. γ.

πιστεύειν δόξαν 551. d.

πιστεύομαί ὑπό τινος, mihi creditur ab aliq. 372. 4.

πιστός, active, 356. Obs.

πλάγιος adverbial, 714. a.

πλάσσειν with acc. 569. 3.

πλεῖν with acc. 559.—with acc. viæ 558.

πλείστος τοῦ χρόνου 442. c.

πλέκειν with acc. 569.

πλείω, πλέον, without ἤ with numerals 780. Obs. 1.—as adverb with numerals ibid.

πλέον with the plural 381. Obs. 3.

πλεονεκτεῖν with acc. 576. 2.

πλέον εἶναι with dat. 596. Obs. 2.

πλέος with gen. 539. 2.

πληγείς τινος 483. Obs. 3.

πλῆθος, acc. 579. 3.

πλήθει, cum multit. 604. 2.—πλήθει πολλοί 899. 1.

πλήθειν with gen. 539. 1.

πληκτίζεσθαι with dat. 601. Obs. 3.

πλήν with gen. 529. 2.

πλήν = ἀλλά 773. Obs. 4.—πλὴν ἤ; πλὴν ἀλλά; πλὴν ἀλλ' ἤ ibid.—after the comparat. 779. Obs. 2.—πλὴν εἰ or πλὴν εἰ μή 860. 7.

πλήρης εἶναι with part. 686.

πλήρης, πληρόω with gen. 539. 1, 2.

πλησιάζειν, πλησίον with gen. 520. 1. c. 526.—with dat. 592.

πλησίον, acc. 558.

(πλήττειν) ἔπεσ. for -εσθα 360.

πλινθεύειν with acc. 569.

πλίνθος for πλίνθοι 354.

πλούσιος with gen. 539. 2.

πλοῦτοι, divitiæ, 355. Obs. 1.

πνεῖν with gen. 484.—with acc. 555. d.

ποθεῖν with gen. and acc. 498. and Obs. 2.

ποθεῖσθαι for ποθεῖν 363. 5.

πόθεν with gen. 527.—πόθεν γάρ; 872.

ποῖ, quo, 605. Obs. 5.—pregnant force for ποῦ (ubi) 646. Obs.

ποιεῖν with gen. materiæ 538.—with acc. 569.—εὖ, κακῶς, with acc. 583. 133.

ποιεῖν εὖ, κακῶς with particip. 689.—with double acc. 583. 133.—*τί τινα, 598. — with inf. 666.—with ὅπως with ind. fut. ib. Obs. — ἡσυχίαν with inf. 668.

ποιεῖν (to represent) with partic. 684. — difference between partic. and inf. ib. Obs. 3. d.

*ποιεῖσθαι ἑαυτοῦ 521.

ποιεῖσθαι with gen. 533. 2. with gen. pret. 517.—

ποικίλλειν with acc. 569. 3.

ποίμνη, of persons, 353. 1.

ποῖος for ὁποῖος in indirect questions 877. Obs. 2.

ποῖός εἰμι with inf. 666.

πολεμεῖν with acc. 564.—with dat. 601. and Obs. 4.

πολιτεύειν with acc. 553.—and -εσθαι 363. 6.

πολλά, πολύ, accus. 578. Obs. 2.—πολλά 579. 4.

πολλάκις with gen. 527.

πολλοῦ δεῖν or πολλοῦ alone 864. 1.

πολλαπλάσιος with gen. 502.—ἤ 503. Obs. 2.

πολλὸν εἶναι, ἐγκεῖσθαι with partic. 690.

πολλοῦ ἡγεῖσθαι, ποιεῖσθαι 517.

πολλῷ, dat. 609.

πολύς, for adverb, 714. c.
πολύς joined by καί, τέ—καί to another adject. 759. Obs. 2.
πολύς (ὁ) τοῦ χρόνου — πολλὴ τῆς χώρας 442.
πολυστεφής with gen. 539.2.
πονεῖν intrans. and trans. 360.—with acc. 563, 569.
πονηρεύειν and -εσθαι 363.6.
πόνος, of a person, 353.
πορεύεσθαι ὁδόν 558.
πορίζειν τι for πορίζεσθαι 363. 3.
ποριστικός with gen. 494.
*πόρρω with gen. 526.
πόσος for ὁπόσος in indirect questions 877. Obs. 2.
πότερα, πότερον, acc. 578. 4.
—πότερον—ἤ in direct questions 875. b.
πότνα θεάων 534. Obs. 2.
ποῦ, πού with gen. 527.
πού 522. Obs. 1.
ποῦ δή 721. 873.
πρᾶγμα with the adj. for the simple neutral adj. 381. Obs. 4.
πρᾶγμα, πράγματα omitted 436.
πραγματεύειν with acc. 559.
πράθεσθαι, seemingly pass. 365. 2.
πράσσειν (to accomplish) with acc. 560. 2.
πράττειν with acc. 560.—-εσθαι (to exact) with double acc. 583. 135.—pass. and acc. ib.
πράττειν εὖ with gen. 483. Obs. 3.
πρέπειν, πρεπόντως with dat. 594. 3.—with dat. and acc. and inf. 674, 676.
πρέπει with partic. 691.
πρεπόντως, πρέπων with gen. 521. 3.—with dat. 594. 3.
πρέσβα θεάων 534. Obs. 2.
πρεσβεία for πρέσβεις 353. 1.
πρεσβεύειν with gen. 504.—with acc. 566.
πρεσβεύματα, of a person, 353. 1.
πρήσσειν ὁδοῖο 522. 2.
πρίασθαι with gen. 515.—*with acc. 576. 2.—with dat. 598.
πρίν — πρίν 795.
πρίν περ 734. 2, 3.—πρίν γε 735. 9.
πρίν, πρὶν ἤ 839.—constr.

848. — πρίν or πρὶν ἤ with conj. for πρὶν ἄν 842. 2.
πρό, prep. with gen. 619.—as adv. 640. 2.
προ- in compos. 619. Obs.
προαιδεῖσθαι with dat. 598.
προαιρεῖσθαι with inf. 665.
προβαίνειν with acc. 558.
προδιδόναι with gen. 535.
προέχειν with gen. 504.
προέχειν with dat. instrum. 609. 1.
προθυμὸν εἶναι, προθυμεῖσθαι with inf. 664.—with ὅπως with ind. fut. 664. Obs. 3.—with τό and inf. 670.
προίεσθαι with gen. 531.—with gen. pret. 516.
προκαλεῖσθαί τινά τι 583. 137.—προκ. χάρμη 592.
προνηστεύειν with dat. 598.
προνοεῖν with gen. 496.
προορᾶν with gen. 496.
προπάλαι 644.
προπάροιθε with gen. 526.
προπέρυσι 642.
προπίνειν with gen. 497.
προρεῖν with acc. 555.
πρός, with gen., dat. and acc. 638.—as adv. 640.—with dat. in pregnant force for acc. 645.
προσαυδᾶν with double acc. 583. 29.
προσβάλλειν with gen. 484.
προσδιδόναι with gen. 535.
προσδοκᾶν with acc. 550.
προσέτι with dat. 644. Obs.
προσεύχεσθαι with dat. 589.
προσήκει different from προσῆκε 858. Obs. 4.
προσήκειν with dat. 594. 3. dat. and acc. with inf. 674, 676.
προσήκει μοι with gen. 509.
προσῆκον, acc. absol. 700. a.
προσήγορος with gen. 494.
πρόσθεν with gen. 526.
προσιέναι προσόδια 559. Obs. 2.
προσκαλεῖσθαι with gen. 501.
*προσσόζειν with gen. 484.
*προσπνεῖν with gen. 484.
προστάττειν with inf. 664.
προστέλλειν with acc. 558.
προσυμβάλλεσθαι with gen. 535.
*προσφερής with gen. 519.
προσφωνεῖν προοίμιον 566.1.

προσχαίνειν with acc. 566. 3.
*πρόσω with gen. 526.
*προταρβεῖν with acc. 550. b.
προτοῦ (πρὸ τοῦ) 444. a.
*προύφάνη τινί ποθοῦντι 599. 3.
προφαίνομαι ἰδέσθαι 667. Obs. 2.
πρόφασιν 579. 3.
προφέρειν with gen. 504.
πρυμνός for adverb 714.
πρωΐ with gen. 527.
πρῶτα, τά, applied to a person, 382.
πρωτεύειν with gen. 504.
πρῶτος with gen. 502. 3.—adverbial 714. a.—difference between πρῶτος and πρῶτον ib. Obs. 3.
πταίειν and compos. for -εσθαι 360.
πτερόν, bird, 353. 2.
*πτώσσειν with acc. 550.
Πυθοῖ 605. Obs. 1.
πυκνός for adverb 714. c.
πύλαι for the sing. 355. Obs. 1.
πυνθάνεσθαι, in sense of perfect, 396.
πυνθάνεσθαι with gen. 485.—with partic. 683.—difference between inf. and partic. ib. Obs.
πυροί 355. b.
πωλεῖν with gen. 515. 2.—with acc. 573.
πωλεῖσθαι with gen. 481.1.
πώμαλα 880. Obs. 2.
πῶς γὰρ ἄν; πῶς δ᾽ οὐκ ἄν; without verb 430.
πῶς γάρ; πῶς γὰρ οὔ; 872.i.
πῶς ἔχειν, ἥκειν with gen. 528.
πῶς δή 723, 872.—πῶς οὖν δή, πῶς δὴ οὖν ibid. and 872.—πῶς δαί 727.—πῶς καί 872.—πῶς μήν 728. 872.

ῥάδιον with dat. 602. 3.
ῥαδίως φέρειν with partic. 685.
Ῥαμνοῦντι 605. Obs. 1.
ῥάπτειν with acc. 569.
ῥαψῳδεῖν with acc. 566.
ῥέζειν (to do) with acc. 560.
ῥεῖν with acc. 555.
ῥέπειν with acc. 558.
ῥηγνύναι πέπλους for ῥήγνυσθαι 363. 3.—φωνήν 566. 1.

*ῥιγεῖν with acc. 550. b.
ῥοφεῖν with acc. 562.
ῥύεσθαι with gen. 531.—
with inf. 664.
ῥύσιος with dat. 602. 3.

σαλπίζει sc. ὁ σαλπιγκτής 373. 2.
σατραπεύειν with gen. 518.
σάττειν with gen. 539. 1.
σαυτοῦ or σεαυτοῦ, uses of, 652. 3.
σέβας in periphrases 442.
σὲ δή elliptic sc. λέγω 581. 2.
σείει sc. ὁ θεός 373. 2.
σημαίνει τῇ σάλπιγγι sc. ὁ σαλπιγκτής 373. 2.—προ-σημαίνει sc. ὁ θεός 373. 3.
σημαίνειν with gen. 578.—with dat. Obs. 3. 589. 3.
σημεῖον δέ 655. Obs. 4.
σημερινός for adv. 714. b.
σήμερον, acc. 577. Obs. 2.
σήσαμα, of a place, 353. 2.
σήτειος for adv. 714. b.
σθένος in periphrases 442.
σιγᾶν λόγον &c. 566.
σίδηρος, iron-mart, 353. 2.
σιτεῖσθαι with acc. 562.
σιωπᾶν with acc. 566.—with dat. 598.
σκεδάζειν with acc. 570.
(σκέπτεσθαι) ἐσκέφθαι pass. 368.
σκευάζειν with acc. 569.
σκοπεῖν and -εῖσθαι 363. 6.
σκοπεῖν with gen. and acc. 485, 487. 1.
(σκοτάζει) συσκοτάζει sc. ὁ θεός 373. 2.
σκοτιαῖος for ἐν σκότῳ 714. b.
σμικροῖς, quum res parvæ sunt, 603. 1.
σοί, dat. of reference, 600. 2.
σοῦ for σός 652. 3.—σοῦ before its substantive for σοί ib. Obs. 4.
σοῦ, σοί, σέ, retrospective, 658.
σόρος, of a person, 353. 1.
σός for σοῦ 652. Obs. 6.
σοφίζεσθαι with acc. 551. 1.
σοφός with gen. 493.—with acc. 579. 2.—πρός τι ib. Obs.
σπανίζειν with gen. 529.
σπάνιος, adverbial, 714. c.
σπείρειν with acc. 569. 2, 570.
σπένδειν with gen. 497.—-εσθαι σπονδάς &c. 560. 2.—with acc. 570.

σπέρχειν for σπέρχεσθαι 360.
σπέρχεσθαι with dat. 601.
σπεύδειν with acc. 560.
σπουδάζειν with acc. 560.—with inf. 664. 1.
σπουδῇ, ægre, 603. 2.
σταγών for ὄνες 354.
στάζειν with acc. 555, 570.
σταθμᾶν and -ᾶσθαι 363. 6.
σταθμᾶσθαί τι τινί 609. 3.
στείχειν with acc. 558.
στέλλειν with acc. 558, 569.
στέμματα for στέμμα 355. Obs. 1.
στενάζειν with acc. 566. 3.—with instrum. dat. 607.
στένειν, στένεσθαι with gen. 488.
στένω μέλος accus. 566. 4.
στέργειν with acc. 549. Obs. 2.—with gen. and dat. 498. Obs. 2.
στέργειν, -εσθαι with in-strum. dat. 607.
στερεῖν with gen. 529. 1.
στερεῖν and -εῖσθαι with gen. 529.—with double acc. 583. 144.
στερήσεσθαι seemingly pas-sive, 364. Obs.
*στεφανοῦσθαι τείρεα 545. 3.—with dat. 596.
στεφανώσασθαι seemingly passive, 364. b.
(στῆναι) καταστῆναι ὑπό τι-νος 359. 3.
στῆναι with acc. 556.—with dat. 601.
(στήσεσθαι) καταστ. seem-ingly passive, 364. a.
στόλῳ cum caterva, 604. 2.
στοχάζεσθαι with gen. 506.
στρατεύειν and -εσθαι 363. 6.—with acc. 564.
στρατηγεῖν with gen. 518.—with dat. ibid. Obs. 3. 596. 2.
στρατηλατεῖν with gen. and dat. 518. and Obs. 3.—with dat. 596. 2.
στρατοπεδεύειν and -εσθαι 363. 5.
στρέφειν and compos. in-transitive, 360.
στρέφεσθαι with acc. 507.—with acc. 551. 1.
στρατῷ, cum exercitu, 604. 2.
*στυγεῖν with acc. 549. c.
στύγος of a person, 353. 1.
σύ use of, 652. (in Homer, ibid. Obs. 1.)

συγγενής with gen. 519.—with dat. 590.
συγγεγνώσκεσθαι with inf. 665.—συγγεγνώσκω dif-ferent constructions of, 682. 2.
συγγνώμων. with gen. 493.
* συγκεράννυσθαι φιλίᾳ 572.
συγχωρεῖν with gen. 530.—with inf. 664. 1.—with ὥστε ib. Obs. 3.
συλᾶν with double acc. 583, 146.
συλλαμβάνειν, -εσθαι with gen. 535.
συλλαμβάνοντι 599.
συμβαίνειν with inf. 669. 1.—construction of, 674.—with inf. 674, 676. b.—with partic. 691.
συμβάλλεσθαι with gen. 535.
συμβουλεύειν with inf. 664.
συμμαχία for σύμμαχοι 353.
συμμίγα with dat. 590.
συμπράσσειν with dat. 596.
συμφέρειν with dat. 596.
συμφέρει with partic. 691.
σύμφορος with gen. 519.—σύμφορόν ἐστι with dat. and acc. with inf. 674.—with partic. 691.
συμφυής with gen. 519.
σύμφυτος with gen. 519.
σύμφωνος with gen. 519.
σύμφωνος, -εῖν, -ία with dat. 594. 2. and Obs. 1.
σύμψηφος with gen. 519.
σύν, ξύν, prep. with dat. 623.—as adverb, 640.
σύν with a subst. of quality instead of the gen. 604. Obs. 2.
συν- in compos. 623. Obs.
συνάγειν τινὰ νηόν, δια-στήριον &c. 559.
συναινεῖν with dat. 594. 1.
συναίρεσθαι with gen. and acc. 536. and Obs. 4.
συναλλάττεσθαι with dat. 590.
συνέβη with ὥστε 669. Obs. 1.
συνειδέναι with gen. 493.
συνελόντι 599.—συνελόν-τι ἁπλῶς εἰπεῖν 864. 1.
συνέπεσθαι with gen. 536.
συνεργός with gen. 519.
συνετρίβη τῆς κεφαλῆς 522. Obs. 3.
συνήθης with gen. 519.

συνήνεικεν with inf. 669.— with ὥστε ibid. Obs. 1.
συνιέναι with gen. 485.— with gen. and acc. ibid. Obs.
συνίστωρ with acc. 581. Obs.
σύννομος with gen. 519.
σύνοιδα with partic. 682. 2.
συντεμόντι 599.
σύνεστι with partic. 691.
σύντροφος with gen. 519.
συντυγχάνειν with gen. 509.
συνῳδός with dat. 594. 2.
συχνά, acc. 578. Obs. 2.
συχνός adverbial, 714. c.
σφαγείς τινος 483. Obs. 3.
σφακελίζειν for -εσθαι 360.
σφάλλειν, σφάλλεσθαι with gen. 511.
σφέτερος for ἡμέτερος, ὑμέτερος 654. c.— σφέτερος for ἐμός, σός, 654. Obs. 3.
Σφηττοῖ 605. Obs. 1.
σφίσιν for ὑμῖν 654. a.
σχεδόν with gen. 526.
σχέσθαι and compos., seemingly passive, 365, 2.
σχέτλιος with gen. 489, 495.
σχῆμα Ἀλκμανικόν (εἰς Ἀχέροντα Πυριφλεγέθων τε ῥέουσιν Κώκυτός τε) 393. 5.
σχῆμα Βοιώτιον or Πινδαρικόν (μελιγάρυες ὕμνοι τέλλεται) 386. 1.
σχῆμα καθ' ὅλον καὶ μέρος in the nominat. 478. — in the accus. 584. 1.
σῴζειν with gen. 531.
σωτήρ, adjective, 439.

τά with the gen. plur. and the verb in plur. 380.
τὰ μὲν ἄρα—, ἀλλά 787. c.
τὰ τοιαῦτα without καί 792. h.
τάδε πάντα 655. 3. — τάδε with adverbs of time and place, ibid. 5.
τάλας with gen. 489.
τἆλλα accus. 579. 4.
τἀμά for ἐγώ 436. Obs. 1.
ταμιεύειν and -εσθαι 363. 6.
τἀναντία accus. 579. 4.
*τανύειν τί τινι, 588. 1.
τανῦν accus. 577. Obs. 2.
τανῦν τάδε 655. 5.
τάξασθαι seemingly passive, 364. b.
τὰ πολλά, acc. 578. Obs. 2.

ταράττειν πόλεμον, στάσεις 583. 147.
*ταρβεῖν with acc. 550. b.
τἀρχαῖον accus. 577. Obs. 2.
ταυροῦσθαι with acc. 554.
ταῦτα applied to a notion or thought, 383. Obs.
ταῦτα, the world, &c. 655. 2.—ταῦτα with an adverb of place or time, ib. 5.—ταῦτα πάντα ib. 3.—ταῦτα prospective use of, 657. 2.
ταῦτα μέν—ταῦτα δέ, accus. 579. 4.
ταῦτ' ἄρα, 579. 4.
ταύτῃ 605. Obs. 1.— hoc modo, 603. 2.
τάχα with indic. of historic tenses without ἄν 859.
τάχος, celeriter 579. 5.
τέ—τέ 754. 1—4.—τέ—δέ; μέν—τέ 754. 5.—τέ alone, 754. 6, 7.—τέ with πολύς 759. Obs. 2.—Epic use of τέ 755.—εἴπερ τέ—τέ;—εἴπερ—τέ;—ἤ τε;—μέντε—δέ τε or ἀλλά τε;—τέ—δέ τε, ἀλλά τε; μέν τε—δέ or ἀλλά;—δέ τε, ἀλλά τε;—δέ—τέ; τέ—δέ; τέ—αὐτάρ;—καί τε;—γάρ τε;—ἤτε;—ἤτε—ἤτε 755. 2.—ὅστε, ὅστις τε, οἷός τε, ὅσος τε, ὥστε, ὡσεί τε, ἅτε, ἠΰτε, ὅπως τε, ὅτε τε, ὄθι τε, ἵνα τε 755. 3.—οἷός τε εἰμί, ὥστε, ὡσείτε, ἔστε in the Attic, ἐπείτε in Herod. 755. 4.
τέ—καί 758.— with πολύς 759. Obs. 2.
τε οὗ for οὔτε 775. Obs. 1.—τε—οὐδέ 776. Obs.
τέ—καί for ὅτε 752. 2.
τέ γε 735. 10.
τέγγειν with acc. 555.
(τείνειν) ξυντ. for -εσθαι 360. — προτείνειν and -εσθαι 363. 6.
τεκμαίρεσθαί τι τινί 609. 3.
τεκμήριον δέ 655. 6.
τεκνοῦν with acc. 569. 2.—parentem esse, 396.
τεκνοῦν, -οῦσθαι with gen. 483.
τειχεῖν, τειχίζειν with acc. 569.
τεκταίνειν with acc. 569.
τελεῖν with acc. 561, 573.
τέλειος with gen. 494.
τελευτᾶν ὑπό τινος 359. 3.

τελευτᾶν, as intrans. 360.
τελευτᾶν with gen. 514.—with acc. 560. 2.
τελευτήσεσθαι seemingly passive, 364.
τελευτῶν, at last, 696. Obs. 1.
τέλος, accus. 577. Obs. 2.
τέμνειν ὅρκια, φιλότητα, συνθεσίας, φίλια 560. 2.
τέμνεσθαι μέρη 583. 43.
τέρπεσθαι with gen. 540.—with acc. 549.— with partic. 686.
τεταρταῖος, on the fourth day, 714. b.
τεύχειν with acc. 569. 1.
τεχνᾶν with acc. 569. 3.
τέως for ἕως 795, 839.—poet. for τότε ib. 4.
τῇ ἀληθείᾳ 603. 2.
τῇ, τῇδε 605. Obs. 1.
τῇδε with gen. 527.
τήκειν with acc. 549. c.—οἰμωγάν with acc. 360. Obs. 3.
(τήκειν) ἐκτ. intrans. 360.
τῆλε, τηλόθι with gen. 526.
τηλίκος εἰμί with inf. 666.
τηλικοῦτος as femin. 390. Obs.
τημελεῖν with gen. 496.
τῆμος, accus. 577. Obs. 2.— τῆμος poet. for τότε 839. 4.
τὴν ἀρχήν 577. Obs. 2.
τὴν ταχίστην, τὴν πρώτην, τὴν ἄλλως, τὴν εὐθεῖαν 558. 1.
τὴν ὥρην, ad tempus, 577. Obs. 1.
τηνίκα poet. for τότε 839. 4.
τηνᾶσθαι with gen. 529. 1.
τῆτες, accus. 577. Obs. 2.
τὶ with the neutr. adject. 381. Obs. 4.
τὶ, in any respect, 579. 4.
τί with the negat. for οὐδέν οὐ in the middle of a sentence, 882. 2.
τί ἄλλο ἤ 895. 2.
τί βουλόμενος—; cur, 697.
τί γὰρ μέλλει; τί δ' οὐ μέλλει; τί δ' οὐκ ἔμελλε; in answers, 880. Obs. 2.
τί δέ μοι or σοι; quid ad me? 590. Obs. 2.
τί δή, τί δή ποτε, τί δὴ οὖν, τί οὖν δή 721.—τί δαί 727.—τί μήν 728.—τί νυ 732.
τὶ εἶναι, aliquid esse, 381. Obs. 3.

τί ἐστί μοί τινι; (κοινόν) 590. *Obs.* 2.

τί λέξεις; 406. 5.

τί μαθών and τί παθών 872. k.

τί μέλλει; in answers, 880. *Obs.* 2.

τί μοι τινός 535. *Obs.* 2.

τί οὐ, τί οὖν οὐ with the aorist 403. 3.

τίεσθαί τινά τινος 500.

τιθέναι and τίθεσθαι νόμους 362. 2.

τιθέναι, -εσθαι with gen. 533. 2.—with dat. 591.

(τίθημι) τιθέντες as femin. 390. *Obs.*

τίκτειν with acc. 569. 2.—*parentem esse*, 396.

τίλλεσθαί τινα 364. 4.

τιμαί of a person, 353. 1.

τιμᾶν, -ᾶσθαι with gen. 517.

τιμᾶσθαι, τετιμῆσθαι, τετιμήσεσθαι seemingly passive, 364. 4.

τιμωρεῖν, -εῖσθαί τινά τινος and ἀντί τινος 500. and *Obs.* 4. — with dat. 596. —τιμώρημα with dat. 596. *Obs.* 2.

τινάξασθαι seemingly passive, 364. 4.

τίνειν with acc. 573.—with dat. 588. 1.

τίπτε 872. a.

τις omitted, 373. 5.

τὶς or πᾶς τις with the II. pers. imper. 390. γ.

τὶς as indefinite article, 446, 659.—position of, 660.

τὶς, τί collective, 659. 1.—for ἐγώ, σύ ib. 2.—with adj., indefinite numerals, and adv. ib. 4.—*eximius quidam*, ib. *Obs.* 1.—with pronouns and cardinal numerals, ib. 5.—ἤ τις ἤ οὐδείς ib. *Obs.* 2.

τίς for ὅστις in indirect questions, 877. *Obs.* 2.

τίς ὅστις οὐ attracted, 824. 2.

τίς ποτε 872.—τίς τε, τίς τ' ἄρ', τίς νυ ib. b.—τίς ἄρα ib. c.—τί δή, τί δήποτε, τί δαί, τίς δὴ οὖν, τί οὖν δή ib. d.—τί μήν ib. f.—τί δέ; τί δ' οὖ; ib. g.—τί καί ib. h. — τίς γάρ, τί γάρ; ib. i.

τίς τ' ἄρ', τί τ' ἄρ' 788. 1. 872. c.

τίσασθαι with gen. 500.—

with δίκην ibid. *Obs.* 1.—construction of, 585.

τιτρώσκεσθαι σφαγάς 583. 124.

τιτύσκεσθαι with gen. 506.

τλήμων with gen. 489.

τλῆναι with acc. 563.—with inf. 664.—with partic. 687.—with inf. ib. *Obs.*

τό with inf. for the inf. alone, 670.

τό, τοῦ, τῷ with inf. or with acc. with inf. 678.—τό with inf. or with acc. with inf. to explain a subst. ib.—τό with inf. or with acc. with inf. in exclamations and questions, 679.

τό with the gen. plur. and the verb in plur. 380. 1.

τὸ αὐτίκα accus. 577. *Obs.* 2.

τὸ δ' ἀληθές accus. 579. 3.

τὸ δὲ μέγιστον, καὶ τὸ μέγιστον, τὸ δὲ δεινότατον, καὶ τὸ ἔσχατον, τὸ τελευταῖον &c. 580. *Obs.* 2.

τὸ δ' ὅλον 579. 4.

τὸ ἐμόν for ἐγώ 436. *Obs.* 1.

τὸ ἐπίπαν acc. of quantity, 578. *Obs.* 2.

τὸ ἑωθινόν accus. 577. *Obs.* 2.

τὸ θάτερον 459. 6.

τὸ καὶ τό, τὸν καὶ τόν 444. b.

τὸ κατά (ἐπί, εἰς) τι or τινα 679. 2.

τὸ κατὰ τοῦτον εἶναι 679. 2.

*τὸ λεγόμενον 580. 2.

τὸ λοιπόν 577. *Obs.* 2. 523.

τὸ μηδέν 745. *Obs.* 4.

τὸ νῦν εἶναι — τὸ τήμερον εἶναι — τὸ ἐπὶ σφᾶς εἶναι — τὸ ἐπ' ἐκείνοις εἶναι — τὸ κατὰ τοῦτον εἶναι 679. 2.

τὸ πέρας, τὸ παλαιόν, τὸ πρῶτον, τὸ πάλαι, τὸ πρίν acc. 577. *Obs.* 2.

τὸ σὸν μέρος, accus. 579. 3.

τὸ ταὐτόν 459. 6.

τὸ τέλος, τὸ τελευταῖον, ad *postremum*, 577. *Obs.* 2.

*τὸ τοῦ ποιητοῦ, 580. 2.

τόδε, *huc*, 655. 1.—τόδε with an adverb of place or time, ib. 5.—prospective use of, 657. 2.

τόδ' ἐκεῖνο 655. 8.

τοί 736.—in answers, 880. f.

τοίγαρ 790. 3.

τοιγάρτοι 790. 4.

τοίνυν 790. 1, 2.

τοῖον, only, 823. *Obs.* 2.

τοιόσδε different from τοιοῦτος 655. 6.—τοιόσδε εἰμι 666.

τοιοῦτος seemingly with dat. 594. *Obs.* 2. — τοιοῦτος different from τοιόσδε 655.6.—τοιοῦτός εἰμι with inf. 666.

τοκεῖς of one parent, 355. *Obs.* 2.

τολμᾶν with acc. 561. 563.—with inf. 664.—with partic. 687.—with inf. ib. *Obs.* 1.

τὸν χρόνον 577.

τόξα for τόξον 355. *Obs.* 1.

τοξεύειν with gen. 506.

τόσον, only, 823. *Obs.* 2.

τοσοῦτον — ὅσον; τοσαύτη —ὅσῳ 870.

τοσοῦτο accus. of quantity, 578. *Obs.* 2.

τότ' ἤδη 719. 4. — τότε δὴ 720. 1.

τοῦ with inf. or with acc. with inf. to explain a subst. 678.—τοῦ and τοῦ μή with inf. or with acc. with inf. to express the aim, 492.

τοῦ λοιποῦ 523.

τοὐναντίον accus. 579. 4.

τοὐπ' ἐμέ, τουτί σε 579. 4.

τοῦτο with adverb of time or place, 655. 5.—τοῦτ' ἐκεῖ ib.—τοῦτ' ἐκεῖνο 8. — τοῦτ' αὐτό 656.—τοῦτο prospective use of, 657. 2.

τοῦτο ὅ, *id quod*, applying to a whole sentence, 836. 2.

τοῦτο μέν—τοῦτο δέ, accus. 579. 4.

τόφρα poet. for ἐν τούτῳ 839. 4.

*τραγῳδεῖν with acc. 566. 1.

τραφείς τινος 483. *Obs.* 3.

τραφῆναι different from θρεφθῆναι 367. *Obs.* 2.

τρέπειν and compos. for τρέπεσθαι 363.

τρέπεσθαι with gen. 530.—with acc. *vias*, 558. 1.—with dat. 591.

τρέφειν with double acc. 583. 154.

τρέχειν with acc. 563.

τρίβειν and compos. for τρίβεσθαι 363.

βῶν with gen. 493. —
with acc. 581. Obs.
ζειν with acc. 566. 3.
ηραρχεῖν with acc. 553.
ηρεσι, cum tri. 605.
ιμμα of a person, 353. 1.
ιπλάσιος with gen. 502.
3.
ιπλοῦς with gen. 502. 3.
ιταῖος. on the third day,
714. b.
ὁπον accus. 580. 1.
οπῷ τοιῷδε 603. 2.
ίψεσθαι seemingly passive, 364. a.
ρομεῖν with acc. 350. 6.
ιόπον, τοῦτον τὸν τρόπον
&c. 580. 1.
ιώγειν with acc. 562.
υγχάνειν seemingly for εἶναι 375. 3.
υγχάνειν with gen. 509.—
with acc. 576. 2.—with
partic. 694.
ὕμβος of a person, 353. 1.
ὕπτειν with double acc.
583. 155.
ὕπτεσθαί τινα 545. 3.
ὕπτεσθαι πολλὰς πληγάς
ibid.
τυραννεῖν, -νεύειν with gen.
518.
τυρός, cheese-shop, 353. 2.
τύχη with inf. 669. β.
τῷ, wherefore, 609. 3.
τῷ ὄντι, τῷ λόγῳ, ἔργῳ 603.
2.
τώς for ὡς 816. 1.

ὑβρίζειν with double acc.
583. 156.
ὕβρισμα of a person, 353. 1.
ὑγιαίνειν τὰς φρένας 579. 1.
ὑγίειαι 355. γ.
ὕει sc. ὁ θεός 373. 2.
ὕειν with acc. 570.
υἷες Ἀχαιῶν 442.
υἱός omitted, 436.
ὑλαῖος for ἐν ὕλῃ 714. a.
ὑλακτεῖν with acc. 566. 3.
ὑλήεντι as femin. 390. Obs.
ὑμέτερον for ὑμεῖς 436. Obs.
1.
ὑμῖν, dative of reference,
600. 2.
ὑμνεῖν with acc. 566. 3.
ὕμνος with dat. 598. Obs.
ὑμνωδεῖν with acc. 566. 3.
ὑπάγειν with gen. 501. and
Obs. 1.
ὑπακούειν with dat. 593.
ὑπανίστασθαι with gen.530.

ὑπαντᾶν, ὑπαντιάζειν with
gen. and acc. 510.
—with dat. 592.
ὕπαρ accus. 577. Obs. 2.
ὑπάρχειν with gen. and acc.
513. and Obs. — with
partic. 688.
ὑπάρχον accus. absol. 700.
ὑπατεύειν with gen. 504.
ὑπείκειν with gen. 530.—
with acc. 548. Obs. 1.—
*with dat. 593. 1.
ὑπέκ 640. 3.
ὑπεκστῆναι with acc. 548.
Obs. 1.
ὑπεκτρέπεσθαι with acc. 548.
Obs. 1.
ὑπεξάγειν πόδα with acc.
548. Obs. 1.
ὑπέρ, prep. with gen. and
acc. 630.
ὑπερ- in compos. 630. Obs.
ὑπεράπω 644.
ὑπερβάλλειν with gen. and
acc. 504. and Obs. 2.—
τινά τινι 609. 1.
ὑπερβατόν 904.
ὑπερέχειν with gen. and acc.
504. and Obs. 2.
ὑπεριδεῖν with gen. 496.
ὑπεροπτίας of a person, 353.
1.
ὑπερπόντιος for ὑπὲρ πόντον
714. a.
ὑπερφέρειν with gen. 504.
ὑπερφυῶς ὡς 823. Obs. 7.
ὑπέρχεσθαι with acc. 548.
Obs. 1.
ὕπεστι with partic. 691.
ὑπήκοος with gen. 487. 4.
ὑπηοῖος, adverbial, 714. b.
ὑπηρετεῖν with acc. 553.—
with dat. 596. 2.
ὕπνου, somni tempore, 523.
ὑπό. prep. with gen., dat.
and acc. 639.—as adverb,
640.—with dat. in pregnant force, with acc. 645.
ὑπό with acc. and partic.
(ὑπὸ νύκτα ἐλθοῦσαν)696.
Obs. 4.
ὑποκάτω 644.
ὑπομένειν with inf. 664.—
with partic. 687.
ὑπομιμνήσκειν, -εσθαι with
gen. and acc. 512. and
Obs.— with double acc.
583. 158.
ὑπονοεῖν with gen. 485.
ὕποπτος transit. 356. Obs.
—with gen. 542. 2.
ὑποστῆναι with dat. 601.

ὑποστραφείς τινος 483. Obs.
3.
ὑποταρβεῖν with acc. 550.
ὑπουργεῖν with acc. 573.
Obs. 2.
ὑποχωρεῖν with gen. 530.—
with acc. 548. Obs. 1.
ὕστατος, adverbial, 714. a.
ὑστερεῖν, ὕστερον εἶναι, ὑστερίζειν with gen. 505.
ὕστερος with gen. 502.—
ὕστερος ἤ 503. Obs. 2.
ὑφαίνειν with acc. 569. 3.
*ὑφέλκειν with gen. 522.
1.
ὑφιέναι, -εσθαι with gen.
531.
ὑφίστασθαι with dat. 601.
ὕψι, in alto, in altum, 605.
Obs. 5.
ὑψόθεν with gen. 526.
ὕψος, accus. 579. 3.

φαγεῖν with gen. and acc.
537. Obs.—with acc. 562.
φαίνειν intrans. 360.—with
acc. 569. 2.
φαίνειν, φαίνεσθαι with partic. 684.—φαίνομαι ποιῶν
τι ib. Obs. 2.
φαίνεσθαι with gen. 521. b.
—with gen. loci. 522.—
—with inf. 665, 684.
φαίνομαι ἰδεῖν 667. Obs. 2.
φάναι with gen. 486.—with
inf. 665.
φανερὸν εἶναι with partic.
684.—φανερός εἰμι ποιῶν
τι ib. Obs. 1.
φανῆναι different from φανθῆναι 367. Obs. 2.
φάσθαι with acc. 566.
φείδεσθαι with gen. 496,
531. Obs. 1.
φενακίζειν with acc. 563.
φέρε applied to more than
one, 390. a.
φέρε with conj. 416.
(φέρειν) διαφ., ὑπερφ. intrans. 360.
φέρειν τι for φέρεσθαι 363.
φέρειν with gen. 530.—with
acc. 573.
φερόμενος, φέρων, maximo
studio, 698. Obs. 1.—φέρων, with, ib. Obs. 2.—
pleonast. ib. Obs. 2.
φεῦ with gen. 489.
φεύγειν ὑπό τινος 359. 3.
φεύγειν with gen. 530.
φεύγειν with gen. as κλοπῆς
501.

φεύγειν with acc. 558.—
δίωγμα 559. *Obs.* 2. 568.
with dat. 598.—with inf.
664.

φεύγειν φυγῇ 899. 1.

φεύγων ἔφυγε 899. 1.

φθάμενος,φθάς,quickly,698.

φθάνειν 694. — with part.
694.—with part. and acc.
of person, followed by
ἤ, πρὶν ἤ ibid. *Obs.* 2.—
with inf. ibid. *Obs.* 4.—
φθάνειν in partic. with
verbum fin. ibid. *Obs.* 3.

φθέγγεσθαι with acc. 566.1.

φθονεῖν with gen. 499.—
with acc. 549.—with dat.
601.—with dat. and acc.
with inf. 674.

φθονεῖν εἰ for ὅτι 804. 8.

φθόνος τινός 499. *Obs.* 1.

φθονοῦμαι ὑπό τινος, invidetur mihi ab aliq. 372. 4.

φθόρος of a person, 353. 1.

φθόρος adjective, 439. 1.

φιλεῖν, solere, 402. *Obs.* 1.

φιλεῖν with double acc. 583.
159.

φιλία τινός 499. *Obs.* 2.

φιλήσεσθαι seemingly pas-
sive, 364. *Obs.*

φίλον ἐστί μοι ποιεῖν τι for
φίλον ἐστί με π. τι 677.

φίλον ἐστί with dat. 602. 3.
with partic. 691.

φίλος with gen. 520.—with
dat. 590.

*φιλοφρονεῖσθαι with dat.
and acc. 594. 4. *Obs.* 2.

φίλτατα, τά of a person,
355. *Obs.* 2.

φιτύειν with acc. 569. 2.

φλόξ of a person, 353. 1.

φλυαρεῖν with acc. 566. 1.

φλυαρεῖς ἔχων 698. *Obs.*

φοβεῖσθαι with acc. 550.—
φοβερόν,φόβος ἐστίν with
inf.664.—φοβεῖσθαι with
τό and inf. 670.

φόβος with inf. 667.

φόβος in periphrases, 442.d.
τινός 499. *Obs.* 2.

φορεῖν with acc. 576. 1.

φράζειν with acc. 486.—
with acc. 566.—with dat.
and acc. with inf. 674.—
with part. 684. *Obs.* 2.

φρίσσειν with acc. 550.

(φρονεῖν) καταφρονοῦμαι ὑπό
τινος 372. 4.

φρονεῖν with acc. 551. 1.—
with part. 683.

φρονήσεις 355. γ.

φρόνιμός τι 579. 2.

φροντίζειν with gen. and acc.
and περί τινος 496. and
Obs. 1, 3.—with ὡς and
gen. absol. 702.

φρόντις τινός with gen. 496.
Obs. 4.

φροντίζειν οὐ with partic.
687.

*φυγάς, φυγή with acc. 581.
Obs.

φυγή for φυγάδες 353. 1.

φύειν intrans. 360.

φύειν with acc. 569. 2.—
φῦναι seemingly for εἶναι
375. 3.—with an adverb,
ibid.—with gen. 483.

φυλακήν accus. 579. 5.

φυλάττεσθαι with gen. 496.

φῦναι with gen. origin.483.
and a subst. with inf.668.

φύξιμος with acc. 581. *Obs.*

φύρειν with gen. 539. 1.

φυσᾶν with acc. 555.

φυτεύειν, -εσθαι with gen.
483.

φωνεῖν, with acc. 566.

χάζεσθαι with gen. 530.

χαίνειν ῥήματα 566. 1.

(χαίρειν) κεχαρῆσθαι for κε-
χαρηκέναι 363. 5.

χαίρειν with acc. 549.—
with dat. instrum. 607.
—χαίρειν λέγειν τινά and
χαίρειν λέγειν, εἰπεῖν, φράζειν τινί 674. — χαίρειν
with partic. 685.

χαλᾶν for -ᾶσθαι 360.

χαλεπαίνειν with gen. 490.
—with acc. 549.—with
dat. 601. 1.

χαλεπός εἰμι with inf. for
χαλεπόν ἐστι with acc.
with inf. 677.

χαλεπῶς φέρειν with dat.
instrum. 607.

χαμαί, humi and humum 605.
Obs. 5.

χανδάνειν with acc. 576. 1.

χαρίζεσθαι with gen. 535.
—with acc. 573.—with
dat. 588.

χάριν, gratiâ, with gen.
621. *Obs.* 2.—χάριν ἐμήν,
σήν ib.—χάριν ἕνεκα ib.

χάρμα, of a person, 353. 1.

χειμερινός adverbial, 714. b.

χεῖν with acc. 570, 571.—
τι τινί 592. 1.

χείρ, of works of art, 353.

χείρ omitted 436.

χειρός, δεξιᾶς, ἀριστερᾶς &c.
530. *Obs.* 1.

χηροῦν with gen. 529. 1.

χθιζός for χθές 714. b.

χιτών, wearing house, 353. 2.

χόλος τινός, de aliquo, 4xc.
Obs. 2.

χολοῦσθαι with gen. and
περί, ἔκ τινος 490. and
Obs. 1.—with dat. 601.

χοῦν with acc. 571.

χορδή omitted 436.

χορεύειν ἀγῶνας, Φρύγιον
556.—τινά 556. *Obs.*

χορηγεῖν with gen. and dat.
518. *Obs.* 3.—with acc.
553.—with dat. 596. 2.

χορτάζειν with double acc.
583. 161.

χορτάζεσθαί τι ibid.

χραισμεῖν with dat. 596.

χρᾶν with dat. 589.

χρᾶσθαι with dat. 591.

χρεία with gen. 529.—with
dat. 596. *Obs.* 2.

χρεώ with gen. 529.

χρεωμένῳ ἀληθεῖ λόγῳ 599.
1.

χρεών, acc. absol. 700.

χρή with gen. 529. 1.
—with dat. 594. 3.—
with inf. 669.—χρή with
dat. and acc. and inf.
674.

χρή different from χρῆν
858. *Obs.* 4.

χρῆμα with the adject. for
the simple neut. adject.
381. *Obs.* 4.

χρῆμα,χρήματα omitted 436.

χρῆμα in periphrases 442.d.

χρῆν and χρῆν ἄν 858. *Obs.*
3.

(χρῆσθαι) χρησθῆναι pass.
368. b.

χρῆσθαί with dat. 591.

χρήσιμος, χρηστός τι 579. 2.

χρόνιος adverbial, 714. b.

χρόνος omitted 436.

χρόνου &c. gen. of time,
523.

χρόνον, χρόνῳ, σὺν χρ. 577.

*χρόνῳ, τῷ χρ. 606.

χρῶμαι ὑπό τινος 372. 4.

χρώμενος, with, 698.

χώεσθαι with gen. 490.

χώρα omitted 436.

χωρεῖν with gen. 530.—
— with acc. 558. — to
hold, with acc. 576.—
with dat. 593. 1.

ὀρίζειν with gen. 530.
ὀρίς with gen. 526, 529. 2.

ἀμάθοι 355. b.
αὔειν with gen. 536.
ἔχειν with gen. and acc.
495. and Obs. 3.—with
double acc. 583. 162.
·εύδειν, -εσθαι with gen.
511.— *ψεύδεσθαι with
dat. 609.
ηφίζειν with acc. 568.
ψηφίζεσθαι) καταψηφίζο-
μαι θανάτου 372. 4.
ιθυρίζειν τινί 589, 1.
ιλός with gen. 529.
ιολοέντος as fem. 390. Obs.
ὑχη 355. γ.
ψυχῳ) καταψυχθέντες as
fem. 390. Obs.

ὁ with vocat., position of,
479. 2, 3.
ὁ, hic and huc 605. Obs. 5.
ὁ μοι τινός 489.
ὅδε ἔχειν, ἥκειν with gen.
528.
ὅδε, hic and huc 605. Obs. 5.
ὅδε, different from οὕτως,
655. 6.
ὅδε with partic. 696. Obs. 6.
ὤν, partic. with adject. or
subst. besides the partic.
705. 6.—omitted ibid.
ὠνεῖν and -εῖσθαι 368. 3.
(ὠνεῖν) ὠνούμενος, ὠνηθεῖ-
σαν, ἐωνῆσθαι pass. 368. 3.
ὠνεῖσθαι with gen. 515. 2.
with acc. 573.
ὥραιος with gen. 494.
ὥρην (τήν), ad tempus, 577.
Obs. 1.
ὡριαῖος adverbial, 714. b.
ὡς, prep., force of, 615. 626.
ὡς, that, with indic. and
opt. 419. 3. See ὅτι.
ὡς, ut, in wishes, (utinam)
418. b.
ὡς, as, 868. sqq.—ὡς ἔοικας
&c. personal for ὡς ἔοι-
κεν, ut videris for ut videtur 869. 6.
ὡς, as, in indirect questions
for ὅπως, 876. Obs. 3.
ὡς, as, in apposition, 467.
Obs. 3.

ὡς with ἴσος, ὁ αὐτός 594.
Obs. 4.
ὡς with superl. 870. Obs. 4.
ὡς with dat.; as, ὡς γε-
ρόντι, ὡς ἐμοί, meo judicio,
ὡς ἐμῇ δόξῃ 599. 4.
ὡς, as, after comparatives,
779. Obs. 2.
ὡς with partic. fut. 690. Obs.
2.
ὡς with partic. and cases
absol. 701. sqq.
ὡς with acc. and partic.,
after a verb of believing
or saying, 703. Obs.
ὡς—ὡς for ὡς—οὕτως 816. e.
ὡς for ὅτι οὕτως 804. 9.
ὡς, final conj., that, 805.
sqq.—with conj. and opt.
805. 2. and 806.—inter-
change of the conj. and
opt. with 809.—ὡς ἄν with
conj. and opt. 810.—ὡς κε
with opt. utinam 810. Obs.
1.—ὡς with indic. fut.
811.—with ind. of hist.
tenses, 813.
ὡς, that, after a verb of fear,
814. Obs. 4.
ὡς for οὕτως 839. 4, 868. 2.
—in wishes and asser-
tions 869. 1.
ὡς, when &c. 839. a. See
ὅτε.
ὡς for ὥστε. See ὥστε.
ὡς ἀληθῶς, ὡς ἀτεχνῶς, ὡς
πάνυ, ὡς μάλα, ὡς ἐπὶ τὸ
πολύ, ὡς ἕκαστοι 870.
Obs. 4.
ὡς ἄν without verb 430.—
ὡς ἄν εἰ ibid.
ὡς ἄν with conj. see ὅταν
after ὅτε.—ὡς with conj.
for ὡς ἄν 842. 2.—since,
see ὅτε.
ὡς ἄρα 788. 2.
ὡς γε 735. 9.
ὡς δή 721. 3.—ironic. ibid.
ὡς εἰ 869. Obs.
ὡς εἰπεῖν and ὡς ἔπος εἰπεῖν
893. d.
ὡς εἰς, ἐπί, πρός with acc.,
ὡς ἐπί with dat. 626.
Obs. 1.
ὡς ἔχειν, ἥκειν with gen.
(ὡς ποδῶν εἶχον) 528.

ὡς μή, see ὡς.
ὡς ὅτε or ὅτ' ἄν with conj.
841, 869. Obs.
ὡς οὖν 791. 1.
ὡς οὗτις or ὡς οὐδεὶς ἄλλος
ellipt. 895. 2.
ὡς τὰ πολλά 578. Obs. 2.
ὡς τί; with what intent?
882. 1.
ὡς ὤφελον, -ες, -ε with inf.
856. Obs. 2.
ὡσαύτως ἔχειν, ἥκειν with
gen. 528.
ὡσαύτως with dat. 594. 2.
ὥσπερ, as, in comparative
adverbial sentences, 868.
3, 4. after ἴσος, ὁ αὐτός
&c. 869. 2.-594. Obs. 4.
ὥσπερ, when, 839. a. See
ὅτε.
ὥσπερ after a comparative,
779. Obs. 2.
ὥσπερ ἄν εἰ, as if, 430,
432. a.
ὥστε, ὥστε δή with partic.
and gen. absol. 704.
ὥστε, so that, with indic.
and inf. 863.—ὥστε, ge-
nerally ὡς with inf. in
parentheses (ὡς ἔπος εἰ-
πεῖν) 864. 1.—with opt.
with and without ἄν 865.
—with indic. of historic
tenses, and ἄν.—with inf.
and ἄν 866. — with im-
perat. 867.
ὥστε μή with inf. after verbs
of fear, 814. Obs. 4.
ὥστε, as, in comparative adverbial sent. 868. 3, 4.
*ὠστίζεσθαι with dat. 592.
ὠφελεῖν with double acc.
583. 164.—with dat. 596.
1.
ὠφελεῖσθαι ἀπό, ἔκ τινος
491. Obs. 2.
ὠφέλημα with dat. 596.
Obs. 2.
ὠφελήσεσθαι, seemingly
passive, 364. Obs.
ὠφέλιμόν ἐστιν with inf.
669. a.
ὠφέλιμος with dat. 596. 3.
ὤφελον for ὤφελον ἄν 858.
3.

ADDENDA ET CORRIGENDA.

§. 356. Add to *Obs.* "Compound verbal adjectives in τός are frequently thus used, ξιφοδηλητός Æsch. Choeph. 729: νυκτιπλαγκτῶν Id. 751."

§. 359. After 4. add, " 5. Many verbs which properly express only an intransitive state or action assume a further transitive force, the effect or operation of the intransitive state or action being considered in its relation to some other object; so λοχᾶν (*insidiari*), δορυφορεῖν, ἐπιτροπεύειν τινά, χορεύειν Φοῖβον *choreis celebrare* Pind. Isthm. I. 8.: Cf. Soph. Antig. 1153: so Eur. Herc. F. 690 ἐλίσσουσαι *saltando celebrantes:* so in the middle, τύπτεσθαι θεόν, to honour, πατέρα, to mourn: cf. §. 362. 8: and a neuter notion is sometimes derived from a passive, as ἐκπλήττεσθαι, to be alarmed (= to fear,) τί.

§. 360. p. 11. After αἴρειν insert "Soph. Phil. 1331."

Ibid. p. 13. Add to *Obs.* 3. "Demosth. p. 53.45. τεθνᾶσι τῷ δέει (=τεθνᾶσι δειμαίνοντες) τοὺς ἀποστόλους: Æsch. Ag. 823 ψήφους ἔθεντο (=ἐψηφίσαντο) 'Ιλίου φθοράς."

§. 372. 4. p. 26. line 3. After " intransitive verbs" add " which take a genitive or dative of the object of the intransitive act or state."

§. 386. 2. p. 39. Add to the examples, Thuc. III. 36 προσξυνελάβετο οὐκ ἐλάχιστον τῆς ὁρμῆς αἱ Πελοποννησίων νῆες (where Duker, προσξυνελάβοντο.)

Page 82. note d. For *Hein.* read *Herm.*

§. 436. *b.* p. 92. Add to the examples Thuc. VI. 59 ἡ πατρός (sc. θυγάτηρ) τε καὶ ἀνδρὸς (sc. γυνὴ) ἀδελφῶν (sc. κασιγνήτη) τ' οὖσα τυράννων καὶ παιδῶν (sc. μήτηρ).

§. 439. 2. p. 94. In the heading, after "Proleptic" add " or Predicative."

§. 472. 3. p. 118. line 7. Instead of " case" read " matter."

§. 480. In the last line but one of *Obs.* after σοι insert τοῦτο, and in the last line, after δίδωμι insert τοῦτο.

§. 481. 1. p. 124. To the examples add Æsch. Sept. 145 Λύκειος γενοῦ στρατῷ δαΐῳ στόνων αὐτᾶς, on account of.

Ibid. Add the following observation : " The genitival suffix θεν is not unfrequently used for the regular inflected genitive, so οὐρανόθεν, σέθεν, &c. : cf. Eur. Ion. 960 : and even prepositions are sometimes joined with these forms, as ἐξ ἀλόθεν, ἐκ Διόθεν."

§. 489. p. 130. Add to the examples Eur. Ion. 960.

§. 495. p. 134. Add to the examples, Arist. Nub. 22. τοῦ δώδεκα μνᾶς Πασίᾳ.

§. 500. line 5. For Æsch. Aj. read Æsch. Ag., and line 6, for ἀγαγῆς read ἀγωγῆς.

§. 501. line 3. For ἐπισκήψεσθαι, read ἐπισκήπτεσθαι, and after κρίνειν insert κρίνεσθαι.

§. 503. line 4. After "e contrario" add ἀλλόκοτος: Soph. Phil. 1191 τί ῥέξοντες ἀλλοκότῳ γνώμᾳ τῶν πάρος.

§. 504. line 22. On ἀνέχεσθαι, see Stallb. ad Plat. Apol. p. 31 B.

§. 509. 1. Add to the examples, Æsch. Choeph. 932 ἐπήκρισε αἱμάτων: Ibid. 1033 τόξῳ προσίξεται πημάτων.

§. 512. To the examples add Eur. Hec. 279 ἐπιλήθομαι κακῶν.

§. 519. Add to the adjectives, ἐφέστιος, ἐπώνυμος, ἧλιξ : and to the examples, Æsch. Eum. 577 δόμων ἐφέστιος: Id. Choeph. 607 ἧλικα παιδός.

§. 521. b. line 6. Dele the example Eur. Hec. 279 ἐπιλήθομαι κακῶν.

§. 522. Obs. 3. line 3. After βόστρυχον add, "and perhaps : Il. η. 59 μέσσου δουρὸς ἑλών : Od. γ, 439 βοῦν ἀγέτην κεράων, et sim."

§. 523. After Obs. add "The temporal force of the genitive is clearly seen in such adverbs as ἐπιπολῆς, ἑξῆς, ἐφεξῆς, ποῦ, αἴφνης, or (with the preposition) ἐξαίφνης, ἐξαπίνης, like de subito:" and to the end of the Obs. add " ἐκ χειρός, ἐκ ποδός, ἐξ ἀγχιμόλοιο, (Il. ω, 352) ἐξ ἀπροσδοκήτου, ἐξ ἑτοίμων, ἀπὸ τοῦ προφανοῦς, &c."

§. 536. To the verbs given add ἐρείδεσθαι.

§. 540. Add to the adverbs ἅδην and ἅλις.

§. 554. c. line 2. For δέργμα read ὄμμα and add Ib. 187 ἀποταυροῦται δέργμα.

§. 556. d. line 2. For φυλακήν read φρουρᾶς, and for φυλάσσων read φρουρῶν.

§. 558. 2. Add, " so ἀΐσσειν χέρα, βάσιν &c."

§. 566. 1. To the instances given add Arist. Ach. 622 κωμῳδήσει τὰ δίκαια : Plat. Cratyl. p. 414. C τραγῳδεῖν τὰ ὀνόματα.

Ib. 2. Last line but two, for δειπάζων read δεννάζων.

Ib. 3. To the instances given add Æsch. Choeph. 655 τρίτον τόδ᾽ ἐκπέραμα δωμάτων καλῶ, the κλῆσις being ἐκπέρα, ἐκπέρα, ἐκπέρα.

§. 568. Add Demosth. p. 48. 39 ἐπιχειροτονεῖν τὰς γνώμας : Thuc. III. 42 προσκατηγοροῦντες ἐπίδειξιν.

§. 573. Add Æsch. Eum. 7. διδόναι δόσιν.

§. 581. Obs. Add Soph. Ant. 788 φύξιμός σε : Eur. Hipp. 1029 φυγὰς χθόνα.

§. 583. To the list of verbs which take a double accusative add "βλάπτω, Plat. Legg. p. 920 C βλάπτοι σμικρότατα τοὺς χρωμένους: Pass. Ibid. p. 696 B μέγιστα ἂν βλάπτοιτο: δηλέομαι, Hdt. IV. 115 δηλησαμένους πολλὰ γῆν : ἐλαύνω, Aristoph. Nub. 29 ἐλαύνεις πολλοὺς δρόμους ἐμέ : ἐξορκόω. Hdt. IV. 74 : κερδαίνω (make a gain of), Eur. Hec. 518 κερδᾶναι δάκρυά με."

Ib. 1. To ἄγω add "so ἐξάγω, Soph. Œ. C. 98."

Ib. 15. For ἀναμνάω read ἀναμιμνήσκω.

Ib. 67. For ἐπικνέομαι read ἐφικνέομαι.

Ib. 86. After ἱστορέω, add ἀνιστορέω.

Ib. 89. After καλέω add, κικλήσκω.

Ib. 104. Add Soph. Ant. 1180 λούσαντες ἁγνὸν λοῦτρόν τινα.

Ib. 124. Add Æsch. Choeph. 640 διανταίαν οὐτᾷ.

Ib. 155. Add, "so Arist. Equit. 5. προστρίβεται πληγὰς τοῖς οἰκέταις, Dind. τοὺς οἰκέτας, Bekk."

§. 589. 2. Add, "so ποιεῖν, δρᾶν, πράττειν &c. take the dat. of the person for whose benefit or hurt any thing is done."

§. 598. p. 225. line 9. Omit the example from Il. κ. 16.

§. 605. 2. line 17. For *us* read *those*. *Obs.* 5. line 2. After "adverbs in η," add, "or ῃ."

§. 709. Add, "and not unfrequently the verb belonging to the participle is implied in what follows, which was in the mind of the speaker when he used the nominative, though for the sake of emphasis he resolves the verb into an independent form : Æsch. Choeph. 520 τὰ πάντα γάρ τις ἐγχέας ἀνθ' αἵματος ἑνός, μάτην ὁ μόχθος = μάτην μοχθεῖ : Id. Sept. c. Theb. 681 ἀνδρῶν δ' ὁμαίμων θάνατος ὧδ' αὐτοκτόνος, οὐκ ἔστι γῆρας τοῦδε τοῦ μιάσματος = οὐκ ἐᾷ τὸ μίασμα γηράσκειν."

§. 711. line 5. for Choeph. 396. read 410.

§. 721. 1. Last line but two, for εἶτα δή read εἴτε δή.

§. 725. In the heading of section, for *Coordinate thoughts*, read *Subordinate thoughts*.

§. 793. Heading, dele *Substantival clauses*.

THE END.

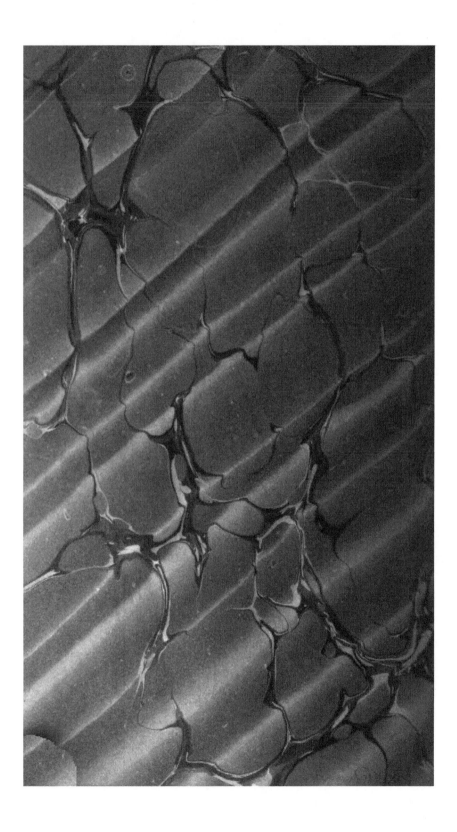